ECONOMICS

Michael Parkin

University of Western Ontario

Addison-Wesley Publishing Company

*Reading, Massachusetts • Menlo Park, California • New York
Don Mills, Ontario • Wokingham, England • Amsterdam
Bonn • Sydney • Singapore • Tokyo • Madrid • San Juan*

Library of Congress Cataloging-in-Publication Data

Parkin, Michael, 1939-
    Economics / Michael Parkin.
        p.   cm.
    Includes index.
    ISBN 0-201-05931-2
    1. Economics.   I. Title.
HB171.5.P313   1990

330—dc19   88-9709
                                       CIP

Reprinted with corrections April, 1990.

CDEFGHIJ-DO-9543210

Senior Sponsoring Editor: **Barbara Rifkind**
Development Manager: **Sue Gleason**
Development Editors: **Janice Byer, Robert McGough**
Managing Editor: **Mary Clare McEwing**
Senior Production Supervisor: **Kazia Navas**
Art and Design Director: **Marshall Henrichs**
Cover and Interior Designer: **Karen Gourley-Lehman**
Production Services Manager: **Herb Nolan**
Art Supervisor: **Nancy Blodget**
Illustrators: **Black Dot Graphics, George Nichols**
Photographer for Interviews: **Marshall Henrichs**
Associate Editor: **Christine O'Brien**
Copyeditor: **Stephanie Magean**
Proofreader: **Cecilia Thurlow**
Layout Artists: **Nancy Blodget, Karen Gourley-Lehman**
Production Administrator: **Loren Stevens**
Permissions Editor: **Mary Dyer**
Indexer: **Alexandra Nickerson**
Manufacturing Supervisor: **Roy Logan**
Senior Marketing Manager: **Mac Mendelsohn**
Promotions Supervisor: **Julia Berkley**
Compositor: **Black Dot Graphics**
Color Separator: **Black Dot Graphics**
Printer: **R.R. Donnelley & Sons**

Text and photo credits appear on p. I-17, which constitutes a
continuation of the copyright page.

About Michael Parkin

Michael Parkin received his training as an economist at the Universities of Leicester and Essex in England. Currently in the Department of Economics at the University of Western Ontario, Canada, Professor Parkin has held faculty appointments at Brown University, the University of Manchester, and the University of Essex. He has served on the editorial boards of the *American Economic Review* and the *Journal of Monetary Economics* and as managing editor of the *Canadian Journal of Economics*. He is the author of *Macroeconomics* (Prentice-Hall). Professor Parkin's research on macroeconomics, monetary economics, and international economics has resulted in 160 publications in journals and edited volumes including the *American Economic Review*, the *Journal of Political Economy*, the *Review of Economic Studies*, the *Journal of Monetary Economics*, and the *Journal of Money, Credit and*

Banking. It became most visible to the public with his work on inflation that discredited the use of wage and price controls. Michael Parkin also spearheaded the movement toward European monetary union. Professor Parkin is an experienced and dedicated teacher of introductory economics.

To Robin

Preface

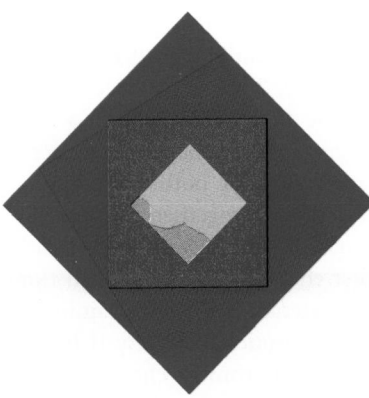

To change the way students see the world: this is my goal in teaching economics and in writing this book.

Economics teaches students to use the economist's lens to view the world more clearly. At every point in the writing, development, and production of this book, I have tried to put myself in the student's place. I have repeatedly recalled my own early struggles to master this discipline, and I have drawn on the learning experiences of the several thousand principles students whom I have been privileged to teach over the past twenty-five years.

Three assumptions (or are they facts?) about students have been my guiding principles in determining the content, organization, features, and visual appearance of this book. First, students are eager to learn, but they are overwhelmed by the seemingly endless claims on their time, interests, and energy. As a result, they want to be told—and in a convincing way—just *why* they are being asked to study a particular body of material. They want to be motivated by a demonstration of its relevance to their everyday experience. Second, once motivated, students want to be presented with a thoughtful, clear, and logical explanation, so that they can understand and begin to apply what they have learned. They do not want to be handed loosely related facts and anecdotes. Third,

students are more interested in the present and future than in the past. They want to learn the economics of the 1980s so that, as they enter the 1990s and the twenty-first century, they will be equipped with the most up-to-date tools available to guide them.

Content and Organization

The core of the principles course has been around for more than one hundred years, and other important elements, especially parts of the theory of the firm and Keynesian macroeconomics, have been with us for more than fifty years. But economics has also been developing and changing rapidly during the past few decades. Although all principles texts pay some attention to these more recent developments, they have not succeeded in integrating the new and the traditional. They have created a patchwork quilt rather than a seamless web. I have worked hard to avoid this patchwork approach and to present new ideas in a new way, incorporating them into the body of timeless principles so as to weave a coherent pattern.

Among the many recent developments that you will find in this book are rational expectations, efficient markets, game theory, the principal-agent problem, public choice theory, aggregate demand and aggregate supply, and real business cycle theory. Yet the presence of modern topics does not translate into "high level." Nor does it translate into "bias." The presentation has been crafted to make recent developments in economics thoroughly accessible to the beginning student. Furthermore, where these modern theories are controversial, the more traditional models are also presented and the two (or more) approaches evaluated and compared. Thus, for example, in macroeconomics, all the alternative "schools"—Keynesian, monetarist, rational expectations, and real business cycle—are given an evenhanded treatment.

But this book does have a point of view. It is that economics is a serious, lively, and evolving science—a science that seeks to develop a body of theory powerful enough to explain the economic world around us and that pursues its task by building, testing, and rejecting economic models. In some areas the science has succeeded in its task, but in others it has some way to go and controversy persists. Where matters are settled, I present what we know in the clearest possible light; where controversy persists, I present the alternative viewpoints.

The existence of controversy has implications for the organization of the principles course. As a consequence, I have paid special attention to ensuring that this book can be used in a variety of ways.

Flexibility

Most fundamentally, there is disagreement about the best order in which to present microeconomics and macroeconomics. I have chosen to do microeconomics first, but the book has been written to accommodate courses that are sequenced in either order. The microeconomics and macroeconomics chapters do not depend on each other; concepts and terms are defined and ideas are developed independently in each of the two halves.

I have also tried to accommodate a wide range of teaching approaches by building flexibility and optionality into the book. In addition to the techniques mentioned below, there are several optional chapter sections, which are indicated with an asterisk (*) on the section title and in the table of contents. These may be omitted with no loss of continuity.

Microeconomics   In the core areas of consumer and producer theory, there are two optional chapters: one on indifference curves (Chapter 8) and the other on isoquants (Chapter 11). I have provided a full chapter rather than appendixes on these topics because it is my belief that more difficult ideas need a gentle and thoughtful treatment. My own teaching experience has led me to the conclusion that placing more difficult material in short appendixes renders that material almost unteachable. The indifference curve chapter may be treated as a complement of or a substitute for the marginal utility chapter (Chapter 7), and for those instructors using both, there is an appendix showing how they fit together. Because many instructors run out of time when they get to factor markets, the first chapter (Chapter 15) in this part contains the core material, and the remaining chapters may be treated as optional. Finally, I have placed all the material on government choices in a single part (Chapters 19, 20, and 21). However, these chapters may be read before those on factor markets (Chapters 15, 16, 17, and 18), and the chapter on regulation (Chapter 21) may be read immediately after those on competition and monopoly (Chapters 12 and 13).

Macroeconomics   In recognition of the diversity in approaches to teaching macroeconomics—and believing strongly that diversity is appropriate in unsettled parts of the discipline—I have paid special attention to writing these chapters so that they can be used in a variety of ways. I think that the most natural way to teach macroeconomics is that in which it is presented here. But several other sequences also work well.

I have long been puzzled by the way principles texts present the aggregate demand and aggregate supply model. *Aggregate* demand and *aggregate* supply analysis is harder than demand and supply analysis. Yet most books devote a full and thoughtful chapter to the demand and supply model and then present the aggregate demand and aggregate supply model in a scant few pages. I have recognized the inherently more difficult nature of the aggregate model and have tried to present an equally careful development of that model, which parallels the development of the microeconomic demand and supply model in Chapter 4. Chapter 24 on aggregate demand and aggregate supply serves as an overview of the rest of the macroeconomics material. Alternately, it can be read as a synthesis of the individual components of aggregate demand and aggregate supply, and can be studied after Chapter 30.

For those instructors who like to teach the *IS-LM* model, it is presented in an appendix, but one that is, I hope, more teachable than is commonly found.

Special Features

Art Program

One of the most important tools for economists is graphical analysis, yet this is often a real stumbling block for students. The development and art editors at Addison-Wesley and I kept this challenge always in mind as we developed the art program.

We began by observing a distinction between diagrams that represent models and those that display data. Model-based diagrams emphasize analysis and abstraction, whereas empirical graphs emphasize shapes, patterns, and visual correlations. It makes good pedagogical sense to differentiate these two kinds of figures in order to help students work with them better. As a signal to students, we set our model-based diagrams on a white background, and the empirical graphs on a manila background.

Our goal in the model-based art (see the representative figure below) is to show clearly "where the economic action is." To achieve this, we observe a consistent protocol in style, notation, and use of color, including

• Highlighting shifted curves, points of equilibrium, and the most important features in red.

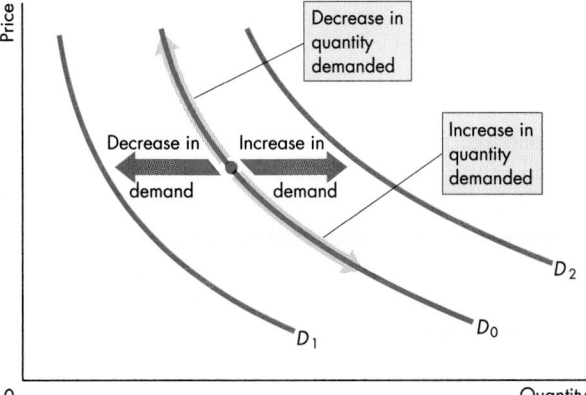

• Using arrows in conjunction with color to lend directional movement to what are usually static presentations.
• Pairing graphs with data tables from which the curves have been plotted.
• Using color consistently to underscore the content, and referring to such color in the text and captions.
• Labeling key pieces of information in graphs with boxed notes.
• Rendering each piece electronically, so that precision is achieved.

The entire art program has been developed with the study and review needs of the student in mind. We have set up the following features, including:

• Marking the most important figures and tables with a red "key" and listing them at the end of the chapter as "Key Figures and Tables." ◆
• Using complete, informative captions that encapsule major points in the graph so that students can preview or review the chapter by skimming through the art.

We undertook extensive tests of the quality of our art program. For example, we had two art reviewers evaluate every graph. Once a style had been developed, we also conducted informal discussions on the use of color and on the rendering technique. And since accuracy of illustrations and their in-text references is vital, we engaged five economists as accuracy reviewers of the manuscript and three of the galleys and page proofs to check words, numbers, and illustrations. These economists assisted the publisher's in-house development editors and proofreaders, who checked every line, point, label, and cross-reference for clarity and accuracy.

The Interviews

An important goal of the principles course is to develop in students the ability to reason like economists. To aid this process, this book enables students to eavesdrop on a series of conversations that I conducted with twelve eminent economists who have changed the way we think about the world. These interviews open each of the book's parts. It has been a great joy to learn something of how these economists view their area of specialization, of their unique contributions to economics, and also of their general insights which are relevant to beginning students.

Each interview has been carefully edited to be self-contained, and the necessary concepts and terms are defined informally within each one. Since each interview discusses topics that are introduced formally in the following chapters, students can use it as a preview to some of the issues they are about to encounter. A more careful reading afterwards will give students a fuller appreciation of the discussion. Finally, the whole series of interviews can be approached as an informal symposium on the subject matter of economics as it is practiced today.

Reading Between the Lines

Another common goal of the principles course is to develop the student's ability to use economics to analyze current events reported in the media. Recognizing this need, I have developed a feature that may, I hope, be a fruitful model. Each "Reading Between the Lines" spread contains three passes at a story. It begins with a facsimile of an actual (sometimes abbreviated) newspaper or magazine article. It then presents a digest of the article's essential points. Finally, it provides an economic analysis of the news story, based on the economic methods presented in that chapter. It is my intention that students, using this feature, will learn how to do more than just notice the relevance of economics to modern life. I hope that they will also develop the ability to ask good questions, to evaluate the quality of information presented in the media, and to use economic models to deepen their understanding of the economic world.

Our Advancing Knowledge

Another group of special essays reveals the birth and development of economic ideas, not just as abstract models, but as intimately tied to the people and circumstances that formed them.

Learning Aids

We have developed a careful pedagogical plan to ensure that this book complements and reinforces classroom learning. Each chapter contains the following pedagogical elements:

- *Objectives.* A list of chapter objectives that enables students to set their goals before embarking on a chapter.
- *Chapter openers.* Economic vignettes, questions, puzzles, or metaphors that motivate the analysis and that are resolved in the chapter.
- *Highlighted in-text reviews.* Succinct summaries at the end of many main sections.
- *Key terms.* Highlighted within the text, these concepts form the first part of a three-tiered review of economic vocabulary. These terms are repeated with page references at chapter ends and compiled in the end-of-book glossary.
- *Key figures and tables.* Identified with the "key" logo and listed at chapter ends. ◆
- *End-of-chapter study material.* Summaries organized around major headings; lists of key terms with page references; lists of key figures and tables with page references; review questions; and problems. We have worked hard to make the problems meaningful and useful for students.

Design

The design has an important place in the overall pedagogical plan. Our mission with the design of special features was to evoke the colorful feeling of nontextbook print media, notably magazines and annual reports, thus reinforcing the connection of economics to the real world. In the text itself, we strove for a scrupulously clear and honest look that would let the models being presented speak for themselves.

The Teaching and Learning Package

The authors of the supplements, Addison-Wesley, and I have put a tremendous amount of effort into ensuring that each component of the package will help students and instructors derive the maximum benefit from the textbook.

Chapter and Page Numbering System We have given great thought to the best way to enumerate the chapters and paginate the hardcover and split paperback versions of the book so that they work well with all the supplements. Our solution to the problem of confusing numbering systems for chapters in the hardcover and paperback versions was to renumber the pages of each paperback (beginning with page 1) but to keep the chapter numbers the same throughout the three books. This system permits the three books and all of the teaching and learning supplements to work together without confusion.

Study Guide   Prepared by David Spencer of Brigham Young University, the Study Guide has been carefully coordinated with the main textbook. Each chapter contains: Chapter in Perspective; Learning Objectives; Helpful Hints; Self-Test (concepts review; true/false, multiple-choice, short-answer questions, and problems) and Answers to Self-Test; and Key Figures and Tables.

Economics in the News   This supplement, prepared by Saul Pleeter and Philip Way of the University of Cincinnati, is a unique workbook that extends the "Reading Between the Lines" feature of the textbook. The book includes eighty-five recent news articles organized according to the topical outline of the textbook. An introductory paragraph, objectives, and preview precede a facsimile of the article itself. After the article, two or more pages of analytical questions actively engage students.

Answers to Economics in the News   This booklet provides answers to the problems in the supplement above and is available to instructors upon request from the Business and Economics Group at Addison-Wesley.

Test Item File   Prepared by Patricia Euzent of the University of Central Florida and David Spencer of Brigham Young University, this file offers over 4000 multiple-choice questions. Each chapter includes a separate section of questions directly from the Study Guide and a section of questions that parallel those in the Study Guide.

Computerized Test Item File   This software for qualified adopters is available for IBM-PC and compatible microcomputers and Macintosh microcomputers.

Instructor's Manual   Prepared by Patricia Euzent of the University of Central Florida, the Instructor's Manual includes detailed chapter outlines and teaching suggestions, a list of acetates, answers to all review questions and problems in the textbook, and a flexibility guide prepared by Michael Parkin.

Acetates   All of the text's key figures are rendered in full color on the acetates. There are 109 acetates for *Microeconomics* and 95 acetates for *Macroeconomics*, and are available to qualified adopters of the textbook by contacting Addison-Wesley.

Graphecon II Software   This software for IBM-PC and compatible microcomputers, prepared by Cols. James R. Golden and L. Donne Olvey of the United States Military Academy at West Point, are menu-driven interactive tutorial and quizzing programs that allow students to work with economic graphs.

Student Edition Software   Full-function versions of leading software adapted for educational use are available from Addison-Wesley, including Student Edition Software for Lotus® 1-2-3®, Second Edition, MathCAD® 2.0, and MINITAB®.

Acknowledgments

One of the great pleasures of writing an introductory text is the opportunity it affords to learn from so many generous friends and colleagues. Although the extent of my debts cannot be fully acknowledged here, it is nevertheless a joy to record my gratitude to the many people who have helped, some without realizing just how helpful they were.

I want to thank those of my colleagues at the University of Western Ontario who have taught me a great deal that can be found in these pages: Jim Davies, Jeremy Greenwood, Ig Horstmann, Peter Howitt, Greg Huffman, David Laidler, Phil Reny, Chris Robinson, John Whalley, and Ron Wonnacott. I want to extend a special thanks to Glenn MacDonald, who worked well beyond the call of duty discussing this project with me from its outset, helping me develop many of its pedagogical features, and reading and commenting in detail on all the micro chapters.

I also want to acknowledge my debt to those who have had a profound influence on my whole view of and approach to economics and whose influence I can see in these pages. Although I never sat in their classrooms, they are in a very real sense my teachers. I am especially grateful to John Carlson (Purdue University), Carl Christ (Johns Hopkins University), Robert Clower (University of South Carolina), Ed Feige (University of Wisconsin at Madison), Herschel Grossman (Brown University), and Sam Wu (University of Iowa). I also want to place on record my enormous debt to the late Karl Brunner. The energy, drive, and entrepreneurship of this outstanding economist provided me and my generation of economists with incredible opportunities to intereact and learn from each other in a wide variety of conference settings both in the United States and in Europe.

It is also a pleasure to acknowledge my debt to the several thousand students to whom I have been privileged to teach introductory economics. The instant feedback that comes from that look of puzzlement or enlightenment has taught me, more than anything else, how to teach economics.

Producing a text such as this is a team effort, and the members of the Addison-Wesley "Parkin Team" are genuine co-producers of this book. I am especially grateful to and have been truly inspired by my sponsoring editor, Barbara Rifkind. Barbara discovered this book when it was no more than an idea in my mind, while she was working as an Addison-Wesley sales representative in Florida. After two promotions, she came onto the project when Addison-Wesley had already designed the book and when I thought I had finished writing it. Barbara liked what she saw, but saw more in its potential than in its realization. She coaxed me into rewriting the entire book one more time and coaxed Addison-Wesley into another complete overhaul of the design. Because of Barbara, this book is really the second edition of *Economics*! Sue Gleason as development editor has had an enormous influence on both the words and the art program. Sue and I have developed cauliflower ears as a result of working with each other on the telephone over the past two years. Kazia Navas, the production editor, has coordinated the entire production process, keeping us all on track and coping cheerfully with my numerous and sometimes outrageous demands.

Great thanks go to Stephanie Magean, Sherry Berg, Nancy Blodget, Janice Byer, Marshall Henrichs, Mary Stuart Lang, Karen Lehman, Mary Clare McEwing, Dick Morton, Christine O'Brien, Loren Stevens, Christine Shuster, and the more than eighty economists (whose names appear separately) who have acted as reviewers or members of focus groups. It is a pleasure to acknowledge my debt to Steven Mautner, the Sponsoring Editor who initiated this project, and to Will Ethridge, who played an important role in the early stages of development. I also wish to express my gratitude to Bob McGough, a superb financial and economic journalist, who provided a thorough and creative edit of my second draft and who also taught me a great deal about how to write more clearly and effectively. David Spencer, Patricia Euzent, Saul Pleeter, and Philip Way were the primary authors of the supplements package and graciously shared their professional insights and teaching expertise with me. I also want to thank the many secretaries who have helped at various stages of this book, typing and retyping its countless drafts and redrafts. They are Yvonne Adams, Lynda Sollazzo, Kendra McKague, and, most recently, Barbara Craig.

I have left until last four people to whom I want to give special thanks. First, my colleague and best friend Robin Bade has been almost a co-author of this work. She has read every word that I have written, commented in detail on every draft of the work, and has helped manage the project from its conception to its conclusion. Without the anticipation of her help and its availability, I could never have contemplated embarking on this project. Finally, I want to acknowledge the help and inspiration of my children, Catherine, Richard, and Ann. Through the years that I have been developing and writing this work, they have been going through various stages of high school and college. They have forced me to craft a book that they can understand and find interesting.

The empirical test of this textbook's value will be made in the classroom. I would appreciate hearing from instructors and students about how I might improve the book in future editions.

Michael Parkin
Department of Economics
University of Western Ontario
London, Ontario N6A 5C2

Reviewers

Manuscript Reviewers

Berhanu Abegaz
College of William and Mary

Lee J. Alston
University of Illinois

Ted Amato
University of North Carolina
at Charlotte

Richard K. Anderson
Texas A & M University

Mohsen Bahmani-Oskooee
University of Wisconsin—Milwaukee

Ian R. Bain
Minnegasco, Inc.

Peter S. Barth
University of Connecticut

Brian R. Binger
University of Arizona

Bruce R. Bolnick
Northeastern University

M. Neil Browne
Bowling Green State University

Clive Bull
Paine Webber

Michael R. Butler
Texas Christian University

Steven Caudill
Auburn University

Steven L. Cobb
University of North Texas

John D. Coupe
University of Maine

Paul N. Courant
University of Michigan

Larry DeBrock
University of Illinois

David Denslow
University of Florida

Donald Dutkowsky
Syracuse University

Nathan Edmonson
Georgia State University

Kenneth G. Elzinga
University of Virginia

Patricia J. Euzent
University of Central Florida

Roger E. A. Farmer
University of California
at Los Angeles

Kevin F. Forbes
Catholic University of America

Lynn G. Gillette
Texas A & M University

Edward Greenberg
Washington University

John Grobey
Humbolt State University

Timothy J. Gronberg
Texas A & M University

John R. Hanson II
Texas A & M University

Stephen Happel
Arizona State University

Elizabeth Hoffman
University of Arizona

Glenn Hueckel
Purdue University

Dennis W. Jansen
Texas A & M University

Bruce E. Kaufman
Georgia State University

Arjo Klamer
University of Iowa

Levis A. Kochin
University of Washington

Don N. MacDonald
Northeast Louisiana University

Michael Magura
University of Toledo

George J. Mailath
University of Pennsylvania

Steven J. Matusz
Michigan State University

Sam Mirmirani
Bryant College

W. Douglas Morgan
University of California,
Santa Barbara

Anthony L. Ostrosky
Illinois State University

Harold Petersen
Boston College

Frank Petrella
Holy Cross College

Thomas J. Pierce
California State University,
San Bernadino

Mark W. Plant
U.S. Department of Commerce

Andrew J. Policano
State University of New York at
Stony Brook

Robert Puth
University of New Hampshire

Krishnamurthy Ramagopal
University of Vermont

J. David Reed
Bowling Green State University

Robert Rosenman
Washington State University

Mark Rush
University of Florida

Allen R. Sanderson
The University of Chicago

Michael P. Shields
Southern Illinois University
at Carbondale

Ronald Soligo
Rice University

David E. Spencer
Brigham Young University

Robert W. Thomas
Iowa State University

Marie Thursby
Purdue University

Arthur L. Welsh
Pennsylvania State University

Walter J. Wessels
North Carolina State University

James N. Wetzel
Virginia Commonwealth University

Jeffrey Wolcowitz
Harvard University

William C. Wood
James Madison University

Gavin Wright
Stanford University

Peter A. Zaleski
Villanova University

Gary Zarkin
Research Triangle Institute

Art Reviewers

Donald Dutkowsky
Syracuse University

Willard W. Radell, Jr.
Indiana University of Pennsylvania

Accuracy Reviewers

Eugene Bland
National Education Center's
Tampa Technical Institute

Robert P. Edwards
County College of Morris (NJ)

Edward Monkman
County College of Morris (NJ)

David Spencer
Brigham Young University

Jeffrey Wrase
Arizona State University

Brief Contents

Contents

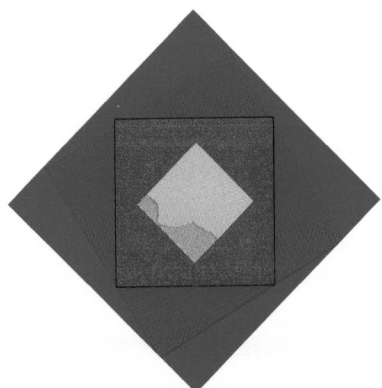

†Summary, Key Concepts, Review Questions, and Problems appear at the end of each chapter.

Part 5 *Markets for Goods and Services*

Talking with HUGO SONNENSCHEIN / 275

Part 7 *Markets and Government*
Talking with ALFRED KAHN / 491

Part 9 *How the Macroeconomy Works*

Talking with ROBERT E. LUCAS, JR. / 639

Part 10 *Macroeconomic Policy*

Talking with PAUL VOLCKER / 863

Part 12 *Growth and Comparative Systems*

Talking with JANOS KORNAI / 973

Part I

Talking
with
Assar
Lindbeck

Assar Lindbeck is a professor of economics and director of the Institute for International Economic Studies at the University of Stockholm. He has been a visiting professor at Columbia University, the University of Michigan, and Yale University. Since 1981, he has been chairman of the committee that annually awards the Nobel Prize for economic science. Michael Parkin talked with Professor Lindbeck about the nature of economics, the economic landscape of the 1990s, and the way economists do their work.

Professor Lindbeck, how did you decide to become an economist?

My father was a politician in northern Sweden, so I was interested myself in studying political science at college. After three semesters, I decided to learn economics as a background. The problem is that I never finished learning economics!

What was it about economics that was so compelling?

I discovered that political science dealt mainly with the forms of political events, the way political decisions are made. But it dealt very little with the consequences of political decisions. Economics, on the other hand, does just that, by looking at how political decisions and economic policy actually affect families, businesses, or nations.

What makes economics different from political science or the other social sciences?

First, economics asks different questions. Questions about employment; output; the allocation of resources, including labor; the distribution of income. Next, economics has been able to build up a general analytical structure. We don't need a special kind of economics to discuss housing or agriculture or education. We apply the same economic principles to each different field. Other social sciences tend to build specific theories for each issue or field. Family sociology is different from criminal sociology, for example. Finally, economics can use narrower assumptions to produce reasonably good predictions. For instance, if you ask me about factors that influence the demand for butter or margarine, I don't have to go into philosophical issues about the basis for human behavior.

Do microeconomics and macroeconomics, the two traditional branches of economics, use the same principles?

Well, there has been a discontinuity between microeconomics and macroeconomics. Macro-

"I wonder if we aren't straining out young people with creativity by forcing them into elaborate analysis."

economics is based on the idea that there are systematic movements of broad aggregates—total output, national economic growth, unemployment, or inflation—and that we can explain one aggregate by another, as a kind of short cut. You don't have to explain all relative prices and the allocation of resources to be able to explain a recession. But it *is* important that what you're saying about these aggregate movements should be consistent with the microeconomic assumptions you would make about the behavior of individual firms or consumers. Milton Friedman, Franco Modigliani, James Tobin, and others started this approach in the 1950s because they were dissatisfied with the absence of microeconomic foundations for the

empirical generalizations that characterized macroeconomics at the time.

If you want to talk about "the economy," you need to work with aggregate concepts because the human brain is just too small to consider all the variables at one time. For economics to be useful to you as an individual, you have to be able to play with the model in your head. You should be able to read the newspaper or watch the TV news and process it mentally. For economics to be useful to society, an economist must be able to talk with journalists and politicians, or to draw diagrams on the blackboard for students. If you cannot transform your thinking into broad categories, you can never communicate outside a group of specialists.

You've been chairman of the committee that awards the Nobel Prize for economic science. What characterizes the great economists?

The Prize Committee—and economists in general—recognize the value both of people who have influential ideas, even if they haven't formalized them into complete models, and of people who formalize ideas borrowed partly from others. There are very few people with both bright ideas and the ability or opportunity to formalize them. I think that today economists with interesting and realistic visions are scarcer than technical economists. I have always been a strong advocate for rigorous training, but I sometimes wonder if we aren't straining out some young people with common sense and creativity by forcing them into elaborate technical analysis.

What do you see as the most important economic issue facing us in the 1990s?

Let me begin by looking back at some of the events that have led us to where we are today. The 25 years after World War II are regarded now as a golden age—expanding world trade, low unemployment, rapid

growth, and prosperity. Unique historical events contributed to that era —workers were available to move from agriculture to industry; prewar trade protectionism gave way; there were great advances in technology after years of stagnation. In the 1960s and 1970s, politicians started to believe, however, that economic growth and prosperity were manna from heaven. And we began to consume the very source of our economic success —by tampering with the efficiency of our market economies. In the 1970s, the OPEC oil shocks came, and, at least in Europe, great explosions in wages. There were also extraordinary policy efforts to squeeze out inflation, which was a basic reason for the depths of the recessions in the 1970s and 1980s. The late 1980s have been a period of recovery from the turmoil of the previous decade. The growth rate has started to improve, unemployment has fallen in the United States and England. What is happening? There's a distinct

possibility that we're finally returning the strength of the market to market economies.

And in the future?

I see the issue of the 1990s as how far deregulation can go without interest groups protesting—many people feel the pinch of deregulation. In global terms, with the European Economic Community, how much control will any

national government give up to international market forces? Will a government be willing to say that they can't do anything about a problem because they've deregulated both the domestic economy and its foreign economic relations? Can a government do that without its domestic population throwing them out of office?

In addressing such difficult issues, can economists really separate scientific analysis from passionate advocacy of policy?

"I see the issue of the 1990s as how far deregulation can go without interest groups protesting."

If someone asks an economist what will be the effects of a tax on imported oil, the answer should be completely independent of his or her

opinion about whether those effects are good or bad. A liberal or a conservative economist should give the same answer if they've each used the same type of economic model. So why don't they always? Perhaps because they have inadvertently been influenced by their political beliefs to choose a model that tends to support a certain political value or world view.

The purpose of science, of economic science, is to discriminate correctly among different models in order to produce an honest assessment. It's never easy to do this, but it's critical to the justification of economics as a positive science.

You've tried in some of your writing to apply positive economics to explain the policy choices made by politicians—

what is called "public choice." Why is this an important area of economic research and what progress have we made in understanding political decision making?

This is a vital area of research. We cannot make economic forecasts without forecasting policies. And we cannot forecast policies without having a theory that predicts how politicians will react to new economic events in the future. But so far, I think that there

are few generally solid results—because politicians naturally have a very complex pattern of behavior that we can't yet really explain. For example, there are often conflicts between the policy agenda that politicians believe they should pursue and the policy decisions they may have to make in order to stay in office. The chief result of research in this area, so far, is that economists have become much more aware of how complicated it really is to give good advice on policy.

What have been the guiding principles that have helped you as an economist and as a person concerned with economic policy?

I like to be inspired by real-world problems. I want to look around and see something that puzzles me, something I don't understand, and try to find a plausible explanation. Next, I sit down at my desk and try to write the problem down. I try to make sense of it in both ordinary words and formal terms, with graphs and equations. I often find out that the answer was different from what I had expected.

What advice would you give to a student in the first weeks of a principles of economics course?

Try to understand the principles intuitively and not just mechanically. Try to understand the common sense, if there is any, of the examples your teachers and textbooks provide. If you only memorize the facts, after two years you'll have forgotten it all. But if you learn economics with your intuition backing you up, you'll keep something of great value.

"We cannot make economic forecasts without forecasting policies."

Chapter 1

What Is Economics?

After studying this chapter, you will be able to:	● State the kinds of questions that economics tries to answer	● Describe the function and the working parts of an economy
	● Explain why all economic questions and economic activity arise from scarcity	● Distinguish between positive and normative statements
	● Explain why scarcity forces people to make choices	● Explain what is meant by an economic theory and how economic theories are developed by building and testing economic models
	● Define opportunity cost	

PRODUCTION, CONSUMPTION, AND TECHNOLOGICAL CHANGE

If you wanted to watch a movie in your home in 1975, you had to rent a movie projector and a screen—as well as the movie itself. The cost of such entertainment would have been as high as what a theater would pay to show the movie to several hundred people. Only the rich chose to watch movies in the comfort of their own homes. ■ In 1976, the video cassette recorder (VCR) became available to consumers. Its typical price tag was $2000 (which in today's dollars is $4000). Since that time, the price of VCRs has steadily fallen so that today you can buy a reliable machine for $200. A video can be rented for a dollar a day and can be bought for less than $30. In just a few years, watching a movie at home changed from a luxury available to the richest few to an event enjoyed by millions. ■ Advances in technology affect the way we consume. We now watch far more movies at home than we did a decade ago because new technologies have lowered the cost. ■ New technologies also affect the way we *produce* things. Johnny Wilder, Jr., was a successful popular musician in the 1970s with such hits as ''Boogie Nights'' and ''Always and Forever.'' A car accident in 1979 left Wilder paralyzed from the neck down. Today, Wilder again produces music but of a new kind. The artist now works with a Macintosh computer and synthesizers controlled by his breath and by beams of light. ■ We hear a great deal these days about lasers. Their most dramatic use may be in futuristic defense systems such as the Strategic Defense Initiative—or ''Star Wars'' as it is popularly known. But lasers already affect us every day. They scan prices at the supermarket checkout. They create holograms on credit cards, making them harder to forge. Neurosurgeons and eye surgeons use them in our hospitals.

■ It is clear that new technologies affect the way that we produce goods and services. The examples that we have given, whether they affect our consumption or production, give rise to the first big economic question:

How do people choose *what* to consume and *how* to produce, and how are these choices affected by the discovery of new ways of doing things—of new technologies?

Wages and Earnings

On a crisp, bright winter day on the ski slopes at Aspen, a bronzed 23-year-old instructs some beginning skiers in the snowplow turn. For this pleasant and uncomplicated work, the young man, who quit school after eleventh grade, is paid $10 an hour.

In a lawyer's office in the center of a busy city, a 23-year-old secretary handles a large volume of correspondence, filing, scheduling, and meetings. She arrives home most evenings exhausted. She has a bachelor's degree in English and has taken night courses in computer science and word processing. She receives $8 an hour for her work.

On September 10, 1988, Steffi Graf and Gabriela Sabatini played a stunning tennis match in the final of the Women's U.S. Open Championship. At the end of the close and hard-fought match, the winner, Steffi Graf, received $275,000; Ms. Sabatini collected only half that amount. A similar phenomenon can be seen in the headquarters of large corporations. Chief executive officers who work no harder (and in some cases, even less hard) than the people immediately beneath them receive far higher salaries than their subordinates.

Situations like these raise the second big economic question:

What determines people's incomes and why do some people receive much larger rewards than others whose efforts appear to be similar?

Unemployment

During the Great Depression, the four years from 1929 to 1933, unemployment afflicted almost one fifth of the labor force in the industrial world. For months and in some cases years on end, many families had no income other than meager payments from the government or from private charities. In the 1950s and 1960s, unemployment rates stayed below 5 percent in most countries and in some, below 2 percent. During the 1970s and early 1980s, unemployment steadily increased so that by late 1982 and early 1983 almost 11 percent of the U.S. labor force was looking for work. But in 1989, the U.S. unemployment rate had fallen to 5 percent.

Unemployment hurts different groups unequally. When the average unemployment rate in the United States was 5 percent—as it was in 1989—the unemployment rate among young people 16 to 19 years old was 19 percent, but for young blacks, it was 43 percent. These facts raise the third big economic question:

What are the causes of unemployment and why are some groups more severely affected than others?

Inflation

Between August 1945 and July 1946, prices in Hungary rose by an average of 20,000 percent per month. In the worst month, July 1946, they rose 419 quadrillion percent (a quadrillion is the number one followed by 15 zeros).

In 1985, the cost of living in Bolivia rose by 11,750 percent. This meant that in downtown La Paz a McDonald's hamburger that cost 20 bolivianos on January 1, cost 2370 bolivianos by the end of the year. That same year, prices rose only 3.2 percent in the United States. But in the late 1970s, prices in the United States were rising at a rate well in excess of 10 percent a year. These facts raise the fourth big economic question:

Why do prices rise and why do some countries sometimes experience rapid price increases while others have stable prices?

Government

The government touches many aspects of life. It maintains the army, air force, navy, and marines for our national defense. It provides law enforcement, health care, insurance, and education. Its agencies regulate food and drug production, nuclear energy, and agriculture.

The cost of government has increased dramatically over the years. In the early 1900s, the federal government took in taxes and spent about 3¢ out of every dollar earned by the average American, and state and local governments took in and spent about 5¢—for a total of about 8¢ for every dollar earned. Government budgets were balanced. In 1987, the federal government collected 20¢ in taxes out of every dollar earned, but it spent 24¢, thereby generating a 4¢ deficit, or a 4¢ excess of spending over taxes for every dollar earned. If you add state and local government spending to that of the federal government, approximately 35¢ of every dollar earned by Americans is spent by the government.

These facts about government raise the fifth big economic question:

How do government spending and taxes influence economic life and what happens when the government has a deficit, as it does at the present time?

International Trade

In the 1960s, almost all the cars and trucks on the highways of the United States were Fords, Chevrolets, and Chryslers. By the 1980s, Toyotas, Hondas, Volkswagens, and BMWs were a common sight on these same highways. As a matter of fact, by 1985 one third of all new cars sold in the United States were imported; in the mid-1950s, less than 1 percent were.

Cars are not exceptional. The same can be said of television sets, clothing, and computers.

Governments regulate international trade in cars and in most other commodities. They impose taxes on imports, called tariffs, and also establish quotas, which restrict the quantities that may be imported. These facts raise the sixth big economic question:

What determines the pattern and the volume of trade between nations and what are the effects of tariffs and quotas on international trade?

Wealth and Poverty

At the mouth of the Canton River in southeast China is a small rocky peninsula and a group of islands with virtually no natural resources. But this bare land supports more than five million people who, though not excessively rich, live in rapidly growing abundance. They produce much of the world's fashion goods and electronic components. They are the people of Hong Kong.

On the eastern edge of Africa bordering the Red Sea, a tract of land a thousand times larger supports a population of 34 million people—only seven times that of Hong Kong. The region suffers such abject poverty that in 1985 rock singers from Europe and North America organized one of the most spectacular worldwide fund-raising efforts ever seen—Live Aid—to help them. These are the desperate and dying people of Ethiopia.

Hong Kong and Ethiopia, two extremes in income and wealth, are not isolated examples. The poorest two thirds of the world's population consumes less than one fifth of all the things produced. A middle income group accounts for almost one fifth of the world's population and consumes almost one fifth of the world's output. A further one fifth of the world's population—living in rich countries such as the United States, Canada, Western Europe, Japan, Australia, and New Zealand—consumes two thirds of the world's output.

These facts raise the seventh big economic question:

What causes differences in wealth among nations, making the people in some countries rich and in others poor?

Big Questions with No Easy Answers

These seven big questions provide an overview of economics. They are *big* questions for two reasons. First, they affect the quality of human life with great intensity. Second, they are hard questions to answer. They generate passionate argument and debate, and just about everybody has an opinion about them. Self-appointed experts abound. One of the hardest things for students of economics, whether beginners or seasoned practitioners, is to stand clear of the passion and emotion, and to approach their work with the detachment, rigor, and objectivity of a scientist.

Later in this chapter, we will explain how economists try to find answers to economic questions. But before doing that, let's go back to the seven big questions. What do these questions have in common? What distinguishes them from non-economic questions?

Scarcity

All economic questions arise from a single and inescapable fact: You can't always get what you want. We live in a world of scarcity. An economist defines **scarcity** to mean that wants always exceed the resources available to satisfy them. A child wants a 75¢ can of soft drink and a 50¢ pack of gum but has only $1.00 in her pocket. She experiences scarcity. A student wants to go to a party on Saturday night but also wants to spend that same night catching up on late assignments. He also experiences scarcity. The rich and the poor alike face scarcity. The U.S. government with its $1 trillion budget faces scarcity. The total amount that the federal government wants to spend on defense, health, education, welfare, and other services exceeds what it collects in taxes. Even parrots face scarcity—there just aren't enough crackers to go around.

Wants do not simply exceed resources; they are unlimited. In contrast, resources are limited, or finite. People want good health and a long life, material comfort, security, physical and mental recreation, and, finally, an awareness and understanding of themselves and their environment.

None of these wants are satisfied for everyone; and everyone has some unsatisfied wants. While many Americans have all the material comfort they want, many do not. No one is entirely satisfied with his or her state of health and length of life. No one feels entirely secure, especially in this nuclear age, and no one—not even the wealthiest person—has the time to enjoy all the travel, vacations, and art that he or she would like. Not even the wisest and most knowledgeable philosopher or scientist knows as much as he or she would like to know.

We can imagine a world that satisfies people's wants for material comfort and, perhaps, even security. But we cannot imagine a world in which people live as long and in as good a state of health as they would like. Nor can we imagine people having all the time, energy, and resources to enjoy all the sports, travel, vacation, and art that they would like. Natural resources and human resources—in the form of time, muscle-power, and brain-power—as well as all the dams, highways, buildings, machinery, tools, and other equipment that have been built by past human efforts amount to an enormous heritage, but they are limited. Our unlimited wants will always outstrip the resources available to satisfy them.

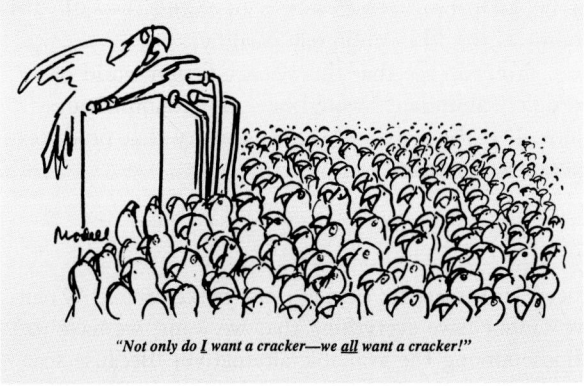

"Not only do I want a cracker—we all want a cracker!"

Drawing by Modell; © 1985 The New Yorker Magazine, Inc.

Economic Activity

The confrontation of unlimited wants with limited resources results in economic activity. **Economic activity** is what people do to cope with scarcity. **Economics**, then, is the study of how people use their limited resources to try to satisfy unlimited wants. Defined in this way, economic activity and economics deal with a wide range of issues and problems. The seven big questions posed earlier are examples of the more important problems economists study. Let's see how those questions could not arise if resources were infinitely abundant and scarcity did not exist.

With unlimited resources, there would be no need to devise better ways of producing more goods. Studying how we all spend our time and effort would not be interesting because we would simply do what we enjoyed without restriction. There would be no wages. We would do only the things that we enjoyed because there would be enough goods and services to satisfy everyone without effort. Unemployment would not be an issue because no one would work—except for people who wanted to work simply for the pleasure that it gave them. Inflation—rising prices—would not be a problem because no one would care about prices. Questions about government intervention in economic life would not arise because there would be no need for government-provided goods and no taxes. We would simply take whatever we wanted from the infinite resources available. There would be no international trade since, with complete abundance, it would be pointless to transport things from one place to another. Finally, differences in wealth among nations would not arise because we would all have as much as we wanted. There would be no such thing as rich and poor countries—all countries would be infinitely wealthy.

You can see that this science fiction world of complete abundance would have no economic questions. It is the universal fact of scarcity that produces economic questions.

Choice

Faced with scarcity, people must make *choices*. When we cannot have everything that we want, we have to choose among the available alternatives. Because scarcity forces us to choose, economics is sometimes called the science of choice—the science that explains the choices that people make and predicts how changes in circumstances affect their choices.

To make a choice, we balance the benefits of having more of one thing against the costs of having less of something else. Balancing benefits against costs and doing the best within the limits of what is possible is called **optimizing.** There is another word that has a similar meaning—*economizing.* **Economizing** is making the best use of the resources available. Once people have made a choice and have optimized, they cannot have more of *everything*. To get more of one thing means having less of something else. Expressed in another way: In making choices, we face costs. Whatever we choose to do, we could always have chosen to do something else instead.

Opportunity Cost

Economists use the term opportunity cost to emphasize that making choices in the face of scarcity implies a cost. The **opportunity cost** of any action is the best alternative forgone. If you cannot have everything that you want, then you have to choose among the alternatives. The best thing that you choose not to do—the alternative forgone—is the cost of the thing that you choose to do. This is the meaning of opportunity cost. We must be careful to measure opportunity cost accurately. To understand how to do this, let's examine a familiar situation.

You are supposed to attend a lecture at 8:30 on a Monday morning. There are two alternatives to attending this lecture: to stay in bed for an hour or to go jogging for an hour. You cannot, of course, stay in bed *and* go jogging for that one same hour. The opportunity cost of attending the lecture is not the cost of an hour in bed *and* the cost of jogging for an hour. If these are the only two alternatives that you

would contemplate, then you have to decide which one you would do if you did not go to the lecture. The opportunity cost of attending a lecture for a jogger is an hour of exercise; the opportunity cost of attending a lecture for a late sleeper is an hour in bed.

Suppose you always have a muffin and a cup of coffee for breakfast. On the day that you go to your lecture, you pick these items up in the college cafeteria as you race to class. If you did not spend $1.50 every day on your breakfast, you would go to the movies more often than you are now able to afford. The movies that you forgo are the opportunity cost of your breakfast. But they are not part of the opportunity cost of going to class—you spend $1.50 on your breakfast every day whether or not you attend your class.

Not all of the opportunity costs that you incur are the result of your own choices. Sometimes others make choices that impose opportunity costs on you. For example, when you cannot get onto a bus at rush hour, you have to bear the cost of the choices made by all the other people who filled the bus.

Everything has an opportunity cost. In choosing one activity, an individual decides that the cost of that activity—the activity forgone—is worth paying. Scarcity not only implies cost, it implies one other fundamental feature of human life—competition.

Competition and Cooperation

Competition If wants exceed resources, wants must compete against each other for what is available. **Competition** is a contest for command over scarce resources. In the case of the child with $1.00 in pocket money who wants a soft drink and gum that add up to $1.25, the soft drink and gum compete for the $1.00 in her pocket. For the student who has allowed assignments to accumulate, the party and the assignments compete with each other for Saturday night. For the government, defense and social services compete with each other for limited tax dollars.

Scarcity also implies competition between people. If it is not possible to have everything that you want, then you must compete with others for what is available. In modern societies, competition has been organized within a framework of almost universally accepted rules that have evolved. This evolution of rules is itself a direct response to the problem of scarcity. Not all societies, even modern societies, employ identical rules to govern competition. For example, the way that economic life is organized in the United States differs greatly from that in the Soviet Union. In Chapter 38, we will examine these differences and compare alternative economic systems. For now, we will restrict our attention to the rules that govern competition in the United States.

A key rule of competition is that people own what they have acquired through voluntary exchange. People can compete with each other by offering more favorable exchanges—for example, selling something for a lower price or buying something for a higher price. But they cannot compete with each other by simply taking something from someone else.

Cooperation Perhaps you are thinking that scarcity does not make competition inevitable and that cooperation would better solve economic problems. **Cooperation** means working with others to achieve a common end. If instead of competing with each other we cooperated, wouldn't that eliminate economic problems? This line of reasoning is appealing because it emphasizes the possibility that we might be able to solve our economic problems by using reason. Unfortunately, cooperation does not eliminate economic problems, because it does not eliminate scarcity. Cooperation may, though, be one way to get the best use of our scarce resources. Indeed, we cooperate when we agree to rules of the game that limit competition to avoid violence.

Other more specific examples of solving economic problems through cooperation abound. Marriage partners cooperate. Most forms of business also entail cooperation. Workers cooperate with each other on the production line; members of a management team cooperate with each other to design, produce, and market their products; management and workers cooperate; business partners cooperate.

Common as it is, cooperative behavior neither solves the economic problem nor eliminates competition. Almost all cooperative behavior implies some prior competition to find the best individuals with whom to cooperate. Marriage provides a good example. Although marriage is a cooperative affair, unmarried people compete intensely to find a marriage partner. Similarly, although workers and management cooperate with each other, firms compete for the best workers and workers compete for the best employers. Professionals such as lawyers and doctors compete with each other for the best business partners.

Competition does not end when a partner has been found. Groups of people who cooperate together compete with other groups. For example, although a group of lawyers may have formed a partnership and may work together, they will be in competition with other lawyers.

R E V I E W

Economics studies the activities arising from scarcity. Scarcity forces people to make choices. Economists try to understand the choices that people make. To make choices, people optimize. To optimize, they evaluate the costs of alternative actions. We call these opportunity costs, to emphasize that doing one thing removes the opportunity to do something else. Scarcity also implies that people must compete with each other. ■

You now know the types of questions that economists try to answer and that all economic questions and economic activity arise from scarcity. In the following chapters, we are going to study economic activity and discover how a modern economy such as that of the United States works. But before we do that, we need to stand back and take an overview of our economy. What exactly do we mean by "the economy"?

The Economy

What is an economy? How does an economy work? Rather than trying to answer these questions directly, let's begin by asking similar questions but on a more familiar subject. What is an airplane? How does an airplane work?

Without delving into the detail that would satisfy an aeronautical engineer, most of us could take a shot at answering these two questions. We would describe an airplane as a flying machine that transports people and cargo. To explain how an airplane works, we would describe its key components—fuselage (or body), wings, and engines, and also perhaps its flaps, rudder, and control and navigation systems. We would also explain that as powerful engines move the machine forward, its wings create an imbalance in air pressure that lifts it into the air.

This example nicely illustrates four things. First, it is hard to explain what something is without saying what it does. To say that an airplane is a machine does not tell us much. We have to go beyond that and say what the machine is for, and how it works.

Second, it is hard to explain how something works without being able to divide it up into components. Once we have described something in terms of its components, we can explain how those components work and how they interact with each other.

Third, it is hard to explain how something works without leaving out some details. Notice that we did not describe an airplane in all its detail. Instead, we isolated the most important parts in order to explain how the whole works. We did not emphasize the inflight movie system, the seat belts, or the color of the paint on the wings. We supposed that these things were largely, or even totally, irrelevant to an explanation of how an airplane works.

Fourth and finally, there are different levels of understanding how something works. We gave a superficial account of how an airplane works. An aeronautical engineer would have given a deeper explanation and experts in the individual components—engines, navigation systems, control system, and so on—would have given an even more detailed and precise explanation than a general engineer.

Now let's return to questions about the economy. What is an economy? How does it work?

What Is an Economy?

An **economy** is a mechanism that allocates scarce resources among competing uses. This mechanism achieves three things:

- What
- How
- For whom

1 *What* goods and services will be produced and in *what* quantities? How many VCRs will be made and how many movie theaters will be built? Will young professionals vacation in Europe or live in large houses? How many high performance cars will be built, and how many trucks and station wagons?

2 *How* will the various goods and services be produced? Will a supermarket operate with three checkout lines and clerks using laser scanners or six checkout lines and clerks keying in prices by hand? Will workers weld station wagons by hand or will robots do the job? Will farmers keep track of their livestock feeding schedules and inventories by using paper and pencil records or personal computers? Will credit card companies use computers to read charge slips in New York or ship paper records to Barbados for hand processing?

3 *For whom* will the various goods and services be produced? The distribution of economic benefits depends on the distribution of income and wealth. Those with a high income and great wealth consume more goods and services than those with low income and little wealth. Who gets to consume what thus depends on income. Will the ski instructor consume more than the lawyer's secretary? Will the people of Hong Kong get to consume more than the people of Ethiopia?

The Economy's Working Parts

To understand how an economy works, we must identify its major working parts and see how they interact with each other. The working parts of an economy and the interrelations between them are illustrated in Fig. 1.1. The working parts of the economy fall into two categories:

- **Decision makers**—any person or organized group of persons that make choices
- **Coordination mechanisms**—arrangements that make the choices of one person or group compatible with the choices of others

Decision Makers   Decision makers fall into three groups:

- Households
- Firms
- Governments

A **household** is any group of people living together as a decision-making unit. Every individ-

Figure 1.1   A Picture of the Economy

The economy has three groups of decision makers: households, firms, and governments. It also has two groups of markets: factor markets and goods markets. Households provide factors of production to both firms and governments through the factor markets. Firms and governments pay households wages, interest, rent, and profits in exchange. Firms supply goods and services to households and to governments through the goods markets. Households and governments pay firms for these goods and services. In addition, governments provide goods and services directly to households and firms. Households and firms pay taxes to governments, and governments make transfer payments—subsidies and benefits—to firms and households. In this figure, money and other expenditures move along the green arrows; goods, services, land, labor, and capital move along the red arrows.

ual in the economy belongs to a household. Some households consist of a single person while others consist either of families or of groups of unrelated individuals, such as two or three students sharing an apartment.

A **firm** is an organization that produces goods and services. All producers are called firms, no matter how big they are or what they produce. Car makers, farmers, banks, and insurance companies are all firms.

A **government** is an organization that has two functions: the provision of goods and services to households and firms and the redistribution of income and wealth. Examples of the goods and services supplied by government are national defense, law enforcement, public health, transportation, and education.

You can see these three groups of decision makers in Fig. 1.1. You can also see in this figure the decisions that they make. Households supply factors of production to firms and governments. **Factors of production** are the economy's productive resources, usually classified under three headings:

• Labor
• Land
• Capital

Labor is the brain-power and muscle-power of human beings; **land** is natural resources of all kinds; **capital** is all the equipment, buildings, tools, and other manufactured goods that can be used in production. Households sell or rent factors of production to firms and governments and receive an income in payment for their supply. Households also receive benefits from the government and pay taxes to the government. With what is left, households buy goods and services produced by firms.

Firms hire factors of production from households and choose how to use them to produce goods and services. They also decide what goods and services to produce and in what quantities. Expenditures by households and governments on goods and services are received by firms. Firms use these receipts to make payments to households for the factors of production supplied. Firms also receive subsidies from and pay taxes to governments.

Governments decide on the scale of purchases of factors of production from households and of goods and services from firms. They also decide on the scale of provision of goods and services to households and firms, as well as on the rates of benefits and subsidies and taxes.

Coordination Mechanisms

Perhaps the most striking thing about the choices made by households, firms, and governments, as illustrated in Fig. 1.1, is that they surely must come into conflict with each other. For example, house-holds choose how much work to do and what type of work to specialize in, but firms choose the type and quantity of labor to employ in the production of various goods and services. In other words, households choose the types and quantities of labor to sell and firms choose the types and quantities of labor to buy. Similarly, in markets for goods and services, households choose the types and quantities of goods and services to buy, while firms choose the types and quantities to sell. Government choices regarding taxes, benefits, subsidies and the provision of goods and services also enter the picture. Taxes taken by the government affect the amount of income that households and firms have available for spending and saving. Also, decisions by firms and households depend on the types and quantities of goods and services governments make available. For example, if the government provides excellent highways but a dilapidated railroad system, households will allocate more of their income to buying motor vehicles and less to buying train rides.

How is it possible for the millions of individual decisions taken by households, firms, and governments to be consistent with each other? What makes households want to sell the same types and quantities of labor that firms want to buy? What happens if the number of households wanting to work as economics professors exceeds the number that universities want to hire? How do firms know what to produce so that households will buy their output? What happens if firms want to sell more hamburgers than households want to buy?

There are two mechanisms that can achieve a coordination of individual economic choices:

• Command mechanism
• Market mechanism

A **command mechanism** is a method of determining *what*, *how*, and *for whom* goods and services are produced, based on the authority of a ruler or ruling body—such as a king or a ruling political party. The best example of a command mechanism in the modern world is in the USSR and some other Eastern European countries. In those economies, a central planning bureau makes decisions about *what* will be produced, *how* it will be produced, and *for whom* it will be produced. We'll study command economies and compare them with other types of economies in the last chapter of this book.

A **market mechanism** is a method of determining *what*, *how*, and *for whom* goods and services are produced, based on individual choices coordinated through markets. In ordinary speech, the word *market* means a place where people buy and sell goods such as fish, meat, fruits, and vegetables. In economics, the word *market* has a more general meaning. A **market** is any arrangement that facilitates the buying and selling (trading) of a good, service, or factor of production.

As an example of a market, consider that in which oil is bought and sold—the world oil market. The world oil market is not a place. It is all the many different institutions, buyers, sellers, brokers and so on who buy and sell oil. The market is a coordination mechanism because it pools together the separate plans of all the individual decision makers who try to buy and sell any particular good. Decision makers do not have to meet in a physical sense. In the modern world, telecommunications have replaced direct contact as the main link between buyers and sellers.

Markets are classified according to the types of things traded in them. Figure 1.1 shows the two types of market. The markets in which goods and services are traded are called **goods markets.** The markets in which factors of production are traded—markets for labor, land, and capital—are called **factor markets.** These markets enable the plans of individual households and firms and the government to be coordinated and made consistent with each other.

The U.S. economy relies extensively on the market as the mechanism for coordinating the plans of individual households and firms. There is, though, an element of command in the U.S. economy. Markets do not operate in isolation of the legal framework established and enforced by the government sector of the economy. In recognition of the role played both by command and market coordination mechanisms, modern economies are referred to as mixed economies. A **mixed economy** is one that uses both market and command mechanisms to coordinate economic activity.

The U.S. economy is a mixed economy but one that relies much more heavily on the market than on a command mechanism. However, actions taken by the government sector modify the allocation of scarce resources, changing *what*, *how*, and *for whom* the various goods and services are produced.

How Market Coordination Works   The market coordinates individual decisions through price adjustments. To see how, think about the market for hamburgers in your local area. Suppose that the quantity of hamburgers being offered for sale is less than the quantity that people would like to buy. Some people who want to buy hamburgers will not be able to do so. To make the choices of buyers and sellers compatible, buyers will have to scale down their appetites and more hamburgers will have to be offered for sale. An increase in the price of hamburgers will produce this outcome. A higher price will encourage producers to offer more hamburgers for sale. It will also curb the appetite for hamburgers and change some lunch plans. Fewer people will buy hamburgers and more will buy hot dogs (or some other alternative to hamburgers). More hamburgers (and more hot dogs) will be offered for sale.

Now imagine the opposite situation. More hamburgers are available than people want to buy. In this case, the price is too high. A lower price will discourage the production and sale of hamburgers, and encourage their purchase and consumption. Decisions to produce and sell, and to buy and consume, are continuously adjusted and kept in balance with each other by adjustments in prices.

In some cases, prices get stuck or fixed. When this happens, some other adjustment has to make the plans and choices of individuals consistent. Customers waiting in lines and stocks of inventories operate as a temporary safety valve when the market price is stuck. If people want to buy more than the quantity that firms have decided to sell, and if the price is temporarily fixed, then one of two things will have to happen. Firms wind up selling more than they would like and their inventories will shrink; or, lines of customers will develop and only those who get to the head of the line before the goods run out will be able to make a purchase. The longer the line or the bigger the decline in inventories, the more prices will have to adjust to keep buying and selling decisions in balance.

We have now seen how the market solves the question of *what* quantity to produce—how many hamburgers to make. The market also solves the question of *how* to produce in similar fashion. For example, hamburger producers can use gas, electric power, or charcoal to cook their hamburgers.

Figure 1.2   International Linkages

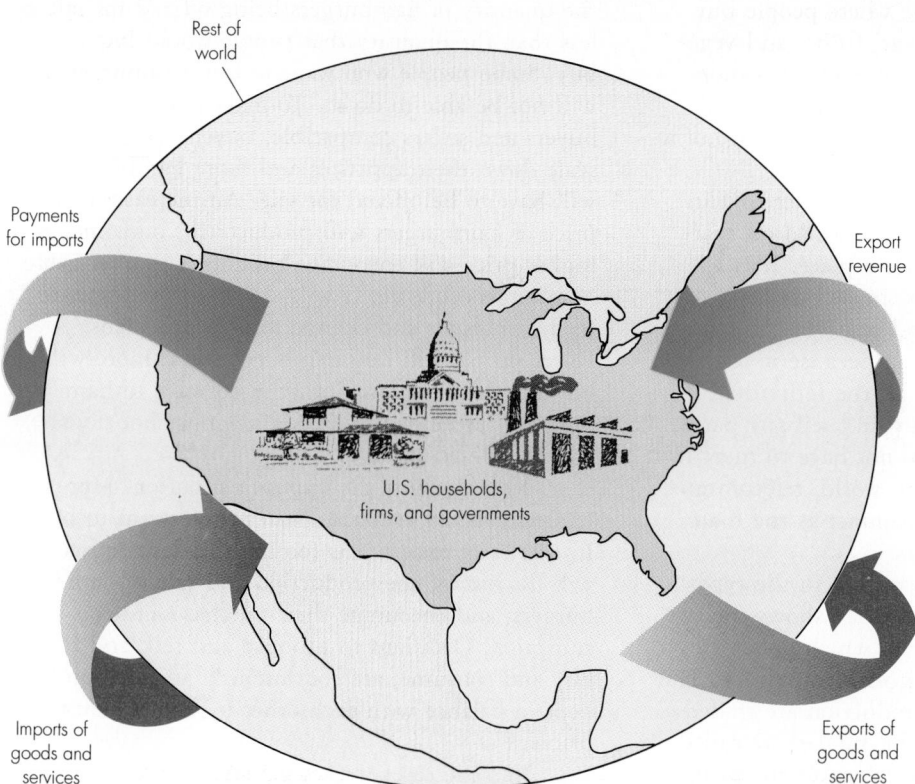

The U.S. economy exports and imports goods and services. It receives a flow of revenue from its exports of goods and services and makes payments for imports. The difference between these two flows is the country's net foreign borrowing or lending. In recent years, the United States has been a net borrower.

Rest of world

Payments for imports

Export revenue

U.S. households, firms, and governments

Imports of goods and services

Exports of goods and services

Which fuel is used depends in part on the flavor that the producer wants to achieve and on the cost of the different fuels. If a fuel becomes very expensive, as did oil in the 1970s, less of it will be used and more of other fuels will be used in its place. By substituting one fuel for another as the costs of the different fuels change, the market solves the question of how to produce.

Finally, the market helps solve the question of *for whom* to produce. Skills, talents, and resources that are in very short supply will command a higher price than those in greater abundance. The owners of rare resources and skills will obtain a larger share of the output of the economy than the owners of those resources in abundant supply.

Closed and Open Economies

The economy depicted in Fig. 1.1 is a closed one. A **closed economy** is one that has no links with any other economy. The only truly closed economy is that of the entire world. The U.S. economy is an open economy. An **open economy** is one that has economic links with other economies. Firms in an open economy export some of their production to other countries, rather than selling only to households within their own country. Firms, households, and governments in an open economy also buy some of the goods and services that they use from firms in other countries. These imports and exports of goods and services are illustrated in Fig. 1.2.

The total values of exports and imports are not necessarily equal to each other. The difference between those two values is the net amount that a country lends to or borrows from the rest of the world.

In the United States, there has been a deficit on international payments in recent years, with the government borrowing more than $100 billion each year. The consequence of our importing more goods and services than we export is that the United States is a net borrower from—not a net lender to—the rest of the world. We will study the international linkages between the U.S. economy and the rest of the world later in this book.

R E V I E W

An economy is a mechanism that determines what is produced, how it is produced, and for whom it is produced. In the U.S. economy, these choices are made by households, firms, and government, and they are coordinated through markets. Governments influence these choices by taxing, subsidizing, regulating, and lawmaking. The U.S. economy is an open economy, having extensive links with other economies. ∎

We have now described an economy in about as much detail as we described an airplane. But we're about to become the economic equivalent of aeronautical engineers! We're going to build economies that fly! To do that, we have to understand the principles of economics as thoroughly as aeronautical engineers understand the principles of flight. To discover these principles, economists approach their work with the rigor and objectivity of natural scientists—they do economic science.

Economic Science

Economic science, like the natural sciences (such as physics and biology) and the other social sciences (such as political science, psychology, and sociology), is an attempt to find a body of laws of nature. All sciences have two components:

- Careful and systematic observation and measurement
- Development of a body of theory to direct and interpret observations

All sciences are careful to distinguish between two types of statements:

- Statements about what *is*
- Statements about what *ought* to be

What Is and What Ought to Be

Statements about what *is* are **positive statements.** Statements about what *ought* to be are **normative statements.** Let's illustrate the distinction between positive and normative statements with two examples.

First, consider the controversy over the Strategic Defense Initiative, or "Star Wars." The question *Is it possible* to build an effective strategic defense system? is positive. The question *Ought* we to try to build a strategic defense system? is normative. Second, consider the economic controversy over tax cuts and cutbacks on social programs. The question *Will* lower taxes and less generous social programs make people work harder? is positive. The question *Should* taxes and social programs be cut? is normative.

Science—whether natural, social, or economic—tries to discover and catalog positive statements that are consistent with what we observe in the world. Science is silent on normative questions. It is not that such questions are unimportant. On the contrary, they are often the most important questions of all. Nor is it that scientists as people do not have opinions on such questions. It is simply that the activity of doing science cannot settle a normative matter and the possession of scientific knowledge does not equip a person with superior moral precepts or norms. A difference of opinion on a positive matter can ultimately be settled by careful observation and measurement. A difference of opinion on a normative matter cannot be settled in that way. In fact, there are no well-defined rules for settling a normative dispute and sometimes reasonable people simply have to agree to disagree.

When they cannot, political and judicial institutions intervene in order for decisions to be made. We settle normative disagreements in the political, not the scientific, arena. The scientific community can, and often does, contribute to the normative debates of political life. But science is a distinct activity. Even though scientists have opinions about what ought to be, those opinions have no part in science itself.

Now let's see how economists attempt to discover and catalog positive statements that are consistent with their observations and that enable them to answer economic questions such as the seven big questions that we reviewed earlier.

Observation and Measurement

Economic phenomena can be observed and measured in great detail. For example, we can catalog the amounts and locations of natural and human resources. We can describe who does what kind of work, for how many hours, and how they are paid. We can catalog the things that people produce, consume, and store, and their prices. We can describe in detail who borrows and who lends and at what interest rates. We can also catalog the things that government taxes and at what rates, the programs it finances and at what cost.

Our list is not exhaustive. It gives a flavor, though, of the array of things that economists can describe through careful observation and measurement of economic activity.

In today's world, computers have given us access to an enormous volume of economic description. Government agencies around the world, national statistical bureaus, private economic consultants, banks, investment advisors, and research economists working in universities generate an astonishing amount of information about economic behavior.

But economists do more than observe and measure economic activity, crucial as that is. Describing something is not the same as understanding it. You can describe your digital watch in great detail, but that does not mean you can explain what makes it work. Understanding what makes things work requires the discovery of laws. That is the main task of economists—the discovery of laws governing economic behavior. How do economists go about this task?

Economic Theory

We can describe in great detail the ups and downs, or cycles, in unemployment, but can we explain *why* unemployment fluctuates? We can describe the fall in the price of a VCR or a pocket calculator and the dramatic increase in its use, but can we explain the low price and popularity of such items? Did the fall in the price lead more people to use pocket calculators, or did their popularity lower the costs of production and make it possible to lower the price? Or did something else cause both the fall in the price and the increase in use?

Questions like these can be answered only by developing a body of economic theory. An **economic theory** is a reliable generalization that enables us to understand and predict the economic choices that people make. We develop economic theories by building and testing economic models. What is an economic model?

Economic Model

You have just seen an economic model. To answer the question What is an economy and how does it work? we built a model of an economy. We did not describe in all its detail all the economic actions that take place in the United States. We concentrated our attention only on those features that seemed important for understanding economic choices, and ignored everything else. You will perhaps better appreciate what we mean by an economic model if you think about more familiar models.

We have all seen model trains, cars, and airplanes. Although we do not usually call dolls and stuffed animals models, we can think of them in this way. Architects make models of buildings, and biologists make models of DNA (the double helix carrier of the genetic code).

A model is usually smaller than the real thing that it represents. But models are not always smaller in scale (e.g., the biologist's model of the components of cells) and, in any case, the scale of a model is not its most important feature. A model also shows less detail than its counterpart in reality. For example, all the models we have mentioned resemble the real thing in *appearance*, but they are not usually made of the same substance nor do they work like the real thing that they represent. The architect's model of a new high-rise shows us what the building will look like and how it will conform with the buildings around it—but it does not contain plumbing, telephone cables, elevator shafts, air conditioning plants, and other interior workings.

All the models that we have discussed (including those that are typically used as toys) represent something that is real, but they lack some key features. The model abstracts from the detail of the real thing. It includes only those features needed for the purpose at hand. It leaves out the inessential or unnecessary. What a model includes and what it leaves out is not arbitrary; it results from a conscious and careful decision.

The models that we have just considered are all "physical" models. We can see the real thing and we can see the model. Indeed, the purpose of those models is to enable us to "visualize" the real thing. Some models, including economic models, are not physical. We cannot look at the real thing and look at the model and simply decide whether the model is a good or bad representation of the real thing. But the idea of a model as an abstraction from reality still applies to an economic model.

An economic model has two components:

- Assumptions
- Implications

Assumptions form the foundation on which a model is built. They are propositions about what is important and what can be ignored; about what can be treated as being constant and, therefore, reliably used to make predictions.

Implications are the outcome of a model. The link between a model's assumptions and its implications is a process of logical deduction.

Let's illustrate these components of a model by building a simple model of your daily journey to school. The model has three assumptions:

1 Class begins at 9:00 A.M.
2 The bus ride takes 30 minutes.
3 The walk from the bus to class takes five minutes.

The implication of this model is that to be in class on time, you have to be on the bus by 8:25 A.M.

The assumptions of a model depend on the model's purpose. The purpose of an economic model is to understand how people make choices in the face of scarcity. Thus in building an economic model, we abstract from the rich detail of human behavior and focus only on behavior that is relevant for coping with scarcity. Everything else is ignored. Economists know that people fall in love and form deep friendships; that they experience great joy and security or great pain and anxiety. But economists assume that in seeking to understand economic behavior, they may build models that ignore many aspects of life. They focus on one and only one feature of the world: People have wants that exceed their resources and so, by their choices, have to make the best of things.

Assumptions of an Economic Model   Economic models are based on four key assumptions:

1 *People have preferences.* Economists use the term **preferences** to denote likes and dislikes and the intensity of those likes and dislikes. People can judge whether one situation is better, worse, or just as good as another one. For example, you can judge whether for you, one loaf of bread and no cheese is better, worse, or just as good as a half a loaf of bread and four ounces of cheese.

2 *People are endowed with a fixed amount of resources and a technology that can transform those resources into goods and services.* Economists use the term **endowment** to refer to the resources that people have and the term **technology** to describe the methods of converting those endowments into goods and services.

3 *People economize.* They choose how to use their endowments and technologies in order to make themselves as well-off as possible. Such a choice is called a rational choice. A **rational choice** is the best possible course of action from the point of view of the person making the choice. Each choice, no matter what it is or how foolish it may seem to an observer, is interpreted, in an economic model, as a rational choice.

Choices are made on the basis of the information available. With hindsight, and with more information, people may well feel that some of their past choices were bad ones. This fact does not make such choices irrational. Again, a rational choice is the best possible course of action, from the point of view of the person making the choice, given that person's preferences and *given the information available when the choice is made.*

4 *People's choices are coordinated.* One person's choice to buy something must be matched by another person's choice to sell that same thing. One person's choice to work at a particular job must be matched by another person's choice to hire someone to do that job. The coordination of individual choices is made either by a market mechanism or a command mechanism.

Implications of an Economic Model   The implications of an economic model are the equilibrium values of various prices and quantities. An **equilibrium** is a situation in which everyone has economized—that is, all individuals have made the best possible choices in the light of their own preferences and given their endowments, technologies, and information—and in which those choices have been coordinated and made compatible with the choices of everyone else. Equilibrium is the solution or outcome of an economic model.

The term equilibrium conjures up the picture of a balance of opposing forces. For example, a balance scale can be said to be in equilibrium if a pound of butter is placed on one side of the balance and a one-pound weight is placed on the other side. The two weights exactly equal each other and so offset each other, leaving the balance arm horizontal. A soap bubble provides another excellent physical illustration of equilibrium. The delicate spherical film of soap is held in place by a balance of forces of the air inside the sphere and the air outside it.

This second physical analogy illustrates a further important feature of an equilibrium. An equilibrium is not necessarily static but may be dynamic—constantly changing. By squeezing or stretching the bubble, you can change its shape, but its shape is always determined by the balance of the forces acting upon it (including the forces that you exert upon it).

An economic equilibrium has a great deal in common with that of the soap bubble. First, it is in a constant state of motion. At each point in time, each person makes the best possible choice, given the endowments and actions of others. But changing circumstances alter those choices. For example, on a busy day in Manhattan, there are more cars looking for parking spaces than the number of spaces available. In this situation, the equilibrium number of free spaces is zero. But people do get to park. Individual cars are leaving and arriving at a

"*And now a traffic update: A parking space has become available on Sixty-fifth Street between Second and Third. Hold it! A bulletin has just been handed me. That space has been taken.*"

Drawing by H. Martin; © 1987 The New Yorker Magazine, Inc.

steady pace. As soon as one car vacates a parking space, another instantly fills it. Being in equilibrium does not mean that everyone gets to park instantly. There is an equilibrium amount of time spent finding a vacant space. People hunting for a space are frustrated and experience rising blood pressure and increased anger. But there is still an equilibrium in the hunt for available parking spaces.

Similarly, an economic equilibrium does not mean that everyone is experiencing economic prosperity. The constraints may be such that some people are very poor. Nevertheless, given their preferences, endowments, the available technologies, and the actions of everyone else, each person has made the best possible choice and sees no advantage in modifying his or her current action.

Microeconomic and Macroeconomic Models

Economic models fall into two categories: microeconomic and macroeconomic. **Microeconomics** is the branch of economics that studies the decisions of individual households and firms. Microeconomics also studies the way that individual markets work and the detailed way that regulation and taxes affect the allocation of labor and of goods and services.

Macroeconomics is the branch of economics that studies the economy as a whole. It seeks to understand the big picture rather than the detailed individual choices. In particular, it studies the determination of the overall level of economic activity—of unemployment, aggregate income, average prices, and inflation.

Of the seven big questions, those dealing with technological change, production and consumption, and wages and earnings are microeconomic. Those dealing with unemployment, inflation, and differences in wealth among nations are macroeconomic.

Model, Theory, and Reality

People who build models often get carried away and start talking as if their model *is* the real world—as if their model is reality. No matter how useful it is, there is no sense in which a model can be said to be reality.

A model is an abstract entity. It lists assumptions and their implications. When economists talk about people who have made themselves as well-off as possible, they are not talking about real people. They are talking about artificial people in an economic model. Do not lose sight of this important but easily misunderstood fact.

Economic theory bridges the gap between an economic model and the real world. Economic theory proposes that the economic behavior of people in actual economies can be predicted by using models in which people who make rational choices interact with each other in an equilibrium. Economics develops models based on this idea to explain all aspects of economic behavior. But economic models have to be tested.

To test an economic model, its implications are matched against actual events in the real world. That is, the model is used to make predictions about the real world. The model's predictions may correspond to or be in conflict with the facts. It is by comparing the model's predictions with the facts that we are able to test a model. The process of developing economic theories by using models is illustrated in Fig. 1.3. We begin by building a model. The model's implications are used to generate predictions about the world. These predictions and their test form the basis of a theory. When predictions are in conflict with the facts, either a theory is discarded in favor of a superior alternative

Figure 1.3   How Theories Are Developed

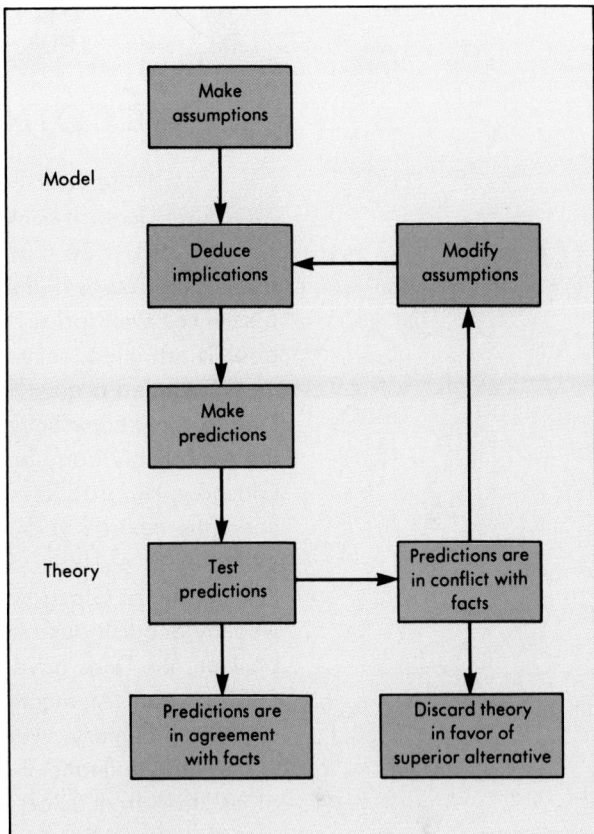

Economic theories are developed by building and testing economic models. An economic model is a set of *assumptions* about what is important and what can be ignored and the *implications* of those assumptions. The implications of a model form the basis of *predictions* about the world. These predictions are tested by being checked against the facts. If the predictions are in conflict with the facts, either the theory is discarded in favor of a superior alternative or the model-building process begins anew with modified assumptions. It is only when predictions are in agreement with the facts that a useful theory has been developed.

or we return to the model building stage, modifying our assumptions and creating a new model. Economics itself provides guidance on how we might discover a better model. It prompts us to look for some aspect of preferences, endowments, technology, or the coordination mechanism that has been overlooked.

Adam Smith and the Birth of Economic Science

I n the year that colonists in far-off America revolted against Britain, a Scottish thinker touched off a different kind of revolution. For it was in 1776 that Adam Smith published *An Inquiry into the Nature and Causes of the Wealth of Nations*, the book that began economics as a science. Even today, more than two hundred years after its publication, the book is reprinted, reinterpreted, and reread repeatedly.

Smith led a quiet, scholarly life. He was born in 1723 in Kirkaldy, Scotland, a small community near Edinburgh where he spent his first 14 years. At the remarkably early age of 14, he became a student at the University of Glasgow. He graduated at 17 and then went on to Oxford University where he spent the next six years. His first major academic appointment, at age 28, was as Professor of Logic, and subsequently as Professor of Logic and Moral Philosophy, at Glasgow. After 13 years at Glasgow, Smith became a tutor to a wealthy Scottish duke who lived in France. After Smith spent two years in that position, the Duke gave him a pension—an income for the rest of his life—of £300 a year. (An income of this size would have bought a great deal in the eighteenth century, when the average wage was about £30 a year.)

With the financial security of a pension, Smith devoted the next ten years of his life—from 1766 to 1776—to his great treatise. He was writing his

Adam Smith

Wealth of Nations at a time when the British economy was undergoing what came to be called the Industrial Revolution. New technologies were being invented and applied to the manufacture of cotton and wool, iron, transportation, and agriculture. The prevailing intellectual climate held that Britain needed to be protected from cheap foreign imports so that the nation could build up its stock of gold and finance its continuing process of industrialization.

Smith scoffed at this idea and developed a massive case against protection and in favor of "free trade." *The Wealth of Nations* argued that when each person makes the best economic choice possible, that choice leads, as if by "an invisible hand," to the best economic outcome for society as a whole. This best possible social outcome arises not because people pay attention to the needs of others but from self-interest. Said Smith, "It is not from the benevolence of

22

the butcher, the brewer, or the baker, that we can expect our dinner, but from their regard to their own interest.''*

The Wealth of Nations proposed that all economic behavior can be understood as the rational pursuit of self-interest. The book begins much like the one that you are now studying, but much more profoundly, for Smith's was the first systematic treatment of these ideas. Smith explained how specialization, exchange, and the development of money lead to massive increases in goods and services. He applied his basic theory to a sweep of human history, starting from the fall of the Roman Empire. He explained the rise and progress of towns and cities, how commerce between towns and farmlands benefits both, and why free international trade leads to improved living standards. He also applied the theory of rational self-interest to explain why the universities of the eighteenth century were organized not for the benefit of the students but, as he put it, ''for the ease of the professors.'' He even used his theory to explain the proliferation of new religions.

Many thinkers had written earlier on economic questions, but Smith was the first to make a science of economics.

> It was Smith who provided so broad and authoritative an account of the known economic doctrine that henceforth it was no longer permissible for any subsequent writer on economics to advance his own ideas while ignoring the state of general knowledge. A science consists of interacting practitioners, and henceforth no one could decently ignore Smith's own work and in due time the work of Malthus, Ricardo, and the galaxy of economists who populated the first half of the nineteenth century.**

This first box on our advancing knowledge in economic science has been devoted to Adam Smith, who stands alone as the founder of this discipline. Subsequent boxes in this series will give you a taste of how various branches of the subject have advanced from this founding father through to the present. The goal is to enable you to see how the science of economics advances and perhaps even to inspire you to become one of that community of scholars seeking to deepen our understanding of economic phenomena.

*Adam Smith, *An Inquiry into the Nature and Causes of the Wealth of Nations*, ed. Edwin Cannan, with a new preface by George J. Stigler (Chicago: University of Chicago Press, 1976), p. 18.
**George J. Stigler, ''Nobel Lecture: The Process and Progress of Economics,'' *Journal of Political Economy* 91 (August 1983): 529–45.

Economics is a young science and a long way from having achieved its goal. Its birth can be dated fairly precisely in the eighteenth century with the publication of Adam Smith's *The Wealth of Nations* (see Our Advancing Knowledge, p. 22). In the closing years of the twentieth century, economic science has managed to discover a sizable number of useful generalizations. In many areas, however, we are still going around the circle—changing assumptions, performing new logical deductions, generating new predictions, and getting wrong answers yet again. The gradual accumulation of correct answers gives most practitioners some faith that their methods will, eventually, provide usable answers to the big economic questions.

As we make progress, though, more and more things become clearer and seem to fit together. Theoretical advances lead to deeper understanding. This feature of economics is shared with scientists in all fields. As Albert Einstein, the great physicist, said: "Creating a new theory is not like destroying an old barn and erecting a skyscraper in its place. It is rather like climbing a mountain, gaining new and wider views, discovering new connections between our starting point and its rich environment. But the point from which we started still exists and can be seen, although it appears smaller and forms a tiny part of our broad view gained by the mastery of the obstacles on our adventurous way up."[1]

■ In the next chapter, we will study some of the tools that economists use to build economic models. Then, in Chapter 3, we'll build an economic model and use that model to understand the world around us and to start to answer some of the seven big economic questions.

---

[1]These words are attributed to Einstein in a letter by Oliver Sacks to *The Listener* 88, no. 2279, 30 Nov. 1972, 756.

SUMMARY

Seven Big Questions

Economics tries to answer difficult questions that affect our daily lives. These questions concern the production and consumption of goods and services; wages and earnings; unemployment; inflation; government spending, taxation, and regulation; international trade; and the distribution of wealth and poverty in the United States and throughout the world. There are no easy answers to the big economic questions, which must be approached in a scientific manner. (pp. 6–8)

Scarcity

All economic questions arise from the fundamental fact of scarcity. Scarcity means that wants exceed resources. Human wants are effectively unlimited but the resources available to satisfy them are finite.

Economic activity is what people do to cope with scarcity. Scarcity forces people to make choices. Making the best choice possible from what is available is called optimizing. In order to make the best possible choice, a person weighs the costs and benefits of the alternatives.

Opportunity cost is the cost of one choice in terms of the best forgone alternative. The opportunity cost of any action is the best alternative action that could have been undertaken in its place. Attending class instead of staying in bed has an opportunity cost—the cost of one hour of rest.

Scarcity forces people to compete with each other for scarce resources. People may cooperate in certain areas, but all economic activity ultimately results in competition among individuals acting alone or in groups. (pp. 9–11)

The Economy

The economy is a mechanism that allocates scarce resources among competing uses, determining *what*, *how*, and *for whom* the various goods and services will be produced.

The economy's working parts are divided into two categories: decision makers and coordination mechanisms. Economic decision makers are households, firms, and governments. Households decide how much of their factors of production to sell to firms and government, and what goods and services to buy from firms. Firms decide what factors of production to hire and which goods and services to produce. Governments decide on the scale of purchases of factors of production from households and of goods and services from firms. They also decide on the scale of provision of goods and services to households and firms, as well as on the rates of benefits and subsidies and taxes.

There are two types of coordination mechanisms: the command mechanism and the market mechanism. The U.S. economy relies mainly on the market mechanism, but the actions taken by the government sector do modify the allocation of scarce resources. The U.S. economy is therefore a mixed economy. (pp. 11–17)

Economic Science

Economic science, like the natural sciences and the other social sciences, attempts to find a body of

laws of nature. Economic science seeks to understand what *is* and is silent about what *ought* to be. Economists try to find economic laws by developing a body of economic theory, and economic theory, in turn, is developed by building and testing economic models. Economic models are abstract, logical constructions that contain two components: assumptions and implications. An economic model has four key assumptions:

1 People have preferences.
2 People have a given endowment of resources and technology.
3 People economize.
4 Peoples' choices are coordinated through market or command mechanisms.

The implications of an economic model are the equilibrium values of various prices and quantities that result from each individual doing the best that is possible, given the individual's preferences, endowments, information, and technology and given the coordination mechanism. (pp. 17–24)

K E Y   C O N C E P T S

Key Figure

R E V I E W   Q U E S T I O N S

1 Give two examples, different from those in the chapter, that illustrate each of the seven big economic questions.

2 Why does scarcity force us to make choices?

3 What do we mean by "rational choice"? Give examples of rational and irrational choices.

4 Why does scarcity force us to optimize?

5 Why does optimization require us to calculate costs?

6 Why does scarcity imply competition?

7 Why can't we solve economic problems by co-operating with each other?

8 Name the main economic decision makers.

9 List the economic decisions made by households, firms, and governments.

10 What is the difference between a command mechanism and a market mechanism?

11 Distinguish between positive and normative statements by listing three examples of each type of statement.

12 What are the four key assumptions of an economic model?

13 Explain the difference between a model and a theory.

P R O B L E M S

1 Which of the following are part of your opportunity cost of attending school? Explain why they are or are not.

   a) The money you spend on haircuts

   b) The vacation you would have taken if you had been working rather than being in school

   c) The tapes and compact discs that you don't have because you've had to spend so much on economics textbooks

   d) The amount you pay for your lunch in the college cafeteria each week

   e) The $20,000 annual salary you could have made in your Uncle Fred's store

2 List some examples of opportunity costs that you have incurred today.

3 Give some examples of opportunity costs you incurred that are the results of someone else's actions. Give some examples of opportunity costs incurred by someone else that are the result of your actions.

4 Which of the following statements are positive and which are normative?

   a) Low rents will restrict the supply of housing.

   b) High interest rates lower the demand for mortgages and new homes.

   c) No family ought to have to pay more than one quarter of its income to rent decent housing.

   d) Owners of apartment buildings ought to be free to charge whatever rent they like.

   e) The government ought to restrict the rents that apartment owners are allowed to charge.

5 You have been hired by a company that makes and markets tapes, records, and compact discs. Your employer is going to start selling these products in a new market that has a population of 100 million people. A survey has revealed that 40 percent of this market buys only popular music and 5 percent of it buys only classical music. No one buys both types of music. The average income of the pop music fan is $10,000 a year and that of the classical fan is $50,000 a year. It has also been discovered that people with low incomes spend one quarter of 1 percent of their income on tapes, records, and CDs while those with high incomes spend 2 percent of theirs. You have been asked to predict how much is likely to be spent in this market on pop music and classical music in one year.

   Build a model to answer this question. List your assumptions and work out their implications. Draw attention to the potential for unreliablility in your answers. Why might your model give wrong answers?

Chapter 2

**Making and
Using Graphs**

*After studying this
chapter, you will be
able to:*

- Make and interpret a
time-series graph and a
scatter diagram

- Distinguish between linear
and nonlinear relation-
ships and relationships
that have a maximum and
a minimum

- Define and calculate the
slope of a line

- Graph relationships
among more than two
variables

Benjamin Disraeli, British prime minister in the late nineteenth century, is reputed to have said that there are three kinds of lies: lies, damned lies, and statistics. One of the most powerful ways of conveying statistical information is in the form of a picture—a graph. Thus graphs, too, like statistics, can tell lies. But the right graph does not lie. Indeed, it reveals data and helps its viewer to see and think about relationships that would otherwise be obscure. ■ Graphs are a surprisingly modern invention. The first graphs appeared in the late eighteenth century, long after the discovery of mathematically sophisticated ideas such as logarithms and calculus. But today, especially in the age of the personal computer and the video display, graphs have

Three Kinds of Lies

become almost more important than words. The ability to make and use graphs is as important as the ability to read and write. ■ How do economists use graphs? What are the different types of graphs that economists use? What do economic graphs reveal and what can they hide? What are the main pitfalls that can result in a graph that lies? ■ It will be clear to you from the seven big questions that you studied in Chapter 1 that the problems that economics seeks to solve are difficult ones. You will also suspect, and rightly so, that hardly anything in economics has a single cause. Variations in the quantity of ice cream consumed are not caused merely by variations in the air temperature or in the price of cream but by at least these two factors and probably several others as well. How can we draw graphs of relationships that involve several variables, all of which vary simultaneously? How can we interpret such relationships? ■ In this chapter, we are going to look at the different kinds of graphs that are used in economics. We are going to learn how to make them and read them.

We are going to look at examples of useful graphs as well as misleading graphs. We are also going to study how we can calculate the strength of the effect of one variable on another.

There are no graphs or techniques used in this book that are more complicated than those explained and described in this chapter. If you are already familiar with graphs, you may want to skip or at least only skim this chapter. Whether you study this chapter thoroughly or give it a quick pass, you should regard it as a handy reference chapter to which you can return if you feel that you need additional help understanding the graphs that you encounter in your study of economics.

Graphing Data

Graphs represent a quantity as a distance. Figure 2.1 gives two examples. Part (a) shows temperature, measured in degrees Fahrenheit, as the distance on a scale. Movements from left to right represent increases in temperature. Movements from right to left represent decreases in temperature. The point marked zero represents zero degrees Fahrenheit. To the right of zero, the temperatures are positive. To the left of zero, the temperatures are negative (as indicated by the minus sign in front of the numbers).

Figure 2.1(b) provides another example. This time altitude, or height, is measured in thousands of feet above sea level. The point marked zero represents sea level. Points to the right of zero represent feet above sea level. Points to the left of zero (indicated by a minus sign) represent depths below sea level.

There are no rigid rules about the scale for a graph. The scale is determined by the range of the variable being graphed and the space available for the graph.

The two graphs in Fig. 2.1 show just a single variable. Marking a point on either of the two scales indicates a particular temperature or a particular height. Thus the point marked *a* represents 32°F, the freezing point of water. The point marked *b* represents 20,320 feet, the height of Mount McKinley, the highest mountain in North America.

Graphing a single variable as we have done does not usually reveal much. Graphs become powerful when they show how two variables are related to each other.

Figure 2.1   Graphing a Single Variable

(a) Temperature

(b) Height

All graphs have a scale that measures a quantity as a distance. The two scales here measure temperature and height. Numbers to the right of zero are positive. Numbers to the left of zero are negative.

Two-Variable Graphs

To construct a two-variable graph, we set two scales perpendicular to each other. Let's continue to use the same two variables as those in Fig. 2.1. We will measure temperature in exactly the same way, but we will turn the height scale to a vertical position. Thus temperature is measured exactly as it was before but height is now represented by movements up and down a vertical scale.

The two scale lines in Fig. 2.2 are called **axes.** The vertical line is called the **y-axis** and the horizontal line is called the **x-axis.** The letters *x* and *y* appear on the axes of Fig. 2.2. Each axis has a zero point shared by the two axes. The zero point, common to both axes, is called the **origin.**

To represent something in a two-variable graph, we need two pieces of information. For example, Mount McKinley is 20,320 feet high and, on a particular day, the temperature at its peak is 20°F. We can represent this information in Fig. 2.2 by marking the height of the mountain on the *y*-axis at 20,320 feet and the temperature on the *x*-axis at 20°F. We can now identify the values of the two variables that appear on the axes by marking point *c*.

Two lines, called coordinates, can be drawn from point *c*. **Coordinates** are lines running from a point on a graph perpendicularly to its axis. The line

Figure 2.2   Graphing Two Variables

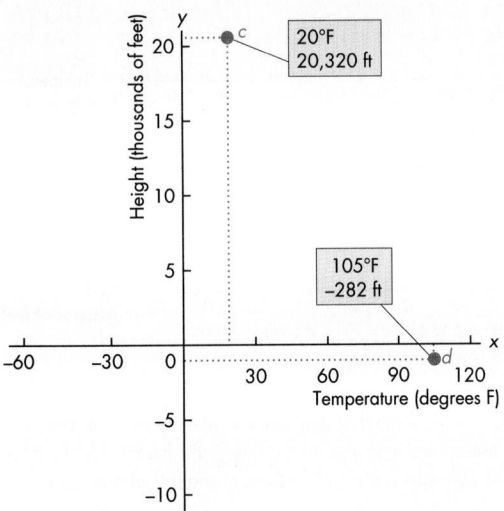

The relationship between two variables is graphed by forming two axes perpendicular to each other. Height is measured here on the y-axis and temperature on the x-axis. Point c represents the top of Mt. McKinley, 20,320 feet above sea level (measured on the y-axis), with a temperature of 20°F (measured on the x-axis). Point d represents Death Valley, 282 feet below sea level, with a temperature of 105°F.

running from *c* to the *x*-axis is the **y-coordinate**, because its length is the same as the value marked off on the *y*-axis. Similarly, the line running from *c* to the vertical axis is the **x-coordinate**, because its length is the same as the value marked off on the *x*-axis.

Now let's leave the top of Mount McKinley, at 20,320 feet and 20°F, and go to Death Valley in the Mojave Desert, the lowest point in the United States at 282 feet *below* sea level. Death Valley is represented by point *d*, which shows that we are 282 feet below sea level (the *y*-coordinate) and that the temperature is 105°F (the *x*-coordinate).

Economists use graphs similar to this one in a variety of ways. Let's look at two examples.

Time-Series Graphs

One of the most common and powerful graphs used in economics is the time-series graph. A **time-series**

graph measures time (for example, in years or months) on the *x*-axis and the variable or variables in which we are interested on the *y*-axis.

Figure 2.3 illustrates a time-series graph. Time is measured in years on the *x*-axis. The variable that we are interested in—the U.S. unemployment rate (the percentage of the labor force unemployed)—is measured on the *y*-axis. The time-series graph conveys an enormous amount of information quickly and easily:

1   It tells us the *level* of the unemployment rate—when it is *high* and *low*. When the line is a long way from the *x*-axis, the unemployment rate is high. When the line is close to the *x*-axis, the unemployment rate is low.

2   It tells us how the unemployment rate *changes*—whether it *rises* or *falls*. When the line slopes upward, as in the early 1930s, the unemployment rate is rising. When the line slopes downward, as in the early 1940s, the unemployment rate is falling.

3   It tells us the *speed* with which the unemployment rate is *changing*—whether it is rising or falling *quickly* or *slowly*. If the line rises or falls very steeply, then unemployment is changing quickly. If the line is not steep, unemployment is rising or falling slowly. For example, unemployment rose sharply between 1930 and 1932. Unemployment went up again in 1933 but more slowly. Similarly, when unemployment was falling in the early 1950s, it fell quickly between 1950 and 1951, but then it began to fall much more gently in 1952 and 1953.

A time-series graph can also be used to depict a trend. A **trend** is a general tendency for a variable to rise or fall. You can see that unemployment had a general tendency to rise from the mid-1940s to the mid-1980s. That is, although there were ups and downs in the unemployment rate, there was an upward trend.

Graphs also allow us to compare different periods quickly. It is apparent, for example, that the 1930s were different from any other period in the twentieth century because of exceptionally high unemployment. You can also see that unemployment fluctuated more violently in the years before 1920 than it did in the years since 1950. The sawtooth pattern is more jagged in the period from 1900 to 1930 than it is in the period after 1950.

Figure 2.3   A Time-Series Graph

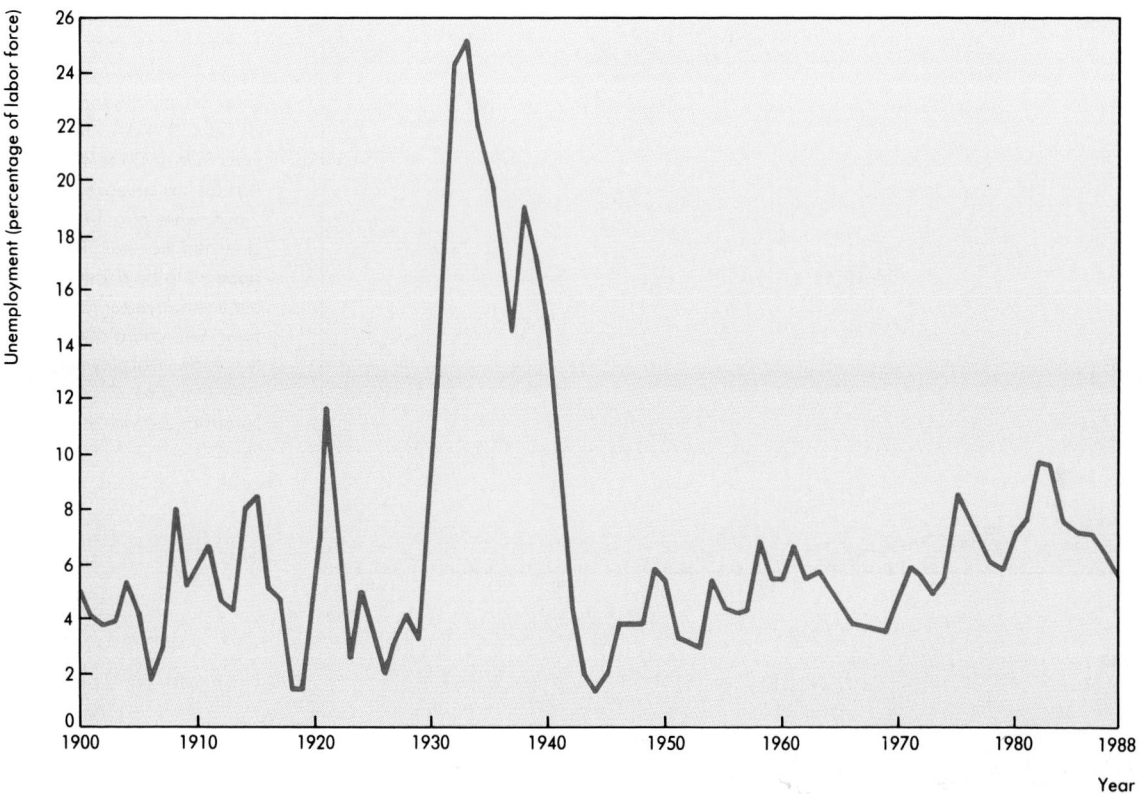

A time-series graph plots the level of a variable on the y-axis against time (day, week, month, or year) on the x-axis. This graph shows the U.S. unemployment rate each year from 1900 to 1988.

We can thus see that not only does Fig. 2.3 convey a wealth of information, it does so in a much shorter space than we have used to describe only some of its features.

Misleading Time-Series Graphs   Although time-series graphs are powerful devices for conveying a large amount of information, they can also be used to distort data and to create a misleading picture.

One common way of misleading is to place two graphs that have different scales, side by side. Figure 2.4 provides an illustration. This figure contains exactly the same information as Fig. 2.3, but the information is packaged in a different way. In part (a), the scale on the y-axis has been compressed; in part (b), it has been expanded. When we look at these two parts as a whole, they suggest that unemployment was pretty stable during the first half of this century but that it has trended upward dramatically in the last 40 years or so.

You may think that this graphical way of distorting data is so outrageous that no one would ever attempt to use it. If you scrutinize the graphs that you see in newspapers and magazines, you will be surprised how common this device is.

Omitting the Origin   Sometimes a graph is drawn with the origin (0 on the axis) omitted. Sometimes omitting the origin is precisely the correct thing to do, as it enables the graph to reveal its information. But there are also times when omitting the origin is misleading.

Figure 2.4   Misleading Graphs: Squeezing and Stretching Scales

(a) 1900–1943

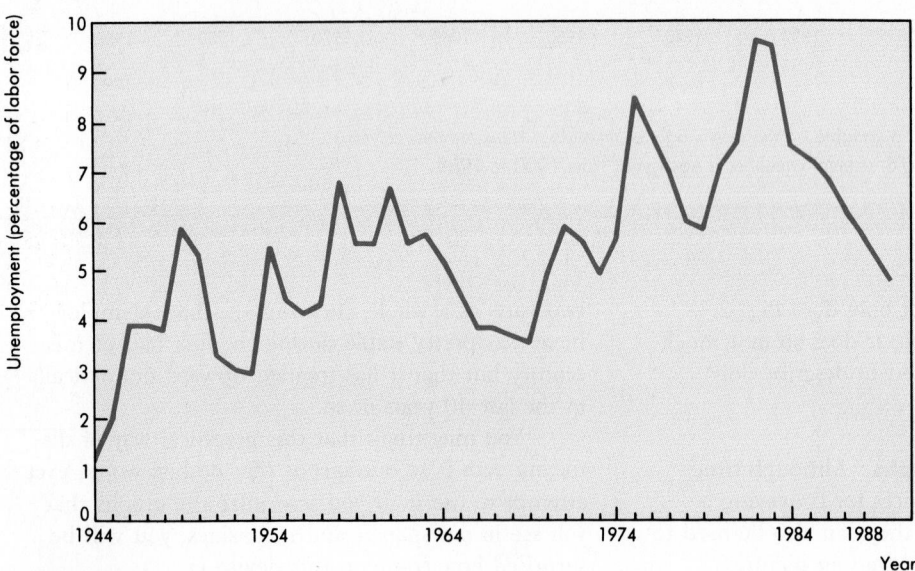

(b) 1944–1988

Graphs can mislead by squeezing and stretching the scales. These two graphs show exactly the same thing as Fig. 2.3—U.S. unemployment from 1900 to 1988. Part (a) has squeezed the y-axis, while part (b) has stretched that axis. The result appears to be a low and stable unemployment rate before 1943 and a rising, highly volatile unemployment rate after that date. Contrast the lie of Fig. 2.4 with the truth of Fig. 2.3.

Figure 2.5 illustrates the effect of omitting the origin. In parts (a) and (b), you can see a graph of the unemployment rate between 1970 and 1988. Part (a) includes the origin, and part (b) does not.

The graph in part (a) provides a clear account of what happened to unemployment over the time period in question. You can use that graph in the same way that we used Fig. 2.3 to describe all the features

Figure 2.5   Omitting the Origin

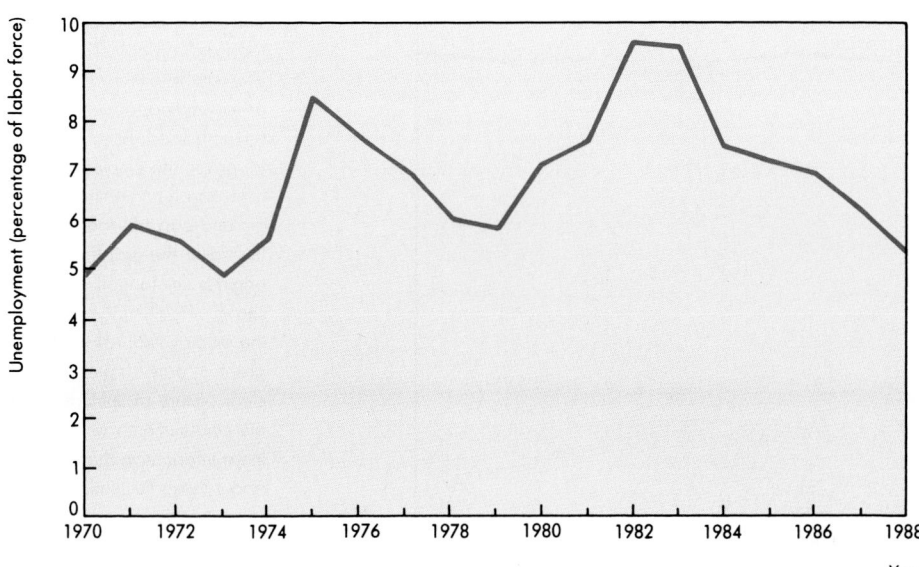

(a) Revealing graph with origin

Sometimes the origin is omitted from a graph. This practice can be either revealing or misleading, depending on how it is used. Parts (a) and (b) graph the U.S. unemployment rate between 1970 and 1988. Part (a) is graphed with the origin and part (b) without it. Part (a) reveals a large amount of information about the level and changes in the unemployment rate over this time period. Part (b) overdramatizes the rises and falls in unemployment and gives no direct visual information about its level.

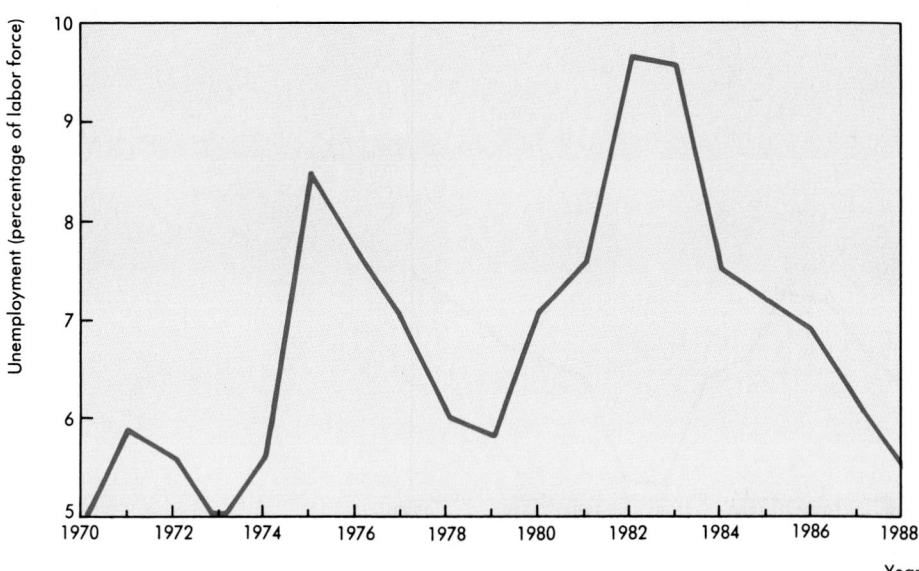

(b) Misleading graph with origin omitted

(Figure 2.5, parts c and d, continued on following page.)

of unemployment during that time period. But the graph in part (b) is less revealing and distorts the picture. It fails to reveal the level of unemployment. It focuses only on, and exaggerates the magnitude of, the increases and decreases in its rate. In particular, the increases in the unemployment rate in 1974–75 and in 1981–82 look enormous when compared with the increases that appear in part (a). By omit-

Figure 2.5   (continued)

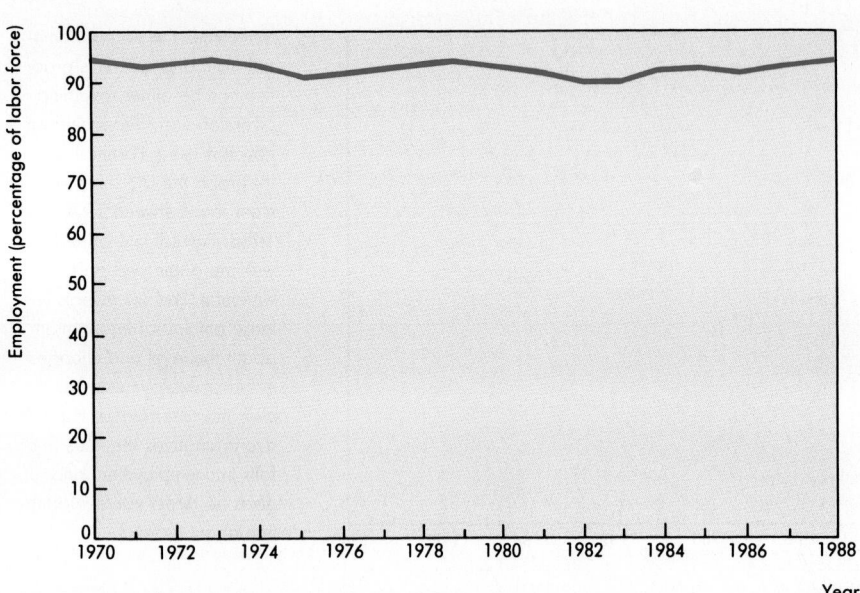

(c) Uninformative graph with origin

Sometimes the origin is omitted from a graph. This practice can be either revealing or misleading, depending on how it is used. Parts (c) and (d) graph the employment rate. Part (c) contains an origin and part (d) does not. In this case, the graph with the origin is uninformative and shows virtually no variation in the employment rate. The graph in part (d) gives a clear picture of fluctuations in the employment rate and is more informative than part (c) about those fluctuations.

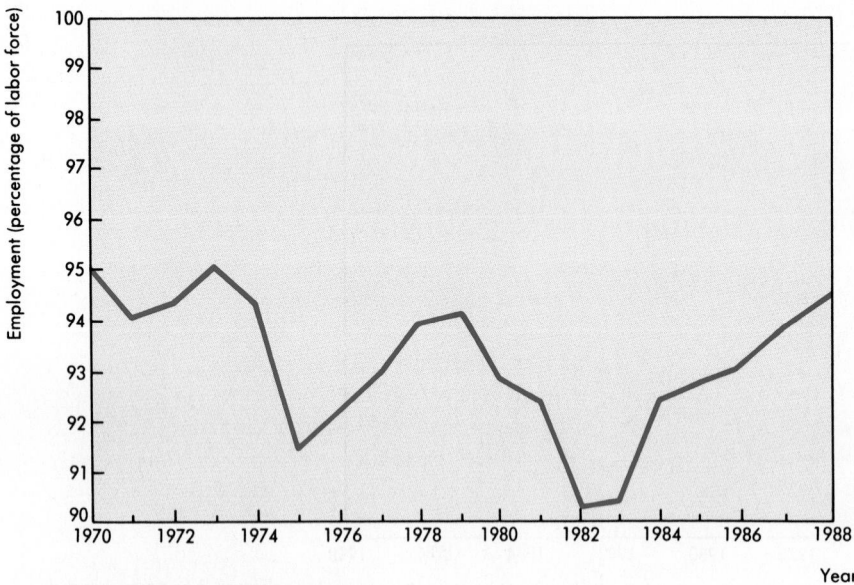

(d) Revealing graph with origin omitted

ting the origin, small percentage changes in unemployment look like many hundredfold changes.

Parts (c) and (d) of Fig. 2.5 graph the employ-

ment rate—the percentage of the labor force employed. Part (c) includes the origin, and part (d) omits it. As you can see, the graph in part (c) reveals very little about movements in the employment rate. It seems to suggest that the employment rate was pretty constant and lying between 90 and 95 percent. The main feature of part (c) is an enormous amount of empty space and an inefficient use of the space available. Part (d) shows the same information but with the origin omitted. The scale begins at 90 percent. In this case, we can see very clearly the ups and downs in the employment rate. This graph does not provide a visual impression of the level of employment but it does provide a clear picture of variations in its rate.

The decision about whether to include or exclude the origin of the graph depends on what the graph is designed to reveal. To convey information about the level of employment and unemployment and variations in their rates, the graphs in parts (a) and (d) of Fig. 2.5 are almost equally revealing. By comparison, the graphs in parts (b) and (c) convey almost no information.

Comparing Two Time-Series   Sometimes we want to use a time-series graph to compare two different variables. For example, suppose you wanted to know how the balance of the government's budget—its surplus or deficit—fluctuated and how those fluctuations compared with fluctuations in the unemployment rate. You can examine two such series by drawing a graph of each of them in the manner shown in Fig. 2.6(a). The scale for the unemployment rate appears on the left side of the figure and the scale for the government's budget surplus appears on the right. The (black) line shows unemployment and the (red) line shows the government's budget. You will probably agree that it is pretty hard work figuring out from Fig. 2.6(a) just what the relationship is between the unemployment rate and the government's budget. But it does look as if there is a tendency for the government's budget to go into a bigger deficit (red line goes downward) when the unemployment rate increases (black line goes upward). In other words, it seems as if these two variables have a tendency to move in opposite directions to each other.

In a situation such as this, it is often more revealing to flip the scale of one of the variables over, and graph it upside-down. Figure 2.6(b) does this. The unemployment rate in part (b) is graphed in exactly the same way as in part (a). But the government's budget has been flipped over. Now, instead of measuring the deficit (a negative number) in the

down direction and the surplus (a positive number) in the up direction, we measure the deficit upward and the surplus downward. You can now "see" very clearly the relationship between these two variables. There is indeed a tendency for the government's deficit to get bigger when the unemployment rate gets higher. But the relationship is by no means an exact one and there are significant periods, clearly revealed in the graph, when the deficit and the unemployment rate move apart. You can "see" these periods as those in which the gap between the two lines widens.

Time-series graphs, whether simple ones with a single variable or more complex ones, such as those in Fig. 2.6 that show two variables, enable us to see how things change over time. But sometimes we are more interested in how variables relate to each other than in how they move over time. To study such relationships, we need to use a different but common kind of graph employed in economics—the scatter diagram.

Scatter Diagrams

A **scatter diagram** plots the value of one economic variable associated with the value of another. It measures one of the variables on the x-axis and the other variable on the y-axis.

Figure 2.7 illustrates three scatter diagrams. Part (a) shows the relationship between average consumption and average income. The x-axis measures average income and the y-axis measures average consumption. Each point represents average consumption and average income in the United States from 1970 to 1988. The years are identified by the two-digit numbers "scattered" within the graph. For example, the point marked 83 tells us that in 1983 average consumption was $9200 and average income was $10,000. The pattern formed by the points in part (a) tells us that when income rises, consumption also rises.

In part (b), the x-axis shows the percentage of households owning a video cassette recorder and the vertical axis shows its average price. The two-digit numbers each represent a year. Thus the point marked 81 tells us that the average price of a VCR in 1981 was $600 and that VCRs were owned by 20 percent of all households. The pattern formed by the points in part (b) tells us that as the price of a VCR falls, more people own one.

Figure 2.6   Seeing Relationships in Time-Series Graphs

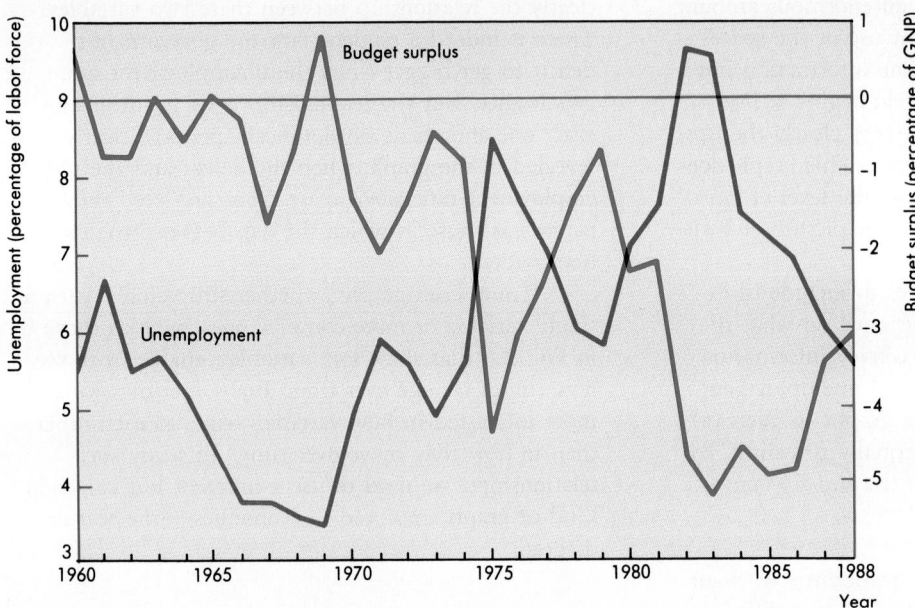

(a) Unemployment and budget surplus

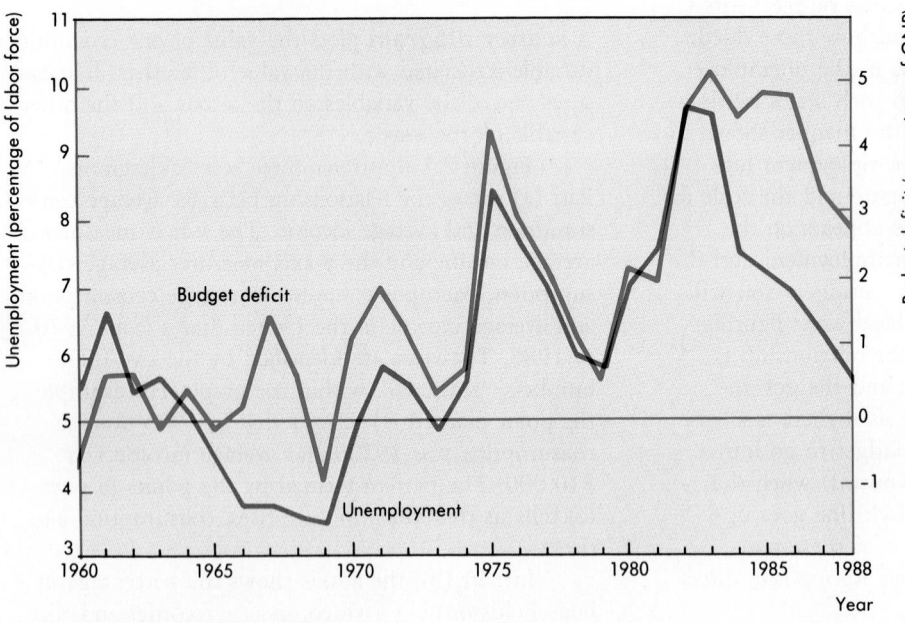

(b) Unemployment and budget deficit

A time-series graph can be used to reveal relationships between two variables. These two graphs show the unemployment rate and the balance of the government's budget between 1960 and 1988. The unemployment line is identical in the two parts. In part (a), the budget balance is shown measuring surpluses upward and deficits downward (as negative numbers) on the right scale. It looks as if the budget goes into a bigger deficit when unemployment rises, but not much else is shown by part (a). Part (b) inverts the scale on which the budget is measured. Now a deficit is measured in the up direction and a surplus in the down direction on the right scale. The relationship between the budget deficit and unemployment is now clearer. There is a tendency for unemployment and the deficit to move together. But there are times, such as 1967–69 and 1984–88, when the variables move apart.

Part (c) is another scatter diagram. Its *x*-axis measures unemployment in the United States and its *y*-axis measures inflation. Again, each two-digit number represents a year. The point marked 85 tells us that in 1985 unemployment was 7.2 percent and inflation was 3.3 percent. The pattern formed by the

Figure 2.7   Scatter Diagrams

(a) Consumption and income

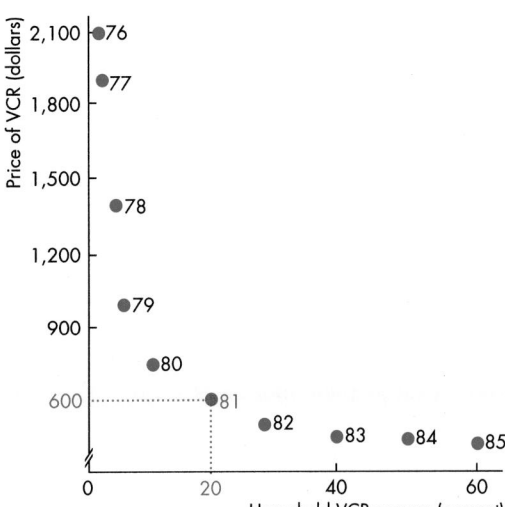

(b) VCR ownership and price

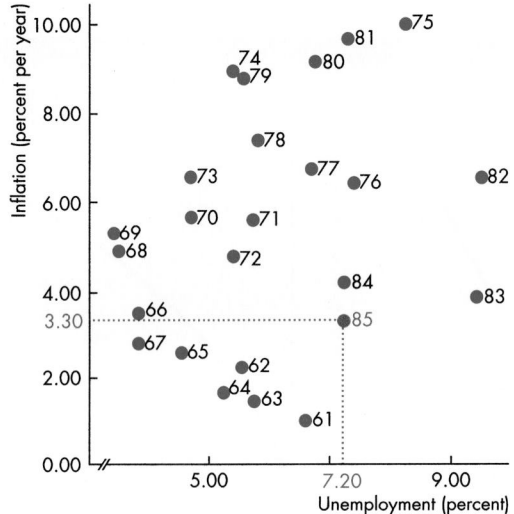

(c) Unemployment and inflation

A scatter diagram shows a relationship between two variables. Each point on these scatter diagrams represents an observation of two variables in a specific year. Part (a) shows that as income increases, so does consumption. Part (b) shows that as the price of a VCR falls, the number of VCRs owned increases. Part (c) shows that there is no relationship between inflation and unemployment.

points in part (c) does not reveal a clear relationship —upward-sloping or downward-sloping—between the two variables. The graph thus informs us, by its lack of a distinct pattern, that there is no relationship between these two variables.

Now that we have seen how we can use graphs in economics to represent economic data and to show the relationship between variables, let us examine how economists use graphs in a more abstract way to construct and analyze economic models.

Graphs Used in Economic Models

Although you will encounter many different kinds of graphs in economics, there are some patterns which, once you have learned to recognize them, will instantly convey to you the meaning of a graph. There are graphs that show each of the following:

- Things that go up and down together
- Things that move in opposite directions
- Things that are not related to each other at all
- Things that have a maximum or a minimum

Let's look at these four cases.

Things That Go Up and Down Together

Graphs that show the relationship between two variables that move up and down together are shown in Fig. 2.8. The relationship between two variables that move in the same direction is called a **positive relationship.** Such a relationship is shown by a line that slopes upward.

Part (a) shows the relationship between the number of miles traveled in 5 hours and speed. For example, the point marked *a* tells us that we will travel 200 miles in 5 hours if our speed is 40 miles an hour. If we double our speed and travel at 80 miles an hour, we will cover a distance of 400 miles. The relationship between the number of miles traveled in 5 hours and speed is represented by an upward-sloping straight line. A relationship depicted by a straight line is called a **linear relationship.** A linear relationship is one that has a constant slope.

Part (b) shows the relationship between distance sprinted and exhaustion (exhaustion being measured by the time it takes the heart rate to return to normal). This relationship is an upward-sloping one depicted by a curved line that starts out with a gentle slope but then becomes steeper.

Part (c) shows the relationship between the number of problems worked by a student and the amount of study time. This relationship is illustrated

Figure 2.8   Positive Relationships

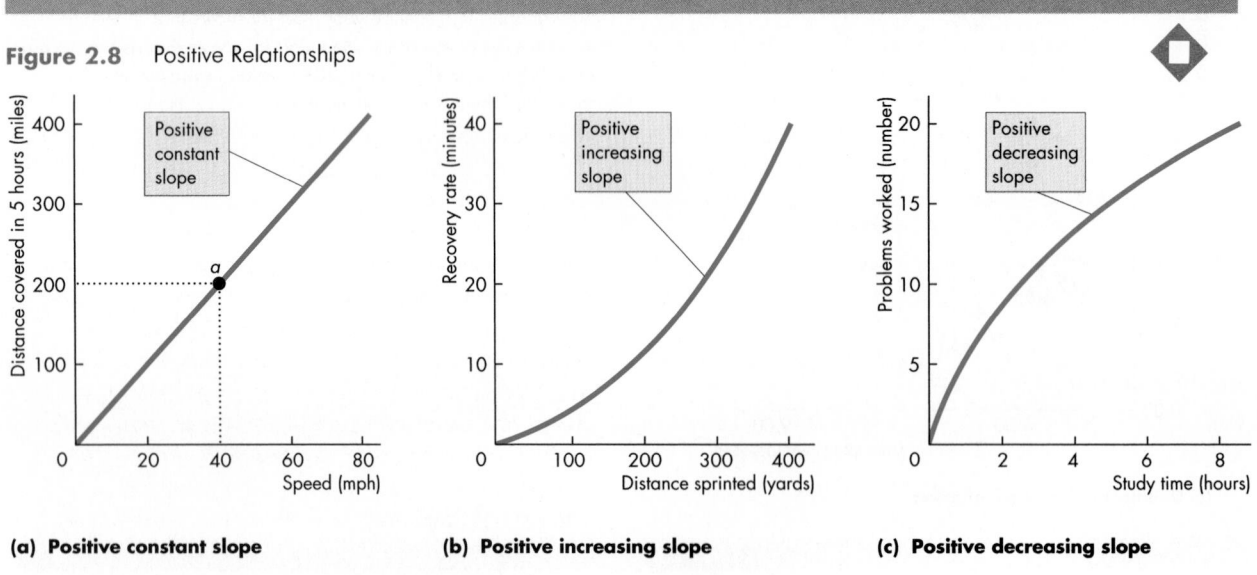

(a) Positive constant slope   **(b) Positive increasing slope**   **(c) Positive decreasing slope**

Each part of this figure shows a positive relationship between two variables. That is, as the value of the variable measured on the x-axis increases, so does the value of the variable measured on the y-axis. Part (a) illustrates a linear relationship—a relationship whose slope is constant as we move along the curve. Part (b) illustrates a positive relationship whose slope becomes steeper as we move along the curve away from the origin. It is a positive relationship with an increasing slope. Part (c) shows a positive relationship whose slope becomes flatter as we move away from the origin. It is a positive relationship with a decreasing slope.

Figure 2.9   Negative Relationships

(a) Negative constant slope   **(b) Negative decreasing slope**   **(c) Negative increasing slope**

Each part of this figure shows a negative relationship between two variables. Part (a) shows a linear relationship—a relationship whose slope is constant as we travel along the curve. Part (b) shows a negative relationship of decreasing slope. That is, the slope of the relationship gets less steep as we travel along the curve from left to right. Part (c) shows a negative relationship of increasing slope. That is, the slope becomes steeper as we travel along the curve from left to right.

by an upward-sloping curved line that starts out with a steep slope but then becomes more gentle.

There are three types of upward-sloping lines in the graphs in Fig. 2.8, one straight and two curved. But they are all called curves. Any line on a graph—no matter whether it is straight or curved—is called a **curve.**

Things That Move in Opposite Directions

Figure 2.9 shows relationships between things that move in opposite directions. A relationship between variables that move in opposite directions is called a **negative relationship.**

Part (a) shows the relationship between the number of hours available for playing squash and the number of hours for playing tennis. One extra hour spent playing tennis means one hour less playing squash and vice versa. This relationship is negative and linear.

Part (b) shows the relationship between the cost per mile traveled and the length of a journey. The longer the journey, the lower is the cost per mile. But as the journey length increases, the cost per mile

decreases at a decreasing rate. This feature of the relationship is illustrated by the fact that the curve slopes downward starting out steep at a short journey length and then becoming flatter as the journey length increases.

Part (c) shows the relationship between the amount of leisure time and the number of problems worked by a student. If the student takes no leisure, 25 problems can be worked. If the student takes 4 hours of leisure, only 20 problems can be worked (point *a*). Increasing leisure time beyond 4 hours produces a large reduction in the number of problems worked and, if the student takes 8 hours of leisure a day, no problems get worked. This relationship is a negative one that starts out with a gentle slope at a low number of leisure hours and becomes increasingly steep as leisure hours increase.

Things That Have a Maximum and a Minimum

Economics is about optimizing, or doing the best with limited resources. Making the highest possible profits or achieving the lowest possible costs of production are examples of optimizing. Economists make

Figure 2.10   Maximum and Minimum Points

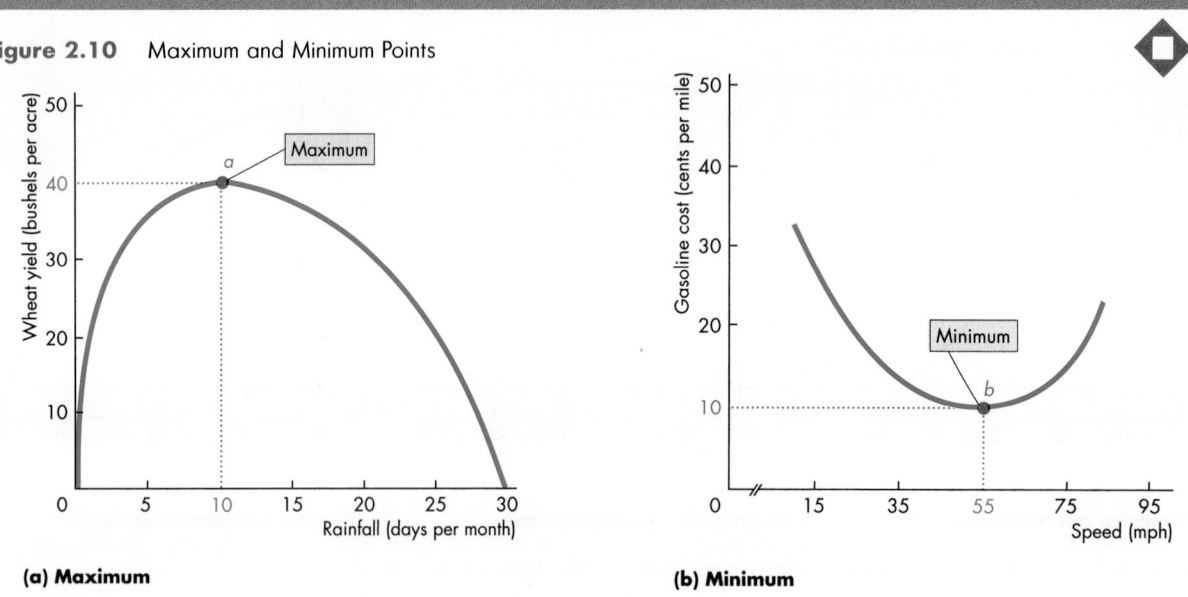

(a) Maximum

(b) Minimum

Part (a) shows a relationship that has a maximum point, *a*. The curve rises at first, reaches its highest point, and then falls. Part (b) shows a relationship with a minimum point, *b*. The curve falls to its minimum and then rises.

frequent use of graphs depicting relationships that have a maximum or a minimum. Figure 2.10 illustrates such relationships.

Part (a) shows the relationship between rainfall and wheat yield. When there is no rainfall, wheat will not grow, so the yield is zero. As the rainfall increases up to 10 days a month, the wheat yield also increases. With 10 rainy days each month, the wheat yield reaches its maximum at 40 bushels an acre (point *a*). Rain in excess of 10 days a month starts to lower the yield of wheat. If every day is rainy, the wheat suffers from a lack of sunshine and the yield falls back almost to zero. This relationship is one that starts out positive, reaches a maximum, and then becomes negative.

Part (b) shows the reverse case—a relationship that begins with a negative slope, falls to a minimum, and then becomes positive. An example of such a relationship is the gasoline cost per mile as the speed of travel varies. At low speeds, the car is creeping along in a traffic snarl-up. The number of miles per gallon is low so the gasoline cost per mile is high. At very high speeds, the car is operated beyond its most efficient rate and, again, the number of miles per gallon is low and the gasoline cost per mile is high. At a speed of 55 miles an hour, the

gasoline cost per mile traveled is at its minimum (point *b*).

Things That Are Independent

There are many situations in which one variable is independent of another. No matter what happens to the value of one variable, the other variable remains constant. Sometimes we want to show the independence between two variables in a graph. Figure 2.11 shows two ways of achieving this. In Fig. 2.11(a), your grade in economics is shown on the vertical axis against the price of bananas on the horizontal axis. Your grade (75 percent in this example) does not depend on the price of bananas. The relationship between these two variables is shown by a horizontal straight line. In part (b), the output of French wine is shown on the horizontal axis and the number of rainy days a month in California is shown on the vertical axis. Again, the output of French wine (3 billion gallons a year in this example) does not change when the number of rainy days in California changes. The relationship between these two variables is shown by a vertical straight line.

Figures 2.8 through 2.11 illustrate ten different shapes of graphs that we will encounter in economic

Figure 2.11   Variables with No Relationship

(a) Unrelated: horizontal

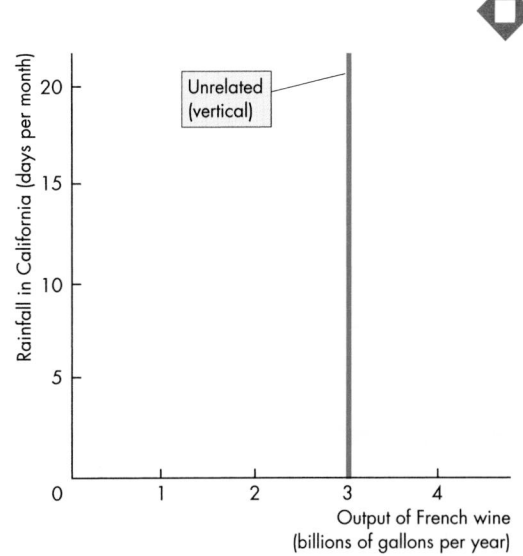

(b) Unrelated: vertical

This figure shows how we can graph two variables that are unrelated to each other. In part (a), a student's grade in economics is plotted at 75 percent regardless of the price of bananas on the x-axis. In part (b), the output of the vineyards of France does not vary with the rainfall in California.

models. In describing these graphs, we have talked about curves that slope upward or slope downward and slopes that are steep or gentle. The concept of slope is an important one. Let's spend a little time discussing exactly what we mean by slope.

The Slope of a Relationship

The Definition of Slope

The **slope** of a relationship is the change in the value of y divided by the change in the value of x. We use the Greek letter Δ to represent "change in." Thus Δy means the change in the value of y, and Δx means the change in the value of x. Therefore, the slope of the relationship between x and y is

$$\frac{\Delta y}{\Delta x}$$

If a large change in y is associated with a small change in x, the slope is large and the curve is steep. If a small change in y is associated with a large

change in x, the slope is small and the curve is flat.

We can make the idea of slope sharper by doing some calculations.

Calculating Slope

A Straight Line   The slope of a straight line is the same regardless of where on the line you calculate it. Thus the slope of a straight line is constant. Let's calculate the slopes of the lines in Fig. 2.12. In part (a), when x increases from 2 to 6, y increases from 3 to 6. The change in x is $+4$—that is, Δx is 4. The change in y is $+3$—that is, Δy is 3. The slope of that line is

$$\frac{\Delta y}{\Delta x} = \frac{3}{4}$$

In part (b), when x increases from 2 to 6, y decreases from 6 to 3. The change in y is *minus* 3—that is, Δy is -3. The change in x is *plus* 4—that is, Δx is $+4$. The slope of the curve is

$$\frac{\Delta y}{\Delta x} = \frac{-3}{4}$$

Figure 2.12 The Slope of a Straight Line

(a) Positive slope

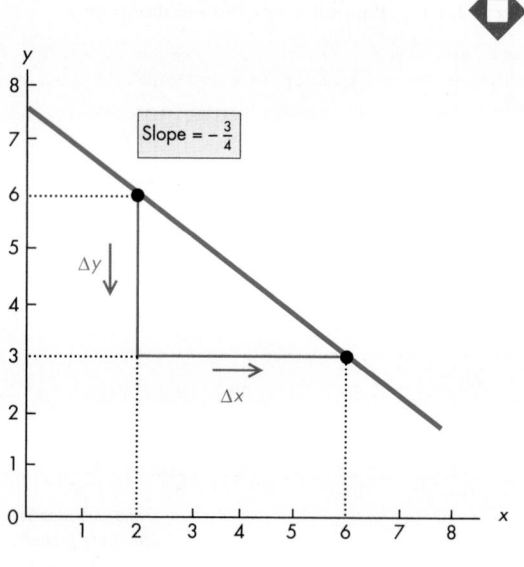

(b) Negative slope

To calculate the slope of a straight line, we divide the change in the value of y by the change in the value of x. Part (a) shows the calculation of a positive slope—where both x and y go up together. When x goes up from 2 to 6, the change in x is 4—that is, Δx equals 4. That change in x brings about an increase in y from 3 to 6, so that Δy equals 3. The slope ($\Delta y/\Delta x$) equals 3/4. Part (b) shows a negative slope (when x goes up, y goes down). When x goes up from 2 to 6, Δx equals 4. That change in x brings about a decrease in y from 6 to 3, so that Δy equals −3. The slope ($\Delta y/\Delta x$) equals −3/4.

Notice that the two slopes have the same magnitude (3/4), but the slope of the line in part (a) is positive ($+3/+4 = 3/4$), while that in part (b) is negative ($-3/+4 = -3/4$). The slope of a positive relationship is positive; the slope of a negative relationship is negative.

A Curved Line Calculating the slope of a curved line is trickier. The slope of a curved line is not constant. Its slope depends on where on the line we calculate it. There are two ways to calculate the slope of a curved line: You can calculate the slope at a point on the line or you can calculate the slope across an arc of the line. Let's look at the two alternatives.

Slope at a point To calculate the slope at a point on a curved line, you need to construct a straight line that has the same slope as the curve at the point in

question. Figure 2.13 shows how such a calculation is made. Suppose you want to calculate the slope of the curve at the point marked *a*. Place a ruler on the graph so that it touches point *a* and no other point on the curve, then draw a straight line along the edge of the ruler. The straight red line in part (a) is such a line. If the ruler touches the curve only at point *a*, then the slope of the curve at point *a* must be the same as the slope of the edge of the ruler. If the curve and the ruler do not have the same slope, the line along the edge of the ruler will cut the curve instead of just touching it.

Having now found a straight line with the same slope as the curve at point *a*, you can calculate the slope of the curve at point *a* by calculating the slope of the straight line. We already know how to calculate the slope of a straight line, so the task is straightforward. In this case, as *x* increases from 0 to

Figure 2.13   The Slope of a Curve

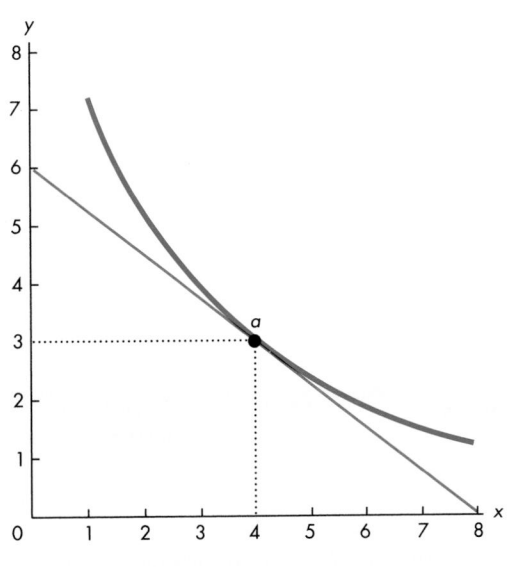

(a) Slope at a point

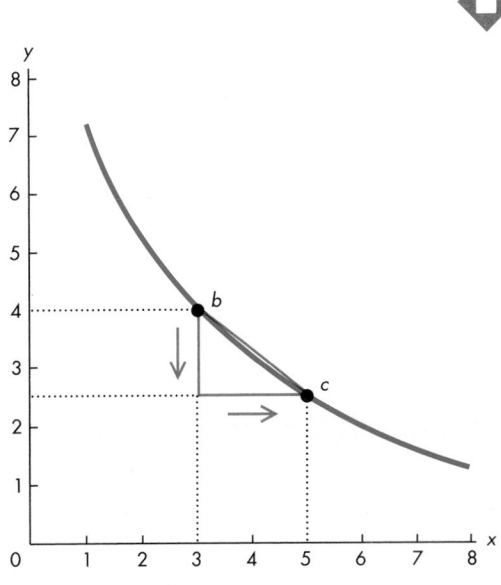

(b) Slope across an arc

The slope of a curve can be calculated either at a point, as in part (a), or across an arc, as in part (b).
The slope at a point is calculated by finding the slope of a straight line that touches the curve only at
one point. One such straight line touches the curve at point a. The slope of that straight line is
calculated by dividing the change in y by the change in x. When x increases from 0 to 8, Δx equals 8.
That change in x is associated with a fall in y from 6 to 0, so Δy equals −6. The slope of the line is
−6/8 or − 3/4. To calculate the slope across an arc, we place a straight line across the curve from
one point to another and then calculate the slope of that straight line. One such line is that from b to c
in part (b). The slope of the straight line bc is calculated by dividing the change in y by the change in
x. In moving from b to c, x goes up by 2, Δx equals 2, and y goes down by 1½, Δy equals −1½. The
slope of the line bc is −1½ divided by 2, or −3/4.

8 ($\Delta x = 8$), y decreases from 6 to 0 ($\Delta y = -6$).
Therefore, the slope of the straight line is

$$\frac{\Delta y}{\Delta x} = \frac{-6}{+8} = \frac{-3}{4}$$

Thus the slope of the curve at point a is $-3/4$.

Slope across an arc   Calculating a slope across an arc is
similar to calculating an average slope. In Fig.
2.13(b), we are looking at the same curve as in part
(a), but instead of calculating the slope at point a,
we calculate the slope for a change in x from 3 to 5.
As x increases from 3 to 5, y decreases from 4 to

2½. The change in y is $-1½$ ($\Delta y = -1½$). The
change in x is $+2$ ($\Delta x = 2$). Therefore, the slope of
the line is

$$\frac{\Delta y}{\Delta x} = \frac{-1½}{2} = \frac{-3}{4}$$

This calculation gives us the slope of the red
line between points b and c. In this particular example, the slope of the arc bc is identical to the slope of
the curve at point a in part (a). Calculating the slope
across an arc does not always work out so neatly. You
might have some fun constructing other examples
that do not give such an outcome.

Figure 2.14   Graphing a Relationship Among Three Variables

(a) Price and consumption at a given temperature

(b) Temperature and consumption at a given price

(c) Temperature and price at a given consumption

Price (cents per scoop)	Ice Cream Consumption (gallons per day)			
	30°F	50°F	70°F	90°F
15	12	18	25	50
30	10	12	18	37
45	7	10	13	27
60	5	7	10	20
75	3	5	7	14
90	2	3	5	10
105	1	2	3	6

The quantity of ice cream consumed (one variable) depends on its price (a second variable) and the air temperature (a third variable). The table provides some hypothetical numbers that tell us how many gallons of ice cream are consumed each day at different prices and different temperatures. For example, if the price is 45¢ per scoop and the temperature is 50°F, 10 gallons of ice cream will be consumed. In order to graph a relationship among three variables, the value of one variable must be held constant. Part (a) shows the relationship between price and consumption, holding temperature constant. One curve holds temperature constant at 90°F and the other at 70°F. Part (b) shows the relationship between temperature and consumption, holding price constant. One curve holds the price at 30¢ and the other at 15¢. Part (c) shows the relationship between temperature and price, holding consumption constant. One curve holds consumption constant at 10 gallons and the other at 7 gallons.

Graphing Relationships Among More Than Two Variables

We have seen that we can graph a single variable as a point on a straight line and we can graph the relationship between two variables as a point formed by the *x*- and *y*-coordinates in a two-dimensional graph. You may be suspecting that although a two-dimensional graph is informative, most of the things in which you are likely to be interested involve relationships among not just two variables but many.

Examples of relationships among more than two variables abound. For example, consider the relationship between the price of ice cream, the air temperature, and the amount of ice cream eaten. If ice cream is expensive and the temperature is low, people eat much less ice cream than when ice cream is inexpensive and the temperature is high. For any given price of ice cream, the quantity consumed varies with the temperature, and for any given temperature, the quantity of ice cream consumed varies with its price.

Other Things Being Equal

Figure 2.14 illustrates such a situation. The table shows the number of gallons of ice cream that will be eaten each day at various temperatures and ice cream prices. How can we graph all these numbers?

To graph a relationship that involves more than two variables, we consider what happens if all but two of the variables are held constant. This device is called ceteris paribus. **Ceteris paribus** is a Latin phrase that means "other things being equal." For example, in Fig. 2.14(a) you can see what happens to the quantity of ice cream consumed when the price of ice cream varies while the temperature is held constant. The line labeled 70°F shows the relationship between ice cream consumption and the price of ice cream when the temperature stays at 70°F. The numbers used to plot that line are those in the third column of the table in Fig. 2.14. The curve labeled 90°F shows the consumption of ice cream when the price varies and the temperature is 90°F.

Alternatively, we can show the relationship between ice cream consumption and temperature while holding the price of ice cream constant, as is shown in Fig. 2.14(b). The curve labeled 30¢ shows how the consumption of ice cream varies with the temperature when ice cream costs 30¢, and a second curve shows the relationship when ice cream costs 15¢. Part (c) shows the combinations of temperature and price that result in a constant consumption of ice cream. One curve shows the combination that results in 10 gallons a day being consumed and the other shows the combination that results in 7 gallons a day being consumed. A high price and a high temperature lead to the same consumption as a lower price and lower temperature. For example, 7 gallons are consumed at 30°F and 45 cents per scoop and at 70°F and 75 cents per scoop.

■ With what you have now learned about graphs, you can move forward with your study of economics. There are no graphs in this book that are more complicated than those that have been explained here.

SUMMARY

Graphing Data

There are two main types of graphs used to represent economic data: time-series graphs and scatter diagrams. A time-series graph plots the value of one or more economic variables on the vertical axis (y-axis) and time on the horizontal axis (x-axis). A well-constructed time-series graph quickly reveals the level, direction of change, and speed of change of a variable. It also reveals trends. Graphs sometimes mislead, especially when scales are stretched or squeezed to exaggerate or understate a variation.

Scatter diagrams plot the value of one economic variable associated with the value of another. These diagrams reveal whether or not there is a relationship between two variables and, if there is a relationship, its nature. (pp. 29–37)

Graphs Used in Economic Models

Graphs are used in economic models to illustrate relationships between variables. There are four cases: positive relationships, negative relationships, relationships that have a maximum or a minimum, and variables that are not related to each other. Examples of these different types of relationships are summarized in Figures 2.8 through 2.11. (pp. 38–41)

The Slope of a Relationship

The slope of a relationship is calculated as the change in the value of y divided by the change in the value of x—$\Delta y/\Delta x$. A straight line has a constant slope, but a curved line has a varying slope. To calculate the slope of a curved line, we either calculate the slope at a point or across an arc. (pp. 41–43)

Graphing Relationships Among More Than Two Variables

To graph a relationship among more than two variables, we hold constant the values of all the variables except two. We then plot the value of one of the variables against the value of another. Holding constant all the variables but two is called the ceteris paribus assumption—other things being equal. (pp. 44–45)

K E Y   C O N C E P T S

Axes, 29
Ceteris paribus, 45
Coordinates, 29
Curve, 39
Linear relationship, 38
Negative relationship, 39
Origin, 29
Positive relationship, 38
Scatter diagram, 35
Slope, 41
Time-series graph, 30
Trend, 30
x-axis, 29
x-coordinate, 30
y-axis, 29
y-coordinate, 30

Key Figures

Figure 2.8   Positive Relationships, 38
Figure 2.9   Negative Relationships, 39
Figure 2.10   Maximum and Minimum Points, 40
Figure 2.11   Variables with No Relationship, 41
Figure 2.12   The Slope of a Straight Line, 42
Figure 2.13   The Slope of a Curve, 43
Figure 2.14   Graphing a Relationship Among Three
              Variables, 44

R E V I E W   Q U E S T I O N S

1 Why do we use graphs?

2 What are the two scale lines on a graph called?

3 What is the origin on a graph?

4 What do we mean by the y-coordinate and x-coordinate?

5 What is a time-series graph?

6 List three things that a time-series graph shows quickly and easily.

7 What do we mean by trend?

8 What is a scatter diagram?

9 Sketch some graphs to illustrate the following:

   a) Two variables that move up and down together

   b) Two variables that move in opposite directions

   c) A relationship between two variables that has a maximum

   d) A relationship between two variables that has a minimum

10 Which of the relationships in question 9 is a positive relationship and which a negative relationship?

11 What is the definition of the slope of a relationship?

12 What are the two ways of calculating the slope of a curved line?

13 How do we graph relationships among more than two variables?

PROBLEMS

1 The rate of inflation in the United States between 1970 and 1987 was as follows:

Year	Inflation Rate	Year	Inflation Rate
1970	5.7	1979	11.3
1971	4.4	1980	13.5
1972	3.2	1981	10.3
1973	6.2	1982	6.2
1974	11.0	1983	3.2
1975	9.1	1984	4.3
1976	5.8	1985	3.6
1977	6.5	1986	1.9
1978	7.6	1987	3.6

Draw a time-series graph of these data; use your graph to answer the following questions:

a) In which year was inflation highest?

b) In which year was inflation lowest?

c) In which years did inflation rise?

d) In which years did inflation fall?

e) In which year did inflation rise/fall the fastest?

f) In which year did inflation rise/fall the slowest?

g) What have been the main trends in inflation?

2 Interest rates on treasury bills in the United States between 1970 and 1987 were as follows:

Year	Interest Rate	Year	Interest Rate
1970	6.5	1979	10.0
1971	4.3	1980	11.5
1972	4.1	1981	14.0
1973	7.0	1982	10.7
1974	7.9	1983	8.6
1975	5.8	1984	9.6
1976	5.0	1985	7.5
1977	5.3	1986	6.0
1978	7.2	1987	5.8

Use these data together with those in problem 1 to draw a scatter diagram showing the relationship between inflation and the interest rate. Use this diagram to determine whether there is a relationship between inflation and the interest rate and whether it is positive or negative.

3 Use the following information to draw a graph showing the relationship between x and y.

x	0	1	2	3	4	5	6	7	8
y	0	1	4	9	16	25	36	49	64

a) Is the relationship between x and y positive or negative?

b) Does the slope of the relationship rise or fall as the value of x rises?

4 Using the data in problem 3,

a) Calculate the slope of the relationship between x and y when x equals 4.

b) Calculate the slope of the arc when x rises from 3 to 4.

c) Calculate the slope of the arc when x rises from 4 to 5.

d) Calculate the slope of the arc when x rises from 3 to 5.

e) What do you notice that is interesting about your answers to (b), (c), and (d), compared with your answer to (a)?

5 Calculate the slopes of the following two relationships between x and y.

a)
x	0	2	4	6	8	10
y	20	16	12	8	4	0

b)
x	0	2	4	6	8	10
y	0	8	16	24	32	40

6 Draw a graph showing the following relationship between x and y:

x	0	1	2	3	4	5	6	7	8	9
y	0	2	4	6	8	10	8	6	4	2

a) Is the slope positive or negative when x is less than 5?

b) Is the slope positive or negative when x is greater than 5?

c) What is the slope of this relationship when x equals 5?

d) Is y at a maximum or at a minimum when x equals 5?

7 Draw a graph showing the following relationship between x and y:

x	0	1	2	3	4	5	6	7	8	9
y	10	8	6	4	2	0	2	4	6	8

a) Is the slope positive or negative when x is less than 5?

b) Is the slope positive or negative when x is greater than 5?

c) What is the slope of this relationship when x equals 5?

d) Is y at a maximum or at a minimum when x equals 5?

Chapter 3

Production, Specialization, and Exchange

After studying this chapter, you will be able to:

- Define the production possibility frontier

- Calculate opportunity cost

- Explain why economic growth and technical change do not provide free gifts

- Explain comparative advantage

- Explain why people specialize and how they gain from trade

- Explain why property rights and money have evolved

Whe live in a style that most of our grandparents could not even have imagined. Medicine has cured diseases that terrified them. Most of us live in better and more spacious homes. We eat more, we grow taller, we are even born larger than they were. Our parents are amazed at the matter-of-fact way we handle computers. We casually use products—microwave ovens, graphite tennis rackets, digital watches—that didn't exist in their youth. Economic growth has made us richer than our parents and grandparents. ■ But economic growth and technical change, and the wealth they bestow, have not liberated us from scarcity. Why not? Why, despite our immense wealth, do we still have to face costs? Why are there no "free lunches"? ■ We see an incredible amount of specialization and trading in the modern world. Each one of us specializes in a particular job—as lawyer, car maker, homemaker. Countries and regions also specialize—Florida in orange juice, Idaho in potatoes, Detroit in cars, and the Silicon Valley in computer-related products. We have become so specialized that one farm worker can feed 100 people. Only one in five of us works in manufacturing. More than half of us work in wholesale and retail trade, banking and finance, other services, and government. ■ Why do we specialize? How do we benefit from specialization and exchange? How do money and the legal institution of private property extend our ability to specialize and increase production? These are the questions that we tackle in this chapter.

■ We will begin by making the idea of scarcity more precise. Then we will go on to see how we can measure opportunity cost. We will also see how, when each individual tries to get the most out of scarce resources, specialization and exchange

Making the Most of It

occur. That is, people will specialize in doing what they do best and exchange their products with other specialists. We are also going to see why such institutions as private property and money exist and how they spring from people's attempts to make the most of their limited resources.

The Production Possibility Frontier

What do we mean by production? **Production** is the conversion of natural, human, and capital resources into goods and services. In defining production, we have used several terms that need to be defined. Let's review them.

Natural resources are all the gifts of nature. They include the air, the water, and the land, and the minerals that lie on top of or beneath the surface of the earth. They are the factor of production called *land*. **Human resources** are all the muscle-power and brain-power of human beings. The voices and artistry of singers and actors, the strength and coordination of athletes, the daring of astronauts, the political skill of diplomats, as well as the physical and mental skills of the many millions of people who make cars and cola, gum and glue, wallpaper and watering cans, are included in this category. They are the factor of production called *labor*.

Capital resources are goods that have been produced and can now be used in the production of other goods and services. Examples include the interstate highway system, the fine buildings of great cities, dams and power projects, airports and jumbo jets, car production lines, shirt factories, and cookie shops. Capital resources also include human capital. **Human capital** is the accumulated skill and knowledge of human beings, which arise from their training and education. These are the factor of production called *capital*.

Goods and services are all the valuable things that people produce. Goods are tangible—cars, spoons, VCRs, and bread. Services are intangible—haircuts, amusement park rides, and telephone calls. There are two types of goods: capital goods and consumption goods. **Capital goods** are goods that are added to our capital resources. **Consumption goods** are goods that are used up as soon as they are produced. **Consumption** is the process of using up goods and services.

The **production possibility frontier** (PPF) marks the boundary between production levels that can and cannot be attained. It is important to understand the production possibility frontier in the real world, but in order to achieve that goal more easily, we will first study an economy—a model economy—that is simpler than the one in which we live.

A Model Economy

Instead of looking at the real world economy with all its complexity and detail, we will build a model of an economy. The model will have features that are essential to understanding the real economy, but we will ignore most of reality's immense detail. Our model economy will be simpler in three important ways:

1 For the time being, we will suppose that everything that is produced is also consumed. This simplification means that, in our model, capital resources neither grow nor shrink. Later we will examine what happens if we consume less than we produce and add to capital resources.

2 In our model economy, there will be just two goods—even though in the real world we use our scarce resources to produce countless goods and services.

3 Although there are approximately five billion people living on this planet, our model economy initially has just one person, Jane, who lives on a deserted island and has no dealings with other people.

Let's suppose that all the resources of Jane's island economy can be used to produce two goods, corn and cloth. Suppose also that Jane can work twelve hours each day. The amount of corn and cloth that Jane can produce will depend on how many hours she devotes to producing them. Table 3.1 sets out Jane's production possibilities for corn and cloth. If she does no work, she produces nothing. Three hours a day devoted to corn farming produces 9 pounds of corn per month. Devoting more hours to corn increases the output of corn, but there is a decline in the extra amount of corn that comes from extra effort. The reason for this decline is that Jane has to use increasingly unsuitable land for growing corn. At first, she plants corn on a lush, flat plain. Eventually, when she has used all the arable land, she has to start planting on the rocky hills and the edge

Table 3.1   Jane's Production Possibilities

Hours worked per day		Corn grown (pounds per month)		Cloth produced (yards per month)
0	either	0	or	0
3	either	9	or	4
6	either	15	or	7
9	either	20	or	9
12	either	25	or	10

If Jane does no work, she produces no corn or cloth. If she works for 3 hours per day and spends the entire amount of time on corn production, she produces 9 pounds of corn per month. If that same time is used for cloth production, 4 yards of cloth are produced but no corn. The last three rows of the table show the amounts of corn or cloth that can be produced per month as more hours are devoted to each activity.

of the beach. The numbers in the second column of the table show how the output of corn rises as the hours devoted to cultivating it rise.

To produce cloth, Jane gathers wool from the sheep that live on the island. Some of the sheep are tame, so the first few hours she works produce a large amount of cloth. As she devotes more hours to collecting wool and making cloth, her output rises but, as in the case of corn, each additional hour produces less wool. Jane has to find and catch less cooperative sheep to make more wool.

If Jane devotes all her time to growing corn, she can produce 25 pounds of corn in a month. In that case, however, she cannot produce any cloth. Conversely, if she devotes all her time to making cloth, she can produce 10 yards a month but will have no time left for growing corn. Jane can devote some of her time to corn and some to cloth but not more than 12 hours a day total. Thus she can spend 3 hours growing corn and 9 hours making cloth or 6 hours on each (or any other combination of hours that add up to 12 hours).

We have defined the production possibility frontier as the boundary between what is attainable and what is not attainable. You can calculate Jane's

production possibility frontier by using the information in Table 3.1. These calculations are summarized in the table in Fig. 3.1 and graphed in that figure as *Jane's production possibility frontier.* To see how we calculated that frontier, let's concentrate first on the table in Fig. 3.1.

Possibility *a* shows Jane devoting no time to cloth and her entire 12-hour working day to corn. In this case, she can produce 25 pounds of corn per month and no cloth. For possibility *b*, she spends 3 hours a day making cloth and 9 hours growing corn, to produce a total of 20 pounds of corn and 4 yards of cloth per month. The pattern continues on to possibility *e*, where she devotes 12 hours a day to cloth and no time to corn. These same numbers are plotted in the graph shown in Fig. 3.1. Yards of cloth are measured on the horizontal axis and pounds of corn on the vertical axis. Points *a*, *b*, *c*, *d*, and *e* represent the numbers in the corresponding row of the table.

Of course, Jane does not have to work in blocks of 3 hours, as in our example. She can work 1 hour or 1 hour and 10 minutes growing corn and devote the rest of her time to making cloth. All other feasible allocations of Jane's 12 hours will result in a series of production possibilities represented by the line that joins points *a*, *b*, *c*, *d*, and *e*. This line shows Jane's production possibility frontier. She can produce at any point on the frontier or inside it, within the orange area. These are attainable points. Points outside the frontier are unattainable. To produce at points beyond the frontier, Jane needs more time than she has. By working 12 hours a day producing both corn and cloth, Jane can choose any point she wishes on the frontier. By working less than 12 hours a day, she produces at a point inside the frontier.

On the Frontier Is Best

Jane produces corn and cloth, not for the fun of it, but so that she can eat and keep warm. The larger the quantities of corn and cloth she produces, the more she can consume. Her wants for corn and cloth outstrip her production possibilities, and the best that she can do is to produce—and, therefore, consume—at a point *on* her production possibility frontier. To see why, consider a point such as *z* in the attainable region. At point *z*, Jane can improve her situation by moving to a point such as *b* or *d* or to a point on the frontier between *b* and *d*, such as point *c*. Jane can have more of everything on the frontier

Figure 3.1   Jane's Production Possibility Frontier

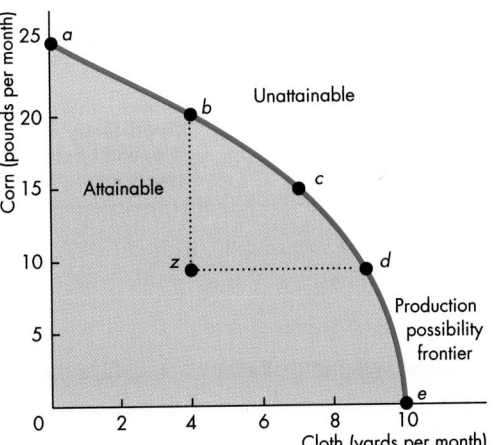

Possibility	Corn (pounds per month)		Cloth (yards per month)
a	25	and	0
b	20	and	4
c	15	and	7
d	9	and	9
e	0	and	10

The table lists five points on Jane's production possibility frontier. Row d tells us that if Jane produces 9 pounds of corn, the maximum cloth production that is possible is 9 yards. These same points are graphed as points a, b, c, d, and e in the figure. The line passing through these points is Jane's production possibility frontier, which separates the attainable from the unattainable. The orange attainable area contains all the possible production points. Jane can produce anywhere inside this area or on the production possibility frontier. Points outside the frontier are unattainable. Jane prefers points on the frontier to any point inside. Points between b and d on the frontier are better than point z inside the frontier because they give Jane more of both goods.

than at points inside it. At point *b*, she can consume more corn and no less cloth than at point *z*. At point *d*, she can consume more cloth and no less corn than at point *z*. At point *c* she can consume more corn and more cloth than at point *z*. Jane will never choose points such as *z* because better choices, such as *c*, will always be available. That is, some point on the frontier is always better than a point inside the frontier.

In comparing points *b*, *c*, and *d* with point *z*, we can see that *z* is an inferior point and one that Jane will not choose. It is easy to see that Jane will want to produce at some point on her production possibility frontier, but she will still be faced with the problem of choosing the best point. In choosing between one point and another, Jane is confronted with opportunity costs. At point *b*, for example, she will have less cloth and more corn than at point *c*. If she chooses point *c*, she will do so because she figures that the extra cloth is worth the corn forgone. Let's go on to explore opportunity cost more closely and see how we can measure it.

Opportunity Cost

We've defined opportunity cost as the best alternative forgone: For a late sleeper, the opportunity cost of attending an early morning class is an hour in bed; for a jogger, it is an hour of exercise. The concept of opportunity cost can be made more precise by using a production possibility frontier such as the one shown in Fig. 3.1. Let's see what that curve tells us.

The Best Alternative Forgone

The production possibility frontier in Fig. 3.1 traces the boundary between attainable and unattainable combinations of corn and cloth. Since there are only two goods, there is no difficulty in working out what is the best alternative forgone. More corn can be grown only by paying the price of having less cloth, and more cloth can be made only by bearing the cost of having less corn. Thus the opportunity cost of cloth is the corn forgone and the opportunity cost of corn is the cloth forgone. Let's put numerical values on the opportunity costs of corn and cloth.

Measuring Opportunity Cost

We are going to measure opportunity cost by using Jane's production possibility frontier. We will calculate how much cloth she has to give up to get more corn and how much corn she has to give up to get more cloth.

If all Jane's time is used to produce cloth, she produces 10 yards of cloth and no corn. If she decides to give up 1 yard of cloth in order to get some corn, how much corn can she produce? You can see the answer in Fig. 3.1. By giving up 1 yard of cloth to produce some corn, Jane moves from e to d and produces 9 pounds of corn. Thus the opportunity cost of the first 9 pounds of corn is 1 yard of cloth.

Consider next the reverse move, from d to e. Jane increases her cloth production by 1 yard but she has to give up 9 pounds of corn. Thus the opportunity cost of the tenth yard of cloth is 9 pounds of corn. The opportunity cost of cloth when moving from d to e is the inverse of the opportunity cost of corn when moving from e to d. If giving up the last 1 yard of cloth allows Jane to produce 9 pounds of corn, then, conversely, getting the last yard of cloth costs her 9 pounds of corn.

We have just worked out the opportunity cost of corn if we move from e to d and the opportunity cost of cloth if we move from d to e in Fig. 3.1. These opportunity costs are recorded in Table 3.2. The first row records the opportunity cost of the first 9 pounds of corn. That opportunity cost is 1 yard of cloth, which means that the opportunity cost of 1 pound of corn is ⅑ of a yard of cloth. The last row of the table records the opportunity cost of the last yard of cloth. That opportunity cost is 9 pounds of corn. Table 3.2 also sets out the opportunity costs of moving between points a, b, c, and d on the production possibility frontier. You may want to work out another example on your own to be sure that you understand what is going on. Calculate Jane's opportunity cost of moving from point b to c, or from c back to b.

Increasing Opportunity Cost

As you can see, opportunity cost varies with the quantity produced. The first 9 pounds of corn cost

Table 3.2 Jane's Opportunity Costs of Corn and Cloth

(a) Opportunity cost of corn

As Jane increases her cloth production:	Opportunity cost of 1 pound of corn (yards of cloth)
First 9 pounds of corn cost 1 yard of cloth	⅑
Next 6 pounds of corn cost 2 yards of cloth	⅓
Next 5 pounds of corn cost 3 yards of cloth	⅗
Last 5 pounds of corn cost 4 yards of cloth	⅘

(b) Opportunity cost of cloth

As Jane increases her cloth production:	Opportunity cost of 1 yard of cloth (pounds of corn)
First 4 yards of cloth cost 5 pounds of corn	1¼
Next 3 yards of cloth cost 5 pounds of corn	1⅔
Next 2 yards of cloth cost 6 pounds of corn	3
Last yard of cloth costs 9 pounds of corn	9

Part (a) shows Jane's opportunity cost of corn. The first 9 pounds of corn cost 1 yard of cloth or 1 pound of corn costs ⅑ of a yard of cloth. The next 6 pounds of corn cost 2 yards of cloth. The opportunity cost of corn rises as Jane produces more corn, with the last 5 pounds of corn costing 4 yards of cloth. Part (b) shows Jane's opportunity cost of cloth. The first 4 yards of cloth cost 5 pounds of corn or 1 yard of cloth costs 1¼ pounds of corn. The opportunity cost of cloth rises as Jane produces more cloth, with the last yard of cloth costing 9 pounds of corn.

only 1 yard of cloth. The next 6 pounds of corn cost 2 yards of cloth. The last 5 pounds of corn cost 4 yards of cloth. Thus the opportunity cost of corn increases as Jane grows more corn.

The same is true for cloth. The first 4 yards of cloth cost 5 pounds of corn. The next 3 yards of cloth also cost 5 pounds of corn. The last yard of cloth costs 9 pounds of corn. Thus the opportunity cost of cloth also increases as Jane makes more cloth.

The Shape of the Frontier

Pay special attention to the shape of the production possibility frontier in Fig. 3.1. When a large amount of corn and not much cloth is produced—between points *a* and *b*—the frontier has a gentle slope. When a large amount of cloth and not much corn is produced—between points *d* and *e*—the frontier is steep. The whole frontier bows outward. These features of the production possibility frontier are a reflection of increasing opportunity cost. Between points *a* and *b*, a large amount of cloth can be obtained by giving up a small amount of corn so that the opportunity cost of cloth is low and the opportunity cost of corn is high. Between points *d* and *e*, a large amount of corn must be given up to produce a small extra amount of cloth. In this region, the opportunity cost of cloth is high and the opportunity cost of corn is low.

Increasing opportunity cost and the outward bow of the production possibility frontier arise from the fact that scarce resources are not equally useful in all activities. For instance, some of the land on Jane's island is extremely fertile and produces a high crop yield, while other land is rocky and barren. The sheep on the island, however, prefer the rocky, barren land.

Jane uses the most fertile land for growing corn and the most barren areas for raising sheep. Only if she wants a larger amount of corn does she try to cultivate relatively barren areas, and only if she wants a larger amount of wool does she start raising sheep on the more fertile corn-growing land. If she uses all her time to grow corn, she has to use some very unsuitable, low-yielding land. Devoting some time to making cloth, and reducing the time spent growing corn by the same amount, produces a small drop in corn production but a large increase in the output of cloth. Conversely, if Jane uses all her time to make cloth, a small reduction in woolgathering yields a large increase of corn production.

Production Possibilities in the Real World

Jane's island is dramatically different from the world that we live in. The fundamental lesson it teaches us, however, applies to the real world. The world has a fixed number of people with a limited time to spend producing things. The world also has a fixed amount of natural and capital resources. Thus there is a limit to the goods and services that can be produced, a boundary between what is attainable and what is not attainable. That boundary is the real-world economy's production possibility frontier. On that frontier, producing more of any one good requires producing less of some other good or goods.

For example, a presidential candidate who promises better welfare and education services must at the same time, to be credible, promise either cuts in defense spending or higher taxes. Higher taxes mean less money left over for vacations and other consumption goods and services. The cost of better welfare and educational services is less of other goods. On a smaller scale but equally important, each time you decide to rent a video you decide not to use your limited money to buy soda, or popcorn, or some other good. The cost of one more video is less of something else.

On Jane's island, we saw that the opportunity cost of a good increased as the output of the good increased. Opportunity costs in the real world increase for the same reasons that Jane's opportunity costs increase. Consider, for example, two goods vital to our well being—food and health care. In allocating our scarce resources, we use the most fertile land and the most skillful farmers to produce food. We use the best doctors and the least fertile land for health care. If we shift fertile land and tractors away from farming and ask farmers to do surgery, the production of food drops drastically and the increase in the production of health care services is small. The opportunity cost of health care services rises. Similarly, if we shift our resources away from health care toward farming, we have to use more doctors and nurses as farmers and more hospitals as hydroponic tomato factories. The drop in health care services is large, but the increase in food production small. The opportunity cost of producing more food rises.

This example is extreme and unlikely, but these same considerations apply to any pair of goods that you can imagine: guns and butter; housing for the needy and diamonds for the rich; wheelchairs and golf carts; television programs and breakfast cereals. We cannot escape from scarcity and opportunity cost. More of one thing always means less of something else, and the more of anything that we have or do, the higher is its opportunity cost.

R E V I E W

The production possibility frontier is the boundary between the attainable and the unattainable. There is always a point on the frontier that is better than any point inside it. Moving from one point on the frontier to another means having less of one good to get more of another. The frontier is bowed outward or, equivalently, the opportunity cost of a good increases as more of it is produced. ■

Changing Production Possibilities

Although the production possibility frontier defines the boundary between what is attainable and what is unattainable, that boundary is not static. It is constantly changing. Sometimes the production possibility frontier shifts *inward,* reducing our production possibilities. For example, droughts or other extreme climatic conditions shift the frontier inward. Sometimes the frontier moves outward. For example, excellent growing and harvest conditions have this effect. Sometimes the frontier shifts outward because we get a new idea. It suddenly occurs to us that there is a better way of doing something that we never before imagined possible—we invent the wheel.

Over the years, our production possibilities have undergone enormous expansion. The persistent expansion of our production possibilities is called **economic growth.** As a consequence of economic growth we can now produce much more than we could 100 years ago and quite a bit more than even ten years ago. By the mid–1990s, if the same pace of growth continues, our production possibilities will be even greater. By pushing out the frontier, can we avoid the constraints imposed on us by our limited resources? That is, can we get our free lunch after all?

The Cost of Shifting the Frontier

We are going to discover that although we can and do shift the production possibility frontier outward over time, we cannot increase the pace at which we

do so without incurring costs. The faster the pace of economic growth, the less we can consume at the present time. Let's investigate the costs of growth by examining why economies grow and prosper.

Two key activities generate economic growth: capital accumulation and technological progress. **Capital accumulation** is the growth of capital resources. **Technological progress** is the development of new and better ways of producing goods and services. As a consequence of capital accumulation and technological progress, we have an enormous quantity of cars and airplanes that enable us to produce more transportation than when we only had horses and carriages; satellites that make transcontinental communications possible on a scale much larger than that produced by the earlier cable technology. But accumulating capital and developing new technology is costly. To see why, let's go back to Jane's island economy.

Capital Accumulation and Technological Change

We know that if Jane spends her entire 12 hours of working time each day producing corn and cloth, she will be somewhere on the production possibility frontier illustrated in Fig. 3.1. If Jane produces at a point on the frontier, she cannot devote any time to making tools or equipment that can be used to grow corn or to make cloth. Her production possibilities for next year will be the same as this year. She will have no more capital and no better technology in the future than she has now. To expand her future production, Jane must produce less corn and cloth today and devote resources to making tools or developing better methods of growing corn and making cloth. The cut in her output of corn and cloth today will be the opportunity cost of expanding her production in the future.

Figure 3.2 provides a more concrete example. The table sets out Jane's production possibilities for producing tools as well as corn and cloth. If she devotes all her working hours to corn and cloth production (row *e*), she produces no tools. If she devotes enough time to produce 1 tool per month (row *d*), her corn and cloth production is cut back to 90 percent of its maximum possible level. She can devote still more time to toolmaking and, as she does so, her corn and cloth production falls by successively larger amounts.

The numbers in the table are graphed in the figure. Each point, from *a* through *e*, represents a row of the table. Notice the similarity between Figs. 3.2 and 3.1. Each shows a production possibility frontier. In the case of Fig. 3.2, the frontier is that between producing tools and producing current consumption goods—corn and cloth. If Jane produces at point *e* in Fig. 3.2, she produces no tools and remains stuck on the production possibility frontier for corn and cloth shown in Fig. 3.1. However, if she moves to point *d* in Fig. 3.2, she can produce 1 tool each month. But to do so, Jane must reduce her production of corn and cloth to 90 percent of what she can produce if all her time is devoted to those activities.

By lowering her production of corn and cloth and producing tools, Jane is able to increase her production possibilities. She will have an increasing stock of tools and can use these tools to become more productive at growing corn and making cloth. She can even use tools to make better tools. As a consequence, Jane's production possibility frontier shifts outward as shown by the shift arrow—she experiences economic growth. The amount by which the frontier shifts out depends on how much time she devotes to toolmaking. If she devotes no time to making tools, the frontier remains at *abcde*—the original production possibility frontier. If she cuts back on the production of corn and cloth and produces one tool (at point *d*), her frontier moves out to the position of the red curve shown in the figure. The less time she devotes to corn and cloth production and the more time to toolmaking, the farther out the frontier shifts. But economic growth is not a free gift for Jane. To make it happen she has to devote more time to producing tools and less to producing corn and cloth. Economic growth is no magic formula for abolishing scarcity.

The Real World Again

The ideas that we have explored in the setting of Jane's island apply with equal force to our real-world economy. If we devote all our resources to producing food, clothing, housing, vacations, and the many other consumer goods that we enjoy, and none to research, development, and accumulating capital, we will have no more capital and no better technologies in the future than we have at present. Our production possibilities in the future will be

Figure 3.2   Jane's Tool Production Possibilities

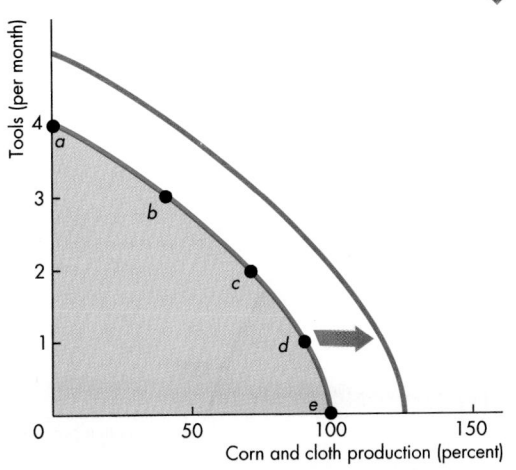

Possibility	Tools (per month)	Corn and cloth production (percent)
a	4	0
b	3	40
c	2	70
d	1	90
e	0	100

If Jane devotes all her time to corn and cloth production, she produces no tools (row *e* of the table). As she devotes more time to tool production, she can produce successively smaller amounts of corn and cloth. If all her time is devoted to tool production (possibility *a*), no corn and cloth and 4 tools are produced. In the figure, the curve *abcde* is Jane's production possibility frontier for tools and consumption goods (corn and cloth). If Jane produces at point *e* (producing no tools), her production possibility frontier remains fixed at *abcde*. If she cuts her production of corn and cloth and makes one tool (producing at point *d*), her future production possibility frontier shifts outward as shown in the figure. The more tools and the less corn and cloth Jane produces, the farther out the frontier shifts. The reduced output of corn and cloth is the opportunity cost of increasing future production possibilities.

exactly the same as those today. If we are to expand our production possibilities in the future, we must produce fewer consumption goods today. The

Figure 3.3   Economic Growth in the United States and Japan

(a) United States   **(b) Japan**

In 1965, the production possibilities per capita in the United States, part (a), were much larger than those in Japan, part (b). But Japan devoted one third of its resources to producing capital goods, while the United States devoted only one fifth. Japan's more rapid increase in capital resources resulted in its production possibility frontier shifting out more quickly than that in the United States. The two production possibilities per capita in 1990 are similar to each other. If Japan produces at point b on its 1990 frontier, it will continue to grow more quickly than the United States. If Japan increases consumption and produces at point c on its 1990 frontier, its growth rate will slow down to that of the United States.

resources we free up today will enable us to accumulate capital and to develop better technologies for producing consumption goods in the future. The cut in the output of consumption goods today is the opportunity cost of economic growth.

The recent experience of the United States and Japan provides a striking example of the effects of our choices on the rate of economic growth. In 1965, the production possibilities per capita in the United States were much larger than those in Japan (see Fig. 3.3). The United States devoted one fifth of its resources to producing capital goods and the other four fifths to producing consumption goods, as illustrated by point *a* in Fig. 3.3(a). But Japan devoted one third of its resources to producing capital goods and only two thirds to producing consumption goods, as illustrated by point *a* in Fig. 3.3(b). Both countries experienced economic growth, but the growth in Japan was much more

rapid than the growth in the United States. Because Japan devoted a bigger fraction of its resources to producing capital goods, its stock of capital equipment grew more quickly than ours, and its production possibilities expanded more quickly. As a result, Japanese production possibilities per capita are now so close to those in the United States that it is hard to say which country has the larger per capita production possibilities. If Japan continues to devote a third of its resources to producing capital goods (at point *b* on its 1990 production possibility frontier), it will continue to grow much more rapidly than the United States and its frontier will move out beyond our own. If Japan increases its production of consumption goods and reduces its production of capital goods (moving to point *c* on its 1990 production possibility frontier), then its rate of economic expansion will slow down to that of our own.

R E V I E W

Economic growth results from the accumulation of capital and the development of better technologies. To reap the fruits of economic growth, we must incur the cost of fewer goods and services for current consumption. By cutting the current output of consumption goods, we can devote more resources to accumulating capital and to the research and development that lead to technological change—the engines of economic growth. Thus economic growth does not provide a free lunch. It has an opportunity cost—the fall in the current output of consumption goods. ■

Gains from Trade

No one excels at everything. One person is more athletic than another, another person may have a quicker mind or a better memory. What one person does with ease, someone else may find difficult.

Comparative Advantage: Jane Meets Joe

Differences in individual abilities mean that there are also differences in individual opportunity costs of producing various goods. Such differences give rise to **comparative advantage**—we say that a person has a comparative advantage in producing a particular good if that person can produce the good at a lower opportunity cost than anyone else.

People can produce for themselves all the goods that they want to consume or they can concentrate on producing one good (or perhaps a few goods) and then exchange some of their own products for the output of others. Concentrating on the production of only one good or a few goods is called **specialization.** We are going to discover how people can gain by specializing in that good at which they have a comparative advantage and then trading their output with others.

Let's return again to our island economy. Suppose that Jane has discovered another island very close to her own on which a fellow voyager named Joe is stranded. Joe's island is much like Jane's. Jane and Joe each have access to a simple boat that is adequate for transporting themselves and their goods between the two islands.

Joe's island, too, can produce only corn and cloth, but its terrain differs from that on Jane's island. While Jane's island has a lot of fertile corn-growing land and a small sheep population, Joe's island has little fertile corn-growing land and plenty of sheep. This important difference between the two islands means that Joe's production possibility frontier is different from Jane's—in fact, it is a mirror image of Jane's. The table in Fig. 3.4 presents the production possibility frontiers of Jane and Joe. Note that if Jane devotes all her time to cloth production, she can make 10 yards of cloth, but if Joe devotes all his time to cloth, he can make 25 yards of cloth. Conversely, if Jane devotes all her time to corn farming, she can produce 25 pounds of corn, but Joe can produce only 10 pounds.

The graph in Fig. 3.4 illustrates the same production possibility frontiers. Jane's frontier, labeled "Jane's PPF," looks different here from the way it looked in Fig. 3.1 because we have had to change the scale on the x-axis to make room for Joe's frontier, labeled "Joe's PPF."

Jane and Joe can be self-sufficient in corn and cloth. **Self-sufficiency** is a state that occurs when people produce only for their own consumption. Suppose that Jane and Joe are each self-sufficient and that each chooses to produce 9 yards of cloth and 9 pounds of corn. (They could have chosen any other point on their own production possibility frontier.) Given this choice, each of them is at point x in Fig. 3.4. Total production of corn and cloth is twice the amount shown at x. That is, Jane and Joe individually produce at point x, which means that total production is at point n. Together, Joe and Jane produce 18 pounds of corn and 18 yards of cloth.

Jane's Comparative Advantage   In which of the two goods does Jane have a comparative advantage? We have defined comparative advantage as a situation in which one person's opportunity cost of producing a good is lower than another person's opportunity cost of producing that same good. Jane, then, has a comparative advantage in producing whichever good she produces at a lower opportunity cost than Joe. What is that good?

Figure 3.4   The Gains from Specialization and Trade

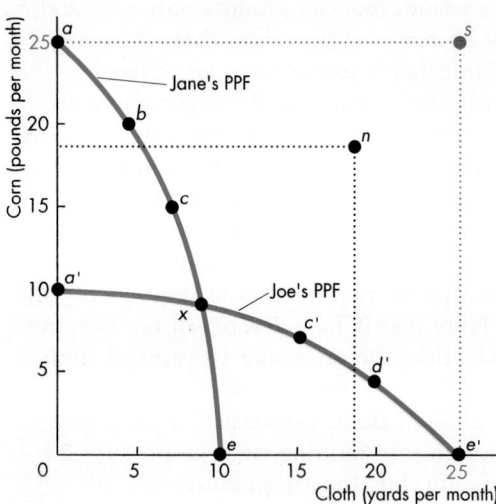

	Jane				Joe		
	Corn (pounds per month)		Cloth (yards per month)		Corn (pounds per month)		Cloth (yards per month)
a	25	and	0	a'	10	and	0
b	20	and	4	b'	9	and	9
c	15	and	7	c'	7	and	15
d	9	and	9	d'	4	and	20
e	0	and	10	e'	0	and	25

Jane's and Joe's production possibility frontiers (PPFs) are shown. Suppose that Joe and Jane each produce at point x. Their total production is at point n. Joe and Jane can do better by specialization and exchange. Jane has a lower opportunity cost of producing corn than Joe, and Joe has a lower opportunity cost of producing cloth than Jane. Jane has a comparative advantage in corn production. If she specializes in corn production, she produces 25 pounds of corn and no cloth. Joe has a comparative advantage in cloth production. If he specializes in that activity, he produces 25 yards of cloth and no corn. That is, Jane chooses row a and Joe chooses row e' of the table. Total production is then 25 pounds of corn and 25 yards of cloth (point s). If Jane exchanges some of her corn for Joe's cloth and if Joe exchanges some of his cloth for Jane's corn, each can consume more corn and cloth than in a state of self-sufficiency. If each exchanges half of his or her output with the other, they will each consume 12.5 pounds of corn and 12.5 yards of cloth. The increased corn and cloth consumption is the gain from specialization and trade.

You can answer the question by looking at the production possibility frontiers for Jane and Joe in Fig. 3.4. If each of them is producing at point x—the point of self-sufficiency—Jane's production possibility frontier is much steeper than Joe's. To produce more corn, Jane gives up much less cloth than Joe. Hence Jane's opportunity cost of a pound of corn is much lower than Joe's. This means that Jane has a comparative advantage in producing corn.

Joe's Comparative Advantage   Joe's comparative advantage is in producing cloth. His production possibility frontier at x—the point of self-sufficiency—is much flatter than Jane's. This means that Joe has to give up much less corn to produce more cloth than Jane does. Joe's opportunity

cost of a yard of cloth is lower than Jane's, so Joe has a comparative advantage in cloth production.

Reaping the Gains from Trade

Can Jane and Joe do better than be self-sufficient? In particular, what would happen if each were to specialize in producing the good at which each has a comparative advantage and then trade with the other?

If Jane, who has a comparative advantage in corn production, puts all her resources into growing corn, she can grow 25 pounds (the amount labeled a on the vertical axis of Fig. 3.4). If Joe, who has a comparative advantage in cloth production, puts all his resources into making cloth, he can make 25 yards (the amount labeled e' on the horizontal axis). By specializing, Jane and Joe together can produce 25 pounds of corn and 25 yards of cloth (the amount labeled s in the figure). Point s shows the production of 25 pounds of corn (all produced by Jane) and 25 yards of cloth (all produced by Joe). Clearly, at point s Jane and Joe produce more cloth and corn than they were producing at point n, when each took care only of his or her own requirements. Point s is a better point than n because, between them, Jane and Joe have more of both corn and cloth than at point n.

To obtain the gains from trade, Jane and Joe must do more than specialize in producing the good at which each has a comparative advantage. They must exchange the fruits of their specialized production. Suppose that Jane and Joe agree to exchange one half of their output. Jane pays Joe 12.5 pounds of corn in exchange for 12.5 yards of cloth. Joe pays Jane 12.5 yards of cloth in exchange for 12.5 pounds of corn. Both Jane and Joe will now have consumption greater than what they had under a self-sufficiency arrangement. Under self-sufficiency, each was consuming 9 pounds of corn and 9 yards of cloth. With specialization and exchange, each is consuming 12.5 pounds of corn and 12.5 yards of cloth. The gain from trade is represented by the increase in consumption of both goods that each person obtains. In this example, the gain from trade is 3.5 pounds of corn and 3.5 yards of cloth for each individual—a gain of almost 39 percent.

Absolute Advantage

Whenever a person can produce more of all goods than anyone else, that person has an **absolute advantage.** In our example, no one has an absolute advantage. Jane and Joe have production possibilities that are mirror images of each other. Jane produces corn as easily as Joe produces cloth, and she is as bad at making cloth as Joe is at growing corn. Suppose that Jane becomes more productive, so that she has an absolute advantage over Joe. In particular, suppose that she becomes twice as productive. Her new production possibilities appear in Table 3.3.

We have already worked out that the gains from trade arise when each person specializes in producing that good with the lower opportunity cost. Joe's opportunity costs remain exactly the same as they were before. What has happened to

Table 3.3   Jane's New Production Possibilities

Possibility	Corn (pounds per month)		Cloth (yards per month)
a	50	and	0
b	40	and	8
c	30	and	14
d	18	and	18
e	0	and	20

Jane's opportunity costs now that she has become twice as productive?

You can work out Jane's opportunity costs by using exactly the same calculation that was used in Table 3.2. Start by looking at Jane's opportunity cost of corn. The first 18 pounds of corn that Jane grows cost her 2 yards of cloth. So the opportunity cost of 1 pound of corn is $\frac{1}{9}$ of a yard of cloth—the same as Jane's original opportunity cost of corn. If you calculate the opportunity costs for Jane's production possibilities a through e, you will discover that each of them has remained the same.

Since the opportunity cost of cloth is the inverse of the opportunity cost of corn, Jane's opportunity costs of cloth also have remained unchanged. Let's work through one example. If Jane moves from a to b to make 8 yards of cloth, she will have to reduce her corn production by 10 pounds—from 50 to 40 pounds. Thus the first 8 yards of cloth cost 10 pounds of corn. The cost of 1 yard of cloth is, therefore, $1\frac{1}{4}$ pounds of corn—again exactly the same as before.

When Jane becomes twice as productive as before, each hour of her time produces more output, but her opportunity cost remains the same. One more unit of corn costs the same in terms of cloth forgone as it did previously. Since Jane's opportunity costs have not changed and since Joe's have not changed, Joe continues to have a comparative advantage in producing cloth. Both Jane and Joe can have more of both goods if Jane specializes in corn production and Joe in cloth production.

The key point to recognize is that it is *not* possible for a person having an absolute advantage to have a comparative advantage in everything.

R E V I E W

Gains from trade come from comparative advantage. Unless two individuals have the same opportunity costs, each has a comparative advantage in some activity. Differences in opportunity costs provide the basis for comparative advantage and the gains from specialization and exchange. Even a person with an absolute advantage gains from specialization and exchange. ■

Exchange in the Real World

In the real world, where there are billions of people specializing in millions of different activities, gains from specialization and trade exist, but they are harder to exploit. Trade has to be organized. To organize trade, we have evolved rules of conduct and mechanisms for enforcing those rules. One such mechanism is private property rights. Another is the institution of money. In the island economy of Jane and Joe, direct exchange of one good with another is feasible. In the real-world economy, direct exchange of one good for another would be very cumbersome. To lubricate the wheels of exchange, societies have created money—a medium that enables indirect exchange of goods for money and money for goods. Let's examine these two aspects of exchange arrangements in more detail.

Property rights

Property rights are social arrangements that govern the ownership, use, and disposal of property. **Property** is anything of value: It includes land and buildings—the things we call property in ordinary speech; it also includes stocks and bonds, durable goods, plant and equipment; it also includes intellectual property. **Intellectual property** is the intangible product of creative effort, protected by copyrights and patents. This type of property includes books, music, computer programs, and inventions of all kinds.

What if property rights did not exist? What would such a social science fiction world be like?

A World Without Property Rights   Without property rights, people could take possession of whatever they had the strength to obtain for themselves. In such a world, people would have to devote a good deal of their time, energy, and resources to protecting what they had produced or acquired.

In a world without property rights, it would be impossible to reap any gains from specialization and exchange. People would have no incentive to specialize in producing those goods at which they each had a comparative advantage. In fact, the more of a particular good someone produced, the bigger the chance that others would simply help themselves to it. Also, if a person could take the goods of others without giving up something in exchange, then there would be no point in specializing in producing something for exchange. In a world without property rights, no one would enjoy the gains from specialization and exchange, and everyone would specialize only in unproductive acts of piracy. It is to overcome the problems that we have just described that property rights have evolved. Let's examine these property rights as they operate to govern economic life in the United States today.

Property Rights in Private Enterprise Capitalism   The U.S. economy operates for the most part on the principles of private enterprise capitalism. **Private enterprise** is an economic system that permits individuals to decide on their own economic activities. **Capitalism** is an economic system that permits private individuals to own the capital resources used in production.

Under the property rights in such an economic system, individuals own what they have made, or what they have acquired in a voluntary exchange with others, or what they have been given. Any attempt to remove the property of someone against that person's will is considered theft, a crime punished by a sufficiently severe penalty to deter most people from becoming thieves.

It is easy to see that property rights based on these ideas can generate gainful trade: People can specialize in producing those goods that, for them, have the least opportunity cost. Some people will specialize in enforcing and maintaining property rights (for example, politicians, judges, and police officers) and all individuals will have the incentive to trade with each other, offering the good in which they have a comparative advantage in exchange for the goods produced by others.

Although the U.S. economic system is based on a system of private property with voluntary exchange, property rights even in this country have limits. Let's look at some of these.

Taxes Limit Private Property Rights   The most important and pervasive limit on people's rights to private property comes from taxes. All of us have to pay taxes to federal, state, and local governments. Many people regard the taxes that they pay as a fair price for the services provided by government. Many others, however, regard the taxes that they pay as exorbitant. Taxing part of the property that people have created limits people's efforts to create more property and reduces their gain from specialized production.

Even though taxes constitute a partial intrusion into private property rights, the taxes themselves are not arbitrary. Everyone faces the same rules and can calculate the effects of their own actions on the taxes for which they will be liable.

Regulation Limits Private Property Rights
Other restrictions on private property rights prohibit certain kinds of voluntary exchange. For example, food and drug manufacturers cannot place a product on the market without first obtaining approval from a government agency. The government controls or prohibits the sale of many types of drugs, and also restricts trading in human beings and their component parts—that is, it prohibits the selling of slaves, children, and human organs.

These restrictions on the extent of private property and on the legitimacy of voluntary exchange, though important, do not, for the most part, seriously impede specialization and gainful trade. Most people take the view that the benefits of regulation—for example, prohibiting the sale of dangerous drugs—far outweigh the costs imposed on the sellers.

Let's now turn to the other major social institution that permits specialization and exchange—the development of an efficient means of exchange.

Money

We have seen that well-defined property rights based on voluntary exchange allow individuals to specialize and exchange their output with each other. In our island economy, we studied only two people and two goods. Exchange in such a situation was a simple matter. In the real world, however, how can billions of people exchange the millions of goods that are the fruits of their specialized labor?

Barter   Goods can be simply exchanged for goods. This system is known as **barter.** However, exchanging goods only through the barter system severely limits the amount of trading that can take place. Imagine that you have roosters, but you want to get roses. First, you must look for someone with roses who wants roosters. Economists call this a **double coincidence of wants**—when person A wants to sell exactly what person B wants to buy, and person B wants to sell exactly what person A wants to buy. As the term implies, such occurrences are coincidences and will not arise frequently. A second way of trading by barter is to undertake a sequence of exchanges. If you have oranges and you want apples, you may have to trade oranges for plums and plums for pomegranates and pomegranates for pineapples and then eventually pineapples for apples.

Cumbersome though it is, quite a large amount of barter trade does take place. For example, when British rock star Rod Stewart played in Budapest, Hungary, in August 1986, he received part of his $30,000 compensation in Hungarian sound equipment, electrical cable, and the use of a forklift truck. Hairdressers in Warsaw, Poland, obtain their barbershop equipment from England in exchange for hair clippings that they supply to London wigmakers.

Although barter exchange does occur, it is an inefficient means of exchanging goods. Fortunately, a better alternative has been invented.

Monetary Exchange   An alternative to barter is **monetary exchange**—a system in which some commodity or token serves as the medium of exchange. A **medium of exchange** is anything that is generally acceptable in exchange for goods and services. **Money** can also be defined as a medium of exchange—something that can be passed on to others in exchange for goods and services. In a monetary exchange system, people exchange money for goods and goods for money, but they do not directly exchange goods for goods.

Overcoming Obstacles to the Gains from Trade

In Romania, Smoking A Kent Cigarette Is Like Burning Money

It isn't true that Romania, a hard-core Communist country, doesn't operate on the market principle. It does. Call it the farmers' market principle, and this is how it works:

As dawn breaks, a crowing rooster on sale at the downtown market signals the opening of an intense round of barter trading. Apples will get you peppers. Cauliflower will get you beets. Turnips will get you garlic. And Kent cigarettes will get you everything.

"Psssst. Mister. With the Kents," whispers a young farmer rushing from behind his fruit and vegetable stand to pursue someone who has just flashed a pack of Kents. Never mind the line of customers at the stand. They can wait; they have only *lei*, the official Romanian currency. The other guy has Kents.

"You sell?" asks the farmer, now being joined by four fellow farmers. He presents his left palm and begins writing on it. "Twenty-five," he writes. That is 25 *lei*, or about $2.20, for one pack of Kents. The man with the Kents sells two packs for 50 *lei* and inquires about the apples on sale.

"You want apples?" asks the farmer. He pulls out a bag hidden at the bottom of the pile. These aren't the yellow apples for the regular customers—the ones with *lei*. These are red apples for the man with the Kents.

Under the farmers' market principle, the fruit and vegetable farmer perhaps will trade away his Kents to get his tractor fixed. The mechanic will use the Kents to get a rare and relatively good cut of meat at the butcher shop. The butcher will pass on the Kents to get a table at a packed restaurant. The maitre d' will use the Kents to pay his doctor. The doctor will flash the Kents at the farmers' market to get some attention. And some farmer, writing on his hand, will come running after.

"In Romania, Kents are the ultimate affirmation of the market theory," says a Western diplomat here. "You've heard of the gold standard. Well this is the Kent standard. Everyone in this country wants Kents." And only Kents. Winston, Marlboro, Pall Mall won't do.

Want to be a big shot in Romania? Flash a pack of Kents. Want a taxi? Wave some Kents. (With the distinctive gold box used for the European Kents, they can be spotted at surprising distances.) Want to get past a troublesome passport officer at the airport? A couple of packs of Kents will do. Kents will open most every door in this country, including the door to the outside world.

The Wall Street Journal, **January 3, 1986**

by Roger Thurow, Staff Reporter

The Essence of the Story

In Romania, people buy and sell goods in three ways:

- By barter—exchanging apples for peppers and cauliflower for beets

- By using their official currency—giving and receiving lei in exchange for goods and services

- By using Kents—giving and receiving packs of Kent cigarettes in exchange for goods and services.

People offering Kents get a better deal than people offering lei. Kents circulate as a medium of exchange:

- The "man with the Kents" buys apples

- The farmer uses Kents to get his tractor fixed

- The mechanic uses Kents to buy meat

- The butcher uses Kents at a restaurant

- The head waiter uses Kents to get medical treatment

- The doctor uses Kents to buy apples—and so on.

Kents thus allow people to undertake a wide variety of trades (or exchanges).

Background and Analysis

Romania is a socialist country in Eastern Europe. Private property rights are restricted and the government controls most aspects of economic life. Some examples of what the government dictates:

- The things that people may produce

- The quantities that may be produced

- The prices at which goods may be sold

Romanians specialize in producing the things at which they have a comparative advantage. If they were to sell their output at the prices fixed by the government, they would receive less than the opportunity cost of production.

For this reason, people try to evade the government's controlled prices by direct barter or by using Kent cigarettes as money. Because people widely accept Kents as a means of payment, these cigarettes have come to serve as a medium of exchange—as money.

Conclusion

The people of Romania have invented the social contract of using Kents as money. By so doing, they have lessened the severity of restricted property rights and removed, at least partly, a major obstacle to achieving the gains from specialization and exchange.

65

Metals such as gold, silver, and copper have long served as money. Most commonly, they serve as money by being stamped as coins. Primitive societies have traditionally used various commodities, such as sea shells, as money. During the Civil War and for several years after, people used postage stamps as money. Prisoners of war in German camps in World War II used cigarettes as money. Even today in Bucharest, the capital of Romania, people use cigarettes as money (see Reading Between the Lines, pp. 64–65).[1] Using cigarettes as a medium of exchange should not be confused with barter. Under the circumstances described, cigarettes play the role of money, and people buy and sell goods by using cigarettes as a medium of exchange.

In modern societies, governments provide paper money. The banking system also provides money in the form of checking accounts. Checking accounts can be used for settling debts simply by writing an instruction—writing a check—to the bank requesting that funds be transferred to another checking account. Electronic links between bank accounts, now becoming more widespread, enable direct transfers between different accounts without any checks being written.

■ You have now begun to see how economists go about the job of trying to answer some important questions. The simple fact of scarcity and the associated concept of opportunity cost allow us to understand why people specialize, why they trade with each other, why they have social conventions that define and enforce private property rights, and why they use money. One simple idea—scarcity and its direct implication, opportunity cost—explains so much!

---

[1]This is the first in a series of "Reading Between the Lines" boxes. Each box begins with an extract from a newspaper or news magazine. The news story is then retold in stripped down form and analyzed by using the tools of economics that have been developed in the chapter.

S U M M A R Y

The Production Possibility Frontier

The production possibility frontier is the boundary between what is attainable and what is not attainable. Production can take place at any point inside or on the production possibility frontier. But it is not possible to produce outside the frontier. There is always a point on the production possibility frontier that is better than a point inside it. (pp. 51–53)

Opportunity Cost

The opportunity cost of any action is the best alternative action forgone. The opportunity cost of acquiring one good is equivalent to the amount of another good that must be given up. The opportunity cost of a good increases as the quantity of it produced increases. (pp. 53–56)

Changing Production Possibilities

Although the production possibility frontier marks the boundary between the attainable and the unattainable, that boundary does not remain fixed. It changes, partly because of natural forces (changes in climate and the accumulation of ideas about better ways of producing) and partly by the choices that we make. If we use some of today's resources to produce capital goods and for research and development we will be able to produce more goods and services in the future. The economy will grow. But growth cannot take place without incurring costs. The opportunity cost of more goods and services in the future is consuming fewer goods and services today. (pp. 56–59)

Gains from Trade

When people have different opportunity costs, they can gain from specialization and exchange. Each person specializes in producing the good for which their opportunity cost is lower than everyone else's —the good in which he or she has a comparative advantage. They then exchange part of their output with each other. (pp. 59–62)

Exchange in the Real World

Property rights and a system of monetary exchange enable people to specialize, exchanging their labor for money and their money for goods, thereby reaping the gains from trade. (pp. 62–66)

KEY CONCEPTS

Absolute advantage, 61
Barter, 63
Capitalism, 62
Capital accumulation, 56
Capital goods, 51
Capital resources, 51
Comparative advantage, 59
Consumption, 51
Consumption goods, 51
Double coincidence of wants, 63
Economic growth, 56
Goods and services, 51
Human capital, 51
Human resources, 51
Intellectual property, 62
Medium of exchange, 63
Monetary exchange, 63
Money, 63
Natural resources, 51

Private enterprise, 62
Production, 51
Production possibility frontier, 51
Property, 62
Property rights, 62
Self-sufficiency, 59
Specialization, 59
Technological progress, 56

Key Figures

Figure 3.1 Jane's Production Possibility Frontier, 53
Figure 3.2 Jane's Tool Production Possibilities, 57

REVIEW QUESTIONS

1 How does the production possibility curve illustrate scarcity?

2 How does the production possibility curve illustrate opportunity cost?

3 Explain what shifts the production possibility frontier outward and what shifts it inward.

4 Explain how our choices influence economic growth. What is the cost of economic growth?

5 Why does it pay people to specialize and trade with each other?

6 What are the gains from trade? How do they arise?

7 Why do social contracts such as property rights and money become necessary?

8 Why is monetary exchange more efficient than barter?

PROBLEMS

1 Suppose that there is a change in the weather conditions on Jane's island that makes the corn yields much higher. This enables Jane to produce the following amounts of corn:

Hours worked per day	Corn (pounds per month)
0	0
3	66
6	96
9	110
12	120

Her cloth production possibilities are the same as those that appeared in Table 3.1.

a) What are five points on Jane's new production possibility frontier?

b) What are Jane's opportunity costs of corn and cloth?

c) Comparing Jane's opportunity cost of corn with that in Table 3.2, has her opportunity cost of corn gone up, down, or remained the same? Explain why.

2 Suppose that Joe has the following production possibilities:

Corn (pounds per month)		Cloth (yards per month)
6	and	0.0
5	and	0.5
4	and	1.0
3	and	1.5
2	and	2.0
1	and	2.5
0	and	3.0

Jane has the following production possibilities:

Corn (pounds per month)		Cloth (yards per month)
3.0	and	0
2.5	and	1
2.0	and	2
1.5	and	3
1.0	and	4
0.5	and	5
0.0	and	6

Find the maximum quantity of corn and cloth that they can produce if each specializes in the activity at which he or she has the lower opportunity cost.

3 Suppose that Jane has become twice as productive and that she can now produce the following quantities:

Corn (pounds per month)		Cloth (yards per month)
6	and	0
5	and	2
4	and	4
3	and	6
2	and	8
1	and	10
0	and	12

a) Show the effect of Jane's increased productivity on her production possibility frontier.

b) Will it still pay Jane to specialize and trade with Joe now that she is twice as productive?

c) Will it still pay Joe to trade with Jane?

Chapter 4

Demand and Supply

After studying this chapter, you will be able to:

- Explain how prices are determined

- Explain why some prices rise, some fall, and some fluctuate

- Explain how quantities bought and sold are determined

- Construct a demand schedule and a demand curve

- Construct a supply schedule and a supply curve

- Make predictions about price changes using the demand and supply model

Disneyland rides? No. Commonly used descriptions of the behavior of prices. ■ There are lots of examples of price slides. One particular example is probably very familiar to you. In 1979, Sony began to market a pocket-sized cassette player that delivered its sound through tiny earphones. They named their new product the Walkman and they gave it a price tag of around $300—more than $500 in today's money. Today Sony has been joined by many other producers of Walkman clones, and you can buy a Walkman (or its equivalent) that's even better than the 1979 prototype, for less than one tenth of the original price. During the time that the Walkman has been with us, the quantity bought has increased steadily each

Slide, Rocket, and Roller Coaster

year. Why has there been a long and steady slide in the price of the Walkman? Why hasn't the increase in the quantity bought kept its price high? ■ Rocketing prices are also a familiar phenomenon. An important recent example is that of rents paid for apartments and houses, especially in central locations in big cities. Huge increases in rents and house prices have not deterred people from living in the centers of cities—on the contrary, their numbers have increased slightly in recent years. Why do people continue to seek housing in city centers when rents have rocketed so sharply? ■ There are lots of price roller coasters—cases in which prices rise and fall from season to season or year to year. Prices of coffee, strawberries, and many other agricultural commodities fit this pattern. Why does the price of coffee roller-coaster even when people's taste for coffee hardly changes at all? ■ Though amusement park rides provide a vivid description of the behavior of prices, many of the things that we buy have remarkably steady prices. The audiocassette tapes that we play in a Walkman are an example. The price of a tape has barely changed over the past ten years.

Nevertheless, the number of tapes bought has risen steadily year after year. Why do firms sell more and more tapes, even though they're not able to get higher prices for them and why do people willingly buy more tapes even though their price is no lower than it was a decade ago?

■ We will discover the answers to these and similar questions by studying demand and supply. We are first going to discover what determines the demand for different goods and the supply of them. Then we are going to discover how demand and supply together determine price. This powerful theory enables us to analyze many important economic events that affect our lives and even to make predictions about future prices.

Demand

The **quantity demanded** of a good or service is the amount that consumers plan to buy in a given period of time. Demands are different from wants. **Wants** are the unlimited desires or wishes that people have for goods and services. How many times have you thought that you would like something "if only you could afford it" or "if it weren't so expensive"? Scarcity guarantees that many — perhaps most — of our wants will never be satisfied. Demand reflects a decision about which wants to satisfy. If you demand something, then you've made a plan to buy it.

The quantity demanded is not necessarily the same amount as the quantity actually bought. The quantity that people actually buy and sell is called the **quantity traded.** Sometimes the quantity demanded is greater than the amount of goods available, so the quantity traded is less than the quantity demanded.

The quantity demanded is measured as an amount per unit of time. For example, suppose a person consumes one cup of coffee a day. The quantity of coffee demanded by that person can be expressed as one cup per day or seven cups per week or 365 cups per year. Without a time dimension, we cannot tell whether a particular quantity demanded is large or small.

What Determines the Quantity Demanded?

The amount that consumers plan to buy of any particular good or service depends on many factors. Among the more important ones are:

- The price of the good
- The prices of other goods
- Income
- Population
- Tastes

The theory of demand and supply makes predictions about the prices at which goods are traded and the quantities bought and sold. Our first focus, therefore, is on the relationship between the quantity demanded and the price of a good. To study this relationship, we hold constant all other influences on consumers' planned purchases. We can then ask: How does the quantity demanded of the good vary as its price varies?

The Law of Demand

The law of demand states:

Other things being equal, the higher the price of a good, the lower is the quantity demanded.

Why does a higher price reduce the quantity demanded? The answer is that each good, although unique, can usually be replaced by some other good. As the price of a good climbs higher, people buy less of that good and more of some substitute that serves almost as well.

Let's consider an example — blank audiocassette tapes, which we'll refer to as "tapes." Many different goods provide a similar service to a tape; for example, records, compact discs, prerecorded tapes, radio and television broadcasts, and live concerts. Tapes sell for about $3 each. If the price of a tape doubles to $6 while the prices of all the other goods remain constant, the quantity of tapes demanded will fall dramatically. People will buy more records and prerecorded tapes and fewer blank tapes. If the price of a tape falls to $1 while the prices of all the other goods stay constant, the quantity of tapes demanded will rise and the demand for records, albums, and prerecorded tapes will fall dramatically.

Figure 4.1   The Demand Schedule and
the Demand Curve

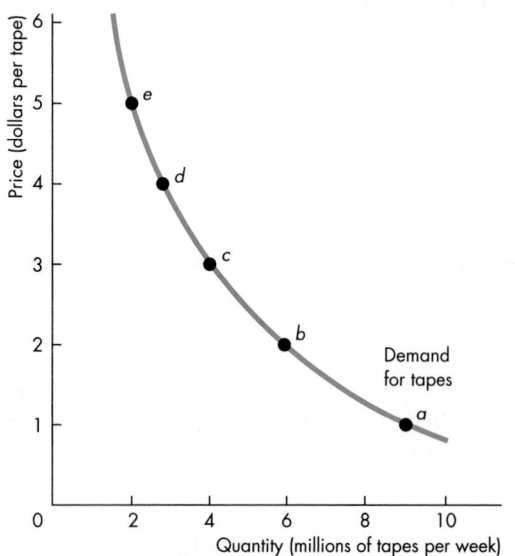

	Price (dollars per tape)	Quantity (millions of tapes per week)
a	1	9
b	2	6
c	3	4
d	4	3
e	5	2

The table shows a demand schedule listing the quantity of tapes demanded at each price if all other influences on buyers' plans are held constant. At a price of $1 a tape, 9 million tapes a week are demanded; at a price of $3 a tape, 4 million tapes a week are demanded. The demand curve shows the relationship between quantity demanded and price, holding everything else constant. The demand curve slopes downward: as price decreases, the quantity demanded increases. The demand curve can be read two ways. For a given price it tells us the quantity that people plan to buy. For example, at a price of $3 a tape, the quantity demanded is 4 million tapes a week. For a given quantity, the demand curve tells us the maximum price that consumers are willing to pay for the last tape bought. For example, the maximum price that consumers will pay for the 6 millionth tape is $2.

Demand Schedule and Demand Curve

A **demand schedule** lists the quantities demanded at each different price, when all the other influences on consumers' planned purchases—such as the prices of other goods, income, population, and tastes—are held constant.

The table in Fig. 4.1 sets out a demand schedule for tapes. For example, if the price of a tape is $1, the quantity demanded is 9 million tapes a week. If the price of a tape is $5, the quantity demanded is 2 million tapes a week. The other rows of the table show us the quantities demanded at prices between $2 and $4.

A demand schedule can be illustrated by drawing a demand curve. A **demand curve** graphs the relationship between the quantity demanded of a good and its price, holding constant all other influences on consumers' planned purchases. The graph in Fig. 4.1 illustrates the demand curve for tapes. By convention, the quantity demanded is always measured on the horizontal axis and the price is measured on the vertical axis. The points on the demand curve labeled *a* through *e* represent the rows of the demand schedule. For example, point *a* on the graph represents a quantity demanded of 9 million tapes a week at a price of $1 a tape.

Willingness to Pay

There is another way of looking at the demand curve: It shows the highest price that people are willing to pay for the last unit bought. If a large quantity is available, that price is low; but if only a small quantity is available, that price is high. For example, if 9 million tapes are available each week, the highest price that consumers are willing to pay for the 9 millionth tape is $1. But if only 2 million tapes are available each week, consumers are willing to pay $5 for the last tape available.

This view of the demand curve may become clearer if you think about your own demand for tapes. If I give you a list of possible prices of tapes, you could write down alongside each price your planned weekly purchase of tapes. On the other hand, if I tell you that there is just one tape available each week, you could tell me how much you'd be willing to pay for it. If I then told you that there is one more tape available, you could tell me the maximum price that you will be willing to pay for that second tape. We could continue this process, increasing the number of tapes by one, with you saying the maximum price that you're prepared to pay for each extra tape. The schedule of prices and quantities that we'd arrive at would be your demand schedule.

A Change in Demand

The term **demand** refers to the entire relationship between the quantity demanded and the price of a good. The demand for tapes is described by both the demand schedule and the demand curve in Fig. 4.1. To construct a demand schedule and demand curve, we hold constant all the other influences on consumers' buying plans. But what are the effects of each of those other influences?

1. Prices of Other Goods   The quantity of tapes that consumers plan to buy does not depend only on the price of tapes. It also depends in part on the prices of other relevant goods. These other goods fall into two categories: substitutes and complements.

A **substitute** is a good that can be used in place of another good. For example, a bus ride substitutes for a train ride; a hamburger substitutes for a hot dog; a pear substitutes for an apple. As we have seen, tapes have many substitutes—records, prerecorded tapes, compact discs, radio and television broadcasts, and live concerts. If the price of one of these substitutes increases, people economize on its use and buy more tapes. For example, if the price of records doubles, fewer records are bought and the demand for tapes increases—there is much more taping of other people's records. Conversely, if the price of one of these substitutes decreases, people use the now cheaper good in larger quantities, and they buy fewer tapes. For example, if the price of prerecorded tapes decreases, people play more of these tapes and make fewer of their own tapes—the demand for blank tapes falls.

The effects of a change in the price of a substitute occur no matter what the price of a tape. Whether tapes have a high or a low price, a change in the price of a substitute encourages people to make the substitutes that we've just reviewed. As a consequence, a change in the price of a substitute changes the entire demand schedule for tapes and shifts the demand curve.

A **complement** is a good used in conjunction with another good. Some examples of complements are hamburgers and french fries, party snacks and drinks, spaghetti and meat sauce, running shoes and jogging pants. Tapes also have their complements: Walkmans, tape recorders, and stereo tape decks. If the price of one of these complements increases, people buy fewer tapes. For example, if the price of a Walkman doubles, fewer Walkmans are bought and, as a consequence, fewer people are interested in buying tapes—the demand for tapes decreases. Conversely, if the price of one of these complements decreases, people buy more tapes. For example, if the price of the Walkman halves, more Walkmans are bought and a larger number of people buy tapes— the demand for tapes increases.

2. Income   Another influence on demand is consumer income. When income increases, consumers demand more of most goods. When income decreases, consumers demand less of most goods. Higher average income means consumers demand more of most goods. Lower average income means consumers demand less of most goods. Rich people consume more food, clothing, housing, art, vacations, and entertainment than do poor people.

Although an increase in income leads to an increase in the demand for most goods, it does not lead to an increase in the demand for all goods. Goods that do increase in demand as income increases are called **normal goods.** Goods that decrease in demand when income increases are called **inferior goods.** Examples of inferior goods are rice and potatoes. These two goods are a major part of the diet of people with very low incomes. As incomes increase, the demand for these goods declines as more expensive meat and dairy products are substituted for them.

3. Population   Demand also depends on the size of the population. The larger the population, the greater is the demand for all goods and services. The smaller the population, the lower is the demand for all goods and services.

4. Tastes   Finally, demand depends on tastes. **Tastes** are an individual's attitudes or preferences toward goods and services. For example, a rock music fanatic has a much greater taste for tapes than does a tone-deaf workaholic. As a consequence, even if they have the same incomes, their demands for tapes will be very different. There is, however, a fundamental difference between tastes and all the other influences on demand. Tastes cannot be directly observed. We can observe the price of a good and of its substitutes and complements. We can observe income and population size. But we cannot observe people's tastes. Economists assume that tastes do not change or that they change only slowly, and that they are independent of all the other influences on demand.

A summary of influences on demand and the direction of those influences is presented in Table 4.1.

Movement Along Versus a Shift in the Demand Curve

Changes in the influences on buyers' plans cause either a movement along the demand curve or a shift in it. Let's discuss each case in turn.

Movement Along the Demand Curve   If the price of a good changes but everything else remains the same, then we say that the quantity demanded of that good has changed. We illustrate the effect as a movement along the demand curve. For example, if

the price of a tape changes from $3 to $5, the result is a movement along the demand curve, from point c to point e in Fig. 4.1.

A Shift in the Demand Curve   If the price of a good remains constant but another influence on buyers' plans changes, we say that there is a change in demand for that good. We illustrate the change in demand as a shift in the demand curve. For example, a dramatic fall in the price of the Walkman—a complement of tapes—increases the demand for tapes. We illustrate this increase in demand for tapes with a new demand schedule and a new demand curve. Consumers demand a larger quantity of tapes at each and every price.

The table in Fig. 4.2 provides some hypothetical numbers that illustrate such a shift. The table sets out the original demand schedule and the new demand schedule resulting from a fall in the price of a Walkman. These numbers record the change in demand. The graph in Fig. 4.2 illustrates the corresponding shift in the demand curve. When the price of the Walkman falls, the demand curve for tapes shifts to the right.

A Change in Demand Versus a Change in Quantity Demanded   The quantity demanded at a given price is shown by a point on a demand curve. The entire demand curve shows demand. It follows, then, that a **change in demand** is a shift in the entire demand curve. It also follows that a movement along a demand curve is a **change in the quantity demanded.** Figure 4.3 illustrates these distinctions. If the price of a good falls but nothing else changes, then there is an increase in the quantity demanded of that good (a movement down the demand curve D_0). If the price rises, but nothing else changes, then there is a decrease in the quantity demanded (a movement up the demand curve D_0). When any other influence on buyers' planned purchases changes, the demand curve shifts and there is a *change* (an increase or a decrease) *in demand*. A rise in income, in population, or in the price of a substitute, or a fall in the price of a complement shifts the demand curve to the right (to the red demand curve D_2). This represents an *increase in demand*. A fall in income, in population, or in the price of a substitute, or a rise in the price of a complement shifts the demand curve to the left (to the red demand curve D_1). This represents a *decrease in demand*.

Table 4.1   The Demand for Tapes

The law of demand

The quantity of tapes demanded

Falls if:	Rises if:
• The price of a tape rises	• The price of a tape falls

Changes in demand

The demand for tapes

Falls if:	Rises if:
• The price of a substitute falls	• The price of a substitute rises
• The price of a complement rises	• The price of a complement falls
• Income falls	• Income rises
• The population decreases	• The population increases

Figure 4.2   A Change in the Demand Schedule and a Shift in the Demand Curve

	Original demand schedule (Walkman $200)			New demand schedule (Walkman $50)	
	Price (dollars per tape)	Quantity (millions of tapes per week)		Price (dollars per tape)	Quantity (millions of tapes per week)
a	1	9	a′	1	13
b	2	6	b′	2	10
c	3	4	c′	3	8
d	4	3	d′	4	7
e	5	2	e′	5	6

A change in any influence on buyers other than the price of the good itself results in a new demand schedule and a shift in the demand curve. Here, a fall in the price of a Walkman—a complement of tapes—increases the demand for tapes. At a price of $3 a tape (row c of table), 4 million tapes a week are demanded when the Walkman costs $200 and 8 million tapes a week are demanded when the Walkman costs only $50. The demand curve shifts to the right, as shown by the shift arrow and the resulting red curve.

Figure 4.3   A Change in Demand Versus a Change in the Quantity Demanded

When the price of a good changes, there is a movement along the demand curve and a *change in the quantity of the good demanded*. For example, if the demand curve is D_0, a rise in the price of the good produces a decrease in the quantity demanded and a fall in the price of the good produces an increase in the quantity demanded. The arrows on demand curve D_0 represent these movements along the demand curve. If some other influence on demand changes, which increases the quantity that people plan to buy, there is a shift in the demand curve to the right (from D_0 to red D_2) and an *increase in demand*. If some other influence on demand changes, which reduces the quantity people plan to buy, there is a shift in the demand curve to the left (from D_0 to red D_1) and a *decrease in demand*.

R E V I E W

The quantity demanded is the amount of a good that consumers plan to buy in a given period of time. Other things being equal, the quantity demanded of a good increases if its price falls. Demand can be represented by a schedule or curve that sets out the quantity demanded at each price. Demand describes the quantity that consumers plan to buy at each possible price, or the highest price that consumers are willing to pay for the last unit bought. Demand increases if the price of a substitute rises, if the price of a complement falls, if income rises, or if the population increases; demand decreases if the price of a substitute falls, if the price of a complement rises, if income falls, or if the population decreases.

If the price of a good changes but all other influences on buyers' plans are held constant, there is a change in the quantity demanded and a movement along the demand curve. All other influences on consumers' planned purchases shift the demand curve. ■

Supply

The **quantity supplied** of a good is the amount that producers plan to sell in a given period of time. The quantity supplied is not the amount a firm would like to sell but the amount it definitely plans to sell. However, the quantity supplied is not necessarily the same amount as the quantity actually sold, or traded. If consumers do not want to buy the quantity a firm plans to sell, the firm's sales plans will be frustrated. Like quantity demanded, the quantity supplied is expressed as an amount per unit of time.

What Determines the Quantity Supplied?

The quantity supplied depends on the number of firms supplying a good and the plans of each firm. The amount of any good that each firm plans to supply depends on many factors. Among the more important ones are:

• The price of the good
• The prices of other goods

• The prices of the resources used to produce the good
• The number of suppliers
• Technology

Since the theory of demand and supply makes predictions about prices and quantities traded, we focus first on the relationship between the price of a good and the quantity supplied. In order to study this relationship, we hold constant all the other influences on the quantity supplied. We ask: How does the quantity supplied of a good vary as its price varies?

The Law of Supply

The law of supply states:

Other things being equal, the higher the price of a good, the greater is the quantity supplied.

Why does a higher price lead to a greater quantity supplied of a good? The key to the answer is profitability. If the prices of the resources used to produce a good are held constant, a higher price for the good means a higher profit for the producer. Higher profits encourage existing producers to increase the quantity they supply. Higher profits also attract additional producers.

Supply Schedule and Supply Curve

A **supply schedule** lists the quantities supplied at each different price, when all other influences on the amount firms plan to sell are held constant. Let's construct a supply schedule. To do so, we examine how the quantity supplied of a good varies as its price varies, holding constant the prices of other goods, the prices of resources used to produce it, and the state of technology.

The table in Fig. 4.4 sets out a supply schedule for tapes. It shows the quantity of tapes supplied at each possible price. For example, if the price of a tape is $1, no tapes are supplied. If the price of a tape is $4, 5 million tapes are supplied each week.

A supply schedule can be illustrated by drawing a supply curve. A **supply curve** graphs the relationship between the quantity supplied and the price of a good, holding everything else constant.

Using the same numbers listed in the table, the graph in Fig. 4.4 illustrates the supply curve for tapes. For example, point *d* represents a quantity supplied of 5 million tapes a week at a price of $4 a tape.

Minimum Supply Price

Just as the demand curve has two interpretations, so too does the supply curve. So far we have thought about the supply curve and the supply schedule as showing the quantity that firms will supply at each possible price. But we can also think about the supply curve as showing the minimum price at which the last unit will be supplied. Looking at the supply schedule in this way, we ask what is the minimum price that brings forth a supply of a given quantity. For firms to supply the 3 millionth tape each week, the price has to be at least $2 a tape. For firms to supply the 5 millionth tape each week, they have to get at least $4 a tape.

A Change in Supply

The term **supply** refers to the entire relationship between the quantity supplied of a good and its price. The supply of tapes is described by both the supply schedule and the supply curve in Fig. 4.4. To construct a supply schedule and supply curve, we hold constant all the other influences on suppliers' plans. Let's now consider these other influences.

1. Prices of Other Goods The supply of a good can be influenced by the prices of other goods. For example, if an automobile assembly line can produce either sports cars or sedans, the quantity of sedans produced will depend on the price of sports cars and the quantity of sports cars produced will depend on the price of sedans. These two goods are substitutes in production. An increase in the price of a substitute in production lowers the supply of the good. Goods can also be complements in production. Complements in production arise when two things are, of necessity, produced together. For example, extracting chemicals from coal produces coke, coal tar, and nylon. An increase in the price of any one of these by-products of coal increases the supply of the other by-product.

Tapes have no obvious complements in production, but they do have substitutes: prerecorded tapes. An increase in the price of prerecorded tapes will decrease the supply of blank tapes.

Figure 4.4   The Supply Schedule and the Supply Curve

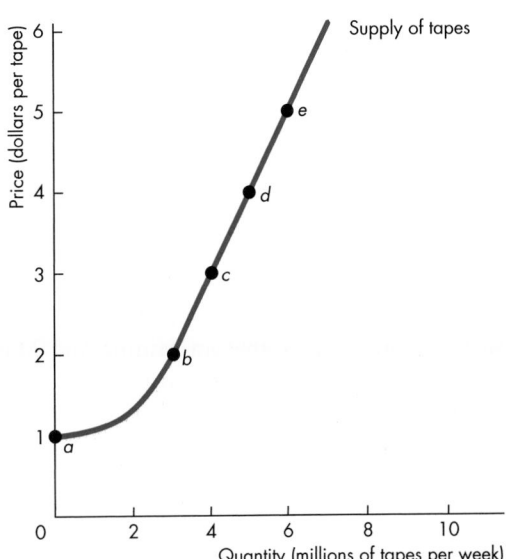

	Price (dollars per tape)	Quantity (millions of tapes per week)
a	1	0
b	2	3
c	3	4
d	4	5
e	5	6

The table shows the supply schedule of tapes. For example, at $2 a tape, 3 million tapes a week are supplied; at $5 a tape, 6 million tapes a week are supplied. The supply curve shows the relationship between the quantity supplied and price, holding everything else constant. The supply curve usually slopes upward: as the price of a good increases, so does the quantity supplied. A supply curve can be read in two ways. For a given price, it tells us the quantity that producers plan to sell. For example, at a price of $3 a tape, producers plan to sell 4 million tapes a week. The supply curve also tells us the minimum acceptable price at which a given quantity will be offered for sale. For example, the minimum acceptable price that will bring forth a supply of 4 million tapes a week is $3 a tape.

2. Prices of Resources   The prices of the resources used to produce a good will exert an important influence on its supply. For example, an increase in the prices of the labor and the capital equipment used to produce tapes decreases the supply of tapes.

3. The Number of Suppliers.   Other things being equal, the larger the number of firms supplying a good, the larger is the supply of the good.

4. Technology   Technology also influences supply. New technologies that enable producers to use fewer resources will lower the cost of production and increase supply. For example, the development of a new technology for tape production by companies such as Sony and Minnesota Mining and Manufacturing (3M) has lowered the cost of producing tapes and increased their supply. A summary of influences on supply and the directions of those influences is presented in Table 4.2.

Table 4.2   The Supply of Tapes

The law of supply

The quantity of tapes supplied

Falls if:	*Rises if:*
• The price of a tape falls	• The price of a tape rises

Changes in supply

The supply of tapes

Falls if:	*Rises if:*
• The price of a substitute in production rises	• The price of a substitute in production falls
• The price of a complement in production falls	• The price of a complement in production rises
• The price of a resource used to produce tapes increases	• The price of a resource used to produce tapes decreases
• The number of firms supplying tapes decreases	• The number of firms supplying tapes increases
	• More efficient technologies for producing tapes are discovered

---

Movement Along Versus a Shift in the Supply Curve

Changes in the influences on producers cause either a movement along the supply curve or a shift in it.

Movement Along the Supply Curve   If the price of a good changes but everything else influencing suppliers' planned sales remains constant, there is a movement along the supply curve. For example, if the price of tapes increases from $3 to $5 a tape, there will be a movement along the supply curve from point c (4 million tapes a week) to point e (6 million tapes a week).

A Shift in the Supply Curve   If the price of a good remains constant but another influence on suppliers' planned sales changes, then there is a change in supply and a shift in the supply curve. For example, as we have already noted, technological advances lower the cost of producing tapes and increase their supply. As a result, the supply schedule changes. The table in Fig. 4.5 provides some hypothetical numbers that illustrate such a change. The table contains two supply schedules: the original, based on "old" technology, and one on "new" technology. With the new technology, more tapes are supplied at each price. The graph in Fig. 4.5 illustrates the resulting shift in the supply curve. When tape-producing technology improves, the supply curve of tapes shifts to the right, as shown by the shift arrow and the red supply curve.

A Change in Supply Versus a Change in Quantity Supplied   The quantity supplied at a given price is shown by a point on a supply curve. The entire supply curve shows supply. A **change in supply** occurs whenever there is a shift in the supply curve. A **change in the quantity supplied** occurs when there is a movement along the supply curve.

Figure 4.6 illustrates and summarizes these distinctions. If the price of a good falls but nothing else changes, then there is a decrease in the quantity supplied of that good (a movement down the supply curve S_0). If the price of a good rises but nothing else changes, there is an increase in the quantity supplied (a movement up the supply curve S_0). When any other influence on sellers changes, the supply curve shifts and there is a

Figure 4.5   A Change in the Supply Schedule and a
Shift in the Supply Curve

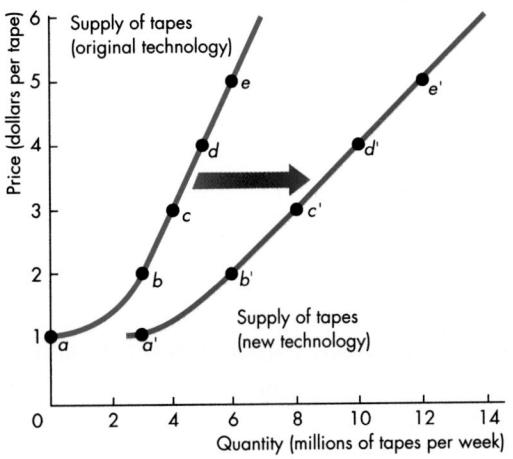

	Original technology		New technology	
	Price (dollars per tape)	Quantity (millions of tapes per week)	Price (dollars per tape)	Quantity (millions of tapes per week)
a	1	0	a'	1	3
b	2	3	b'	2	6
c	3	4	c'	3	8
d	4	5	d'	4	10
e	5	6	e'	5	12

If the price of a good remains constant but another influence on its supply changes, there will be a
new supply schedule and the supply curve will shift. For example, if Sony and 3M invent a new,
cost-saving technology for producing tapes, the supply schedule changes, as shown in the table.
At $3 a tape, producers sell 4 million tapes a week with the old technology and 8 million tapes a
week with the new technology. Improved technology increases the supply of tapes and shifts the
supply curve of tapes to the right.

Figure 4.6   A Change in Supply Versus a Change in the Quantity Supplied

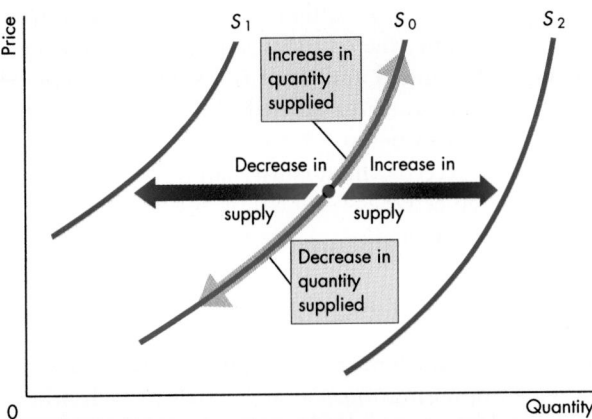

When the price of a good changes, there is a movement along
the supply curve and a *change in the quantity of the good
supplied*. For example, if the supply curve is S_0, a rise in the
price of the good produces an increase in the quantity supplied
and a fall in the price produces a decrease in the quantity
supplied. The arrows on curve S_0 represent these movements
along the supply curve. If some other influence on supply
changes, which increases the quantity that producers plan to
sell, there is a shift in the supply curve to the right (from S_0 to
red S_2) and an *increase in supply*. If some other influence on
supply changes, which reduces the quantity that producers
plan to sell, there is a shift to the left in the supply curve (from
S_0 to red S_1) and a *decrease in supply*.

change in supply. If the supply curve is S_0 and there
is, say, a technological change that reduces the
amounts of the resources needed to produce the

good, then supply increases and the supply curve
shifts to S_2. If production costs rise, supply decreases
and the supply curve shifts to S_1.

R E V I E W

The quantity supplied is the amount of a good that producers plan to sell in a given period of time. Other things being equal, the quantity supplied of a good increases if its price rises. Supply can be represented by a schedule or a curve that shows the relationship between the quantity supplied of a good and its price. Supply describes the quantity that will be supplied at each possible price or the lowest price at which producers will supply the last unit. Supply increases if the price of a substitute in production falls, if the price of a complement in production rises, if the prices of the resources used to produce the good fall, or when technological advances lower the cost of production. If the price of a good changes but all other influences on producers' plans are held constant, there is a change in the quantity supplied and a movement along the supply curve. A change in any other influence on producers' plans shifts the supply curve. Changes in the prices of substitutes and complements in production, changes in the prices of resources, or improvements in technology shift the supply curve and are said to change supply. ■

Now that we have studied demand and supply, let's bring these two concepts together and see how prices are determined.

Price Determination

We have seen that when the price of a good rises, the quantity demanded decreases and the quantity supplied increases. We are now going to see how adjustments in price achieve an equality between the quantities demanded and supplied.

Price as a Regulator

The price of a good regulates the quantities demanded and supplied. If the price is too high, the quantity supplied exceeds the quantity demanded. If the price is too low, the quantity demanded exceeds the quantity supplied. There is one price, and only one price, at which the quantity demand-ed equals the quantity supplied. We are going to work out what that price is. We are also going to discover that natural forces operating in a market move the price toward the level that makes the quantity demanded equal the quantity supplied.

The demand schedule shown in the table in Fig. 4.1 and the supply schedule shown in the table in Fig. 4.4 appear together in the table in Fig. 4.7. If the price of a tape is $1, the quantity demanded is 9 million tapes a week but no tapes are supplied. The quantity demanded exceeds the quantity supplied by 9 million tapes a week. In other words, at a price of $1 a tape, there is a shortage of 9 million tapes a week. This shortage is shown in the final column of the table. At a price of $2 a tape, there is still a shortage but only of 3 million tapes a week. If the price of a tape is $5, the quantity supplied exceeds the quantity demanded. The quantity supplied is 6 million tapes a week, but the quantity demanded is only 2 million. There is a surplus of 4 million tapes a week. There is one price and only one price at which there is neither a shortage nor a surplus. That price is $3 a tape. At that price the quantity demanded is equal to the quantity supplied—4 million tapes a week. That quantity is also the quantity traded.

The market for tapes is illustrated in the graph in Fig. 4.7. The graph shows both the demand curve of Fig. 4.1 and the supply curve of Fig. 4.4. The demand curve and the supply curve intersect when the price is $3 a tape, and the quantity traded is 4 million tapes a week. At prices above $3 a tape, the quantity supplied exceeds the quantity demanded and there is a surplus of tapes— shown by the blue area labeled "Surplus" in the figure. At prices below $3 a tape, the quantity demanded exceeds the quantity supplied and there is a shortage of tapes—shown by the red area labeled "Shortage."

Equilibrium

We defined *equilibrium* in Chapter 1 as a situation in which opposing forces exactly balance each other and in which no one is able to make a better choice given the available resources and actions of others. So, in an equilibrium, the price is such that opposing forces exactly balance each other. The **equilibrium price** is the price at which the quantity demanded equals the quantity supplied. To see why this situation is an equilibrium, we

Figure 4.7   Equilibrium

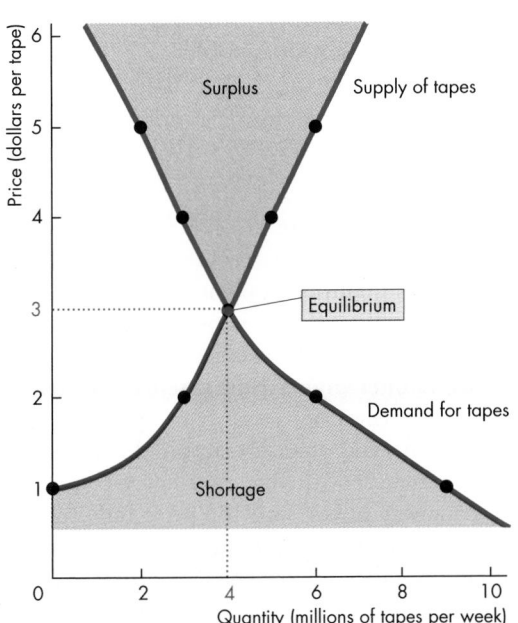

The table lists the quantities demanded and quantities supplied as well as the shortage or surplus of tapes at each price. (Note that the numbers in the final column of the table represent the shortages as negative numbers and the surpluses as positive numbers.) If the price of a tape is $2, 6 million tapes a week are demanded and 3 million are supplied. There is a shortage of 3 million tapes a week and the price rises. If the price of a tape is $4, 3 million tapes a week are demanded but 5 million are supplied. There is a surplus of 2 million tapes a week and the price falls. If the price of a tape is $3, 4 million tapes a week are demanded and 4 million are supplied. There is neither a shortage nor a surplus. Neither buyers nor sellers have any incentive to change the price. The price at which the quantity demanded equals the quantity supplied is the equilibrium price.

Price (dollars per tape)	Quantity demanded (millions of tapes per week)	Quantity supplied (millions of tapes per week)	Shortage (−) or surplus (+) (millions of tapes per week)
1	9	0	−9
2	6	3	−3
3	4	4	0
4	3	5	+2
5	2	6	+4

need to examine the behavior of buyers and sellers a bit more closely. First, let's look at the behavior of buyers.

The Demand Curve and the Willingness to Pay

Suppose the price of a tape is $2. In such a situation, producers plan to sell 3 million tapes a week. Consumers cannot force producers to sell more than they want to sell, so the quantity sold will also be 3 million tapes a week. What is the highest price that buyers are willing to pay for the 3 millionth

tape each week? The answer can be found on the demand curve in Fig. 4.7—it is $4 a tape.

If the price remains at $2 a tape, the quantity of tapes demanded is 6 million tapes a week—3 million tapes more than are available. In such a situation, the price of a tape does not remain at $2. Because people want more tapes than are available at that price and because they are willing to pay up to $4 a tape, the price rises. If the quantity supplied stays at 3 million tapes a week, the price rises all the way to $4 a tape.

In fact, the price doesn't have to rise by such a large amount because at higher prices the quantity supplied increases. The price will rise from $2 a tape to $3 a tape. At that price, the quantity supplied is 4 million tapes a week, and $3 a tape is the highest price that consumers are willing to pay. At $3 a tape, buyers are able to make their planned purchases and producers are able to make their planned sales. Therefore no one has an incentive to bid the price higher.

The Supply Curve and the Minimum Supply Price   Suppose that the price of a tape is $4. In such a situation, the quantity demanded is 3 million tapes a week. Producers cannot force consumers to buy more than they want, so the quantity bought is 3 million tapes a week. Producers are willing to sell 3 million tapes a week for a price lower than $4 a tape. In fact, you can see on the supply curve in Fig. 4.7 that suppliers are willing to sell the 3 millionth tape each week at a price of $2. At $4 a tape, they would like to sell 5 million tapes each week. Because they want to sell more than 3 million tapes a week at $4 a tape, and because they would be willing to sell the 3 millionth tape for as little as $2, they will continuously undercut each other in order to get a bigger share of the market. They will cut their price all the way to $2 a tape if only 3 million tapes a week can be sold.

In fact, producers don't have to cut their price to $2 a tape because the lower price brings forth an increase in the quantity demanded. When the price falls to $3, the quantity demanded is 4 million tapes a week, which is exactly the quantity that producers want to sell at that price. So, when the price reaches $3 a tape, producers have no incentive to cut the price any further.

The Best Deal Available for Buyers and Sellers   Both situations we have just examined result in price changes. In the first case, the price starts out at $2 and is bid upward. In the second case, the price starts out at $4 and producers undercut each other. In both cases, prices change until they hit the price of $3 a tape. At that price, the quantity demanded and the quantity supplied are equal and no one has any incentive to do business at a different price. Consumers are paying the highest acceptable price and producers are selling at the lowest acceptable price.

When people can freely make bids and offers and when they seek to buy at the lowest price and sell at the highest price, the price at which they trade is the equilibrium price—the quantity demanded equals the quantity supplied.

R E V I E W

The equilibrium price is the price at which the plans of buyers and sellers match each other—the price at which the quantity demanded equals the quantity supplied. If the price is below equilibrium, the quantity demanded exceeds the quantity supplied, buyers offer higher prices, sellers ask for higher prices, and the price rises. If the price is above equilibrium, the quantity supplied exceeds the quantity demanded, buyers offer lower prices, sellers ask for lower prices, and the price falls. Only when the price is such that the quantity demanded and the quantity supplied are equal are there no forces acting on the price to make it change. Therefore that price is the equilibrium price. At that price, the quantity traded is also equal to the quantity demanded and the quantity supplied. ∎

The theory of demand and supply that you have just studied, is now a central part of economics. But that was not always so. Only 100 years ago, the best economists of the day were quite confused about these matters, which today even students in introductory courses find relatively easy to get right (see Our Advancing Knowledge on pp. 84–85).

As you'll discover in the rest of this chapter, the theory of demand and supply enables us to understand and make predictions about changes in prices—including the price slides, rockets, and roller coasters described in the chapter opener.

Predicting Changes in Price and Quantity Traded

The theory we have just studied provides us with a powerful way of analyzing influences on prices and quantities traded. According to the theory, a change in price stems from either a change in demand or a change in supply. Let's look first at the effects of a change in demand.

Figure 4.8   The Effect of a Change in Demand

If the price of a Walkman is $200, the quantity of tapes demanded and the quantity traded is 4 million tapes a week at a price of $3 a tape. If the price of a Walkman falls from $200 to $50, the quantity of tapes demanded at a price of $3 is 8 million tapes a week. If the price stays at $3, there is a shortage of 4 million tapes a week. The quantities of tapes demanded and supplied are equal when the price is $5 a tape and the quantity traded is 6 million tapes a week. The increase in demand raises the equilibrium price by $2 and raises the equilibrium quantity traded by 2 million tapes a week.

Price (dollars per tape)	Quantity demanded (millions of tapes per week)		Quantity supplied (millions of tapes per week)
	Walkman $200	Walkman $50	
1	9	13	0
2	6	10	3
3	4	8	4
4	3	7	5
5	2	6	6

A Change in Demand

What happens to the price of tapes and the quantity traded if demand for tapes increases? We can answer this question with a specific example. If the price of a Walkman falls from $200 to $50, the demand for tapes will increase as is shown in the table in Fig. 4.8. The original demand schedule and the new one are set out in the first three columns of the table. The table also shows the supply schedule.

The original equilibrium price was $3 a tape. At that price, 4 million tapes a week were demanded and supplied. When demand increases, the price that makes the quantity demanded equal the quantity supplied is $5 a tape. At this price 6 million tapes are traded each week. When demand

increases, the price rises and the quantity traded increases.

We can illustrate these changes in the graph in Fig. 4.8. The graph shows the original demand for and supply of tapes. The original equilibrium price is $3 a tape and the quantity traded is 4 million tapes a week. When demand increases, the demand curve shifts to the right. The equilibrium price rises to $5 a tape and the quantity traded increases to 6 million tapes a week, as is highlighted in the figure.

The exercise that we've just conducted can easily be reversed. If we start at a price of $5 a tape, trading 6 million tapes a week, we can then work out what happens if demand falls back to its original level. You will see that a fall in demand lowers price and decreases the quantity traded.

Discovering the Laws of Demand and Supply

How are the prices of goods and services determined? Why are some vital-to-life resources, such as the air that we breathe and the water that we drink, virtually free while luxurious but inessential commodities such as diamonds are so expensive? For centuries, people have puzzled over these and similar questions. The questions were finally answered when the theories of demand, supply, and equilibrium price, which you have been studying in this chapter, were discovered and refined. But this discovery was not completed until the 1890s.

Let's transport ourselves back in time to the early part of the nineteenth century. We are planning to make a sizable investment in railroads and we are using the prevailing theory of prices to guide our decision. Economists believe that prices are determined by costs of production. So we predict that the price of railroad transportation will stay in line with production costs and that a reasonable rate of return will be made on our investment. As a result, we (and millions of others) invest heavily in this new mode of transportation. Rates of return turn out to be much lower than we predicted. Why? What went wrong? Ignorant of the laws of demand and supply, we failed to realize that a massive increase in the supply of railroad transportation services would drive their prices down and therefore lower the returns on investing in them. Let's look at the main milestones on the road to discovering the theory of demand and supply.

The road begins with the work of Antoine-Augustin Cournot. Cournot (1801–1877) was born near Dijon, France. In 1834, he became professor of mathematics at the University of Lyon. Four years later he published a book entitled *Recherches sur les principes mathématiques de la théorie des richesses* (*The Mathematical Principles of the Theory of Wealth*). In that book Cournot wrote down the law of demand. But he wrote it in abstract mathematical language. Cournot's book was a work of amazing clarity, but, because it used a mathematical language unfamiliar at that time to most students of economics, and because the book was in French, it did not have much influence until many years later.

The first person to draw a demand curve was Arsène-Jules-Emile Juvenal Dupuit (1804–1866). Like Cournot, Dupuit was a Frenchman. He made profound contributions as both an engineer and an economic theorist. Dupuit's demand curve,

Cournot

which he called "the curve of consumption" (*courbe de consommation*) appeared in 1844.

The law of demand was independently discovered a few years later, and given its first practical application by Dionysius Lardner (1793–1859), an Irishman who was professor of philosophy at the University of London. In his book *Railway Economy*, published in 1850, Lardner drew and used a demand curve for transportation services.

The first person to draw a demand and supply curve together and to use demand and supply theory to determine price was Fleeming Jenkin (1833–1885), an Englishman who was also a professor of philosophy at the University of London. Jenkin's demand and supply curves appeared in a paper entitled "The Graphic Representation of the Laws of Supply and Demand," published in 1870. Jenkin also was the first to use the theories of demand and supply to make predictions about the effects of taxes, in a paper entitled "On the Principles Which Regulate the Incidence of Taxes," published in 1872.

Many others had a hand in the refinement of the theory of demand and supply, but the first thorough and complete statement of the theory, in terms sufficiently modern for it to be recognized as the same theory that you have studied in this chapter, was provided by Alfred Marshall (1842–1924). Marshall was a professor of political economy at the University of Cambridge, and in 1890, he published a monumental treatise—*Principles of Economics*. Marshall's *Principles* was *the* textbook on this subject for almost half a century. In the preface to *Principles*, Marshall acknowledged his own debt to Cournot. He also expressed his view that the theory of demand and supply provides a unifying analysis applicable to all aspects of economics.

Marshall

Although Marshall was an outstanding mathematician, he kept mathematics and even diagrams in the background. His own supply and demand diagram and discussion of how the equilibrium price arises appears only in a footnote. It is reproduced here. Although Marshall's diagram is far less striking than those you have been studying, note the strong similarities it has with Fig. 4.7.

Figure 4.9   The Effect of a Change in Supply

When the supply schedule changes as a result of introducing a new technology, the quantity of tapes supplied at $3 a tape exceeds the quantity demanded at that price. The quantity supplied is 8 million tapes at a price of $3. The table shows that the quantity demanded equals the quantity supplied when the price of tapes falls to $2. At this price, 6 million tapes are demanded and supplied each week. The new technology results in a shift in the supply curve to the right. The original technology supply curve intersects the demand curve at a price of $3 and at a quantity traded of 4 million tapes a week. The new technology supply curve intersects the demand curve at a price of $2 and a quantity traded of 6 million tapes a week. The increase in supply lowers the price of tapes by $1 and increases the quantity traded by 2 million tapes a week.

Price (dollars per tape)	Quantity demanded (millions of tapes per week)	Quantity supplied (millions of tapes per week)	
		Original technology	New technology
1	9	0	3
2	6	3	6
3	4	4	8
4	3	5	10
5	2	6	12

We can now make our first two predictions:

- When demand increases, the price rises and the quantity traded increases.
- When demand decreases, the price falls and the quantity traded decreases.

Reading Between the Lines on pp. 90–91 provides further illustration of demand and supply in action—explaining what happened when a massive but temporary rise in demand for boat rides around Liberty Island occurred on the Fourth of July in 1986.

A Change in Supply

Let's ask what happens if supply changes. Again, we'll start out with a price of $3 a tape and 4 million tapes a week being traded. Suppose that Sony and 3M have just introduced a new cost-saving technology in their tape-production plants. The new technology shifts the supply schedule and the supply curve. The new supply schedule (the same one that was shown in Fig. 4.5) is presented in the table in Fig. 4.9. What is the new equilibrium price and quantity traded? The answer is highlighted in the table: The price falls to $2 a tape and the number of tapes traded rises to 6 million a week. You can see why by looking at the quantities demanded and supplied at the old price of $3 a tape. The quantity supplied at that price is 8 million tapes a week and there is a surplus of tapes. The price falls. Only when the price is $2 a tape is the quantity supplied equal to the quantity demanded.

The graph in Fig. 4.9 illustrates the effect of an increase in supply. The graph shows the demand curve for tapes and the original and new supply curves. The initial equilibrium price is $3 a tape and the original quantity traded is 4 million tapes a week. When the supply increases, the supply curve shifts to the right. The new equilibrium price is $2 a tape and the quantity traded is 6 million tapes a week, highlighted in the figure.

The exercise that we've just conducted can easily be reversed. If we start out at a price of $2 a tape with 6 million tapes a week being traded, we can work out what happens if the supply curve shifts back to its original position. You can see that the fall in supply increases the equilibrium price to $3 a tape and decreases the quantity traded to 4 million tapes a week. Such a fall in supply could arise from an increase in the cost of labor and raw materials. We can now make two more predictions:

• When supply increases, the quantity traded increases and the price falls.
• When supply decreases, the quantity traded decreases and the price rises.

Reading Between the Lines on pp. 92–93 shows the effects of increases in the supply of compact discs and CD players on their prices and quantities traded.

Changes in Both Supply and Demand

In the above exercises, we changed either demand or supply but only one at a time. If we change just one of these, we can predict the direction of change of the price and the quantity traded. If we change both demand and supply, we cannot always say what will happen to both the price and the quantity traded. For example, if both demand and supply increase, we know that the quantity traded increases but we cannot predict whether the price will rise or fall. To make such a prediction, we need to know the relative importance of the increase in demand and supply. If demand increases and supply decreases, we know that the price rises but we cannot predict whether the quantity traded will increase or decrease. Again, to be able to make a prediction about the quantity traded, we need to know the relative magnitudes of the changes in demand and supply.

As an example of a change in both supply and demand, let's take one final look at the market for tapes. We've seen how demand and supply determine the price and quantity of tapes traded; how an increase in demand resulting from a fall in

the price of a Walkman both raises the price of tapes and increases the quantity traded; how an increase in the supply of tapes resulting from an improved technology lowers the price of tapes and increases the quantity traded. Let's now examine what happens when both of these changes—a fall in the price of a Walkman (which increases the demand for tapes) and an improved production technology (which increases the supply of tapes)— occur together.

The table in Fig. 4.10 brings together the numbers that describe the original quantities demanded and supplied and the new quantities demanded and supplied after the fall in the price of the Walkman and the improved tape production technology. These same numbers are illustrated in the graph. The original demand and supply curves intersect at a price of $3 a tape and a quantity traded of 4 million tapes a week. The new supply and demand curves also intersect at a price of $3 a tape but at a quantity traded of 8 million tapes a week. In this example, there is an equal increase in both demand and supply. As a result, the rise in price brought about by an increase in demand is offset by the fall in price brought about by an increase in supply—so the price does not change. An increase in either demand or supply increases the quantity traded. Therefore, when both demand and supply increase, so does the quantity traded. Note that if demand had increased slightly more than shown in the figure, the price would have risen. If supply had increased by slightly more than shown in the figure, the price would have fallen. But in both cases the quantity traded would have increased.

Walkmans, Apartments, and Coffee

At the beginning of this chapter, we looked at some facts about prices and quantities traded of Walkmans, apartments, and coffee. Let's use the theory of demand and supply that we have just studied to explain the movements in the prices and the quantities traded of those goods. Figure 4.11 illustrates the analysis.

First, let's consider the Walkman, shown in part (a). In 1980, using the original technology, the supply of Walkmans is described by the supply curve S_0. The 1980 demand curve is D_0. The quantities supplied and demanded in 1980 are equal at

Figure 4.10   The Effect of a Change in Both Demand and Supply

When a Walkman costs $200, the price of a tape is $3 and the quantity traded is 4 million tapes a week. A fall in the price of a Walkman increases the demand for tapes and improved technology increases the supply of tapes. The new technology supply curve intersects the higher demand curve at $3, the same price as before, but at a higher quantity traded of 8 million tapes a week. The simultaneous increase in both demand and supply increases the quantity traded but leaves the price unchanged.

Price (dollars per tape)	Original Quantities (millions of tapes per week)		New Quantities (millions of tapes per week)	
	Quantity demanded (Walkman $200)	Quantity supplied (Original technology)	Quantity demanded (Walkman $50)	Quantity supplied (New technology)
1	9	0	13	3
2	6	3	10	6
3	4	4	8	8
4	3	5	7	10
5	2	6	6	12

Q_0 and the price is P_0. Advances in technology and the building of additional production plants increase supply and shift the supply curve from S_0 to S_1. At the same time, increasing incomes increase the demand for Walkmans but not by nearly as much as the increase in supply. The demand curve shifts from D_0 to D_1. With the new demand curve D_1 and supply curve S_1, the equilibrium price is P_1 and the quantity traded is Q_1. The large increase in supply combined with a smaller increase in demand results in an increase in the quantity of Walkmans traded and a dramatic fall in their price.

Next, let's consider apartments in the center of the city, as in part (b). The supply of apartments is described by supply curve S. The supply curve is steep, reflecting the fact that there is a fixed amount of land and a fixed number of apartment buildings. As the number of young urban professionals increases and the number of two-income families increases, the demand for urban apartments increases sharply. The demand curve shifts from D_0 to D_1. As a result, the price increases from P_0 to P_1 and the quantity traded also increases but not as dramatically as price.

Figure 4.11   More Changes in Supply and Demand

(a) Walkmans

(b) Apartments

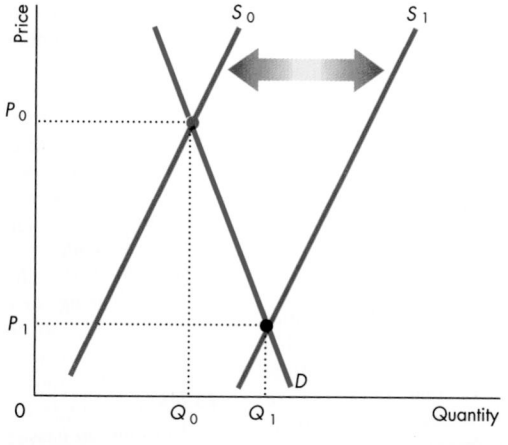

(c) Coffee

A large increase in the supply of Walkmans, from S_0 to S_1, combined with a small increase in demand, from D_0 to D_1, results in a fall in the price of the Walkman, from P_0 to P_1, and an increase in the quantity traded, from Q_0 to Q_1 (part a). An increase in the demand for apartments produces a large increase in the price, from P_0 to P_1, but only a small increase in the quantity traded, from Q_0 to Q_1 (part b). Variations in the weather and in growing conditions lead to fluctuations in the supply of coffee, between S_0 and S_1, which produce fluctuations in the price of coffee, between P_0 and P_1, and in the quantity traded, between Q_0 and Q_1 (part c).

Finally, let's consider the market for coffee, shown in part (c). The demand for coffee is described by curve D. The supply of coffee fluctuates between S_0 and S_1. When growing conditions are good, the supply curve is S_1. When there are adverse growing conditions such as frost, the supply decreases and the supply curve is S_0. As a consequence of fluctuations in supply, the price of coffee fluctuates between P_0 (the maximum price) and P_1 (the minimum price). The quantity traded fluctuates between Q_0 and Q_1.

■ By using the theory of demand and supply, you will be able to explain past fluctuations in prices and quantities traded and make predictions about future fluctuations. But you will want to do more than predict whether prices are going to rise or fall. In your study of microeconomics, you will learn to predict *by how much* they will change. In your study of macroeconomics, you will learn to explain fluctuations in the economy as a whole. In fact, the theory of demand and supply can help answer almost every economic question.

Demand and Supply in Action: A Temporary Increase in Demand

Planning Early for the 4th of July

Let others grouse about Christmas coming so early in the year. New Yorkers are frantically making plans for the Fourth of July.

The city's chronic scramble for space—space to walk, space to dine, space to rent—focuses now on finding a spot to view the historic, histrionic relighting of the Statue of Liberty on July 4 and related extravaganzas, Frank Sinatra and an armada of tall ships among them.

Some hotels and restaurants are already booked. Rudy Montgomery has been offered $3,600—three times his monthly rent—to sublet his modest Brooklyn Heights apartment, a short walk from the Promenade and a view of the statue, for the four-day holiday weekend.

Boats that normally charge $25 to $50 per person for trips around the harbor have raised their fees to $1,000 per person or more. Neiman Marcus has made a Fourth of July harbor excursion one of its extravagant Christmas catalogue items. And the scramble for a place at the bar at Windows On The World has begun. . . .

One of the unanswered questions is: Is there enough water in the harbor? The Coast Guard estimates that there will be at least 25,000 private pleasure boats in the harbor to observe the flotilla and fireworks. "You will be able to walk across the hulls," said one boater. "It will be a bumper-boat situation."

"Everything that floats is being rented," said Bill Sills, another boater. "Some of the boats ain't much more than a piece of driftwood."

Marilyn Vogel, commodore of the Sebago Canoe Club of Brooklyn, said that a boat at the 79th Street Marina that doesn't even run was rented for the holiday weekend for $7,000.

She said the canoe club receives requests to rent canoes for that weekend, and that the club is considering becoming part of the festivities. "It would be their last outing . . . gridlock on the waters."

"The only thing they forgot," said Mr. O'Keefe [owner of the River Cafe] is that there is nowhere to embark and disembark. You figure 1,000 yachts minimum and maybe, just maybe, Manhattan's three marinas can service 15 extra boats, so what do the other 985 do?"

"This will be 10 times the colossal jam caused by the boats at the Brooklyn Bridge celebration," he said. "That was a New York party. This is national and international. I get five calls a day from Florida, Texas, the Carribean and everywhere to tie up at our restaurant." "You will see launch services springing up to take people out to the boats," he said.

Captain Parker [of The Ethel] is leasing some dock space for $2,500 for the weekend and plans to rent it out at high rates: about $3,000 for a single 100-foot boat to pick up passengers. He will hire security guards to make sure only customers use the space. "Boats will be landing wherever they can," he said. "This will look like Dunkirk."

The New York Times, November 6, 1985

by William E. Geist

The Essence of the Story

Background and Analysis

- A unique and massive spectacular was held in the waters surrounding Liberty Island, on the weekend of the Fourth of July in 1986. The refurbished Statue of Liberty was illuminated amidst fireworks, tall ships, and "related extravaganzas."

- The demand for space to view these events was extraordinarily high. Boats, restaurants, and any places with a view of the Liberty celebrations were demanded on a scale much larger than the demand for those same facilities on an ordinary day.

- The prices increased astronomically and the quantities available increased (to the point of total congestion).

The events of this weekend illustrate the effects of a large temporary increase in the demand for boat rides. The figure on the left shows what happened.

- The demand curve for boat rides and places with a view of the Liberty celebrations shifted to the right.

- The quantity of boat rides and viewing places supplied increased but could not do so without limit.

- The increase in demand produced a large price rise (to P_F) but only a small increase in the quantity of boat rides and viewing places traded (to Q_F).

After the Fourth of July weekend, demand returned to its normal level and so did the price and the quantity traded—to P_N and Q_N.

Demand and Supply in Action: An Increase in Supply

A Compact Sonic Boom

Listen to this: *Bam*. Sssh, now wait for this: *Tinkle*. And get a load of what's next: *Twang*. Whether they're playing thundering Tchaikovsky, delicate Debussy or stand-on-your-feet Springsteen, music fans love what they get from their new compact-disc systems —and that enthusiasm is producing a resounding result for the home-electronics industry: *Boom*.

Compact-disc players and recordings only hit the market in early 1983, but the takeoff has been astonishing. . . . This year [1985] retail sales are expected to total a hefty $500 million—2½ times 1984 sales—and they may double in 1986 to $1 billion. Leslie Rosen, executive director of the Compact Disc Group, a trade association, claims compact-disc products are the fastest-selling consumer electronics merchandise ever. "It took VCR's seven years to get to the point where we got in just two years," she says.

The big beneficiaries of the surge are Philips of Holland and Japan's Sony, which copioneered the CD system, and other Japanese companies such as Matsushita and Hitachi that al-

ready dominate other areas of the American consumer-electronics market. For the industry, the disc boom came just in time. Sales of recorded music and stereo equipment were stagnating in 1983. The fast growth of prerecorded cassettes eased some of the pain, but other innovations like quadrophonic sound and eight-track tapes had failed to help. At first, manufacturers were nervous about the prospect for CD products. With players typically priced at $1000 and discs selling for more than $20, sales did begin as a trickle. As in the case of VCR's, it took a price break to open the floodgates. Today the average player sells for about $225, discs go for $11 and up, and customers are grabbing everything in sight.

Happily for consumers, they don't have to choose between competing CD technologies as they do with VCR's. That's because the manufacturers banded together in the Compact Disc Group at the outset to settle on a single standard. . . . One thing the trade group couldn't do was put an end to disc and player shortages. There are only 10 ma-

jor disc-making plants in the world—only one in the United States—and they typically have back orders of 18 months. Some relief is in sight. The one American plant, in Terre Haute, Ind., has been expanded. CBS, which is selling its interest in the Indiana plant to its partner, Sony, says it may build another facility of its own. And Philips and Du Pont plan a joint plant in North Carolina.

The first buyers of CD players tended to be classical-music buffs, and now almost all new classical recordings come in disc form. Pop music on CDs got off to a slower start—partly because the multitrack recording process favored by pop artists is more complicated. But increasingly, the list of best-selling CDs mimics that of top-selling

LPs and tapes. Record companies are also reissuing old favorites in digital versions—but the supply of oldies is limited by the availability of good master recordings. . . .

Given the voracious appetites of CD fans, disc supplies may continue to be tight for some time. A few nervous companies like Motown and Warner Brothers, however, fear that sales growth may taper off to more reasonable levels and some retail inventories may begin to pile up next year. It seems more likely that . . . when off-brand manufacturers from South Korea and elsewhere begin to flood the market, . . . player prices may dip as low as $99, against today's low-ball price of $140.

NEWSWEEK, December 16, 1985

David Pauly with Penelope Wang in New York, Patricia King in Chicago, and bureau reports.

The Essence of the Story

- Compact disc players and recordings were first offered for general sale in 1983. Players were priced at more than $1000 and discs at more than $20. Sales were low.

- Even in 1983, prices began to fall, and the discount prices were $750 for CD players and $16 for discs.

- Prices continued to fall rapidly and by 1985 CD players averaged $225 and sold at discount for $140. Disc prices fell to $11. Sales grew quickly.

- Large increases in the supply of players (especially from Korea) are expected, so prices are expected to fall still further, to less than $100.

Background and Analysis

- The quantity of CD players demanded depends on the price of CD players. In 1983, the demand for CD players was D_{83} (Fig. a).

- The quantity of discs demanded depends on the price of discs. In 1983, the demand for discs was D_{83} (Fig. b).

- In 1983, the supply of both players and discs was low (S_{83} in Figs. a and b).

- In 1983 the demand and supply curves for players intersected at a price of $750 and at a quantity traded of 30,000 players (Fig. a). The demand and supply curves for discs intersected at a price of $16 and at a quantity traded of 800,000 discs (Fig. b).

- After 1983, the supply of both players and discs increased. The supply curves for 1986 (consistent with the predictions in the story) are those marked S_{86}.

- Compact disc players and discs are complements. The lower the price of a player, the greater is the demand for discs; the lower the price of discs, the greater is the demand for players. All CD players use a single technolo-

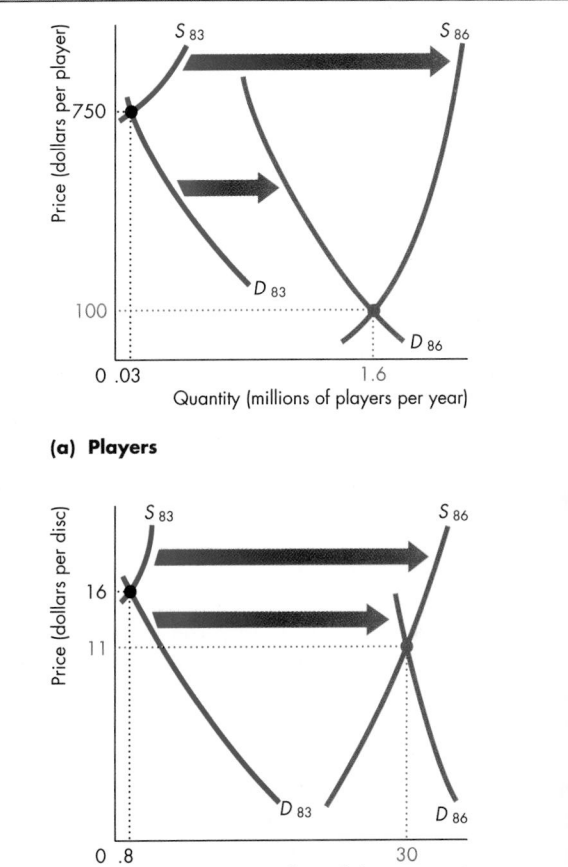

(a) Players

(b) Discs

gy standard (unlike VCRs, which use two technologies —VHS and Beta). This single standard reinforces the complementarity between players and discs.

- In Fig. a, the lower prices of discs shifted the demand for players from D_{83} to D_{86} for 1986. In Fig. b, lower prices of players shifted the demand for discs from D_{83} to D_{86} for 1986.

- In Fig. a, the price of players in 1986 is predicted to be $100 and the quantity traded 1.6 million players.

- In Fig. b, the price of a disc in 1986 is predicted to be $11 and the quantity traded 30 million discs. (The story does not predict the price of discs in 1986, but if the supply of discs increases more than the increase in demand, the price will fall.)

S U M M A R Y

Demand

The quantity demanded of a good or service is the amount that consumers plan to buy in a given period of time. Demands are different from wants. Wants are unlimited, whereas demands reflect decisions to satisfy specific wants. The quantity that consumers plan to buy of any good depends on:

- The price of the good
- The prices of other goods—substitutes and complements
- Income
- Population
- Tastes

The demand schedule lists the quantities that will be demanded at each price, holding constant all other influences on consumers' planned purchases.

A demand curve graphs the quantity demanded at each price, holding everything else constant. A change in the price of a good produces a movement along the demand curve for that good. Such a movement is called a change in the quantity demanded. Changes in things other than the price of a good shift the demand curve. Such changes are said to change demand. (pp. 71–76)

Supply

The quantity supplied of a good or service is the amount that producers plan to sell in a given period of time. The quantity that producers plan to sell of any good or service depends on:

- The price of the good
- The prices of other goods
- The prices of the resources used to produce the good
- The number of suppliers
- Technology

The supply schedule lists the quantities that will be supplied at each price, holding constant all other influences on producers' planned sales. The supply curve graphs that relationship. Changes in the price of the good produce movements along the supply curve of that good. Such movements are called changes in the quantity supplied. Changes in variables other than the price shift the supply curve. Such shifts are called changes in supply. (pp. 76–80)

Price Determination

Price regulates the quantities supplied and demanded. The higher the price, the greater is the quantity supplied and the smaller is the quantity demanded. At high prices, there is a surplus—an excess of the quantity supplied over the quantity demanded. At low prices, there is a shortage—an excess of the quantity demanded over the quantity supplied. There is one price and only one price at which the quantity demanded equals the quantity supplied. That price is the equilibrium price. At that price, buyers have no incentive to offer a higher price and suppliers have no incentive to sell at a lower price. (pp. 80–82)

Predicting Changes in Price and Quantity Traded

Changes in demand and supply lead to changes in price and in the quantity traded. An increase in demand leads to a rise in the price and to an increase in the quantity traded. A decrease in demand leads to a fall in price and to a decrease in the quantity traded. An increase in supply leads to an increase in the quantity traded and to a fall in price. A decrease in supply leads to a decrease in the quantity traded and a rise in price. (pp. 82–89)

K E Y   C O N C E P T S

Key Figures and Tables

R E V I E W   Q U E S T I O N S

1 Define the quantity demanded of a good or service.

2 Define the quantity supplied of a good or service.

3 Define the quantity traded and distinguish between the quantities demanded, supplied, and traded.

4 What determines the quantity demanded of a good? List the more important factors and say whether an increase in the factor increases or decreases the amount that consumers plan to buy.

5 What determines the quantity supplied? List the more important factors and say whether an increase in that factor increases or decreases the quantity that firms plan to sell.

6 State the law of demand and the law of supply.

7 The demand curve shows the quantity of a good demanded at each price. If a fixed amount of the good is available, what does the demand curve tell us about the price that consumers are willing to pay for that fixed quantity?

8 The supply curve shows the quantity supplied at each price. If consumers are only willing to buy a certain fixed quantity, what does the supply curve tell us about the price at which firms will supply that quantity?

9 Distinguish between:
a) A change in demand and a change in the quantity demanded
b) A change in supply and a change in the quantity supplied

10 Why is the price at which the quantity demanded equals the quantity supplied the equilibrium price?

11 What happens to the price and the quantity traded of a good if:
a) Demand increases
b) Supply increases
c) Both demand and supply increase
d) Demand decreases
e) Supply decreases
f) Both demand and supply decrease

P R O B L E M S

Suppose that one of the following events occur:

a) The price of gasoline rises.

b) The price of gasoline falls.

c) All speed limits on highways are abolished.

d) A new fuel-effective engine that runs on cheap alcohol is invented.

e) The population doubles.

f) Robotic production plants lower the cost of producing cars.

g) A law banning car imports from Japan is passed.

h) The rates for auto insurance double.

i) The interstate highway system is greatly improved.

j) The minimum age for drivers is increased to 19 years.

k) A massive and high-grade oil supply is discovered in Mexico.

l) The environmental lobby succeeds in closing down all nuclear power stations.

m) The price of cars rises.

n) The price of cars falls.

o) The summer temperature is ten degrees higher than normal and the winter temperature is ten degrees lower than normal.

p) GM stops making cars.

State which of the preceding events will:

1 Increase the quantity of gasoline demanded.

2 Decrease the quantity of gasoline demanded.

3 Increase the quantity of cars demanded.

4 Decrease the quantity of cars demanded.

5 Increase the quantity of gasoline supplied.

6 Decrease the quantity of gasoline supplied.

7 Increase the quantity of cars supplied.

8 Decrease the quantity of cars supplied.

9 Increase the demand for gasoline.

10 Decrease the demand for gasoline.

11 Increase the demand for cars.

12 Decrease the demand for cars.

13 Increase the supply of gasoline.

14 Decrease the supply of gasoline.

15 Increase the supply of cars.

16 Decrease the supply of cars.

17 Increase the price of gasoline.

18 Decrease the price of gasoline.

19 Increase the price of cars.

20 Decrease the price of cars.

21 Increase the quantity of gasoline purchased.

22 Decrease the quantity of gasoline purchased.

23 Increase the quantity of cars purchased.

24 Decrease the quantity of cars purchased.

Part 2

How Markets Work

Milton Friedman spent most of his career at the University of Chicago, where he was one of the most forceful exponents of the Chicago view of economics. Currently a senior fellow at the Hoover Institution at Stanford University, he has made contributions to the theories of consumption, money, the functioning of markets, and comparative economic systems, and to the methods of scientific inquiry in economics. In 1977, Dr. Friedman was awarded the Nobel Prize in economic science.

Professor Friedman, what brought you to economics?

I took my first courses in economics in 1930 and 1931, during the depths of the Depression. The choice for me was very easy, since the Depression was clearly the single most important issue facing the world.

What was your college experience in economics like?

I was lucky enough to study with two people who had a great influence on me: Homer Jones, a student of Frank Knight's, and Arthur Burns, later chairman of the Fed. I took a seminar with Burns that was devoted entirely to poring over his Ph.D. thesis on U.S. production trends, sentence by sentence. It was probably the best research training I ever got!

Your lifetime contributions have spanned an enormous breadth. What is the unifying theme in all your work?

Most important is taking economics seriously. There are two ways to look at economics, I believe. One is to regard it as a game, a mathematical recreation judged by its elegance. Some of that is very impressive intellectually and contributes to our understanding of the world. The other approach descends from Alfred Marshall and his idea that economics is an engine for analyzing concrete problems. That's how I

approach economics. In practice, it always comes down to trying to understand the forces of demand and supply, based

on the idea of using scarce resources to achieve alternative goals. There is no major economic problem that ultimately does not reduce to this.

Can you give some examples that illustrate how economic problems of all sorts reduce to demand and supply?

When people decide what fraction of their income to consume, it's clear that they have scarce resources that they'd like to apply to alternative ends. In the realm of macroeconomics, when you're deciding how to conduct monetary policy, the paper on which currency is printed may be, in effect, unlimited, but the resources

that they command are scarce. You have to decide how they should be applied. It's the same

approach that Gary Becker originally used, in his dissertation, to study racial discrimination. People have scarce resources and can use them to discriminate against people. That's one goal—you may not like it, but that's a different question. So finally, my approach includes the belief that economics is capable in principle of being value-free. It's a technique of analysis, not a begging of the question of what's good or bad.

Your approach includes a methodology that some people have criticized—that you say that assumptions don't matter. Is this fair?

What I've said is that the crucial test of any hypothesis is found in its predictions, not in its assumptions. I'll give you an analogy from outside economics. I hypothesize,

"It always comes down to trying to understand the forces of demand and supply."

for example, that if I drop a ball from a building, it will hit the ground in an amount of time given by a certain formula. The formula only gives an accurate answer in a perfect vacuum. So am I actually assuming that there's a vacuum all around me as I drop the ball from the rooftop? No, of course not. I know there isn't a vacuum. But it doesn't make any difference. How do I know? There's only one way to tell. I predict that the ball will hit the ground in so much time. You tell me what range of error you'll permit. Then we drop the ball. If it

hits the ground within the range you set, then I'm getting correct results by *assuming* that there is a vacuum.

Another use of assumptions is to let them stand in for a body of complex propositions.

For example, I can predict the density of distribution of leaves on a tree by supposing that the leaves deliberately position themselves to get maximum sunlight. Now that gives me good predictions, but I obviously don't really believe that the leaves do this. In economics, we say that people in business behave as if they know

what their production functions are. It's just a shorthand—a good one if it works.

By the way, the article in which I made these comments about assumptions has given rise to more comments and attacks than any other I've written. I never replied to any of them, because I decided that I'd rather spend my time doing economics than

talking about how economics should be done.

You've studied the effectiveness of markets. What do we know about how markets work?

I always say that economists may not know much, but we know one thing very well, and that's how to create shortages and surpluses. Just tell us which you want! If you want a shortage, all we have to do is to set a price that's below the market price and I'll guarantee you a shortage. If you want a

> "The crucial test of any hypothesis is in its predictions, not its assumptions."

surplus, set a price too high and you'll have your surplus.

The contrast between the taxicab markets in

York, while there are almost always cabs available in Washington. But the most important effect, in my mind, is that

the public choice approach, and the revival of money as an important factor in macroeconomics. In the world of economics, there's no doubt that the most important change is the complete loss of faith in socialism. The triumph of capitalism over socialism as an ideology, though not as an actual practice. In fact, there's been very little change in practice, but there's been the enormous change that practically nobody believes that a centrally planned economy is the right way to get prosperity. Twenty years ago that wasn't true.

> "What's true for the individual is the opposite of what's true for the society."

New York and Washington, D.C., is a good example with many implications. In Washington, because government officials, who control the city, want cheap taxicab rides, entry into the taxicab industry is virtually free. Prices are fixed, but also elastic and responsive to change. In New York, however, there is essentially a taxicab cartel, a limit on the number of taxicab medallions. A breakdown of the market. Therefore, these licenses have a very high value—somewhere over a hundred thousand dollars. One consequence is that it's often difficult to find a cab in New

the fraction of black and Latin cab drivers and owners is high in Washington but very low in New York. That's because many members of minority groups can't afford to break into the business. And that's a tragedy.

What have been the most important developments in economics of the past 20 years?

Let's divide that question into developments in the theoretical discipline and in the world of economics. In the discipline, I'd say the rational expectations revolution,

What advice would you share with a student studying economics for the first time?

Try to get a feel for the central principles of demand and supply, for how these two forces are reconciled with each other. Work to understand the function of prices and the price system. Don't worry about all the intricate details of the banking system or the institutions you're familiar with now. I'd also propose the statement that it's generally correct that what's true for the individual is the opposite of what's true for the society. Find out why that's so.

Chapter 5

Elasticity

After studying this chapter, you will be able to:

- Define and calculate the price elasticity of demand

- Explain what determines the elasticity of demand

- Distinguish between short-run demand and long-run demand

- Use elasticity to determine whether a price change will increase or decrease revenue

- Define and calculate other elasticities of demand and supply

- Distinguish between momentary supply, long-run supply, and short-run supply

If the supply of a good falls, its price rises. But by how much? To answer this question, you will have to don a flowing caftan: You have just been named chief economic strategist for OPEC—the Organization of Petroleum Exporting Countries. You want to bring more money into OPEC. Would you restrict the supply of oil to raise prices? Or would you produce more oil? ■ You know that a higher price will bring in more dollars per barrel, but lower production means that fewer barrels will be sold. Will the price rise high enough to offset the smaller quantity that OPEC will sell? ■ As OPEC's economic strategist, you need to know about the demand for oil in great detail. For example, as the world economy grows, how will that growth translate into an increasing demand for oil? What about substitutes for oil? Will we discover inexpensive methods to convert coal and tar sands into usable fuel? Will nuclear energy become safe and cheap enough to compete with oil?

OPEC's Dilemma

■ In this chapter, you will learn how to tackle questions such as the ones just posed. You will learn how we can measure in a precise way the responsiveness of the quantities bought and sold to changes in prices and other influences on buyers or sellers.

Price Elasticity of Demand

Let's begin by looking a bit more closely at your task as OPEC's economic strategist. You are trying to decide whether to advise a cut in output to shift the supply curve and raise the price of oil. To make this decision, you need to know how the quantity of oil demanded responds to a change in price. You also need some way to measure that response.

Two Possible Scenarios

To understand the importance of the responsiveness of the quantity of oil demanded to a change in its price, let's compare two possible (hypothetical) sce-narios in the oil industry, shown in Fig. 5.1. In the two parts of the figure, the supply curves are identical, but the demand curves differ.

Focus first on the supply curve labeled S_0 in each part of the figure. This curve represents the initial supply. Notice that S_0 cuts the demand curve, in both cases, at a price of \$10 a barrel and a quantity traded of 40 million barrels a day.

Now suppose that you contemplate a cut in supply that shifts the supply curve from S_0 to S_1. In part (a), the new supply curve S_1 cuts the demand curve D_a at a price of \$30 a barrel and a quantity traded of 23 million barrels a day. In part (b), the same shift in the supply curve results in the new supply curve cutting the demand curve D_b at a price of \$15 a barrel and a quantity traded of 15 million barrels a day.

Figure 5.1 Demand, Supply, and Revenue

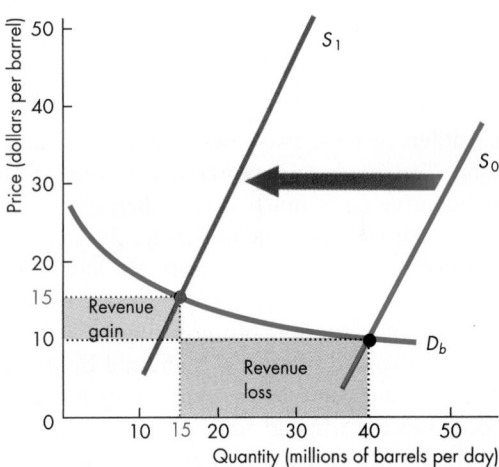

(a) More revenue

(b) Less revenue

If supply is cut from S_0 to S_1, the price rises and the quantity traded falls. In part (a), revenue—quantity multiplied by price—rises from \$400 million to \$690 million a day (the increase in revenue from a higher price—blue area—exceeds the decrease in revenue from lower sales—red area). In part (b), revenue falls from \$400 million to \$225 million a day (the increase in revenue from a higher price—blue area—is smaller than the decrease in revenue from lower sales—red area). These two different responses in revenue arise from different responses of the quantity demanded to a change in price. In the figure, revenue increases when the demand curve is steep; it falls when the demand curve is flat. To compare the responsiveness of two demand curves, we must draw them on the same scale. Changing the scale or the units of measurement will change the slope of the demand curve, thus creating the illusion of a different degree of responsiveness.

You can see that in part (a) the price rises by more and the quantity traded falls by less than it does in part (b). What happens to the revenue of the oil producers in these two cases? The **revenue** from the sale of a good equals the price of the good multiplied by the quantity sold.

An increase in price has two opposing effects on revenue. The higher price brings in more revenue on each unit sold (blue area) and the higher price leads to a decrease in the quantity sold, which in turn results in less revenue (red area). In case (a) the first effect is larger (blue area exceeds red area), so revenue rises. In case (b) the second effect is larger (red area exceeds blue area), so revenue falls.

You can confirm these results by doing some multiplication. In both cases, the original revenue was $400 million a day ($10 a barrel multiplied by 40 million barrels a day). What happens to the revenue after the supply is reduced? In part (a), revenue goes up to $690 million a day ($30 a barrel multiplied by 23 million barrels a day). In part (b), revenue falls to $225 million a day ($15 a barrel multiplied by 15 million barrels a day).

Slope Depends on Units of Measurement

What differs in these two cases is how the quantity demanded responds to a change in the price of oil. Demand curve D_a is much steeper than demand curve D_b. For the same cut in supply, the steeper demand curve causes a higher price rise and a smaller drop in the quantity traded. The steepness of the demand curve is one way of measuring how the quantity demanded of a good is affected by its price. A steep demand curve means that the quantity demanded does not respond much to price changes. A relatively flat demand curve means that the quantity demanded will change greatly with price changes.

But the slope of a demand curve depends on the units that we put on the axes of the diagram. In Fig. 5.1, we use the same units in both parts so that we can compare the demand curves D_a and D_b. However, we could easily make the demand curve D_b look as steep as D_a by changing the units on the axes of the figure. If, in part (b), we measured quantity in hundreds of millions of barrels a day, the demand curve D_b would be almost vertical. It would "look" much steeper than demand curve D_a, but the appearance would be an illusion. If, again in part (b), we

measured the price in cents per barrel, the demand curve D_b would appear as a much steeper curve than D_a. Again, the appearance would be an illusion.

Since we can influence the slope of a demand curve purely by our choice of the units in which we measure prices and quantities, we cannot hope to find a rule that tells us how revenue responds to a price change that is based on the slope of the demand curve. What we need is a measure of response that is independent of our units of measurement of prices and quantities. Elasticity is such a measure.

A Units-Free Measure of Response

Price elasticity of demand measures the responsiveness of the quantity demanded of a good to a change in its price. It measures responsiveness by calculating the percentage change in the quantity demanded divided by the percentage change in its price.

Price elasticity of demand is represented by the Greek letter *eta* (η). We use the following formula to calculate the price elasticity of demand:

$$\eta = \frac{\text{Percentage change in quantity demanded}}{\text{Percentage change in price}}$$

When the price of a good rises, the quantity demanded falls. If the percentage change in price is positive, the percentage change in quantity demanded will be negative. As a consequence, the price elasticity of demand will be a negative number. Because the price elasticity of demand is always negative, we adopt the convention of dropping the minus sign and speaking only of the magnitude of the elasticity. Also, for simplicity (provided no ambiguity will result), we often drop the word *price* and simply refer to the elasticity of demand. Whenever we use the term **elasticity of demand,** we mean *price* elasticity of demand. Let's practice using the formula for the elasticity of demand.

Calculating Elasticity

In order to calculate an elasticity, we need to know the quantities demanded at different prices. We also need some reasonable assurance that when the price changes, nothing else that influences consumers' buying plans changes. As an example, let's assume we have the relevant data on prices and quantities de-

Table 5.1   Calculating the Price Elasticity of Demand

	Numbers	Symbols and Formulas*
Prices (dollars per barrel)		
Original price	$ 9.50	P_0
New price	$10.50	P_1
Change in price	$ 1.00	$\Delta P = P_1 - P_0$
Average price	$10.00	$P = (P_0 + P_1)/2$
Percentage change in price	10%	$(\Delta P/P) \times 100$
Quantities (millions of barrels per day)		
Original quantity demanded	41	Q_0
New quantity demanded	39	Q_1
Change in quantity demanded	2	$\Delta Q = Q_0 - Q_1$
Average quantity demanded	40	$Q = (Q_0 + Q_1)/2$
Percentage change in quantity demanded	5%	$(\Delta Q/Q) \times 100$
Price elasticity of demand	0.5	$\eta = (\Delta Q/Q)/(\Delta P/P)$

*The Greek letter *delta*, (Δ), stands for "change in."

manded for the oil industry. The calculations that we will perform are summarized in Table 5.1. You can use the symbols and the formulas shown in the final column of the table to perform the same calculations on any set of numbers.

At $9.50 a barrel, 41 million barrels a day are sold. As the price increases to $10.50 a barrel, the quantity demanded falls to 39 million barrels a day. When the price rises by $1 a barrel, the quantity demanded falls by 2 million barrels a day. To calculate the elasticity of demand, we have to express changes in price and quantity demanded as percentage changes. But there are two prices and two quantities—the original and the new. Which price and which quantity do we use for calculating the percentage change? By convention, we use the *average* price and the *average* quantity. The formula for calculating

a percentage change (in either the price or the quantity) is:

$$\text{Percentage change} = \frac{\text{Change in value}}{\text{Average value}} \times 100$$

Let's use this formula to calculate the percentage changes in price and quantity. The original price was $9.50 and the new price is $10.50, so the average price is $10. When the price rises by $1, it changes one tenth, or 10 percent, of the average price. The original quantity was 41 million barrels and the new quantity is 39 million barrels, so the average quantity demanded is 40 million barrels. When the quantity falls by 2 million barrels a day, it changes by one twentieth, or 5 percent, of the average quantity.

Remember, price elasticity of demand (η) is the ratio of the percentage change in the quantity demanded to the percentage change in the price. That is,

$$\eta = \frac{\Delta Q/Q}{\Delta P/P} = \frac{5\%}{10\%} = 0.5$$

Notice three things about the calculation of the price elasticity of demand:

1 The change in price and the change in the quantity demanded are both recorded as positive numbers. It is true that as the price increases, the quantity demanded decreases. Usually, a rise in something is called a positive change and a fall in something is a negative change. Since the quantity demanded *always* falls when the price rises (other things being equal), there is no need to attach a negative sign. The elasticity, a positive number, tells us the responsiveness of a quantity *fall* to a price *rise* or of a quantity *rise* to a price *fall*.

2 The changes in prices and quantities demanded are expressed as percentages of the *average* price and *average* quantity demanded. We do this to avoid the awkwardness of having two values for the elasticity, depending on whether we move from the original price to the new price or from the new price back to the original price. The price and quantity demanded change by the same amount in each case—in our example, $1 a barrel and 2 million barrels a day. But whereas $1 is 10.5 percent of $9.50, it is only 9.5 percent of $10.50. Furthermore, 2 million barrels a day is 4.9 percent of 41 million barrels but 5.1 percent of 39 million barrels. If we use these numbers to calculate the elasticity, we get a value of 0.54 for a price rise from $9.50 to $10.50 and 0.47 for a price cut from $10.50 to $9.50. By using the average price and quantity demanded, we calculate an elasticity that is the same, 0.5, regardless of whether the price rises or falls.

3 Although it is convenient to think of elasticity as the ratio of the *percentage* change in the quantity demanded to the *percentage* change in the price, it is also, equivalently, the *proportionate* change in the quantity demanded divided by the *proportionate* change in the price. In Table 5.1, notice that although the formula multiplies both the change in price and the change in quantity demanded by 100, to create a percentage, those hundreds cancel when we divide.

REVIEW

Elasticity is a units-free measure of response. The price elasticity of demand—or simply, the elasticity of demand—is calculated as the percentage change in the quantity demanded divided by the percentage change in price. ∎

Elastic and Inelastic Demand

The elasticity that we have just calculated in our example is 0.5. Is that a large or a small value for an elasticity? The size of the elasticity of demand can range between zero and infinity. The elasticity of demand would be zero if the quantity demanded did not change when the price changed. You can see that by assuming that the percentage change in the quantity demanded is zero and then doing a little calculation. It doesn't matter what the percentage change in the price is because if we divide zero by any positive number, we get zero. An example of a good that has a very low elasticity of demand (perhaps zero) is insulin. This commodity is of such importance to many diabetics that they would buy the quantity they need for their health at almost any price.

If a price rise causes a fall in the quantity demanded, the elasticity is greater than zero. When the percentage change in the quantity demanded is less than the percentage change in price, the elasticity is a fraction (the example that we calculated in Table 5.1 is such a case).

If the percentage change in the quantity demanded exactly equals the percentage change in price, then the elasticity of demand is 1. If the percentage change in the quantity demanded exceeds the percentage change in price, then the elasticity is greater than 1.

In an extreme case, the quantity demanded may be infinitely sensitive to price changes. At a particular price, people demand any quantity of a good, but if the price rises by one cent, then the quantity demanded will drop to zero. In this case, an almost zero percentage change in the price produces an infinite percentage change in the quantity demanded, so the elasticity of demand is infinity. An example of a good whose elasticity is infinite is Schweppes soda. If the price of Schweppes soda increased, while all other prices, including the pric-

Table 5.2   Elastic and Inelastic Demand (effects of a 10% price change)

	Original quantity demanded	New quantity demanded	Change in quantity demanded	Average quantity demanded	Percentage change in quantity demanded	Elasticity of demand
Inelastic	41	39	2	40	5	0.5
Unit elastic	42	38	4	40	10	1.0
Elastic	50	30	20	40	50	5.0

es of competing sodas, remained constant, there would be an indefinitely large decrease in the quantity of Schweppes soda consumed. Other sodas are almost perfect substitutes for Schweppes soda.

For elasticities between zero and 1, demand is called **inelastic.** When the elasticity is greater than 1, demand is said to be **elastic.** The dividing line between inelastic and elastic demand is called **unit elastic demand.** When elasticity is equal to infinity, demand is sometimes called **perfectly elastic;** when elasticity is equal to zero, demand is called **perfectly inelastic.**

Table 5.2 shows examples of inelastic, elastic, and unit elastic demands. We can see in this table the changes in quantities demanded for a 10 percent change in price. The first row simply reproduces the calculations that you worked through in Table 5.1. The second row shows the case of a unit elastic demand. The initial quantity demanded was 42 million barrels a day and the new quantity demanded is 38. Thus the average quantity demanded is 40 and the change in the quantity demanded is 4. The percentage change in the quantity demanded is 10 percent—the same as the percentage change in price. Therefore the elasticity is 1. The final case is one where the original quantity demanded was 50 but the new quantity demanded is 30. The average quantity demanded is still 40 but the change in quantity demanded is now 20, which is 50 percent. In this case, the elasticity is 50 percent divided by 10 percent, which is 5.

Elasticity is not just a number calculated by economists. Whether demand is elastic or inelastic is of enormous importance to each of us on an individual level. In the 1970s, when OPEC did in fact cut back on the supply of oil, Americans discovered that their demand for oil was inelastic. Despite the lower supplies, we still demanded a lot of oil and gasoline, which led to cuts in spending on other things—people took fewer vacations; vast companies were thrown into a panic as they tried to adjust; schools had to cut the salaries of teachers so that they could pay for heating oil; speed restrictions were imposed and angry car owners had to face the premature obsolescence of their gas guzzlers.

Elasticity and the Slope of the Demand Curve

Elasticity is not the same as slope, but the two are related. However, that connection is not entirely straightforward. To understand the relation better, we'll consider the elasticity along a demand curve that has a constant slope. Such a demand curve is a straight line.

Let's calculate the elasticity of the straight-line demand curve shown in Fig. 5.2. To do so, we first pick an initial price and quantity demanded. Next, we change the price and observe the change in the quantity demanded. Finally, we combine the information on prices and quantities to calculate elasticity by using the formula (summarized in Table 5.1, page 105):

$$\eta = (\Delta Q/Q)/(\Delta P/P)$$

Let's start with a price of $50 a barrel. What is the elasticity if we lower the price from $50 to $40? The change in the price is $10 and the

Figure 5.2   Elasticity Along a Straight-Line Demand Curve

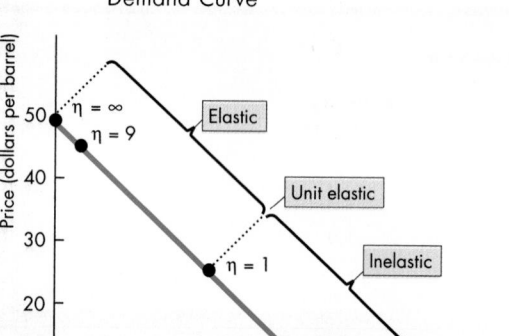

On a straight-line demand curve, elasticity falls as the price falls and the quantity demanded rises. Demand is unit elastic at the midpoint of the demand curve (elasticity is 1). Above the midpoint, demand is elastic (elasticity is greater than 1); below the midpoint, demand is inelastic (elasticity is less than 1).

average price is $45 (average of $50 and $40), which means that the proportionate change in price is:

$$\Delta P/P = 10/45$$

The original quantity demanded was zero and the new quantity demanded is 10 million barrels a day, so the change in the quantity demanded is 10 million barrels a day and the average quantity is 5 million barrels a day (the average of 10 million and zero). We can use these numbers to calculate the proportionate change in the quantity demanded as:

$$\Delta Q/Q = 10/5$$

To calculate the elasticity of demand, we divide the proportionate change in the quantity demanded by the proportionate change in the price. That is:

$$\eta = (\Delta Q/Q)/(\Delta P/P) = (10/5)/(10/45) = 9$$

Using this same formula, we can calculate the elasticity of demand when the price of a barrel is cut repeatedly by $10—from $45 to $35, from $40 to $30, from $35 to $25, and so on. You can verify the elasticity of demand at each point on the demand curve in Fig. 5.2. Notice that on a straight-line demand curve, the elasticity falls as the price falls.

Figure 5.3   Demand Curves with Constant Elasticity

(a) Zero elasticity

(b) Unit elasticity

(c) Infinite elasticity

Each demand curve shown here has a constant elasticity. The demand curve in part (a) has zero elasticity. The demand curve in part (b) has unit elasticity. The demand curve in part (c) has infinite elasticity.

At the midpoint of the demand curve, where the price is $25 a barrel and the quantity demanded is 25 million barrels a day, elasticity is exactly 1. Above the midpoint, the elasticity is bigger than 1 and it rises as the price rises. Below the midpoint, the elasticity is less than 1 and it falls as the price falls.

Elasticity is infinity when the price is $50 a barrel and the quantity demanded is zero, and elasticity is zero when the quantity demanded is 50 million barrels a day and the price is zero. By using the formula for elasticity, you will be able to verify these calculations.

A demand curve can have a constant elasticity. A perfectly inelastic demand curve has a constant elasticity of zero ($\eta = 0$) and is vertical. A perfectly elastic demand curve has a constant elasticity of infinity ($\eta = \infty$) and is horizontal. Other constant elasticity demand curves are *curved*. Figure 5.3 illustrates three constant elasticity demand curves—the cases of zero, unity, and infinity.

The example we gave earlier, of a good with very low elasticity of demand (shown as zero in part a of the figure) is insulin. Regardless of the price, the quantity demanded remains constant in part (a). An example of a good whose elasticity is close to 1 (part b) is electricity. As its price increases, the quantity demanded decreases by the same percentage amount. The example we gave of a good whose elasticity is infinite (part c) is Schweppes soda. Schweppes is bought only if its price equals that of identical competing sodas. If the price of Schweppes exceeds the price of competing sodas, the quantity of Schweppes demanded is zero. If the price of competing soda exceeds that of Schweppes, Schweppes is the only soda bought. When the prices are equal, there is no unique quantity demanded.

Actual Elasticities   Actual values of elasticities of demand have been estimated from the average spending patterns of consumers and some examples are set out in Table 5.3.

The Size of the Elasticity of Demand

What makes the demand for some goods elastic and the demand for others inelastic? Elasticity depends on:

Table 5.3   Some Price Elasticities in the U.S. Economy

Industry	Elasticity
Elastic demands	
Metals	1.52
Electrical engineering products	1.39
Mechanical engineering products	1.30
Furniture	1.26
Motor vehicles	1.14
Instrument engineering products	1.10
Professional services	1.09
Transportation services	1.03
Inelastic demands	
Gas, electricity, and water	0.92
Oil	0.91
Chemicals	0.89
Beverages (all types)	0.78
Tobacco	0.61
Food	0.58
Banking and insurance services	0.56
Housing services	0.55
Clothing	0.49
Agricultural and fish products	0.42
Books, magazines, and newspapers	0.34
Coal	0.32

Source: Ahsan Mansur and John Whalley, "Numerical Specification of Applied General Equilibrium Models: Estimation, Calibration, and Data," in *Applied General Equilibrium Analysis*, eds. H.E. Scarf and J.B. Shoven (New York: Cambridge University Press, 1984), 109.

- The ease with which one good can be substituted for another
- The proportion of income spent on the good
- The amount of time elapsed since the price change

Substitutability   Substitutability depends on the nature of the good itself. For example, oil, a good with an inelastic demand, certainly has substitutes but none that are very close (imagine a steam-driven, coal-fueled car or a nuclear-powered jetliner). On the other hand, metals, a group of goods with elastic demands, have very good substitutes in the form of plastics.

The degree of substitutability between two goods depends on how narrowly (or broadly) we define them. For example, even though oil does not have a close substitute, different types of oil substitute for each other without much difficulty. Oils from different parts of the world differ in weight and chemical composition. Let's consider a particular kind of oil—called Saudi Arabian Light. Its elasticity will be relevant if you happen to be the economic advisor to Saudi Arabia (as well as the OPEC economic strategist!). Suppose Saudi Arabia is contemplating a unilateral price rise, which means that prices of other types of oil will stay the same. Although Saudi Arabian Light has some unique characteristics, other oils can easily substitute for it, and most buyers will be very sensitive to its price relative to the prices of other types of oil. Demand in this case is highly elastic.

This example, which distinguishes between oil in general and different types of oil, has broad applications. For example, the elasticity of demand for meat in general is low while the elasticity of demand for beef, lamb, or pork is high. The elasticity of demand for personal computers is low, but the elasticity of demand for an IBM, Zenith, or Apple is high.

Proportion of Income Spent on a Good   Other things being equal, the higher the elasticity, the higher is the proportion of income spent on a good. If only a small fraction of income is spent on a good, then a change in its price will have little impact on the consumer's overall budget. In contrast, even a small rise in the price of a good that commands a large part of a consumer's budget will induce the consumer to undertake a radical reappraisal of expenditures.

To appreciate the importance of the proportion of income spent on a good, consider your own elasticity of demand for textbooks and chewing gum. If the price of textbooks doubled (increased 100 percent) there would be an enormous fall in the quantity of textbooks bought. There would be an increase in sharing and in illegal photocopying. If the price of chewing gum doubled, also a 100 percent increase, there would be almost no change

in the quantity of gum demanded. Why the difference? Textbooks take a large proportion of your budget while gum takes only a tiny portion. You don't like either price increase, but you hardly notice the effects of the increased price of gum, while the increased price of textbooks blows you away!

Time   Elasticity also depends on the amount of time elapsed since a price change. In general, the greater the lapse of time, the higher the elasticity of demand. The reason is related to substitutability. The greater the passage of time, the more it becomes possible to develop substitutes for a good whose price has increased. Thus at the moment of a price increase, the consumer often has little choice but to continue consuming similar quantities of a good. However, given enough time, the consumer finds alternatives or cheaper substitutes and gradually lowers the rate of purchase of items that have become more expensive.

R E V I E W

The elasticity of demand ranges between zero and infinity. Goods that have a high elasticity of demand are those that have close substitutes and on which a large proportion of income is spent. Goods that have a low elasticity of demand are those that do not have good substitutes and on which a small portion of income is spent. Elasticity also is higher, the longer the time lapse since a price change.   ∎

Two Time-Frames for Demand

To take account of the importance of time on the elasticity of demand, we distinguish between two time-frames for demand—the short run and the long run. Let's examine them now.

Short-run Demand

The **short-run demand curve** describes the initial response of buyers to a change in the price of a good. The short-run response depends on whether the price change is seen as permanent (or, at least, long-lasting) or temporary. A price change that is believed to be temporary produces a highly elastic buyer response. Why would you pay a higher price now if you can get the same thing for a lower price a few days from now? And if the price is temporarily low, why wouldn't you take advantage of it and buy a lot before the price goes up again?

Examples of temporary price changes abound. For example, you can make telephone calls at much lower rates on weekends than during the week. The drop in price on Saturday and the rise in price on Monday produces a large change in the quantity demanded—demand is highly elastic. Of course, many calls are made during normal business hours, but the lower price on the weekend induces a large switch from business day calling to weekend calling. Other examples are seasonal variations in the price of travel and of certain fresh fruits and vegetables.

When a price change seems permanent, the quantity bought does not change much in the short run. That is, short-run demand is inelastic. The reason is that people find it hard to change their buying habits. More importantly, they often have to adjust their consumption of other complementary goods, an expensive and time-consuming undertaking.

An example of a permanent, or at least a long-lasting, price change occurred in the market for oil in the early 1970s. At the end of 1973 and the beginning of 1974, the price of oil increased fourfold, leading in turn to a sharp rise in the costs of home heating and of gasoline. Initially, consumers had little choice but to accept the price increases and maintain consumption at more or less their original levels. Home heating equipment and cars may not have been the most energy-efficient, but there was nothing else available. Drivers could lower their average speed and economize on gasoline. Thermostats could be turned down but that too imposed costs—costs of discomfort. As a consequence, there were severe limits in the extent to which people felt it worthwhile cutting back on their consumption of the now much more costly fuel, oil, and gasoline. The short-run buyer response in the face of this sharp price increase was inelastic.

Long-run Demand

The **long-run demand curve** describes the response of buyers to a change in price after all possible

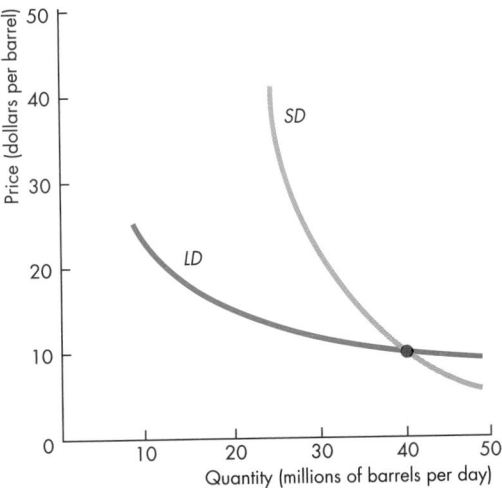

Figure 5.4   Short-run and Long-run Demand

The light blue short-run demand curve (SD) shows the initial response of the quantity demanded to a change in the price of a good, before buyers have had sufficient time to make all possible adjustments. The dark blue long-run demand curve (LD) shows how the quantity demanded varies with the price of a good when buyers have made all possible adjustments to their buying plans.

adjustments have been made. Long-run demand is more elastic than short-run demand. The 1974 rise in the price of oil and gasoline produced a clear demonstration of the distinction between long-run and short-run demand. Initially, buyers responded to higher gasoline and oil prices by using their existing capital equipment—furnaces and gas guzzlers—in a way that economized on the more expensive fuel. With a longer time to respond, people bought more energy-efficient capital equipment. Cars became smaller and more fuel-efficient, car engines also became more efficient.

Two Demand Curves

The short-run and long-run demand curves for oil in 1974 appear in Fig. 5.4. The light blue short-run demand curve (SD) shows the initial response of the quantity demanded to a permanent change in price. The dark blue long-run demand curve (LD) shows the change in the quantity demanded after buyers have made all possible adjustments.

The price of a barrel of oil in 1974 was $10 and the quantity of oil traded in that year was 40 million barrels a day. The two demand curves have been drawn to intersect at that price and quantity. At that point of intersection, the long-run demand curve is more elastic than the short-run demand curve.

In Chapter 6, we'll use the short-run and long-run demand curves to work out what happens in a market when supply changes.

Elasticity, Revenue, and Expenditure

We've defined *revenue* as the price of a good multiplied by the quantity sold. **Expenditure** is the price of a good multiplied by the quantity *bought*. Thus revenue and expenditure are two sides of the same coin— revenue is the receipts of the sellers while expenditure is the outlays of the buyers. When the price of a good rises, the quantity sold falls. What happens to revenue (and expenditure) depends on the extent to which the quantity sold falls as the price rises. If a 1 percent rise in the price reduces the quantity sold by less than 1 percent, revenue increases. If a 1 percent rise in price lowers the quantity sold by more than 1 percent, revenue falls. If a 1 percent rise in price lowers the quantity sold by 1 percent, the price rise and the quantity fall just offset each other and revenue stays constant. But we now have

a precise way of linking the percent change of the quantity sold to the percent change in price—the elasticity of demand. When the price of a good rises, the size of the elasticity of demand determines whether revenue rises or falls. Table 5.4 provides some examples based on the three cases in Table 5.2.

In case *a,* the elasticity of demand is 0.5. When the price goes up from $9.50 to $10.50, the quantity sold falls from 41 million to 39 million barrels a day. Revenue, which is equal to price multiplied by quantity sold, was originally $9.50 multiplied by 41 million, which is $389.50 million a day. After the price rises, revenue rises to $409.50 million a day. Thus a rise in the price leads to a *rise* in revenue of $20 million a day.

In case *b,* the elasticity of demand is 1. The quantity sold falls from 42 million to 38 million barrels a day as the price rises from $9.50 to $10.50. Revenue in this case is the same at each price, $399 million a day. Thus when the price changes and the elasticity of demand is 1, revenue *does not change.*

In case *c,* the elasticity of demand is 5. When the price rises by $1, the quantity sold falls by 20 million barrels a day. The original revenue was $475 million a day but the new revenue is $315 million a day. Thus in this case, a rise in the price leads to a *fall* in revenue of $160 million a day.

Elasticity and revenue are closely connected. When the elasticity of demand is greater than 1, the percentage fall in the quantity demanded exceeds the percentage rise in price and therefore revenue falls. When the elasticity of demand is less

Table 5.4   Elasticity of Demand, Revenue, and Expenditure

	Elasticity	Price (dollars per barrel)		Quantity demanded (millions of barrels per day)		Revenue/Expenditure (millions of dollars per day)		
		Original	New	Original	New	Original	New	Change
a	0.5	9.50	10.50	41	39	389.50	409.50	+ 20.00
b	1.0	9.50	10.50	42	38	399.00	399.00	0
c	5.0	9.50	10.50	50	30	475.00	315.00	−160.00

Figure 5.5 Income Elasticity of Demand

(a) Elasticity greater than 1

(b) Elasticity between zero and 1

(c) Elasticity less than 1 and becomes negative

There are three ranges of values for income elasticity of demand. In part (a), income elasticity of demand is greater than 1. In this case, as income increases, the quantity demanded increases but by a bigger percentage than the increase in income. In part (b), income elasticity of demand is between zero and 1. In this case, as income increases, the quantity demanded increases but by a smaller percentage than the increase in income. In part (c), the income elasticity of demand is positive at low incomes but becomes negative as income rises above the level m. Maximum consumption occurs at the income m.

than 1, the percentage fall in the quantity demanded is less than the percentage rise in price and therefore revenue rises. When the elasticity of demand is 1, the percentage fall in the quantity demanded equals the percentage rise in price and revenue remains constant. Extra revenue from a higher price is exactly offset by the loss in revenue from the smaller quantities sold.

As we have seen, long-run demand curves are more elastic than short-run demand curves. It is possible, therefore, that an increase in price will result in an increase in revenue in the short run but not in the long run. If the short-run elasticity is less than 1 but the long-run elasticity is greater than 1, this outcome will occur.

The price elasticity of demand that you have just learned to calculate and interpret is the most important of all the elasticities. Whenever economists refer to the elasticity of demand without qualification, they mean the price elasticity of demand. There are, however, some other elasticities of demand. Let's now turn our attention to them.

More Demand Elasticities

The quantity demanded of any good (or service or factor of production) is influenced by many things other than its price. It depends on, among other things, incomes and the prices of other goods. We can calculate elasticities of demand with respect to these other variables as well. Let's now examine some of these additional elasticities.

Income Elasticity of Demand

As income grows, how will the demand for a particular good change? The answer depends on the income elasticity of demand for the good. The **income elasticity of demand** is the percentage change in the quantity demanded divided by the percentage change in income. It is represented by η_y.

Table 5.5   Some Income Elasticities of Demand

Elastic		Unit Elasticity	
Airline travel	5.82	Dentists' services	1.00
Movies	3.41	**Inelastic**	
Foreign travel	3.08		
Drugs and medicines	3.04	Shoes and other footwear	0.94
Housing services	2.45	Car repairs	0.90
Toys	2.01	Tobacco	0.86
Electricity	1.94	China, glassware, and utensils	0.77
Intercity buses	1.89	Shoe repairs	0.72
Stationery	1.83	Alcoholic beverages	0.62
Restaurant meals	1.61	Water	0.59
Books and maps	1.42	Furniture	0.53
Local buses and trains	1.38	Clothing	0.51
Gasoline and oil	1.36	Newspapers and magazines	0.38
Haircutting	1.36	Telephone	0.32
Car insurance	1.26		
Household appliances	1.18		
Taxicabs	1.15		
Physicians' services	1.15		
Cars	1.07		

Source: H.S. Houthakker and Lester D. Taylor, *Consumer Demand in the United States* (Cambridge, Mass.: Harvard University Press, 1970).

That is:

$$\eta_y = \frac{\text{Percentage change in quantity demanded}}{\text{Percentage change in income}}$$

Income elasticities of demand can be positive or negative; however, there are three interesting ranges for the income elasticity of demand:

- Greater than 1 (income elastic)
- Between zero and 1 (income inelastic)
- Less than zero (negative income elasticity)

These three cases are illustrated in Figure 5.5. Part (a) shows an income elasticity of demand that is greater than 1. As income rises, the quantity demanded rises, but the quantity demanded rises faster than income. The curve slopes upward and has an increasing slope. Goods that fall into this category include ocean cruises, custom clothing, international travel, jewelry, and works of art.

Part (b) shows an income elasticity of demand that is between zero and 1. In this case, the quantity demanded rises as income rises, but income rises faster than the quantity demanded. The curve slopes upward but the slope declines as income rises. Goods that fall into this category include basic food, clothing, housing, and local bus transportation.

Part (c) illustrates a third category of goods that is a bit more complicated. For these goods, as income rises, the quantity demanded increases until it reaches a maximum at income *m*. Beyond that point, as income continues to rise, the quantity demanded declines. The elasticity of demand is positive but less than 1 up to point *m*. Beyond *m*, the income elasticity of demand is negative. Examples of goods in this category include one-speed bicycles, small motorbikes, potatoes, and rice. Low income consumers buy most of these goods. At low income levels, the demand for such goods rises as income rises. Eventually, income reaches a level (at point *m*) where consumers replace these goods with superior alternatives. For example, a small car replaces the motorbike; fruit, vegetables, and meat begin to appear in a diet that was heavy in rice or potatoes.

Goods whose income elasticities of demand are positive are called *normal goods*. Goods whose income elasticities of demand are negative are called *inferior goods*. These goods are "inferior" in the sense that as income increases they are replaced with "superior," but more expensive substitutes.

Let's now look at some estimates of actual income elasticities of demand in the United States. Table 5.5 provides a summary. The various goods and services are listed in three groups. The first group lists goods and services whose income elasticity is greater than 1. The second group, in which there is just one example, has a unit elasticity. The third group lists goods whose income elasticity is less than 1 and whose demands are said to be income inelastic.

By using estimates of income elasticity of demand, we can translate projections of average income growth rates into growth rates of demand for particular goods and services. For example, if average incomes grow by 3 percent a year, the demand for gasoline and oil will grow by 4 percent a year (3 percent multiplied by the income elasticity of demand for gasoline and oil which, as shown in Table 5.5, is 1.36).

Cross Elasticity of Demand

The quantity of any good demanded depends on the prices of its substitutes and complements. The responsiveness of the quantity demanded of a particular good to the prices of its substitutes and complements is measured by **cross elasticity of demand**, which is represented by η_x. The cross elasticity of demand is calculated as the percentage change in the quantity demanded of one good divided by the percentage change in the price of another good (a substitute or a complement).

That is:

$$\eta_x = \frac{\text{Percentage change in quantity demanded of one good}}{\text{Percentage change in the price of another good}}$$

Figure 5.6   Cross Elasticities: Substitutes and Complements

(a) Substitutes

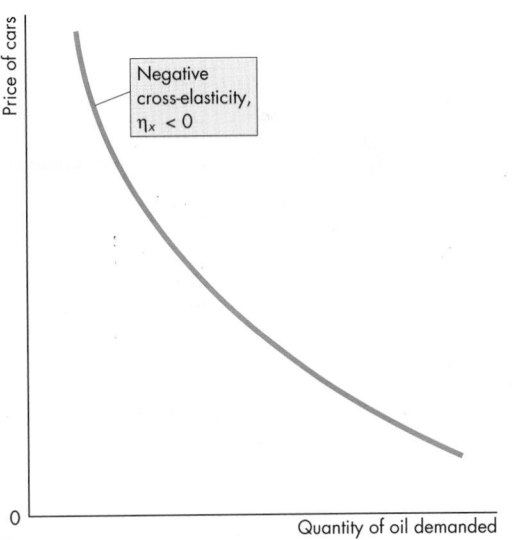

(b) Complements

Part (a) shows the cross elasticity of demand with respect to the price of a substitute. When the price of coal increases, the quantity of oil demanded also increases. Part (b) shows the cross elasticity of demand with respect to the price of a complement. When the price of cars increases, the quantity of oil demanded decreases.

Table 5.6 A Compact Glossary of Elasticities of Demand

Price elasticities (η)

When η is:	The relationship is described as:	Which means that:
Infinity	Perfectly elastic or infinitely elastic	The smallest possible price rise (fall) causes an infinitely large fall (rise) in the quantity demanded.
Less than infinity but greater than 1	Elastic	The percentage rise (fall) in the quantity demanded exceeds the percentage fall (rise) in price.
1	Unit elasticity	The percentage rise (fall) in the quantity demanded equals the percentage fall (rise) in price.
Greater than zero but less than 1	Inelastic	The percentage rise (fall) in the quantity demanded is less than the percentage fall (rise) in price.
Zero	Perfectly inelastic or completely inelastic	The quantity demanded is the same at all prices.

Income Elasticities (η_y)

When η_y is:	The relationship is described as:	Which means that:
Greater than 1	Income-elastic (normal good)	The percentage rise (fall) in the quantity demanded is greater than the percentage rise (fall) in income.
Less than 1 but greater than zero	Income-inelastic (normal good)	The percentage rise (fall) in the quantity demanded is less than the percentage rise (fall) in income.
Less than zero	Negative income elasticity (inferior good)	When income rises, quantity demanded falls.

Cross Elasticities (η_x)

When η_x is:	The relationship is described as:	Which means that:
Infinity	Perfect substitutes	The smallest possible rise (fall) in the price of one good causes an infinitely large rise (fall) in the quantity demanded of the other good.
Less than infinity but greater than zero	Substitutes	If the price of one good rises (falls), the quantity demanded of the other good also rises (falls).
Zero	Independent	The quantity demanded of one good remains constant regardless of the price of the other good.
Less than zero (negative)	Complements	The quantity demanded of one good falls (rises) when the price of the other good rises (falls).

The cross elasticity of demand with respect to the price of a substitute is positive. The cross elasticity of demand with respect to the price of a complement is negative. Figure 5.6 makes it clear why. When the price of coal (a substitute for oil) rises, the demand for oil rises. When the price of cars (a complement with oil) rises, the demand for oil declines. The degree to which demand changes depends on how close the substitute or complement is. That is, the more easily coal and oil substitute for each other, the bigger the cross elasticity of demand between them. The more complementary are cars and oil, the more negative the cross elasticity of demand for oil with respect to the price of a car.

Table 5.6 provides a compact summary of all the different kinds of demand elasticities you've just studied, and Reading Between the Lines (pp. 118–119) gives an example of how these elasticities may be used in practical calculations.

Let's now turn our attention to the supply curve and study the concept of the elasticity of supply.

Elasticity of Supply

We have seen that the concept of elasticity of demand may be used to determine the extent to which price and the quantity traded change when there is a change in supply. But suppose we want to predict the effects on price and the quantity traded of a change in demand. To make such a prediction, we need to know how responsive the quantity supplied is to the price of a good. That is, we need the concept of the elasticity of supply.

The **elasticity of supply** is the percentage change in the quantity supplied of a good divided by the percentage change in its price. It is represented by η_s. That is:

$$\eta_s = \frac{\text{Percentage change in quantity supplied}}{\text{Percentage change in price}}$$

The supply curves that we have considered in this chapter (and those in Chapter 4) all slope upward. When the price increases, the quantity supplied increases. Upward-sloping supply curves have a positive elasticity.

There are two interesting cases of the elastici-

ty of supply. If the quantity supplied is fixed regardless of the price, the supply curve is vertical. In this case, the elasticity of supply is zero. An increase in price leads to no change in the quantity supplied. If there is a price below which nothing will be supplied and at which suppliers are willing to sell any quantity demanded, the supply curve is horizontal. In this case, the elasticity of supply is infinite. The small fall in price would reduce the quantity supplied from an indefinitely large amount to zero.

The magnitude of the elasticity of supply depends on:

* The technological conditions governing production
* The amount of time elapsed since the price change

The importance of technological conditions is best illustrated by considering two extreme examples. Some goods, such as a painting by Georgia O'Keeffe, are unique. There is just one of each of her paintings. Its supply curve is vertical and its elasticity of supply is zero. At the other extreme, the supply of sand for making silicon chips is available in indefinitely large quantities at a virtually constant cost of production. Its supply curve is horizontal and its elasticity of supply is infinitely large.

To study the influence of the length of time elapsed since a price change, we distinguish three time-frames of supply: momentary, short-run, and long-run.

Momentary Supply

When the price of a good rises or falls in a sudden, unforeseen way, we use the momentary supply curve to describe the initial change in the quantity supplied. The **momentary supply curve** shows the response of the quantity supplied immediately following a price change.

For many goods, the momentary supply curve is perfectly inelastic—which means that the supply curve is vertical. Consider perishable fruits and vegetables. The amounts that can be supplied depend on crop planting decisions made several months earlier. In the case of fruit such as oranges, for example, the planting decisions have to be made many years in advance. All crops and all animal products take *some* time to grow, and so the

Warning: Travel with Care

Terrorism Spurs U.S. Tourists to Change Their Vacation Plans in Droves

It is Eastertide in Rome, April in Paris and the eve of Passover in Jerusalem. But suddenly, for millions of American tourists, this is chiefly the season for caution in making travel plans. In 1986, in sharp contrast to the overseas-travel surge of a year ago, Americans and their sought-after dollars are making themselves scarce in many parts of Western Europe and the Mediterranean. The phones of travel agents are as busy as ever, but many of the callers now want to change their vacation plans. Some are canceling their trips abroad entirely. Others are choosing more circuitous means and routes to reach their destinations, rather than having to pass through airports in Rome, Athens and other cities along the Mediterranean littoral. The fear of terrorism has suddenly become an important factor in the $250 billion U.S. travel industry.

Many U.S. holidaymakers are hurriedly lining up presumably safer summer excursions, including Caribbean cruises and even charter tours to Moscow. But above all, Americans this year are deciding that they would rather take in the splendors of their own land, on motor-home jaunts to Disney World, camping trips to U.S. national parks, and surfing safaris to Hawaii. The travel industry expects a jump of 10% or more in domestic bookings this year. Says Harold Van Sumeren, president of the Chamber of Commerce in Traverse City, Mich., a boating and camping mecca: "We're really anticipating one of the biggest and finest summer seasons we've ever had."

The apprehension over travel to Europe and the Mediterranean is a direct result of the recent rash of bloody attacks directed against U.S. citizens in Italy and West Germany, of rioting in Egypt and of random bombings in France. Last week travelers had further cause to be spooked by the harsh words and bellicose gestures flying between the U.S. and Libya. Reasons other than the terrorism scare, such as a sharp decline in the value of the U.S. dollar abroad and an abundance of cheap gasoline at home, are also involved in the shuffle of itineraries. Even so, says Sam Massell, an Atlanta travel agent, "if you're going on vacation, you want to start off happy. You're not supposed to go where you have to think about stress management."

The change in U.S. traveling patterns is already starting to have substantial effects. Until late last year, U.S. travel to Europe and the Mediterranean was setting records, thanks partly to the buying power of the strong dollar. Some 6.4 million Americans visited European countries in 1985, up from 5.8 million the previous year. Now the trade magazine *Travel Industry Monthly* expects European tourism by Americans to fall by about 25% in 1986.

Time, **April 21, 1986**

By Stephen Koepp, reported by Thomas McCarroll/New York, with other bureaus

The Essence of the Story

Facts

- In 1984, 5.8 million Americans visited Europe.

- In 1985, 6.4 million Americans visited Europe, a 10 percent increase.

- In April 1986, it was predicted that European tourism by Americans would fall by 25 percent of its 1985 level.

- In April 1986, the U.S. travel industry expected a rise of 10 percent in domestic business.

- In 1986, the U.S. dollar fell in value—i.e., it bought fewer goods abroad than in 1985.

- In 1986, the price of gasoline fell.

- In the winter of 1985 and the spring of 1986, there was a wave of terrorism directed at U.S. citizens in several European and Mediterranean countries.

Alleged explanation

- People switched from European to domestic vacations mainly because of the rise in anti-American terrorism and partly because of the drop in the value of the dollar and in the price of gasoline.

Background and Analysis

Prices

- A fall in the price of a good leads to an increase in the quantity demanded.

- An increase in the price of a substitute leads to an increase in demand.

- In 1985, the price of a European vacation fell by 1.8 percent. (The dollar cost of a European vacation rose by 1.7 percent but prices in the United States rose by 3.5 percent so that the relative price (opportunity cost) of a European vacation fell by the difference—1.8 percent).

- In 1986 the price of a European vacation increased by 18.2 percent. (In that year the dollar fell in value resulting in an increased dollar cost of a European vacation of 21.3 percent. Prices rose in the United States by 3.1 percent so the relative price (opportunity cost) of a European vacation rose by the difference—18.2 percent).

Incomes

- In 1985 disposable income per head rose by 1 percent.

- In 1986 disposable income per head rose by 2 percent.

Elasticities

- The income elasticity of demand for foreign travel is estimated to be 3 (see Table 5.5, p. 114).

- The price elasticity of demand for European vacations is not known but is likely to be much bigger than 1 because vacations in Europe, Asia, Latin America, Canada, and the United States are close substitutes for each other.

- The formula used for predicting the percentage change in the quantity demanded of a good is:

  Percent rise in quantity demanded =

  Price elasticity × percent fall in price +

  Income elasticity × percent rise in income

- The table gives predicted percentage changes in the quantity of European vacations demanded for three different values of the price elasticity of demand and for an income elasticity of demand of 3.

- If the price elasticity of demand is about 2, then the price and income changes in 1985 and 1986 come close to predicting the actual changes in travel.

- The rise in the quantity demanded in 1985 is slightly bigger than would have been predicted, but the fall in the quantity demanded in 1986 is smaller than predicted.

- The puzzle raised by the numbers in the table is not that European travel by Americans fell in 1986. Rather, it is that European travel fell by so little! It is thus plausible that terrorism had no effect.

- But why would European travel fall by only 25 percent when the relative price had risen by 18 percent? Perhaps something else changed.

- Since vacations in Japan and the Far East are substitutes for vacations in Europe, a rise in the price of an Asian vacation would lead to a rise (or a smaller fall) in the demand for European vacations.

- Prices in Japan rose by 1.6 percent, but the dollar *fell* in value against the Japanese yen by 26.3 percent, so the dollar cost of a Japanese vacation rose by 27.9 percent.

- Since European travel costs, in dollars, rose by only 18.2 percent, the price of a European vacation relative to that of a Japanese vacation *fell* by almost 10 percent.

- The rise in the cost of a Japanese vacation relative to that of a European vacation would moderate the fall in the quantity demanded of European vacations.

Conclusion

- The journalists reporting this story probably overemphasized the importance of terrorism and underemphasized the importance of price and income changes in explaining the changes in the vacation plans of Americans.

	1985	1986
Elasticity		
1	+ 4.8%	−12.2%
2	+ 6.6%	−30.4%
3	+ 8.4%	−48.6%
Actual	+10%	−25%

momentary supply curve for these goods is always perfectly inelastic.

Other goods have elastic momentary supply curves. One such good is electricity. If we all turned on our TV sets and air conditioners simultaneously, there would be a big surge in the demand for electricity. If the supply of electricity were inelastic, this surge in demand would cause a sharp rise in price and no change in the quantity of electricity actually bought. Surges in demand are common, but when they occur, the quantity bought increases and the price remains constant. Electricity producers can usually anticipate fluctuations in demand and bring more generators into operation to ensure that the quantity supplied equals the quantity demanded without raising the price. (There is, of course, an upper limit to what can be produced, but normally increased output can meet the extra demand.) In this example, the momentary supply is perfectly elastic. But the momentary supply curve for most goods is inelastic, perhaps perfectly inelastic.

Let's now look at the other extreme—the long run.

Long-run Supply

The **long-run supply curve** shows the response of the quantity supplied to a change in price after all the technologically possible ways of adjusting supply have been exploited. In the case of oranges, the long run is the time it takes new plantings to grow to full maturity—about 15 years. In some cases, the long-run adjustment occurs only after a completely new production plant has been built and workers have been trained to operate it—typically a process that may take several years.

Between the momentary and the long-run time-frames, there are many intermediate time-frames. We call these the short run.

Short-run Supply

The **short-run supply curve** shows how the quantity supplied responds to a price change when only *some* of the technologically possible adjustments to production have been made. The first adjustment that is usually made is in the amount of labor employed. To increase output in the short-run, firms work their labor force overtime and perhaps hire additional workers. To decrease their output in the

Figure 5.7   Supply: Momentary, Short-run, and Long-run

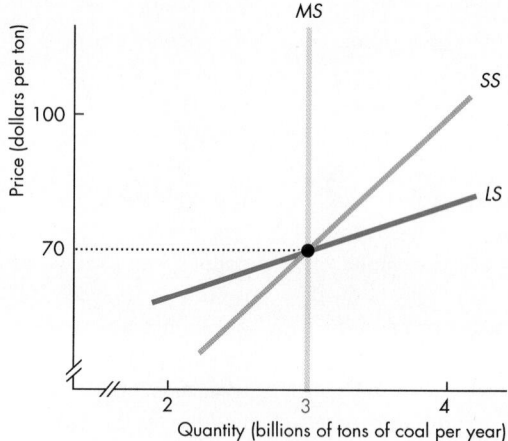

The momentary supply curve (*MS*) shows how quantity supplied responds to a price change the moment that it occurs. The light blue momentary supply curve shown here is perfectly inelastic. The medium blue short-run supply curve (*SS*) shows how the quantity supplied responds to a price change after some adjustments to production have been made. The dark blue long-run supply curve (*LS*) shows how the quantity supplied responds to a price change when all the technologically possible adjustments to the production process have been made.

short-run, firms lay off workers or reduce their hours of work. With the passage of more time, firms can make additional adjustments, perhaps training additional workers or buying additional tools and other equipment. The short-run response to a price change, unlike the momentary and long-run responses, is not a unique response but a sequence of adjustments.

Three Supply Curves

Three supply curves corresponding to the three time-frames are illustrated in Fig. 5.7. They are the supply curves in the world market for coal in a year in which the price is $70 a ton and the quantity of coal produced is 3 billion tons. The three supply curves all pass through that point. The light blue momentary supply curve (*MS*) is perfectly inelastic at 3 billion tons. The dark blue long-run supply curve (*LS*) is the most elastic of the three curves.

The medium blue short-run supply curve (SS) lies between the other two curves. In fact, there is a series of successively more elastic short-run supply curves between the momentary and the long-run curves. As more time elapses following a price change, more changes can be made in the method of production to increase output. The short-run supply curve (SS) shown in Fig. 5.7 is an example of one of these short-run supply curves.

The momentary supply curve (MS) is vertical because, at a given moment in time, no matter what the price of coal, producers cannot change their output. They have a certain labor force and a certain amount of coal mining equipment in place and there is a given amount of output that can be

produced. But as time elapses, coal producing companies can increase their capacity. They can hire and train more miners and buy more equipment. In the long run, they can sink new mines, discover more accessible coal deposits, and increase the quantity supplied even more in response to a given price rise.

■ You have now studied the theory of demand and supply, and you have learned how to measure the responsiveness of the quantities demanded and supplied to changes in price and income. In the next chapters we are going to use what we have learned, to study some real world markets—markets in action.

S U M M A R Y

Price Elasticity of Demand

Price elasticity of demand is a precise measure of the responsiveness of the quantity demanded of a good to a change in its price. It enables us to calculate the effect of a change in supply on price, quantity traded, and revenue. Price elasticity of demand (η) is calculated using the formula:

$$\eta = \frac{\text{Percentage change in quantity demanded}}{\text{Percentage change in price}}$$

When elasticity is between zero and 1, demand is inelastic. When elasticity is 1, demand is unit elastic. When elasticity is greater than 1, demand is elastic.

Elasticity varies along a straight-line demand curve. The elasticity falls as the price falls and the quantity demanded rises.

The size of the elasticity depends on how easily one good may serve as a substitute for another, on the proportion of income spent on the good, and on the time that has elapsed since the price change. (pp. 103–110)

Two Time-Frames for Demand

We use two time-frames to analyze demand: short-run and long-run. Short-run demand describes the initial response of buyers to a price change. Long-run demand describes the response of buyers to a price change after all possible adjustments have

been made. Short-run demand is usually less elastic than long-run demand. (pp. 110–112)

Elasticity, Revenue, and Expenditure

If the elasticity of demand is less than 1, a decrease in supply leads to an increase in revenue—the percentage increase in price is greater than the percentage decrease in the quantity traded. If the elasticity of demand is greater than 1, a decrease in supply leads to a decrease in revenue—the percentage increase in price is less than the percentage decrease in the quantity traded. (pp. 112–113)

More Demand Elasticities

Income elasticity of demand measures the responsiveness of demand to a change in income. Income elasticity of demand is calculated as the percentage change in the quantity demanded divided by the percentage change in income. Income elasticities may be greater than 1 (income elastic), between zero and 1 (income inelastic), or less than zero (negative income elasticity). Income elasticities are greater than 1 for items typically consumed by the rich; they are positive but less than 1 for more basic consumption items. Income elasticities are less than zero for inferior goods—goods that are consumed only at low incomes and that disappear as budgets increase.

Cross elasticity of demand measures the responsiveness of demand for one good to a change in the price of another good. Cross elasticity of demand is calculated as the percentage change in the quantity demanded of one good divided by the percentage change in the price of another good (a substitute or a complement). The cross elasticity of demand with respect to the price of a substitute is positive. The cross elasticity of demand with respect to the price of a complement is negative. (pp. 113–117)

Elasticity of Supply

The elasticity of supply measures the responsiveness of the quantity supplied to a change in price. Elasticity of supply is calculated as the percentage change in the quantity supplied of a good divided by the percentage change in its price. Supply elasticities are usually positive but range between zero (vertical supply curve) and infinity (horizontal supply curve).

We classify supply according to three different time-frames: momentary, long-run, and short-run. Momentary supply refers to the response of suppliers to a price change at the instant that it happens. Long-run supply refers to the response of suppliers to a price change when all the technologically feasible adjustments in production have been made. Short-run supply refers to the response of suppliers to a price change after some adjustments in production have been made. For many goods, the momentary supply curve is perfectly inelastic. Supply becomes more elastic as suppliers have more time to respond to price changes. (pp. 117–121)

KEY CONCEPTS

Key Figures and Tables

REVIEW QUESTIONS

1 Define the price elasticity of demand.

2 Why is elasticity a more useful measure of responsiveness than slope?

3 Draw a graph of, or describe the shape of, a demand curve that along its whole length has an elasticity of:

   a) Infinity

   b) Zero

   c) Unity

4 What three factors determine the size of the elasticity of demand?

5 What do we mean by short-run demand and long-run demand?

6 Explain why the short-run demand curve is usually less elastic than the long-run demand curve.

7 What is the connection between elasticity and revenue? If the elasticity of demand is 1, by how much does a 10 percent price increase change revenue?

8 Define the income elasticity of demand.

9 Give an example of a good whose income elasticity is:

a) greater than 1

b) positive but less than 1

c) less than zero

10 Define the cross elasticity of demand. Is the cross elasticity of demand positive or negative?

11 Define the elasticity of supply. Is the elasticity of supply positive or negative?

12 Give an example of a good whose elasticity of supply is

a) Zero

b) Greater than zero but less than infinity

c) Infinity

13 What do we mean by momentary, short-run, and long-run supply?

14 Why is the momentary supply curve perfectly inelastic for many goods?

15 Why is the long-run supply curve more elastic than the short-run supply curve?

P R O B L E M S

1 The demand schedule for videotape rentals is:

Price (dollars)	Quantity demanded per day
0	120
1	100
2	80
3	60
4	40
5	20
6	0

a) At what price is the elasticity of demand equal to

(i) 1

(ii) infinity

(iii) zero

b) What price brings in the most revenue per day?

c) Calculate the elasticity of demand for a rise in price from $3 to $4.

2 Assume that the quantity of videotape rentals demanded in problem 1 increases by 10 percent at each price.

a) Draw the old and new demand curves.

b) Calculate the elasticity of demand for a rise in the rental price from $3 to $4. Compare your answer with that of problem 1(c).

3 Which item in each of the following pairs has the larger elasticity of demand:

a) Daily newspapers or *The New York Times*

b) Exercise equipment or rowing machines

c) Soda or Diet Pepsi

4 You have been hired as an economic consultant by OPEC and given the following schedule showing the world demand for oil:

Price (dollars per barrel)	Quantity demanded (millions of barrels per day)
10	60,000
20	55,000
30	45,000
40	20,000
50	5,000

Your advice is needed on the following questions:

a) If the supply of oil is cut back so that the price rises from $10 to $20 a barrel, will the revenue from oil sales rise or fall?

b) What will happen to revenue if the supply of oil is cut back further and the price rises to $30 a barrel?

c) What will happen to revenue if the supply of oil is cut back further still so that the price rises to $40 a barrel?

d) What is the price that will achieve the highest revenue?

e) What quantity of oil will be sold at the price that answers problem 4(d)?

f) What are the values of the price elasticity of demand for price changes of $10 a barrel at average prices of $15, $25, $35, and $45 a barrel?

g) What is the elasticity of demand at the price that maximizes revenue?

5 State the sign (positive or negative) and, where possible, the range (less than 1, 1, greater than 1) of the following elasticities:

a) The price elasticity of demand for coal at the point of maximum revenue

b) The cross elasticity of demand for coal with respect to the price of oil

c) The income elasticity of demand for diamonds

d) The income elasticity of demand for toothpaste

e) The elasticity of supply of Maine lobsters

f) The cross elasticity of demand for floppy discs with respect to the price of personal computers

6 The following table gives some data on the quantities of chocolate chip cookies demanded:

Price (cents per cookie)	Quantity demanded (thousands per day)	
	Short-run	Long-run
10	700	1,000
20	500	500
30	200	0

Using 20¢ as the average price of a cookie and 500,000 cookies a day as the average quantity, calculate:

a) The short-run elasticity of demand

b) The long-run elasticity of demand

7 The following table gives some data on the quantities of chocolate chip cookies supplied:

Price (cents per cookie)	Quantity supplied (thousands per day)		
	Momentary	Short-run	Long-run
10	500	200	0
20	500	500	500
30	500	700	10,000

Using 20¢ as the average price of a cookie and 500,000 cookies a day as the average quantity, calculate:

a) The momentary elasticity of supply

b) The short-run elasticity of supply

c) The long-run elasticity of supply

Chapter 6

Markets in Action

After studying this chapter, you will be able to:

- Explain the short-run and long-run effects of a change in supply on price and the quantity traded

- Explain the short-run and long-run effects of a change in demand on price and the quantity traded

- Explain the effects of price controls

- Explain why price controls can lead to black markets

- Explain how people cope with uncertainty and make decisions in the face of unpredictable fluctuations in demand and supply

- Explain how inventories and speculation limit price fluctuations

On April 18, 1906, San Francisco suffered a devastating earthquake. From April 18 to April 20, massive fires destroyed countless buildings on 3400 acres in the heart of the city. Despite the extreme destruction of property, fewer than 1000 people died. The remaining population somehow had to fit into a vastly smaller number of houses and apartments. How did the San Francisco housing market cope with this enormous shock? What happened to rents and to the quantity of housing services available? ■ Almost every day, new machines and techniques are being invented that save labor and increase productivity. But the invention and adoption of new technologies doesn't reduce the demand for labor—it changes its

Turbulent
Times

composition. The simplest tasks performed by the least skilled workers are the ones most easily mechanized. So the march of technological change brings a persistent decrease in the demand for the least skilled types of labor. But ever more sophisticated equipment needs ever more sophisticated management and maintenance. As a consequence, it brings a steady increase in the demand for more highly skilled types of labor. How do labor markets cope with the changing patterns in demand for labor and what happens to the wages of the unskilled in the process? Does falling demand make those wages fall lower and lower? ■ Wages and housing costs are the two most important items in the budget of every household. Because of this fact, politicians take a great interest in the markets for housing and labor. If rents get too high, rent controls are introduced. If wages get too low, minimum wage laws are introduced. What are the effects of rent controls and minimum wage laws? How do rent controls affect the rents that people pay and the housing services that are available? How do minimum wages affect wages and employment prospects? ■ When the winter is severe and the summer is hot and humid, there is an increase in the number of days on which people run furnaces and air conditioners. The number of such days in the year has an important effect on the total demand for electricity and, in turn, for fuels used to generate electricity. As we all know from experience, fluctuations in the weather cannot be forecast with any real accuracy—at least not a whole season ahead. We know the range of possibilities, but there is no way of predicting whether the coming winter will turn out to be mild or severe. Producers of electricity and of the fuels they use must devise ways of coping with the inherent unpredictability in the demand for their products. How do these producers cope with uncertainty about demand? What are the effects of unpredictable fluctuations in demand on prices and the quantities traded?

The weather also creates unpredictable fluctuations in supply. The output of virtually every agricultural product is subject to unpredictable fluctuations of weather—hours of sunshine, rainfall, and temperature—and their effect on growing conditions. For example, the grain yield in 1982 was very high, but in 1988 it was extremely low as crops were devastated by the drought.

Fluctuations in demand and supply cause fluctuations in the price of a good and the quantity traded. In some cases, the price fluctuates a great deal and the quantity traded hardly changes. In other cases, the quantity traded fluctuates dramatically and price changes very little. What determines the amount by which price and quantity traded fluctuate?

Every day, the pages of any newspaper—from your local daily to the *Wall Street Journal*—report the latest fortunes of the stock market. Attention focuses on various indexes, such as the Dow-Jones industrial average. On one particular day—October 19, 1987—a page in history was written. The Dow-Jones average fell by more than 36 percent from its peak value. A movement of this magnitude is, of course, unusual. Nevertheless, stock prices do go up and down—and they do so much more than the prices of most of the ordinary goods and services we buy. Why are stock prices so volatile? Is it speculation that makes the stock market fluctuate so much?

■ In this chapter, we use the theory of demand and supply (of Chapter 4) and the concept of elasticity (of Chapter 5) to answer questions such as those we have

just asked. We'll study how unregulated markets work, and we'll study government intervention to regulate prices. We'll see how such regulation can produce black markets and unemployment. We'll extend the demand and supply model to take account of the fact that production decisions made today often do not affect output until a later date. For example, if a producer decides today to grow more oranges, the actual supply of oranges will not increase until the new orange trees mature—in about 15 years. In a situation such as this, suppliers have to make today's production decisions on the basis of forecasts of future prices. We'll see how they go about making such forecasts. A final extension of the demand and supply model that we'll make takes account of the fact that many goods can be stored. We'll study the way in which inventories of goods, and changes in those inventories, affect the prices of goods and the quantities traded. We'll emerge from this chapter with a richer model of demand and supply that explains many features of the real world.

Let's begin by studying how a market responds to a severe supply shock in both the short run and the long run. We'll see how an unregulated market responds and also we'll see what happens when the government intervenes in the market to limit price changes.

Housing Markets and Rent Ceilings

To see how an unregulated market copes with a massive supply shock, let's transport ourselves to the city of San Francisco in April 1906 as the city is facing the effects of its massive earthquake and fire. You can sense the enormity of San Francisco's problems by reading some headlines from *The New York Times* on the first days of the crisis.

On April 19, 1906:

Over 500 Dead, $200,000,000 Lost in San Francisco Earthquake.

Nearly Half the City Is in Ruins and 50,000 Are Homeless.

On April 20, 1906:

Army of Homeless Fleeing from Devastated City.

200,000 Without Shelter and Facing Famine.

And again on April 21, 1906:

San Francisco's New Peril; Gale Drives Fire Ferryward.

Fighting Famine and Disease Among the 200,000 Refugees.

San Francisco Multitudes Camped Out Shelterless and in Want.

The commander of the federal troops in charge of the resulting emergency described the magnitude of the problem:

Not a hotel of note or importance was left standing. The great apartment houses had vanished . . . two-hundred-and-twenty-five thousand people were . . . homeless.[1]

Almost overnight, more than half the people in a city of 400,000 had lost their homes. Temporary shelters and camps alleviated some of the problem, but it was also necessary to utilize the apartment buildings and houses left standing. As a consequence, they had to accommodate 40 percent more people than they had prior to the earthquake.

The *San Francisco Chronicle* was not published for more than a month after the earthquake. When the newspaper reappeared on May 24, 1906, the city's housing shortage—what would seem like a major news item that would still be of grave importance—was not mentioned. Milton Friedman and George Stigler describe the situation:

There is not a single mention of a housing shortage! The classified advertisements listed sixty-four offers of flats and houses for rent, and nineteen of houses for sale, against five advertisements of flats or houses wanted. Then and thereafter a considerable number of all types of accommodation except hotel rooms were offered for rent.[2]

[1]Reported in Milton Friedman and George J. Stigler, "Roofs or Ceilings? The Current Housing Problem," in *Popular Essays on Current Problems,* vol. 1, no. 2 (New York: Foundation for Economic Education, 1946), 3–15, 3.

[2]*Ibid., 3.*

How did San Francisco cope with such a devastating reduction in the supply of housing?

The Market Response to an Earthquake

We can work out how the unregulated San Francisco housing market responded to the earthquake of 1906 by using the theory of demand and supply that we studied in Chapters 4 and 5. Figure 6.1 analyzes this market. Part (a) shows the situation before the earthquake and parts (b) and (c), after the earthquake. The horizontal axis of each part measures the quantity of housing units and the vertical axis measures the monthly rent of a unit of housing.

Look first at the situation before the earthquake (part a). The demand curve for housing is *D*. There are two supply curves: the short-run supply curve, which is labeled *SS* and the long-run supply curve, which is labeled *LS*. The short-run supply curve shows how the quantity of housing supplied varies as the price (rent) varies, while the number of houses and apartment buildings remains constant. This supply response arises from a variation in the intensity with which existing buildings are used. The quantity of housing supplied increases as families rent out rooms or parts of their houses and apartments to others, and the quantity supplied decreases as families occupy a larger number of the rooms under their control.

The long-run supply curve shows how the quantity supplied varies after enough time has elapsed for new apartment buildings and houses to be erected or existing buildings to be destroyed. The long-run supply curve is shown as being perfectly elastic. We do not actually know that the long-run supply curve is perfectly elastic, but it is a reasonable assumption. It implies that the cost of building an apartment is pretty much the same regardless of whether there are 50,000, 100,000, or 150,000 apartments in existence.

The equilibrium price and quantity traded are determined at the point of intersection of the short-run supply curve and the demand curve. Before the earthquake, that equilibrium rent is $110 a month and the quantity of housing units traded is 100,000. In addition (but only because we are assuming it to be so), the housing market is on its long-run supply curve, *LS*. Let's now look at the situation immediately after the earthquake.

Figure 6.1   The San Francisco Housing Market in 1906

(a) Before earthquake

(b) After earthquake

(c) Long-run adjustment

Before the earthquake, the San Francisco housing market is in equilibrium with 100,000 housing units being traded each month at an average rent of $110 a month. This equilibrium is at the intersection of demand curve D, short-run supply curve SS, and long-run supply curve LS. After the earthquake, the short-run supply curve shifts from SS to SS_A (part b). The equilibrium rent rises to $120 a month and the number of housing units available falls to 74,000 a month. The rent rises because only 44,000 units of housing will be supplied at the old rent of $110 a month, and the price that demanders will willingly pay for the forty-four thousandth unit is $130 a month. With rents at $120 a month, there is profit in building new apartments and houses. As the building program proceeds, the short-run supply curve shifts to the right. As it does so (part c), rents gradually fall back to $110 a month and the number of housing units available increases gradually to 100,000. Note that we use a special arrowed line to indicate such gradual movements along a curve.

After the Earthquake

After the earthquake and the subsequent fires, housing for 56 percent of the population is destroyed. Figure 6.1(b) reflects the new situation by shifting the short-run supply curve SS to the left by 56,000 units, to become the short-run supply curve SS_A (A

for after the earthquake). If people use the remaining housing units with the same intensity as before the earthquake and if the rent remains at $110 a month, only 44,000 units of housing are available.

But rents do not remain at $110. With only 44,000 units of housing available, the maximum rent that will willingly be paid for the last available apartment is $130 a month. Since people value the available housing more highly than the long-run price of $110 a month, they offer to pay higher rents. At higher rents, people with accommodations economize on their use of space and make their spare rooms, attics, and basements available to others. Thus the quantity of housing units offered increases. The market achieves a new, short-run equilibrium at a rent of $120 a month, where 74,000 units of housing are available. In this new short-run equilibrium, approximately 20 percent of the population has left the city and a further 6 percent has been housed in temporary camps.[3]

You've now seen how the housing market reacts, almost overnight, to a devastating shock. When supply decreases, the intersection point of the new short-run supply curve and the demand curve determines the price and the quantity traded. The price rises; those willing to pay the higher price find housing, and those with housing are willing to economize on its use. People who are unwilling or unable to pay the higher rents either leave the city or are housed in temporary shelters.

Long-run Adjustments   The new equilibrium depicted in Fig. 6.1(b) is not the end of the story. The long-run supply curve tells us that with sufficient time for new apartment buildings and houses to be constructed, housing will be supplied at a rent of $110 a month. Since the current rent of $120 a month is higher than the long-run supply price of housing, there will be a rush to build and supply new apartments and houses. As time passes, more apartments and houses are built, and the short-run supply curve starts moving back gradually to the right.

Figure 6.1(c) illustrates the long-run adjustment. As the short-run supply curve shifts back to the right, it intersects the demand curve at lower rents and higher quantities. The market follows the arrows down the demand curve. The process ends when there is no further profit in building new housing units. Such a situation occurs at the original rent of $110 a month and the original quantity of 100,000 units of housing.

[3] *Ibid., 3.*

REVIEW

An earthquake reduces the short-run supply, raising rents and lowering the quantity traded. Higher rents immediately bring forth an increase in the quantity of housing supplied as people economize on their own use of space and make rooms available for rent to others. High rents also lead to increased building activity, which causes the short-run supply curve to shift gradually back to the right. As this process continues, the price of housing falls and the quantity rises. The original (pre-earthquake) equilibrium eventually is restored (because nothing has happened in the meantime to shift the long-run supply curve or the demand curve). ■

A Regulated Housing Market

We've just seen how the housing market of San Francisco coped with a massive supply shock. One of the things that happened was that rents increased sharply. Let's now suppose that the San Francisco city government imposed a **rent ceiling.** A rent ceiling is a regulation making it illegal to charge a rent higher than a specified level. What would have happened if a rent ceiling of $110 a month—the rent before the earthquake—had been imposed? This question is answered in Fig. 6.2.

First let's work out what will happen to the quantities supplied and demanded. The quantity supplied at the controlled rent of $110 a month is 44,000 units. The quantity demanded at that rent is 100,000 units. When the quantity demanded exceeds the quantity supplied, what determines the quantity actually bought and sold? The answer is the smaller of the quantities demanded and supplied. At a monthly rent of $110, the suppliers of housing only want to supply 44,000 units. They cannot be forced to supply more. The demanders would like to rent 100,000 units at that price, but they cannot do so. The difference between the quantity demanded and the quantity supplied is called the excess quantity demanded.

When a rent ceiling of $110 a month is imposed, the quantity of housing available falls to 44,000 units, but the quantity demanded remains constant at 100,000 units. There is an excess demand of 56,000 units. Is that the end of the story? Is this situation an equilibrium? To answer this question, we need to explore a bit more closely what the demanders are doing.

If the rent really is $110 a month, a lot of people who would like to rent more housing will not be able to do so. Moreover, some people would be willing to pay much more than $110 a month to get an apartment. To understand why, recall that there are two ways of interpreting a demand curve. One interpretation is that the curve tells us the quantities demanded at each price. But the demand curve also tells us the highest price that demanders will pay for the last unit available. What is the highest price that people will pay for the last apartment available? The answer, which can be read from the demand curve, is $130 a month. Since the people who are not able to find housing are willing to pay more than the rent ceiling, the situation that we have just described is not an equilibrium. Two mechanisms come into play in an unbalanced situation such as this one to achieve equilibrium. They are search activity and black markets.

Search Activity

Even when the quantity demanded exceeds the quantity supplied, some suppliers have goods available. But many are sold out. In these circumstances, buyers spend time looking for a supplier with whom they can do business. The time and effort spent in searching for someone with whom to do business is called **search activity.** Even in markets where prices are permitted to fluctuate to bring equality between the quantities demanded and supplied, search activity takes place. But when price is regulated, search activity increases.

The time spent searching for available supplies imposes costs on buyers. Adjustments in the time spent searching bring about an equilibrium. You can see why by thinking about the total amount that the demanders are willing to pay for the last unit of housing available. With only 44,000 housing units available, demanders are willing to pay $130 a month. But the rent is restricted to $110. How does the buyer spend another $20? The answer is by using $20 worth of time in the business of searching for an available apartment. That is, the total cost of housing—the price actually paid for housing obtained—is equal

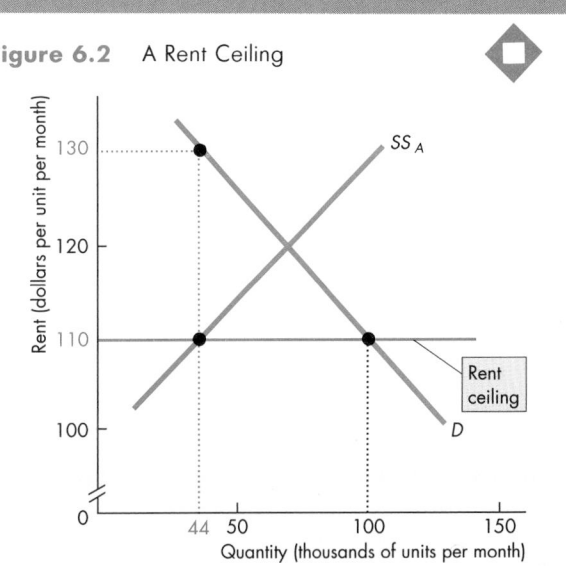

Figure 6.2   A Rent Ceiling

If there had been a rent ceiling of $110 a month following the earthquake, the quantity of housing supplied would have been stuck at 44,000 units. People would willingly pay $130 a month for the forty-four thousandth unit. The difference between the rent ceiling and the maximum price that will willingly be paid is the value of the time used up in searching for an available apartment. The individuals doing the searching are those with the lowest opportunity cost of time. Those whose value of time is high avoid search costs by buying on an illegal black market.

to the rent paid to the owner plus the opportunity cost of time spent searching for the available supply.

Black Markets

Opportunity cost (the value of the best opportunity forgone) enables us to predict *who* will search for available housing. Some people earn high wages and others earn low wages. If it takes one hour to find an apartment, the total price paid is higher for a high-wage earner than a low-wage earner. Therefore the lowest paid people will be those who devote the most time to searching out available supplies. High-wage earners will devote time to search activity only if they place a much higher value on the good than does a low-wage earner.

A person with a high opportunity cost of time has another way of obtaining a good—buying it from someone whose opportunity cost of time is lower. The person with a low wage can devote time to searching out the available supplies and then resell to someone whose opportunity cost of searching is higher. Buying goods in this way is illegal and creates what is known as a black market. A **black market** is an illegal trading arrangement in which buyers and sellers do business at a price higher than the legally imposed price ceilling. The functioning of a black market depends on how tightly the government polices its price regulations, on the chances of being caught violating them, and on the scale of the penalties imposed for violations.

At one extreme, the chance of being caught violating a rent ceiling is small. In this case, the black market will function similarly to an unregulated market, and the black market rent and quantity traded will be close to the unregulated equilibrium. At the other extreme, where policing is highly effective and where large penalties are imposed on violators, the rent ceiling will restrict the quantity traded to 44,000 units. The small number of black marketeers operating in the market will buy at the controlled rent of $110 a month and sell at $130 a month. The government will constantly try to detect and punish such people. The equilibrium in the black market will be such that anyone can obtain an apartment for $130 a month and the profit for the black marketeer is just sufficient compensation for the risk of being caught and punished.

There are many examples of markets, other than housing markets, that are regulated in some way and in which economic forces result in black market trading. One example is the market for personal computers in Poland and other Eastern European countries. (See Reading Between the Lines, pages 134–135.)

We've just looked at what would have happened in a hypothetical situation if there had been rent ceilings following the San Francisco earthquake. But San Francisco actually did have rent ceilings 45 years later—following World War II—so we can see how rent ceilings operated in practice. Let's take a look at that episode in the history of the San Francisco housing market.

Rent Ceilings in Practice

By 1940, the population of San Francisco had increased to 635,000. At that time, only 93 percent of the city's houses and apartments were occupied.

The situation stayed much the same throughout World War II. Then, after the war, the population increased by 30 percent, but the number of houses and apartments increased by only 20 percent. As a result, each dwelling unit had to house 10 percent more people in 1946 than one year earlier. The housing problems that San Francisco suffered in 1946 were only a quarter of the magnitude of the problems that followed the earthquake in 1906. Yet the 1946 housing shortage was a major political problem.

> On January 8 [1946] the California State Legislature was convened, and the Governor listed the housing shortage as "the most critical problem facing California." During the first five days of the year there were altogether only four advertisements offering houses or apartments for rent . . . [and] . . . there were thirty advertisements per day by persons wanting to rent houses or apartments. . . .[4]

The key difference between San Francisco in 1906 and in 1946 was the way in which scarce housing was rationed. In 1906, the scarce housing was allocated by an unregulated market. Rent increases achieved an equilibrium between the quantity of housing supplied and the quantity demanded and resulted in a steady increase in the quantity of housing available. In 1946, rent ceilings were in place. Scarce housing was allocated by people devoting time and effort to searching out and advertising for available houses and apartments. The actual cost of housing, taking account of the frustration and effort involved in finding accommodation, exceeded the controlled rent level and even exceeded the rents that would have prevailed in an unregulated market.

We've now studied the way in which a market responds, in both the short run and the long run, to a change in supply and how a regulated market would work in the face of such a supply shock. Let's now study how a market responds, both in the short run and the long run, to a change in demand. We'll study how an unregulated market handles such a shock and the effects of government intervention to limit price movements.

[4]*Ibid.*, 4.

The Labor Market and Minimum Wage Regulation

L abor-saving technology is constantly being invented and, as a result, the demand for certain types of labor, usually the least skilled types, is constantly decreasing. How does the labor market cope with this continuous decrease in the demand for unskilled labor? Doesn't it mean that the wages of the unskilled will constantly be falling? To study this question, let's examine the market for unskilled labor.

Figure 6.3(a) shows this market. The quantity of labor (millions of hours per year) is measured on the horizontal axis and the wage rate (dollars per hour) on the vertical axis. The demand curve is D. There are two supply curves: the upward-sloping short-run supply curve SS and the horizontal long-run supply curve LS.

Figure 6.3   A Market for Unskilled Labor

(a) Before invention

(b) After invention

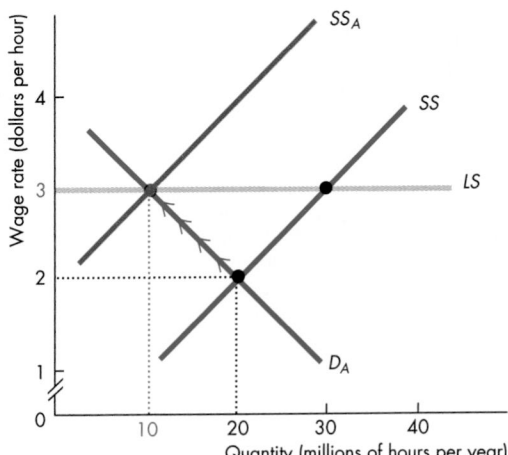

(c) Long-run adjustment

A market for unskilled labor is in equilibrium (part a) at a wage rate of $3 an hour with 30 million hours of labor a year being traded. The short-run supply curve (SS) slopes upward because employers have to pay a higher wage to get more hours out of a given number of workers. The long-run supply curve (LS) is perfectly elastic because workers will eventually enter this labor market if the wage rate is above $3 an hour or leave it if the wage rate is below $3 an hour. The invention of a labor-saving machine shifts the demand curve from D to D_A (part b). The wage rate falls to $2 an hour and employment falls to 20 million hours a year. With the lower wage, workers begin to leave this market to undertake training for other types of work. As they do so, the short-run supply curve shifts to SS_A (part c). As the supply curve shifts, the wage rate gradually increases and the employment level decreases. Ultimately, wages return to $3 an hour and employment falls to 10 million hours a year.

A Black Market for Personal Computers

High Tech Leak: Astute Poles Purchase Capitalist Computers, Sell Them to the State

What would a Polish bus conductor do if he had a couple of IBM-compatible mother boards, each with a 16-MHz 386 processor, 2MB of RAM, an FDD/HDD controller and a TEAC 360KB floppy disk drive?

Sell them to buy a taxi.

What would a Polish taxi driver do with the above, fitted out with EGA cards, enhanced keyboards and 40MB SEAGATE hard disks?

Sell them to build a house.

Capitalist computers have become hot items for nimble Polish entrepreneurs seeking quick profits in the complicated world of embargoes, export licenses, and black-market currencies. A quick computer killing takes just a few fancy steps, a bribe or two and a buyer willing to pay in Polish zlotys at triple the dollar's black market rate.

Thus, a $2,000 computer will cost two million zlotys (the price of those dollars in the black market) and sell here for six million. The seller pays a tax of one million zlotys and comes away three million zlotys richer. It takes most Poles 10 years to make that much.

Desperate Desire

But who in Poland would be fool enough to pay three times the black-market rate for a personal computer? It would have to be a customer with a desperate desire to enter the high-tech age, plenty of zlotys, and not a dollar to spare. A customer, in short, like the Polish state.

"The government gets the computers free," says Marek Kaluzny, a software writer who hands out the perfumed business cards of a Taiwanese clone maker. "It just prints zlotys." Its shrewder citizens then parlay that paper into more computers. Says a man who buys PCs for the state: "It's big money. Everybody benefits."

This isn't quite what the industrial democracies had in mind when they embargoed high-technology exports to the Soviet bloc. Nor is it what the Soviet bloc has in mind now that it is setting out to build PCs of its own.

Relatives' Dollars

Always on the lookout for loopholes, the Poles have become the East bloc's biggest PC traders, thanks largely to the greenbacks provided by their Polish-American relatives. One Taiwan company shipped 1,500 machines to Poland in 1986. Amstrad computers from Britain account for 70% of the air freight between London and Warsaw. On Warsaw airport's import dock, close to 100 PCs pile up daily.

A Polish dealer figures that tens of thousands arrive in a year. "We are talking," he says, "about tens of millions of dollars." Since the boom began in 1985, PC prices have actually fallen in Poland. The cause isn't a drop in demand but a surge of supply.

All of which has made life easier in the Warsaw University physics department. Private middlemen have delivered 50 powerful PCs from Taiwan to Roman Szwed (a young physicist), who is in the market for 50 more.

"I'd prefer to buy direct from the U.S.," he says, standing in the doorway of the department's basement computer center, "but it's my duty to keep things going in our little environment."

Work stations fill the room before him, each with a PC and a number-crunching researcher. Beyond them, in a room behind a glass wall, stands a big mainframe from Czechoslovakia. The room is dark. Nobody goes in there anymore.

The Wall Street Journal, January 7, 1988
By Barry Newman, staff reporter
Reprinted by permission of *The Wall Street Journal*,

The Essence of the Story

- The industrial countries that produce PCs have placed an embargo on the shipment of computers to the Soviet Union and Eastern European countries such as Poland.

- There is a large demand for PCs in Poland, much of it by the state and the universities.

- Computers are illegally shipped into Poland on a very large scale and sold on a black market.

- A PC that costs $2000 in the United States sells for $6000 on the Polish black market, but since 1985 the price has fallen.

- Scientists and others make heavy use of their PCs and have stopped using inferior mainframe computers made in Czechoslovakia.

Background and Analysis

- The black market for computers in Poland is illustrated in the figure. The demand curve for PCs is labeled D. The light blue horizontal supply curve labeled S_N is the (assumed) supply curve of PCs in Poland without restrictions.

- If no PCs get into Poland, there will be a large unsatisfied demand. People will be willing to pay a much higher price than the $2000 that PCs cost in the United States.

- Finding ways around embargoes takes time and effort and is also risky. But it is profitable. Black-market traders, evading the embargo, had a supply curve in 1985 labeled S_{1985}.

- In 1985, the equilibrium price in Poland for PCs was $8000 and the equilibrium quantity traded was 10,000.*

- As more people sought to profit from the illegal trade in PCs, the supply curve shifted to the right so that, by 1988, it was

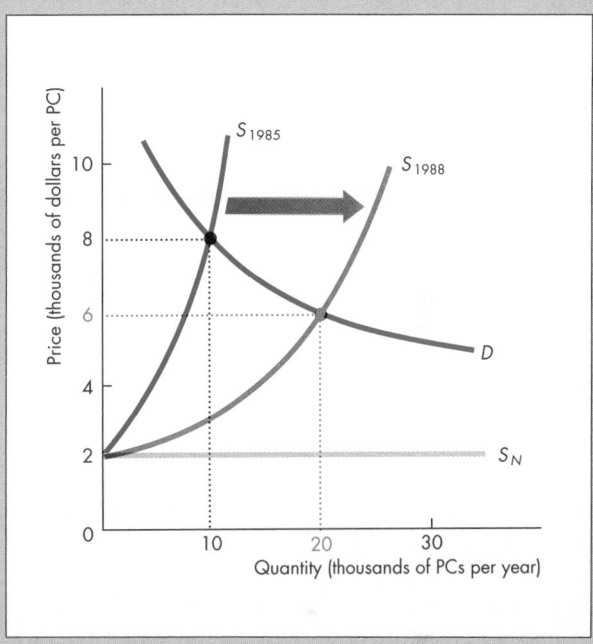

S_{1988}. The price fell and the quantity traded increased.

- In 1988, the equilibrium price of PCs was $6000 and the quantity traded was 20,000. (The price of $6000 is the actual price reported in the article. The quantity traded is not specified exactly in the article, but we are told that "tens of thousands arrive in a year.")

- As the world supply of PCs increases, and as the number of supply

sources increases, we may predict that the supply curve for PCs in Poland will continue to shift to the right. As a consequence, the price will continue to fall and the quantity traded will continue to increase.

—————

*The prices used in this analysis come from the article but the quantities are hypothetical. The article does not contain enough information to locate the positions of the supply curve and the demand curve.

The short-run supply curve shows how the hours of labor supplied by a given number of workers varies as the wage rate varies. To get workers to work longer hours, firms have to offer higher wages. The long-run supply curve shows the relationship between the quantity of labor supplied and the wage rate when the number of workers in the market varies. The number of people in this unskilled labor market depends on the wage in this market compared with other opportunities. If the wage is high enough, people will enter this market. If the wage is too low, people will leave this unskilled labor market and seek training to enter a different, more skilled market. The long-run supply curve tells us the conditions under which workers supply labor in this unskilled market after enough time has passed for people to have acquired new skills and moved to new types of jobs.

The labor market is initially in equilibrium at a wage rate of $3 an hour and with 30 million hours of labor being supplied. We're now going to analyze what happens in the labor market if the demand for this particular type of labor falls as a result of the invention of some labor-saving technology. Figure 6.3(b) shows the short-run effects of such a change. The demand curve before the new technology is introduced is D. After the introduction of the new technology, the demand curve shifts to the left, to D_A. The wage rate falls to $2 an hour and the quantity of labor employed falls to 20 million hours. This short-run effect on wages and employment is not the end of the story.

People who are now earning only $2 an hour look around for other opportunities. They see, for example, that the new labor-saving equipment doesn't always work properly and, when it breaks down, it is maintained by more highly paid, highly skilled workers. There are many other jobs (in markets for other types of skills) paying higher wages than $2 an hour. One by one, workers decide to quit this particular market for unskilled labor. They go back to school or they take jobs that pay less but offer on-the-job training. As a result of these decisions, the short-run supply curve begins to shift to the left.

Figure 6.3(c) shows the long-run adjustment. As the short-run supply curve shifts to the left, it intersects the demand curve D_A at higher wage rates and lower levels of employment. In the long run, the short-run supply curve will have shifted all

the way to SS_A. At this point, the wage has returned to $3 an hour, and the level of employment has fallen to 10 million hours.

Sometimes, the adjustment process that we have just described will take place quickly. At other times, it will be a long drawn-out affair. If the adjustment process is long and drawn out and wages remain low for a prolonged period, there will be a temptation on the part of government to intervene in the market, setting a minimum wage to protect the incomes of the lowest-paid workers. What are the effects of imposing a minimum wage?

The Minimum Wage

Suppose that when the demand for labor decreases from D to D_A, as illustrated in Fig. 6.3(b), and the wage falls to $2 an hour, the government passes a minimum wage law. A **minimum wage law** is a regulation that makes trading labor below a specified wage illegal. In particular, suppose that the government declares that the minimum wage is $3 an hour. What are the effects of this law?

The answer can be found by studying Fig. 6.4. In that figure, the minimum wage is shown as the horizontal red line labeled "Minimum wage." At the minimum wage, only 10 million hours of labor are demanded (point a). But there are 30 million hours of labor available at that wage (point b). Because the number of hours demanded is less than the number of hours supplied, 20 million hours of available labor go unemployed.

What are the workers doing with their unemployed hours? They are looking for work. It pays to spend a lot of time searching for work. With only 10 million hours of labor being employed, there are many people willing to supply their labor for wages much lower than the minimum wage. In fact, the ten-millionth hour of labor will be supplied for as little as $1. How do we know that there are people willing to work for as little as $1 an hour?

Look again at Fig. 6.4. As you can see, when there are only 10 million hours of work available, the lowest wage at which workers will supply that ten-millionth hour—read off from the supply curve—is $1. Someone who manages to find a job will earn $3 an hour—$2 an hour more than the lowest wage at which someone is willing to work.

Figure 6.4   The Minimum Wage and Unemployment

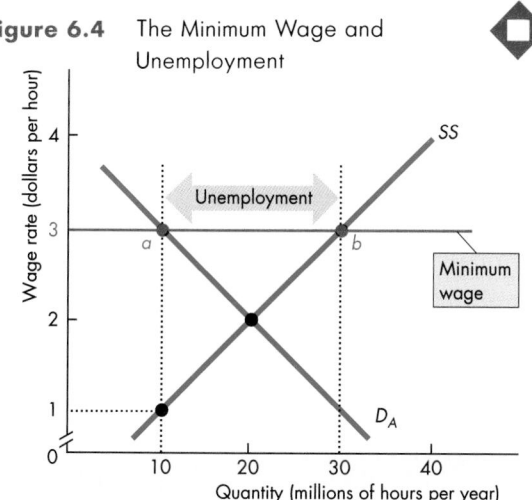

The demand curve for labor is D_A and the supply curve is SS. In an unregulated market, the wage rate is $2 an hour and 20 million hours of labor a year are employed. If a minimum wage of $3 an hour is imposed, only 10 million hours of labor are hired but 30 million hours are available. This results in unemployment—ab—of 20 million hours of labor a year. With only 10 million hours of labor being demanded, workers will willingly supply that ten millionth hour for $1. It will pay such suppliers to spend the difference between the minimum wage and the wage for which they are willing to work—$2 an hour—in time and effort looking for a job.

It pays the unemployed, therefore, to spend a considerable amount of time and effort looking for work. Even though only 10 million hours of labor actually find employment, each person will spend time and effort searching for one of the scarce jobs.

The severity of the unemployment generated by a minimum wage depends on the demand and supply for labor. You can see that if the supply curve were farther to the left, unemployment would be less. In fact, if the supply curve cut the demand curve at point *a*, the minimum wage would be the same as the unregulated wage. In such a situation, there would be no unemployment. Also, the farther to the right is the demand for labor, the smaller is the amount of unemployment. If the demand curve cut the supply curve at point *b*, then, again, the minimum wage would be the same as the unregulated wage, and there would be no unemployment.

The Minimum Wage in Reality

The **Fair Labor Standards Act** makes it illegal to hire an adult worker for less than $3.35 an hour. Economists are not in agreement on the effects of the minimum wage or on how much unemployment it causes. However, they do agree that minimum wages bite hardest on the unskilled. Since there is a preponderance of unskilled workers among the young—the young have had less opportunity to obtain work experience and acquire skills—we would expect the minimum wage to cause more unemployment among young workers than among older workers. And that is exactly what happens. The unemployment for teenagers is more than twice the average rate. Although there are many factors other than the minimum wage influencing unemployment among young people, it is almost certainly the case that part of the higher unemployment among the young arises from the impact of minimum wage laws.

REVIEW

Governments intend minimum wages to protect the incomes of the lowest paid. But a minimum wage lowers the quantity of labor demanded and hired. Some people will want to work, but they will be unemployed and will spend time searching for work. The young and the unskilled are hit hardest by the minimum wage. ∎

We have now studied how changes in either supply or demand bring about changes—in the short run and the long run—in price and in the quantity traded. But the examples that we've studied are of shocks that come like bolts from the blue—an earthquake lowers the supply of housing or a technological change lowers the demand for unskilled labor. But many changes in demand and supply are predictable. How do predictable changes in demand and supply affect prices and quantities traded? And how do people go about making predictions? Let's now study these questions.

Anticipating the Future

Producers are especially concerned about two uncertainties: the price at which they will be able to sell their product and the conditions affecting how much of their product will be produced. Farmers provide a clear illustration of the importance of these two uncertainties. First, when farmers decide how many acres of corn to plant, they do not know the price at which the corn will be sold. Knowing the price of corn today does not help them make decisions about how much seed to sow today. Today's planting becomes tomorrow's crop, and so tomorrow's price determines how much revenue farmers get from today's sowing decisions. Second, when farmers plant corn, they do not know what the growing conditions will turn out to be. Conditions may be excellent, producing a high yield and a bumper crop, or conditions such as drought and inadequate sunshine may lead to a low crop yield and disaster.

Uncertainty about the future price of a good can arise from uncertainty about its future demand or its future supply. We have just considered some uncertainties about supply. There are also many uncertainties about demand. We know that demand for a good depends on the prices of its substitutes and complements, income, population, and tastes. Demand varies as a result of fluctuations in all these influences on buyers' plans. Since these influences *do* fluctuate and are impossible to predict exactly, the level of future demand is always uncertain.

Uncertainties about future supply and demand also make future prices uncertain. But producers must make decisions today even though they do not know the price at which their output will be sold. In making such decisions, they have no choice but to rely on a forecast of the future price.

The higher the expected price, the greater is the amount that each producer will supply. The total market supply combines the supplies of all producers and it too depends on the expected future price. In Fig. 6.5, the market supply curve (*ES*) shows how the quantity supplied one year in the future responds to producers' current expectations or forecasts of the price of a good—not to next year's price of that good. To determine what actions to take today to influence the quantity supplied next year, producers must first form expectations of next year's price. How do they do that?

Figure 6.5   Supply and Expected Prices

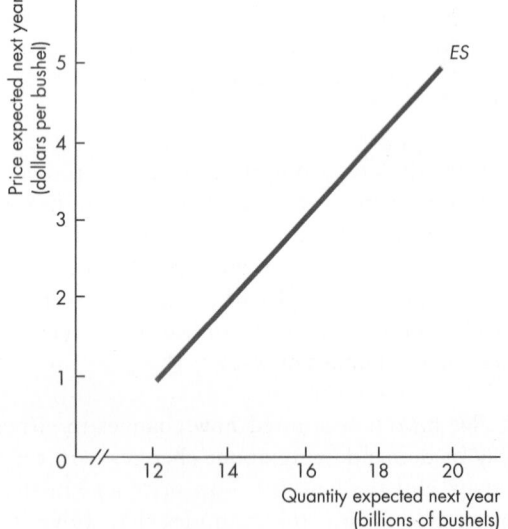

When the quantity supplied depends on past production decisions, quantity supplied depends on the price expected at the time the production decision is made rather than on the actual price. Expected supply is represented by the supply curve *ES*. The expected future quantity supplied rises as the expected future price rises.

Making Forecasts

The time and effort devoted to making forecasts varies considerably from one individual to another. Most people devote hardly any time to this activity at all. Instead, they follow rules of thumb that, most of the time, seem to work well. But in important matters that directly affect their incomes, people will try to do better than that. One way of doing better is to simply imitate the actions of others who have a track record of success. Another way of doing better is to buy forecasts from specialists. A large number of forecasting agencies exist—from investment advisors and stock and commodity brokers to professional economic forecasting agencies. Such agencies have a strong incentive to make their forecasts correct, at least on the average.

The particular methods used to make forecasts are, of course, highly diverse, but our task is not to describe all of the actual methods used to make forecasts. Instead, our task is to build a model of forecasting. To build such a model, we use the fundamental assumption of economics—the assumption that people are seeking to get the most they can out of their scarce resources. In pursuit of that goal, forecasts will be correct on the average and forecasting errors will be as small as possible. If any information is available that can improve a forecast, that information will be used. The forecast that uses all of the relevant information available about past and present events and that has the least possible error is called a **rational expectation.**

How does an economist go about calculating a rational expectation? The answer is by using an economic model. The economic model that explains prices is the model of demand and supply. Therefore, we use the demand and supply model to forecast prices—to calculate a rational expectation of a future price. We know that the point at which next year's demand curve intersects next year's supply curve determines next year's price. But until next year arrives, we don't know where those demand and supply curves will be located. However, we do know the factors that determine their position and by forecasting those factors we can forecast next year's demand and supply curves and forecast their point of intersection—next year's price. Let's work out a rational expectation of the future price of corn.

Expected Demand and Expected Supply Our goal is to make the best forecast we can of the future price of corn. To make that forecast, we must forecast the positions of next year's demand and supply curves for corn. We learned earlier that the position of the demand curve for a good depends on the prices of its substitutes and complements, income, population, and tastes. The expected position of a demand curve, therefore, depends on the expected values of all these variables. In order to form an expectation about the future position of the demand curve of corn, it is necessary to forecast the future prices of corn's substitutes and

complements, of income, of population, and of current trends that might influence tastes. By taking into account every conceivable piece of available information that helps forecast such variables, farmers—or the specialists from whom farmers buy forecasts—can form a rational expectation of next year's demand for corn.

We also learned earlier that the position of the supply curve of a good depends on the prices of its substitutes and complements in production, the prices of the resources used to produce the good, and technology. An important part of the technology of farming is the biological process that converts seed to crop. That process, of course, depends in an important way on the temperature, the amount of sunshine, and the amount of rain. Expected supply depends on the expected values of all these variables. In order to form an expectation about the future supply of corn it is necessary to forecast the future prices of corn's substitutes and complements in production, the prices of the resources used to produce the corn (the wages of farm workers and the prices of seed and fertilizers) as well as any current trends in weather patterns that might influence growing conditions. By taking into account every available piece of information that helps forecast such variables, people can form a rational expectation of the next year's corn supply.

Calculating a Rational Expectation A rational expectation of next year's price of corn can be formed by bringing together expectations about next year's demand and supply. Figure 6.6 illustrates how to accomplish this. The quantities measured on the two axes are expectations of next year's price and quantity. The curve labeled *ED* is the best forecast available of next year's demand for corn. The curve labeled *ES* is the best forecast available of next year's supply of corn.

What do people expect the price of corn to be next year? They expect it to be $3 a bushel. That is the price at which expected quantity demanded equals the expected quantity supplied. People also can forecast next year's quantity traded. That forecast is 16 billion bushels. The price of $3 a bushel is the rational expectation of next year's price of corn. It is the forecasted price based on all the available relevant information. Producers use that forecast of the price to decide how many acres of corn to plant.

Figure 6.6   A Rational Expectation of Price

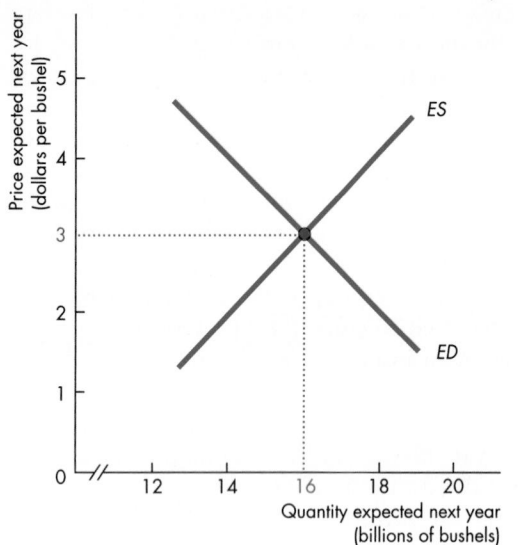

Since actual price is determined by actual supply and demand, expected price is determined by expected supply and expected demand. The point where expected demand (*ED*) cuts expected supply (*ES*) determines the rational expectation of the price ($3 a bushel) and quantity traded (16 billion bushels).

REVIEW

The rational expectation of a future price is the best forecast that can be made using all the available information. It is the price at which the expected quantity demanded equals the expected quantity supplied. Expected demand and expected supply are themselves the best forecasts available of the positions of the supply and demand curves. ∎

We have seen how people form a rational expectation of a future price. What determines the actual future price?

Demand Fluctuations

Producers make the best forecast they can of future demand and future price—but almost certainly they will turn out to be wrong. The future hardly

ever turns out to be exactly as expected. Let's suppose that the demand for corn fluctuates between a high level (D_1) and a low level (D_0) but that on the average it is *ED* (expected demand). These demand curves are shown in Fig. 6.7(a). Let's also suppose that it is impossible to forecast the fluctuations in demand. The best that people can do in forecasting demand is to suppose that demand will be at its average level. The rational expectation of this year's demand for corn is the demand curve *ED*. But this expectation was made last year. The curves D_0 and D_1 are possible actual demand curves for the current year.

We will be able to understand the effects of fluctuations in demand if we focus exclusively on that source of future uncertainty. To do that, let's suppose just for the moment that there is no uncertainty about supply. Expecting the price next year to be $3 a bushel, farmers plant enough acres of corn for the actual output to equal the actual output they expected—16 billion bushels. Growing conditions turn out to be exactly the same as they forecasted, so not only did they plan to produce 16 billion bushels, they actually achieve that plan. Since the quantity of corn actually produced is 16 billion bushels, the momentary supply curve of corn (*MS*) is completely inelastic.

Price Determination   If demand turns out to be exactly as expected, the price of corn this year will be exactly the same as was forecasted a year ago. That is, with this year's demand turning out to be *ED* and with this year's momentary supply curve *MS*, the quantity demanded equals the quantity supplied at a price of $3 a bushel—exactly the same price that was forecasted a year ago and shown in Fig. 6.6.

Let's now look at the two other cases where demand is either higher or lower than expected, both shown in Fig. 6.7(a). First, suppose that demand is D_1. In this case, demand and momentary supply intersect at a price of $5 a bushel. When demand is higher than expected, the price turns out to be higher than it was forecasted to be. If demand is D_0, then the demand and momentary supply curves intersect at a price of $1 a bushel. When demand is lower than expected, the price turns out to be lower than it was forecasted to be.

It is interesting to note that suppliers are disappointed with the outcome whenever demand turns out to be different from its expected level. If

Figure 6.7   The Effects of Temporary Fluctuations in Demand

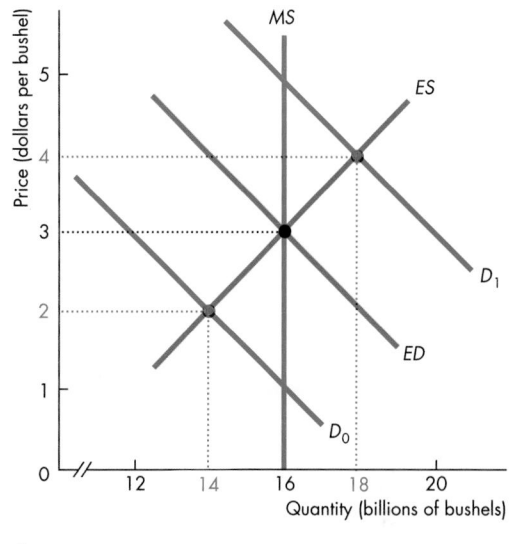

(a)   **(b)**

Demand fluctuates between D_0 and D_1, but on the average, demand is as expected, *ED*. Expected supply is *ES*. The rational expectation of the price is $3 a bushel. Producers plan to produce 16 billion bushels. Actual supply equals planned supply and the momentary supply curve is *MS*. As demand fluctuates, the price fluctuates. In part (a), when demand is D_0, the price falls to $1 a bushel. When demand is D_1, the price rises to $5 a bushel. In part (b), if suppliers could anticipate the demand fluctuations correctly, the quantity supplied would fluctuate along curve *ES* and price fluctuations would be less severe than those that actually occur. But because the future is uncertain, suppliers can do no better than produce 16 billion bushels and put up with the price fluctuations that result.

demand is D_1, then suppliers will regret that they did not plant a bigger acreage to produce a bigger quantity. They would have liked, in this case, to have produced 18 billion bushels and sold them for $4 a bushel, as shown in Fig. 6.7(b). This point is where the demand curve D_1 intersects the expected supply curve *ES*. That is, if they could have correctly forecasted demand at D_1, they would have forecasted a price of $4 a bushel and produced 18 billion bushels. At a price of $5 a bushel, farmers have produced less than they would have liked to produce. But bygones are bygones. They couldn't do any better than forecast demand at *ED* and so, at the time they made their planting decision, they made the correct decision.

If demand turns out to be D_0, then suppliers will regret that they did not plant a smaller acreage which would have produced 14 billion bushels of

corn and sold at $2 a bushel, in Fig. 6.7(b). This quantity and price are at the point where the demand curve D_0 intersects the expected supply curve *ES*. That is, if farmers could have correctly forecasted demand at D_0, they would have forecasted a price of $2 a bushel and planted sufficient acres to grow 14 billion bushels. At a price of $1 a bushel, farmers would have liked to produce less than they did. Again, bygones are bygones. They did the best they could at the time they had to make their decisions.

Supply Fluctuations

Let's now study the effects of supply fluctuations on price and the quantity traded. We'll understand these effects more clearly if we isolate supply as the only source of uncertainty. To do this, let's suppose

Figure 6.8   The Effects of Temporary Fluctuations in Supply

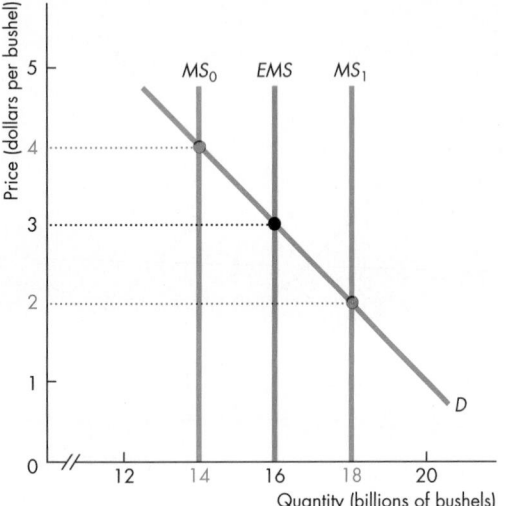

Growing conditions fluctuate and momentary supply fluctuates between MS_0 and MS_1. Expected momentary supply is EMS. Demand is expected to be and actually turns out to be D. The rational expectation of the price is $3 a bushel. When supply is low (MS_0), the quantity produced falls to 14 billion bushels and the price rises to $4 a bushel. When supply is high, (MS_1), the quantity produced increases to 18 billion bushels and the price falls to $2 a bushel.

that demand is forecasted correctly. The actual demand curve turns out to be the same one that was expected. What is uncertain now is the size of the crop.

There are three possibilities regarding growing conditions: First, they may turn out to be excellent, resulting in a bumper crop. Although ideal growing conditions do sometimes occur, farmers cannot forecast them. When they do happen, farmers grow more corn than they originally planned or expected. Second, growing conditions may turn out to be unusually poor, resulting in a crop yield much lower than expected. Third, growing conditions may turn out to be average, resulting in a crop yield equal to what was expected.

Figure 6.8 illustrates how each of these situations affects price. The demand curve D is the same as the demand curve that was forecasted a year ago. The figure contains three momentary sup-

ply curves: the curve EMS arises if growing conditions are average; the curve MS_0 arises if there is a drought and a low crop yield results; the curve MS_1 describes the situation when excellent growing conditions occur and a bumper crop results.

Price Determination   The price is determined at the point of intersection of the momentary supply curve and the demand curve. In a drought, that price will be $4 a bushel, with a bumper crop it will be $2 a bushel, and, on the average, when expectations are correct, it will be $3 a bushel.

Notice that when supply is correctly forecasted, the actual price equals the forecasted price. If supply turns out to be lower than its forecasted level, the price is higher than it was forecasted to be; if supply turns out to be higher than its forecasted level, the price is lower than forecasted.

In the examples that we've just worked through, momentary supply is perfectly inelastic, so price fluctuations have to do all of the work to achieve an equilibrium. What happens to these price fluctuations if corn is stored in inventories? We will now spend a bit of time examining this common situation.

*Inventories

Many goods, including a wide variety of agricultural products, can be stored. These inventories provide a cushion between production and consumption. If demand increases or if production decreases, goods can be sold from inventory; if demand decreases or if production increases, goods can be put into inventory.

Inventory holders speculate. They try to buy at a low price and sell at a high price. That is, they try to buy goods and put them into inventory when the price is low, and sell them from inventory when the price is high. Their aim is to make a profit equal to the difference between their buying price and selling price, minus the cost of storage.[5]

_____

*This section is more demanding and may be omitted.

[5]We will suppose that the cost of storage is so small that we can ignore it. This assumption, though not essential, enables us to see more sharply the effects of inventory holders' decisions on prices.

But how do inventory holders know when to buy and when to sell? How do they know whether the price is high or low? To decide whether a price is high or low, and to make their buying and selling decisions, inventory holders have to forecast future prices. To do this, they form a rational expectation of the future price. If the price is above its expected future level, they sell goods from inventory. If the price is below its expected future level, they buy goods to put into inventory.

Selling goods from inventory is equivalent to increasing supply. Buying goods to put into inventory is equivalent to decreasing supply. If the price is one penny above the inventory holder's rational expectation, goods will be supplied from inventory. If the price is one penny below the inventory holder's rational expectation, the supply available to the market will be reduced as the inventory holder puts goods into inventory. This behavior by the inventory holder makes the supply curve perfectly elastic at the inventory holder's rational expectation of the price.

In a market that has inventories, we need to distinguish the producer's supply, the inventory holder's supply, and the market supply. Let's now work out what happens to the price and quantity traded when there are unexpected fluctuations in demand and in producers' supply in a market in which inventories are held. We'll study demand fluctuations first.

Demand Fluctuations

To make things concrete, we'll continue to study the market for corn. Figure 6.9(a) illustrates the analysis of demand fluctuations. We'll suppose, for the moment, that the producer's supply of corn is perfectly inelastic and determined by the momentary supply curve MS at 16 billion bushels. The rational expectation of the price level is $3 a bushel. Therefore, the inventory holders' supply curve SI, highlighted in red, is perfectly elastic at that price. Demand fluctuates between D_1 and D_0.

In the absence of inventories, the quantity traded stays fixed at 16 billion bushels and the price fluctuates to maintain equality between the quantity demanded and the fixed quantity supplied. But things turn out very differently when there are inventory holders. If demand is D_0 (a low level of demand), the quantity bought by consumers falls to 14 billion bushels. Producers still supply 16 billion bushels. The difference between the

quantity supplied by producers and the quantity demanded by consumers is taken off the market and put into inventory. Thus inventories increase, in this example by 2 billion bushels. If the demand is high (D_1), consumers buy 18 billion bushels. Farmers produce 16 billion bushels and the additional 2 billion bushels come from inventory. Demand fluctuations lead to fluctuations in the quantity bought and to fluctuations in the size of inventory holdings, but the price stays constant at the inventory holder's rational expectation of its future level. The expectation of the future price becomes the actual price.

Now let's consider fluctuations in supply.

Supply Fluctuations

Supply fluctuations are analyzed in Fig. 6.9(b). Here the demand curve is expected to be and actually turns out to be D. The rational expectation of the price level is $3 again, so inventory holders' supply curve (SI) is perfectly elastic at that price. The producers' momentary supply now fluctuates between MS_0 and MS_1. Recall that without inventories, when supply fluctuates, the price and the quantity traded fluctuate, the price falling when supply increases and rising when supply decreases.

With inventories, there are no price fluctuations. When supply is low (at MS_0), the quantity supplied by producers falls to 14 billion bushels. The quantity bought remains 16 billion bushels and inventory holders supply the 2 billion bushels that make up the difference. When producers' supply is high (at MS_1), producers sell 18 billion bushels. Consumers continue to buy 16 billion bushels and 2 billion bushels are taken into inventory. Again, the actual price is equal to the inventory holders' expectations of the future price.

The model of a market with inventories that we have reviewed is the simplest possible. It serves to show how inventories and inventory holders' expectations about future prices reduce price fluctuations. In the above example, the price fluctuations are entirely eliminated. When there are costs of carrying inventories and when inventories become almost depleted, some price fluctuations do occur, but these fluctuations are much smaller then those occurring in a market without inventories.

People's holdings of stock are similiar to holdings of inventories. They are also a good example of an inventory that in fact does have a zero (or almost zero) cost of storage—you can store shares

Figure 6.9 How Inventories Limit Price Changes: When Demand Fluctuates

(a) Demand fluctuations

(b) Supply fluctuations

The rational expectation of the price is $3 a bushel. Inventory holders supply from inventory if the price rises above $3 and take goods into inventory if the price falls below $3. The inventory holders' supply curve is the perfectly elastic curve SI at the rationally expected price of $3 a bushel. When demand fluctuates between D_0 and D_1, the price stays constant at $3 a bushel, as shown in part (a). When demand is low (at D_0), production exceeds consumers' purchases by 2 billion bushels and that amount is taken into inventory. When demand is high (at D_1), consumers buy more than producers are supplying and the difference is made up from inventories. Fluctuations in supply lead to fluctuations in the producers' momentary supply curve between MS_0 and MS_1, as shown in part (b). The price stays constant at $3 a bushel and consumers buy a constant 16 billion bushels. When supply falls to 14 billion bushels, 2 billion bushels are supplied from inventory. When supply increases to 18 billion bushels, 2 billion bushels are taken into inventory.

of IBM or AT&T at virtually zero cost. Do inventories of stocks work like inventories of corn to reduce the range of price fluctuations? And if they do, why do the prices on the stock market fluctuate so dramatically?

The Stock Market

The stock market is the market on which the stocks of corporations are traded. Fig. 6.10 illustrates how a stock price is determined. The horizontal axis measures the quantity expected next period. The vertical axis measures the price expect-

ed next period and the actual price this period. This period's expectations of next period's demand and supply curves are shown as ED and ES. The intersection point of those curves determines the rational expectation of next period's price, EP. If the actual price rose by a penny above that expected price, people would supply stocks from their inventories. If the price fell to a penny below that price, people would put stocks into their inventory. Thus the supply of stocks, taking into account inventory behavior, is the perfectly elastic supply curve SI at the price level that is rationally expected for next period. The actual price (P) is equal to the expected price (EP). No matter how the demand and supply curves actually fluctuate, as long as the expected demand and expected supply curves are those shown in the figure, inventory holders supply from inventory or take stock into inventory and, by so doing, keep the price at its expected level.

We have seen that a rational expectation is an expectation that uses all the available information that is relevant for forecasting a future price. Since the actual stock price is equal to the rational expectation of the future stock price, that stock price also embodies all the relevant information that is available. A market in which the actual price embodies all currently available relevant information is called an **efficient market.** In an efficient market, it is impossible to forecast changes in price. Why? If your forecast is that the price is going to rise next period, you will buy now (since the price is low today compared with what you predicted it is going to be in the future). Your action of buying today acts like an increase in demand today and increases today's price. It's true that your action—the action of a single trader—is not going to make much difference to a huge market like the New York Stock Exchange. But if traders in general expect a higher price next period and they all act today on the basis of that expectation, then today's price will rise. It will keep on rising until it reaches the expected future price. For only at that price do traders see no profit in buying more stock today.

There is an apparent paradox about efficient markets. Markets are efficient because people try to make a profit. They seek a profit by buying at a low price and selling at a high price. But the very act of buying and selling to make a profit means that the market price moves to its expected future value. Having done that, no one, not even those who are seeking to profit, can *predictably* make a profit. Every profit opportunity seen by a trader leads to an action that produces a price change that removes the profit opportunity for others.

Thus an efficient market has two features:

- Its price equals the expected future price and embodies all the available information

- There are no forecastable profit opportunities available

The key thing to understand about an efficient market such as the stock market is that if something can be anticipated, it will be and the anticipation will be acted upon.

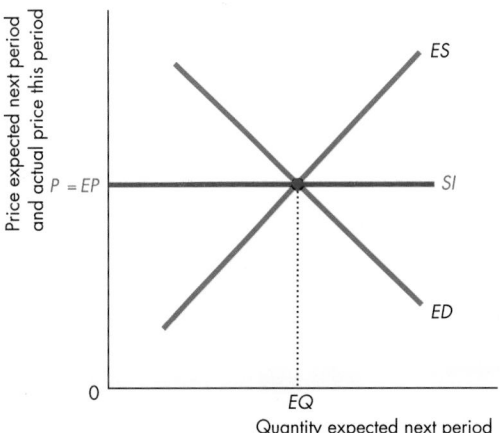

Figure 6.10 The Stock Market

Holders of stocks behave like inventory holders. They form a rational expectation of the future price of a stock (EP) at the point of intersection of the expected demand curve (ED) and the expected supply curve (ES). If the price is a penny above their expectation of the future price, stockholders sell. If the price is a penny below their expectation of the future price, they buy. These transactions keep the actual price (P) equal to the expected future price. Such a market is called an efficient market. In an efficient market, it is not possible to forecast a future price change and profit from that forecast. A foreseen price change is acted on immediately, and the actual price adjusts to eliminate the profit opportunity.

Volatility in Stock Prices

If the price of a stock is always equal to its expected future price, why is the stock market so volatile? The answer must be that expectations themselves are subject to fluctuation. Expectations depend on the information available. As new information becomes available, stock traders form new expectations about the future state of the economy and in turn new expectations of future stock prices. Expectations about the economy are of crucial importance: Is the economy going to enjoy sustained rapid expansion? Or is it going to suffer a recession? The macroeconomic events, such as expansion and recession, influence stock prices. Individual stock prices are influenced by technological change, which in turn influences the supply of and demand for particular goods and services. Since new information is being accumulated daily about all these

"Drat! I suppose the market has already discounted this, too."

all these matters, expectations about the future price of a stock are constantly being re-evaluated. It is this process of re-evaluation that leads to high volatility in the stock market. As expectations change from being optimistic to pessimistic, the stock market can plunge many percentage points— as it did dramatically on October 19, 1987. On the other hand, a sustained period of increasing optimism can produce a long upswing in stock prices. The five-year run from mid-1982 to mid-1987 is an example of such stock market behavior.[6]

■ We've now completed our study of demand and supply and its applications. You've seen how this powerful model enables us to make predictions about prices and quantities traded and also how it enables us to understand a wide variety of markets and situations.

We're now going to start digging a bit more deeply into people's economic choices, and, in the next section, we'll study the economic choices of households.

---

[6]We will study the stock market in more detail in Chapter 17.

SUMMARY

Housing Markets and Rent Ceilings

A sudden decrease in the supply of housing shifts the short-run supply curve to the left. Rents increase. In the short run, higher rents bring forth an increase in the quantity of housing supplied as people economize on the available space. In the long run, the higher rents stimulate building activity, resulting in a shift to the right in the short-run supply curve. Through this process, rents gradually decrease, and the quantity of housing available gradually increases.

If a rent ceiling prevents rents from increasing, the quantity of housing supplied is lower, in both the short run and the long run, than it would be in an unregulated market. There is no inducement to economize on space in the short run and no incentive to build new houses and apartments in the long run. Equilibrium is achieved by people spending time searching for housing. The total cost of housing, including the value of the time spent searching, exceeds the cost in an unregulated market. (pp. 127–132)

The Labor Market and Minimum Wage Regulation

A decrease in the demand for unskilled labor lowers wages and reduces employment in the short run. Low wages encourage people to quit a particular market and to acquire skills and seek different, more highly paid work. As they do so, the short run supply curve for unskilled labor shifts to the left. As it does so, it intersects the demand curve at higher wages and lower levels of employment. Eventually, the wage will return to its previous level but at a much lower employment level.

If the government imposes a minimum wage, a decrease in the demand for labor will result in an increase in unemployment and an increase in the amount of time spent searching for a job. Minimum wages bite hardest on people having the fewest skills and such workers tend to be young persons. The unemployment rate among young people is more than twice the average rate. (pp. 133–137)

Anticipating the Future

Producers have to make decisions about how much of a good to supply before they know the price at which they can sell it. In order to make supply decisions, producers form expectations about future prices. There is uncertainty about both demand and supply.

Producers form rational expectations about future prices based on their forecasts of future demand and supply. The actual price fluctuates around its expected level. Higher-than-expected demand produces a higher-than-expected price. Higher-than-expected supply produces a lower-than-expected price. (pp. 138–142)

Inventories

Goods that can be stored in inventory have smaller price flucutations than those that cannot be stored.

If demand or supply fluctuate, such goods can be put into or taken out of inventory. When goods are put into inventory, the supply to the market is reduced; when goods are taken out of inventory, the supply to the market is increased. Inventory holders try to buy at a low price and sell at a high price. To do so, they forecast the future price—they make a rational expectation—and sell when the price is above that expectation and buy when it is below it. Inventory holders' supply curves are perfectly elastic at their expected price (if we ignore the costs of holding inventories).

Actual prices are determined by inventory holders' rational expectations. Inventories fluctuate in response to fluctuations in demand and in producers' supply.

A rational expectation embodies all relevant information that is available. In a market in which the price equals its rational expectation, that price embodies all relevant information. Such a market is called an efficient market. Since the actual price equals the expected price, no systematic profit can be made in such a market. The actual price fluctuates in an efficient market because new information leads to a revision of the rational expectation of the price. (pp. 142–146)

KEY CONCEPTS

Black market, 132
Efficient market, 145
Fair Labor Standards Act, 137
Minimum wage law, 137
Rational expectation, 139
Rent ceiling, 130
Search activity, 131

Key Figures

REVIEW QUESTIONS

1 Describe what happens to rent and to the quantity of housing available if an earthquake suddenly and unexpectedly reduces the supply of housing. Trace the evolution of the rent and the quantity traded over time.

2 In the situation described in question 1, how

will things be different if a rent ceiling is imposed?

3 Describe what happens to the price and quantity traded in a market in which there is a sudden and unforeseen increase in supply. Trace the evolution of the price and quantity traded in the market over time.

4 Describe what happens to the price and quantity traded in a market in which there is a sudden and unforeseen increase in demand. Trace the evolution of the price and quantity traded in the market over time.

5 Describe what happens to the wage rate and quantity of labor employed when there is a sudden and unforeseen increase in demand for labor. Trace the evolution of the wage rate and employment over time.

6 In the situation described in question 5, how are things different if a minimum wage is introduced?

7 When a government regulation prevents a price from changing, what forces come into operation to achieve an equilibrium?

8 What are the main uncertainties that producers face?

9 What is a rational expectation?

10 How are the price and quantity traded of a good determined in a market in which expectations are rational but the good cannot be stored in inventory?

11 How are the price and quantity traded of a good determined in a market in which expectations are rational but the good can be stored in inventory?

12 What determines the price per share of a corporation's stock? Why will the actual price always equal the expected price?

13 Why is the stock market so volatile?

P R O B L E M S

You may find it easier to answer some of these problems by drawing the supply and demand curves on graph paper.

1 You have been given the following information about the market for rental housing in your town:

Rent (dollars per month)	Quantity demanded	Quantity supplied
50	20,000	0
100	15,000	5,000
150	10,000	10,000
200	5,000	15,000
250	2,500	20,000
300	1,500	25,000

a) What is the equilibrium rent?

b) What is the equilibrium quantity of housing traded?

2 Now suppose that a rent ceiling of $100 a month is imposed in the housing market described in problem 1:

a) What is the quantity of housing demanded?

b) What is the quantity of housing supplied?

c) What is the excess quantity of housing demanded?

d) What is the maximum price that demanders are be willing to pay for the last unit available?

e) Suppose that the average wage rate is $5 per hour. How many hours a month will a person spend looking for housing?

3 The demand for and supply of teenage labor are as follows:

Wage rate (dollars per hour)	Hours demanded	Hours supplied
1	3000	1000
2	2500	1500
3	2000	2000
4	1500	2500
5	1000	3000

(continued)

a) What is the equilibrium wage rate?

b) What is the level of employment?

c) What is the level of unemployment?

d) If the government imposes a minimum wage of $2.50 an hour for teenagers, how many hours do teenagers work?

e) If the government imposes a minimum wage of $3.50 an hour for teenagers, what are the employment and unemployment levels?

f) If there is a minimum wage of $3.50 an hour and demand increases by 500 hours, what is the level of unemployment?

4 Why does a minimum wage create unemployment?

5 The following table illustrates three supply curves for train travel:

Price (cents per passenger mile)	Quantity supplied (billions of passenger miles)		
	Momentary	Short run	Long run
10	500	300	100
20	500	350	200
30	500	400	300
40	500	450	400
50	500	500	500
60	500	550	600
70	500	600	700
80	500	650	800
90	500	700	900
100	500	750	1000

a) If the price is 50 cents per passenger mile, what is the quantity supplied

(i) In the long run

(ii) In the short run

b) Suppose that the price is initially 50 cents but that it then rises to 70 cents. What will be the quantity supplied

(i) Immediately following the price rise

(ii) In the short run

(iii) In the long run

6 Suppose that the supply of train travel is the same as in problem 5. The following table gives two demand schedules—original and new:

Price (cents per passenger mile)	Quantity demanded (billions of passenger miles)	
	Original	New
10	10,000	10,300
20	5,000	5,300
30	2,000	2,300
40	1,000	1,300
50	500	800
60	400	700
70	300	600
80	200	500
90	100	400
100	0	300

a) What is the original equilibrium price and quantity?

b) After the increase in demand has occurred, what is

(i) The momentary equilibrium price and quantity

(ii) The short-run equilibrium price and quantity

(iii) The long-run equilibrium price and quantity

7 The short-run and long-run demand for travel is as follows:

Price (cents per passenger mile)	Quantity demanded (billions of passenger miles)	
	Short run	Long run
10	700	10,000
20	650	5,000
30	600	2,000
40	550	1,000
50	500	500
60	450	400
70	400	300
80	350	200
90	300	100
100	250	0

The supply of train travel is the same as in problem 5.

a) What is the long-run equilibrium price and quantity of train travel?

b) Serious floods destroy one fifth of the train tracks and rolling stock, and supply falls by 100 billion passenger miles. What happens to the price and the quantity of train travel

  (i) In the short run

  (ii) In the long run

8 Assume that corn is not stored. The demand for corn and the supply of corn are expected to be as follows:

Price (dollars)	Expected quantity demanded	Expected quantity supplied
1	700 *800*	100 *0*
2	600 *700*	200 *100*
3	500 *600*	300 *200*
4	400 *500*	400 *300*
5	300 *400*	500 *400*
6	200 *300*	600 *500*
7	100 *200*	700 *600*

a) The average levels of demand and supply are expected to remain constant, and farmers expect no unusual events. What is their rational expectation of the price of corn?

b) A drought occurs and corn production is 100 units less than expected.

  (i) What is the actual quantity of corn traded?

  (ii) What is the actual price of corn at that quantity?

  (iii) How much corn will producers like to have supplied if they had been able to forecast the drought accurately?

c) Growing conditions turn out to be exactly as expected, and actual supply equals average supply. At the same time, a drought in the Soviet Union increases Soviet demand for U.S. corn by 100 units.

  (i) What is the actual price of corn?

  (ii) What is the actual quantity of corn traded?

  (iii) How much corn will U.S. growers like to have produced if they had been able to predict the rise in Soviet demand?

9 Assume that corn *is* stored and that the average demand and supply described in problem 8 still apply.

a) If farmers expect the average levels of demand and supply, and they forecast no unusual events, what is their rational expectation of

  (i) The price of corn

  (ii) The quantity of corn

b) A drought occurs and corn production is 100 units less than expected.

  (i) What is the actual price of corn?

  (ii) What is the actual quantity of corn traded?

  (iii) How much corn will producers like to have supplied if they had been able to forecast the drought accurately?

  (iv) Is corn added to inventories or taken out of inventories? By how much do inventories change?

c) Growing conditions turn out to be exactly as expected, and actual supply equals average supply. At the same time, a drought in the Soviet Union increases Soviet demand for U.S. corn by 100 units.

  (i) What is the actual price of corn?

  (ii) What is the actual quantity of corn traded?

  (iii) How much corn will U.S. growers like to have produced if they had been able to predict the rise in Soviet demand?

  (iv) Is corn added to inventories or taken out of inventories? By how much does the inventory level change?

Part 3

G ary Becker has devoted much of his lifetime research to applying the economic way of thinking to problems traditionally studied by sociologists. Professor Becker holds professorships in the departments of economics and sociology at the University of Chicago. Michael Parkin spoke with him about how the economics of human behavior sheds light on social issues.

Professor Becker, can we really hope to explain all human choices by using models that were invented to explain and predict choices about the allocation of income among alternative consumer goods?

All human decisions involve scarcity. Should I watch television or read a book? Should I go out on a date or drink beer with my friends? Should I get married now or remain single? In all these problems, I'm deciding how to allocate my money, my time, my effort, and my love among various uses. We live in a rich society, but we're not rich in time or energy. We're limited even in money. It's natural to ask, how do people make their choices? Do they make different types of choices when they decide what to watch on television than when they plan how to spend their money in a grocery store? Do they make different types of choices in deciding whether to get divorced or what job they should take? When I try to understand what people are doing, I do not believe that they make rational choices

Talking
with
Gary
Becker

"I don't believe that people make rational choices sometimes and irrational choices other times."

sometimes and at other times they make irrational choices. It's far more natural to suspect that they use the same criteria in making all their decisions. That's really the economic approach to choice, or what's called the rationality assumption.

Other social sciences consider social issues and problems. How do they differ from economics?

Economics is, uniquely I believe, a way of thinking about social issues. I think it's fair to say that economics is the most powerful of all the social sciences in providing a general organizing theory. In other respects, it's inferior to the other social sciences. Sociologists are more ingenious at conducting surveys. Anthropologists are wonderful observers and recorders of information. Psychologists are good experimenters. So all the social sciences contribute, but economics' main contribution is its analytical framework.

In this economic framework, which principles have been most fruitful for your own work?

I like to stress four principles. First, that people maximize—that's what economists sometimes associate with rational behavior. People try to do the best they can given limited income or time. They want to use their time and resources effectively. Next, people's goals are stable over time and don't shift around. If people's goals changed readily, it would be very hard for us to talk about their behavior. And third, people try to anticipate the adverse consequences of their behavior. If I'm going to smoke, what's going to happen to me? I may still do it, but I try to anticipate the consequences. Finally, at the group level, these different individuals, interact and end up with some aggregate solution, or what we call equilibrium. These are the basic principles. They sound simple, but it's a little more complicated to see all their implications.

What are the achievements of the economics of human behavior? To what questions do we have convincing answers?

We have answers to many questions! For example, if we raise the tax on cigarettes, we can predict with confidence not only that the consumption of cigarettes will decline but by how

much. If the price goes up, people consume less. Even those addicted to cigarettes will consume less. We can predict outcomes in labor markets, and say, for example, that when firms have to provide paid child care, the wages of women will fall. Or perhaps firms will try not to hire women.

I'm willing to say we also know a good deal about less conventional areas. We know that if you increase the likelihood that you'll catch criminals and stiffen their punishment, you get less crime. Lots of recent studies demonstrate that. We know that if you have unemployment you'll increase the amount of crime.

When you first suggested that children could be treated as durable consumer goods, the suggestion was treated with derision. Thirty years later, what are the concrete payoffs gained from making that assumption?

Thirty years later many more economists are taking this approach. And it's accepted not only by economists but by groups who didn't accept it then, by sociologists, demographers, and the like. Let me give you an example of its success. What would the economic approach emphasize in looking at the demand for children? It would naturally look at the benefits and costs of having children, including the value of the mother's time. You would predict with this approach that if the value of the mother's time went up, it would raise the cost of having children and mothers would have fewer children. Now some people would say, that's such a materialistic view. People have children because they love them. Well, of course people have children because of love. We wouldn't have any children with all the difficulties of raising kids if we didn't love them, but love has its price.

Now, if you're a skeptic, you'll want to see the evidence. And the evidence shows that as the value of the time of women has gone up, they have fewer children, in every country that I know of. The theory also says that you might substitute. When people have fewer children, they give them more education, they may spend more time with each child. For example, China has had an official "one child policy" of family planning. There's much discussion now in Chinese newspapers about the so-called Emperor Child. The child who gets lots of toys, whose parents are pushing him to get him into the best nursery school. That's just what the theory predicts. This substitution between quantity and quality.

Some people think it's immoral to reduce choices of a deeply personal nature to mere economic calculations. How do you respond to this objection?

First of all, when we use an economic approach, we don't concentrate on money alone. I never claim that people marry only according to how much money they're going to get out of it, or that when they have children, they reckon up each child as a profit or loss. That's ridiculous. Money is just a part of it. There have certainly been lots of family fights over money, but it's not the whole of life or any human behavior. The economic approach

> "As the value of the time of women has gone up, they have fewer children."

doesn't say it's the whole of life. It just says that people maximize. What they're maximizing may include love toward children or a spouse. I think it's a great virtue to say, life is short and full of hardships, so let's try to get as much out of life as we can. Not the least, but the most.

Many people who are not economists don't believe that the "rationality assumption" should be taken seriously. They look inside themselves, examine their own behavior, and don't find it rational. So how can you fairly assume that other people behave rationally?

> "When people solve problems rationally, they don't look at their marginal utility any more than Orel Hershiser is Einstein."

I disagree with the premise of that question. I believe that, on reflection, people will say that a lot of the things they do are in fact rational. Let me pose some simple questions. You're a college student and you're thinking of going to the movies and a happy hour. You're worried about how much the evening will cost. You say, of course I'm going to think about the cost. Suppose there's no student discount and the movie will cost $6. Will you change your behavior? Well if you don't think you can afford $6, you'll maybe go and watch television. Are you behaving rationally? Are you thinking about the consequences? Yes. That's rationality.

I'd ask more questions of this 19-year-old: How many beers are you going to have at the happy hour? Well, the legal drinking age is 21, but maybe you have a fake ID, so you get in under age. But suppose you're caught by campus security. You've got to spend the night in jail and get thrown out of school. Do you think you'd be willing to try to get in under age? Well, you might very well answer, what's my chance of being caught? And that's exactly a rational choice. Worrying about your chances of being caught and about the likely punishment.

But even if you don't actually analyze your actions in these terms doesn't mean you're acting irrationally. Let me give you another example. Orel Hershiser is a top baseball player. He effectively knows all the laws of motion, of eye and hand coordination, about the speed of the bat and the ball, and so on. He's in fact solving a complicated physics problem when he steps up to pitch, but obviously he doesn't have to know physics to do that. Likewise, I'm saying that when people solve problems rationally, they're really not thinking that, well, I have this budget and I read this textbook, and I look at my marginal utility or my indifference curve. They don't do that, but it doesn't mean they're not being rational any more than Orel Hershiser is Einstein.

Chapter 7

After studying this chapter, you will be able to:

- Explain the connection between individual demand and market demand

- Define utility and marginal utility

- Explain the marginal utility theory of consumer choice

- Use the marginal utility theory to predict the effects of changing prices

- Use the marginal utility theory to predict the effects of changing income

- Define and calculate consumer surplus

- Explain the paradox of value

We need water to live. We don't need diamonds for much besides decoration. If the benefits of water far outweigh the benefits of diamonds, why, then, does water cost practically nothing while diamonds are terribly expensive? ■ When OPEC restricted its sale of oil in 1973, it created a dramatic rise in price, but people continued to use almost as much oil as they had before. Our demand for oil was inelastic. But why? ■ When Sony introduced the Walkman in 1979, it cost about $300, and consumers didn't buy very many of them. Since then, the price has decreased dramatically, and people are buying them in enormous quantities. Our demand for portable audio headsets is elastic. But

Water, Water, Everywhere

why? What makes the demand for some things elastic while the demand for others is inelastic? ■ Over the past 15 years, incomes have increased by 40 percent. Over that same period, expenditure on electricity has increased by 66 percent, while expenditure on transportation has increased by only 18 percent. Thus the proportion of income spent on electricity has increased while the proportion spent on transportation has decreased. Why, as incomes rise, does the proportion of income spent on some goods rise and on others fall?

■ In the last three chapters, we've seen that demand has an important effect on the price of a good. But we have not analyzed what exactly shapes a person's demand. This chapter explains why demand is elastic for some goods and inelastic for others. It also explains why the prices of some things, such as diamonds and water, are so out of proportion with their benefits.

Individual Demand and Market Demand

When we studied how demand and supply determine price and the quantity bought and sold, we used the concept of **market demand**—the relationship between the total quantity of a good demanded and its price. Goods and services are demanded, though, by individuals. The relationship between the quantity demanded by a single individual and the price of a good is called **individual demand.**

Obviously, there is a relationship between market demand and individual demand. In fact, market demand is the sum of all individual demands. The table in Fig. 7.1 illustrates the relationship between

individual demand and market demand. In this example Lisa and Chuck are the only people. The market demand is the total demand of Lisa and Chuck. At $3 a movie, Lisa demands 5 movies and Chuck 2, so that the total quantity demanded by the market is 7 movies.

We can represent the relationship between individual and market demands in a diagram such as that in Fig. 7.1. Here Lisa's demand curve for movies appears in part (a) and Chuck's appears in part (b). The market demand curve, shown in part (c), adds Chuck's quantity demanded to Lisa's quantity demanded at each price.

The market demand curve is the sum of the quantities demanded by each individual at each price.

Figure 7.1   Individual and Market Demand Curves

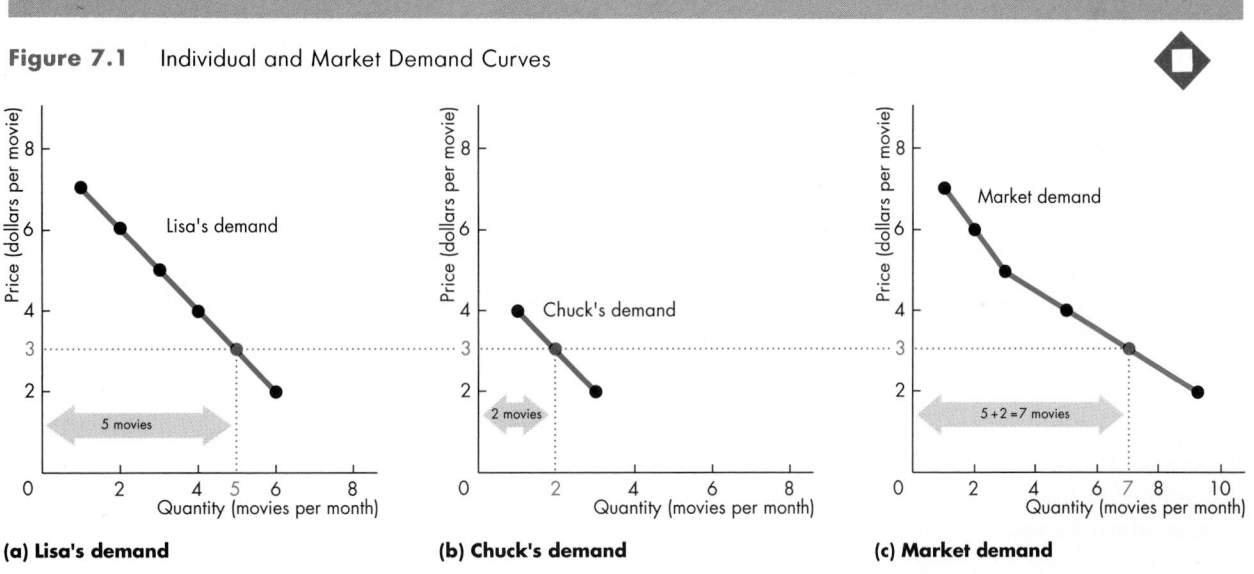

(a) Lisa's demand   **(b) Chuck's demand**   **(c) Market demand**

The table and diagram illustrate how the quantity of movies demanded varies as the price of a movie varies. The market demand is the sum of the individual demands. For example, at a price of $3, Lisa demands 5 movies and Chuck demands 2 movies, so the total quantity demanded in the market is 7 movies.

Price (dollars per movie)	Quantity (movies per month)		
	Lisa	Chuck	Market
7	1	0	1
6	2	0	2
5	3	0	3
4	4	1	5
3	5	2	7
2	6	3	9

Let's now investigate an individual demand curve by studying how an individual household makes its consumption choices.

Household Consumption Choices

Suppose that a household has a certain amount of money to spend and that it cannot influence the prices of the goods and services that it buys. How does the household choose the consumption goods on which to spend its income? The answer to this question that you're about to study is called the marginal utility theory. It was invented almost 100 years ago by Alfred Marshall (see Our Advancing Knowledge on pp. 84–85)

To study the marginal utility theory, we'll examine Lisa's consumption choices. Lisa has a monthly income of $30, and spends all of it on only two goods—movies and soda. Movies cost $6 each and soda costs 50 cents a can or $3 for a six-pack. How does Lisa divide her $30 between these two goods? The answer depends on her likes and dislikes—on what economists call *preferences*. The marginal utility theory of consumption choice has a particular way of describing preferences—it uses the concept of utility.

Utility

The benefit or satisfaction that a person gets from the consumption of a good or service is called **utility.** But what exactly is utility and in what units can we measure it? Utility is an abstract theoretical concept and units of utility are chosen arbitrarily, just like the units in which we measure temperature.

Temperature—an Analogy   Temperature is a concept with which you are familiar. You know when you feel hot and when you feel cold. But you can't *observe* temperature. You can observe water turning to steam if it is hot enough or turning to ice if it is cold enough. You can construct an instrument, called a thermometer, that will predict when such changes of state will occur. The scale on the thermometer is what we call temperature. But the units in which we measure temperature are arbitrary. For example, we can accurately predict that when a Fahrenheit thermometer shows a temperature of 32°, water will turn to ice. But the units of measurement do not matter, because this same event will also occur when a centigrade thermometer shows a temperature of zero.

The concept of utility helps us make predictions about consumption choices in much the same way that the concept of temperature helps us make predictions about physical phenomena. It has to be admitted, though, that the marginal utility theory is not as precise as the theory that enables us to predict when water will turn to ice or steam.

Let's now see how we can use the concept of utility to describe preferences.

Utility and Consumption

The amount of utility that a person gets depends on the person's level of consumption—more consumption gives more utility. Table 7.1 gives an example of Lisa's utility derived from consuming different quantities of movies and soda. If she sees no movies, she gets no utility from movies. If she sees 1 movie in a month, she gets 50 units of utility. As the number of movies she sees in a month increases, her utility increases so that if she sees 10 movies a month, she gets 250 units of utility. The other part of the table shows Lisa's utility from soda. If she drinks no soda, she gets no utility. As the amount of soda she drinks rises, her utility increases.

Table 7.1   Lisa's Utility from Movies and Soda

Movies		Soda	
Quantity per month	Utility	Six-packs per month	Utility
0	0	0	0
1	50	1	30
2	88	2	57
3	121	3	81
4	150	4	102
5	175	5	122
6	196	6	141
7	214	7	159
8	229	8	176
9	241	9	192
10	250	10	207

Figure 7.2   Utility and Marginal Utility

Quantity	Utility	Marginal utility
0	0	
		50
1	50	
		38
2	88	
		33
3	121	
		29
4	150	
		25
5	175	
		21
6	196	
		18
7	214	
		15
8	229	
		12
9	241	
		9
10	250	

(a) Utility

(b) Marginal utility

The table shows that as Lisa's consumption of movies increases, so does the utility she derives from movies. For example, 4 movies gives 150 units of utility while 5 movies give 175 units. The table also shows her marginal utility—the change in utility resulting from the last movie seen. Marginal utility declines as consumption increases. For example, the marginal utility from the fourth movie is 29 units while that from the fifth movie is 25 units. Lisa's utility and marginal utility from movies are graphed in the figure. Part (a) shows the extra utility gained from each additional movie as an orange bar. Part (b) shows the marginal utility of each new movie as a declining series of steps.

Marginal Utility

Marginal utility is the additional utility derived from the last unit of a good consumed. We calculate marginal utility as the change in utility that occurs when one more unit of a good is consumed. Such a calculation is shown in the table in Fig. 7.2. When Lisa's consumption of movies increases from 4 to 5 movies a month, her utility from movies increases from 150 units to 175 units. Thus the marginal utility of Lisa's fifth movie each month is 25 units. The table displays calculations of marginal utility for each level of movie consumption. Notice that the units of marginal utility appear midway between the quantities of consumption. It is the *change* in consumption from 4 to 5 movies that produces the *marginal* utility of 25 units.

Lisa's utility and marginal utility can be illustrated in a graph. Figure 7.2(a) illustrates the utility that Lisa gets from movies. As you can see, the more movies Lisa sees in a month, the more utility she gets. Part (b) illustrates her marginal utility. This graph tells us that as Lisa sees more movies, the marginal utility that Lisa gets from watching movies falls. For example, her marginal utility from the first movie is 50 units, from the second, 38 units, and from the third, 33 units. We call this decline in marginal utility as the consumption of a good increases the principle of **diminishing marginal utility.**

Marginal utility is positive but diminishes as the consumption of a good increases. Why does marginal utility have these two features? In Lisa's case, she likes movies, and the more she sees the better. That's why marginal utility is positive. The benefit that Lisa gets from the last movie seen is its marginal utility. To see why marginal utility diminishes, think about how you'd feel in the following two situations: In one, you've just been studying for 29 evenings in a row. An opportunity arises to see a movie. The utility that you get from that movie is the marginal utility from seeing one movie in a month. In the second situation, you've been on a movie binge. For the past 29 nights, you have not even seen an assignment or test. You are up to your eyeballs in movies. You are happy enough to go to a movie on yet one more night. But the kick that you get out of that thirtieth movie in 30 days is not very large. It is the marginal utility of the thirtieth movie in a month.

REVIEW

Lisa divides her income of $30 a month between movies that cost $6 each and soda that costs $3 a six-pack. Lisa's preferences are described by using the concept of utility: The more movies Lisa sees in a given month, the more utility she gets; the more cans of soda she drinks in a month, the more

utility she gets. The increase in utility that results from the last unit of a good consumed is called marginal utility. As the quantity of a good consumed increases, marginal utility decreases. ∎

Utility Maximization

Utility maximization is the attainment of the greatest possible utility. But a household's income and the prices that it faces limit the utility that it can obtain. We assume that a household consumes in a way that maximizes its utility, taking into consideration its income and the prices that it faces. In Lisa's case, we examine how she allocates her spending between movies and soda to maximize her utility, assuming that movies cost $6 each, soda costs $3 a six-pack, and Lisa only has $30 a month to spend.

The Utility-Maximizing Choice   Let's calculate how Lisa spends her money to maximize her utility by constructing a table. Table 7.2 has two parts. Part (a) records Lisa's expenditure and part (b), her utility. Part (a) shows six ways in which Lisa can allocate her $30 of income between movies and soda. For example, she can buy 2 movies at a cost of $12, in which case she will be able to buy 6 six-packs for a cost of $18. Each row in part (a) shows the combinations of movies and soda that exhaust her income.

Part (b) considers the same affordable combinations of movies and soda that are set out in part (a). Part (b) records three things: first, the number of movies consumed and the utility derived from them (the left side of the table); second, the number of six-packs of soda consumed and the utility derived from them (the right side of the table); and third, the total utility derived from both movies and soda (the middle column of the table).

Consider, for example, the first row. It shows Lisa watching no movies, getting no utility from them but getting 207 units of utility from drinking 10 six-packs of soda. Her total utility, in this case, is 207 units.

Now consider the second row. Lisa watches 1 movie, getting 50 units of utility from it, and drinks 8 six-packs of soda, getting another 176 units of utility. In this case, her total utility is the sum of 50 units from movies and 176 units from soda, or 226 units. The rest of part (b) is constructed in exactly the same way.

Table 7.2 Lisa's Utility Maximizing Combinations of Movies and Soda

(a) Expenditure

Movies			Soda	
Quantity	Expenditure (dollars)	Total expenditure (dollars)	Expenditure (dollars)	Six-packs
0	0	30	30	10
1	6	30	24	8
2	12	30	18	6
3	18	30	12	4
4	24	30	6	2
5	30	30	0	0

(b) Utility

Movies			Soda	
Quantity	Utility	Total utility	Utility	Six-packs
0	0	207	207	10
1	50	226	176	8
2	88	229	141	6
3	121	223	102	4
4	150	207	57	2
5	175	175	0	0

Notice also that Table 7.2 does not consider allocations in which Lisa consumes odd numbers of six-packs of soda (1, 3, 5, 7, or 9). The reason is that she cannot buy half a movie. She has to buy movies in whole numbers and, since movies cost $6, twice as much as a six-pack of soda, she can only consume 0, 2, 4, 6, 8, or 10 six-packs of soda if she spends all her income on these two goods.

The consumption of movies and soda that maximizes Lisa's utility is highlighted in part (b) of the table. When Lisa consumes 2 movies and 6 six-packs of soda, she gets 229 units of utility. This is the best Lisa can do given that she has only $30 to spend and given the prices of movies and six-packs. If she buys 8 six-packs of soda, she can see only 1 movie and gets 226 units of utility, 3

less than the maximum attainable. If she sees 3 movies and drinks only 4 six-packs, she gets 223 units of utility, 6 less than the maximum attainable. Thus Lisa can do no better than consume 2 movies and 6 six-packs—the allocation of her $30 that maximizes her utility.

The situation that we've just described is a consumer equilibrium. A **consumer equilibrium** is a situation in which a consumer has allocated his or her income in a manner that maximizes utility. In calculating Lisa's consumer equilibrium, we have measured her total utility from the consumption of movies and soda. There is another, better way of determining a consumer equilibrium that does not involve measuring total utility at all. Let's look at this alternative.

Equalizing Marginal Utility per Dollar Spent

Another way to find out the allocation that maximizes a consumer's utility is to make the marginal utility per dollar spent equal for all goods. The **marginal utility per dollar spent** on a good is the marginal utility obtained from the last good consumed divided by the price of the good. For example, Lisa's marginal utility from consuming the first movie is 50 units of utility. The price of a movie is $6, which means that the marginal utility per dollar spent on movies is 50 units divided by $6, or 8.33 units of utility per dollar.

Table 7.3 sets out Lisa's marginal utilities per dollar spent for both movies and soda. Again, the table has been arranged so that each row represents an allocation of Lisa's income that uses up her $30. You can see that Lisa's marginal utility per dollar spent on either good, like marginal utility itself, declines as consumption of the good rises. The marginal utility per dollar spent on movies falls from 8.33 for the first movie to 6.33 for the second to 4.16 for the fifth. The marginal utility per dollar spent on soda is 9.00 for 2 six-packs, 7.00 for 4 six-packs, 6.33 for 6 six-packs, and 5.00 for 10 six-packs.

Notice that when Lisa consumes 2 movies and 6 six-packs of soda, she gets the same marginal utility per dollar spent from movies as she does from soda. This allocation of her income maximizes her utility. It is the same allocation that we calculated in Table 7.2.

Utility is maximized when the marginal utility per dollar spent is equal for all goods.

In calculating the utility-maximizing allocation of income in Table 7.3, we have not used the concept of total utility at all. All the calculations have been performed using marginal utility and price. By making the marginal utility per dollar spent equal for both goods, we know that we have maximized utility but we have not calculated what the maximum level of utility is. As a matter of fact, we do not need to know what the level of utility is. We need only to know that the maximum utility has been attained. This way of viewing maximum utility is important; it means that the units in which utility is measured do not matter. We could double or halve all the numbers measuring utility, or multiply them by any other positive number, or square them, or take their square roots. None of these transformations of the units used to measure utility will make any difference to the outcome. Utility is maximized when the marginal utility per dollar spent is equal for all goods. It is in this respect that utility is analogous to temperature. Our prediction about the freezing of water does not depend on the temperature scale; our prediction about maximizing utility does not depend on the units of utility.

Table 7.3   Maximizing Utility by Equalizing Marginal Utilities per Dollar Spent

Movies ($6 each)			Soda ($3 per six-pack)		
Quantity	Marginal utility	Marginal utility per dollar spent	Six-packs	Marginal utility	Marginal utility per dollar spent
0	0		10	15	5.00
1	50	8.33	8	17	5.66
2	38	6.33	6	19	6.33
3	33	5.50	4	21	7.00
4	29	4.83	2	27	9.00
5	25	4.16	0	0	

You can see why the rule "equalize marginal utility per dollar spent on all goods" works by considering what happens if Lisa spends differently. Suppose that instead of consuming 2 movies and 6 six-packs of soda, Lisa consumes 1 movie and 8 six-packs of soda (the second row of Table 7.3). She will then get 8.33 units of utility from the last dollar spent on movies and 5.66 units of utility from the last dollar spent on soda. It will pay Lisa to spend less on soda and more on movies. Spending a dollar less on soda lowers her utility by 5.66 units, while spending the extra dollar on movies gives her an additional 6.33 units. Lisa's utility rises if she spends less on soda and more on movies.

Or, suppose that Lisa consumes 3 movies and only 4 six-packs of soda (the fourth row of the table). In this situation, she will get 5.50 units of utility from the last dollar spent on movies and 7.00 units of utility from the last dollar spent on soda. It will now pay Lisa to cut her spending on movies, at a cost of 5.50 units of utility per dollar, and raise her spending on soda, where she gets 7.00 units of utility per dollar. When Lisa's marginal utility per dollar spent on both goods is equal, she cannot get more utility by spending differently. Her utility is maximized.

R E V I E W

Consumers maximize utility. A consumer spends his or her income in order to make the marginal utility per dollar spent on each good equal. In such a situation, the consumer cannot reallocate spending to get more utility. The absolute level of utility is irrelevant—all that matters is its maximization. The units in which utility is measured are irrelevant—all that matters is that the marginal utility per dollar is equal for all goods. ■

Predictions of Marginal Utility Theory

Now let's go on to use marginal utility theory to make some predictions. In particular, let's see what happens to Lisa's con-

sumption of movies and soda when their prices change and also when her income changes.

First, we'll work out what happens to Lisa's consumption if the price of a movie drops by half, to $3. Next, we'll work out what happens if the price of a movie stays at $3 and the cost of soda doubles to $6 per six-pack.

The Effects of Changes in Prices

To determine the effects of changes in prices on consumption requires three steps. First, we need to determine the combinations of movies and soda that can be bought at the new prices. Second, we need to calculate the new marginal utilities per dollar spent. Third, we need to determine the consumption of each good that makes the marginal utility per dollar spent on each good equal and that just exhausts the money available for spending. Table 7.4 works out the answers for two price changes: first halving the price of a movie (from $6 to $3) and then doubling the price of soda (from $3 to $6) while the price of a movie remains at $3.

A Fall in the Price of Movies Case 1 in Table 7.4 shows ways of consuming movies at $3 each and soda at $3 a six-pack. Once again, each row of the table shows quantities consumed that exactly use up the $30 of income available. The marginal utility per dollar spent is marginal utility of the good divided by its price. Marginal utility, which was shown in the table in Fig. 7.2, describes Lisa's preferences. Her preferences do not change when prices change, so her marginal utility schedule remains the same as that in Fig. 7.2. But now we divide her marginal utility from movies by $3, the new price of a movie, to get the marginal utility per dollar spent on movies. You can see that Lisa's marginal utility per dollar spent on movies declines from 16.67 at 1 movie all the way down to 3.00 at 10 movies.

Lisa's marginal utility per dollar spent on soda declines from 10.00 at 1 six-pack to 5.00 at 10 six-packs. The marginal utilities per dollar spent on movies and on soda are each equal to 7.00 when Lisa watches 6 movies and drinks 4 six-packs.

What has been the effect of the fall in the price of a movie on Lisa's consumption? You can find the answer by comparing Lisa's utility-maxi-

Table 7.4   How a Change in Price Affects Lisa's Choices

Case 1: Movies $3.00 each Soda $3.00 per six-pack				Case 2: Movies $3.00 each Soda $6.00 per six-pack			
Movies		**Soda**		**Movies**		**Soda**	
Quantity	Marginal utility per dollar spent	Six-packs	Marginal utility per dollar spent	Quantity	Marginal utility per dollar spent	Six-packs	Marginal utility per dollar spent
0		10	5.00	0		5	3.33
1	16.67	9	5.33	2	12.67	4	3.50
2	12.67	8	5.67	4	9.67	3	4.00
3	11.00	7	6.00	6	7.00	2	4.50
4	9.67	6	6.33	8	5.00	1	5.00
5	8.33	5	6.67	10	3.00	0	
6	7.00	4	7.00				
7	6.00	3	8.00				
8	5.00	2	9.00				
9	4.00	1	10.00				
10	3.00	0					

mizing allocation shown in Case 1 in Table 7.4 with her allocation in Table 7.3. You can see that as a result of the fall in the price of a movie, Lisa watches more movies (up from 2 to 6 a month) and she drinks less soda (down from 6 six-packs to 4 six-packs a month).

A Rise in the Price of Soda   Let us now look at Case 2 in Table 7.4. The price of a movie stays at $3, but the price of soda doubles to $6 a six-pack. The rows of the table show the possible ways of consuming soda and movies at these new prices. Because soda now costs $6, Lisa cannot consume more than 5 six-packs. Five six-packs of soda cost $30, exactly the amount that Lisa has available. Since we are assuming that a six-pack cannot be split into single cans, Lisa can consume only 0, 2, 4, 6, 8, or 10 movies. Because movies cost the same in Case 1 and Case 2, the marginal utility per dollar spent on movies remains the same. You

can see that if Lisa sees 2 movies, her marginal utility per dollar spent on movies is 12.67 in both cases. If Lisa sees 10 movies, her marginal utility per dollar spent on movies is 3.

Lisa's marginal utility per dollar spent on soda is the marginal utility of soda divided by the new price of soda ($6). These marginal utilities per dollar spent are set out in the extreme right-hand column of Table 7.4. As you can see in Case 2, the marginal utility per dollar spent on movies and on soda are equal when Lisa watches 8 movies and drinks 1 six-pack a month. You can calculate the effects of the rise in the price of soda on Lisa's consumption by comparing Case 2 with Case 1. Lisa's consumption of soda has fallen from 4 six-packs to 1 six-pack and her consumption of movies has increased from 6 to 8 a month. For Lisa, soda and movies are substitutes. When there is a rise in the price of soda, Lisa substitutes movies for soda. She sees more movies and drinks less soda.

R E V I E W

Let's review how Lisa changes her consumption when prices change. When the price of a movie falls but the price of soda stays constant, Lisa increases her consumption of movies and cuts her consumption of soda. When the price of a movie stays constant but the price of soda increases, Lisa cuts her consumption of soda and increases her consumption of movies. When the price of a movie falls or the price of soda rises, with unchanged consumption, the marginal utility per dollar spent on movies exceeds that on soda. To restore the equality of the marginal utility per dollar spent on each good, the consumption of movies must rise and the consumption of soda must fall. ■

Marginal utility theory predicts these two results: When the price of a good rises, the quantity demanded falls. When the price of one good rises, the demand for another good that can serve as a substitute increases. Does this sound familiar? It should. These predictions of marginal utility theory correspond to the assumptions that we made about consumer demand in Chapter 4. There we *assumed* that the demand curve for a good sloped downward, and we *assumed* that a rise in the price of a substitute increased demand. Marginal utility theory predicts these responses to price changes. It makes these predictions by assuming three things: First, that consumers maximize utility. Second, that they get more utility as they consume more of a good. Third, as consumption increases, marginal utility declines.

Thus the assumption of diminishing marginal utility implies the law of demand. But this is not the only implication of diminishing marginal utility. It also has implications for the response of consumption to a change in income. Let's see how by studying the effects of a change in Lisa's income on her consumption.

The Effects of a Rise in Income

Let's suppose that Lisa gets a raise of $12 a month, which means that she now has $42 a month to spend on movies and soda. Let's also suppose that movies cost $3 each and a six-pack costs $3 (as in

Case 1 in Table 7.4). We now want to compare Lisa's consumption of movies and soda at her original income of $30 with her consumption at her new income of $42. The calculations for such a comparison are presented in Table 7.5. Case 1 (which is identical to Case 1 in Table 7.4) shows Lisa's utility-maximizing consumption of movies and soda when she earns $30. Case 2 shows what happens when Lisa's income goes up to $42. With $42, Lisa can buy 14 movies a month and no soda or 14 six-packs a month and no movies or any combination of the two goods shown in the rows of Table 7.5.

We can calculate the marginal utility per dollar spent on movies and soda in exactly the same way as we did before. Only now, because Lisa has more income, she can consume more soda for any given consumption of movies or, equivalently, more movies for any given consumption of soda. For example, Lisa can watch 1 movie and drink 13 six-packs of soda when she earns $42. When her income is $30, however, she can buy only 9 six-packs of soda if she sees 1 movie. Lisa maximizes her utility when the marginal utilities per dollar spent on movies and on soda are equal. At an income of $42, such a situation occurs when the marginal utility per dollar spent on each good is 6 units. Lisa watches 7 movies a month and drinks 7 six-packs of soda.

By comparing Case 2 with Case 1, we can see another important prediction of the marginal utility theory of consumption. When Lisa earns more income, she increases her consumption of both goods—but she does not increase her consumption of both goods by the same amount. She consumes 3 more six-packs of soda but sees only 1 more movie each month. Lisa's response arises from her preferences, as described by her marginal utilities of movies and soda.

For Lisa, soda and movies are normal goods. When her income rises, Lisa buys more of both goods. This prediction of the marginal utility theory corresponds to another assumption that we made when studying the theory of demand in Chapter 4. There we *assumed* that demand rises when income rises. Here we have obtained that result as a prediction of marginal utility theory.

The marginal utility theory of consumption is summarized in Table 7.6. We can use the marginal utility theory of consumer behavior to make sense

Table 7.5   How a Change in Income Affects Lisa's Choices

Case 1: Income $30

Movies ($3 each)		Soda ($3 per six-pack)	
Quantity	Marginal utility per dollar spent	Six-packs	Marginal utility per dollar spent
0		10	5.00
1	16.67	9	5.33
2	12.67	8	5.67
3	11.00	7	6.00
4	9.67	6	6.33
5	8.33	5	6.67
6	7.00	4	7.00
7	6.00	3	8.00
8	5.00	2	9.00
9	4.00	1	10.00
10	3.00	0	

Case 2: Income $42

Movies ($3 each)		Soda ($3 per six-pack)	
Quantity	Marginal utility per dollar spent	Six-packs	Marginal utility per dollar spent
0		14	
1	16.67	13	
2	12.67	12	
3	11.00	11	
4	9.67	10	5.00
5	8.33	9	5.33
6	7.00	8	5.67
7	6.00	7	6.00
8	5.00	6	6.33
9	4.00	5	6.67
10	3.00	4	7.00
11		3	8.00
12		2	9.00
13		1	10.00
14		0	

of some of the features of the world described at the beginning of this chapter. For example, it explains why the demand for some goods, such as audio headsets, are elastic and others, such as oil, are inelastic. It also explains why, as income increases, the proportion of income spent on some goods, such as electricity, increases, while the proportion spent on other goods, such as transportation, decreases. These effects occur because of our preferences. The speed with which our marginal utility for each good diminishes as we increase our consumption of the good affects the way in which we reallocate our income in response to price changes and the way in which our spending responds to a change in income. The calculations that we've performed for Lisa illustrate these effects.

Criticisms of Marginal Utility Theory

Marginal utility theory helps us to understand the choices people make, but there are some criticisms of this theory. Let's look at them.

Utility Can't Be Observed or Measured

Agreed—we can't observe utility. But we do not need to observe it to use it. We can and do observe the quantities of goods and services that people consume, the prices of those goods and services, and people's incomes. Our goal is to understand the consumption choices that people make and to predict the effects of changes in prices and incomes on these choices. To make such predictions, we *assume* that people derive utility from their consumption, that more consumption yields more utility, and that marginal utility diminishes. From these assumptions, we make predictions about the directions of change in consumption when prices and incomes change. As we've already seen, the actual numbers we use to express utility do not matter. Consumers maximize utility by making the marginal utility per dollar spent on each good equal. As long as we use the same scale to express utility for all goods, we'll get the same answer regardless of the units on our scale. In this regard, utility is similar to temperature—water freezes when it's cold enough, and that occurs independently of the temperature scale used.

"People Aren't That Smart"

Some critics maintain that marginal utility theory assumes that people are super-computers. It requires people to look at the marginal utility of every good at every different quantity they might consume, divide those numbers by the prices of the goods, and then calculate the quantities at which the marginal utility of each good divided by its price is equal.

But such criticism of marginal utility theory confuses the actions of people in the real world with those of people in a model economy. A model economy is no more an actual economy than a model railway is an actual railway. The people in the model economy perform the calculations that we have just described. People in the real world just consume. We observe their consumption choices, not their mental gymnastics. The marginal utility theory proposes that the consumption patterns that we observe in the real world are similar to those implied by the model economy in which people do compute the quantities of goods that maximize utility. We test how closely the marginal utility model resembles reality by checking the predictions of the theory against observed consumption choices.

Marginal utility theory also has some broader implications that provide an interesting way of testing its usefulness. Let's examine two of these.

Table 7.6   Marginal Utility Theory

Assumptions

(a) A consumer derives utility from the goods consumed.

(b) Each additional unit of consumption yields additional utility; marginal utility is positive.

(c) As the quantity of a good consumed increases, marginal utility decreases.

Implication

Utility is maximized when the marginal utility per dollar spent is equal for all goods.

Predictions

(a) Other things being equal, the higher the price of a good, the lower is the quantity bought (the law of demand).

(b) The higher the price of a good, the higher is the consumption of substitutes for that good.

(c) The higher the consumer's income, the greater is the quantity demanded of normal goods.

Some Implications of Marginal Utility Theory

We all love bargains—paying less for something than its usual price. One implication of the marginal utility theory is that we almost *always* get a bargain when we buy something. That is, we place a higher total value on the things we buy than the amount that it costs us. Let's see why.

Consumer Surplus and the Gains from Trade

In Chapter 3, we saw how people can gain by specializing in the things at which they have a comparative advantage and then trading with each other. Marginal utility theory provides a precise way of measuring the gains from trade.

When Lisa buys movies and soda, she exchanges her income for them. Does Lisa profit from

Figure 7.3   Consumer Surplus   ◇

Lisa is willing to pay $7 to watch her first movie, $6 to watch her second, $5 to watch her third, and $4 to watch her fourth. She actually has to pay only $3 for each movie. At that price, she sees 5 movies. She has a consumer surplus on the first four movies equal to $10—the difference between the highest price she is willing to pay and the price actually paid ($4 + $3 + $2 + $1).

this exchange? Are the dollars she has to give up worth more or less than the movies and soda are worth to her? As we are about to discover, the principle of diminishing marginal utility guarantees that Lisa, and everyone else, gets more value from the things they buy than the amount of money they give up in exchange.

Calculating Consumer Surplus

The **value** of a good is the maximum amount that a person would be willing to pay for it. The amount that a person has actually paid for a good is its price. **Consumer surplus** is the difference between the value of a good and its price. The principle of diminishing marginal utility guarantees that a consumer always makes some consumer surplus. To understand why, let's look again at Lisa's consumption choices.

As before, let's assume that Lisa has $30 a month to spend, that movies cost $3 each, and that she watches 6 movies each month. Now let's look at Lisa's demand curve for movies, shown in Fig. 7.3. We can see from Lisa's demand curve that if she were able to watch only 1 movie a month she would be willing to pay $7 to see it. She would be willing to pay $6 to see a second movie, $5 to see a third, and so on.

Luckily for Lisa, she has to pay only $3 for each movie she sees. Although she values the first movie she sees in a month at $7, she pays only $3—$4 less than she would be willing to pay. The second movie she sees in a month is worth $6 to her. The difference between the value she places on the movie and what she has to pay is $3 in this case. The third movie she sees in a month is worth $5 to her—$2 more than she has to pay for it, and the fourth movie is worth $4—$1 more than she has to pay for it. You can see this progression in Fig. 7.3, which highlights the difference between the price she pays ($3) and the higher value she places on the first, second, third, and fourth movies. These differences are a gain to Lisa. Let's calculate her total gain.

The total amount that Lisa is willing to pay for the 5 movies that she sees is $25 (the sum of $7, $6, $5, $4, and $3). She actually pays $15 (5 movies multiplied by $3). The extra value she receives from the movies is therefore $10. This amount is the value of Lisa's consumer surplus. From watching 5 movies a month, she gets $10 worth of value in excess of what she has to spend to see them.

Let's now look at another implication of the marginal utility theory.

The Paradox of Value

More than 200 years ago, Adam Smith posed a paradox that we also raised at the start of this chapter. Water, which is essential to life itself, costs little, but diamonds, which are useless compared to water, are expensive. Why? Adam Smith could not solve the paradox. Not until the theory of marginal utility had been invented could anyone give a satisfactory answer.

You can solve Adam Smith's puzzle by distinguishing between total utility and marginal utility. The total utility that we get from water is enormous. But remember, the more we consume of something, the smaller is its marginal utility. We use so much water that the marginal utility—the benefit we get from one more glass of water—diminishes to a tiny value. Diamonds, on the other hand, have a small total utility relative to water, but because we buy few diamonds, they have a high marginal utility.

Our theory also tells us that consumers spend in a way that makes the marginal utility from each good divided by its price equal for all goods. This also holds true for their spending on diamonds and water: Diamonds have a high marginal utility divided by a high price, while water has a low marginal utility divided by a low price. In each case, the marginal utility per dollar spent is the same.

■ We've now completed our study of the marginal utility theory of consumption. We've used that theory to examine how Lisa allocates her income between the two goods that she consumes—movies and soda. We've also seen how the theory can be used to resolve the paradox of value. Furthermore, we've seen how the theory can be used to explain our real-world consumption choices.

In the next chapter, we're going to study an alternative theory of household behavior. To help you see the connection between the marginal utility theory of this chapter and the more modern theory of consumer behavior of the next chapter, we'll continue with the same example. We'll meet Lisa again and discover another way of understanding how she gets the most out of her $30 a month.

S U M M A R Y

Individual Demand and Market Demand

Individual demand represents the relationship between the price of a good and the quantity demanded by a single individual. Market demand is the sum of all individual demands. (pp. 157–158)

Household Consumption Choices

The marginal utility theory explains how people divide their spending between goods and services. The theory is based on a model that assumes certain characteristics about the consumer: The consumer derives utility from the goods consumed. This utility rises as consumption of the good increases. The change in utility resulting from a one-unit increase in the consumption of a good is called marginal utility. Marginal utility declines as consumption rises. The consumer's goal is to maximize total utility, which occurs when the marginal utility per dollar spent on each good is equal. (pp. 158–163)

Predictions of Marginal Utility Theory

Marginal utility theory predicts how prices and income affect the amounts of each good consumed.

First, it predicts the law of demand. That is, other things being equal, the higher the price of a good, the lower is the quantity demanded of that good. Second, it predicts that, other things being equal, the higher the consumer's income, the greater is the consumption of all normal goods. (pp. 163–166)

Criticisms of Marginal Utility Theory

Some people criticize marginal utility theory because utility cannot be observed or measured. However, the size of the units of measurement of utility do not matter. All that matters is that the ratio of the marginal utility from each good to its price is equal for all goods. Any units of measure consistently applied will do. The concept of utility is analogous to the concept of temperature—it cannot be directly observed but it can be used to make predictions about events that are observable.

Another criticism of marginal utility theory is that consumers can't be as smart as the theory implies. In actuality, the theory makes no predictions about the thought processes of consumers. It only makes predictions about their actions and assumes that people spend their income in what seems to them to be the best possible way. (pp. 166–167)

Some Implications of Marginal Utility Theory

Marginal utility theory implies that every time we buy goods and services we get more value for our expenditure than the money we spend. We benefit from consumer surplus, which is equal to the difference between the maximum amount that we are willing to pay for a good and the price that we actually pay.

Marginal utility theory resolves the paradox of value: Water is extremely valuable but cheap, while diamonds are less valuable though expensive. When we talk loosely about value, we are thinking of total utility. The total utility of water is higher than the total utility of diamonds. The marginal utility of water, though, is lower than the marginal utility of diamonds. People choose the amount of water and diamonds to consume so as to maximize utility. In maximizing utility, they make the marginal utility per dollar spent the same for water as for diamonds. (pp. 167–169)

K E Y   C O N C E P T S

Consumer equilibrium, 161
Consumer surplus, 168
Diminishing marginal utility, 160
Individual demand, 157
Marginal utility, 159
Marginal utility per dollar spent, 162
Market demand, 157
Utility, 158
Utility maximization, 160
Value, 168

Key Figures and Tables

Figure 7.1   Individual and Market Demand Curves, 157
Figure 7.2   Utility and Marginal Utility, 159
Figure 7.3   Consumer Surplus, 168
Table 7.6   Marginal Utility 'teory, 167

R E V I E W   Q U E S T I O N S

1 What is the relationship between individual demand and market demand?

2 How do we construct a market demand curve from individual demand curves?

3 What do we mean by utility?

4 What is marginal utility?

5 How does marginal utility change as the level of consumption of a good changes?

6 Susan is a consumer living in Chicago. When is Susan's utility maximized? Explain your answer.

 a) When she has spent all her income

 b) When she has spent all her income and marginal utility is equal for all goods

 c) When she has spent all her income and the marginal utility per dollar spent is equal for all goods

7 What does the marginal utility theory predict about the effect of a change in price on the quantity of a good consumed?

8 What does the marginal utility theory predict about the effect of a change in the price of one good on the consumption of another good?

9 What does the marginal utility theory predict about the effect of a change in income on consumption?

10 How would you answer someone who says that the marginal utility theory is useless because utility cannot be observed?

11 How would you respond to someone who tells you that the marginal utility theory is useless because people are not smart enough to compute a consumer equilibrium in which the marginal utility per dollar spent is equal for all goods?

12 What is consumer surplus? How is consumer surplus calculated?

13 What is the paradox of value? How does the marginal utility theory resolve it?

14 Calculate Lisa's marginal utility from soda from the numbers given in Table 7.1. Draw two graphs, one of her utility and the other of her marginal utility from soda. Your graphs should look similar to those for movies in Fig. 7.2.

P R O B L E M S

1 Shirley's demand for yogurt is given by the following:

Price (dollars per pound)	Quantity (cartons per week)
1	9
2	7
3	5
4	3
5	2

a) Draw a graph for Shirley's demand for yogurt.

Dan also likes yogurt. His demand for yogurt is given by the following:

Price (dollars per pound)	Quantity (cartons per week)
1	5
2	4
3	3
4	2
5	1

b) Draw a graph of Dan's demand curve.

c) If Shirley and Dan are the only two individuals, construct the market demand schedule for yogurt.

d) Draw a graph of the market demand for yogurt.

e) Draw a graph to show that the market demand curve is the horizontal sum of Shirley's demand curve and Dan's demand curve.

2 Max enjoys windsurfing and snorkeling. He obtains the following utility from each of these sports:

Half-hours per month	Utility from windsurfing	Utility from snorkeling
1	60	20
2	110	38
3	150	53
4	180	64
5	200	70
6	210	70

a) Draw graphs showing Max's utility from windsurfing and from snorkeling.

b) Compare the two utility graphs. Can you say anything about Max's preferences?

c) Draw graphs showing Max's marginal utility from windsurfing and from snorkeling.

d) Compare the two marginal utility graphs. Can you say anything about Max's preferences?

3 Max has $35 to spend. Equipment for windsurfing rents for $10 a half-hour while snorkeling equipment rents for $5 a half-hour. Use this information together with that given in problem 1 to answer the following questions:

a) What is the marginal utility per dollar spent on snorkeling if Max snorkels for
  (i) Half an hour
  (ii) One and a half hours

b) What is the marginal utility per dollar spent on windsurfing if Max windsurfs for
  (i) Half an hour
  (ii) One hour

c) How long can Max afford to snorkel if he windsurfs for
  (i) Half an hour
  (ii) One hour
  (iii) One and a half hours

d) Will Max choose to snorkel for one hour and windsurf for one and a half hours?

e) Will he windsurf for more or less than one and a half hours?

f) How long will Max choose to windsurf and to snorkel?

4 Max's sister gives him $20 to spend on his leisure pursuits, so he now has $55 to spend. How long will Max windsurf and snorkel?

5 If Max has only $35 to spend and the rent on windsurfing equipment doubles to $20 a half-hour, how will Max now spend his time windsurfing and snorkeling?

6 Does Max's demand curve for windsurfing slope downward or upward?

7 Max takes a Club Med holiday, the cost of which includes unlimited sports activities—including windsurfing, snorkeling, and tennis. There is no extra charge for any equipment. Max decides to spend two hours each day on both windsurfing and snorkeling. How long does he windsurf? How long does he snorkel?

8 Sara also enjoys windsurfing. Her demand for windsurfing is given by the following:

Price (dollars per half-hour)	Time windsurfing (half-hours per month)
2.50	8
5.00	7
7.50	6
10.00	5
12.50	4
15.00	3
17.50	2
20.00	1

a) Windsurfing costs $10.00 a half-hour. If Sara windsurfs for a half an hour, what is her consumer surplus?

b) If Sara windsurfs for two and a half hours, what is her consumer surplus?

Chapter 8

(Alternative to Chapter 7)

Possibilities, Preferences, and Choices

After studying this chapter, you will be able to:

- Calculate and graph a household's budget line

- Work out how the budget line changes when prices and income change

- Make a map of preferences by using indifference curves

- Calculate a household's optimal consumption plan

- Predict the effects of price and income changes on the pattern of consumption

- Explain why the workweek gets shorter as wages rise

- Explain how budget lines and indifference curves can be used to understand all household choices

The past 30 years have seen great changes in how we spend our incomes. Some goods—from home videos to microwave popcorn—that now regularly appear on our shopping lists didn't exist before. Other goods, such as Davy Crockett coonskin caps and horse-drawn carriages, have virtually disappeared. Yet other goods, such as miniskirts, appear, disappear, and reappear in cycles of fashion. ■ But the glittering surface of our consumption obscures deeper and slower changes in how we spend. In the last few years, we've seen a proliferation of gourmet food shops and designer clothing boutiques. Yet we spend a smaller percentage of our income today on food and clothing than we did in 1950. Despite the proliferation of jet travel and interstate highways, we spend about the same percentage of our income on transportation today as we did 40 years ago. At the same time, the percentage of our income spent on fuel, housing, and medical care has grown steadily. Like the continents floating on the earth's mantle, our spending patterns change steadily over time. On such subterranean movements, business empires rise and fall. Why does consumer spending change over the years? How do people react to changes in income and changes in the prices of the things they buy? ■ There are similar subterranean movements governing most aspects of household behavior. For example, the average workweek has fallen steadily from 70 hours a week in the nineteenth century down to 35 hours a week today. Why has the average workweek declined? Similarly, there have been steady trends in fertility, marriage, education, crime, and social interactions. Why do the habits and social mores of one generation become the old-fashioned ideas of another?

Subterranean Movements

■ We're going to study a model of household behavior that has predictive power over an enormous range of choices. We'll first use the model to study consumption choice. We'll learn how to predict the way in which people spend their income and how spending changes when income and prices change. Then we'll see how this same model helps us to understand people's choices of hours of work and leisure, borrowing and lending, and even such sociological issues as fertility and the incidence of crime.

Consumption Possibilities

How does a household divide its income among the goods and services available? We are going to study a model of household behavior that can answer this question and that predicts how consumption patterns change when income and prices change. Our first step is to examine the constraint on the household's possible choices.

Constraint

A household's consumption choices are constrained by the household's income and by the prices of the goods and services available. We're going to study a household that has a given amount of income to spend and that cannot influence the prices of the goods and services that it buys. It has to take those prices as given.

The limits to a household's consumption choices are described by its **budget line.** In order to make the concept of the household's budget line as clear as possible, we'll consider the example of Lisa, who has an income of $30 a month to spend.[1] She buys two goods—movies and soda. Movies cost $6 each; soda costs $3 for a six-pack. If Lisa spends all of her income, she will reach the limits to her consumption of movies and soda.

---

[1]If you have read the preceding chapter on marginal utility theory, you have already met Lisa. This tale of her thirst for soda and zeal for movies will sound familiar to you—up to a point. But in this chapter, we're going to use a different method for representing preferences—one that does not require us to resort to the idea of utility. The appendix to this chapter explains the differences and the connections between the marginal utility approach and the approach of this chapter.

Figure 8.1   The Budget Line

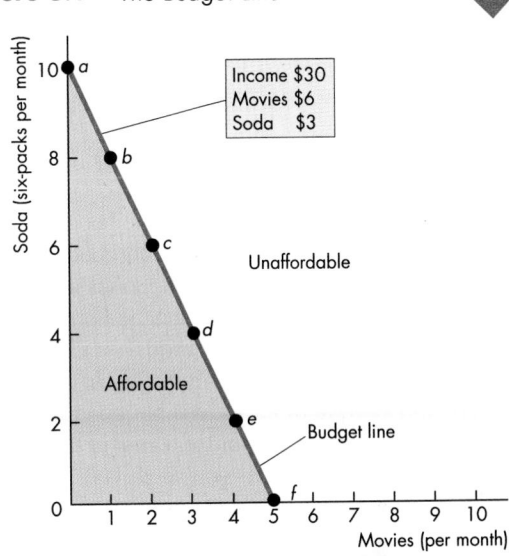

Consumption possibility	Movies (per month)	Soda (six-packs per month)
a	0	10
b	1	8
c	2	6
d	3	4
e	4	2
f	5	0

Lisa's budget line shows the boundary between what Lisa can and cannot afford. The table lists Lisa's affordable combinations of movies and soda when she has an income of $30 and when soda costs $3 a six-pack and movies cost $6 each. For example, row a tells us that Lisa can buy 10 six-packs and see no movies—a combination that exhausts her $30 income. The figure graphs Lisa's budget line. Points a through f on the graph represent rows of the table. For divisible goods, the budget line is the continuous line af.

In Fig. 8.1, each row of the table shows an affordable way for Lisa to consume movies and soda. Row a indicates that she can buy 10 six-packs of soda and see no movies. You can see that this combination of movies and soda exhausts her monthly income of $30. Now look at row *f*. It says that Lisa can watch 5 movies and drink no soda—another combination that exhausts the $30 available. Each of the other rows in the table also exhausts Lisa's income. (Check that each of the other rows costs exactly $30.) The numbers in the table define Lisa's consumption possibilities. We can graph Lisa's consumption possibilities as points *a* through *f*.

Divisible and Indivisible Goods   Some goods can be bought in any quantity desired. Such goods are called divisible. Examples of divisible goods are gasoline and electricity, both of which can be bought in almost any quantity at all. Other goods—called indivisible goods—can be bought only in whole units. Movies are an example of an indivisible good. Although you can watch a fraction of a movie (as presumably you've done when you've picked a loser), you can buy movies only in whole units.

We can best understand the model of consumer behavior that we are about to study if we suppose that all goods and services are divisible. In this case, the consumption possibilities are not just the points *a* through *f* shown in Fig. 8.1, but those points plus all the intermediate points that form a continuous straight line running from *a* to *f*. Such a line is a budget line. Thus, for example, if instead of movies and soda we measure gallons of gasoline on the vertical axis and yards of cloth on the horizontal axis, Lisa can buy at any point along the line, consuming any fraction of a gallon or a yard.

Though Lisa can consume at only one of the six points represented by each row of the table in our example, we'll develop the model so that it can deal with the more general case in which goods are divisible into any desired units.

Lisa's budget line is a constraint on her choices. It marks the boundary between what is affordable and what is unaffordable. She can afford all the points on the line and inside it. She cannot afford points outside the line. The constraint on her consumption depends on prices and on her income, and the constraint changes when prices and her income change.

The Budget Equation

To discover how the constraint on consumption changes when prices and income change, we need to describe the budget line in the form of an equation. Such an equation is called the budget equation. The **budget equation** states the limits to consumption

for a given income and for given prices. We're going to work out such an equation and, to keep things tidy, we'll summarize our calculations in Table 8.1.

The left side of the table works out the budget equation by using symbols that apply to any consumer; the right side of the table works out the equation by using numbers that describe Lisa's situation. The first section of the table lists the variables that affect a household's budget. Those variables are income, the prices of the goods consumed, and the quantities consumed. To make our calculations clear, we have assigned symbols to each of these variables. In Lisa's case, her income is $30, the prices are $6 for movies and $3 for soda, and Lisa will choose the quantities of movies and soda to consume.

The consumer's budget is set out in the second section of the table. It states that expenditure (on the left side of the equation) equals income (on the right side of the equation). Look at the elements of expenditure. Expenditure is equal to the sum of the expenditures on each of the goods. Expenditure on any one good equals its price multiplied by the quantity consumed. In Lisa's case, income (on the right side) is $30, and the most that she can spend (on the left side of the equation) is the amount of soda consumed (Q_s) multiplied by the price of a soda ($3) plus the number of movies consumed (Q_m) multiplied by their price ($6).

The third section of the table shows you how to derive the budget equation from the consumer's budget. There are just two steps. First, divide both sides by the price of soda. Second, subtract $(P_m/P_s)Q_m$ from both sides of the resulting equation. The result is the budget equation shown in the last line of the table. This equation tells us how the consumption of one good varies as consumption of the other good varies. To interpret the equation, let's go back to the budget line of Fig. 8.1.

Let's first check that the budget equation that we have derived in Table 8.1 delivers the graph of the budget line in Fig. 8.1. Begin by setting Q_m equal to zero. In this case, the budget equation tells us that Q_s will be 10. This combination of Q_s and Q_m is the same as that shown in row *a* of the table in Fig. 8.1. Setting Q_m equal to 5 makes Q_s equal to zero (row *f* of the table in Fig. 8.1). Check that you can derive the other rows of the table in Fig. 8.1.

The budget equation contains two variables under the control of the individual (Q_m and Q_s) and two numbers outside the individual's control. Let's look more closely at the two numbers outside the individual's control (y/P_s and P_m/P_s).

Table 8.1   Calculating the Budget Equation

In General		In Lisa's Case
1. The variables		
Income	$= y$	$y = \$30$
Price of movies	$= P_m$	$P_m = \$6$
Price of soda	$= P_s$	$P_s = \$3$
Quantity of movies	$= Q_m$	$Q_m =$ Lisa's choice
Quantity of soda	$= Q_s$	$Q_s =$ Lisa's choice

2. The budget

$$P_s Q_s + P_m Q_m = y \qquad\qquad \$3Q_s + \$6Q_m = \$30$$

3. Calculating the budget equation

- Divide by P_s to obtain:

$$Q_s + \frac{P_m}{P_s} Q_m = \frac{y}{P_s}$$

- Subtract $(P_m/P_s)Q_m$ from both sides to obtain:

$$Q_s = \frac{y}{P_s} - \frac{P_m}{P_s} Q_m$$

- Divide by $3 to obtain:

$$Q_s + 2\,Q_m = 10$$

- Subtract $2\,Q_m$ from both sides to obtain:

$$Q_s = 10 - 2\,Q_m$$

The first number y/P_s, or 10 in Lisa's case, is the maximum number of six-packs that can be bought. It is called real income in terms of soda. **Real income** is income expressed in units of goods. Real income in terms of a particular good is income divided by the price of that good. In Lisa's case, her real income is 10 six-packs. In Fig. 8.1, the budget line intersects the vertical axis at Lisa's real income in terms of soda. That is, if Lisa spends all her income on soda, she can buy 10 six-packs.

Let's now look at the second number in the budget equation that is outside the consumer's control (P_m/P_s), or 2 in Lisa's case. This number shows the relative price of the two goods. A **relative price** is the price of one good divided by the price of another good. In the equation, P_m/P_s is the relative price of movies in terms of soda. For Lisa, that relative price is 2. That is, in order to see one more movie, she has to give up 2 six-packs.

You can see the relative price of movies to soda in Fig. 8.1 (p. 175) as the magnitude of the slope of the budget line. To calculate the slope of the budget line, recall the formula for slope that was introduced in Chapter 2: Slope equals the change in soda divided by the change in movies. In Lisa's case, the change in movies is 5 and the change in soda is -10. (As movies increase from 0 to 5, soda falls from 10 to 0.) Therefore the slope of the budget line is $-10/5$, or -2. The flatter the slope of the budget line, the less expensive is the good measured on the horizontal axis relative to the good measured on the vertical axis. The steeper the line, the more expensive is the good measured on the horizontal axis relative to the one on the vertical axis. In other words, the slope of the budget line is the relative price of the good whose quantity appears on the horizontal axis.

The relative price of one good in terms of another is the opportunity cost of the first good in terms of the second. In Lisa's case, the opportunity cost of one movie is 2 six-packs of soda. Equivalently, the opportunity cost of 2 six-packs of soda is one movie.

Changes in Prices and Income

Let's now work out what happens to the budget line when prices and income change. We'll begin with a change in the price of one good.

A change in the price of movies   Suppose that the price of movies rises. What happens to Lisa's budget line? To make things vivid, let's suppose that the price of movies halves to $3 a movie. By working through the calculations in Table 8.1, you can work out Lisa's budget line with the new price of movies. Recall that the budget equation is

$$Q_s = \frac{y}{P_s} - \frac{P_m}{P_s} Q_m.$$

Nothing has happened to income (y) or the price of soda (P_s). Lisa's real income in terms of soda remains 10. But the price of movies has fallen and is now equal to the price of soda. Therefore the relative price of movies P_m/P_s has decreased to 1. Lisa's new budget equation is

$$Q_s = 10 - Q_m.$$

Let's check that this new budget equation works. With movies costing $3 each, Lisa can see as many

Figure 8.2   Prices, Income, and the Budget Line

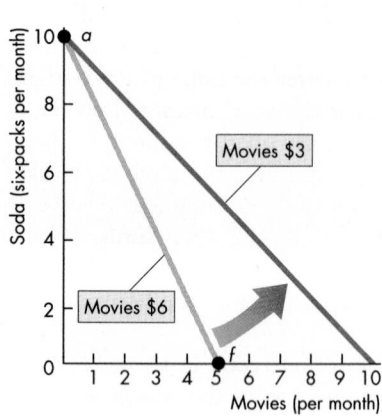

(a) A fall in the price of movies

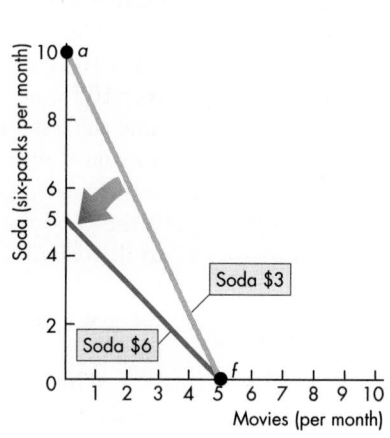

(b) A rise in the price of soda

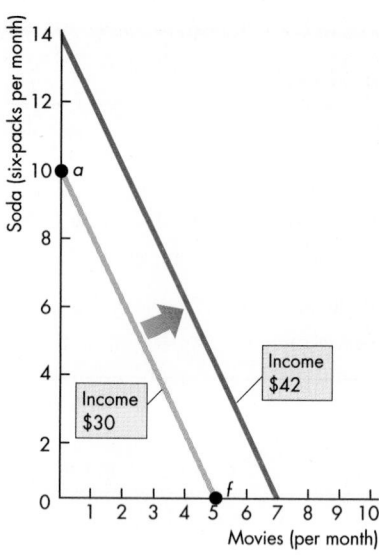

(c) A rise in income

In part (a), the price of a movie falls from $6 to $3. In part (b), the price of a six-pack of soda
increases from $3 to $6. In part (c), income increases from $30 to $42, but prices remain constant.
The arrow in each part indicates the shift in the budget line.

as 10 movies with her income. Using Lisa's new
budget equation, you will see that substituting 10 for
Q_m results in zero for Q_s. We know that this answer
is correct because if Lisa sees 10 movies, she spends
all her income on movies and has nothing left for
soda.

Figure 8.2(a) shows how the fall in the price of
movies affects the budget line. Because the price of
movies has gone down, the new budget line is flatter
than budget line *af*. But notice that point *a* has not
changed. If Lisa spends all her income on soda, she
can still buy 10 six-packs. In other words, Lisa's real
income in terms of soda has not changed. Only the
price of movies has changed. Movies have become
cheaper in terms of soda. Previously, 1 movie was
worth 2 six-packs. In the new situation, the relative
price or opportunity cost of 1 movie is 1 six-pack.

Let's see what happens to the budget line when
the price of soda changes.

A Change in the Price of Soda   Let's go back to
the original situation in which movies cost $6 each
and soda $3 a six-pack. What happens to Lisa's

budget line if the price of a six-pack rises? Let's
suppose that the price goes up from $3 to $6. If Lisa
spends all her income on soda, she can buy 5 six-
packs. Her real income in terms of soda has gone
down. Since movies cost $6 each and soda costs $6 a
six-pack, the relative price of movies is 1, the same
as in the previous example. The opportunity cost of
1 movie is 1 six-pack of soda. We can work out the
new budget line by using the budget equation:

$$Q_s = \frac{y}{P_s} - \frac{P_m}{P_s} Q_m.$$

The price of soda P_s is now $6. Lisa's income is still
$30 and the price of a movie is still $6. So Lisa's
budget equation is

$$Q_s = \frac{30}{6} - \frac{6}{6} Q_m,$$

or $Q_s = 5 - Q_m.$

Figure 8.2(b) shows the new budget line. Notice this
time point *f* has not moved. If Lisa spends all her income on movies, she can still see only 5 movies. Her
real income in terms of movies has not changed.

Look at the new budget lines in parts (a) and (b). In part (a), both movies and soda cost $3; in part (b), they both cost $6. Lisa earns $30 in both cases. Therefore in part (b), she can consume less of everything than in part (a), but movies have the same opportunity cost in the two cases—to see 1 more movie she must give up 1 six-pack of soda. Notice that the new budget line in part (b) has the same slope as the new budget line in part (a).

Let's now see what happens to the budget line when income changes.

A Change in Income   If prices remain constant and income rises, a person can then consume more of all goods. Go back to the initial situation when Lisa had an income of $30, a movie cost $6, and a six-pack cost $3. Keeping the prices of the two goods constant, let's work out what happens if Lisa's income goes up from $30 to $42. Again, recall the budget equation:

$$Q_s = \frac{y}{P_s} - \frac{P_m}{P_s} Q_m.$$

Let's put into this equation the numbers for prices and for the new income. The price of soda (P_s) is $3 and the price of movies (P_m) is $6. Income ($y$) is $42. Putting these numbers into the equation gives

$$Q_s = \frac{42}{3} - \frac{6}{3} Q_m,$$
$$\text{or } Q_s = 14 - 2 Q_m.$$

Lisa's real income has gone up because her money income has gone up, while the prices of movies and soda have stayed the same. Her real income in terms of soda has gone up from 10 to 14. That is, if she spends all her income on soda, she can now buy 14 six-packs. Her real income in terms of movies has also gone up. If she spends all her income on movies, she can see 7 movies.

The shift in Lisa's budget line is shown in Fig. 8.2(c). The initial budget line is the same one that we began with in parts (a) and (b) when Lisa's income was $30. The new budget line shows Lisa able to consume more of each good. The new line is parallel to the old one but farther out. The two budget lines are parallel, or have the same slope, because the relative price is the same in both cases. With movies costing $6 each and a six-pack $3 each, Lisa must give up 2 six-packs to see 1 movie. The new budget line is farther out than the initial one because her real income has risen.

The budget line describes the maximum amounts of consumption that a household can undertake given its income and the prices of the goods that it buys. A change in the price of one good changes the slope of the budget line. If the price of the good measured on the horizontal axis rises, the budget line gets steeper. A change in income makes the budget line shift, but its slope does not change. ■

Let's now leave the budget line and look at the second ingredient in the model of consumer choice: preferences.

Preferences

P references are a person's likes and dislikes. There are three fundamental assumptions about preferences:

- Preferences do not depend on the prices of goods.
- Preferences do not depend on income.
- More of any good is preferred to less of that good.

The first two assumptions amount to the proposition that people's likes and dislikes do not depend on what they can afford to buy. This assumption does *not* mean that people's preferences do not change over time. Nor does it mean that their preferences are not influenced by the things that they have consumed and experienced. It *does* mean that just because income increases or the price of a good decreases, people do not, *for one of those reasons,* suddenly decide that they like a particular good more than they did before.

The third assumption—more of any good is preferred to less of that good—is just a different way of saying that wants are unlimited. Of course, in reality, you can imagine having enough of any one good to want no more of it, but there will always be something that you will prefer to have more of—that you will not prefer to have less of.

We are going to discover in this section a very neat idea—that of drawing a map of a person's preferences.

Figure 8.3   Mapping Preferences

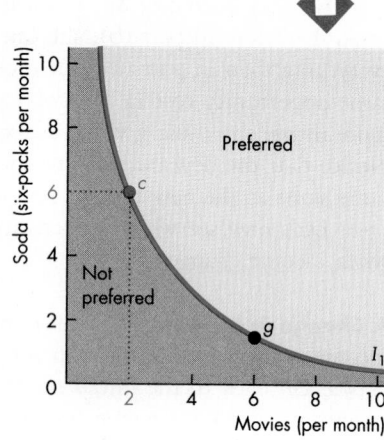

(a) A consumption point   **(b) Preference relations**   **(c) Indifference curve**

If Lisa consumes 6 six-packs of soda and 2 movies, she consumes at point c in part (a). Lisa prefers more goods to fewer goods. This fact is illustrated in part (b). She prefers any point at which she consumes more of both soda and movies to point c (all the points in the yellow area). She prefers point c to any point at which fewer movies and six-packs are consumed (all the points in the gray area). If she sees more movies but has less soda than at point c, whether she prefers c or not depends on how many more movies and how much less soda she has. Similarly, if she consumes more soda and sees fewer movies than at point c, whether she prefers that situation to c depends on how much more soda and how many fewer movies she has. The boundary between points that she prefers to points c and those to which c is preferred is shown in part (c). That boundary is called an indifference curve. Lisa is indifferent between points such as g and c on the indifference curve. She prefers any point above the indifference curve (yellow area) to any point on it, and she prefers any point on the indifference curve to any point below it (gray area).

A Preference Map

Let's see how we can draw a map of a person's preferences by constructing a map of Lisa's preferences for movies and soda. This map, which appears in Fig. 8.3, measures the number of movies seen on the horizontal axis and the number of six-packs consumed on the vertical axis. Let's start with Fig. 8.3(a) and focus on point c, where Lisa sees 2 movies and consumes 6 six-packs of soda. We will use this point as a reference and ask how Lisa likes all the other points in relation to point c.

Figure 8.3(b) takes us to the next step. It is divided into four areas. The area shaded orange has, at each point, more movies and more soda than at point c. Lisa prefers all the points in this area to point c. The area shaded gray has, at each point, fewer movies and less soda than at point c. She prefers point c to all the points in this area.

Points in the two white areas have either more movies and less soda than point c or more soda and fewer movies than point c. How does Lisa rank points in these areas against point c? To answer this question, we need to take the final step in constructing a map of Lisa's preferences.

Figure 8.3(c) takes the final step. It contains a line—I_1—passing through point c and through what were the two white areas. That line defines the boundary between points that Lisa prefers to point c and points she regards as inferior to point c. Lisa is indifferent between point c and the other points on line I_1 such as point g. The line itself is called an indifference curve. An **indifference curve** is a line that shows all combinations of two goods among which the consumer is indifferent. The indifference curve shown in Fig. 8.3(c) shows all the combinations of movies and soda among which Lisa is indifferent.

The indifference curve shown in Fig. 8.3(c) is just one of a whole family of such curves. This indifference curve appears again in Fig. 8.4. It is labeled I_1, and passes through points c and g. Two other indifference curves are I_0 and I_2. Lisa prefers any point on indifference curve I_2 to those on indifference curve I_1 and she prefers any point on I_1 to those on I_0. We refer to I_2 as being a higher indifference curve to I_1 and I_1 as higher than I_0.

Indifference curves never intersect each other. To see why, consider indifference curves I_1 and I_2 in Fig. 8.4. We know that point j is preferred to point c. We also know that all points on indifference curve I_2 are preferred to all points on indifference curve I_1. If these indifference curves did intersect, the consumer would be indifferent between the combination of goods at the intersection point and combinations c and j. But we know that point j is preferred to point c, so such a point cannot exist. Hence the indifference curves never intersect.

A preference map consists of a series of indifference curves. The indifference curves shown in Fig. 8.4 are only a part of Lisa's preference map. Her entire map consists of an infinite number of indifference curves, all of them sloping downward and none of them intersecting. They resemble the contour lines on a map measuring the height of mountains. An indifference curve joins points representing combinations of goods among which a consumer is indifferent in much the same way that contour lines on a map join points of equal height above sea level. By looking at the shape of the contour lines on a map, we can draw conclusions about the terrain. In the same way, by looking at the shape of a person's indifference curves we can draw conclusions about preferences. But interpreting a preference map requires a bit of work. It also requires some way of describing the shape of the indifference curves. In the next two sections, we'll learn how to "read" a preference map.

Indifference Curves and Preferences

We use the concept of the marginal rate of substitution to describe the shape of an indifference curve. The **marginal rate of substitution** (or **MRS**) is the rate at which a person will give up good y in order to get more of good x and at the same time remain indifferent. The marginal rate of substitution is measured from the slope of an in-

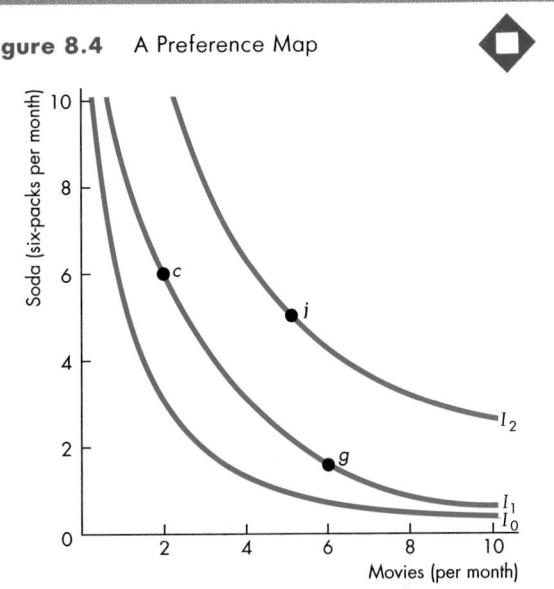

Figure 8.4   A Preference Map

A preference map consists of an infinite number of indifference curves. Here, we show just three — I_0, I_1, and I_2 — that are part of Lisa's preference map. Each indifference curve shows points among which Lisa is indifferent. For example, she is indifferent between point c and point g on indifference curve I_1. But Lisa prefers point j to points c or g; she prefers all the points on indifference curve I_2 to all the points on indifference curve I_1. Points on a higher indifference curve are preferred to points on a lower curve.

difference curve. If the indifference curve is steep, the marginal rate of substitution is high. The person is willing to give up a large quantity of good y (measured on the vertical axis) in exchange for a small quantity of good x (measured on the horizontal axis) while remaining indifferent. If the indifference curve is flat, the marginal rate of substitution is low. The person is willing to give up only a small amount of good y and must be compensated with a large amount of good x to remain indifferent.

Let's work out the marginal rate of substitution in two cases, both illustrated in Fig. 8.5. The curve labeled I_1 is one of Lisa's indifference curves. Suppose that Lisa drinks 6 six-packs of soda and watches 2 movies (point c in the figure). What is her marginal rate of substitution at this point? It is calculated by measuring the magnitude of the slope of the indifference curve at that point. To measure the slope, place a straight line against, or tangential

Figure 8.5   The Marginal Rate of Substitution

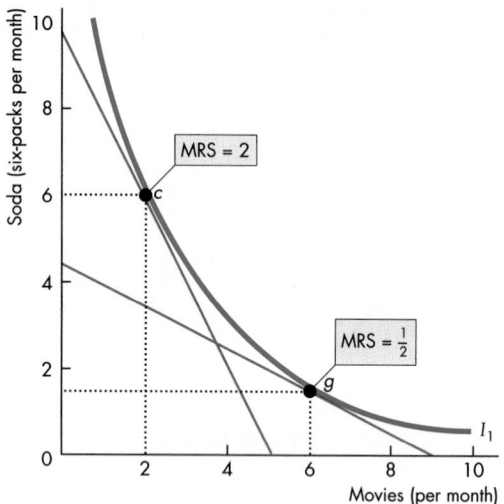

The slope of an indifference curve is called the marginal rate of substitution, or MRS. The marginal rate of substitution measures how much of one good a person is willing to give up to gain more of another good, while remaining indifferent. The marginal rate of substitution at point c is 2; at point g it is ½.

to, the indifference curve at that point. The slope of that line is the change in soda divided by the change in movies. As movies increase by 5, soda falls by 10. The slope of that line is −2. Thus when Lisa is consuming 2 movies and 6 six-packs of soda, her marginal rate of substitution is 2.

Now, suppose that Lisa is consuming 6 movies and 1.5 six-packs (point g in Fig. 8.5). What is her marginal rate of substitution at this point? The answer is found by calculating the slope of the indifference curve at that point. That slope is the same as the slope of the straight line that is drawn tangential to the point. Again, the slope equals the change in soda divided by the change in movies. As movies increase by 9, soda falls by 4.5. The slope of the line is −1/2. Thus when Lisa sees 6 movies and consumes 1.5 six-packs of soda, she is willing to substitute movies for soda at the rate of half a six-pack per movie while remaining indifferent. Her marginal rate of substitution is 1/2.

Notice that if Lisa drinks a lot of soda and does not see many movies, her marginal rate of substitution is high. If she watches a lot of movies and does not drink much soda, her marginal rate of substitution is low. This feature of the marginal rate of substitution is the central assumption of the theory of consumer behavior and is referred to as diminishing marginal rate of substitution. The assupmption of **diminishing marginal rate of substitution** is the general tendency for the marginal rate of substitution to diminish as the consumer moves along an indifference curve, increasing consumption of good x and decreasing consumption of good y.

You may be able to appreciate why we assume that the marginal rate of substitution diminishes by thinking about your own preferences. Imagine two situations: In one, you are watching 3 movies a night but have no soda. In the other, you have 6 six-packs of soda and no movies. In the first situation, you will probably willingly give up seeing 1 movie if you can get just a small amount of soda in exchange. In the second situation, you will probably be willing to give up quite a lot of soda to watch just 1 movie. Your preferences satisfy the assumption of diminishing marginal rate of substitution.

The shape of the indifference curves incorporates the assumption of diminishing marginal rate of substitution because these curves are bowed toward the origin. The tightness of the bend of an indifference curve tells us how willing a person is to substitute one good for another while remaining indifferent. Let's look at some examples that will clarify this point.

Degree of Substitutability

Most of us would not regard movies and soda as being close substitutes for each other. We probably have some fairly clear ideas about how many movies we want to see each month and how many cans of soda we want to drink. Nevertheless, to some degree, we are willing to substitute between these two goods. No matter how big a soda freak you are, there is surely some increase in the number of movies you can see that will compensate you for being deprived of a can of soda. Similarly, no matter how addicted you are to the movies, surely some number of cans of soda will compensate you

Figure 8.6 The Degree of Substitutability

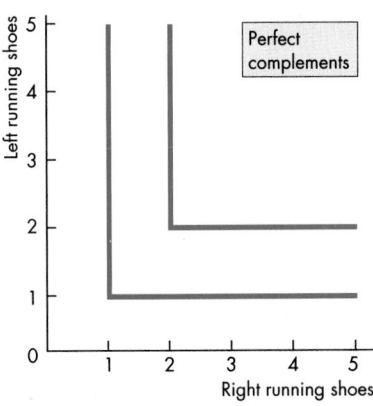

(a) Ordinary goods   **(b) Perfect substitutes**   **(c) Perfect complements**

The shape of the indifference curves reveals the degree of substitutability between two goods. Part (a) shows the indifference curves for two ordinary goods: movies and soda. To remain indifferent as less soda is consumed, one must see more movies. The number of movies that compensates for a reduction in soda increases as less soda is consumed. Part (b) shows the indifference curves for two perfect substitutes. For the consumer to remain indifferent, one fewer can of Schweppes diet soda must be replaced by one extra can of Canada Dry diet soda. Part (c) shows two perfect complements—goods that cannot be substituted for each other at all. Two left running shoes with one right running shoe is no better than one of each. But two of each is preferred to one of each.

for being deprived of seeing one movie. A person's indifference curves for movies and soda might look something like those shown in Fig. 8.6(a).

Close Substitutes Some goods substitute so easily for each other that most of us do not even notice which we are consuming. A good example concerns different brands of personal computers. Zenith, Leading Edge, and Tandy are all clones of the IBM PC—but most of us can't tell the difference between the three clones and indeed the IBM machine itself. The same holds true for soda. Except for a few connoisseurs, most of us don't care whether we are drinking Canada Dry or Schweppes diet soda. When two goods are perfect substitutes for each other, their indifference curves are straight lines that slope downward, as illustrated in Fig. 8.6(b). The marginal rate of substitution between perfect substitutes is constant.

Complements Some goods cannot substitute for each other at all. Instead they are complements. The complements in Fig. 8.6(c) are left and right running shoes. Indifference curves of perfect complements are L-shaped. One left running shoe and one right running shoe are as good as one left shoe and two right ones. Two of each is preferred to one of each, but two of one and one of the other is no better than one of each.

The extreme cases of perfect substitutes and perfect complements shown here don't often happen in reality. They do, however, illustrate that the shape of the indifference curve shows the degree of substitutability between two goods. The more perfectly substitutable the two goods, the more nearly are their indifference curves straight lines and the less quickly does the marginal rate of substitution fall. Poor substitutes for each other have tightly curved indifference curves, approaching the shape of those shown in Fig. 8.6(c).

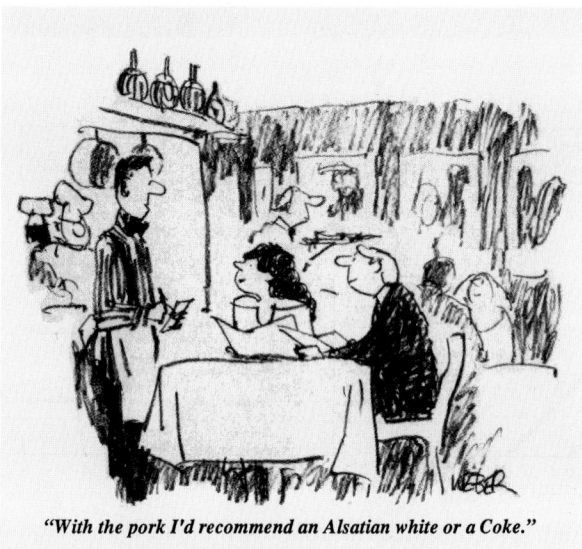

"With the pork I'd recommend an Alsatian white or a Coke."

Drawing by Weber; © 1988 The New Yorker Magazine, Inc.

As you can see in the cartoon, according to the waiter's preferences, Coke and Alsatian white wine are perfect substitutes for each other and are each complements with pork. We hope the customers agree with him.

R E V I E W

A person's preferences can be represented by a preference map. A preference map consists of a series of indifference curves. Indifference curves slope downward, bow toward the origin, and do not intersect each other. The slope of an indifference curve is called the marginal rate of substitution. The marginal rate of substitution falls as a person consumes less of good y and more of good x. The tightness of an indifference curve tells us how well two goods substitute for each other. Indifference curves that are almost straight lines indicate that the goods are close substitutes. Indifference curves that are tightly curved and that approach an L-shape indicate that the two goods complement each other. ∎

The two components of the model of consumer behavior are now in place: the budget line and the preference map. We will now use these two components to work out the consumer's choice.

Choice

Recall that Lisa has $30 to spend and she buys only two goods: movies (at $6 each) and soda (at $3 a six-pack). We've learned how to construct Lisa's budget line, which summarizes what she can buy, given her income and the prices of movies and soda (Fig. 8.1). We've also learned how to characterize Lisa's preferences in terms of her indifference curves (Fig. 8.4). We are now going to bring Lisa's budget line and indifference curves together and discover her best affordable way of consuming movies and soda.

The analysis is summarized in Fig. 8.7. You can see in that figure the budget line from Fig. 8.1 and the indifference curves from Fig. 8.4. Let's first focus on point h on indifference curve I_0. That point is on Lisa's budget line, so we know that she can afford it. But does she prefer this combination of movies and soda over all the other affordable combinations? The answer is no, she does not. To see why not, consider point c where she consumes 2 movies and 6 six-packs. Point c is also on Lisa's budget line, so we know she can afford to consume at this point. But point c is on indifference curve I_1, a higher indifference curve than I_0. Therefore we know that Lisa prefers point c to point h.

Are there any affordable points that Lisa prefers to point c? The answer is that there are not. All Lisa's other affordable consumption points—all the other points on or below her budget line—lie on indifference curves that are below I_1. Indifference curve I_1 is the highest indifference curve on which Lisa can afford to consume.

Let's look more closely at Lisa's best affordable choice.

Properties of the Best Affordable Point

Two properties of point c need to be highlighted. First, the best affordable point is *on* the budget line. If Lisa chooses a point inside the budget line, she will have an affordable point on the budget line where she can consume more of both goods. Lisa prefers that point to the one inside the budget line. The best affordable point cannot be outside the budget line because Lisa cannot afford such a point.

Second, the chosen point is where the highest attainable indifference curve has the same slope as the budget line. Stated another way, the marginal

Figure 8.7   The Best Affordable Point

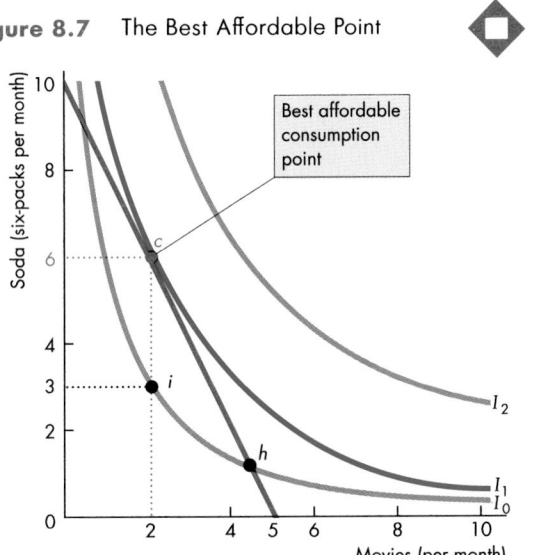

Lisa's best affordable point is c. At that point, she is on her budget line and so spends her entire income on the two goods. She is also on the highest attainable indifference curve. Indifference curves above I_1 (such as I_2) do not touch her budget line and so she cannot afford any point on them. At point c, the marginal rate of substitution (the slope of the indifference curve) equals the relative price of movies (the slope of the budget line). A point such as h on the budget line is not Lisa's best affordable point because at that point she is willing to give up more movies in exchange for soda than she has to. She can move to a point such as i, which she regards as being just as good as point h and which allows her to still have some income left over. She can spend that income and move to c, a point that she prefers to point i.

rate of substitution between the two goods (the slope of the indifference curve) equals their relative price (the slope of the budget line).

To see why this condition describes the best affordable point, consider point h, which Lisa regards as inferior to point c. At point h, Lisa's marginal rate of substitution is less than the relative price—indifference curve I_0 has a flatter slope than Lisa's budget line. As Lisa gives up movies for soda and moves up indifference curve I_0, she moves inside her budget line and has some money left over. She can move to point i, for example,

where she consumes 2 movies and 3 six-packs and has $9 to spare. She is indifferent between the combination of goods at point i and at point h. But she prefers point c to point i, since at c she has more soda than at i and sees the same number of movies.

By moving along her budget line from point h toward point c, Lisa passes through a whole array of indifference curves (not shown in the figure) located between indifference curves I_0 and I_1. All of these indifference curves are higher than I_0 and therefore any point on them is preferred to point h. Once she gets to point c, Lisa has reached the highest attainable indifference curve. If she keeps moving along the budget line, she will now start to encounter indifference curves that lie below I_1.

R E V I E W

The consumer has a given income and faces fixed prices. The consumer's problem is to allocate that fixed income in the best possible way. Affordable combinations of goods are described by the consumer's budget line. The consumer's preferences are represented by indifference curves. The consumer's best allocation of income occurs when all income is spent (on the budget line) and when the marginal rate of substitution (the slope of the indifference curve) equals the relative price (the slope of the budget line). ∎

We will now use this model of consumer choice to make some predictions about the effects of changes in prices and income on consumption patterns.

Predicting Consumer Behavior

Let's examine how consumers respond to changes in prices and income. We'll start by looking at the effect of a change in price. By studying the effect of a change in price on a consumer's choice, holding all other effects constant, we are able to derive a consumer's demand curve.

Figure 8.8   The Price Effect and the Demand Curve

(a) Price effect

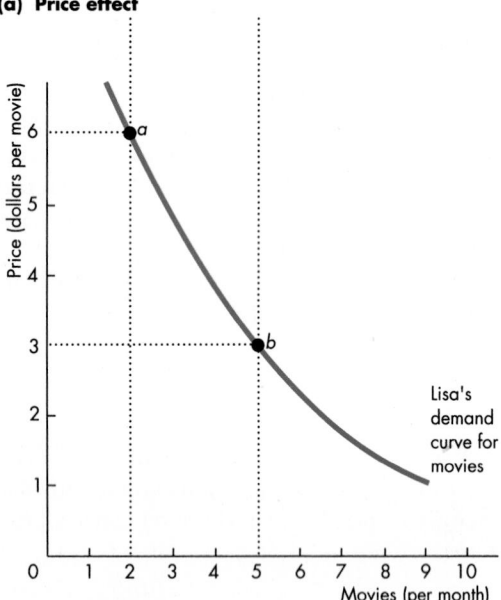

(b) Demand curve

Initially, Lisa consumes at point c (part a). If the price of a movie falls from $6 to $3, she consumes at point j. The increase in the consumption of movies from 2 to 5 per month is the price effect. When the price of a movie falls, Lisa consumes more movies. She also consumes less soda. Lisa's demand curve for movies is shown in part (b). When the price of movies is $6, she consumes 2 a month, at point a. When the price of movies falls to $3, she consumes 5 a month, at point b. The demand curve is traced by varying the price of movies and calculating Lisa's best affordable consumption of movies for each different price.

A Change in Price: The Demand Curve

The effect of a change in price on the quantity of a good consumed is called the **price effect.** Let's work out the price effect of a fall in the price of movies and derive Lisa's demand curve for movies. We'll start out with movies costing $6 each, soda costing $3 a six-pack, and with Lisa's income being $30 a month. In this situation, she consumes at point c (Fig. 8.8a) where her budget line is tangential to her highest attainable indifference curve, I_1. She consumes 6 six-packs and 2 movies a month.

Now suppose that the price of a movie falls to $3. We've already seen how a change in price (in Fig. 8.2a) affects the budget line. With a lower price of movies, the budget line moves outward and becomes less steep. You can see the new budget line (dark red) in Fig. 8.8(a).

Lisa's new best affordable point is j, where she consumes 5 movies and 5 six-packs of soda. As you can see, Lisa drinks less soda and watches more movies now that movies cost less. Her soda consumption has been cut from 6 to 5 six-packs, and her movie consumption has gone up from 2 to 5.

This analysis of the effect of a change in the price of movies enables us to derive Lisa's demand curve for movies. Lisa's demand curve is derived by gradually lowering the price and calculating the best affordable point at each different price. Figure 8.8(b) highlights just two prices and two points that lie on Lisa's demand curve for movies. When the price of movies is $6, Lisa consumes two movies a month at point a. When the price falls to $3, she increases her consumption to 5 movies a month at point b. The entire demand curve is made up of the two points that we've derived plus all the other points that tell us Lisa's best affordable consumption of movies at each price—above $6, between $6 and $3, and below $3. As you can see, Lisa's demand curve for movies slopes downward—the lower the price of a movie, the more movies she watches each month.

Next, let's examine what happens when Lisa's income changes.

A Change in Income

We've already seen, earlier in this chapter, how a change in income shifts the budget line. We worked out and illustrated (in Fig. 8.2c) that a rise in income shifts the budget line outward, with its slope unchanged.

Figure 8.9   The Income Effect

(a) Normal goods

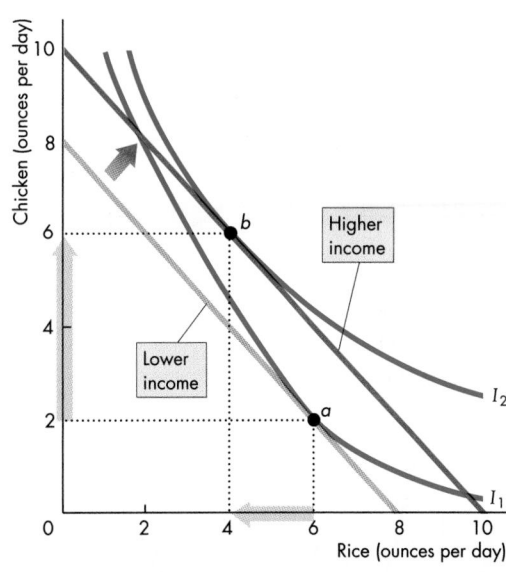

(b) Inferior good

An increase in income increases the consumption of most goods. These goods are normal goods. In part (a), Lisa consumes more of both soda and movies (as shown by the orange arrows) as her income increases.

Soda and movies are normal goods, but some goods are inferior goods. The consumption of inferior goods decreases as income increases. In part (b), as income increases, the consumption of rice decreases (and more chicken is consumed), again shown by the orange arrows. For this consumer, rice is an inferior good.

It will be clear to you that, as income rises, a person can consume more of all goods. But being able to consume more of all goods does not mean that a person will consume more of all goods. Goods are classified into two groups: normal goods and inferior goods. *Normal goods* are goods whose consumption increases as income increases. *Inferior goods* are goods whose consumption decreases as income increases. As the name implies, most goods are normal goods. A few examples of inferior goods, however, do exist. Rice and potatoes are perhaps the most obvious. People with low incomes have a heavy rice or potato component to their diet. As incomes rise, people substitute chicken or beef—normal goods—for rice and potatoes. Thus

as income increases, the consumption of chicken and beef increases but that of rice and potatoes decreases.

The effect of a change in income on consumption is called the **income effect.** The income effect for a normal good is positive. That is, a rise in income produces a rise in consumption of a normal good. If all goods are normal, then the consumption of each good rises as income rises. In Lisa's case, both movies and soda are normal goods. Therefore as Lisa's income rises, she consumes more movies and more soda.

Parts (a) and (b) of Fig. 8.9 illustrate the two types of income effect. Part (a) shows the income effect for normal goods, using Lisa's consumption

Figure 8.10   Price Effect, Substitution Effect, and Income Effect

(a) Price effect

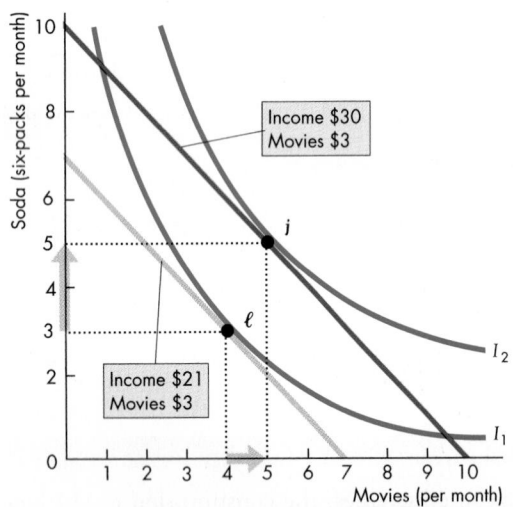

(c) Income effect

The price effect can be separated into a substitution effect and an income effect. The price effect is shown in part (a) and is the same as that in Fig. 8.8(a).

The substitution effect in part (b) is calculated by imagining that Lisa's income falls at the same time as the fall in the price of a movie, so that when she chooses her best affordable point ℓ, she is indifferent between that and the original situation. The move from c to ℓ is the substitution effect. The substitution effect of a price change always results in more consumption of the good whose price has fallen. The orange arrows show the changes in consumption.

The income effect (part c) is calculated by reversing the imaginary pay cut. Income is increased while holding prices constant at their new level. The budget line moves outward and more of both goods is consumed, as shown by the orange arrows. The move from ℓ to j is the income effect.

as an example. With an income of $30 and with movies costing $6 each and soda $3 for a six-pack, she consumes at point c—2 movies and 6 six-packs. If her income goes up to $42, she consumes at point k—consuming 3 movies and 8 six-packs. Thus with a higher income, Lisa consumes more of both goods. Part (b) of Fig. 8.9 shows the income

effect for an inferior good—rice. At the initial income level, the household consumes at point a, by consuming 2 ounces of chicken and 6 ounces of rice a day. When income increases, chicken consumption increases to 6 ounces a day, but rice consumption decreases to 4 ounces a day, at point b.

A Change in Price: Income and Substitution Effects

We've now worked out the effects of a change in the price of movies and the effects of a change in Lisa's income on the consumption of movies and soda. We've discovered that when her income increases, she increases her consumption of both goods. When the price of movies falls, she increases her consumption of movies and decreases her consumption of soda. Movies and soda are *normal goods*. For a normal good, a fall in its price leads to an increase in consumption of that good, as well as to a decrease in the consumption of the substitutes for that good. In this example, a fall in the price of movies leads to an increase in the consumption of movies and to a decrease in the consumption of soda, a substitute for movies. To see why these changes in spending patterns occur when there is a change in price, we separate the effect of the change into two parts. One part is called the substitution effect; the other part is called the income effect. You will discover that the income effect of a price change is exactly the same as the effect of a change in income such as the one that we have already studied. But first let's study the substitution effect.

The Substitution Effect   The **substitution effect** is the effect of a change in price on the quantities consumed when the consumer (hypothetically) remains indifferent between the original and the new combinations of goods consumed. To work out Lisa's substitution effect, we have to imagine that when the price of movies falls, Lisa's income also falls by an amount that is just enough to leave her on the same indifference curve as before.

The substitution effect is illustrated in Fig. 8.10(b). When the price of movies falls from $6 to $3, let's suppose (hypothetically) that Lisa's income falls to $21. What's special about $21? It is the income that is just enough, at the new price of movies, to enable Lisa to buy 4 movies and 3 six-packs, a combination at ℓ, which is on the same indifference curve as her initial consumption point c. Lisa's budget line in this situation is the light red line shown in Fig. 8.10(b). With the new price of movies and the new lower income, Lisa's best affordable point is ℓ on indifference curve I_1. The move from c to ℓ isolates the substitution effect of a price change. The substitution effect of

the fall in the price of movies is an increase in the consumption of movies from 2 to 4 and a decrease in the consumption of soda. The direction of the substitution effect never varies: when the relative price of a good falls, the consumer substitutes more of that good for the other good.

Income Effect   To calculate the substitution effect, we gave Lisa a $9 pay cut. Now let's give Lisa her money back. This means shifting Lisa's budget line, as shown in Fig. 8.10(c). That move does not involve any change in prices. The budget line moves outward but its slope does not change. This change in the budget line is similar to the one that occurs in Fig. 8.9 where we study the effect of income on consumption. As Lisa's budget line shifts outward, her consumption possibilities expand and her best affordable point becomes j on indifference curve I_2. The move from ℓ to j isolates the income effect of a price change. In this example, the increase in income increases the consumption of both movies and soda; they are normal goods.

Price Effect   We have separated the effect of a change in price, as Fig. 8.10(a) illustrates, into two parts—part (b) keeps the consumer indifferent between the two situations (by making a hypothetical income change at the same time) and looks at the substitution effect of the price change; part (c) keeps prices constant and looks at the effect of undoing the hypothetical change in income. The substitution effect always works in the same direction—the consumer buys more of the good whose price has fallen. The direction of the income effect depends on whether the good is normal or inferior. By definition, normal goods are ones whose consumption rises as income rises. In our example, movies and soda are normal goods because the income effect raises their consumption. Both the income effect and the substitution effect raise Lisa's consumption of movies.[2]

---

[2]The example that we have just studied is that of a normal good. The effect of the change in price of an inferior good is different. Recall that an inferior good is one whose consumption falls as income increases. For an inferior good, the income effect is negative. It is not always the case that a lower price leads to an increase in the quantity demanded of an inferior

(continued)

The substitution and income effects of a price change are marked off on the axes in parts (b) and (c) of Fig. 8.10. The move from point c to ℓ is the substitution effect, and the move from point ℓ to point j is the income effect.

Reading Between the Lines (pp. 192–193) takes a look at some recent real-world examples of income and price changes and their effects on consumption patterns.

Model, Theory, and Reality

We have built a model of household behavior that makes predictions about consumption choices and how those choices are affected by changes in income and prices. This model leads to a theory of consumer behavior that helps us to understand past spending patterns and to predict future ones. Let's summarize this model.

The Model

All models begin with assumptions. By using logic, we work out the implications of those assumptions.

---

good. A lower price has a substitution effect that tends to increase the quantity demanded. But the lower price raises real income and the higher real income lowers the demand for an inferior good. Thus the income effect offsets the substitution effect to some degree.

It has been suggested that the negative income effect is so large for some goods that it dominates the substitution effect. As a result, a lower price leads to a decrease in the quantity demanded for such a good. Goods of this type are called "Giffen" goods, named after Sir Robert Giffen, an Irish economist. During a potato famine in Ireland in the nineteenth century, Giffen noticed that when the price of potatoes increased, the quantity of potatoes consumed also increased. Potatoes made up such a large part of the diets of these impoverished people that when the price of potatoes rose, consumers couldn't afford to buy meat or other more expensive foods. Though it is likely that there are many inferior goods, Giffen goods are very uncommon. Thus even though some goods do have a negative income effect, that negative income effect is usually not large enough to offset the substitution effect. So the law of demand still operates—when the price of a good falls, the quantity of that good consumed rises.

Let's look at the assumptions and implications in the model of consumer choice.

Assumptions

- A household has a fixed income to allocate among various goods.
- The prices of goods cannot be influenced by the household.
- The household has preferences and can compare alternative combinations of goods as preferred, not preferred, or indifferent.
- Preferences can be represented by indifference curves.
- Indifference curves bow toward the origin—the marginal rate of substitution falls as consumption of good x rises and consumption of good y falls.
- The household chooses its best affordable combination of goods.
- Preferences do not change when prices and incomes change. *Choices* change but the new choices result from given preferences and changed constraints.

Implications

- The chosen consumption point is affordable and is *on* the budget line.
- The chosen consumption point is on the highest attainable indifference curve.
- At the chosen consumption point, the slope of the indifference curve equals the slope of the budget line. Expressed in another way, the marginal rate of substitution equals the relative price of the two goods.
- For normal goods, a rise in income raises demand.
- For inferior goods, a rise in income lowers demand.
- For any good, a rise in its price has a substitution effect that lowers the quantity demanded of it.
- For a normal good, a rise in its price lowers the quantity demanded of it—the income effect and the substitution effect reinforce each other. This is the law of demand.
- For an inferior good, a rise in its price can lead to a rise in the quantity demanded of it if the income effect is bigger than the substitution effect.

The above, in a nutshell, is the model of consumer choice that we have studied in this chapter. That model provides a basis for developing a theory that explains the patterns of consumption.

The Theory

The theory of consumer choice can be summarized as follows:

- The choices made by real people resemble the choices made by the artificial people in the model economy.
- Spending patterns in the model look like the actual spending patterns in the real world.

What the Theory Is Not

- The theory of consumer choice does *not* say that people compute marginal rates of substitution and then set them equal to relative prices to decide how much of each good to buy.
- Economists do not have a theory about the mental processes people use to arrive at their choices.

Back to the Facts

We started this chapter by observing how consumer spending has changed over the years. The theory of consumption choice studied in this chapter can be used to explain those changes. Spending patterns are interpreted as being the best choices households can make, given their preferences and incomes and given the prices of the goods they consume. Changes in prices and in income lead to changes in the best possible choice—changes in consumption patterns.

Models based on the same ideas that you've studied here are used to explain the actual changes that occur and to measure the response of consumption to changes in prices and in income—the price and income elasticities of demand. You met some measures of these elasticities in Chapter 5. Most of those elasticities were measured by using models of exactly the same type that we've studied here (but models that have more than two goods).

But the model of household choice can do much more than explain consumption choices. It can be used to explain a wide range of other aspects of household behavior. Let's look at some of these.

Other Household Choices

Households make many choices other than those about how to spend their income on the various goods and services available. There are two key choices that households must make:

- The type and amount of work to do
- How much to consume and how much to save

Time Allocation and Labor Supply

Every day, we have to allocate our 24 hours between leisure, working for ourselves, and working for someone else. When we work for someone else, we are supplying labor.

We can understand our labor supply decisions by using the theory of household choice. Supplying more labor is exactly the same thing as consuming less leisure. Leisure is a good, just like movies and soda. Other things being equal, a situation that has more leisure is preferred to one that has less leisure. We have indifference curves for leisure and consumption goods similar to those we've already studied. For example, we can relabel the axes of Fig. 8.4 so that instead of soda, we measure all consumption goods on the vertical axis and instead of movies, we measure leisure on the horizontal axis.

We can't have as much leisure and consumption as we'd like. Our choices are constrained by the wages that we can earn. For a given hourly wage rate, increasing our consumption of goods and services is only possible if we decrease our leisure time and increase our supply of labor. The wage rate that we can earn determines how much extra consumption we can undertake by giving up an extra hour of leisure. The slope of our indifference curve tells us the marginal rate of substitution—the rate at which we will be willing to give up consumption of goods and services to get one more hour of leisure while remaining indifferent. Our best choice of consumption and leisure has exactly the same properties as our best choice of movies and soda. We get onto the highest possible indifference curve by making the marginal rate of substitution between consumption and leisure equal to the wage rate relative to the price of consumption goods.

Growing Pains at 40

As They Approach Mid-Life, Baby Boomers Struggle to Have It All

The generation that wanted to stay forever young is entering middle age. This year the leading edge of the Baby Boom, the 76 million Americans born in the fecund years between 1946 and 1964, reaches mid-life. Former White House Wunderkind David Stockman and Actor Sylvester Stallone (Rocky, Rambo) turn 40 in 1986. So do ex-Mouseketeer Carl ("Cubby") O'Brien, Arms Control and Disarmament Agency Director Kenneth Adelman, and Real Estate Mogul Donald Trump.

The generation idealized by Madison Avenue for its superior muscle tone and free-spending habits is ruefully discovering that, contrary to the promise of the ads, it cannot have it all. . . . Says Mern Wildcat, 30, . . . in Olathe, Kans., "People want a home, two cars and all the new technologies, like VCRs, but it's hard to afford it all."

The Baby Boom, says Richard C. Michel of the Urban Institute, was hit by a quadruple whammy: inflation, fierce competition for jobs, exorbitant housing costs and the recessions of the '70s and early '80s. "They grew up with the expectation that they would live better than their parents no matter what they did," says Michel. "The 1970s ended that. It was a time of tremendous economic disillusionment for many people." Between 1973 and 1983 the median real income of a typical young family headed by a person aged 25 to 34 fell by 11.5% . . . "If you can't afford a home, you want the best espresso machine you can buy," observes Los Angeles Psychologist Shelley Taylor, 39. Manhattan Ad Executive Julianne Hastings, 39, wears designer clothes and jets off to the Caribbean for vacations. But she lives in an apartment "the same size as the bedroom I grew up in."

Time, **May 19, 1986**

By Evan Thomas, reported by Ann Blackman/Washington, Cathy Booth/New York, and Jon D. Hull/Los Angeles
(Copyright 1986 Time Inc. Reprinted by permission.)

- No matter what our aspirations, there are limits to what we can consume: Scarcity is a fact of life for everyone.

- The following four negative factors have lowered consumption possibilities: inflation, a competitive job market, high housing prices, and recession.

- The net result of the four negative factors is a cut in real income of 11.5% for a typical family headed by a person aged 25 to 34.

- People would prefer to have avoided a fall in real income.

- Even for people whose real income has risen, their demand for housing has remained fairly constant while their demand for other goods — such as designer clothes, Caribbean vacations, VCRs and espresso machines — has increased.

Background and Analysis

- We can use the theory of consumer choice to analyze this article. The household's budget line defines the limit of the household's consumption possibilities. Points beyond that line are not attainable.

- Between 1973 and 1983, two things happened to the budget line of the median family: It shifted inward and the relative price of housing increased.

- The top figure illustrates these changes. The horizontal axis measures the consumption of housing and the vertical axis measures the consumption of other goods such as VCRs, Caribbean vacations, designer clothes, and espresso machines.

- People prefer to be on the 1973 budget line rather than on the 1983 one.

- Income for some people increased between 1973 and 1983, but housing costs also increased. The bottom figure illustrates the situation facing such individuals. (For example, Julianne Hastings in the story.)

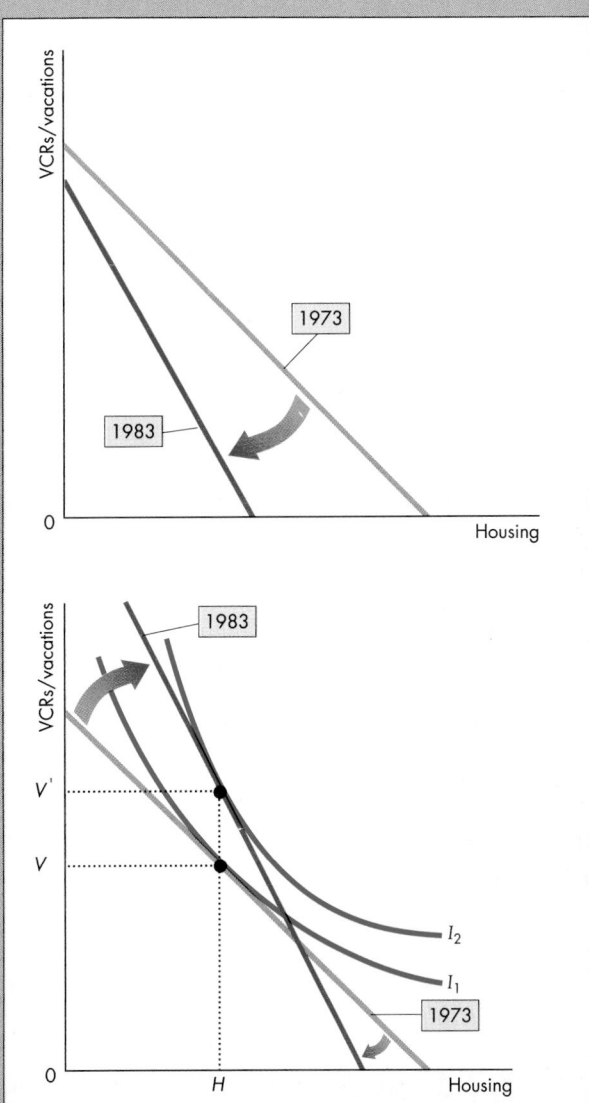

Conclusion

- "Growing Pains at 40" is an interesting and clear example of scarcity and how the behavior of mid-life baby boomers can be entirely predicted by an economic model of consumer choice.

- In 1973, the budget line was the light red line; in 1983, it was the dark red line.

- In 1973, consumption of housing was H and of other goods V.

- A rise in income produces a rise in the demand for all goods.

- A rise in the price of housing produces a substitution effect away from housing toward other goods.

- For some people, the combination of a rise in the price of housing and a rise in income results in a larger quantity demanded of designer clothes and Caribbean vacations (V'), but no change in the quantity of housing demanded (H).

Understanding Human Behavior

T he past 20 years have seen incredible advances in applying economic analysis to human behavior. Though many people have made contributions to our advancing knowledge in this area, one person stands out: Gary Becker of the University of Chicago.

But the economic approach to human behavior did not begin with his work. Adam Smith (see "Our Advancing Knowledge" in Chapter 1) used the approach to understand political choices. The approach was also taken by one of Smith's contemporaries, Jeremy Bentham. Bentham lived in London, England, throughout his life—from 1748 to 1832. He believed that what he called the pleasure-pain calculus was applicable to all human behavior: "Nature has placed mankind under the governance of two sovereign masters, *pain and pleasure*. It is for them alone to point out what we ought to do, as well as to determine what we shall do. . . . They govern us in all we do, in all we say, in all we think."*

Many years passed between the writings of Bentham and Becker with little development in the economics of human behavior. In the last 20 years, many scholars have worked to extend the economic approach to a variety of nontraditional problems. The economics of the family and the economics of crime are just two such areas.

The economics of the family have attracted a lot of attention and a good deal of controversy. The Chicago view, led by Gary Becker (see "Talking with Gary Becker" on pages 151–154), is that we must seek explanations of family behavior as the outcome of given preferences and changing constraints. Chicago students of the economics of the family, such as Robert Michael and Robert J. Willis (both at the University of Chicago's National Opinion Research Center), have used this approach to conduct extensive studies of fertility designed to understand the postwar baby boom (and its subsequent bust).

A competing view, sometimes called the "Pennsylvania school," inspired primarily by Richard Easterlin of the University of Pennsylvania, assumes that preferences have changed in a systematic way to affect postwar fertility.

Among the more active investigators of the economics of crime are Isaac Ehrlich (State University of New York at Buffalo), Stephen Layson (University of North Carolina at Greensboro), Mitchell A. Polinsky (Stanford Law School), and Steven Shavell (Harvard Law School). These scholars are attempting to discover what might be called "supply of offenses" and "demand for enforcement or protection" curves that can be used to provide guidance on how best to design a system of law and enforcement that balances the gains from low crime rates against the costs of achieving them.

Jeremy Bentham

---

*The Bentham quotation is from Gary Becker, *The Economic Approach to Human Behavior* (Chicago: University of Chicago Press, 1976), p. 8.

Changes in wages affect our choice of consumption and leisure in a similar way to that in which a change in the price of movies affects our consumption of movies and soda. A higher wage rate makes leisure more expensive. There is a substitution effect encouraging us to take less leisure and work longer hours, thereby consuming more goods and services. But a higher wage rate also has an income effect. A higher wage leads to a higher income, and with a higher income we consume more of all normal goods. Leisure is a normal good. Other things being equal, the higher the income, the more leisure we take.

People who can earn only a very low hourly wage rate tend to work fewer hours, or perhaps not at all. As the wage rate increases, the substitution effect encourages less leisure and more work to be undertaken. But as the wage rate keeps on increasing, eventually, the income effect comes to dominate the substitution effect. The higher wage leads to higher consumption of goods and services and to additional leisure. It is the ultimately dominant role of the income effect that has resulted in the workweek getting steadily shorter despite the fact that wages have increased.

Consumption and Saving

We don't have to spend all our income here and now. Nor are we constrained to consuming only our current income. We can consume less than our current income, saving the difference for future consumption. Or we can consume more than our current income, borrowing the difference but putting ourselves in a position where we must consume less later in order to repay our loan. Choosing when to consume, how much to save, and how much to borrow can also be understood by using the same theory of household choice that explained Lisa's allocation of her income to movies and soda.

Other things being equal, more consumption today is preferred to less. Also, other things being equal, more consumption in the future is preferred to less. As a consequence, we have indifference curves for consumption now and in the future that are similar to our indifference curves for any pair of goods. Of course, we cannot consume as much as we'd like to today or in the future. Our choices are constrained. The constraint on our choices is our income, and the interest rate that we can earn on our savings or that we have to pay on our borrowings. The interest rate is a relative price—the relative price of consumption today versus consumption in the future. We make our choice of the timing of consumption (and the amount of saving or borrowing to undertake) by making the marginal rate of substitution between current and future consumption equal to the interest rate. Thus high interest rates will discourage borrowing and lead to lower current consumption and higher future consumption.

Other Choices

Many other choices can be understood by using this same theory of household behavior. Some of these choices are discussed in Our Advancing Knowledge (p. 194).

■ We've now completed our study of household choices. We've seen how we can derive, from a model of household choice, the law of demand. We've also seen how that same model can be applied to a wide range of other choices, including the demand for leisure and the supply of labor.

In Part 4, we're going to study the choices made by firms. We'll see how, in the pursuit of profit, firms make choices governing the supply of goods and services and the demand for factors of production (inputs).

After completing these chapters, we'll then bring the analysis of households and firms back together again, studying their interactions in markets for goods and services and factors of production.

S U M M A R Y

Consumption Possibilities

A household's budget line shows the limits to consumption given the household's income and the prices of goods. The budget line is the boundary between what the consumer can and cannot afford.

Changes in prices and changes in income produce changes in the budget line. The slope of the budget line equals the relative price. The point at which the budget line intersects each axis marks the consumer's real income in terms of the good measured on that axis. (pp. 175–179)

Preferences

A consumer's preferences can be represented by indifference curves. An indifference curve joins all the combinations of goods among which the consumer is indifferent. A consumer prefers points above an indifference curve to the points on it and points on an indifference curve to all points below it. Indifference curves bow toward the origin.

The slope of an indifference curve is called the marginal rate of substitution. A key assumption is the diminishing marginal rate of substitution. In other words, the marginal rate of substitution falls as the consumption of good y falls and the consumption of good x increases. The more perfectly two goods substitute for each other, the straighter are the indifference curves. The less easily they substitute, the more tightly curved are the indifference curves. Goods that are always consumed together are complements and have L-shaped indifference curves. (pp. 179–184)

Choice

A household consumes at the best affordable point. Such a point is on the budget line and on the highest attainable indifference curve. At that point the indifference curve and the budget line have the same slope—the marginal rate of substitution equals the relative price. (pp. 184–185)

Predicting Consumer Behavior

Goods are classified into two groups: normal goods and inferior goods. Most goods are normal. When income increases, a consumer buys more normal goods and fewer inferior goods. If prices are held constant, the change in consumption resulting from a change in income is called the income effect.

The change in consumption resulting from a change in the price of a good is called the price effect. The price effect can be divided into a substitution effect and an income effect. The substitution effect is calculated as the change in consumption resulting from the change in price accompanied by a (hypothetical) change in income that leaves the

consumer indifferent between the initial situation and the new situation. The substitution effect of a price change always results in an increase in consumption of the good whose prices have decreased. The income effect of a price change is the effect of (hypothetically) restoring the consumer's original income but keeping the price of the good constant at its new level. For a normal good, the income effect reinforces the substitution effect. For an inferior good, the income effect offsets the substitution effect. (pp. 185–190)

Model, Theory, and Reality

A model of household behavior based on the assumption that households' preferences can be represented by indifference curves that bow toward the origin (that have a diminishing marginal rate of substitution) has the implication that the household will choose to consume on its budget line at a point at which the marginal rate of substitution and relative price are equal. A change in price or a change in income leads to a new choice that corresponds to the law of demand: When the price of a good falls, the quantity consumed increases; when income increases, the demand for (normal) goods increases.

The theory of consumer behavior based on this model is that the choices made in the real world correspond to choices made in the model economy. Such a model is used to measure the response of consumption to changes in price and income—the price and income elasticities of demand that appeared in Chapter 5. (pp. 190–191)

Other Household Choices

The model of household behavior also enables us to understand other household choices such as the allocation of time between leisure and work, the allocation of consumption over time, and decisions regarding borrowing and saving. (pp. 191–195)

K E Y   C O N C E P T S

Key Figures and Tables

R E V I E W   Q U E S T I O N S

1 What determines the limits to a household's consumption choices?

2 What is the budget line?

3 What determines the intercept of the budget line on the vertical axis?

4 What determines the slope of the budget line?

5 What do all the points on an indifference curve have in common?

6 What is the marginal rate of substitution?

7 How can you tell by looking at the consumer's indifference curves how closely two goods substitute for each other?

8 What two conditions are satisfied at the best affordable consumption point?

9 What is the effect of a change in income on consumption?

10 What is the effect of a change in price on consumption?

11 Distinguish between the income effect and the substitution effect of a price change.

P R O B L E M S

1 Marc has a monthly income of $20. Beer costs $1 a can and chips cost 50 cents a bag. He consumes 10 cans of beer and 20 bags of chips.

a) What is the relative price of beer in terms of chips?

b) What is the opportunity cost of a can of beer?

c) What is Marc's budget equation?

d) Is Marc on his budget line?

e) What is his marginal rate of substitution of beer for chips?

2 Now suppose that the price of beer rises to $1.50 a can and the price of chips falls to 25 cents a bag.

a) Can Marc still buy the same quantities of beer and chips as before if he wants to?

b) Will he want to?

c) If he changes his consumption, which good does he buy more of and which less?

d) Which situation does Marc prefer: beer at $1 a can and chips at 50 cents a bag or beer at $1.50 and chips at 25 cents?

Appendix to Chapter 8

Utility and Preferences

If you have studied both Chapters 7 and 8, you know that they both explain people's consumption choices. Each chapter presents a different model of consumer choice but they both do the same job. They even use the same example—Lisa and her consumption of movies and soda. This appendix deals with the connection between the two models. When you have read this appendix, you will be able to reinterpret each model in terms of the other.

Utility and Indifference Curves

A key element in each theory of choice is its way of describing the consumer's preferences. The marginal utility theory of Chapter 7 describes preferences in terms of the utility derived from consumption. In the indifference curve theory of Chapter 8, indifference curves represent preferences. You can understand how the two models relate to each other by thinking of an indifference curve as connecting points of equal utility. Let's say that Lisa is indifferent between watching 3 movies and drinking 4 six-packs of soda and watching 2 movies and drinking 6 six-packs of soda. Another way of saying that she is

indifferent is that she gets equal utility from the two.

You can literally see the connection between utility and indifference curves by looking at the two parts of Fig. A8.1. Part (a) of this figure has three dimensions: the quantity of soda consumed, the quantity of movies watched, and the level of utility. Part (b) has just two dimensions—the quantities of soda and movies consumed.

The utility that Lisa gets from soda alone (with no movies) appears here as the left-hand yellow line. It shows that as Lisa's consumption of soda rises, so does the utility she gets from soda. Lisa's utility from movies, which appeared in Fig. 7.2, appears as the right-hand yellow line. It shows that as Lisa's consumption of movies rises, so does the utility she gets from movies. Lisa's indifference curve for movies and soda is also visible in both parts of the figure. It appears as the blue line in part (b). It can also be seen in part (a). There it appears as a contour line on a map that shows the height of the terrain. Viewed in this way, an indifference curve is a contour line that measures equal levels of utility.

We can work either with utility curves, as we did in Chapter 7, or with indifference curves, as we did in Chapter 8. They each give the same answers. There are, though, some interesting differences between the two theories.

Figure A8.1   Utility and Indifference Curves

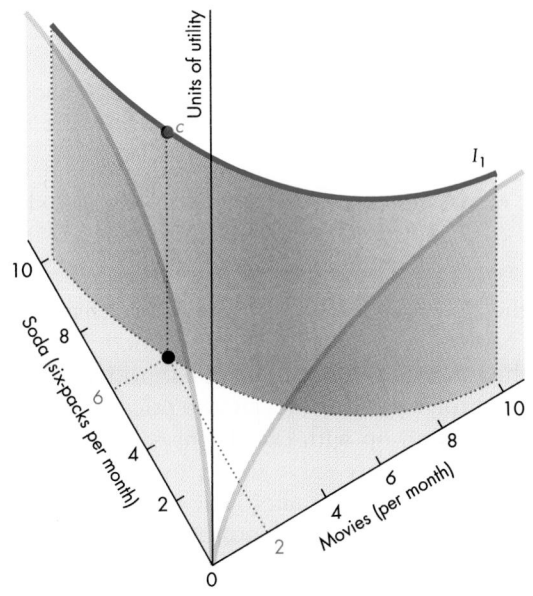

(a) Utility from soda and movies

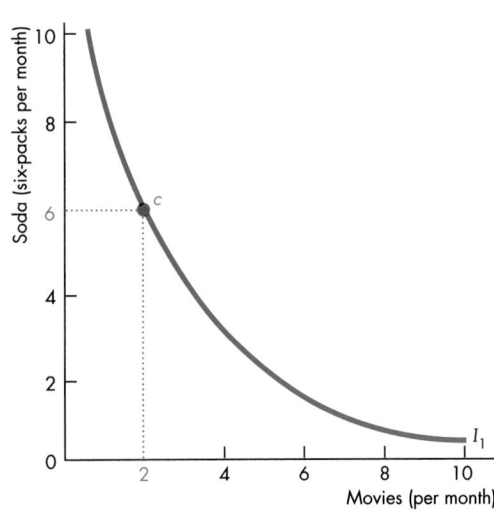

(b) Indifference curve for soda and movies

We can represent preferences in two ways: by using utility curves or indifference curves. These two methods are different ways of looking at the same thing. Part (a) shows the utility received from soda when no movies are consumed (the left-hand yellow curve) and the utility received from movies when no soda is consumed (the right-hand yellow curve). It also shows an indifference curve that tells us the combinations of soda and movies that give equal (constant) utility (the blue curve).

Part (b) shows an indifference curve for movies and soda. You can see that it is the same as the indifference curve in part (a). Point c in part (a) is exactly the same as point c in part (b). The indifference curve in part (b) is what you would see if you looked straight down on top of the three-dimensional diagram shown in part (a).

Maximizing Utility and Choosing the Best Affordable Point

According to marginal utility theory, the consumer maximizes utility by dividing the available income among different goods and services so that the marginal utility per dollar spent on each is equal. In Lisa's case, she maximizes utility by making the marginal utility of a dollar spent on movies equal to the marginal utility of a dollar spent on soda. Her choice of movies and soda satisfies the following equation:

$$\frac{\text{Marginal utility of movies}}{\text{Price of movies}} = \frac{\text{Marginal utility of soda}}{\text{Price of soda}}.$$

According to the indifference curve theory, the best consumption point is chosen by making the marginal rate of substitution between the two goods equal to their relative price. In terms of our example, Lisa makes her marginal rate of substitution of movies for soda equal to the relative price of movies in terms of soda. That is, her choice of movies and soda satisfies the following equation:

$$\text{Marginal rate of substitution} = \frac{\text{Price of movies}}{\text{Price of soda}}.$$

In Chapter 8, we learned how to calculate the marginal rate of substitution as the slope of the indifference curve. The marginal rate of substitution is, therefore, the change in the quantity of movies divided by the change in the quantity of soda, such that Lisa remains indifferent.

Indifference in the indifference curve theory means the same thing as constant utility in the marginal utility theory. The two situations that derive the same utility are two situations between which Lisa is indifferent. The marginal rate of substitution, therefore, is the change in the consumption of movies divided by the change in the consumption of soda, holding utility constant. But, according to the utility theory, when consumption levels change utility changes. Total utility, in fact, changes in accordance with the following equation:

$$\text{Change in utility} = \text{Marginal utility of movies} \cdot \Delta Q_m + \text{Marginal utility of soda} \cdot \Delta Q_s.$$

where Δ stands for "change in." If Lisa is indifferent, the change in utility must be zero, which means that

$$\text{Marginal utility of soda} \cdot \Delta Q_s = -\text{Marginal utility of movies} \cdot \Delta Q_m.$$

If we divide both sides of the above equation by the ΔQ_m, and both sides by the marginal utility of soda, we get

$$\frac{\Delta Q_s}{\Delta Q_m} = \frac{-\text{Marginal utility of movies}}{\text{Marginal utility of soda}}.$$

We've just calculated the change in soda divided by the change in movies, while holding utility constant or, equivalently, while staying on an indifference curve. Therefore what we've calculated is nothing other than the marginal rate of substitution. That is,

$$\text{Marginal rate of substitution} = \frac{\text{Marginal utility of movies}}{\text{Marginal utility of soda}}.$$

(Recall that we ignore the minus sign when talking about the magnitude of the marginal rate of substitution.)

You are now ready to see directly the connection between the two theories. The utility theory says that Lisa chooses her consumption of movies and soda to ensure that

$$\frac{\text{Marginal utility of movies}}{\text{Price of movies}} = \frac{\text{Marginal utility of soda}}{\text{Price of soda}}$$

The indifference curve theory says that Lisa chooses her consumption of movies and soda to ensure that

$$\text{Marginal rate of substitution} = \frac{\text{Marginal utility of movies}}{\text{Marginal utility of soda}} = \frac{\text{Price of movies}}{\text{Price of soda}}.$$

All that you now have to do is to notice that you can manipulate the marginal utility condition by dividing both sides by the marginal utility of soda and multiplying both sides by the price of movies. Thus you wind up with exactly the same equation that the indifference curve theory uses to characterize the consumer's best affordable choice.

Equivalently, you can go the other way and start with the indifference curve equation. Multiply both sides by the marginal utility of soda and divide both sides by the price of movies and you arrive at the condition for maximizing utility. Thus the condition for maximizing utility, according to the marginal utility theory, and the condition for choosing the best affordable consumption point, according to the indifference curve theory, are equivalent to each other.

Differences Between the Theories

The key difference between the two models of consumer choice is that the indifference curve approach does not require us to use the concept of utility. We merely have to talk about preferences between different pairs of goods. We have to say whether the consumer prefers one combination to another or is indifferent between the two combinations. We don't have to say anything about *how* the consumer makes such evaluations. Though the indifference curve theory does not require the concept of utility, as we've seen, it is not inconsistent with marginal utility theory.

Part 4

Talking
with
Oliver
Williamson

Oliver Williamson, the author of *Markets and Hierarchies* and *The Economic Institutions of Capitalism*, is one of the architects of what is called the "new institutional economics." Now a professor of economics at the University of California, Berkeley, he has worked in the antitrust division of the U.S. Department of Justice. Michael Parkin spoke with Professor Williamson about the nature of markets and firms, and how the internal structure and organization of firms affects their behavior.

What are some of the basic issues that you consider when you look at economic organizations?

One issue is when people engage in an economic activity within a firm rather than contract for the same thing in the market. When the job is done, you have the same product but how you get it may make a real difference. Even within the firm there are different internal structures, some more advantageous and some less. The science of organizations looks at a firm's composition and limitations, its formal and informal structure.

What was the course of events that brought you to the study of economic organizations?

I was an undergraduate at M.I.T. studying chemical engineering and business administration.

I then went to work for the government as a project engineer and got exposed to the way engineering projects get shaped, the way contracts are made. Dealing with private firms—large and small—that were doing R&D, and with the government gave me an incredible appreciation for bureaucracy. Later when I took courses in organizational theory, the courses meant a great deal more to me because I had seen bureaucracy in motion. After an M.B.A. and graduate school in economics, when I was teaching at Berkeley, I inherited a course of Julie [Julius] Margolis's on the pricing of public services. This course got me deeply into the market failure literature. Trying to puzzle out what's behind market failure and why it's important. I worked with Julie Margolis again at the University of Pennsylvania when I was asked to teach organization theory. The field was new to me, so I decided to teach it by reexamining market failure. That got me thinking in more microanalytic terms—were organizational and contractual issues behind some of these market failures?

In your work, you've distinguished between two

"When the job is done, you have the same product, but how you get it may make a real difference."

concepts of the firm— what you call a "governance structure" and a "production function." Why do you think that viewing the firm as a governance structure is more revealing than thinking of it as a production function?

The production function describes the firm as a transformation of inputs into outputs. It looks at things like the choice of labor and capital, the effect of taxes, and how firms set prices. This approach assumes that the firm's business activities can be taken as givens. We are producing shoes and we have certain kinds of relationships with suppliers and contractors.

The concept of a governance structure says that there are a variety of ways to produce any

particular good or service. The firm can produce it internally, can buy it from another firm, can engage in a joint venture, or can have a long-term or a short-term contract. The notion here is that organization matters, that some kinds of contracting relations work well for some purposes and poorly for others. Some contracts are subject to hazards. If we take these transactions out of markets and organize them internally, we may be able to introduce additional protections against breakdown of the contract. There are two extremes. One is spot contracting and using court-enforced contracts. The other is internal organization and using administration to control contracts. These are alternative ways of governing a contractual relation, or two different governance structures.

How do we observe governance structures in real business practice?

A classic case was the contract between Fisher Body and General Motors in the 1920s. GM originally produced cars with wooden bodies that were supplied by Fisher. But then wooden body technology was replaced by metal body technology, which required new and expensive specialized plant investments. The two companies had contracting problems in conjunction with this move from wooden body construction to metal. GM wanted Fisher to do some things that Fisher didn't want to do. When the two firms were unable to work these things out, what had been a good contracting relationship was eventually replaced by an ownership relation. Fisher Body became a division of the General Motors Corporation.

The notion here is that there is a logic to making and buying and selling. This logic is determined less by technological considerations than it is by contracting considerations.

You never encountered him in the classroom,

but you've said that you always thought of Ronald Coase as one of your teachers. Coase suggested that transactions costs were the key factor that determined whether an activity would be carried out within a firm or by individuals coordinated through markets. What are transactions costs and why are they important?

Kenneth Arrow calls them the costs of running the economic system. I like to think about transactions costs mainly from a contractual point of view. Things don't get done simply because we agree to them. That is, it's costly to write and negotiate a contract. Next, there are all kinds of surprises and adjustments in life. Sometimes people renege

on agreements. So, it's costly to enforce a contract. The really critical transactions costs are those that make a difference as to whether you organize in one way or another. Of special importance are the costs of adaptation. These costs principally come up when the parties to the contract want to change the terms of the contract because of unanticipated events.

What effect do the costs of adaptation have on the relative effectiveness of firms and markets?

The principle is that there is an underlying tradeoff between incentive intensity and adaptability. Markets provide stronger incentives—for cost control, for many forms of innovation—than do large firms. The problem with firms in

> "Bureaucratic organizations can't pay commensurate rewards to those who make huge contributions."

terms of incentives is that bureaucratic forms of organization simply can't deliver on promises to pay commensurate rewards to those who make huge contributions. Markets are therefore superior to firms in this respect.

But firms are superior to markets in terms of adaptability when the parties have no choice but to work things out between themselves. Where a dependency builds up between parties, as in the case of Fisher Body and General Motors, markets have limitations. Markets therefore give way to firms when specialized investments in human and physical capital are called for.

"Not everything a manager does contributes equally to improve the firm's earnings and stock prices."

Let's turn from questions about how *a firm functions to* why *it functions. You, among other economists, have questioned the notion that firms actually seek to maximize profits by suggesting that the objectives of owners or stockholders and the objectives of managers are different and sometimes*

in conflict. What does this suggest about a firm's ability to maximize profits?

I would say that managers are like everyone else. They're neither better nor worse. They behave in a principled way, but they also have their own interests in mind. Put differently, they're not given to faultless behavior. If you tell a manager to maximize profits, he may not really know what that means. Even if he does, if it runs counter to his own purposes he'll provide you with a mixture of his preferences and yours. As a profession, we've almost abandoned the notion of profit maximization as far as managers go.

Managers, as I said, are like everyone else. Maybe they have a bit more energy. Maybe a bit more ambition, but basically they're interested in income, security, prestige, power, an easy life. Shareholders, in contrast, have a simple relation to the firm. They derive satisfaction from dividends and stock prices and they favor activities that en-

hance them. That's it. Not everything a manager does contributes equally to improve the firm's earnings and stock prices. That's when there's a problem.

What are some of the professional applications of studies in the economics of organizations? Where do people trained in these studies work in the business world?

Corporations need people that understand how economic organizations work. People that can shed light on important organization questions. In marketing, questions like how do you organize your distribution systems? How do you pay your salespeople? Financial questions such as what are the tradeoffs between debt and equity, in terms of transactions costs. Management issues that involve strategic behavior. Obviously, legal questions, antitrust work, about whether there are underlying economic rationales for mergers and acquisitions.

Chapter 9

Organizing Production

After studying this chapter, you will be able to:

- Explain what a firm is, and describe the economic problems that *all* firms face

- Describe and distinguish between different forms of business organization

- Explain how firms raise the money to finance their operations

- Calculate and distinguish between a firm's historical costs and opportunity costs

- Define technological efficiency and economic efficiency and distinguish between them

- Explain why firms solve some economic problems and markets solve others

E very day tens of thousands of trees are harvested and a similar number of new seedlings are planted. Billions of individual trees become one day older. The forest looks much the same from one day to the next, but the evolution of the birth and death of trees means that the individual trees that make up the forest are continuously changing. It is much the same with businesses. Every day thousands of new businesses are born and a similar number die. From one day to the next, the industries that produce the goods and services we consume look much the same, but the individual firms that make up those industries are constantly changing. ■ On a July day in 1977, a tiny new firm was born that grew into and remains a

Trees, Forests, and Apples

giant—Apple Computer. Apple began its life when Steven Jobs and Stephen Wozniak—two Stanford University students working out of a garage—bought a few components and produced the world's first commercially successful personal computer, the Apple. From that modest start, Apple Computer has grown into a giant, with revenue in 1987 of $2.7 billion. But neither founder now works at Apple: both have gone off and founded new companies. ■ As Apple grew, it passed through several stages of organization, much as a growing tree passes from seed to sapling to maturity. Just as a tree needs nourishment to grow, so does a business. The main form of nourishment that encourages business growth is financial, and it is obtained from investors. Why do companies take different forms? How does a company get the money it needs to build plants and to do research? What do investors expect in return when they put money into a company? ■ At the same time that Apple was growing, other computer companies were dying. You may have heard of Entre Computer Center, ECS Computers, Abacus Computer Centers, and ComputerWorks, but don't try applying for jobs there. They are all firms that fizzled! Sometimes disaster can follow hard on the heels of success. Worlds of Wonder, Inc., a toymaker that created a talking bear, was one of the fastest growing companies in history in 1986. In 1987, it filed for bankruptcy. How does an economist measure a firm's health? What happens to owners and investors of business organizations that die?   ■ Economists call business organizations firms. Some 16.5 million firms operate in the United States today in a startling diversity of forms. They range from multinational giants such as IBM, Exxon, and Sony to small family businesses such as painters, gardeners, and restaurants. Some types of business can be done in several forms: Some bookstores have single owners, others belong to corporations. Three quarters of all firms are operated by their owners, as Apple once was. But corporations (like Apple today) account for 90 percent of all business sales. Why are owner-operated firms so predominate in number, but corporations predominate in sales?   ■ We have learned that the market is an amazing instrument for coordinating the economic actions of millions of individuals. Firms are another type of instrument for coordinating individual activity. Why do we need firms to organize and coordinate activity? Why don't people simply buy everything they need from other individuals in markets?

■ In this chapter, we are going to address the questions that have just been posed. Although we are going to learn about the many different types of firms, we will understand better the behavior of all firms if we focus on the things they have in common.

The Firm's Economic Problem

The 16.5 million firms in the United States differ enormously in size, in what they do, and in their survival power. What do they have in common? What is the distinguishing characteristic of a firm? What are the different ways in which firms are organized? Why are there different forms of organization? These are the questions that we will tackle first.

What Is a Firm?

A **firm** is an institution that buys or hires factors of production and *organizes* these resources to produce and sell goods and services. The important word in the definition of a firm is "organizes." Someone, or some hierarchy of managers, runs the firm.

What Firms Have in Common

Firms exist because of scarcity. We use firms to get as much as we can out of our scarce resources. Each firm has to solve its own economic problem. That is, each firm has to get the most it can out of the scarce resources under its control. To do so, a firm has to decide on the following:

• What to produce and in what quantities
• Which techniques of production to use
• The quantities of each factor of production to employ
• Its organization and management structure
• The arrangements for compensating factors of production

A firm's receipts from the sale of goods and services are called *revenue*. The total payment made by a firm for the services of factors of production is called **cost**. The difference between a firm's revenue and cost is its **profit** (if revenue exceeds cost) or its **loss** (if cost exceeds revenue). A firm's revenue, cost, and profits (or losses) are obviously affected by the choices that a firm makes to solve its economic problem. Though all firms face common problems, they do not solve those problems in the same way. In particular, the management arrangements and the arrangements for compensating factors of production vary and lead to different forms of business organization. Let's look at these different forms.

Forms of Business Organization

There are three main forms of business organization:

• Proprietorship
• Partnership
• Corporation

Which form a firm takes influences both its management structure and how it compensates factors of production. It also affects how much tax the firm and its owners have to pay. Finally, it affects who receives the firm's profits and who is liable for its debts in the event that it has to go out of business.

Proprietorship   Most firms are proprietorships. Corner stores, computer programmers, and freelance editors and artists are all examples of proprietorships. A **proprietorship** is a firm with a single owner—a proprietor—who has unlimited liability. **Unlimited liability** is the legal responsibility for all the debts of a firm up to an amount equal to the entire wealth of the owner. If a proprietorship cannot pay its debts, the personal property of the owner can be claimed by those to whom the firm owes money.

The management structure of a proprietorship is very simple. The sole owner makes all the management decisions—what to produce, in what quantities, and with what techniques; what capital equipment to buy and how much labor to hire; how much money to put into the firm and how much to borrow from others. The proprietor is also the firm's sole residual claimant. A firm's **residual claimant** is the agent or agents who receive the firm's profits and are responsible for its losses.

The profits of a proprietorship are treated as the income of the proprietor. They are simply added to any other income that the proprietor has and taxed as personal income. The proprietorship does not pay taxes in its own right. Profits are taxed just once, when the owner receives them.

Partnership   Partnerships are the second most common type of business organization. Most law firms and accounting firms are partnerships. A **partnership** is a firm with two or more owners who have unlimited liability. A partnership has a more complicated management structure than a proprietorship. The partners must agree on an appropriate management structure and how to run the firm. They also must agree on how to divide the firm's

Table 9.1   The Pros and Cons of Different Types of Firms

Type of firm	Pros	Cons
Proprietorship	• Easy to set up • Simple decision making • Profits taxed only once as owner's income	• Bad decisions not checked by need for consensus • Owner's entire wealth at risk • Firm dies with owner • Capital is expensive • Labor is expensive
Partnership	• Easy to set up • Diversified decision making • Can survive withdrawal of partner • Profits taxed only once as owners' incomes	• Achieving consensus may be slow and expensive • Owners' entire wealth at risk • Withdrawal of partner may create capital shortage • Capital is expensive
Corporation	• Owners have limited liability • Large scale, low-cost capital available • Professional management not restricted by ability of owners • Perpetual life • Long-term labor contracts cut labor costs	• Complex management structure can make decisions slow and expensive • Profits bear corporation tax and dividends are taxed as income of stockholders

profits among themselves. As in a proprietorship, the profits of a partnership are taxed as the personal income of the owners. But each partner is legally liable for all the debts of the partnership (only limited by the wealth of an individual partner). Liability for the full debts of the partnership is called **joint unlimited liability.**

Corporation   Corporations are the best known types of business organizations, though they are not the most common. IBM, Exxon, and Sony are all examples of corporations. Many corporations, including these three, are multinational giants. A **corporation** is a firm owned by one or more limited liability stockholders. **Limited liability** means the owners have legal liability only for the value of their initial investment. Furthermore, the stock of a corporation is divided into shares. A **share** is a fraction of the stock of a corporation. Shares in some corporations are held privately and can be bought and sold only by mutual agreement between two people. Shares in other corporations can be bought and sold on stock markets like the New York Stock Exchange. Only larger corporations, however, have shares traded on major stock exchanges. The shares of smaller corporations are bought and offered for sale by individual stockbrokers.

The management structures of corporations vary enormously. Some corporations, no bigger than a proprietorship, have just one effective owner. Such corporations are managed in exactly the same way as a proprietorship. Large corporations have elaborate management arrangements. Typically, they have an organization structure headed by a chief executive officer. Below that officer, there are usually senior vice-presidents responsible for such areas as production, finance, marketing, and perhaps research. These senior executives are in turn served by a series of specialists and subspecialists. Each layer in the management structure knows enough about what happens in the layer below to exercise control, but the entire management consists of specialists who concentrate on a narrow aspect of the corporation's activities.

The corporation receives much of its money from its owners—the stockholders. The stockholders' compensation comes in part from dividends and in part from changes in the market price of their shares. Corporations also raise money by issuing bonds (see pages 211–215). Bondholders are compensated by an agreed fixed interest payment.

For as long as a corporation makes profits, the residual claimants to those profits are the stockholders. If a corporation incurs losses on such a scale that it becomes bankrupt, the residual loss is absorbed by the banks and other corporations to whom the troubled corporation is in debt. The stockholders themselves, by virtue of their limited liability, are responsible for the debt of the corporation only up to the value of their initial investment.

Government taxes the profits of a corporation independently of the incomes of the stockholders. The rate of tax on corporations is 34 percent. Corporate profits are, in effect, taxed twice. After the corporation has paid tax on its profits, the stockholders themselves pay taxes on their dividend income. The rate of tax paid by the stockholder depends on that individual stockholder's total income.

Other Types of Firms   Although most firms are proprietorships, partnerships, or corporations, there are two other less common types of firms—not-for-profit firms and government firms.

A **not-for-profit** firm is an organization that either chooses or is required to have equal costs and revenue. Examples are universities and colleges, churches, and some insurance companies called mutual insurance companies. A **government firm** is a firm that is owned and operated by a government. Common examples of government firms are those in industries such as water supply, garbage collection, and in some countries airlines, railroads, and utilities.

What are the pros and cons of the various different forms of business organization?

The Pros and Cons of the Different Forms

Since each of the three main types of firms exists in large numbers, each type obviously has advantages in particular situations. Each type also has its disadvantages, which explains why it has not driven out the other two. Table 9.1 summarizes the pros and cons of each type of firm. Let's see how the advantages and disadvantages balance out for each type of business, beginning with a proprietorship.

Proprietorship   The pros and cons of a proprietorship balance out in favor of this form of business organization mainly for small operations in which the proprietor is an expert. Though the risk of a bad

Table 9.2   The Relative Importance of the Three Main Types of Firms in Various Industries in 1982

Industry	Percentage of firms in industry			Percentage of industry revenues		
	Proprietorship	Partnership	Corporation	Proprietorship	Partnership	Corporation
Agriculture, forestry, and fishing	91	5	4	59	4	37
Mining	61	24	15	8	11	81
Construction	79	4	17	15	6	79
Manufacturing	54	4	42	1	1	98
Transportation and public utilities	77	3	20	4	1	95
Wholesale trades	40	5	55	2	2	96
Retail trades	74	6	20	14	3	83
Finance, insurance, and real estate	44	34	22	6	16	78
Services	80	5	15	21	13	66
All industries	73	9	18	7	4	89

Almost three quarters of all firms are proprietorships. The least common type of firm is a partnership (accounting for less than 10 percent of all firms). Corporations account for 18 percent of all firms. In contrast to the percentage of firms, the percentage of industry revenues is by far the largest for corporations (except in agriculture, forestry, and fishing).

Source: U.S. Bureau of the Census, *Statistical Abstract of the United States: 1987*, 107th ed. (Washington, D.C.: 1986): 504 and 623.

decision always exists, the expertise of the proprietor keeps mistakes to a minimum. For example, experienced computer programmers with a good grasp of their field often work as proprietorships. The proprietorship also works well in businesses that require relatively low-skilled labor and where a high rate of labor turnover does not hurt efficiency. Most farms, which require the expertise of the owners but which also use unskilled labor, are proprietorships.

Table 9.2 shows the relative importance of the three main types of firms in various industries. As illustrated in the table, proprietorships are particularly important in agriculture, forestry, and fishing and in the service sector.

Proprietorships are often a step on the way to becoming a corporation—the first step in the evolution of a firm. Proprietorships are risky. Those with

profitable ideas and expert abilities can earn a large income. Those whose ideas don't fly die quickly. The survivors, with the wealth coming from their success, may go on to create and manage corporations.

For example, the largest greeting card company in the United States—Hallmark Cards—started out as a proprietorship. Its founder, Joyce Hall, kept his first greeting cards under a bed in his room at the YMCA in Kansas City. Today Hallmark is a corporation with annual sales of more than a billion dollars.

Partnership   The partnership suits skilled professionals who share a body of knowledge and discipline such as accounting, architecture, law, and medicine. The common viewpoint and background of a group of lawyers, for example, usually means that they can reach a consensus easily. Partnerships have thrived in professions. Table 9.2 shows that partnerships are important in finance, insurance, and real estate, as well as in the services sector. Somewhat surprisingly, a significant percentage of mining firms are partnerships—mainly small prospecting firms.

Corporation   The corporation has become the dominant form of business organization in the modern economy because of its advantages in financing, in hiring professional managers, and in hiring and training labor. Although there are far more proprietorships, as you can see in Table 9.2, corporations account for more than 50 percent, and in many cases more than 90 percent, of industry revenue except in agriculture, forestry, and fishing.

R E V I E W

A firm is an organization that organizes factors of production to produce goods and services. There are three main types of firm: proprietorships, partnerships, and corporations. Each has its advantages and each plays a role in every sector of the economy. The pros and cons of the different types of firm are summarized in Table 9.1 and the importance of each type of firm in the various sectors of the economy are summarized in Table 9.2. ∎

Business Finance

Now let's look at some financial aspects of firms. First we will examine the ways in which firms raise money. Then we will see how we can measure their costs. And finally, we will look at the ways in which accountants measure costs and compare them with the economist's concept of cost—opportunity cost.

How Firms Raise Money

All firms get some of their money from their owner. The owner's stake in a business is called **equity** or **equity capital.** Proprietorships and partnerships raise additional money by borrowing from the bank or from friends. This limits the amount of money that they can raise. Corporations raise

much more money than partnerships and proprietorships. An airline, for example, may raise hundreds of millions of dollars to buy a bigger fleet of jets. A steel manufacturer may raise hundreds of millions of dollars to build a new plant. The more permanent structure of corporations gives them two important ways of raising large sums of money that are not generally available to households and unincorporated businesses.

• Selling bonds
• Issuing stock

Let's look at these two ways in which corporations raise billions of dollars each year.

Selling Bonds   A **bond** is a legally enforceable obligation to pay specified sums of money at specified future dates. Usually a corporate bond specifies that a certain sum of money called the **redemption value** of the bond will be paid at a certain future date called the **redemption date.** In addition, another sum will be paid each year between the date of issue of the bond and the redemption date. The sum of money paid each year is called the **coupon payment.**

Let's look at the example shown in Fig. 9.1. On June 25, 1987, the General Cinema Corporation raised more than $100 million by selling bonds. On that day, General Cinema obligated itself to make a payment on the redemption date, July 1, 1997, of $125 million plus any interest then owing. It also committed itself to making a coupon payment of 9⅜ percent on July 1 each year. General Cinema did not expect to get $125 million on July 1, 1987. The bonds were sold for 99¼ percent. That is, General Cinema was to receive $99.25 in 1987 for every $100 that it promised to pay back in 1997.

Let's suppose that the bonds issued by General Cinema are divided into lots that have a redemption value of $100. An investor buys one of these $100 bonds from General Cinema, and each year until 1997 General Cinema makes a coupon payment to the investor. The flow of cash between bond issuer and bond holder is set out in Table 9.3. As you can see, General Cinema receives $99.25 on July 1, 1987, and then makes coupon payments of $9.37 (9⅜ percent of $100) each year through 1996. Finally, in 1997 it redeems the bond for $100 and makes the coupon payment for the last year. At that time, General Cinema will

Figure 9.1   Selling Bonds

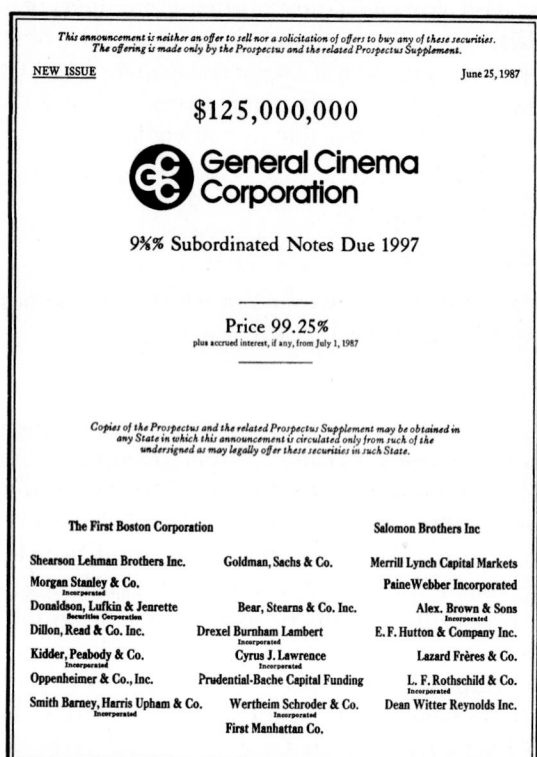

This announcement is neither an offer to sell nor a solicitation of offers to buy any of these securities.
The offering is made only by the Prospectus and the related Prospectus Supplements.

NEW ISSUE   June 25, 1987

$125,000,000

General Cinema Corporation

9⅜% Subordinated Notes Due 1997

Price 99.25%

plus accrued interest, if any, from July 1, 1987

Copies of the Prospectus and the related Prospectus Supplement may be obtained in
any State in which this announcement is circulated only from such of the
undersigned as may legally offer these securities in such State.

The First Boston Corporation		Salomon Brothers Inc
Shearson Lehman Brothers Inc.	Goldman, Sachs & Co.	Merrill Lynch Capital Markets
Morgan Stanley & Co. Incorporated		PaineWebber Incorporated
Donaldson, Lufkin & Jenrette Securities Corporation	Bear, Stearns & Co. Inc.	Alex. Brown & Sons Incorporated
Dillon, Read & Co. Inc.	Drexel Burnham Lambert Incorporated	E. F. Hutton & Company Inc.
Kidder, Peabody & Co. Incorporated	Cyrus J. Lawrence Incorporated	Lazard Frères & Co.
Oppenheimer & Co., Inc.	Prudential-Bache Capital Funding	L. F. Rothschild & Co. Incorporated
Smith Barney, Harris Upham & Co. Incorporated	Wertheim Schroder & Co. Incorporated	Dean Witter Reynolds Inc.
	First Manhattan Co.	

A bond is an obligation to make coupon payments and a redemption payment. General Cinema issued bonds in 1987 promising to pay 9⅜ percent each year as a coupon payment. For each $100 of redemption value, General Cinema received $99.25.

have paid out $94.50 per bond more than it received from the bondholder. For all bondholders, the net outflow will come to slightly more than $118 million. In other words, General Cinema receives about $124 million in 1987 (99¼ percent of the $125 million bond issue) and it contracts, over the next 10 years, to pay back that $124 million plus another $118 million.

On the face of it, this appears to be a terrible way of doing business. Why would General Cinema find that a worthwhile deal? To answer this question, we need to understand a fundamental principle of business (and indeed personal) finance.

Discounting and Present Value   We have seen that a bond is an obligation to make a series of *future* payments. Also, a bond is sold for a *current* receipt. Money flows into General Cinema in 1987 and out in 1988 through 1997.

If you were given the choice between a dollar today and a dollar a year from today, you would choose a dollar today. The same is true for General Cinema. A dollar in 1987 is worth more to General Cinema than that same dollar in 1988 and even more still than that same dollar in 1997. A dollar today is worth more than a dollar in the future because today's dollar can be invested to earn interest.

The next two paragraphs contain a hefty load of calculations, but they are well worth sticking with. There are many situations in your own life where an understanding of this material will help you to make the right decisions—decisions about whether to rent or to buy a videotape or a VCR, whether to buy for cash or buy on credit, whether to buy in bulk or buy more frequently in smaller quantities. Any calculation that involves comparing a sum of money today with a different sum of money at a later date involves calculating a present value. Let's learn how to do such a calculation.

Suppose that the interest rate is 10 percent a year. One hundred dollars invested this year at 10 percent produces $110 one year from now. We can turn the tables and say that $110 a year from now is worth $100 today. The **present value** of a future sum of money is the amount which, if invested today, will grow as large as that future sum, taking into account the interest that it will earn. Let's express this idea with an equation:

$$\text{Future sum} = \text{Present value} \times (1 + r).$$

If you have $100 today and the interest rate (r) is 10 percent a year (r = 0.1), one year from today you will have $110. Check that the above formula delivers that answer. One hundred dollars multiplied by 1.1 equals $110.

The formula that we have just used calculates a future sum from the present value and an interest rate. To calculate the present value, we just have to work backward. Instead of multiplying the present value by (1 + r), we divide the future sum by (1 + r). That is,

$$\text{Present value} = \frac{\text{Future sum}}{(1 + r)}.$$

You can use this formula to calculate present value. Calculating present value is called discounting. **Discounting** is the conversion of a future sum of money to its present value. Let's check that we can use the present value formula by calculating the present value of $110 one year from now when the interest rate is 10 percent a year. You'll be able to guess that the answer is $100 because we just calculated that $100 invested today at 10 percent a year becomes $110 in one year. Thus it follows immediately that the present value of $110 in one year's time is $100. But let's use the formula. Putting the numbers into the above formula we have

$$\text{Present value} = \frac{\$110}{(1 + 0.1)}$$
$$= \frac{\$110}{1.1}$$
$$= \$100.$$

Calculating the present value of a sum of money one year from now is the easiest case. But we can also calculate the present value of a sum any number of years in the future. As an example, let's see how we calculate the present value of a sum of money available two years from now.

Suppose that you invest $100 today for two years at an interest rate of 10 percent a year. The money will earn $10 in the first year, which means that by the end of the first year you will have $110. If the interest of $10 is invested, then the interest earned in the second year will be a further $10 on the original $100 plus $1 on the $10 interest. Thus the total interest earned in the second year will be $11. The total interest earned overall will be $21 ($10 in the first year and $11 in the second year). After two years, you will have $121. From the definition of present value, you can see that the present value of $121 two years hence is $100. That is, $100 is the present sum which, if invested at 10 percent interest, will grow to $121 two years from now.

To calculate the present value of a sum of money two years in the future we use the formula

$$\text{Present value} = \frac{\text{Sum of money two years in future}}{(1 + r)^2}.$$

Let's see if the formula works by calculating the present value of $121 two years in the future when the rate of interest is 10 percent a year.

Putting these numbers into the above formula gives:

$$\text{Present value} = \frac{\$121}{(1 + 0.1)^2}$$
$$= \frac{\$121}{(1.1)^2}$$
$$= \frac{\$121}{1.21}$$
$$= \$100.$$

We can calculate the present value of a sum of money any number of years in the future by using a formula based on the two that we've already used. The general formula is

$$\text{Present value} = \frac{\text{Money available } n \text{ years in future}}{(1 + r)^n}$$

For example, if the rate of interest is 10 percent a year, $100 received 10 years from now will have a present value of $38.55. That is, if $38.55 is invested today at an interest rate of 10 percent, it will accumulate to $100 in 10 years. (You may want to check that calculation on your pocket calculator.)

Now that you understand and can calculate a present value, we can return to the main question: Why does it pay General Cinema to borrow $124 million in 1987 and pay out $242 million over the next 10 years?

The Present Value of a Bond First, General Cinema isn't planning to pay out $242 million on a $124 million loan just for fun. It plans to use the money for its business. Let's suppose that General Cinema plans to build $124 million worth of movie theaters in college towns across the country. It doesn't have $124 million in its pocket to spare. It can borrow the money from the bank for 9.5 percent interest. Alternatively, it can sell the bonds that we have just been describing. Let's suppose it sells the bonds.

You know from what you have learned about discounting that a sum of money paid two or five or 10 years in the future is worth a smaller sum today. Discounting tells you that the money General Cinema pays in future years to its bondholders is worth less today. How much less? To find out, let's calculate the present value of the bond payments.

We will use the formulas that we have just learned. To begin, we need to list the sums of

Table 9.3   General Cinema Corporation Bonds
(per $100 of redemption value)

Year	Cash flow (dollars)	Present value at 9½% (dollars)
1987	+99.250	+99.250
1988	−9.375	−8.562
1989	−9.375	−7.819
1990	−9.375	−7.141
1991	−9.375	−6.521
1992	−9.375	−5.955
1993	−9.375	−5.439
1994	−9.375	−4.967
1995	−9.375	−4.536
1996	−9.375	−4.141
1997	−109.375	−44.134
Net	−94.500	0.035

money that General Cinema is going to receive and to pay out. Such a list appears in Table 9.3, in the column headed "Cash Flow." A plus sign (+) means that money flows into General Cinema and a minus sign (−) means that money flows out from General Cinema. In 1987, General Cinema receives $99.25 on each $100 worth of bonds. Between 1988 and 1996, the company makes coupon payments of $9.375. In 1997, the company makes a final coupon payment of $9.375 and redeems each bond for $100; so it makes a total payment of $109.375. To calculate the present value of this stream of receipts and payments, we divide each item by $(1 + r)^n$. The variable n is the number of years in the future that the money is paid and r is the interest rate. Since General Cinema could have borrowed the money that it needs from the bank for 9.5 percent, that is the interest rate that we will use for calculating the present value of a bond. The interest rate (r) is 0.095.

The results of our calculations are set out in Table 9.3, in the column headed "Present Value." The present value of a sum of money today is the sum itself. So for 1987, the present value of the cash flow is $99.25. The present value of $9.375 one year hence is $8.562. How did we arrive at that figure? We used our formula

$$\text{Present value} = \frac{\$9.375}{1 + 0.095}$$
$$= \frac{\$9.375}{1.095}$$
$$= \$8.562.$$

You can use your pocket calculator to verify this calculation. The further out we go into the future, the smaller are the present values. In the final year when General Cinema makes a $100 payment to redeem the bond plus the coupon payment of $9.375 for the last year, the present value of that payment is $44.134.

The sum of the present values is called the net present value. The **net present value** of a stream of future payments is the sum of the present values of the payments in each year. As you can see, the net present value per $100 worth of bonds is 3.5 cents when the rate of interest is 9.5 percent. Expressed another way, the present value of the future payments General Cinema will make is almost equal to the $124 million it borrowed. To be precise, since the net present value of each $100 worth of bonds is 3.5 cents, the net present value of the bond issue of $124,000,000 equals approximately $44,000. That is, the present value of the payments is $44,000 less than the amount received in the first place.

Now you can see that General Cinema was not so crazy to take in $124 million in 1987 and pay out $242 million over the next 10 years. The present value of its future payments is far smaller than $242 million. In our example, we used an interest rate of 9.5 percent to calculate the present value. Using other interest rates will yield different results. But if a bank loan at an interest rate of 9.5 percent is the alternative, issuing the bond is better than borrowing from the bank. The wisdom of borrowing at all will finally depend on the profits of the new college town movie theaters. General Cinema will want the theaters to earn enough profits to meet the payments on the bonds.

The Attractions of Bonds   Bonds provide a corporation with predictable long-term financing at guaranteed cost. Large corporations typically sell some bonds every year or two and redeem others in sequence so that the firm has a fairly constant maturity structure of bonds outstanding. The **maturity structure** of bonds is the distribution of future dates on which bonds are to be redeemed.

Bonds are attractive to purchasers because of the security they provide. Just as they give the corporation predictable interest costs, so do they provide the investor with predictable interest income. Bonds are risky in the sense that if a corporation goes bankrupt it may not be able to pay the bondholders. Nevertheless, the bondholders get paid with any residual value of the corporation before stockholders get any payments. Though bondholders have a prior claim on the residual value of the company in the event of bankruptcy, they have less control over the company than stockholders do. They have no rights to select the directors who oversee management or to select the management that runs the corporation.

Issuing Stock   The second major way in which corporations raise money is by issuing stock. Money raised in this way is the corporation's *equity capital* because the stockholders of a corporation are its owners. They have bought shares of the corporation's stock.

There are three types of corporate stock:

- Common stock
- Preferred stock
- Convertible stock

Common stock gives voting rights at stockholders' meetings but gives a claim to a dividend only if the directors vote to pay one and at a variable rate, determined by the directors and varying according to the firm's profits.

Preferred stock gives no voting rights but gives a prior claim on dividends at a fixed rate, regardless of the profit level. Preferred stockholders stand before common stockholders but after bondholders if the corporation cannot meet all its obligations.

Convertible stock is not quite a bond and not quite a stock. Its owner receives a fixed coupon payment, as a bondholder does, but has the privilege of being able to convert the bond into a fixed number of shares of common stock.

Corporations issue billions of shares of their stock and these shares regularly trade on stock exchanges. A **stock exchange** is an organized market for trading in stock. The most important

Figure 9.2   Issuing Stock

Wisconsin Toy issued stock in 1987 at $9 a share. The price of a share is the present value of the expected future dividends, based on the company's profits.

stock exchanges in the United States are the New York Stock Exchange (NYSE) and the American Stock Exchange (ASE) in New York City. Although only the NYSE is physically located on Wall Street, in the parlance of finance they are both "on Wall Street." Other major stock exchanges are in Boston, Philadelphia, Chicago, and San Francisco.

The Price of a Share of Stock   In June 1987, Wisconsin Toy Company, Inc., sold 1.4 million shares of common stock for $9 a share (see Fig. 9.2). What determined the price for the shares of Wisconsin Toy's common stock? Why couldn't it get $10 a share? Why were people willing to pay more than $8 a share?

To answer these questions, we need to examine common stock as an investment. The holder of a share receives a dividend each year. That dividend may be zero. If the dividend is zero and is expected to be zero forever, the value of the stock will be exactly zero! Suppose that a corporation is expected to pay a dividend of $110 a share one year from now and nothing thereafter. What will such a share be worth? You probably guessed it: The share will be worth the present value of $110 one year from now. If the interest rate is 10 percent a year, the present value of $110 one year from now is $100. People will be willing to pay $100 for the share today. If the share sells for less than $100, there will be a strong demand for it since the expected return on the share will exceed 10 percent, the prevailing rate of interest. For example, if you can buy the stock for $90, and you receive $110 next year, you will have earned $20, or 22 percent, on your initial $90 investment. If someone tries to sell the share for more than $100, no one will buy it. No one will pay more than $100 for a claim to $110 one year from now if the interest rate is 10 percent. You will do better by simply putting $100 in the bank and collecting $110 in one year's time.

In general, the price of a share is the present value of its expected future dividends. To drive this fact home, let's consider another example. Suppose that investors expect a corporation to pay a dividend of $10 a share each and every year into the indefinite future. Suppose also that the interest rate is 10 percent a year. What will that corporate share be worth? The answer is $100. An investment of $100 in the share will produce $10 a year, or a return of 10 percent a year. That is the same as the interest rate available on other things. The net present value of $10 a year forever, discounted at a 10 percent interest rate, is $100.[1]

Investors can estimate future dividends, but they cannot know them for sure, and their estimates can change. These changing expectations cause share prices to fluctuate dramatically. Because corporations pay dividends out of their profits, news about a corporation's profitability can change investors expectations of future dividends.

One number that investors pay attention to is called the price-earnings ratio. The **price-earnings ratio** is the current price of a stock divided by the current profit per share. A high price-earnings ratio means that investors are willing to pay a high price for a share compared to the profits that the share is currently earning. Such a situation arises when the firm's future profits are expected to be high relative to its current profits. A low price-earnings ratio means that investors are willing to pay only a low price for a share relative to its current earnings. This situation arises when future profits are expected to be low compared with current profits.

In this example, we have worked out how the price of a share of common stock is determined. The prices of preferred stock and convertible stock are determined in a similar manner and depend on the expected future stream of payments that will be made to the holders of those stocks.

Cost: Accountant's and Economist's Measures

What is cost? Cost is the total payment made by a firm for the services of factors of production. There are two ways of measuring cost — the accountant's way and the economist's way.

Accountants measure historical cost. **Historical cost** values resources at the prices actually

---

[1] If you are comfortable with algebra you may find the following demonstration of this result helpful. First, write out the formula for the present value of $10 forever, at an interest rate of 10 percent (0.1):

$$PV = \frac{\$10}{1.1} + \frac{\$10}{(1.1)^2} + \cdots\cdots + \frac{\$10}{(1.1)^n} + \cdots\cdots.$$

The dots stand for the years between year 2 and year n and the years beyond year n. Next, divide this equation by (1.1) to give

$$\frac{PV}{1.1} = \frac{\$10}{(1.1)^2} + \cdots\cdots + \frac{\$10}{(1.1)^n} + \cdots\cdots.$$

Now subtract the second equation from the first to give

$$PV - \frac{PV}{1.1} = \frac{\$10}{1.1}.$$

Multiply both sides of the equation by 1.1 to give

$$(1.1)PV - PV = \$10 \quad \text{or} \quad (0.1)PV = \$10.$$

Finally divide both sides of the previous equation by 0.1 to give

$$PV = \frac{\$10}{(0.1)} = \$100.$$

So, the present value of $10 forever at an interest rate of 10 percent is $100.

paid for them. Economists measure opportunity cost. Opportunity cost is the best forgone alternative. For example, the opportunity cost of an hour in the classroom is an hour of swimming, if that is the best alternative forgone. Although opportunity cost is something real, it is convenient, when analyzing the costs of firms, to talk about the dollar equivalent of opportunity cost. Thus we can ask how many dollars would we have had available to spend on a good if we had not produced some quantity of another good. Here we'll value opportunity cost in terms of dollars. But don't lose sight of the fact that such a measure is just a convenience. When we calculate the opportunity cost of producing something, we're really asking another question: What did we give up to produce this good? We're using dollars as a convenient unit of accounting.

In some cases, historical cost and opportunity cost measures are the same. In others, important differences arise. Let's look first at the cases where they are the same.

When Historical Cost Equals Opportunity Cost

Historical cost equals opportunity cost when a company uses up resources soon after buying them. The historical cost is the money paid for those resources. The opportunity cost (expressed in dollars) is the same as the historical cost because the money could have bought other resources to produce something else or could have bought the goods directly from someone else. Examples of such resources are labor, raw materials, and services such as gas, electricity, and water consumed in production.

When Historical Cost and Opportunity Cost
Differ There are two main sources of difference between historical cost and opportunity cost:

- Durable input costs
- Costs of inputs not directly purchased

Durable inputs are factors of production that are not entirely used up in a single production period. They are bought in a lump and then used gradually over a prolonged period of time. A firm may spend a large sum of money on buildings, plant, and equipment in a single year and then spend nothing on them for another five years. Similarly, a firm may carry large inventories of raw materials and semifinished products that it does not use up completely in a single year. It may use items that it bought a year or two earlier. What is the opportunity cost of using capital equipment bought several years earlier? What is the opportunity cost of taking inputs from inventory? We'll answer these questions below.

A second difference between historical cost and opportunity cost occurs when a firm uses inputs that it does not directly pay for. Examples are the time of the owner and the owner's reputation for reliable service.

Let's examine the differences by looking first at plant and machinery costs, then inventory costs, and finally at the costs of inputs not directly purchased.

Plant and Machinery

Historical Cost Measures The historical cost of buildings, plant, and equipment is calculated by applying a conventional depreciation rate to the original purchase price. **Depreciation** is the fall in the value of a durable input over a given period of time. For buildings, a conventional depreciation allowance is 5 percent a year. Thus if a firm builds a factory for $100,000, the accountant will regard 5 percent of that amount, $5000, as a cost of production in the first year. At the end of the first year, the accountant will record the value of the building as $95,000 (the original cost minus the 5 percent depreciation). In the next year, the accountant will regard $4750 as a cost of production (5 percent of the remaining $95,000 value of the building), and so on. The accountant uses different depreciation rates for different types of inputs. Fifteen percent is a common rate for plant and equipment.

If a firm borrows money to buy a building, plant, or equipment the accountant will also count the interest on the borrowing as a cost of production. So, in this case, if the firm borrows the entire $100,000 and if the interest rate is 10 percent a year, the accountant will treat the $10,000 interest payment as a cost of production. If the firm has not borrowed anything to build the factory but instead has used its own previously earned profits, the accountant will regard the interest cost incurred in production as zero.

Opportunity Cost Measures To measure opportunity cost, we calculate the implicit rental rate of the inputs. The **implicit rental rate** is defined as the rent that the firm implicitly pays to itself for the use of the durable inputs that it owns. You are familiar with the idea of renting equipment. People commonly rent houses, apartments, cars, televisions, VCRs, videotapes; firms commonly rent earthmoving equipment, satellite launching services, etc. When someone rents a piece of equipment, that person pays an *explicit* rent. When an owner uses a piece of equipment rather than renting it out, the economist notes that the owner could have rented the equipment out instead. By not doing so, owners *implicitly* rent from themselves.

Another term that is sometimes used to describe an implicit cost or rent is an imputed cost. An **imputed cost** is an opportunity cost that does not require an actual expenditure of cash. How does the economist work out the implicit (or imputed) cost of a firm using such durable inputs as its own buildings, plant, and equipment?

Economic Depreciation   **Economic depreciation** is the change in the market price of a durable input over a given period. For example, economic depreciation over a year is calculated as the market price of the input at the beginning of the year minus its market price at the end of the year. That amount is part of the implicit cost of using the input. The original cost of the equipment is not directly relevant to this calculation. The equipment could have been sold at the beginning of the year for the market price then prevailing. The opportunity cost of hanging on to the equipment, therefore, is the value lost by not selling it. If a firm has kept the equipment for a year and used it, the difference between its market prices at the beginning of the year and at the end of the year tells us how much of its value has been used up in production.

Interest Costs   The other cost of using durable inputs is interest. Whether a firm borrows to buy its buildings, plant, and equipment or uses previously earned profits to pay for them, it makes no difference to the opportunity cost of the funds tied up in the productive assets. If a firm borrows the money, then it makes an interest payment. That's the payment the accountant picks up using the historical cost method. If a firm uses its own funds, then the opportunity cost is the amount that could have been earned by using those funds for something else. The firm could have sold the equipment at the beginning of the year and used the funds from the sale for some other purpose. At the very least, the firm could have put the money in the bank and earned interest. The interest passed up is the opportunity cost of the funds tied up in equipment, regardless of whether that money is borrowed or not. So, the implicit interest cost of a durable resource is the value of the input at the beginning of the year multiplied by the current year's rate of interest.

The implicit cost of the firm using its own buildings, plant, and equipment is the sum of their depreciation and interest costs—that is, the change in their market value over the year, plus their market value at the beginning of the year multiplied by the interest rate prevailing during the year.

Inflation   Inflation complicates the calculation of opportunity cost. A change in prices that results purely from inflation—a rise in all prices—does not affect opportunity cost. To avoid being misled by inflation, we measure opportunity cost in terms of the prices prevailing in a single year. As a result of the high inflation rates experienced in the 1970s and early 1980s, accountants also have begun to pay attention to the distortions that inflation can cause in measuring historical cost and comparing costs between one year and another.

Sunk Costs   A situation sometimes arises in which a firm has bought some capital equipment and the equipment is in place, functioning well, but has no resale value. The historical cost of buying that equipment is called a sunk cost. A **sunk cost** is the historical cost of buying plant and machinery that have no current resale value. The opportunity cost of using such equipment is zero.

Inventory Costs   **Inventories** are stocks of raw materials, semifinished goods, and finished goods held by firms. Some firms have small inventories or inventories that turn over very quickly. In such cases, the accountant's historical cost and the economist's opportunity cost are the same. When a production process requires inventories to be held for a long time, the two measurements differ and possibly in important ways.

Historical Cost Measures   To measure the cost of using inventories, accountants use a historical cost method called FIFO, which stands for "First In,

First Out." This method of pricing the use of inventories assumes, as a convenient fiction, that the first item placed into the inventory is literally the first one out. An alternative accountant's measure that is used in some cases is called LIFO, which stands for "Last In, First Out." This measure, though not quite opportunity cost, is sometimes close to it.

Opportunity Cost Measures   The opportunity cost of using inventories is their current replacement cost. If an item is taken out of inventory, it will have to be replaced by a new item. The cost of that new item is the opportunity cost of using the inventory. Again, we have to be careful to avoid contaminating our measure with the effects of inflation. If the cost of some inventory item has risen purely because the prices of all things have risen, then the higher dollar cost does not reflect a higher opportunity cost.

Other Costs

Owners' Wages   The owner of a firm often puts a great deal of time and effort into working for the firm but rarely takes an explicit wage payment for this work. Instead, the owner withdraws cash from the business to meet living expenses. Accountants regard such withdrawals of cash as the owner taking "profits" from the business and they do not take into account the cost of the owner's time. But the owner could have worked at some other activity and earned a wage. The opportunity cost of the owner's time is the income forgone by the owner by not working in the best alternative job.

Patents, Trademarks, and Names   Many firms have patents, trademarks, or a name that has come to be associated with reliability, service, or some other desirable characteristic. Sometimes firms have acquired these things by their own past efforts. In other cases, they have bought them. A firm always has the option of selling its patents, trademarks, or name to other firms.

In calculating historical cost, these items are ignored unless the firm actually bought them. But they have an opportunity cost regardless of whether or not they were bought. The opportunity cost of a firm's patents, trademarks, or name used in this year's production is the change in their market value—the change in the best price for which they

could be sold. If their value falls over the year, there is an additional opportunity cost of production. If their value rises, there is a negative opportunity cost, or a reduction in the opportunity cost of production.

The Bottom Line   What does all this add up to? Is the historical measure of cost higher or lower than the opportunity cost measure? And what about the bottom line—the profit or loss of the firm. Does the accountant come up with the same answer as the economist or is there a difference in the measurement of profit as well?

In general, opportunity cost includes more things than historical cost, so the historical measure of cost understates the opportunity cost of production. There is no difference in the accountant's measure and the economist's measure of a firm's receipts or revenue. Profit is the difference between revenue and cost. Since opportunity cost is bigger than historical cost, economic profit is thus lower than profit calculated on the basis of historical cost.

To see how this works out, let's look at an example. Rocky owns a shop that sells bikes. His revenue, cost, and profit for last year appear in Table 9.4. The historical view of Rocky's cost and profit is on the left-hand side and the economic view is on the right-hand side.

Rocky sold $300,000 worth of bikes during the year. This amount appears as his sales revenue. The wholesale cost of bikes was $150,000, he bought $20,000 worth of utilities and other services, and paid out $50,000 in wages to his mechanic and sales clerk. Rocky also paid $12,000 in interest to the bank. All of the items just mentioned appear in both the accountant's and the economist's statement. The remaining items differ between the two statements and some notes at the foot of the table explain the differences. The only additional cost taken into account by the accountant is depreciation, which the accountant calculates as a fixed percentage of Rocky's assets. The economist imputes a cost to Rocky's time and money invested in the firm and also calculates depreciation based on the change in the market value of Rocky's assets. The historical cost method puts Rocky's cost at $254,000 and his profit at $46,000. In contrast, the opportunity cost of Rocky's year in business was $293,500 and his "economic" profit was $6,500.

Table 9.4   Rocky's Mountain Bikes Revenue, Cost, and Profit Statement

The accountant		The economist	
Item	Amount	Item	Amount
Sales revenue	$300,000	Sales revenue	$300,000
Costs:		Costs:	
Wholesale cost of bikes	150,000	Wholesale cost of bikes	150,000
Utilities and other services	20,000	Utilities and other services	20,000
Wages	50,000	Wages	50,000
		Rocky's wages (imputed)[a]	40,000
Depreciation	22,000	Fall in market value of assets[b]	10,000
Bank interest	12,000	Bank interest	12,000
		Interest on Rocky's money[c] invested in firm (imputed)	11,500
Total costs	$254,000	Total costs	$293,500
Profit	$46,000	Profit	$6,500

Notes:

(a) Rocky could have worked elsewhere for $40 an hour, but he worked 1000 hours on the firm's business, which means that the opportunity cost of his time is $40,000.
(b) The fall in the market value of the assets of the firm gives the opportunity cost of not selling them one year ago. That is part of the opportunity cost of using them for the year.
(c) Rocky has invested $115,000 in the firm. If the current rate of interest is 10% a year, the opportunity cost of those funds is $11,500.

REVIEW

Firms raise money by selling bonds and issuing stock. Bondholders receive a fixed income stream. Stockholders receive a future dividend based on the firm's profitability.

A firm's "economic" profit is the difference between its revenue and the opportunity cost of production. Opportunity cost differs from historical cost. Historical cost measures cost as the dollars spent to buy inputs. Opportunity cost measures cost as the value of the best forgone alternative. The most important differences between the two measures arise when assessing the cost of durable inputs and of inputs that the firm does not directly buy, such as the labor of the owner. ∎

We are interested in measuring the opportunity cost of production, not for its own sake, but so that we can compare the efficiency of alternative methods of production. What do we mean by efficiency?

Economic Efficiency

Firms make decisions about *how* to produce their output. There is almost always more than one way of making a product. For example, cars can be made on assembly lines that make extensive use of robots but hardly use any people. Cars can also be made without any robots but with a larger number of workers. The first case uses more capital than the second but less labor.

How does a firm choose among alternative methods of production? What is the most efficient way of producing? There are two concepts of efficiency: technological efficiency and economic efficiency. **Technological efficiency** occurs when it is not possible to increase output without increasing inputs. **Economic efficiency** occurs when the cost of producing a given output is as low as possible.

Technological efficiency is an engineering matter. Given what is technologically feasible, something can or cannot be done. Economic efficiency goes further than technological efficiency. It depends on the prices of inputs. Something that is technologically efficient may not be economically efficient. But something that is economically efficient is always technologically efficient.

Let's examine the differences and the connection between technological efficiency and economic efficiency by looking at an example.

Suppose that there are four ways of making TV sets:

- *Method a:* Robot assembly line
- *Method b:* Human assembly line, with each person specializing in a small part of the job as the emerging TV set passes by
- *Method c:* Human assembly line, with each person following the TV set along the assembly line and performing each and every task and using the appropriate piece of machinery as it is needed
- *Method d:* Hand-tooled assembly, with each TV set fashioned by hand tools and assembled completely by each worker who uses just a few hand tools on a bench to build an entire TV set without the help of any machinery

Table 9.5 sets out the amount of labor and capital required to make 10 TV sets a day by each of these four methods. Are all of these alternative methods technologically efficient? By inspecting the numbers in the table you will be able to see that method *c* is not technologically efficient. It requires 100 workers and 10 units of capital to produce 10 TV sets. Those same 10 TV sets can be produced by method *b* with 10 workers and the same 10 units of capital. Therefore method *c* is not technologically efficient.

Are any of the other methods not technologically efficient? The answer is no: Each of the other three methods is technologically efficient. Method *a* uses less labor and more capital than method *b*,

Table 9.5   Four Ways of Making 10 TV Sets a Day

		Quantities of inputs	
	Method	Labor	Capital
a	Robot assembly line	1	1000
b	Human assembly line	10	10
c	Human assembly line	100	10
d	Hand-tooled assembly	1000	1

and method *d* uses more labor and less capital than method *b*.

What about economic efficiency? Are all three methods economically efficient? To answer that question, we need to know what the labor and capital costs are. Let's suppose that labor costs $75 per person-day and that capital costs $250 per machine-day. Recall that economic efficiency occurs with the least expensive production process. Table 9.6 calculates the costs of using the four different methods of production. As you can see, the least expensive method of producing a TV set is *b*. Method *a* uses less labor but more capital. The combination of labor and capital needed by method *a* winds up costing much more than method *b*. Method *d*, the other technologically efficient method, uses much more labor and hardly any capital. Like method *a*, it winds up costing far more to make a TV set than method *b*.

Method *c* is technologically inefficient. It uses the same amount of capital as method *b* but 10 times as much labor. It is interesting to notice that although method *c* is technologically inefficient, it costs less to produce a TV set using method *c* than it does using methods *a* and *d*. But method *b* dominates method *c*. Because method *c* is not technologically efficient, there is always a lower cost method available. That is, a technologically inefficient method is never economically efficient.

Although *b* is the economically efficient method in this example, in other circumstances methods *a* or *d* could be economically efficient. Let's see when.

First, suppose that labor costs $150 a person-day and capital only $1 a machine-day. Table 9.7 now shows the costs of making a TV set. In this

Table 9.6 The Costs of Four Ways of Making 10 TV Sets a Day

Method	Labor cost ($75 per day)		Capital cost ($250 per day)		Total cost	Cost per TV set
a	$75	+	$250,000	=	$250,075	$25,007.50
b	750	+	2,500	=	3,250	325.00
c	7,500	+	2,500	=	10,000	1,000.00
d	75,000	+	250	=	75,250	7,525.00

case, Method *a* is economically efficient. Capital is now sufficiently cheap relative to labor that the method using the most capital is the winner.

Now, suppose that labor costs only $1 a day while capital costs $1000 a day. Table 9.8 shows the costs in this case. As you can see, method *d,* which uses a lot of labor and little capital, is now the economically efficient method.

A firm that does not use the economically efficient method of production makes a smaller profit and may attempt to sell its output for higher prices than firms that do use the economically efficient method. Natural selection favors firms that choose the economically efficient method of production and goes against firms that do not. In extreme cases, an inefficient firm may go bankrupt or be taken over by another firm that can see the possibilities for lower cost and greater profit. Efficient firms will be stronger and better able to survive temporary adversity than inefficient ones.

Firms and Markets

At the beginning of this chapter, we defined a firm as an institution that buys or hires factors of production and organizes these resources to produce and sell goods and services. In organizing production, firms coordinate the economic activities of many individuals. But a firm is not the only institution that coordinates economic activity. Coordination can also be achieved by using the market. In Chapter 1, we defined the market as a mechanism for coordinating people's buying and selling plans. By buying inputs and services in many individual markets, each one of us can organize the production of the goods and services that we consume. Consider, for example, two ways in which you might get your creaking car fixed.

- *Firm coordination:* You take the car to the garage. Parts and tools as well as automechanic time are

Table 9.7 The Costs of Three Ways of Making 10 TV Sets a Day: High Labor Costs

Method	Labor cost ($150 per day)		Capital cost ($1 per day)		Total cost	Cost per TV set
a	$150	+	$1000	=	$1,150	$115
b	1,500	+	10	=	1,510	151
d	150,000	+	1	=	150,001	15,000

Table 9.8   The Costs of Three Ways of Making 10 TV Sets a Day: High Capital Costs

Method	Labor cost ($1 per day)		Capital cost ($1000 per day)		Total cost	Cost per TV set
a	$1	+	$1,000,000	=	$1,000,001	$100,000
b	10	+	10,000	=	10,010	1,001
d	1,000	+	1,000	=	2,000	200

coordinated and organized by the garage owner and your car gets fixed. You pay one bill for the entire job.

- *Market coordination:* You hire an automechanic who diagnoses the problems and makes a list of the parts and tools needed to fix them. You buy the parts from the local wrecker's yard and rent the tools from ABC Rentals. You hire the automechanic again to fix the problems. You return the tools and pay your bills—wages to the automechanic, rental to ABC, and the wrecker for the parts used.

What determines the method that you use? The answer is cost. Taking account of the opportunity cost of your own time as well as the costs of the other inputs that you'd have to buy, you will use the method that costs least. In other words, you will use the economically efficient method.

Firms coordinate economic activity when they can perform a task more efficiently than markets. In such a situation, it will pay someone to set up a firm. If markets can perform a task more efficiently than a firm, people will use markets and any attempt to set up a firm to replace such market coordination will be doomed to failure.

Why Firms?

There are three key reasons why, in many instances, firms are more efficient than markets as coordinators of economic activity. Firms achieve:

- Lower transactions costs
- Economies of scale
- Economies of team production

Transactions Costs   The idea that firms exist because there are activities in which they are more efficient than markets was first suggested by University of Chicago economist Ronald Coase.[2] Coase focused on the firm's ability to reduce or eliminate transactions costs. **Transactions costs** are the costs arising from finding someone with whom to do business, of reaching an agreement about the price and other aspects of the exchange, and of ensuring that the terms of the agreement are fulfilled. *Market* transactions require buyers and sellers to get together and negotiate the terms and conditions of their trading. Sometimes lawyers have to be hired to draw up contracts. A broken contract leads to still more expenses. A *firm* can lower such transactions costs by reducing the number of individual transactions undertaken.

For example, consider the two ways of getting your car fixed that we've just described. The first method requires that you undertake only one transaction with one firm. It's true that the firm has to undertake several transactions—hiring labor and buying the parts and tools required to do the job. But the firm doesn't have to undertake those transactions simply to fix your car. One set of such transactions enables the firm to fix hundreds of cars. Thus, there is an enormous reduction in the number of individual transactions that take place if people get their cars fixed at the garage rather than going through the elaborate sequence of market transactions that we described above.

---

[2]Ronald H. Coase, "The Nature of the Firm," *Economica* (November 1977): 386–405.

Economies of scale   Economies of scale exist when the cost of producing a unit of a good falls as its output rate increases. Many industries experience economies of scale, and automobile and television manufacturing are two examples. Economies of scale can only be reaped by a large organization; thus, they give rise to firm coordination rather than market coordination.

Team Production   Team production is a production process in which a group of individuals each specializes in mutually supportive tasks. Sport provides the best example of team activity. Some specialize in pitching and some in batting, some in defense and some in offense. But there are many examples of team activity in the production of goods and services. For example, production lines in automobile and TV manufacturing plants work most efficiently when individual activity is organized in teams, each worker specializing in a small task. You can also think of an entire firm as being a team. The team has buyers of raw material and other inputs, production workers, and salespersons. There are even subspecialists within these various groups. Each individual member of the team specializes, but the value of the output of the team and the profit that it earns depend on the coordi-

nated activities of all the team's members.

The idea that firms arise as a consequence of the economies of team production was first suggested by Armen Alchian and Harold Demsetz, of the University of California at Los Angeles.[3]

Because firms can economize on transactions costs, reap economies of scale, and organize efficient team production, it is firms rather than markets that coordinate most of our economic activity. There are, however, limits to the economic efficiency of firms. If firms become too big or too diversified in the things that they seek to do, the cost of management and monitoring per unit of output begins to rise and, at some point, the market becomes more efficient at coordinating the use of resources.

■   In the next two chapters, we are going to study the choices of firms. We will study their production decisions, how they minimize costs, and how they choose the amounts of the various inputs to employ.

---

[3]Armen Alchian and Harold Demsetz, "Production, Information Costs, and Economic Organization," *American Economic Review* 57, 5 (December 1972): 777–795.

S U M M A R Y

The Firm's Economic Problem

A firm is an institution that organizes the production of goods and services. Firms and markets are alternative mechanisms for coordinating economic activity. All firms have to make certain decisions: what to produce and in what quantities; the techniques of production to use; the quantities of each factor of production to employ; their organization and management structure; and the arrangements for compensating the factors of production.

There are three main forms of business organization: proprietorship, partnership, and corporation. Each has its advantages and disadvantages.

Proprietorships are easy to set up and they face lower taxes than corporations, but they are risky and they face higher costs of capital and of labor. Partnerships can draw on diversified expertise but they can also involve decision conflicts. Corporations have limited liability so they can obtain large scale capital at relatively low cost. They hire professional management, but complex management structures can slow down decisions. Corporations pay taxes on profits and their stockholders pay taxes on dividends. Proprietorships are the most common form of business organization, but corporations account for most of the economy's production. (pp. 207–211)

Business Finance

Firms raise money by selling bonds and issuing stock. Bondholders receive a guaranteed annual interest income and face less risk from bankruptcy than do stockholders. Stockholders are the owners of a corporation. The holders of common stock vote at meetings and elect directors. Their liability is limited, but they do not receive dividends unless voted by the directors.

Business profit is calculated as the difference between revenue and cost. Accountants and economists measure cost in different ways. Accountants measure historical cost, economists measure opportunity cost. Opportunity cost usually exceeds historical cost because it includes imputed costs not counted as part of historical cost. The different measures of cost lead to different measures of profit. Economic profit equals revenue minus opportunity cost. (pp. 210–220)

Economic Efficiency

There are two concepts of efficiency: technological efficiency and economic efficiency. A method of production is economically efficient when the cost of producing a given output is as low as possible. Economic efficiency requires technological efficiency. Economic efficiency also takes into account the relative prices of inputs. Economically efficient firms have a better chance of surviving than do inefficient ones. (pp. 220–222)

Firms and Markets

Firms coordinate economic activities when they are able to achieve lower costs than coordination through markets. Firms are able to economize on transactions costs and to achieve the benefits of economies of scale and of team production. (pp. 222–224)

K E Y   C O N C E P T S

Key Tables

REVIEW QUESTIONS

1 What is a firm?

2 What are the economic problems that all firms face? List the main forms of business organization and their advantages and disadvantages.

3 List the main ways firms can raise money.

4 What is a bond?

5 What is a share?

6 What do we mean by net present value?

7 What determines the value of a bond?

8 What determines the value of a share?

9 Distinguish between historical cost and opportunity cost. What are the main items of opportunity cost that don't get counted as part of historical cost?

10 Define economic efficiency.

11 Distinguish between economic efficiency and technological efficiency.

12 Why do firms, rather than markets, coordinate such a large amount of economic activity?

PROBLEMS

1 Soap Bubbles, Inc., has a bank loan of $1 million on which it is paying an interest rate of 10 percent a year. The firm's financial advisor suggests paying off the loan by selling bonds. Soap Bubbles, Inc., has to offer bonds with a redemption value two years in the future of $1,050,000 and a coupon payment of 9 percent to raise $1 million.

a) Does it pay Soap Bubbles to sell the bonds to repay the bank loan?

b) What is the present value of the profit or loss that would result from repaying the bank loan and selling the bonds?

2 One year ago, Jack and Jill set up a vinegar bottling firm (called JJVB).

• Jack and Jill put $50,000 of their own money into the firm.

• They bought equipment for $30,000 and an inventory of bottles and vinegar for $15,000.

• They hired one employee for an annual wage of $20,000.

• JJVB's sales for the year were $100,000.

• Jack gave up his previous job, at which he earned $30,000, and spent all his time working for JJVB.

• Jill kept her old job, which paid $30 an hour, but gave up 10 hours of leisure each week (for 50 weeks) to work for JJVB.

• The cash expenses of JJVB were $10,000 for the year.

• The inventory at the end of the year was worth $20,000.

• The market value of the equipment at the end of the year was $28,000.

• JJVB's accountant depreciated the equipment by 20 percent a year.

a) Construct JJVB's profit and loss account as recorded by their accountant.

b) Construct JJVB's profit and loss account based on opportunity cost rather than historical cost concepts.

3 There are three methods that you can use for doing your tax return: a personal computer, a pocket calculator, or a pencil and paper. With a PC, you complete the job in an hour; with a pocket calculator, it takes 12 hours; and with a pencil and paper, it takes two days. The PC and its software cost $1000; the pocket calculator costs $10; and the pencil and paper cost $1.

a) Which, if any, of the above methods are technologically efficient?

b) Which of the above methods is economically efficient: (1) if your wage rate is $5 an hour? (2) if your wage rate is $50 an hour? (3) if your wage rate is $500 an hour?

Chapter 10

After studying this chapter, you will be able to:

- Explain the objective of a firm

- Explain what limits a firm's profitability

- Explain the relationship between a firm's output and its costs

- Define short-run cost and derive a firm's short-run cost curves

- Explain how cost changes when a firm's plant size changes

- Define long-run cost and derive a firm's long-run average cost curve

- Explain why some firms operate with excess capacity and others over-utilize their plants.

S ize does not guarantee success in business. Of the 100 largest companies in the United States in 1917, according to Forbes magazine, only 22 still remained in that league in 1987. Of the other 78, some had been surpassed in size or swallowed up in takeovers by other companies and some, such as Colorado Fuel & Iron, Studebaker, Willys-Overland—all giants in their day—had gone into bankruptcy. ■ What were all these businesses striving for? If it was for size alone, it didn't ensure their survival. What goals do their successors set for themselves today? How do they decide how to produce and what resources to use? Does a pharmaceutical firm arrive at these decisions the way that a chain of discount stores does or the corner pizza parlor? Or do such businesses

Survival of the Fittest

have nothing in common except the earning of profits? ■ Every firm tries to keep its costs under control. You would think that to keep costs under control firms would want to have production plants that were fully utilized almost all the time. But most car makers in the United States can produce far more cars than they can sell. Why do car makers have expensive equipment lying around that isn't fully used? In other industries, such as electric power production, there isn't always enough production equipment on hand to meet demand. Firms often have to buy power from other producers. Why don't such firms have a bigger production plant so that they can supply the market themselves?

■ We are going to answer these and similar questions in this chapter. To do so, we are going to study the economic decisions that all firms make about how much to produce and how to keep their costs as low as possible. Although many firms are giants—for example, Exxon and Coca-Cola, or even Willys-Overland—we will make better progress if we concentrate our attention on a small, imaginary firm—Swanky, Inc., a producer of knitted sweaters. The firm is owned and operated by Sidney. By studying Swanky's economic problems and the way Sidney solves them, we will be able to get a clear view of the key problems that face all firms—small ones like Swanky as well as the giants.

Firms' Objectives and Constraints

To understand and predict the behavior of firms, we will start by describing a firm's objectives—what it is trying to achieve.

The Objective: Profit Maximization

The firm that we will study has a single objective: profit maximization. **Profit maximization** can be defined as striving for the highest possible profit. As you know, the fundamental problem from which all economic activity springs is scarcity. Profit maximization is a direct consequence of scarcity. Seeking to make the best possible use of scarce resources is the same thing as trying to make the highest possible profit. A firm that does not try to maximize profit will not survive in a competitive environment. Firms have high birth and death rates. They also frequently get taken over. A firm that does not seek to maximize profit will either lose the competitive race to firms that do or it will be taken over by such a firm.

In studying Swanky, we will suppose that Sidney is constantly striving to make the highest possible profits. However, there are limits to, or constraints on, the profits that a firm can make. What are they?

Constraints

There are two types of constraints that limit the profits a firm can make: market constraints and a technology constraint.

Market Constraints A firm's **market constraints** are the conditions under which it can buy its inputs and sell its output. On the output side, people have a limited demand for each good or service and will buy additional quantities only at lower prices. Firms have to recognize this constraint on how much they can sell. A small firm competing with many other firms in a large market has no choice but to sell its

output at the same price as everyone else. It cannot, through its own actions, influence the market price. A large firm that dominates the market for a particular good can manipulate the price to its own advantage. But in so doing, it has to accept the fact that it will sell lower quantities at higher prices.

On the input side, people have a limited supply of the factors of production that they own and will supply additional quantities only at higher prices. Most firms, even large ones, compete with many other firms in the markets for factors of production and have no choice but to buy their inputs at the same prices as everyone else. Except in rare circumstances, firms cannot manipulate the market prices of their factors of production through their own actions.

We will study the output market constraints on firms more thoroughly in Chapters 12 through 14 and the input market constraints in Chapters 15 through 17. Swanky, the firm that we will study in this chapter, is small and cannot influence the prices at which it sells its sweaters or at which it buys the inputs used to make them.

Technology Constraint Firms use inputs to produce outputs. Any feasible way that inputs can be converted into output is called a **technique**. For example, one technique that Swanky can adopt to produce sweaters uses workers equipped with knitting needles. A second technique uses labor and hand-operated knitting machines. A third technique uses automated knitting machines that require a small amount of labor to set them going and to reset them for different sizes and styles of sweaters. A fourth technique uses robotic knitting machines controlled by computers that automatically adjust the size, type, and color of the sweaters with human intervention only at the point of programming the computer. These different techniques use different amounts of labor and capital. But they are all capable of producing the same total output.

Some techniques are capital intensive and some are labor intensive. A **capital-intensive technique** uses a relatively large amount of capital and a relatively small amount of labor. A computer-controlled automated knitting machine is an example of a capital-intensive technique. A **labor-intensive technique** uses a relatively large amount of labor and a relatively small amount of capital. Knitting sweaters by hand—where the only capital equipment used is knitting needles—is an example of a labor-intensive technique.

To maximize profit, a firm will choose a *technologically efficient* production method. Recall the definition of technological efficiency that you encountered in Chapter 9—a state in which no more output can be produced without using more inputs. Technological efficiency does not necessarily require the use of up-to-date or sophisticated equipment. When knitters are working flat out, even if they are using only needles, sweaters are being produced in a technologically efficient way. To produce more sweaters will require more knitters. No resources are being wasted. Similarly, when a computerized automated knitting plant is operating flat out, sweaters are also being produced in a technologically efficient way.

A firm can do no better than use an efficient technique. But it must determine which efficient technique to employ, for not all technologically efficient methods of production are economically efficient. Furthermore, the possibilities open to the firm will depend on the length of the planning period over which the firm is making its decisions. A firm that wants to change its output rate overnight has far fewer options than one that can plan ahead and change its output rate several months in the future. In studying the way a firm's technology constrains its actions, we distinguish between two planning horizons—the short run and the long run.

The Short Run and the Long Run

The **short run** is a period of time in which the quantities of some inputs are fixed and others can be varied. The **long run** is a period of time in which the quantities of all inputs can be varied. Inputs whose quantity can be varied in the short run are called **variable inputs.** Inputs whose quantity cannot be varied in the short run are called **fixed inputs.**

There is no fixed time that can be marked on the calendar to separate the short run from the long run. The short-run and long-run distinction varies from one industry to another. For example, if an electric power company decides that it needs a bigger production plant, it will take several years to implement its decision. If United Airlines decides that it needs 100 additional Boeing 737s, it will take a few years for Boeing to turn out the new planes needed to accommodate United's demand. The short-run for these firms is several years in length. At the other extreme, a laundromat or a copying service has

a short run of just a month or two. New premises can be acquired and new machines installed and made operational quickly.

Swanky has a fixed amount of capital equipment in the form of knitting machines and to vary its output in the short run it has to vary the quantity of labor that it uses. For Swanky, labor is the variable input. The quantity of knitting machinery is fixed in the short run and this equipment is Swanky's fixed input. In the long run, Swanky can vary the quantity of both knitting machines and labor employed.

Let's look a bit more closely at how Sidney makes his output decisions in the short run.

*The Short-run Production Function

A firm's **short-run production function** describes how the maximum attainable output varies as the quantity of labor employed in a given production plant varies. In our example, Swanky can produce more sweaters if it employs more workers. The short-run production function for sweaters shows how the output rate of a fixed number of knitting machines varies as the number of workers varies. There are three ways of describing the short-run production function:

- Total product curve
- Marginal product curve
- Average product curve

Total, Marginal, and Average Product Curves

Swanky's short-run production function appears first in Fig. 10.1. The table shows us how the firm's total quantity produced (output)—the number of sweaters that can be knitted in a day—varies as the quantity of labor employed varies. As you can see, when employment is zero, no sweaters are knitted. As employment rises, so does the number of sweaters knitted. The total quantity produced is called **total product.**

---

*The reader who is anxious to move more quickly to a study of costs may omit this section and jump immediately to the section entitled "Short-run Cost."

Figure 10.1   Total Product

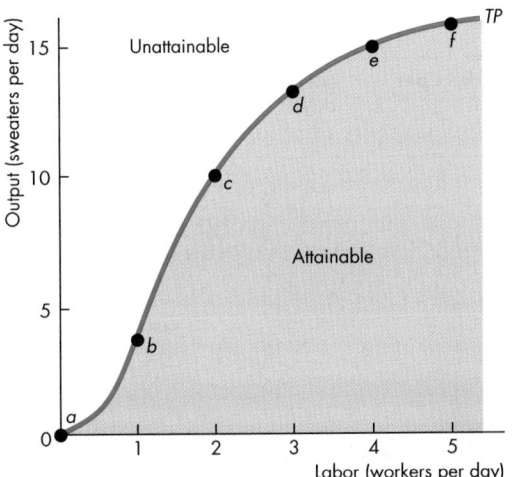

	Labor (workers per day)	Output (sweaters per day)
a	0	0
b	1	4
c	2	10
d	3	13
e	4	15
f	5	16

The numbers in the table show how, with one knitting machine, Swanky can vary the total output of sweaters by varying the amount of labor it employs. For example, 1 worker (row *b*) produces 4 sweaters a day; 2 workers (row *c*) produce 10 sweaters a day. The short-run production function is graphed here as the total product curve (*TP*). Points *a* through *f* on the curve correspond to the rows of the table. The total product curve separates the attainable output from the unattainable.

Total product can be illustrated as a total product curve. The **total product curve** shows the maximum output attainable with a given amount of capital as the amount of labor employed is varied. The total product curve for Swanky is graphed in Fig. 10.1 and labeled *TP*. Points *a* through *f* on the curve correspond to the same rows in the table. The

total product curve separates the attainable output levels from those that are unattainable. All the points above the curve are unattainable. The points below the curve, in the orange area, are attainable, but they are inefficient.

The **marginal product** of any input is the increase in total product resulting from an increase of one unit of that input. The **marginal product of labor** is the change in total product resulting from a one-unit increase in the quantity of labor employed, holding the quantity of capital constant. In Swanky's case, the marginal product of labor is the additional number of sweaters knitted each day that results from hiring one additional worker. The magnitude of that marginal product depends on how many workers Swanky is employing. Swanky's marginal product of labor is calculated in the table in Fig. 10.2. The first two columns of the table are the same as the table in Fig. 10.1. The last column shows the calculation of marginal product. For example, when the quantity of labor rises from 1 to 2 workers, total product rises from 4 to 10 sweaters. The change in total product—6 sweaters—is the marginal product of the second worker.

Swanky's marginal product of labor is illustrated in the two parts of Fig. 10.2. Part (a) reproduces the total product curve that you met in Fig. 10.1. Part (b) shows the marginal product curve (labeled *MP*). In part (a), the marginal product of labor is illustrated by the orange bars. The height of each bar measures marginal product. Marginal product is also measured as the slope of the total product curve. Recall that the slope of a curve is measured as the change in *y*—output—divided by the change in *x*—labor input. A 1-unit increase in labor input, from 1 to 2 workers, increases output from 4 to 10 sweaters, so the slope from point *b* to point *c* is 6, exactly the same as the marginal product that we've just calculated.

Notice the relationship between the total and marginal product curves. The steeper the *slope* of the total product curve, the higher is the *level* of the marginal product curve. The total product curve in part (a) shows that a rise in employment from 1 to 2 workers raises output from 4 to 10 sweaters (an increase of 6). The increase in output of 6 sweaters appears on the vertical axis of part (b) as the marginal product of the second worker. We plot that marginal product at the midpoint between 1 and 2 workers per day. Notice that marginal product shown in Fig. 10.2(b) reaches a peak at 1 unit of labor and at that point marginal product is more than 6. The

Figure 10.2   Total Product and Marginal Product

(a) Total product

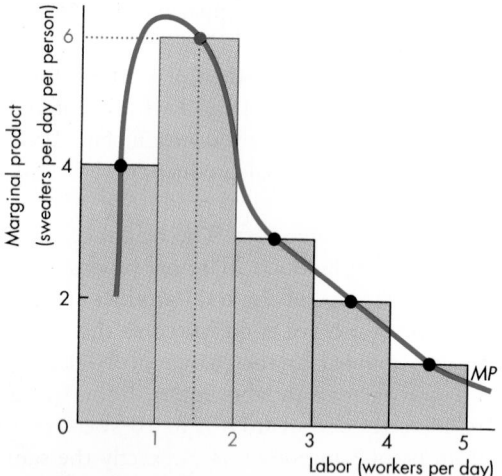

(b) Marginal product

	Labor (workers per day)	Output (sweaters per day)	Marginal product (sweaters per day per person)
a	0	0	
			4
b	1	4	
			6
c	2	10	
			3
d	3	13	
			2
e	4	15	
			1
f	5	16	

The table calculates marginal product as the change in total product resulting from a one-unit increase in labor input. For example, when labor increases from 1 to 2 workers (row *b* to row *c*), total product increases from 4 to 10 sweaters a day. Marginal product is 6 sweaters. (Marginal product is shown midway between the rows to emphasize that it is the result of *changing* inputs—moving from one row to the next.)

Marginal product is illustrated in both parts of the figure by the orange bars. The height of the bars indicates the size of the marginal product. For example, when labor increases from 1 to 2, marginal product is the highlighted orange bar whose height is 6 sweaters (visible in each part of the figure). The steeper the slope of the total product curve (*TP*), in part (a), the higher the marginal product (*MP*) in part (b). Marginal product rises to a maximum (when 1 worker is employed in this example) and then declines—diminishing marginal product.

peak occurs at 1 unit of labor because the total product curve is steepest at 1 unit of labor.

Average product is total product per unit of variable input. In Swanky's case, average product is the total number of sweaters produced each day, divided by the number of workers employed. Swanky's average product is calculated in the table in Fig. 10.3. For example, 3 workers can knit 13 sweaters a day, so the average product is 13 divided by 3, which is 4.33 sweaters per day.

Average product is illustrated in the two parts of Fig. 10.3. First, average product can be measured in part (a) as the slope of a line from the origin to a point on the total product curve. For example, at point *d*, 3 workers knit 13 sweaters. The slope of the red line from the origin to point *d* is equal to the level of output—13 sweaters—divided by the quantity of labor used—3 workers. The result is an average product for 3 workers of 4.33 sweaters a day. You can use this method of calculating average prod-

Figure 10.3   Total, Marginal, and Average Product

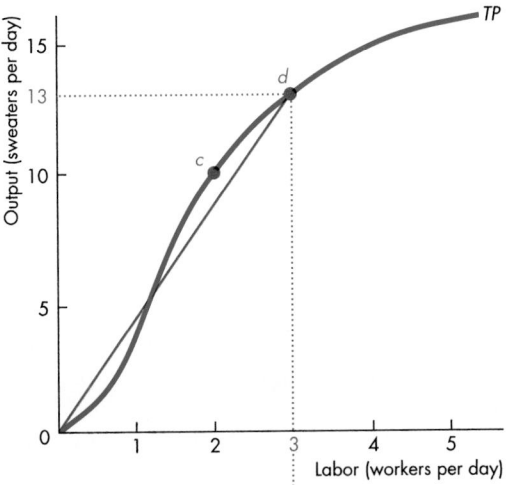

(a) Total product

(b) Marginal and average product

	Labor (workers per day)	Output (sweaters per day	Average product (sweaters per day per person)
b	1	4	4.00
c	2	10	5.00
d	3	13	4.33
e	4	15	3.75
f	5	16	3.20

Average product—total product per unit of labor—is calculated in the table by dividing total product by the quantity of labor employed. For example, 3 workers produce 13 sweaters a day, so the average product of 3 workers is 4.33 sweaters a day. The two parts of the figure show two ways of representing average product on a graph. In part (a), average product is measured as the slope of a straight line from the origin to a point on the total product curve. The straight line to point d is such a line. The slope of that line is 4.33 (13 sweaters a day divided by of 3 workers). Part (b) graphs average product. Points b through f on the average product curve, AP, correspond to the rows of the table. Part (b) also shows the connection between the average product and marginal product curves. Marginal product is above average product when average product is rising and below it when average product is falling. Average product and marginal product are equal at the maximum average product. Part (b) also shows that marginal product increases from 0 to 1 worker and decreases thereafter and that average product increases from 0 to 2 workers and decreases thereafter.

uct to check that point *c* is the point of maximum average product. The steepest line from the origin that touches the total product curve touches only at point *c*. Place a ruler on the curve and check that. Since the slope of such a line measures average product and this line is steepest when 2 workers are employed, average product is at a maximum at that point.

Part (b) graphs the average product curve, *AP*, and also shows the relationship between average product and marginal product. Points *b* through *f* on

the average product curve correspond to those same rows in the table. Average product rises from 1 to 2 workers (its maximum value at point *c*), but then falls as yet more workers are employed. Notice also that the highest average product occurs where average and marginal product are equal to each other. That is, the marginal product curve cuts the average product curve at the point of maximum average product. When the average product curve is rising, marginal product is higher than average product. When the

Table 10.1   Average and Marginal Test Scores

Test	Test score	Aggregate score	Average score	Marginal score
Sidney				
1	55	55	55	
2	65	120	60	 65
3	75	195	65	 75
4	85	280	70	 85
Steve				
1	85	85	85	
2	75	160	80	 75
3	65	225	75	 65
4	55	280	70	 55
Sam				
1	70	70	70	
2	70	140	70	 70
3	70	210	70	 70
4	70	280	70	 70

On the second test, Sidney scores 65 percent. After the first two tests, Sidney has an average score of 60 percent. On the third test, Sidney scores 75 percent. Sidney's marginal score is the change in his aggregate score as the result of doing one more test. The marginal score after three tests is 75 percent. This score is located midway between the scores for the second and third tests to emphasize that it is associated with doing one more test. His marginal score now exceeds his previous average (60 percent), which means that his average after three tests is higher (65 percent). Steve's marginal score is below his average score, so his average falls. Sam's marginal score equals his average score, so his average remains constant.

average product curve is falling, marginal product is below average product.

Why does Swanky care about diminishing marginal and average product? Because they have an important influence on the costs of producing sweaters and the way those costs vary as the production

rate varies. We will examine these matters soon, but first we will take one more look at how marginal product and average product are related, for you will meet this type of relationship many times in your study of economics. You can also see it in your everyday life.

Relationship Between Marginal and Average Values   We have seen, in Fig. 10.3, that when marginal product exceeds average product, average product is rising and when marginal product is below average product, average product is falling. We have also seen that when marginal product equals average product, average product is neither rising nor falling —it is at its peak and it is constant. These relationships between the average and marginal product curves are a general feature of the relationship between the average and marginal values of any variable. Let's look at a familiar example.

Sidney (the owner of Swanky) attends an introductory economics class with his friends Steve and Sam. They each receive a grade of 70 percent in the course the first semester, but they achieved this in different ways. Table 10.1 illustrates how. They took four tests, each worth a quarter of the final mark. Sidney, preoccupied with managing Swanky, started out disastrously with 55 percent but then steadily improved. Steve started out brilliantly but then nosedived, while Sam scored 70 percent on every test.

We can calculate the average and the marginal scores of these three students. The average score is simply the total marks obtained divided by the number of tests written. After two tests, Sidney has an aggregate score of 55 percent plus 65 percent, which is 120 percent, so his average score is 60 percent. A student's marginal score is the score on the last test written. After two tests, Sidney's marginal score is 65 percent.

Over the four tests, Sidney's marginal score rises, Steve's falls and Sam's is constant. But notice what the average scores are doing. For Sidney, the average is rising. His marginal score is higher than his average score and his average rises. For Steve, the marginal score falls. So, too, does his average. Steve's marginal score is always below his average score and pulls his average down. Sam's marginal score equals his average score, so his average stays constant.

These examples of an everyday relationship between marginal and average values agree with the relationship between marginal and average product that we have just discovered. Average product rises when marginal product exceeds average product (Sidney). Average product falls when marginal product is below average product (Steve). Average product is at a maximum and constant (it neither rises nor falls) when marginal product equals average product (Sam).

The Shape of the Short-run Production Function

Now let's get back to studying production. Pretty obviously, the short-run production function, as described by the total, marginal, and average product curves, will be different for different firms and different types of goods. Ford Motor Company's production function will be different from that of Jim's Burger Stand, which in turn will be different from that of Sidney's sweater factory. But the shape of the product curves will be similar, because almost every production process incorporates two features:

• Increasing marginal returns initially
• Diminishing marginal returns eventually

Increasing Marginal Returns   Increasing marginal returns occur when the marginal product of an additional worker exceeds the marginal product of the previous worker. If Sidney employs just one worker at Swanky, that person has to learn all the different aspects of sweater production: running the knitting machines, fixing breakdowns, packaging and mailing sweaters, buying and checking the type and color of the wool. All of these tasks must be done by that one person. If Sidney hires a second person, the two workers can specialize in different parts of the production process. As a result, two workers produce more than twice as much as one. This is the range over which marginal returns are increasing.

Diminishing Marginal Returns   Diminishing marginal returns occur when the marginal product of an additional worker falls short of the marginal product of the previous worker. If Sidney hires a third worker, output increases but not by as much as it did when he added the second worker. With a third worker, the factory produces more sweaters, but the equipment is being operated closer to its limits. Furthermore, there are times when the third worker has nothing to do because the plant is running without the need for further attention. Adding yet more and more workers continues to increase output but by successively smaller amounts. This is the range over

which marginal returns are diminishing. This phenomenon is such a pervasive one that it is called "the law of diminishing returns." The **law of diminishing returns** states that:

As a firm uses more of a variable input, with the quantity of fixed inputs constant, its marginal product eventually diminishes.

Because marginal product eventually diminishes, so does average product. Recall that average product falls when marginal product is below average product. If marginal product is falling, it must eventually fall below average product and, when it does so, average product begins to decline.

R E V I E W

The short-run production function shows how the output rate of a given plant varies as the input of labor is varied. Three curves—total product, marginal product, and average product—describe the short-run production function. As the amount of labor rises but the total labor input is small, average and marginal product rise. With larger amounts of labor, average and marginal product fall. Average product rises when marginal product exceeds average product. Average product falls when marginal product is below average product. Marginal product and average product are equal at the point at which average product begins to decline. ■

Short-run Cost

We have seen how a firm's *output* can be varied in the short run by varying its labor inputs. We now examine how a firm's *costs* vary as it varies its output. Swanky cannot influence the prices of its inputs and has to pay the market price for them. Given the prices of its inputs, Swanky's lowest attainable cost of production for each output level is determined by its short-run production function. Let's see how.

Figure 10.4   Short-run Costs

(a) Total costs

(b) Marginal and average costs

Labor (workers per day)	Output (sweaters per day)	Total fixed cost (TFC)	Total variable cost (TVC)	Total cost (TC)	Marginal cost (change in dollars per change in output) (MC)	Average fixed cost (AFC)	Average variable cost (AVC)	Average total cost (ATC)
		(dollars per day)				(dollars per sweater)		
0	0	25	0	25		..	..	..
					...... 6.25			
1	4	25	25	50		6.25	6.25	12.50
					...... 4.17			
2	10	25	50	75		2.50	5.00	7.50
					...... 8.33			
3	13	25	75	100		1.92	5.77	7.69
					......12.50			
4	15	25	100	125		1.67	6.67	8.33
					......25.00			
5	16	25	125	150		1.56	7.81	9.38

Short-run costs are calculated in the table and illustrated in the graphs. At each level of employment and output in the table, total variable cost (TVC) is added to total fixed cost (TFC) to give total cost (TC). The change in total cost per unit change in output gives marginal cost (MC). Average costs are calculated by dividing total costs by output.

The firm's total cost curves are shown in part (a). Total cost (TC) increases as output increases. Total fixed cost (TFC) is constant—it graphs as a horizontal line—and total variable cost (TVC) increases in a similar way to total cost. The vertical distance between the TC and TVC curves equals total fixed cost (TFC) as illustrated by the green arrows.

The average and marginal cost curves are shown in part (b). Average fixed cost (AFC) falls as the constant total fixed cost is divided by ever higher output levels. The curves showing average total cost (ATC) and average variable cost AVC are U-shaped. The vertical distance between them is equal to average fixed cost, which gets smaller as output increases. The marginal cost curve (MC) is also U-shaped. It cuts the average variable cost curve and the average total cost curve at their minimum points.

Total, Marginal, and Average Cost

Total cost (TC) is the sum of the costs of all the inputs used in production. Total cost is divided into two categories: fixed cost and variable cost. A **fixed cost** is a cost that is independent of the output level. A **variable cost** is a cost that varies with the output level. A fixed cost cannot be avoided, whereas a variable cost can. **Total fixed cost** (TFC) is the cost of all the fixed inputs. **Total variable cost** (TVC) is the cost of all the variable inputs.

Swanky's total cost and its division into total fixed cost and total variable cost appears in the table in Fig. 10.4. The first two columns show the short-run production function from Fig. 10.1. Swanky has fixed inputs in the form of knitting machines and factory space. Let's suppose that the cost of these fixed inputs—total fixed cost—is $25 a day. Furthermore, let's suppose that a worker costs $25 a day (the wage rate). Total variable cost rises as the quantity of labor rises. For example, when Swanky employs 3 workers, total variable cost is $75 (3 multiplied by $25). Total cost is the sum of total fixed cost and total variable cost. For example, when Swanky employs 3 workers, total variable cost is $75, total fixed cost is $25, and total cost is $100.

Marginal cost is the increase in total cost resulting from a unit increase in output. To calculate marginal cost, we find the change in total cost and divide it by the change in output. For example, when output (total product) goes up from 4 to 10 sweaters, total cost rises from $50 to $75. The change in output is 6 sweaters and the change in total cost is $25. The marginal cost of one of those 6 sweaters is $4.17 ($25 divided by 6).

Average cost is the cost per unit of output. There are three average costs:

- Average fixed cost (AFC),
- Average variable cost (AVC), and
- Average total cost (ATC).

Average fixed cost is total fixed cost per unit of output. **Average variable cost** is total variable cost per unit of output. **Average total cost** is total cost per unit output. Average fixed cost plus average variable cost equals average total cost. For example, in the table in Fig. 10.4 when output is 10 sweaters, average fixed cost is $2.50

($25 divided by 10), average variable cost is $5.00 ($50 divided by 10), and average total cost is $7.50 ($75 divided by 10 or, equivalently, $2.50 average fixed cost plus $5.00 average variable cost).

Short-run Cost Curves

We can illustrate Swanky's short-run costs as short-run cost curves (Fig. 10.4a). Total fixed cost is a constant $25. It appears in the figure as the horizontal green curve labeled TFC. Total variable cost and total cost both increase with output. They are graphed as the purple total variable cost curve (TVC) and the blue total cost curve (TC) in the figure. The vertical distance between those two curves is equal to total fixed cost—as indicated by the arrows.

There is a close relationship between the total variable cost curve in Fig. 10.4(a) and the total product curve of Fig. 10.1. They both slope upward. But the more gently sloped the product curve, the more steeply sloped is the variable cost curve. The more gently sloped the total product curve, the slower output rises with a given increase in labor. But cost and labor input changes are proportional, so, turning it around, the faster variable cost rises for a given rise in output, the more steeply sloped is the total variable cost curve.

The average cost curves appear in Fig. 10.4(b). The green average fixed cost curve (AFC) slopes downward. As output rises, the same constant fixed cost is spread over a larger output: When Swanky produces only 4 sweaters, average fixed cost is $6.25; when it produces 16 sweaters, average fixed cost is $1.56.

The blue average total cost curve (ATC) and the purple average variable cost curve (AVC) are U-shaped curves. The vertical distance between the average total cost and average variable cost curves is equal to average fixed cost—as indicated by the arrows. That distance shrinks as output rises, since average fixed cost falls with rising output.

Figure 10.4(b) also illustrates the red marginal cost curve. It is the red curve labeled MC. That curve is also U-shaped. It cuts the average variable cost curve and the average total cost curve at their minimum points. That is, when marginal cost is above average cost, average cost is rising and when marginal cost is below average cost, average cost is falling. This relationship holds for both the ATC curve and the AVC curve. You may wonder

Table 10.2   A Compact Glossary on Product and Cost

Term	Symbol	Equation	Definition
Fixed input			An input whose quantity used cannot be varied in the short run
Variable input	L		An input (labor in our examples) whose quantity used can be varied in the short run
Total product	TP		Output produced
Marginal product	MP	$MP = \Delta TP \div \Delta L$	Change in total product resulting from a unit rise in variable input (equals change in total product divided by change in variable factor)
Average product	AP	$AP = TP \div L$	Total product per unit of variable input (equals total product divided by number of units of variable factor)
Point of maximum average product			Output rate above which average product diminishes
Point of maximum marginal product			Output rate above which marginal product diminishes
Fixed cost			Cost that is independent of the output level
Variable cost			Cost that varies with the output level
Total fixed cost	TFC		Cost of the fixed inputs (equals their number times their unit price)
Total variable cost	TVC		Cost of the variable inputs (equals their number times their unit price)
Total cost	TC	$TC = TFC + TVC$	Cost of all inputs (equals fixed costs plus variable costs)
Marginal cost	MC	$MC = \Delta TC \div \Delta TP$	Change in total cost resulting from a unit rise in total product (equals the change in total cost divided by the change in total product)
Average fixed cost	AFC	$AFC = TFC \div TP$	Total fixed cost per unit of output (equals total fixed cost divided by total product)
Average variable cost	AVC	$AVC = TVC \div TP$	Total variable cost per unit of output (equals total variable cost divided by total product)
Average total cost	ATC	$ATC = AFC + AVC$	Total cost per unit of output (equals average fixed cost plus average variable cost)

why the marginal cost curve cuts both the average total cost curve and the average variable cost curve at their minimum points. It does so because the source of the change in total cost, from which we calculate marginal cost, is variable cost. For average variable cost to fall, marginal cost must be less than average variable cost and for average variable cost to rise, marginal cost must be higher than average variable cost. Similarly, for average total cost to fall, marginal cost must be below average total cost, and for average total cost to rise, marginal cost must be above average total cost. This is exactly the same relationship that we found when studying students' grades in Table 10.1.

There is an interesting and important relationship between the average and marginal product curves, shown in Fig. 10.3(b), and the average and marginal cost curves, shown in Fig. 10.4(b). The average and marginal cost curves are like the flip side of the relationship between the average and marginal product curves. Average variable cost is at a minimum at the same output at which average product is at a maximum (10 sweaters). The output range over which average variable cost is decreasing is the same as that over which average product is increasing. Similarly, the output range over which average variable cost is increasing is the same as that over which average product is decreasing.

The product and cost concepts that we have just studied are summarized in Table 10.2.

Real World Short-run Costs

Swanky's costs are a lot like the costs of a real world firm. Let's confirm this fact by looking at the costs of a group of real firms, the New England Power Pool (NEPOOL). NEPOOL is an association of 92 electric power companies serving more than 5 million customers in the six New England states. If the NEPOOL producers work their production plants to their physical limits, they can generate about 18,500 megawatt-hours of electric power.

NEPOOL's actual production is never that high. It fluctuates between 11,500 and 17,000 megawatt-hours, depending partly on the time of day, partly on the day of the week, and partly on the temperature. To vary their output in the short run, the power producers vary the amount of fuel that they use. Fuel is the variable input of a power producer. The power source with the lowest fuel cost in the New England system is nuclear. Large coal-burning and oil-burning generators come next. The power sources with the highest fuel cost are small gas-turbine generators that use the same kind of fuel as jet aircraft.

NEPOOL operates the New England Power Exchange (NEPEX), whose master control center is in West Springfield, Massachusetts. Engineers equipped with powerful computers make minute by minute decisions to turn power generators on and off in order to minimize the total cost of production. The engineers bring generators into operation to meet demand by choosing the remaining power source with the lowest fuel cost. That is, to increase the amount of electricity, the engineers tap into the power source with the lowest marginal cost. Only at the peak of demand do they use the generators with the highest marginal cost.

On January 28, 1987, a fairly cold winter day, the hour by hour output of the NEPOOL producers and the marginal cost per 1000 megawatt-hours fluctuated in the manner shown in Fig. 10.5. As you can see, there are two cycles over a 24-hour period in electric power production. From 1:00 A.M. to 6:00 A.M., output (shown by the blue curve) is between 11,500 and 12,000 megawatt-hours. Then between 6:00 A.M. and 7:00 A.M., output rises as we all turn on morning TV shows, toasters, and coffeemakers. Output reaches a peak at 9:00 A.M. and then falls off slightly during the day to a low point at 4:00 P.M. In the early evening, there is another TV viewing and meal-preparation peak, and then a gradual fall through to midnight as people go to bed. The marginal cost of production follows a similar cycle and fluctuates between $29 a megawatt-hour at the trough and $44 a megawatt-hour at the peak.

The relationship between output and marginal cost is not perfect. Mechanical failure or maintenance shutdowns often make it impossible to use the idle generator with the lowest marginal cost. Nevertheless, the relationship between output and marginal cost is pretty close. To see how close, let's plot NEPOOL's marginal cost curve—shown in Fig. 10.6. Each point in that figure represents the marginal cost and output at a particular hour. For example, you can see in Fig. 10.5 that, between 10.00 P.M. and 11.00 P.M., 14,000 megawatt-hours were produced at a marginal cost of $32 a megawatt-hour. That output and marginal cost generate point a in Fig. 10.6. The continuous red curve labeled MC is the marginal cost curve for NEPOOL.

Notice the similarity between the marginal cost curves for NEPOOL and Swanky. All production processes have marginal cost curves that have the features of those that we have just studied.

Swanky adjusts its rate of sweater production by varying the amount of labor it employs and varying the extent to which it utilizes its fixed

Figure 10.5   New England Power Pool Output and Cost

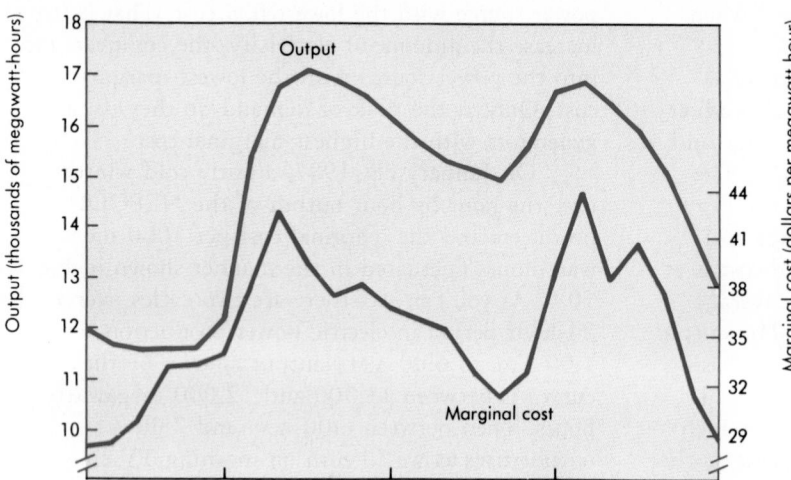

During a 24-hour period, electric power production fluctuated between 11,500 and 17,000 megawatt-hours. Over the same period, marginal cost fluctuated between $29 and $44 per megawatt-hour. The empirical relationship between output and marginal cost is not exact because of maintenance scheduling and uncontrollable factors such as plant breakdowns.

amount of knitting machinery—its physical plant. NEPOOL meets fluctuations in the production of electric power by varying the fuel input and varying the output of a fixed physical generating plant. Over the long run, as the demand for sweaters grows, Swanky might increase output by installing additional knitting machines. Similarly, as the demand for electric power grows, NEPOOL might produce additional output by installing new generators. When does it pay Swanky to install new knitting machines and the New England power producers to install new and larger generators? It is this type of question to which we now turn.

Plant Size, Cost, and Capacity

We have studied how the cost of production varies for a given sweater plant when different quantities of labor are used. The output rate at which a plant's average total cost is at a minimum is called the **capacity** of the plant. If a plant's output is below the point of minimum average total cost—that is, if it produces a lower amount than its capacity—it is said to have **excess capacity.** If a plant's output is above the point of minimum average total cost—that is, if it produces a higher amount than its capacity—it is said to have **overutilized capacity.**

The economist's use of the word capacity differs from the everyday use. It seems more natural to talk about a plant operating at capacity when it cannot produce anymore. However, when we want to refer to the maximum output that a plant can produce, we call that output the **physical limits** of the plant.

The cost curves that were shown in Fig. 10.4 apply to a plant size of one knitting machine that has a fixed cost of $25. There is a set of short-run cost curves, like those shown in Fig. 10.4, for each

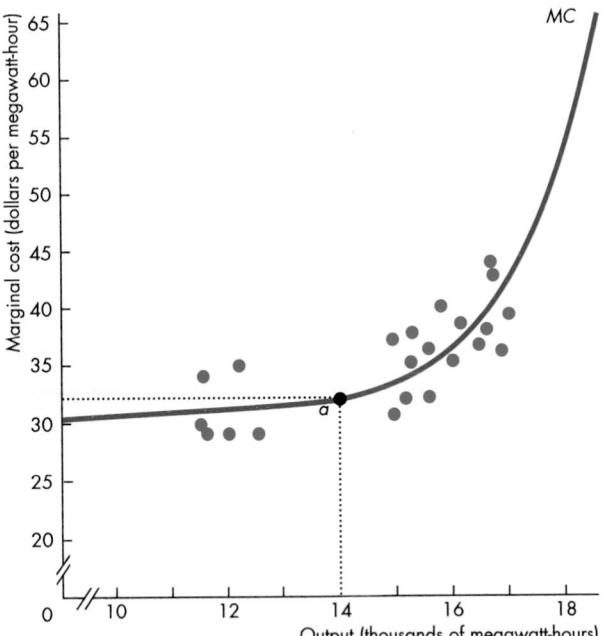

Figure 10.6 New England Power Pool Marginal Cost Curve

Each point in the figure represents marginal cost at a particular hour on January 28, 1987. For example, point a represents a marginal cost of $32 per megawatt-hour and an output rate of 14,000 megawatt-hours. The marginal cost curve for electric power in New England rises steeply as output approaches the physical limits of the generating plant.

different plant size. In the short run, a firm will be economically efficient if it produces at a point on the short-run cost curve for its given plant. In the long run, though, the firm can do better. It can choose its plant size and therefore can create a different short-run cost curve on which it will operate.

The Capacity Utilization Puzzle

The producers of electric power in the New England Power Pool sometimes operate their plant at outputs above capacity and close to their physical limits. Their situation is not uncommon. High-quality gardeners, plumbers, electricians, painters, and other suppliers of services often work so hard

that they produce at an average total cost that is higher than their minimum average cost. To get the work done, they have to hire extra help at overtime wage rates and work evenings and weekends, thereby incurring high marginal costs of production.

Operating with increasing average total cost looks uneconomic. Why don't such firms buy more capital equipment and increase the scale of their business to meet the obvious high demand for their output? Is there an economic reason why they don't?

In contrast, it is not uncommon in many industries to have an almost permanent excess capacity. Steel production is an example. Excess capacity also occurs in the auto industry, in many mining operations, and in a host of other industries. These producers claim that they could increase their output if the demand for their product was higher and, as a result, could produce at a lower average total cost.

It sounds as if these firms have invested in too big a production plant. It seems as if the steel producers and automakers would be better off if they had smaller plants so that they could produce closer to the point of minimum average total cost. Is this in fact the case? Or is there some economic explanation for why firms in such industries persistently have excess capacity? This section, provides a large part of the answers to these questions.

You have already studied how a firm's costs change when it varies its use of labor, while holding constant the size of its production plant. This cost behavior is described by the firm's short-run cost curves. Now we are going to study how a firm's costs vary when *all* its inputs vary—both labor and the scale of the production plant. These variations in costs are described by the firm's long-run cost curves.

Although we want to understand the behavior of real firms, we will, as before, spend most of our time studying the long-run costs of our imaginary firm—Swanky, Inc. We will then use the insights that we get from Sidney's sweater factory to make sense of the behavior of real firms.

Short-run Cost and Long-run Cost

Short-run cost is made up of the fixed cost of a fixed plant and the variable cost of labor. The

Figure 10.7   The Production Function

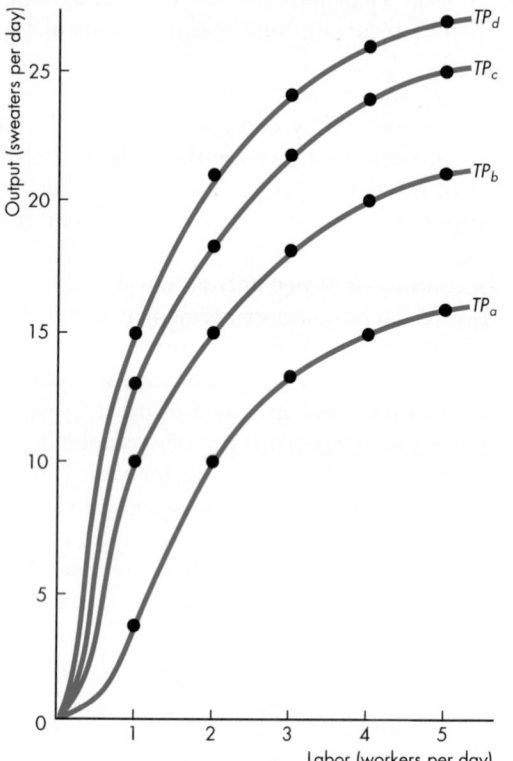

Labor (workers per day)	Plant size (number of knitting machines)			
	1	2	3	4
1	4	10	13	15
2	10	15	18	21
3	13	18	22	24
4	15	20	24	26
5	16	21	25	27

The table shows four different short-run production functions for four different plant sizes. These production functions are plotted in the graph and are labeled TP_a (1 knitting machine), TP_b (2 knitting machines), TP_c (3 knitting machines), and TP_d (4 knitting machines). Each total product curve displays diminishing marginal product. The bigger the plant, the higher is the total product for any given amount of labor employed. The highlighted numbers in the table show what happens as the firm changes its scale of production. Doubling the scale from 1 machine and 1 worker to 2 machines and 2 workers more than doubles the output—increasing returns to scale. Increasing the scale again from 2 workers and 2 machines to 3 workers and 3 machines and to 4 workers and 4 machines increases output by a smaller percentage than the increase in inputs—decreasing returns to scale.

behavior of short-run cost depends on the short-run production function. **Long-run cost** is the cost of production when a firm uses the economically efficient plant size. The behavior of long-run cost depends on the firm's production function. A **production function** is the relationship between the maximum output attainable and the quantities of inputs used.

The Production Function

Swanky's production function is shown in Fig. 10.7. In the table, we look at four different plant sizes and five different quantities of labor input. Perhaps you will recognize the numbers in the column for a plant size of one knitting machine. This is the sweater factory whose short-run product

and cost curves we have just studied. With one knitting machine, output varies as the labor input is varied, as described by the numbers in that column. The table also shows three other plant sizes—two, three, and four times the size of the original one. If Sidney doubles the plant size (to two knitting machines), the various amounts of labor can produce the outputs shown in the second column of the table. The other two columns show the outputs of yet larger plants. Each of the columns of the table is a short-run production function. The production function itself is just the collection of all the short-run production functions.

The total product curves for these four different plant sizes appear in Fig. 10.7. As you can see, each total product curve has the same basic shape, but the bigger the sweater plant, the larger is the number of sweaters knitted each day by a given number of workers. One of the fundamental technological facts reflected in the shape of a total product curve is the law of diminishing returns.

Diminishing Returns

Diminishing returns occur in all four plants as the labor input increases. You can check that fact by doing calculations for the larger plants similar to those done in Fig. 10.2. Regardless of the size of the plant, the larger the labor input, the lower (eventually) its marginal product.

Just as we can calculate the marginal product of labor for each plant size, we can also calculate the marginal product of capital for each quantity of labor. The **marginal product of capital** is the change in total product resulting from a one-unit increase in the quantity of capital employed, holding the quantity of labor constant. It is calculated in a similar way to the marginal product of labor. Also, it behaves in a similar way to the marginal product of labor. That is, if the labor input is held constant as the capital input is increased, the marginal product of capital diminishes.

The law of diminishing returns tells us what happens to output when a firm changes one input, either labor or capital, and holds the other input constant. What happens to output if a firm changes both labor and equipment?

Returns to Scale

A change in scale occurs when there is an equal percentage change in the use of all the firm's inputs. For example, if Swanky has been employing one worker and has one knitting machine and then doubles its use of both inputs (to use two workers and two knitting machines), the scale of the firm doubles. **Returns to scale** are the increases in output that result from increasing all inputs by the same percentage. There are three possible cases.

- Constant returns to scale
- Increasing returns to scale
- Decreasing returns to scale

Constant Returns to Scale Constant returns to scale occur when the percentage increase in a firm's output is equal to the percentage increase in its inputs. If constant returns to scale are present, when a firm doubles all its inputs, its output exactly doubles. Constant returns to scale occur if a rise in output is achieved by replicating the original production process. For example, General Motors can double its production of Cavaliers by doubling its production facility for those cars. It can build an identical production line and hire an identical number of workers. With the two identical production lines, GM will produce exactly twice as many cars.

Increasing Returns to Scale Increasing returns to scale (also called **economies of scale**) occur when the percentage increase in output exceeds the percentage increase in inputs. If economies of scale are present when a firm doubles all its inputs, its output more than doubles. Economies of scale occur in production processes where increased output enables a firm to use a more productive technology. For example, if GM produces only 100 cars a week, it will not pay to install an automated assembly line. The cost per car will be lower if instead GM uses skilled, but expensive, workers equipped only with inexpensive hand tools. But at an output rate of a few thousand cars a week, it will pay GM to install an automated assembly line. Workers will each specialize in a few tasks at which they will become highly proficient. General Motors may use 100 times more capital and labor, but the number of cars it can make will increase much more than a hundredfold. It will experience increasing returns to scale.

Decreasing Returns to Scale Decreasing returns to scale (also called **diseconomies of scale**) occur when the percentage increase in output is less than the percentage increase in inputs. For example, if inputs double and output increases by 50 percent, diseconomies of scale are present. Diseconomies of scale occur in all production processes at some output rate, but perhaps at a very high one. The most common source of diseconomies of scale is the increasingly complex management and organizational structure required to control a large firm. The larger the organization, the larger the number of layers in the management pyramid and the greater the costs of monitoring and maintaining control of all the various stages in the production and marketing process.

Scale Economies at Swanky   Swanky's production possibilities, which were presented in Fig. 10.7, display both economies of scale and diseconomies of scale. If Sidney has 1 knitting machine and employs 1 worker, his factory will produce 4 sweaters a day. If he doubles the firm's inputs to 2 knitting machines and 2 workers, the factory's output will rise almost fourfold to 15 sweaters a day. If he increases his inputs another 50 percent to 3 knitting machines and 3 workers, output will rise to 22 sweaters a day—an increase of less than 50 percent. Doubling the scale of Swanky from 1 to 2 units of each input gives rise to economies of scale, but the further increase from 2 to 3 units of each input gives rise to diseconomies of scale.

Whether a firm experiences increasing, constant, or decreasing returns to scale has an important effect on its long-run costs. Let's see how.

Plant Size and Cost

Earlier in this chapter, we worked out Swanky's short-run costs when the firm has a fixed amount of capital—one knitting machine—and a variable number of workers. We can also work out the short-run costs of different plant sizes. It takes longer to change the size of the production plant than to change the size of the plant's work force. That is why we speak of a short run for each different plant size. But Sidney can buy another knitting machine and put it into his existing factory. He will then have a different size of plant. He can vary the amount of labor employed in that plant and, as he does so, we can trace the short-run cost curves associated with those different levels of the variable input.

Let's look at the short-run costs for different plants and see how plant size itself affects the short-run cost curves.

Four Different Plants

We've already studied the costs of a plant with 1 knitting machine. We'll call that plant *a*. The table in Fig. 10.8 sets out the costs for plant *a* and for 3 other plants—what we will call plants *b, c,* and *d*. Plant *b* has 2 knitting machines; plant *c* has 3 knitting machines; and plant *d* has 4 knitting machines.

The average total cost curves associated with the original plant and these 3 larger plants appear in Fig. 10.8(a). The average total cost curve for each of the 4 plant sizes has the same basic U-shape. Which of these cost curves Swanky operates on depends on its plant size. For example, if Swanky has plant *a*, then its average total cost curve will be ATC_a and it will cost $7.69 per sweater to knit 13 sweaters a day. But Swanky can produce 13 sweaters a day with any of these 4 different plant sizes. If it uses plant *b*, the average total cost curve is ATC_b and the average total cost of a sweater is $6.80. If it uses plant *c*, the average cost curve is ATC_c and the average total cost is the same as plant *a*—$7.69. And if it uses plant *d*, the average total cost curve is ATC_d and the average total cost of a sweater is $9.50. If Swanky wants to produce 13 sweaters a day, the economically efficient plant is plant *b*—the one with the lowest average total cost at that level of output.

Long-run Average Cost Curve

The **long-run average cost curve** traces the relationship between the lowest attainable average total cost and output when both capital and labor inputs can be varied. This curve is illustrated in Fig. 10.8(b) as *LRAC*. The curve is derived from the 4 short-run average total cost curves that we have just reviewed in Fig. 10.8(a). As you can see, from either part (a) or (b), and highlighted in red in the table, plant *a* has the lowest average total cost for all output rates up to 10 sweaters a day. Plant *b* has the lowest average total cost for output rates between 10 and 18 sweaters a day. Between output rates of 18 and 24 sweaters a day, plant *c* has the lowest average total cost. Finally, for output rates above 24 sweaters a day, plant *d* has the lowest average total cost. The segments of the four average total cost curves for which each plant has the lowest average total cost are highlighted in Fig. 10.8(b). The scalloped curve made up of these four segments is the long-run average cost curve.

Swanky will be on its long-run average cost curve if it does the following: to produce up to 10 sweaters a day, it uses 1 knitting machine; to produce between 11 and 18 sweaters a day, it uses 2 knitting machines; to produce between 19 and 24 sweaters a day, it uses 3 knitting machines; and, finally, to produce more than 24 sweaters a day, it uses 4 knitting machines. Within these ranges, it varies its output by varying the number of workers employed.

Long-run Cost and Returns to Scale There is a connection between the long-run average cost curve and returns to scale. Figure 10.9 shows this connection. When long-run average cost falls, there are increasing returns to scale (or economies of scale). When long-run average cost rises, there are decreasing returns to scale (or diseconomies of scale). At outputs up to 15 sweaters a day, Swanky experiences economies of scale; at 15 sweaters a day, long-run average cost is at a minimum. When output rises above 15 sweaters a day, Swanky experiences diseconomies of scale.

The long-run average cost curve derived for Swanky has two special features that will not always be found in a firm's long-run cost curve. First, Swanky is able to adjust its plant size only in big jumps. We can imagine varying the plant in tiny increments so that there is an infinite number of plant sizes. In such a situation, there will be an infinite number of short-run average total cost curves, one for each plant. Second, Swanky's long-run average cost curve is either falling (economies of scale) or rising (diseconomies of scale). Some production processes will have constant returns to scale over some intermediate range of output.

Figure 10.10 illustrates this alternative situation in which there is an infinite number of plant sizes and output ranges over which returns to scale are increasing (up to Q_1), constant (between Q_1 and Q_2), and decreasing (above Q_2). To keep the figure clear, only one of the infinite number of short-run average total cost curves, labeled *SRAC,* is shown. Each short-run average total cost curve touches the long-run average cost curve (*LRAC*) at a single point (one output). Thus for each output, there is a unique, economically efficient plant size. The short-run average total cost curve shown in Fig. 10.10 is for the plant that can produce output rate Q_0 at minimum average total cost, ATC_0.

The first time the long-run average cost curve appeared in print, it was drawn incorrectly. Take a look at Our Advancing Knowledge (p. 250) to see why. You will understand the connection between short-run and long-run average cost curves more thoroughly after you have studied the material in that box.

Long-run Costs Are Total Costs When we examine short-run costs, we distinguish between fixed, variable, and total cost. We make no such distinctions for long-run costs. All inputs vary in the long run, so there are no long-run fixed costs. Since there are no long-run fixed costs, long-run total cost and long-run variable cost are the same thing. The long-run average variable cost is the long-run average cost.

There is a long-run marginal cost curve that goes with the long-run average cost curve. The relationship between the long-run average cost curve and the long-run marginal cost curve is similar to that between the short-run average total cost curve and the short-run marginal cost curve. When long-run average cost is falling, long-run marginal cost is below long-run average cost. When long-run average cost is rising, long-run marginal cost is higher than long-run average cost, and when long-run average cost is constant, long-run marginal cost is equal to long-run average cost.

Shifts in Cost Curves

Both short-run and long-run cost curves depend on two things: the production function and input prices. A change in technology shifts the production function and thus shifts the cost curves. Technological advances increase the output that can be produced from given inputs. They also shift the total product curve as well as the average and the marginal product curves upward, and they shift the cost curves downward. For example, advances in genetic engineering are making it possible to increase the milk production of a cow without increasing the amount of food that it eats—a technological advance that lowers the cost of milk production.

Resource or input prices also affect the cost curves. If the price of an input increases, it directly increases cost and shifts the cost curves upward.

Returns to Scale in Reality

Let's close this chapter by looking at some real world examples and see why there is a great deal of excess capacity in some industries while in others firms are operating "flat-out."

Excess Capacity

It has been estimated that one vacuum cleaner factory could produce a quarter of all the vacuum

Figure 10.8   Short-run and Long-run Costs

(a) Short-run average cost

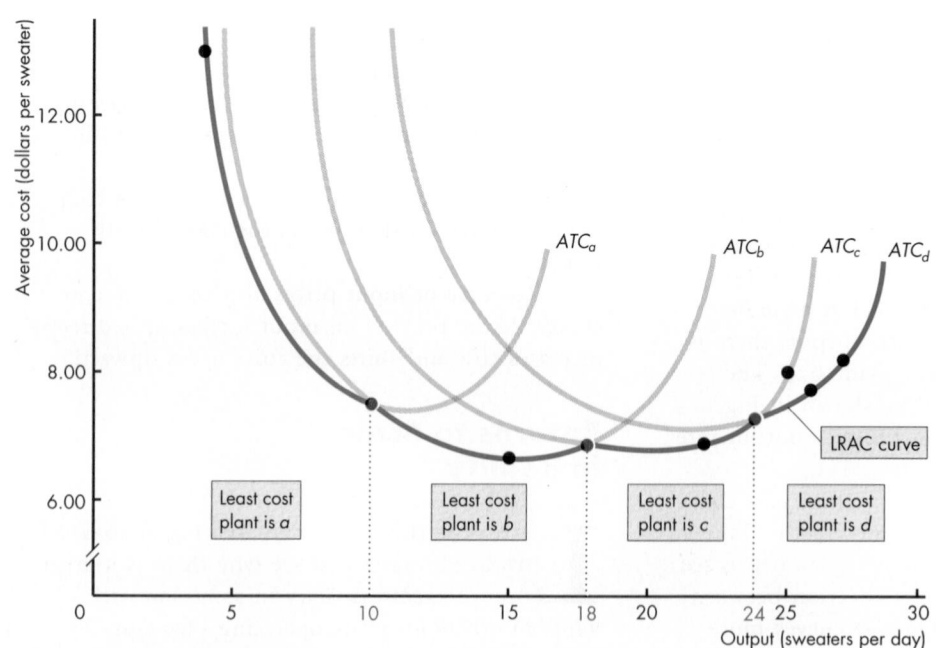

(b) Long-run average cost

The table (opposite page) shows the short-run costs of four different plants. Each plant has a different fixed cost. Plant *a* has 1 knitting machine and a fixed cost of $25; plant *b* has 2 knitting machines and a fixed cost of $50; plant *c* has 3 knitting machines and a fixed cost of $75; and plant *d* has 4 knitting machines and a fixed cost of $100. The short-run average total cost curve for each plant is graphed in part (a). Part (b) illustrates the construction of the long-run average cost curve. This curve traces the lowest attainable costs of production at each output when both capital and labor inputs are varied. On the long-run average cost curve, and highlighted in the table, Swanky uses plant *a* to produce up to 10 sweaters a day; plant *b* to produce between 11 and 18 sweaters a day; plant *c* to produce between 19 and 24 sweaters a day; and plant *d* to produce more than 24 sweaters a day.

Figure 10.8   (Continued)

Labor (workers per day)	Output (sweaters per day)	Total fixed cost	Total variable cost	Total cost	Average total cost (dollars per sweater)
			(dollars per day)		

Plant a: 1 unit of capital—total cost of capital = $25

Labor	Output	TFC	TVC	TC	ATC
1	4	25	25	50	12.50
2	10	25	50	75	7.50
3	13	25	75	100	7.69
4	15	25	100	125	8.33
5	16	25	125	150	9.38

Plant b: 2 units of capital—total cost of capital = $50

Labor	Output	TFC	TVC	TC	ATC
1	10	50	25	75	7.50
2	15	50	50	100	6.67
3	18	50	75	125	6.94
4	20	50	100	150	7.50
5	21	50	125	175	8.33

Plant c: 3 units of capital—total cost of capital = $75

Labor	Output	TFC	TVC	TC	ATC
1	13	75	25	100	7.69
2	18	75	50	125	6.94
3	22	75	75	150	6.82
4	24	75	100	175	7.29
5	25	75	125	200	8.00

Plant d: 4 units of capital—total cost of capital = $100

Labor	Output	TFC	TVC	TC	ATC
1	15	100	25	125	8.33
2	21	100	50	150	7.14
3	24	100	75	175	7.29
4	26	100	100	200	7.69
5	27	100	125	225	8.33

cleaners produced in the United States before its long-run average cost would fall to a minimum.[1]

[1]James V. Koch, *Industrial Organization and Prices,* 2nd ed. (Englewood Cliffs, N.J.: Prentice-Hall, 1980), 123–134.

But there are more than four vacuum cleaner factories in the United States, so each factory is operating at an output rate below that at which long-run average cost is at a minimum. The situation also holds for TV picture tubes and for steel, cars, and

Figure 10.9 Returns to Scale

When the long-run average cost curve (*LRAC*) slopes downward, there are increasing returns to scale (or economies of scale). When the long-run average cost curve slopes upward, there are decreasing returns to scale (or diseconomies of scale).

Figure 10.10 Short-run and Long-run Average Costs

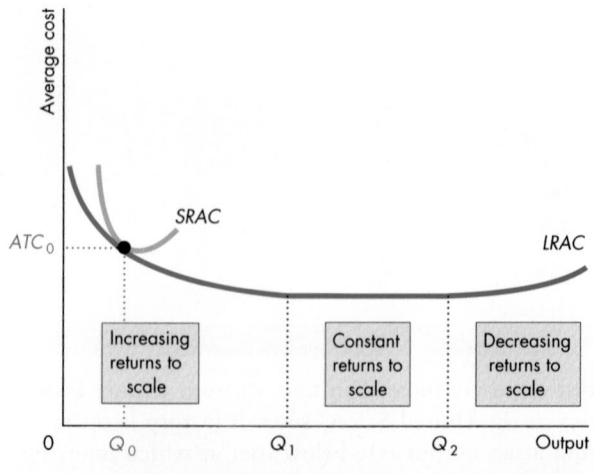

If the capital input can be varied in small units, there are not just four different plant sizes, as in Figure 10.8, but an infinitely large number of them. There are also an infinitely large number of short-run average total cost curves. Each short-run average total cost curve touches the long-run average cost curve at a single point. For example, the short-run average total cost curve (*SRAC*) touches the long-run average cost curve (*LRAC*) at the output rate Q_0 and average total cost ATC_0. The short-run average total cost curve shown is representative of the infinite number of others, each with only one point touching the long-run average cost curve. The long-run average cost curve also illustrates the possibility of constant returns to scale: For outputs up to Q_1, there are increasing returns to scale; between Q_1 and Q_2, there are constant returns to scale; above Q_2, there are decreasing returns to scale.

Figure 10.11 Excess Capacity

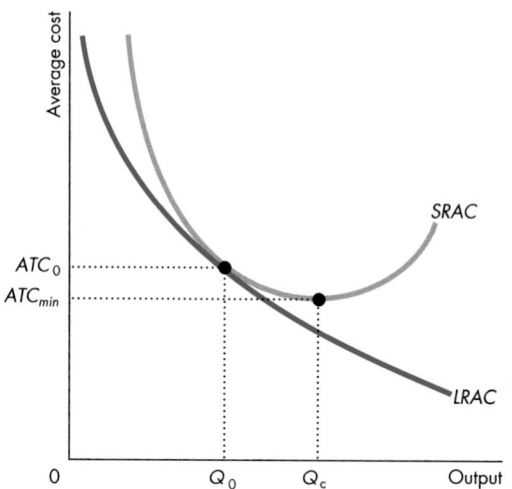

The size of the market limits a firm's output to Q_0. At output Q_0, the long-run average cost curve is downward sloping—there are economies of scale. To produce Q_0 at least cost, the firm installs a plant with a capacity of Q_c and operates the plant below capacity. This situation prevails in many industries, including those manufacturing vacuum cleaners, TV picture tubes, steel, cars, petroleum refining, typewriters, cigarettes, semiconductors and matches.

petroleum refining. Economies of scale also exist for typewriters, cigarettes, semiconductors, and matches.

Figure 10.11 illustrates the situation that prevails in those industries that can lower their average production costs if the market is big enough to permit them to expand to their most efficient scale. Output, limited by the extent of the market, is Q_0. The firm is producing efficiently at an average total cost of ATC_0. But the firm has excess capacity. It can lower its costs to ATC_{min} even with its existing plant if output can be increased to Q_c, and it can lower its costs even more by switching to a bigger plant. But the firm can't sell more than Q_0. So, even when it is operating as efficiently as possible, the firm has excess capacity. The production of vacuum cleaners, TV picture tubes, steel cars, and the other products mentioned above are examples of industries in which the situation shown in Fig. 10.11 prevails.

Operating "Flat-Out"

When we examined the short-run marginal cost of NEPOOL, we discovered that its marginal cost increases as it produces more power. As we saw in Figure 10.6, NEPOOL's marginal cost curve slopes upward and becomes extremely steep at output rates in excess of 17,000 megawatt hours. Why don't the companies in NEPOOL build additional plants? We can answer this question by applying the lessons that you've just learned about the relationship between short-run and long-run costs.

Figure 10.12 shows NEPOOL's short-run marginal cost curve (MC) as well as its short-run average total cost curve (ATC). Two points are

Figure 10.12 Overutilizing Capacity

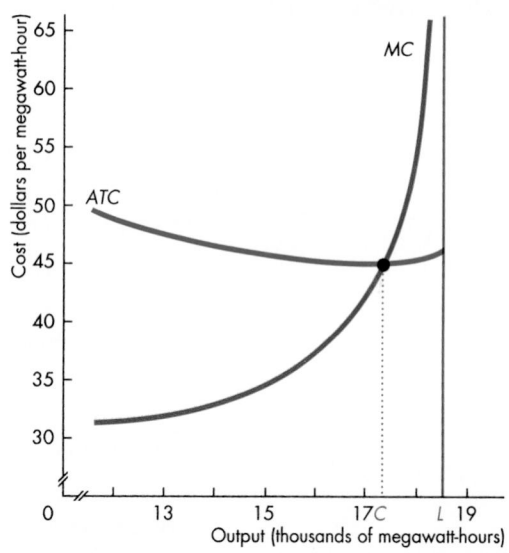

Although NEPOOL producers face steeply increasing marginal costs, their average total cost declines up to output C. The capacity (minimum cost) of NEPOOL'S plant is output C. Output L is the physical limit of their plant. Between C and L, average total cost rises. When demand increases so that NEPOOL is producing in the range between C and L for a significant amount of time, it will be efficient to increase its plant size to meet the additional demand. It will not be efficient to build a bigger plant to meet current demand even though, at peak demand, NEPOOL is operating "flat-out." Although marginal cost can be lowered with a larger plant, average total cost cannot.

Cost Curves

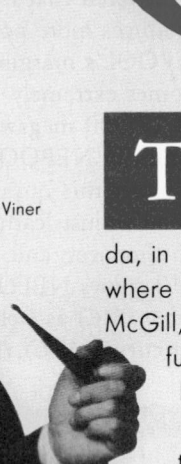

Jacob Viner

T he cost curves that you have studied in this chapter were first expressed in their current form in 1931 by Jacob Viner in an article entitled "Cost Curves and Supply Curves."* Viner, the son of poor immigrant parents from Eastern Europe, was born in Montreal, Canada, in 1892. He did his undergraduate studies at McGill University in Montreal, where he was taught economics by Steven Leacock, the famous humorist. From McGill, Viner went to Harvard where he earned a Ph.D. in 1922. He became a full professor at the University of Chicago at the age of 32. In 1946, he left Chicago for Princeton, where he stayed until his death in 1970.

Viner wrote many important books and articles, mostly on international economic issues. It was his article on cost curves, though, that became his most widely known work. His analysis of cost and cost curves is now studied by every beginning student of economics.

Short-run Cost Curves

Viner's account of the behavior of short-run cost is so clear that it provides a beautifully compact review of what you have studied in this chapter. The following is the essence of Viner's own presentation:

• The short run is a period long enough to permit any desired change of output that is technologically possible without altering the scale of plant but not long enough to permit any adjustment of scale of plant.
• Inputs are classified in two groups—those necessarily fixed in amount in the short run and those freely variable.
• Scale of plant means the amount of the inputs that are fixed in the short run.
• Scale of plant is measured by the output that it produces when average total cost is at a minimum.
• Costs associated with fixed factors are called fixed costs.
• Costs associated with variable factors are called variable costs.**

Viner's diagram of short-run cost curves is reproduced below.†

Viner pointed out the following features of the cost curves:

• Average fixed cost (AFC) declines as output rises.
• Average variable cost (AVC) rises as output rises.
• Marginal cost (MC) rises and equals average cost (ATC) at the lowest point of average total cost.
• Average cost is the vertical sum of average fixed cost and average variable cost and is necessarily U-shaped "for all industries having any substantial fixed costs."

Long-run Cost Curves

Viner also showed how the short-run cost curves and long-run cost curves are related to each other. In this exercise, he made what has become a famous mistake and one which can reinforce your understanding of the long-run average cost curve. The figure below shows the relation between the long-run average cost curve *(LRAC)* and short-run average total cost curve *(SRAC)* in part (a) and Viner's version in part (b).

When instructing his draftsman, a brilliant Chinese mathematician at the University of Chicago, Viner asked that the long-run average cost curve do two things:

• Pass through the minimum point of each *SRAC* curve.

• Not rise above any *SRAC* curve at any point

Notice that in part (a) the *SRAC* curve is never below the *LRAC* curve. Part (a) thus satisfies Viner's second instruction—that the *LRAC* curve not rise above any *SRAC* curve at any point. But it does not satisfy Viner's first instruction—that the long-run average cost curve pass through the minimum point of each *SRAC* curve.

In part (b), you can see what purports to be a long-run average cost curve and that curve does pass through the minimum points of the *SRAC* curves. This curve satisfies Viner's first condition but not the second.

Viner had given his draftsman what he subsequently called a "technically impossible and economically inappropriate assignment." It is possible to draw a curve that never rises above a *SRAC* curve and that *does not* pass through the points of minimum short-run average total cost [part a] or it is possible to draw a curve that passes through the points of minimum short-run average total cost and that *does* rise above the *SRAC* curve (part b), but it is not possible to draw a curve that does both of these things. The curve in part (a) is a long-run average cost curve and the curve in part (b) is not.

Such is the stuff of advancing knowledge. A great economist like Jacob Viner, struggling with a new idea, makes a mistake. Today, a student in an introductory economics course would feel embarrassed to make such an error.

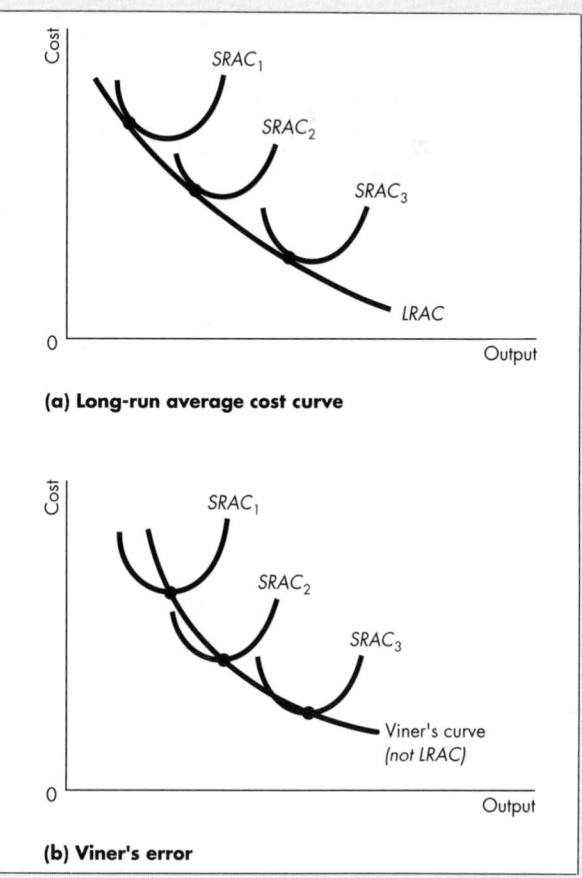

(a) Long-run average cost curve

(b) Viner's error

---

*One of most accessible sources for Viner's article is George J. Stigler and Kenneth E. Boulding (eds.), *Readings in Price Theory* (Chicago: Richard D. Irwin, 1952), 198–232. The brief Viner quotations that appear in this box are taken from this source. The article was first published in *Zeitschrift für Nationalökonomie*, vol. III (1931) pp. 23–46.

**Viner called variable costs "direct costs."

†The figure shown here is a simplified version of the one that appeared in the original article.

marked on the Output axis. Point *C* is NEPOOL's capacity. (The word *capacity* is being used here in its economic sense as the output rate that minimizes average total cost.) The other point marked is *L*, the physical limits of the output of the existing plant.

NEPOOL's marginal cost curve slopes upward very steeply because as its output approaches its physical limits, generators are brought into operation that use very expensive fuel (similar to that used by jet aircraft). But the average total cost curve has a much more gentle slope. Why? Because the bulk of NEPOOL's costs are not variable fuel costs at all but fixed costs. NEPOOL's fixed resources—capital equipment and skilled labor—cannot be varied to meet hourly shifts in demand for power. The great proportion of total costs coming from these fixed resources smoothes out NEPOOL's average total cost. NEPOOL's output fluctuates between 11,500 and 17,000 megawatt-hours (see Fig. 10.6). NEPOOL producers operate on the rising part of the marginal cost curve, but they also operate on a falling part of their average total cost curve. Occasionally, output rises above capacity and therefore moves into the range in which average total cost rises. But such cases are rare—occurring only at the peak of demand for the year.

As the demand for electric power gradually rises, the NEPOOL producers will be able to achieve greater economic efficiency by increasing their plant size. Currently, output fluctuates between 11,500 megawatt-hours and 17,000 megawatt-hours. If demand fluctuates between 17,000 and 19,000 megawatt-hours, production will be taking place on the rising part of the short-run

average total cost curve and, on some occasions, it will be necessary for NEPOOL to operate "flat-out"—at its physical limits—and to import power from neighboring power pools to meet the demand. It will pay NEPOOL producers to increase their production capacity to meet the additional demand.

It does not pay to increase capacity to meet demand fluctuations in the range shown in the figure. An increased plant will increase the fixed costs and shift the average total cost curve upward. The new average total cost curve will only fall below the current one at higher outputs than can be sold. Thus, it pays the NEPOOL power companies to stick with their existing plants and operate them "flat-out" to meet the peak demand.

■ We have now studied the way in which a firm's costs vary as it varies its inputs and output rate. We've seen how the fact that marginal product eventually diminishes gives rise to eventually increasing average and marginal cost. We've also seen how long-run cost curves take their shape from economies and diseconomies of scale—long-run average cost decreasing as output increases with economies of scale and long-run average cost increasing as output increases with diseconomies of scale.

In the next chapter, we're going to probe a firm's costs and input decisions more closely, studying the way in which its demands for inputs at a given output are affected by input prices. With this model, we'll be able to understand why we see variations in techniques employed and why some industries are much more capital-intensive than others.

S U M M A R Y

Firms' Objectives and Constraints

Firms aim to maximize profit. Profit maximization stems directly from scarcity. Only firms that maximize profits can survive in a competitive environment.

Constraints are imposed on profit maximization by the market and by technology. Some firms operate in such competitive markets that they have

no choice but to sell their output at the going price. Other firms can choose the price of their output. However, at higher prices, they will sell less. Most firms are unable to influence the markets for their inputs and have to buy them at the going prices. Technology limits the production process of firms. If firms are technologically efficient, then they can increase their output only by using more inputs.

In the short run, some inputs cannot be changed. In most cases, the capital input is fixed in the short run while labor can be varied. (pp. 229–230)

The Short-run Production Function

The short-run production function describes the limits to output as a firm changes the quantity of a variable input such as labor. The short-run production function is described by the total, average, and marginal product curves. Total product is the output produced in a given period. Average product is total product per unit of variable input. Marginal product is the change in total product resulting from a one-unit increase in the variable input. As the variable input is increased, average and marginal product rise at first until they reach a peak, and thereafter they fall—diminishing returns begin. When average product rises, marginal product exceeds average product. When average product falls, marginal product is less than average product. When average product is at its maximum, marginal product equals average product. (pp. 230–235)

Short-run Cost

Total cost is divided into total fixed cost and total variable cost. As output rises, total cost rises because total variable cost rises. Marginal cost is the additional cost of producing one more unit of output. Average total cost is total cost per unit of output.

Costs depend on how much a firm produces. Average fixed cost falls as output rises. Average variable cost and average total cost are U-shaped. Marginal cost is also U-shaped. When average cost is falling, marginal cost is below average cost, and when average cost is rising, marginal cost exceeds average cost. When average product is at a maximum, average variable cost is at a minimum. When average product is rising, average variable cost is falling and when average product is falling, average variable cost is rising. (pp. 235–240)

Plant Size, Cost, and Capacity

Plant capacity is the output rate with the lowest average total cost. Firms that produce a smaller amount than their capacity are said to have excess capacity; those that produce a larger amount than their capacity are said to have overutilized their capacity.

Long-run cost is the cost of production when all inputs—labor as well as plant and equipment—have been adjusted to their economically efficient levels. The behavior of long-run cost depends on the firm's production function. As a firm uses more labor while holding capital constant, it eventually experiences diminishing returns. When it uses more capital while holding labor constant, it also experiences diminishing returns. When it varies all its inputs in equal proportions, it experiences returns to scale. Returns to scale can be constant, increasing, or decreasing. (pp. 240–244)

Plant Size and Cost

There is a set of short-run cost curves for each different plant size. There is one least-cost plant for each output. The higher the output, the larger is the plant that will minimize average total cost.

The long-run average cost curve traces the relationship between the lowest attainable average total cost and output when both capital and labor inputs can be varied. With constant returns to scale, the long-run average cost curve is horizontal. With increasing returns to scale, the long-run average cost curve slopes downward. With decreasing returns to scale, the long-run average cost curve slopes upward.

There is no distinction between fixed cost and variable cost in the long run. Since all inputs are variable, all costs are also variable.

Cost curves shift when either input prices or technology change. An improvement in technology raises the output from a given set of inputs and shifts the cost curves downward. A rise in input prices shifts the cost curves upward. (pp. 244–245)

Returns to Scale in Reality

Some firms, including those that make vacuum cleaners, TV picture tubes, and cars, have increasing returns to scale (economies of scale). Usually economies of scale exist when the total market is too small to allow the efficient scale of production. In such industries, firms operate efficiently with excess capacity.

Some firms overutilize their plants, operating

them at an output rate that exceeds capacity. The NEPOOL power producers are an example. Though the marginal cost of electric power rises as output rises, only rarely does NEPOOL produce so much power that producers are operating on the upward-sloping section of their short-run average total cost curves. Only if a firm persistently operates on the upward-sloping part of its short-run average total cost curve is it efficient to increase its plant size. (pp. 245–252)

KEY CONCEPTS

Average fixed cost, 237
Average product, 232
Average total cost, 237
Average variable cost, 237
Capacity, 240
Capital-intensive technique, 229
Constant returns to scale, 243
Decreasing returns to scale or diseconomies of scale, 243
Diminishing marginal returns, 235
Excess capacity, 240
Fixed cost, 237
Fixed inputs, 230
Increasing marginal returns, 235
Increasing returns to scale or economies of scale, 243
Labor-intensive technique, 229
Law of diminishing returns, 235
Long run, 230
Long-run average cost curve, 244
Long-run cost, 242
Marginal cost, 237
Marginal product, 231
Marginal product of capital, 243
Marginal product of labor, 231
Market constraints, 229
Overutilized capacity, 240

Physical limits, 240
Production function, 242
Profit maximization, 229
Returns to scale, 243
Short run, 230
Short-run production function, 230
Technique, 229
Total cost, 237
Total fixed cost, 237
Total product, 230
Total product curve, 231
Total variable cost, 237
Variable cost, 237
Variable inputs, 230

Key Figures and Tables

REVIEW QUESTIONS

1 Why do we assume that firms maximize profit?

2 What are the main constraints on a firm's ability to maximize profit?

3 Distinguish between the short run and the long run.

4 Define total product, average product, and marginal product. Explain the relationships between a total product curve, average product curve, and marginal product curve.

5 State the law of diminishing returns. What does this law imply about the shapes of the total, marginal, and average product curves?

6 Define total cost, total fixed cost, total variable cost, average total cost, average fixed cost, average variable cost, and marginal cost.

7 What is the relationship between the average total cost curve, the average variable cost curve, and the marginal cost curve?

8 Define the long-run average cost curve. What is the relationship between the long-run average cost curve and the short-run average total cost curves?

9 What does the long-run average cost curve tell us?

10 Define economies of scale. What effects do economies of scale have on the shape of the long-run average cost curve?

11 When does the long-run average cost curve touch the minimum point of a short-run average total cost curve?

12 When does the long-run average cost curve touch a point on the short-run average total cost curve to the left of its minimum point?

13 When does the long-run average cost curve touch a point on the short-run average total cost curve to the right of its minimum point?

14 Why might long-run average cost decline? Why might long-run average cost rise?

15 What makes the short-run cost curves shift (a) upward or (b) downward?

P R O B L E M S

1 The short-run production function of Rubber Duckies, Inc., a firm making rubber boats, is described by the following:

Labor (number of persons employed per week)	Output (rubber boats per week)
1	1
2	2
3	4
4	7
5	11
6	14
7	16
8	17
9	18
10	18

a) Draw the total product curve.

b) Calculate average product and draw the average product curve.

c) Calculate marginal product and draw the marginal product curve.

d) What is the relationship between average product and marginal product at output rates below 16 boats per week? Why?

e) What is the relationship between average product and marginal product at outputs above 16 boats per week? Why?

2 Suppose that the price of labor is $400 per week, total fixed costs are $10,000 a week, and the production possibilities are those presented in question 1.

a) Calculate the firm's total cost, total variable cost, and total fixed costs for each of the outputs given.

b) Draw the total cost, total variable cost, and total fixed cost curves.

c) Calculate the firm's average total cost, average fixed cost, average variable cost, and marginal cost at each of the outputs given.

d) Draw the following cost curves: average total cost, average variable cost, average fixed cost, and marginal cost.

3 Suppose that total fixed costs rise to $11,000 a week. How will this affect the firm's average total cost, average fixed cost, average variable cost, and marginal cost curves in question 2.

4 Suppose that total fixed costs remain at $10,000 a week, but that the price of labor rises to $450 a week. Using these new costs, rework questions 2(a) and (b) and draw the new cost curves.

Chapter 11

(Optional)

Producing at Least Cost

After studying this chapter, you will be able to:

- Define and calculate the marginal rate of substitution between two inputs

- Explain what an isoquant measures

- Explain what an isocost line measures

- Calculate the least-cost technique of production

- Predict the effect of a change in input prices on the least-cost technique

- Explain variations in capital intensity across industries and countries

If you journey to the right part of Amazonia, deep in the interior of Brazil, you will encounter a scene straight from medieval times. As you approach by helicopter, you can see through the mist an enormous pit, several hundred feet wide, dug into the earth. As you draw closer, you can see crude wooden ladders scaling the pit's terraces. Finally, you distinguish the muddy, exhausted shapes of thousands of men scaling the ladders with sacks of dirt on their backs. The scene you are watching is an enormous gold mine, being dug largely by hand by laborers paid little more than a dollar a day. ■ The scene is different at a strip mine in North America. There, far fewer workers, who receive far higher pay, operate earthmovers so large that they make ordinary cars and trucks look like toys. ■ Why do such differences exist? Why do gold mines in Amazonia employ such large numbers of people, risking their lives daily on rickety ladders? Why don't Brazilian mines use the efficient, labor-saving equipment of North American mines? ■ The capital equipment used by all the firms operating in the United States is worth close to three trillion dollars—or $26,000 per person employed. The processed food industry—producing packaged meat and frozen fruits and vegetables—uses about the average amount of capital per worker. Manufacturers of chemicals, especially of plastic materials and industrial gases, use eight times the average amount of capital per person; manufacturers of shirts and other clothing use around one tenth the average capital per person. Why don't shirtmakers use more machinery? Why do plastics makers use so much capital equipment?

■ Capital per person employed varies because different industries, and even different countries, use different techniques of production. The choice of a technique of

A Dollar a
Day in
Amazonia

Figure 11.1   Swanky's Production Function

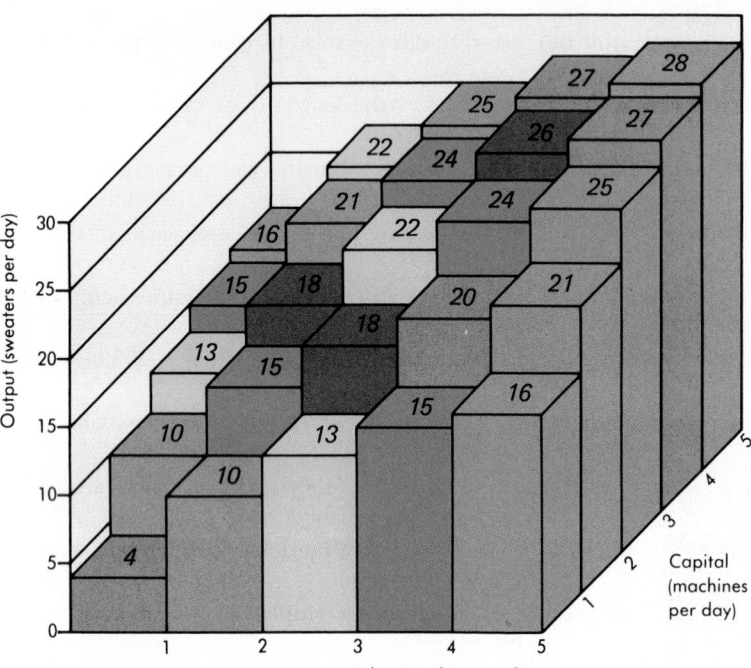

The figure shows how many sweaters can be produced a day by various combinations of labor and capital input. For example, by using 4 workers and 2 knitting machines, Swanky can produce 20 sweaters.

production is a crucial decision to be made by a firm. This chapter examines the way in which firms make such decisions. It also introduces you to some powerful tools of analysis that are well worth the effort required to master them.

Input Substitution

You would be hard-pressed to think of many goods that can be produced in only one way. Just about every good and service can be produced by using a large amount of labor and a small amount of capital or a large amount of capital and a small amount of labor. For example, cars can be made with computer-controlled robotic assembly lines that use enormous amounts of capital and hardly any labor, or they can be built by skilled labor using only hand tools; highways and dams can be built using giant earth-moving machines operated by a small amount of labor or by hoards of workers using picks, shovels, and wheelbarrows.

A production technique that uses a lot of capital per worker is called a *capital-intensive technique.* One that uses a lot of labor and a little capital per worker is called a *labor-intensive technique.* Capital intensity is the ratio of capital to labor employed in a production process. Labor intensity is the ratio of labor to capital.

The technically feasible range of production possibilities is described by the production function. An example of a production function is shown in Fig. 11.1. This production function is that of Swanky, Inc. (the sweater factory owned by Sidney that was introduced in Chapter 10). The figure records the maximum daily output of sweaters that can be produced by using different combinations of labor and capital. For example, if Swanky has 3 knitting machines and employs 1 worker, it can produce 13 sweaters a day. With 3 knitting machines and 5 workers, it can produce 25 sweaters a day.

If you study the numbers in Fig. 11.1, you will see that it shows three ways of producing 15 sweaters a day. It also shows two ways of producing 10, 13, 16, 18, 21, 22, 24, 25, and 27 sweaters a day.

Table 11.1   Substituting Between Capital and Labor to Produce 15 Sweaters a Day

Method	Capital (K)	Labor (L)	Fall in capital (−ΔK)	Rise in labor (ΔL)	Marginal rate of substitution of capital for labor (−ΔK/ΔL)
a	4	1			
		 2	2	1	2
b	2	2			
		 1	1	2	1/2
c	1	4			

Switching from method a to method b involves cutting capital (−ΔK) by 2 machines and raising the labor (ΔL) by 1 worker. The marginal rate of substitution of capital for labor—which is the ratio of the fall in capital (−ΔK) to the rise in labor (ΔL)—is 2. Switching from method b to method c involves cutting capital by 1 machine and raising labor by 2 workers, which means that the marginal rate of substitution of capital for labor is 1/2.

The production function in Fig. 11.1 can be used to calculate the marginal product of labor and the marginal product of capital. As we learned in Chapter 10, *marginal product of labor* is the change in total product per unit change of labor, holding the amount of capital constant. We've already learned how to calculate the marginal product of labor in Chapter 10 and so we will not repeat the calculations here. The *marginal product of capital* is the change in total product per unit change in capital, holding the amount of labor constant. Although we have not calculated examples of marginal products of capital, there is no new principle involved in such calculations. They are performed in exactly the same way as the calculation of the marginal product of labor that you studied in the previous chapter. Furthermore, the law of diminishing returns applies to capital just as it does to labor. That is, holding labor input constant, the marginal product of capital diminishes as the capital input increases.

It's easy to see why the law of diminishing returns applies to capital by imagining this scene in Swanky's knitting factory. Suppose that there is 1 worker with 1 machine. Output (as shown in Fig. 11.1) is 4 sweaters a day. If an extra machine is installed, the one worker can still easily handle the 2 machines. One machine can be set to knit blue

sweaters and the other, red sweaters. There's no need to stop the machines to change the wool color. Output more than doubles to 10 sweaters a day. But if a third machine is added, a single worker finds it hard to cope with the increasingly complex factory. For example, there are now three times as many breakdowns as there were with just 1 machine. The worker has to spend an increasing amount of time fixing problems. Output only increases to 13 sweaters a day.

Although all goods and services can be produced by using a variety of alternative methods of production, the ease with which capital and labor can be substituted for each other varies from industry to industry. The production function reflects the ease with which inputs can be substituted for each other. Also, the production function can be used to calculate the degree of substitutability between inputs. Such a calculation involves a new concept—that of the marginal rate of substitution of capital for labor.

The Substitutability of Capital and Labor

The **marginal rate of substitution of capital for labor** is the decrease in capital needed per unit increase in labor that keeps output constant. Table 11.1 illustrates how to calculate the marginal rate of substitution of capital for labor. As we saw in Fig. 11.1, there are three ways of producing 15 sweaters a day. Let's call those methods *a*, *b*, and *c*. They appear again in Table 11.1. A daily output of 15 sweaters can be produced with 4 knitting machines and 1 worker, 2 units of each input, or 1 knitting machine and 4 workers.

Changing the method of production from *a* to *b* reduces the capital input by 2 machines and raises the labor input by 1 worker. The marginal rate of substitution is the ratio of the fall in capital to the rise in labor and, for the switch from technique *a* to *b* equals 2. Switching from method *b* to *c* reduces capital by 1 machine and raises labor by 2 workers. Again, the marginal rate of substitution is the ratio of the fall in capital to the rise in labor, so, for the move from method *b* to *c* the marginal rate of substitution is ½.

The marginal rates of substitution that we have just calculated obey the **law of diminishing marginal rate of substitution** which states that:

The marginal rate of substitution of capital for labor falls as the amount of capital decreases and the amount of labor increases.

You can see that the law of diminishing marginal rate of substitution makes sense by considering Swanky's sweater factory. With 1 worker racing between 4 knitting machines, desperately trying to keep them all operating, coping with breakdowns, and keeping the wool from tangling, output can be held constant by getting rid 1 machine and hiring only a small additional amount of labor. The marginal rate of substitution is high. At the other extreme, 4 workers are falling over each other to operate 1 machine. In this situation, output can be kept constant by laying off 2 workers and installing 1 additional machine. The marginal rate of substitution is low. This principle of the diminishing marginal rate of substitution applies to (almost) all production processes.

Isoquants

Suppose that we want to graph the different combinations of labor and capital that produce 15 sweaters a day. Such a graph would be an isoquant. An **isoquant** is a curve that shows the different combinations of labor and capital required

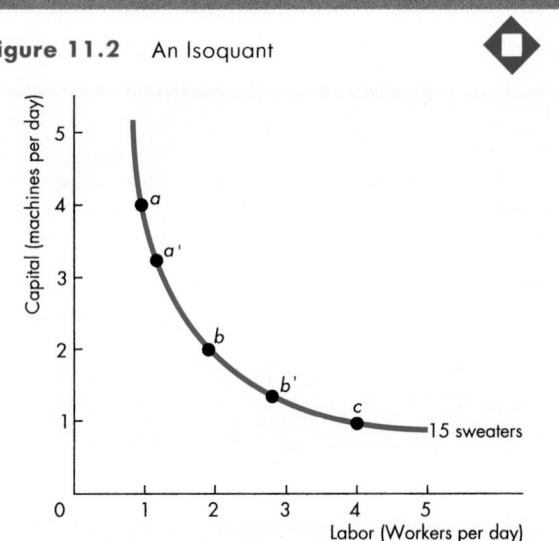

Figure 11.2   An Isoquant

This isoquant shows the different techniques of production, or combinations of capital and labor, that can produce 15 sweaters a day. For example, point a tells us that 4 machines and 1 worker can produce 15 sweaters a day. The same output level can be produced by 2 machines and 2 workers (point b) or 1 machine and 4 workers (point c). Each of these points can be found in Fig. 11.1. The isoquant also shows combinations not found in Fig. 11.1, such as a' and b'.

to produce a given quantity of output. The word *isoquant* means "equal quantity"— *iso* meaning equal and *quant* meaning quantity. Fig. 11.2 illustrates an isoquant. Each point (*a*, *b*, and *c*) represents a technique of production—a combination of workers and knitting machines—that can produce 15 sweaters a day. These three techniques are the same as those that appear in Table 11.1 (and are extracted from Fig. 11.1).

The isoquant in Fig. 11.2 shows more than the three techniques of production set out in the table. It shows *all* the combinations of capital and labor capable of producing 15 sweaters a day. For example, between *a* and *b* there is *a'*. The technique *a'* combines 3.2 knitting machines with 1.2 workers to produce 15 sweaters a day. Between *b* and *c* is *b'*. Technique *b'* combines 1.4 units of capital and 2.8 units of labor to produce 15 units of output. (You might think it's strange to talk about fractions of knitting machines and workers. If so, think of Swanky as using three machines full time and another one for one fifth of its time—0.2—so that 3.2 machines are used in total. Similarly, think of Swanky hiring one full-time worker and one part-time worker.)

Marginal Rate of Substitution and Isoquant

The marginal rate of substitution equals the magnitude of the slope of the isoquant. Fig. 11.3 illustrates this relationship. The figure shows the isoquant for 13 sweaters a day. Pick any point on this isoquant and imagine increasing labor by the smallest conceivable amount and decreasing capital in order to keep output constant at 13 sweaters. As we lower the capital input and raise the labor input, we travel along the isoquant. If the isoquant is steep (as at point *a*), the capital input falls by a large amount relative to the rise in the labor input. The marginal rate of substitution is high. But if the isoquant has a gentle slope (as at point *b*), the fall in capital is small relative to the rise in labor and the marginal rate of substitution is small.

The marginal rate of substitution at point *a* is the slope of the straight red line that is tangent to the isoquant at point *a*. The slope of the isoquant at point *a* is the same as the slope of the line. To calculate that slope, use the formula Δy divided by Δx. Along the red line, if capital (*y*) falls by 5 knitting machines, labor (*x*) rises by 2.5 workers. The magnitude of the slope is 5 divided by 2.5, which equals 2. Thus when using technique *a* to produce 13 sweaters a day, the marginal rate of substitution of capital for labor is 2.

The marginal rate of substitution at point *b* is the slope of the straight red line that is tangent to the isoquant at point *b*. This line has the same slope as the isoquant at point *b*. That slope is 2.5 knitting machines (Δy) divided by 5 workers (Δx), which equals ½. Thus when using technique *b* to produce 13 sweaters a day, the marginal rate of substitution of capital for labor is ½.

You can now see that the law of diminishing marginal rate of substitution is embedded in the shape of the isoquant. When the capital input is large and the labor input is small, the isoquant is steep. As the capital input decreases and the labor input increases the slope of the isoquant diminishes. Only curves that are bowed toward the origin have this feature; hence, isoquants are always bowed toward the origin.

Figure 11.3   The Marginal Rate of Substitution

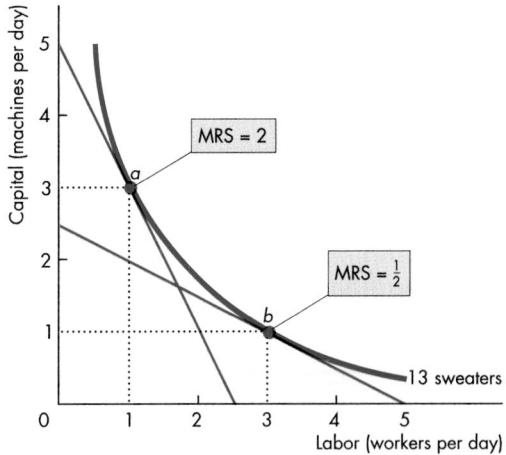

The marginal rate of substitution is measured by the magnitude of the slope of the isoquant. To calculate the marginal rate of substitution at point *a*, use the red line that is tangential to the isoquant at point *a*. Calculate the slope of that line to find the slope of the isoquant at point *a*. The magnitude of the slope at point *a* is 2. Thus at point *a*, the marginal rate of substitution of capital for labor is 2. The marginal rate of substitution at point *b* is found from the slope of the line tangential to the isoquant at that point. That slope is ½. Thus, the marginal rate of substitution of capital for labor at point *b* is ½.

The Isoquant Map

An **isoquant map** shows a series of isoquants, each for a different output. You have already seen two different isoquants in Figs. 11.2 and 11.3 (for 15 and 13 sweaters a day respectively). Figure 11.4(a) shows an isoquant map. It has three isoquants: one for 10 sweaters, the one for 15 sweaters that appears in Fig. 11.2, and one for 21 sweaters. Isoquants for higher outputs are farther from the origin. That is because for any given capital input, to produce more output you need more labor, and for any given labor input, to produce more output you need more capital. Thus starting on any given isoquant if you move to the right (more labor) or upward (more capital) or to the right and upward (more of both capital and labor), you get more output. Each of the isoquants shown in Fig. 11.4(a) is based on the production function presented in Fig. 11.1. But Fig. 11.4(a) does not show all the isoquants.

Figure 11.4   An Isoquant Map

(a) Isoquants

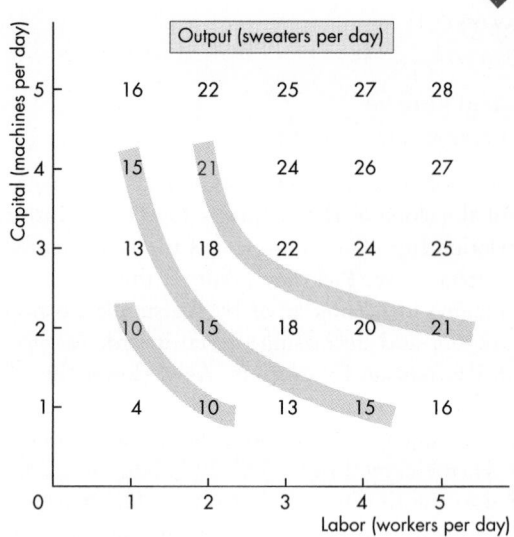

(b) Production function table

Part (a) is an isoquant map but one that shows only 3 isoquants—those for 10, 15, and 21 sweaters a day. Part (b) highlights from Fig. 11.1 the different ways of producing these output levels. The different ways of producing a given output are connected in part (b) with the light blue curves. These curves correspond to the isoquants in part (a). Each of the points on the isoquants can be found in part (b). For example, point *a* uses 2 machines and 1 worker to produce 10 sweaters, and point *b* uses 4 machines and 2 workers to produce 21 sweaters.

Now, let's make sure that we can see the relationship between the isoquant map in Fig. 11.4(a) and the numbers describing the production function in Fig. 11.1. Figure 11.4(b) is designed to help us do so. It extracts from Fig. 11.1 the three output levels shown by the isoquants in Fig. 11.4(a). Each output level, represented by a number in Fig. 11.4(b), corresponds to a point on an isoquant, and equal outputs are traced by light blue curves that correspond to the isoquants. Let's identify two points on the isoquant map in Fig. 11.4(a) and find them in Fig. 11.4(b). First, consider point *a* on the isoquant for 10 sweaters a day. At point *a*, 2 knitting machines and 1 worker produce the 10 sweaters. We can see that this same information appears in Fig. 11.4(b). Second, consider point *b* on the isoquant for 21 sweaters a day. At point *b*, 4 machines and 2 workers produce 21 sweaters a day. We can also see that this same information appears in Fig. 11.4(b).

REVIEW

A firm's production function can be shown as an isoquant map. An isoquant shows all the alternative combinations of capital and labor that can produce a given level of output. The slope of an isoquant measures the marginal rate of substitution. The marginal rate of substitution of capital for labor diminishes as the capital input is decreased and the labor input is increased. There is a separate isoquant for each distinct level of output. Thus isoquants are bowed toward the origin. ∎

Isoquants are very nice, you might be saying to yourself, but what do we do with them? The answer is that we use them to work out a firm's least-cost technique of production. But to do so, we need a way of illustrating the firm's costs in the same sort of diagram as that containing the isoquants.

Isocost Lines

An **isocost line** shows all the combinations of capital and labor that can be bought for a given total cost. To make the concept of the isocost line as clear as possible, we'll consider the following example. Swanky is going to spend a total of $100 a day producing sweaters. Knitting-machine operators can be hired for $25 a day. Knitting machines can be rented for $25 a day. (We'll consider what happens, below, when these

Figure 11.5 Swanky's Input Possibilities

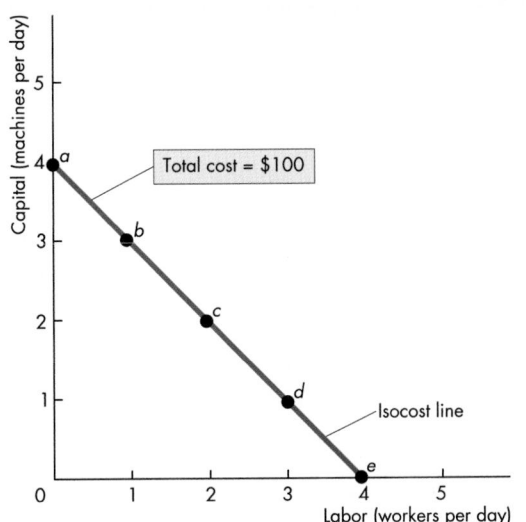

	Capital (machines per day)	Labor (workers per day)
a	4	0
b	3	1
c	2	2
d	1	3
e	0	4

For a given total cost, Swanky's input possibilities depend on input prices. If labor and capital each cost $25 a day, for a total cost of $100 Swanky can employ the combinations of capital and labor presented in the table. These combinations are also graphed in the figure. The line passing through points a through e is an isocost line for a total cost of $100.

Table 11.2 Calculating the Isocost Equation

In general			In Swanky's case
1. The variables			
Total cost	=	TC	TC = $100
Price of labor (daily wage rate)	=	P_L	P_L = $25
Price of capital (daily rental rate of machine)	=	P_K	P_K = $25
Quantity of labor (number of knitting machine operators)	=	L	L = Swanky's choice
Quantity of capital (number of knitting machines)	=	K	K = Swanky's choice

2. Firm's total cost

$P_L L + P_K K = TC$ $25L + $25K = $100

3. Calculating the isocost equation

- Divide by P_K to give:

  $(P_L/P_K)L + K = TC/P_K$

- Subtract $(P_L/P_K)L$ from both sides to give:

  $K = TC/P_K - (P_L/P_K)L$

- Divide by P_K to give:

  $L + K = 4$

- Subtract L from both sides to give:

  $K = 4 - L$

input prices vary.) The table in Fig. 11.5 lists five possible combinations of labor and capital that Swanky can employ for a total cost of $100. For example, row *b* shows that Swanky can use 3 machines (costing $75) and 1 worker (costing $25). The numbers in the table are graphed in the figure and each point, *a* through *e*, represents the corresponding row in the table. If Swanky can employ workers and machines for fractions of a day, then any of the combinations along the line *ae* can be employed for a total cost of $100. This line is Swanky's isocost line for a total cost of $100.

The Isocost Equation

The isocost line can be described by an isocost equation. An **isocost equation** states the relationship between the quantities of inputs that can be hired for a given total cost. Table 11.2 works out the isocost equation by using symbols that apply to any firm and numbers that describe Swanky's situation. The first section of the table lists the variables that affect the firm's total cost. The variables are total cost itself, the prices of the inputs, and the quantities of the inputs employed. We have assigned symbols to each of these variables. In Swanky's case, we're going to look at the amount of labor and capital that can be employed when these two inputs each cost $25 a day and when total cost is $100.

The firm's total cost is set out in the second section of the table. It defines the isocost equation for a given level of total cost. That is, total cost (TC) equals the price of labor (P_L) multiplied by the quantity of labor employed (L) plus the price of capital (P_K) multiplied by the quantity of capital employed (K). In Swanky's case, TC is $100 and the two input prices are $25 each.

The third section of the table shows you how to calculate the isocost equation. There are two steps. First, divide the firm's total cost by the price of capital. Second, subtract $(P_L/P_K)L$ from both sides of the resulting equation. The result is the isocost equation. This equation tells us how the capital input varies as the labor input varies, holding total cost constant. You can check that Swanky's isocost equation corresponds to the isocost line that is graphed in Fig. 11.5. If L is 0, K is 4, which is point a in the figure. If L is 1, K is 3, which is point b in the figure, and so on.

Figure 11.6   Input Prices and the Isocost Line

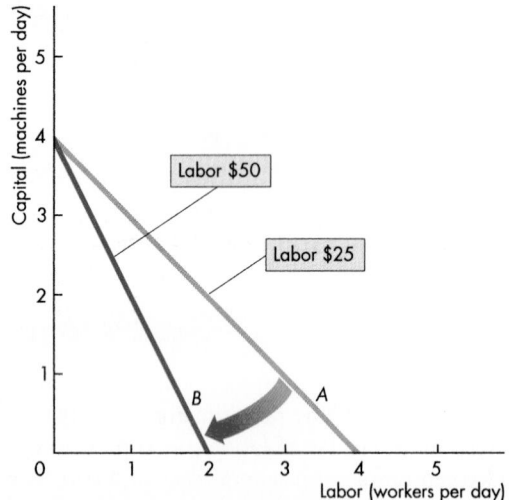

(a) An increase in the price of labor

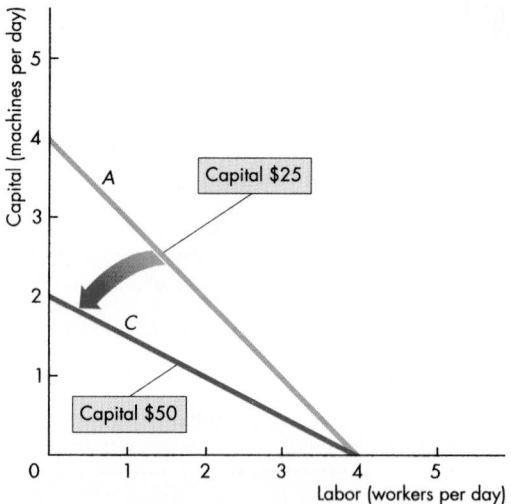

(b) An increase in the price of capital

The slope of the isocost line depends on the relative input prices. When all the inputs have the same price, the isocost line has a slope of 1. The line labeled A shows the isocost line for a total cost of $100 when capital and labor each cost $25 a day. If the price of labor doubles to $50 but the price of capital remains constant at $25, the isocost line for a total cost of $100 will be B in part (a). Its slope is twice that of isocost line A. If the price of capital doubles to $50 but the price of labor stays at $25, the isocost line for a total cost of $100 will be C in part (b). The slope of line C is half that of A.

Isocost line	Price of capital (rental rate per day)	Price of labor (wage per day)	Isocost equation
A	$25	$25	$K = 4 - L$
B	25	50	$K = 4 - 2L$
C	50	25	$K = 2 - (½)L$

The Effect of Input Prices

Along the isocost line that we have just calculated, capital and labor each cost $25 a day. Because these input prices are the same, in order to increase labor by 1 unit, capital must be lowered by 1 unit. The isocost line shown in Fig. 11.5 has a slope of −1. That slope tells us that adding 1 unit of labor costs 1 unit of capital. Isocost lines always slope downward—their slope is always negative. Again, because we know the slope is always negative, we drop the negative sign and talk about the magnitude of the slope. The magnitude of the slope of the isocost line in Fig. 11.5 is 1.

Next, let's consider some different prices, as shown in the table for Fig. 11.6. If the daily wage rate is $50 and the daily rental rate for knitting machines remains at $25, then 1 worker costs the same as 2 machines. Holding total cost constant at $100, to use 1 more worker now requires using 2 fewer machines. With the wage rate double that of the machine rental rate, the isocost line is line B in Fig. 11.6(a), and its slope is 2. That is, in order to hire 1 more worker and keep total cost constant, Swanky must give up 2 knitting machines.

If the daily wage rate remains at $25 and the daily rental rate of a knitting machine rises to $50, then 2 workers cost the same as 1 machine. In this case, in order to hire 1 more worker and keep total cost constant, Swanky must give up only half a knitting machine. The slope of the isocost line is now ½—as for line C in Fig. 11.6(b).

The higher the relative price of labor, the steeper is the slope of the isocost line. The magnitude of the slope of the isocost line measures the relative price of labor in terms of capital—that is, the price of labor divided by the price of capital.

The Isocost Map

An **isocost map** shows a series of isocost lines, each for a different level of total cost. Obviously, the higher the total cost, the larger the quantities of all inputs that can be employed. Figure 11.7 illustrates an isocost map. In that figure, the middle isocost line is the original one that appears in Fig. 11.5. It is the isocost line for a total cost of $100 when both capital and labor cost $25 a day

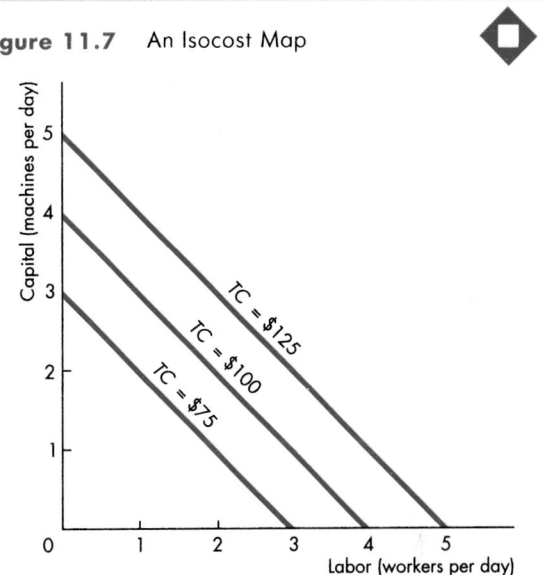

Figure 11.7   An Isocost Map

There is an isocost line for each level of cost, and the lines shown here are just a sample. This isocost map shows three isocost lines, one for a total cost of $75, one for $100, and one for $125. For each isocost line, the prices of capital and labor are $25 each. The slope of the lines in an isocost map is determined by the relative price of the two inputs—the price of labor divided by the price of capital. The higher the total cost, the further is the isocost line from the origin.

each. The other two isocost lines in Fig. 11.7 are for a total cost of $125 and $75, holding the prices of the inputs constant at $25 each.

R E V I E W

An isocost line shows all the combinations of capital and labor that can be bought for a given total cost. The slope of an isocost line is the relative price of the two inputs—the price of labor divided by the price of capital. An isocost map shows a series of isocost lines, one for each level of total cost. ∎

We now have all the tools that we need to calculate the firm's least-cost technique of production.

The Least-Cost Technique

The **least-cost technique** is the combination of inputs that minimizes total cost of producing a given output. Let's suppose that Swanky wants to produce 15 sweaters a day. What is the least-cost way of doing this? The answer can be seen in Fig. 11.8. The isoquant for 15 sweaters is shown and three points on that isoquant (marked *a*, *b*, and *c*) illustrate the three techniques of producing 15 sweaters that were shown earlier in Fig. 11.1. The figure also contains two isocost lines—each drawn for a price of capital and a price of labor of $25. One isocost line is for a total cost of $125 and the other is for a total cost of $100.

Figure 11.8   The Least-Cost Technique of Production

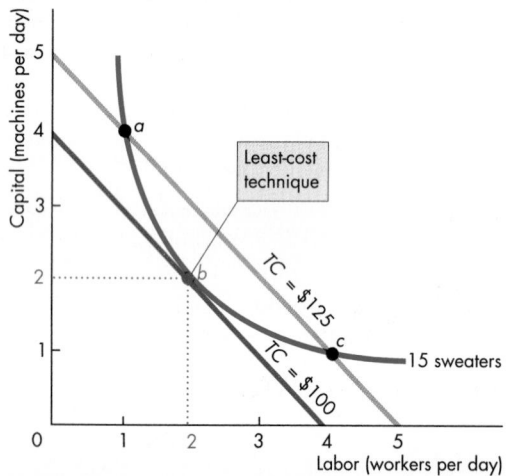

The least-cost technique of producing 15 sweaters occurs when 2 machines and 2 workers are employed at point *b*. An output of 15 sweaters can be produced with the technique illustrated by point *a* (4 machines and 1 worker) or with the technique illustrated by point *c* (1 machine and 4 workers). With either of these techniques, the total cost is $125 and exceeds the total cost at *b* of $100. At *b*, the isoquant for 15 sweaters is tangential to the isocost line for $100. The isocost line and the isoquant have the same slope. If the isoquant intersects the isocost line—for example at *a* and *c*—the least-cost technique has not been found. With the least-cost technique, the marginal rate of substitution (slope of isoquant) equals the relative price of the inputs (slope of isocost line).

First, consider point *a*, which is on the isoquant for 15 sweaters and also on the isocost line with a total cost of $125. Swanky can produce 15 sweaters at point *a* by using 1 worker and 4 machines. The total cost, using this technique of production, is $125. Point *c*, which uses 4 workers and 1 machine, is similar to point *a*, except that it shows another technique by which the firm can produce 15 sweaters for a cost of $125.

Next look at point *b*. At this point, Swanky uses 2 machines and 2 workers to produce 15 sweaters at a total cost of $100. Point *b* is the *least-cost technique* or *the economically efficient technique* for producing 15 sweaters, when knitting machines and workers each cost $25 a day. At those input prices, there is no way that Swanky can produce 15 sweaters for less than $100.

There is an important feature of point *b*, the least-cost technique. At that point, the isoquant on which Swanky is producing (the isoquant for 15 sweaters) has a slope equal to that of the isocost line. The isocost line (for a total cost of $100) is tangential to the isoquant (for 15 sweaters).

Notice that although there is only one way that Swanky can produce 15 sweaters for $100, there are several ways of producing 15 sweaters for more than $100. Techniques shown by point *a* and point *c* are two examples. All the points between *a* and *b* and all the points between *b* and *c* are also ways of producing 15 sweaters for a cost that exceeds $100 but is less than $125. That is, there are isocost lines between those shown, for total costs falling between $100 and $125. Those isocost lines cut the isoquant for 15 sweaters at the points between *a* and *b* and between *b* and *c*. Swanky can also produce 15 sweaters for a cost that even exceeds $125. That is, the firm can change its technique of production by moving to a point on the isoquant higher than point *a* and use a more capital-intensive technique than at point *a* or by moving to a point on the isoquant lower than point *c* and use a more labor-intensive technique than at point *c*. All of these ways of producing 15 sweaters are economically inefficient.

You can see that Swanky cannot produce 15 sweaters for less than $100 by imagining the isocost line for $99. That isocost line will not touch the isoquant for 15 sweaters. That is, the firm cannot produce 15 sweaters for $99. At $25 for a unit of each input, $99 will not buy the inputs required to produce 15 sweaters.

Marginal Rate of Substitution Equals Relative Input Price

When a firm is using the least-cost technique of production, the marginal rate of substitution between the inputs equals their relative price. Recall that the marginal rate of substitution is the slope of an isoquant. Relative input prices are measured by the slope of the isocost line. We've just seen that producing at least cost means producing at a point where the isocost line is tangential to the isoquant. Since the two curves are tangential, their slopes are equal. Hence the marginal rate of substitution (the slope of isoquant) equals the relative input price (the slope of isocost line).

You will perhaps better appreciate the importance of relative input prices if we examine what happens to the least-cost technique when those prices change.

Changes in Input Prices

The least-cost technique of production depends in an important way on the relative prices of the inputs. The case that we've just studied is one in which capital and labor each cost $25 a day. Let's look at two other cases: one where capital costs twice as much as labor and the other where labor costs twice as much as capital.

If knitting machines cost $25 a day and a worker is paid $50 a day, the isocost line becomes twice as steep as the one in Fig. 11.8. That is, to hire one more worker, while holding total cost constant, Swanky has to operate two fewer knitting machines. Let's see how this change in input prices changes the least-cost production technique. Figure 11.9(a) illustrates this. You can see in that figure the isoquant for 15 sweaters a day and the initial inputs of 2 knitting machines and 2 workers. When wages are $50 a day and knitting machines $25 a day, the isocost line becomes steeper. Also, to continue producing 15 sweaters a day, total cost has to rise. That is, the minimum total cost for producing 15 sweaters is higher than originally. The new, steeper isocost line in the figure is that for the minimum cost at which 15 sweaters can be produced at the new input prices. Along that isocost line, Swanky is spending $140. This is the least-cost method of producing 15 sweaters a day; it is achieved by using 3 machines and 1.3 workers

Figure 11.9   Changes in Input Prices

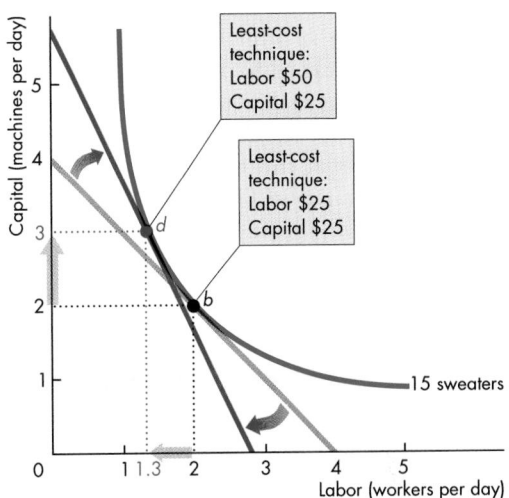

(a) An increase in wages

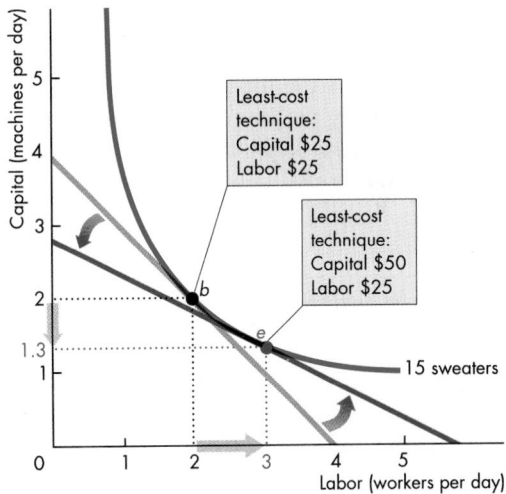

(b) An increase in the price of capital

If the price of labor doubles while the price of capital is held constant, the isocost line becomes twice as steep (part a). The least-cost method of producing 15 sweaters a day changes from point b to point d (using one more machine and 0.7 fewer workers per day). If the price of capital doubles, while the price of labor is held constant, the isocost line becomes half as steep (part b). The least-cost method of producing 15 sweaters a day now changes from point b to point e. One additional worker is hired and 0.7 fewer machines are used.

a day. (These inputs cost $140: 3 machines × $25 = $75 and 1.3 workers × $50 = $65).

Next, let's see what happens if wages stay constant but the cost of a machine increases. In particular, suppose that knitting machines cost $50 a day while wages stay at $25 a day. In this case, the isocost line becomes less steep. Swanky now has to give up only half a worker-day to get one more machine. The effect of this change on the least-cost technique is illustrated in Fig. 11.9(b). Again, the initial isocost line and least-cost technique are shown in the figure. When the cost of capital increases, the isocost line flattens. The least-cost method of producing 15 sweaters a day now uses 1.3 machines and 3 workers a day. This combination again costs Swanky $140 a day, but it is the least-cost method of producing 15 sweaters a day when machines cost $50 and labor $25 a day.

A change in input prices leads to input substitution. Less of the input whose price has increased and more of the other input are used to produce a given output level. The size of this substitution depends on the technology itself. If the inputs are very close substitutes for each other, the isoquants will be almost straight lines and substitution will be large. If the inputs are not close substitutes for each other, the isoquants will be curved very tightly and quite large changes in input prices would lead to only small substitution effects.

R E V I E W

The least-cost technique of producing a given output is the combination of inputs that minimizes total cost. With the least const technique:

• The slope of the isoquant equals the slope of the isocost line.

• The marginal rate of substitution of capital for labor equals the ratio of the price of labor to the price of capital.

• The higher the price of an input, the less of that input is used to produce a given output. ∎

Let's now return to some of the questions with which this chapter opened and see how we can ust the ideas that you've studied here to explain variations in capital intensity, both across different industries and from country to country.

Real World Choice of Technique

We began this chapter by noting that the amount of capital used per unit of labor —capital intensity—varies enormously from one industry to another. We also observed that capital intensity varies across countries. With the tools that you have just discovered, you can interpret these facts.

Industry Variations in Capital Intensity

Variations in capital intensity across industries in a given country arise because of differences in production functions. All firms buy their inputs in common markets, so they have to pay similar input prices. As a result, firms face similar isocost lines. But the isoquants that describe their technologies differ. Figure 11.10 shows possible shapes of isoquants for three industries: plastics, frozen foods, and shirts. With each industry facing a similar isocost line, the least-cost technique chosen varies considerably from one industry to another. In plastics, the chosen point is a, a technique using a high capital-labor ratio. Faced with the same input prices, firms producing frozen foods choose point b, with an average ratio. Faced with those same input prices, shirt producers choose point c, a technique with a low capital-labor ratio.

As input prices change, the least-cost technique changes. The most important such change, over our industrial economic history, has been a steady increase in the relative price of labor. As wages have increased, the isocost line has become steeper over time. As a consequence, firms have substituted capital for labor—they have chosen a more capital-intensive technique. This tendency to increased capital intensity does not only occur in industries such as plastics. It affects all industries.

Differences Across Countries

The differences in capital intensity across countries is explained mainly by differences in wages. In a high-wage country, the isocost lines are steep; in a low-wage country, they are gently sloped. Figure 11.11 shows two isocost lines—one in part (a) for a country in which wages are high and the other in part (b) for a country in which wages are low.

Figure 11.10   Variations in Capital and Labor Inputs Across Industries

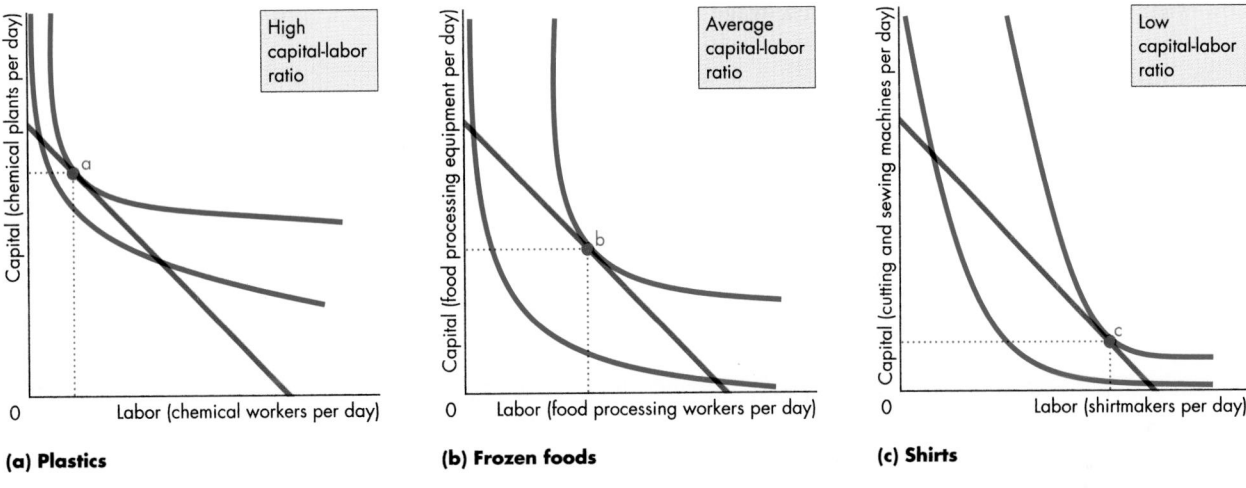

(a) Plastics   **(b) Frozen foods**   **(c) Shirts**

Variations in the relative amounts of capital and labor employed in different industries arise from differences in technologies. Industries face the same relative input prices (the isocost line) but have different isoquants. Isoquants for plastics (part a), frozen foods (part b), and shirts (part c) are shown in the figure. The least-cost technique for plastics (point a) uses a high capital-labor ratio; that for frozen food (point b) uses an average capital-labor ratio; and that for shirts (point c) uses a low capital-labor ratio.

In contrast with the wages, the isoquants for the two countries are similar. Their similarity arises from the fact that all firms, no matter where they are located, have access to the same technology.

(This is true in most cases, but it might not be so if some techniques are protected by patents.) In general, the isoquants in a particular industry are therefore the same for both high-wage and

Figure 11.11   Capital and Labor Inputs in High-Wage and Low-Wage Countries

(a) High-wage country

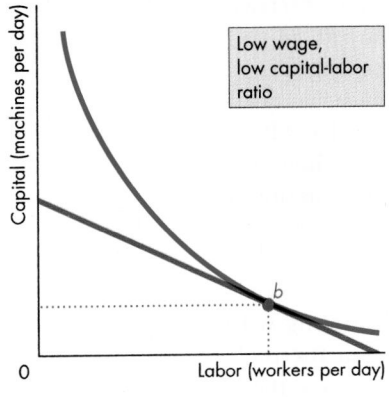

(b) Low-wage country

In high-wage countries, the isocost line is steep (part a), and in low-wage countries, its slope is gentle (part b). The same technologies are available in all countries, so the isoquants are the same for both countries. The least-cost technique in a high-wage country (point a) uses a high capital-labor ratio. The least-cost technique in a low-wage country (point b) uses a low capital-labor ratio.

low-wage countries. One such isoquant is shown in Fig. 11.11. For the high-wage country, the least-cost technique of production is at point *a;* for the low-wage country, it is at point *b.* In low-wage countries, firms use a more labor-intensive technique than in high-wage countries, where a more capital-intensive technique is adopted. As wages rise in poorer countries, firms gradually slide along their isoquants and use a more capital-intensive technique of production. If in high-wage countries wages rise further, relative to the cost of capital, then firms in these countries, too, will use an even more capital-intensive technique of production.

You can now see why gold mines in Amazonia look very different from strip mines in North America. With low wages and a high cost of capital, it pays Brazilian gold mine operators to use a very labor-intensive production technique. With a high wage rate and a low cost of capital, it pays the mining companies of the United States to use a highly capital-intensive technique of production. As wages gradually rise in Brazil, more and more capital will be substituted for labor and those Amazonian gold mines will look like strip mines in the United States.

Marginal Product and Marginal Cost

When we studied short-run and long-run cost in Chapter 10, we learned about the connection between the marginal product curve of a variable input and the marginal cost curve. In the output range over which marginal product increases, marginal cost decreases; in the output range over which marginal product decreases, marginal cost increases. We also learned, in Chapter 10, that it will pay a firm to change its plant size if a different plant can produce the firm's desired output at a lower short-run cost than the existing plant. In this chapter, we learned how to calculate the firm's cost-minimizing combination of capital (plant) and labor. Thus our discussion of product curves and cost curves in Chapter 10 and of isocost lines, isoquants, and least-cost techniques of production in this chapter are both dealing with the same problem. But they're looking at the problem from different viewpoints. Let's examine the connection between these two approaches to the firm's cost minimization problem.

First, we're going to learn about the relationship between the marginal rate of substitution and marginal product.

Marginal Rate of Substitution and Marginal Products

The marginal rate of substitution and the marginal products are linked together in a simple formula:

The marginal rate of substitution of capital for labor equals the marginal product of labor divided by the marginal product of capital.

A few steps of reasoning are needed to establish this fact. First, we know that output changes when a firm changes the amount of labor and capital employed. Furthermore, we know that the effect on output of a change in one of the inputs is determined by the marginal product of the input. That is:

$$\text{Change in output} = \text{Marginal product of labor} \cdot \Delta L + \text{Marginal product of capital} \cdot \Delta K$$

That is, the change in output is equal to the change in the labor input multiplied by its marginal product plus the change in the capital input multiplied by its marginal product.

Suppose now that the firm wants to remain on an isoquant—that is, Swanky wants to produce the same number of sweaters when it changes its labor and capital inputs. To remain on an isoquant, the change in output must be zero. We can make the change of output zero in the above equation, and doing so yields the equation

$$\text{Marginal product of labor} \cdot \Delta L = - \text{Marginal product of capital} \cdot \Delta K.$$

This equation tells us what must happen to the capital and labor inputs for Swanky to stay on an isoquant. If the labor input rises, the capital input must fall or, equivalently, if the labor input falls, the capital input must rise. Thus we can write this equation in a slightly different way to state that

$$\text{Marginal product of labor} \cdot \text{Rise in labor input} = \text{Marginal product of capital} \cdot \text{Fall in capital input}$$

If we divide both sides of the above equation by the rise in the labor input and also divide both sides by the marginal product of capital, we get

$$\frac{\text{Fall in capital}}{\text{Rise in labor}} = \frac{\text{Marginal product of labor}}{\text{Marginal product of capital}}.$$

This equation tells us that, when Swanky remains on an isoquant, the fall in its capital input divided by the rise in its labor input is equal to the marginal product of labor divided by the marginal product of capital. But we have defined the marginal rate of substitution of capital for labor as the fall in capital divided by the rise in labor when we remain on a given isoquant. What we have discovered, then, is that the marginal rate of substitution of capital for labor is the ratio of the marginal product of labor to the marginal product of capital.

Marginal Cost

We can use the fact that we have just discovered—that the marginal rate of substitution of capital for labor equals the ratio of the marginal product of labor to the marginal product of capital—to work out an important implication of cost minimization. A few steps are needed and Table 11.3 provides a guide to those steps.

Part (a) defines some symbols. Part (b) reminds us that the marginal rate of substitution of capital for labor is the slope of the isoquant, which in turn equals the ratio of the marginal product of labor (MP_L) to the marginal product of capital (MP_K). Part (b) also reminds us that the slope of the isocost line equals the ratio of the price of labor (P_L) to the price of capital (P_K). Part (c) of the table summarizes some propositions about a firm that is using the least-cost technique of production.

The first of these propositions is that when the least-cost technique is employed, the slope of the isoquant and the slope of the isocost line are the same. That is,

$$MP_L/MP_K = P_L/P_K$$

The second proposition is that total cost is minimized when the marginal product per dollar spent on labor equals the marginal product per dollar spent on capital. To see why, just rearrange the above equation in the following way. First, multiply both sides by the marginal product of capital and then divide both sides by the price of labor.

Table 11.3	The Least-Cost Technique	

(a) Symbols

Marginal rate of substitution of capital for labor	MRS
Marginal product of labor	MP_L
Marginal product of capital	MP_K
Price of labor	P_L
Price of capital	P_K

(b) Definitions

Slope of the isoquant (MRS)	MP_L/MP_K
Slope of the isocost line	P_L/P_K

(c) The least-cost technique

Slope of the isoquant = Slope of the isocost line

Therefore:

$$MP_L/MP_K = P_L/P_K$$

Equivalently:

$$MP_L/P_L = MP_K/P_K$$

That is,

Total cost is minimized when the marginal product per dollar spent on labor equals the marginal product per dollar spent on capital.

Equivalently, flipping the last equation over:

For least-cost technique

$$P_L/MP_L = P_K/MP_K$$

That is,

Marginal cost with fixed capital and a change in labor input equals marginal cost with fixed labor and a change in capital input.

We then get:

$$MP_L/P_L = MP_K/P_K$$

This equation says that the marginal product of labor per dollar spent on labor is equal to the marginal product of capital per dollar spent on capital. In other words, the extra output from the last dollar spent on labor equals the extra output from the last dollar spent on capital. This makes sense. If the extra output from the last dollar spent on labor exceeds the extra output from the last dollar spent on capital, it will pay the firm to use less capital and use more labor. By doing so, it could produce the same output at a lower total cost. Conversely, if the extra output from the last dollar spent on capital exceeds the extra output from the last dollar spent on labor, it will pay the firm to use less labor and use more capital. Again, by so doing, it lowers the cost of producing a given output. A firm achieves the least-cost technique of production only when the extra output from the last dollar spent on all the inputs is the same.

The third proposition is that marginal cost with fixed capital and variable labor equals marginal cost with fixed labor and variable capital. To see this proposition, simply flip the last equation over and write it as

$$P_L/MP_L = P_K/MP_K.$$

Expressed in words, this equation says that the price of labor divided by its marginal product must equal the price of capital divided by its marginal product. But what is the price of an input divided by its marginal product? The price of labor divided by the marginal product of labor is marginal cost when the capital input is held constant. To see why this is so, first recall the definition of marginal cost: *Marginal cost* is the change in total cost resulting from a unit increase in output. If output rises because one more unit of labor is employed, total cost rises by the cost of the extra labor, and output rises by the marginal product of the labor. So marginal cost is the price of labor divided by the marginal product of labor. For example, if labor costs $25 a day and if the marginal product of labor is 2 sweaters, then the marginal cost of a sweater is $12.50 ($25 divided by 2).

The price of capital divided by the marginal product of capital has a similar interpretation. The price of capital divided by the marginal product of capital is marginal cost when the labor input is constant. As you can see from the above equation, with the least-cost technique of production, marginal cost is the same regardless of whether the capital input is constant and more labor is used, or the labor input is constant and more capital is used.

REVIEW

If a firm wants to increase output, it looks at the various methods available for achieving that end. If one of the methods of increasing output adds less to cost than some other method does, then that method is used. Even if the firm doesn't want to increase output, if the marginal cost of production using one input exceeds that of using another, it will pay the firm to decrease its use of the input whose contribution to marginal cost is highest and increase the use of the input whose contribution to marginal cost is lowest. Only when all inputs have the same impact on marginal cost has the firm achieved the minimum cost method of production. ■

■ We have now seen how firms choose their capital and labor inputs to minimize the cost of producing a given level of output. We've also seen how that choice is influenced by the relative prices of capital and labor. Our next task is to study the interactions of firms and households in markets for goods and services and see how prices, output levels, and profits are determined.

SUMMARY

Input Substitution

A given amount of output can be produced by using a small amount of capital and a large amount of labor (a labor-intensive technique) or a small amount of labor and a large amount of capital (a capital-intensive technique). The production func-

tion describes the maximum output that can be produced by different combinations of capital and labor. The marginal rate of substitution of capital for labor measures the decrease in capital per unit increase in labor that keeps output constant. (pp. 258–260)

Isoquants

An isoquant is a curve that shows the different combinations of inputs that can produce a fixed amount of output. The magnitude of the slope of the isoquant equals the marginal rate of substitution. An isoquant map shows a series of isoquants, each for a different level of output. Isoquants for larger outputs are farther from the origin. (pp. 260–262)

Isocost Lines

An isocost line shows the combinations of capital and labor that can be bought for a given total cost. An isocost map shows a series of isocost lines, each for a different level of total cost. The slope of an isocost line is the ratio of the price of labor to the price of capital—the relative price of labor. (pp. 263–265)

The Least-Cost Technique

The least-cost technique of production is the least expensive combination of inputs that produces a given output. The least-cost technique of producing a given output occurs where an isocost line is tangential to the isoquant. With the least-cost technique, the marginal rate of substitution of capital for labor equals the ratio of the price of labor to the price of capital.

A change in input prices changes the least-cost production technique. The higher the price of an input, the smaller is the quantity of that input used in the least-cost technique. (pp. 266–268)

Real World Choice of Technique

Variations in capital intensity across industries occur because of differences in production functions. Some industries have isoquants that lead them to choose a capital-intensive technique as the least-cost technique of production. Others have isoquants that lead to a labor-intensive technique of production.

Capital intensity varies in different countries mainly because of differences in wages. In a high-wage country, the isocost lines are steeper; in a low-wage country, they are more gently sloped. Thus firms in high-wage countries use capital-intensive techniques while those in low-wage countries adopt labor-intensive techniques. (pp. 268–270)

Marginal Product and Marginal Cost

The marginal rate of substitution of capital for labor also equals the ratio of the marginal product of labor to the marginal product of capital. When total cost is minimized, the ratio of the marginal product of labor to the marginal product of capital equals the ratio of the price of labor to the price of capital. This fact implies that when the least-cost technique of production is used, the marginal product of labor per dollar spent on labor is equal to the marginal product of capital per dollar spent on capital. (p. 270–272)

KEY CONCEPTS

Key Figures and Tables

R E V I E W   Q U E S T I O N S

1 What is a production function?

2 Define the marginal rate of substitution.

3 How is the marginal rate of substitution calculated?

4 What is an isoquant?

5 What does the slope of an isoquant measure?

6 What is an isocost line?

7 What does the slope of an isocost line measure?

8 Describe the conditions that are satisfied when a firm has chosen the least-cost technique for producing a given output.

9 How does the least-cost technique change when input prices change?

10 Why do we observe variations in capital intensity across industries in a given country?

11 Why do we observe variations in capital intensity between countries?

12 What is the relationship between the marginal rate of substitution and the marginal product of labor and capital?

13 When costs are minimized, what is the relationship between the marginal cost of increasing output by using more capital and that from using more labor?

P R O B L E M S

1 The following table shows the output per hour of a doughnut producer, using alternative combinations of capital and labor.

Units of capital	Units of Labor		
	1	2	3
3	280	430	490
2	190	280	320
1	100	160	190

Sketch the isoquants for 190 and 280 doughnuts an hour and identify two points on each isoquant.

2 Calculate the marginal rate of substitution of capital for labor in problem 1 if the firm switches the method of production from:

   a) 1 unit of labor and 3 units of capital to 2 units of each.

   b) 2 units of capital and 1 unit of labor to 1 unit of capital and 3 units of labor.

3 Suppose that labor costs $10 an hour and capital rents for $15 an hour. Calculate the isocost equation.

4 Given the information in problems 1 and 3, what is the least-cost technique of producing:

   a) 190 doughnuts an hour

   b) 280 doughnuts an hour

   (Use only whole units, not fractions of units, of labor and capital.)

5 When the least-cost technique is being used in problem 4, what is the marginal cost of labor and of capital?

6 Suppose that labor costs rise to $15 an hour and the cost of capital equipment falls to $10 an hour. Calculate the isocost equation.

7 Given the information in problem 6, what is the doughnut producer's least-cost technique of producing:

   a) 190 doughnuts an hour

   b) 280 doughnuts an hour

   (Use only whole units, not fractions of units, of labor and capital.)

8 When the least-cost technique is being used in problem 7, what is the marginal cost of labor and of capital?

9 Compare your answers to problems 3 and 6. What do they tell us about the effect of relative input prices on the slope of the isocost line?

10 Compare your answers to problems 4 and 7. What do they tell us about the effects of relative input prices on the least-cost technique of production?

Part 5

Markets for
Goods and
Services

Talking
with
Hugo
Sonnenschein

Hugo Sonnen-
schein is a mi-
croeconomic
theorist whose research
has focused on general
equilibrium and game
theory. For many years a
professor of economics at
Princeton University, he
is now the Dean of Arts
and Sciences at the Uni-
versity of Pennsylvania.
Michael Parkin spoke
with Dean Sonnenschein
about how he became
interested in economics
and his view of the im-
portance of economic
theory.

***Dean Sonnenschein,
what brought you to the
study of economics?***

My first course in eco-
nomics, if the truth be
told, was not entirely
satisfactory. It was definitely not a case of love

at first sight. As a senior
I enrolled in a statistics
course for social scientists
to satisfy a distribution
requirement, though as a
mathematics major, I
had actually taken ad-
vanced statistics by then.
When my professor dis-
covered that I was sub-
stantially overprepared,
he suggested that I go to
the university library,
find the journal *Econometrica,* and write some
critical reviews of papers
that used interesting
mathematical methods
to do economics. I
quickly found an article
about Kenneth Arrow's
general possibility theo-
rem. It so fascinated me
that I tore up my ac-
ceptances to mathematics
graduate school and set
off for graduate school
in economics instead. I
have never regretted this
decision.

What was it about this work that so appealed to you?

It involves mathematics but within the context of real people in social relationships. I hadn't seen that in my introductory economics courses. Perhaps I should have, but I didn't. Instead, I saw a lot of demand and supply curves. The big picture of "what is to be

"Economics involves mathematics but within the context of real people in social relationships."

produced, the method of production, and the distribution of output" was not at first apparent to me. Economics is concerned with social equilibrium, how people interact, sometimes working together, and sometimes opposing each other. When I finally understood this I started really to love economics.

How do you like to think about social relationships, about how people interact in markets?

My attraction was first to ideas that are similar to game theory, although I didn't recognize that at

the time. I am drawn to problems that have two or three people coming together with different goals, controlling different possible actions, but who will share some kind of outcome as a result of their interaction. When the problem is put this way, it is as much sociology or political science as it is economics. Approaching this setting in formal terms is where economists and game theorists have made particular contributions.

Can you define game theory for us in your own terms?

Game theory tries to explain how individuals behave in situations with elements of both cooperation and conflict. It explains how they *might* behave and also suggests

how they *should* behave. It suggests what the outcome of cooperation and conflict will be.

For a long time before game theory, there were well-developed aspects of decision theory that considered how individuals operating independently should act in a situation that had more than one

option, with consequences associated with each option. Everything changes when you speak about how agents will or should behave when there is more than one agent making choices. With many agents, what each individual should do depends on what he believes others will do. In economics, this feature is central to our simplest descriptions of what happens in markets when there are a small number of buyers or sellers.

You've also been known for your work in general equilibrium theory. What does this approach tell us about markets and competition?

General equilibrium is based on the explicit realization that the price of any good is determined not only by traits that are specific to it, such as how much of some other commodity an agent will be willing to surrender for one unit of it, or how much of other commodities are needed to produce it. Instead the price of each commodity is determined by the total menu of trade-offs of every commodity versus every other one by all consumers, the total menu of trade-offs in production, and the distribution of wealth among individuals. As a result, changes in taste or technology, which may to the untrained eye appear to influence only a single market, will have ripple effects throughout the economy. Prices will not settle down until all of these ripples dissipate.

Can you give an example of how general equilibrium theory looks at the world?

Let's say that it has been discovered that grapes in a certain region are being sprayed with a chemical that's harmful to humans if eaten. When the news is reported on television, some consumers become worried and stop buying grapes. They may, for example, prefer cherries at the existing prices. A decrease in the demand for grapes and an increase in the demand for cherries will

decrease the price of grapes and increase the price of cherries. Cherries are harvested with specialized machinery and the demand for the machinery will rise. This will lead to an increase in the production of cherry-picking machines. At the same time you'd expect to see research on safer ways to spray grapes. The demand for biochemists and entomologists will be affected. This may even have some small effect on the demand for Deans of Arts and Sciences. All of these changes and many more from a single economic event, and their impact will depend on a lengthy menu of tradeoffs.

Are game theory and general equilibrium theory compatible approaches?

Yes. I view general equilibrium theory and game theory as complementary. Also, in many ways they are similar in spirit. A major lesson of both approaches is that in economics everything depends on everything else. In general equilibrium the lesson is that what I pay for a commodity depends on other people's tastes, the distribution of income, and the production processes for many different commodities. In game theory the lesson is that what I should choose depends on what others choose, because their actions influence the consequences of my own actions.

One of the most important uses of general

"In economics everything depends on everything else."

equilibrium theory has been to explore Adam Smith's idea that individuals serving their own interests, and not intending to help others, will somehow promote the social good. This problem has been studied for many decades. Currently the best statement of conditions under which self-interested behavior serves to promote the social good is based on the 1950s work of Kenneth Arrow and Gerard Debreu. Game theory has enabled us to appreciate more fully the restrictive nature of their results. It has at the same time led to models that support the general equilibrium theory. One could argue that the most important developments in general equilibrium theory over the past 30 years are a collection of results that provide game theory underpinnings for the general equilibrium theory of competitive markets.

> "There are not many areas in which economists can predict what lies more than a few feet down the road."

Our discussion has been largely about insights and principles, not about things that have empirical results. Do you have to be interested only in theory to do your kind of economics? Is there any practical value to it?

Insights and principles are not to be disparaged. They are what enable us to put rockets into the air and grow crops more efficiently. They can help a manager to run a firm with success and a legislator to understand more fully the likely impact of proposed quotas and taxes. Theory can be useful and provide powerful insights or it can be vacuous and uninformative. Similarly, some empirical work is meaningless, since it concerns the measurement of quantities which are ill-defined or can only be measured by imposing implausible structural hypotheses.

Empirical work is *per se* no more or less relevant than theory. Even with the best of our theories and the best of our empirical work, there are not many areas in which economists can predict very well what lies more than a few feet down the road. Economics is not for those who are attracted to real-world problems which have simple and clear solutions. For these individuals I recommend astrology. In economics we are fortunate when one or two important aspects of a problem under study have reasonably tractable solutions.

I look at it this way. For economics to be applied well, one must pick carefully the aspects that will be exposed to formal analysis. Theoretical and empirical methods, used with judgment and skill, can often shed important light. Economic theory is especially exciting today, because we are making great strides in our ability to organize ideas that are quite clearly relevant to everyday affairs.

Chapter 12

After studying this chapter, you will be able to:

- Define perfect competition

- Explain why a perfectly competitive firm cannot influence the market price

- Explain how a competitive industry's output changes when price changes

- Explain why firms sometimes shut down temporarily and lay off workers

- Explain why firms enter and leave an industry

- Predict the effects on an industry and on a typical firm of a change in demand and of a technological advance

- Explain why farmers have had such a bad time in recent years

- Explain why perfect competition is efficient

Ice cream is big business. In 1988, close to one billion gallons were bought—an average of four gallons per person—at a cost of more than $7 billion. Of the two basic kinds of ice cream—"economy" and "super premium"—the market for economy is the largest but that for super premium is growing fastest. ■ Competition in the ice cream industry is fierce. Great Midwestern Ice Cream, named the best in America by *People* and *Playboy* magazines, nevertheless had to cut back ambitious expansion plans when it discovered that supermarkets were not willing to carry its product. Competition is especially fierce in the super premium category. National names, such as Häagen-Dazs and Frusen Glädjé, are competing with other national, regional, and local

Hot Rivalry in Ice Cream

brands. Ben and Jerry's, Steve's, Larry's, Emack & Bolio's, Hilary's, Dave's, Damian's, Bart's, and Annabel's are all battling for a place in a crowded market. ■ In this fiercely competitive environment, new firms are entering and trying their luck while other firms are being squeezed out of the business. Some are growing and disappearing in a matter of months. One example is Steve's Homemade Ice Cream, Inc., of Bloomfield, New Jersey. After growing 56 percent in 1987, sales became stagnant in 1988. Although the firm still exists, ice cream is no longer its major product. Steve's is now moving into microwave sundaes and other products. Many other ice cream producers are moving into frozen yogurt. Baskin Robbins has even changed its name to Baskin Robbins Ice Cream and Yogurt.[1] ■ How does competition affect prices and profits? What causes some firms to leave an industry and others to enter it? What are the effects on profits and prices of new firms entering and old firms leaving an industry?

---

[1] This account of the ice cream industry is based on "Ice Cream Makers' Rivalry Heating Up" by Lawrence Ingrassia, *Wall Street Journal,* (December 21, 1988): p. B1.

■ In 1982 and 1983, more than ten million people were unemployed. Of these, six million were unemployed because they had lost their jobs. Many of these job losers had worked for firms that had gone out of business. But most of them were laid off by firms seeking to trim their costs and avoid bankruptcy. Ice cream producers, car producers, computer manufacturers, and firms in almost every sector of the economy were laying off their workers on a massive scale. Those years were unusually harsh ones, but even in a typical year, more than three million people are unemployed as a result of firms trimming back the scale of their labor force. Why do firms lay off workers? When will a firm temporarily shut down, laying off all its workers? ■ Over the past few years, there has been a dramatic fall in the prices of all kinds of consumer goods, such as VCRs, Walkmans, pocket calculators, and personal computers. What exactly goes on in an industry when the price of its output falls dramatically? What causes the price to fall and what happens to the profits of the firms that produce such goods? ■ American farms have been in the news a great deal in recent years. Most farmers have fallen on very hard times. Many of them have gone out of business. What is happening in the farm sector that is creating such serious problems?

■ With what you learn in this chapter you will be able to make sense of the phenomena that we have just described and the questions that we have posed. To tackle these issues, we have to look beyond the individual firm standing in isolation and think about how firms interact with each other. Most goods are produced by more than one firm, so the firms themselves compete with each other. Each firm tries to outdo its rivals by producing at a lower cost and by selling a larger output, thereby making the biggest possible profit. We will study markets in which firms are locked together in such stiff competition with each other that the best a firm can do is to match its rivals in terms of quality and price. We will study other types of markets in the following two chapters. But what we learn in this chapter will help us to understand a wide variety of business situations including the facts and puzzles we have just reviewed.

Perfect Competition

In order to study competitive markets, we are going to build a model of a market in which competition is as fierce and extreme as possible.

Economists call the most extreme form of competition perfect competition. **Perfect competition** occurs in a market where:

- There are many firms, each selling an identical product.
- There are many buyers.
- There are no restrictions on entry into the industry.
- Firms in the industry have no advantage over potential new entrants.
- Firms and buyers are completely informed about the prices of the products of each firm in the industry.

Therefore, in perfect competition no single firm can exert a significant influence on the market price of a good. Firms in such markets are said to be price takers. A **price taker** is a firm that cannot influence the price of its product.

Perfect competition does not occur frequently in the real world, but in many industries competition is so fierce that the model of perfect competition that we are about to study is of enormous help in predicting the behavior of the firms in these industries. Ice cream making and retailing, farming, fishing, wood pulping and paper milling, the manufacture of paper cups and plastic shopping bags, grocery retailing, photo-finishing, lawn service, plumbing, painting, and dry cleaning and the provision of laundry services are all examples of industries that are highly competitive.

When a Firm Can't Influence Price

Perfectly competitive or, equivalently, price-taking behavior occurs in markets in which a single firm produces a small fraction of the total output of a particular good. Imagine for a moment that you are a wheat farmer in Kansas. You have a thousand acres under cultivation—which sounds like a lot. But then you go on a drive, first heading west. The flat lands turn into rolling hills as you head toward the Rocky Mountains, but everywhere you look you see thousands and thousands of acres of wheat. The sun goes down in the west behind millions of acres of golden plants. The next morning, it rises in the east above the same scene. Driving to Colorado, Oklahoma, Texas, back up to Nebraska and the Dakotas, reveals similar vistas. You also find unbroken stretches of wheat in Canada, Argentina, Australia, and the Soviet Union. Your thousand acres is a drop in the bucket. To be accurate, it's a molecule in a bucket.

Table 12.1   A Fishery's Elasticity of Demand

(a) Data[1]

- World output of fish is 169 billion pounds a year.[2]
- The average U.S. fishery produces 1.8 million pounds a year.[3]
- The average price of fish is 37.5 cents a pound.[4]
- The elasticity of demand for fish and fish products η_m is 0.42.

(b) Effect on world price

- If an average U.S. fishery raises output by 100 percent, world output rises by 1.8 million pounds—0.00107 percent.

- To calculate change in world price, use the formula

$$\eta_m = \frac{\text{Percentage change in quantity}}{\text{Percentage change in price,}}$$

which means that

$$\text{Percentage change in price} = \frac{\text{Percent change in quantity}}{\eta_m}$$

- To find the fall in price, use the formula

$$\text{Percentage change in price} = 0.00107/0.42$$
$$= 0.00254 \text{ percent}$$

So, a price fall of 0.00254 percent is a fall of 0.00095 cents.

- When a firm doubles its output, the price falls by 0.00095 cents.

(c) Fishery's elasticity of demand

- The firm's elasticity of demand (η_f) is given by

$$\eta_f = \frac{\text{Percentage change in firm's output sold}}{\text{Percentage change in price}}$$
$$= 100/0.00254$$
$$= 39{,}370$$

Part (a) provides some data about the market for fish. Most fish is sold frozen and the market for fish is a world-wide market. Part (b) calculates the effects on the world market price of fish if one U.S. fishery doubles its output. If one fishery doubles its output, world output will rise by 1.8 million pounds or change by approximately 0.001 percent. As a result of this increase in output, the world price of fish falls by 0.00254 percent or 0.00095¢ a pound. Part (c) calculates the individual producer's elasticity of demand, η_f. That elasticity is almost 40,000!

[1]The quantity and price data refer to 1982 and are from U.S. Bureau of the Census, *Statistical Abstract of the United States: 1986*, 106th ed. (Washington, D.C.: 1985): 681–9. The estimate of the elasticity of demand for fish products is that in Table 5.3.
[2]*Statistical Abstract*, 683.
[3]In 1982, 3600 fishery shore establishments caught 6367 million pounds (6367 million/3600 = 1.77 million). *Statistical Abstract*, 682–3.
[4]*Statistical Abstract*, 682.

You are a price taker. Nothing makes your wheat any better than any other farmer's. If everybody else sells their wheat for $3 a bushel, and you want $3.10, why would people buy from you? They can simply go to the next farmer, and the one after that, and the next, and buy all they need for $3.

Industry and Firm Elasticity of Demand

A price-taking firm faces a demand curve that is perfectly elastic. To see why this is so, let's consider an example. Suppose that there are 1000 firms of equal size producing a good. Even if one firm doubles its output (a big change for an individual firm), industry output will rise by only 0.01 percent (one thousandth is 0.01 percent). Suppose that the industry elasticity of demand for the good is 0.5, then this

increase in industry output results in a 0.02 percent fall in price. To put things in perspective, a price change of this magnitude is $1 on a $500 television set, 10¢ on a $50 dress, or a penny on a $5 movie ticket. But these price changes, although small, are much larger than the ones that result from changes in output of a magnitude that a firm might actually make. Therefore, when a firm changes its output rate, the effect of that change on price is tiny and the firm ignores it. The firm behaves as if its own actions have no effect on the market price.

Table 12.1 works through a real world example —the market for fish—and shows the relationship between the elasticity of demand facing an individual competitive fishery and the fish market as a whole. The market elasticity of demand for fish is 0.42 but the elasticity of demand facing an individual producer is almost 40,000.

When we studied the concept of elasticity in Chapter 5, we discovered that a horizontal demand curve has an elasticity of infinity. An elasticity of 40,000 is not quite infinity, but it is very large. A firm whose demand has such an elasticity has, for all practical purposes, an infinitely elastic demand. Such a firm's demand curve is horizontal. The firm is a price taker.

Competition in Everyday Life

We have defined perfect competition as a market where a firm has no choice but to be a price taker. Even massive percentage changes in a firm's own output have only a negligible effect on the market price. In such a situation, there is little point in a firm attempting to set its own price at a level different from the market. If a firm tries to charge a higher price, no one will buy its output; if it offers its goods for a lower price, it will sell them, but it can sell them for the market price so there is no point in price cutting.

The inability of a perfectly competitive firm to compete by price cutting makes it seem as if a perfectly competitive market is not, in fact, very competitive at all. If firms don't compete on price, in what sense are they competing with each other?

Firms compete with each other in much the same way as athletes or football teams do. Firms try to find new tricks that will give them the edge over their competitors and enable them to win. Sometimes, though, the competition that they face is so stiff that they are left with little room to maneuver. This happens in sporting events, too. For example, when two wrestlers are closely matched, they compete with each other, but neither of them has much room to maneuver. They are locked in such fierce competition that the best they can do is to match each other's moves, try not to make a mistake, and accept the inevitable—that the outcome will be close and may even be a tie.

Like evenly matched athletes, firms in perfect competition are locked in such a fierce competitive struggle with each other that they have no choice other than to mimic each other's actions—producing a comparable quality good at a comparable price—and to put up with an outcome analogous to a tie.

Let's now study the behavior of a perfectly competitive industry, beginning with an examination of the choices made by a typical firm in such an industry.

Firms' Choices in Perfect Competition

A perfectly competitive firm has to make three key decisions:

- Whether to stay in the industry or to leave it
- If the decision is to stay in the industry, whether to produce or to temporarily shut down
- If the decision is to produce, how much to produce

In studying the competitive firm's choices, we will continue to look at a model firm whose single objective is to maximize its profit. We'll first consider a situation in which a firm decides to produce. We will then look at the other cases—firms that decide to shut down production temporarily or to leave the industry altogether.

Profit and Revenue

Profit is the difference between a firm's total revenue and total cost. We defined and studied the behavior of total cost in the last two chapters. But what is total revenue? Let's begin by looking at the concepts of revenue.

Total revenue is the value of a firm's sales. It equals the price of the firm's output multiplied by the number of units of output sold (price times quantity). **Average revenue** is total revenue divided by the total quantity sold—revenue per unit sold. Since total revenue is price times quantity sold, average revenue (total revenue divided by quantity sold) equals price. **Marginal revenue** is the change in total revenue resulting from a one-unit increase in the quantity sold. Since, in the case of perfect competition, the price remains constant when the quantity sold changes, the change in total revenue is equal to price multiplied by the change in quantity. Therefore, in perfect competition, marginal revenue equals price.

An example of these revenue concepts is set out for Swanky, Inc., in Fig. 12.1. The table shows three different quantities of sweaters sold. For a price taker, as the quantity sold varies, the price stays constant—in this example at $25. Total revenue is equal to price multiplied by quantity. For example, if Swanky sells 8 sweaters, total revenue is 8 times $25, which equals $200. Average revenue is total revenue divided by quantity. Again, if Swanky sells 8 sweaters, average revenue is total revenue ($200) divided by

Figure 12.1   Demand, Price, and Revenue in Perfect Competition

(a) Sweater industry

(b) Swanky's demand, average revenue, and marginal revenue

(c) Swanky's total revenue

Quantity (Q) (sweaters per day)	Price (P) (dollars per sweater)	Total revenue (TR = P × Q) (dollars)	Average revenue (AR = TR/Q) (dollars per sweater)	Marginal revenue (MR = ΔTR/ΔQ) (dollars per sweater)
7	25	175	25	
				25
8	25	200	25	
				25
9	25	225	25	

In perfect competition, price is determined where the industry demand and supply curves intersect. Such an equilibrium is illustrated in part (a) where the price is $25 and 7000 sweaters are bought and sold. Swanky, a perfectly competitive firm, faces a fixed price, $25 in this example, regardless of the quantity it produces. The table calculates Swanky's total, average, and marginal revenue. For example, when 7 sweaters are sold, total revenue is $175, and average revenue is $25. When sales increase from 7 sweaters to 8 sweaters, marginal revenue equals $25. The demand curve faced by Swanky is perfectly elastic at the market price and is shown in part (b) of the figure. Swanky's demand curve is also its average revenue curve and marginal revenue curve (AR = MR). Swanky's total revenue curve (TR) is shown in part (c). Point a on the total revenue curve corresponds to the first row of the table.

quantity (8), which equals $25. Marginal revenue is the change in total revenue resulting from a one-unit change in quantity. For example, when the quantity sold rises from 7 to 8, total revenue rises from $175 to $200, so marginal revenue is $25. (Notice that in the table, marginal revenue appears *between* the lines for the quantities sold. This arrangement presents a visual reminder that marginal revenue results from the *change* in the quantity sold.)

Suppose that Swanky is one of a thousand similar small producers of sweaters. The demand and supply curves for the entire sweater industry are shown in Fig. 12.1(a). Demand curve D intersects supply curve S at a price of $25 and a quantity of 7000 sweaters. Figure 12.1(b) shows Swanky's demand curve. Since the firm is a price taker, its demand curve is perfectly elastic—the horizontal line at $25. The figure also illustrates Swanky's total, average, and marginal revenues, calculated in the table. The average revenue curve and marginal revenue curve are the same as the firm's demand curve. That is, the firm's demand curve tells us the revenue per sweater sold and the change in total revenue that results from selling one more sweater. Swanky's total revenue curve (part c) shows the total revenue for each quantity sold. For example, when Swanky sells 7 sweaters, total revenue is $175 (point *a*). Since each additional sweater sold brings in a constant amount —in this case $25—the total revenue curve is an upward-sloping straight line.

R E V I E W

A firm in a perfectly competitive market is a price taker. The firm's demand curve is perfectly elastic at the market price. The firm's average revenue and marginal revenue are each equal to price so that the marginal revenue and average revenue curves are the same as the firm's demand curve. Total revenue rises as the quantity sold rises. ■

Profit-maximizing Output

Profit is the difference between a firm's total revenue and total cost. Maximizing profit is the same thing as maximizing the difference between total revenue and total cost. Even though a perfectly competitive firm cannot influence its price, it can influence its profit by choosing its level of output. As we have just seen, a perfectly competitive firm's total revenue changes when its output changes. Also, as we discovered in Chapter 10, a firm's total cost varies as its output varies. By changing its inputs and its output, a firm can change its cost. In the *short run,* a firm can change its output by changing its variable inputs and by changing the intensity with which it operates its fixed inputs. In the *long run,* a firm can vary all its inputs. Let's work out how a firm maximizes profit in the short run.

Total Revenue, Total Cost, and Profit   Figure
12.2 shows Swanky's total revenue, total cost, and profit both as numbers (in the table) and as curves (in the graphs). Part (a) of the figure shows Swanky's total revenue and total cost curves. These

curves are graphs of the numbers shown in the first three columns of the table. The total revenue curve *(TR)* is the same as that in Figure 12.1(c). The total cost curve *(TC)* is similar to the one that you met in Chapter 10. Notice that Swanky's total cost is $25 when output is zero. This amount is Swanky's fixed cost—the cost that is incurred even if nothing is produced and sold. As output increases, so does total cost.

The difference between total revenue and total cost is profit. As you can see in Fig. 12.2(b), Swanky will make a profit at any output above 4 and below 12 sweaters a day. At outputs below 4 sweaters, Swanky makes a loss. A loss is also made if output exceeds 12 sweaters a day. At outputs of 4 sweaters and 12 sweaters, total cost equals total revenue. An output at which total cost equals total revenue is called a **break-even point.**

Swanky's profit, calculated in the final column of the table, is graphed in part (b) of the figure. Notice the relationship between the total revenue, total cost, and profit curves. Profit is measured by the vertical distance between the total revenue and total cost curves. When the total revenue curve in part (a) is above the total cost curve, between 4 and 12 sweaters, the firm is making a profit and the profit curve in part (b) is above the horizontal axis. At the break-even point, where the total cost and total revenue curves intersect, the profit curve cuts the horizontal axis.

When the profit curve is at its highest, the distance between *TR* and *TC* is greatest. In this example, profit maximization occurs at an output of 9 sweaters a day. At this output, profit is $40 a day.

Marginal Calculations

In working out Swanky's profit-maximizing output, we examined its cost and revenue schedules and from all the possibilities picked out the point at which profit is at a maximum. There is a quicker, neater, and more powerful way of figuring out the profit-maximizing output. All Swanky has to do is to calculate its marginal cost and marginal revenue and compare the two. If marginal revenue exceeds marginal cost, it pays to produce more. If marginal revenue is less than marginal cost, it pays to produce less. When marginal revenue and marginal cost are equal, profit is maximized. Let's convince ourselves that this rule works.

Figure 12.2   Total Revenue, Total Cost, and Profit

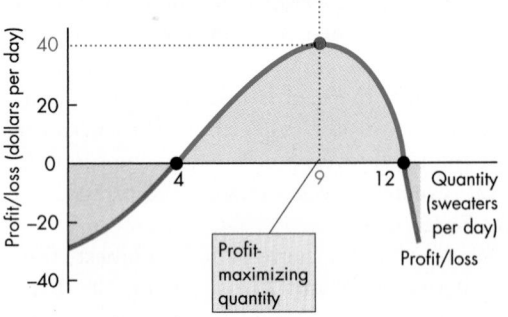

(a) Revenue and cost

(b) Profit and loss

Quantity (Q) (sweaters per day)	Total revenue (TR) (dollars)	Total cost (TC) (dollars)	Profit (TR − TC) (dollars)
0	0	25	−25
1	25	49	−24
2	50	69	−19
3	75	86	−11
4	100	100	0
5	125	114	11
6	150	128	22
7	175	144	31
8	200	163	37
9	225	185	40
10	250	212	38
11	275	246	29
12	300	300	0
13	325	360	−35

The table lists Swanky's total revenue, total cost, and profit. Part (a) graphs the total revenue and total cost curves. Profit is seen in part (a) as the blue area between the total cost and total revenue curves. The maximum profit, $40 a day, occurs when 9 sweaters are produced—where the vertical distance between the total revenue and total cost curves is at its largest. At outputs of 4 sweaters a day and 12 sweaters a day, Swanky makes zero profit—these are break-even points. At outputs below 4 and above 12 sweaters a day, Swanky makes a loss. Part (b) of the figure shows Swanky's profit curve. The profit curve is at its highest when profit is at a maximum and it cuts the horizontal axis at the break-even points.

Look at the table in Fig. 12.3. It records Swanky's marginal cost and marginal revenue. Recall that marginal cost is the change in total cost per unit change in output. For example, when output rises from 8 to 9 sweaters, total cost rises from $163 to $185, a rise of $22, which is the marginal cost of changing the output rate from 8 to 9 sweaters a day. Marginal revenue is the change

Figure 12.3   Marginal Revenue, Marginal Cost, and Profit-Maximizing Output

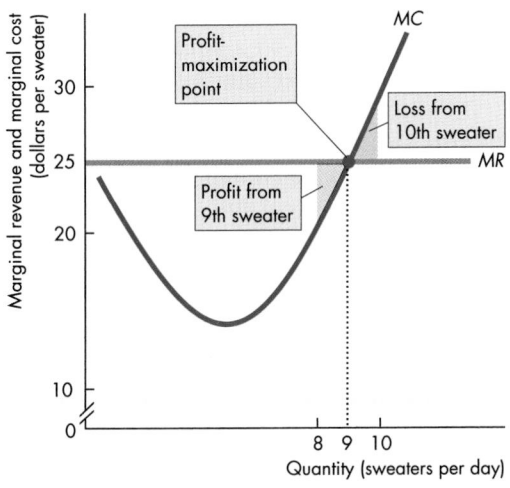

Another way of finding the profit-maximizing output is to determine where marginal revenue equals marginal cost. The table shows that if output rises from 8 to 9 sweaters, marginal cost is $22, which is less than the marginal revenue of $25. If output rises from 9 to 10 sweaters, marginal cost is $27, which exceeds the marginal revenue of $25. The figure shows that marginal cost and marginal revenue are equal when Swanky produces 9 sweaters a day. If marginal revenue exceeds marginal cost, an increase in output increases profit. If marginal revenue is less than marginal cost, an increase in output lowers profit. If marginal revenue equals marginal cost, profit is maximized.

Quantity (Q) (sweaters per day)	Total revenue (TR) (dollars)	Marginal revenue (MR) (dollars per sweater)	Total cost (TC) (dollars)	Marginal cost (MC) (dollars per sweater)	Profit (TR − TC) (dollars)
0	0		25		−25
		25		24	
1	25		49		−24
		25		20	
2	50		69		−19
		25		17	
3	75		86		−11
		25		14	
4	100		100		0
		25		14	
5	125		114		11
		25		14	
6	150		128		22
		25		18	
7	175		144		31
		25		19	
8	200		163		37
		25		22	
9	225		185		40
		25		27	
10	250		212		38
		25		34	
11	275		246		29
		25		54	
12	300		300		0
		25		60	
13	325		360		−35

in revenue per unit change in the quantity sold and is, for a perfectly competitive firm, the same as its price. In this case, marginal revenue is $25. The marginal cost and marginal revenue curves corresponding to the table appear in Fig. 12.3.

Now focus on the highlighted row of the table. When output rises from 8 to 9 sweaters, marginal cost is $22. Since marginal revenue is $25, the rise in total revenue exceeds the rise in total cost. Profit goes up by the difference—$3. By looking at the last column of the table, you can see that profit does indeed rise by $3. Because marginal revenue exceeds marginal cost, it pays to expand output from 8 to 9 sweaters. At 8 sweaters a day, profit is $37 and at 9 sweaters a day it is $40—$3 more.

Suppose that output is expanded yet further to 10 sweaters a day. Marginal revenue is still $25, but marginal cost is now $27. Marginal cost exceeds marginal revenue by $2, so expanding output to 10 sweaters increases total cost by $2 more than total revenue and profit falls by $2. So, to maximize profit, all Swanky has to do is to compare marginal cost and marginal revenue. As long as marginal revenue exceeds marginal cost, it pays to increase output. Swanky keeps increasing output until the cost of producing one more sweater equals the price at which the sweater can be sold. At that point, it is making maximum profit. If Swanky makes one more sweater, that sweater will cost more to produce than the revenue it will bring back in, so Swanky will not produce it.

Profits in the Short Run

We've just seen that we can calculate a firm's profit-maximizing output by comparing marginal revenue with marginal cost. But maximizing profit is not the same thing as *making* a profit. Maximizing profit can mean minimizing loss. We cannot tell whether a firm is actually making a profit only by comparing the marginal revenue and marginal cost curves. To check whether a firm is making a profit, we need to look at total revenue and total cost, as we did before, or we need to compare average total cost with price. When a firm makes a profit, average total cost is lower than price. If average total cost exceeds price, the firm makes a loss. When average total cost equals price, the firm breaks even.

Three Possible Profit Outcomes   The three possible profit outcomes in the short-run are illustrated in Fig. 12.4. In part (a), Swanky is making an economic profit. At a price of $25, marginal revenue equals marginal cost at an output of 9 sweaters a day. That is, the profit-maximizing output is 9 sweaters a day. Average total cost is lower than the market price and economic profit is represented by the blue rectangle. The height of that rectangle is

the gap between price and average total cost, or economic profit per sweater. Its length shows the quantity of sweaters produced. So the rectangle's area measures Swanky's economic profit: profit per sweater (its height—$4.44 a sweater) multiplied by the number of sweaters produced (its length—9 sweaters) equals total profit (its area—$40).

In part (b), Swanky breaks even. At a price of $20, Swanky's profit-maximizing output is 8 sweaters. The average total cost of producing this output level is $20, the same as its price. It is also the minimum average total cost. The maximum profit that Swanky can make in this case is zero.

In part (c), Swanky incurs an economic loss. At a price, of $17, the profit-maximizing output is 7 sweaters. At that output, average total cost is $20.57, so the firm is losing $3.57 a sweater and incurring a total loss of $25.

Temporary Plant Shutdown

There are some situations in which a firm's profit-maximizing decision will be to shut down temporarily, lay off its workers, and produce nothing. Such a situation arises when the price is so low that total revenue is not even enough to cover the variable costs of production. A firm cannot escape its fixed costs. These costs are incurred even at a zero output. A firm that shuts down and produces no output makes a loss equal to its total fixed cost. But this loss is the maximum loss that a firm will make. If the price just equals the average variable cost of production, total revenue equals total variable cost and the loss equals total fixed cost. But if price is below minimum average variable cost, total revenue does not even cover total variable cost and the loss exceeds total fixed cost if the firm produces anything at all. It is in such a situation that the firm minimizes its losses by shutting down, incurring a loss equal to its total fixed cost.

The **shutdown point** is the point at which a firm's maximum profit is the same regardless of whether the firm produces a positive amount of output or produces nothing—temporarily shuts down. The shutdown point is reached when the market price falls to a level equal to the minimum of average variable cost. Table 12.2 illustrates what happens at the shutdown point. The table has two parts: Part (a) shows a case in which it just pays the firm to keep producing, and part (b) shows a case in which it just pays the firm to shut down.

Figure 12.4   Three Possible Profit Outcomes in the Short Run

(a) Economic profit

(b) Zero economic profit

(c) Economic loss

In the short run, a firm's economic profit may be positive, zero (a breakeven), or negative (a loss). If the market price is greater than the average total cost of producing the profit-maximizing output, the firm makes a profit (part a). If price equals minimum average total cost, the firm breaks even (part b). If the price is below minimum average total cost, the firm makes a loss (part c). The firm's profit is shown as the blue rectangle and the firm's loss is the red rectangle.

The table shows Swanky's total fixed cost, total variable cost, and total cost of producing 6, 7, and 8 sweaters. It also shows the average variable cost and marginal cost. The cost data are the same in both parts (a) and (b) of the table.

Next let's look at the revenue. In part (a), the price of a sweater is $17. To find Swanky's total revenue, multiply the price by the quantity sold. We calculate the profit or loss (and they are all losses in this case) by subtracting total cost from total revenue. For example, if Swanky sells 7 sweaters at $17 each, then total revenue is $119. Total cost is $144, so the loss equals $144 minus $119, which is $25. We calculate the loss from producing 6 sweaters or 8 sweaters in a similar way.

The minimum loss occurs when 7 sweaters are produced. You can see that fact directly by looking at the profit or loss column. You can also check that the loss is minimized by looking at marginal cost and marginal revenue. Increasing output from 6 to 7 sweaters has a marginal cost of $16 but a marginal revenue of $17, so total revenue rises by more than total cost. Increasing output still further, from 7 to 8 sweaters, has a marginal

cost of $19, which exceeds marginal revenue, so profit falls (loss rises).

Swanky's loss when producing 7 sweaters exactly equals its total fixed cost—$25. Alternatively, if Swanky produces nothing, it will also lose its $25 of total fixed cost. So, at a price of $17 Swanky is indifferent between producing and shutting down—it makes a loss equal to its fixed cost.

In part (b) the price is $16.99—a lower price but by just a penny. Costs are unchanged. We calculate total revenue and profit in the same way as before. The output that maximizes profit (minimizes loss) is still 7 sweaters but, in this case, the minimum possible loss is $25.07. Swanky loses 7 cents more than it would if it produced nothing at all. The firm will shut down. Its minimum average variable cost is $17. At $17, it just pays to produce and at $16.99 it just pays to shut down. The minimum output that it pays Swanky to produce is 7 sweaters.

Real World Shutdowns Shutdowns occur in the real world either because of a fall in price or be-

Table 12.2   The Shutdown Point

(a) Swanky keeps producing

Output (sweaters per day)	Total fixed cost (dollars)	Total variable cost (dollars)	Total cost (dollars)	Average variable cost (dollars per sweater)	Marginal cost (dollars per sweater)	Price (dollars per sweater)	Total revenue (dollars)	Marginal revenue (dollars per sweater)	Profit(+) loss(−) (dollars)
6	25	103	128	17.17		17	102		−26
					16			17	
7	25	119	144	17.00		17	119		−25
					19			17	
8	25	138	163	17.25		17	136		−27

(b) Swanky shuts down

Output (sweaters per day)	Total fixed cost (dollars)	Total variable cost (dollars)	Total cost (dollars)	Average variable cost (dollars per sweater)	Marginal cost (dollars per sweater)	Price (dollars)	Total revenue (dollars)	Marginal revenue (dollars per sweater)	Profit(+) loss(−) (dollars)
6	25	103	128	17.17		16.99	101.94		−26.06
					16			.....16.99	
7	25	119	144	17.00		16.99	118.93		−25.07
					19			.....16.99	
8	25	138	163	17.25		16.99	135.92		−27.08

The shutdown point occurs at the point of minimum average variable cost. If price equals minimum average variable cost, Swanky is indifferent between producing at the shutdown point and producing nothing. If price falls below minimum average variable cost, it pays Swanky to produce nothing. Minimum average variable cost is $17 and occurs at 7 units of output. If the price is $17 and Swanky produces 7 sweaters, its loss equals its total fixed cost of $25 (part a). If the price falls to $16.99, even when it produces at the point of minimum average variable cost, the firm makes a loss that is bigger than its total fixed cost, and so it pays to shut down (part b).

cause of a rise in costs. Shutdowns occur most frequently in raw material producing sectors as a result of fluctuating prices. For example, if the price of gold falls, gold mines temporarily stop producing. If the price of nickel falls, nickel mines shut down. Shutdowns also occur in many industries—such as those producing ice cream, cars, and air transportation services.

A famous example of an airline shutdown occurred in 1982. Braniff, a Dallas-based airline, had grown rapidly following the deregulation of the airline business in 1982. When 1000 new domestic routes became available, Braniff's aggressive chairman, Harding Lawrence, applied for 624

of them, spreading over the Southwest and Southeast. The company also added routes to Asia, Europe, and the Middle East. If airfares had remained stable, the company's expansion plans would have been highly profitable. But the airlines became embroiled in a fare-cutting orgy, and at a time when fuel prices were rising sharply. Braniff, vastly overextended, lost more than $40 million in 1979 and by 1981 it was losing $160 million. In May 1982, after 54 years in the airline business, Braniff laid off all its workers and stopped flying. Because the firm was losing more than its total fixed cost and with no prospect of the situation improving, it shut down.

REVIEW

In perfect competition, a firm's marginal revenue equals its price. A firm maximizes profit by producing the output at which marginal cost equals marginal revenue (equals price). The lowest output a firm will produce is that at which average variable cost is at a minimum. If price falls below the minimum of average variable cost, the best a firm can do is to stop producing and make a loss equal to its total fixed cost. Maximizing profit is not the same thing as making a profit. In the short run, a firm can make a profit, break even, or make a loss. The maximum loss that a firm will make is equal to its total fixed cost. ∎

The Firm's Supply Curve

A **perfectly competitive firm's supply curve** shows how a firm's profit-maximizing output varies as the market price varies. We are now going to derive Swanky's supply curve. Actually, we have already calculated three points on Swanky's supply curve. We discovered that when the price is $25, Swanky produces 9 sweaters a day; when the price is $20, Swanky produces 8 sweaters a day; and when the price is $17, Swanky is indifferent between producing 7 sweaters a day and shutting down. We are now going to derive Swanky's entire supply curve. Figure 12.5 illustrates the analysis.

Figure 12.5(a) shows Swanky's marginal cost and average variable cost curves and Fig. 12.5(b) shows its supply curve. There is a direct connection between the marginal cost and average variable cost curves and the supply curve. Let's see what that connection is.

The smallest quantity that Swanky will supply is at the shutdown point. When the price is equal to the minimum average variable cost, the marginal revenue curve is MR_0 and the firm produces the output at its shutdown point—point s in the figure. If the price falls below minimum average variable cost, Swanky produces nothing. As the price rises above its minimum average variable cost, Swanky's output rises. Since Swanky maximizes profit by producing the output at which marginal cost equals price, we can determine from its marginal cost curve how much the firm produces at each price. At a price of $25, the marginal revenue curve is MR_1. Swanky maximizes profit by produc-

Figure 12.5 Swanky's Supply Curve

(a) Marginal cost and average variable cost

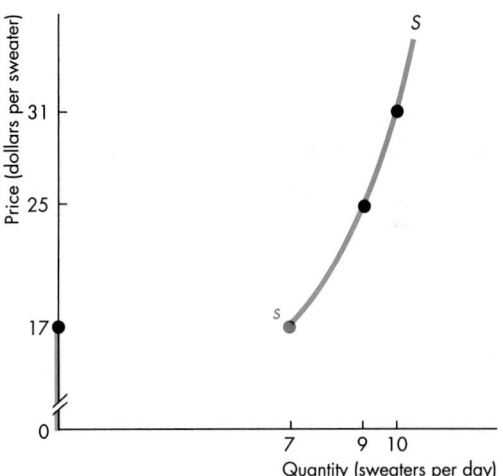

(b) Firm's supply curve

Part (a) shows Swanky's profit-maximizing output at each market price. At $25 a sweater, Swanky produces 9 sweaters. At $17 a sweater, Swanky produces 7 sweaters. At any price below $17 a sweater, Swanky produces nothing. Swanky's shutdown point is at s. Part (b) shows Swanky's supply curve—the number of sweaters Swanky will produce at each price. Swanky's supply curve is made up of its marginal cost curve (part a) at all points above the average variable cost curve and the vertical axis at all prices below minimum average variable cost.

Figure 12.6   Firm and Industry Supply Curves

(a) Swanky, Inc.

(b) Sweater industry

The industry supply schedule is the sum of the supply schedules of all individual firms. An industry that consists of 1000 identical firms has a supply schedule similar to that of the individual firm. But the quantity supplied by the industry is 1000 times as large as that of the individual firm (see table). At the shutdown price, the firm produces either 0 or 7 sweaters per day. The industry supply curve is perfectly elastic at the shutdown point. Part (a) shows Swanky's supply curve, S_F, and part (b), the sweater industry supply curve, S_I. Points a, b, c, and d correspond to the rows of the table. Note that the unit of measurement on the horizontal axis for the industry supply curve is 1000 times the unit for Swanky.

	Price (dollars per sweater)	Quantity supplied by Swanky, Inc. (sweaters per day)	Quantity supplied by industry (sweaters per day)
a	17	0 or 7	0 to 7,000
b	20	8	8,000
c	25	9	9,000
d	31	10	10,000

ing 9 sweaters. At a price of $31, the marginal revenue curve is MR_2 and Swanky produces 10 sweaters. The supply curve, shown in Fig. 12.5(b), has two separate parts. First, in the range of prices that exceed the minimum of average variable cost, the supply curve is the same as the marginal cost curve—above the shutdown point (s). Second, at prices below minimum average variable cost, Swanky shuts down and produces nothing and its supply curve runs along the vertical axis.

So far, we have studied a single firm in isolation. We have seen that the firm's profit-maximizing actions depend on the market price—which the firm takes as given. The higher the price, the larger is the quantity that the firm will choose to produce—the firm's supply curve is up-

ward sloping. But how is the market price determined? To answer this question, we need to study not one firm in isolation but the market as a whole.

Short-run Equilibrium

Market price is determined by industry demand and industry supply. It is the price that makes the quantity demanded equal the quantity supplied. But the quantity supplied depends on the supply decisions of all the individual firms in the industry. Those supply decisions, in turn, depend on the market price.

A short-run equilibrium prevails in a competitive market when each firm operates its plant to produce the profit-maximizing output level and when the total quantity produced by all the firms in the market equals the quantity demanded at that price. To find the short-run equilibrium, we first need to construct the short-run industry supply curve.

Short-run Industry Supply Curve

The **short-run industry supply curve** shows how the total quantity supplied in the short run by all firms in an industry varies as the market price varies. The quantity supplied in the short run by the industry at a given price is the sum of the quantities supplied in the short run by all firms in the industry at that price. To construct the industry supply curve, we sum horizontally the supply curves of the individual firms. Let's see how we do that.

Suppose that the competitive sweater industry consists of 1000 firms exactly like Swanky. The relationship between a firm's supply curve and the industry supply curve, for this case, is illustrated in Fig. 12.6. Each of the 1000 firms in the industry has a supply schedule like Swanky's, set out in the table. At a price below $17, every firm in the industry will shut down production so that the industry will supply nothing. At $17, each firm is indifferent between shutting down and producing 7 sweaters. Since each firm is indifferent, some firms will produce and others will shut down. Industry supply will be anything between 0 (all firms shut down) and 7000 (all firms producing 7 sweaters a day each). Thus at $17, the industry supply curve is horizontal—it is perfectly elastic. As the price rises above $17, each firm increases its quantity supplied and the industry quantity supplied also increases, but by 1000 times that of each individual firm.

The supply schedules set out in the table form the basis of the supply curves that are graphed in Fig. 12.6. Swanky and every other firm has the supply curve S_F shown in Fig. 12.6(a); the industry supply curve S_I is shown in Fig. 12.6(b). Look carefully at the units on the horizontal axes of parts (a) and (b) and note that in part (a) the units are individual sweaters while in part (b) they are thousands of sweaters. But there are two important

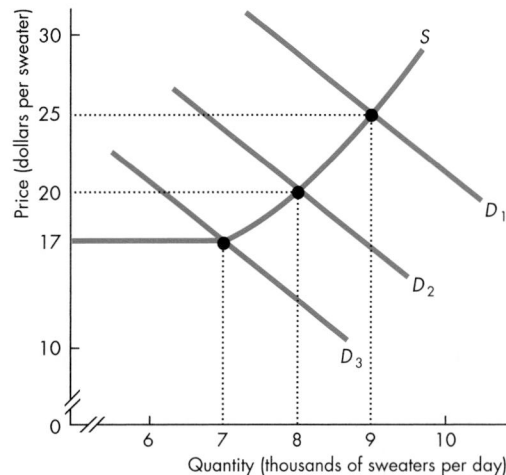

Figure 12.7 Three Short-run Equilibrium Positions for a Competitive Industry

The competitive sweater industry's supply curve is S. If demand is D_1, the price is $25 and the industry produces 9000 sweaters. If demand is D_2, the price is $20, and industry output is 8000 sweaters. If demand is D_3, the price is $17, and industry output is 7000 sweaters. To see what is happening to the individual firms, look back at Fig. 12.4. When the price is $25, the firms are making a profit; when the price is $20, they are breaking even (making zero profit) and when the price is $17, they are incurring a loss. Even when they make a loss, the firms are maximizing profit (minimizing loss).

differences. First, at each price, the quantity supplied by the industry is 1000 times the quantity supplied by a single firm. Second, at a price of $17, the firm supplies either nothing or 7 sweaters a day. There is no individual firm supply curve between those two numbers. But for the industry, any quantity between zero and 7000 will be produced, so the industry supply curve is perfectly elastic over that range.

Short-run Competitive Equilibrium

Price and industry output are determined by industry demand and supply. Three different possible short-run competitive equilibrium positions are shown in Fig. 12.7. The supply curve (S) is the same as S_I, which we derived in Fig 12.6. If the demand curve is D_1, the equilibrium price is $25 and industry output is 9000 sweaters a day. If the demand curve is D_2, the price is $20 and industry output is 8000 sweaters a day. If the demand curve is D_3, the price is $17 and industry output is 7000 sweaters a day.

To see what is happening to each individual firm and its profit in these three situations, you need to check back to Fig. 12.4. With the demand curve D_1, the price is $25 a sweater, each firm produces 9 sweaters a day and makes a profit as shown in Fig. 12.4(a); if the demand curve is D_2, the price is $20 a sweater, each firm produces 8 sweaters a day and makes a zero profit, as shown in Fig. 12.4(b); and if the demand curve is D_3, the price is $17 a sweater, each firm is indifferent between producing 7 sweaters a day and shutting down and, in either event, is making a loss equal to total fixed cost, as shown in Fig. 12.4(c). If the demand curve shifts farther to the left than D_3, the price will remain constant at $17 since the industry supply curve is horizontal at that price. Some firms will continue to produce 7 sweaters a day and others will shut down. Firms will be indifferent between these two activities and, whichever they choose, will make a loss equal to their total fixed cost. The number of firms continuing to produce will just be enough to satisfy the market demand at a price of $17.

R E V I E W

In a competitive industry, the price and quantity traded are determined by industry supply and industry demand. Industry supply is the sum of the supplies of all the individual firms. The price determined by industry demand and supply cannot be influenced by the actions of any one individual firm. Each firm takes the market price and, given that price, maximizes profit. The firm maximizes its profit by producing the output at which marginal cost equals marginal revenue (equals price), as long as price is not lower than minimum average variable cost. If the price falls below minimum average variable cost, the firm shuts down and incurs a loss equal to its total fixed cost. ∎

Long-run Equilibrium

We have seen that in short-run equilibrium a firm might make a profit, a loss, or break even. Though each of these three situations is a short-run equilibrium, only one of them is a long-run equilibrium. To see why, we need to examine the dynamic forces at work in a competitive industry. An industry adjusts over time in two ways. First, the number of firms in the industry changes; second, the existing firms change the scale of their plants, thereby shifting their short-run cost curves. Let's study the effects of these two dynamic forces in a competitive industry.

Entry and Exit

Entry is the act of setting up a new firm in an industry. **Exit** is the act of closing down a firm and leaving an industry. When will a new firm enter an industry or an existing one leave? How do entry and exit affect the market price, profit, and output in an industry? Let's first look at the causes of entry and exit.

Profits and Losses as Signals   What triggers entry and exit? The prospect of profit triggers entry and the prospect of continuing losses triggers exit. Temporary profits and temporary losses that are purely random, like the winnings and losings at a casino, do not trigger entry or exit, but the prospect of profits or losses for some foreseeable future period does. An industry making economic profits attracts new entrants; one making economic losses induces exits; and an industry in which neither economic losses nor economic profits are being made stimulates neither entry nor exit. Thus profits and losses are the signals to which firms respond in making entry and exit decisions.

What are the effects of entry and exit on price and profits?

Effects of Entry and Exit on Price and Profits
The immediate effect of entry and exit is to shift the industry supply curve. If more firms enter an industry, the industry supply curve shifts to the right: supply increases. If firms exit an industry, the industry supply curve shifts to the left: supply falls. The effects of entry and exit on price and on

Figure 12.8   Entry and Exit

(a) Effect of entry

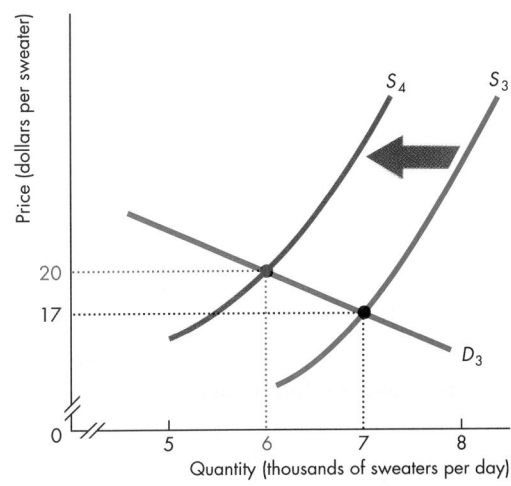

(b) Effect of exit

When new firms enter the sweater industry, the industry supply curve shifts to the right, from S_1 to S_2 (part a). The equilibrium price falls from $25 to $20, and the quantity traded rises from 9000 to 10,000 sweaters. When firms exit the sweater industry, the industry supply curve shifts to the left, from S_3 to S_4 (part b). The equilibrium price rises from $17 to $20, and the quantity traded falls from 7000 to 6000 sweaters.

the total quantity traded in the sweater industry are shown in Fig. 12.8.

Entry   First, let's look at what happens when new firms enter an industry. Suppose that the demand curve for sweaters is D_1 and the industry supply curve is S_1, so sweaters sell for $25 and 9000 sweaters are being bought and sold. Now suppose that some new firms enter the industry. As they do so, the industry supply curve shifts to the right to become S_2. With the higher supply and unchanged demand, there is a fall in price from $25 to $20 a sweater and a rise in the quantity of sweaters traded from 9000 to 10,000.

As the price falls, Swanky and the other firms in the industry will react by lowering their output. That is, for each existing firm in the industry, its profit-maximizing output falls. Since the price falls, and since each firm sells less, profit falls for each firm. You can see this reduction of profit by glancing back at Fig. 12.4. Initially, when the price is

$25, each firm makes a profit and is in the situation shown in Fig. 12.4(a). When the price falls to $20, the firm's profit disappears and it is in the situation shown in Fig. 12.4(b).

You have just discovered an important result:

As new firms enter an industry, the price falls and the profit of each existing firm falls.

A good example of this process has occurred in the last few years in the personal computer industry. When IBM introduced its first personal computer in the early 1980s, the price of PCs gave IBM a big profit. Very quickly thereafter new firms such as Compaq, Zenith, Leading Edge, and a host of others entered the industry with machines technologically identical to the IBM. In fact, they were so similar that they came to be called "clones." The massive wave of entry into the personal computer industry shifted the supply curve to the right and lowered the price and the profits for all firms.

Exit   Let's see what happens when firms leave an industry. Again, the impact of a firm leaving is to shift the industry supply curve, but this time to the left. Figure 12.8(b) illustrates. Suppose that initially the demand curve is D_3 with an industry supply curve S_3, so the market price is \$17 and 7000 sweaters are being sold. As firms leave the industry, the supply curve shifts to the left and becomes S_4. With the fall in supply, industry output falls from 7000 to 6000 sweaters and the price rises from \$17 to \$20.

To see what is happening to Swanky, go back again to Fig. 12.4. With the demand curve D_3 and a price of \$17, Swanky is in a situation like that illustrated in Fig. 12.4(c). Price is lower than average total cost and Swanky is making a loss. Some firms exit and Swanky (and some others) hang in. As firms exit, the price rises from \$17 to \$20, so the firms that remain increase their output and their losses vanish. They are then back in a situation like that illustrated in Fig. 12.4(b).

Figure 12.9   Changes in Plant Size

Swanky has a plant whose short-run cost curves are *SRMC* and *SRAC*. The price of a sweater is \$20, so average revenue and marginal revenue (*AR = MR*) are \$20. The profit-maximizing short-run output is 8 sweaters a day. Swanky's long-run costs are described by the long-run average cost curve (*LRAC*). The firm will want to expand its plant to take advantage of lower average costs and make a bigger profit—it will want to move into the blue area. As firms expand, the industry supply increases and the price falls.

You have just worked out the second important result:

As firms leave an industry the price rises and so do the profits of the remaining firms.

An example of a firm leaving an industry is International Harvester, a manufacturer of farm equipment. For decades, people associated the name "International Harvester" with tractors, combines, and other farm machines. But International Harvester wasn't the only maker of farm equipment. The industry became intensely competitive and the firm began losing money. Now the company has a new name, Navistar International, and it doesn't make tractors anymore. After years of losses and shrinking revenues, it got out of the farm business in 1985. Now it makes trucks. Another example is Singer sewing machines. The name "Singer" still means sewing machines to millions of people but Singer no longer makes these machines. It makes electronic equipment for jet aircraft and the like.

Both Singer and International Harvester exited because they were losing money on their operations. Their exits lowered supply and made it possible for the remaining firms in those two industries to break even.

Equilibrium   We've seen that the prospect of profit triggers entry and the prospect of continuing loss triggers exit. We have also seen that entry into an industry lowers the profits of the existing firms and that exit from an industry increases the profits of the remaining firms. Long-run equilibrium results from the interaction of profits and losses as signals to entry and exit and the effects of entry and exit on profits and losses.

Long-run equilibrium occurs in a competitive industry when economic profits are zero. If an industry makes economic profits, firms enter the industry and the supply curve shifts to the right. As a result, the market price falls and so do profits. Firms continue to enter and profits continue to fall as long as the industry is earning positive economic profits.

In an industry with economic losses, some firms will exit. As those firms leave the industry, the supply curve shifts to the left and the market price rises. As the price rises, the industry's losses shrink. As long as losses continue, some firms will leave the industry. Only when losses have been eliminated and zero economic profits are being made will firms stop exiting.

Let's now examine the second way in which the competitive industry adjusts in the long run— by existing firms changing their plant size.

Changes in Plant Size

A firm will change its plant size whenever it can increase its profit by doing so. A situation in which a firm can profitably expand its output by increasing its plant is illustrated in Fig. 12.9. In that figure the price (and marginal revenue) is $20. With its current plant, Swanky's marginal and average total cost—its short-run costs—are shown by the curves *SRMC* and *SRAC*. Swanky maximizes profit by producing 8 sweaters a day but with its existing plant, Swanky makes zero economic profit.

Swanky's long-run average cost curve is *LRAC*. By installing more knitting machines—increasing its plant size—Swanky can lower its costs and operate at a positive economic profit. For example, if Swanky increases its plant size so that it operates at point *m*, the minimum of its long-run average cost, it lowers its average cost from $20 to $14 and makes a profit of $6 a sweater. Since Swanky is a price taker, expanding output from 8 to 12 sweaters does not lower the market price and so would be a profitable thing for Swanky to do. Because it takes time to change the production plant, the short-run equilibrium prevails. Nevertheless, over time, the firm will gradually expand its plant.

As firms expand their plants, the short-run industry supply curve starts to shift to the right. (Recall that the industry supply curve is the sum of the supply curves of all the individual firms.) With increases in supply and a given demand, the price gradually falls. As the price falls, so do profits. It will pay firms to expand as long as expansion increases profits. Only when no economic profits are being made will firms stick with their existing plant size. There is only one possible plant size that is consistent with long-run equilibrium in a competitive industry and that is the one associated with the minimum long-run average cost (point *m*) in Fig. 12.9.

Figure 12.10   The Long-run Equilibrium of a Firm

As firms expand their plant, industry supply increases and the price falls. Long-run equilibrium occurs when the price equals $14 and each firm is producing at point *m*, its point of minimum long-run average cost.

Figure 12.10 illustrates the long-run competitive equilibrium. It occurs at a price of $14 with each firm producing 12 sweaters a day. Each firm in the industry has the plant size such that its marginal cost and average total cost curves are *SRMC* and *SRAC*. Each firm produces the output at which its short-run marginal cost equals price. No firm can change its output in the short run and make more profit. As each firm is producing at minimum long-run average cost (point *m* on *LRAC*), no firm has an incentive to expand or contract its production plant—a bigger plant or a smaller plant will lead to a higher long-run average cost and an economic loss. Finally, no firm has an incentive to leave the industry or to enter it.

R E V I E W

Long-run competitive equilibrium is described by three conditions:

• Firms maximize short-run profit so that marginal cost equals marginal revenue (equals price).

- Economic profits are zero so that no firm has an incentive to enter or to leave the industry
- Long-run average cost is at a minimum so that no firm has an incentive to expand or to contract its plant ■

Predictions

Let's now use the theory of perfect competition to make some predictions.

A Permanent Decrease in Demand

There are many examples in the real world of a permanent decrease in demand. Increased awareness of the health hazard of smoking has caused a decrease in the demand for tobacco and cigarettes. The development of inexpensive car and air transportation has caused a huge decrease in the demand for long-distance trains and buses. Solid-state electronics have caused a large decrease in the demand for TV and radio repair. There has been a decrease in the demand for American-made cars as a result of high-quality alternatives from Japan. What happens in a competitive industry when there is a permanent decrease in demand?

Let's suppose that an industry starts out in long-run competitive equilibrium, shown in Fig. 12.11(a). The demand curve labeled D_0 and the supply curve labeled S_0 represent the initial demand and supply in the market. The price initially is P_0 and the total industry output is Q_0. A single firm is shown in Fig. 12.11(b). Initially, it produces the quantity q_0 and makes zero economic profit.

Now suppose that demand decreases to D_1, as shown in part (a). This decrease in demand causes the price to drop to P_1. At this lower price, each firm produces a smaller output (q_1) and the quantity supplied by the industry decreases from Q_0 to Q_1 as the industry slides down its short-run supply curve (S_0). The industry is now in short-run equilibrium but not long-run equilibrium. It is in short-run equilibrium because each firm is maximizing profit. But it is not in long-run equilibrium because each firm is making an economic loss—its average total cost exceeds the price.

In this situation, firms will leave the industry. As they do so, the industry supply curve starts

shifting to the left, the quantity supplied shrinks, and the price gradually rises. At each higher price, the profit-maximizing output is higher, so the firms remaining in the industry raise their output as the price rises. Each slides up its marginal cost or supply curve (part b). Eventually, enough firms will have left the industry for the supply curve to have shifted to S_1 (part a). When that has happened, the price will have returned to its original level (P_0). At that price, the firms remaining in the industry will produce the same amount as they did before the fall in demand (q_0). No firms will want to leave the industry because of losses and none will want to enter. The industry supply curve settles down at S_1 and total industry output is Q_2. The industry is again in long-run equilibrium.

The difference between the initial long-run equilibrium and the final long-run equilibrium is the number of firms in the industry. Fewer firms remain after the adjustment. Each remaining firm produces the same output in the new long-run equilibrium as it did initially. While moving from the original equilibrium to the new one, firms that remain in the industry suffer losses. But they keep their losses to a minimum because they adjust their output to keep price equal to marginal cost.

A Permanent Increase in Demand

There are many examples of industries that have experienced a permanent increase in demand. The most spectacular examples stem from technological change. For example, the development of the microwave oven has produced an enormous increase in demand for paper, glass, and plastic cooking utensils, and for plastic wrap. The demand for almost all products is steadily increasing as a result of increasing population and increasing incomes. What happens in a competitive industry when the demand for its product increases? Let's begin the story again in long-run equilibrium, as shown in Fig. 12.12(a). With demand curve D_0 and supply curve S_0, the market price is P_0 and quantity Q_0 is sold by the industry. Figure 12.12(b) shows a single firm. At price P_0, the firm is making zero economic profit and producing an output of q_0. Now suppose that the demand for the industry's output increases from D_0 to D_1. The increased demand raises the price to P_1. The quantity supplied by the industry rises from Q_0 to Q_1 as each

Figure 12.11   A Decrease in Demand

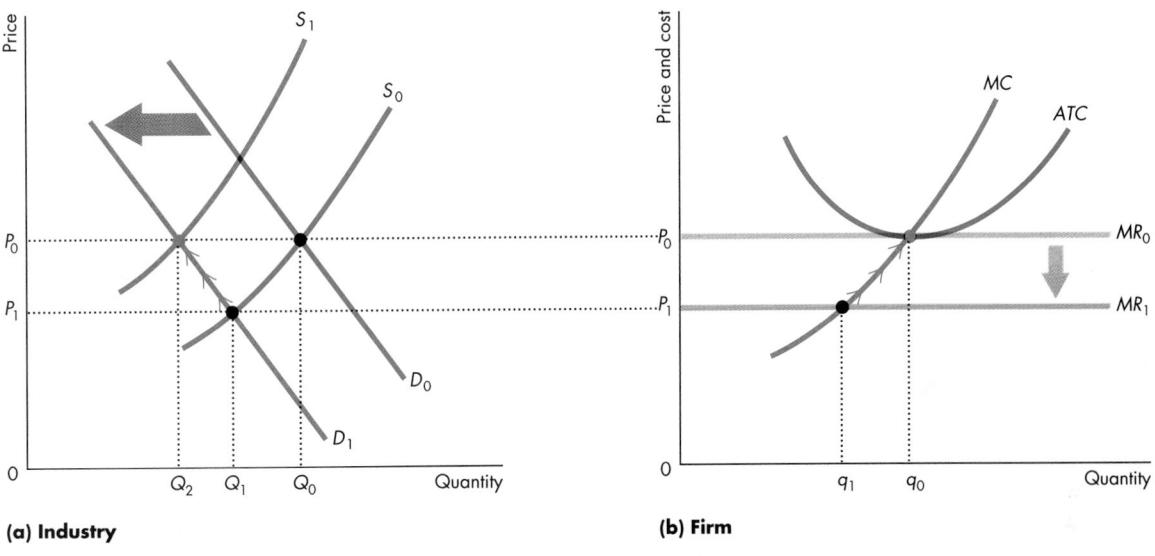

(a) Industry

(b) Firm

An industry starts out in long-run competitive equilibrium. Part (a) shows the industry demand curve D_0, the industry supply curve S_0, the equilibrium quantity Q_0 and the market price P_0. Each firm sells at price P_0, so its marginal revenue curve is MR_0 in part (b). Each firm produces q_0 and makes a zero profit. Demand decreases from D_0 to D_1 (part a). The equilibrium price falls to P_1, each firm lowers its output to q_1 (part b) and industry output falls to Q_1. In this new situation, firms are making losses and some firms will leave the industry. As they do so, the industry supply curve gradually shifts to the left, from S_0 to S_1. This shift gradually raises the industry price from P_1 back to P_0. While the price is below P_0, firms are making losses and some are leaving the industry. Once the price has returned to P_0, the smaller number of firms whose supply curves add up to the industry supply curve (S_1) will each be making a zero profit. There will be no further incentive for any firm to leave the industry. Each firm produces q_0 and industry output is Q_2.

firm increases its output from q_0 to q_1 (part b). At price P_1 and quantity Q_1, the industry is in short-run equilibrium but not in long-run equilibrium. Firms in the industry are making economic profits. These economic profits will attract new firms into the industry.

As new firms enter, the industry supply curve starts shifting to the right, and as it does so it intersects the demand curve at lower and lower prices and higher and higher quantities. Firms in the industry react to the falling price by cutting their output. That is, in Fig. 12.12(b) each firm slides back down its marginal cost curve in order to maximize profit at each successively lower price. Eventually, enough new firms enter the industry to shift the industry supply curve all the way to S_1.

By that time, the market price falls to P_0, the original price, and each firm cuts its output back to its original level, q_0. Each firm is again making zero economic profit and no firms enter or exit the industry. This new situation is a long-run equilibrium. During the adjustment process from the initial long-run equilibrium to the new one, all firms —both those firms that were in the industry originally and those that entered—make economic profits.

External Economies and Diseconomies   One feature of the predictions that we have just generated seems odd: In the long-run, regardless of whether demand increases or decreases, the price returns to its original level. Is that outcome inevitable? In

Figure 12.12   An Increase in Demand

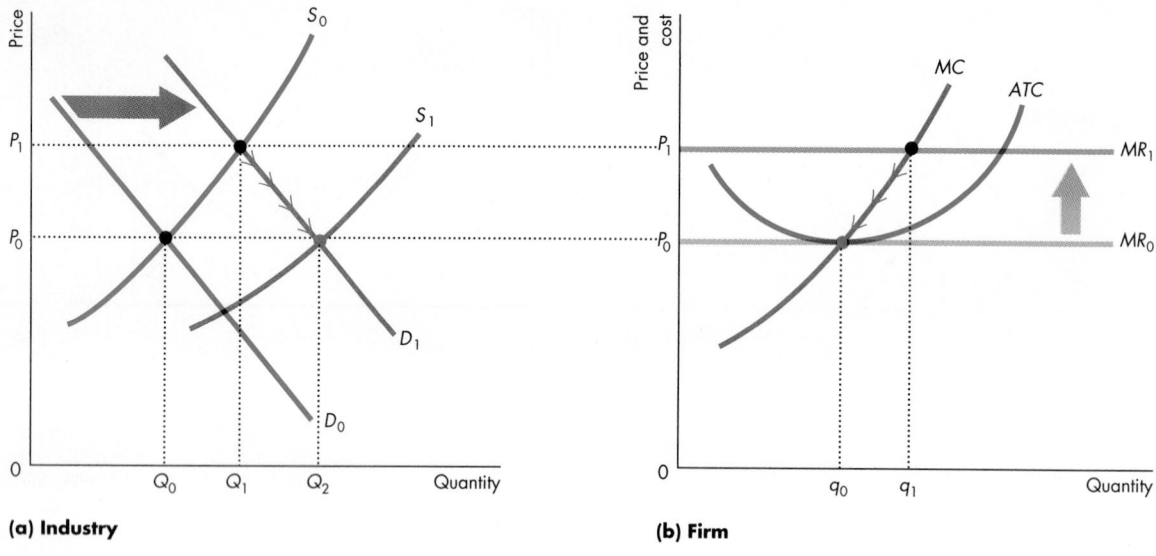

(a) Industry   **(b) Firm**

A competitive industry is in long-run equilibrium. The demand curve is D_0 and the supply curve S_0 (part a). The quantity traded is Q_0 and the market price is P_0. Each firm faces the marginal revenue curve MR_0 and maximizes profit by producing q_0 (part b). Demand increases from D_0 to D_1. The price rises to P_1 and industry output rises to Q_1. Each firm increases its output to q_1. In this situation, firms are making a profit (price is greater than average total cost). New firms will enter the industry and as they do so, the industry supply curve shifts to the right. As the supply curve shifts to the right, the price gradually falls and each individual firm gradually cuts its output from q_1 back to q_0. Since firms are entering the industry, total industry output rises even though each firm's output is cut back. The new equilibrium occurs when enough firms have entered the industry for the supply curve to have moved to S_1 with the price restored to its original level, P_0, and with each firm making zero profit. At this point, industry output is at Q_2. Since each firm is making a zero profit, there is no further tendency for new firms to enter the industry, so the supply curve remains stationary at S_1.

fact, it is not. It is possible for the long-run equilibrium price to either rise, fall, or stay the same. Figure 12.13 illustrates these three cases. In part (a), the long-run supply curve (LS_A) is perfectly elastic. In this case, an increase in demand from D_0 to D_1 (or a decrease in demand from D_1 to D_0) results in a change in the quantity traded but an unchanged price. This is the case that we have just analyzed. In part (b), the long-run supply curve (LS_B) slopes upward. In this case, when demand increases from D_0 to D_1, the price increases, and when demand decreases from D_1 to D_0, the price decreases. Finally, part (c) shows a case in which the long-run supply curve (LS_C) slopes downward. In this case, an increase in demand from D_0 to D_1

results in a fall in the price in the long run. A decrease in demand from D_1 to D_0 results in a higher price in the long run.

Whichever outcome occurs depends on external economies and external diseconomies. **External economies** are factors beyond the control of an individual firm that lower its costs as industry output rises. **External diseconomies** are factors outside the control of a firm that raise its costs as industry output rises.

There are many examples of external economies and diseconomies. They are both well illustrated in the agricultural sector. As farm output increased in the nineteenth and early twentieth centuries, the services available to farmers expanded

Figure 12.13   Long-run Price and Quantity Changes

(a) Constant cost industry

(b) Increasing cost industry

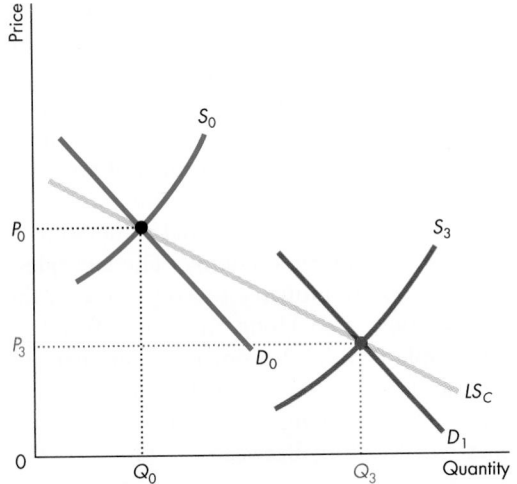

(c) Decreasing cost industry

Three possible long-run changes in price and quantity are illustrated. When demand increases from D_0 to D_1, entry occurs and the industry supply curve shifts from S_0 to S_1. In part (a), the long-run supply curve LS_A is horizontal. The quantity increases from Q_0 to Q_1 and the price remains constant at P_0. In part (b), the long-run supply curve is LS_B; the price increases to P_2 and the quantity traded increases to Q_2. This case occurs in industries with external diseconomies. In part (c), the long-run supply curve is LS_C; the price decreases to P_3 and the quantity traded increases to Q_3. This case occurs in an industry with external economies.

and their costs fell. Farm machinery, fertilizers, transportation networks, storage, and marketing facilities all improved, lowering farm costs. As a consequence, as the demand for farm products has increased, the quantity produced has increased but the price has fallen (as in Fig. 12.13c).

One of the best examples of external diseconomies is congestion. The airline industry pro-

vides a good illustration. With bigger airline industry output, there is greater congestion of both airports and airspace, which results in longer delays and extra waiting time for passengers and airplanes. These external diseconomies mean that as the demand for air transportation continues to increase, eventually (in the absence of further technological change), prices will rise.

Technological Change

Industries are constantly discovering lower-cost techniques of production. Most cost-saving production techniques cannot be implemented, however, without investing in new plant and equipment. As a consequence, it takes time for a technological advance to spread through an industry. Some firms whose plants are on the verge of being replaced will be quick to adopt the new technology, while other firms whose plants have recently been replaced will continue to operate with older technology until they can no longer cover their average variable cost. Once average variable cost cannot be covered, it pays a firm to scrap even a relatively new plant (embodying the original technology) in favor of a plant with the new technology.

Let's work out exactly what happens to the output and profit of each firm in an industry reshaped by a new technology. Figure 12.14(a) shows the demand curve for an industry (D) and an initial supply curve (S_0). The price is P_0 and the quantity Q_0. Initially there are only original technology firms in existence (Fig. 12.14b). Each firm has a marginal cost curve MC_O and an average total cost curve ATC_O. At the market price, P_0, each firm faces a marginal revenue curve MR_0, produces an output q_0^O, and makes zero economic profit. The industry is in long-run competitive equilibrium.

New technology allows firms to produce at substantially lower cost than the existing technology. The cost curves of firms with the new technology are shown in part (c). Suppose that one firm with the new technology enters the industry. Since the industry is competitive, this one firm will be a negligible part of the total industry and will hardly affect the industry supply, so that the supply curve remains at S_0. The price remains at P_0 and the new technology firm produces a profit-maximizing output of q_0^N and makes a positive economic profit.

Gradually, more new technology firms enter the industry and, after a period, enough have entered to shift the industry supply curve to become S_1 in part (a). By this time, the market price has fallen to P_1 and the industry output has risen to Q_1. Each firm takes the price P_1 and maximizes its profit. Each new technology firm, in part (c), maximizes profit by producing the output q_1^N and continues to make a positive economic profit. Each original technology firm, in part (b), minimizes its loss by producing the output q_1^O.

More new technology firms will continue to enter since the new technology is profitable. Original technology firms will begin to leave the industry or switch to the new technology because the original technology is unprofitable. Eventually all the firms in the industry will be new technology firms and, by this time, the industry supply curve will have moved to S_2. The supply curve S_2 is based on the marginal cost curves of the new technology firms. The supply curve S_0 is based on the marginal cost curves of the original technology firms. The supply curve S_1 is based on the marginal cost curves for both original technology and new technology firms. With supply curve S_2, the market price is P_2 and the industry output Q_2. At price P_2, the new technology firms produce a profit-maximizing output of q_2, making zero profits. The industry long-run equilibrium price is P_2.

The process that we have just analyzed is one in which some firms experience economic profits and others economic losses. It is a period of dynamic change for an industry. Some firms do well and others do badly. Often a change of the kind that we have just examined will have a geographical dimension to it. For example, the new technology firms may be located in a new industrial region of a country, while the original technology firms may be located in a traditional industrial region. Alternatively, the new technology firms might be in a foreign country, while the original technology firms are in the domestic economy. The struggles of the American textile industry to keep up with the fierce competition from Hong Kong and Taiwan is a good example of this phenomenon. Another example is the dairy industry, which is undergoing a major technological change arising from the use of hormones (see Reading Between the Lines, p. 304).

Farms in Distress

In 1981, there were 2.4 million farms in the United States. The average farm had 425 acres. The population of farms has been steadily declining over the years. In the five years between 1976 and 1981, that decline was close to 1 percent a year. But in the five years between 1981 and 1986, 220,000 farms (9 percent of the total) disappeared —more than three times the number that went out of business in the preceding five years. At the same time, the average size of farms increased by 7 percent to 455 acres. Through the early to mid-

Figure 12.14   Technological Change in a Competitive Industry

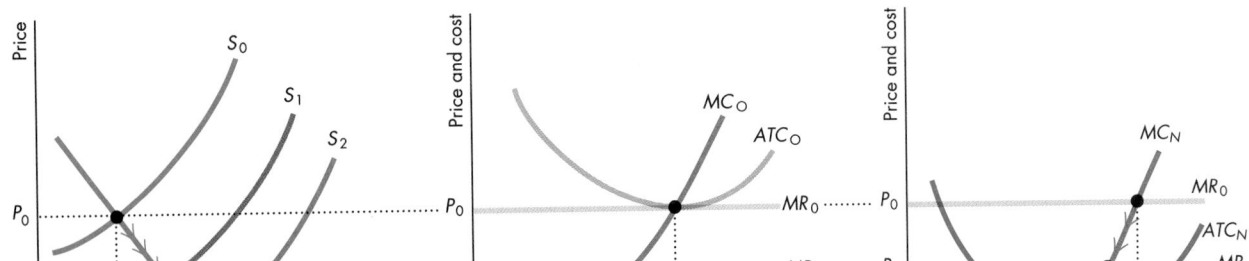

(a) Industry   **(b) Original technology firms**   **(c) New technology firms**

Initially the industry supply curve is S_0 and the demand curve is D, so the equilibrium price is P_0 and quantity traded is Q_0 (part a). Each individual firm, shown in part (b), produces q_0^O and makes a zero profit. A new technology is developed. The costs associated with the new technology (ATC_N and MC_N) are shown in part (c) and are lower than those for the original technology. A new technology firm, faced with the price P_0, produces a profit-maximizing output of q_0^N and makes a profit. Since the new technology is profitable, more and more firms will use it. As they do so, the industry supply curve begins to shift to the right, from S_0 to S_1. With an increase in industry supply, industry output rises to Q_1, but the price falls to P_1. As a result, new technology firms will cut their output from q_0^N to q_1^N, but they will still be making a profit. Original technology firms will cut their output from q_0^O to q_1^O. They will be making losses. As firms with the original technology begin to close down and more new technology firms enter the industry, the industry supply curve continues to shift to the right, from S_1 to S_2. At S_2, the price is P_2 and industry output is Q_2. Each new technology firm is now producing q_2 and making a zero profit and there are no firms using the original technology.

The effect of the introduction of the new technology has been to raise output and lower price. In the process, firms that adopted the new technology early made profits while firms that stuck with the original technology for too long incurred losses.

1980s, there were many indications of financial distress in the farm sector. By 1985, more than 5 percent of farms were unable to meet their bank loan repayment schedules; almost 40 percent had borrowed up to their loan limits; close to 5 percent a year were going out of business and close to 4 percent were in bankruptcy. Why have American farms gone through a period of such tremendous financial distress? Why have so many farms gone out of business? Why, after such a shakeout, is the remaining farm larger, on the average?

The farm problem is a complex one. In fact, there is no single "farm problem" but many individual problems varying from region to region,

crop to crop, and a host of other factors. But there is a single, common problem that affected all farmers to some degree during the early 1980s. It's on this problem that we'll focus.

Although some farmers are wealthy, many are not. They have to buy their land and farm buildings and equipment by borrowing from the bank. In the early 1980s, the cost of bank borrowing increased on an unprecedented scale. Bank loans that in the 1970s had cost an average of 7 or 8 percent a year, suddenly were costing an average of 13 percent and climbed briefly to 20 percent in 1981. The cost remained high at 15 percent a year through 1982. This massive increase in the cost of

Biotechnology in the Milk Industry

After Years of Hype, High Tech Starts to Transform the Business of Farming

After years of hype, the first commercial fruits of biotechnology are nearing the market; the computer is already having an impact in the fields. Over the next two decades, economists and scientists say, these twin technologies will transform agriculture just as mechanization and applied chemistry changed it earlier in this century. . . .

Although elephantine cows and drought-resistant corn remain years away, several companies have used biotechnology to create diagnostic kits, curatives and vaccines for a number of livestock diseases. A hormone that can boost a cow's milk production as much as 40% is expected to hit the market within two years. And a recent General Accounting Office survey showed that nearly five dozen genetically altered plants and organisms will be ready for field tests by 1990. . . .

Produced in animals' pituitary glands, growth hormones play a central role in regulating growth and milk production. Although scientists have known about the powerful effect of these hormones since the 1930s, only genetic engineering allowed them to produce the chemicals in quantities large enough to be commercially applicable. Now, such agribusiness giants as Monsanto Co., American Cyanamid Co., and International Minerals & Chemical Corp. are racing to bring the hormones to the market. Bovine somatotropine, used in dairy cows, is expected to be commercially available by 1988, followed shortly by hormones for hogs, and ultimately byproducts for sheep and beef cattle.

The new hormones will lead to dramatic production spurts, reshaping their respective industries. Bovine somatotropine could boost U.S. milk production by 20% within three years, dropping milk prices by 10% to 15% and eventually forcing 1/4 of the nation's dairy farmers out of business says Cornell University agricultural economist, Robert Kalter. . . .

Wall Street Journal, **November 10, 1986**

by Wendy L. Wall

The Essence of the Story

- Biotechnology enables the production of growth hormones that can increase a cow's milk production by up to 40 percent.

- It is predicted that within three years (of the date of the article) the use of such hormones will increase U.S. milk production by 20 percent, resulting in milk prices falling by between 10 and 15 percent.

- It is predicted that 25 percent of the nation's dairy farmers will eventually go out of business.

Background and Analysis

- The model of a perfectly competitive industry predicts what will happen to dairy farmers as the new hormone technology is adopted.

- A dairy farmer using the current technology has an average total cost curve ATC_0 and a marginal cost curve MC_0, as shown in part (a) of the figure.

- The market demand curve D and the market supply curve S_0 intersect to determine the equilibrium price, P_0 (part b).

- At the price P_0, the farmer maximizes profit by producing q_0 gallons of milk a day.

- The average total cost curve with the new hormone technology is ATC_N. The marginal cost curve with the new technology is MC_N.

- The hormone can boost production by 40 percent, so the output that minimizes average total cost with the new technology (q_N) is 40 percent larger than q_0.

- Some farmers immediately adopt the new technology and have cost curves ATC_N and MC_N.

- Some stick to original technology and have cost curves ATC_0 and MC_0.

- As farmers adopt new technology, the short-run industry supply curve gradually shifts from S_0 to S_N (part b).

- The market price gradually falls.

- When the price has fallen to P_N, farmers using

the new technology break even and those using the original technology make an economic loss.

- Those with the original technology gradually go out of business.

- When all dairy farmers have the new technology, the industry short-run supply curve is S_N, the price is P_N, and farmers make zero economic profit.

- In the new long-run equilibrium, the industry produces Q_N millions of gallons of milk and each farmer remaining in business produces q_N gallons.

- The number of dairy farmers will have fallen by approximately 25 percent.

(a) Dairy farmer

(b) Milk industry

305

Figure 12.15   The Effects of High Interest Rates on Farm Profits and Prices

(a) High interest rates cause losses

(b) Exit raises prices—eventually

Initially, an individual farm has an average total cost curve ATC, and at a price of P_0 its profit-maximizing output is q_0 (part a). Fixed costs increase, shifting the average total cost curve upward to ATC'. Marginal cost and price remain constant and so does the profit-maximizing output. Farms now make a loss shown by the red rectangle. As some farms exit, the industry supply curve shifts to the left and the price begins to rise from P_0 to P_1. The profit-maximizing output increases from q_0 to q_1 (part b). The process of adjustment is not instantaneous and farms make losses for a prolonged period.

borrowing represented an increase in the fixed costs of a farm. Recall that fixed costs are those incurred independently of the volume of output. Even if a farm produces nothing, it has to pay the bank the interest on its loans.

We can analyze the effects of an increase in fixed costs in the farm sector by using the model of a perfectly competitive industry that we've just been studying. Figure 12.15 shows you what happens. In part (a), a farm's average total cost curve is *ATC* and its marginal cost curve is *MC*. The market price is P_0 and the farm's marginal revenue curve is *MR*. The farm's profit-maximizing output is q_0. The initial situation shown in part (a) is a long-run equilibrium with the farm making zero economic profit.

An increase in total fixed cost shifts the average total cost curve upward but does not change the marginal cost curve. (Recall that marginal cost is the cost of producing one additional unit of

output. Since the increase in interest charges increases fixed cost but not variable cost, marginal cost is unchanged.) Suppose that the increased fixed cost shifts the average total cost curve to *ATC'*. If the price remains P_0, the farm's profit-maximizing output remains at q_0. But the farm is now losing money. In part (a) of Fig. 12.15, the loss is equal to the red rectangle.

The size of a farm's loss depends on its financial situation. Farms with large debts make the largest losses. Nine percent of farms have loans that exceed 70 percent of the value of their land and buildings. It is these farms that incur the largest losses. These are the farms that will begin to leave the industry. As farms go out of business, the supply curve for farm products starts to shift to the left and the price of farm products begins to increase. Figure 12.15 (b) shows what happens in the long run. When enough farms have left the industry, the price will have increased from P_0 to P_1. At the higher price, farm output increases from q_0 to q_1 and farms are no longer losing money. Individual farm outputs are now bigger than before, which means that the average farm uses more inputs—more labor, machines, and land.

But the situation shown in part (b) takes a long time to come about. The price does not rise quickly from P_0 to P_1. The main factor slowing the rise in price is the fact that even with a large exit of U.S. farms, they represent but a small fraction of the world market for most agricultural products. As a consequence, farms make losses for a prolonged period of time, during which the adjustment process takes place.

You've now studied how a competitive market works and have used the model of perfect competition to interpret and explain a variety of aspects of real world economic behavior. The last topic that we'll study in this chapter is the efficiency of perfect competition.

Competition and Efficiency

In perfect competition, freedom of entry ensures that firms produce at the least possible cost. Also, the fact that each firm is a price taker, facing a perfectly elastic demand curve, results in firms producing a quantity such that marginal cost equals price. These features of a perfectly competitive market have important implications for the efficiency of such a market.

Allocative Efficiency

Allocative efficiency occurs when no resources are wasted—when no one can be made better off without someone else being made worse off. If someone can be made better off without making someone else worse off, a more efficient allocation of resources can be achieved. Three conditions must be satisfied to achieve allocative efficiency:

- Economic efficiency
- Consumer efficiency
- Equality of marginal social cost and marginal social benefit

We defined economic efficiency in Chapter 9 as a situation in which the cost of producing a

given output is minimized. Economic efficiency involves technological efficiency—producing the maximum possible output from given inputs—as well as using inputs in their cost-minimizing proportions. Economic efficiency occurs whenever firms maximize profit. Since firms in perfect competition maximize profit, perfect competition is economically efficient.

Consumer efficiency occurs when consumers cannot make themselves better off by reallocating their budget. A consumer's best possible budget allocation is summarized in the consumer's demand curves. That is, a demand curve tells us the quantity demanded at a given price when the consumer has made the best possible use of a given budget. Thus when the quantity bought at a given price is a point on the demand curve, the allocation satisfies consumer efficiency.

The third condition occurs in perfect competition if there are no external costs and benefits. **External costs** are those costs not borne by the producer but borne by other members of society. Examples of such costs are the costs of pollution and congestion. **External benefits** are those benefits accruing to people other than the buyer of a good. Examples of such benefits are the pleasure we get from well-designed buildings and beautiful works of art. As long as *someone* buys these things, *everyone* can enjoy them.

Marginal social cost is the cost of producing one additional unit of output, including external costs. **Marginal social benefit** is the dollar value of the benefit from one additional unit of consumption, including any external benefits. Allocative efficiency occurs when marginal social cost equals marginal social benefit. Figure 12.16 illustrates such a situation. The marginal social benefit curve is MSB and the marginal social cost curve is MSC. Allocative efficiency occurs at a quantity Q^* and price P^*. In this situation, there is no waste. No one can be made better off without someone else being made worse off. If output is above Q^*, marginal social cost will exceed marginal social benefit. The cost of producing the last unit will exceed its benefit. If output is below Q^*, marginal social benefit will exceed marginal social cost. Producing one more unit will bring more benefit than it costs.

There are some circumstances in which perfect competition delivers allocative efficiency, as shown in Fig. 12.16. Those circumstances are ones in

Figure 12.16 Allocative Efficiency

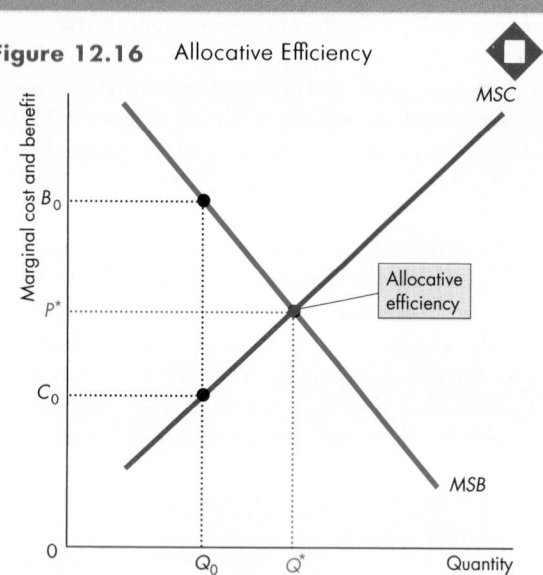

Allocative efficiency, which occurs when no resources are wasted, requires that marginal social cost (MSC) be equal to marginal social benefit (MSB). Allocative efficiency occurs at output Q^*. If output is Q_0, marginal social cost (C_0) will be less than marginal social benefit (B_0). The benefit from one additional unit of output exceeds its cost. A perfectly competitive market delivers allocative efficiency when there are no external costs and benefits. In such a situation, the marginal social cost curve is the industry supply curve and the marginal social benefit curve is the industry demand curve. The price is P^* and the quantity traded Q^*.

which there are no external costs and benefits. In such a case, all the benefits accrue to the buyers of a good and the costs are borne by its producer. In that case, the marginal social benefit curve is the same as the market demand curve. Also, the marginal social cost curve is the market supply curve. With perfect competition, price and quantity are determined at the point of intersection of the demand and supply curves. Hence, a perfectly competitive market produces an output Q^* at a price P^*. Perfect competition delivers allocative efficiency.

To check that in this situation no resources are being wasted—no one can be made better off without someone being made worse off—consider what will happen if output is restricted to Q_0. At that output, marginal social cost is C_0 but marginal social benefit is B_0. Everyone can be made better off by increasing output. Producers will willingly sup-

ply more of the good for a price higher than C_0. Consumers will willingly buy more of the good for a price lower than B_0. Everyone would like to trade more. But once output has increased to Q^*, there are no further available gains from increasing the output of this good. The benefit to the consumer of the last unit produced exactly equals the cost to the producer of the last unit.

The Invisible Hand

The founder of economic science, Adam Smith, suggested that a competitive market acts like an invisible hand to guide buyers and sellers to achieve the best possible social outcome. Each participant in a competitive market is, according to Smith, "led by an invisible hand to promote an end which was no part of his intention." You can see the invisible hand at work in the cartoon on page 309. Adam Smith was not able to work out his conclusion with the clarity and precision with which we are able to do so today. It is the work of Léon Walras and Vilfredo Pareto, and more recently, Nobel Prize-winning American economists Kenneth Arrow and Gérard Debreu that demonstrated the precise conditions under which perfect competition and maximum social welfare coincide.

Obstacles to Efficiency

There are two main obstacles to allocative efficiency:

- External costs and external benefits
- Monopoly

External costs and external benefits mean that many goods cannot be efficiently produced even in perfectly competitive markets. Such goods as national defense, the enforcement of law and order, the provision of clean drinking water and the disposal of sewage and garbage are all examples of goods in which there are enormous external benefits. Left to competitive markets, we would have too small a production of such goods. There are also many examples of goods that impose high external costs. The production of steel and chemicals generate air and water pollution. Perfect competition will result in an overproduction of such goods. One of the key functions of government is to modify the outcome of competitive markets in cases such as these. Government institutions (which we study in Chapters 19 to 21) arise, in part, because of external costs and benefits.

Another obstacle to allocative efficiency is the existence of monopoly. Monopoly, which we study in the next chapter, results in the restriction of output below its competitive level in order to increase price and make a larger profit. Precisely how monopoly achieves this outcome is the subject of the next chapter.

■ We have now completed our study of perfect competition. We have seen how a firm in a perfectly competitive market chooses its profit-maximizing output. We have seen how the actions of all the firms in a market combine to determine the market supply curve and how the market supply and demand curves determine the price and quantity. We have seen how a competitive industry operates in the short run, and we have studied the dynamic forces that move such a market to a long-run equilibrium. We have used the model of perfect competition to understand several important features of real world markets. Finally, we have seen that under some specific circumstances, perfect competition delivers an economically efficient allocation of resources.

Although many markets approximate the model of perfect competition, many do not. Our next task, in Chapters 13 and 14, is to study markets that depart from perfect competition. When we have completed this study, we'll have a toolkit of alternative models of markets that will enable us to study all the possible situations that arise in the real world. We begin, in the next chapter, by going to the opposite extreme of perfect competition—pure monopoly. Then, in Chapter 14, we'll study the markets between perfect competition and pure monopoly—monopolistic competition and oligopoly (competition among a few producers).

Drawing by M. Twohy; ©1985 The New Yorker Magazine, Inc.

SUMMARY

Perfect Competition

Perfect competition occurs in a market in which a large number of firms produce an identical good; there are many buyers; firms face competition from potential new entrants; and all firms and buyers are fully informed about the prices charged by each firm. In perfect competition, each firm sells its good for the same price and no single firm can influence the market price. Even if one firm doubles its output, the industry output will change by a tiny percentage and the market price will hardly be affected at all. (pp. 281–283)

Firms' Choices in Perfect Competition

A competitive firm takes the market price and has to choose how much to produce, when to temporarily shut down, and when to permanently leave an industry. The firm's choices are motivated by its desire to maximize profit.

A firm's maximum profit is not necessarily a positive profit. If price is above average total cost, the firm makes a profit. If price equals total average cost, the firm breaks even. If price is below average total cost, the firm makes a loss. If price is low enough, the firm maximizes profit by temporarily shutting down and laying off its workers. It pays to shut down production if price is below minimum average variable cost. When price equals minimum average variable cost, the firm makes a loss equal to its total fixed costs whether it produces the profit maximizing output or shuts down.

The firm's supply curve is the upward-sloping part of its marginal cost curve, at all points above the point of minimum average variable cost and runs along the vertical axis at all prices below minimum average variable cost. (pp. 283–292)

Short-run Equilibrium

The short-run industry supply curve shows how the total quantity supplied in the short run by all the firms in an industry varies as the market price varies.

The market price occurs where the quantity supplied and the quantity demanded are equal. Each firm takes the market price as given and chooses the output that maximizes profit. In short-run equilibrium, each firm can make an economic profit or an economic loss, or it can break even. (pp. 292–294)

Long-run Equilibrium

If the firms in an industry make positive economic profits, existing firms will expand and new firms will enter the industry. If the firms in an industry make economic losses, some firms will leave the industry and the remaining firms will produce less. Entry and exit shift the industry supply curve. As firms enter, the industry supply curve shifts to the right. As firms leave, the industry supply curve shifts to the left. Entry causes profits of existing firms to fall and exit causes profits of existing firms to rise (or losses to fall). In long-run equilibrium,

firms make zero economic profit. No firm wants to enter or leave the industry and no firm wants to expand or contract its production plant. Long-run competitive equilibrium occurs when each firm maximizes its short-run profit (marginal cost equals marginal revenue equals price); economic profit is zero, so that there is no entry or exit; and each firm produces at the point of minimum long-run average cost; so it has no incentive to change its plant size. (pp. 294–298)

Predictions

In a perfectly competitive market, a permanent decrease in demand leads to a lower industry output and a smaller number of firms in the industry. A permanent increase in demand leads to a rise in industry output and an increase in the number of firms in the industry. If there are no external economies or diseconomies, the market price remains constant in the long-run, as demand changes. If there are external economies, price falls in the long-run as demand rises. If there are external diseconomies, price rises in the long-run as demand rises.

New technology increases the industry supply, and in the long run the market price falls and the quantity traded rises. The number of firms in the industry falls. Firms that are slow to change to the new technology will make losses and eventually will go out of business. Firms that are quick to adopt the new technology will make economic profits initially, but in the long run they will make zero economic profit.

The farm problem of the 1980s, although a complex one, has one central feature that can be understood using the model of perfect competition. A large increase in interest rates increased farms' fixed costs. As a result, their average total cost curves shifted upward. Increased average total cost brought losses. These losses, in turn, forced many farms out of business. As the number of farms declines, the supply curve of farm products shifts to the left and prices increase. But this process takes time—time during which persistent losses occur in the farm sector. Eventually, after the adjustment process is complete, a smaller number of farms will break even. (pp. 298–307)

Competition and Efficiency

Allocative efficiency occurs when no one can be made better off without making someone else worse off. Three conditions for allocative efficiency—economic efficiency, consumer efficiency, and equality of marginal social cost and marginal social benefit—occur in perfect competition when there are no external costs and benefits. It is this situation that Adam Smith was describing when he talked of the economy being led by an "invisible hand."

There are two main obstacles to the achievement of allocative efficiency—the existence of external costs and external benefits and of monopoly. (pp. 307–309)

KEY CONCEPTS

Allocative efficiency, 307
Average revenue, 283
Break-even point, 285
Entry, 294
Exit, 294
External benefits, 307
External costs, 307
External diseconomies, 300
External economies, 300
Marginal revenue, 283
Marginal social benefit, 307
Marginal social cost, 307
Perfect competition, 281
Perfectly competitive firm's supply curve, 291
Price taker, 281

Short-run industry supply curve, 293
Shutdown point, 288

Key Figures

Figure 12.2   Total Revenue, Total Cost, and Profit, 286
Figure 12.3   Marginal Revenue, Marginal Cost, and Profit-Maximizing Output, 287
Figure 12.5   Swanky's Supply Curve, 291
Figure 12.6   Firm and Industry Supply Curves, 292
Figure 12.13   Long-run Price and Quantity Changes, 301
Figure 12.16   Allocative Efficiency, 308

REVIEW QUESTIONS

1 What are the main features of a perfectly competitive industry?

2 Why can't a perfectly competitive firm influence the industry price?

3 List the three key decisions that a firm in a perfectly competitive industry has to make in order to maximize profit.

4 Why is marginal revenue equal to price in a perfectly competitive industry?

5 When will a perfectly competitive firm temporarily stop producing?

6 What is the connection between the supply curve and marginal cost curve of a perfectly competitive firm?

7 What is the relationship between a firm's supply curve and the short-run industry supply curve in a perfectly competitive industry?

8 When will firms enter an industry and when will they leave it?

9 What happens to the short-run industry supply curve when firms enter a competitive industry?

10 What is the effect of entry on the price and quantity produced?

11 What is the effect of entry on profit?

12 Trace the effects of a permanent increase in demand on price, quantity traded, number of firms, and profit.

13 Trace the effects of a permanent decrease in demand on price, quantity traded, number of firms, and profit.

14 Under what circumstances will a perfectly competitive industry have:

a) A perfectly elastic long-run supply curve

b) An upward-sloping long-run supply curve

c) A downward-sloping long-run supply curve

15 Use the model of a perfectly competitive industry to explain why such a large number of farms went out of business in the 1980s.

16 What is allocative efficiency and under what circumstances does it arise?

P R O B L E M S

1 Suppose that a firm produces one thousandth of an industry's output. The industry's elasticity of demand is 3. What is the firm's elasticity of demand?

2 Pat's Pizza Kitchen has the following hourly costs:

Output (pizzas per hour)	Total cost (dollars per hour)
0	10
1	12
2	16
3	22
4	30
5	40

a) If pizzas sell for $9 (and Pat is a price taker), what is his profit-maximizing output per hour?

b) What is Pat's shutdown point?

c) Derive Pat's supply curve.

d) What price will cause Pat to leave the pizza industry?

e) What price would cause other firms with costs identical to Pat's to enter the industry?

f) What is the long-run equilibrium price of pizzas?

3 Why have the prices of pocket calculators and VCRs fallen?

4 What has been the effect of a rise in world population on the wheat market and the individual wheat farmer?

5 How has the diaper service industry been affected by the fall in the U.S. birth rate and the development of disposable diapers?

6 The market demand schedule for record albums is as follows:

Price (dollars per album)	Quantity demanded (albums per week)
0.75	440,000
1.75	430,000
2.75	420,000
3.75	410,000
4.75	400,000
5.75	390,000
6.75	380,000
7.75	370,000
8.75	360,000
9.75	350,000
10.75	340,000
11.75	330,000
12.75	320,000

The market is perfectly competitive and each firm has the same cost structure described by the following table:

Output (albums per week)	Marginal cost (dollars)	Average variable cost (dollars)	Average total cost (dollars)
150	4.82	8.80	15.47
200	4.09	7.69	12.69
250	4.63	7.00	11.00
300	6.75	6.75	10.07
350	9.75	6.91	9.75
400	13.95	7.50	10.00
450	19.62	8.52	10.74
500	26.57	9.97	11.97

There are 1000 firms in the industry.

a) What is the industry price?

b) What is the industry quantity traded?

c) What is the output of each firm?

d) What is the economic profit of each firm?

e) What is the shutdown point?

7 The same demand conditions as those in problem 6 prevail, but total fixed cost increases by $500.

a) What is the short-run profit-maximizing output for each firm?

b) Do firms enter or exit the industry?

c) What is the new long-run equilibrium price?

d) What is the new long-run equilibrium number of firms in the industry?

8 The same cost conditions as those in problem 6 prevail, but the falling price of compact discs decreases the demand for record albums and the demand schedule becomes as follows:

Price (dollars per album)	Quantity demanded (albums per week)
0.75	360,000
1.75	350,000
2.75	340,000
3.75	330,000
4.75	320,000
5.75	310,000
6.75	300,000
7.75	290,000
8.75	280,000
9.75	270,000
10.75	260,000
11.75	250,000
12.75	240,000

a) What is the short-run profit-maximizing output for each firm?

b) Do firms enter or exit the industry?

c) What is the new long-run equilibrium price?

d) What is the new long-run equilibrium number of firms in the industry?

Chapter 13

Monopoly

After studying this chapter, you will be able to:

- Define monopoly

- Explain the conditions under which monopoly arises

- Distinguish between legal monopoly and natural monopoly

- Explain how a monopoly determines its price and output

- Define price discrimination

- Explain why price discrimination leads to a bigger profit

- Compare the performance of a competitive and a monopolistic industry

- Define rent seeking and explain why it arises

- Explain the conditions under which monopoly is more efficient than competition

You have been hearing a lot in this book about firms that want to maximize profit. But perhaps you've been looking around at some of the places where you do business and wondering if they are really so intent on profit. After all, don't you get a student's discount when you get a haircut? Don't museums and movie theaters give discounts to students, too? And what about the airline that gives a discount for buying a ticket in advance? Are your barber and movie theater owner, as well as the museum and airline operators, simply generous folks to whom the model of profit-maximizing firms does not apply? Aren't they simply throwing profit away by cutting ticket prices and offering discounts? ■ When you want a phone line installed, you really have only one choice—you have to call the local phone company. If you live in New York City and want to buy cable TV service, you only have one option: Buy from Manhattan Cable. Regardless of where you live, you have no choice about the supplier of your local phone service, gas, electricity, or water. If you want to mail a letter, there is only one producer of letter-carrying services (aside from expensive couriers), the U.S. postal service. These are all examples of a single producer of a good or service controlling its supply. Such firms are obviously not like firms in perfectly competitive industries. They don't face a market determined price. They can choose their own price. How do such firms behave? How do they choose the quantity to produce and the price at which to sell it? How does their behavior compare with firms in perfectly competitive industries? Do such firms charge prices that are too high and that damage the interests of consumers? And do such firms bring any benefits?

The Profits of Generosity

■ This chapter studies markets in which individual firms can influence the quantity of goods supplied and, as a consequence, exert some influence on price. Whether a firm is a single producer such as the U.S. postal service, or a single producer in a particular location such as a public utility, the firm does not take the market price for its output as given but chooses its price. We begin by studying the conditions under which a single producer controls a market. Then we analyze the price and quantity decisions of such a firm when it sells its output for a single price to all its customers. After that, we study markets in which a firm can charge a higher price to some customers than others. Finally, we ask whether a market controlled by a single firm achieves the same allocative efficiency that arises when a market is perfectly competitive.

How Monopoly Arises

A monopoly is an industry in which there is one supplier of a good, service, or resource that has no close substitutes, and in which there is a barrier preventing the entry of new firms. The supply of local phone services, gas, electricity, and water are examples of local monopolies—monopolies restricted to a given location. The U.S. postal service is an example of a national monopoly—a sole supplier of letter-carrying service.

Barriers to Entry

The key feature of a monopoly is the existence of barriers preventing the entry of new firms. **Barriers to entry** are legal or natural impediments protecting a firm from competition from potential new entrants.

Legal Barriers to Entry   Legal barriers to entry give rise to legal monopoly. **Legal monopoly** occurs when a law, license, or patent restricts competition by preventing entry. The first legal barrier to entry is a public franchise. A **public franchise** is an exclusive right granted to a firm to supply a good or service. An example of a public franchise is the U.S. postal service, which has the exclusive right to carry first class mail. Another common form of public franchise occurs on freeways and turnpikes where particular firms are given exclusive rights to sell gasoline and food services.

The second legal barrier is a government license. A **government license** controls entry into particular occupations, professions, and industries. Government licensing in the professions is the most important example of this type of barrier to entry. For example, a license is required to practice medicine, law, dentistry, schoolteaching, architecture, and a variety of other professional services and industries. Licensing does not create monopoly, but it does restrict competition.

A third legal restriction on entry is a patent. A **patent** is an exclusive right granted by the government to the inventor of a product or service. A patent is valid for a limited time period that varies from country to country, in the United States it is 17 years. Patents are designed to protect inventors and thereby encourage invention (by preventing others from copying an invention until sufficient time has elapsed for the inventor to have reaped some benefits).

Natural Barriers to Entry   Natural barriers to entry give rise to natural monopoly. **Natural monopoly** occurs when there is a unique source of supply of a raw material or when one firm can supply the entire market at a lower price than two or more firms can. As the definition of natural monopoly implies, natural barriers to entry take two forms. First, a single firm may own and control the entire supply of a mineral or natural resource. This type of monopoly occurs in the production of particular types of mineral water, for which there is just a single, unique source, and for some raw materials such as diamonds and chromium. De Beers, a South African company, for example, owns and controls four fifths of the world's diamond mines. Also, all the sources of chromium, again concentrated in southern Africa, are controlled by a small number of producers.

Natural monopoly can also arise because of economies of scale. When a single producer can supply the entire market at a lower average total cost of production than can two or more firms, then only a single firm can survive in the industry. Examples of natural monopoly arising from economies of scale are public utilities, such as the distribution of electricity, natural gas, and water.

Most monopolies in the real world, whether legal or natural, are regulated in some way by government or by government agencies. We will study such regulation in Chapter 21. Here we will consider an unregulated monopoly for two important reasons.

First, we can better understand why governments regulate monopolies and the effects of regulation if we also know how an unregulated monopoly would behave. Second, even in industries with more than one producer, firms often have an element of monopoly power, arising from locational advantages or from important differences in product quality protected by patents. The theory of monopoly sheds important light on the behavior of such firms and industries.

We will begin by studying the behavior of a single-price monopoly. A **single-price monopoly** is a monopoly that charges the same price for each and every unit of its output. How does a single-price monopoly determine the quantity to produce and the price to charge for its output?

Single-Price Monopoly

The starting point for understanding how a single-price monopoly chooses its price and output is to work out the relationship between the demand for the good produced by the monopoly and the monopoly's revenue.

Demand and Revenue

Since in a monopoly there is only one firm, the demand curve facing that firm is the industry demand curve. Let's look at an example: Bobbie's Barbershop, the sole supplier of haircuts in Cairo, Nebraska. The demand schedule that Bobbie faces is set out in Table 13.1. At a price of $20, Bobbie sells no haircuts. The lower the price, the more haircuts per hour Bobbie is able to sell. For example, at a price of $12, consumers demand 4 haircuts per hour (row *e*) and at a price of $4, they demand 8 haircuts per hour (row *i*).

Total revenue (TR) is the price (P) multiplied by the quantity sold (Q). For example, in row *d*, Bobbie sells 3 haircuts at $14 each, so total revenue is $42. *Marginal revenue (MR)* is the change in total revenue (ΔTR) resulting from a one-unit rise in the quantity sold. For example, if the price falls from $18 (row *b*) to $16 (row *c*), the quantity sold rises from 1 to 2 haircuts. Total revenue rises from $18 to $32, so the change in total revenue is $14. Since the quantity sold rises by 1 haircut, marginal revenue equals the change in total revenue and is $14. When recording

Table 13.1 Single-Price Monopoly's Revenue

	Price P (dollars per haircut)	Quantity demanded Q (haircuts per hour)	Total revenue TR = P × Q (dollars)	Marginal revenue MR = $\Delta TR/\Delta Q$ (dollars per haircut)
a	20	0	0	
				18
b	18	1	18	
				14
c	16	2	32	
				10
d	14	3	42	
				6
e	12	4	48	
				2
f	10	5	50	
				−2
g	8	6	48	
				−6
h	6	7	42	
				−10
i	4	8	32	
				−14
j	2	9	18	
				−18
k	0	10	0	

The table shows Bobbie's demand schedule—the number of haircuts demanded per hour at each price. Total revenue (TR) is price multiplied by quantity sold. For example, row c shows that when the price is $16 a haircut, two haircuts are sold for a total revenue of $32. Marginal revenue (MR) is the change in total revenue resulting from a one-unit rise in the quantity sold. For example, when the price falls from $16 to $14 a haircut, the quantity sold increases from 2 to 3 haircuts and total revenue increases by $10. The marginal revenue of the third haircut is $10. Total revenue rises through row f, where 5 haircuts are sold for $10, and it falls thereafter. In the output range over which total revenue is increasing, marginal revenue is positive; in the output range over which total revenue is decreasing, marginal revenue is negative.

marginal revenue, it is written between the two rows to emphasize that marginal revenue relates to the *change* in the quantity sold.

Figure 13.1 shows Bobbie's demand curve (D). Each row of Table 13.1 corresponds to a point on the demand curve. For example, row *d* in the table and point *d* on the demand curve tell us that at a price of $14, Bobbie sells 3 haircuts. The figure also shows Bobbie's marginal revenue curve (MR). Notice that the marginal revenue curve is below the demand

Figure 13.1   Demand and Marginal Revenue
for a Single-Price Monopoly

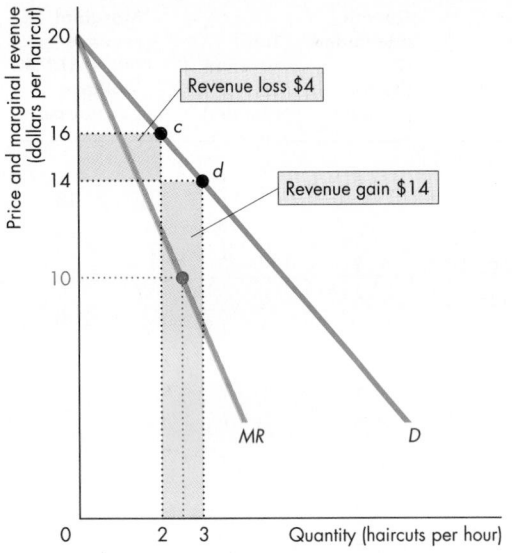

The monopoly demand curve (D) is based on the numbers in Table 13.1. At a price of $16 a haircut, Bobbie sells 2 haircuts an hour. If she lowers the price to $14, she sells 3 haircuts an hour. The sale of the third haircut brings a revenue gain of $14 (the price charged for the third haircut). But there is a revenue loss of $4 ($2 per haircut) on the 2 haircuts that she could have sold for $16 each. The marginal revenue (extra total revenue) from the third haircut is the difference between the revenue gain and the revenue loss—$10. The marginal revenue curve (MR) shows the marginal revenue at each level of sales. Marginal revenue is lower than price.

curve. That is, at each level of output marginal revenue is less than price. Why is marginal revenue less than price? It is because when the price is lowered to sell one more unit, there are two opposing effects on total revenue. The lower price results in a revenue loss and the increased quantity sold results in a revenue gain. For example, at a price of $16 Bobbie sells 2 haircuts (point c). If she reduces the price to $14, she sells 3 haircuts and has a revenue gain of $14 on the third haircut. But she receives only $14 on the first two as well—$2 less than before—so her revenue loss on the first 2 haircuts is $4. She has to deduct this amount from the revenue gain of $14. Marginal revenue—the difference between the revenue gain and the revenue loss—is $10.

Figure 13.2 shows Bobbie's demand curve, marginal revenue curve *(MR),* and total revenue curve *(TR)* and illustrates the connections between them. Again, each row in Table 13.1 corresponds to a point on the curves. For example, row *d* in the table and point *d* on the graphs tell us that when 3 haircuts are sold for $14 each (part a) total revenue is $42 (part b). Notice that as the quantity sold rises, total revenue rises to a peak of $50 (point *f*) and then declines. To understand the behavior of total revenue, notice what happens to marginal revenue as the quantity sold increases. Over the range 0 to 5 haircuts, marginal revenue is positive. When more than 5 haircuts are sold, marginal revenue becomes negative. The output range over which marginal revenue is positive is the same as that over which total revenue is rising. The output range over which marginal revenue is negative is the same as that over which total revenue declines. When marginal revenue is 0, total revenue is at a maximum.

Revenue and Elasticity   When we studied elasticity in Chapter 5, we discovered a connection between the elasticity of demand and the effect of a change in price on total expenditure or total revenue. Let's refresh our memories of that connection.

Recall that the elasticity of demand is the percentage change in the quantity demanded divided by the percentage change in price. If the elasticity of demand is greater than 1, a 1 percent decrease in price results in a greater than 1 percent increase in the quantity demanded. If the elasticity of demand is less than 1, a 1 percent decrease in price results in a less than 1 percent increase in the quantity demanded.

But the responsiveness of the quantity demanded to a change in price also influences the change in total revenue. If a 1 percent decrease in price results in an increase in the quantity demanded of more than 1 percent, total revenue increases. We've seen that the output range over which total revenue increases when the price decreases is the same as that over which marginal revenue is positive. Thus the output range over which marginal revenue is positive is also the output range over which the elasticity of demand is greater than 1. The output range over which total revenue decreases when price decreases is the same as that over which marginal revenue is negative. Thus the output range over which marginal revenue is negative is also the output range over which the elasticity of demand is less than 1.

Figure 13.2   A Single-Price Monopoly's Revenue Curves

(a) Demand and marginal revenue curves

(b) Total revenue curve

Bobbie's demand curve (D) and marginal revenue curve (MR), shown in part (a), and total revenue curve (TR), shown in part (b), are based on the numbers in Table 13.1. For example, at a price of $14, Bobbie sells 3 haircuts an hour (point d in part a) for a total revenue of $42 (point d in part b). Over the range 0 to 5 haircuts an hour, total revenue is increasing and marginal revenue is positive, as shown by the blue bars. Over the range 5 to 10 haircuts an hour, total revenue declines—marginal revenue is negative, as shown by the red bars. Over the output range for which marginal revenue is positive, the elasticity of demand is greater than 1—demand is elastic. Over the output range for which marginal revenue is negative, the elasticity of demand is less than 1—demand is inelastic. At the output at which marginal revenue is zero, total revenue is at a maximum and the elasticity of demand equals 1—point f.

We've seen what happens to marginal revenue and total revenue when the elasticity of demand is greater than 1 and when it is less than 1. If the elasticity of demand is exactly 1, the percentage decrease in price equals the percentage increase in the quantity demanded. In this case, a price change results in no change in total revenue. Marginal revenue is zero. Thus when the elasticity of demand is 1, total revenue is at its maximum and marginal revenue is zero.

The relationship that you have just discovered has an interesting implication: A profit-maximizing monopoly will never produce an output in the inelastic range of its demand curve. If it does so, marginal revenue will be negative—each additional unit sold will lower total revenue. In such a situation, it will always pay to charge a higher price and sell a smaller quantity. But exactly what price and quantity does a profit-maximizing monopoly firm choose?

Price and Output Decision

Profit is the difference between total revenue and total cost. To determine the output level and price that maximize a monopoly's profit, we need to study the behavior of both revenue and costs as output varies.

A monopoly faces the same types of technology and cost constraints as a competitive firm. The monopoly has a production function that is subject to diminishing returns. The monopoly buys its inputs in competition with other firms, at prices that it cannot influence. The sole difference between the monopoly that we'll study here and a perfectly competitive firm lies in the market constraint for the output that each firm faces. The competitive firm is a price taker, whereas the monopoly supplies the entire market. Because the monopoly supplies the entire market, its output decision affects the price at which that output is sold. It is this fact that gives rise to the difference between the decisions faced by these two types of firm.

We have already looked at Bobbie's revenue in Table 13.1 and Figs. 13.1 and 13.2. The revenue information contained in Fig. 13.3 is extracted from Table 13.1. The figure also contains information on Bobbie's costs and profit.

Total cost (*TC*) rises as output rises and so does total revenue (*TR*). Profit equals total revenue minus total cost. As you can see in the table, the maximum profit ($12) occurs when Bobbie sells 3 haircuts for $14 each. If she sells 2 haircuts for $16 each or 4 haircuts for $12 each, her profit will be only $8.

Figure 13.3   A Single-Price Monopoly's Profit-Maximizing Output and Price

(a) Total revenue and total cost curves

(b) Total profit curve

(c) Demand and marginal revenue and cost curves

Figure 13.3   A Single-Price Monopoly's Profit-Maximizing Output and Price

Price P (dollars per haircut)	Quantity demanded Q (haircuts per hour)	Total revenue $TR = P \times Q$ (dollars)	Marginal revenue $MR = \Delta TR/\Delta Q$ (dollars per haircut)	Total cost TC (dollars)	Marginal cost $MC = \Delta TC/\Delta Q$ (dollars per haircut)	Profit $TR - TC$ (dollars)
20	0	0		20		−20
			18		1	
18	1	18		21		−3
			14		3	
16	2	32		24		+8
			10		6	
14	3	42		30		+12
			6		10	
12	4	48		40		+8
			2		15	
10	5	50		55		−5

The table adds information about total cost *(TC)*, marginal cost *(MC)*, and profit *(TR − TC)* to the information on demand and revenue in Table 13.1. For example, at a price of $16, 2 haircuts will be sold for a total revenue of $32. The total cost of producing 2 haircuts is $24, so profit equals $8 ($32 − $24). Profit is at a maximum in the row highlighted in red.

The numbers in the table are graphed in the three parts of the figure. The total cost and total revenue curves appear in part (a). The vertical distance between total revenue *(TR)* and total cost *(TC)* equals total profit. Maximum profit occurs at 3 haircuts an hour. Part (b) shows the total profit curve. This curve reaches a maximum at 3 haircuts an hour. The total profit curve is at a maximum (part b) when the vertical distance between the total revenue and total cost curves is also at a maximum (part a). Where total revenue equals total cost (in part a), the total profit curve cuts the horizontal axis (in part b). Part (c) shows that at the profit-maximizing output of 3 haircuts, marginal cost *(MC)* equals marginal revenue *(MR)*. The monopoly sells the output for the maximum possible price as determined by its demand curve. In this case, that price is $14. The monopoly's profit is illustrated in part (c) by the blue rectangle. That profit is $12—the profit per haircut ($4) multiplied by 3 haircuts.

You can see why 3 haircuts is the profit-maximizing output by looking at the marginal revenue and marginal cost columns. When Bobbie raises output from 2 to 3 haircuts, marginal revenue is $10 and marginal cost is $6. Profit increases by the difference—$4. If Bobbie increases output yet further, from 3 to 4 haircuts, she generates a marginal revenue of $6 and a marginal cost of $10. In this case, marginal cost exceeds marginal revenue by $4, so profit falls by $4. It always pays to produce more if marginal revenue exceeds marginal cost and to produce less if marginal cost exceeds marginal revenue. It pays to produce neither more nor less when marginal cost and marginal revenue are equal to each other. Thus the profit-maximizing output occurs when marginal revenue equals marginal cost.

The information set out in the table is shown graphically in Fig. 13.3. Part (a) shows Bobbie's total revenue curve *(TR)* and total cost curve *(TC)*. Profit is the vertical distance between *TR* and *TC*. Bobbie maximizes her profit at 3 haircuts an hour—profit is $42 minus $30, or $12. Part (b) shows how Bobbie's profit varies with the number of haircuts sold.

Figure 13.3(c) shows the demand curve *(D)* and the marginal revenue curve *(MR)* along with the marginal cost curve *(MC)* and average total cost curve *(ATC)*. The profit-maximizing output is 3 haircuts, where marginal cost equals marginal revenue. The price charged is found by reading from the demand curve the price at which 3 haircuts can be sold. That price is $14. When Bobbie produces 3 haircuts, average total cost is $10 (read from the *ATC* curve).

Figure 13.4 Short-run Profit, Costs, and Demand

(a) Zero profit   **(b) Loss**

In the short run, a monopoly can make zero profit or even a loss. Part (a) shows a monopoly making zero profit. At the profit-maximizing output—3 haircuts an hour—average total cost and price are each $14. Part (b) shows a monopoly making a short-run loss. In this case, at the profit-maximizing output (again 3 haircuts an hour) average total cost is $16 and price is $14, so the firm incurs a loss of $6. The loss is represented by the red rectangle.

Her profit per haircut is $4 ($14 minus $10). Bobbie's total profit is indicated by the blue rectangle, which equals the profit per haircut ($4) multiplied by the number of haircuts (3), for a total profit of $12. Since price always *exceeds* marginal revenue and at the profit-maximizing output marginal revenue equals marginal cost, price always exceeds marginal cost.

Bobbie makes a positive profit. But there is nothing to guarantee that a monopoly will be able to make a profit. A monopoly can make a zero profit or even, in the short run, a loss. Figure 13.4 shows the conditions under which these other two outcomes will occur.

If Bobbie's average total cost is ATC_a, as shown in Fig. 13.4(a), then the profit-maximizing output, where marginal revenue equals marginal cost, will be 3 haircuts. At this output, average cost just equals price, so both the profit per haircut and total profit are zero. If Bobbie's average total cost curve is ATC_b, as shown in Fig. 13.4(b), then marginal cost equals

marginal revenue at 3 haircuts and average total cost is $16. But 3 haircuts can only be sold for $14 each, so Bobbie makes a loss of $2 a haircut. That loss, however, is the minimum possible loss, so Bobbie is still maximizing profit. A monopoly that makes a loss will only do so in the short run. If the situation shown in Fig. 13.3(b) were permanent, Bobbie would go out of business.

When we studied a competitive firm, we checked to see whether price was higher or lower than average variable cost. With a price below average variable cost, it pays a firm to shut down temporarily and produce nothing. It makes a loss equal to total fixed cost. Like a competitive firm, Bobbie also needs to check her average variable cost to see whether it pays to shut down temporarily. There is no point in any firm, competitor or monopoly, making a loss that exceeds total fixed cost.

If firms in a perfectly competitive industry are making a positive economic profit, new firms enter. That does not happen in a monopoly industry. Barriers to entry prevent new firms from entering. So a firm can make a positive economic profit and continue to do so indefinitely in a monopoly industry. Sometimes that profit is large, as in the cable TV industry (see Reading Between the Lines, pp. 324–325.)

No Monopoly Supply Curve   Unlike a perfectly competitive firm, a monopoly does not have a supply curve. Recall that a supply curve shows the quantity supplied at each different price. A change in demand in a competitive industry results in the industry moving along its supply curve and each firm moving along its marginal cost curve. A change in demand in a monopoly also produces a change in price and quantity, but the monopoly does not slide along a supply curve. Instead, given the new demand conditions, the monopoly picks the combination of output and price that maximizes profit, given its cost curves. As in competitive conditions, the monopoly chooses to sell a quantity such that marginal revenue equals marginal cost. But the relationship between price and marginal revenue, and between price and marginal cost, depends on the shape of the demand curve. For a given profit-maximizing quantity, the steeper the demand curve, the higher is the price at which that quantity is sold. It is for this reason that there is no unique relationship between the monopoly's profit-maximizing quantity and price, and therefore no such thing as a monopoly's supply curve.

R E V I E W

A single-price monopoly maximizes profit by producing an output at which marginal cost equals marginal revenue. At that output, the monopoly charges the highest price that consumers are willing to pay. Since a monopoly's price exceeds its marginal revenue, its price also exceeds its marginal cost. But there is no guarantee that a monopoly will make a profit in the short run. Depending on its cost curves and the demand for its output, the monopoly might make a positive economic profit, or a zero profit, or incur a loss. But a monopoly can make a positive economic profit even in the long run since there are barriers to the entry of new firms. There is no unique relationship between the quantity that a monopoly produces and its price— there is no monopoly supply curve. ∎

Price Discrimination

Price discrimination is the practice of charging some customers a higher price than others for an identical good or of charging an individual customer a higher price on a small purchase than on a large one. An example of price discrimination is the practice of charging children or students a lower price than adults to see a movie. Another example is the common practice of barbers and hairdressers giving discounts to senior citizens and students. Price discrimination can be practiced in varying degrees. **Perfect price discrimination** occurs when a firm charges a different price for each unit sold and charges each consumer the maximum price that he or she is willing to pay for each unit. Though perfect price discrimination does not happen in the real world, it shows the limit to which price discrimination can be taken.

Not all price *differences* imply price *discrimination*. In many situations, goods that are similar but not identical have different costs and sell for different prices *because* they have different costs. For example, we saw in Chapter 12 that the marginal cost of producing electricity depends on the time of day. If an electric power company charges a higher price for consumption between 7:00 and 9:00 in the morning and between 4:00 and 7:00 in the evening than it does at other times of the day, this practice is not called price discrimination. Price discrimination charges varying prices to consumers, not because of differences in the cost of producing the good, but because different consumers have different demands for the good.

At first sight, it appears that price discrimination contradicts the assumption of profit maximization. Why would a movie operator allow children to see movies at half price? Why would a hairdresser or barber charge students and senior citizens less? Aren't these producers losing profit by being nice guys?

Deeper investigation shows that far from losing profit, price discriminators actually make a bigger profit than they would otherwise. Thus a monopoly has an incentive to try to find ways of discriminating among groups of consumers and charging each group the highest possible price. Some people may pay less with price discrimination, but others pay more. Let's see how price discrimination brings in more total revenue.

Local Monopoly in Cable TV

With America Well Wired, Cable Industry Is Changing

With most of the nation now wired for reception, the cable television industry is entering a new phase, aiming for an even greater surge of growth based on better programming and more aggressive marketing.

The hope is to make cable television, in the words of one industry spokesman, as prevalent as air-conditioning in American homes. . . .

Inception in 1948

Cable existed only as a delivery service for broadcast channels at its inception in 1948, until the mid-1970's when programming services like Ted Turner's station in Atlanta became widely available through satellite distribution.

Still, through the mid-1980's, cable television was widely regarded as the minor league of the medium, a limited refuge for network reruns, old movies and fringe sports events. Today, however, it represents a threat to the broadcast networks' traditional dominance of the industry.

The industry has increased subscriber fees and has experienced a sharp rise in advertising revenues, a dual-income stream that the industry has exploited to great advantage over the broadcast networks. With that financial base, cable is taking a more aggressive marketing approach to add subscribers.

A $15.4-Billion-a-Year Business

More than half the homes in the United States now pay a fee, averaging $24.26 a month for both the basic fee and the cost of premium channels, to receive cable.

In sports, the coveted programming once carried exclusively by the networks, more and more of the action has switched to cable. Cable television now carries many games in major league baseball, the National Football League, and National Hockey League. In 1992, some events of the Olympics will be carried on cable for the first time.

In the process, cable's annual revenues from advertising and fees have grown from $6.5 billion in 1983 to an estimated $15.4 billion in 1989. Unlike the broadcast networks, which are losing viewers and scratching for profits, cable is making substantial annual gains in subscribers, revenues, profits and national attention.

Shift in Audience Attention

In the 1988-89 television season, the share of the prime-time audience controlled by NBC, ABC and CBS fell three percentage points from the previous season, to an all-time low of 61 percent, as measured by the A. C. Nielsen Company. . . .

Local Monopolies Prevalent

Most cable systems are local monopolies. They gain an exclusive franchise from a local governing body to deliver cable to homes in that area. On some occasions local groups have protested a cable system's service and sought either to have the franchise turned over to new owners or to invite a different system to compete with the original franchise holder.

But in the vast majority of cases, a cable system sells its service locally without competition.

Though there are more than 9,000 individual cable systems in the United States, and they carry programming provided by almost 100 different channels, the cable television industry is concentrated, at least in terms of who controls most of it.

The Acknowledged Giant

One company, Tele-Communications Inc., is the acknowledged giant of the business, with interests in systems that reach more than 11 million of the 50 million national subscribers.

This concentration in relatively few hands has prompted heightened interest in Congress about possible abuse of that power. The industry has defended itself by saying that concentration results in improved quality on television. That successful system operators have financial interests in channels that produce programming enables them to invest system profits in superior programming, they argue.

The New York Times, July 9, 1989

The Essence of the Story

- Cable television service began in 1948 as a method of delivering broadcast television channels.

- In the mid-1970s, the Turner Broadcasting System in Atlanta started supplying television programming services distributed via satellite to local cable companies.

- At first, most programming offered by cable companies was limited to network reruns, old movies, and special interest sporting events. But by 1989, cable programming companies were offering top sporting attractions, and material similar to that on the broadcast networks.

- Cable fees have increased to an average of $24.26 a month; advertising revenue has grown from $6.5 billion in 1983 to an estimated $15.4 billion in 1989; and cable companies' profits are substantial.

- The prime time audience is switching from NBC, ABC, and CBS to the cable channels, and cable television is now in more than 50 million homes.

- Cable television services are operated by local monopolies that gain exclusive franchises from a local government body.

- There are 9000 individual cable systems carrying almost 100 different channels, but some very big companies service a significant proportion of the market and make much of the programming.

- The industry defends monopoly and large-scale producers, saying that large profits are used to make better programs, thereby improving the quality of television.

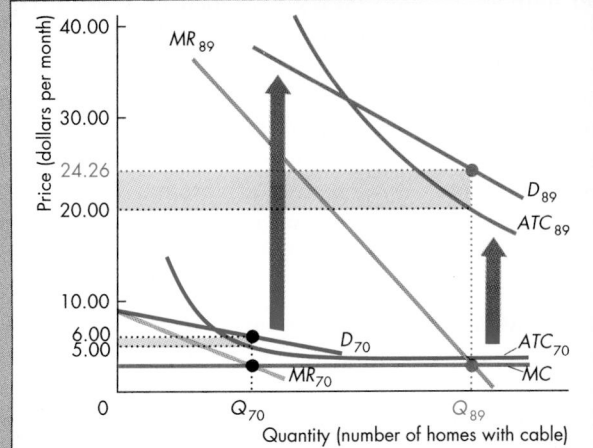

Background and Analysis

- Until the mid-1970s, all television programming could be received (in major population centers) by either broadcast or cable. Hence cable was a close substitute for broadcasting, and the demand for cable services was low, as shown in the figure by demand curve D_{70}. The marginal revenue curve was MR_{70}.

- The marginal cost of adding homes to cable service is low (shown as MC in the figure) and in the mid-1970s average total cost was ATC_{70}.

- In the 1970s, profit was maximized by providing cable service to Q_{70} homes at a price of $6.00 a month. Profits were modest, as shown by the smaller blue-shaded rectangle in the figure.

- The development of satellite technology made it possible for cable programmers to sell via cable services that were not available by broadcast. As a result, the cable companies created improved-quality television services, available exclusively on cable. Consequently, the demand for cable service increased, and the demand curve shifted to D_{89}. The marginal revenue curve shifted to MR_{89}

- The increased cost of providing the improved cable services shifted the average total cost curve to ATC_{89}, but the marginal cost of adding homes to cable service (probably) did not change, so the marginal cost curve remained at MC.

- The profit-maximizing situation in 1989 was for cable service to be sold to Q_{89} homes—the quantity that makes marginal cost and marginal revenue equal—at a price of $24.26 a month. Profits were high (large blue rectangle).

- Cable programming companies do not "invest their profits in superior programming," as they are reported to argue. To maximize profit, they operate on two margins—the number of homes serviced and the quality of programming. Superior programs cost more but increase demand and bring in more revenue. To maximize profit, cable programmers make the marginal cost of superior programs equal to the marginal revenue they generate.

Figure 13.5   Total Revenue and Price Discrimination

(a) **One price**   (b) **Two prices**   (c) **Many prices**

If Bobbie sells 4 haircuts for the same price—$12 each—her total revenue is $48, as shown by the blue rectangle in part (a). If she charges two prices—$16 each for the first 2 haircuts and $12 each for the next 2—her total revenue will be $56, as shown by the blue area in part (b). If Bobbie charges four different prices—$18 for the first haircut, $16 for the second haircut, $14 for the third haircut, and $12 for the fourth haircut—her total revenue will be $60, as shown by the blue area in part (c). The more finely a monopoly can discriminate, the larger the total revenue from a given level of sales.

Price Discrimination and Total Revenue

The total revenue received by a single-price monopoly equals the quantity sold multiplied by the single price charged. That revenue is illustrated in Fig. 13.5(a). Suppose that Bobbie sells 4 haircuts for a single price of $12 each. Bobbie's total revenue, $48, is the area of the blue rectangle—the quantity sold, 4 haircuts, multiplied by the price, $12.

Now suppose that Bobbie can sell some haircuts for one price and some for another, higher price. Figure 13.5(b) illustrates this case. The first 2 haircuts are sold for $16 each and then two more are sold for the original price, $12. In this case, Bobbie has greater total revenue than when she charges a single price. The extra revenue earned on the first 2 haircuts sold has to be added to the original revenue. Total revenue, the blue area shown in part (b), is $56 (2 at $12 plus 2 at $16).

What will happen if Bobbie can perfectly price discriminate? The answer is shown in Fig. 13.5(c). Each haircut is sold for the maximum

possible price. The first haircut sells for $18, the next for $16, the third for $14, and the fourth for $12. Total revenue, the blue area in part (c), is $60.

Price Discrimination and Consumer Surplus

Demand curves slope down because the value that an individual places on a good falls as the quantity consumed of that good rises. When all the units consumed can be bought for a single price, consumers make a surplus—*consumer surplus*. (If you need to refresh your understanding of consumer surplus, flip back to Chapter 7, p. 167.) Price discrimination can be seen as an attempt by a monopoly to capture the consumer surplus (or as much of the surplus as possible) for itself.

Discriminating among Units of a Good   One form of price discrimination charges each single buyer a different price on each unit of a good bought. An example of this type of discrimination is a discount for bulk buying. The larger the order, the larger is the discount—and the lower is the price. This type of price discrimination works because each individual's demand curve slopes downward. For example, suppose that Lisa is willing to pay $7 to see one movie a month, $6 to see two, and $5 to see three. If movies cost $5, she sees three and pays $5 for each. But the value to her of the first movie is $7—$2 more than she pays for it. And the value to her of the second movie is $6—$1 more than she pays for it. Lisa's consumer surplus is $3.

Now imagine that a movie theater offers the following monthly subscription. For $7, you can see one movie a month; for $13, you can see two a month; for $18, you can see three movies a month. If Lisa opts for the three-movie package, the movie theater extracts from Lisa her entire consumer surplus. But to extract every dollar of consumer surplus from every buyer, the monopolist would have to offer each individual customer a separate contract based on that customer's own demand curve. Clearly such price discrimination cannot be carried out in practice, because a firm does not have sufficient information about each individual consumer's demand curve to be able to do the necessary calculations. But by making arrangements of the type just described that extract most of the consumer surplus of a typical customer, firms can move somewhere toward perfect price discrimination.

Discriminating among Individuals   Even when it is not possible to charge each individual a different price for each unit bought, it may still be possible to discriminate among individuals. This possibility arises from the fact that some people place a higher value on consuming one more unit of a good than do other individuals. By charging such an individual a higher price, the producer can obtain some of the consumer surplus that would otherwise accrue to their customers.

Let's look a bit more closely at the price and output decisions of a monopoly that practices price discrimination.

Price and Output Decisions
with Price Discrimination

Price discrimination often takes the form of discriminating between different groups of consumers on the basis of age, employment status, or other easily distinguished characteristics. Price discrimination works only if each group has a different price elasticity of demand for the product. If one group has a high elasticity and the other a low elasticity, then a firm can increase profit by charging a lower price to the group with the high elasticity and a higher price to the group with a low elasticity.

Let's stick with the example of haircuts. Bobbie suspects that the students and the elderly of Cairo have a higher elasticity of demand for haircuts than do other people—they do not seem to care as much about getting a bit shaggy as the business people and homemakers. Let's see how Bobbie exploits these differences in demand and raises her profit by price discriminating. Until now, Bobby has sold 3 haircuts an hour at $14 a haircut, for a total revenue of $42. With a total cost of $30 an hour, Bobbie makes an hourly profit of $12. Bobbie's costs, revenues, and profit were shown in the table in Fig. 13.3.

Bobbie has noticed that students and elderly customers come in less frequently than other clients. In fact, of the 3 haircuts she does each hour, 2 are for business people or homemakers and only 1 for an elderly customer or a student. Bobbie also suspects that the business people and homemakers will still turn up for haircuts at the rate of 2 an hour, even if she charges them a higher price. She knows that to get more students and seniors, she has to lower the price she charges them. Bobbie decides to try price discriminating between the two groups. But she has to figure out what price to charge each group to maximize her profit. Table 13.2 sets out the calculations that Bobbie performs. It shows Bobbie's estimates of the demand schedules for her two groups of customers. It also shows the total revenue and marginal revenue calculations for the two separate groups. Bobbie's marginal costs are the same for both groups—hair is hair, whether it belongs to a student or a homemaker. But marginal revenue differs between the two groups of customers. For example, when the price falls from $18 to $16, the marginal revenue from students and the elderly is zero, while for others, it is $14. When the price falls from $16 to $14, the marginal revenue from students and the elderly is $14, while that from others is *minus* $4.

Bobbie maximizes her profit by lowering the price and increasing output when marginal revenue exceeds marginal cost and by raising the price and

Table 13.2   Profiting from Price Discrimination

Price P (dollars per haircut)	Students and the elderly				Others			
	Quantity demanded Q (haircuts per hour)	Total revenue TR (dollars)	Marginal revenue MR (dollars per haircut)		Quantity demanded Q (haircuts per hour)	Total revenue TR (dollars)	Marginal revenue MR (dollars per haircut)	
20	0	0			0	0		
			0				18	
18	0	0			1	18		
			0				14	
16	0	0			2	32		
			14				.............−4	
14	1	14			2	28		
			10				.............−4	
12	2	24			2	24		
			6				.............−4	
10	3	30			2	20		

Profit Calculation
Profit = $TR - TC$
$= (\$12 \times 2) + (\$16 \times 2) - \$40$
$= \$16$

As a single-price monopoly, Bobbie sells 3 haircuts an hour for $14 each and makes a maximum profit of $12, as was shown in Fig. 13.3. By discriminating between two groups of customers—the first group consisting of students and the elderly and the second group consisting of all other customers—Bobbie is able to make a bigger profit. She raises the price of regular haircuts to $16 and lowers the price for students and the elderly to $12. Her sales rise to 4 haircuts an hour and her profit rises to $16.

decreasing output when marginal cost exceeds marginal revenue. In this example, Bobbie calculates her profit-maximizing prices and output in the following way. She knows that the marginal cost of the third haircut that she is producing, without price discrimination, is $6. (To see this, look back at the table for Fig. 13.3.) If her output increases, with price discrimination, the marginal cost of the fourth haircut is $10. She looks at her marginal revenues and compares them with this $10 marginal cost. She notices that by charging her business and homemaking customers $16, this group buys 2 haircuts an hour for a marginal revenue of $14. If she charges her students and elderly customers $12, that group buys 2 haircuts an hour and brings in a marginal revenue of $10. Thus when she sells a total of 4 haircuts (2 to students

and elderly and 2 to other customers) the marginal revenue from the students and elderly, $10, just equals the marginal cost of the fourth haircut.

But she can see that if she lowers the price to either group, marginal revenue will fall short of marginal cost. Marginal cost will climb to $15 for a fifth haircut and marginal revenue will fall to $6 if an extra haircut is sold to students and the elderly. Other customers have an inelastic demand curve and will not buy any more than 2 haircuts, so that marginal revenue from lowering the price to that group is negative. Thus Bobbie can make no more profit than that arising from charging students and the elderly $12 and other customers $16 and producing 4 haircuts an hour. The profit from such price discrimination is $16. (The calculation is set out at the foot of Table 13.2.)

Figure 13.6   Output and Profit with Perfect Price Discrimination

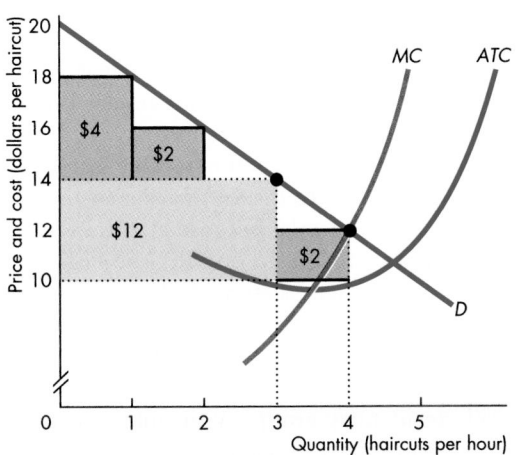

Bobbie's profit as a single-price monopoly, shown by the the light blue area, is $12. With perfect price discrimination, Bobbie charges $18 for the first haircut, $16 for the second, $14 for the third, and $12 for the fourth. Marginal revenue equals price in each case because, with perfect price discrimination, the marginal revenue curve is the same as the demand curve. Profit is maximized when the demand curve intersects the marginal cost curve. It does not pay Bobbie to sell a fifth haircut because its marginal revenue (price) is less that its marginal cost. Bobbie's additional profit as a perfect price discriminator, shown by the dark blue areas, is $8. Her maximum total profit with perfect price discrimination is $20.

Maximum profit with single price:			$12	Quantity: 3 haircuts
add	extra profit from 1st haircut		+4	
add	extra profit from 2nd haircut		+2	
add	extra revenue from 4th haircut	$12		
less	marginal cost of 4th haircut	−10		
add	extra profit from 4th haircut		+2	
equals	maximum profit with price discrimination		$20	Quantity: 4 haircuts

Perfect Price Discrimination

Suppose that Bobbie is able to devise a means of being a perfect price discriminator. How much profit can she make in this case? Bobbie's demand and cost curves are shown in Fig. 13.6. As a single-price monopoly, she produces 3 haircuts, sells them for $14 each, and makes a profit of $12—the light blue rectangle. (Refresh your memory if necessary by referring back to Fig. 13.3c.) If Bobbie can get each of her customers to pay the maximum price that each is willing to pay for a haircut, then she can sell the first haircut for $18. She makes an extra profit of $4 ($18 minus $14) from that first haircut sold. She can sell the second haircut for $16, $2 more than before. She will still sell the third for $14, since that is the maximum price that the third customer is willing to pay for a haircut. If Bobbie continues to produce 3 haircuts, her profit rises to $18, an increase of $6.

But Bobbie will not stop at 3 haircuts an hour. To see why, consider the marginal revenue from selling a fourth haircut and the marginal cost of producing it. The fourth haircut can be sold for $12. The marginal cost of the fourth haircut, from the table in Fig. 13.3, is only $10. So by producing a fourth haircut and selling it for $12, Bobbie makes a further $2 profit. The maximum profit with price discrimination occurs when Bobbie sells 4 haircuts, each for the maximum price that the consumers are willing to pay. That profit is illustrated in the figure as the sum of the light blue and the dark blue rectangles. The table in the figure summarizes the calulation.

When a firm practices perfect price discrimination, its output exceeds that of a single-price monopoly. It produces up to the point at which the marginal cost curve cuts the demand curve. The less perfect the price discrimination, the smaller is the additional output produced.

R E V I E W

Price discrimination increases a monopoly's profit by increasing its total revenue. By charging the highest price for each unit of the good that each person is willing to pay, a monopoly perfectly price discriminates and captures all of the consumer surplus. Much price discrimination takes the form of discriminating among different groups of customers, charging a higher price to some and a lower price to others. Such price discrimination increases total revenue and profit, but it is possible only if the two groups have different elasticities of demand. A price-discriminating monopoly produces a larger output than a single-price monopoly. ∎

Discrimination among Groups

You can now see why it pays to price discriminate. The sign in Bobbie's window—"Haircuts $16: Special for students and seniors, only $12"—is no generous gesture. It is profit-maximizing behavior. The model of price discrimination that you have just studied explains a wide variety of familiar pricing practices, even by firms that are not pure monopolies. For example, airlines offer lower fares for advance-purchase tickets than for last-minute travel. Last-minute travelers usually have a low elasticity of demand, while vacation travelers who can plan ahead have a higher elasticity of demand. Retail stores of all kinds hold seasonal "sales" when they reduce their prices, often by substantial amounts. These "sales" are a form of price discrimination. Each season, the newest fashions carry a high price tag but retailers do not expect to sell all their stock at such high prices. At the end of the season, they sell off what is left at a discount. Thus such stores discriminate between buyers who have an inelastic demand (for example, those who want to be instantly fashionable) and buyers who have an elastic demand (for example, those who pay less attention to up-to-the-minute fashion and more attention to price).

Limits to Price Discrimination

Since price discrimination is profitable, why don't more firms do it? Why don't we see senior citizen discounts on speeding tickets? What are the limits to price discrimination?

Profitable price discrimination can take place only under certain conditions. First, it is possible to price discriminate only if the good cannot be resold. If a good can be resold, then customers who get the good for the low price can resell it to someone willing to pay a higher price. Price discrimination breaks down. It is for this reason that price discrimination usually occurs in markets for services rather than in markets for storable goods. One major exception, price discrimination in the sale of fashion clothes, works because at the end of the season when the clothes go on sale, the fashion plates are looking for next season's fashions. People buying on sale have no one to whom they can resell the clothes at a higher price.

Second, a price discriminating monopoly must be able to identify groups with different elasticities of demand. The characteristics used for discrimination must also be within the law. These requirements usually limit price discrimination to cases based on either age or employment status, or on the timing of the purchase.

Despite these limitations, there are some ingenious criteria used for discriminating. For example, TWA discriminates between five different passenger groups on many of its international flights. The economy class alternatives between New York and London at one point in 1989 were:

- $1730—no restrictions
- $821—14-day advance purchase
- $771—14-day advance purchase mid-week only
- $658—30-day advance purchase
- $608—30-day advance purchase mid-week only

These different prices discriminate between different groups of customers with different elasticities of demand.

Comparing Monopoly and Competition

We have now studied a variety of ways in which firms and households interact in markets for goods and services. In Chapter 12, we saw how perfectly competitive firms behave and discovered the price and output at which they operate. In this chapter, we have studied the price and output of a single-price monopoly and a monopoly that price discriminates. How do

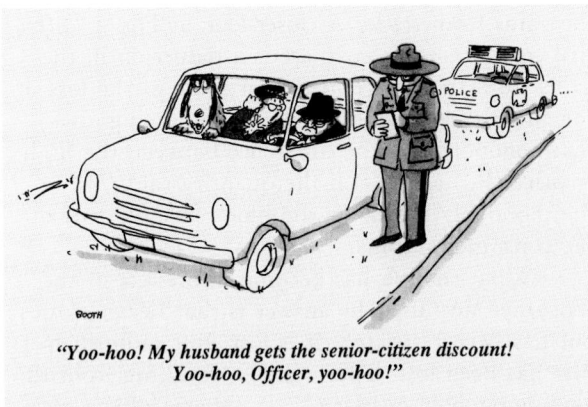

"Yoo-hoo! My husband gets the senior-citizen discount! Yoo-hoo, Officer, yoo-hoo!"

Drawing by Booth; ©1989 The New Yorker Magazine, Inc.

the quantities produced, prices, and profits of these different types of firms compare with each other?

To answer this question, let's imagine an industry made up of a large number of identical competitive firms. We will work out what the price charged and quantity traded will be in that industry. Then we will imagine that a single firm buys out all the individual firms and creates a monopoly. We will then work out the price charged and quantity produced by the monopoly, first when it charges a single price, and second when it price discriminates.

Price and Output

We will conduct the analysis by using Fig. 13.7. The industry demand curve is D and the industry supply curve is S. In perfect competition, the market equilibrium occurs where the supply curve and the demand curve intersect. The quantity produced by the industry is C and the price is P_C.

Each firm takes the price P_C and maximizes its profit by producing the output at which its own marginal cost equals the price. Since each firm is a small part of the total industry, there is no incentive for any firm to try to manipulate the price by varying its output.

Now suppose that this industry is taken over by a single firm. No changes in production techniques occur, so the new combined firm has identical costs to the original separate firms. The new single firm recognizes that by varying output it can influence price. It also recognizes that its marginal revenue curve is MR. To maximize profit, the firm chooses an output at which marginal revenue equals marginal cost. But what is the monopoly's marginal cost curve? To answer this question, you

need to recall the relationship between the marginal cost curve and the supply curve of a competitive firm. The supply curve of an individual competitive firm is its marginal cost curve. The supply curve of a competitive industry is derived from the supply curves of each individual firm. The industry supply curve tells us how the sum of the quantities supplied by each firm varies as the price varies. Thus the industry supply curve is also the industry's marginal cost curve. (The supply curve has also been labeled MC to remind you of this fact.) Therefore, when the industry is taken over by a single firm, that firm's marginal cost curve is the

Figure 13.7   Monopoly and Competition Compared

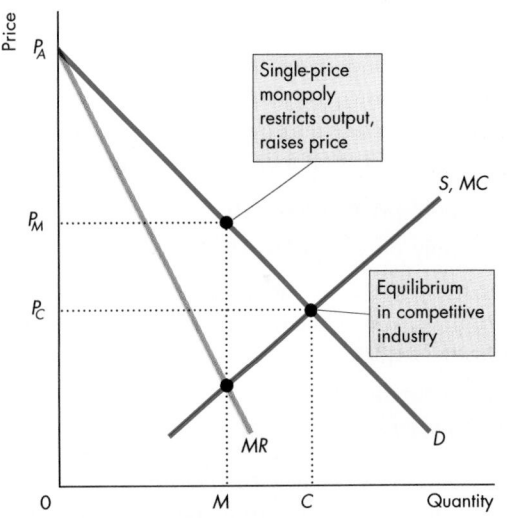

A competitive industry has a demand curve D and a supply curve S. Equilibrium occurs where the quantity demanded equals the quantity supplied at quantity C and price P_C. If all the firms in the industry are taken over by a single producer who sells the profit-maximizing output for a single price, marginal revenue is MR and the supply curve of the competitive industry, S, becomes the monopoly's marginal cost curve, MC. The monopoly produces the output at which marginal revenue equals marginal cost. A single-price monopoly produces M and sells that output for the price P_M. A perfectly price-discriminating monopoly produces C and charges a different price for each unit sold. The prices charged range from P_A to P_C. Monopoly restricts output and raises the price. But the more perfectly a monopoly can price discriminate, the closer its output gets to the competitive output.

same as what used to be the competitive industry's supply curve.

A competitive industry operates at the point of intersection of its supply and demand curves—in Fig. 13.7, at a price of P_C and quantity C. The single-price monopoly maximizes profit by restricting output to M, where marginal revenue equals marginal cost. Since the marginal revenue curve is below the demand curve, output M will always be smaller than output C. The monopoly charges the highest price for which output M can be sold, and that price is P_M.

If the monopoly can perfectly price discriminate, it will charge a different price on each unit sold and increase output to C. The highest price charged is P_A and the lowest price charged is P_C, the price in a competitive market. The price P_A is the highest that is charged because at yet higher prices nothing can be sold. The price P_C is the lowest charged because when a monopoly perfectly price discriminates, its marginal revenue curve is the same as the demand curve and at prices below P_C marginal cost exceeds marginal revenue.

The key price and output differences between competition and monopoly are the following:

• Monopoly price exceeds the competitive price.

• Monopoly output is less than competitive output.

• The more perfectly the monopoly can price discriminate, the closer its output gets to the competitive output.

Allocative Efficiency

Monopoly is less efficient than competition. It prevents some of the gains from trade from being achieved. To see why, look at Fig. 13.8. The maximum price that consumers are willing to pay for each unit is shown by the demand curve. The difference between the maximum price that they are willing to pay for each unit bought and the price they do pay is *consumer surplus*. Under perfect competition (part a), consumers have to pay only P_C for each unit bought and obtain a consumer surplus represented by the green triangle.

A single-price monopoly (part b) restricts output to M and sells that output for P_M. Consumer surplus is reduced to the smaller green triangle. Consumers lose partly by having to pay more for what is available and partly by getting less of the good. But is the consumers' loss equal to the monopoly's gain? Is there simply a redistribution of

the gains from trade? A closer look at Fig. 13.8(b) will convince you that there is a reduction in the gains from trade. It is true that some of the loss in consumer surplus does accrue to the monopoly— the monopoly gets the difference between the higher price (P_M) and P_C on the quantity sold *(M)*. So the monopoly has taken the blue rectangle part of the consumer surplus.

What though has become of the rest of the consumer surplus? The answer is that because output has been restricted, it is lost. But more than that has been lost. The total loss resulting from the lower monopoly output *(M)* is the area of the gray triangle in Fig. 13.8(b). The part of the gray triangle above P_C is the loss of consumer surplus and that part of the triangle below P_C is a loss to the producer—a loss of producer surplus. **Producer surplus** is the difference between a producer's revenue and the opportunity cost of production. It is calculated as the sum of the differences between price and the marginal cost of producing each unit of output. Under competitive conditions, the producer sells the output between M and C for a price of P_C. The marginal cost of producing each extra unit of output through that range is shown by the supply curve. Thus the vertical distance between the marginal cost curve and price represents a producer surplus. Part of the producer surplus is lost when a monopoly restricts output below its competitive level.

The gray triangle, which measures the total loss of both consumer and producer surplus, is called the deadweight loss. **Deadweight loss** measures allocative inefficiency as the reduction in consumer and producer surplus resulting from a restriction of output below its efficient level. A monopoly's reduced output and higher price results in the monopoly capturing some of the consumer surplus. It also results in the elimination of the producer surplus and consumer surplus on that output that a competitive industry would have produced but which the monopoly does not.

We have seen that a single-price monopoly creates a deadweight loss by restricting output. What is the deadweight loss if the monopoly practices perfect price discrimination? The answer is zero. A perfect price discriminator produces the same output as the competitive industry. The last item sold costs P_C, the same as its marginal cost. Thus from the point of view of allocative efficiency, a perfect price-discriminating monopoly achieves the same result as perfect competition.

Figure 13.8   The Allocative Inefficiency of Monopoly

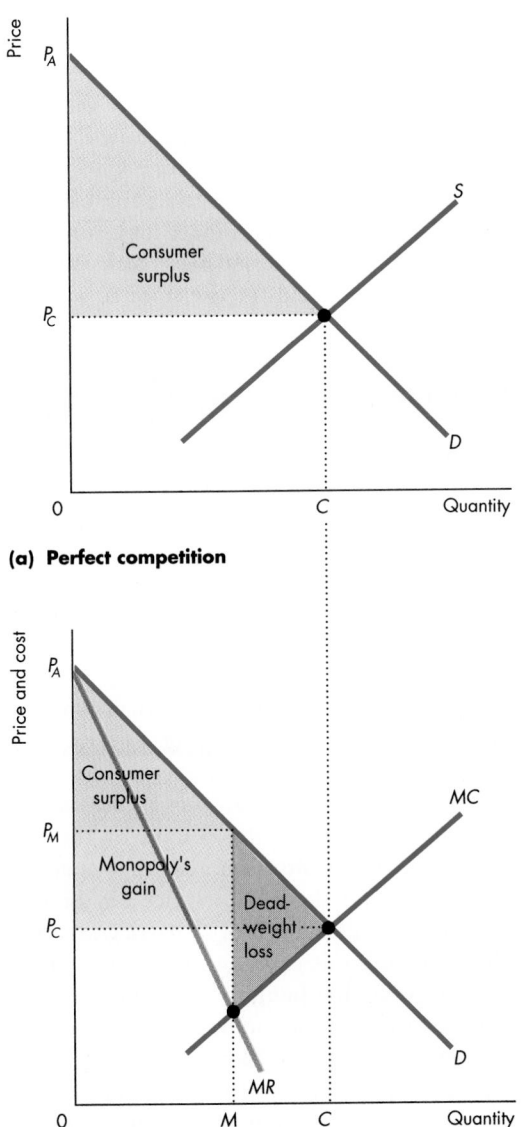

(a) Perfect competition

(b) Monopoly

In perfect competition (part a), demand curve D intersects supply curve S at quantity C and price P_C. Consumer surplus is represented by the green triangle. With free entry, firms' profits in long-run equilibrium are zero. Consumer surplus is maximized. Under a single-price monopoly (part b), output is restricted to M and the price increases to P_M. Consumer surplus is reduced to the smaller green triangle. The monopoly takes the blue rectangle for itself, but the gray triangle is a deadweight loss. Part of the deadweight loss (above P_C) is a loss of consumer surplus, and part (below P_C) is a loss of producer surplus.

Redistribution

Under perfect competition, the consumer surplus is the green triangle in Fig. 13.8(a). With free entry, the long-run equilibrium economic profit of each perfectly competitive firm is zero. We've just seen that the creation of monopoly reduces consumer surplus. Further, in the case of a single-price monopoly, a deadweight loss arises. But what happens to the distribution of surpluses between producers and consumers? The answer is that the monopoly always wins. In the case of a single-price monopoly (Fig. 13.8b), the monopoly gains the blue rectangle at the expense of the consumer. It has to offset against that gain its loss of producer surplus—its share of the deadweight loss. But there is always a net positive gain for the monopoly and a net loss for the consumer. We also know that because there is a deadweight loss, the consumer loses more than the monopoly gains.

In the case of a perfect price-discriminating monopoly, there is no deadweight loss but there is an even larger redistribution away from consumers to the monopoly. In this case, the monopoly captures the entire consumer surplus, the green triangle in Fig. 13.8(a).

R E V I E W

The creation of a monopoly results in a redistribution of economic gains away from consumers and to the monopoly producer. If the monopoly can perfectly price discriminate, it captures the entire consumer surplus. If the monopoly cannot perfectly price discriminate, a deadweight loss results from restricting output below its perfectly competitive level. The monopoly gains and the consumer loses, but the loss of the consumer exceeds the gain of the monopoly. ■

Rent Seeking

Operating a monopoly is more profitable than operating a firm in a perfectly competitive industry. Economic profit can be made in a competitive industry in the short run but not in the long run. Freedom of entry brings new firms into a profitable industry and results in economic profit being competed away. Barriers to entry prevent this process in a monopoly industry, so a monopoly can enjoy economic profit even in the long run. Because monopoly is more profitable than perfect competition, there is an incentive to attempt to create monopoly. The activity of creating monopoly is called **rent seeking.** The name rent seeking arises from the fact that another name for consumer surplus and producer surplus is rent. We've just seen that a monopoly makes its profit by diverting part of the consumer surplus to itself. Thus pursuing maximum monopoly profit is the same thing as diverting consumer surplus, or rent seeking.

Rent seeking is not a costless activity. To obtain a monopoly right, resources have to be used. Furthermore, everyone has an incentive to seek monopoly power, so there will be competition for monopoly rights. There are two ways in which people compete for monopoly rights—they buy an existing right or they create a new one. But existing monopoly rights had to be created at some time, so ultimately, competition for monopoly rights is a process that uses productive resources in order to establish a monopoly right. What is the value of the resources that a person will use to obtain a monopoly right? The answer is any amount up to the monopoly's profit. If the value of resources spent trying to acquire a monopoly exceeds the monopoly's profit, the net result is an economic loss. But as long as the value of the resources used to acquire a monopoly falls short of the monopoly's profit, there is a profit to be earned. If there is no barrier to entry, the value of the resources used up in rent seeking will, in equilibrium, equal the monopoly's profit.

Because of rent seeking, monopoly imposes costs that exceed the deadweight loss that we calculated earlier. To calculate that cost, we must add to the deadweight loss the value of resources used in rent seeking. That amount equals the entire monopoly profit since that is the value of the resources that it pays to use in rent seeking. Thus the cost of monopoly is the deadweight loss plus monopoly profit.

What exactly are the resources used in rent seeking? What do rent seekers do? One form of rent seeking is the searching out of existing monopoly rights that can be bought for a lower price than the monopoly's economic profit—that is, seeking to acquire existing monopoly rights. This form of rent seeking results in a market price for monopoly rights that is close to the economic prof-

it. There are many real world examples of this type of rent-seeking activity. One that is well known is the purchase of taxicab licenses. In most cities, taxicabs are regulated. The city restricts both the fares and the number of taxis that are permitted to operate. Operating a taxi is profitable—resulting in economic profit or rent being earned by the operator. A person who wants to operate a taxi has to buy the right to do so from someone who already has that right. Competition for that right leads to a price sufficiently high to eliminate long-run economic profit. For example, in New York City, the price that has to be paid for the right to operate a taxi is close to $100,000.[1]

Another example occurred in the airline industry. In 1986, United Airlines bought the rights to all the international air routes across the Pacific Ocean that had previously been owned and operated by Pan American Airlines. United paid Pan Am $500 million for the exclusive rights to these routes. Pan Am had originated these Pacific routes, and other U.S. airlines were prohibited from competing on them by an international air transportation agreement entered into by the United States and other governments. To acquire these routes, United had to pay Pan Am a price that provided as much profit as Pan Am hanging onto the rights and operating the routes themselves would have made. Competition among airlines to buy these rights resulted in them being bought by the most efficient potential operator, because that operator was willing to offer the highest price for them.

Although a great deal of rent-seeking activity involves searching out existing monopoly rights that can be profitably bought, much of it is devoted to the creation of monopoly. This type of rent-seeking activity takes the form of lobbying and seeking to influence the political process. Such influence is sometimes sought by making campaign contributions in exchange for legislative support or in the form of indirectly seeking to influence political outcomes through publicity in the media or more direct contacts with politicians and bureaucrats. (This type of rent seeking is discussed and explained more fully in Chapters 20 and 21.)

[1] Taxis do not earn $100,000 in a single year; if they did, there would be fewer economics professors and far more cabbies. Since profits on a taxi will be earned over several future years, the $100,000 price tag on the right to operate a taxi is the *present value* of the expected future profits—see Chapter 9.

REVIEW

When rent seeking is taken into account, there are no guaranteed long-run profits, even from monopoly. Competition for monopoly rights results in the use of resources to acquire those rights equal in value to the potential monopoly profit. As a consequence, monopoly imposes costs equal to the deadweight loss plus the monopoly's economic profit. ∎

Gains from Monopoly

In our comparison of monopoly and competition, monopoly comes out in a pretty bad light. If monopoly is so bad, why do we put up with it? Why don't we have laws that crack down on monopoly so hard that it never rears its head? As we'll see in Chapter 21, we do indeed have laws that limit monopoly power. We also have laws that regulate those monopolies that exist. But monopoly is not all bad. Let's look at its potential advantages and some of the reasons for its existence.

The main reasons for the existence of monopoly are:

- Economies of scale and economies of scope
- Incentive to innovate

Economies of Scale and Scope   You met economies of scale in Chapters 9 and 10. There, we defined *economies of scale* as decreases in average total cost resulting from increasing a firm's scale. The scale of a firm increases when it increases all its inputs—capital, labor, and materials—in the same proportions. For example, if all inputs double, total cost also doubles. If output more than doubles, average total cost declines or, equivalently, the firm has economies of scale.

Economies of scope are decreases in average total cost made possible by increasing the number of different goods produced. For example, McDonald's can produce both hamburgers and French fries at an average total cost that is lower than what it would cost two separate firms to produce the same goods. Economies of scope are important when highly skilled (and expensive) technical inputs can be shared by different goods.

For example, computer programmers and designers and marketing experts can apply their skills to producing a variety of goods, thereby spreading their costs and lowering the cost of production of each of the goods.

Large-scale firms that have control over supply and can influence price—and that therefore behave like the monopoly firm that we've been studying in this chapter—can reap these economies of scale and scope. Small, competitive firms cannot. As a consequence, there are situations in which the comparison of monopoly and competition that we made earlier in this chapter is not a valid one. Recall that we imagined the takeover of a large number of competitive firms by a single monopoly firm. But we also assumed that the monopoly would use exactly the same technology as the small firms and have the same costs. But if one large firm can reap economies of scale and scope, its marginal cost curve will lie below the supply curve of a competitive industry made up of thousands of small firms. It is possible for such economies of scale and scope to be so large as to result in a higher output and lower price under monopoly than a competitive industry would achieve.

Figure 13.9 illustrates such a situation. Here, the demand curve and the marginal revenue curve are the same regardless of whether the industry is a competitive one or a monopoly. With a competitive industry, the supply curve is S, the quantity produced is C, and the price is P_C. With a monopoly that can exploit economies of scale and scope, the marginal cost curve is MC_M. The monopoly maximizes profit by producing the output (M) at which marginal revenue equals marginal cost. The price that maximizes profit is P_M. By exploiting a superior technology not available to each of the large number of small firms, the monopoly is able to achieve a higher output and lower price than the competitive industry.

There are many examples of industries in which economies of scale are so important that they lead to an outcome similar to that shown in Fig. 13.9. Public utilities such as gas, electric power, water, local telephone service, and garbage collection are all such cases. There are also many examples where a combination of economies of scale and economies of scope are important. Examples are the brewing of beer, the manufacture of refrigerators and other household appliances, pharmaceuticals, and the refining of petroleum.

Figure 13.9   When Economies of Scale and Scope
Make Monopoly More Efficient

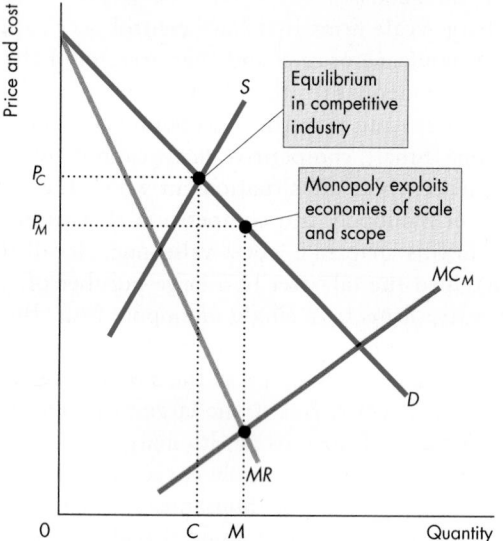

In some industries, economies of scale and economies of scope result in the monopoly's marginal cost curve (MC$_M$) lying below the competitive industry supply curve (S). In such a case, it is possible that the single-price monopoly output (M) exceeds the competitive output (C) and that the monopoly price (P$_M$) is below the competitive price (P$_C$).

Innovation   Innovation is the first-time application of new knowledge in the production process. Innovation may take the form of developing a new product or a lower-cost way of making an existing product. Controversy has raged among economists over whether large firms with monopoly power or small competitive firms lacking such monopoly power are the most innovative. It is clear that some monopoly power (temporary monopoly power) arises from innovation. A firm that develops a new product or process and patents it obtains exclusive right to that product or process for the term of the patent. But does the granting of a monopoly, even a temporary one, to an innovator increase the pace of innovation? One line of reasoning suggests that it does. With no protection, an innovator is not able to enjoy the profits from innovation for very long. Thus the incentive to innovate is weakened. A contrary argument is that monopolies can afford

to be lazy while competitive firms cannot. Competitive firms must strive to innovate and cut costs even though they know that they cannot hang on to the benefits of their innovation for long. But that knowledge spurs them on to greater and faster innovation.

A matter such as this one cannot be resolved by listing arguments and counterarguments. It requires a careful empirical investigation. Many such investigations have been conducted. But the evidence that they bring to bear on this question is mixed. They show that large firms do much more research and development than do small firms. They also show that large firms are significantly more prominent at the development end of the research and development process. But measuring research and development is measuring the volume of inputs into the process of innovation. What matters is not input but output. Two measures of the output of research and development are the number of patents and the rate of productivity growth. On these measures, there is no clear evidence that big is best. But there is a clear pattern in the process of diffusion of technological knowledge. After innovation, a new process or product spreads gradually through the industry. Whether an innovator is a small firm or a large firm, large firms jump on the bandwagon more quickly than do the remaining small firms. Thus large firms are important in speeding the process of diffusion of technological advances.

In determining public policy toward monopoly (matters discussed in Chapter 21), laws and regulations are designed that balance these positive aspects of monopoly against the deadweight loss and redistribution that they also generate.

■   We've now studied two models of market structure—perfect competition and monopoly. We've discovered the conditions under which perfect competition achieves allocative efficiency and we've compared the efficiency of competition with that of monopoly. We've also used these two models to make predictions about the effects on prices and quantities of changing cost and demand conditions.

Although there are examples of markets in the U.S. economy that are highly competitive or highly monopolistic, the markets for most goods and services lie somewhere between these two extremes. In the next chapter, we're going to study this middle ground between monopoly and competition. We're going to discover that many of the lessons that we learned from these two extreme models are still relevant and useful in understanding behavior in real world markets.

S U M M A R Y

How Monopoly Arises

Monopoly arises because of barriers to entry that prevent competition. Barriers to the entry of new firms may be legal or natural. Legal barriers take the form of public franchises, government licenses, or patents. Natural barriers exist when a single firm possesses total control of a mineral or natural resource or when economies of scale are so large that a single firm can supply an entire market at a lower average total cost than can several firms. (pp. 316–317)

Single-Price Monopoly

A monopoly is an industry in which there is a single supplier of a good, service, or resource. A single-price monopoly is a firm that charges the same price for each unit of output. The monopoly's demand curve is the market demand curve for the good. For a single-price monopoly, marginal revenue is less than price. Total revenue rises at first, but above some output level it begins to decline. When total revenue is rising, marginal revenue is positive. When total revenue is falling, marginal revenue is negative. When marginal revenue is positive (total revenue rising), the elasticity of demand is greater than 1. The elasticity of demand equals 1 when total revenue is at a maximum.

A monopoly's technology and costs behave in a way similar to those of any other type of firm. The monopoly maximizes profit by producing the output that makes marginal revenue equal to marginal cost, and by charging the maximum price that consumers are willing to pay for that output. The price charged always exceeds marginal cost. There is no supply curve in a monopoly. (pp. 317–323)

Price Discrimination

Price discrimination is the practice of charging some consumers a higher price than others for an identical item or charging an individual customer a higher price on a small purchase than on a large one. Price discrimination is an attempt by the monopoly to convert consumer surplus into profit. Perfect price discrimination extracts all the consumer surplus. Such a monopoly charges a different price for each unit sold and obtains the maximum price that each consumer is willing to pay for each unit bought. With perfect price discrimination, the monopoly's marginal revenue curve is the same as its demand curve and the monopoly produces the same output as would a perfectly competitive industry.

A monopoly can discriminate between different groups of customers on the basis of age, employment status, or other distinguishable characteristics. Such price discrimination increases the monopoly's profit if each group has a different elasticity of demand for the product. To maximize profit with price discrimination, the monopoly produces an output such that marginal cost equals marginal revenue, but then charges each group the maximum price that it is willing to pay.

Price discrimination can be practiced only when it is impossible for a buyer to resell the good and when consumers with different elasticities can be identified. (pp. 323–330)

Comparing Monopoly and Competition

If a monopoly takes over all the firms in a perfectly competitive industry and if the technology and input prices in the industry remain unchanged, the monopoly charges a higher price and produces a lower quantity than would prevail in a perfectly competitive industry. If the monopoly can perfectly price discriminate, it produces the competitive quantity and sells the last unit for the competitive price.

Monopoly is less efficient than competition because it prevents some of the gains from trade from being achieved. A monopoly captures some part of the consumer surplus, but to do so it has to restrict output so that when it maximizes profit it creates a deadweight loss. The more a monopoly is able to price discriminate, the smaller the deadweight loss but the larger the monopoly profit and the smaller the consumer surplus.

Monopoly redistributes away from consumers toward the producer. The more perfectly a monopoly can price discriminate, the smaller the deadweight loss but the larger the reallocation of surpluses from consumers to the producer.

Monopoly imposes costs that equal its deadweight loss plus the cost of the resources devoted to rent seeking—searching out profitable monopoly opportunities. It pays to use resources equal in value to the entire monopoly profit that might be attained. As a result, the cost of monopoly equals its deadweight loss plus the entire monopoly profit.

There are some industries in which a monopoly is more efficient than a large number of perfectly competitive firms. Such industries are those in which economies of scale and scope are so large that the monopoly's output is higher and price lower than those that would arise if the industry had a large number of firms. There are also situations in which monopoly may be more innovative than competition, resulting in a faster pace of technological change. (pp. 330–336)

KEY CONCEPTS

REVIEW QUESTIONS

1 What is a monopoly? What are some examples of monopoly in your state?

2 How does monopoly arise?

3 Distinguish between a legal monopoly and a natural monopoly. Give examples of each type.

4 Explain why marginal revenue is always less than average revenue for a single-price monopoly.

5 Why does a monopoly's profit increase as output rises initially but eventually decrease when output gets too big?

6 Explain how a monopoly chooses its output and price.

7 Does a monopoly operate on the inelastic part of its demand curve? Explain why it does or does not.

8 Explain why a monopoly produces a smaller output than an equivalent competitive industry.

9 Is monopoly as efficient as competition?

10 What is deadweight loss?

11 Can any monopoly price discriminate? If yes, why? If no, why not?

12 Show graphically the deadweight loss under perfect price discrimination.

13 As far as allocative efficiency is concerned, is single-price monopoly better or worse than perfect price discrimination? Why?

14 Explain why people indulge in rent-seeking activities.

15 When taking account of the cost of rent seeking, what is the social cost of monopoly?

16 What are economies of scale and economies of scope? What effects, if any, do they have on allocative efficiency of monopoly?

17 Monopoly redistributes consumer surplus. Explain why the consumer loses more under perfect price discrimination than under single-price monopoly.

PROBLEMS

1 Minnie's Mineral Springs, a single-price monopoly, faces the following demand schedule for bottled mineral water:

Price (dollars per bottle)	Quantity demanded (bottles)
5	0
4	1
3	2
2	3
1	4
0	5

a) Calculate Minnie's total revenue schedule.

b) Calculate its marginal revenue schedule.

c) At what price is the elasticity of demand equal to one?

2 Minnie's has the following total cost:

Quantity produced (bottles)	Total cost (dollars)
0	1
1	2
2	4
3	7
4	11
5	16

Calculate the profit-maximizing levels of

a) Output

b) Price

c) Marginal cost

d) Marginal revenue

e) Profit

3 Suppose that Minnie's can perfectly price discriminate. What is its profit-maximizing

a) Output

b) Total revenue

c) Profit

4 How much would someone be willing to pay Minnie's for a license to operate its mineral spring?

5 Two demand schedules for round-trip flights between New York and Los Angeles are set out below. The schedule for weekday travelers is for those making round-trips on weekdays and returning within the same week. The schedule for weekend travelers is for those who stay through the weekend. (The former tend to be business travelers and the latter vacation and pleasure travelers.)

Weekday travelers		Weekend travelers	
Price (dollars per round trip)	Quantity demanded (thousands of round trips)	Price (dollars per round trip)	Quantity demanded (thousands of round trips)
1500	0	500	0
1000	10	250	10
500	20	125	10
250	25	0	20
125	27.5		
0	30		

The marginal cost of a round trip is $125. If a single-price monopoly airline controls the New York–Los Angeles route, use a graph to find out the following:

a) What price is charged?

b) How many passengers travel?

c) What is the consumer surplus?

6 If the airline in problem 5 discriminates between round-trips within a week and round-trips through the weekend:

a) What is the price for the round-trip within the week?

b) What is the price of the airline ticket with a weekend stay?

c) What is the consumer surplus?

7 Barbara runs a truck stop on the prairies, miles from anywhere. She has a monopoly and faces the following demand for meals:

Price (dollars per meal)	Quantity demanded (meals per week)
1.00	160
1.50	140
2.00	120
2.50	100
3.00	80
3.50	60
4.00	40
4.50	35
5.00	30
5.50	25

Barbara's marginal cost and average total cost are a constant $1 per meal.

a) If Barbara charges all customers the same price for a meal, what price is it?

b) What is the consumer surplus of all the customers who buy a meal from Barbara?

c) What is the producer surplus?

d) What is the deadweight loss?

8 Barbara discovers that some of the people stopping for meals are truck drivers and some are tourists. She estimates that the demand schedules for the two groups are:

Price (dollars per meal)	Quantity demanded (meals per week)	
	Truck drivers	Tourists
1.00	70	90
1.50	65	75
2.00	60	60
2.50	55	45
3.00	50	30
3.50	45	15
4.00	40	0
4.50	35	0
5.00	30	0
5.50	25	0

If Barbara price discriminates between the two,

a) What price does she charge truck drivers?

b) What price does she charge tourists?

c) What is her output per week, and is it higher, lower, or the same as when she did not price discriminate?

d) What is her weekly profit, and is it higher, lower, or the same as when she did not price discriminate?

Chapter 14

Monopolistic Competition and Oligopoly

After studying this chapter, you will be able to:

- Describe and distinguish among market structures that lie between perfect competition and monopoly

- Define monopolistic competition

- Explain how price and output are determined in a monopolistically competitive industry

- Define oligopoly and duopoly

- Explain what game theory is

- Explain the prisoner's dilemma game

- Explain duopoly and oligopoly as games that firms play

- Predict the price and output behavior of duopolists

- Make predictions about price wars and competition among small numbers of firms

Every week, we receive a newspaper stuffed with supermarket fliers describing this week's "specials," providing coupons and other enticements, all designed to grab our attention and persuade us that A & P, Kroger, Safeway, Alpha Beta, Winn Dixie, Stop & Shop, Shop 'n' Save, and H.E.B.'s have the best deals in town. Supermarkets are not the only businesses that cut prices in order to attract customers. Every few months, clothing and furniture stores hold sales designed partly to clear space for the new season's inventory, but also partly to attract new customers. ▪ Firms do not only compete with each other on price. They also compete on product quality. Millions of dollars are spent on TV and magazine advertising, all designed to

Fliers and War Games

enable us to pick the best brand and, having picked it, to keep buying it again and again, even if its price is slightly higher than that of some competing brands. ▪ How do firms that are locked in fierce competition with other firms set their prices, pick their product, and choose the quantities to produce? How are the profits of such firms affected by the actions of other firms? ▪ Suddenly in 1973, the prices that people paid for gasoline, heating oil, and other petroleum products depended on the whims of the Organization of Petroleum Exporting Countries (OPEC). In that year, OPEC acted like a monopoly, restricting the production of oil and raising prices. For almost a decade, the price of oil kept rising until, in 1982, it stood at 11 times the price of a decade before. Horrified consumers speculated about the day when it would cost $50, $60, $70 a barrel. ▪ Equally suddenly, and to the surprise of millions of people, OPEC fell apart. Oil prices faltered for a bit, and then, in a matter of months, they fell by more than half. Headlines in early 1986 screamed, "The Price War Is Here," and "Frenzied Gas Wars Push Down Pump Prices." ▪ Why did OPEC's stranglehold on oil prices, which had brought its members enormous riches, suddenly disappear? Not only did OPEC stop raising prices, it saw them fall dramatically. Why did prices suddenly break? Will OPEC ever control oil prices again? ■ Price-fixing arrangements such as those practiced by OPEC are illegal in the United States. This means that any conspiracies by firms to fix prices have to be undertaken in secrecy. As a result we get to know about such agreements only after they have been cracked by the Justice Department. One famous price-fixing arrangement, involving almost 30 firms, has been called "the incredible electrical conspiracy."[1] For most of the 1950s, 30 producers of electrical equipment, including such giants as General Electric and Westinghouse, fixed prices "on items ranging from $2 insulators to huge turbine generators costing several million dollars."[2] Though the electrical equipment pricing conspiracy operated throughout the 1950s, the individual firms conspiring often changed. In particular, General Electric sometimes participated in the price-fixing agreement and sometimes dropped out, undercutting the agreed price and dragging down the industry price and profit. ■ Why do firms start price wars and drag down the industry's profit? Do competitors always follow suit? When do price wars end?

■ The theories of monopoly and perfect competition, which we studied in Chapters 12 and 13, do not predict the kind of behavior that we've just described. There are no fliers and coupons or price wars in perfect competition because each firm is a price taker. There are none in monopoly either because each monopoly firm has the entire market to itself and so never needs to fear the actions of a competitor. To understand fliers, coupons, discounts, sales, price-fixing agreements, and price wars, we need richer models of the behavior of firms in markets than those of perfect competition and monopoly. This chapter presents such models. The industries that we're going to study lie between the two extremes of perfect competition and monopoly. We'll study two cases: One in which there are many firms but each

produces a slightly different product from the others so that, although the firms are in competition with each other, each has a small element of monopoly power arising from the uniqueness of its own product. This model will enable us to understand markets such as those for food and clothing, soft drinks and plastics, printing and book publishing. The second model applies to industries that contain only a few firms. These few firms are locked in an unusual game. Each one has to keep a wary eye on how its competitors are acting. And in choosing its own actions, each firm must work out what its competitors' response will be and what its own best response is to its competitors' actions. Our model of the competition that arises in this type of situation will enable us to understand industries like oil and electrical equipment supply. ■ But first, before turning to these two additional models, we are going to describe the characteristics of different types of markets so that we can identify those to which each model applies.

Varieties of Market Structure

We have studied two types of market structure—perfect competition and monopoly. In perfect competition, a large number of firms produce identical goods and there are no barriers to the entry of new firms into the industry. In this situation, each firm is a price taker and, in the long run, there is no economic profit. The opposite extreme, monopoly, is an industry in which there is one firm. That firm is protected by barriers preventing the entry of new firms. The firm sets its price to maximize profit and the firm enjoys economic profit even in the long run.

Although there are some industries in the real world that have the characteristics of a perfectly competitive or a monopoly industry, most do not. Most industries lie somewhere between these two extreme cases. There are many situations in which firms are in fierce competition with a large number of other firms but they do have some power to set prices. There are other cases in which the industry consists of very few firms and each firm has considerable power in price determination. In order to tell how close to the competitive or monopolisitic extreme an industry comes, economists have developed a measure of industrial concentration. This measure is designed to indicate

[1]Richard A. Smith, "The Incredible Electrical Conspiracy," Part I and Part II, Fortune (April 1961): 132 and (May 1961): 161.

[2]James V. Koch, Industrial Organization and Prices, 2nd ed. (Englewood Cliffs, N.J.: Prentice-Hall, 1980): 423.

Table 14.1   Concentration Ratio Calculations (hypothetical)

Tiremakers		Printers	
Firm	Sales (millions of dollars)	Firm	Sales (millions of dollars)
Top, Inc.	200	Fran's	2.5
ABC, Inc.	250	Ned's	2.0
Big, Inc.	150	Tom's	1.8
XYZ, Inc.	100	Jill's	1.7
Top 4 sales	700	Top 4 sales	8.0
Other 10 firms	175	Other 1000 firms	1592.0
Industry sales	875	Industry sales	1600.0

Four-firm concentration ratios:

Tiremakers:	700/875	=	80%
Printers:	8/1600	=	0.5%

the degree of control that a small number of firms have over a market. The most commonly used measure of concentration is called the four-firm concentration ratio. The **four-firm concentration ratio** is the percentage of the value of sales accounted for by the largest four firms in an industry. (Concentration ratios are also defined and measured for the largest eight, 20, and 50 firms in an industry.) Table 14.1 sets out two hypothetical concentration ratio calculations, one for tires and one for printing. In this example, there are 14 firms in the tire industry. The biggest four have 80 percent of the sales of the industry, so the four-firm concentration ratio for that industry is 80 percent. In the printing industry, with 1004 firms, the top four firms account for only 0.5 percent of total industry sales. In that case, the four-firm concentration ratio is 0.5 percent.

Using data on each firm's sales, the Department of Commerce calculates concentration ratios for a large number of industry groups. Some industries, such as commercial printing, plastic products, and soft drinks have low concentration ratios. These industries are highly competitive. At the other extreme

are industries with a high concentration ratio—such as electric light bulbs, motor vehicles, and household refrigerators. These are examples of industries in which there is competition but among a small number of firms, each of which has considerable control over its price. Medium concentration ratios exist in the newspaper, pharmaceutical preparation, and meat packing industries.

The idea behind calculating concentration ratios is to provide information about the degree of competitiveness of a market: A low concentration ratio indicates a high degree of competition and a high concentration ratio indicates an absence of competition. In the extreme case of monopoly, the concentration ratio is 100—the largest (and only) firm makes the entire industry sales. But there are problems with concentration ratios as measures of competitiveness and, although the ratios themselves are useful, they have to be supplemented by other information. There are three key problems:

1. Geographical Scope of Market   Concentration ratio data are based on a national view of the market.

Many goods are indeed sold on a national market but some are sold on a regional market and some on a global one. The newspaper industry is a good example of one in which the local market is more important than the national market. Thus although the concentration ratio for newspapers is not high, there is nevertheless a high degree of concentration in the newspaper industry in most cities. The automobile industry is an example of one for which there is a global market. Thus although the biggest four U.S. car producers account for 92 percent of all cars sold by U.S. producers, they account for a much smaller percentage of the total U.S. car market (including imports) and an even smaller percentage of the global market for cars.

2. Barriers to Entry and Turnover Measures of concentration do not tell us how severe are the barriers to entry in an industry. Some industries, for example, are highly concentrated but have virtually free entry and experience an enormous amount of turnover of firms. A good example is the market in local restaurants. Many small towns have few restaurants. But there are no restrictions on entering the restaurant industry and indeed firms do enter and exit with great regularity.

3. Market and Industry The classifications used to calculate concentration ratios allocate every firm in the U.S. economy to a particular industry. Markets for particular goods do not always correspond exactly to particular industries. For example, Westinghouse is classified by the Department of Commerce as being in the electrical goods and equipment industry. That is indeed the main product line of Westinghouse. But Westinghouse also produces, among other things, gas-fired incinerators and plywood. Thus this one firm operates in three quite separate markets. Furthermore, the market or markets in which a firm operates depend on the profit opportunities that exist. There are many spectacular examples of firms that have built their initial organization on one product but then diversified into a wide variety of others.

Nevertheless, concentration ratios, combined with information about the geographical scope of the market, barriers to entry, and the extent to which large, multiproduct firms straddle a variety of markets, do provide the basis for classifying industries. The less concentrated an industry and the lower its barriers to entry, the more closely it approximates the perfect competition case. The more concentrated an industry and the higher the barriers to entry, the more it approximates the monopoly case.

But there is a great deal of space between perfect competition and monopoly. That space is occupied by two other market types that we'll now identify. The first of these is monopolistic competition. **Monopolistic competition** is a market type in which a large number of firms compete with each other by making similar but slightly different products. Making a product slightly different from the product of a competing firm is called **product differentiation.** Because of product differentiation, a monopolistically competitive firm has an element of monopoly power. The firm is the sole producer of the particular version of the good in question.

For example, in the market for microwave popcorn, only Nabisco makes Planters Premium Select, only General Mills makes Pop Secret, and only American Popcorn makes Jolly Time. Each of these firms has a monopoly on a particular brand of microwave popcorn. Differentiated products are not necessarily different in an objective sense. For example, the different brands of microwave popcorn may actually be only different ways of packaging an identical commodity. What matters is that consumers perceive products to be differentiated. In fact, there are claims that the different brands of microwave popcorn are different in ways other than their packaging—for example, in popability.

Oligopoly is a market type in which a small number of producers compete with each other. There are hundreds of examples of oligopolistic industries. Oil and gasoline production, the manufacture of electrical equipment, and international air transportation are but a few. In some oligopolistic industries, each firm produces an almost identical product while in others products are differentiated. For example, oil and gasoline are essentially the same whether they are made by Texaco or Exxon. But Chrysler's Plymouth Reliant is a differentiated commodity from Chevrolet's Celebrity and Ford's Mercury Topaz.

Table 14.2 summarizes the characteristics of the two market types that we're going to study in this chapter, monopolistic competition and oligopoly, along with those of perfect competition and monopoly.

Table 14.2   Market Structure

Characteristic	Perfect competition	Monopolistic competition	Oligopoly	Monopoly
Number of firms in industry	Many	Many	Few	One
Product	Identical	Differentiated	Either identical or differentiated	No close substitutes
Barriers to entry	None	Some	Scale and scope economy barriers	Scale and scope economics or legal barriers
Firm's control over price	None	Some	Considerable	Considerable or regulated
Concentration ratio (0 to 100)	0	Low	High	100
Examples	Wheat, corn	Food, clothing	Automobiles, cereals	Local phone service, electric and gas utilities

Monopolistic Competition

Three conditions define a monopolistically competitive industry:

- Each firm faces a downward-sloping demand curve.
- There is free entry.
- There are a large number of firms in the industry.

Because each firm faces a downward-sloping demand curve, it has to choose its price as well as its output. Also a firm's marginal revenue curve is different from its demand curve. These features of monopolistic competition are also present in monopoly. The important difference between monopoly and monopolistic competition lies in free entry.

In monopoly, there is no entry. In monopolistic competition, there is free entry and, as a consequence, though monopolistic competition enables economic profits to occur in the short run, they cannot persist forever. When profits are available, new firms will enter the industry. Such entry will result in lower prices and lower profits. When losses are being incurred, firms will leave the industry. Such exit will increase prices and increase profits. In long-run equi-

librium, firms will neither enter nor leave the industry, and firms will be making a zero economic profit.

Because the industry consists of a large number of firms, no one firm can effectively influence what other firms will do. That is, if one firm changes its price, that firm is such a small part of the total industry that it will have no effect on the actions of the other firms in the industry.

Price and Output in Monopolistic Competition

To see how price and output are determined by a firm in a monopolistically competitive industry, let's look at Fig. 14.1. Part (a) deals with the short run and part (b) the long run. To keep things simple, we will suppose that the industry consists of a large number of firms with a differentiated product and that all firms in the industry have identical demand and cost curves. Let's concentrate initially on the short run. The demand curve D is the demand curve for the firm's own variety of the product. For example, it is the demand for Bayer aspirin rather than for aspirin in general; or for McDonald's hamburgers rather than for hamburgers in general. The curve MR is the marginal revenue curve associated with the

Figure 14.1 Monopolistic Competition

(a) Short run

(b) Long run

Under monopolistic competition, a firm faces a downward-sloping demand curve and so has to choose its price and the quantity to produce. Profit is maximized where marginal revenue equals marginal cost. Part (a) of the figure shows a short-run profit-maximizing situation. The quantity produced is Q_S, the price is P_S, average total cost is C_S, and profit is represented by the blue rectangle.

Profit encourages new entrants, and so the firm's demand curve begins to shift to the left, as shown in part (b). As the demand curve shifts to the left, so too does the firm's marginal revenue curve. When the demand curve has shifted all the way from D to D', the marginal revenue curve is MR', and the firm is in a long-run equilibrium. The output that maximizes profit is Q_L and the price is P_L. Profit, in long-run equilibrium, is zero. There is no further entry into the industry.

demand curve. The firm's average total cost *(ATC)* and marginal cost *(MC)* are also shown in the figure. A firm maximizes profit in the short run by producing output Q_S, where marginal revenue equals marginal cost, and charging the price P_S. The firm's average total cost is C_S and the firm makes a short-run profit, as measured by the blue rectangle.

So far, the monopolistically competitive firm looks just like a monopoly. It produces the quantity at which marginal revenue equals marginal cost and then charges the highest possible price for that quantity. The key difference between monopoly and monopolistic competition lies in what happens next. There is no restriction on entry so, with economic profit being earned, new firms will enter the industry. As new firms enter the industry, they take some of the market away from the existing firms. As they do

so, the firm's demand curve starts to shift to the left. The marginal revenue curve also starts to shift to the left. At each point in time, the firm will seek to maximize its short-run profit. That is, output will be chosen so that marginal revenue equals marginal cost and the highest possible price will be charged for the good. But as the demand curve shifts to the left, the profit-maximizing quantity and price fall. In the long run, shown in part (b), the firm produces Q_L and sells it at a price of P_L. In this situation, the firm is making a zero economic profit. Average total cost exactly equals price.

Excess Capacity Notice that in the long run the firm in monopolistic competition always has excess capacity in that it produces a lower output than that which minimizes average total cost. This result arises from the fact that the firm faces a downward-sloping demand curve. Only if the demand curve facing the firm is perfectly elastic will the long-run equilibrium be at the point of minimum average total cost. The demand curve slopes down because of product differentiation. If each firm produces an identical product, each firm's output will be a perfect substitute for the outputs of all other firms and so the demand curve will be perfectly elastic. Thus it is product differentiation that produces excess capacity.

Efficiency of Monopolistic Competition

When we studied a perfectly competitive industry, we discovered that in some circumstances, such an industry achieves allocative efficiency. A key feature of allocative efficiency is that price equals marginal cost. Recall that price measures the value placed on the last unit bought by the consumer and marginal cost measures the opportunity cost of producing the last unit. We also discovered that monopoly is allocatively inefficient because it restricts output below the level at which price equals marginal cost. As we have just discovered, monopolistic competition shares this feature with monopoly. Even though there is zero profit in long-run equilibrium, the monopolistically competitive industry produces an output at which price equals average total cost and exceeds marginal cost.

Does this feature of monopolistic competition mean that this market structure, like monopoly, is allocatively inefficient? It does not. It is true that if the firms in a monopolistically competitive industry each produce an identical product, so that they are perfect substitutes, then each firm will face a perfectly elastic demand curve and will produce, in the long run, at the point of minimum average total cost and charge a price equal to marginal cost. But achieving that outcome will itself have a cost. The cost is the absence of product differentiation. Variety is valued by consumers but variety is only achievable if firms make differentiated products. The loss in allocative efficiency occurring in monopolistic competition has to be offset against the gain of greater product variety.

Product Innovation

Another source of gain from monopolistically competitive industries is product innovation. Monopolisti-

cally competitive firms are constantly seeking out new products that will provide them with a competitive edge, even if only temporarily. A firm that manages to introduce a new and differentiated variety will temporarily face a steeper demand curve than before and will be able to temporarily increase its price. Entry of new firms will, eventually, compete away the profit arising from this initial advantage.

Advertising

Monopolistically competitive firms seek to differentiate their products partly by designing and introducing products that actually are different from those of the other firms in the industry. But they also attempt to differentiate the consumer's perception of the product. Advertising is the principal means whereby firms seek to achieve this end. But advertising increases the monopolistically competitive firm's costs above those of a competitive firm or a monopoly that does not advertise.

To the extent that advertising provides consumers with information about the precise nature of the differentiation of products, it serves a valuable purpose to the consumer, enabling a better product choice to be made. But the opportunity cost of the additional information through advertising has to be offset against the gain to the consumer from making a better choice.

The bottom line on the question of allocative efficiency of monopolistic competition is ambiguous. In some cases, the gains from extra product variety unquestionably offset the costs in the form of advertising and excess capacity. The tremendous varieties of books and magazines, of clothing, food, and drink are examples of such gains. It is less easy to see the gains from being able to buy brand name drugs that have an identical chemical composition to a generic alternative. But some people do willingly pay more for the brand name alternative.

REVIEW

A firm in a monopolistically competitive industry faces a downward-sloping demand curve and so has to choose its price as well as the quantity to produce. Such firms also compete on product variety and by advertising. A lack of barriers to entry into such industry ensures that economic profit is competed away. In long-run equilibrium, firms make zero economic profit, charging a price equal to average total cost. But price exceeds marginal cost and the quantity produced is below that which minimizes average total cost. The cost of monopolistic competition is excess capacity and high advertising expenditure; the gain is a wide product variety. ■

We can use the model of monopolistic competition to interpret and analyze many real world industries. One such industry is that for microwave popcorn (see Reading Between the Lines, pp. 350–352). Although this industry has a small number of producers that dominate the market (it has a high concentration ratio), it does have differentiated products and there are no obvious restrictions on the entry of new firms. Thus it is an industry in which entry may result in economic profit being competed away in the long run. There are some industries, however, in which barriers to entry prevent such an outcome. In such industries, competition is restricted to a small number of firms, each of whose actions affect not only its own profits but those of the other firms in the industry. This is the case of oligopoly, to which we now turn.

Oligopoly

We have defined oligopoly as a market in which a small number of producers compete with each other. In such a market, each producer is interdependent. The sales of any one producer depends upon that producer's price and the prices charged by the other producers. If one firm lowers its price, its own sales increase but the sales of the other firms in the industry decrease. In such a situation, the other firms will, most likely, lower their prices, too. Then the price cuts of the other firms will lower the profits of the first firm. So, before deciding to cut its prices, the first firm tries to predict how other firms will react and attempts to calculate the effects of those reactions on its own profit.

The situation faced by firms in an oligopolistic industry is not unlike that faced by military planners. For example, in deciding whether to build additional weapons or to dismantle existing

ones, U.S. military planners have to take into account the effects of U.S. actions on the behavior of the Soviet Union. Similarly, in making its plans, the Soviet Union has to take into account the reactions of the United States. Neither side can assume that its rival's behavior will be independent of its own actions.

Whether we're studying price wars or star wars, we need a method of analyzing choices that takes into account the interactions between agents. Such a method has been developed and is called game theory.

Game Theory

Game theory is a method of analyzing strategic interaction. **Strategic interaction** is acting in a way that takes into account the expected behavior of others and the mutual recognition of interdependence. Game theory was invented by John von Neumann in 1937 and further extended by von Neumann and Oskar Morgenstern in 1944 (see Our Advancing Knowledge, pp. 354–355). It is the topic of a massive amount of current research.

Game theory seeks to understand oligopoly as well as political and social rivalries by using a method of analysis specifically designed to understand games of all types, including the familiar games of everyday life. We will begin our study of game theory, and its application to the behavior of firms, by considering those familiar games.

Familiar Games: What They Have in Common

What is a game? At first thought, the question seems silly. After all, there are many different games. There are ball games and parlor games, games of chance and games of skill. What do games of such diversity and variety have in common? In answering this question, we will focus on those features of games that are relevant and important for game theory and for analyzing oligopoly as a game. All games have three things in common:

• Rules

• Strategies

• Payoffs

Let's see how these common features of ordinary games apply to oligopoly.

Monopolistic Competition in Action

Microwave Key to Popcorn War

Poor Orville Redenbacher. The executives of General Mills, Pillsbury and Nabisco Brands are out to get the king of popcorn.

Their passion for popcorn—or to be more precise, microwave popcorn—is easy to understand. In the last four years, the nation has developed a seemingly insatiable appetite for microwave popcorn, making it the fastest-growing segment of the popcorn business.

Five years ago, microwave popcorn did not exist. In 1983, the first full year that microwave popcorn was available nationally, it generated retail sales of $53 million, according to Packaged Facts, a New York-based consumer research concern. Last year, consumers popped an estimated $250 million worth of the stuff, according to the Popcorn Institute, a Chicago-based trade group.

One pattern in the highly competitive packaged-snack-food industry is that, where there is demand, an abundance of supply will surely follow. Indeed, there are now five major brands slugging it out: Pillsbury's Microwave Popcorn, General Mills' Pop Secret, American Pop Corn's Jolly Time, Nabisco's Planters Premium Select and, of course Beatrice's Orville Redenbacher's Microwave Popping Corn. Several smaller companies, including the food concern of the actor Paul Newman, have also jumped into the fray.

Calling the market "keenly competitive," Donald L. Knutzen, the general manager of the General Mills snack food division said: "This is easily the hottest microwave product General Mills has ever introduced."

Two consumer trends are responsible for microwave popcorn's rise: the health craze and the growing popularity of microwave ovens.

Since popcorn (at least in its unadulterated form) is low in calories and sodium and high in fiber, Americans are now annually gobbling up 675 million pounds of all types, or an average of 46 quarts a person—twice the amount consumed in 1970.

65% of Homes Have Microwaves

With microwave ovens now in about 65 percent of households in the United States, popcorn that can be prepared in those ovens is increasingly the kind of popcorn that Americans are eating. Total popcorn retail sales (popped and unpopped) are expected to double to $2 billion by 1990. And the microwave variety, which now accounts for 44 percent of unpopped popcorn sold, will probably become the dominant form in its category, with retail sales of $430 million by 1990, said Dennis P. Mitchell, managing editor of Snack Food Magazine.

Given these projections, it is easy to understand why some of the biggest guns of the packaged-foods industry have entered the business.

Consumers are willing to pay an average of $2 for a package of microwave popcorn—substantially more than the 89 cents that a much larger generic bag of regular popcorn typically costs. Even with their high technology and marketing costs, microwave-popcorn manufacturers have margins of 10 to 20 percent or more, according to several makers.

Pillsbury introduced the first popcorn geared for microwaves in 1982, when it came out with a frozen microwave popcorn. But Orville Redenbacher, the dominant power in the traditional unpopped-popcorn market, burst onto the microwave scene in 1983. By 1985, Redenbacher, a Beatrice Companies unit, had taken the lead in the microwave segment.

Since then, General Mills' Betty Crocker Pop Secret has caught up with Redenbacher. Each company now holds about 26 percent of the market, measured in retail dollars.

General Mills promoted Pop Secret as the first popcorn appropriate for all microwave ovens—no matter what the wattage. More of Pop Secret's kernels will pop than the competition's, General Mills says.

Some of General Mills' competitors disagree—and for understandable reasons. Because packaging is pretty much the same, "popability" is a big deal.

Redenbacher asserts that virtually every single one of its kernels pops. Nabisco Brands U.S.A. makes the same claim for its Planters Premium Select Popcorn.

The Essence of the Story

One With Butter

For its part, the American Pop Corn Company is trying to distinguish its fourth-ranked Jolly Time Microwave Popcorn from the pack by noting that Jolly Time is the only microwave popcorn to contain butter. Meanwhile, all the big contenders have introduced salt-free versions for health-conscious consumers.

Despite the growing popularity of microwave popcorn, many in the industry are already predicting a shakeout. "Like wine coolers, two or three winners will entrench in the microwave market, which will become a big, mainstream staple," said Faith B. Popcorn, chairman of Brainreserve, a marketing consulting firm in New York. "All the others will fall into the ocean."

Microwave Popcorn Sales Are Surging

The market share for microwave popcorn is charted in percent, and the dollar value of sales for each year is inset.

- 1983: $53 Million (about 17%)
- 1984: $97 Million (about 29%)
- 1985: $158 Million (about 39%)
- 1986: $250 Million (about 43%)

Market share (percentage)

The New York Times, June 22, 1987

Copyright© 1987 by The New York Times Company. Reprinted by permission.

- Popcorn that pops in a microwave oven became available in 1982.

- Between 1983 and 1986, sales of microwave popcorn grew from $53 million (18 percent of popcorn market) to $250 million (44 percent of popcorn market).

- Growth in demand has been generated by increased awareness of health value of popcorn, and the spread of microwave ovens (to 65 percent of homes by 1986).

- Projected microwave popcorn sales by 1990 are $430 million.

- Price of a package of microwave popcorn is $2, more than twice the price of regular popcorn.

- Manufacturers' profit is at least 10 percent and perhaps more than 20 percent of total cost.

- In 1982, there was only one producer of microwave popcorn—Pillsbury. In 1983, Orville Redenbacher entered the market and by 1985 had become the biggest producer.

- There were five major producers of microwave popcorn by 1986 (see table below).

- The producers attempt to distinguish their products from each other on the basis of "popability" and additives (or their absence).

- Some industry observers are predicting that despite further growth in demand, the number of major producers will settle down to two or three.

(Continued on next page.)

Producer	Brand name	Sales in 1986 (if known)
Pillsbury	Microwave Popcorn	—
Orville Redenbacher	Microwave Popping Corn	$ 65 million*
Betty Crocker (General Mills)	Pop Secret	$ 65 million*
American Pop Corn	Jolly Time	—
Nabisco	Planters Premium	—
		$250 million

*About 26 percent of market according to the article.

351

Background and Analysis

(Continued)

▪ The microwave popcorn industry may be studied using the model of monopolistic competition: While a small number of firms dominate the market, there is product differentiation and free entry.

▪ In 1983, there were two major producers, Pillsbury and Orville Redenbacher. A typical firm sold 13.25 million packages of popcorn at $2 a package and had a total revenue of $26.5 million.

▪ The revenue, cost, and profit of a typical producer in 1983 are shown in the first figure below.

— The demand curve is *D*
— The marginal revenue curve is *MR*
— The average total cost curve is *ATC*
— The marginal cost curve is *MC*

— The producer maximizes profit by producing 13.25 million packages of microwave popcorn (the quantity that makes marginal revenue equal marginal cost)
— Price is $2 a package
— Profit, the blue area, is 20 percent of total cost.

▪ After 1983, demand continued to grow; existing firms expanded their plant; new firms entered the industry.

▪ By 1986, the biggest firms were producing 32.5 million packages of popcorn a year and making profits in excess of 20 percent.

▪ A typical producer in 1986 had cost and revenue curves similar to those shown in the figure but at larger scales of production than those shown there.

▪ While profit opportunities are available, existing firms will expand and/or new firms will enter the industry.

▪ The prediction reported in the article is that there will be no new entry but that existing firms will expand. Furthermore, two or three of the existing firms will expand so successfully that the others will be unable to survive.

▪ The second figure illustrates a possible situation after the predicted "shake-out." Three firms produce 72 million packages each. Their average total cost curve (*ATC*) just touches their demand curve (*D*) at that quantity. Maximum profit is being earned but that profit is zero. In such a situation, there is no further incentive to expand or for new firms to try to

enter the industry. The industry has excess capacity as a consequence of product differentiation. Each firm is selling 72 million packages at $2 a package for a total revenue of $144 million and industry revenue is three times that amount, the $430 million predicted by Dennis P. Mitchell in the article.

▪ In both figures, the cost curves and demand curves have been *assumed* to change so that the price stays constant at $2 a package. Nothing in the article predicts a constant price. The diagrams have been drawn to generate a constant price so that the analysis is neutral in that regard. It is possible that the price will rise or fall depending on exactly how the demand and cost curves shift over time.

(a)

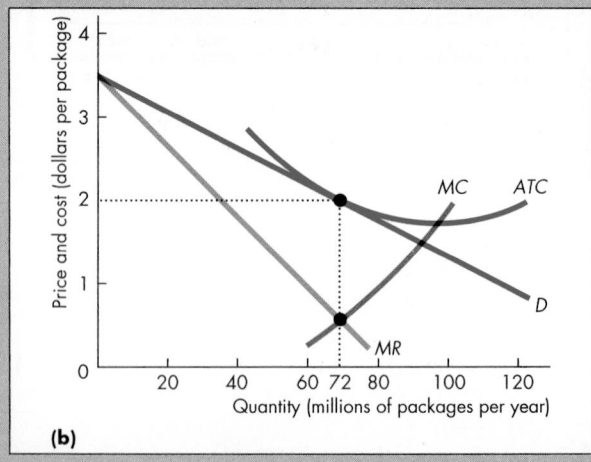

(b)

Rules of the Oligopoly Game

The rules of the oligopoly game have not been written down by the "National Oligopoly League." They arise from the economic, social, and political environment in which the oligopolists operate.

One rule of the oligopoly game is the number of players—the number of firms in the market. Another rule is the method of calculating the score. This rule states that the score of each player is the player's economic profit or loss. The goal of each player of the oligopoly game is to make the largest possible profit. The remaining rules of the oligopoly game are determined by the framework of laws within which the oligopolists are operating. Oligopolists' actions are restricted only by the legal code.

Strategies in the Oligopoly Game

In game theory as in ordinary games, **strategies** are all the possible actions of each player. A comprehensive list of strategies in the oligopoly game would be very long, but it would include, for each player, such actions as:

- Raise price, lower price, hold price constant.
- Raise output, lower output, hold output constant.
- Increase advertising, cut advertising, hold advertising constant.
- Enhance features of product, simplify product, leave product unchanged.

Payoffs in the Oligopoly Game

In game theory, the score of each player is called the **payoff.** In the oligopoly game, the payoffs are the profits and losses of the players. These payoffs are determined by the oligopolists' strategies and by the constraints that they face. Constraints come from customers who determine the demand curve for the product of the oligopoly industry, from the technology available, and from the prices of the resources used by the oligopolists.

To understand how an oligopoly game works, it is revealing to study a special case of oligopoly called duopoly. **Duopoly** is a market structure in which there are two producers of a commodity competing with each other. There are few cases of duopoly on a national and international scale but many cases of local duopolies. For example, in some communities, there are two suppliers of milk, two local newspapers, two taxi companies, two car rental firms. But the main reason for studying duopoly is not its "realism" but the fact that it captures all the essential features of oligopoly and yet is more manageable to analyze and understand. Furthermore, there is a well-known game called "the prisoner's dilemma" that captures some of the essential features of duopoly and that provides a good illustration of how game theory works and how it leads to predictions about the behavior of the players. Let's now turn our attention to studying a duopoly game, beginning with the prisoner's dilemma.

The Prisoner's Dilemma

Alf and Bob have been caught red-handed stealing a car. Facing airtight cases, they will receive a sentence of two years each for their crime. During his interviews with the two prisoners, the district attorney begins to suspect that he has stumbled on the two people who were responsible for a multimillion-dollar bank robbery some months earlier. The district attorney also knows, however, that this is just a suspicion. He has no evidence on which he can convict them of the greater crime unless he can get each of them to confess. The district attorney comes up with the following idea.

He places the prisoners in separate rooms so that they cannot communicate with each other. Each prisoner is told that he is suspected of having carried out the bank robbery and that if he and his accomplice both confess to that crime, each will receive sentences of three years. Each is also told that if he alone confesses and his accomplice does not, he will receive an even shorter sentence of one year while his accomplice will receive a ten-year sentence. The prisoners know that if neither of them confesses, then they will only be tried for and convicted of the lesser offense of car theft, which carries a two-year prison term. How do the prisoners respond to the district attorney?

Models of Oligopoly

Economists have studied oligopoly and duopoly since the time of Cournot (see Our Advancing Knowledge, p. 84). The earliest models were based on assumptions about the beliefs of each firm concerning the reactions of another firm (or firms) to its own actions. A particularly influential model was proposed in the 1930s by Paul M. Sweezy, editor of the *Monthly Review* for the past 40 years.

Sweezy's concern was to explain why prices did not fall more quickly during the years of the Great Depression. He proposed a theory based on the following propositions about the beliefs held by firms:

• If we increase our price, we will be on our own—others will not follow us.
• If we decrease our price, so will everyone else.

If these beliefs are correct, a firm faces a demand curve for its product that has a kink occurring at the current price, P (see figure). At prices above P the demand curve is relatively flat, reflecting the belief that if the firm increases its price, it will be out of line with all of the other firms and so will experience a large fall in the quantity demanded. At prices below P, the demand curve is relatively steep, reflecting the belief that since all other firms are matching the price cut, the increase in the quantity demanded will not be as large as the decrease in the quantity demanded resulting from a price rise.

The kink in demand curve D results in a break in the marginal revenue curve (MR). The profit-maximizing output (Q) is where the marginal cost curve passes through the discontinuity in the marginal revenue curve—the gap ab. If marginal cost fluctuates between a and b, an example of which is shown in the figure with the marginal cost curves, MC_0 and MC_1, the firm will change neither its price nor its quantity of output. Only if marginal cost fluctuates outside the range ab will the firm change its price and quantity produced.

There are two problems with Sweezy's model:

• It does not tell us how the price, P, is determined
• It does not tell us what happens if firms discover that their belief about the demand curve is incorrect.

Suppose, for example, that marginal cost increased by enough to cause the firm to increase its price and that all firms experience the marginal cost increase. In such a case, all firms increase their prices together and the belief that other firms will not match the price increase is incorrect. The firm's beliefs are inconsistent with reality and the demand and marginal revenue curves, which summarize those beliefs, are

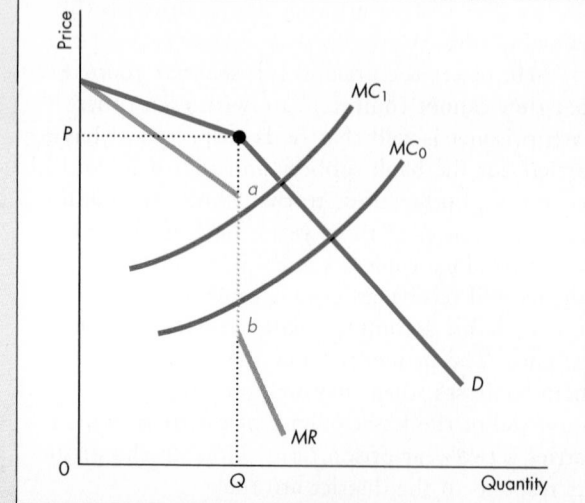

not the correct ones for the purpose of calculating the new profit-maximizing price and output. A widespread dissatisfaction with the state of the theory of oligopoly was a primary impetus to the development of game theory.

Game theory was invented in 1928 by John von Neumann, a brilliant mathematician, physicist, and pioneer in mathematical economics. He established the logical basis for the computer and built the first modern computing machine. He also worked on the "Manhattan Project," which developed the atomic bomb in Los Alamos, New Mexico. Born in Budapest, Hungary, in 1903, von Neumann studied in Budapest and Zurich, and from 1931 worked at the Institute for Advanced Study at Princeton University.

Von Neumann's mathematical brilliance was recognized at an early age and his first mathematical publication which grew out of lessons with his tutor appeared when he was only 18. But it was at the age of 25, in 1928, that von Neumann published an article that started a flood of research in game theory. In that article, von Neumann studied a game with two players in which the sum of the payoffs is zero—what one player gains the other player loses. Bargaining for shares of a fixed pie is an example. Such a game is called a zero-sum game, a phrase which has entered common usage in English. He proved that there existed, in a zero-sum game, a best strategy for each player. In 1944, von Neumann and his collaborator Oskar Morgenstern published *Theory of Games and Economic Behavior*, a book in which they extended von Neumann's earlier results to games involving any number of players and to cases where the payoffs added up to more than zero.

John von Neumann

Von Neumann strongly believed that the social sciences would progress by applying mathematical tools, but he also believed that they required completely different mathematical tools from the physical sciences.

The next major step in the development of game theory was taken in 1951 by John F. Nash, Jr., a mathematician at MIT, who developed the equilibrium concept that now bears his name and that you have learned about in this chapter.

Today there is an enormous volume of research being done on game theory, and a large number of brilliant economists and mathematicians are at work on the subject. Among these is John Harsanyi who teaches decision science—the mathematical analysis of economic decisions—at the University of California at Berkeley. Harsanyi has studied games in which the players are not fully informed and each knows some things that the others do not know. Another interesting contribution is by Eric Maskin of Harvard and Jean Tirole of MIT, who have recently shown that even the kinked demand curve theory of Sweezy can be viewed as the outcome of a game. The particular game is one in which firms take turns at determining the market price and all other firms accept the price that has been set. The model proposed by Maskin and Tirole overcomes all the problems of the original Sweezy theory: Firms' beliefs, on the average, are correct, and the model even predicts where the kink in the demand curve will occur—at the monopoly profit-maximizing price and quantity point.

Game theory has now firmly established itself as one of the main tools of analysis in mathematical economics.

First, notice that the prisoner's dilemma is a game with two players. Each player has two strategies: To confess to the multimillion-dollar bank robbery or to deny the charge. Because there are two players, each with two strategies, there are four possible outcomes.

1 Neither player confesses.
2 Both players confess.
3 Alf confesses but Bob does not.
4 Bob confesses but Alf does not.

Each prisoner can work out exactly what will happen to him—his payoff—in each of these four situations. We can tabulate the four possible payoffs for each of the prisoners in what is called a payoff matrix for the game.

The Payoff Matrix

A **payoff matrix** is a table that shows the payoffs for every possible action by each player for every possible action by each other player.

Table 14.3 shows a payoff matrix for Alf and Bob. The squares show the payoffs for each prisoner—A for Alf and B for Bob. If both prisoners confess (top left), they each get a prison term of 3 years. If Bob confesses but Alf denies (top right), Alf gets a 10-year sentence and Bob gets a 1-year sentence. If Alf confesses and Bob denies (bottom left), Alf gets a 1-year sentence and Bob gets a 10-year sentence. Finally, if both of them deny (bottom right), neither can be convicted of the bank robbery charge but both are sentenced for the car theft—a 2-year sentence.

The Dilemma   The dilemma is seen by considering the consequences of confessing and not confessing. Each prisoner knows that if he and his accomplice remain silent about the bank robbery, they will only be sentenced to 2 years for stealing the car. Neither prisoner, however, has any way of knowing that his accomplice will remain silent and refuse to confess. Each knows that if the other confesses and he denies, the other will receive only a 1-year sentence while the one denying will receive a 10-year sentence. Each poses the following questions: Should I deny and rely on my accomplice to deny so that we may both get only 2 years? Or should I confess in the hope of getting just 1 year (providing my accomplice denies), but knowing that if my

Table 14.3   Prisoner's Dilemma Payoff Matrix

		Alf's strategies	
		Confess	Deny
Bob's strategies	Confess	A 3 years / B 3 years	A 10 years / B 1 year
	Deny	A 1 year / B 10 years	A 2 years / B 2 years

Each square shows the payoffs for the two players, A for Alf and B for Bob, for each possible pair of actions. For example, if both confess, the payoffs are in the top left square. Alf reasons as follows: If Bob confesses, it pays me to confess because then I get 3 years rather than 10. If Bob denies, it pays me to confess because then I get 1 year rather than 2. Regardless of what Bob does, it pays me to confess. Alf's dominant strategy is to confess. Bob reasons similarly: If Alf confesses, it pays me to confess and get 3 years rather than 10. If Alf denies, it pays me to confess and get 1 year rather than 2. Bob's dominant strategy is to confess. Since each player's dominant strategy is to confess, the equilibrium of the game is for both players to confess and to each get 3 years.

accomplice does confess we will both get 3 years in prison? Resolving the dilemma involves finding the equilibrium for the game.

Equilibrium

The equilibrium of a game is called a Nash equilibrium: It is so named because it was first proposed by John Nash (see Our Advancing Knowledge, pp. 354–355). A **Nash equilibrium** occurs when A takes the best possible action given the action of B and B takes the best possible action given the action of A. In the case of the prisoner's dilemma, the equilibrium occurs when Alf makes his best choice given Bob's choice and when Bob makes his best choice given Alf's choice.

The prisoner's dilemma is a game that has a special kind of Nash equilibrium. Its equilibrium is called a dominant strategy equilibrium. A **domi-**

nant strategy is a strategy that is the same regardless of the action taken by the other player. In other words, there is a unique best action regardless of what the other player does. A **dominant strategy equilibrium** occurs when there is a dominant strategy for each player. The equilibrium in the prisoner's dilemma is an example of a dominant strategy equilibrium. In the prisoner's dilemma, no matter what Bob does, Alf's best strategy is to confess, and no matter what Alf does Bob's best strategy is to confess. Thus each player confessing is the equilibrium of the prisoner's dilemma.

If each prisoner plays the prisoner's dilemma game in his own individual best interest, the outcome of the game will be that each confesses. To see why each player confesses, let's consider again their strategies and the payoffs from the alternative courses of action.

Strategies and Payoffs

Look at the situation from Alf's point of view. Alf realizes that his outcome depends on the action Bob takes. If Bob confesses, it pays Alf to confess also, for in that case, he will be sentenced to 3 years rather than 10 years. But if Bob does not confess, it still pays Alf to confess (in that case he will receive 1 year rather than 2 years). Alf reasons that regardless of Bob's action, his own best action is to confess.

The dilemma from Bob's point of view is identical to Alf's. Bob knows that if Alf confesses, he will receive 10 years if he does not confess or 3 years if he does. Therefore if Alf confesses, it pays Bob to confess. Similarly, if Alf does not confess, Bob will receive 2 years for not confessing and 1 year if he confesses. Again, it pays Bob to confess. Bob's best action, regardless of Alf's action, is to confess.

Each prisoner sees that regardless of what the other prisoner does, his own best action is to confess. Since each player's best action is to confess, each will confess, each will get a 3-year prison term, and the district attorney has solved the bank robbery. This is the equilibrium of the game.

A Bad Outcome

The equilibrium of the game, where each player confesses, is not for the prisoners the best outcome.

A better outcome would be for neither of them to confess, because they would each get only 2 years for the lesser crime. Isn't there some way in which this better outcome can be achieved? It seems that there is not, because the players cannot communicate with each other. Each player can put himself in the other player's place and, as a result, each player can figure out that there is a dominant strategy for each of them. The prisoners are indeed in a dilemma. Each prisoner knows that he can serve 2 years only if he can trust the other not to confess. Each prisoner also knows, however, that it is not in the best interest of the other to not confess. Thus each prisoner knows that he has to confess, thereby delivering a bad outcome for both.

Let us now see how we can use the ideas that we have just developed to understand price fixing, price wars, and the behavior of duopolists.

A Duopoly Game

To study a duopoly game, we're going to build a model of a duopoly industry. The model is inspired by "the incredible electrical conspiracy." But don't lose sight of the fact that what follows is a model. It is not a description of a real historical episode.

Suppose that only two firms make a particular kind of electric switchgear. We will call the firms Trick and Gear. Our goal is to make predictions about the prices charged and the outputs produced by each of the two firms. We are going to pursue that goal by constructing a duopoly game that the two firms will play. To set out the game, we need to specify the strategies of the players and the payoff matrix.

We will suppose that the two firms enter into a collusive agreement. A **collusive agreement** is an agreement between two (or more) producers to restrict output in order to raise prices and profits. Such an agreement is illegal and is undertaken in secret. A group of firms that has entered into a collusive agreement to restrict output and increase prices and profits is called a **cartel**. The strategies that firms in a cartel can pursue are to:

• Comply
• Cheat

Complying simply means sticking to the agreement. Cheating means breaking the agreement in a manner designed to benefit the cheating firm and harm the other firm.

Since each firm has two strategies, there are four possible combinations of actions for the two firms:

- Both firms comply.
- Both firms cheat.
- Trick complies and Gear cheats.
- Gear complies and Trick cheats.

We need to work out the payoffs to each firm from each of these four possible sets of actions. To do that we need to explore the cost and demand conditions in the industry.

Cost and Demand Conditions

The cost of producing switchgears is the same for both Trick and Gear. The average total cost curve

(*ATC*) and the marginal cost curve (*MC*) for each firm are shown in Fig. 14.2(a). The market demand curve for switchgears (*D*) is shown in Fig. 14.2(b). Each firm produces an identical switchgear product, so one firm's switchgear is a perfect substitute for the other's. The market price of each firm's product, therefore, is identical. The quantity demanded depends on that price—the higher the price, the lower is the quantity demanded.

Notice that in this industry, there is room for only two firms. For each firm the *minimum efficient scale* of production is 3000 switchgear units a week. When the price equals the average total cost of production at the minimum efficient scale, total industry demand is 6000 switchgear units a week. Thus there is no room for three firms in this industry. If there were only one firm in the industry, it would make an enormous profit and invite competition. If there were three firms, at least one of them would make a loss. The number of firms that an industry can sustain depends on the relationship between cost and the industry's demand conditions. In the model industry that we're study-

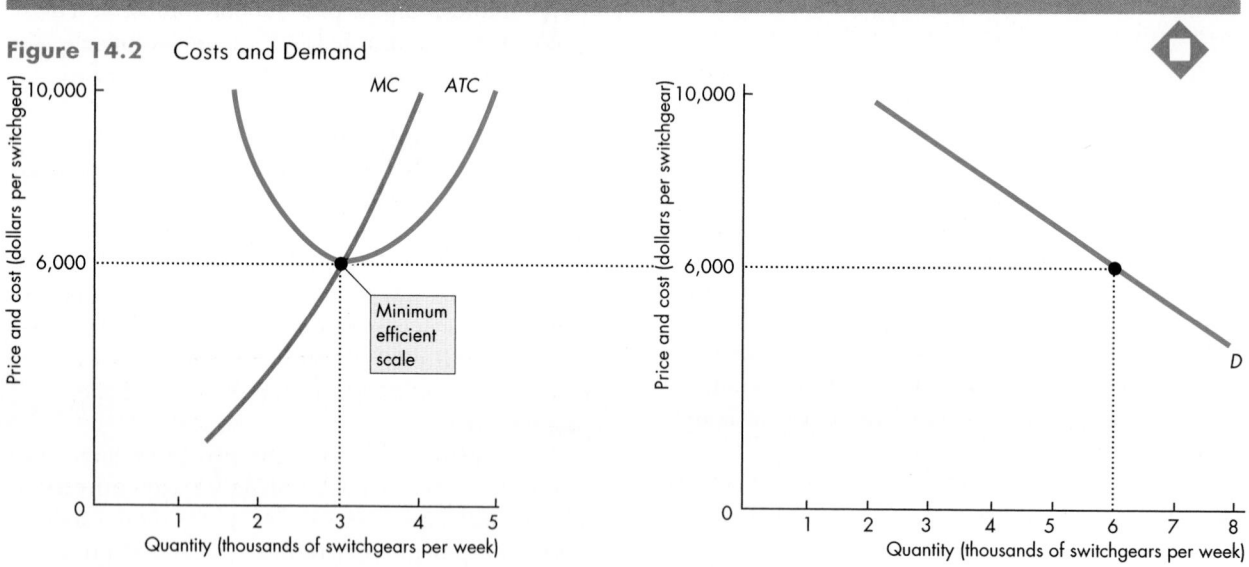

Figure 14.2   Costs and Demand

(a) Individual firm

(b) Industry

Part (a) shows the costs facing Trick and Gear, two duopolists who make switchgears. Each firm faces identical costs. The average total cost curve for each firm is *ATC* and the marginal cost curve is *MC*. For each firm, the minimum efficient scale of prduction is 3000 units per week and the average total cost of producing that output is $6000 a unit. Part (b) shows the industry demand curve. At a price of $6000 a unit, the quantity demanded is 6000 units per week. There is room for only two firms in this industry.

Figure 14.3   Colluding to Make Monopoly Profits

(a) Individual firm

(b) Industry

If Trick and Gear come to a collusive agreement, they can act as a single monopolist and maximize profit. Part (a) shows the consequences of reaching such an agreement for each firm and part (b) shows the situation in the industry as a whole.

To maximize profit, the firms first calculate the industry marginal cost curve (MC_I) shown in part (b)—the horizontal sum of the two firms' marginal cost curves (MC) in part (a). Next they calculate the industry marginal revenue, MR in part (b). They then choose the output rate that makes marginal revenue equal to marginal cost (4000 units per week). They agree to sell that output for a price of $9000, the price at which 4000 switchgear units are demanded.

The costs and profit of each firm are seen in part (a). Each firm produces half the total output—2000 units per week. Average total cost is $8000 per unit, so each firm makes a profit of $2 million (blue rectangle)—2000 units multiplied by $1000 profit per unit.

ing here, the particular cost and demand conditions assumed are designed to generate an industry in which two firms can survive in the long run. In real world oligopoly and duopoly, barriers to entry may arise from economies of scale of the type featured in our model industry but there are other possible barriers as well (as discussed in Chapter 13, pp. 316–317).

Colluding to Maximize Profits

Let's begin by working out the payoffs to the two firms if they collude to make the maximum industry profit—the profit that would be made by a single monopoly. The calculations that the two firms will perform are exactly the same calculations

that a monopoly performs. (You have already studied such calculations in the previous chapter, pp. 320–321.) The only additional thing that the duopolists have to do is to agree on how much of the total output each of them will produce.

The price and quantity that maximizes industry profit for the duopolists is shown in Fig. 14.3. Part (a) shows the situation for each firm and part (b) for the industry as a whole. The curve labeled MR is the industry marginal revenue curve. The curve labeled MC_I is the industry marginal cost curve if each firm produces the same level of output. That curve is constructed by adding together the outputs of the two firms at each level of marginal cost. That is, at each level of marginal cost, industry output is twice as much as the output of each individual firm. Thus the curve MC_I in part

(b) is twice as far to the right as the curve MC in part (a).

To maximize industry profit, the duopolists agree to restrict output to the rate that makes the industry marginal cost and marginal revenue equal. That output rate, as shown in part (b), is 4000 switchgear units a week. The highest price for which the 4000 units can be sold is $9000 each. Let's suppose that Trick and Gear agree to split the market equally so that each firm produces 2000 switchgear units a week. The average total cost (ATC) of producing 2000 units a week is $8000, so the profit per unit is $1000 and the total profit is $2 million (2000 units × $1000 per unit). The profit of each firm is represented by the blue rectangle in Fig. 14.3(a).

We have just described one possible outcome for the duopoly game: The two firms collude to produce the monopoly profit-maximizing output and divide that output equally between themselves. From the industry point of view, this solution is identical to a monopoly. A duopoly that operates in this way is indistinguishable from a monopoly. The profit that is made by a monopoly is the maximum profit that can be made by colluding duopolists.

Cheating on a Collusive Agreement

Under a collusive agreement, the colluding firms restrict output to make their joint marginal revenue equal to their joint marginal cost. They set the highest price for which the quantity produced can be sold—a price higher than marginal cost. In such a situation, each firm recognizes that if it cheats on the agreement and raises its output, even though the price will fall below that agreed to, more will be added to revenue than to cost, so its profit will increase. Since each firm recognizes this fact, there is a temptation for each firm to cheat. There are two possible cheating situations: One in which one firm cheats and one in which both firms cheats. What happens if one of the firms cheats on the agreement?

One Firm Cheats   What is the effect of one firm cheating on a collusive agreement? How much extra profit does the cheating firm make? What happens to the profit of the firm that sticks to the agreement in the face of cheating by the other firm? Let's work out the answers to these questions.

There are many different ways for a firm to cheat. We will work out just one possibility. Suppose that Trick convinces Gear that there has been a fall in industry demand and that it cannot sell its share of the output at the agreed price. It tells Gear that it plans to cut its price in order to sell the agreed 2000 switchgear units each week. Since the two firms produce a virtually identical product, Gear has no alternative but to match the price cut of Trick.

In fact, there has been no fall in demand and the lower price has been calculated by Trick to be exactly the price needed to sell the additional output that it plans to produce. Gear, though lowering its price in line with that of Trick, restricts its output to the previously agreed level.

Figure 14.4 illustrates the consequences of Trick cheating in this way: Part (a) shows what happens to Gear (the complier); part (b) shows what happens to Trick (the cheat); and part (c) shows what is happening in the industry as a whole.

Suppose that Trick decides to raise output from 2000 to 3000 units a week. It recognizes that if Gear sticks to the agreement to produce only 2000 units a week, total output will be 5000 a week and, given demand in part (c), the price will have to be cut to $7500 a unit.

Gear continues to produce 2000 units a week at a cost of $8000 a unit, and so incurs a loss of $500 a unit or $1 million. This loss is represented by the red rectangle in part (a). Trick produces 3000 units a week at an average total cost of $6000 each. With a price of $7500, Trick makes a profit of $1500 a unit and therefore a total profit of $4.5 million. This profit is the blue rectangle in part (b).

We have now described a second possible outcome for the duopoly game—one of the firms cheats on the collusive agreement. In this case, the industry output is larger than the monopoly output and the industry price is lower than the monopoly price. The total profit made by the industry is also smaller than the monopoly's profit. Trick (the cheat) makes a profit of $4.5 million and Gear (the complier) incurs a loss of $1 million, and the industry makes a profit of $3.5 million. Thus the industry profit is $0.5 million less than the maximum profit would be with a monopoly outcome. But that profit is distributed unevenly. Trick makes an even bigger profit than it would under the collusive agreement, while Gear makes a loss.

Figure 14.4   Cheating on a Collusive Agreement

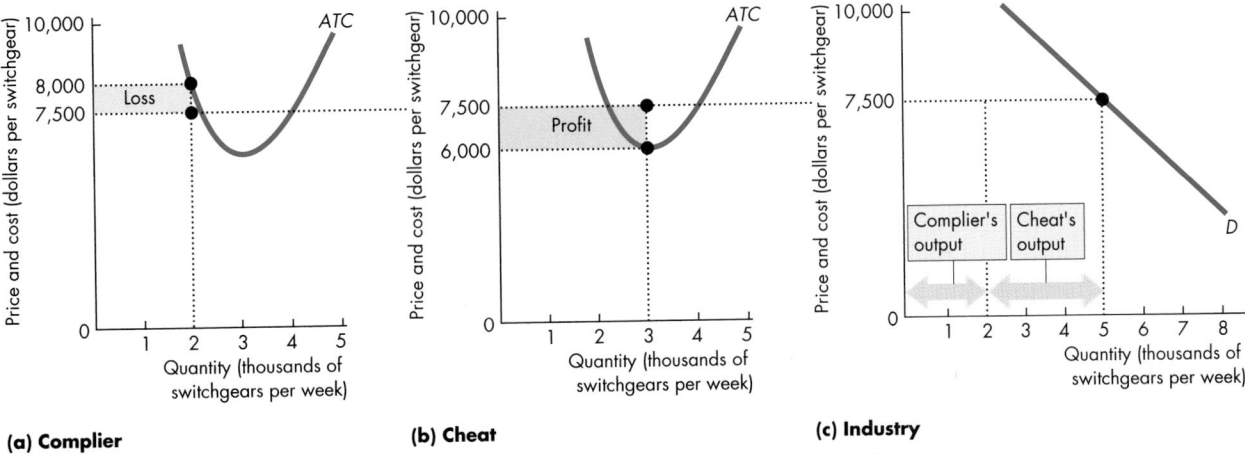

(a) Complier   **(b) Cheat**   **(c) Industry**

In part (a), one firm complies with the agreement. In part (b), the other firm cheats by raising output above the agreed limit to 3000 switchgears per week. Either firm can be the complier and the other the cheat. In part (c), the effect on the industry price of the actions of the cheat are shown. As a result of cheating, industry output rises to 5000 units a week and the market price falls to $7500—the price at which 5000 switchgear units can be sold.

Part (a) describes the complier's situation. Output remains at 2000 units and average total cost remains at $8000 per unit. The firm loses $500 per switchgear and makes a total loss of $1 million (red rectangle). Part (b) describes the cheat's situation. Average total cost is $6000 per unit and profit per switchgear is $1500, so the cheat's total profit is $4.5 million (blue rectangle).

We have just worked out what happens if Trick cheats and Gear complies with the collusive agreement. There is another similar outcome that would arise if Gear cheated and Trick complied with the agreement. The industry profit and price would be the same but in this case Gear (the cheat) would make a profit of $4.5 million and Trick (the complier) a loss of $1 million.

There is yet another possible outcome: Both firms cheat on the agreement.

Both Firms Cheat   Suppose that instead of just one firm cheating on the collusive agreement, both firms cheat. In particular, suppose that each firm behaves in exactly the same way as the cheating firm that we have just analyzed. Each firm tells the other that it is unable to sell its output at the going price and that it plans to cut its price. But since both firms are cheating, each will propose a successively lower price. They will only stop proposing lower prices when the price has reached $6000. That is the price that equals minimum

average cost. At a price of less than $6000, each firm will make a loss. At a price of $6000, each firm will cover all its costs and make zero economic profit. Also, at a price of $6000, each firm will want to produce 3000 units a week, so that the industry weekly output will be 6000 units. Given the demand conditions, 6000 units can be sold at a price of $6000 each.

The situation just described is illustrated in Fig. 14.5. Each firm, shown in part (a) of the figure, is producing 3000 units a week, and this output level occurs at the point of minimum average total cost ($6000 per unit). The market as a whole, shown in part (b), operates at the point at which the demand curve (D) intersects the industry marginal cost curve. This marginal cost curve is constructed as the horizontal sum of the marginal cost curves of the two firms. Each firm has lowered its price and increased its output in order to try to gain an advantage over the other firm, and they have each pushed this process as far as they can without incurring losses.

Figure 14.5   Both Firms Cheat

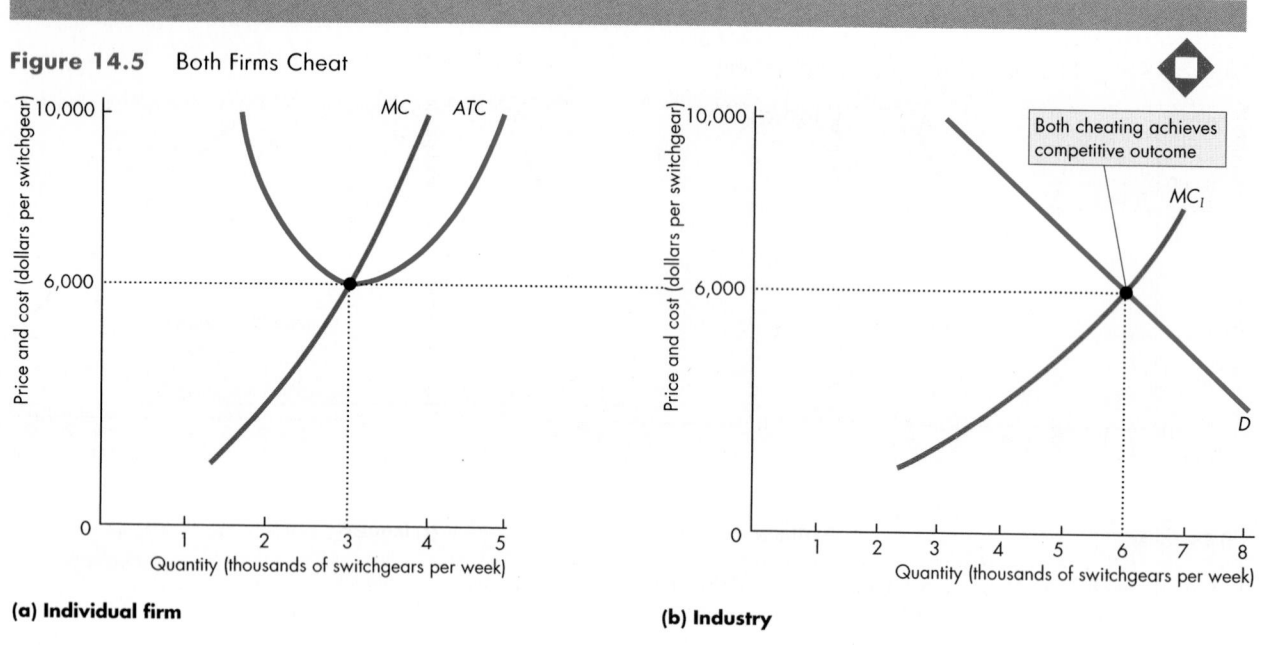

(a) Individual firm

(b) Industry

If both firms cheat by raising their output and lowering the price, the collusive agreement completely breaks down. The limit to the breakdown of the agreement is the competitive equilibrium. Neither firm will want to cut the price below $6000 (minimum average total cost), for to do so will result in losses.

Part (a) shows the situation facing each firm. At a price of $6000, the firm's profit-maximizing output is 3000 units. At that output rate, price equals marginal cost, and it also equals average total cost. Economic profit is zero. Part (b) describes the situation in the industry as a whole. The industry marginal cost curve (MC$_I$)—the horizontal sum of the individual firms' marginal cost curves (MC)—intersects the demand curve at 6000 switchgear units per week and at a price of $6000. This output and price is the one that would prevail in a competitive industry.

We have now described a third possible outcome of this duopoly game—both firms cheat. If both firms cheat on the collusive agreement, the output of each firm is 3000 units a week and the price is $6000. Each firm makes zero profit.

The Payoff Matrix and Equilibrium

Now that we have described the strategies and payoffs in the duopoly game, let's summarize the strategies and the payoffs in the form of the game's payoff matrix and then calculate the equilibrium.

Each firm has two possible actions—cheat or comply. Since each firm has two possible actions and there are two firms, there are four possible outcomes:

- Both firms cheat.
- Both firms comply.
- Gear complies and Trick cheats.
- Trick complies and Gear cheats.

What are the payoffs from these alternative actions? Table 14.4 sets out the payoff matrix for this game. It is constructed in exactly the same way as the payoff matrix for the prisoner's dilemma in Table 14.3. The squares show the payoffs for the two firms—Gear and Trick. In this case, the payoffs are profits. (In the case of the prisoner's dilemma, the payoffs were losses.)

The table shows that if both firms cheat (top left), they achieve the perfectly competitive outcome—each firm makes zero economic profit. If both firms comply (bottom right), the industry makes the monopoly profit and each firm earns a profit of $2 million. The top-right and bottom-left squares show what happens if one firm cheats while the other complies. The firm that cheats collects a profit of $4.5 million and the one that complies makes a loss of $1 million.

This duopoly game is, in fact, the same as the prisoner's dilemma that we examined earlier in this chapter; it is a duopolist's dilemma. You will see this once you have determined what the equilibrium of this game is.

To find the equilibrium, let's look at things from the point of view of Gear. Gear reasons as follows: Suppose that Trick cheats. If we comply with the agreement, we make a loss of $1 million. If we also cheat, we make a zero profit. Zero profit is better than a $1 million loss, so it will pay us to cheat. But suppose Trick complies with the agreement. If we cheat, we will make a profit of $4.5 million, and if we comply, we will make a profit of $2 million. A $4.5 million profit is better than a $2 million profit so it would again pay us to cheat. Thus regardless of whether Trick cheats or complies, it pays us to cheat. Gear's dominant strategy is to cheat.

Trick comes to the same conclusion as Gear. Therefore both firms will cheat. The equilibrium of this game then is that both firms cheat on the agreement. Although there are only two firms in the industry, the price and quantity is the same as in a competitive industry.

Although we have done this analysis for only two firms, it would not make any difference (other than to increase the amount of arithmetic) if we were to play the game with three, four, or more firms. In other words, though we have analyzed duopoly, the game theory approach can also be used to analyze oligopoly. The analysis of oligopoly is much harder, but the essential ideas that we have learned apply to oligopoly.

Repeated Games

The first game that we studied, the prisoner's dilemma, was played just once. The prisoners did not have an opportunity to observe the outcome of the game and then play it again. The duopolist game that we have just studied was also played just once. But unlike the duopolists that we have just studied, real world duopolists do get an opportunity to

Table 14.4   Duopoly Payoff Matrix

		Gear's strategies	
		Cheat	Comply
Trick's strategies	Cheat	Gear $0 Trick $0	Gear −$1.0m Trick +$4.5m
	Comply	Gear +$4.5m Trick −$1.0m	Gear +$2.0m Trick +$2.0m

Each square shows the payoffs from a pair of actions. For example, if both firms comply with the collusive agreement, the payoffs are recorded in the square at the bottom right corner of the table. Gear reasons as follows: If Trick cheats, it pays me to cheat and make a zero economic profit rather than a $1 million loss. If Trick complies, it pays me to cheat and make a $4.5 million profit rather than a $2 million profit. Cheating is Gear's dominant strategy. Trick reasons similarly: If Gear cheats it pays me to cheat and make a zero profit rather than a $1 million loss. If Gear complies, it pays me to cheat and make a $4.5 million profit rather than a $2 million profit. The equilibrium is a Nash equilibrium in which both firms cheat.

play repeatedly against each other. This fact suggests that real world duopolists might find some way of learning to cooperate so that their efforts to collude are more effective. If Gear cheats this week, won't Trick cheat next week? Shouldn't Gear take account of the possibility of Trick cheating next week before it decides to cheat this week?

If a game is played repeatedly, one player always has the opportunity to penalize the other player for previous "bad" behavior. If Trick refuses to cooperate this week, then Gear can refuse to cooperate next week (and vice versa).

What is the equilibrium of this more complicated prisoner's dilemma game when it is repeated indefinitely? Actually there is more than one possibility. One is the Nash equilibrium that we have just analyzed. Both players cheat with each making zero profit forever. In such a situation, it will never pay one of the players to start complying unilaterally, for to do so would result in a loss for that

Table 14.5   Repeated Duopoly Game

Period of play	Collude		Cheat with tit-for-tat strategy	
	Trick	Gear	Trick	Gear
	(Profit in millions of dollars)		(Profit in millions of dollars)	
1	2	2	2.0	2.0
2	2	2	4.5	−1.0
3	2	2	−1.0	4.5
4	2	2	2.0	2.0
.	.	.	.	.
.	.	.	.	.
.	.	.	.	.

If duopolists repeatedly play the "cooperate" strategy, they each make $2 million in each period. If one player cheats in one period, the other player cheats in the following period—tit-for-tat. The profit from cheating can be made only for a single period. In the following period, the other player cheats and the first player must cooperate if the cooperative agreement is to be restored in period 4. The profit from cheating, calculated over 4 periods of play, is lower than that from colluding. Under collusion, each player makes $8 million; with a single cheat responded to with a tit-for-tat, each makes a profit of $7.5 million. It pays each player to cooperate, so cooperation is an equilibrium.

player and a profit for the other. The price and quantity will remain at the competitive levels forever.

But another equilibrium is possible in which the players make and share the monopoly profit. How might this equilibrium come about? Why wouldn't it always pay each firm to try to get away with cheating? The key to answering this question is the fact that when a prisoner's dilemma game is played repeatedly, the players have an increased array of strategies. Each player can punish the other player for previous actions. There are two extremes of punishment. The smallest penalty that one player can impose on the other is what is called "tit-for-tat". A **tit-for-tat strategy** is one in which a player cooperates in the current period if the other player cooperated in the previous period but cheats in the current period if the other player cheated in

the previous period. The most severe form of punishment that one player can impose on the other arises in what is called a trigger strategy. A **trigger strategy** is one in which a player cooperates if the other player cooperates but plays the Nash equilibrium strategy forever thereafter if the other player cheats. Since a tit-for-tat strategy and a trigger strategy are the extremes of punishment—the most mild and most severe—there are evidently other intermediate degrees of punishment. For example, if one player cheats on the agreement, the other player could punish by refusing to cooperate for a certain number of periods. In the duopoly game between Gear and Trick, it turns out that a tit-for-tat strategy keeps both players cooperating and earning monopoly profits. Let's see why.

Table 14.5 sets out the profits that each firm will make in each period of play under two sets of conditions: First, if they cooperate and second, if cheating is responded to with a tit-for-tat strategy. As you can see, as long as both firms stick to the collusive agreement, they make the monopoly profit ($2 million per period each). Suppose that Trick contemplates cheating in period 2. The cheating produces a quick $4.5 million profit and inflicts a $1 million loss on Gear. The next period Gear will hit Trick with its tit-for-tat response and cheat. If Trick reverts to cooperating (to induce Gear to cooperate in period 4), Gear now makes a profit of $4.5 million and Trick makes a loss of $1 million. Adding up the profits over two periods of play, Trick comes out ahead by cheating ($6.5 million compared with $4 million). But if we run the game forward for four periods, Trick would be better off having cooperated. In that case, it would have made $8 million in profit compared with $7.5 million from cheating and generating Gear's tit-for-tat response.[3]

Though we have just worked out what happens if Trick cheats, we can turn the tables and perform the same thought experiment for Gear cheating. We will come up with the same conclusion—it pays Gear to collude. Since it pays both firms to stick with the collusive agreement, both firms will do so and the monopoly price, quantity, and profit will prevail in the industry. This equilibrium is called a **cooperative equilibrium**—an equilibrium resulting from each player responding rationally to the credible threat of the other player to inflict heavy damage if the agreement is broken. But in order for this strategy to work, the threat must be credible: That is, each player must recognize that it is in the interest of the other player to respond with a tit-for-tat. The tit-for-tat and the trigger strategies are credible because if one player cheats, it clearly does not pay the other player to continue complying. So the threat of cheating in response to cheating is credible and sufficient to support the monopoly equilibrium outcome.

---

[3]In calculating Trick's profits from colluding compared with cheating, we've ignored the fact that future profits have a smaller *present value* than current profits (see pp. 214–216). However, provided that the interest rate at which future profits are discounted is not too high, it will still pay Trick to cooperate rather than cheat.

Uncertainty

In reality, there are random fluctuations in demand and in costs that make it impossible for one firm to detect whether the other firm is cheating. For example, a fall in demand can also lower the industry price. One firm increasing its output can also lower the industry price. If a firm observes only that the industry price has fallen, it cannot tell which of these forces caused it. If it knew that the price resulted from a fall in demand, its profit-maximizing action would be to continue cooperating with the other firm to maintain the monopoly agreement. But if the price fall resulted from the other firm cheating and increasing its output, the profit-maximizing response will be to hit the other firm with a tit-for-tat in the next period. But, by only observing the price fall, neither firm can tell whether the other firm has cheated. What can the firms do in a situation such as this one?

If they each always *assume* that whenever the price falls it is because the other firm has cheated, the monopoly agreement will repeatedly break down and the firms will fail to realize the potentially available monopoly profits. If, on the other hand, one firm assumes that the other firm is always cooperating and that any price falls have resulted from market forces beyond the control of either firm, then that other firm will have an incentive to cheat. (Recall that with one firm cheating and the other cooperating, the cheat makes even bigger profits than when they both cooperate.) To remove that incentive to cheat, each firm will assume that the other is cooperating, provided the price does not fall by more than a certain amount. If the price does fall below that predetermined amount, each firm will react as if the other firm had cheated. When market forces take the price back up above the critical level, the firms will cooperate again.

Other Oligopoly Models

The oligopoly model that we have studied in this section, based on the prisoner's dilemma game, is only one of several models that have been suggested for understanding this important type of market. But it is the approach that dominates current research in the area. Earlier attempts to understand oligopoly are briefly explained and reviewed in Our Advancing Knowledge, pp. 354–355.

Games and Price Wars

Let's see whether the theory of price and output determination under duopoly can help us understand real world behavior and, in particular, price wars. Suppose that two (or more) producers reach a collusive agreement and set their prices at the monopoly profit-maximizing level and that the agreement is enforced by each firm pursuing a strategy that involves cooperating in the agreement unless the price falls below a certain critical level, as described above. Fluctuations in demand will lead to fluctuations in the industry price and output. Most of the time, these fluctuations will be small ones and the price, although it will rise and fall, will not normally fall far enough to make either firm depart from the agreement. Occasionally, however, a large decrease in demand will bring about a large decrease in price. When the price falls by a large enough amount, each firm will respond by abandoning the agreement. The events that take place in such a situation will look exactly like a price war. For it is extremely unlikely that each firm would abandon the agreement, lowering its price, at exactly the same moment. It will appear as if one firm abandoned the agreement and then the other abandoned it in retaliation. But what is actually happening is that each firm is reacting to the large price fall in a manner that maintains a credible threat to the other firm that preserves the monopoly cooperative equilibrium in normal demand conditions. When demand increases again and market forces increase the price, the firms revert to their cooperative behavior reaping the monopoly profit.

Thus there will be cycles of price wars and the restoration of collusive agreements. The behavior of prices and outputs in the oil industry (see Reading Between the Lines, pp. 368–369) can be explained by the type of game that you have just studied.

Preserving Secrecy

Because collusion is illegal, one special problem that colluding firms face is hiding the fact of their collusion and preserving secrecy. The real world 1950s case of "the incredible electrical conspiracy" provides a fascinating view of one way in which

this problem has been solved. The particular device used in this conspiracy was called the "phases of the moon" pricing formula.

> [These pricing formulas were listed on] sheets of paper, each containing a half dozen columns of figures. . . . One group of columns established the bidding order of the seven switchgear manufacturers—a different company, each with its own code number, phasing into the priority position every two weeks (hence "phases of the moon"). A second group of columns, keyed into the company code numbers, established how much each company was to knock off the agreed-upon book price. For example, if it were No 1's (G.E.'s) turn to be low bidder at a certain number of dollars off book, then all Westinghouse (No 2), or Allis-Chalmers (No 3) had to do was look for their code number in the second group of columns to find how many dollars they were to bid *above* No 1. These bids would then be fuzzed up by having a little added to them or taken away by companies 2, 3, etc. Thus, there was not even a hint that the winning bid had been collusively arrived at.[4]

Before stumbling on the "phases of the moon" papers, the Justice Department was having a very hard time proving conspiracy but, with the formula in hand, they were able to put the conspiracy under the spotlight and end it.

Other Strategic Variables

We have focused here on firms that play a simple game and consider only two possible strategies—complying and cheating—concerning two variables—price and quantity produced. However, the approach that we have used can be extended to deal with a much wider range of choices facing firms. For example, a firm has to decide whether to enter or leave an industry; whether to mount an expensive advertising campaign; whether to modify its product; how reliable to make its product (the more reliable a product, usually, the more expensive it is to produce);

---

[4]Richard A. Smith, "The Incredible Electrical Conspiracy," Part II, *Fortune* (May 1961): 210.

whether to price discriminate and if so among which groups of customers and to what degree; whether to undertake a large research and development (R&D) effort aimed at lowering production costs. All of these choices that firms make can be analyzed by using game theory. The basic method of analysis that you have studied can be applied to these problems by working out the payoff for each of the alternative strategies and then finding the equilibrium of the game. Let's look at an example —based on an important, real world case—of an R&D game.

An R&D Game in the Disposable Diaper Industry

Disposable diapers were first marketed in 1966. The two market leaders from the start of this industry have been Procter & Gamble (makers of Pampers) and Kimberly-Clark (makers of Huggies). Procter & Gamble has 60 to 70 percent of the total market while Kimberly-Clark has 25 percent. The disposable diaper industry is fiercely competitive. When the product was first introduced in 1966, it had to be cost-effective in competition against reusable, laundered diapers. A massive research and development effort resulted in the development of machines that could make disposable diapers at a low enough cost to achieve that initial competitive edge. But, as the industry has matured, a large number of firms have tried to get into the business and take market share away from the two industry leaders and the industry leaders themselves have battled against each other to maintain or increase their own market share.

The disposable diaper industry is one in which technological advances that result in small decreases in the average total cost of production can provide an individual firm with an enormous competitive advantage. The current machines can produce disposable diapers at a rate of 3000 an hour—a rate that represents a tenfold increase on the output rate just a decade earlier. The firm that develops and uses the least-cost technology gains a competitive edge, undercutting the rest of the market, increasing its market share, and increasing its profit. But the research and development effort that has to be undertaken to achieve even small cost reductions is itself very costly. This cost of research and development has to be deducted from the profit resulting from the increased market share

Table 14.6 Pampers versus Huggies: An R&D Game

		Procter & Gamble's strategies	
		R&D	No R&D
Kimberly-Clark's strategies	R&D	K-C $ 5m P&G $45m	K-C $85m P&G −$10
	No R&D	K-C −$10m P&G $85m	K-C $30m P&G $70m

If both firms undertake R&D, their payoffs are those shown in the top left square. If neither firm undertakes R&D, their payoffs are in the bottom right square. When one firm undertakes R&D and the other one does not, their payoffs are in the top right and bottom left squares. The dominant strategy equilibrium for this game is for both firms to undertake R&D. The structure of this game is the same as that of the prisoner's dilemma.

that lower costs achieve. If no firm does R&D, every firm can be better off, but if one firm initiates the R&D activity, all must.

Each firm is in a research and development dilemma situation. Table 14.6 illustrates the dilemma (with hypothetical numbers) for the R&D game that Kimberly-Clark and Procter & Gamble are playing. Each firm has two strategies: to spend $25 million a year on R&D, or to spend nothing on R&D. If neither firm spends on R&D, they make a joint profit of $100 million, $30 million for Kimberly-Clark and $70 million for Procter & Gamble (bottom right square in payoff matrix). If each firm conducts R&D, market shares are maintained but each firm's profit is lower, by the amount spent on R&D (top left square of payoff matrix). If Kimberly-Clark pays for R&D but Procter & Gamble does not, Kimberly-Clark gains a large part of Procter & Gamble's market. Kimberly-Clark profits and Procter & Gamble loses (top right square of payoff matrix). Finally, if Procter & Gamble invests in R&D, and Kimberly-Clark does not, Procter & Gamble gains market share from Kimberly-Clark, increasing its profit while Kimberly-Clark makes a loss.

Oligopoly in Action

The Price War Is Here

Saudi Arabia's Oil-production Binge May Cost Its Competitors Dearly

When petroleum prices were doubling and redoubling during the 1970s, oil buyers wondered whether the increases would ever hit a ceiling. Last week the problem was reversed: as global prices continued to plummet, traders despaired about the lack of a firm floor. "The market is in a careening tailspin," said one Manhattan oil-futures analyst. Warned another: "Put on your hard hat. The sky is falling." The price for next month's delivery of West Texas Intermediate, a major U.S. crude, plunged $3.39 on Monday and Tuesday to $15.44 per bbl., its lowest point since 1979 and a nearly 50% decline from just three months ago. Only toward the end of the week did the markets calm down a bit, and the price recovered part of its losses, to finish at $17.68.

The steep slide early in the week occurred when members of the Organization of Petroleum Exporting Countries confirmed that the group has in effect abandoned any effort to curb its production, thus ensuring a worsening global glut. Meeting in Vienna under dark snow clouds, a committee of oil ministers from five OPEC nations—Venezuela, Indonesia, Iraq, Kuwait and the United Arab Emirates—declined to propose any new output limit for the 13-member group. Their decision goes along with the strategy being pursued by Saudi Arabia, Kuwait and other wealthy oil producers, who are flooding the market with excess petroleum. . . .

How did OPEC go from a strategy of one-for-all to a free-for-all? The cartel's disintegration began in 1981, when prices started sliding because of worldwide overproduction, partly caused by consumption cutbacks in many oil-dependent nations. To sop up the surplus, OPEC imposed output limits on its members. But that only provided a chance for such new producers as Mexico and Britain to steal business from OPEC countries, whose market share consequently dropped from 63% in 1979 to 38% currently.

Saudi Arabia tried for years to set an example of self-restraint in OPEC. The country slashed its production from a peak 10.3 million bbl. a day in 1981 to a low of 2 million bbl. a day last June. But gradually the Saudis began to feel that they were being played for a sucker by other OPEC members like Colonel Muammar Gaddafi's Libya, which has exceeded its quotas, and by some non-OPEC countries, which were producing at peak capacity. Finally fed up, the Saudis quietly began opening their spigots last autumn, when a seasonal increase in demand temporarily camouflaged the additional supply. By now the kingdom has more than doubled its output, to nearly 4.5 million bbl. a day.

Time, February 17, 1986
By Stephen Koepp. Reported by Robert Ball/Vienna and Raji Samghabadi/New York, with other bureaus

The Essence of the Story

Background and Analysis

- In the 1970s, oil prices rose sharply.

- In 1986, OPEC abandoned its efforts to curtail production and oil prices fell quickly.

- OPEC's cartel came under pressure in 1981, but Saudi Arabia kept total production limited and maintained high prices by cutting its own output from 10.3 million barrels a day in 1981 to 2 million barrels a day in 1985.

- Other OPEC members produced more than their agreed output, and by 1985 Saudi Arabia decided to abandon its efforts to single-handedly restrain OPEC production.

- OPEC is made up of 13 countries (Algeria, Ecuador, Gabon, Indonesia, Iran, Iraq, Kuwait, Libya, Nigeria, Qatar, Saudi Arabia, United Arab Emirates, and Venezuela) and seeks to achieve the best available returns for its members' exports of crude oil and petroleum products.

- The world oil industry is an oligopoly.

- In 1973, the OPEC producers controlled two thirds of the world's oil supply. In that year, they entered into a collusive agreement to restrict world oil production and raise its price.

- The OPEC producers stuck to their agreement from the early 1970s until 1982.

- Faced with a fall in demand and lower profits, individual OPEC members began to abandon the collusive agreement. By 1985, all members except Saudi Arabia were cheating. In 1985, Saudi Arabia also abandoned the agreement.

- The events just summarized can be understood in terms of the game that we have analyzed in this chapter. The OPEC members are playing an oligopoly game similar to the duopoly game that we have studied.

- They began by colluding and stuck to the agreement for a remarkable length of time. Eventually, responding to falling profits, the smaller producers abandoned the agreement. Ultimately the big producer, Saudi Arabia, abandoned its production limits in order to punish its partners who had previously abandoned their own part of the agreement.

- Although at this writing it has not happened, OPEC has a strong incentive to try to restore its collusive agreement and again restrict output and raise the world price of oil.

369

The two firms, confronted with the payoff matrix in Table 14.6, calculate their best strategies. Kimberly-Clark reasons as follows: If Procter & Gamble does not undertake R&D, we make $85 million if we do and $30 million if we do not; therefore it pays to conduct R&D. If Procter & Gamble conducts R&D, we lose $10 million if we don't and make $5 million if we do. Again, R&D pays off. Thus conducting R&D is a dominant strategy for Kimberly-Clark. It pays Kimberly-Clark to do R&D regardless of Procter & Gamble's decision. Procter & Gamble reasons similarly: If Kimberly-Clark does not undertake R&D, we make $70 million if we follow suit and $85 million if we conduct R&D. It therefore pays to conduct R&D. If Kimberly-Clark does undertake R&D, we make $45 million by doing the same and lose $10 million by not doing R&D. Again, it pays to conduct R&D. So, for Procter & Gamble, R&D is also a dominant strategy. Since R&D is a dominant strategy for both players, it is the Nash equilibrium. The outcome of this game is that both firms conduct R&D. They make lower profits than they would if they could collude to achieve the cooperative outcome of no R&D.

In this real world situation, there are actually more players than Kimberly-Clark and Procter & Gamble. There are a large number of other firms sharing a small portion of the market all of them ready to eat into the share of Procter & Gamble and Kimberly-Clark. So, the R&D effort by these two firms not only serves the purpose of maintaining shares in their own battle, but helps to keep barriers to the entry of other firms high enough to preserve their joint market share.

■ We have now studied the four main market types—perfect competition, monopolistic competition, oligopoly, and monopoly—and discovered how prices and outputs, revenue, cost, and profit are determined in these industries. We have used the various models to make predictions about behavior and to assess the efficiency of alternative market structures. A key element in our analysis of the markets for goods and services is the behavior of costs. Costs are determined partly by technology and partly by the prices of factors of production. We have treated those factor prices as given. It is now time to turn our attention to an examination of the way in which factor prices are themselves determined. Factor prices interact with the goods market that we have just studied in two ways. First, they determine the firm's production costs. Second, they determine household incomes and therefore influence the demand for goods and services. Factor prices also have an important effect upon the distribution of income. The firms that we've been studying in the past five chapters decide *how* to produce; the interactions of households and firms in the markets for goods and services decide *what* will be produced. But the factor prices determined in the markets for factors of production determine *for whom* the various goods and services are produced.

S U M M A R Y

Varieties of Market Structure

Most industries in the real world lie between the extremes of perfect competition and monopoly. The degree of competition is sometimes measured by the concentration ratio. The four-firm concentration ratio measures the percentage of the value of the sales of an industry accounted for by its four largest firms. High concentration ratios indicate a relatively low degree of competition and vice versa, with some important qualifications. There are three key problems related to concentration ratios: (1) con-

centration ratios refer to the national market, but some industries are local while others are international; (2) concentration ratios do not tell us about the degree of turnover of firms and the ease of entry; and (3) some firms classified in one particular industry operate in several others.

There are two models of industries that lie between monopoly and perfect competition: monopolistic competition and oligopoly. Monopolistic competition is a market type where a large number of firms compete, each making a slightly differentiated product from the others by competing on price, quality, and advertising. Oligopoly is a market type in which a small number of firms compete with each other and in which the actions of any one firm have an important impact on the profit of the others. (pp. 343–346)

Monopolistic Competition

Monopolistic competition occurs when a large number of firms compete with each other by making slightly different products. Under monopolistic competition, each firm faces a downward-sloping demand curve and so has to choose its price as well as its output level. Because there is free entry, in long-run equilibrium zero economic profit is earned. When profit is maximized, with marginal cost equal to marginal revenue, average cost also equals price in the long run. But average cost is not at its minimum point. That is, in monopolistic competition firms operate with excess capacity. (pp. 346–349)

Oligopoly

Oligopoly is a situation in which a small number of producers compete with each other. The key feature of oligopoly is that the firms strategically interact. Each firm has to take into account the effects of its own actions on the behavior of other firms and the effects of the actions of other firms on its own profit.

Game theory is a method of analyzing strategic interaction. Game theory focuses on three aspects of a game:

• Rules
• Strategies
• Payoffs

The rules of the oligopoly game specify the permissible actions by the players. These actions are limited only by the legal code and involve such things as raising or lowering prices; raising or lowering output; raising or lowering advertising effort; enhancing or not enhancing the product. The strategies in the oligopoly game are all the possible actions that each player can take given the action of the other player. The payoff of the oligopoly game is the player's profit or loss. It depends on the actions of both the players and on the constraints imposed by the market, technology, and input costs. (pp. 349–353)

The Prisoner's Dilemma

Duopoly is a market structure in which there are two producers of a good competing against each other. Duopoly is a special case of oligopoly. The duopoly game is similar to the prisoner's dilemma game. Two prisoners are faced with the problem of deciding whether or not to confess to a crime. If neither confesses, they are tried for a lesser crime and receive a light penalty. If both confess, they receive a higher penalty. If one confesses and the other does not confess, the one confessing receives the lightest of all penalties and the one not confessing receives a very heavy penalty.

The prisoner's dilemma has a dominant strategy Nash equilibrium. That is, regardless of the action of the other player there is a unique best action for each player—to confess. (pp. 353–357)

A Duopoly Game

A duopoly game can be constructed in which two firms contemplate the consequences of colluding to achieve a monopoly profit or of cheating on the collusive agreement to make a bigger profit at the expense of the other firm. Such a game is identical to the prisoner's dilemma. The equilibrium of the game will be one in which both firms cheat on the agreement. The industry output will be the same in this case as it would be if the industry was perfectly competitive. The industry price will also be the competitive price and firms will make zero economic profit. If the firms are able to enforce the collusive agreement, the industry will look exactly like a monopoly industry. Price, output, and profit will be the same as in a monopoly.

If a game is repeated indefinitely, there is an opportunity for one player to punish another player for previous "bad" behavior. In such a situation, a tit-for-tat strategy can produce an equilibrium in which both firms stick to the agreement. A tit-for-tat strategy is one in which the players begin by colluding. If one player cheats, the other player responds at the next play by also cheating. Since each knows that it pays the other to respond in this manner, no one cheats. This equilibrium is a cooperative equilibrium—one in which each player cooperates because such behavior is a rational response to the credible threat of the other to inflict damage if the agreement is broken. Uncertainty makes it possible for such an equilibrium to break down from time to time. (p. 357–365)

Games and Price Wars

Price wars can be interpreted as the outcome of a repeated duopoly game. The competing firms comply with the agreement unless market forces bring about a sufficiently large fall in price. A large fall in price is responded to as if it had resulted from the other firm cheating. Only by responding in this manner can each firm maintain the credible threat that it will punish a cheat and thereby ensure that the ever-present temptation to cheat is held in check and the monopoly agreement maintained. When market conditions bring about an increase in price, the firms revert to their cooperative behavior. Industries will go through cycles, starting with a monopoly price and output and occasionally, when demand falls by enough, temporarily pursuing non-cooperative actions. At these times, the industry price and output will be the competitive ones. (p. 366)

Other Strategic Variables

Firms in oligopolistic industries have to make a large range of decisions: Whether to enter or leave an industry; how much to spend on advertising; whether to modify its product; whether to price discriminate; whether to undertake research and development. All these choices result in payoffs for the firm and the other firms in the industry and a game can be constructed to predict the outcome of such choices.

An interesting real world example is the research and development game played between producers of disposable diapers. The equilibrium of that game results in a large amount of research and development being undertaken and lower profits than would emerge if the firms could collude somehow to keep out new entrants and undertake less research and development. Thus that game is similar to the prisoner's dilemma. (pp. 366–370)

KEY CONCEPTS

Key Figures and Tables

REVIEW QUESTIONS

1 What are the main varieties of market structure? What are the main characteristics of each of those market structures?

2 What is a four-firm concentration ratio? If the four-firm concentration ratio is 90 percent, what does that mean?

3 Give some examples of U.S. industries that have a high concentration ratio and of U.S. industries that have a low concentration ratio.

4 What are barriers to entry? Give some examples of barriers to entry that exist in the U.S. economy?

5 Explain how a firm can differentiate its product.

6 What is the difference between monopolistic competition and perfect competition?

7 Is monopolistic competition more efficient or less efficient than perfect competition?

8 What is the difference between duopoly and oligopoly?

9 What is the essential feature of both duopoly and oligopoly?

10 List the key features that all games have in common with each other.

11 What are the features of duopoly that make it reasonable to treat duopoly as a game between two firms?

12 What is the prisoner's dilemma?

13 What is a dominant strategy equilibrium?

14 What is meant by a repeated game?

15 Explain what a tit-for-tat strategy is.

16 What is a price war? What is the effect of a price war on the profit of the firms in the industry and on the profitability of the industry itself?

PROBLEMS

1 A monopolistically competitive industry is in long-run equilibrium as illustrated in Fig. 14.1(b). An increase in demand for the industry's product shifts the demand curves of each firm to the right. Using diagrams similar to those in Fig. 14.1, analyze the short-run and long-run effects on price, output, and profit of this change in demand.

2 Another monopolistically competitive industry is in long-run equilibrium, as illustrated in Fig. 14.1(b), when it experiences a large increase in wages which raises the costs of all the firms. Using diagrams similar to those in Fig. 14.1, analyze the short-run and long-run effects on price, output, and profit of this change in costs.

3 Describe the game known as the prisoner's dilemma. In describing the game:

a) Make up a story that motivates the game.

b) Work out a payoff matrix.

c) Describe how the equilibrium of the game is arrived at.

4 Consider the following game. There are two players and they are each asked a question. They can answer the question honestly or they can lie. If they both answer honestly, they each receive a payoff of $100. If one answers honestly and the other lies, the liar gains at the expense of the honest player. In that event, the liar receives a profit of $500 and the honest player gets nothing. If they both lie, then they each receive a payoff of $50.

a) Describe this game in terms of its players, strategies, and payoffs.

b) Construct the payoff matrix.

c) What is the equilibrium for this game?

5 Explain the behavior of oil prices by using a repeated prisoner's dilemma game.

Part 6

Talking
with
Orley
Ashenfelter

O rley Ashenfelter is a professor of economics at Princeton University and director of the Industrial Relations Section of the Woodrow Wilson School. He has held visiting appointments in the U.S. Department of Labor. His work has covered various aspects of the labor market, including the relationship between racial discrimination and trade union behavior and the determinants of labor supply. He also works in the area of dispute resolution and arbitration systems. Michael Parkin spoke with Dr. Ashenfelter about labor economics and about the nature of empirical economics.

Professor Ashenfelter, what first drew you to economics?

I enjoyed economics from the very first course I took. I found it easy, if you can believe that. I went to graduate school on the recommendation of the professor who taught me labor economics, who claimed that academia was the only place you could do economics where there was a demand for—and payment for—honest opinions. I've always valued that.

Why do you think economics seemed easy to you?

Beginning students are often troubled by the powerful hypothesis that people act in their own self-interest, but that assumption always seemed perfectly natural to me. The practical conse-

"Academia was the only place you could do economics where there was a demand for honest opinions."

quences of rational self-interest didn't seem harmful. Sometimes students get this economic assumption confused with the moral judgments people make in other contexts about whether it's wrong to act in your own self-interest. But if you find it a hospitable assumption in the context of economic analysis, then you'll find that the questions your professors ask you on exams will also seem completely natural.

How did you become interested in labor economics in particular?

I think my family background contributed. My father belonged to a trade union most of his life. I worked in a factory in the summers during college. At that time, in the late 1950s, there was substantial unemployment in my part of California. When a human resource—a person—is underutilized—out of work or in the wrong job—it has always seemed to me to be more of a waste, in human terms, than when a machine is down. Labor problems have always seemed to be a more important set of concerns than most others.

One of the most controversial issues in the labor market deals with discrimination of all kinds. Against blacks, or women, or young people, for example. Are economic tools useful in studying the extent and effects of discrimination?

The study of discrimination originated as a study of an anomaly in the labor market. As an economist, if you look at equally qualified workers, you expect to find that their wage rates would be unrelated to race, sex, or any such personal characteristic. But the data have shown many times that there *has* historically been a correlation between pay and race or sex. If you think that employers are acting in their self-interest, then any difference in wage rates between equally qualified groups of workers ought to lead rational employers to hire only the workers who are discriminated *against*. Once they have hired the workers that had been earning less, the difference in pay between the two groups should disappear. In other words, most economic theories imply that there isn't actually discrimination in the long run. But that doesn't explain the facts.

How do you, as an economist, explain the facts?

The economic model doesn't work that well here, probably because employers abide by cultural constraints. I'll give you an example. Jim Heckman, at Yale, has studied the employment of black workers in the South Carolina textile industry. Apparently, employers used the 1964 Civil Rights Act to break down racial discrimination, which was a cultural institution that forced them to act against their own self-interest. Until 1965, there were no black workers to speak of in that industry, even though there had been a terrific labor shortage of white workers since 1954. Naturally, the wage rates of the white workers were increasing dramatically. Many employers would have liked to hire black workers, and ease the labor shortage, but they didn't. Not until 1965, when the employers announced that the government was forcing them to hire black workers—which was in their interest also. All of a sudden, there was an enormous increase in the hiring of black workers in the textile industry. Wages began to level off. The labor shortage disappeared. The only way you can account for these events is by looking at the cultural factors.

What about the role of labor unions?

I have studied in great detail the occurrence of discrimination against blacks in the labor unions themselves. My experience in looking at these issues reveals how important I think empirical economics is. In the 1960s, I began to wonder whether black workers would be as likely as white workers to belong to trade unions. I couldn't get any data, no numbers, on that question. There wasn't much progress on this question until the late 1960s when the Office of Economic Opportunity sponsored a government survey. That information suggested that black workers are better off with trade unions, or at least not worse off.

The union movement has been in decline in recent years. Why is that?

No one really knows. To understand unions, you have to realize that unions act as agents for workers. Everyone would like to have the kinds of agents that movie stars have, but they're expensive. A union is a cost-effective way of providing agents for workers. Of course, agents have drawbacks. The interests of the agent may not be precisely the same as the interests of the people they represent. It may be that workers today in new industries and occupations don't see the value of unions acting as their agents. My personal belief is that the union movement will grow again if it can find a way of providing cost-effective services as agents for the new kinds of jobs in service, high-tech, and government sectors.

"Economic theories imply that there isn't discrimination in the long run. But that doesn't explain the facts."

What are some of the ways to do empirical economics and get solid answers?

Experiments in the field —where you actually take an idea and test it with real people in a real economy—have much higher credibility than any other kind of work in empirical economics. Of course, they're very hard to carry out. Recently, one remarkable field experiment, the Illinois Unemployment Insurance Bonus, looked at ways to lower unemployment insurance payments and simultaneously help unemployed workers. Some economists have wondered whether people look hard enough for a

new job when they're collecting unemployment insurance. So in this experiment, half the people

in certain unemployment offices were offered the following: If you get a job within 10 weeks of collecting your unemployment benefits and keep it for six months, you'll get your insurance *and* a $500 bonus. There was a dramatic drop in unemployment among the people that were offered the bonus.

What principles have been most important to you and your work?

I've always tried to understand the fundamental tension between any

simple economic model and the real world. To recognize the limitations of any model by measuring variations in the real world. Understanding those variations deepens and expands your original model. It allows you to quantify your predictions as a probability. And if you predict right more often than not, then you're improving economic policy.

What advice would you give to a student

interested in studying economics?

I'd say that you should study economics because you love it, not because of any vocational reason. Ninety percent of an economist's job is doing the work, not getting the answers. If you care about the problems that economics tries to deal with and if you like doing the work itself, then you'll do really interesting research. Of course, then it's hard to keep your strong feelings from influencing your work. I'll pass on the advice that my former teacher, Richard Musgrave, shared with me—let your interests and passions guide you in choosing the questions you ask, but keep those passions out of the answers you form.

"Ninety percent of an economist's job is doing the work, not getting the answers."

Chapter 15

Pricing and Allocating Factors of Production

After studying this chapter, you will be able to:

- Explain how firms choose the quantities of labor, capital, and land to employ in their production activities

- Explain how households choose the quantities of labor, capital, and land to supply

- Explain how wages, interest, and rent are determined in competitive factor markets

- Explain the concept of economic rent

- Distinguish between economic rent and transfer earnings

I t may not be your birthday and, even if it is, chances are that you are spending most of the day working. But at the end of the week, or month (or, if you're devoting all your time to college, when you graduate), you will receive the *returns* from your labor. ■ Of course, those returns vary a lot from one person to another and from one kind of job to another. An average person in full-time employment in 1987 earned $21,000—about $12 an hour. Most of us are clustered around that average. Such a person is Pedro Lopez. Pedro spends his day in a small container, suspended by cables attached to the top of Chicago's John Hancock Tower. With the wind whipping off Lake Michigan, and with chilly toes, fingers and ears, Pedro cleans the several acres of glass that form

Many Happy Returns

the windows of that skyscraper. Pedro works hard for his $12 an hour, but when those happy returns come in at the end of the week, it all seems worthwhile. ■ For some workers, the returns are very happy indeed. Dan Rather is one such work-er. Dan collects a cool $3.6 million a year for that 30-minute news show he puts on each weekday evening. And he's not alone on those dizzy heights of happy paychecks. Barbara Walters, Tom Brokaw, Bryant Gumbel, and Diane Sawyer are all up there with him in the million-dollar plus annual pay range. ■ At the other extreme are those working for the minimum wage and, in some cases, for even less than the minimum wage. Student help at McDonald's and farm workers in the fields of southern California labor away for just a few dollars an hour. But even for those workers, the returns are worthwhile. Sure they'd like more, but they prefer working for low wages than not working at all and having no income. ■ What determines the wages that we are paid? What determines the kinds of jobs we do? How does our economy allocate its labor resources to the many thousands of different tasks that must be performed?

■ Most of us have little trouble spending our pay. But most of us manage to save some of what we earn. Some of our savings we put on deposit in the bank or at the savings and loan. With some we buy bonds and stocks. The returns that we get on our savings depend on which of these various things we do with them. If we put the money in the bank or in a savings and loan, we earn interest on it. If we buy bonds and stocks, we're paid a dividend and enjoy stock price increases—or suffer decreases. The size of our return on a stock depends on the company whose stock we've bought. We may be lucky and get a huge return or unlucky and get little or nothing at all. For example, the people who invested in Service Merchandise, a Nashville-based retail company, made a staggering 400 percent return in 1988; those investing in Borman's, Inc., the Detroit-based supermarket chain, doubled their money; and those investing in Murray Ohio, a bicycle maker, almost doubled theirs. But the people buying Texas American Bancshares, a troubled Texas bank, and Berkey, Inc., a photographic processing concern in White Plains, New York, gave their money away. The value of those investments fell by 90 percent. ■ What determines the amount of saving that people do and the returns they make on that saving? How do the returns on saving influence the allocation of savings across the many industries and activities that use our capital resources? ■ Savings can also be used to buy land. That use of a person's savings generates a return in the form of rent. The amount of rent earned varies enormously with the location and quality of land. For example, if you buy an acre of farmland in Iowa, you will be able to rent it out for something approaching $1000 a year. If you buy a block on Chicago's "Magnificent Mile," you'd collect several million dollars a year in rent income. ■ What determines the rent that people are willing to pay for different blocks of land? Why are rents so enormously high in big cities and so relatively low in the great farming regions of the nation? ■ It is not only land rents that are much higher in cities than in other parts of the country. Many of the things we buy are more expensive in a city than in a small town. For example, a cup of coffee that costs a quarter in your university cafeteria costs 50¢ in a central city snack bar, $1.25 in New York City, and $2 in Tokyo. Why? Obvious, you answer. High rent leads to high cost, so coffee shops in high rent areas have to charge high prices for their coffee. But wait! Is it high rents that lead to high prices of coffee in big cities, or is it that a high demand for coffee leads to high prices which in turn lead to high rents?

■ In this and the following three chapters, we deal with the kinds of questions that have just been posed. We study markets for factors of production—for labor, capital, and land—and learn how the prices of these factors of production are determined. This first chapter provides an overview of all three types of factor markets and also introduces you to the important concept of economic rent. It begins by introducing you to the terminology of factor markets and setting out the link between factor prices and incomes.

Factor Prices and Incomes

Factors of production are divided into three broad categories: *labor, capital,* and *land.* (We defined these factors of production in Chapter 1, p. 14.) The owners of factors of production receive an income from the firms that use those factors as inputs into their production activities. These incomes are *wages* paid for labor, *interest* paid for capital, and *rent* paid for land. Wages include all labor income including salaries, commissions, and any other supplementary forms of income paid in compensation for labor. Interest includes all forms of capital income including dividends paid by firms. Rent is the income paid for the use of land and natural resources. Apartment rents include an element of rent and also an element of interest—a payment for the use of capital.

Labor is by far the most important factor of production and generates about 70 percent of all income, and that percentage has been steadily increasing over the years.

In the rest of this chapter, we're going to build a model of a factor market. We'll use that model to determine factor prices, the quantities of factors traded, and the incomes that factors of production earn.

An Overview

Factor prices are determined in factor markets, and we can understand those prices by using the model of demand and supply. The quantity of a factor of production demanded depends upon the factor's price. That is, the quantity of labor demanded

Figure 15.1   Demand and Supply in a
Factor Market

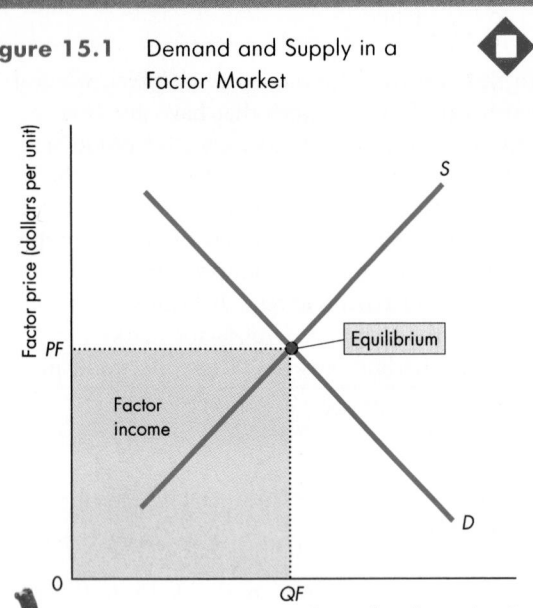

The demand curve for a factor of production (D) slopes downward and the supply curve (S) slopes upward. Where the demand and supply curves intersect, the factor price (PF) and the
quantity of a factor traded (QF) are determined. The factor
income is the product of the factor price and the quantity, as
represented by the blue rectangle of the factor.

depends on the wage rate, the quantity of capital
demanded depends on the interest rate, and the
quantity of land demanded depends on the rent. The
law of demand applies to factors of production just as
it applies to all other economic entities. Thus as the
price of a factor of production decreases, the quantity
of the factor demanded increases. The demand curve
for a factor of production is shown in Fig. 15.1 as
the curve labeled D.

The quantity supplied of a factor of production
depends on its price. With some exceptions that we'll
identify later in this chapter, the law of supply applies to factors of production, so that as the price of a
factor of production increases, the quantity of the
factor supplied increases. The supply of a factor of
production is shown in Fig. 15.1 as the curve
labeled S.

The equilibrium factor price is determined at
the point of intersection of the factor demand and
factor supply curves. Figure 15.1 shows such an equilibrium—QF is the quantity of the factor of production traded and PF is the factor price.

The income earned by a factor of production is
its price multiplied by the quantity traded. In this
case, the price is measured by the distance from the
origin to PF in Fig. 15.1, and the quantity traded is
measured by the distance from the origin to QF. The
factor income is the product of these two distances
and it is equivalent to the blue shaded area in the
figure.

All the influences on the quantity of a factor
bought other than its price result in a shift in the
factor demand curve. We'll study what those influences are in the next section. For now, let's simply
work out the effects of a change in the demand for a
factor of production. An increase in demand for a
factor of production, as illustrated in Fig. 15.2(a),
shifts the demand curve to the right, leading to an
increase in the quantity of the factor traded and an
increase in its price. Thus when the demand curve
shifts from D_0 to D_1, the quantity traded increases
from QF_0 to QF_1 and the price increases from PF_0 to
PF_1. An increase in the demand for a factor of
production increases that factor's income. The dark
blue area in Fig. 15.2(a) illustrates the increase in
income.

When the demand for a factor of production
decreases, its demand curve shifts to the left. Figure
15.2(b) illustrates the effects of a decrease in demand: the demand curve shifts to the left from D_0 to
D_2; the quantity traded decreases from QF_0 to QF_2;
and the price decreases from PF_0 to PF_2. When the
demand for a factor of production decreases, the
income of that factor also decreases. The light blue
area in Fig. 15.2(b) illustrates the decrease in income.

The extent to which a change in the demand
for a factor of production changes the factor price and
the quantity traded depends on the elasticity of supply. If the supply curve is very flat (supply is elastic),
the change in the quantity traded is large and the
change in price is small. If the supply curve is very
steep (supply is inelastic), the change in the price is
large and the change in the quantity traded
is small.

A change in the supply of a factor of production also changes the price and quantity traded as
well as the income earned by those supplying the
factor. An increase in supply results in an increase in
the quantity traded and a decrease in the factor price.
A decrease in supply results in a decrease in the
quantity traded and an increase in the factor price.
But whether a change in supply increases or decreases
income depends on the elasticity of demand for the
factor.

Figure 15.2   Changes in Demand

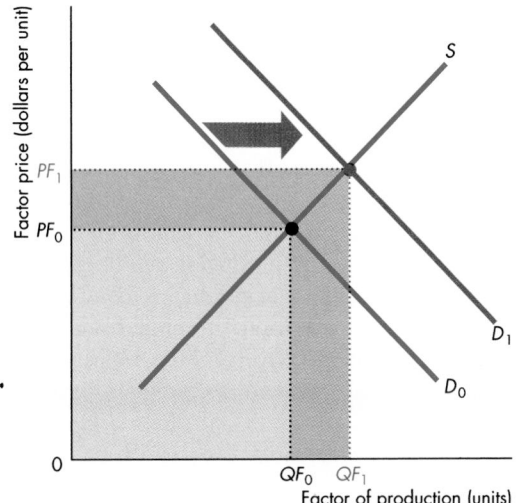

(a) An increase in demand

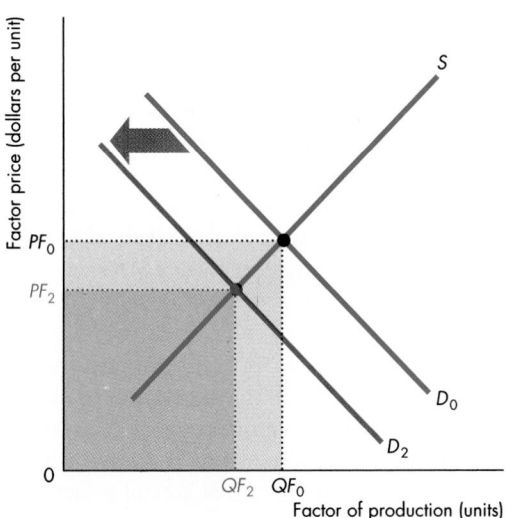

(b) A decrease in demand

An increase in the demand for a factor of production (part a) shifts its demand curve to the right — from D_0 to D_1. The quantity traded increases from QF_0 to QF_1 and the price increases from PF_0 to PF_1. The factor income increases, and that income increase is shown by the dark blue area. A decrease in the demand for a factor of production, from D_0 to D_2, results in a decrease in the quantity traded, from QF_0 to QF_2, and a decrease in the factor price, from PF_0 to PF_2. The decrease in demand results in a decrease in the factor income. That decrease in income is illustrated by the light blue area.

Figure 15.3   Factor Income and Demand Elasticity

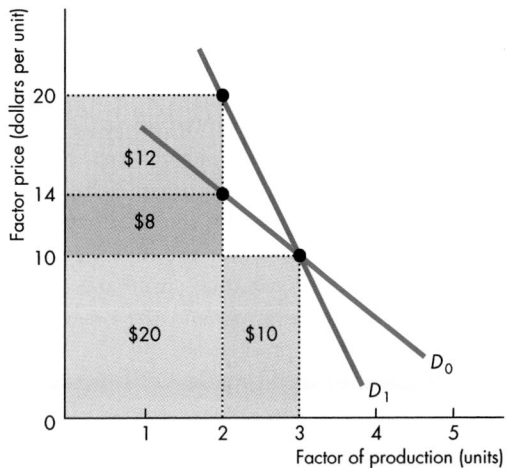

A decrease in the quantity traded of a factor of production may result in a decrease or an increase in the factor's income. If the demand curve is D_0 (an elastic demand curve over the relevant range), a decrease in the quantity traded, from 3 to 2, results in a decrease in the factor income, from $30 to $28. If the demand curve is D_1 (an inelastic demand curve over the relevant range), a decrease in the quantity traded, from 3 to 2, results in an increase in the factor's income, from $30 to $40.

Suppose that the quantity traded of the factor of production illustrated in Fig. 15.3 decreases from 3 units to 2 units. Initially, the price is $10 a unit. If the demand curve is D_0, the decrease in supply results in an increase in the price of the factor but a decrease in the income of those supplying this factor of production. You can see that income decreases by multiplying the factor price by the quantity traded. Initially, when 3 units are traded at a price of $10 each, the income earned by the suppliers of this factor of production is $30 (the $20 light blue area plus the $10 red area). When the quantity traded decreases to 2 units and the price increases to $14, income decreases (by the $10 red area) but increases (by the $8 dark blue area), for a net decrease to $28. Over the range of the price change that we've just considered, the demand curve D_0 is elastic — its elasticity is greater than 1.

Conversely, suppose that the demand curve is D_1. In this case, when the quantity traded decreases to 2 units, the price increases to $20 a unit. Income increases to $40. The smaller quantity traded lowers income by $10 (red area), but the higher factor price increases income by $20 (dark blue plus green areas). Over the range of the price change that we've just considered, the demand curve D_1 is inelastic—its elasticity is less than 1.

The markets for factors of production determine factor prices in much the same way as goods markets determine the prices of goods and services. These markets also determine factor incomes. Factor income is the factor price multiplied by the quantity of the factor traded. Thus to work out the influences on incomes we have to pay attention simultaneously to the determination of the prices and the quantities traded of the factors of production.

We're going to spend the rest of this chapter exploring more closely the influences on the demand for and supply of factors of production. We're also going to discover what determines the elasticities of supply and demand for factors. These elasticities are important because of their effects on factor prices and the incomes earned. Let's begin by studying the demand for inputs.

Demand for Factors

The demand for any factor of production is a derived demand. A **derived demand** is a demand for an input not for its own sake but in order to use it in the production of goods and services. A firm's derived demand for inputs depends on the constraints the firm faces—its technology constraint and its market constraint. It also depends on the firm's objective. The objective of the model firms that we have studied is to maximize profit. We'll continue to study the behavior of such firms.

A firm's demand for factors stems from its profit-maximization decision. *What* to produce and *how* to produce it are the questions that the firm must answer in order to make maximum profit. Those choices have implications for the firm's demand for inputs, which we'll now investigate.

Profit Maximization

A firm's inputs fall into two categories: fixed and variable. In most industries, the fixed inputs are capital (i.e., plant, machinery, and buildings) and land; and the variable inputs are labor and raw materials. A firm meets permanent changes in output by changing the scale of its inputs of capital and land. It meets short-run variations in output by varying its labor and raw material inputs.

Profit-maximizing firms produce the output at which marginal cost equals marginal revenue. This principle holds true whether the firm is in a perfectly competitive industry, in monopolistic competition, in oligopoly, or a monopoly. If one more unit of output adds less to total cost than it adds to total revenue, the firm can increase its profit by producing more. A firm maximizes profit by producing the output at which the additional cost of producing one more unit of output equals the additional revenue from selling it. If we shift our perspective slightly, we can also state the condition for maximum profit in terms of the marginal cost of an input and the marginal revenue that input generates. Let's see how.

Marginal Revenue Product and Factor Price

The change in total revenue resulting from employing one more unit of any factor is called the factor's **marginal revenue product.** The concept of marginal revenue product sounds a bit like the concept of marginal revenue that you have met before. These concepts are indeed related but there is an important distinction between the two. *Marginal revenue product* is the extra revenue generated as a result of employing one extra unit of a factor; *marginal revenue* is the extra revenue generated as a result of selling one additional unit of output.

A profit-maximizing firm hires the quantity of a factor that makes the marginal revenue product of the factor equal to the marginal cost of the factor. For a firm that buys its factors of production in competitive factor markets, the marginal cost of a factor is the factor's price. That is, in a competitive factor market, each firm is such a small demander of the factor that it has no influence on its price. The firm simply has to pay the going factor price—market wage rate for labor, interest rate for capital, and rent for land. We have defined the additional revenue resulting from employing one more unit of a factor as the factor's marginal revenue product. We have seen that in competitive factor markets, the marginal cost of a factor equals its price. Therefore a profit-maximizing firm—a firm that makes the marginal revenue product equal to the marginal cost of each input —hires each factor up to the point at which its

Table 15.1   Marginal Revenue Product and Average Revenue Product at Max's Wash 'n' Wax

	Quantity of labor L (workers)	Output Q (cars washed per hour)	Marginal product of labor MP = ΔQ/ΔL (washes per worker)	Total revenue TR = P × Q (dollars)	Marginal revenue product MRP = ΔTR/ΔL (dollars per worker)	Average revenue product ARP = TR/L (dollars per worker)
a	0	0		0		
			5		20	
b	1	5		20		20
			4		16	
c	2	9		36		18
			3		12	
d	3	12		48		16
			2		8	
e	4	14		56		14
			1		4	
f	5	15		60		12

The marginal revenue product of labor is the change in total revenue that results from a one-unit increase in labor input. To calculate marginal revenue product, first work out total revenue. If Max hires 1 worker (row b), output is 5 washes an hour, and total revenue, at $4 a wash, is $20. If he hires 2 workers (row c), output is 9 washes an hour, and total revenue is $36. By hiring the second worker, total revenue rises by $16—the marginal revenue product of labor is $16. The average revenue product of labor is total revenue per unit of labor employed. For example, when Max employs 2 workers, total revenue is $36, and average revenue product is $18 ($36 divided by 2).

marginal revenue product equals the factor's price. As the price of a factor varies, the quantity demanded of it also varies. The lower the price of a factor, the larger is the quantity demanded of that factor. Let's illustrate this proposition by working through an example—that of labor.

The Firm's Demand for Labor

Labor is a variable input. A firm can change the quantity of labor it employs in both the short run and the long run. Let's focus first on a firm's short-run demand for labor.

A firm's short-run technology constraint is described by its *short-run production function*. Table 15.1 sets out the production function for a car wash operated by Max's Wash 'n' Wax. (This production function is similar to the one that we studied in Chapter 10, Fig. 10.1.) The numbers in the first two columns of the table tell us how the maximum number of car washes each hour varies as the amount of labor

employed varies. The third column shows the *marginal product of labor*—the change in output resulting from a one-unit increase in labor input. (Since marginal product refers to a *change* in the quantity of labor employed, these numbers appear midway between the two levels of employment from which they are calculated.) Max's market constraint is the demand curve for his product. If in the goods market a firm is a monopoly or engaged in monopolistic competition or oligopoly, it faces a downward-sloping demand curve for its product. If a firm is perfectly competitive, it faces a fixed price for its product regardless of its output level and therefore faces a horizontal demand curve for its product. We will assume that Max operates his car wash in a perfectly competitive market and can sell as many washes as he chooses at a constant price of $4 a wash. Given this information, we can calculate Max's total revenue (fourth column) by multiplying the number of cars washed per hour by $4. For example, if 9 cars are washed each hour (row c), total revenue is $36.

Table 15.2   A Compact Glossary of Factor Market Terms

Factors of production	Labor, capital, and land (including raw materials)
Factor prices	Wages—price of labor; interest—price of capital; rent—price of land
Marginal product	Output produced by last unit of input hired; e.g., the marginal product of labor is additional output produced by employing one more person
Average product	Output per unit of input; e.g., average product of labor is output divided by labor input
Marginal revenue	Revenue resulting from selling one additional unit of output
Marginal revenue product	Revenue resulting from hiring one additional unit of a factor of production; e.g., the marginal revenue product of labor is the additional revenue resulting from selling the output produced by employing one more person.
Average revenue product	Total revenue per unit of input; calculated as total revenue divided by labor input

The fifth column shows the calculation of marginal revenue product of labor—the change in total revenue per unit change in labor input. For example, if Max hires a second worker (row c), total revenue increases from $20 to $36, so marginal revenue product is $16. There is an alternative way of calculating the marginal revenue product of labor—multiply marginal product by marginal revenue. To see that this method gives the same answer, multiply the marginal product of hiring a second worker—4 cars an hour—by marginal revenue—$4 a car—and notice that we get the same $16 as before.

Total revenue divided by the quantity of the factor hired is called the **average revenue product** of the factor. Thus average revenue product is the average contribution of each unit of an input to the firm's total revenue. The last column of Table 15.1 shows the average revenue product of labor. For example, when Max employs 3 workers (row d), total revenue is $48. Thus the average revenue product of labor is $48 divided by 3 workers, which is $16 per worker.

Notice that as the quantity of labor rises, the marginal revenue product of labor falls. When Max hires the first worker, the marginal revenue product of labor is $20. If Max hires a second worker, the marginal revenue product of labor is $16. Marginal revenue product of labor continues to decline as Max hires more workers.

Marginal revenue product diminishes as Max hires more workers because of the principle of dimin-

ishing returns that we first studied in Chapter 10. With each additional worker hired, the marginal product of labor falls and so brings in a smaller marginal revenue product. Because Max's Wash 'n' Wax is a perfectly competitive firm, the price of each additional car wash is the same and brings in the same marginal revenue. If instead Max had a monopoly, he would have to lower his price to sell more washes. In such a case, the marginal revenue product of labor diminishes even more quickly than in perfectly competitive conditions. Marginal revenue product diminishes because of diminishing marginal product of labor and also because of diminishing marginal revenue. Table 15.2 provides a compact glossary of factor market terms.

We can illustrate the marginal revenue product and average revenue product of labor as curves. The **average revenue product curve** shows the average revenue product of a factor at each quantity of the factor hired. The **marginal revenue product curve** shows the marginal revenue product of a factor at each quantity of the factor hired. Figure 15.4(a) shows the marginal revenue product and average revenue product curves for workers employed by Max. Let's study this figure.

The horizontal axis measures the number of workers that Max hires and the vertical axis measures the marginal and average revenue product of labor. The curve labeled *ARP* is the average revenue product curve and is based on the numbers in Table 15.1. For example, point d on the *ARP* curve represents

Figure 15.4   Marginal Revenue Product and
the Demand for Labor at Max's
Wash 'n' Wax

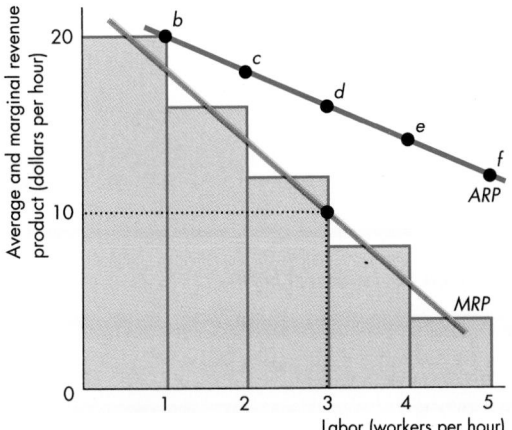

(a) Average and marginal revenue product

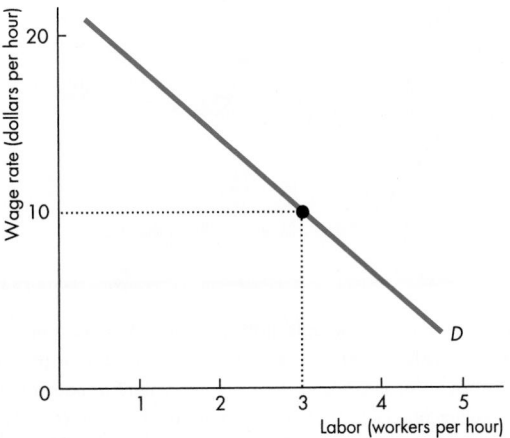

(b) Demand for labor

Part (a) shows the average and marginal revenue product
curves for Max's Wash 'n' Wax. Points *b* through *f* on the
average revenue product curve correspond to the rows of Table
15.1. The blue bars representing marginal revenue product are
also based on the numbers in that table. (Each point is plotted
midway between the labor inputs used in its calculation.) Average revenue product and marginal revenue product decline and
the marginal revenue product curve is always below the average revenue product curve. Part (b) shows Max's demand for
labor curve. It is identical to his marginal revenue product curve.
Max demands labor up to the point at which the wage rate (the
worker's marginal cost) equals marginal revenue product.

row *d* in the table. Max employs 3 workers and the
average revenue product of labor is $16 a worker.
The blue bars show the marginal revenue product of
labor as Max employs more workers. These bars correspond to the numbers in Table 15.1. The curve
MRP is the marginal revenue product curve.

The firm's demand for labor curve is based on
its marginal revenue product curve. You can see
Max's demand for labor curve (*D*) in Fig. 15.4(b).
The horizontal axis measures the number of workers
hired—the same as part (a). The vertical axis measures the wage rate in dollars per hour. The demand
for labor curve is exactly the same as the firm's
marginal revenue product curve. For example, when
Max employs 3 workers an hour, his marginal revenue product is $10 an hour, as in Fig. 15.4(a); and
at a wage rate of $10 an hour, Max hires 3 workers
an hour, as in Fig. 15.4(b).

But why is the demand for labor curve identical
to the marginal revenue product curve? Because the
firm hires the profit-maximizing quantity of labor. If
the cost of hiring one more worker—the wage rate—
is less than the additional revenue that worker will
bring in—the marginal revenue product of labor—
then it pays the firm to employ one more worker.
Conversely, if the cost of hiring one more worker is
greater than the additional revenue that worker will
bring in—the wage rate exceeds the marginal revenue product—then it does not pay the firm to employ one more worker. When the cost of the last
worker hired equals the revenue brought in by that
worker, the firm is making the maximum possible
profit. Such a situation occurs when the wage rate
equals the marginal revenue product. Thus the quantity of labor demanded by the firm is such that the
wage rate equals the marginal revenue product of
labor.

R E V I E W

A firm chooses the quantity of labor to hire so that
its profit is maximized. The additional total revenue generated by hiring one additional worker is
called the marginal revenue product of labor. It is
the change in total revenue generated by a one-unit
change in labor input. In a competitive industry,
the marginal cost of labor is the wage rate. Profit is

maximized when the marginal revenue product of labor equals the wage rate. The marginal revenue product of labor curve is the firm's demand for labor curve. The lower the wage rate, the higher is the quantity of labor demanded. ■

Two Conditions for Profit Maximization When we studied firms' output decisions, we discovered that a condition for maximum profit is that marginal revenue equals marginal cost. We've now discovered another condition for maximum profit—that marginal revenue product equals the factor price. How can there be two conditions for a maximum profit? There are two conditions for a maximum profit because they are equivalent to each other. That marginal revenue equals marginal cost is the condition that tells us the quantity of goods a firm produces; and that marginal revenue product equals the factor price is the condition that tells us the quantity of a factor that a firm hires to produce its profit-maximizing output. The equivalence of the two conditions is set out in Table 15.3.

We have just derived the law of demand as it applies to the labor market. Let's now study the influences that result in a change in the demand for labor and, therefore, in a shift in the demand for labor curve.

Shifts in the Firm's Demand for Labor Curve
The position of the demand for labor curve depends on three factors:

- The price of the firm's output
- The prices of other inputs
- Technology

The higher the price of a firm's output, the greater is the quantity of labor demanded by the firm, other things being equal. The price of output affects the demand for labor through its influence on marginal revenue product. A higher price for the firm's output increases marginal revenue which, in turn, increases the marginal revenue product of labor. A change in the price of a firm's output leads to a shift in the firm's demand for labor curve. If the output price increases, the demand for labor increases.

The other two influences on the demand for labor have their main effects not in the short run but in the long run. The **short-run demand for**

Table 15.3   Two Conditions for Maximum Profit

Symbols

Marginal revenue	MR
Marginal cost	MC
Marginal revenue product	MRP
Factor price	PF

Two conditions for maximum profit

1. MR = MC
2. MRP = PF

Equivalence of conditions

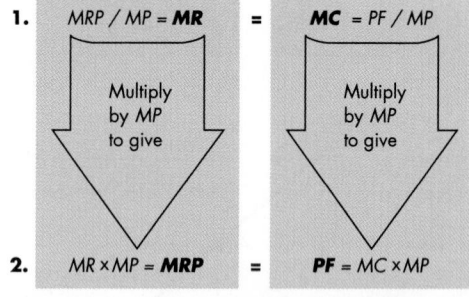

Marginal revenue (MR) equals marginal cost (MC), and marginal revenue product (MRP) equals the price of the factor (PF). The two conditions for maximum profit are equivalent because marginal revenue product (MRP) equals marginal revenue (MR) multiplied by marginal product (MP), and the factor price (PF) equals marginal cost (MC) multiplied by marginal product (MP).

labor** is the relationship between the wage rate and the quantity of labor demanded when the firm's capital is fixed and labor is the only variable input. The **long-run demand for labor** is the relationship between the wage rate and the quantity of labor demanded when all inputs can be varied. A change in the relative price of inputs—such as the relative price of labor and capital—leads to a substitution away from the input whose relative price has increased and toward the input whose relative price has decreased. Thus if the price of using capital decreases relative to that of using labor, the firm substitutes capital for labor, increasing the quantity of capital demanded and decreasing its demand for labor.

Finally, a technological change that influences the marginal product of labor also affects the demand for labor. Again, this effect is felt in the long run when the firm takes the opportunity to adjust all its inputs and incorporate the new technology into its production process. A technological change that decreases the marginal product of labor results in a decrease in the demand for labor, and one that increases the marginal product of labor results in an increase in the demand for labor. Table 15.4 summarizes the influences on a firm's demand for labor.

As we saw earlier, Fig. 15.2 illustrates the effects of a change in the demand for a factor. If that factor is labor, then Fig. 15.2 shows the effects of a change in the demand for labor on the wage rate and the quantity of labor hired. But we can now say why the demand for labor curve shifts. For example, an increase in the price of the firm's output, an increase in the price of capital, or a technological change that increases the marginal product of labor shifts the demand for labor curve from D_0 to D_1 in Fig. 15.2(a). Conversely, a decrease in the price of the firm's output, a decrease in the price of capital, or a technological change that lowers the marginal product of labor shifts the demand curve for labor from D_0 to D_2 in Fig. 15.2(b).

Market Demand

So far, we've studied only the demand for labor by an individual firm. Let's now look at the market demand. The market demand for a factor of production is the total demand for that factor by all firms. The market demand curve for a given factor is obtained by adding up the quantities demanded of that factor by each firm at each given factor price. Thus the concept of the market demand for labor curve is exactly like the concept of the market demand curve for a good or service. In the case of a good or service, the market demand curve is obtained by adding together the quantities demanded of that good by all households at each

Table 15.4   A Firm's Demand for Labor

The law of demand

The quantity of labor demanded by a firm

Decreases if:	Increases if:
• The wage rate increases	• The wage rate decreases

Changes in demand

A firm's demand for labor

Decreases if:	Increases if:
• The firm's output price decreases	• The firm's output price increases
• The prices of other inputs decrease	• The prices of other inputs increase
• A technological change decreases the marginal product of labor	• A technological change increases the marginal product of labor

price. In the case of labor, the market demand curve is obtained by adding together the quantities of labor demanded by all firms at each wage rate.

Elasticity of Demand for Labor

The elasticity of demand for labor measures the responsiveness of the quantity of labor demanded to the wage rate. We calculate this elasticity in the same way that we calculate a price elasticity: the elasticity of demand for labor equals the percentage change in the quantity of labor demanded divided by the percentage change in the wage rate. The elasticity of demand for labor depends on the elasticity of demand for the good that the firm is producing and on the properties of the firm's production function. However, there is a slight difference in the things that affect the elasticity of demand for labor in the short run and the long run.

Short-run Elasticity   The term **short-run elasticity of demand for labor** is the percentage change in the quantity of labor demanded divided by the percentage change in the wage rate when labor is the only variable input. Since the quantity of labor demanded always falls when the wage rate rises, there is no need to attach a negative sign. The elasticity of demand for labor, in positive numbers, tells us the responsiveness of a quantity *fall* to a wage rate *rise*. A higher elasticity means a more responsive demand. The short-run elasticity of demand for labor depends on three things:

1 *The short-run elasticity of demand for the product.* If the demand for the good that labor produces is elastic, then a small change in the price of the good creates a large change in the quantity demanded of the good. One thing that can change the price of the good is a change in costs, and costs change in the short-run if the wage rate changes. For a given wage rate change, the price changes, and the larger the elasticity of demand for the good, the larger is the change in the quantity of the good demanded and, therefore, the larger is the change in the labor input used to produce that good. Other things being equal, the higher the elasticity of demand for the product, the higher is the elasticity of demand for labor.

2 *Labor intensity.* The proportion of labor in the production of a good—the labor intensity of the production process—also affects the elasticity of demand for labor. Suppose that the cost of labor is 90 percent of the total cost of producing a good. In such a situation, a 10 percent change in the cost of labor generates a 9 percent change in total cost. Conversely, if the cost of labor is only 10 percent of the total cost, then a 10 percent change in the cost of labor produces only a 1 percent change in total cost. The larger the percentage change in total cost, the larger is the percentage change in price and, for a given elasticity of demand for the product, the larger is the percentage change in output. The larger the change in output, the larger is the change in labor input. So, the larger the proportion of total cost coming from labor (labor intensity), the more elastic is the demand for labor, other things being equal.

3 *The slope of the marginal product of labor curve.* The slope of the marginal product of labor curve depends on the production technology. In some processes, marginal product diminishes quickly; in others, it remains fairly constant as a firm hires more workers. The steeper the slope of the marginal product curve, the more responsive is the marginal revenue product to a change in labor input. When the revenue brought in by an extra worker diminishes quickly, a firm will not hire many new workers to produce more of its product. Therefore, the steeper the marginal product curve, the less elastic is the firm's demand for labor.

Long-run Elasticity The **long-run elasticity of demand for labor** is the percentage change in the quantity of labor demanded divided by the percentage change in the wage rate when all inputs are varied. Long-run elasticity, like short-run elasticity, depends on the elasticity of demand for the product in the long run rather than in the short run, and on *labor intensity*. In addition, the long-run elasticity depends on the *substitutability of capital for labor*. The more easily capital can be substituted for labor in production, the larger is the long-run elasticity of demand for labor. For example, it is fairly easy to substitute robots for assembly line workers in car factories and automatic picking machines for labor in vineyards and orchards. At the other extreme, it is difficult (though not impossible) to substitute robots for newspaper reporters, bank loan officers, and stockbrokers. The more readily can capital be substituted for labor, the more elastic is the firm's demand for labor.

REVIEW

The short-run elasticity of demand for labor depends on three factors:

- The short-run elasticity of demand for the product
- Labor intensity
- The slope of the marginal product of labor curve

The long-run elasticity of demand for labor also depends on three factors:

- Long-run elasticity of demand for the product
- Labor intensity
- Substitutability of capital for labor ∎

Supply of Factors

The supply of factors is determined by the decisions of households. Households allocate the factors of production that they own to their most rewarding uses. The quantity supplied of any factor of production depends on its price. Usually, the higher the price of a factor of production, the larger is the quantity supplied. There is an important possible exception to this general law of supply concerning the supply of labor. It arises from the fact that labor is the single most important factor of production and the source of the largest portion of household income.

Let's examine household factor supply decisions, beginning with the supply of labor.

Supply of Labor

A household chooses how much labor to supply as part of its time allocation decision. Time is allocated between two broad activities:

• Market activity
• Nonmarket activity

Market activity is the same thing as supplying labor. **Nonmarket activity** consists of leisure and nonmarket production activities including education and training. The household obtains an immediate return from market activities in the form of an income. Nonmarket activities generate a return in the form of goods and services produced in the home, in the form of a higher future income, or in the form of leisure, which is valued for its own sake and which is classified as a good.

In deciding how to allocate its time between market activity and nonmarket activity, a household weighs the returns that it can get from the different activities. We are interested in the effects of the wage rate on the household's allocation of its time and on how much labor it supplies.

Wages and Quantity of Labor Supplied To induce a household to supply labor, it must be offered a high enough wage rate. Nonmarket activities are valued by households either because the time is used in some productive activity or because of the value they attach to leisure. In order for it to be worthwhile to supply labor, a household has to be offered a wage rate that is at least equal to the value it places on the last hour it spends in nonmarket activities. This wage rate—the lowest one for which a household will supply labor to the market—is called its **reservation wage.** At wage rates below the reservation wage, the household supplies no labor. Once the wage rate reaches the reservation wage, the household begins to supply labor. As the wage rate rises above the reservation wage, the household varies the quantity of labor that it supplies. But a higher wage rate has two offsetting effects on the quantity of labor supplied—a *substitution effect* and an *income effect.*

1. Substitution Effect Other things being equal, the higher the wage rate, the more will people economize on their nonmarket activities and increase the time they spend working. As the wage rate rises, the household will discontinue any nonmarket activity that yields a return that is less than the wage rate; instead, the household will switch to market activity. For example, a household might use some of its time to cook meals and do laundry—nonmarket activities—that can, alternatively, be bought for $10 an hour. If the wage rate available to the household is less than $10 an hour, the household will cook and wash for itself. If the household's wage rate rises above $10 an hour, it will be worthwhile for the household to work more hours and use part of its income ($10) to buy laundry services and to eat out. The higher wage rate induces a switch of time from nonmarket activities to market activities.

2. Income Effect The higher the household's wage rate, the higher is its income. A higher income, other things being equal, induces a rise in demand for most goods. Leisure, a component of nonmarket activity, is one of those goods. Since an increase in income creates an increase in the demand for leisure, it also creates a decrease in the amount of time allocated to market activities and, therefore, to a fall in the quantity of labor supplied.

Backward-bending Household Supply of Labor Curve
The substitution effect and the income effect work in opposite directions. The higher the wage rate, the higher is the quantity of labor supplied via the substitution effect, but the lower is the quantity of labor supplied via the income effect. At low wage rates, the substitution effect is larger than the in-

Figure 15.5   The Supply of Labor

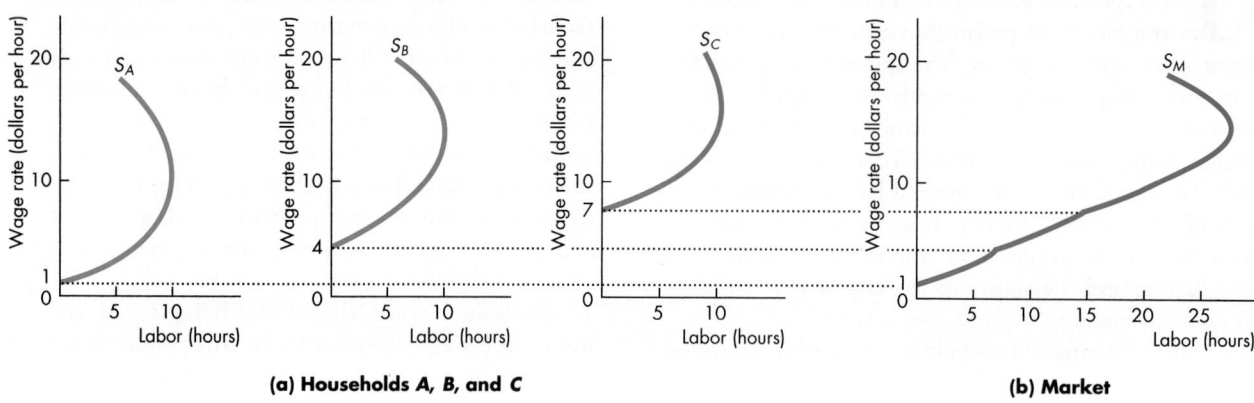

(a) Households A, B, and C   **(b) Market**

Part (a) shows the labor supply curves of three households (S_A, S_B, and S_C). Each household has a reservation wage below which it will supply no labor. As the wage rises above the reservation wage, the quantity of labor supplied rises to a maximum. If the wage continues to rise, the quantity of labor supplied begins to decline. Each household's supply curve eventually bends backward. When the quantity of labor supplied increases as the wage increases, the substitution effect dominates the income effect. When the quantity of labor supplied begins to fall as the wage rate increases, the income effect (which leads people to demand more leisure) dominates the substitution effect.

Part (b) shows how, by adding together the quantities of labor supplied by the individual households at each wage rate, we derive the market supply curve of labor (S_M). The market supply curve also eventually bends backward, but in the real world at a higher wage rate than that currently experienced. The upward-sloping part of the labor supply curve before it bends backward is the part along which the market operates.

come effect. As the wage rate rises, the household supplies more labor. But as the wage rate continues to rise, there comes a point at which the substitution effect and the income effect just offset each other. At that point, a change in the wage rate has no effect on the quantity of labor supplied. If the wage rate continues to rise, the income effect begins to dominate the substitution effect and the quantity of labor supplied declines. The household's supply of labor curve does not slope upward throughout its entire length but begins to bend back on itself. This curve is called a backward-bending supply curve.

Three individual household labor supply curves are shown in Fig. 15.5(a). Each household has a different reservation wage. Household A has a reservation wage of $1 an hour, household B of $4 an hour, and household C of $7 an hour. Each household's labor supply curve is backward-bending.

Market Supply   The quantity of labor supplied to the entire market is the total quantity supplied by all households. The market supply of labor curve is the sum of the supply curves of all the individual households. Figure 15.5(b) shows the market supply curve (S_M) derived from the supply curves of the three households (S_A, S_B, S_C) in Fig. 15.5(a). At wage rates of less than $1 an hour, the three households do laundry and cook, but they do not supply any market labor. The household most eager to supply market labor has a reservation wage of $1 an hour. As the wage rate rises to $4 an hour, household A increases the quantity of labor that it supplies to the market. The reservation wage of household B is $4 an hour, so as the wage rate rises above $4 an hour, the quantity of labor supplied in the market is the sum of the labor supplied by households A and B. When the wage rate reaches $7 an hour, household C begins to supply some labor to the market. At wage rates above $7 an hour, the quantity supplied in the market is equal to the sum of the quantities supplied by the three households.

Notice that the market supply curve S_M, like the individual household supply curves, eventually bends backward. But the market supply curve has a long upward-sloping section. The reason why the market supply curve slopes up for such a long stretch is that the reservation wages of individual households are not equal and at higher wage rates additional households are confronted with their reservation wage and so begin to supply labor.

Though the market supply curve eventually bends backward, no real world economy has reached a wage rate so high that it operates on the backward-bending portion of its labor supply curve. Many individual households are on the backward-bending portion of their own labor supply curve. Thus as wage rates rise, some people work fewer hours. But higher wage rates induce those workers who are on the upward-sloping part of their labor supply curve to supply more hours and induce additional workers to enter the work force. The response of these workers to higher wage rates dominates that of those whose work hours decline as wage rates rise. Therefore, for the economy as a whole, the labor supply curve slopes upward. For this reason, we will restrict our attention to the upward-sloping part of the labor supply curve in Fig. 15.5(b).

Supply to Individual Firms We've studied the labor supply decisions of individual households and seen how those decisions add up to the total market supply. But how is the supply of labor to each individual firm determined? The answer to this question depends on the degree of competitiveness in the labor market.

In a perfectly competitive labor market, each firm faces a perfectly elastic supply of labor curve. This situation arises because the individual firm is such a small part of the total labor market that it has no influence on the wage rate.

Some labor markets are noncompetitive in the sense that firms can and do influence the price of the labor that they hire. In these cases, firms face an upward-sloping supply of labor curve. The more labor they wish to employ, the higher is the wage rate they have to offer. We examine how this type of labor market operates in Chapter 16. Here, we deal only with the case of perfectly competitive input markets.

REVIEW

A household chooses the quantity of labor to supply as part of its time allocation decision. If the wage rate is below the household's reservation wage, the household supplies no labor to the market and uses all its time for nonmarket activities. At wage rates above the household's reservation wage, the household supplies some labor to the market. A rising wage has two opposite effects on the quantity of labor that the household supplies: a substitution effect and an income effect. Other things being equal, the higher wage rate induces the household to economize on leisure and other nonmarket time and to work more hours—the substitution effect. The higher wage rate also raises the household's income, which increases its demand for most goods including leisure. More time taken for leisure means less labor is supplied. That is, other things being equal, the higher wage rate induces the household to spend more time on leisure and work fewer hours—the income effect.

The market supply of labor is the total quantity of labor supplied by all households. The market supply curve, like a household's supply curve, bends backward above a certain wage rate. Actual economies operate on the upward-sloping part of the market supply of labor curve. The supply of labor curve faced by each individual firm depends on the degree of competitiveness of the labor market. In a perfectly competitive labor market, each firm faces a perfectly elastic supply curve. ■

Next, let's examine the supply of capital.

Supply of Capital

Households supply capital to firms by consuming less than their income—they save. Thus the scale on which a household supplies capital depends on how much of its income it saves.

The most important factors determining a household's savings are:

• Its current income in relation to its expected future income
• The interest rate

Current and Future Income A household with a current income that is low compared with its expected future income saves little and might even

Figure 15.6   Short-run and Long-run Supply of Capital

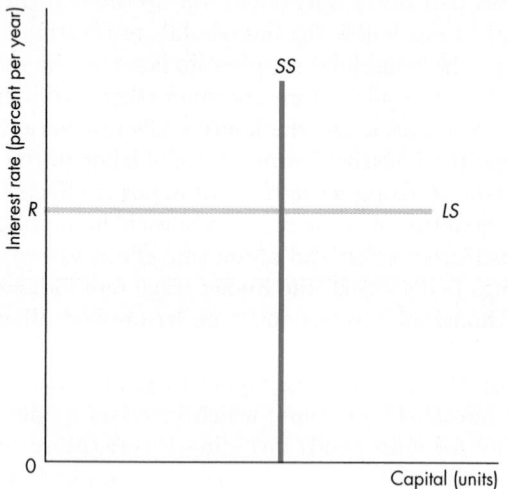

The long-run supply of capital (LS) is highly elastic (perfectly elastic in this figure). If the interest rate is above R, households increase their saving and increase the total amount of capital supplied. If the interest rate is below R, households decrease their saving and reduce the amount of capital supplied. The short-run supply of capital (SS) is highly inelastic (perfectly inelastic in the figure). For the economy as a whole and for individual firms in the short run, once capital is put in place, it is difficult to vary its quantity easily and quickly. Thus, no matter what the interest rate, at a given point in time there is a given amount of capital supplied.

have negative saving. A household with a current income that is high compared with its expected future income saves a great deal in the present in order to be able to consume more in the future. The stage in the household's life cycle is the main factor influencing whether current income is high or low compared with expected future income. Young households typically have a low current income compared with their expected future income, while older households have a high current income relative to their expected future income. The consequence of this pattern in income over the life cycle is that young people have negative saving and older people have positive saving. Thus the young incur debts (such as mortgages and consu-

mer credit) to acquire durable goods and to consume more than their income, while older people save and accumulate assets (often in the form of pension and life insurance arrangements) to provide for their later retirement years.

Interest Rate and Capital Supply Curve   A household's supply of capital is the stock of capital that it has accumulated as a result of its past saving. The household's supply curve of capital shows the relationship between the quantity of capital supplied and the interest rate. Other things being equal, a higher interest rate encourages people to economize on current consumption in order to take advantage of the higher return available from saving. Thus the higher the interest rate, the greater is the quantity of capital supplied.

Market Supply   The market, or aggregate, quantity of capital supplied is the sum of the supplies of all the individual households. The market supply curve of capital shows how the aggregate quantity of capital supplied varies as the interest rate varies. The market supply curve of capital is likely to be highly elastic and might even be perfectly elastic. Such a market supply curve is shown in Fig. 15.6 as that labeled LS. At interest rates above R, enough households are willing to save so that the total stock of capital supplied increases. At interest rates below R, a sufficient number of households plan to consume more than their income, and the total quantity of saving supplied decreases.

Supply to Individual Firm   When studying the supply of capital to an individual firm, it is important to distinguish between the short-run and long-run supply of capital. Recall the distinction between the short run and the long run. The short run is a period during which a firm can vary its labor input but not its capital input. Thus in the short run, the firm's capital input is fixed. The long run is a period during which a firm can vary all its inputs. Thus in the long run, the firm can vary its capital as well as its labor inputs. In the long run, a firm operating in a competitive capital market can obtain any amount of capital at the going market interest rate. Thus it faces a perfectly elastic supply curve of capital. In the short run, the firm has acquired a specific set of assets. For example, an auto producer has acquired a production assembly line; a laundromat operator has

Figure 15.7   The Supply of Land

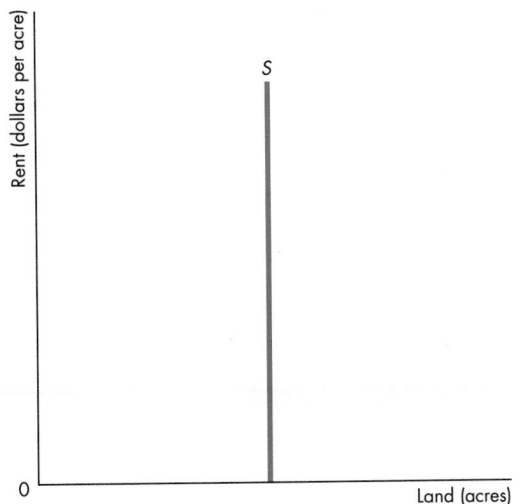

The supply curve of a given piece of land is perfectly inelastic. No matter what the rent, no more land than exists can be supplied.

acquired a number of washing machines and dryers; the campus print shop has acquired a number of photocopying and other printing machines. In the short run, the supply of capital facing an individual firm can be highly inelastic. Specific pieces of machinery and equipment have been bought and have been bolted in place. They cannot be quickly disposed of or added to. In the extreme case, the short-run supply of capital is perfectly inelastic. Such a case is illustrated as the vertical line (*SS*) in Fig. 15.6.

The inelastic short-run supply and the elastic long-run supply of capital have important implications for the returns obtained from different types of capital. We'll explore those implications later in this chapter when we study equilibrium in the capital market. But before that, let's complete our analysis of the supply of factors of production by examining the supply of land.

Supply of Land

Land is the stock of natural resources and its aggregate quantity supplied cannot be changed by any individual decisions. Individual households can vary the amount of land they own, but whatever land is acquired by one household is sold by another so that the aggregate quantity of land supplied of any particular type and in any particular location is fixed regardless of the decisions of any individual household. This fact means that the supply of each particular piece of land is perfectly inelastic. Figure 15.7 illustrates such a supply. Regardless of the rent available, the quantity of land supplied on Chicago's Magnificent Mile is a fixed number of square feet.

Expensive land can be, and is, used more intensively than inexpensive land. For example, high rise buildings enable land to be used more intensively. However, to use land more intensively, it has to be combined with another factor of production—capital. Increasing the amount of capital per block of land does nothing to change the supply of land itself.

Although the supply of each type of land is fixed and its supply is inelastic, each individual firm, operating in competitive land markets, faces an elastic supply of land. That is, each firm can acquire the land that it demands at the going rent, as determined in the marketplace. Thus provided land markets are highly competitive, firms are price takers in these markets, just as they are in the markets for other factors of production.

REVIEW

The supply of capital is determined by households' saving decisions. Other things being equal, the higher the interest rate, the greater is the amount of capital supplied. The supply of capital to individual firms is highly inelastic in the short run but elastic in the long run.

Individual households can vary the amount of land that they supply but the aggregate supply of land is determined by the fact that there is a given, fixed quantity of it available. Thus the supply of each particular piece of land is perfectly inelastic. In a competitive land market, each firm faces an elastic supply of land at the going rent. ■

Let's now see how factor prices and quantities are determined.

Figure 15.8   Labor Market Equilibrium

(a) News anchors

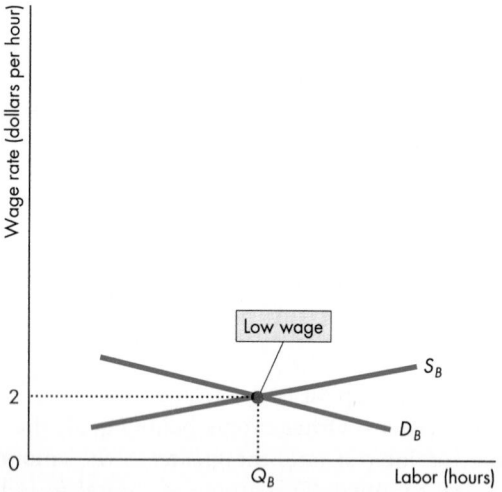

(b) Babysitters

News anchors (part a) have a high marginal revenue product, which is reflected in the high demand for their services—curve D_N. The number of people with the talents required for this job is few and the supply curve is S_N. Equilibrium occurs at a high hourly wage rate of $500 and a low quantity traded, Q_N. The marginal revenue product of babysitters (part b) is low, so the demand curve is D_B. There is a huge supply of babysitters and the supply curve is S_B. Equilibrium occurs in this market at a low wage rate of $2 an hour and a high quantity traded, Q_B.

Competitive Equilibrium

The price of a factor of production and the quantity of it traded are determined by the interaction of the demand for the factor and its supply. We'll illustrate competitive equilibrium by looking at the markets for labor, capital, and land and by looking at two examples of each.

Labor Market Equilibrium

Figure 15.8 shows two labor markets. That in part (a) is the labor market for national news anchors. Such people have a very high marginal revenue product and this is reflected in the demand curve for their services, curve D_N. The supply of individuals with the required talents for this kind of job is low, and this fact is reflected in supply curve S_N. Equilibrium occurs at a high hourly wage rate ($500 in this example) and a low quantity traded, Q_N.

Figure 15.8(b) shows another market, that for babysitters. Although people value the output of babysitters, the marginal revenue product of these services is low, a fact reflected in demand curve D_B. There are many households, typically those with high school students, willing to supply these services and the supply curve is S_B. This market achieves an equilibrium at a low wage rate ($2 an hour in this example) and at a relatively high quantity traded, Q_B.

If there is an increase in the demand for news anchors, the demand curve D_N in Fig. 15.8(a) shifts to the right, increasing their wage and increasing the quantity traded. The higher wage rate will induce more households to offer their services in this activity. If there is an increase in demand for babysitters, the demand curve D_B in Fig. 15.8(b) shifts to the right, increasing their wage rate and increasing the quantity traded. Again, a higher wage rate will induce an increase in the quantity supplied. Movements in wage rates occur to achieve a balance between the quantities demanded and supplied in each individual labor market. Changes in demand result in changes in the wage rate that achieve a reallocation of the labor force.

Capital Market Equilibrium

Figure 15.9 shows capital market equilibrium. In Fig. 15.9(a), we illustrate that part of the capital

Figure 15.9   Capital Market Equilibrium

(a) Steel industry

(b) Computer industry

The long-run supply curve of capital (LS) in the steel industry (part a) and the computer industry (part b) is perfectly elastic. The number of steel mills in place is fixed at Q_1, so the short-run supply curve in the steel industry is SS_1. The demand curve for steel mills is D_1. The interest rate on capital invested in steel is R_1. The amount of computer-producing equipment in place is fixed at Q_3, so the short-run supply curve in the computer industry is SS_3. The demand curve for computer-producing equipment is D_2. The interest rate in the computer industry is R_2. With a higher interest rate in the computer industry, capital leaves the steel industry and goes into the computer industry. The short-run supply curves shift. In the steel industry, the short-run supply curve shifts to the left, to SS_2, and the interest rate rises. In the computer industry, the short-run supply curve shifts to the right, to SS_4, and the interest rate falls. In long-run equilibrium, interest rates are the same in both industries.

market in the steel industry—the market for steel mills. The long-run supply of capital to the steel industry is shown as the perfectly elastic supply curve *LS*. But the actual quantity of steel mills in place is Q_1, and the short-run supply curve is SS_1. The demand curve for steel mills, determined by their marginal revenue product, is D_1. The interest rate earned by the owners of steel mills—the stockholders in U.S. Steel and similar firms—is R_1.

Figure 15.9(b) shows that part of the capital market in the computer industry. Again, the long-run supply curve is *LS*, the same curve as in the steel industry. That is, in the long run, capital is supplied to each of these industries at an interest rate R. But the amount of computer-producing capital in place is Q_3, and the short-run supply

curve is SS_3 in part (b). The interest rate earned by the owners of computer production equipment—the stockholders of IBM and similar firms—is R_2.

You can see that the interest rate paid to owners of capital in the steel industry is lower than that in the computer industry. This inequality of interest rates on capital sets up an interesting dynamic adjustment process that gradually lowers the stock of capital in the steel industry and increases the stock of capital in the computer industry. With a low interest rate on capital in the steel industry and a high interest rate on capital in the computer industry, it pays people to take their investments out of the steel industry and to put them into the computer industry. But physical plant and equipment have been built in the steel industry and

Figure 15.10   Land Market Equilibrium

(a) Magnificent Mile

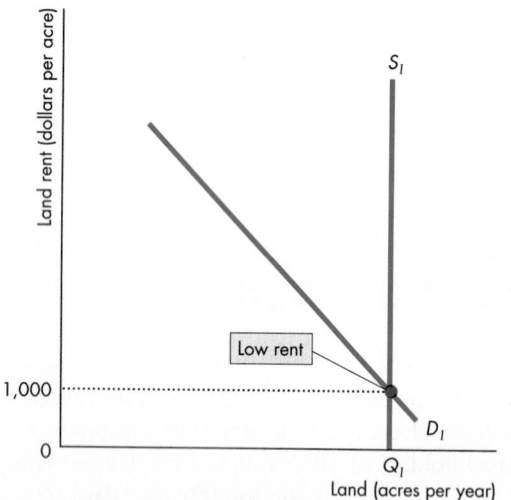

(b) Iowa farmland

The marginal revenue product of land on Chicago's Magnificent Mile gives rise to the demand curve D_M (part a). The quantity of land on the Magnificent Mile is fixed at Q_M, so the supply curve is S_M. Equilibrium occurs at an annual rent of $10,000 a square foot. The marginal revenue product of farmland in Iowa (part b) gives rise to a demand curve D_I. The quantity of farmland in Iowa is fixed at Q_I and the supply curve is S_I. Equilibrium occurs at an annual rent of $1000 an acre.

cannot be readily transformed into computer-making equipment. Its owners must wait until their investment has worn out. But as capital equipment depreciates in the steel industry, it is not replaced and so the capital stock declines. The short-run supply curve shifts to the left, to SS_2. Conversely, as capital is freed up and additional saving is made, it is directed toward the computer industry, so that its short-run supply curve shifts to the right, to SS_4. The interest rates adjust in the two industries during this process. The interest rate increases in the steel industry and decreases in the computer industry. Eventually, in long-run equilibrium, the interest rate on capital in the two industries will have equalized at R.

Land Market Equilibrium

Equilibrium in the land market occurs at rents that allocate the fixed amounts of land available to their highest value uses. Figure 15.10 illustrates two land markets. Part (a) shows the market for land on Chicago's Magnificent Mile. Its marginal revenue product gives rise to the demand curve D_M. There are a fixed number of square feet of land (Q_M), so the supply is inelastic, as shown by the curve S_M. Equilibrium occurs at a rent of $10,000 a square foot a year.

Figure 15.10(b) illustrates the market for farmland in Iowa. Here, the marginal revenue product produces the demand curve D_I. There is a vast amount of land available but again, only a fixed quantity—in this case, Q_I. Thus the supply curve lies a long way to the right but is vertical—perfectly inelastic—at S_I. Here the equilibrium rent occurs at $1000 an acre a year.

We've now studied the markets for the three factors of production and seen how wages, interest, and rent are determined. We now turn to our final task in this chapter—defining and distinguishing between economic rent and transfer earnings.

Economic Rent and Transfer Earnings

The total income of a factor of production is made up of its economic rent and its transfer earnings. **Economic rent** is an income received by the owner of a factor over and above the amount required to induce that owner to offer the factor for use. The income required to induce the supply of a factor of production is called **transfer earnings.**

These concepts of economic rent and transfer earnings are illustrated in Fig. 15.11. The figure shows the market for a factor of production. It could be *any* factor of production—labor, capital, or land. The demand curve for the factor of production is *D* and its supply curve is *S*. The factor price is *PF* and the quantity traded *QF*. The income of the factor is the sum of the yellow and green areas. The yellow area below the supply curve measures transfer earnings and the green area below the factor price but above the supply curve measures economic rent.

To see why the area above the supply curve measures economic rent, recall that a supply curve can be interpreted in two different ways. The standard intepretation is that a supply curve indicates the quantity supplied at a given price. But the alternative interpretation of a supply curve is that it shows the minimum price at which a given quantity is willingly supplied. If suppliers receive only the minimum amount required to induce them to supply each unit of the factor of production, they will be paid a different price for each unit and the prices will trace the supply curve and the income received is entirely transfer earnings—the yellow area in Fig. 15.11.

The concept of economic rent is similar to the concept of consumer surplus that you met in Chapter 7, pp. 167–168. Consumer surplus, recall, is the difference between the price the household pays for a good and the maximum price it would be willing to pay, as indicated by the demand curve. In a parallel sense, economic rent is the difference between the factor price a household actually receives and the minimum factor price at which it would be willing to supply a given amount of a factor of production.

It is important to distinguish between *economic rent* and *rent*. Rent is the price paid to the factor of production, land. Economic rent is a component of the income received by every factor of production.

The portion of the income of a factor of production that consists of economic rent depends on the elasticity of the supply of the factor of production. When the supply of a factor of production is inelas-

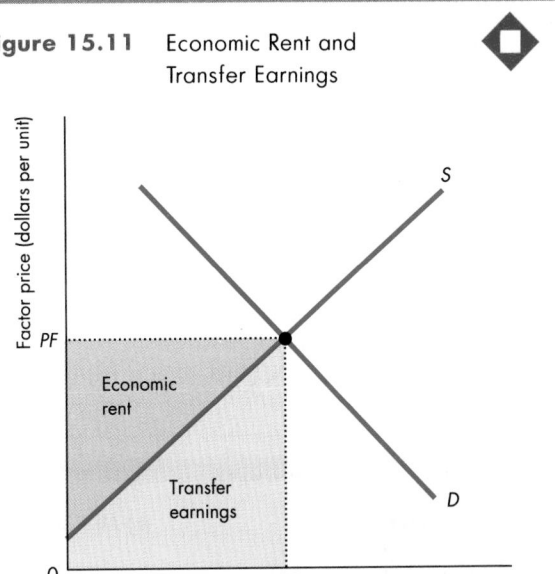

Figure 15.11   Economic Rent and Transfer Earnings

The total income of a factor of production is made up of its economic rent and its transfer earnings. Transfer earnings are measured by the yellow area under the supply curve and economic rent, by the green area above the supply curve and below the factor price.

tic, its entire income is economic rent. When the supply of a factor of production is perfectly elastic, none of its income is economic rent. In general, when the supply curve is neither perfectly elastic nor perfectly inelastic (like that illustrated in Fig. 15.11), some part of the factor income is economic rent and and the other part transfer earnings.

Figure 15.12 illustrates the three possibilities. Part (a) of the figure shows the market for a particular parcel of land in New York City. The land is fixed in size at *L* square yards. Therefore the supply curve of the land is vertical—perfectly inelastic. No matter what the rent on the land is, there is no way of increasing the quantity that can be supplied.

The demand for that block of land is determined by its marginal revenue product. The marginal revenue product in turn depends on the uses to which the land can be put. In a central business district such as Manhattan, the marginal revenue

Figure 15.12   Economic Rent and Supply Elasticity

(a) All economic rent   **(b) All transfer earnings**   **(c) Intermediate case**

When the elasticity of supply is zero (the supply curve is vertical) as in part (a), the entire factor income is economic rent. When the supply of the factor of production is perfectly elastic, as in part (b), the factor's entire income is transfer earnings. When a factor supply curve slopes upward, as in part (c), part of the factor income is economic rent and part is transfer earnings. Land is the example shown in part (a); unskilled labor in poor countries such as India and China in part (b); and rock singers in part (c).

product is high because a large number of people are concentrated in that area, making it a prime place for conducting valuable business. Suppose that the marginal revenue product of this block of land is shown by the demand curve in Fig. 15.12(a). Then it commands a rent of R. The entire income accruing to the owner of the land is the green area in the figure. This income is *economic rent*. The rent charged for this piece of land depends entirely on its marginal revenue product— on the demand curve. If the demand curve shifts to the right, the rent rises. If the demand curve shifts to the left, the rent falls. The quantity of land supplied remains constant at L.

The conclusion that we have just reached concerning the determination of the rent of a block of land in Manhattan answers one of the questions posed at the beginning of this chapter: Is coffee expensive in New York City because rents are high or are rents high because people are willing to pay a high price for coffee in New York City? We've seen that the rent of a New York City block is determined entirely by the demand for it and that

the demand, in turn, is determined by marginal revenue product. Land has a high marginal revenue product only if people are willing to pay a high price to use the land. Of course, from the point of view of McDonald's, they feel that they have to charge a high price for their coffee at their 57th Street restaurant because of the high rent they pay there. But the rent wouldn't be high if McDonald's (and other potential users) did not have a high marginal revenue product "attached" to that land, making them willing to pay those high rents.

Figure 15.12(b) shows the market for a factor of production that is in perfectly elastic supply. An example of such a market might be that for unskilled labor in a poor country such as India or China. In those countries, large amounts of labor flock to the cities and are available for work at the going wage rate (in this case, W). Thus, in these situations, the supply of labor is almost perfectly elastic. The entire income earned by this labor is transfer earnings. They receive no economic rent.

Figure 15.12(c) shows the market for rock singers. To induce a rock singer to sing at a larger number of concerts, a higher income has to be offered—the rock singer's supply curve is upward-sloping. The demand curve—measuring the marginal revenue product of the rock singer—is that labeled D in the figure. Equilibrium occurs where the rock singer receives a wage of W and sings in C concerts. The green area above the rock singer's supply curve is economic rent and the yellow area below the supply curve is the rock singer's transfer earnings. If the rock singer is not offered at least the amount of the transfer earnings, then the singer will withdraw from the rock concert market and perform some alternative activity.

■ We've now studied the market for the three factors of production—labor, capital, and land—

and we've seen how the returns to these factors of production—wages, interest, and rent—are determined. We've seen the crucial role played in determining the demand for a factor of production by the factor's marginal revenue product. We've seen how the interaction of demand and supply determines factor prices and factor incomes. We've also seen how changes in these prices and incomes come about from changes in demand and supply. Finally, we've distinguished between economic rent and transfer earnings.

In the next chapter, we're going to examine some detailed features of the labor market more closely, explaining differences in wage rates among the skilled and the unskilled, males and females, and racial and ethnic minorities.

S U M M A R Y

Factor Prices and Incomes

The factors of production—labor, capital, and land—earn a return—wages, interest, and rent. Labor is the most important source of income. Factor prices are determined by the demand for and supply of factors of production. Incomes are determined by the prices of factors of production and the quantities traded. An increase in the demand for a factor of production increases the factor's price and income; a decrease in the demand for a factor of production decreases its price and income. An increase in supply increases the quantity traded of a factor of production but decreases its price. A decrease in supply decreases the quantity traded and increases the factor's price. Whether an increase in supply leads to an increase or decrease in the income of a factor of production depends on the elasticity of demand of the factor. When elasticity of demand is greater than 1, an increase in supply leads to an increase in the factor's income. When the elasticity of demand for a factor is less than 1, an increase in supply leads to a decrease in the factor's income. (pp. 381–384)

Demand for Factors

A firm's demand for a factor stems from its desire to maximize profit. The extra revenue generated by

hiring one more unit of a factor is called the marginal revenue product of the factor. A firm's demand curve for a factor is derived from that factor's marginal revenue product curve. A firm demands an input up to the point at which the marginal revenue product of the factor equals the factor's price.

A firm's labor input is variable in both the short run and the long run. The firm's capital input may be varied only in the long run. The elasticity of the demand for labor in the short run depends on the short-run elasticity of demand for the firm's product, on the labor intensity of the production process, and on the slope of the marginal product of labor curve. The long-run elasticity of a firm's demand for labor depends on the long-run elasticity of demand for the product, on labor intensity, and on the ease with which capital can be substituted for labor.

The market demand for labor is the sum of the demands by each individual firm. (pp. 384–390)

Supply of Factors

The supply of factors is determined by households' decisions on the allocation of their time and the division of their income between consumption and saving. In choosing how much time to allocate to market activities, each household compares the wage rate that can be earned with the value of its time in other nonmarket activities. The household will supply no market labor at wage rates below its reservation wage. At wage rates above the household's reservation wage, the quantity of labor supplied rises as long as the substitution effect of the higher wage rate is larger than the income effect. As the wage rate continues to rise, the income effect, which leads to more time taken for leisure, becomes larger than the substitution effect, and the quantity of labor supplied by the household falls.

The market supply curve of labor is the sum of the supply curves of all households. Like the household's labor supply curve, the market supply of labor curve eventually bends backward. However, the response to higher wage rates of those on the upward-sloping part of the labor supply curve dominates the response of those on the backward-bending part, and the market supply curve slopes upward over the range of wage rates that we experience.

Households supply capital by saving. Saving increases as the interest rate increases. The supply of capital to an individual firm is highly inelastic in the short run but highly elastic in the long run.

The supply of land is fixed and independent of its rent. (pp. 391–395)

Competitive Equilibrium

In a competitive factor market, the factor price and quantity traded are determined at the point of intersection of the demand and supply curves. High factor prices occur for factors of production that have a high marginal revenue product and a low supply. Low factor prices occur for factors of production with a low marginal revenue product and a high supply. (pp. 396–398)

Economic Rent and Transfer Earnings

Economic rent is that part of the income received by a factor owner over and above the amount needed to induce the owner to supply the factor of production for use. The rest of a factor's income is transfer earnings. When The supply of a factor is perfectly inelastic, its entire income is made up of economic rent. Factors that have a perfectly elastic supply receive only transfer earnings. In general, the supply curve of a factor of production is upward-sloping, and part of the income received is transfer earnings (below the supply curve) and part is ceonomic rent (above the supply curve but below the factor price). (pp. 398–401)

K E Y   C O N C E P T S

Key Figures and Tables

R E V I E W   Q U E S T I O N S

1 Explain what happens to the price of a factor of production and its income if the following occurs:

a) There is an increase in demand for the factor.

b) There is an increase in the supply of a factor.

c) There is a decrease in demand for the factor.

d) There is a decrease in supply of the factor.

2 Explain why the effect of a change in supply of a factor on a factor's income depends on the elasticity of demand for the factor.

3 Define marginal revenue product and distinguish between marginal revenue product and marginal revenue.

4 Why does marginal revenue product decline as the quantity of a factor employed increases?

5 What is the relationship between the demand curve for a factor of production and its marginal revenue product curve? Why?

6 Show that the condition for maximum profit in the product market—marginal cost equals mar-

ginal revenue—is equivalent to the condition for maximum profit in the factor market—marginal revenue product equals marginal cost of factor (equals factor price in a competitive factor market).

7 Review the main influences on the demand for a factor of production—the influences that shift the demand curve for a factor.

8 What determines the short-run and the long-run elasticity of demand for labor?

9 What determines the supply of labor?

10 Why might the supply of labor curve bend backward at a high enough wage rate?

11 What determines the supply of capital?

12 Define economic rent and transfer earnings and distinguish between these two components of income.

13 Suppose that a factor of production is in perfectly inelastic supply. If the marginal revenue product of the factor decreases, what happens to its price, quantity traded, income, transfer earnings, and rent?

P R O B L E M S

1 Wendy owns an apple orchard. She employs students to pick the apples. Students can pick the following amounts of apples in an hour:

Number of students	Quantity of apples (pounds)
1	20
2	50
3	90
4	120
5	145
6	165
7	180
8	190

a) Draw the average and marginal product curves of these students.

b) If Wendy can sell her apples for 50 cents a

pound, draw the average and marginal revenue product curves.

c) Draw Wendy's demand for labor curve.

d) If all apple growers in Wendy's neighborhood pay their pickers $7.50 an hour, how many students will Wendy hire?

2 The price of apples falls to 33.33¢ a pound, and apple pickers' wages remain at $7.50 an hour.

a) What happens to Wendy's average and marginal product curves?

b) What happens to her average and marginal revenue product curves?

c) What happens to her demand for labor curve?

d) What happens to the number of students that she hires?

3 Apple pickers' wages increase to $10 an hour but the price of apples remains at 50¢ a pound.

   a) What happens to the average and marginal revenue product curves?

   b) What happens to Wendy's demand curve?

   c) How many pickers does Wendy hire?

4 Using the information provided in problem 1, calculate Wendy's marginal revenue and marginal cost, marginal revenue product, and marginal cost of labor. Show that when Wendy is making maximum profit, marginal cost equals marginal revenue and marginal revenue product equals the marginal cost of labor.

5 You are given the following information about the labor market in an isolated town in the Rocky Mountains. Everyone works for logging companies, but there are many logging companies in the town. The market for logging workers is perfectly competitive. The town's labor supply is given as follows:

Wage rate (dollars per hour)	Quantity of labor supplied (hours)
2	120
3	160
4	200
5	240
6	280
7	320
8	360

The market demand for labor from all the logging firms in the town is as follows:

Wage rate (dollars per hour)	Quantity of labor demanded (hours)
2	400
3	360
4	320
5	280
6	240
7	200
8	160

   a) What is the competitive equilibrium wage rate and the quantity of labor employed?

   b) What is total labor income?

   c) How much of that labor income is economic rent and how much is transfer earnings? (You may find it easier to answer this question by drawing graphs of the demand and supply curves and then finding the economic rent and transfer earnings as areas on the graph in a manner similar to what was done in Fig. 15.11.)

Chapter 16

Labor Markets

After studying this chapter, you will be able to:

- Explain why college graduates earn more, on the average, than high school graduates

- Explain why skilled workers earn more, on the average, than unskilled workers

- Explain why union workers earn higher wages than nonunion workers

- Explain why, on the average, men earn more than women and whites earn more than minorities

- Predict the effects of a comparable worth program

- Explain why some people are paid by the hour and others by formulas based on performance

- Explain how performance-related compensation rules induce greater effort and higher profit

As you well know, college is not just a ball. Those exams, quizzes, tests, and problem-sets require a lot of hard work. Are they worth all the effort that goes into them? What is the payoff? Part of the payoff is a higher income. At age 22, college graduates earn 30 percent more, on the average, than high-school graduates, and when they reach middle age their earnings are more than 50 percent higher than high school graduates and three times the level of those who attended elementary school only. But have you ever wondered why? After all, an accountant or a lawyer or even an economist doesn't sweat as hard as a person who works as a laborer. Why do they earn more? ■ Suppose that you do earn more after college.

The Sweat of Our Brows

Ignoring the many cultural and social benefits of college, and focusing only on money, let's ask a simple question: How much more income will you have to earn after graduation to make up for four years of tuition, room and board, and lost wages? (You could, after all, be washing dishes now instead of slogging through this economics course.) ■ Many workers, both blue collar and white collar, belong to labor unions. Usually, union workers earn a higher wage than nonunion workers in comparable jobs. Why? How are unions able to get higher wages for their members than the wages that nonunion workers are paid? ■ Among the most visible and persistent differences in earnings are those between men and women and between whites and minorities. White men, on the average, earn incomes that are one third higher than the incomes earned by black men. Black men earn more, in descending order, than Hispanic men, white women, black women, and Hispanic women, who earn only 56 cents for each dollar earned by the average white man. Certainly a lot of individuals defy the averages. But why do minorities and women so consistently earn less than white men? Is it because of discrimination and exploitation? Or could it be because of economic factors? Or is it a combination of the two? ■ Equal pay legislation has resulted in comparable-worth programs, which try to ensure that jobs of equivalent value receive the same pay regardless of the pay set by the market. Can comparable-worth programs bring economic help to women and minorities? ■ Most people work for an hourly wage rate. The total amount earned depends on the total hours worked. But not everyone is paid in this way. For example, some doctors get paid by the number of X-rays or appendectomies they perform. Garment workers receive an income based on the number of shirts they make. Sales people receive a percentage of the value of their sales. Senior managers often get to share in their company's profits. Tennis players and boxers are compensated by prize money. Managers and production workers sometimes receive bonuses for achieving target profits or output levels. Why is there such variety in the ways in which people are compensated for their work? Why don't we all get an hourly wage rate?

■ In this chapter, we study the way labor markets work and answer questions such as these. We begin by using the model of a competitive labor market, such as that developed in Chapter 15, to analyze the effects on wages of differences in education and training. We then extend the model to explain differences in union and nonunion wages, in pay among men, women, and minorities, and to analyze the effects of comparable-worth laws. Finally, we study compensation arrangements based not on hours of work but on performance. We explain how such schemes lead to greater effort and higher profits. We'll even discover that chief executives and tennis stars get paid in a similar way.

Skill Differentials

Differences in earnings between workers with varying levels of education and training can be explained using a model of competitive labor markets. In the real world, there are many different levels and varieties of education and training. To keep our analysis as clear as possible, we'll study a model economy in which there are just two different levels that result in two types of labor, what we will call skilled labor and unskilled labor. We'll

study the demand for and supply of these two types of labor and see why there is a difference in their wages and what determines that difference. Let's begin by looking at the demand for the two types of labor.

The Demand for Skilled and Unskilled Labor

Skilled workers can perform a wide variety of tasks that unskilled workers would perform badly or perhaps could not even perform at all. Imagine an untrained, inexperienced person performing surgery or piloting an airplane. Because skilled workers perform complex tasks, they have a higher marginal revenue product than unskilled labor. As we learned in Chapter 15, the demand for labor curve is derived from the marginal revenue product curve. The higher the marginal revenue product of labor, the higher is the demand for labor.

Figure 16.1(a) shows the demand curves for skilled and unskilled labor. At any given level of employment, firms are willing to pay a higher wage to a skilled worker than to an unskilled worker. The gap between the two wages is the difference between the marginal revenue products of a given number of skilled and unskilled workers. This difference is the marginal revenue product of skill. For example, at an employment level of 2000 hours, firms are willing to pay $12.50 for a skilled worker and only $5 for an unskilled worker. The difference in the marginal revenue product of the two workers is $7.50 an hour. Thus the marginal revenue product of skill is $7.50 an hour.

The Supply of Skilled and Unskilled Labor

Skills are costly to acquire. Furthermore, a worker pays the cost of acquiring a skill before benefiting from a higher wage. For example, attending college usually leads to a higher income, but the higher income is not earned until after graduation. These facts make the acquisition of skills similar to investment. To emphasize the investment nature of acquiring a skill, we call that activity an investment in human capital. **Human capital**, as we defined it in Chapter 3, is the accumulated skill and knowledge of human beings. The value of a person's human capital is the *present value* of the extra earnings *received* as a result of acquiring skill and knowledge. (The concept

Figure 16.1   Skill Differentials

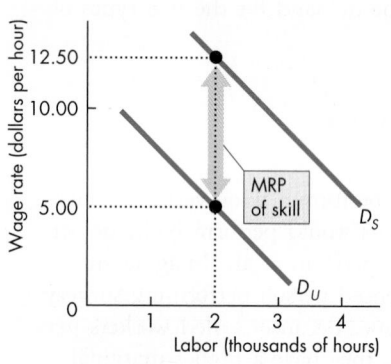

**(a) Demand for skilled
and unskilled labor**

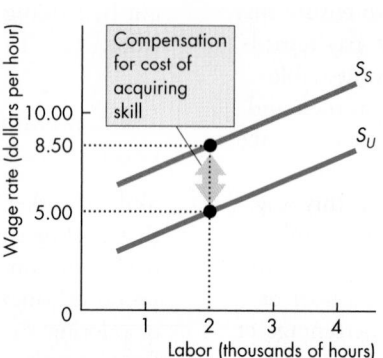

**(b) Supply of skilled
and unskilled labor**

**(c) Markets for skilled
and unskilled labor**

Part (a) illustrates the marginal revenue product of skill. Unskilled workers have a marginal revenue product that gives rise to the demand curve marked D_U. Skilled workers have a higher marginal revenue product than unskilled workers. Therefore the demand curve for skilled workers (D_S) thus lies to the right of D_U. The vertical distance between these two curves is the marginal revenue product of skill.

Part (b) shows the effects of the cost of acquiring skills on the supply curves of labor. The supply curve for unskilled workers is S_U. Skilled workers have to incur costs in order to acquire their skills. Therefore they will only supply labor services at a wage rate that exceeds that of unskilled labor. The supply curve for skilled workers is S_S. The vertical distance between these two curves is the required compensation for the cost of acquiring a skill.

Part (c) shows the determination of the equilibrium levels of employment and the skilled and unskilled wage differential. Unskilled workers earn the wage rate $5 an hour where the quantities demanded and supplied of unskilled workers are equal. The employment level of unskilled workers is 2000 hours. Skilled workers earn the wage rate $10 an hour where the quantities demanded and supplied of skilled workers are equal. The employment level of skilled workers is 3000 hours. Wages for skilled workers are always greater than those for unskilled workers.

of present value is explained in Chapter 9.) It is equivalent to a sum of money which, if invested today at the average interest rate, will yield a stream of income equivalent to the extra earnings resulting from a person's acquired knowledge and skills.

The cost of acquiring a skill includes actual expenditures on such things as tuition and room and board, and also costs in the form of lost or reduced earnings while the skill is being acquired. When a person goes to school full time, that cost is the total earnings foregone. However, some people acquire skills on the job. Such skill acquisition is called on-the-job training. Usually a worker undergoing on-the-job training is paid a lower wage than one doing a comparable job but not undergoing training. In such a case, the cost of acquiring the skill is the

difference between the wage paid to a person not being trained and that paid to a person being trained.

Supply Curves of Skilled and Unskilled Labor
The position of the supply curve of skilled workers reflects the cost of acquiring the skill. Figure 16.1(b) shows two supply curves, one for skilled workers and the other for unskilled workers. The supply curve for skilled workers is S_S and for unskilled workers S_U.

The skilled worker's supply curve lies above the unskilled worker's supply curve. The vertical distance between the two supply curves is the compensation for the cost of acquiring the skill. (The difference is the amount that has a present value equal to the cost of acquiring the skill.) For example, suppose that the quantity of unskilled labor supplied is 2000 hours at a wage rate of $5 an hour. This wage rate compensates the unskilled workers purely for their time on the job. Consider next the supply of skilled workers. To induce 2000 hours of skilled labor to be supplied, firms have to pay a wage rate of $8.50 an hour. This wage rate for skilled labor is higher than that for unskilled labor since skilled labor must be compensated not only for the time on the job but also for the time and other costs of acquiring the skill.

Wage Rates of Skilled and Unskilled Labor

To work out the wage rates of skilled and unskilled labor, all we have to do is bring together the effects of skill on the demand and supply of labor. Figure 16.1(c) shows the demand curves and the supply curves for skilled and unskilled labor. These curves are exactly the same as those plotted in parts (a) and (b). Equilibrium occurs in the market for unskilled labor where the supply and demand curves for unskilled labor intersect. The equilibrium wage rate is $5 an hour and the quantity of unskilled labor employed is 2000 hours. Equilibrium in the market for skilled workers occurs where the supply and demand curves for skilled workers intersect. The equilibrium wage rate is $10 an hour and the quantity of skilled labor employed is 3000 hours.

As you can see in part (c), the equilibrium wage rate of skilled labor is higher than that of unskilled labor. There are two reasons why this occurs: First, skilled labor has a higher marginal revenue product than unskilled labor; second, skills are costly to acquire. The wage differential (in this case $5 an hour) depends on both the marginal revenue product of the skill and the cost of acquiring it. The higher the marginal revenue product of the skill, the larger is the vertical distance between the demand curves for skilled and unskilled labor. The more costly it is to acquire a skill, the larger is the vertical distance between the supplies of skilled and unskilled labor. The higher the marginal revenue product of the skill and the more costly it is to acquire, the larger is the wage differential between skilled and unskilled workers.

Do Education and Training Pay?

There are large and persistent differences in earnings based on the degree of education and training. An

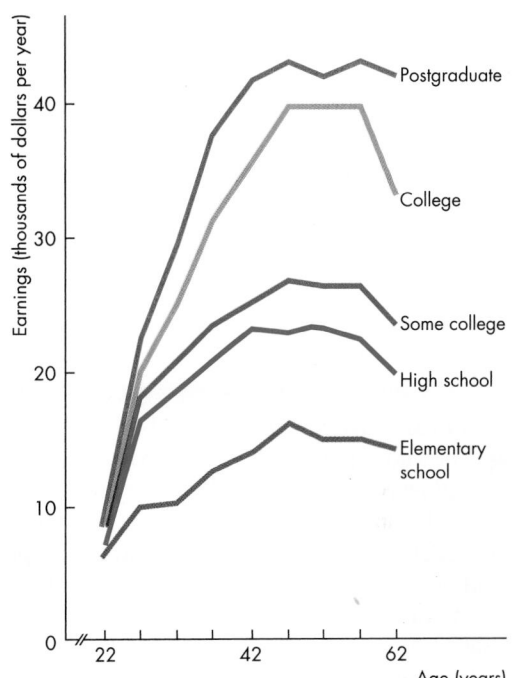

Figure 16.2 Education and Earnings

Earnings of male employees at various ages and with varying school levels are shown. Earnings increase with length of education and also with age, but only up to the mid-forties. Beyond that age, earnings decrease. These differences show the importance of experience and education in influencing skill differentials.

indication of those differences can be seen in Fig. 16.2. This figure highlights two important sources of earnings differences. The first is the degree of education itself. The higher the level of education, other things being equal, the higher are a person's earnings. The second source of earnings differences apparent in Fig. 16.2 is age. Age is strongly correlated with experience and the degree of on-the-job training a person has had. Thus as a person gets older, up to middle age, earnings increase.

We can see, from Fig. 16.2, that going through high school, college, and postgraduate education leads to higher incomes. But do they pay in the sense of yielding a higher income that compensates for the cost of education and for the delay in the start of earnings? For most people, college does indeed pay. Rates of return have been calculated suggesting that a college degree is a better investment than almost any other that a person can undertake. Rates of return as high as 15 percent, after allowing for inflation, are not uncommon.

Differences in education and training are an important source of differences in earnings. But they are not the only source. Another is the activities of labor unions. Let's see how unions affect wages and why, on the average, union wages exceed nonunion wages.

Union-Nonunion Wage Differentials

A **labor union** is an organized group of workers whose purpose it is to increase wages and influence other job conditions. A labor union acts in the labor market like a monopolist in the product market. The union seeks to restrict competition and, as a result, raises the price at which labor is traded. A compact glossary on unions can be found in Table 16.1.

There are two main types of union: craft unions and industrial unions. A **craft union** is a group of workers who have a similar range of skills but work for many different firms in many different industries and regions. An example of a craft union is the carpenters' union. An **industrial union** is a group of workers who have a variety of skills and job types but work for the same firm or industry. The United Auto Workers (UAW) is an example of an industrial union.

Most unions are members of the AFL-CIO. The AFL-CIO was created in 1955 when two labor organizations combined: the American Federation of Labor (AFL), which was founded in 1886 to organize craft unions, and the Congress of Industrial Organizations (CIO), founded in 1938 to organize industrial unions. The AFL-CIO acts as the national voice of organized labor in the media and in politics. Unions vary enormously in size. Craft unions are the smallest and industrial unions the biggest.

Union strength peaked in the 1950s when 35 percent of the work force belonged to unions. That percentage has declined steadily since 1955 and is now less than 20 percent. Changes in union membership, however, have been uneven. Some unions have declined dramatically while others, especially those in government, have increased in strength.

Table 16.1   A Compact Glossary on Unions

Labor union	An organized group of workers that attempts to increase wages and improve other conditions of employment
AFL-CIO	A federation of unions formed in 1955 by a merger of the American Federation of Labor (AFL) and the Congress of Industrial Organizations (CIO); acts as the voice of organized labor in media and political arenas
Craft union	A union in which workers have a similar range of skills but work for many firms and in many different industries
Industrial union	A union in which workers have a variety of skills and job types but work in same industry
Local	A sub-unit of a union that organizes individual workers. In craft unions, the local is geographical; in industrial unions, the local is based on a plant or a company
Open shop	A place of work that has no union restriction on who can work in the shop; here, the union bargains for its members but not for nonmembers
Closed shop	A place of work where only union members may be employed; illegal since 1947, when Congress passed the Labor-Management Relations Act (the Taft-Hartley Act)
Union shop	A place of work that may hire nonunion workers but only if they join the union within a specified period; illegal in 20 states where "right-to-work" legislation has been passed
Right-to-work law	A law that protects the right of an individual to work without joining a union
Collective bargaining	Negotiations between representatives of employers and unions on wages and other employment conditions
Strike	A group decision to refuse to work under prevailing conditions
Lockout	A firm's refusal to allow its labor force to work
Binding arbitration	Determination of wages and other employment conditions by a third party (an arbitrator) acceptable to both parties

Union organization is based on a subdivision known as the local. The **local** is a sub-unit of a union that organizes the individual workers. In craft unions, the local is based on a geographical area, while in industrial unions the local is based on a plant or an individual firm.

There are three possible forms of organization for a local: an open shop, a closed shop, or a union shop. An **open shop** is an arrangement in which workers have a right to be employed without joining the union—there is no union restriction on who can work in the "shop." A **closed shop** is an arrangement in which only union members may be employed by a firm. Closed shops have been illegal since the passage of the Taft-Hartley Act in 1947. A **union shop** is an arrangement in which a firm may hire nonunion workers, but in order for such workers to remain employed they must join the union within a brief period specified by the union. Union shops are illegal in the 20 states that have passed "right-to-work" laws. A **right-to-work law** allows an individual to work at any firm without joining a union.

Unions negotiate with employers or their representatives in a process called **collective bargaining.** The main weapons available to the union and the employer in collective bargaining are the strike and the lockout. A **strike** is a group decision to refuse to work under prevailing conditions. A **lockout** is a firm's refusal to operate its plant and employ its workers. Each party uses the threat of a strike or a lockout to try to get an agreement in its own favor. Sometimes when the two parties in the collective bargaining process cannot agree on wages and other conditions of employment, they agree to put their disagreement to binding arbitration. **Binding arbitration** is a process in which a third party—an arbitrator—determines wages and other employment conditions on behalf of the negotiating parties.

Though not labor unions in a legal sense, professional associations act, in many ways, like labor unions. A **professional association** is an organized group of professional workers such as lawyers, dentists, or doctors that seeks to influence the compensation and other labor market conditions affecting its members. An example of a professional association is the American Medical Association (AMA).

Unions' Objectives and Constraints

Unions have three broad objectives:

* Improving compensation
* Improving working conditions
* Improving employment prospects

Each of these objectives contains a series of more detailed goals. For example, in seeking to improve its members' compensation unions operate on a variety of fronts: wages, fringe benefits, retirement pay, and such things as vacation allowances. In seeking to improve working conditions, unions are concerned with occupational health and safety as well as the environmental quality of the workplace. In seeking to improve employment prospects, unions try to obtain greater job security for existing union members and to expand their job opportunities.

A union's ability to pursue its objectives is restricted by two sets of constraints—one on the supply side and the other on the demand side of the labor market. On the supply side, the union's activities are limited by how well it can restrict nonunion workers from offering their labor. The larger the fraction of the work force controlled by the union, the more effective the union can be. For example, unions find it difficult to be effective in markets for unskilled farm labor in southern California because of their inability to control the flow of nonunion, often illegal, labor from Mexico. At the other extreme, unions in the construction industry can better pursue their goals because they can influence the number of people obtaining skills as electricians, plasterers, and carpenters. Those best able to restrict supply are the professional associations for such groups as lawyers, dentists, and doctors. These groups control the number of qualified workers by controlling the examinations that new entrants must pass.

The constraint facing a union on the demand side of the labor market arises because the union cannot force firms to hire more labor than they demand. Anything that raises wages or other employment costs will lower the quantity of labor demanded. Unless the union can take actions that shift the demand curve for the labor that it represents, it will have to accept the fact that the higher wage can be obtained only at the price of lower employment. Recognizing the importance of the demand for labor curve, unions try to make the demand for their labor inelastic and to increase the demand for labor. Here are some of the methods that they employ:

* Encouraging import restrictions
* Supporting minimum wage laws
* Supporting immigration restrictions
* Increasing product demand
* Increasing the marginal product of union members

Figure 16.3   A Union in a Competitive Labor Market

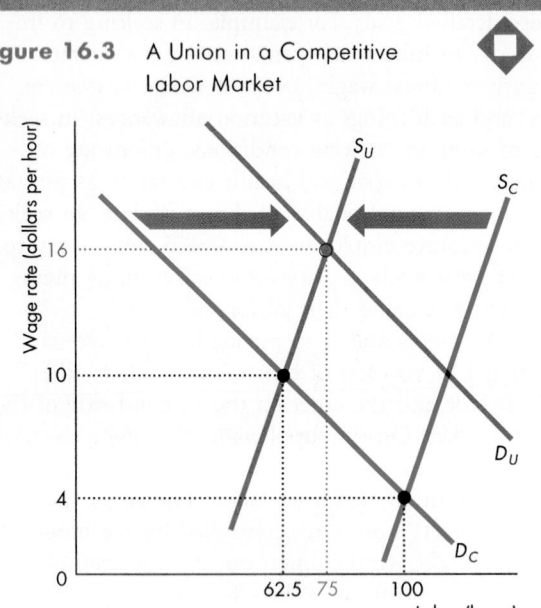

In a competitive labor market, the demand curve is D_C and the supply curve S_C. Competitive equilibrium occurs at a wage rate of $4 an hour with 100 hours employed. By restricting employment below its competitive level, the union shifts the supply of labor to S_U. If the union can do no more than that, the wage rate will rise to $10 an hour, but employment will fall to 62.5 hours. If the union can increase the demand for labor (by increasing the demand for the good produced by the union members or by raising the price of substitute labor) and shift the demand curve to D_U, then it can raise the wage rate still higher to $16 an hour and achieve employment of 75 hours.

One of the best examples of import restrictions is the support by the United Auto Workers union for import restrictions on foreign cars. Unions support minimum wage laws in order to increase the cost of unskilled labor, a substitute for skilled union labor. Supporting restrictive immigration laws leads indirectly to an increase in the wages of unskilled workers and again increases the cost of labor that might otherwise be substituted for the higher cost union labor. Increasing product demand indirectly increases the demand for labor. The best examples of attempts by unions in this activity are in the textile and auto industries. Garment workers are encouraged to buy union-made clothes and auto workers to buy only U.S.-produced cars. Increasing the marginal product of union members directly shifts the demand curve for their services. Unions use apprenticeship, training, and professional certification to increase the marginal product of their members.

Unions in a Competitive Labor Market

When a union operates in an otherwise competitive labor market, it seeks to raise wages and other compensation and to limit employment reductions by increasing demand for the labor of its members.

Figure 16.3 illustrates a labor market. The demand curve is D_C and the supply curve is S_C. If the market is a competitive one with no union, the wage rate is $4 an hour and 100 hours of labor will be employed. Suppose that a union is formed to organize the workers in this market and that the union has sufficient control over the supply of labor to be able to artificially restrict that supply below its competitive level—to S_U. If that is all the union does, employment will fall to 62.5 hours of labor and the wage rate will rise to $10 an hour. If the union can also take steps that increase the demand for labor to D_U, it can achieve an even bigger rise in the wage rate with a smaller fall in employment. By maintaining the restricted labor supply at S_U, the union raises the wage rate to $16 an hour and achieves an employment level of 75 hours of labor.

An example of a union operating in an industry with a competitive output market is that of coal mining. Some recent developments in that industry are analyzed in Reading Between the Lines on pp. 414–416.

We next turn our attention to the case in which employers have considerable influence in the labor market.

Monopsony

A **monopsony** is a market structure in which there is just a single buyer. With the growth of large-scale production over the last century, large manufacturing plants such as coal mines, steel and textile mills, and car manufacturers became the major employer of labor in some regions, and in some places a single firm employed almost all the labor. Such a firm is a monopsonist in the labor market.

A monopsonist can make a bigger profit than a group of firms that have to compete with each other for their labor. Figure 16.4 illustrates how a monopsonist operates. The monopsonist's marginal revenue product curve is *MRP*. This curve tells us the extra revenue from selling the output produced by the last hour of labor hired. The curve labeled *S* is the supply curve of labor. This curve tells us how many hours are supplied at each wage rate. It also tells us the minimum wage that is acceptable at each level of labor supplied.

In deciding how much labor to hire, the monopsonist recognizes that to hire more labor it must pay a higher wage or, equivalently, by hiring less labor the monopsonist can get away with paying a lower wage. The monopsonist takes account of this fact when calculating its marginal cost of labor. The marginal cost of labor is shown by the curve *MCL*. The relationship between the marginal cost of labor curve and the supply curve is similar to the relationship between the marginal cost and average total cost curves that you studied in Chapter 10. The supply curve is like the average total cost of labor curve. For example, in Fig. 16.4 the firm can hire 50 hours of labor at $5 an hour, so its average total cost is $5 an hour. The total cost of labor is $5 an hour multiplied by 50 hours, which equals $250 an hour. But suppose that the firm hires slightly less than 50 hours of labor, say 49 hours. The wage rate at which 49 hours of labor can be hired is $4.90 an hour. The firm's total labor cost is 49 multiplied by $4.90, which equals $240.10. Hiring the fiftieth hour of labor raises the total cost of labor from $240.10 to $250, which is almost $10. The curve *MCL* shows the $10 marginal cost of hiring the fiftieth hour of labor.

To calculate the profit-maximizing quantity of labor to hire, the firm sets the marginal cost of labor equal to the marginal revenue product of labor. That is, the firm wants the cost of the last worker hired to equal the extra revenue brought in. In Fig. 16.4, this outcome occurs when the monopsony employs 50 hours of labor. To hire 50 hours of labor, the firm has to pay $5 an hour. The marginal revenue product of labor, however, is $10 an hour, which means that the firm makes an economic profit of $5 on the last hour of labor that it hires. Each worker gets paid $5, and marginal revenue product is $10. So the firm gets an extra $5 economic profit out of the last hour of labor hired.

The ability of a monopsonist to make an economic profit depends on the elasticity of labor supply. The more elastic the supply of labor, the less opportunity a monopsonist has to make an economic profit.

Figure 16.4   A Monopsony Labor Market

A monopsony is a market structure in which there is a single buyer. A monopsonist whose marginal revenue product curve is *MRP* faces a labor supply curve *S* and has a marginal cost of labor curve *MCL*. Profit is maximized by making the marginal cost of labor equal to marginal revenue product. The monopsonist hires 50 hours of labor and pays the lowest wage for which that labor will work — $5 an hour.

If this labor market were competitive, the wage rate would be $7.50 and the level of employment would be 75 hours. Compared with a competitive labor market, employment and the wage rate are lower under monopsony.

Monopsony Tendencies   With today's low costs of transportation, it is unlikely that many pure monopsonists remain. Workers can easily commute long distances to a job, and so for most people there is not just one potential employer. Nevertheless, many firms still face an upward-sloping supply of labor curve. Though they are not monopsonists, there is a monopsony tendency in their market in the sense that to attract more workers they have to offer higher wages. A firm's monopsony element may come from its location, if it is more conveniently reached by some workers than others. Firms compete with each other for labor by offering wages that not only compensate their workers for time on the job but also for commuting time. The more workers a firm hires, the longer the commute for the marginal worker and,

A Labor Union Faces a Fall in Demand

Weaker UMW's Hard Task

The master labor contract, which covers the workers who produce roughly half of the nation's coal supply, will expire next Jan. 31 [1988], an event for which the industry is already preparing. Although formal negotiations have yet to begin, at least 10 of the 30 or so coal producers in the Bituminous Coal Operators Association, the industry bargaining group, have already dropped out, thinking they can cut a better deal with the union on their own. These companies are meeting with union representatives on their own timetable, and some have even signed preliminary agreements.

Dwindling Membership

The defections will almost certainly weaken a union that has been steadily losing ground, industry and labor experts say. The U.M.W.'s dues-paying membership has dwindled to about 73,000 from 144,000 in 1980 according to Leo Troy, a Rutgers University expert on unions. And in a decade when demand for coal has been weakened by the wide availability and low price of oil, the union, like its counterpart in the automobile industry, will have to make job security a top priority in upcoming talks. At the same time, it plans not to give up any of its wage gains, although it hasn't articulated its pay demands as yet.

"Trumka's [U.M.W. president] got a tough assignment," said Bud Ogden, head of the Island Creek Coal Company, the coal subsidiary of the Occidental Petroleum Corporation.

Island Creek, which broke away from the B.C.O.A. in 1984, has decided to go it alone again this year. By negotiating on his own, Mr. Ogden is hoping to customize the industry contract to address the particular needs of some of Island Creek's operations. "Working through the association leaves us once removed at best," he said.

As it has in the steel industry, the deterioration of industrywide bargaining has caused concern among union leaders and labor experts. Charles R. Perry, an associate professor at the University of Pennsylvania's Wharton School who has written extensively on coal mining, said the trend toward fragmentation could stretch the union's resources. "It makes their life more complicated because now they have to deal with a more fragmented bargaining structure."

Thomas A. Grames, a miner in Price, Utah, who serves part-time as president of his union local, agreed. "We have limited numbers of people capable of doing the negotiation, and if the companies are playing hardball and making you negotiate each one of them, it makes it hard," he said.

Threats Foreign and Domestic

Such a scenario would have been unthinkable in the Lewis era.* Back then, nearly all the nation's coal was produced by U.M.W. mines, and the industry considered a master contract in its best interests. It was expedient, and it assured all producers of the same labor costs.

Coal Miners' Pay Exceeds Some Other Workers'...

Source: Bureau of Labor Statistics

...But the United Mine Workers Union Is Losing Members

While the number of domestic mine workers is decreasing, the number of dues-paying U.M.W. members is dropping faster.

Source: Leo Troy, Rutgers University, Bureau of Labor Statistics

That level playing field no longer suffices because the B.C.O.A. companies are not the only coal producers. Foreign coal not represented by the B.C.O.A. has made inroads, but the bigger threat is homegrown. Nonunion mines can produce coal for $2 to $5 a ton less than similar union operations. A ton typically costs about $20, but the price can range from as little as $3 in some of the newer Western surface mines to $35 in some of the older Eastern mines. The result: Union coal now accounts for only 60 percent of all bituminous, or soft, coal mined in the United States, according to the U.M.W., and independent estimates are closer to 40 percent.

Making the U.M.W.'s task all the more daunting is the coal industry's failing health. Producers are still reeling from a decade of overexpansion, fueled by an anticipated growth in demand that was expected to accompany soaring oil prices. That surge in demand never materialized. "People back in the 1970's believed some of their own press releases," said Richard M. Holsten, the president of the Pittsburg and Midway Coal Mining Company, based in Denver, which has never been in the B.C.O.A.

Lower oil prices and a slump in the steel industry,

the second-largest user of coal after utilities, have caused prices to fall 33 percent since 1982 and led to layoffs. "The industry is definitely in a lot of trouble and in a period of stagnation," said Forrest Hill, a consultant based in Annapolis, Md.

At the same time, productivity has soared, although management and labor disagree about who deserves the credit. Island Creek officials, for instance, said new mining methods had helped to raise production at its Virginia Pocahontas No. 6 mine near Rowe, Va.

Five years ago, using continuous mining machines to scoop out the coal, the mine produced 12 tons of coal per worker per eight-hour shift. It now averages 19.8 tons, relying primarily on $10 million long-wall mining machines that can extract the coal from a 600-foot panel in about 20 minutes by remote control. "Just like your microwave," said George King, the mine's superintendent, demonstrating the push-button device.

And as long as productivity continues to outpace sluggish demand, mine workers will keep losing their jobs. . . .

———————
*John L. Lewis was the founder of the U.M.W. and its leader for 40 years.

The Essence of the Story

- The Bituminous Coal Operators Association (B.C.O.A.), an association of mine employers, traditionally has negotiated a "master labor contract," governing all its members, with the United Mine Workers Union (U.M.W.).

- In mid-1987, as the existing contract approached its expiration date (January 31, 1988), 10 of the 30 members of B.C.O.A. decided to bargain separately with the U.M.W.

- The U.M.W. is in a weak bargaining position because of several reasons:

  —Its membership is declining, down from 144,000 in 1980 to 73,000 in 1987.
  —The demand for coal has fallen as a result of a lower price of oil and a slump in the steel industry.
  —Competition from foreign and nonunion domestic producers has reduced domestic union-produced coal to 60 percent of the market.

  —Costs in nonunion mines are $2 to $5 a ton less than costs in union mines.
  —New but expensive machines have raised output per worker from 12 tons a shift in 1982 to 19.8 tons a shift in 1987.
  —Productivity growth is faster than the growth in demand and the number of jobs available is declining.

- Job security is the U.M.W.'s top priority, though it also wants to maintain the wage gains that it has achieved in the past (see illustration in the news article comparing wages in mining with steel and construction).

(Continued on next page)

The New York Times, August 10, 1987

By Alison Leigh Cowan

Background and Analysis

(Continued from previous page)

- The ability of the U.M.W. to maintain wage and employment levels depends on the demand for coal miners, which in turn is determined by the marginal revenue product of coal miners.

- The marginal revenue product of coal miners depends on:

  —The marginal revenue of coal producers
  —The marginal product of coal miners

- Coal mining is a competitive industry and no single mine can exert a significant influence on the price of coal. As a consequence, a coal producer's marginal revenue is equal to the price of coal.

- The price of coal is determined by supply and demand in the market for coal. The demand for coal has been falling because of two factors:

  —The price of oil, a substitute for coal, has been falling.
  —The price of steel, a major user of coal, has been falling.

- The price of coal has fallen by 33 percent since 1982.

- The marginal product of coal miners depends on the technology used for coal production. The installation of long-wall mining machines has increased average productivity by 65 percent in the past five years.

- The figure illustrates what has been happening to the demand for coal miners in the past few years. In 1982, the marginal revenue product (and demand) was the curve labeled MRP_{82}. The industry operated at the point marked 1982 on that demand curve, employing 200,000 workers at a wage rate of $13 an hour.

- If there had been no technical advances in coal mining, the fall in the price of coal (33 percent) between 1982 and 1986 would have lowered the marginal revenue product of coal miners, and the demand for coal, to the line labeled MRP_0.

- Between 1982 and 1986, technological changes in coal mining resulted in massive productivity gains. The introduction of long-wall machines raised the marginal revenue product of miners. As a consequence, the marginal revenue product curve and, equivalently, the demand curve shifted to that labeled MRP_N. The average wage rate rose to $15.50 an hour and 150,000 coal miners were employed (the point marked 1986).

- The combination of the two factors—the fall in the price of coal and the rise in the productivity of coal miners resulting from the use of long-wall machines—only slightly lowered the demand for coal miners.

- The U.M.W. pushed up coal miners' wages in the period since 1982 and accepted a cut in employment. To have maintained employment at 200,000 miners, it would have been necessary to accept a pay cut. If wages had been held constant at $13 an hour, employment would have fallen but by less than the fall that oc--curred with higher wages.

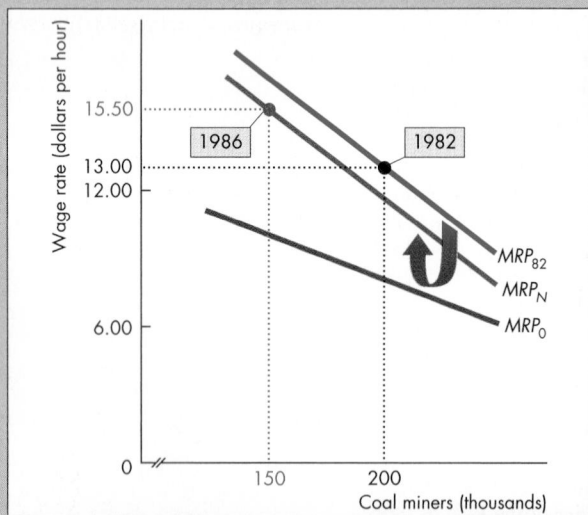

therefore, the higher the wage that the firm has to pay to attract that worker. How strong such a monopsony tendency is depends on the size and density of the urban area in which the labor market is situated. Next, let's see the effects of minimum wage laws and unions in a monopsonistic labor market.

Monopsony, Minimum Wage, and Unions

In Chapter 6, we saw how a minimum wage usually decreases employment. However, in a situation where a firm is a monopsonist, minimum wage regulations can actually raise both the wage rate and employment. A union can also raise the wage rate and employment. Let's see how.

Minimum Wages and Monopsony   Suppose that the labor market is that shown in Fig. 16.5 and that the wage rate is $5 an hour with 50 hours of labor being employed. The government now passes a minimum wage law that prohibits anyone from hiring labor for less than $7.50 an hour. Firms can hire labor for $7.50 an hour or more but not for less than that wage. The monopsonist in Fig. 16.5 now faces a perfectly elastic supply of labor at $7.50 an hour up to 75 hours. Above 75 hours, a higher wage than $7.50 an hour has to be paid to hire additional hours of labor. Since the wage rate is a fixed $7.50 an hour up to 75 hours, the marginal cost of labor is also constant at $7.50 up to 75 hours. Beyond 75 hours, the marginal cost of labor rises above $7.50 an hour. To maximize profit, the monopsonist sets the marginal cost of labor equal to its marginal revenue product. That is, the monopsonist hires 75 hours of labor at $7.50 an hour. The minimum wage law has made the supply of labor perfectly elastic and made the marginal cost of labor the same as the wage rate up to 75 hours. The law has not affected the supply of labor curve or the marginal cost of labor at employment levels above 75 hours. The minimum wage law has succeeded in raising wages by $2.50 an hour and raising the amount of labor employed by 25 hours.

Monopsony and Unions   When we studied monopoly in Chapter 13, we discovered that a single seller in a market is able to determine the price in that market. We have just studied monopsony—a market with a single buyer—and discovered that in such a market the buyer is able to determine the price. Suppose that a union starts to operate in a

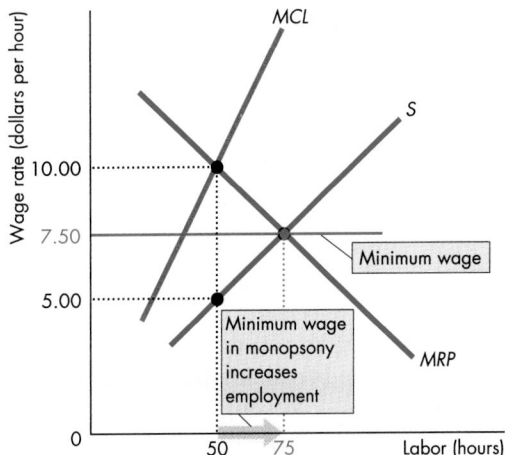

Figure 16.5   Minimum Wage in Monopsony

In a monopsony labor market, the wage rate is $5 an hour. If a minimum wage law raises the wage rate to $7.50 an hour, employment rises to 75 hours. Equivalently, if a union enters the market, it will attempt to increase the wage rate to above $5 an hour. If the union is all-powerful, the highest wage rate it can achieve is $10 an hour. If the union and the firm are equally powerful, they will bargain and agree to a wage rate of $7.50 an hour—the wage rate that splits the difference between marginal revenue product and the lowest wage for which labor will work equally.

monopsony labor market. A union is like a monopoly. It controls the supply of labor and acts like a single seller of labor. If the union (monopoly seller) faces a monopsony buyer, the situation is one of **bilateral monopoly.** In bilateral monopoly, the wage rate is determined by bargaining between the two traders. Let's study the bargaining process.

We saw that if the monopsony in Fig. 16.4 is free to determine the wage rate and the level of employment, it hires 50 hours of labor for a wage rate of $5 an hour. If a union that represents the workers can maintain employment at 50 hours but charge the highest wage rate acceptable to the employer, the wage rate will be $10 an hour. That is, the wage rate will equal the marginal revenue product of labor. If the monopsonist and the union bargain over the wage rate, the result will be a wage rate between $10 an hour (the maximum that the union can achieve) and $5 an hour (the minimum that the firm can achieve).

The actual outcome of the bargaining depends on the costs that each party can inflict on the other as a result of a failure to agree on the wage rate. The firm can shut down the plant and lock out its workers and the workers can shut down the plant by striking. Each party knows the strength of the other and knows what it has to lose if it does not agree to the demands of the other. If the two parties are equally strong, and they realize it, they will split the difference and agree to a wage rate of $7.50 an hour. If one party is stronger than the other—and both parties know that—the agreed wage will favor the stronger party. Usually, an agreement is reached without a strike or a lockout. The threat—the knowledge that such an event can occur—is usually enough to bring the bargaining parties to an agreement. When strikes or lockouts do occur, it is because one party has misjudged the situation.

The Scale of Union-Nonunion Wage Differentials

We have seen that unions can influence the wages of their members partly by restricting the supply of labor and partly by manipulating the demand for labor. How much of a difference to wage rates do unions make in practice?

In 1985, union wage rates were, on the average, 33 percent higher than nonunion wage rates. In mining and financial services, union and nonunion wages are similar, and in services, manufacturing, and transportation the differential is between 11 and 19 percent. But in the wholesale and retail trades the differential is 42 percent and in construction it is 77 percent.

These union-nonunion wage differentials do not give a true measure of the effects of unions on wages, however. In some industries, union wages are higher than nonunion wages because union members do jobs that involve greater skill. Even without a union, those who perform such tasks receive a higher wage. To calculate the effects of unions, we have to examine the wages of unionized and nonunionized workers who do nearly identical work. The evidence suggests that after allowing for the effects of skill differentials, the union-nonunion wage differential lies between 10 percent and 25 percent. For example, airline pilots who belong to the Airline Pilots' Union earn about 25 percent more than nonunion pilots with the same level of skill.

Wage Differentials between Sexes and Races

There are persistent earnings differences between the sexes and the races. Figure 16.6 provides a snapshot of these differences in 1984. The wages of each race and sex group are expressed as a percentage of the wages of white men. By definition, then, the wages of white men are 100. As you can see, the wages of each group fall progressively from 81 percent for other men down to 64 percent for women of Hispanic origin.

Why do the differentials shown in Fig. 16.6 exist, and why do they persist? Do they arise because there is discrimination against women and members of minority races, or is there some other explanation? These controversial questions generate an enormous amount of passion. It is not my intention to make you angry, but that may happen as an unintended consequence of this discussion. The objective of this section is to show you how to use economic analysis to address controversial and emotionally charged issues.

We are going to examine three possible explanations for these earnings differences:

- Discrimination
- Differences in human capital
- Differences in degree of specialization

Discrimination

To see how discrimination can affect earnings, let's look at an example—the market for investment advisors. Suppose that there are two groups of investment advisors who are identical in terms of picking good investments. One group consists of black females and the other of white males. The supply curve of black females (S_{BF}) is shown in Fig. 16.7(a). The supply curve of white males (S_{WM}) is shown in Fig. 16.7(b). These supply curves are identical. The marginal revenue product of investment advisors, whether they are black female or white male is also identical and is shown by the two curves labeled MRP in parts (a) and (b). (Their revenues are the fees their customers pay for investment advice.)

Suppose that everyone in this society is free of prejudice about color and sex. The market for black female investment advisors determines a wage rate of $40,000 a year and there are 2000 black female investment advisors. The white male investment ad-

Figure 16.6   Sex and Race Differentials

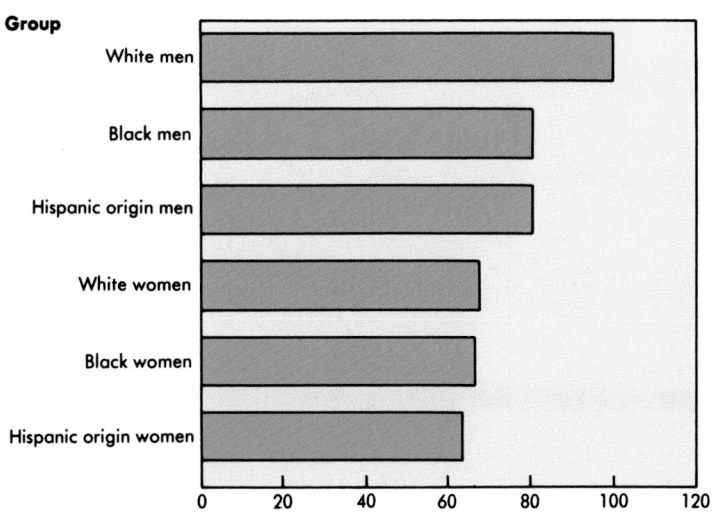

Median hourly wages are shown as percentages of white male income. These differentials have persisted over many years.

Source: Statistical Abstract of the United States: 1987, 107th ed., p. 404.

visor market also clears at a wage rate of $40,000 a year, and there are 2000 white male investment advisors.

In contrast to the previous situation, suppose that the customers of investment houses are prejudiced against women and against members of racial minorities. The two types are equally able, as before, but the degree of prejudice is so strong that the customers are not willing to pay as much for investment advice given by a black female as they will pay for advice from a white male. Because of the differences in the amounts that people are willing to pay, based purely on their prejudices, the marginal revenue products of the two groups are different. The ability of the two groups is the same but the value that prejudiced consumers place on their outputs is not the same. Suppose that the marginal revenue product of the black females, when discriminated against, is the line labeled MRP_{DA} — DA standing for discriminated against. Suppose that the marginal revenue product for white males, the group discriminated in favor of, is MRP_{DF} — DF standing for discriminated in favor of. Given these marginal revenue product curves, the markets for the two groups of investment advisors will now determine very different wages and employment levels. Black females will earn $20,000 a year and only 1000 will work as invest-

ment advisors. White males will earn $60,000 a year and 3000 of them will work as investment advisors. Thus, purely on the basis of the prejudice of the demanders of investment advice, black women will earn one third the wages of white men, and three quarters of all investment advisors will be white men and only one quarter will be black women.

The case that we have just examined is a hypothetical example of how prejudice can produce differences in earnings. But economists disagree about whether or not prejudice actually causes wage differentials for a simple but difficult reason: You can recognize prejudice when you see it, but you cannot easily measure it. Our model shows that sex and race differentials may come from prejudice. But without a way of measuring prejudice in the real world, we cannot easily test that model to see if it is true.

We need to make another point as well. Our model of prejudice, like all economic models, is in an equilibrium, albeit an unhappy one. But simply because a model is in equilibrium does not mean that such a real situation is either desirable or inevitable. Economic theory makes predictions about the way things will be, not moral statements about the way things ought to be. Policies designed to bring equal wages and employment prospects to women and minorities can be devised. But to be successful, such

Figure 16.7   Discrimination

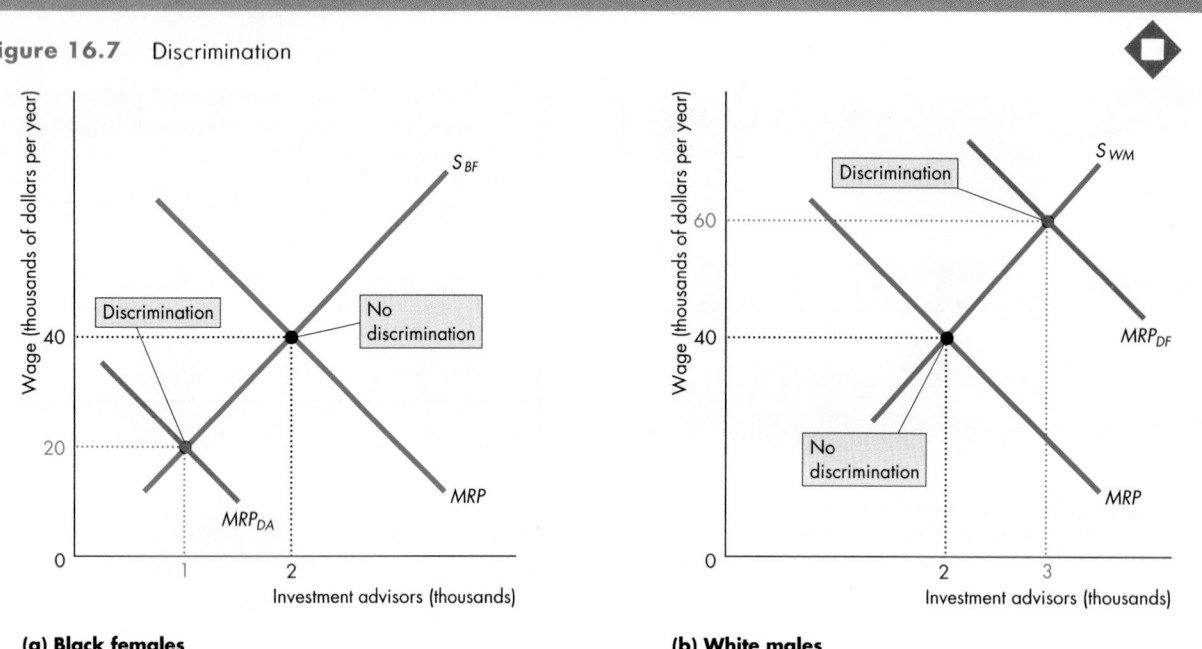

(a) Black females   **(b) White males**

The supply curve for black female investment advisors is S_{BF} in part (a) and the supply curve for white male investment advisors is S_{WM} in part (b). If the marginal revenue product of both groups of investment advisors is MRP (the same curve in each part), then the equilibrium wage rate for each group is $40,000 a year and 2000 of each type of advisor are employed. If there is discrimination against blacks and women, the marginal revenue product curve is to the left of the original curve. It is the curve labeled MRP_{DA}—DA standing for discriminated against. There is discrimination in favor of white males, so their marginal revenue product curve is MRP_{DF}—DF standing for discriminated in favor of. The wage rate for black women falls to $20,000 a year and only 1000 are employed. The wage rate for white males rises to $60,000 a year and 3000 are employed.

policies must be based on careful economic analysis. Good intentions are not enough to bring about equality.

Human Capital Differences

As we saw above (pp. 407–410), wages are compensation, in part for time spent on the job and in part for the cost incurred in acquiring skill—in acquiring human capital. The more human capital a person supplies, the higher is that person's earnings, other things being equal. Measuring human capital with any precision is difficult. But there are some rough indicators. One such indicator is the number of years of schooling that a person has had. A second indicator is the number of years of work experience. The most recent figures indicate that the median years in

school for all races and both sexes are almost equal at about 12½ years. But this equality in median years of schooling is recent. In 1960, whites, on the average, spent about 11 years in school while blacks, on the average, had about 8 years of schooling. By 1970, that differential had been cut to two years and today it has virtually disappeared.

A third possible indicator of human capital is the number of job interruptions. Interruptions to a career disrupt and reduce the effectiveness of job experience and slow down the accumulation of human capital. Also, during a job interruption, it is possible that human capital depreciates through lack of use. Traditionally, women's careers have been interrupted more frequently than men's, usually for bearing and rearing children. This factor is a possible source of lower wages, on the average, for women.

Just as education differences are virtually disappearing, so career interruptions for women are becoming less severe. Maternity leave and day-care facilities are providing an increasing number of women with uninterrupted employment that makes their human capital accumulation indistinguishable from that of men.

Thus it seems that human capital differences possibly can account for earnings differentials among races and sexes in the past and some of the differentials that still remain. The trends, however, suggest that wage differentials from this source will eventually disappear.

Degrees of Specialization

People undertake two kinds of production activities: They supply labor services to the market (market activities) and they undertake household production (nonmarket activities). **Household production** creates goods and services to be consumed within the household rather than to be supplied to the market. Such activities include cooking, cleaning, minor repair work, education, and various organizational services such as arranging vacations and other leisure activities. Bearing and rearing children is another important nonmarket activity.

In Chapter 3, we discovered that people can gain from specializing in particular activities and trading their output with each other. Specialization and the gains from trade do not operate exclusively in the marketplace. They also operate within the household and among its members. It is not uncommon for one member of a household to specialize in shopping, another in cleaning, another in laundry, and so on. Specialization in bearing children is a biological necessity, although rearing them is not.

Consider, for example, a household that has two members—Bob and Sue. Bob and Sue have to decide how they will allocate their time between various nonmarket household production activities and market activity. One solution is for Bob to specialize in market activity and Sue to specialize in nonmarket activity. Another solution is to reverse the roles and have Sue specialize in market activity and Bob in nonmarket activity. Alternatively, one or both of them can become diversified doing some market and some nonmarket activity. A completely egalitarian allocation will have them each share the nonmarket tasks equally and each devote the same amount of time and energy to market activity. But unequal allocations of time are also possible with one of the household members specializing in market activity and the other being diversified.

In deciding which of the many alternative time allocations to choose, Bob and Sue will take into consideration their future plans for having children. The particular allocation chosen by Bob and Sue will depend on their preferences and on the market earning potential of each of them. An increasing number of households are choosing the egalitarian allocation with each person diversified between nonmarket household production and market activity. Most households, however, still choose an allocation that would have Bob almost fully specialized in market activity and Sue covering a greater diversity of tasks both in the job market and the household. What are the effects of this more common assignment of market and nonmarket tasks? Though there will always be exceptions, on the average, it seems likely that if Bob specializes in market production and Sue diversifies between market and nonmarket production, Bob will have higher earning potential in the marketplace than Sue. If Sue is devoting a great deal of productive effort to ensuring Bob's mental and physical well-being, the quality of Bob's market labor will be higher than if he were undertaking his household production tasks on his own. If the roles were reversed, Sue would be able to supply market labor capable of earning more than Bob.

Economists have attempted to test whether the degree of specialization can account for earnings differentials between the sexes by examining the wages of men and women where, as far as possible, the degree of specialization is held constant. For example, if the degree of specialization is an important factor influencing a person's wage, then men and women of identical ages and educational backgrounds in identical occupations will be paid different wages depending on whether they are single, married to a spouse who specializes in household production, or married to a spouse who works. Single men and women who live alone and who are equally specialized in household and market production and who have the same amounts of human capital and who do similar jobs will be paid the same wage. To make nonmarket factors as similar as possible, two groups have been chosen for analysis. They are "never married" men and women. The available evidence suggests that, on the average, when they have the same amount of human capital—measured by years of schooling, work experience, and career interruptions—the wages of these two groups are not identical but they are much closer than the difference between average wages for men and women. As we saw in Fig. 16.6(b), women are paid on the average about 66 percent of the wages of men. When allowance is made for degree of specialization and human capital, this wage differential comes down to between 5 and 10 percent, by some estimates. Some economists suspect the remaining discrepancy stems from discrimination against women, although the difficulty of measuring such discrimination makes this hypothesis hard to test.

Most of the difference in men's and women's wages arises from the fact that men and women do different jobs and, for the most part, men's jobs are better paid than women's jobs. There are, however, an increasing number of women entering areas that were traditionally the preserve of men. This trend is particularly clear in professions such as architecture, medicine, economics, law, accounting, and pharmacology where the percentage of total enrollments in university courses in these subjects for women has increased from less than 20 percent in 1970 to approaching, and in some cases exceeding, 50 percent today.

Comparable-Worth Laws

In 1963, Congress passed the Equal Pay Act and in 1964 the Civil Rights Act. These acts require equal pay for equal work. They are attempts to remove the most blatant forms of discrimination between men and women and whites and minorities. But many people believe that these acts do not go far enough. In their view, getting paid the *same* wage for doing the *same* job is just the first tiny step that has to be taken. What's important is that *comparable* jobs receive the *same* wages regardless of whether they are done by men or women, or by blacks or whites. Paying the same wage for different jobs that are judged to be comparable is called **comparable worth.**

Advocates of comparable-worth laws argue that wages should be determined by analyzing the characteristics of jobs and determining their worth on objective grounds. However, such a method of determining wage rates does not achieve the objectives sought by supporters of wage equality. Let's see why.

Figure 16.8 shows two markets: that for oil rig operators in part (a) and that for nurses in part (b).

The marginal revenue product curves (MRP_R and MRP_N) and the supply curves (S_R and S_N) are shown for each type of labor. Competitive equilibrium generates a wage rate W_R for oil rig operators and W_N for nurses.

Suppose that the knowledge and skills required in those two occupations—the mental and physical demands, the responsibilities and the working conditions—result in a judgment that these two jobs are of comparable worth. Suppose that the wage rate that is judged to apply to each of them is W_C. Suppose that a court enforces that wage rate as part of a comparable-worth ruling. What will happen? First, there will be a shortage of oil rig operators. Oil rig companies will be able to hire only S_r workers at the wage rate W_C. They will have to cut back their production or build more expensive labor-saving oil rigs. There will also be a fall in nursing employment. But this fall occurs because hospitals will demand fewer nurses. At the higher wage W_C, hospitals will demand only D_n nurses. The quantity of nurses supplied will be S_n and the difference between S_n and D_n will be the number of unemployed nurses looking for jobs.

Thus legislated comparable wages for comparable work may have serious and costly unintended consequences.

R E V I E W

Differences in earnings based on skill or education level arise because skilled labor has a higher marginal revenue product than unskilled labor and because skills are costly to acquire. Union workers have higher wages than nonunion workers because unions are able to control the supply of labor and, indirectly, influence the marginal revenue product of their members. Wage differences between the sexes and the races are harder to explain. They may arise from discrimination and from differences in human capital. Sex differentials may also in part arise from differences in the degree of specialization. Comparable worth law cannot, on its own, eliminate wage differentials. Differentials will be reduced only if differences in marginal revenue product are reduced. The process of equalization of human capital and of the degree of specialization will lead to lower differentials and possibly will eliminate them. ∎

Figure 16.8   The Problem with Comparable Worth

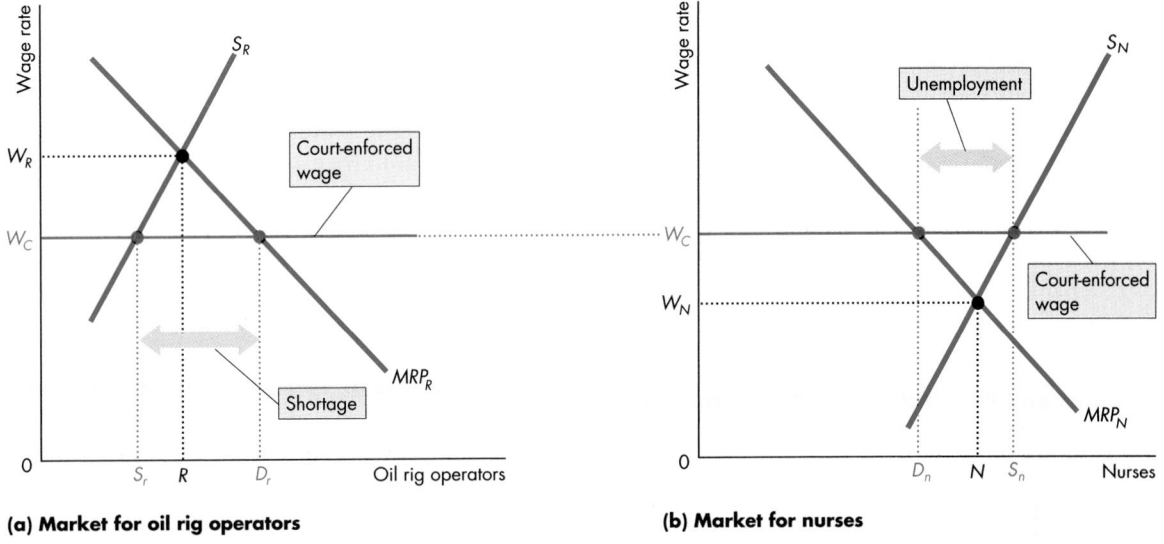

(a) Market for oil rig operators   **(b) Market for nurses**

The demand for and supply of oil rig operators (MRP_R and S_R) are shown in part (a) and for nurses (MRP_N and S_N) in part (b). The competitive equilibrium wage rate for oil rig operators is W_R and for nurses it is W_N. If an evaluation of the two jobs finds that they have comparable worth and it is ruled that the wage rate W_C be paid to both types of workers, there will be an excess demand for oil rig operators and an excess supply of nurses. There will be $S_n - D_n$ nurses unemployed and a shortage of $D_r - S_r$ oil rig operators. Oil producers will have to find other ways of producing oil (that are more expensive) and nurses will have to find other jobs (that are less desirable to them and less well paid).

Our next task is to study alternative compensation arrangements—those based on workhours and those based on performance.

Alternative Compensation Rules

A **compensation rule** is a formula for calculating a person's income. There are four commonly used compensation rules:

- Time-related payments
- Performance-related payments
- Payments based on the performance of a team or group
- Payments based on the performance of one person compared with that of another

Non-standard compensation arrangements have become increasingly common in recent years (see Reading Between the Lines, pp. 428–429). Let's look at the four basic alternatives.

Time-related Compensation Rules

Time-related compensation rules are called time rates. **Time rates** are compensation rules based on the number of hours an individual works; they are expressed in dollars per hour. Many occupations are compensated on a time basis and almost all production line jobs are rewarded in this way.

Performance-related Compensation Rules

There are three measures of performance that are commonly used as the basis for performance-related compensation rules. They are:

- Physical production (piece rates)
- Value of sales (commissions and royalties)
- Profit (profit-sharing)

Piece Rates   A compensation rule based on the amount of output a worker produces is called a **piece rate.** Workers are paid a dollar amount for each piece they produce. The piece may be a very simple item such as a shirt sleeve, or a more complicated service such as performing an appendectomy or writing a will. In all of these cases, the worker gets paid for the number of units of output produced, not for the number of hours worked.

Commissions and Royalties   **Commissions and royalties** are a form of compensation based on the value of sales. This method of compensation is common among salespersons, realtors, stockbrokers, pop singers, and authors. In all these cases, the person buying the output does not observe the amount of time that the individual works and the amount of effort exerted.

Profit-Sharing   **Profit-sharing** is a compensation rule that allocates a certain fraction of a firm's profit to its employees. Such compensation schemes are not as common as the others that we have just considered, and they are usually reserved for senior executives of corporations. Each year, newspapers and magazines publish lists of the top money-making executives of the year. Usually most of their multimillion dollar income is not from salary but from profit-sharing.

Team Performance

In some production situations with teams of workers, the output of the entire team decides the compensation of each of the members of the team. This method of compensation is used in some team sports, for example, where a win results in higher pay for each member of the team. It is also used in team production where a bonus is paid if the team achieves particular target output levels.

Besides bonuses, there are also penalties for failure. For example, a price is sometimes agreed to provided delivery takes place by a certain time. Failure to meet the agreed deadline results in a penalty being paid by the supplier. Such penalty

clauses are not common in labor contracts but they are common in transactions between firms.

Comparative Performance

Compensation rules based on comparative performance are a major form of compensation in professional sports. The winner of a tennis tournament typically is paid twice as much as the runner-up, who in turn receives twice as much as the defeated semifinalists. They in turn earn twice as much as the defeated quarterfinalists, and so on. As we'll see below, compensation of senior executives in firms can also be interpreted as having a ''prize element'' for winning.

Our goal is to work out why firms use compensation schemes based on performance. To achieve that understanding, we study what is known as the principal-agent model.

Principals and Agents

A **principal** is an individual who sets a compensation rule to motivate an agent to choose activities advantageous to the principal. An **agent** is a person who works for a principal and performs various activities, some of which are not observable by the principal. A principal may hire just one or many agents.

The compensation rule chosen by the principal will contain appropriate incentives. An **incentive** is an inducement to an agent to behave in a particular way. The word incentive is derived from Latin and means ''setting the tune.'' Thus an incentive can be thought of as a ''tune'' that induces an agent to ''sing the appropriate song.''

The observation of an agent's actions by a principal is called **monitoring.** A principal cannot monitor an agent without incurring costs. Such costs are called **monitoring costs.** In some situations, monitoring costs are modest; in others they are high. There are even situations in which no matter how much is spent on monitoring, the relevant actions of an agent cannot be observed. An example of low monitoring costs occurs in quality control work. A quality control worker's effort can be checked by observing how many defective items are missed. An example of expensive monitoring costs (which we don't observe in reality) would occur on a car assembly line. If an auto manufacturer hires a second worker to monitor every assembly line worker, it will probably go broke. An example of a situation in which monitoring is impossible is in the work of designers, film makers, and other creative artists.

Where monitoring is impossible, a principal has no choice but to use a compensation rule based on those parts of the agent's actions that can be observed. Where monitoring is possible but costly, the principal may be able to avoid monitoring costs by using a compensation rule based on only those aspects of an agent's behavior that can be observed at low cost. Let's look more closely at the monitoring of an agent's actions.

There are many situations where getting a job done presents problems of monitoring either the output of the worker or the effort that the worker is exerting. Often it is fairly easy to observe output but virtually impossible to measure effort.

Observing Output

Some of the best examples where we can observe output but not effort are those of professional services. Doctors, dentists, lawyers, and accountants provide services that in many cases are easily observed and evaluated by their clients. Performing an appendectomy, crowning a tooth, drawing up a will, or preparing an income tax return are all reasonably well defined activities that can be monitored and observed by the client. The client cannot observe how much effort the doctor, dentist, lawyer, or accountant exerts to produce the service. These are all cases where the quantity and quality of the product is known to the buyer, but the time and effort needed to produce the product is known only to the supplier—the worker.

Other examples concern the effort of people who work in a different geographical location from their employer, such as salespersons. These people are hired to sell as much as they can. Their output, measured in sales, can be readily observed by their employers, but not the time and energy they put into their job. It would be easy for a salesperson to take off a day or two, or to mix pleasure with business to the point where no business was being done. Provided the salesperson's output, measured in terms of sales, was large, the employer would never discover the low volume of effort.

There are other cases in which it is possible to observe effort but hard or impossible to observe output.

Observing Effort

It is often easy to observe effort but impossible to observe an individual's output when people work together as a team. The team effort produces the output. No one individual can produce the output alone and the contribution of any one individual to the final output cannot be determined.

Individual effort can be observed, however, when there are precise standards by which to judge it. These standards are present when the output is controlled by some objective circumstance, such as the speed at which a production line is running. In such a case, an individual worker has no choice but to put in the effort required to keep up with the production line. Examples of jobs in which effort can be observed are car assembly lines and steel rolling mills.

In some cases, neither the output nor the effort of an individual can be observed. Let's now consider these.

Observing neither Output nor Effort

The best examples of cases in which it is difficult or impossible to observe either the effort being exerted or the output achieved by a single individual is in the area of sports. The effort exerted by a tennis player, a boxer, a football player, and so on is known only to the individual player. The output is a sports event the quality of which depends on the joint efforts and interactions of all the players. Each individual player's contribution to the output is virtually impossible to assess. And it is also not possible to calculate each player's contribution to the commercial successes of the event, the revenue from selling tickets and broadcast rights.

Although sporting examples are the most obvious ones, there are many other cases in which neither individual effort nor output can be easily monitored. The effort exerted in the board rooms and executive suites of large corporations by chief executives is virtually impossible for their employers, the shareholders of the company, to monitor. The value of the executive's output, the extent to which his or her effort increases the profitability of the corporation, cannot be calculated directly.

If we cannot observe effort and output, how can we compensate people so that they do nevertheless supply the right amount of effort and a high quality output? In a nutshell, how can a principal devise a compensation rule that spurs an agent to take an action that is not observed but brings maximum attainable benefit to the principal?

Efficient Compensation Rules

Efficient compensation rules have two characteristics. The first characteristic is that the compensation rule delivers a maximum expected profit for the principal. A compensation rule that does not maximize the principal's expected profit (net of monitoring costs) can be improved upon. Profit-maximizing principals will constantly seek out an efficient compensation rule in each situation. A second characteristic of an efficient compensation rule is that it is acceptable to the agent. That is, whatever rule the principal proposes, it delivers a compensation package that the agent is willing to accept. In a competitive environment, an agent will have alternative job possibilities. An efficient compensation rule makes the agent at least as well off as in the best available alternative job. Let's consider an example.

Jenny has invented a revolutionary new vacuum cleaner—the Dustbeater—and she is going to hire a salesperson to go on the road and sell her product. She knows that a salesperson can put in a great deal of effort or take a lot of leisure on the job. The salesperson who takes leisure on the job is not going to encounter many potential customers and sales will be low. The salesperson who works hard might have bad luck and do no better than the lazy salesperson but might also have good luck and find a lot of customers with filthy rugs and worn out vacuum cleaners. But Jenny does not have the time to follow the salesperson around checking on the amount of effort being expended. How is she to tell the difference between a hardworking salesperson who has bad luck and a lazy one?

She structures the compensation package for the salesperson in such a way as to induce him to exert an effort that maximizes her expected income.

In figuring out the appropriate contract, she begins by working out the effects of the effort of the salesperson on her income.

Income, Effort, and Luck

Suppose that the total income of Jenny and the salesperson depends on two things: the effort of the salesperson and luck; let's also suppose that there are two levels of effort—"work" and "shirk"—and that there are two levels of luck—"good" and "bad." Income depends on the combination of effort and luck. The incomes arising from each of these considerations are set out in Table 16.2. Income is $60 if the agent shirks, regardless of whether there is good or bad luck. If the agent works, income is $140 if there is good luck and $60 if there is bad luck. The probability (or chance) of good luck occurring is 50 percent, or one half.

Jenny, the principal, can figure out the four possible outcomes shown in Table 16.2, but she cannot observe the effort of the agent nor tell whether the agent had good or bad luck. The agent—the salesperson—knows whether or not he is shirking but has no incentive to tell Jenny.

Jenny's problem is to figure out how to compensate the salesperson given the possible outcomes shown in the table. Her next step is to figure out what the salesperson's next best alternative employment prospect is.

Agent's Preferences and Alternatives   The agent has alternative employment prospects (selling encyclopedias or brushes) and also has preferences that Jenny has to take into account when designing the compensation rule. Let's suppose that the agent places a $20 value on shirking. That is, he prefers shirking to working but a day of working compensated with $20, or a day of shirking, are equally acceptable to him.

The agent does not have to sell vacuum cleaners. Let's suppose that selling encyclopedias will yield him an income of $70 a day but that $20 worth of work has to be expended to earn to $70, so the net gain to the agent is $50 a day. To attract the agent, the principal has to offer compensation worth at least $50. Jenny compares two compensation rules: Rule 1 is a daily wage and Rule 2 is a commission.

Table 16.2   Compensation Schemes for Dustbeater Salespersons

Incomes, effort, and luck

Luck	Effort	
	Work	Shirk
Good	$140	$60
Bad	$ 60	$60

There is an equal (50 percent) chance of good luck or bad luck.

Agent's preferences and alternative employment

Value of time spent working is $20 per day.

Income from alternative employment is $70 per day.

Value of work is $70 minus $20, which is $50 per day.

Compensation rules and outcomes

Rule 1: Principal pays $50.

	Value to agent
If the agent works:	$50 − $20 = $30
If the agent shirks:	$50 − $ 0 = $50

Outcome:
Agent's choice is to shirk.

Total income = Principal's income + Agent's income
$$\$60 \quad = \quad \$10 \quad + \quad \$50$$

Rule 2: Principal pays agent $20 plus 51 percent of value of output.

	Value to agent
If the agent works:	$20 + 0.51\left(\dfrac{\$140}{2} + \dfrac{\$60}{2}\right) - \$20 = \$51.00$
If the agent shirks:	$20 + 0.51(\$60) \qquad - \$ 0 = \$50.60$

Outcome:
Agent's choice is to work.

Total income = Principal's income + Agent's income
$$\$100 \quad = \quad \$29 \quad + \quad \$71$$

Under Rule 1, Jenny pays the agent $50 a day. The agent calculates the value of working and shirking. If the agent works, that value is $30—the $50 paid by Jenny minus $20 worth of work effort. If the agent shirks, that value is $50. Nothing has to be subtracted from the wage for work effort. In this situation, the agent chooses to shirk. Table 16.2 shows the outcome. Total income generated is $60. That income is divided between Jenny and the salesperson in accordance with the compensation rule. Jenny gets $10 and the salesperson $50. Tough luck for Jenny.

Under Rule 2, Jenny pays the salesperson $20 a day plus 51 percent of the total income generated. Let's look at the salesperson's choices under this scheme. If the agent shirks, regardless of his luck, he generates a total income for Jenny and himself of $60. He is paid 51 percent of that income—$30.60—plus the fixed payment of $20. Thus his income from shirking is $50.60. If the agent works, his income depends on whether he has good or bad luck. So he calculates his expected or average income. With good luck, total income is $140 but with bad luck, it is $60. Since there is an equal chance of good luck and bad luck, total income on the average is $100. The agent gets 51 percent of this amount or, $51. Over and above this amount, Jenny pays $20 a day but this payment is offset by the value of the effort expended by the agent in working. Thus the expected net value of work under this compensation scheme is $51.

The agent compares the outcome from working, $71, with that from shirking, $50.60, and concludes that work yields a sufficiently higher income than shirking to induce him to work. Since expected total income is $100, and the salesperson is paid an average income of $71, Jenny has an average income of $29.

Let's compare Rule 1 with Rule 2 from the point of view of both Jenny and the salesperson. Under Rule 1, the salesperson has an income of $50. Under Rule 2, the salesperson has an income of $71 on the average, but because he has to work, its value is only $51. Still, even when accounting for the distaste of having to work, the salesperson has $1 more under Rule 2 than under Rule 1. Jenny has an average income under Rule 1 of $10 and under Rule 2 of $29. She is better off under Rule 2 by $19. Since both the salesperson and

Bonus Schemes in Action

Bonuses Replace Wage Rises and Workers Are the Losers

Seeking to hold down labor costs, thousands of companies are changing the way they increase workers' pay. Instead of the traditional annual increase, millions of workers in industries as diverse as supermarkets and aerospace are receiving cash bonuses—and this new form makes a big difference.

While many corporate executives are promoting the bonus programs as a tool to share the wealth and increase productivity, the plans clearly mean less money for most workers.

The bonuses take many forms and names. . . . But virtually all of them have two things in common: They can vary with a company's fortunes, disappearing in hard times, and they are not permanent. . . .

In a recent survey, 1,120 of the 1,600 companies that responded had one or more of these bonus plans, and 69 percent of those companies had instituted the plans in the last five years, according to the American Productivity Center, a research organization. . . .

"The new bonus raise is contributing to a flattening of wages nationally," said Robert Reich, a Harvard economist. "We don't know how important the contribution is yet, but it is a factor." Total compensation—pay plus benefits, adjusted for inflation—grew by a scant three-tenths of 1 percent for all American workers in the year ended March 31 and only 1.8 percent in the previous year, the Labor Department reported.

The vast change developing in pay practices should, on the face of it, have labor unions up in arms. But unions, more concerned about losing jobs to nonunion companies and foreign countries with lower labor costs, are reluctant to fight the trend. . . .

Stephen P. Yokich, a United Automobile Workers vice president, insists that standard wage increases must be restored to the Ford and General Motors agreements in the contract negotiations that start July 22. Such increases have been absent since 1982, replaced by profit-sharing formulas that produced an average bonus of $2,100 a worker at Ford for 1986, but not a penny for G.M. workers.

The U.A.W. gave in on wage increases in 1982 because of the trauma of thousands of layoffs in the auto industry, and job security is still the main concern. "Wages don't mean a hill of beans if you don't have a job," Mr. Yokich said. "Wages are not the most important thing anymore; job security is." . . .

The New York Times, **June 26, 1987**

By Louis Uchitelle

The Essence of the Story

- A 1987 survey revealed that 70 percent of companies (1,120 out of 1,600) had profit-sharing bonus schemes and 69 percent of them had started such schemes between 1982 and 1987.

- Real wages increased very slowly during this period, and the more widespread use of bonus schemes was partly responsible for the slow wage growth.

- All the schemes have two things in common. Bonuses:

  —vary with company profits
  —are not built into base pay.

- Unions did not oppose the trend to greater use of profit-sharing bonuses, believing them to contribute to job security.

Background and Analysis

- Profit sharing is used when team effort is important and when the principal cannot observe the effort of each individual agent.

- It is unlikely that changes in the importance of team effort and in the cost of monitoring individual workers can explain the scale of the increase in profit sharing in the years since 1982.

- Also, it is unlikely that profit sharing has much effect on average wage rates (as claimed in the article). For a principal must reward an agent with the market average wage rate; otherwise the agent will quit and seek work with another principal.

- Slow growth in real wages between 1982 and 1987 can be explained by the forces of demand and supply. During those years, both demand and supply increased, increasing employment but keeping real wages steady.

- Profit sharing enables wages to adjust quickly when demand changes, and its spread in the 1980s may have arisen because demand changes have been large.

- With no bonus (top figure), the wage rate consists entirely of base pay. With a demand curve LD_0

and a supply curve LS, the wage rate is W_0 and employment is L_0. If demand decreases to LD_1, and if the wage rate does not fall, employment falls to L_1. To restore equilibrium, the base pay rate eventually falls.

- In the bottom figure, the same equilibrium wage rate, W_0, is made up of base pay and a bonus.

- In this case, if demand decreases to LD_1, the bonus shrinks, the wage rate falls to W_1, and employment falls to L_2, a smaller decrease than if wages failed to fall.

- Bonuses that make wage rates adjust quickly reduce the effects of demand fluctuations on employment.

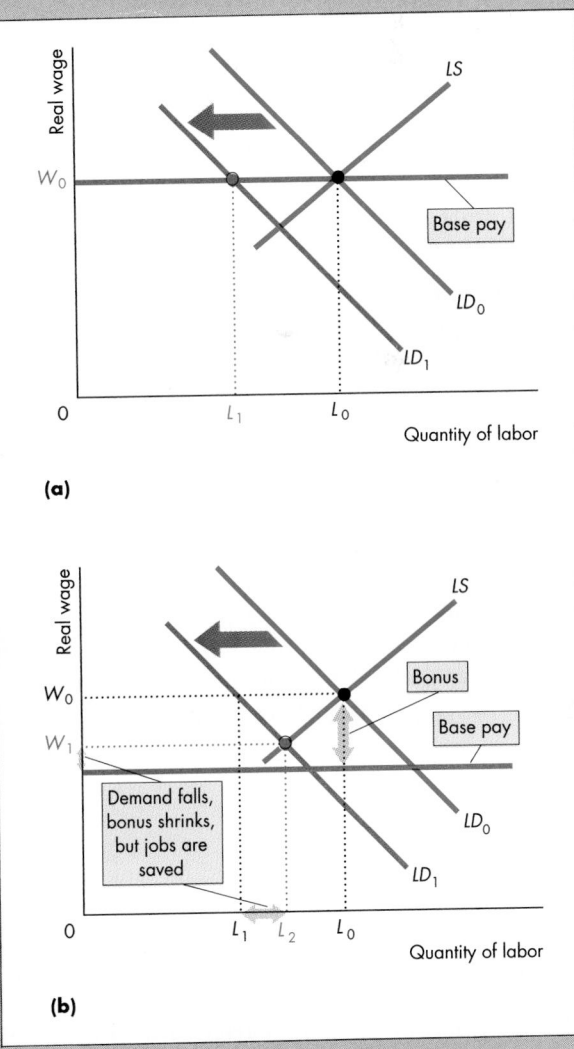

(a)

(b)

429

Jenny gain by using Rule 2, that is the compensation rule Jenny offers. This example illustrates why most salespersons are compensated for their work by a commission rather than a fixed daily wage rate. It also explains why piece rates are used to compensate textile workers and why royalties compensate authors. All of these cases are examples in which output—the value of the final product—can be measured but the effort of the individual worker in producing that output cannot.

Compensation Rules and Teams   The compensation scheme that we have just considered arises in a situation in which effort cannot be observed but an agent's output can. There are some situations in which neither individual effort nor individual output can be directly observed. These situations occur when the production process involves a team whose combined efforts determine how much is produced and at what cost. In these cases, performance-related compensation rules can be employed, but they have to be based on the total output of the team rather than on the effort of any one individual. The most comprehensive team compensation rule is profit-sharing.

Profit-Sharing   The objective of any firm is to maximize profit. Since that is the objective, why isn't *everyone* paid by a profit share? Profit sharing is, in fact, becoming more common (see Reading Between the Lines, p. 428), but there are many situations in which there is only a loose connection between profit and an *individual* agent's output where profit sharing is not used. Profit is the consequence of the joint output of all the firm's inputs. But profit gives a good indication of the effectiveness of senior management. It is their job to co-ordinate the other inputs to achieve maximum profit. That is why profit-sharing arrangements are usually seen in compensation rules for senior managers.

**Compensation Rules
Based on Rank**

Compensation rules that are based on rank deliver a payment related not to the *absolute* output performance of an agent but on the performance of one agent *relative* to another. This type of compensation rule is also common in sports, and because of this, such a rule is usually referred to as a rank-tournament compensation rule. A **rank-tournament compensation rule** is one in which the payment to the agent depends on the agent's rank in the tournament.

Let's see how rank-tournament compensation rules work. Table 16.3 contains an example that we'll use in our exploration of such rules. Suppose that there are ten agents, each of whom generates a value of output based on effort and luck in the same way as the agent in Table 16.2. Each agent has the same preferences as before and has the opportunity, from alternative employment, to generate a net return of $50. Compensation Rule 1 simply has the principal paying each agent $50. The agents accept this compensation rule but shirk. Total income is $600 (10 × $60); the principal pays the agents $500 and makes $100 of income.

Now consider Rule 2. The principal pays a prize of $260 to the agent with the highest output —the agent that comes first in rank—and pays $50 each to all the other agents. If two or more agents tie in producing the highest output, the prize is shared. How does the agent respond to this compensation rule? The answer is worked out in the final part of Table 16.3.

Each agent figures that by working there is a one in ten chance of winning the prize and nine in ten chances of not winning the prize. Therefore, the agent who works will expect an income of $71 (1/10 of $260 plus 9/10 of $50). The cost of working as opposed to shirking is $20, so subtracting that from the expected income leaves the working agent with an expected dollar value of work effort of $51. If the agent shirks, there is no chance of winning the prize, so income is $50. In this situation, each agent will choose to work. Since they all work, they will in fact all share the prize, so they will each receive an income of $71. This income is made up of $50, the income for coming in second, plus 1/10 of $210, the excess of the prize income over the normal income.

The total value of the work done by the agents, and therefore the principal's income, depends on whether good or bad luck occurs. On the average, the value of the output of a single agent is $100 (the average of $140 and $60). The total income generated by the 10 agents is, on the average, $1000 ($100 multiplied by 10). The agents receive $710 and the principal $290.

Comparing the outcome of Rule 1 with that of Rule 2, it is clear that both the principal and

Table 16.3   Rank-Tournament Compensation Scheme

Value of output of each agent

	Effort	
Luck	Work	Shirk
Good	$140	$60
Bad	$ 60	$60

There is an equal (50 percent) chance of good or bad luck.
There are 10 agents and the output of each agent is observable.

Compensation rules and outcomes

Rule 1: Principal pays each agent $50.

Outcome:
Each agent's choice is to shirk.

Total income = Principal's income + Agent's income
$600   = $100   + $500

Rule 2: Principal pays a prize of $260 to the agent with highest output and $50 to each other agent (a tie results in sharing the prize).

	Value to each agent
If the agent works:	$\frac{1}{10}(\$260) + \frac{9}{10}(\$50) - \$20 = \$51$
If the agent shirks:	$= \$50$

Outcome:
Each agent's choice is to work.

Total income = Principal's income + Agent's income
$1000   = $290   + $710

the agents gain by operating under Rule 2 rather than Rule 1.

Though rank tournaments in practice usually involve somebody winning outright rather than agents tying, rank tournaments work for exactly the same reason that this example works. By giving the agent the incentive to try for the prize, the agent finds it advantageous to work, thereby raising the income of the principal as well as that of the agent.

Professional tennis illustrates this type of compensation rule very well. If Martina Navratilova and Steffi Graff were paid by the hour, it would be in their interest to play a match where the game length was such that the cost to each of them of the last hour played equaled the hourly wage rate. If the wage rate was fairly high, they would play a long and boring game. If the wage rate was low, the game would be short (and probably equally boring). It wouldn't matter to either of them who won—they could even agree on the winner before the game began. Compensating such people with a prize for the best player induces each to try to be the best and produces a greater total output. In this case, it produces a greater total output by generating a higher quality and more exciting game of tennis that people are willing to pay more to watch.

Similar situations can be found in network newsrooms. Newscasters such as Tom Brokaw, Peter Jennings, and Dan Rather receive compensation packages well in excess of $1 million a year. They are talented broadcasters. But there are dozens of other talented broadcasters, working with them in their newsrooms and news-gathering organizations around the world. It is hard to monitor the activities of reporters, but the quality of the job that they do influences such things as total audience size and total revenue that can be generated from advertising during the newscasts. In such a situation, the news-gathering and reporting business can be treated like a tennis match. Though the rules are less precise and the rules for scoring are more complicated, those who perform best win the prize of being promoted to the most prestigious position in the news organization. The top prize, anchor on the nightly news, has to be worth enough to keep the people below that position working hard and competing for it.

The same considerations apply to the executive suites and boardrooms of large corporations. By having large differences in compensation between the chief executive officer and the people on the next rung below that level and so on down the executive ladder, a competitive environment similar to that of tennis or other sports tournaments is created. The result is an average level of effort that, though not observed and monitored by anyone, is higher than it otherwise would be. Paying the chief executive twice as much as everybody else makes everybody work harder!

Many individuals are compensated by a combination of the schemes we have just reviewed. For example, some senior executives are rewarded partly with a prize for winning a tournament, partly with profit-sharing, and partly on an hourly basis.

We have now seen how simple compensation rules based on observable characteristics of performance can spur agents to work hard for the principal, even when much of their effort cannot be observed. Where it is impossible to observe the agent's actions, the principal has no choice but to use such compensation rules. But in some situations, the principal can monitor the agent, at a cost, and make sure that the agent behaves in the principal's interest. An implication of the compensation rules that we have just examined is that sometimes, with appropriate compensation rules, principals can avoid monitoring costs.

Avoiding Monitoring Costs

To see why a principal can avoid monitoring costs, let's go back to the example of Jenny's vacuum cleaner summarized in Table 16.2. Suppose that by spending $1, Jenny can monitor the salesperson's effort. If a principal can monitor an agent's effort, then it is possible to base the agent's compensation on that effort. Suppose that Jenny incurs the cost of $1 to monitor the salesperson and offers the following compensation rule: If you work, I will pay you $71. If you shirk, I will pay you $50. The salesperson knows that Jenny can monitor his actions and therefore computes the value of working and shirking in the following way:

- If I work, I receive an income of $71 but incur a cost of working of $20; so the net value of my effort is $51.
- If I shirk, I receive an income of $50 but avoid the cost of working; so the net value I receive is $50.
- It pays me to work.

The salesperson works and receives an income of $71. Jenny receives an average income of $28. This income is arrived at in the following way. The average income generated by the agent that works is $100 (the average of $140 for good luck and $60 for bad luck). Jenny pays $71 to the salesperson and incurs a $1 monitoring cost. Subtracting these costs from the average total income of $100 leaves her with an average of $28.

Now compare the results in the case that we have just worked through with the example in Table 16.2 if Rule 2 is employed. Recall that under Rule 2 Jenny pays the salesperson $20 plus 51 percent of the value of the output. The salesperson works and receives an income, on the average, of $71. Jenny receives an average income of $29. The only difference between monitoring and not monitoring is Jenny's income. Her income falls by the cost of monitoring. The salesperson earns the same income in both situations. This example shows that a compensation rule can encourage an agent to work hard for a principal without the principal having to incur the cost of monitoring the agent's efforts.

Labor Market Equilibrium

You may be wondering, in light of this discussion of performance-related compensation, what has become of the idea that wages and employment are determined by equilibrium in the labor market. We have simply added a more detailed account of the labor market and one that requires a more detailed notion of labor market equilibrium.

Workers supply their time and effort in whatever way makes them best off. They have a variety of choices concerning not only the type of job to take and the number of hours to work but also the type of compensation scheme to accept. On the demand side of the market, firms decide not only how much of each type of labor to hire but also what to choose among the available compensation schemes for paying those workers. An equilibrium in the labor market consists of wage rates for different types of jobs, employment quantities in different jobs and industries, and a list of compensation rules that are actually used in each different type of employment. In labor market equilibrium, no individual worker (agent) can switch from one job to another or from one compensation rule to another and become better off. Moreover, no firm (principal) can offer a different compensation rule that will raise profit.

This description of equilibrium does not mean that clever principals cannot devise new, previously unthought of compensation rules that work better than existing compensation rules. There is technical progress in devising compensation rules just as there is technical progress in devising ways of getting cows to produce milk or tomato plants to produce fruit. But at any given point in time, given the alternative rules that have been invented, the best available compensation rule for each situation is being used. That is the compensation rule that provides the agent with at least as good a deal as the next best alternative employment and which maximizes the principal's profit.

■ In this chapter, we have extended and applied the factor markets model to understand a wide variety of phenomena in labor markets such as wage differentials and alternative compensation schemes. In the next chapter, we apply and extend the factor markets model to deal with markets for capital and for natural resources.

S U M M A R Y

Skill Differentials

Skill differentials arise partly because skilled labor has a higher marginal product than unskilled labor and partly because skills are costly to acquire. The higher marginal product of skilled workers results in a higher marginal revenue product. Since the demand for labor curve is derived from the marginal revenue product curve, the higher the marginal revenue product of skilled labor, the greater is the demand for skilled labor.

Skills are costly to acquire because households have to invest in human capital to become skilled. Investment sometimes means direct payments such as tuition and other training fees and sometimes means working for a lower wage during on-the-job training. Because skills are costly to acquire, households supply skilled labor on terms that compensate them for both the time spent on the job and the costs of acquiring the skills. Thus the supply curve of skilled labor lies above the supply curve of unskilled labor.

Wage rates of skilled and unskilled labor are determined by demand and supply in the two labor markets. The equilibrium wage rate for skilled labor exceeds that for unskilled labor. The difference in wages reflects the higher marginal product of skill and the cost to acquire skill. (pp. 407–410)

Union-Nonunion Wage Differentials

Labor unions influence wages by controlling the supply of labor. In competitive labor markets, unions obtain higher wages only at the expense of lower employment. Even so, unions can increase the total wage bill by forcing firms to hire at the point on their marginal revenue product curve where the

demand for labor is less elastic. Unions in competitive industries also influence the marginal revenue product of their members by restricting imports, raising minimum wages, supporting immigration restrictions, increasing demand for their product, and increasing the marginal product of their members.

In a monopsony—a market in which there is a single buyer—unions increase wages without sacrificing employment. Bilateral monopoly occurs when the union is a monopoly seller of labor, the firm is a monopsony buyer of labor, and the wage rate is determined by bargaining between the two parties.

In practice, union workers earn an estimated 10 to 25 percent more than comparable nonunion workers. (pp. 410–418)

Wage Differentials between Sexes and Races

There are persistent differentials in earnings between men and women and whites and minorities. Three possible explanations for these differentials are discrimination, differences in human capital, and differences in degree of specialization.

Discrimination results in lower wages and lower employment for those discriminated against and higher wages and higher employment levels for those discriminated in favor of. Human capital differences result from differences in schooling and work experience. Differentials based on schooling have been falling and have almost been eliminated. Differentials based on work experience have kept women's pay below that for men because women's careers have traditionally been interrupted more frequently than those of men, resulting on the average in a smaller accumulation of human capital. This difference is less important today than in the past. Differentials arising from different degrees of specialization are probably important and may persist. Men have traditionally been more specialized in market activity, on the average, than women. Women have traditionally undertaken both nonmarket, household production activities, as well as market activities. Attempts to test for the importance of the degree of specialization suggest that it is an important source of the difference between the earnings of men and women. (pp. 418–422)

Comparable-Worth Laws

Comparable-worth laws determine wages by assessing the value of different types of jobs on objective characteristics rather than on what the market will pay. Determining wages through comparable worth will result in a cut in the number of people employed in those jobs where the market places a lower value, and shortages of those workers that the market values more highly. Thus the attempt to achieve comparable wages for comparable work has costly, unintended consequences. (pp. 422–423)

Alternative Compensation Rules

There are four commonly used compensation rules:

• Time-related payments
• Performance-related payments
• Payments based on the performance of a team or group
• Rank-related payments (pp. 423–424)

Principals and Agents

Compensation rules are studied by using a principal-agent model. A principal is a person who specifies the compensation rule and the agent is a person who works for a principal and receives an income determined by the compensation rule. The principal's goal is to devise a compensation rule that will spur the agent to maximize the principal's profit.

There are many production situations in which observing or monitoring a person's effort or output is either expensive or impossible. In some situations, output is easily observed but effort is

not. In other situations, effort is easily observed but output is not. In some cases, neither output nor effort is readily observable. For situations in which either effort or output or both are unobservable, principals have to devise compensation rules that induce agents to work in a profit-maximizing way. (pp. 424–426)

Efficient Compensation Rules

Compensation rules have two characteristics: acceptability to the agent and profit maximization for the principal. When an individual agent's effort can be easily monitored but output is harder to observe, principals commonly use time rates of pay. When effort is not easily measured but output is, a compensation rule based on the agent's output can result in maximum profit for the principal. By paying an agent an amount that varies with output, or some fraction of the value of the agent's output, the principal can induce the agent to work harder and produce more.

Even when the principal can at some expense monitor the agent, it may still be possible to use a compensation rule that enables the principal to make maximum profit while avoiding the monitoring costs.

In labor market equilibrium, no individual worker or firm can become better off by adopting a different compensation rule. On the supply side, workers determine how much time and effort to supply, but they also decide which compensation scheme to accept. On the demand side, firms decide not only how much labor to hire but also what compensation schemes to offer. Labor market equilibrium consists of wage rates for different types of labor, the amount of employment in different jobs and industries, and a list of compensation rules for each different type of job. (pp. 426–433)

K E Y   C O N C E P T S

Agent, 424
Bilateral monopoly, 417
Binding arbitration, 411
Closed shop, 411
Collective bargaining, 411
Commissions and royalties, 424
Comparable worth, 422
Compensation rule, 423
Craft union, 410
Human capital, 407
Household production, 421
Incentive, 424
Industrial union, 410
Labor union, 410
Local, 410
Lockout, 411
Monitoring, 424
Monitoring costs, 424
Monopsony, 412
Open shop, 411
Piece rate, 424
Principal, 424
Professional association, 411
Profit-sharing, 424
Rank-tournament compensation rule, 430

Right-to-work law, 411
Strike, 411
Time rates, 423
Union shop, 411

Key Figures and Tables

R E V I E W   Q U E S T I O N S

1 Explain why skilled workers are paid more than unskilled workers.

2 What are the main types of labor union?

3 How does a labor union try to influence wages?

4 What can a union do in a competitive labor market?

5 How might a union increase the demand for its members' labor?

6 Under what circumstances would a minimum wage increase employment?

7 How big are the union-nonunion wage differentials in the United States today?

8 What are the three main reasons why sex and race differentials in earnings exist?

9 How do comparable-worth laws work and what are their predicted effects?

10 What are the main alternative compensation schemes?

11 Define and distinguish between a principal and an agent.

12 What are monitoring costs?

13 Why are student helpers at McDonald's paid by the hour rather than by the number of hamburgers they sell?

14 Why does Dan Rather make a higher wage than the news cameraman filming the war-torn streets of Beirut for the evening news?

P R O B L E M S

1 Wendy owns an apple orchard. She employs students to pick the apples. They can pick the following amounts of apples in an hour:

Number of students	Quantity of apples (pounds)
1	20
2	50
3	90
4	120
5	145
6	165
7	180
8	190

a) Draw the average and marginal product curves of these students.

b) If Wendy can sell her apples for 50 cents a pound, draw Wendy's average and marginal revenue product curves.

c) Draw Wendy's demand for labor curve.

d) If all apple growers in Wendy's neighborhood pay their pickers $7.50 an hour, how many students will Wendy hire?

2 Assume that fruit pickers become unionized and student pickers are outlawed. If the union gets the wage increased to $10 an hour, how many unionized pickers will Wendy hire?

3 In a small isolated town in the Rocky Mountains the only firm hiring workers is a logging company. The firm's demand for labor and the town's supply of labor are given by:

Wage rate (dollars per hour)	Quantity demanded (hours)	Quantity supplied (hours)
2	400	120
3	360	160
4	320	200
5	280	240
6	240	280
7	200	320
8	160	360

a) What is the wage rate and how much labor does the firm hire?

b) If the townspeople form a union that is more powerful than the logging company in the labor market, what is the wage rate and how much labor does the firm hire?

4 The value of the output of labor in a particular production is as follows:

Marginal revenue products

	Work hard	Average effort	Shirk
Lots of bugs	$100	$ 70	$ 70
Average bugs	140	100	70
No bugs	180	140	100

An agent might work hard, give average effort, or shirk and the production process may have lots of bugs, average bugs, or no bugs. Depending on which combination of these situations prevail, the marginal revenue product of a worker will be one of the numbers set out in the table.

From the worker's point of view, shirking has no cost. Supplying average effort has a cost of $10, and working hard has a cost of $20. The worker has to be offered a compensation arrangement that is worth at least $50. Devise a compensation scheme that will make the maximum possible profit for the principal.

5 Suppose that there are three national football leagues: the Time League, the Goal Difference League, and the Bonus for Win League. The difference between the three leagues is in the way the players are paid. In the first league, the players are paid by the hour for time spent practicing and time spent playing. In the second league, the players are paid an amount that depends on the number of points that the team scores minus the number of points scored against it. In the third league, the players are paid one wage for a loss, a higher wage for a draw, and the highest wage of all for a win.

Provide a brief description of the predicted differences in the quality of the game in each of these three football leagues. Which league will be the most attractive and generate the biggest profits?

Chapter 17

Capital and Natural Resource Markets

After studying this chapter, you will be able to:

- Define and distinguish among financial and real assets, capital, and investment

- Define and distinguish between saving and portfolio choice

- Describe the structure of capital markets in the United States today

- Explain how interest rates and stock prices are determined and why the stock market fluctuates

- Define natural resources and explain how their prices are determined

- Explain how markets regulate the pace at which we use exhaustible resources such as oil

An air of panic filled the cavernous New York Stock Exchange on Monday, October 19, 1987. It had taken five years, from August 1982, for the average price of a common stock to climb 200 percent. But on that single day, stock prices fell an unheard of 22 percent—knocking billions of dollars off the value of people's investments. The crash touched off other stock market plunges from Tokyo to London. Why did the stock market boom for five years and then crash so suddenly and so spectacularly? ■ If you had bought $1000 worth of the stock of Circuit City Stores in August 1982, five years later your $1000 would have grown in value to an impressive $3,337,300. In contrast, if in 1982 you had bought $1000 worth

Boom and Bust

of the stock of Brock Hotel Corporation, you would, by August 1987, have had only $17 left. Why do some companies' stocks boom and others slump? What determines the prices of individual companies' stocks? ■ The New York Stock Exchange, large as it is, is only a part of the enormous capital market of the United States. And the capital market of the United States is just a part of an even more enormous worldwide capital market. Every year, billions of dollars are saved and flow into the nation's and the world's capital markets. Savings flow by various channels—through banks, insurance companies, and stock exchanges—and end up financing the purchases of machinery, factory and office buildings, cars, homes, and a host of other capital goods. How does a dollar saved and placed on deposit in a bank help a firm to finance the purchase of a shiny new machine? How does your purchase of life insurance result in your savings enabling Pepsi-Cola to open a new bottling plant? ■ Giant firms, such as Shell Oil, and household names, such as Revlon and E. F. Hutton, have been taken over by other companies in recent years. Other firms, such as Sperry and

Burroughs, two computer makers, have merged to pool their strength. Takeovers and mergers affect the jobs of hundreds of thousands of people and change the competitive balance in entire industries. Why do firms merge or get taken over? ■ Many of our natural resources are exhaustible and yet we are using up these resources at an alarming rate. Every year we burn billions of cubic feet of natural gas and petroleum. We burn millions of tons of coal, we extract bauxite to make aluminium, and iron ore and other minerals to make steel. Aren't we one day going to run out of natural gas, oil, coal, bauxite, iron ore, and other natural resources? How do markets allocate these exhaustible resources? How are their prices determined? And do their prices adjust to encourage us to conserve such resources, or does the market need help to ensure that we do not pillage the exhaustible endowments of nature?

■ In this chapter, we're going to study capital and natural resource markets. We'll find out why people save as much or as little as they do, and why firms buy the amount of new capital equipment that they do. We will find out how interest rates and stock values are determined. In our study of natural resource markets, we'll discover that these markets obey some of the same economic laws as capital markets. We'll pay special attention to markets for exhaustible resources and discover how market forces act to encourage conservation.

Capital, Investment, and Saving

Let's begin with some capital market vocabulary and define three key terms:

• Asset
• Liability
• Balance sheet

An **asset** is anything of value that a household, firm, or government *owns*. A **liability** is a debt—something that a household, firm, or government *owes*. A **balance sheet** is a list of assets and liabilities.

Table 17.1 shows an example of a balance sheet—that for Rocky's Mountain Bikes. It lists three assets—cash in the bank, an inventory of bikes, and

fixtures and fittings—that add up to $243,000. The balance sheet contains two liabilities—a bank loan of $120,000 and Rocky's equity of $123,000. Rocky's equity is the amount that the company owes to Rocky.

Financial Assets and Real Assets

Assets fall into two broad classes: financial and real. **Financial assets** are sophisticated IOUs—pieces of paper that represent a claim against another household, firm, or government. When you hold an IOU, it means that somebody else owes you money. Similarly, if you own a financial asset, someone else has a financial liability—owes you money. For example, the savings deposit that you own (your asset) is a liability of your bank. The difference between financial assets and financial liabilities is called **net financial assets**. Net financial assets are the net value of the paper claims that one household, firm, or government has against everyone else.

Real assets are physical things such as buildings, plant and equipment, inventories, and consumer durable goods. Real assets are also called capital. **Capital** is the real assets owned by a household, firm, or government.

Table 17.2 illustrates the distinction between financial assets and real assets by again presenting the information contained in the balance sheet of Rocky's Mountain Bikes. But this time the information is sorted into financial and real items. The financial items in the balance sheet are the cash in bank (an asset) and the bank loan and Rocky's equity (liabilities). To calculate net financial assets, we have to subtract financial liabilities from financial assets, so the bank loan and Rocky's equity appear with negative signs. The net financial assets of Rocky's Mountain Bikes are −$225,000. The real assets are the inventory of bikes and the fixtures and fittings—the firm's capital—which add up to $225,000.

Capital and Investment

All the assets and liabilities recorded in a balance sheet are stocks. A **stock** is a quantity measured at a point in time. An example of a stock is the amount of water in Lake Powell at a given moment. Capital is a stock because it is the quantity of buildings, plant, and machinery in existence at a given point in time.

Table 17.1   Balance Sheet of Rocky's Mountain Bikes

Assets		Liabilities	
Cash in bank	$ 18,000	Bank loan	$120,000
Inventory of bikes	15,000	Rocky's equity	123,000
Fixtures and fittings	210,000	Total liabilities	$243,000
Total assets	$243,000		

A related concept to the stock of capital is the flow of investment. A **flow** measures a quantity per unit of time. An example of a flow is the number of gallons of water per hour passing from the San Juan and Colorado Rivers into Lake Powell. It is a flow that adds to the stock of water in the lake. **Investment** is the amount of new capital equipment purchased in a given time period. It is a flow that adds to the stock of capital.

There is another flow that reduces the stock of capital—like the water flowing out of Lake Powell into the Colorado River. That flow is called depreciation. **Depreciation** is the fall in the value of capital resulting from its use and from the passage of time. Investment adds to the capital stock; depreciation

Table 17.2   Financial Assets and Real Assets of Rocky's Mountain Bikes

Financial assets	
Cash in bank	$ 18,000
Bank loan	− 120,000
Rocky's equity	− 123,000
Net financial assets	−$225,000

Real assets	
Inventory of bikes	$ 15,000
Fixtures and fittings	210,000
Capital	$225,000

lowers the capital stock. The net change in the capital stock is the difference between investment and depreciation. To emphasize this fact, we distinguish between **gross investment,** the value of all the new capital purchased in a given time period and **net investment,** which equals gross investment minus depreciation.

Saving and Portfolio Choice

The quantity of capital supplied results from people's saving decisions. Saving is the opposite of consuming. **Saving** is income minus consumption. The sum of a household's past saving, together with any inheritances it has received, is the household's **wealth.** Wealth is allocated across a variety of financial and real assets in a manner described by the household's balance sheet. A household's choice regarding how much to hold in various assets and how much to owe in various liabilities is called a **portfolio choice.** For example, if a household decides to borrow $100,000 from a bank and to use that $100,000 to buy stocks in a corporation, the household is making a portfolio choice. It is choosing the amount of an asset (the equity in a corporation) and the amount of a liability (the bank loan).

In everyday language, we often refer to the purchase of stocks and bonds as investment. That everyday use of the word investment can cause confusion in economic analysis. It is to avoid that confusion that we use the term *portfolio choice* to refer to the choices that households make in allocating their wealth across the various assets available to them. We reserve the word *investment* to refer to the purchases of new real assets by firms and households.

We can illustrate the concepts of saving, wealth, and portfolio choice by looking at Rocky's *personal*

Table 17.3   Rocky's Income, Consumption, Saving, and Wealth

	Income	Consumption	Savings	Wealth
Initial net worth				$150,000
Year 1	$58,000	$50,000	$8000	158,000

situation—at Rocky's household balance sheet. Rocky has an initial wealth of $150,000 (see Table 17.3). During year 1, Rocky earns an income of $58,000, consumes $50,000, and saves $8000. His wealth rises to $158,000.

How has Rocky allocated his wealth among the various assets and liabilities? Table 17.4 separates out Rocky's financial assets and liabilities from his real assets. His financial assets include, first of all, his equity in Rocky's Mountain Bikes. Second, Rocky has some cash in the bank. This is his own personal bank account and is completely separate from the cash in the bike business. Third, Rocky has a mortgage on his home of $140,000 and a bank loan of

Table 17.4   Rocky's Financial Assets and Real Assets at End of Year 1

Financial assets

Equity in Rocky's Mountain Bikes	$123,000
Cash in bank	10,000
Mortgage	− 140,000
Car loan	− 10,000
Net financial assets	−$ 17,000

Real assets

House	$160,000
Car	15,000
Capital	$175,000

Wealth	$158,000

$10,000 secured by the value of his car. Rocky's personal net financial assets are −$17,000. Note the minus sign. It tells us that Rocky *owes* $17,000 more than he owns—his net financial assets are negative.

Rocky's real assets are his house (valued at $160,000), and his car (valued at $15,000), so his capital stock is $175,000. Rocky's wealth is the sum of his capital stock and his net financial assets. Since Rocky's net financial assets are negative (he owes more than he owns), his wealth is his capital stock minus what he owes—$158,000.

With exactly the same savings, investment, and wealth, Rocky could have chosen a different portfolio allocation. For example, he could have used his bank deposit to pay off part of his bank loan or part of his mortgage. Alternatively, he could have taken a bigger mortgage and a smaller bank loan. Savings and investment decisions determine how much wealth a person has. Portfolio decisions determine how that wealth is held and financed.

R E V I E W

There are two kinds of assets: financial and real. Financial assets are the paper claims that lenders have on borrowers. One person's financial asset is another person's financial liability. Real assets are buildings, plant and equipment, and inventories. Physical capital is the stock of real assets in existence at a point in time. Additions to the stock of capital are called investment. Capital wears out over time. This process is called depreciation. The quantity of capital supplied results from people's saving decisions. Saving is income minus consumption. The accumulated sum of past saving is wealth. The allocation of wealth among different assets and liabilities is called a portfolio choice. ■

Capital Markets in the United States Today

Capital markets are the channel whereby savings are translated into investment—into the accumulation of capital. There are three broad ways in which investment takes place:

- Households buy capital.
- Firms buy capital and finance it by selling stocks and bonds to households.
- Firms buy capital and finance it by loans from financial intermediaries who in turn take in households' savings.

Figure 17.1 illustrates the structure of capital markets and the financing of investment. The green arrows in the figure show that households can employ their savings (allocate their portfolio of wealth) in the three ways just listed.

- They can directly own firms (proprietorships and partnerships).
- They can buy stocks or bonds issued by firms.
- They can place deposits with financial intermediaries.

Financial intermediaries are firms whose principal business is taking deposits, making loans, and buying securities. The best known type of financial intermediary is a commercial bank. A **commercial bank** is a financial intermediary that takes deposits and makes loans. There is another important type of bank called an investment bank. An **investment bank** is a bank that trades in firms' equities and bonds. (The distinction between a commercial bank and an investment bank is a legal one made by the Glass-Steagall Act passed in 1932.)

Other important types of financial intermediaries are insurance companies and savings and loan associations. Insurance companies take in the savings of households and provide life insurance and pen-

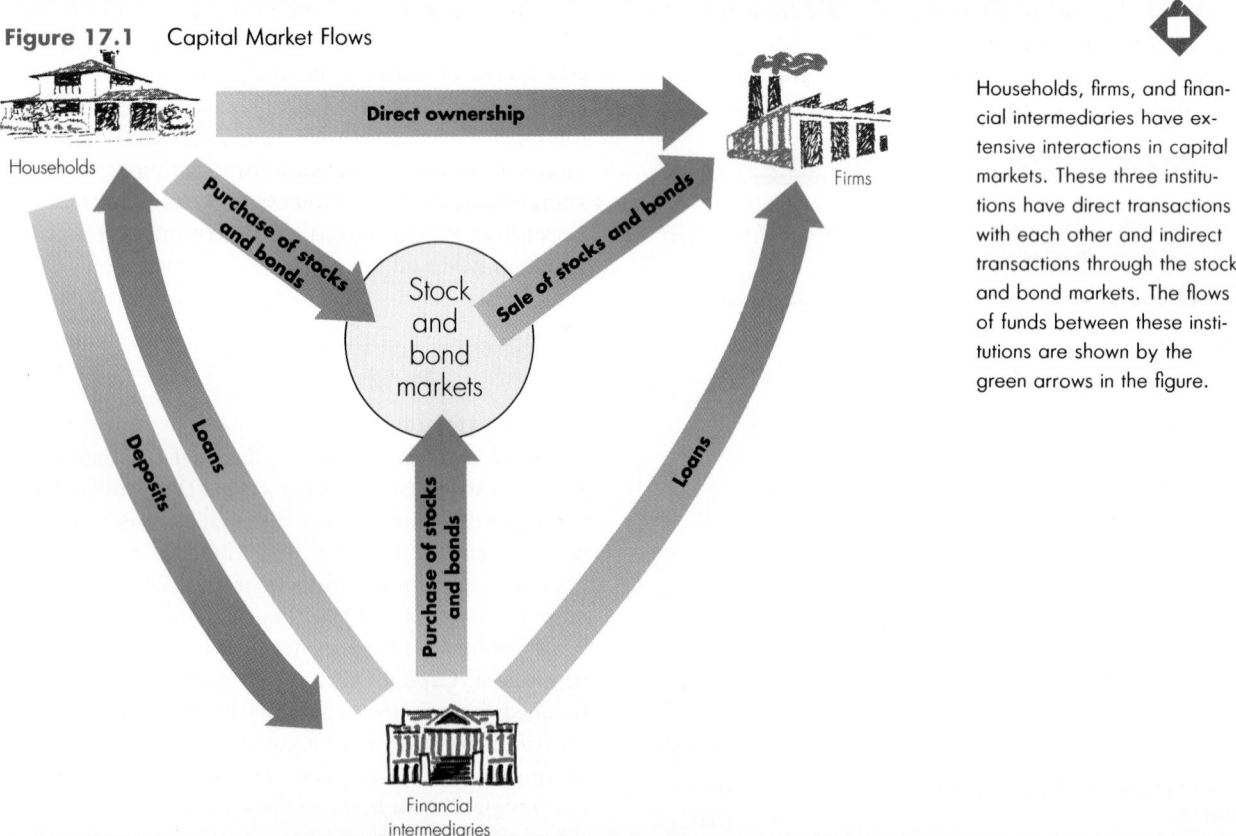

Figure 17.1   Capital Market Flows

Households

Direct ownership

Purchase of stocks and bonds

Sale of stocks and bonds

Stock and bond markets

Deposits

Loans

Purchase of stocks and bonds

Loans

Firms

Financial intermediaries

Households, firms, and financial intermediaries have extensive interactions in capital markets. These three institutions have direct transactions with each other and indirect transactions through the stock and bond markets. The flows of funds between these institutions are shown by the green arrows in the figure.

sions. They lend the money received from households to firms by buying equity or bonds. Savings and loan associations take in savings from households and make loans, mainly back to households in the form of mortgages.

Coordinating the actions of households, firms, and financial intermediaries are the markets for stocks and bonds. The **stock market** is the market in which the equities of firms are traded. The **bond market** is the market in which the bonds issued by firms and governments are traded. (Governments are not shown in the figure but are important participants in the bond market.) The distinction between equity and bonds was made in Chapter 9 (pp. 211–216). Firms sell stocks and bonds in exchange for money to finance their investment. Governments also sell bonds to finance their budget deficits. Households and financial intermediaries buy new stocks and bonds and also buy and sell existing stocks and bonds.

The direct ownership of capital by a household is the riskiest portfolio choice. It is placing all one's eggs in a single basket. For instance, if Rocky's bike firm fails, his household loses its wealth. If the bike firm succeeds, Rocky can earn an enormous return. Buying stocks such as shares in IBM or bonds in General Electric, is the second most risky way of allocating one's wealth. By holding a diverse collection of stocks, a household can spread its risk and avoid the extremes that can occur from lending to a single firm or a single project. Even so, there is still some risk because stock prices fluctuate. When stock prices fall, a household loses some of its wealth. Nevertheless, buying stocks is a much safer portfolio choice than putting everything into a single firm or project.

Bonds are less risky than stocks but their prices also fluctuate, so they are not a completely safe group of assets to hold.

The safest place to put one's wealth is depositing it into a financial intermediary. The risk associated with this portfolio choice is that a financial intermediary may make bad loans and be unable to repay its depositors. Although financial intermediaries fail on occasion, such failures are rare. Furthermore, deposit insurance provides guarantees in the event of a failure.

The Nation's Balance Sheet

How large are the U.S. capital markets? How big a role do the various elements play? The borrowing and lending pictured in Fig. 17.1 can be measured in the nation's balance sheet. This balance sheet lists the assets and liabilities of each of the major groups of agents in the economy—households, financial intermediaries, firms and governments. Figure 17.2 provides a picture of those balance sheets. The data, in trillions of dollars, are from December 31, 1984, and are the most recent available. Assets are shown in blue and liabilities in red. The green arrows show the direction of the flow of funds.

First look at the households. They have financial assets in the form of deposits with financial intermediaries, savings in life insurance and pension funds, and holdings of equity and bonds. The total of these items is $6.2 trillion. Households have financial liabilities in the form of mortgages and consumer credit totalling $1.7 trillion. Total financial assets of households exceed their liabilities by $4.5 trillion, that is $6.2 trillion less $1.7 trillion. Households own real assets in the form of houses and consumer durable goods valued at a total of $4.2 trillion ($3.0 trillion in houses plus $1.2 trillion in consumer durables). Total household wealth is the sum of net financial assets and real assets and is $8.7 trillion.

Next look at the financial intermediaries. Their liabilities are the deposits and life insurance and pension funds, which we have just seen as the assets of households. They are liabilities of financial intermediaries because the financial intermediaries "owe" them to households. The assets of financial intermediaries represent loans by these institutions to households, firms, and governments. Financial intermediaries make loans to households in the form of mortgages and consumer credit. The financial intermediaries make loans to firms and governments as a result of purchasing bonds issued by these institutions. Financial intermediaries also make mortgage loans to firms. These bond purchases and mortgages provide firms and governments with funds to buy real assets. The financial assets and liabilities of financial intermediaries are each $4.2 trillion.

The financial liabilities of firms—bonds ($1.3 trillion), mortgages ($0.4 trillion), and equity ($1.5 trillion)—totaling $3.2 trillion—are matched by their capital (real assets)—plant and equipment ($1.5 trillion) and buildings ($1.7 trillion).

Government financial liabilities (bonds) generate funds to finance the purchase of plant and equipment and buildings. The value of the government sector's real assets exceeds the value of its liabilities, and the difference is the wealth of the government sector.

Figure 17.2   The Nation's Balance Sheet

The nation's balance sheet records the indebtedness between the sectors of the economy—households, financial intermediaries, firms, and governments. The financial assets (blue) and liabilities (red) are shown in the top part of the figure, and real assets or capital (orange) appear in the bottom part. All numbers are trillions of dollars.

Households' financial assets are deposits with financial intermediaries, life insurance and pension funds, equity, and bonds. These assets are the liabilities of financial intermediaries, firms, and governments. Financial intermediaries take deposits and life insurance and pension fund contributions from households. Then they lend some of these funds back to households as mortgages and consumer credit; the remainder is lent to firms and governments in the form of bonds and mortgages. Both firms and governments borrow from financial intermediaries and households.

Capital (real assets) consists of houses and consumer durables owned by households and of plant and equipment and buildings owned by firms and governments.

Source: Statistical Abstract of the United States: 1986, 106th ed. p. 488.

The numbers in Fig. 17.2 give you an idea of the scale of the operations of the various elements in the capital markets. But they do not provide a flavor of the huge volume of transactions that take place—the flow of activity each day—nor of the dynamic change over time in the scale of capital market transactions. The daily turnover in the ownership of stocks and bonds is enormous. On an average day in 1987, more than 200 million individual stocks changed hands on the New York Stock Exchange. On what has come to be called Black Monday—October 19, 1987—a record 605 million shares were traded.

Demand for Capital

The demand for capital, like the demand for any other input, stems from firms' profit-maximization choices. As a firm increases the quantity of capital employed, other things being equal, the marginal revenue product of capital diminishes. To maximize profit, a firm uses additional amounts of capital until the marginal revenue product of capital equals the opportunity cost of a unit of capital. That is, the firm increases its capital stock until the additional total revenue generated by one extra unit of capital equals the opportunity cost of one unit of capital. When a firm rents capital equipment, its calculations are identical to those made to choose its labor input. The firm faces an hourly rate for renting a machine and it simply calculates the marginal revenue product of the machine per hour and compares that number with the hourly rental rate. Many machines are rented—for example, earth-moving equipment, cars, and airplanes—so these calculations are relevant in such cases.

But most capital is not rented. Firms *buy* buildings, plant, and equipment and operate them for several years. To decide how much capital equipment to buy, the firm must compare the price of the equipment to be paid, here and now, with the returns—the marginal revenue products—that the equipment will generate over its entire life. To see how a firm decides how much capital to buy, we need to convert the future stream of marginal revenue products into its present value so that it can be directly compared with the price of buying a new piece of capital equipment. You have already met the concept of present value in Chapter 9 (pp. 212–213)

and you may like to flip back to it to refresh your memory before moving on.

Net Present Value of Investment

Let's calculate the present value of the marginal revenue product of a capital input and see how we can use the result to make an investment decision. Table 17.5 summarizes the data that we'll use.

Tina runs a firm called Taxfile, Inc. The firm sells advice to taxpayers designed to minimize the taxes that they have to pay. Tina is considering buying a new computer that will cost $10,000. The computer has a life of two years, after which it will be worthless. Although Tina works hard all year

Table 17.5   Net Present Value of an Investment—Taxfile, Inc.

(a) Data

Price of computer	$10,000
Life of computer	2 years
Marginal revenue product	$5900 at end of each year
Interest rate	4% a year

(b) Present value of the flow of marginal revenue product

$$PV = \frac{MRP}{1+r} + \frac{MRP}{(1+r)^2}$$
$$= \frac{\$5900}{1.04} + \frac{\$5900}{(1.04)^2}$$
$$= \$5673 + \$5455$$
$$= \$11,128$$

(c) Net present value of investment

$$NPV = PV \text{ of Marginal revenue product} - \text{Cost of computer}$$
$$= \$11,128 - \$10,000$$
$$= \$1128$$

studying tax law and writing sophisticated computer programs that will enable her to corner a good share of the market, she generates an income only once each year—at tax filing time. If she buys the computer that she is now evaluating, Tina expects to be able to sell tax advice in each of the next two years that will bring in $5900 at the end of each year. The interest rate that she has to pay is 4 percent a year.

We can calculate the present value of the marginal revenue product of Taxfile's computer by using a formula similar to the one that you met on p. 213. The formula is set out in Table 17.5(b). The present value *(PV)* of $5900 one year in the future is $5900 divided by 1.04 (one plus the interest rate expressed as a proportion—4 percent as a proportion is 0.04). The present value of $5900 two years in the future is $5900 divided by $(1.04)^2$. Working out those two present values and then adding them gives the present value of the flow of marginal revenue product from the machine as $11,128.

To decide whether or not to buy the computer, Tina compares the present value of its stream of marginal revenue product with its price. She makes this comparison by calculating the net present value *(NPV)* of the investment. The **net present value of an investment** is the present value of the stream of marginal revenue product generated by the investment minus the cost of the investment. If the net present value of an investment is positive, it pays to buy the item. If the net present value is negative, it does not pay to buy this item. Only investments that have a positive net present value increase a firm's net worth. Part (c) of Table 17.5 shows this calculation. The net present value of Tina's investment in a computer is $1128. Therefore the investment is worth undertaking and Tina buys the computer.

Whenever the net present value of an investment is positive, a firm will increase its net worth by making the investment. Like all other inputs, capital is subject to diminishing marginal returns. The more capital is added, the lower is its marginal product and the lower is its marginal revenue product. We have seen in the above example that it pays the firm to buy one machine because that investment yields a positive net present value. Should Tina invest in two computers or three? To answer this question, she must do more calculations similar to those summarized in Table 17.5.

Suppose, in particular, that Taxfile's investment opportunities are as set out in Table 17.6. Tina can buy any number of computers. They each cost

---

Table 17.6   Taxfile's Investment Decision

(a) Data

Price of computer	$10,000
Life of computer	2 years
Marginal revenue product:	
Using 1 computer	$5900 a year
Using 2 computers	$5600 a year
Using 3 computers	$5300 a year

(b) Present value of the stream of marginal revenue product

If r = 0.04 (4% a year):

Using 1 computer: $PV = \dfrac{5900}{1.04} + \dfrac{5900}{(1.04)^2} = \$11,128$

Using 2 computers: $PV = \dfrac{5600}{1.04} + \dfrac{5600}{(1.04)^2} = \$10,562$

Using 3 computers: $PV = \dfrac{5300}{1.04} + \dfrac{5300}{(1.04)^2} = \$9996$

If r = 0.08 (8% a year):

Using 1 computer: $PV = \dfrac{5900}{1.08} + \dfrac{5900}{(1.08)^2} = \$10,521$

Using 2 computers: $PV = \dfrac{5600}{1.08} + \dfrac{5600}{(1.08)^2} = \$9986$

If r = 0.12 (12% a year):

Using 1 computer: $PV = \dfrac{5900}{1.12} + \dfrac{5900}{(1.12)^2} = \$9971$

$10,000 and have a life of two years. The marginal revenue product generated by each computer depends on how many Taxfile operates. If it operates just one computer, it has a marginal revenue product of $5900 a year (the case just reviewed). If Taxfile uses a second computer, marginal revenue product falls to $5600 a year, and in the case of a third computer to $5300 a year. Part (b) calculates the present value of the marginal revenue product of each of these three levels of investment in computers.

We have seen that with an interest rate of 4 percent it pays to invest in the first computer—the net present value of that computer is positive. It also pays to invest in a second computer. The present value of the marginal revenue product resulting from using two computers, $10,562, exceeds the cost of the second machine by $562. You can also see that it does *not* pay to invest in a third computer. The present value of the marginal revenue product resulting from using three computers is $9996. But the computer costs $10,000, so the net present value of the third computer is −$4. Tina buys a second computer but does not buy a third one. If she does, the net worth of Taxfile will fall by $4.

We have just discovered that at an interest rate of 4 percent a year it pays Tina to buy two computers but not three. Suppose that the interest rate is higher than 4 percent a year—say, 8 percent a year. In this case, the present value of one machine (see calculations in Table 17.6b) is $10,521. Therefore it still pays to buy the first machine. But its net present value is smaller when the interest rate is 8 percent than at the lower 4 percent interest rate. At an 8 percent interest rate, the net present value resulting from using two machines is negative. The present value of the marginal revenue product, $9986, is less than the $10,000 that the second computer costs. Therefore at an interest rate of 8 percent it pays Tina to buy one computer but not two.

Suppose that the interest rate is even higher, say, 12 percent a year. In this case, the present value of the marginal revenue product of one computer is $9971 (see Table 17.6b). At this interest rate, it does not pay to buy even one computer.

The calculations that you have just reviewed trace out Taxfile's demand schedule for capital. The demand schedule for capital shows the number of computers demanded by Taxfile at each rate of interest. As the interest rate falls, the quantity of capital demanded increases. At an interest rate of 12 percent a year, the firm demands no computers. At an interest rate of 8 percent a year, one computer is demanded; at 4 percent a year, the quantity demanded is two; and at an interest rate below 4 percent a year, the quantity demanded is three. (Although we have stopped our calculations at three computers, at lower interest rates Tina would buy yet more machines.)

Demand Curve for Capital

A firm's demand curve for capital relates the quantity of capital demanded to the interest rate. Figure 17.3 illustrates the demand for computers *(D_F)* by Tina's firm. The horizontal axis measures the number of computers that Taxfile owns and the vertical axis measures the interest rate. Points *a, b,* and *c* correspond to the example that we have just worked

Figure 17.3   A Firm's Demand for Capital

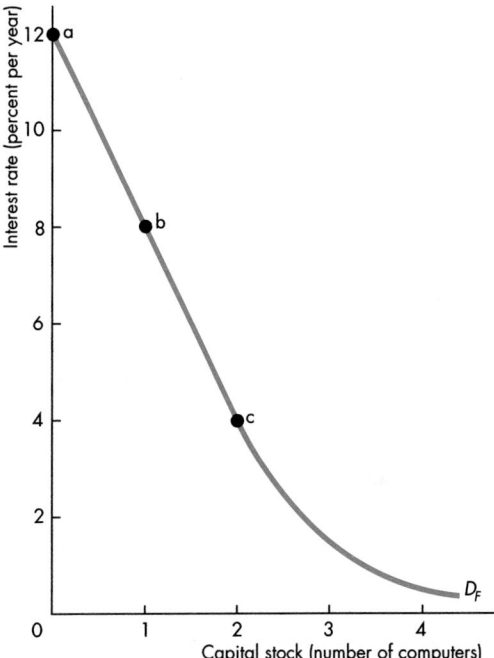

Taxfile demands capital (computers) until the present value of the stream of marginal revenue product of computers equals the price of a computer. The present value depends on the interest rate. The lower the interest rate, the higher the number of computers demanded. At an interest rate of 12 percent a year, Taxfile demands no computers (point a). At an interest rate of 8 percent, the firm demands 1 computer (point b). At an interest rate of 4 percent, the firm demands 2 computers (point c). If computers of different types (fractions of a $10,000 computer) can be bought, a demand curve that passes through points a, b, and c is generated.

through. At an interest rate of 12 percent a year, it does not pay Tina to buy any computers—point *a*. At an interest rate of 8 percent, it pays to buy 1 computer—point *b*. At an interest rate of 4 percent, it pays to buy 2 computers—point *c*.

In our example, we've only considered one type of computer—that which costs exactly $10,000. In practice, Tina could consider buying a different type of computer the power of which could be expressed as a multiple or fraction of one of the $10,000 computers that we've been considering here. For example, there may be a $5000 computer that has half

Figure 17.4   The Market Demand for Capital

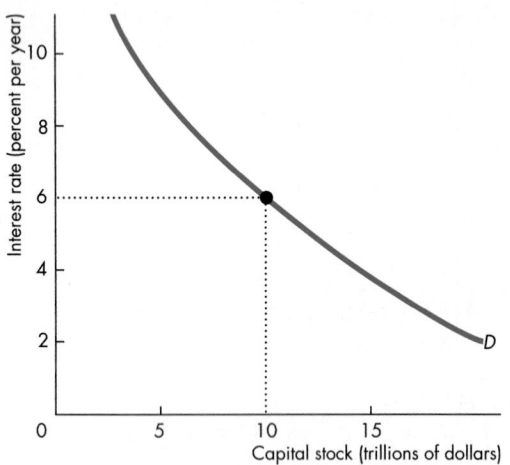

The market demand curve for capital is obtained by adding together the demand curve for capital of all the firms in the economy. An example of a market demand curve is *D*. On this demand curve, the quantity of capital demanded is $10 trillion when the interest rate is 6 percent a year, and the quantity of capital demanded falls as the interest rate rises, other things being equal.

the power of a $10,000 machine. Or a bigger machine costing $12,500 that has one and a quarter times the power of a $10,000 machine. If we consider all the different types of computers that Tina can buy, we will generate not just the three points *a, b,* and *c* but an entire demand curve like that shown in the figure.

The market demand curve for capital is obtained by adding all the individual firm's demand curves. Since different firms demand different types of machines (and since even the same firm demands different types of machines), we have to use common units of measurement to calculate the market demand curve for capital. The dollar value is a convenient unit. The market demand curve is shown in Fig. 17.4. It measures the total quantity of capital demanded (in trillions of dollars) on the horizontal axis and the interest rate on the vertical axis. On that curve, at an interest rate of 6 percent per year the quantity of capital demanded is $10 trillion. Like the firm's demand curve, the market demand curve slopes down.

Changes in the Demand for Capital

The demand for capital is constantly changing and the demand curve for capital is constantly shifting. Also, the composition of the demand for capital is constantly changing, the demand for some types of capital increases while the demand for other types decreases. Technological change is the main force generating these changes in the demand for capital. For example, the development of diesel engines for railroad transportation resulted in a decrease in demand for steam engines, an increase in demand for diesel engines, and not much change in the overall demand for capital in the railroad industry. In contrast, the development of desktop computers has led to a large increase in demand for office and research computing equipment.

The general trend resulting from the development of new technology and its exploitation through innovation is for the demand for capital to steadily increase over time with a steady rightward shift of the demand curve for capital.

R E V I E W

The demand for capital is determined by firms' profit-maximizing choices. The marginal product of capital declines as the amount of capital used rises. As a consequence, the marginal revenue product of capital declines as more capital is used. Capital is demanded up to the point where the present value of its stream of marginal revenue products equals its price. The interest rate is an important factor in the present value calculation. The higher the interest rate, the lower is the present value of the stream of marginal revenue products.

The demand curve for capital is the relationship between the quantity of capital demanded and the interest rate. The higher the interest rate, the lower is the present value of the stream of marginal products and the smaller is the quantity of capital demanded by a firm. The demand curve for capital slopes downward. The demand for capital changes as a result of technological change. There is a general tendency for the demand for capital to increase over time with the demand curve for capital shifting to the right.   ■

The Supply of Capital

The quantity of capital supplied results from the saving decisions of households. The most important factors determining a household's savings are:

• The household's current income in relation to its expected future income
• The interest rate

The stage in the household's life cycle is the major factor influencing whether current income is high or low compared with expected future income. Households typically smooth their consumption over the life cycle. Consumption smoothing is one of the main influences on the savings of a household. As we saw in Chapter 15 some young households typically have low current income compared with their expected future income, and older households have high income relative to expected future income; young people incur debts, older people save and accumulate assets. A household's savings depends on how much it smoothes its consumption over the life cycle.

Interest Rate

There are two distinct effects of interest rates on the level of savings:

• Substitution effect
• Income effect

Substitution Effect   A higher interest rate increases the future payoff from today's saving. It therefore increases the opportunity cost of current consumption. Thus a higher interest rate encourages people to economize on current consumption and take advantage of the higher interest rate available on savings. As the interest rate rises, people substitute higher future consumption for current consumption, and savings increase.

Income Effect   A change in the interest rate changes people's incomes. Other things being equal, the higher a person's income, the higher is the level of current consumption and the higher are the levels of future consumption and of saving.

The effect of a change in the interest rate on income depends on whether a person is a borrower or a lender. For a lender—a person with positive net financial assets—an increase in interest rates increases income, so the income effect is positive. The income effect reinforces the substitution effect and a higher interest rate results in higher savings.

For a borrower—a person with negative net financial assets—an increase in interest rates decreases the income available for consumption. In this case, the income effect is negative—higher interest rates lower consumption and savings. The income effect works in a direction opposite to that of the substitution effect and savings may decrease.

Supply Curve of Capital

The supply of capital is the total stock of accumulated savings by a household. The supply curve of capital shows the relationship between the quantity of capital supplied and the interest rate. We've seen that this relationship depends on the relative strengths of the income effect and the substitution effect, and for an individual household may be either positive or negative. For the economy as a whole, however, the substitution effect is stronger than the income effect, so a higher interest rate encourages saving and the supply curve of capital is upward-sloping. Figure 17.5 illustrates the supply curve of capital. On that

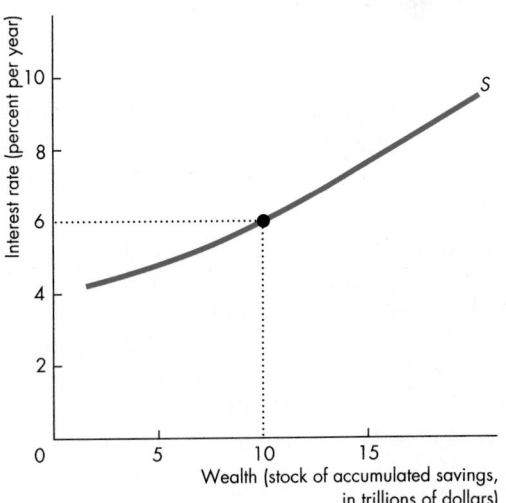

Figure 17.5   The Supply of Capital

The higher the interest rate, the more capital households supply—the supply curve of capital slopes upward. At an interest rate of 6 percent a year, the quantity of capital supplied is $10 trillion.

curve, at an interest rate of 6 percent per year, the quantity of capital supplied is $10 trillion.

Changes in the Supply of Capital

The supply of capital changes constantly. The main influences on the supply of capital are demographic. As the population changes and as its age distribution changes, so does the supply of capital. A population with a larger proportion of young people has a smaller supply of capital than a population with a larger proportion of middle-aged people. The age distribution of the population affects the supply of capital as a result of the life-cycle consumption smoothing described above.

Another influence on the supply of capital is the average income level. The higher the level of income, the larger is the supply of capital. A growing population and steadily rising income result in the supply of capital curve gradually shifting to the right over time.

Portfolio Choices

Households have to choose not only how much to save (the total quantity of capital to supply) but also how to allocate their savings across various financial assets—which financial assets to hold.

In making portfolio choices, households take account of two primary factors:

• Relative interest rates
• Relative degrees of risk

Relative Interest Rates Other things being equal, the higher the interest rate on a particular asset, the more of that asset and the less of other assets will households choose to hold. For example, if the interest rate on bonds is 10 percent a year and on equities 5 percent a year, households will want to switch their portfolios away from holding equities and into holding bonds. If the gap widens even further so that bonds are yielding 12 percent a year and equities 3 percent a year, households will want to switch out of equities and hold even more bonds.

If the interest rates on equities and bonds are identical and if all other things are equal, then households will be indifferent between putting their wealth into bonds or equities.

Relative Degrees of Riskiness In general, when comparing two securities, there are more things to take into account than their interest rates. The certainty with which those interest rates are available is also an important consideration. To make this clear, suppose that you have the following two choices:

1 Put your money in the bank for a guaranteed interest rate of 5 percent a year.

2 Lend your money to a friend who has an exciting business idea. If his business succeeds, he will pay you back with interest at a rate of 150 percent. If his business fails, not only will he pay you no interest, he will not even give you your original money back.

The first option has no risk. For every dollar you put in the bank you will have $1.05 one year from now for sure. The second option has a great deal of risk. To compare this second risky project with the first safe project, you need to calculate the expected interest rate that you would make and also to make some assessment of the degree of risk. Suppose that your friend has been involved in several other business ventures and you know from experience that half of them succeeded and the other half failed. Let's suppose also that you have no reason to expect this project to be any different from the others. If you were to put your savings into a large number of your friend's projects, half of the time you'd lose your savings and the other half of the time you'd receive $2.50 on every dollar put into these projects. On the average, you would receive $1.25 on each dollar. You will expect an interest rate of 25 percent on your financial stake in your friend's projects. Whether an interest rate of 25 percent with a lot of risk is better or worse than an interest rate of 5 percent with no risk is something that only you can decide. It depends on your attitude toward risk. Some people feel that the risk is worth taking. Others would rather sleep well at night. In general, the wealthier the person and the larger the number of projects they can put their savings into, the more willing they are to take risks on any individual project. But one thing is clear: The higher the degree of risk, the higher is the interest rate required to make a project worthwhile.

REVIEW

The quantity of capital supplied is determined by households' saving decisions. Savings depend on the amount of consumption smoothing the household undertakes over its life cycle and the interest rate. The more the household smoothes its consumption and the higher the interest rate, the larger the amount people save. The supply curve of capital is the relationship between the interest rate and the quantity of capital supplied. It slopes upward — the higher the interest rate, the larger the quantity of capital supplied, other things being equal. The supply of capital changes as a result of changes in the population and its age composition, and the level of income. Increasing population and increasing income result in a steady increase in the supply of capital — with the supply curve shifting steadily to the right.

People allocate their savings to different types of assets depending on relative interest rates and relative degrees of risk. Other things being equal, the higher the interest rate and the lower the riskiness of a particular asset, the larger the amount of savings people will allocate to that asset. ∎

Now that we have studied the demand for and supply of capital, we can bring these two sides of the capital market together and study the determination of interest rates and asset prices. We'll then be able to answer some of the questions posed at the beginning of this chapter about the stock market and understand the forces that produce stock market booms and crashes.

Interest Rates and Asset Prices

Households' saving plans and firms' investment plans are coordinated through capital markets. Asset prices and interest rates adjust to make these plans compatible. We are now going to study the way in which these market forces work. And we are going to discover what determines the stock market value of a firm.

Two Sides of the Same Coin

Interest rates and asset prices can be viewed as two sides of the same coin. We'll look first at interest rates, then at asset prices, and finally at the connection between them. Some assets, such as bank deposits, earn a guaranteed interest rate. Other assets, such as bonds and shares in the stocks of firms, do not. The interest rates on these assets are usually called bond yields and stock yields. A **bond yield** is the interest on a bond, expressed as a percentage of the price of the bond. A **stock yield** is the income from a share in the stock of a firm, expressed as a percentage of the price of the share — the stock market price. A bond earns a guaranteed dollar income, but its market price fluctuates and hence its yield also fluctuates. A share in the stock of a firm earns a dividend based on the profitability of the firm. Also the stock market value of the share fluctuates. Thus a stock yield fluctuates for two reasons — fluctuations in the dividend and fluctuations in its stock market price.

Let's now look at the two sides of the same coin — the price of an asset and its yield or interest rate. To calculate a bond yield or stock yield, we divide the earnings of the asset by the price paid for it. For example, if Taxfile, Inc., pays a dividend of $5 a share and if a share can be bought for $50, the stock yield will be 10 percent ($5 divided by $50, expressed as a percent). It follows from this calculation that for a given amount of earnings, the higher the price of an asset, the lower its yield. For example, if the price of a share in Taxfile increases to $100 but its dividend remains constant at $5, its yield falls to 5 percent. This connection between the price of an asset and its yield or interest rate means that we can study the market forces in capital markets as simultaneously determining asset yields (interest rates) and asset prices. We will first look at capital market equilibrium in terms of interest rate (or yield) determination and then in terms of the stock market value of a particular firm.

Equilibrium Interest Rate

Figure 17.6 brings together the relevant parts of the previous analysis of the demand for and supply of capital. The diagram shows the entire capital market. The horizontal axis measures the total quantity of capital. Notice that the axis is labeled "Capital stock

Figure 17.6   Capital Market Equilibrium

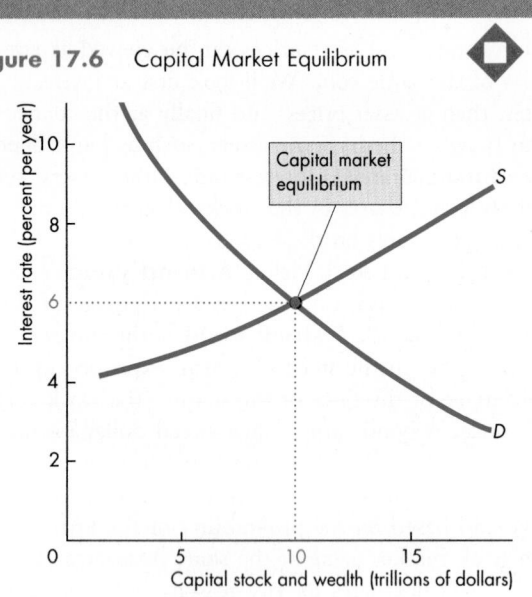

Capital market equilibrium occurs when the interest rate is such that the quantity of capital demanded equals the quantity of capital supplied. The demand curve is *D* and the supply curve is *S*. These curves intersect at an interest rate of 6 percent a year and a capital stock of $10 trillion.

and wealth." This label emphasizes the fact that the value of the capital stock and of wealth are equivalent. The vertical axis measures the interest rate. The demand curve (*D*) is the market demand for capital that you met in Fig. 17.4. The supply curve (*S*) is the market supply of capital shown in Fig. 17.5.

Capital market equilibrium occurs where the quantity of capital supplied equals the quantity of capital demanded. In Fig. 17.6, this equilibrium occurs at an interest rate of 6 percent a year where $10 trillion of capital is supplied and demanded. The market forces that bring about the equilibrium are exactly the same as those that we have discussed in the context of the markets for goods and services. In the case of the capital market, there are organized institutions, banks, insurance companies, and specialized dealers that constantly trade, thus maintaining equality between the quantity of capital demanded and quantity supplied.

The interest rate determined in Fig. 17.6 is the *average* interest rate. Interest rates on individual assets will be distributed around that average, based on the relative degree of riskiness of individual assets. An asset with a high degree of risk will earn an interest rate that exceeds the average and a very safe asset will earn an interest rate that is below the average. For example, if the average interest rate is 6 percent a year as shown in Fig. 17.6, the interest rate on a bank deposit might be 4 percent a year (a safer asset) and that on equities 8 percent a year (riskier assets).

We've now seen how asset yields or interest rates are determined. Let's look at the other side of the coin—asset prices. To determine asset prices, we will change our focus and look not at the capital market in aggregate but at the stock market value of an individual firm.

Stock Market Value of a Firm

We've seen that there is a connection between an asset's yield (or interest rate) and that asset's price. The yield is the earnings on the asset divided by its price (expressed as a percent). Let's use this fact to work out the stock market value of a firm. Suppose that a firm finances its purchases of capital by selling shares of its stock. What determines the price of a share? What determines the total value of all the shares sold?

The value of a share depends on the total value of the firm and on the number of shares sold. The value of one share is equal to the value of a firm divided by the number of shares sold, or, equivalently, the value of the firm is equal to the value of one share multiplied by the number of shares sold. So for a firm with a given number of shares, asking what determines the price of a share is the same as asking what determines the value of the firm?

When a person buys a share in the stock of a firm, that person becomes entitled to receive a profit each year. The price of a share depends on the expected future profit to be paid out by the firm. As we discovered in Chapter 9 (pp. 215–216) when we looked at the value of a share in Wisconsin Toy, the price of a share is the present value of its expected future profit. If a firm is expected to pay out no profits at all in the future, its shares will be worthless. If it is expected to pay out $10 a year on a share and if the interest rate is 10 percent a year, its shares will be worth $100 each. If it is expected to pay out $20 a year on a share and the interest rate is 10 percent, its shares will be worth $200 each.

The price of a share is determined by current expectations of the future profitability of the firm. Stockholders must therefore form expectations about future profit. How do they go about that task?

Rational Expectations

We defined a rational expectation in Chapter 6 (pp. 139) as the best forecast that can be made on the basis of all the available and relevant information. To make a rational expectation about future profit, it is necessary to make a forecast of the future profitability of the firm.

Stockholders calculate the profitability of a firm by making forecasts of conditions in the firm's output markets, input markets, and the technological developments that will influence the firm. For example, forecasts are made of the demand for the firm's product, the degree of competition that it faces, new cost-saving technologies that might become available to it, and the prices of the inputs that it employs to produce a good. Armed with forecasts of all these things, stockholders can forecast the future profit of the firm. By discounting the forecasted future profit, stockholders can calculate the price that it is worth paying today for a share of the stock of the firm.

Price-Earnings Ratio

A commonly used measure to describe the performance of a firm's stock is its price-earnings ratio. A *price-earnings ratio* is the current price of a share in a firm's stock divided by the most recent year's profit per share. In 1982, the average price-earnings ratio of the stocks that formed the Dow-Jones Industrial Average was 8.1. By 1987, the price-earnings ratio had risen to 20.5, but that was a peak year. The ratio then fell off and, at the beginning of 1989, stood at about 12.

What determines a price-earnings ratio? Why, at the beginning of 1989, was Ford's price-earnings ratio only 5 while Sony's was 33?

We have seen that the price of a share of stock is determined by the present value of the expected future profit of the firm. The higher the *expected future* profit, the higher is *today's* price. The price-earnings ratio of a firm depends on its current profit in relation to its expected future profit. When expected future profit is high relative to current profit, the price-earnings ratio is high. When expected future profit is low relative to current profit, the price-earnings ratio is low. Fluctuations in the price-earnings ratio arise from fluctuations in expected future profit relative to current profit.

Stock Market Volume and Prices

Sometimes the prices quoted on the stock market rise or fall with little trading taking place. At other times, stock market prices rise or fall with an enormous volume of trading. On yet other occasions, there is little change in the stock prices but there is an enormous volume of trading. Why do stock prices rise or fall and what determines the volume of trading on the stock market?

Stock prices rise and fall because of changes in expectations of future profit. Consider the firm whose profit per share is $1. Suppose that the interest rate on assets that are as risky as a share of this firm's stock is 8 percent a year. Further suppose that the firm's profit in each future year is expected to be exactly the same as this year's. The price of the firm's stock will adjust until a share can be bought for the price that makes the stock yield equal to 8 percent a year. That price is $12.50. People will buy shares in this company for $12.50 and expect, on the average, to make $1 a share each year, or a stock yield of 8 percent ($1 is 8 percent of $12.50). The price-earnings ratio will be 12.5—today's price ($12.50) divided by last year's profit ($1 per share).

Suppose that market conditions change and people now expect the firm's profit to double to $2 per share starting next year. With an expected profit of $2 a share, the stock market price jumps to $25. It's true that at $25 a share this year's profit ($1 per share) represents only a 4 percent stock yield ($1 is 4 percent of $25), but with profit expected to be $2 per share next year and every year thereafter, the expected yield is 8 percent a year—the interest rate available on other assets of similar risk. This price jump to $25 occurs with no change in the current year's profitability of the firm. It occurs entirely because people observe some event today that leads them to expect higher profit in the future.

Suppose that the change in market conditions leading to expected higher future profit is so obvious that everyone can see it and everyone agrees that this firm's earnings are indeed going to double next year. In such a situation, the market value of the firm's shares rises to $25 but no one buys or sells shares. Stockholders are happy with the shares that they already hold. If the price does not rise to $25, everyone will want to buy some shares. If the price rises to more than $25, everyone will want to sell some shares. If the price rises to exactly $25, everyone will be indifferent between hanging on to those shares or buying some other shares that are currently yielding 8 percent a year.

On the other hand, suppose that the event that changed expectations about this firm's profitability is difficult to interpret. Some people think the event will lead to a rise in the firm's profit and others think it will not have any effect on profit. Let's call the first group optimists and the second group pessimists. The optimists will want to buy the stock and will be willing to do so as long as its price is less than $25. The pessimists will sell the stock as long as its price is above $12.50. In such a situation, the pessimists will sell out and the optimists will buy in. The price will not necessarily change, but there will be a large volume of trading activity. What causes the trading activity is the disagreement, not the event that triggered the change in expected profitability. High volume of trading on the stock market implies a large amount of disagreement. Large price changes with low volume of trading imply a great deal of agreement that something fundamental has changed. A large volume of trading with hardly any price change means that the underlying changes are difficult to interpret: Some people predict that things will move in one direction while others predict the opposite.

Reading Between the Lines (pp. 456–458) looks at the long upswing in the stock market that occurred between 1982 and 1987 and illustrates some of the principles that you've just studied.

Takeovers and Mergers

The theory of capital markets that you've now studied can be used to explain why takeovers and mergers occur. A **takeover** is the purchase of the stock of one firm by another firm. A takeover occurs when the stock market value of a firm is lower than the present value of the expected future profit from operating the firm. For example, suppose that Taxfile Inc., has a stock market value of $120,000. But suppose also that the present value of the future profit of the firm is $150,000. It will pay for someone to try to take over the firm. Takeover activity affects the price of a

firm and often the threat of a takeover drives the price to the point at which the takeover is no longer profitable.

There are other takeover situations in which the expected future profit of a firm depends on the firm taking it over. A recent example illustrates this point very well. The Atari Computer Company was having difficulty in breaking into the retail computer market on the scale that it desired. To overcome its problems, Atari searched out, surprisingly, a retail chain that was losing money. The present value of a firm that is making a loss is less than the value of its plant and equipment. So, Atari was able to buy retail outlets for a lower price from its current owners than it could have done by starting afresh. Atari believed that by buying the firm and using its retail stores to sell Atari computers, Atari could convert that firm's loss into a profit.

A **merger** is the combining of the assets of two firms to form a single, new firm. Mergers take place when two firms perceive that by combining their assets, they can increase their combined stock market values. For example, the merger of Piedmont and U.S. Air enabled the resulting firm to increase its profit by integrating their routes and schedules.

R E V I E W

Saving plans and investment plans are coordinated through capital markets. Adjustments in asset prices and interest rates make the saving plans and investment plans compatible. Interest rates and asset prices are two sides of the same coin. The interest rate on an asset is the income on the asset divided by its price. The average interest rate makes the quantity of capital demanded equal to the quantity of savings supplied.

The value of a share of a firm's stock is determined by the firm's current and expected future profit. Expected future profit is based on rational expectations of future prices, costs, and technologies that the firm will face. The stock market value of a firm is often expressed as a ratio of the firm's current profit per share—the price-earnings ratio. The price-earnings ratio depends on expected profit growth.

Stock market prices sometimes move dramatically and the volume of trading on the stock market is sometimes high and sometimes low. Prices change quickly when there are changes in expectations of future profitability. The volume of stock market trading rises when people disagree strongly about the future.

Mergers and takeovers occur when the stock market value of a firm is lower than the present value of the future profit stream that another firm believes it could generate with the first firm's assets. ■

The lessons that we've just learned about capital markets have wider application than explaining fluctuations in the stock market. They also enable us to understand how natural resource markets operate. These lessons are particularly important and interesting in the cases of exhaustible natural resources—resources that we are using up and will eventually use up completely. Let's now turn to this important range of issues.

Natural Resource Markets

Natural resources are the nonproduced factors of production with which we are endowed. Natural resources fall into two categories: exhaustible and nonexhaustible. **Exhaustible natural resources** are natural resources that can be used only once and that cannot be replaced once used. Examples of exhaustible natural resources are coal, natural gas, and oil—the so-called hydrocarbon fuels. **Nonexhaustible natural resources** are natural resources that can be used repeatedly without depleting what's available for future use. Examples of nonexhaustible natural resources are land, sea, rivers and lakes, rain and sunshine. Plants and animals are also examples of nonexhaustible natural resources. By careful cultivation and husbandry, more of these natural resources can be produced to replace those used up in production and consumption activities.

Natural resources have two important economic dimensions—a stock dimension and a flow dimension. There is a stock of each natural resource determined by nature and by the previous rate of use of the resource. The flow of a natural resource is the rate at which it is being used. This flow is determined by human choices and those choices determine whether a given stock of natural resources is used up quickly, slowly, or not at all. In studying the operation of

natural resource markets, we'll begin by considering the stock dimension of a natural resource.

Supply and Demand in a Natural Resource Market

The stock of a natural resource supplied is the amount of the resource in existence. For an exhaustible natural resource, that amount is not influenced by the price of the resource. In such a case, the supply of the stock of the natural resource is perfectly inelastic. Its position depends on the amount of the resource available initially, and on the rate at which it has been used up in the past. The smaller the initial stock and the faster the rate of use, the smaller is the stock of a resource available.

The demand for a stock of a natural resource is one aspect of portfolio choice. People own stocks of natural resources as an alternative to owning equities in corporations, other financial assets such as bonds, or other real assets such as plant, equipment, and buildings.

The demand for a stock of a natural resource is determined in the same way as the demand for any other asset—by the income that it is expected to earn, expressed as an interest rate or yield. If the expected yield—or interest rate—on a stock of a natural resource exceeds that on other assets (with comparable risk), people will allocate more of their net worth to owning the natural resource and less to other assets. Conversely, if the expected interest rate on a natural resource falls short of that on other assets (with comparable risk), portfolios will be reallocated by selling the stock of a natural resource and buying other assets. When the yield, or interest rate, from owning a stock of a natural resource equals the yield on other comparably risky assets, there will be no tendency for people to either buy or sell stocks of natural resources or other assets. People will be satisfied with their existing portfolio allocation and with the quantity of the stock of the natural resource that they are holding.

Equilibrium occurs in the market for a stock of a natural resource when the price of the resource is *expected* to rise over time, at a rate equal to the interest rate. This proposition is known as the **Hotelling Principle.**[1] Why is the price of a

---

[1] The Hotelling Principle, discovered by Harold Hotelling, first appeared in "Economics of Exhaustible Resources," *Journal of Political Economy* 39 (April 1931): 137–75.

A Stock Market Boom

How Much Power Is Left in the Bull?

Conventional wisdom on Wall Street says the bull market began in August 1982. But not everyone agrees.

One respected market analyst dates the move from December 1974. Another professional views the five-year advance as part of a supercycle that began in 1932. Still another takes his cues from the stars and the moon, rather than rates and the economy; he sees the market's movements as a series of celestial-based cycles lasting three to eight weeks. . . .

Several experts say the market may go through a wrenching correction in the next few months, giving investors a rough ride. They differ on exactly when and where the market will top out, and they're more ready to say how high it will go than when it's going to get there. In many cases, their thoughts on when the bull market will end are linked to when they believe it began. Here's a sample of when some of them think that was, and what they see for the future.

1932: The current bull market is really the final phase of a big stock market move that began 55 years ago, says Mr. Prechter, author of an investment newsletter based on the Elliott wave theory, the mathematical application of crowd psychology to market behavior.

Yardsticks for the Rally

	CHG FROM 8/12/82	P/E 8/7/87
DJIA	+233.6%	20.5
S&P 500	+215.4	19.8
NYSE Composite	+207.6	18.9
Wilshire 5000	+202.4	19.6
Amex	+204.3	24.1
Nasdaq Composite	+171.3	23.5

Source: Wilshire Associates

He says large stock market moves occur in a series of five waves. If the trend is up, there are five sub-waves: up, down, up, down, up. . . .

The first wave was from 1932 to 1937, an advance that carried the stock market out of the Great Depression. From 1937 to 1942, the Dow Jones Industrial Average declined more than 50%. In the next 24 years, ending in 1966, stocks enjoyed a prolonged bull market. Mr. Prechter sees the 1966 to 1982 experience as "a sideways market." The fifth wave began in August 1982. Mr. Prechter . . . believes the Dow Jones Industrial Average can eventually reach 3600 to 3700 before the 1932 supercycle ends. But, the rally could be interrupted by a substantial correction, he warns. . . .

1974: Robert Farrell, chief technical analyst at Merrill Lynch Capital Markets, sees the bull market as a series of "theme stages.". . .

The first theme stage began in late 1974 and lasted through 1980. It was led by companies that benefited from accelerating inflation and the energy crisis, but that didn't make this stage "any less of a bull market," Mr. Farrell contends.

. . . The second stage [starting] in late 1981 [and] lasting through 1986 was the era of disinflation and lower interest rates and leaps in stock values. Low inflation made investors willing to pay more for companies' future profits. The market is now beginning a third stage, where earnings growth is the key, he says.

1982: The first sign this bull market started five years ago, says Philip Erlanger, a technical analyst with Advest Inc. in Hartford, Conn., was that the Dow Jones Transportation Average finally broke through a level it had been bumping against for 15 years.

Mr. Erlanger reasons that transportation companies foreshadow major positive shifts in the economy. The fortunes of railroads, truckers and airlines begin to brighten as they start to haul the raw materials that manufacturers need. Later on, they transport the finished goods.

His charts showed the action in the transportation stocks was similar to the start of what he calls the 1949–1966 bull market. So he estimated this advance could be as strong and long-lived.

Archibald Crawford, an investment newsletter writer in New York City, believes the heavens dictated the start of the bull market in 1982. And now he's expecting some momentous happenings in the galaxy to signal an eventful close in the weeks ahead. Among the powerful events in the sky, Mr. Crawford says, there will be a solar eclipse on the fall equinox and five planets will be lined up in a tight conjunction for six days. "We'll be in for a decline," he declares.

Whatever the causes of great market moves, the stars may be as good as any other guide for charting their beginnings and ends. On Aug. 13, 1982—Friday the 13th —the Dow Jones Industrial Average closed at 788.05, up 11.13. It was the first daily gain in a week, but on that day, most seers saw gloom, not hope. Many were forecasting a renewed decline to as low as 700. Hardly a one would have believed, much less foretold, that a run to 2600 or beyond had just begun.

Wall Street Journal, **August 10, 1987**

By Beatrice E. Garcia

Reprinted by permission of *The Wall Street Journal,*
©Dow Jones & Company, Inc. 1987. All Rights Reserved.

Bull's Run

Stock prices have soared more than 200% in the past five years, but national output has increased barely 40% before inflation—and only 20% if inflation is taken into account.

The stock market "strikes me as being all by itself," says Charles P. Kindleberger, emeritus professor of economics at Massachusetts Institute of Technology. "There is no real industrial investment boom behind it. It's a puzzle."

Stock Market's Advance...

	8/12/82	8/7/87	PCT CHG
DJIA	776.92	2592.00	+233.6%

...vs. Economy's Gains

	3rd QTR 1982	2nd QTR 1987	PCT CHG
Real GNP[1]	$3.15	$3.80	+20.3%
Consumer spending[1]	2.05	2.49	+21.3
After-tax income[1]	2.26	2.65	+17.2

	AUG. '82	LATEST	PCT CHG
Industrial production index ('77=100)	102.0	128.2	+25.7%
Employment[2] (in millions)	101.2	114.4	+13.0
Jobless rate[2]	9.7%	5.9%	−39.2

[1] Seasonally adjusted annual rate, in trillions of 1982 dollars
[2] Based on total employment

Wall Street Journal, August 10, 1987

By Tim Metz

The Essence of the Stories

- The U.S. stock market rose by more than 200 percent in the five years from August 1982 to August 1987.

- In the same five year period, national output grew by 20 percent, industrial production by 25 percent, employment by 13 percent, consumer spending by 21 percent, and after tax income by 17 percent.

- Some economists, such as Professor Kindleberger, are puzzled by the fact that the stock market has advanced on a scale 10 times greater than most indicators of underlying real economic performance.

- Stock market analysts differ in their explanations for the rise and their predictions about the stock market's future course:

  —Wave theorist Prechter sees the advance as the last upward sub-wave of a 55-year trend and predicts a further 40 percent rise before the peak is reached.

  —Technical analyst Farrell identifies a series of "theme stages"—rising inflation and the energy crisis in the 1970s and falling inflation in the 1980s as the source of movements and predicts that earnings growth is now the key to the future performance of the stock market.

  —Technical analyst Erlanger emphasizes the performance of transportation stocks.

  —Celestial-based cycle theorist Crawford looks to solar eclipses and planetary conjunctions.

- For all their differences, virtually no one predicted on August 13, 1982 that day 1 of a sustained five-year upward movement in the stock market had begun.

(continued on next page)

Background and Analysis

What Are All Those Indexes of Stock Market Performance?

■ Here is a brief description of all the different indexes in the table "Yardsticks for the Rally."

—DJIA: the Dow Jones Industrial Average, an index made up from the value of 30 industrial stocks including such household names as American Express, Coca-Cola, IBM, and McDonald's
—S&P 500: Standard and Poor's index of 500 securities
—NYSE Composite: an index compiled by the New York Stock Exchange covering a broad range of stocks
—Wilshire 5000: an index constructed by Wilshire Associates
—Amex: an index of prices on the American stock exchange
—Nasdaq Composite: an index compiled by the National Association of Security Dealers Automated Quotations, for stock not traded on any particular stock exchange

■ Each index gives a slightly different measure of the change in the stock market, but they all agree that the percent change in the five years ending August 1982 was around 200 percent.

What Is a Bull Market?

■ A bull market is simply a rising market. The opposite of a bull market is a bear market. A bear market is a falling market.

Why Was There Such a Strong Bull Market between 1982 and 1987?

■ In 1982, the U.S. economy was in a depressed state, there had been no economic growth for a fourth successive year, and income per head was declining. People were pessimistic about the future and were predicting poor earnings performance for U.S. industry.

■ Starting in the final quarter of 1982, the U.S. economy made a spectacular recovery. Real income grew by 7 percent during the next seven quarters.

■ Bit by bit, industry by industry, it became clear that the pessimistic expectations that had prevailed in 1982 were inappropriate. Optimism replaced pessimism.

■ People's assessments of the present value of expected future earnings increased, so they placed higher values on corporate equity.

■ There is no mystery or puzzle about the strong rise in the stock market substantially outpacing the underlying change in the economy. The economic theory of the value of an asset predicts a relationship between the price of a stock and the expected future growth rate in its earnings. A change in expectations about growth rates has a large effect on the value of a stock. Replacing an expected decline of 4 percent by an expected rise of 1 percent, combined with a moderate fall in interest rates, is enough to produce a 200 percent rise in the value of stocks.

Where Is the Stock Market Heading?

■ No one forecasted the current 1980s upsurge in the stock market.

■ The analysis that we have just performed is a rationalization of what happened but could not have been used to make a prediction ahead of time.

■ As a matter of fact, it is an implication of the economic theory of the value of stocks that it is impossible to forecast future changes.

■ The current price is based on forecasts about future earnings. There are no better forecasts available than the ones that people have made.

■ Therefore we cannot use economic theory to predict that the stock market is going to rise further or that it is going to crash.

■ But we can use the theory to calculate the implications of different assumptions about earnings and interest rates. For example, historically the interest rate in the United States has been 5 percent a year and earnings have grown at about 2 percent a year. If these conditions emerged in the United States economy, the price-earnings ratio would be 34. With a price-earnings ratio of 34 and with earnings at their current level, the Dow Jones Industrial Average would be 4300.

■ This last statement is not a prediction. But it does serve to show that the bull market was not really extraordinary.

natural resource expected to grow at a rate equal to the interest rate? It is to make the expected yield on the natural resource equal to the yield available on other comparably risky assets. But the yield (or interest rate) on a stock of a natural resource is the rate of change in the price of the resource. If you buy a stock of a natural resource, you buy it at today's price. If you sell your natural resource stock a year later, you sell it at the price prevailing at that time. The percentage change in the price of the resource over the year is your yield or interest rate. Thus the more rapid the increase in the price of a natural resource, other things being equal, the larger is the yield on that natural resource.

But there is only one yield that is consistent with an equilibrium portfolio allocation. That yield is the same as the interest rate or yield on other comparably risky assets. Thus the equilibrium yield on a stock of a natural resource occurs when the price of the natural resource rises at a rate equal to the interest rate. Of course, when making a portfolio allocation decision, future prices are not known and decisions are based on expectations. Thus when the price of a natural resource is expected to rise at a rate equal to the interest rate, the portfolio allocation is in equilibrium.

The supply of and demand for the stock of a natural resource determines the yield or interest rate from owning that stock. That yield is determined by the expected rate of increase in the price of the natural resource. But the supply of and demand for the stock of the resource does not determine the current *level* of the price—only its future expected rate of change. To determine the level of the price of a natural resource, we have to consider not only the supply of and demand for the stock of the resource but also the demand for its flow—the rate at which the resource is used up.

The Price of a Natural Resource

To determine the price of a natural resource, we first consider the influences on the demand for the flow of the natural resource and then we study the equilibrium that emerges from the interaction of the demand for the flow with the available stock.

Demand for a Flow   The demand for a flow of a natural resource is determined in the same way as the demand for any other input. It arises from firms'

profit-maximization decisions. A firm maximizes profit when the marginal revenue product of an input equals the marginal cost of the input. In a perfectly competitive market, the marginal cost of an input equals the factor price. The quantity demanded of a flow of a natural resource is the amount that makes the marginal revenue product of that flow equal to the price of the resource. As in the case of all other inputs, the marginal revenue product of a natural resource diminishes as the quantity of the resource used increases. Thus the lower the price of a resource, the greater is the quantity demanded of the flow of the natural resource—as illustrated in Fig. 17.7.

There is one special feature of the demand for a flow of a natural resource. For any resource, there is a high price at which it does not pay anyone to use the resource. The price at which it no longer pays to use a natural resource is called the **choke price**. Figure 17.7 shows a choke price of P_C. Everything has substitutes and at a high enough price, a substitute is used. For example, we do not have to use aluminum to make cans for soft drinks; we can use plastic

Figure 17.7   Demand for a Flow of a Natural Resource

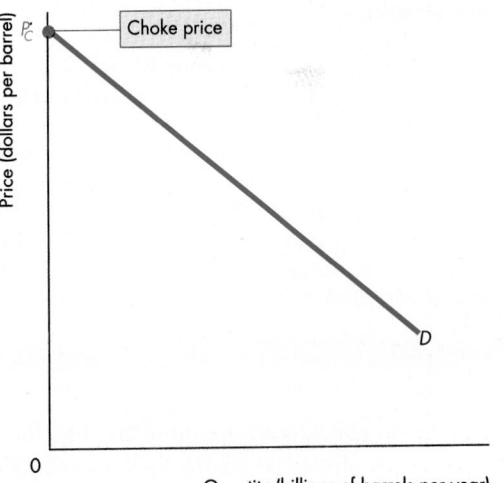

Natural resources have substitutes. If the price of a natural resource is too high, then a substitute will be used. At P_C, none of this resource is demanded and a substitute will be used. At a price below P_C, the quantity demanded is positive and the lower the price, the larger is the quantity demanded. The price P_C is called the choke price.

Figure 17.8   An Exhaustible Natural Resource Market

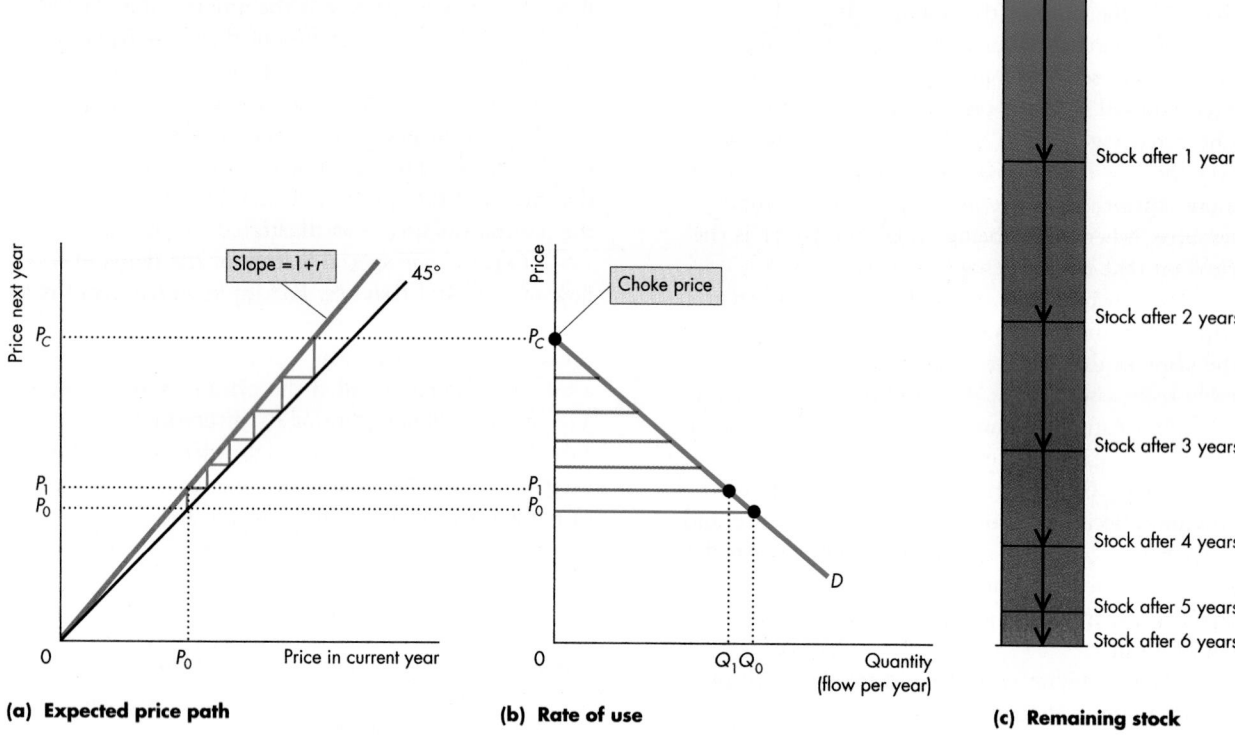

(a) Expected price path   **(b) Rate of use**   **(c) Remaining stock**

The expected rate of increase in the price of a natural resource equals the interest rate. Starting at P_0 in part (a), the price increases at first to P_1 and eventually to P_C. The price path follows the steps shown, with each step bigger than the previous one. Part (b) shows the rate at which the resource is used up. Its demand curve *(D)* determines the quantity demanded for use (a flow) at each price. Initially, when the price is P_0, that flow is Q_0. As the price increases, the flow decreases. When the price reaches P_C, the choke price, the flow is zero. Part (c) illustrates the remaining stock after each year. The initial stock is used up in decreasing amounts until, after six years, the stock is exhausted. The price P_0 is the equilibrium price because it achieves equality between the sum of the flows in each year and the initial stock.

instead. We do not have to use oil as the fuel for cars; we can use alcohol or electric cars instead. We do not have to use gas and electric power to heat our homes; we can use solar energy instead. The natural resources that we *do* use are the least expensive resources available. They cost us less than the next best alternative would.

Equilibrium Stock and Flow   The price and the flow of a natural resource depend on three things:

• The interest rate

• The demand for the flow

• The stock of the resource remaining

Figure 17.8 shows how these three factors combine to determine the price of a natural resource, the expected path of that price, the rate at which the resource is used up, and the stock of the resource remaining. Let's take in the figure one part at a time.

In part (a), you can see the expected price path of the natural resource. That path is determined by the interest rate *r*. The line with a slope of $1 + r$ shows the relationship between the price in the current year and the price next year if the price rises at a rate equal to the interest rate. Suppose that initially the price is P_0. Next year, the price will rise to P_1, the price that is r percent higher than P_0. You can see the rise in price by following the "steps" between the 45° line and the line with a slope of $1 + r$. Each step represents a price increase. The steps become larger but the height of each step is a constant percentage of the previous year's price. Since the price keeps rising, eventually it reaches the choke price, identified as P_C in the figure.

Next, consider Fig. 17.8(b), which shows the rate at which the resource is used up. The demand for the flow, based on the marginal revenue product of the natural resource, is illustrated by the curve D. In the initial year, at a price of P_0 the quantity Q_0 is used. In the following year, we know from part (a) that the price increases to P_1. At this price, the quantity used up is Q_1. As the price increases each year, the quantity used each year decreases. When the price reaches P_C, the choke price, the quantity used is zero.

Figure 17.8(c) shows the remaining stock. The initial stock is identified in the figure and the stock remaining after each year is also identified. For example, the stock after one year is the initial stock minus Q_0, the amount used up in the first year. In this example, after six years, there is no stock left. The price has increased from P_0 to the choke price P_C and the quantity used in each year has declined until, in the final year, it has become zero—the quantity of the flow of natural resources demanded at the choke price.

How do we know that P_0 is the current price? It is because it is the price that achieves an equilibrium between the remaining stock and the current year's flow and the future years' expected flows. That is, it is the only current price that leads to a sequence of future prices (growing at the interest rate) that generate a sequence of flows such that the stock is exhausted in the same year that the choke price is reached. If the current price is higher than P_0 and if the future prices are expected to rise at the interest rate, the choke price will be reached before the stock is exhausted. If the current price is below P_0 and, again, if the future prices are expected to rise at the interest rate, the stock will be exhausted before the choke price is reached.

We can now see how the current price is determined by the three factors that we identified above. First, the higher the interest rate, the lower is the current price of a natural resource. The higher interest rate means that the price is going to increase more quickly. Thus starting from the same initial price, the choke price will be reached sooner. But if the choke price is reached sooner, the stock available will not be used up at that point in time. Thus the initial price has to be lower when the interest rate is higher to ensure that by the time the price does reach the choke price, the total stock available has been used.

Second, the higher the marginal revenue product of the natural resource—the higher the demand for the flow of the natural resource—the higher is the current price of the resource. You can see why this relationship exists by looking again at Fig. 17.8(b). If the demand for the flow of the resource were higher than that shown in this figure, the demand curve would lie to the right of the demand curve shown. In this case, the current price would be higher than P_0.

Third, the larger the initial stock of the natural resource, the lower the current price. You can also see why this relationship holds by considering Fig. 17.8(c). If the initial stock is larger than that shown in the figure, P_0 cannot be the equilibrium price for it leads to a sequence of prices that generate a sequence of quantities demanded that do not exhaust the stock by the time the choke price is reached. Thus the initial price would have to be below P_0 to ensure that the larger stock is exhausted by the time that the choke price is reached.

Equilibrium in the market for a natural resource determines the current price of the natural resource and the expected path of future prices. But the price path actually followed is rarely the same as its expected path. For example, in 1984 expectations about the future price of oil were that it would rise at a rate equal to the interest rate. Opinions differed about the long-term average interest rate, so projections ranged from a low growth rate of 1.8 percent a year to a high growth rate of 7.1 percent a year. But, as events have turned out, the price of oil fell after 1984 (see Fig. 17.9).

Why do natural resource prices change unexpectedly, sometimes even falling rather than following their expected path?

Unexpected Price Changes

The price of a natural resource depends on expectations about future events. It depends on expectations about the interest rate, the future demand for the flow of the resource, and the size of the remaining stock. Natural resource markets are constantly being product of an input are harder to document but, for example, the development of energy-efficient automobile and airplane engines represents a technological change that increases the marginal revenue product of capital—engines—and decreases the marginal revenue product of the exhaustible resource—the oil that those engines burn.

An additional force leading to price changes in natural resource markets in general and in the oil market in particular is the degree of competitiveness in the markets. The model market that we have been studying is a perfectly competitive one. But the real world market for oil has oligopolistic elements (some of which we analyzed in Chapter 14, pp. 349–366). Oligopolistic influences on price can produce price fluctuations over and above the fluctuations arising from the forces at work in a competitive market. Furthermore, in forecasting the future price of a natural resource, it is necessary to forecast future changes in market structure. Adding this complication to an already complex forecasting problem makes it clear that the fluctuations in prices of natural resources such as oil are, for the most part, unforecastable.

Conservation and Doomsday

The analysis that you have just reviewed concerning the price of a natural resource and its expected change over time has important implications for the popular debate concerning natural resources and their use. Many people fear that we are using the earth's exhaustible natural resources at such a rapid pace that we shall eventually (and perhaps in the not very distant future) run out of important sources of energy and of other crucial raw materials. Such people urge a slowing down in the rate of use of exhaustible natural resources so that the limited stocks available will last longer.

This topic is an emotional one and generates passionate debate. It is also a matter that involves economic issues that can be understood using the economic model of a depletable natural resource that you have just studied.

The economic analysis of an exhaustible natural resource market predicts that doomsday—the using up of the entire stock of a natural resource—will eventually arise if our use of natural resources is organized in competitive markets. The economic model also implies that a competitive market will provide an automatic conservation program arising from a steadily rising price. As a natural resource gets

Figure 17.9   Unfulfilled Expectations

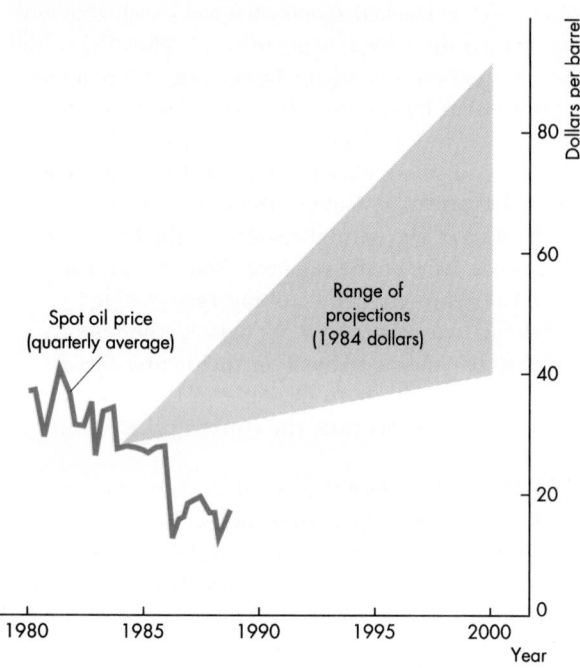

In 1984, the price of oil was expected to increase at a rate equal to the interest rate. There were different views of the future interest rate, so there was a range of expected price increases. The events of the 1980s unfolded in a way that was different from what had been expected in 1984. Higher interest rates, the discovery of increased reserves, and new energy-saving technologies all contributed to a falling price of oil. The breakup of the OPEC cartel also contributed significantly to falling oil prices.

Source: "Future Imperfect," *The Economist:* Feb. 4, 1989, p. 67. © 1989 The Economist Newspaper Limited. Reprinted with permission.

bombarded by new information that leads to new expectations. For example, new information about the stock of a resource or the technologies available for its use can lead to sudden and perhaps quite large changes in the price of a natural resource.

All of these forces have been at work in many of the markets for exhaustible natural resources in recent years. The market for oil illustrates these effects very well. Increased interest rates and the discovery of new supply sources have taken place in recent years, and at the same time the price of oil, far from rising at a rate equal to the interest rate, has actually fallen. Changes in the marginal revenue closer and closer to being depleted, its price gets closer to the choke price—the price at which no one wants to use the resource any more. Each year, as the price rises, the quantity demanded of the flow declines.

But what if the resource gets completely used up? Don't we have a real problem then? We have the problem of scarcity but in no more acute a form than we had it before. The resource that is no longer available was used because to use it was more efficient than to use some alternative. Once that resource is completely used up, then and only then does it pay to turn to using a more expensive substitute. So, the market economy handles the depleting stocks of natural resources by persistently forcing up their prices. Higher prices cause us to ration our use and eventually drive the quantity demanded of the flow to zero when the supply of the stock disappears.

There is an important economic issue as to whether or not a competitive market leads us to use our scarce exhaustible natural resources at an efficient rate. Recall that we have studied the allocative efficiency of a perfectly competitive market in Chapter 12 (pp. 307–309). There we discovered that perfectly competitive markets achieve allocative efficiency if there are no external costs and benefits. The same conclusion applies to markets for natural resources. If there are no external costs or benefits impinging upon these markets, then the rate of use determined in a

perfectly competitive exhaustible natural resource market is the allocatively efficient rate of use. But if there are external costs associated with the use of the natural resource, allocative efficiency will result from a slowdown in the rate of use of the resource compared with that arising in the competitive market. For example, if burning hydrocarbon fuels increases the carbon dioxide in the atmosphere and a warming of the earth's atmosphere results—the so-called greenhouse effect—the costs associated with this atmospheric change have to be added to the costs of using oil and coal as fuels. When these costs are taken into account, the allocatively efficient rate of use of these fuels is lower than that resulting from a perfectly competitive market. We examine ways in which government intervention can achieve allocative efficiency in such a situation in Chapter 19.

■ We have now studied the way in which factor markets allocate scarce productive resources—labor, capital, and land—and the determination of factor prices and factor incomes. The outcome of the operation of the factor markets is the determination of the distribution of income among individuals and families—the determination of *for whom* goods and services are produced. We are now going to examine that distribution and discover the main features and sources of income and wealth inequality in our economy.

S U M M A R Y

Capital, Investment, and Saving

There are two kinds of assets: financial and real. Financial assets are all the paper claims of one economic agent against another. Real assets, or capital, are the stock of all the productive assets owned by households and firms. Investment is the flow of additions to the stock of capital. Depreciation is the flow reduction in the stock of capital through use or the passage of time.

The quantity of capital supplied results from people's saving decisions. Saving equals income minus consumption. People allocate their savings to a variety of alternative financial and real assets. (pp. 439–441)

Capital Markets in the United States Today

Capital markets provide the link between the savings decisions of households and the investment decisions of firms and governments. Households finance firms' investment by buying equity and bonds or by making deposits in financial intermediaries who in turn make loans to firms. Households also make loans to governments by buying bonds and indirectly through deposits with financial intermediaries. (pp. 442–445)

Demand for Capital

The demand for capital is determined—like the demand for factors—by firms' profit-maximization choices. The quantity of capital demanded by a firm is such that the marginal revenue product of capital equals its opportunity cost. A firm can make the comparison between marginal revenue product and cost by calculating the present value of marginal revenue product and comparing that present value with the price of a new piece of capital.

The quantity of capital demanded by a firm depends on the interest rate. The higher the interest rate, the lower is the present value of the future stream of marginal revenue products, and the smaller is the quantity of capital equipment a firm buys. The lower the interest rate, the greater is the quantity of capital demanded—the demand curve for capital is downward sloping. The demand curve for capital shifts steadily to the right as a result of technological change and the general tendency to exploit innovations over time. (pp. 445–448)

The Supply of Capital

The quantity of capital supplied results from the saving decisions of households. Savings depend on how much households smooth their consumption over the life cycle and on the interest rate. The particular assets into which people will put their savings depend on the relative rates of return. Relative rates of return, in turn, reflect differing degrees of riskiness. The supply curve for capital is upward sloping—as interest rates rise, the quantity of capital supplied increases. The supply curve of capital shifts over time as a result of changes in the population, and its age composition, and the level of income. (pp. 449–451)

Interest Rates and Asset Prices

Interest rates and asset prices can be viewed as two sides of the same coin. Interest rates and asset prices adjust to achieve equality between the quantity of capital demanded and the quantity supplied. Interest rates on particular assets are distributed around the average rate according to the degree of riskiness of different types of assets.

The stock market value of a firm depends on the firm's current profit and expectations of its future profit. The higher the expected growth rate of a firm's profit, the higher is the price of a share of its stock. The price-earnings ratio is the ratio of the current price of a share in a firm's stock to its current profit per share. That ratio depends on the expected growth rate of profit.

The volume of trading on the stock market is determined by the extent of the divergence of expectations of the future. When everyone agrees about the future, volume of trading is low. When there is widespread disagreement, volume of trading is high. There can be large changes in prices with low or high volume of trading. Price changes occur when there is a change in expectations about profit growth.

Mergers and takeovers occur as part of the process of maximizing profit. If a firm's stock market value is lower than the value of its assets when used by another firm, it will pay that other firm to take over the first firm. Mergers occur when there is a mutually agreed benefit from combining the assets of two (or more) firms. (pp. 451–455)

Natural Resource Markets

Natural resources are the nonproduced factors of production with which we are endowed. The price of a natural resource is determined by the interest rate, its marginal revenue product (which determines the demand for its flow), and the stock of the natural resource (which determines the supply of its stock). The price of a natural resource is such that its future price is expected to rise at a rate equal to the interest rate and to reach the choke price at the time at which the resource is exhausted. The actual price is constantly changing to take into account new information. Even though the future price is expected to increase, the actual price often decreases as a result of new information leading to an increase in the estimate of the remaining stock or to a decrease in the demand for the flow of the resource. (pp. 455–463)

K E Y   C O N C E P T S

Asset, 439
Balance sheet, 439
Bond market, 443

Bond yield, 451
Capital, 439
Choke price, 459

Key Figures and Tables

R E V I E W   Q U E S T I O N S

1 Why does the quantity of capital demanded by a firm rise as the interest rate falls?

2 Set out the key reasons for differences in interest rates on different types of assets.

3 What is the relationship between interest rates and asset prices?

4 Explain how the stock market value of a firm is determined.

5 Define the price-earnings ratio and explain how it is determined.

6 Why are there some occasions on which stock market prices change a lot but with little trading and other times when prices are stable but trading volumes are high?

7 Why do mergers and takeovers occur?

8 Distinguish between the stock and the flow of an exhaustible natural resource.

9 Explain why the price of an exhaustible natural resource is expected to rise at a rate equal to the interest rate.

10 What determines the price of a natural resource?

11 Why are most of the fluctuations in the price of a natural resource unforecastable?

P R O B L E M S

1 At the end of 1989, a firm had a production plant worth $1 million. The plant depreciated during 1990 by 10 percent. During the same year, the firm also bought new capital equipment for $250,000. What is the value of the firm's stock of capital at the end of 1990? What was the firm's gross investment during 1990? What was the firm's net investment during 1990?

2 You earn $10,000 per year for three years and you spend $8000 each year. How much do you save each year? What happens to your wealth during this three-year period?

3 What are the different ways in which a holder of wealth can channel capital into firms?

4 How can a holder of wealth lower the risk of supplying capital to firms?

5 Why is a deposit in a financial intermediary less risky than buying equity or bonds?

6 A firm is considering buying a new machine. It is estimated that the marginal revenue product of the machine will be $1000 a year for five years. The machine will have a scrap value at the end of five years of $1000. The interest rate is 10 percent a year.

a) What is the maximum price that the firm will pay for the machine?

b) If the machine costs $4000, will the firm buy the machine at an interest rate of 10 percent? What is the highest interest rate at which the firm will buy the machine?

Chapter 18

The Distribution of Income and Wealth

After studying this chapter, you will be able to:

- Describe the distribution of income and wealth in the United States today

- Explain why the data on wealth distribution show greater inequality than the data on income distribution

- Explain how the distribution of income arises from the prices of productive resources and the distribution of endowments

- Explain how the distribution of income and wealth is affected by individual choices

- Explain the different views about fairness in the distribution of income and wealth

- Explain the effects of redistribution policies on the distribution of income and wealth

Fifty-three stories above Manhattan there is for sale a 3363 square foot penthouse with unobstructed views of Central Park, the Hudson River, and the city skyline: The price? $4 million. "Now, you can be one of the enviable few to fly Around the World by Supersonic Concorde. Less than 400 Americans have done it before. Space very limited. $26,800 per person," trumpets an advertisement in the *New Yorker*. What kind of people can afford homes and vacations as costly as these? Obviously only the very richest. And there are some very rich people in the United States today. It has been estimated that the richest 1 percent of families own more than 40 percent of the nation's wealth and the richest 20 percent earn over 40 percent of the nation's income. ■ At the other end of the scale there is abject poverty. Not quite within view of the $4 million penthouse, but not far from it, is Fort Washington Armory in Upper Manhattan. What was opened as a temporary shelter in 1981 now permanently houses 850 men sleeping in one huge room. "As the men at Fort Washington stretch out on cots on the coarse wooden drill floor in a room the size of a football field, there is pervasive fear—fear of AIDS and tuberculosis, fear for physical survival. And there is widespread despair over the future. . . . There, side by side, are predators and their prey, the mentally ill, alcoholics, men with limbs thinned by disease and malnutrition, others with muscles trained through exercise in prison."[1] ■ Though Fort Washington is an extreme example of poverty and despair, many thousands of families, often with a single (and usually female) parent, struggle to obtain even such basics as adequate food, clothing, and shelter. It is estimated that the poorest 50 percent of the families in the United States own a mere 1 percent of the nation's net assets. The

Riches and Rags

---

[1]*New York Times* (February 18, 1988): 1, 42.

poorest 20 percent of families earn only 5 percent of the nation's income. ■ What determines the distributions of wealth and income? Why are some people exceedingly rich while others earn very little and own almost nothing? Are there any trends in the distribution of income? Is the distribution becoming more equal or more unequal? Is it fair that some people should be so incredibly rich while others live in miserable poverty? And what do we mean by fairness?

■ In this chapter, we study the sources of income and wealth inequality. We'll see how factor prices and the quantities of factors hired, as determined in factor markets, result in unequal incomes. We'll study the connection between income and wealth and discover why the distribution of wealth is much more uneven than that of income. We'll also see how inequality results in part from the choices that people make. ■ Most of the chapter deals with positive issues—with trying to understand the world as it is—and not normative matters—commenting on or making judgments about what is desirable. Nevertheless, in the final section of the chapter we do review some of the key contributions to the perennial search for a widely acceptable concept of fairness. ■ Let's begin by looking at some facts about the distributions of income and wealth.

Distributions of Income and Wealth in the United States Today

The incomes earned by the factors of production are the wages (including salaries and other forms of compensation) paid to labor, the interest (and dividend) income paid to the owners of capital, and the rental incomes received by the owners of land and minerals. Labor earns the largest share of total income and that share has increased slightly over the years.

The distribution of income among individuals and families depends on the amount of labor, capital, and natural resources that they supply and on the wage rates, interest and dividend rates, and rental rates they receive. The resource that everyone has in identical amounts is time. But the price at which a person can sell his or her time, the wage rate, depends on the individual's marginal product. That

marginal product in turn depends partly on natural ability, partly on luck or chance, and partly on the amount of human capital that the individual has built up. The income from working is a mixture of a return on human capital as well as a compensation for forgoing leisure.

There is a great deal of inequality in the distribution of ownership of all other factors of production. We will more closely examine that inequality shortly. For now, let's just note that the total income of a family depends on its labor income (including its returns on human capital) as well as its income from other assets.

In 1987, the median U.S. household income was $30,853. The median household is located in the middle of the income distribution—50 percent of households have higher incomes and 50 percent have lower incomes than the median income. Twenty-three percent of all households had incomes of $50,000 or more.[2] One fifth of all households had incomes of less than $15,000.

Figure 18.1 illustrates the distribution of income. It shows the percentage of total income received by each of five equal-sized groups from the poorest 20 percent to the richest 20 percent of families. The 20 percent of families with the lowest incomes receive just 5 percent of total income. The second lowest 20 percent received 11 percent of total income. You can continue reading across the figure to see the percentages of income received by families that are increasingly better off. The 20 percent of families with the highest incomes received 43 percent of total income.

Although the data on the distribution of income display considerable inequality, a picture of even greater inequality emerges from the data on the distribution of wealth. Wealth and income are linked in a way that we will examine shortly, but it's important to remember the distinction: Income is what you earn, wealth is what you own. Data on the wealth distribution measure the value of individual and family holdings of real estate and financial assets. These data are expensive to collect and are updated only infrequently. The most comprehensive data available measure the wealth of families in 1973. In that year, the average family owned net assets of $37,657. The range about that average was enormous. The poorest 40 percent of families owned only

[2]The most recent year for which complete data on income distribution are available is 1987.

Figure 18.1   Family Income Shares

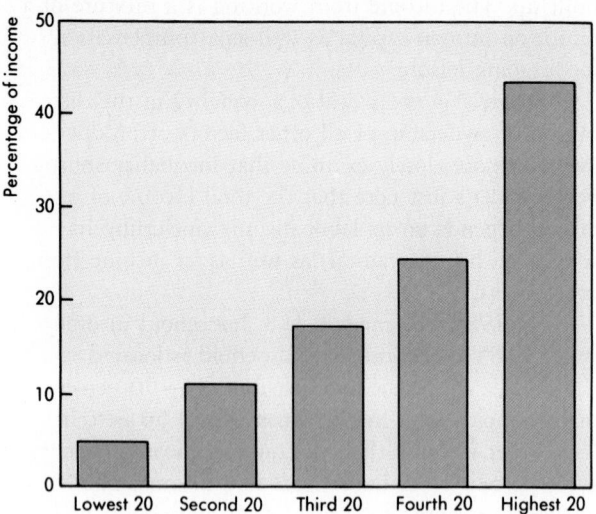

One way of measuring income inequality is to calculate the percentage of total income earned by a given percentage of families, starting with the poorest. The figure shows us that the poorest 20 percent of families earn only 5 percent of the income while the richest 20 percent earn 43 percent of the income. The richest 20 percent are almost nine times as well off, on the average, as the poorest 20 percent.

Source: U.S. Bureau of the Census, *Current Population Reports*, Series P-60.

0.1 percent of the total wealth. The richest 10 percent owned almost 70 percent of total wealth.

Figure 18.2 provides a picture of the distribution of wealth in the United States in 1973. The figure is arranged in a way that enables you to compare the distribution of wealth with the distribution of income.

As in the case of the distribution of income, there is considerable inequality in the distribution of wealth. But there is even more inequality in the case of wealth than of income. For example, the poorest 80 percent of families own 15.4 percent of the wealth but earn 57 percent of total income. The highest 20 percent own 84.6 percent of the wealth and earn 43 percent of total income.

The amount of inequality in the distribution of wealth is even greater if we break down the richest

group. Within that group, the richest 1 percent of all families own 33 percent of total wealth. The next 1 percent own 10 percent of the wealth, and the next 3 percent own 15 percent of the wealth.

Lorenz Curves for Income and Wealth

Another way of describing the distributions of income and wealth is presented in Fig. 18.3. The table records the cumulative percentages of income and wealth of various cumulative percentages of families. For example, row *a* of the table shows the percentages of income and wealth of the lowest 20 percent of families; row *b* shows the data for the lowest 40 percent of families, and so on. These data can be illustrated graphically in what is called a Lorenz curve. A **Lorenz curve** shows the cumula-

Figure 18.2   Income and Wealth Distributions

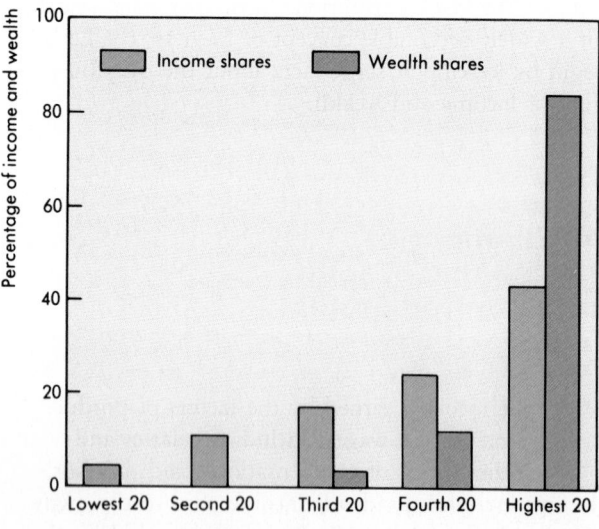

Wealth is distributed even more unequally than income. The poorest 40 percent of the population owns only 0.1 percent of the wealth in the economy. The richest 20 percent owns more than 80 percent of total wealth. Even the middle 20 percent of the population owns only 3.5 percent of total wealth.

Sources: Wealth: Lars Osberg, *Economic Inequality in the United States* (Armonk, N.Y.: M.E. Sharpe, 1983) 44. Income: *Statistical Abstract of the United States: 1987,* 107th ed., p. 437

Figure 18.3   Lorenz Curves for Income and Wealth

The cumulative percentages of income and wealth are graphed against the cumulative percentage of families. If income and wealth were distributed equally, each 20 percent of families would have 20 percent of the income and wealth—the line of equality. Points a through e on the Lorenz curve for income correspond to the rows of the table showing family income and points a' through e on the Lorenz curve for wealth correspond to the rows of the table showing family wealth. Wealth is distributed more unequally than income.

	Cumulative percentage of families	Cumulative percentage of income	Cumulative percentage of wealth	
a	Lowest: 20	5	0	a'
b	40	16	0	b'
c	60	33	4	c'
d	80	57	15	d'
e	100	100	100	e'

Sources: Income: *Statistical Abstract of the United States: 1987*, 107th ed., p. 437. The data are for 1985. Wealth: Lars Osberg, *Economic Inequality in the United States* (Armonk, N.Y.: M.E. Sharpe, 1983) 44. The data are for 1973.

tive percentage of income or wealth of any given cumulative percentage of families. The Lorenz curve derives its name from its founder, Konrad Lorenz, who devised this type of figure in 1905.

The horizontal axis of the figure measures the cumulative percentages of families ranked from the poorest to the richest. For example, the point marked 40 on the horizontal axis represents the 40 percent of families with the lowest income and wealth. The

vertical axis measures the cumulative percentages of income and wealth. For example, the point marked 40 indicates 40 percent of total income or total wealth.

If each family had the same amount of income and wealth, the cumulative percentages of income received and wealth owned by the cumulative percentages of families would fall along the straight line labeled "Line of equality." The actual distributions of income and wealth are shown by the two curves labeled "Income" and "Wealth." The points on the income distribution curve labeled *a* through *e* correspond to the family income shares shown in the table. The points on the wealth distribution curve labeled *a'* through *e* correspond to family wealth shares shown in the table.

The advantage of using Lorenz curves to describe the distribution of income and wealth is that they provide a graphic illustration of the degree of inequality. The closer the Lorenz curve is to the line of equality, the more equal the distribution. As you can see from the two Lorenz curves in Fig. 18.3, the distribution of wealth is much more unequal than the distribution of income. That is, the Lorenz curve for the wealth distribution is much farther away from the line of equality.

The numbers in the table tell the same story. For example, the poorest 60 percent of all families own only 4 percent of the total wealth but earn 33 percent of total income. The poorest 80 percent of all families own only 15 percent of the wealth but earn 57 percent of the income.

Lorenz curves, and the data from which they are drawn, are useful not only for comparing two different distributions, such as that of income and of wealth, but also for comparing distributions at different points in time. Such comparisons reveal whether the distribution of income has become more or less equal over time.

Inequality over Time

Let's take a look at the distribution in the United States 30 years earlier than the numbers that we have just been studying. Table 18.1 provides a comparison. It shows the cumulative percentage of income shares in 1955 and compares those numbers with the same income shares in 1985 (the figures in Fig. 18.3). As you can see from Table 18.1, there was remarkably little change in the distribution of income in the 30 years between 1955 and 1985.

We have seen that there is a great deal of inequality in income and wealth. But *who* are the rich and *who* are the poor? What are the key characteristics of rich and poor families? Let's now turn our attention to these questions.

Who Are the Rich and the Poor?

The poorest person in the United States today is most likely to be a black woman living on her own, probably widowed, who is over 65 years of age, has had less than eight years of elementary school, and lives in the South. The highest income family in the United States today is likely to be a married couple, between ages 45 and 54, with two children. The adult household members in this family have had four years or more of college education, are white, and live in California. These snapshot profiles are the extremes in Fig. 18.4. That figure illustrates the importance of education, marital status, size of household, age of householder, race, and region of residence in influencing the size of a family's income.

Education is the single most important factor. On the average, those with less than eight years of elementary school earn around $10,000 a year while those with four years or more of college earn nearly $40,000 a year. Marital status is also important. Widowed females or those living without a husband, on the average, have incomes of less than $10,000 a year while married couples earn an average income of more than $30,000 a year. Household size has an obvious effect on household income but the house-

Table 18.1   A Comparison of the Distribution of Income in 1955 and 1985

Cumulative percentage of families	Cumulative percentage of income	
	1955	1985
Lowest: 20	5	5
40	16	16
60	32	33
80	55	57
100	100	100

The distributions of income in 1955 and 1985 are remarkably similar. At the low end, they are identical. The 1985 distribution has a slightly lower degree of inequality than the 1955 distribution. The richest 20 percent of families had 45 percent of the income in 1955 but only 43 percent by 1985.

Source: The 1955 figures are from *Historical Statistics of the United States, Colonial Times to 1957*, p. 166; the 1985 figures are from *Statistical Abstract of the United States*, 107th ed., p. 437.

Figure 18.4   The Distribution of Income of Families by Selected Family Characteristics in 1985

Family income (dollars per year)

Education	
40,000 — ● 4 years or more college	
Size of household	**Age of householder**
35,000 —	● 45 – 54
	● 4 persons
Marital status	
● Male, married, wife present	● 5 persons
	● 6 persons
30,000 — ● Female, married, husband present	● 3 persons
● 1–3 years college	● 7 or more persons
	● 55 – 64
	● 25 – 34
25,000 —	**Race** · **Region**
	● White · ● West · ● Northeast
	Median income
	● Midwest
	● 2 persons
● 4 years high school	
● Male, divorced	● South
20,000 — ● Male, single	
● Male, married, wife absent	● Hispanic
● Female, divorced	
● Female, single	● 15 – 24
15,000 — ● 1–3 years high school	● Black
● Male, widowed	
● 8 years elementary school	● 65 and over
	● 1 person
10,000 — ● Less than 8 years elementary school	● Female, married, husband absent
	● Female, widowed

Education is the single biggest factor affecting family income distribution, but marital status, size of household, and age of householder are also very important. Race and region of residence also play a role.

Source: Statistical Abstract of the United States: 1988.

hold size at which income is highest is four persons. Age also is important, with the oldest and youngest households having the lowest incomes and middle-aged households the highest. Race and region of residence also influence the income distribution but on a smaller scale than the other characteristics that we have just examined. Black families have an average income of $15,000 while white families have an average income of $25,000. Incomes are lowest in the South and highest in the West, with those in the Northeast fairly close to those in the West and incomes in the Midwest lying midway between these two.

Poverty   Families at the bottom end of the income distribution are so poor that they are considered to be living in poverty. **Poverty** is an income level measured by a poverty index first calulated by the Social Security Administration in 1964. The index is based on Department of Agriculture assessments of the minimum consumption requirements of families based on their size and composition. In 1987, the poverty level for a two-person family was $7397. For a four-person family, it was $11,611. The distribution of poverty is very unequal by race, with 11 percent of white families and 31 percent of black families being below the poverty level. Poverty is also heavily influenced by family status. More than a third of families where the householder is a female and no husband is present is below the poverty level, while less than 10 percent of other families are.

Extreme wealth   We've seen that there are a large number of very poor families—families living in poverty. Are there a similarly large number of extremely rich families? The answer is no. Extremely rich families are rare compared with extremely poor families. For example, in 1985 there were only 32,000 families in the United States whose wealth exceeded $5 million, and those families had an average wealth of $10 million each. There were, in that same year, only 375,000 families with wealth of more than $1 million but less than $5 million. These families had average wealth of almost $2 million each.

Income Redistribution

Because poverty is so dreadful for those experiencing it and so fearful for everyone else, there is almost universal agreement that the government can play the role of a kind of giant insurance company (a sort of institutionalized Robin Hood, taking from the rich and giving to the poor). There are two main ways in which governments redistribute income in the United States today:

- Income taxes
- Welfare programs

Income Taxes   The amount and nature of the redistribution achieved through income taxes depend on the form that the income taxes take. Income taxes may be progressive, regressive, or proportional. A **progressive income tax** is one that taxes income at a marginal rate that rises with the level of income. The term "marginal," applied to income tax rates, refers to the fraction of the last dollar earned that is paid in taxes. A **regressive income tax** is one that taxes income at a marginal rate that falls with the level of income. A **proportional income tax** is one that taxes income at a constant rate regardless of the level of income.

The income tax rates that apply in the United States are composed of two parts: federal and state taxes. There is a good deal of variety in the detailed tax arrangements in the individual states but the tax system, at both the federal and state levels, is progressive. However, tax reforms introduced in 1986 have reduced the amount of progressiveness. Under the 1986 tax law, there are just two federal income tax rates, one of 15 percent for low income households and 28 percent for all others.

Welfare Programs   A second way governments redistribute income is by making direct payments to those at the low end of the income distribution. The detailed arrangements vary from state to state. Using California as an example (with data from 1982), Table 18.2 provides the details of the monthly value of Aid to Families with Dependent Children (AFDC) payments and food stamp programs that were available to families with zero or very low earnings. Although the figures in the table refer to just one state in one year, the key point that this table makes is not affected by either the state or year chosen. The situation is similar in all the states.

Notice two key things about the numbers in this table. First, the poor receive benefits from the government on a scale that ensures that no family has an income that falls below a certain level. In California in 1982, that level was $669 a month or $8028 a year. Second, the poor face astonishingly high "taxes" on anything that they might earn. It is true that the poor don't actually pay taxes to the government. Instead, the government withdraws benefits as the earnings of the poor increase. But the effect is the same as paying taxes. Imagine giving every family $669 a month, regardless of their earned income, and then imposing a tax on them as their income rises successively by the amounts shown in the first column of Table 18.2. Looked at in this way, we can calculate the marginal tax rates faced by the poor.

The change in earnings (fourth column) is simply the rise in monthly earnings given in the first column. The change in total income is the rise in the total income given in the third column. When earnings rise from nothing to $200 a month, total income rises by less than that amount—it rises by $78 a month. The reason why income only goes up by $78 a month while earnings go up by $200 a month is that the value of the AFDC and food stamp benefits fall by $122 a month. If income rises by another $200 a month, from $200 to $400 a month, an even larger reduction in AFDC and food stamps occurs. This time total income rises by only $17 a month, with a reduction of AFDC and food stamps of $183 a month. A similar thing happens as

Table 18.2   Welfare Payments and Earnings in California in 1982

Monthly earnings	AFDC and food stamps	Total income	Change in earnings	Change in total income	Marginal tax rate (percent)
0	$669	$669	—	—	—
$200	547	747	$200	$78	61
400	364	764	200	17	92
600	201	801	200	37	82

Welfare payments can be thought of as negative taxes (taxes that the government pays to a household). When household earnings rise, welfare benefits fall. The change in benefits divided by the change in income is similar to the marginal tax rate (negative tax rate). Marginal tax rates for welfare recipients are among the highest—even exceeding 90 percent in some cases.

Source: Lars Osberg, Economic Inequality in the United States (Armonk, N.Y.: M. E. Sharpe, 1983), 244.

income rises from $400 to $600. In this event, AFDC and food stamp benefits fall by $163 a month, leaving the family with an extra $37 a month.

We can consider the initial $669 of AFDC and food stamps as a kind of negative tax paid *to* families rather than paid *by* families. We can consider the reduction of benefits as a positive tax paid by families as their incomes rise. We can calculate the marginal tax rate paid by these poor families in the final column in the table. The rise in monthly earnings from nothing to $200 results in benefits falling by $122; this fall is similar to paying a 61 percent tax. The rise in monthly earnings from $200 to $400 results in a drop in benefits of $183, which is similar to paying a tax of almost 92 percent. The rise in monthly earnings from $400 to $600 results in a drop in benefits of $163, which is similar to paying a tax of almost 82 percent.

Marginal income tax rates as high as those shown in Table 18.2 substantially exceed the marginal income tax rates faced by the earners of the highest incomes. Such tax rates act as a considerable disincentive for the poor to seek employment. As a consequence of tax rates of this magnitude, some economists have advocated introducing an explicit *negative income tax.* Such a scheme would pay every family a

bare minimum income of, say, $669 a month. Any earnings that the family makes over and above that would be taxed at a constant, flat rate, regardless of the magnitude of those earnings. A tax rate of perhaps 25 or 30 percent might be applied. Such a scheme would lower the disincentives faced by the poor and encourage them to seek additional employment.

Other Policies that Redistribute   In addition to income taxes and welfare programs, governments undertake other measures not primarily aimed at redistributing income but having that effect. The most important of these measures is the provision of public education and subsidized health care. Because of such programs, the poor are better educated and healthier and so have more human capital and are able to increase their earnings.

The Scale of Income Redistribution   The distribution of income that would prevail in the absence of government policies is called the **market distribution.** The income distribution that takes account of government policies is called the **distribution after taxes and transfers.** Calculating the effects of all the many tax and transfer arrangements in place is a

Figure 18.5   The Effect of Taxes and Transfers on the Distribution of Income

(a) Redistribution of income

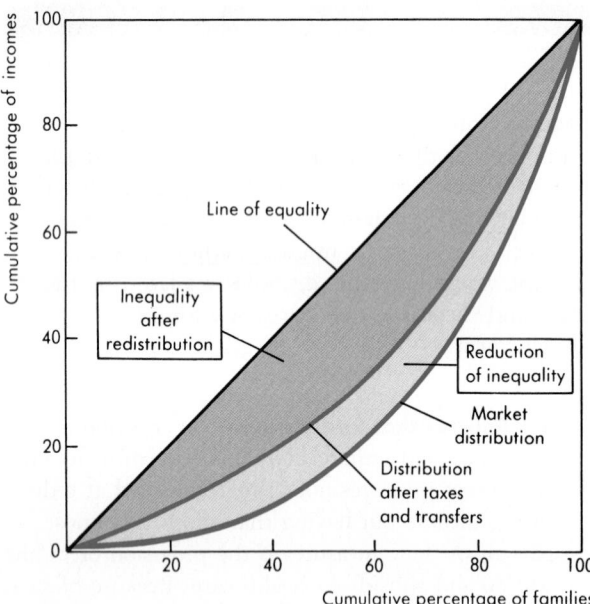

(b) Lorenz curves before and after redistribution

Taxes and transfers reduce the degree of inequality that the market generates. Part (a) shows that 10 percent of income is taken from the richest fifth of the population and 2 percent from the second-richest fifth and redistributed to the poorest two fifths. The poorest fifth receives 8 percent and the second-poorest fifth, 4 percent. The middle income group breaks even. Part (b) shows the effects of this redistribution on the Lorenz curve for income.

complicated matter and the most recent year for which we have a thorough analysis is 1976. Figure 18.5 (a) illustrates the scale of redistribution. The amount of redistribution that takes place between the five groups is 12 percent of total income. Of this, 10 percent is taken from the richest group and 2 percent from the second-richest group. The poorest group receives 8 percent and the second-poorest group receives 4 percent. The middle group just about breaks even. The effects of redistribution policies may also be seen by comparing the Lorenz curves for the market distribution of income and the distribution after taxes and transfers. Figure 18.5 (b) shows these Lorenz curves. As you can see, there is a considerable amount of redistribution undertaken, especially to boost the incomes of the very poor, but a great deal of inequality remains after redistribution.

Another measure of the scale of redistribution is provided by an examination of the sources of income of families at different points on the income distribution scale. The poorest families receive almost two thirds of their income in the form of payments from the government—called transfer income. Even the second 20 percent of families receives a third of its income in government transfers. In contrast, the richest 20 percent receive hardly anything from the government but receive a third of their income from capital—interest and dividends from financial assets. The fraction of income from that source for the other 80 percent of families is remarkably constant at about 8 percent.

We have now examined the distributions of income and wealth in the United States and have seen that a considerable amount of inequality exists. We've seen that the distribution of wealth is much more unequal than that of income. We've also looked at some of the characteristics of rich and poor families and, finally, we have examined the role of redistribution. We've also looked at some of the characteristics of rich and poor families and, finally, we have examined the role played by government in redistributing income.

But what is the reason for the enormous inequality that exists? And why is the distribution of wealth so much more unequal than that of income? Which of these two distributions paints the more accurate picture concerning the degree of inequality? In the next section, we examine the reasons for the *differences* in the degree of inequality as measured by wealth and income. After that we study some of the reasons for inequality itself.

Comparing Like with Like

In order to determine just how much inequality there is, it is necessary to make the correct comparisons. But what are the correct comparisons? Should we be looking at income or should we be looking at wealth? And should we, as we have been doing, look at annual income or should we look at income over some other time period—for example, over a family's lifetime?

Wealth versus Income

The main reason wealth is distributed much more unequally than income is that the data on wealth and income measure different things. The wealth data refer only to nonhuman capital—tangible assets that are traded on capital markets (such as those items analyzed in Chapter 17). The data on income distribution refer to income from all sources, not only from nonhuman capital but also from human capital. Let's explore the sources of these differences a bit more closely by looking at an example. We will begin however by refreshing our memory on the distinction between *income* and *wealth*.

Income and Wealth: Flow and Stock
Income and wealth can be considered different ways of looking at precisely the same thing. *Wealth* is the *stock* of assets owned by an individual. *Income* is the *flow* of earnings received by an individual. *Income* is the *flow of earnings* that results from the *stock of wealth*. It is easiest to see the relationship between income and wealth by considering an example. Suppose that Lee owns assets worth $1 million. Thus Lee's wealth is $1 million. If the rate of return on assets is 5 percent a year, then Lee will receive an income of $50,000 a year from his assets of $1 million. We can describe Lee's economic condition by saying that he has either wealth of $1 million or an income of $50,000. If the rate of return is 5 percent, these two statements are equivalent to each other.

In order to talk about the distribution of income and wealth, let's consider two individuals: Lee, who has wealth of $1 million and income of $50,000, and Peter, who has assets of $500,000. Peter and Lee have the same investment opportunities and they invest their assets at the same rate of return—5 percent a year. Peter has an income of $25,000 (5 percent of $500,000). We can now talk about the distribution of wealth and income between Peter and Lee. Lee has wealth of $1 million compared with Peter's wealth of $500,000. Thus Lee has twice as much wealth as Peter. Lee has an income of $50,000 and Peter has an income of $25,000. Again, Lee's income is twice as much as Peter's. Regardless of whether we compare Peter and Lee on the basis of their wealth or their income, we reach the same conclusion: Lee is twice as rich as Peter, both in terms of wealth and income.

Human Capital

So far, we have discussed only the earnings that Peter and Lee receive from their nonhuman wealth. We sometimes refer to physical and financial assets as *tangible assets* or, to contrast them with human capital, as *nonhuman capital*. What about their work effort? The earnings received from work are partly a compensation for giving up leisure time and partly a return on *human capital*. Although human capital represents intangible things like skills, we can put a value on it. We value human capital by looking at the earnings that a person can make from working over and above what would be earned by someone who has had no education or training. The extra earnings are the income from human capital. The value of human capital is the amount of money that a person would have to be given today so that, if invested, it would generate an interest income equal to the income from that individual's human capital.

Consider Peter and Lee again. Suppose now that each of them has no assets other than their productive skills. Lee earns $50,000 a year and if the interest rate is 5 percent a year, then Lee has $1 million of human capital. A million dollars invested at an interest rate of 5 percent a year will earn $50,000 a year. Peter earns $25,000 a year and, again, if the interest rate is 5 percent a year, Peter has human capital of $500,000. Lee earns twice as much income as does Peter and Lee has twice as much human capital.

Human and Nonhuman Capital

We have now considered the distributions of income and wealth in two extreme cases. In the first case, Lee and Peter owned no human capital so their entire income was generated by their financial and real assets. In the second case, Lee and Peter had only human capital—their productive skills. Most people have both nonhuman and human capital. Wealth, correctly measured, includes both of these types of capital.

No matter what the source of income—whether human capital or nonhuman capital—the distribution of wealth and income is the same when we count both the human and nonhuman capital. In both cases that we have just examined, Lee has twice the wealth and twice the income of Peter. So the distribution of wealth between Lee and Peter is identical to the distribution of income between them.

Let's finally examine the case in which Peter and Lee have both human capital and nonhuman capital. For a reason that will become apparent shortly, however, let's suppose that Peter has much more human capital than does Lee and that Lee has more nonhuman capital than does Peter. Table 18.3 sets out some hypothetical numbers to illustrate this case. As before, Lee has twice the total wealth and twice the total income of Peter. Lee's human capital is only $200,000, so Lee's labor income is just $10,000. But Lee has nonhuman capital of $800,000, which generates an income of $40,000. In contrast, Peter's wealth is almost exclusively human capital. Peter earns $24,950 of income from $499,000 worth of human capital. Peter has only $1000 worth of tangible assets (nonhuman capital), which generates an annual income of $50.

Suppose that a national wealth and income surveyor is examining this economy comprised of Peter and Lee and observes their incomes of $25,000 and

$50,000 respectively. The surveyor concludes that on the basis of income, Lee is twice as rich as Peter. The surveyor then measures their assets. The only assets that are measured are tangible assets. The surveyor observes that Lee owns $800,000 worth of such assets and Peter has $1000 worth. The assets are listed in a distribution of wealth table and the national surveyor concludes that, in terms of assets, Lee is 800 times as wealthy as Peter. The national survey concludes that wealth is much more unevenly distributed than income.

You can see that the national survey techniques measure the distribution of wealth in a way that does not include human capital. The distribution of income takes into account human capital and is the correct measure of the distribution of economic resources. Measured wealth distributions that ignore the distribution of human capital overstate the inequality among individuals.

Annual or Lifetime Income and Wealth?

The income distributions that we have examined earlier in this chapter are based on annual incomes. And the wealth distributions are based on measuring family wealth in a given year. There are many sources of inequality in annual income and in wealth in a given year, but these do not imply inequality over a family's entire lifetime. For example, young people earn less, on the average, than middle-aged people. Thus in a given year, a young family has a lower income

Table 18.3   Capital, Wealth, and Income

	Lee		Peter	
	Wealth	Income	Wealth	Income
Human capital	$ 200,000	$10,000	$499,000	$24,950
Nonhuman capital	800,000	40,000	1,000	50
Total	$1,000,000	$50,000	$500,000	$25,000

When wealth is measured to include the value of human capital as well as nonhuman capital, the distribution of income and the distribution of wealth display the same degree of inequality.

than a middle-aged family. But when the young family becomes middle-aged itself, its income will be no different, on the average, from the current middle-aged family. This is an example of an inequality in annual income that does not reflect an inequality across families over their entire lifetimes. The case of wealth is more extreme. Most young families have few assets and often have debts that exceed those assets. Families with people between middle age and retirement age are at a stage in life when they're building up their assets to provide for a retirement income. Again, the older family looks wealthier than the younger family but, by the time the younger family reaches that same later stage in the life cycle, it will have accumulated assets similar in scale to those of the existing older family.

In order to compare the income and wealth situation of one family with another, it is important that we take into account the family's stage in the life cycle and not be misled by differences arising purely from that factor. To illustrate the importance of this source of inequality, we'll work through an example.

Figure 18.6 shows a family's income, consumption, and wealth over its entire life cycle. The horizontal axis of each part measures age. The vertical axis measures thousands of dollars of income and consumption in part (a) and of wealth in part (b).

Part (a) shows the pattern of income and consumption. This family consumes at a steady rate of $20,000 a year throughout its life. The family's income from employment starts out at $18,000 a year. It gradually rises until, just before retirement, the family is earning $30,000 a year. After retirement, the family's income from work is zero but it continues to receive an income in the form of interest on the capital that it has accumulated in the years before retirement. (Some of the transactions of this hypothetical family are being ignored—for example, the purchase of a house, an automobile, and other consumer durable goods. For the purpose of this example, let's imagine that when the family bought these items, it financed their purchase by borrowing. Thus any real assets owned by the family had offsetting financial liabilities and therefore did not change the family's wealth).

Part (b) shows the family's nonhuman wealth. At first, the family has to borrow to sustain its consumption level. As it does so, it incurs debt and also has to pay interest on the debt. The family is at its deepest point of debt at age 35. After that age,

Figure 18.6   Life-Cycle Income, Consumption, and Wealth

(a) Income and consumption

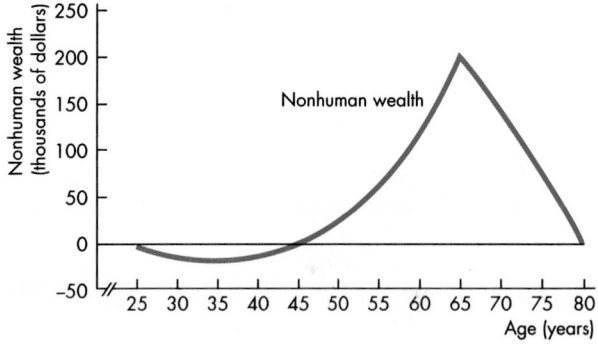

(b) Nonhuman wealth

Part (a) of the figure shows the consumption and income of a household. Consumption is constant at $20,000 a year throughout the lifetime. Labor income starts at $18,000 and gradually increases to $30,000 at retirement. After retirement, the household has no labor income. Total income is labor income plus interest on capital (on nonhuman wealth). Part (b) shows the household's nonhuman wealth. In its early years, the household is consuming more than its income and going into debt. At age 35, the household is at its maximum debt. After that time, the household gradually gets out of debt and begins to accumulate nonhuman wealth up to retirement age. After retirement, the household spends its nonhuman wealth throughout the rest of its life. An economy populated by households like this one but with each household at a different stage in its life cycle will have highly unequal distributions of annual income and wealth. The small fraction of the population close to (both before and after) retirement will own almost all the economy's nonhuman wealth.

Figure 18.7   Lorenz Curves for Imaginary and
Actual Economies

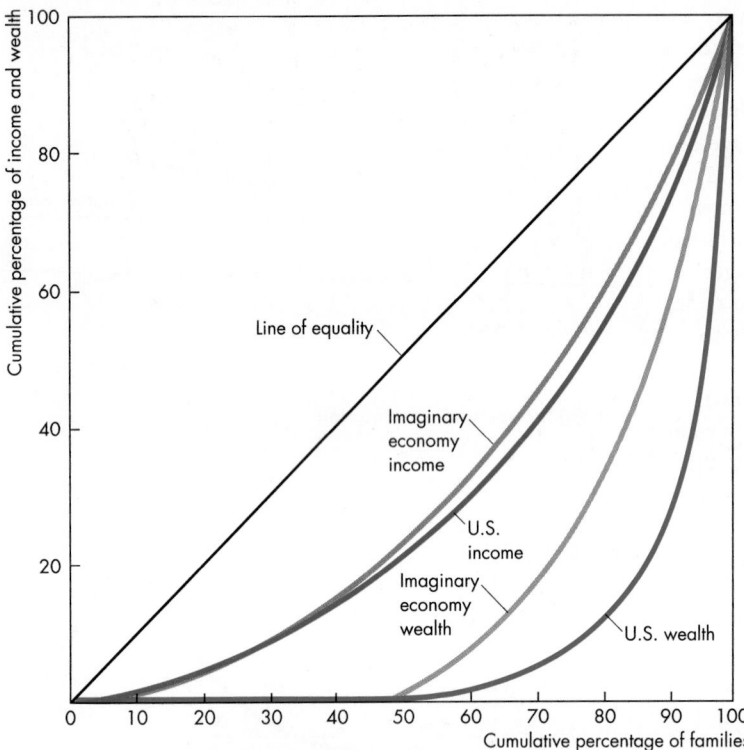

The Lorenz curves for income and wealth in the U.S. economy are shown alongside those for an imaginary economy in which everyone has the same lifetime income and consumption. The degree of lifetime inequality is exaggerated by looking only at the distribution of annual income and the distribution of nonhuman wealth.

the family gradually gets out of debt and through its sixties starts accumulating a great deal of nonhuman wealth. After retirement, that nonhuman wealth is spent on postretirement consumption.

Now suppose that there are two families identical to the one that we've looked at here but at different stages of the life cycle. One of these families is 25 years old and the other is 66. If all we look at is income, we will conclude that the 25-year-old family is almost twice as well off as the 66-year-old family. If all we look at is nonhuman wealth, we will conclude that the 66-year-old family, which has accumulated assets worth $200,000, is much better off than the 25-year-old family. Yet from the point of view of consumption, these two families are identical.

If the entire population of this imaginary economy is made up of families that are identical except for their stage of the life cycle, and if there are an equal number of people at each age, we discover some startling facts about the distributions of wealth

and annual income. First, let's look at the distribution of nonhuman wealth in this imaginary economy. That distribution is illustrated in Fig. 18.7. For comparison, the wealth distribution in the United States is also shown. As you can see, the Lorenz curve for the imaginary economy's wealth distribution lies inside that for the actual U.S. economy, so wealth in the United States is more unequally distributed than wealth in the imaginary economy. This means that although inequality in wealth arising from measuring different families at different points in the life cycle accounts for some of the inequality in the real world, it does not account for it all.

Second, let's consider the distribution of annual income. The Lorenz curve for the imaginary economy is plotted against that for the U.S. economy, again in Fig. 18.7. As you can see, there is more inequality in the United States than in the imaginary economy, but the difference is smaller than it appears when we do not take account of the differences in the stage of the life cycle.

The example through which we have just worked shows that some of the measured inequality in income and wealth arises purely from the fact that different families are at different stages in the life cycle. It also shows, however, that there are important remaining inequalities in income and wealth in the United States today. In the next two sections, we're going to explore the sources of those inequalities.

Factor Prices and Endowments

Each individual owns factors of production and sells the services of those factors to provide an income. A person's income is the price paid for the use of each factor multiplied by the quantity supplied. Factor prices are determined by the forces that we analyzed in Chapters 15 through 17. The amount of each factor service that an individual supplies depends partly on the endowment of the factor owned by the individual and partly on the choices that individual makes. Let's now examine the extent to which differences in income arise from differences in factor prices and from differences in the quantity of factors that people supply.

Labor Market and Wages

We've seen that the biggest single source of income is labor. To what extent do variations in wage rates account for the unequal distribution of income? Table 18.4 helps answer this question. It sets out the average hourly earnings of private sector employees in seven industry groups in the United States in 1985. Average hourly earnings for all industries are $8.57. As a group, those working in construction earn $12.31, substantially more than the average, and those working in the retail trades earn $5.94, substantially less than the average. Within the seven groups, there is a large variation in individual wage rates. For example, in the mining group the highest paid work is in coal mining ($15.25 an hour) and the lowest paid work is in nonmetallic minerals ($10.19 an hour). In the lowest paid industry, retail trades, the highest-paid work is in food stores ($7.35 an hour), while the lowest-paid work is in eating and drinking places ($4.33 an hour).

We can measure the spread between the highest- and lowest-paid workers in these employment categories. Take the highest-paid group of workers,

Table 18.4 Average Hourly Earnings in 1985

Industry	Average hourly earnings (dollars)
Mining	**11.98**
Coal mining	15.25
Non-metallic minerals	10.19
Manufacturing	**9.53**
Primary, nonferrous metals	13.75
Children's outerwear	5.07
Construction	**12.31**
Transportation	**11.40**
Pipeline transport	15.26
Local transit	7.69
Retail trade	**5.94**
Food stores	7.35
Eating and drinking places	4.33
Finance, insurance, and real estate	**7.94**
Services	**7.89**
Motion pictures	12.08
Hotels and lodging places	5.83
Average, all industries (private sector)	**8.57**

There is considerable inequality in average hourly earnings across different occupations. But the range of inequality is much lower than inequality of income. For example, the highest paid group, pipeline transportation workers, earns only 3½ times the income of the lowest-paid group, those who work in eating and drinking places.

Source: Statistical Abstract of the United States: 1987, 107th ed., pp. 396–398.

those in pipeline transport who earn $15.26 an hour on the average, and divide that wage by the wage of the lowest-paid group, those working in eating and

Figure 18.8   A Normal Distribution

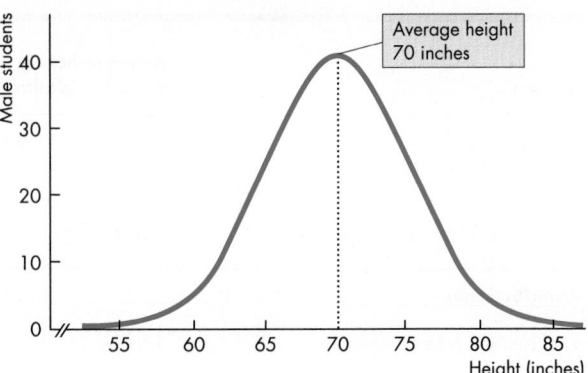

A normal distribution is shaped like a bell and is symmetric around the average. The distribution shown here is the height of a group of male students. The average height is 70 inches. For every person with a height above 70 inches, there is a mirror-image person with a height an equal distance below 70 inches. A symmetric, bell-shaped distribution describes a large number of human characteristics.

drinking places who earn $4.33 an hour. That calculation, which we call a wage differential, is 15.26 divided by 4.33, which is (approximately) 3.5. This differential says that the highest-paid group of workers earns 3.5 times as much as the lowest-paid group.

One of the things that a wage differential undoubtedly includes is the difference in skills, or human capital. For example, the most highly paid people in manufacturing work in nonferrous metals (copper, brass, and aluminum), while the least-paid workers make children's outerwear. The wage differential between those two categories probably reflects, to some degree, differences in training and skill. Similarly, in transportation, operating highly sophisticated pipeline-transport networks requires more skill than driving a local train or bus. Again, this difference in human capital is reflected in the wage differential. You can see other examples in the table.

The distribution of income is generated not only by differences in wage rates but also by differences in the endowments or abilities of individuals. Let's now consider this source of difference.

Distribution of Endowments

Ability   Although we are all endowed with equal amounts of time, we are not endowed with equal abilities. Physical and mental differences (some inherited, some learned) are such an obvious feature of human life that they hardly need mentioning. But these differences produce differences in earnings and, therefore, differences in income and wealth.

It is impossible to know for sure how such an intangible thing as "earnings potential based on ability" is distributed among the population. There are, however, many measurable characteristics of people that probably influence their earnings. For example, physical attributes such as height, weight, strength, and endurance can all be measured objectively. All of these measurable attributes appear to have what is called a normal distribution in the population. For example, Fig. 18.8 shows the distribution of heights of male students. The horizontal axis measures those heights in inches. The average height is 70 inches (5'10"). The vertical axis measures the number of students at each height. The curve in the figure traces the percentage of students at each height. The distribution is symmetric. That is, for each person above the average height there is another person who is below the average by the same amount so that the two are like a mirror image of each other. There are more people at the average and clustered around the average than there are at the two extremes.

Figure 18.9   The Distribution of Income

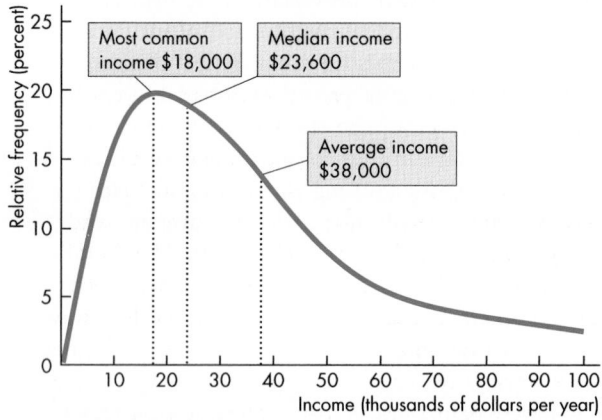

The distribution of income is unequal and is not symmetric around the average. There are many more people below the average than above the average. Also, the distribution has a long thin upper tail representing the small number of people earning very large incomes.

The range of individual ability is a major source of differences in income and wealth. But it is not the only source. If it were, the distributions of income and wealth would look like the bell-shaped curve that describes the distribution of heights in Fig. 18.8. In fact, the distribution of income looks like Fig. 18.9. Figure 18.9 shows different levels of income on the horizontal axis and the percentage of the population on the vertical axis. The median income is shown as $23,600. There are many more people below the average than above it and a relatively small number of people receive extremely high incomes. Because of this, the most common income is below the median—at $18,000—and the average income is above the median—at $38,000. The asymmetric shape of the distribution of income and wealth has to be explained by something more than the distribution of individual abilities.

Choices and the Distribution of Income and Wealth

A person's income and wealth depend in part on the choices that he or she makes. Households get paid for supplying factors of production—labor services, capital, and natural resources. The income received depends partly on the price of those factors of production and partly on the quantities that the household chooses to supply. In most cases, people can't influence the prices of the factors of production. They can't go to a bank and demand that it pay a higher interest rate, or to the New York Stock Exchange and demand that stocks improve their performance. People can't demand higher wages than the equilibrium wage rate for their babysitting, truck driving, car washing, or taxation advice work. An investment banker earns more than a parking lot attendant because of differences in human capital, but the market still determines the wages at which labor is traded.

In contrast, people can and do choose how much of each factor to supply. They also choose whether to baby-sit or to work in a bank, whether to put their savings in the bank or in stocks. Each individual chooses how much of each factor to supply. So the distribution of income depends not only on factor prices but also on people's choices about supplying factors.

We are going to discover that the choices that people make exaggerate the differences among individuals. Their choices make the distribution of income more unequal than the distribution of abilities and also make the distribution of income skewed. A skewed distribution is one in which there are a larger number of people on one side of the average than on the other. In the case of income distribution, there are more people below the average than above the average.

Let's now go on to see why people's choices lead to an unequal and skewed income distribution.

Wages and the Supply of Labor

A family's supply curve of labor shows the relationship between the quantity of labor the household supplies and the wage rate. Suppose that a family has a labor supply curve like the one shown in Fig. 18.10. At a wage rate at or below $1 an hour, the household supplies no labor. As the wage rate in-

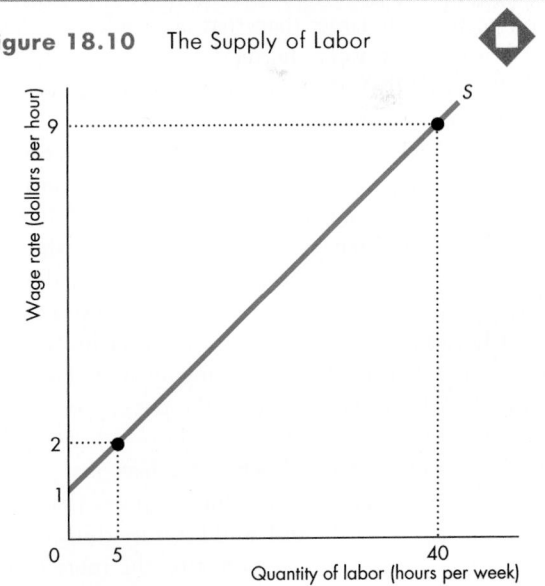

Figure 18.10   The Supply of Labor

As the wage rate increases so does the quantity of labor supplied. A person facing a wage rate of $2 an hour works for 5 hours and so earns $10 a week. A person facing a wage rate of $9 an hour works for 40 hours and earns $360 a week. The wage rate of the second person is 4.5 times that of the first, but the second person's income is 36 times larger.

creases, the quantity of labor supplied increases, and at a wage rate of $9 an hour, 40 hours a week of labor are supplied. The fact that the quantity of labor supplied increases as the wage rate increases results in the distribution of income being more unequal than the distribution of hourly wages. It also results in the distribution of income being skewed even if the distribution of wages is symmetric. To see why these features of the income distribution occur, let's imagine a population of 1000 people, each one of whom has a labor supply curve like the one shown in Fig. 18.10.

Although everyone has the same labor supply curve, suppose that they each have a different marginal revenue product of labor and so are paid a different wage rate (see pp. 407–410). Figure 18.11 describes this artificial economy. Part (a) shows the distribution of marginal revenue products—and hourly wage rates—for the 1000 people. This distribution is a normal curve—bell-shaped, like the distribution of students' heights. The average wage rate is $5 an hour and the wage ranges from $1 an hour to $9 an hour.

Figure 18.11(b) shows the distribution of weekly income. Since people who earn a higher hourly wage work longer hours, their weekly income is disproportionately larger than that of people with low hourly wages who work shorter hours. As you can see from Fig. 18.11(b), the most common income is $100 a week, but the average income is $128 a week. Those who earn $2 an hour only work 5 hours a week for a weekly wage of $10. Those who earn $9 an hour work 40 hours a week for a wage of $360. Thus the range of income from the highest to the lowest is 36 to 1. In contrast, the wage rate of the highest paid is only 4.5 times that of the lowest paid.

Choices also make the distribution of income skewed. You can see this by looking again at Fig. 18.11(b). A larger proportion of the population has an income below the average than above the average.

The example through which we have just worked is, of course, artificial. But the point that it illustrates applies in the real world. Other things being equal, the higher the wage rate, the more labor will a person supply; therefore the distribution of income is more unequal than the underlying distribution of abilities. Even if the distribution of abilities is symmetric, the distribution of income will be skewed. More people will have incomes below the average than above the average.

How important is this source of income inequality? It is impossible to give a firm and precise answer to this question, but we can get some idea of its importance by comparing the distribution of hours of work with the distribution of income. The poorest 20 percent of the population has 5 percent of the income but does only 2 percent of the hours of work. The richest 20 percent receives 43 percent of the income but does only 35 percent of the work. It is the middle groups who do a larger percentage of the work than the percentage of income that they receive. There is a direct relationship between the percentage of the work performed and the percentage of income received by each of the five groups. But the poorest and the richest groups each obtain a bigger fraction of the income than the fraction of the work that they perform, while the middle groups perform a bigger fraction of the work than the fraction of the income that they receive. This feature of the distribution of income and work reflects the fact that the poorest families receive a large amount of their income directly from the government while the richest receive a large amount of their income in the form of dividends and interest.

Another choice that makes for unequal distributions in income and wealth is savings and bequests. Let's now look at this source of inequality.

Savings and Bequests

A **bequest** is a gift from one generation to the next. The wealthier the family, the more that family tends to save and bequeath to later generations. By making a bequest, a family can spread good and bad luck across the generations.

Savings and bequests are not inevitably a source of increased inequality. Savings that merely redistribute uneven income over the life cycle to enable consumption to be constant are an example of savings having no effect on inequality. A generation that is lucky might make a bequest to a generation that is unlucky, in which case the bequest would be a source of equality not inequality. But there are two important features of bequests that do make intergenerational transfers of wealth a source of increased inequality:

• Debts cannot be bequeathed
• Mating is assortative

Bequeathing debts Though a person may die with debts in excess of assets, those debts cannot be forced onto the remaining members of the family of the deceased debtor. Also, as a rule, it is difficult to incur

Figure 18.11   The Distribution of Wages, Hours, and Income

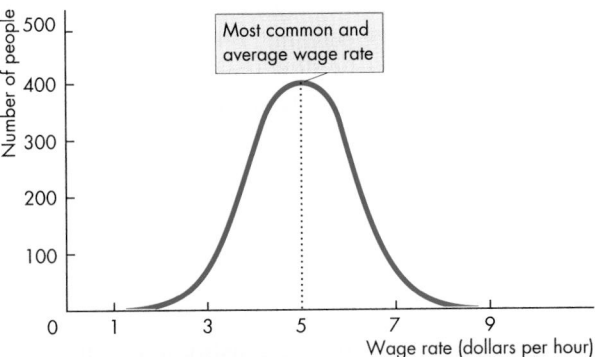

(a) Distribution of wage rates

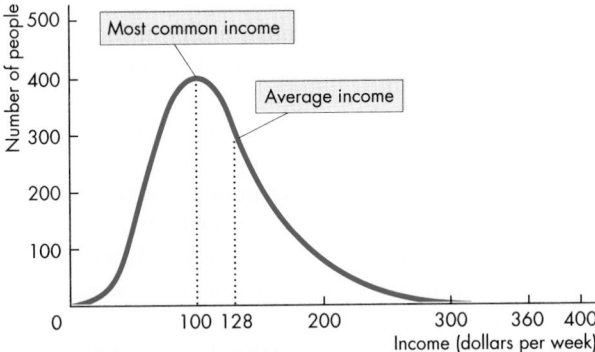

(b) Distribution of weekly incomes

Economic choices create a skewed income distribution. Part (a) graphs the distribution of wages. It is symmetric around the average wage rate of $5 an hour. Part (b) graphs the distribution of weekly income. A majority of the people earn less than the average income. The higher the wage rate, the more labor will a person supply; therefore the distribution of income is more unequal and not symmetric around the average. The range of inequality in wage rates—$1 to $9—is accentuated in the inequality of weekly income—$0 to $360.

debts in excess of assets. It is hard to find anyone willing to lend if there is not some kind of security either in the form of assets that could be seized and sold or in the form of a future earnings potential.

Because a zero inheritance is the smallest inheritance that anyone can receive, savings and bequests

can only add to future generations' wealth and income potential. The vast majority of people inherit nothing or a very small amount from the previous generation. A tiny number of people inherit enormous fortunes. As a result of bequests, the distribution of income and wealth is not only more unequal than the distribution of ability and job skills but also more persistent. A family that is poor in one generation is more likely to be poor in the next. A family that is enormously wealthy in one generation is more likely to be enormously wealthy in the next. But there is a tendency for income and wealth to converge, across the generations, to the average. Though there can be long runs of good luck or bad luck, or good judgment or bad judgment, across the generations, such long runs are uncommon. However, one additional feature of human behavior slows down convergence to the average and makes wealth and income inequalities persist—assortative mating.

Assortative Mating   **Assortative mating** means that people tend to marry within their own socioeconomic class. In the vernacular, "like attracts like." Although there is a good deal of folklore that "opposites attract," perhaps such Cinderella tales appeal to us because they are so rare in reality. Marriage partners tend to have similar socioeconomic characteristics. Wealthy individuals seek wealthy partners. The consequence of assortative mating is that inherited wealth becomes more unequally distributed.

We've now completed our positive analysis of inequality in the distribution of income and wealth. We've described the extent of inequality and have identified some of the reasons that it exists. But we have not attempted to make any assessment about fairness or justice in the distribution of income and wealth. Is it fair that some people can be so incredibly rich and others so abjectly poor? In the final section of this chapter, we examine the way in which economists and philosophers have tried to wrestle with this type of question.

Ideas about Fairness

We all have views about fairness and what constitutes a "fair" distribution of income and wealth. These views are diverse, and they are a source of political and philosophical debate. Throughout the ages, moral philosophers have tried to find a satisfactory theory of distributive justice. A **theory of distributive justice** is a set of principles against which we can test whether a particular distribution of economic well-being is fair. There are two broad classes of theories of distributive justice: end-state theories and process theories.

An **end-state theory of distributive justice** focuses on the justice or fairness of the outcomes or ends of economic activity. A **process theory of distributive justice** focuses on the justice or fairness of the *mechanisms* or *means* whereby the ends are achieved. For example, the belief that everyone should have exactly the same income and wealth is an end-state theory. The belief that everyone should have the same *opportunity* to earn and accumulate wealth is a process theory. Equality of income and wealth requires an equality of outcomes or ends. That is, when the process is over, everyone has to have the same income and wealth. Requiring that people have equal opportunity does not imply that they will have equal income and wealth because people will use their opportunities in different ways. Depending on how they use their opportunities and on a variety of chance events (good and bad luck), unequal income and wealth will emerge.

End-State Theories

The two leading end-state theories of distributive justice are the utilitarian and Rawlsian theories.

The **utilitarian theory** is that the fairest outcome is the one that makes the sum of the utilities of all the individuals in a society as large as possible. If Rob gets less utility than does Ian from the last dollar spent, then fairness requires that a dollar be taken from Rob and given to Ian. The reduction in Rob's utility is less than the gain in Ian's utility, so society is better off. Redistribution should take place until the marginal utility of the last dollar spent by each individual is the same. Utilitarian theories of fairness were developed in the eighteenth and nineteenth centuries by such economists as David Hume, Adam Smith, Jeremy Bentham, and John Stuart Mill.

The **Rawlsian theory of fairness** is that the fairest distribution is that which gives the least well-off member of society the biggest income possible. In the Rawlsian view, if the poorest person can be made better off by taking income from any other person, justice requires that such redistribution take place. The Rawlsian theory of fairness was developed

in the 1960s by John Rawls, a contemporary philosopher at Harvard University, and published in his classic work, *A Theory of Justice*, in 1971.[3]

As you can see, the two end-state theories of justice differ in what they regard as the desirable end-state or desirable outcome: For the utilitarian, it is the average or sum of all the individuals that counts; for Rawls, it is the least well-off individual or individuals that count.

How Much Inequality Is Consistent with End-State Theories?

It used to be thought that an end-state theory of justice implied that complete equality in the distribution of income was the best outcome. This conclusion was reached by reasoning along the following lines. First, people are pretty much alike in their capacity for enjoyment. (In the technical language of economics, they have the same marginal utility of income schedule.) Second, marginal utility declines with income. Therefore by taking a dollar from a rich person and giving it to a poorer person, the marginal utility lost by the rich person is less than the marginal utility gained by the poorer person. Thus, taking from the rich and giving to the poor increases total utility. Maximum utility occurs when each individual has the same marginal utility, a point that is reached, only when incomes—after redistribution—are equal. When incomes have been equalized, total utility of the society has been maximized and "fair shares" have been achieved.

The Big Tradeoff

Although it used to be thought that justice implied complete equality, it is now recognized that there exists what has been called a "big tradeoff" between fairness and economic efficiency. The term comes from the title of a book[4] by Arthur Okun, chairman of the Council of Economic Advisors to President Lyndon Johnson.

The big tradeoff is based on the following idea. Greater equality can be achieved only by taxing productive activities. Taxing people's income from their

---

[3]John Rawls, *A Theory of Justice* (Cambridge: Harvard University Press, 1971).

[4]Arthur Okun, *Equality and Efficiency: The Big Tradeoff* (Washington, D.C.: Brookings Institution, 1975).

work and savings lowers the after-tax income they receive. This lower income makes them work and save less. In economic terms, lower after-tax factor prices result in reduced factor supplies. Lower factor supplies result in smaller output and the smaller output results in less consumption not only for the rich but also, possibly, for the poor. According to this line of reasoning, the correct amount of redistribution to undertake depends on the balance between greater equality and lower average level of consumption.

It also must be recognized that taking resources from the rich to give to the poor cannot be achieved without using resources to administer the redistribution. Tax-collecting agencies such as the Internal Revenue Service as well as all the tax accountants, auditors, and lawyers together with the welfare-administering agencies use massive quantities of skilled labor and capital equipment, such as computers, to do their work. A dollar collected from a rich person does not translate into a dollar received by a poor person. The bigger the scale of redistribution, the greater are the costs of administering the process.

When these aspects of redistribution are taken into account, it is not obvious that taking a dollar from a rich person to give to a poor person increases the welfare of the poor person. The wealth available for redistribution could be reduced to the point where everyone is worse off. Taking account of the disincentive effects of redistribution and the resource costs of administering the redistribution is what produces the "big tradeoff." A more equally shared pie results in a smaller pie.

The Process View of Justice

The process view of distributive justice was given its most recent statement by Harvard philosopher Robert Nozick in his book *Anarchy, State, and Utopia*.[5] Nozick argues that no end-state theory of justice can be valid and that a theory of justice must be based on the justice of the mechanisms through which the distribution of income and wealth arises. Nozick argues for the justice of a system based on private property rights, where private property can be acquired and transferred only through voluntary exchange. His argument can be illustrated with the following story.

We start out with a distribution that you personally regard as the best possible. Now suppose that your favorite rock singer enters into a contract with a recording company and a rock concert organizer. The deal is that she will get 5 cents on every record sold and 50 cents for every ticket sold to her rock concerts. In a given year, she sells 5 million records and 500,000 people attend her concerts. Her total income is half a million dollars. This income is much larger than the average and much larger than she had under the original "ideal" distribution.

Is she entitled to this income? Is the new distribution unfair? The original distribution was fair. You and five million other fans contributed 5-cent and 50-cent pieces to the income of this successful singer. Was there something illegitimate about you buying a record and attending a rock concert? Nozick believes that she is entitled to the income and that there is nothing illegitimate about you and your friends buying records and attending rock concerts. According to Nozick's definition of fairness, the new distribution is also fair.

The philosophical debate continues and will perhaps never be settled. This state of affairs is no deterrent to those in the practical world of politics. While moral philosophers continue their disagreement about fairness, politicians are creating and implementing policies designed to chop off the extremes of the distribution of income and achieve a greater measure of equality.

■ We have examined the distributions of income and wealth in the United States and seen that there is a large amount of inequality across families and individuals. Some of that inequality arises from comparing families at different stages in the life cycle. But even taking a lifetime view, there remains a great deal of inequality. Some of that inequality arises from differences in rates of pay. But economic choices accentuate those differences. Also, savings and bequests result in the growth of huge wealth concentrations over the generations.

The topic that we have examined in this chapter is highly political and, as we've seen, governments attempt to redistribute income to alleviate the worst aspects of poverty. In the next three chapters, we're going to undertake a systematic study of a broad range of political economic issues and of the economic behavior of government. We'll return to questions concerning the distribution of income and wealth as part of that broader study.

[5]Robert Nozick, *Anarchy, State, and Utopia* (New York: Basic Books, 1974).

SUMMARY

Distribution of Income and Wealth in the United States Today

Labor's share in income is the largest and it has grown slightly over the years. It is approximately three quarters of total income. The distribution of wealth and income among individuals is uneven. The richest 1 percent of Americans own almost one third of the total wealth in the country. The poorest 50 percent own only 1 percent of the total wealth. Income is distributed less unevenly than wealth. The income distribution has changed only slightly over time and in the direction of a lower degree of inequality. The poorest people in the United States are most likely to be older, single, black women, with less than eight years of schooling, living in the South. The richest are most likely to live on the West Coast and to be college-educated, middle-aged, white families with husband and wife living together. Income tax and social welfare programs result in a redistribution of income, taking more from the rich than the poor and, to some degree, alleviating poverty. (pp. 469–476)

Comparing Like with Like

In order to judge the extent of inequality, it is important that we make valid comparisons. The measured distribution of wealth exaggerates the degree of inequality because it fails to take into account the distribution of human capital. The distributions of annual income and wealth exaggerate the degree of lifetime inequality because they do not take into account the stage in a family's life cycle. (pp. 477–481)

Factor Prices and Endowments

Differences in income and wealth arise partly from differences in individual endowments and partly from differences in factor prices. Wage rates vary considerably, depending on skill and other factors. But these differences, on their own, are not enough to account for differences in the distribution of income and wealth. Those differences get exaggerated by the economic choices that people make. (pp. 481–483)

Choices and the Distribution of Income and Wealth

The economic choices that people make have an important influence on income and wealth. Attitudes toward work result in some people taking a larger amount of leisure, earning a smaller income than others, and consuming a smaller amount of goods. Also, savings and bequests affect wealth across the generations. Because of assortative mating—the tendency for wealthy individuals to seek wealthy marriage partners—bequests accentuate inequality. (pp. 483–485)

Ideas about Fairness

People disagree on what constitutes a fair distribution of income. Moral philosophers have tried to resolve the issue by finding principles on which we can all agree, but agreement still has not been reached. Two broad groups of theories have been developed: end-state theories and process theories. End-state theories of fairness assert that it is the outcome that matters. Process theories assert that it is equality of opportunity that matters. (pp. 485–487)

KEY CONCEPTS

Assortative mating, 485
Bequest, 484
Distribution after taxes and transfers, 476

End-state theory of distributive justice, 486
Lorenz curve, 470
Market distribution, 475

Key Figures

REVIEW QUESTIONS

1 Which of the following describe the distributions of personal income and wealth in the United States today?

  a) The distributions of income and wealth are best represented by normal or bell-shaped curves.

  b) The richest people are more than 800 times as wealthy as the poorest people, but there is the same percentage of people at each different level of wealth.

  c) More than 50 percent of the population is wealthier than the average.

  d) More than 50 percent of the population is poorer than the average.

2 Which is more unequally distributed, income or wealth? In answering this question, pay careful attention both to the way in which income and wealth are measured by official statistics and to the fundamental concepts of income and wealth.

3 What is wrong with the way in which the official statistics measure the distribution of wealth?

4 Explain why the work/leisure choices made by individuals can result in a distribution of income and consumption that is more unequal than the distribution of ability. If ability is distributed normally (bell-shaped), will the resulting distribution of income also be bell-shaped?

5 Explain how the distribution of income and wealth is influenced by bequests and assortative mating.

6 What is a Lorenz curve? How does a Lorenz curve illustrate inequality? Explain how the Lorenz curves for the distributions of income and wealth in the United States economy differ from each other?

PROBLEMS

1 Imagine an economy in which there are five people who are identical in all respects. They each live for 70 years. For the first fourteen of those years, they earn no income. For the next 35 years, they work and earn $30,000 a year from their work. For their remaining years, they are retired and have no income from labor. To make the arithmetic easy, let's suppose that the interest rate in this economy is zero; the individuals consume all their income during their lifetime and at a constant annual rate. What are the distributions of income and wealth in this economy if the individuals have the following ages:

  a) All are 45

  b) 25, 35, 45, 55, 65

Is case (a) one of greater inequality than case (b)?

2 You are given the following information about income and wealth shares:

	Income shares (percent)	Wealth shares (percent)
Lowest 20%	5	0
Second 20%	11	1
Third 20%	17	3
Fourth 20%	24	11
Highest 20%	43	85

Draw the Lorenz curves for income and wealth for this economy. Explain which of the two variables—income or wealth—is more unequally distributed.

3 An economy consists of 10 people, each of whom has the following labor supply schedule:

Hourly wage rate (dollars per hour)	1	2	3	4	5
Hours worked per day	0	1	2	3	4

The people differ in ability and earn different wage rates. The distribution of *wage rates* is as follows:

Wage rate (dollars per hour)	1	2	3	4	5
Number of people	1	2	4	2	1

a) Calculate the average wage rate.

b) Calculate the ratio of the highest to the lowest wage rate.

c) Calculate the average daily income.

d) Calculate the ratio of the highest to the lowest daily income.

e) Sketch the distribution of hourly wage rates.

f) Sketch the distribution of daily incomes.

g) What important lesson is illustrated by this problem?

Part 7

During his ca-
reer, Alfred E.
Kahn has been
the chairman of the New
York Public Service
Commission and has re-
ceived presidential ap-
pointments as chairman
of the Civil Aeronautics
Board, chairman of the
Council on Wage and
Price Stability, and Ad-
visor on Inflation. Dr.
Kahn is a professor of
political economy at Cor-
nell University. Michael
Parkin spoke with him
about his experience in
public service and about
his views on regulation
and deregulation.

*Professor Kahn, how
did you become an
economist?*

I was a French major,
and also interested,
vaguely, in going into
the theater. I also loved
mathematics, but decid-
ed, foolishly, that it had
no practical usefulness.
Then I took a course in
economics and found it
terribly interesting. I
went to school during
the Depression, when the
world's worst problems
seemed to be economic;
and I wanted to make a
difference in the world. I
always thought—even
12 years after my Ph.D.
—that I would go to
law school, so as to be
able to participate actively in public policy.

Just at that time,
however, I was invited to
be a member of the At-
torney General's Nation-
al Committee to Study
the Antitrust Laws, since
my second book was in
that field, and shortly after that to the senior
staff of the Council of
Economic Advisers; and

Talking
with
Alfred
Kahn

I realized that I could be involved in making policy in the real world and be an academic economist as well.

In 1978, as chairman of the Civil Aeronautics Board, you helped bring about the deregulation of the airline industry. How does airline deregulation look to you today?

Although there have been surprises and disappointments, it has done most of the things I expected it would do. The principal purpose by far was to unleash competition. Regulation had thoroughly cartelized the industry; the result was monstrous inefficiency, and a failure to give travelers the benefits of price competition.

> "Prohibit involuntary bumping, and require airlines to solicit volunteers. How? Offer bribes."

And this has been accomplished?

The industry is unquestionably far more competitive than it was under regulation, even with the disappearance of low-cost carriers like People Express. The release of the existing airlines to invade one another's markets, and the removal of restraints on pricing has produced savings to travelers amounting to $10 to $15 billion a year. And under the pressures of

price competition, some of the worst inefficiencies encouraged by regulation have been eliminated—overscheduling, half-empty planes, inefficient route structures and work practices—while accident rates are down 35 to 45 percent.

But there have been problems?

Of course. There has been enormous turmoil and confusion. That was no surprise; competition is much messier and more turbulent than regulation, but that's because it is also much more creative.

While the explosion of competitive entry was beyond my wildest hopes, the rapid departure of most of the new airlines has left us with a handful of carriers with

significant monopoly power. Travelers in and out of hubs that are dominated by a single carrier, especially travelers whose demand is inelastic, are probably being exploited; discretionary travelers, who can stay over a weekend, can still get real bargains.

Of course, we all now sit around in airports much longer. Is this a consequence of deregulation?

Yes, but in large part it is a measure of its success. It is the result of the fantastic response of travelers to the bargain fares that are now available. But we have not had a corresponding response on the supply side. We rely on government agencies for the supply of safety inspectors and air traffic con-

trollers and for the availability of air channels
and airport space; and
those agencies have been
grossly delinquent in ex-
panding capacity.

**Had you anticipated
these problems when
you set out to deregu-
late the industry?**

Yes, indeed. Back in
1977 and 1978 I warn-
ed the Federal Aviation
Administration that with
more people and new
airlines flying, they were
going to need bigger
budgets to fulfill their
responsibilities for air
safety. I also warned
them about airport con-
gestion. If you see air-
planes waiting for an
hour on a runway for the
chance to take off, ele-
mentary economics will
tell you that it reflects
one of two failures—a
failure to expand supply
efficiently or a failure to
price correctly.

**Was a background in
economics good training
for a new chairman of
the Civil Aeronautics
Board?**

I think it was indispen-
sable. I'll give you an example. In one of my ear-
ly cases, transatlantic
cargo carriers wanted to
charge lower rates per
pound for flights, as I
recall, from east to west
than from west to east,

because they had a lot of
empty space on their
planes going that way.
The CAB lawyers op-
posed such differences as
discriminatory. But ele-
mentary economics tell
us that price differences
are not discriminatory if
the marginal costs differ;
and the marginal cost of
space in a plane that
would otherwise be par-
tially empty could be
as low as zero. The CAB's
requirement of uni-
form charges prevented
the carriers from filling
their planes on the back
hauls.

**Were there other oppor-
tunities to apply ele-
mentary economics?**

Yes, consider the rules
we established for
bumping passengers on
overbooked flights. The
board had been trying

for years to set equitable
bumping priorities. But
there are no acceptable
principles.

I pointed out that al-
locating the scarce seats
was a problem of eco-
nomic efficiency, with a
simple market solution.
All we needed to do was
prohibit involuntary
bumping, and require
the airlines instead to so-
licit volunteers. How? By
offering bribes. The ele-
gant result is that no-
body to whom the value
of staying on the plane,
or the cost of getting off,
exceeds the bribe, need
give up the seat. And
nobody takes the bribe
unless its value to him
or her exceeds that cost.

**Has the climate for de-
regulation changed?
Are there new indus-
tries that are candi-
dates for deregulation,
or are we done with it?**

"If
competition is
to work,
government
has a vital role
to play."

The process of liberalization, once begun, tends to become cumulative: I think we will see continued infusion of competition and deregulation, for example, in telecommunications and in the electric and gas utilities.

On the other hand, in some ways we may be coming to the end of the era, partly because the failure of governments to do their job has resulted in severe dissatisfactions. In the case of the airlines, the major derelictions have been in strenuous enforcement of the antitrust laws and expanding air traffic capacity. In case of the

savings and loan institutions, it has been a failure to close down recklessly run or insolvent banks, or to force their owners to put up more capital, leaving them free to continue to

> "Regulation had thoroughly cartelized the airline industry. The result was monstrous inefficiency."

attract depositors: why should depositors worry, so long as their dollars are federally insured?

The failure to recognize that in many ways deregulation can mean increased responsibilities of government has been discrediting deregulation itself.

What guiding principles of economics do you apply to your work?

First, the importance of economic efficiency, which calls for prices equated to marginal cost. That carries you a tremendous distance. But, second, it doesn't answer the question of what institutional mechanisms are best adapted to give you the efficient result, including the incentive constantly to improve efficiency. The answer is competition, wherever it is remotely feasible.

Third, if competition is to work, government has a vital role to play— for example, in enforcing the antitrust laws, protecting consumers from deception, protecting the environment, and in hundreds of other ways.

Finally, we must never

forget that economics is only a means to an end; the end is a good society and a good life for its people. We are never going to make good policy if we ignore the requirements of economic efficiency; but we are never going to make it either unless we keep clearly in mind the social goals and ultimate values we are trying to serve.

What advice would you give to young people today who are interested in pursuing careers in the public sector?

I don't see how anybody can participate intelligently in the making of public policy without an understanding of economics. But do not study only economics; study also politics, history, and literature. Like every other discipline, economics is limited by its own implicit assumptions and goals. We all look for keys lost in the dark under the street lamp familiar to us, because that's the only place we have any hope of finding them; but they may not be under that lamp at all. The particular principles and hypotheses that most economists employ are one kind of street lamp. It sheds a great deal of light; but we should always be open to the challenge of looking under other people's street lamps as well.

Chapter 19

After studying this chapter, you will be able to:

- Describe the range of economic actions governments undertake

- Outline the structure of the government sector of the United States economy

- Distinguish between a normative and a positive analysis of government economic behavior

- Define market failure and explain how it might be overcome by government action

- Distinguish between private goods and public goods

- Explain the free-rider problem

- Explain how government provision of public goods avoids the free-rider problem

- Explain how property rights and taxes and subsidies may be used to achieve a more efficient allocation of resources when externalities are present

Government is big business—one of the biggest. In 1989, the U.S. federal government employed more than 5 million people and spent more than $1 trillion. State and local governments employed a further 14 million people, spending $0.7 trillion between them. Independent government agencies employed yet another million people. What do all these people and all these dollars do for us? Is the government sector of our economy doing more than it should? Is it simply too big? Is government, as President Ronald Reagan often suggested, "the problem"? Or, despite its enormous size, is government doing less than it should? Is government too small? Is more government activity and intervention the solution to many outstanding problems? ■ Governments provide an enormous array of goods and services. Some are intangibles like laws and their enforcement; others are tangibles like schools and highways. Why does government supply some goods and not others? You've probably seen a Wells Fargo security truck delivering cash to your local bank. Why does Wells Fargo, a private company, supply security services to banks while the local police department provides similar services to residential neighborhoods, streets, and highways? What is so special about roads and highways, nuclear weapons, and judicial services that results in such services always being provided by government and never by private firms? ■ We've been hearing a lot recently about our endangered planet. The massive quantities in which we burn fossil fuels—coal, natural gas, and oil—have some obvious and immediate effects on the atmosphere that result in acid rain. And there are harder to measure but potentially more serious effects on the chemical balance of the earth's atmosphere, increasing the proportion of carbon dioxide and reducing the proportion of other elements. It is predicted that the continuation of

Government— the Solution or the Problem?

this process will result in a gradual warming up of the planet—the so-called greenhouse effect. It is also predicted that the persistent and large-scale use of chlorofluorocarbons (CFCs) will cause irreparable damage to the earth's ozone layer, thereby exposing us to an increased amount of radiation. These environmental issues are simultaneously everybody's problem and nobody's problem. Everyone is put at risk by the continued damage to our atmosphere and yet no one individual can take the necessary action to protect the environment. What, if anything, might government do to protect our environment? How can the government help us to take account of the damage that we cause others every time we turn on our heating or air conditioning systems?

■ We have spent a great deal of time studying the economic choices of households and firms. We have seen how households make choices governing the allocation of the factors of production that they own and how those choices determine their incomes. We've also seen how they choose their spending and saving. We've seen how firms choose the quantities of goods and services to produce and the techniques with which to produce them. We've seen how households and firms interact in markets for goods and services and for factors of production. ■ We've also seen that households and firms do not make their choices in a political vacuum. Their choices are influenced by actions taken by government. For example, rent controls and minimum wage laws influence the way competitive markets operate. We've also seen that many markets are not competitive. They have monopoly elements, and those elements often arise from legal restrictions on competition. ■ In this chapter and the next two, we turn our attention to the economic choices that governments make and to the effects of those choices on the economy. In this chapter, our main concern is to describe the government sector and explain how the market economy, in the absence of a government, would fail to achieve an efficient allocation of resources. We also provide a brief sketch of the economic theory of government behavior that serves as an outline that will be elaborated and applied in the subsequent two chapters on this broad and important topic.

■ We begin by describing the main components of the government sector of the economy and by looking at the size of government and the way in which it has grown over the past 50 years.

The Government Sector

We'll begin by describing the anatomy of the government sector.

The Structure and Scale of Government

The government sector of the U.S. economy consists of more than 80,000 separate organizations, some tiny like the Yuma, Arizona, School District, and some enormous like the U.S. federal government. The total government sector of the U.S. economy accounts for 35 percent of spending on goods and services and 36 percent of total employment.

There are three levels of government in the United States: federal, state, and local. The federal government spends more than the state and local governments do—about $1 trillion a year—but local government has the highest number of employees—close to 10 million. Each level of government is organized into branches and departments. The branches of government are the legislature, judiciary, and executive, and the departments are the bureaucracies that take care of the day-to-day business of government. The bulk of government economic activity takes place in the Departments of Defense, Health, and Treasury. Including military personnel, the Defense Department employs almost two thirds of total government-sector employees and spends almost one third of the budget. The Department of Health and Human Services, which administers welfare programs (including social security), spends more than one third of the total budget. Even the Treasury Department spends close to one fifth of the budget (mainly on debt interest and tax collection).

The Scale and Growth of Government

The scale of government has changed dramatically over the years. In 1940, for example, government-sector expenditure accounted for less than 20 percent of the economy's total expenditure, while in 1990 it had reached 35 percent. But the growth of government expenditure over the past 50 years probably understates the growth of the importance of government in economic life. That importance stems partly from the government's expenditure and partly from the extent of the laws and regulations passed by government that affect the economic actions of individual households and firms. We look at this aspect of government in Chapter 21 where we study regulation and antitrust.

Our main task in this chapter is not to describe the anatomy of government and the pace at which it has grown but to analyze the failure of markets to achieve *allocative efficiency* and to explore the role of government in coping with market failure. Before we embark on that main task, we're going to take an overview of the alternative approaches that economists use to study the economic behavior of government.

The Economic Theory of Government

We all have opinions on political matters and some of those opinions are strongly held. As students of economics, our task is to understand, explain, and predict the economic choices that the government sector makes. Although we cannot suppress our political views, it is important, if we are to make progress in studying political behavior, to continually remind ourselves of the important distinction between positive and normative analysis. We first reviewed that distinction in Chapter 1 (pp. 17–18). But because the distinction is so important for the economic study of political behavior, let's remind ourselves of what that distinction is.

Positive and Normative Analysis   An economic analysis of government choices may be either *positive* or *normative*. The positive analysis of government seeks to explain the reasons for and effects of government economic choices. A normative analysis seeks to evaluate the desirability of a government action and argues for or against some particular proposal. Positive analysis seeks to understand what is; normative analysis seeks to reach conclusions on what *ought* to be. The economic analysis used in both of these activities is similar. But the use to which the analysis is put differs. Here we undertake a positive study of government action; that is, we seek to understand the reasons for and the effects of the actions that we see being undertaken by governments in the United States today. We do not seek to establish the desirability of any particular course of action or to argue for or against any particular policy.

All government economic action stems from two aspects of economic life:

- Market failure
- Redistribution

Market Failure   One explanation for government intervention in the economy is market failure. **Market failure** is the inability of an unregulated market to achieve, in all circumstances, allocative efficiency. There are three types of situations in which market failure arises:

- The provision of goods and services that we consume in common with everyone else
- The production of goods and services where *external costs* or *external benefits* are present
- The restriction of output by monopolies and cartels

In all three cases, the unregulated market produces waste in the sense that a different allocation would result in producing more of some goods without producing less of others and could make someone better off without making anyone worse off. It is important not to take this last statement as being normative. The presence or absence of waste is a positive matter. It is a statement about what *is*. A prediction that government action will (or will not) occur to eliminate such waste is also a positive statement. The proposition that government *ought* (or ought not) to intervene to eliminate waste is normative. In dealing with market failure, it is the positive aspects that will be our concern.

Redistribution   Another explanation for government intervention in the economy is to redistribute income and wealth. Such redistribution is usually justified on the basis of some notion of equity or distributive justice, which we discussed in Chapter 18. But not all redistribution is explained in this way. The creation of monopoly and government protection of cartels also results in the redistribution of income and wealth. And the *rent-seeking* activities that we described in Chapter 13 have an important political dimension.

Again, it is important to keep the distinction between positive and normative aspects of the redistributive role of government clear. The proposition that most people believe that the market distributions of income and wealth are unfair is positive. The proposition that government intervention can redistribute income from the rich to the poor is also positive. The statement that the government *ought* to redistribute income and wealth is normative. We have described the scale of income redistribution in Chapter 18 and we will study it further in Chapter 20. When we do so, our focus will be entirely on its positive aspects.

Public Interest and Public Choice   There are two broad classes of economic theories of government behavior:

- Public interest theories
- Public choice theories

A **public interest theory** of government behavior predicts that government action will take place to eliminate waste and achieve an efficient allocation of resources. A **public choice theory** predicts that the behavior of the government sector of the economy is the outcome of individual choices made by voters, politicians, and bureaucrats interacting with each other in a political marketplace. According to the public interest theory of government, whenever there is market failure, government action can be designed to eliminate the consequences of that failure and to achieve allocative efficiency. According to the public choice theory, matters are not that simple. Not only is there the possibility of market failure (arising in the situations that we have outlined above), but there is also the possibility of "government failure." That is, it is possible that when voters, politicians, and bureaucrats each pursue their own best interests and interact in the political "marketplace," the resulting "public choice" no more achieves the elimination of waste and the attainment of allocative efficiency than does an unregulated market. Understanding why not is the main topic of Chapter 20.

In the next section, we're going to explain more fully the economic role of the government arising from two of the sources of market failure—the provision of goods and services that we consume in common with everyone else, and the production of goods and services where external costs or external benefits are present. The other source of market failure, arising from monopoly and cartels, and the government regulation of such industries, is dealt with in Chapter 21.

Public Goods

Why does the government provide certain goods and services such as a legal system, a system of national defense, schools and highways, and public health services? Why don't we simply leave the provision of these goods and services in the hands of private firms that sell their output in markets? How much national defense would we have if a private firm, Star Wars, Inc., had to compete for our dollars in the marketplace in the same way that McDonald's and Coca-Cola do?

Most of the answers to these questions lie in the distinction between private goods and public goods.

Private Goods and Public Goods

A **private good** is a good or service each unit of which is consumed by only one individual. An example of a private good is a can of soda. There are two important features of a private good. The first feature is called *rivalry*. Rivalry emphasizes the idea that one person's consumption can take place only at the expense of another person's. If you increase your consumption of soda by one can, other things being equal, someone else has to consume one can less. The second feature of a private good is called *excludability*. Once you have bought a can of soda, the soda is yours to do with as you choose. You can exclude others from using it.

A **pure public good** is a good or service each unit of which is consumed by everyone and from which no one can be excluded. An example of a pure public good is the national defense system. There are two important features of a pure public good that parallel the two features that we identified concerning a private good. The first feature is called *nonrivalry*. One person's consumption of a pure public good does not reduce the amount available for someone else. For example, your consumption of the security provided by a national defense system does not decrease the security of anyone else. The second feature is called *nonexcludability*. No one can be excluded from the additional security that every citizen enjoys from the national defense system.

Many goods lie between a pure public good and a private good. Such goods are called **mixed goods.** An example of a mixed good is a highway. A highway is like a pure public good until it becomes congested. One more car or truck on a highway with plenty of space on it does not reduce the consumption of highway services of anyone else. But once the highway is congested, the addition of one more user lowers the quality of the service available for everyone else—it becomes like a private good.

Pure public goods and mixed goods with a large public element—all referred to as public goods —give rise to what is called the free-rider problem.

Free Riding

A **free rider** is someone who consumes a good without paying for it. The **free-rider problem** is the tendency for the scale of provision of a public good to be too small if it is produced and sold privately. The free-rider problem arises because there is no incentive for a person to pay for a good if the payment makes no difference to the quantity of the good that the person is able to consume. Public goods are such goods. To see why, let's look at an example.

Imagine that an effective, antimissile laser weapon has been developed. One of these new weapons can attack and destroy 400 intercontinental ballistic missiles within seconds of their being launched. The larger the number of antimissile laser weapons deployed, the larger is the number of missiles destroyed. Potential enemies have 1500 missile launchers and four of the new weapons can eliminate all of them. Three can do a pretty good job and even two can severely limit the amount of damage that will be inflicted by missiles that get through the laser defense.

But the new weapons system is very expensive. To build it, resources have to be diverted from peaceful space programs and from the development of other productive uses of lasers in medicine. As a result, the larger the number of weapons installed, the greater is their marginal cost.

Our task is to work out the scale on which to install this new defense system to achieve allocative efficiency. We'll then examine whether private provision can achieve allocative efficiency and we'll discover that it cannot—that there is a free-rider problem.

Benefits and Costs

The benefits provided by a weapons system are based on the preferences and beliefs of the consumers of the services of that system. The costs are based on technology and the prices of the factors of production used to produce the system. When studying private goods, we observed that the value of a good to an individual is the maximum amount that the person is willing to pay for one more unit of the good. We worked out this value from the individual's demand curve. That is, the demand curve tells us the quanti-

ty demanded at a given price, or for a given quantity, the maximum price that is willingly paid for the last unit bought. We can work out the value a person places on a public good in a similar manner. That is, the value that a person places on a public good is the maximum amount willingly paid for one additional unit of the good.

To calculate the maximum amount that a person is willing to pay for one more unit of a public good, we first need to establish that person's total benefit schedule. **Total benefit** is the total dollar value that a person places on a given level of provision of a public good. The greater the scale of provision, the larger is the total benefit. The table in Fig. 19.1 sets out an example of the total benefits to Lisa and Max of different scales of provision of the proposed antimissile lasers. Lisa and Max believe that the weapons system reduces the chance of a nuclear war occurring and, if it does occur, increases the chance of preventing nuclear warheads from reaching their targets. The more lasers there are in place, the greater is the degree of security, but up to a maximum level. Each additional laser is believed to provide less additional security than the previous one. The increase in total benefit resulting from a unit increase in the scale of provision of a public good is called its **marginal benefit.** The marginal benefits to Lisa and Max are calculated in the table in Fig. 19.1 As you can see, the greater the scale of provision, the smaller is the marginal benefit. By the time 4 lasers are deployed, Lisa perceives no additional benefits, and Max perceives only $10 worth. Lisa's and Max's marginal benefits are graphed as MB_L and MB_M, respectively, in parts (a) and (b) of the figure.

The marginal benefit of a public good is the maximum amount that a person is willing to pay for one more unit of the good. This maximum amount varies with the quantity of the good consumed. The greater the quantity, the smaller is the maximum amount that will be paid for one more unit.

Part (c) of the figure shows the economy's marginal benefit curve, MB (where the economy has only two people, Lisa and Max). The marginal benefit curve of a public good for an individual is similar to the demand curve for a private good. But there is an important difference between the economy's marginal benefit curve for a public good and the market demand curve for a private good. To obtain the market demand curve for a private good, we add up the quantities demanded by each individual at each price. In other words, we sum the individual demand curves horizontally (see Fig. 7.1, p. 157). In contrast,

Figure 19.1   Benefits of a Public Good

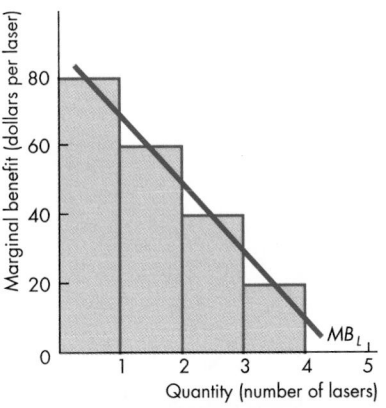

(a) Lisa's marginal benefit curve

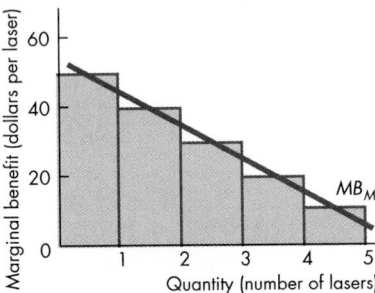

(b) Max's marginal benefit curve

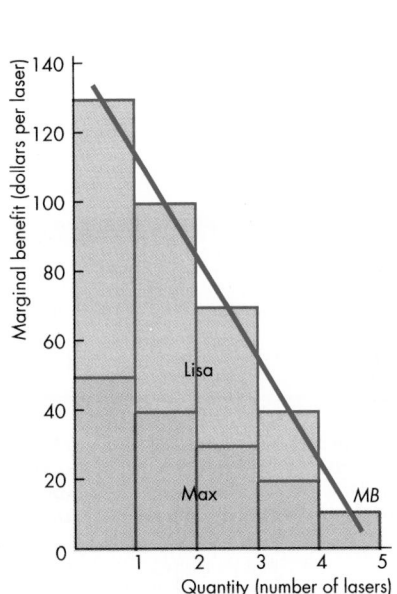

(c) Economy's marginal benefit curve

The table shows various scales of provision of an antimissile laser defense system. It also lists the total benefits accruing to Lisa, Max, and the economy (comprised of only Lisa and Max) of different scales of provision. The table also calculates the marginal benefit—the change in total benefit resulting from a unit increase in the scale of provision—to Lisa, Max, and the economy. The marginal benefits are graphed in the figure, for Lisa in part (a) and for Max in part (b). The marginal benefit to the economy at each level of provision is the sum of the marginal benefits to each individual and is shown in part (c). The marginal benefit curves are MB_L for Lisa, MB_M for Max, and MB for the economy.

	Lisa		Max		Economy	
Quantity (number of antimissile lasers)	Total benefit (dollars)	Marginal benefit (dollars per laser)	Total benefit (dollars)	Marginal benefit (dollars per laser)	Total benefit (dollars)	Marginal benefit (dollars per laser)
0	0		0		0	
		80		50		130
1	80		50		130	
		60		40		100
2	140		90		230	
		40		30		 70
3	180		120		300	
		20		20		 40
4	200		140		340	
		 0		10		 10
5	200		150		350	

to find the economy's marginal benefit curve of a public good, we sum the marginal benefits to each individual at each quantity of provision. That is, we sum the individual marginal benefit curves vertically. The resulting marginal benefit for the economy comprised of just Lisa and Max is calculated in the table,

Figure 19.2   The Efficient Scale of Provision of a Public Good

(a) Total benefit and total cost curves

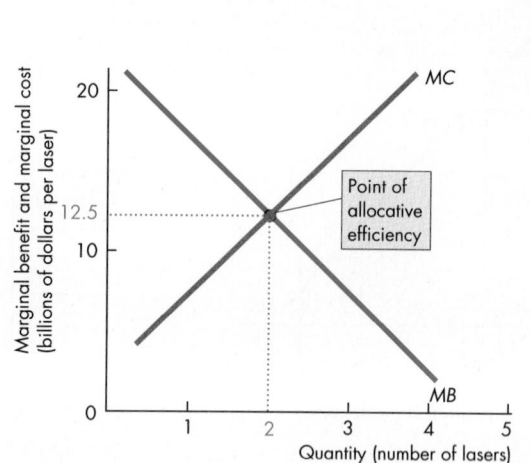

(b) Marginal benefit and marginal cost curves

Quantity (number of antimissile lasers)	Total benefit (billions of dollars)	Marginal benefit (billions of dollars)	Total cost (billions of dollars)	Marginal cost (billions of dollars)	Net benefit (billions of dollars)
0	0		0		0
		20		5	
1	20		5		15
		15		10	
2	35		15		20
		10		15	
3	45		30		15
		5		20	
4	50		50		0
		0		25	
5	50		75		−25

The table shows the total benefit and marginal benefit to the entire economy of various scales of provision of a laser weapons system. It also shows the total cost and marginal cost of the various scales of provision. Total benefit and total cost are graphed in part (a) as the total benefit curve, *TB*, and the total cost curve, *TC*. Net benefit is visible as the vertical distance between these two curves and is maximized when 2 lasers are installed. Part (b) shows the marginal benefit curve, *MB*, and marginal cost curve, *MC*. Where marginal cost equals marginal benefit, net benefit is maximized and allocative efficiency is achieved.

and the economy's marginal benefit curve is graphed in part (c)—the curve labeled *MB*.

An economy with just two people would certainly not buy any antimissile lasers—their total benefits fall far short of their cost. But an economy with 250 million people might. To determine the efficient scale of provision, consider the example set out in Fig. 19.2. The first two columns of the table show the hypothetical total and marginal benefits to the entire economy (consisting of 250 million people).

The next two columns show the total and marginal cost of producing antimissile lasers. These costs are opportunity costs and are derived in exactly the same way as the costs associated with the production of sweaters that we studied in Chapter 10. The final column of the table shows net benefit. **Net benefit** is total benefit minus total cost. The efficient scale of provision is the one that maximizes net benefit.

Total benefit and total cost are graphed as the total benefit curve, TB, and total cost curve, TC, in part (a). Net benefit is also visible in that part of the figure as the vertical distance between the two curves. Net benefit is maximized when that distance is at its largest, a situation that occurs at a scale of provision of 2 lasers. This is the efficient scale of provision.

Another way of describing the efficient scale of provision is in terms of marginal benefit and marginal cost. The marginal benefit and marginal cost of lasers are graphed as the marginal benefit curve, MB, and marginal cost curve, MC, in part (b). When marginal benefit exceeds marginal cost, net benefit increases if the quantity produced increases. When marginal cost exceeds marginal benefit, net benefit increases if the quantity produced decreases. When marginal benefit equals marginal cost, net benefit cannot be increased—it is at its maximum possible level. Thus when marginal benefit equals marginal cost, allocative efficiency has been achieved.

Now that we have worked out the efficient scale of provision of a public good, let's go on to see how much of such a good would be provided by a private producer.

Private Provision

We have now worked out the scale of provision of a national defense system that maximizes net benefit. Would a private firm—Star Wars, Inc.—deliver that scale of provision? It would not. To do so, it would have to collect $15 billion to cover its costs—or $60 from each of the 250 million people in the economy. But no one would have any incentive to buy his or her "share" of the laser weapon system. Each person would reason as follows: The number of antimissile lasers provided by Star Wars, Inc., is not going to be affected by my $60. But my own private consumption is going to be affected by whether or not I pay. If I do not pay, I will enjoy the same level of security from the laser weapons and more of other goods. Therefore it pays me to keep my $60 and spend it

on other goods, my consumption of which is affected by my spending on them. In other words, it pays me to free ride on the public good and buy private goods.

Since everyone reasons in the same manner, Star Wars has zero revenue and zero production.

Public Provision

Suppose that the people in this economy have instituted a government that makes the following proposition: The government will collect $60 from each person and will spend the resulting $15 billion to provide 2 antimissile lasers. Will the people vote for this proposition? Clearly they will. If there is no antimissile system (the output of Star Wars, Inc.), the marginal benefit of installing one laser greatly exceeds its marginal cost. By proposing to provide 2 antimissile lasers, the government is offering each voter a level of security that maximizes net benefit. The voters obtain a benefit of $35 billion—$140 each—for a total cost of $15 billion—$60 each. Since the voters recognize this as an improvement over the zero provision by Star Wars, Inc., they will vote for it.

Whether or not actual governments produce public goods on a scale that maximizes net benefit is something that we examine in Chapter 20. But we have established a key proposition: A government is able to provide any public good on a scale larger than that provided by a private producer.

REVIEW

If people make their own decisions about the provision of public goods and buy those goods in private markets, there is a free-rider problem. It is in everyone's individual interest to free ride, with the result that the scale of provision of the goods is smaller than that required for allocative efficiency. A government that balances marginal cost and marginal benefit provides the public good on a scale that achieves allocative efficiency. ∎

Let's now turn to the second source of market failure, externalities.

Externalities

An **externality** is a cost or a benefit arising from an economic transaction that falls on a third party and that is not taken into account by those who undertake the transaction. For example, when a chemical factory dumps its waste products into a river and kills the fish, it imposes an externality—in this case, an external cost—on the fisherman who lives downstream. Since these costs are not borne by the chemical factory, they are not taken into account in deciding whether to dump waste into the river, and if so, how much. When a person in Los Angeles drives a car that burns leaded gasoline and does not have a catalytic converter, an externality—again, an external cost—is imposed on everyone who tries to breathe the unbreathable air. When a homeowner fills her garden with beautiful spring bulbs, she generates an externality—in this case an external benefit—for all the joggers and walkers who pass by. In deciding how much to spend on this lavish display, she takes into account only the benefits accruing to herself.

Two particularly dramatic externalities have received a lot of attention in recent years. The first arises from the use of chlorofluorocarbons (CFCs). These man-made chemicals are used in a wide variety of products—from coolants in refrigerators and air conditioners, to plastic phones, to cleaning solvents for computer circuits. Though the precise chemistry of the process is not understood, and even the subject of dispute, many atmospheric physicists believe that the consumption of CFCs damages the atmosphere's protective ozone layer. Discoveries of depleted ozone over Antarctica in 1983 have heightened fears of extended ozone depletion. The National Academy of Sciences has estimated that a 1 percent drop in ozone levels might cause a 2 percent rise in the incidence of skin cancer. Diminished ozone is also believed to be a possible cause of cataracts.

The second externality arises from burning fossil fuels that add carbon dioxide and other gases to the atmosphere, which prevents infrared radiation from escaping, resulting in what has been called the "greenhouse effect." If the greenhouse scenario turns out to be correct, it is predicted that much of the Midwest will become a dustbowl and many eastern and Gulf Coast regions will disappear under an expanded Atlantic Ocean (see Reading Between the Lines, pp. 506–508.)

When you take a cold drink from the refrigerator or switch on the air conditioner on a steamy August evening, you do not take into account the consequences of your actions on global atmospheric matters. You compare the private benefits to yourself of drinking the cold can of soda or having a comfortable night's sleep with the cost that *you* have to incur. You do not count the costs of an increase in the incidence of skin cancer as part of the price that has to be paid for the cold soda.

Externalities are not always negative—they are not always external costs. In fact, many activities bring external benefits. Education is a good example. Not only do more highly educated people derive benefits for themselves in the form of higher incomes and the enjoyment of a wider range of artistic and cultural activities, but they also bring benefits to others through social interaction. But in deciding how much schooling to undertake, we make our calculations on the basis of the costs borne by us and the benefits accruing to us as individuals. We do not take into account the extra benefits that we're creating for others.

Health services also create external benefits. The pursuit of good health and personal hygiene reduces the risk that people with whom we come into contact will be infected by transmitted diseases. Again, in making economic choices about the scale of resources to devote to health and hygiene, we take account of the costs borne by ourselves and the benefits accruing to ourselves and not the greater benefit that our actions bring to others.

The existence of externalities—both costs and benefits—is another source of market failure. There are two possible types of action that governments can take to achieve a more efficient allocation of resources in the face of externalities:

• Establish and enforce private property rights.

• Tax those activities producing external costs and subsidize those that bring external benefits.

First, let's briefly consider the use of private property rights for dealing with externalities.

Private Property Rights and Externalities

There are some cases in which externalities arise because of an absence of private property rights. A **private property right** is a legally established title to the sole ownership of a scarce resource. A private property right is enforceable in the courts.

The creation of externalities in the absence of private property rights is illustrated well by the example of the chemical factory and a private fishing club. Members of a private fishing club use a particular stretch of a stream that is well stocked with excellent fish. A chemical factory opens upstream from the fishing club. It has to make a decision about how it will dispose of some of its waste products.

Consider two different legal situations. In the first, no one owns the stream. If the chemical factory dumps its waste products in the stream, its cost of waste disposal is zero. But the waste kills the fish and the fishing club goes out of business.

In the second situation, there are property rights established in the stream. The fishing club owns its stretch of the stream and the fish that swim in it. The chemical factory might still dump its waste into the stream but if it does so, and if it kills the fish, the fishing club will successfully bring a lawsuit against the chemical plant for damages. The damages paid to the fishing club are the cost to the chemical company of disposing of the chemical waste by dumping it in the river. If some other method of waste disposal is available that has a lower cost than killing the fish, the chemical factory will choose that alternative.

Whenever externalities arise from the nonexistence of property rights that can easily be established and enforced, this method of dealing with externalities is a natural one for governments to contemplate. But there are many situations in which private property rights simply cannot be established and enforced. In these cases, governments resort to the alternative method of coping with externalities—using taxes and subsidies. Let's see how these government tools work.

Taxes and External Costs

As we've just noted, every time you burn fossil fuel you release CO_2 into the atmosphere. These CO_2 emissions impose unintended costs on others. Let's see how the government might modify your choices and encourage you to take account of the potential costs that you're imposing on others.

One activity that creates CO_2 is driving a gasoline-fuelled vehicle. To study the demand for this activity, we'll examine the market for transportation services. Fig. 19.3 illustrates this market. The demand curve is also the marginal benefit curve, the curve $D = MB$. It tells us how much consumers value each different level of output. Curve MPC measures

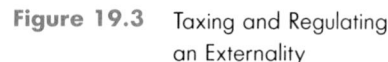

Figure 19.3 Taxing and Regulating an Externality

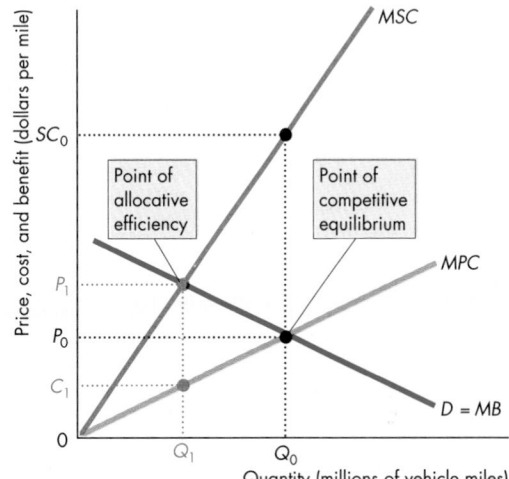

The demand curve for transportation services is also the marginal benefit curve ($D = MB$). The marginal private cost curve is MPC. Because of congestion and environmental pollution, the marginal cost of providing transportation services exceeds the marginal private cost. Marginal social cost is shown by curve MSC. If the market is competitive, output is Q_0 and the price is P_0. Marginal social cost is SC_0. If a tax is imposed to confront producers of transportation services with their full marginal social cost, the MSC curve becomes the relevant marginal cost curve for suppliers' decisions. The price increases to P_1 and the quantity decreases to Q_1. Allocative efficiency is achieved.

the marginal private cost of producing transportation services. **Marginal private cost** is the marginal cost directly incurred by the producer of a good. Thus the MPC curve shows the marginal cost directly incurred by the producers of transportation services. But there are externalities in transportation. The fact that fossil fuels are burned creates atmospheric pollution and contributes to the greenhouse effect. It also causes other, more immediate health problems. Furthermore, one person's decision to use a highway imposes congestion costs on others. These costs also are external costs. When all the external costs are added to the private costs, we obtain the marginal social cost of transportation services. **Marginal social cost** is the marginal cost incurred by the pro-

The Greenhouse Effect

Feeling the Heat

For more than a decade, many scientists have warned that cars and factories are spewing enough gases into the atmosphere to heat up the earth in a greenhouse effect that could eventually produce disastrous climatic changes. But until recently, the prophets of global warming garnered about as much attention as the religious zealots who insist that Armageddon is near.

Unfortunately, scientists cannot agree on how much global warming has occurred, how much more is on the way and what the climatic consequences will be, giving policymakers an excuse for delay. But no one disputes the fact that the amount of CO_2 in the atmosphere has risen and continues to increase rapidly. The possible consequences are so scary that it is only prudent for governments to slow the buildup of CO_2 through preventive measures, from encouraging energy conservation to developing alternatives to fossil fuels.

Recent research has confirmed that [the CO_2 buildup] is more than just theory. By drilling deep into Antarctic and Arctic ice, scientists have been able to measure the amount of CO_2 in air bubbles trapped in ancient layers of snow. They have also looked at fossilized plant tissues for clues as to how warm the air was during the same period. The conclusion: CO_2 levels and global temperatures have risen and fallen together, over tens of thousands of years. And there is evidence from space: Mars, which has little CO_2 in its atmosphere, has a surface temperature that reaches $-24°$ F at best, while Venus, with lots of CO_2, is a hellish $850°$ F.

Carbon dioxide is released in large quantities when wood and such fossil fuels as coal, oil and natural gas are burned. As society industrialized, coal-burning factories began releasing CO_2 faster than plants and oceans, which absorb the gas, could handle it. In the early 1900s, people began burning oil and gas at prodigious rates. And increasing population led to the widespread cutting of trees in less developed countries. These trees are no longer available to soak up excess CO_2, and whether they are burned or left to rot, they instead release the gas. By the late 1800s atmospheric CO_2 had risen to between 280 and 290 parts per million. Today it stands at 350 p.p.m., and by 2050 it could reach 500 to 700 p.p.m., higher than it has been in millions of years.

By far the most efficient and effective way to spur conservation is to raise the cost of fossil fuels. Current prices fail to reflect the very real environmental costs of pumping carbon dioxide into the air. The answer is a tax on CO_2 emissions—or a CO_2 user fee, if that is a more palatable term. The fee need not raise a country's overall tax burden; it could be offset by reductions in income taxes or other levies.

Imposing a CO_2 fee would not be as difficult as it sounds. It is easy to quantify how much CO_2 comes from burning a gallon of gasoline, a ton of coal or a cubic yard of natural gas. Most countries already have gasoline taxes; similar fees, set according to the amount of CO_2 produced, could be put on all fossil-fuel sources. At the same time, companies could be given credits against their CO_2 taxes if they planted trees to take some of the CO_2 out of the air.

A user fee would have benefits beyond forcing a cutback in CO_2 emissions. The fuels that generate carbon dioxide also generate other pollutants, like soot, along with nitrogen oxides and sulfur dioxide, the primary causes of acid rain. The CO_2 tax would be a powerful incentive for consumers to switch from high-CO_2 fuels, such as coal and oil, to power sources that produce less CO_2, notably natural gas.

Ultimately, though, the world must move away from fossil fuels for most of its energy needs. Said Berrien Moore, director of the Institute for the Study of the Earth, Oceans and Space at the University of New Hampshire: "Even if you cut emissions of CO_2 in half, the atmospheric concentration will keep going up. You're still adding CO_2 faster than you're withdrawing it, so the balance keeps rising."

Of all the known nonfossil energy sources, only two are far enough along in their development to be counted on: solar and nuclear, neither of which generates any greenhouse gases at all. Solar power is especially attractive. It produces no waste, and it is inexhaustible. Not all solar power comes directly from the sun: both wind and hydroelectric power are solar, since wind is created by the sun's uneven warming of the atmosphere and since the water that collects behind dams was originally rain, which in turn was water vapor evaporated by solar heating.

But wind and hydroelectric power can be generated at only a relatively few sites, and so governments should redouble financing for research to develop efficient, low-cost photovoltaic power. Photovoltaic cells, which produce electric current when bathed in sunlight, were briefly in vogue during the energy crises of the 1970s, and while public attention and Government funding have waned, research into the technology has continued. "The capital costs have come down from about $50 a peak watt to $5," said [Gus] Speth [of the World Resources Institute]. If they drop to $1, solar power will become competitive. That could happen without significant Government research support—but it will happen sooner with it.

Time, January 2, 1989

By Michael D. Lemonick

The Essence of the Story

- The amount of carbon dioxide (CO_2) in the earth's atmosphere has been increasing and continues to do so.

- In the late 1800s, atmospheric CO_2 was between 280 and 290 p.p.m.; in the late 1900s, it has been 350 p.p.m.; by 2050, it could reach 500 to 700 p.p.m.

- Although there is disagreement among scientists, many predict that these increasing concentrations of CO_2 are leading, and will continue to lead, to an increase in the earth's average temperature.

- The relationship between CO_2 and temperature is suggested by evidence from CO_2 air bubbles in ancient snow layers and fossilized plant tissue. Evidence is also provided by the relationship between CO_2 content and surface temperature on the neighboring planets of Mars and Venus.

- There are two ways government can intervene to control the greenhouse effect:
  —Imposing a tax on CO_2 emission
  —Subsidizing the development of solar energy

Background and Analysis

- The marginal private cost of generating electricity by using fossil fuels is the curve MPC (in each figure). The marginal cost of generating electricity using solar power is the curve MC.

- The power generated by solar energy has no externalities.

- The power generated by fossil fuel creates a carbon dioxide buildup with a possible greenhouse effect.

- The greenhouse effect imposes potentially large social costs: By changing weather patterns and land use patterns, it will increase the cost of food production; by melting the polar ice caps, it will raise the ocean levels, reducing the amount of usable land.

- The marginal social cost of generating electricity by using fossil fuels, including the external costs of the greenhouse effect, is the curve MSC.

- The market demand curve for electricity is D.

- With no intervention (Fig. a), the market supply curve is S; this curve is made from the MPC curve for fossil fuels and the MC curve for solar power.

- Equilibrium occurs at price P_0 and quantity Q_0; only fossil fuels are used; the marginal social cost is MSC_0, which exceeds the price; there is an allocative inefficiency—too much electricity is generated.

(Continued on next page.)

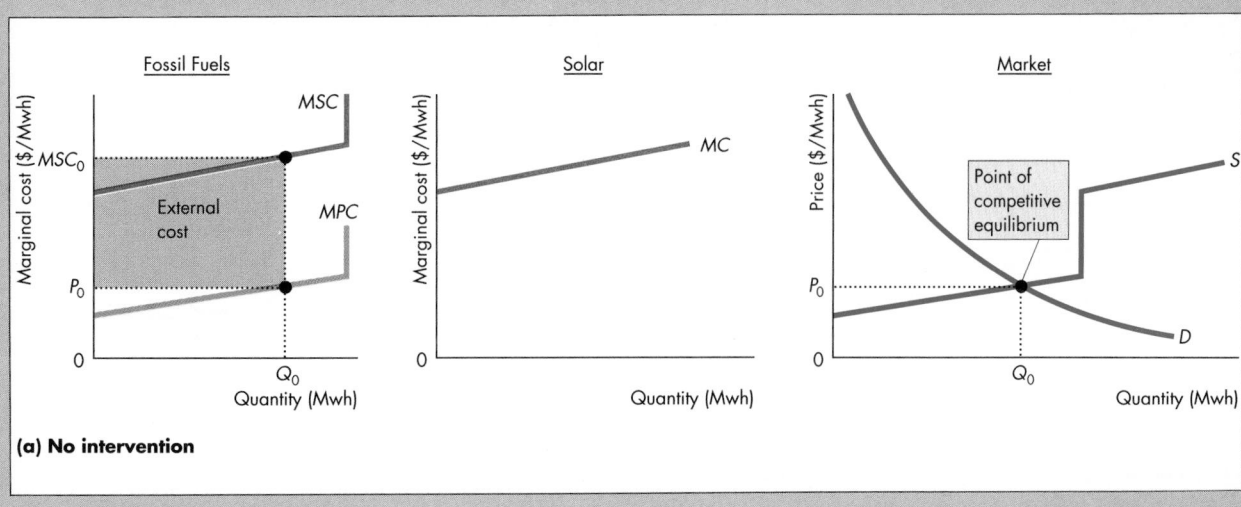

(a) No intervention

Background and Analysis (cont.)

Conclusion

- If a CO_2 tax is imposed (Fig. b) equal to the external costs, fossil fuel producers of electricity face costs shown by the curve "$MPC + tax = MSC$."

- The market supply curve becomes curve "$S + tax$."

- Equilibrium occurs at price P_1 and quantity Q_1; Q_{1F} is produced by fossil fuels and Q_{1S} by solar energy; marginal social cost is MSC_1, which equals the price P_1; allocative efficiency is achieved.

- If the development of solar energy is subsidized and fossil fuels are not taxed, (Fig. c), fossil fuel producers of electricity face the marginal cost curve MPC and solar producers face the marginal cost curve "$MC - subsidy$."

- The market supply curve is "$S - subsidy$."

- Equilibrium occurs at price P_2 and quantity Q_2; Q_{2F} is produced using fossil fuels and Q_{2S} using solar energy.

- Marginal social cost is MSC_2, which exceeds price P_2 and an allocative inefficiency remains; too much electric power is generated.

- A similar parallel analysis can be applied to CFCs and other atmospheric pollutants.

- To achieve allocative efficiency in the face of an externality, the externality has to be identified and its magnitude assessed.

- If a tax is imposed equal to the external marginal cost, allocative efficiency is achieved.

- Subsidizing a substitute activity that does not have external costs is not equivalent to taxing an activity that does have an external cost and does not achieve allocative efficiency.

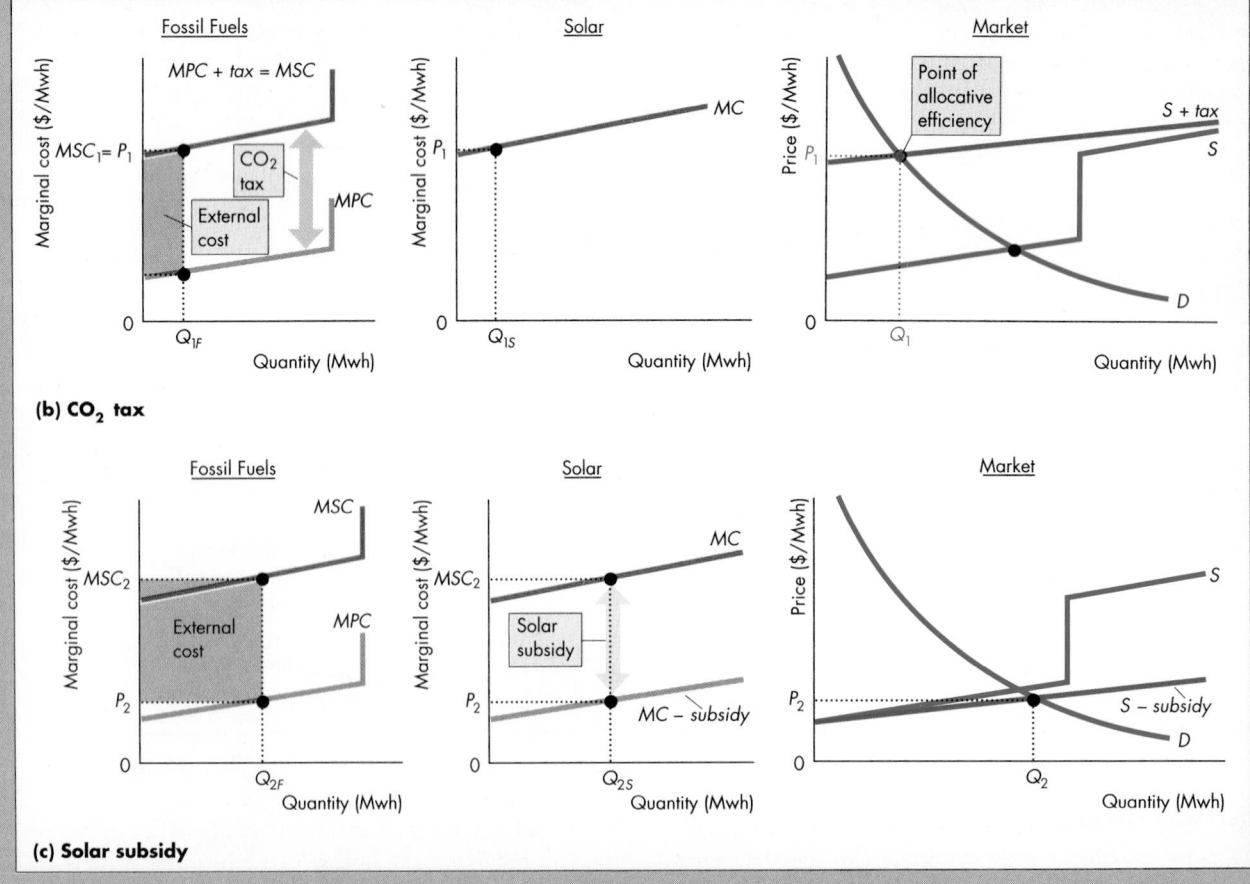

(b) CO₂ tax

(c) Solar subsidy

ducer of a good together with the marginal cost imposed as an externality on others. Marginal social cost is illustrated by the curve *MSC* in the figure.

Suppose that the transportation market is competitive and unregulated. People will balance the marginal private cost against the marginal benefit and travel Q_0 million miles at a price of P_0 per mile. At this scale of travel, a large amount of external costs will be borne. The marginal social cost is SC_0. The difference between P_0 and SC_0 represents the marginal cost imposed on others—the external marginal cost.

Suppose that the government taxes transportation and that it sets the tax equal to the external marginal cost. By imposing such a tax, the government raises the marginal private cost—the original marginal private cost *plus* the tax—to equal the marginal social cost. The *MSC* curve is now the relevant marginal cost curve for each person's decision since each person now faces a marginal cost of transportation equal to its marginal social cost. The market supply curve shifts upward to become the *MSC* curve. The price rises to P_1 and the amount of travel falls to Q_1. The marginal cost of the resources used in producing Q_1 million miles of travel is C_1 but the marginal external cost generated is P_1 minus C_1. That external marginal cost is paid by the consumer through the tax.

The situation depicted at the price P_1 and the quantity Q_1 is allocatively efficient. At an output rate above Q_1, social marginal cost exceeds the marginal benefit; at an output below Q_1, social marginal cost is less than the marginal benefit. In the first situation, producing less reduces costs by more than it reduces benefits and increases the net benefit. In the second situation, by producing more, marginal benefit exceeds marginal cost and net benefit increases.

Subsidies and External Benefits

Some goods bring external benefits—benefits to people who do not directly consume the good. In some cases, the government induces additional consumption of such goods by subsidizing them. A **subsidy** is a payment made by the government to producers that depends on the level of output. Figure 19.4 shows how subsidized education can increase the amount of education and achieve allocative efficiency. Suppose that the marginal cost of producing education is shown by the curve *MC* (assuming there is no difference between marginal private cost and marginal

Figure 19.4   Subsidizing an External Benefit

The demand curve for education also measures the marginal private benefit to education (D = MPB). The marginal cost of education is shown by curve *MC*. If education is provided in a competitive market with no government intervention, the price of education is P_0 and the quantity bought Q_0. But education produces a social benefit and the marginal social benefit is shown by the curve *MSB*. Allocative efficiency is achieved if the government provides education services on a scale such that marginal social cost equals marginal social benefit. This scale of provision is Q_1, which is achieved if the government subsidizes education, making it available for a price of P_1. The quantity demanded at a price of P_1 is Q_1, and at that quantity marginal cost equals marginal social benefit at a level of C_1.

social cost). The demand curve for education tells us the quantity of education demanded at each price when people are free to choose the amount of education that they undertake and have to pay for it themselves. It also measures the marginal private benefit—the benefit perceived by the individual undertaking education. That curve is $D=MPB$. A private competitive education market will produce an output of Q_0 at a price of P_0.

Suppose that the external benefit—the benefit derived by people other than those undertaking education—results in marginal social benefits described by the curve *MSB*. Allocative efficiency occurs where marginal cost equals marginal social benefit, at output Q_1. By providing the quantity of education Q_1 and by making it available at a price P_1, the government can achieve allocative efficiency in the education sector. In this case, by providing education at a low price, the government is able to encourage people to undertake the amount of education that makes its marginal social benefit equal to its marginal cost, rather than making the marginal private benefit equal to marginal cost.

We've now looked at two examples of the way in which government action can achieve an economic outcome different from that of a private unregulated market, by helping market participants take account of the external costs and benefits deriving from their actions. We've also illustrated government interventions that achieve allocative efficiency where the unregulated market fails to do so—where there is market failure. Because we can design a level of government intervention that achieves allocative efficiency in an economic model, it does not automatically mean that actual governments are able to achieve this outcome. Just as in the case of public goods, it is possible that the political equilibrium resulting from the interactions of voters, politicians, and bureaucrats leads to an outcome other than one of allocative efficiency. We'll explore this possibility in the next chapter.

R E V I E W

When externalities are present, the market allocation is not efficient. Sometimes an efficient allocation can be achieved by establishing private property rights. But in many cases, private property rights simply cannot be established and enforced. In such cases, if the government confronts people with taxes equivalent to the external marginal costs, or subsidies equivalent to external marginal benefits, it induces people to produce goods on a scale that achieves allocative efficiency, even in the face of externalities. ∎

∎   We've seen that markets do not always achieve allocative efficiency. When the market fails, we can describe an allocation that is efficient. But showing an efficient allocation is not the same thing a designing institutions to achieve one. Do governments in fact achieve allocative efficiency? Or are there economic problems arising from the functioning of a political system leading to "government failure" and preventing the attainment of an efficient allocation of resources? These questions are dealt with in the next chapter.

S U M M A R Y

The Government Sector

The government sector of the U.S. economy accounts for 35 percent of all expenditure on goods and services and 36 percent of total employment. The biggest departments of government deal with the provision of defense and health services. The Treasury Department is also a large one. The government share of the economy has grown over the years, increasing from less than 20 percent in 1940 to more than 35 percent in 1990.

But when economists study political behavior, they are careful to maintain the distinction between positive and normative analysis. Their main focus is on positive matters—on what *is* and on how the political system works rather than on what *ought* to be and how the political system *ought* to function.

All government economic actions stem from either market failure or the redistribution of income and wealth. Market failure arises from the provision of public goods and services, from externalities, and from monopolies and cartels. The redistribution of income and wealth arises partly from notions of equity and justice and partly from rent-seeking activities.

There are two broad approaches to the economic analysis of government—public interest theories and public choice theories. Public interest theories emphasize the idea of government as an eliminator of waste and an achiever of allocative efficiency. Public choice theories emphasize the idea that government operates in a political marketplace in which politicians, bureaucrats, and voters interact with each other. According to the public choice view, government failure to achieve allocative efficiency is as real as the possible failure of the market. (pp. 497–499)

Public Goods

Pure public goods have two features: nonrivalry and nonexcludability. One person's consumption does not reduce the amount available for someone else (nonrivalry) and no one can be kept from sharing the consumption of such a good (nonexcludability). An example of a pure public good is the national defense system.

The existence of public goods gives rise to the free-rider problem. This problem is the tendency for the scale of provision of a public good to be too small if it is produced and sold privately. The free-rider problem arises because there is insufficient incentive for a person to pay for a good if that payment has no effect on the quantity of the good the person consumes. It thus pays everyone to free ride, so with private provision no revenue can be raised from the sale of a public good. In such a situation, no public goods will be produced. In contrast, the government can produce a public good, paying for it out of taxation. People will vote for taxes and a public good provided that the net benefits are positive. The government is able to provide any public good on a scale larger than that provided by a private producer, but it does not necessarily produce an allocatively efficient amount of a public good. (pp. 499–503)

Externalities

An externality is a cost or a benefit arising from an economic transaction that falls on a third party and that is not taken into account by those undertaking the transaction. When external costs are present, allocative efficiency requires a reduction in the scale of output below what the market will produce. When external benefits are present, allocative efficiency requires an increase in output. There are two ways in which government can deal with externalities: Establishing and enforcing private property rights or using taxes and subsidies. If the government uses taxes and subsidies, it imposes taxes where there are external costs and gives subsidies where there are external benefits. (pp. 504–510)

K E Y   C O N C E P T S

Externality, 504
Free rider, 500
Free-rider problem, 500
Marginal benefit, 500
Marginal private cost, 505
Marginal social cost, 505
Market failure, 498
Mixed good, 499
Net benefit, 503
Private good, 499
Private property right, 504
Public choice theory, 499
Public interest theory, 499

Pure public good, 499
Subsidy, 509
Total benefit, 500

Key Figures

R E V I E W   Q U E S T I O N S

1 How big is the government sector of the U.S. economy today?

2 Set out the main economic functions of government.

3 Provide an example of each function.

4 What is a pure public good?

5 Name examples of three goods: a pure public good, a private good, and a mixed good.

6 What is the free-rider problem and how does government help overcome it?

7 What is an externality?

8 Give three examples of externalities.

PROBLEMS

1 You are given the following information about a sewage disposal system that a city of 1 million people is considering installing:

Capacity (thousands of gallons a day)	Marginal private benefit to one person (dollars)	Total cost (millions of dollars)
0		0
	50	
1		5
	40	
2		15
	30	
3		30
	20	
4		50
	10	
5		75

a) What is the capacity that achieves maximum net benefit?

b) How much will each person have to pay in taxes in order to pay for the efficient capacity level?

c) What are the total and net benefits?

2 A chemical factory dumps waste in a river. Damage is done to the local fish stock and member-ship fees at a nearby fishing club are lowered by the following amounts:

Output of chemical plant (gallons per hour)	Lost fees to fishing club
0	0
100	10
200	30
300	70
400	210

a) The local government plans to tax the chemical factory. Devise a tax that will achieve allocative efficiency.

b) How might private property rights be used in this situation?

3 Explain why your state government should operate a university system and permit students to attend for a tuition fee below the full cost of the education provided.

Chapter 20

Public Choice

After studying this chapter, you will be able to:

- Describe the components of the political market-place

- Define a political equilibrium

- Explain how the main political parties choose an economic policy platform

- Explain how government bureaucracy interacts with politicians to determine the scale of provision of public goods and services

- Explain why we vote for redistributions of income and wealth

- Explain why we tax some goods at much higher rates than others

- Predict the effects of taxes on prices, quantities produced, and profits

- Explain why we subsidize the producers of some goods

- Predict the effects of subsidies on prices, quantities produced, and profits

Franklin Delano Roosevelt was elected president in 1932, at the depths of the greatest depression in history. During the election campaign, Roosevelt set forth a program for economic recovery and reform that came to be called the New Deal. Roosevelt promised to provide aid for farmers and millions of other Americans and to strengthen the forces of competition. He promised that the increase in government spending would not increase the government deficit. Rather, his New Deal would result in an economic recovery that would bring in extra taxes and a balance in the government's budget. ■ Ronald Reagan was elected president in 1980, at a time of severe and stubborn inflation. Reagan's main economic theme was smaller

Rhetoric and Reality

government and lower taxes. Reagan argued that lower tax rates would not lead to a bigger government deficit. Instead, he predicted that with lower revenue, the spending plans of Congress would be kept under firmer discipline. Furthermore, he believed that lower tax rates would stimulate such a large upsurge in economic activity that sufficient additional revenue would flow into the government to balance its budget. ■ Despite dramatic differences in the economic environment of 1932 and 1980, and despite differences in the details of the political rhetoric, political reality resulted in outcomes different from those promised and foreseen. In the 1930s, the promised recovery was slow to arrive and the government's budget remained in deficit through most of that decade. In the 1980s, government spending was not curtailed—in fact it increased—and, although there was an unprecedented expansion of economic activity, tax revenue did not catch up with spending and the budget deficit persisted. ■ One important difference between the 1980s and the 1930s is in the scale of government. In the 1930s, the government undertook less than one fifth of all economic activity. In the 1980s, the government's budget represented two fifths of the nation's total expenditure. What determines the scale of government? What are the forces that generate the level of provision of public goods and services and why has government grown over the years to command an increasing fraction of the economy's resources? ■ Government pervades many aspects of our lives. It is present at our birth, supporting the hospitals in which we are born and training the doctors and nurses who deliver us. It is present throughout our education, supporting schools and colleges and training our teachers. It is present throughout our working lives, taxing our incomes, regulating our work environment, and paying us benefits when we are unemployed. It is present throughout our retirement, paying us a small income, and when we die, taxing our bequests. But the government does not make all our economic choices. We decide for ourselves what work to do, how much to save, and what to spend our income on. Why does the government intervene in some aspects of our lives but not others? Why doesn't the government provide more of our health services? Why doesn't it provide less of our education services? ■ There are many situations in which it is obvious why the government intervenes. Attempting to stem the flow of dangerous drugs is an example. But there are other areas in which the government does not intervene and yet many people believe it should. One such area is the protection of the quality of our air. Why doesn't the government do more to protect air quality? ■ Republicans and Democrats battle to dominate politics. Yet many people complain that there aren't really all that many differences in their policies. Why do two opposing political parties take similar positions on most topics? ■ Almost everyone grumbles about government bureaucracy. The poor single mother complains about the treatment that she receives from bureaucrats that administer the social welfare programs that she uses; the wealthy taxpayer complains about her treatment by the bureaucrats at the Internal Revenue Service; and even presidents, senators, and representatives complain that the bureaucracy is too big, too slow, and inefficient. Why is the bureaucracy so unpopular and the target of so much scorn? How do government bureaus operate to deliver the many public services for which they are responsible? ■ Government taxes almost all the goods and services that we buy. Some of these taxes are very high—for example, those on gasoline, alcohol, and tobacco products. A few items that we buy are not taxed and their producers are even subsidized by the government. Examples are milk and wheat. Why does government impose heavy taxes on some goods and subsidies on others? What are the effects of taxes on prices, on the quantities bought and sold, and on the amount of revenue raised by the government?

■ In this chapter, we study the economic interactions of voters, politicians, and bureaucrats and discover how the scale and variety of government economic activity are determined. Our focus here is on the provision of public goods and services, the taxation needed to pay for those services, the control of externalities, and the redistribution of income. In Chapter 21, we'll apply the same basic theory of government economic behavior to the regulation and control of monopolies and cartels.

The Political Marketplace

Government is not a huge computer that grinds out solutions to resource allocation problems plagued with free riders and externalities. It does not simply calculate and balance marginal social costs and benefits, automatically achieving allocative efficiency. Rather, it is a complex organization made up of thousands of individuals. These individuals have their *own* economic objectives, and government policy choices are the outcome of the choices made by these individuals. To analyze these choices, economists have developed a theory of the political marketplace that parallels theories of ordinary markets—*public choice theory*.

There are three types of actors in the economic model of the marketplace:

• Voters
• Politicians
• Bureaucrats

Voters are the consumers of the outcome of the political process. In ordinary markets for goods and services, people express their demands by their willingness to pay. In the political marketplace, voters express their demands in three principal ways. First, they express them by a willingness to vote, either in an election or on a referendum issue. Second, and less formally, they express their demands through campaign contributions. Third, they express their demands by lobbying. **Lobbying** is the activity of bringing pressure to bear on government agencies or institutions through a variety of informal mechanisms. The pro-life and pro-choice lobbies are two of the most prominent examples of such organizations in the United States today.

Politicians are the elected officials in federal, state, and local government—from chief executives (the president, state governor, or mayor) to members of the legislatures (state and federal senators and representatives, city councilors). Politicians are chosen by voters.

Bureaucrats are the appointed officials who work at various levels in the many government departments, again at the federal, state, and local levels. The most senior bureaucrats are appointed by politicians. Junior bureaucrats are appointed by senior ones.

Voters, politicians, and bureaucrats make their economic choices in a way that best furthers their own objectives, but they each face two types of constraints. First, each group is constrained by the preferences of the others. Bureaucrats are constrained by the preferences of politicians; politicians are constrained by the preferences of bureaucrats and voters; and voters are constrained by the preferences of bureaucrats and politicians. Second, voters, bureaucrats, and politicians cannot ignore technological constraints. They can only do things that are technologically feasible. We are going to examine the objectives of voters, politicians, and bureaucrats and the constraints they face when making their choices. We're also going to study the interactions among the three types of actors. In so doing, we are going to discover how the political system actually works.

The predictions of an economic model of voter, politician, and bureaucrat behavior are the equilibrium of the political process—the political equilibrium. A **political equilibrium** is a situation in which the choices of voters, politicians, and bureaucrats are all compatible and in which no one group of agents will be better off by making a different choice. Thus a political equilibrium has the same characteristics as an equilibrium in the markets for goods and services and factors of production.

The theory of public choice that we are about to study is a relatively new branch of economics that has grown rapidly in the past 30 years. It was recently recognized by the awarding of the Nobel Prize for economics to one of its principal architects, James

Buchanan (see Our Advancing Knowledge, pp. 518-519).

Let's begin our study of public choice theory by looking at the behavior of politicians.

The Behavior of Politicians and Voters

All kinds of people go into politics. Some have noble ideals and want to make a lasting contribution to improving the conditions of their fellow citizens. Others are single-minded in pursuit of their own self-interest and profit. Most politicians, no doubt, blend these two extremes. Economic models of public choice are based on the assumption that in a democratic political system their central objective is to get enough votes to be elected and to keep enough support to remain in office. Votes, to a politician, are similar to dollars to a private firm. In order to obtain enough votes, politicians form coalitions with each other; we call these coalitions political parties. A political party is simply a collection of politicians who have banded together for the purpose of achieving and maintaining office. A political party attempts to develop policies that appeal to a majority of the voters.

Public choice theory assumes that voters support policies that they believe make them better off and oppose policies that they believe make them worse off. They neither oppose nor support—they are indifferent among—policies that they believe have no effect on them. Voters' *perceptions* rather than reality are what guide their choices.

To obtain the support of voters, a politician (or political party) must offer a package of policies that voters believe will make them better off than the policies proposed by the opposing political parties. There are two ways in which a political program can seek to make a voter better off. One way is to implement policies that make *everyone* better off. Providing national defense or protecting the environment are examples of such policies. Another way is to implement policies that make some voters worse off but that make at least 50 percent of the voters better off. Redistributing income in such a way that at least one half of the electorate reaps net benefits is one example. Supporting or opposing abortion is another and supporting or opposing gun control yet another.

Political programs that make everyone better off feature in the platforms of all parties. Policies that favor one group against another differ from party to party and depend on which segment of the population or particular interest group a political party wants to appeal to. Let's see how politicians and voters interact and how the policy platforms of political parties emerge by examining how the political process handles the provision of public goods and external costs and benefits.

Public Goods   In Chapter 19, we compared the scale of provision of public goods that achieves allocative efficiency with the scale that would be provided through the private marketplace. Now we want to work out the scale of provision of public goods that a political system will actually deliver.

For the moment, let's ignore differences among individual voters and suppose that people have identical views about the benefits of public goods and externalities. We'll consider what happens when people disagree and have different preferences shortly. To be concrete, let's stick with the example of national defense that we studied in Chapter 19.

Suppose that the total costs and total benefits of producing antimissile lasers are the ones shown in Fig. 20.1. (These are the same costs and benefits that we used in Chapter 19, p. 504.) Suppose also that there are two political parties. Let's call one the Hawks and the other the Doves. Suppose that the Hawks and the Doves propose exactly the same policy platform in all respects except for national defense. The Hawks offer a high level of national defense. They propose to provide 4 antimissile lasers at a cost of $50 billion, with benefits of $50 billion and a net benefit of zero. The Doves propose to provide just 1 laser at a cost of $5 billion, with a benefit of $20 billion and a net benefit of $15 billion ($20 billion total benefit minus $5 billion total cost).

In an election in which voters are presented with the two platforms just described, the Doves will win. Recall that we assumed that both parties are offering identical programs in every respect except for defense. The defense program of the Doves provides the voters with a net benefit of $15 billion over and above the taxes that they are asked to pay, while the Hawks are offering no net benefit, so the Doves will get all the votes.

Now suppose that the Hawks, contemplating the election outcome that we have just described, realize that their party is offering too high a level of defense—that it is too hawkish—to get elected. It figures that it has to offer net benefits in excess of $15 billion if it is to beat the Doves. It therefore

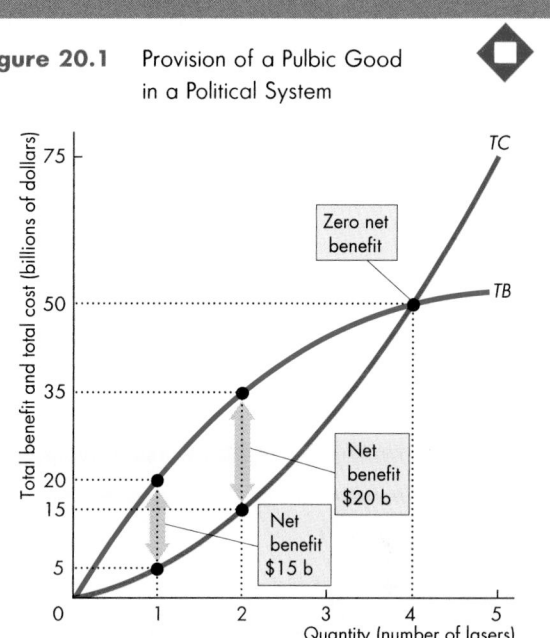

Figure 20.1   Provision of a Pulbic Good in a Political System

The total benefit curve for an antimissile laser weapon is TB, and the total cost curve is TC. Net benefit is maximized if 2 antimissile lasers are installed, with a total benefit of $35 billion and a total cost of $15 billion. There are two political parties offering platforms on this defense systems: the Doves and the Hawks. Their platforms are identical on all matters except defense. The Doves propose to install 1 antimissile laser and the Hawks 4. In an election, the Doves will win since their proposal generates a larger net benefit than the Hawks' proposal. But if the Hawks propose to install 2 lasers, they will beat the Doves since the net benefit resulting from 2 lasers exceeds that from 1. To get even, the Doves will have to match the Hawks. If voters are well informed and in general agreement about the value of a public good, competition between political parties for their votes can achieve an efficient scale of provision.

scales back its plans and proposes to build 2 antimissile lasers. At this level of provision, the total cost is $15 billion and total benefit is $35 billion, so net benefit is $20 billion. The Hawks are now offering a package that the voters prefer to the one offered by the Doves. Now in an election, the Hawks will win.

The Doves, contemplating this outcome, realize that the best they can do is to match the Hawks. They too propose to provide 2 lasers on exactly the same terms as the Hawks. The voters are now indifferent between the proposals of the two parties and are indifferent about which one they vote for.

Public Choice

T he past 30 years have seen an enormous growth in work on the economic choices of government and on the interactions of politicians, bureaucrats, and voters. The result of this work is a well-recognized discipline within economics called *public choice theory.*

The father of modern public choice is Duncan Black. Born in Motherwell, Scotland, in 1908, Black studied first mathematics and physics and then economics and politics at the University of Glasgow (where, 150 years earlier, Adam Smith had worked). Black's work is monumental. His vision was to develop a science of politics—having the same rigor as economics—based on a theory of committees. In Black's model, consumers' preferences are replaced by the preferences of committee members; goods and services are replaced by motions or propositions before a committee. Black's work of the 1940s and 1950s was summarized in his book *The Theory of Committees and Elections* (Cambridge University Press, 1958).

An example of one of Black's discoveries is the possibility of *cyclical voting.* Such a possibility is illustrated in the accompanying table. There are three people and three possible income distributions. If the distribution is 1, then Ben and Con vote for distribution 2. Ann opposes distribution 2, but in a majority vote she loses. If the distribution is 2, Ann and Con vote for distribution 3. Ben votes against that distribution but, again, if the majority decides the day, Ben loses. But if the distribution is 3, Ann and Ben vote for distribution 1 while Con opposes that distribution. Again, majority vote results in distribution 1 winning. But we are now back where we started. Ben and Con can now vote that distribution down and so the whole cycle begins again.

The possibility of voting cycles is just one potential flaw in democracy. Another was suggested by Kenneth Arrow. Arrow, a Nobel Prize winner in economic science in 1972, was born in New York City in 1921 and studied at Columbia and the University of Chicago. He has taught at Harvard and at Stanford, where he currently holds two positions—professor of economics and of operations research. Arrow's contributions to economics span an amazing range (as his dual professorship signifies), but in the public choice area his book *Social Choice and Individual Values* (John Wiley & Sons, 1951) has been of substantial influence. In that book, Arrow demonstrates what has come to be called the "Arrow impossibility theorem." In simplified terms, the theorem states that it is not, in general, possible

Cycles in Voting

	Possible income distribution		
	1	2	3
Ann	150	50	100
Ben	100	150	50
Con	50	100	150

Kenneth Arrow

to aggregate the preferences of individuals to arrive at social preferences that can be used to guide government choice.

One of the major contributors to modern public choice theory is James Buchanan, whose work was recognized by his being awarded the Nobel Prize in economic science in 1986. Born in Murfreesboro, Tennessee, in 1919, Buchanan received his Ph.D. at the University of Chicago in 1948. Buchanan has devoted his lifetime to understanding political decision-making by using the same tools of analysis that economists use to understand all economic choices. Buchanan's ideas are given their most extensive development in *The Calculus of Consent: Logical Foundation of Constitutional Democracy* (University of Michigan Press, 1962) which he wrote with his colleague, Gordon Tullock. In this book, Buchanan and Tullock analyze the effects of different voting systems: for example, simple majority versus qualified majority—qualified majority being two-thirds majority or unanimity—and the effects of having two legislative chambers—a congress and a senate. The authors also examine the economics and ethics of pressure groups, special interests, and the constitution.

Two other Americans have made important contributions that we are studying in this chapter. They are Anthony Downs and William Niskanen.

Downs, born in Evanston, Illinois, in 1930, received his Ph.D. at Stanford in 1956. His doctoral thesis turned into what has become a great classic: *An Economic Theory of Democracy* (Harper and Row, 1957). In that book, Downs first set out the "median voter theorem." He also pointed out what has come to be called the "paradox of voting." The paradox centers on a question: Why do we bother to vote? From a purely economic point of view, voting seems silly. If the political parties offer the policies that best benefit the median voter, no one individual's vote is going to make any difference to the outcome of an election. Since it takes time and effort to vote, the individually rational thing to do is to stay home and give the election a miss. The fact that most of us do vote implies either that the economic theory of voting is overlooking an important aspect of economic behavior or that voting is not to be understood purely and narrowly in economic terms.

William Niskanen, born in Bend, Oregon, in 1933, received his Ph.D. at the University of Chicago in 1962. Niskanen has had an interesting and highly varied career: He has worked as an economist in the Department of Defense and in the armed forces and has been a professor at the University of California at Berkeley and Los Angeles. He also served as head of the economic division of the Ford Motor Company and as a member of the Council of Economic Advisors to President Reagan. With this rich variety of experience, Niskanen has made significant advances in the theory of bureaucracy. His classic book *Bureaucracy and Representative Government* (Aldine-Atherton) was published in 1971. It is in this work that Niskanen proposes the theory of budget maximization that we have studied in this chapter.

Competition for votes among political parties, even when there are only two of them, produces a political platform that maximizes the perceived net benefit accruing to the voters. For this outcome to occur, it is necessary that the voters be able to evaluate the alternatives. We'll see below that this condition is not necessarily going to be satisfied.

Externalities

The example that we have just worked through deals with a situation in which the voters are in agreement about and can calculate the benefits arising from different proposals. The same line of reasoning applies to policies concerning the control of externalities. Provided the voters are in agreement about the benefits and can evaluate them, the political party that offers the level of control of externalities that maximizes net benefits will be the one that wins an election. The political party that proposes a total ban on the production of CFCs or sulfur dioxide emission will lose an election to a party that proposes more limited controls. A party that proposes a free-for-all on CFCs and sulfur dioxide emissions will lose an election to a party that proposes restraint in the production of goods that generate these external costs. Competition for votes will force each party to find the degree of control that maximizes net benefit.

In the examples of public goods and externalities that we have just worked out, we have ignored differences of opinion among the voters. We'll now go on to consider cases in which the preferences of voters differ and in which these differences are crucial in determining the outcome of the political process.

Interest Groups and Redistribution

Most matters decided in the political arena are ones on which people have different opinions. Some people favor a large national defense program while others urge disarmament; some favor a large scale of income redistribution while others urge tax cuts; some want massive government intervention to protect the environment while others want more limited environmental controls. Faced with this diversity of opinion, no political party can propose a platform that pleases everyone. But to attain office, a party must put together a package that attracts a majority of the votes. To do so, each party has to deliver a package that makes a majority of the voters better off (as the voters perceive it) than under the policies proposed

Figure 20.2 The Principle of Minimum Differentiation

A beach stretches from A to B. Sunbathers are distributed at even intervals along the whole beach. An ice cream seller sets up a stand at point C. The distance that people have to walk for ice cream is the same no matter on which side of the ice cream stand they are located. If a second ice cream seller sets up a stand, it will pay to place it exactly next to C in the middle of the beach. If the second stand is placed at D, only the customers on the beach between E and B will buy ice cream from D. Those between A and E will go to C. By moving as close to C as possible, the second ice cream vendor picks up half of the ice cream customers.

by the opposing party (or parties). This search for a majority results in each political party offering policies that are very close to the policies of the others. This tendency toward similar policies is known as the principle of minimum differentiation.

The Principle of Minimum Differentiation The **principle of minimum differentiation** is the tendency for competitors to make themselves almost identical in order to appeal to the maximum number of clients or voters. Let's study the principle of minimum differentiation by looking at a problem that is more familiar and concrete than that faced by political parties.

There are two ice cream vendors on a beach. The beach is one mile long and is illustrated in Fig. 20.2 as the distance from A to B. Sunbathers lounge at equal intervals over the entire beach. One of the ice cream vendors comes along and sets up a stand. Where will she locate? The answer is at position C—exactly halfway between A and B. By locating in this position, the farthest that anyone has to walk to buy an ice cream is a mile (half a mile to the ice cream stand and half a mile back to the beach towel).

Now suppose that a second ice cream vendor comes along. Where will he place his ice cream stand? The answer is right next to the original one at point *C*. To understand why, imagine that the second vendor locates his stand at point *D*—halfway between *C* and *B*. How many customers will he attract and how many will go to the stand at *C*? The stand at *D* will pick up all the customers on the beach between *B* and *D*, because this stand is closer for them. It will also pick up all the customers between *D* and *E* (the point halfway between *C* and *D*), because they too will have a shorter trip for an ice cream by going to *D* than by going to *C*. All the people between *A* and *C* and all those between *C* and *E* will go to stand *C*. So the ice cream stand located at *C* will pick up all the people on the beach between *A* and *E* and the stand located at *D* will pick up all the people located between *E* and *B*.

Now suppose that the vendor with a stand at *D* moves to *C*. There are now two stands at *C*. Half the customers will go to the first vendor and the other half to the second vendor. Only by each locating bang in the center of the beach can each pick up half the customers. If either of them moves slightly away from the center, then that vendor picks up less than half the customers and the one remaining at the center picks up a majority of the customers.

This example illustrates the principle of minimum differentiation. By having no differentiation in location, both ice cream vendors do as well as they can and share the market evenly.

The principle of minimum differentiation has been applied to explain a wide variety of choices—how supermarkets choose their locations; how the makers of automobiles and microwave popcorn design their products; and how political parties choose their platforms.

The principle of minimum differentiation predicts that political parties will be similar to each other. But it does not tell us which policies they will favor, only that they will favor similar ones. In the case of the ice cream vendor, the location is determined by technological considerations—minimizing the distance that the bathers have to walk. But what determines a political party's choice of platform? Let's now address this question.

The Median Voter Theorem An interesting proposition about a political party's choice of platform is provided by the median voter theorem. The **median**

voter theorem states that political parties will pursue policies that maximize the net benefit of the median voter. (The median of a distribution of, say, student heights is the height of the student in the middle. One half of the students are taller and one half of the students are shorter than the median.) Let's see how the median voter theorem applies to the question of how large a tax to impose on sulfur dioxide emissions that cause acid rain.

Imagine arranging all the voters along a line running from *A* to *B*, as shown in Fig. 20.3. The voter wanting the highest tax is at *A* and the one wanting no tax is at *B*, and all the other voters are arranged along the line based on the level of the tax that they favor. The curve in the figure shows the tax

Figure 20.3   The Median Voter Theorem

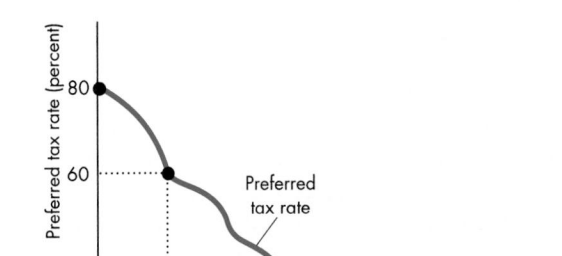

A political party can win an election by proposing policies that appeal to the median voter and to all the other voters on one side of the median. If the median mildly favors a policy, that policy will be proposed. In the figure, voters have different preferences concerning the rate at which to tax an externality. They are ranked from *A* to *B* in descending order of their preferred tax. There are two political parties. If one proposes a 61 percent tax and the other a 59 percent tax, the lower tax party will win the election—voters between *A* and *C* will vote for the high tax and those between *C* and *B* for the low tax. If both parties propose low taxes—11 percent and 9 percent—the party proposing the higher tax will win. It will pick up the votes between *A* and *D*, leaving only the votes between *D* and *B* for the lower tax party. Each party will have an incentive to move toward the tax rate preferred by the median voter. At that point, each party picks up a half of the votes and neither can improve its share.

rate favored by each voter between *A* and *B*. As shown in the graph, the median voter favors a tax rate of 30 percent.

Suppose that two political parties propose similar but not quite identical taxes on emissions of sulfur dioxide. One party proposes a tax of 61 percent and the other of 59 percent. All the voters lying between *A* and *C* prefer the higher tax and will vote for it. All the voters lying between *C* and *B* prefer the lower tax and will vote for it. The lower tax party will win the election.

Alternatively, suppose that the two political parties offer a low tax rate—and again, slightly different rates. One party offers a rate of 11 percent and the other of 9 percent. The voters between *A* and *D* will vote for the higher tax rate and those between *D* and *B* for the lower rate. This time, the higher tax party will win.

But each party, in either of these situations, will see that it can win the election by moving closer to the tax rate preferred by the median voter. Once the two parties are offering that tax rate, however, neither will be able to increase its share of the vote by changing its proposal. One party will get the votes between *A* and the median and the other the votes between the median and *B*. All the voters except the median will be dissatisfied—for those between *A* and the median the tax rate is too low and for those between *B* and the median the tax is too high. But no political party can propose a tax other than 30 percent and expect to win the election. Of course, if the

two parties proposed exactly 30 percent, the voters will be indifferent and will either not bother to vote or will flip a coin to decide which party to vote for.

The principle of minimum differentiation and the median voter theorem seem to imply that all political parties will be identical in all respects. If that is so, it is too bad for the principle and the theorem. The world that we live in has political parties that certainly do differ. Many of us are heated in our support for and opposition to particular parties and policy proposals. It is in the area of the redistribution of income and wealth that one of the major differences in political parties arises. Let's use the principle of minimum differentiation and the median voter theorem to see if we can understand why all political parties favor some redistribution but why, also, there are differences in the parties in this respect.

Voting for Income Redistribution

The first model of redistribution that we'll consider is one that results in voting cycles. Imagine a society with 100 voters. These voters are divided into four different income groups, as set out in Table 20.1. Twenty-five of the voters earn $10,000 a year, another 25 earn $20,000 a year, another 25 earn $40,000 a year, and the richest 25 earn $90,000 a year. The average income in this community is $40,000 a year.

Suppose that a political party proposes to tax the richest 25 people $5000 and the second richest

Table 20.1   Voting for Income Redistribution: A Tie

Number of voters	Income before redistribution (thousands of dollars)	Income after redistribution (thousands of dollars)	Gain (+)/loss (−) (thousands of dollars)
25	10	15	+5
25	20	23	+3
25	40	37	−3
25	90	85	−5
Total 100	Averages: 40	40	0

Table 20.2   Voting for Income Redistribution: The Rich Lose

Number of voters	Income before redistribution (thousands of dollars)	Income after redistribution (thousands of dollars)	Gain (+)/loss (−) (thousands of dollars)
25	10	15	+5
25	20	23	+3
25	40	40	0
25	90	82	−8
Total 100	Averages: 40	40	0

$3000. It proposes to make transfers of $5000 to the poorest 25 people and $3000 to the next poorest 25. The incomes resulting from the tax and transfers in this proposal are set out in the third column of Table 20.1. The average income is still $40,000. The final column of the table shows the gains and losses to each income group. The poorest gain and the richest lose.

Suppose that there is a second political party in this society that opposes the redistribution scheme just described. Which party will win the election? The answer is that it will be a tie. The party proposing the redistribution scheme will pick up 50 percent of the votes—those of the poorer half of the electorate. The party opposing the redistribution scheme will pick up the other half of the votes (those at the wealthier end of the income distribution).

Now suppose that one of the parties offers the modified scheme set out in Table 20.2. The proposal is to tax the richest quarter of the people not $5000 but $8000, and not to tax the second richest quarter at all. Under this scheme, the two poorest groups of people will receive benefits of $5000 and $3000 respectively. One party supports these measures and the other opposes them and proposes no redistribution at all. Which party will win? The answer is the party supporting redistribution. All the people with original incomes of $10,000 and $20,000 will vote for the scheme. Those with incomes of $30,000 will be indifferent between the two parties so we may suppose that half will vote for one party and half the other. The party opposing the redistribution scheme

will collect the votes of the richest quarter of the people plus half of those in the second richest group.

This example shows one particular redistribution proposal that could gain the support of the majority of voters. But there will be many other proposals that could also gain majority support (but with different people making up the majority in each case). There is no end to the different proposals that could win a majority. As these different schemes are proposed, there are cycles in the voting similar to those described in Our Advancing Knowledge, pp. 518–519.

Why do we not observe voting cycles in reality? Why do we see a tendency for redistribution policies to remain in place for very long periods of time? The answer is suggested by a second model of redistribution—a median voter model. A key feature of this model is what has been called the "big tradeoff" (see Chapter 18, pp. 486–487). The greater the amount of income that is redistributed, the smaller is the incentive to work and the lower is the average level of income. As a consequence, redistributive taxes have two effects on the median voter: They raise the median voter's income by taking from those above the median and redistributing to those at and below the median; they also lower the median voter's income by reducing the incentive to work, which lowers average income. Which of these two opposing effects is stronger depends on the scale of redistribution. At low tax rates, the disincentive effects are small, so an increase in taxes makes the median voter better off. The higher income resulting from transfers from the rich is more than enough to offset the lower income resulting from disincentive effects. If tax rates are set too high, a cut in taxes will make the median voter better off. In this case, the lower income resulting from smaller transfers from the rich is more than made up for by the higher average income resulting from improved incentives. But there is a level of taxes and an amount of redistribution that is exactly right from the point of view of the median voter. This scale of redistribution is the one that balances these two considerations and maximizes the median voter's income. This amount of redistribution is a possible political equilibrium.

Model and Reality

We've now looked at two models of equilibrium redistribution—a voting cycles model and a median voter model. In the voting cycles model, there is a never-ending sequence of different majorities for different directions of redistribution. In the median voter model, there is a unique equilibrium that maximizes the net benefit to the median voter.

Which of these models best fits the facts about income redistribution? The median voter model comes closest. Its strengths lie in its predictions that the political parties will differ in their rhetoric but be very close to each other in the actual redistribution measures for which they vote. This prediction accords well with reality and especially well with what occurred in 1986, the most recent occasion on which a major change in redistributive taxes took place. (See Reading Between the Lines, pp. 526–527). In contrast, the voting-cycles model predicts a sequence of different majorities for different directions of redistribution that we do not observe in reality.

R E V I E W

Politicians seek to obtain enough votes to achieve and maintain power. They do this by appealing to slightly more than half of the electorate. The key voter is the median voter. To appeal to the median voter, political parties offer programs that favor a majority of the electorate. Each party tries to outdo the other by appealing to the median voter. In part, that

appeal results from the political parties proposing income-increasing policies. It also, in part, results from the redistribution of income to the point where no one can invent a way of raising the income of the median voter. ■

We have analyzed the behavior of politicians but not that of the bureaucrats who translate the choices of the politicians into programs. Let's now turn to an examination of the economic choices of bureaucrats.

The Behavior of Bureaucrats

An interesting model of the behavior of bureaucrats has been suggested by William Niskanen (see Our Advancing Knowledge, pp. 518–519). In that model, bureaucrats aim to maximize the budget of the agency in which they work. The bigger the budget of the agency, the greater is the prestige of the agency chief and the larger is the opportunity for promotion for people further down the bureaucratic ladder. Thus all the members of an agency have an interest in maximizing the agency's budget. In seeking to obtain the largest budget it can, each government agency and department marshals its best arguments for why it should have more funds to spend. Since each agency does its best to obtain more funds, the net result is upward pressure for expenditure on all publicly provided goods and services.

The constraints on maximizing the budget of a government department or agency are the taxes that the politician has to levy and the implications of those taxes for the politician's own ability to win votes. But government departments and agencies recognize and appreciate the interplay between their own objectives and those of the politician and so do their best to help the politician appreciate the vote-winning consequences of spending more on their own particular department or agency. Thus budget maximization, to some degree, translates itself into political campaigns designed to explain to voters why they need more defense, more health services, and so on.

Let's examine the consequences of bureaucratic budget maximization for the provision of public goods and their cost by looking again at the example of national defense. We've studied this example twice before. The first time (in Chapter 19, p. 504) our concern was to establish that a government could overcome the free-rider problem and produce a larger quantity of a public good than would be produced by the private market. In this chapter, (on pp. 517–520), we examined the way in which political parties competing for votes determine the scale of provision of a public good in a situation in which the voters are in agreement about the benefits of the public good and in which they are able to assess the costs and benefits of different scales of provision. In that example, no bureaucrats intervene in the process.

But the creation and operation of weapons and defense systems require the establishment of a large and complex government bureaucracy. How does the defense bureaucracy influence the scale and cost of the defense program? Let's answer this question by returning to the example of the installation of an antimissile laser defense system.

Take a look at Fig. 20.4. You will recognize it as being similar to Fig. 20.1. The horizontal axis shows the number of antimissile lasers and the vertical axis their total benefit and total cost. The curve labeled *TB* shows the total benefit as perceived by all the individuals in the economy and the curve labeled *TC* shows the total cost.

We saw earlier that the level of provision that maximizes net benefit is 2 lasers. This level of defense costs $15 billion, and it yields a total benefit of $35 billion and a net benefit of $20 billion. A political party that proposes installing 2 lasers will win an election because there is no higher net benefit possible. But will the Pentagon press Congress to vote for 2 lasers? According to Niskanen's model of bureaucracy, it will not. The Pentagon will push to expand the scale of provision and budget for national defense to the largest possible level. If it is able to increase the number of antimissile lasers to 4, for example, it can increase the budget to $50 billion. In this situation, total benefit equals total cost and net benefit is zero. If the Pentagon is able to increase defense to an even higher level, its budget increases yet further and net benefit becomes negative.

But how would it be possible for the Pentagon to get away with pressing the politicians for a scale of defense spending in excess of that which maximizes net benefit? Won't it always pay the politicians to take control of the Pentagon and cut back on the scale of military spending?

We've already seen that when there are two political parties competing for votes, the party that gets closest to maximizing net benefit is the one that picks up the most votes. Don't these forces of competition for votes dominate the wishes of the bureau-

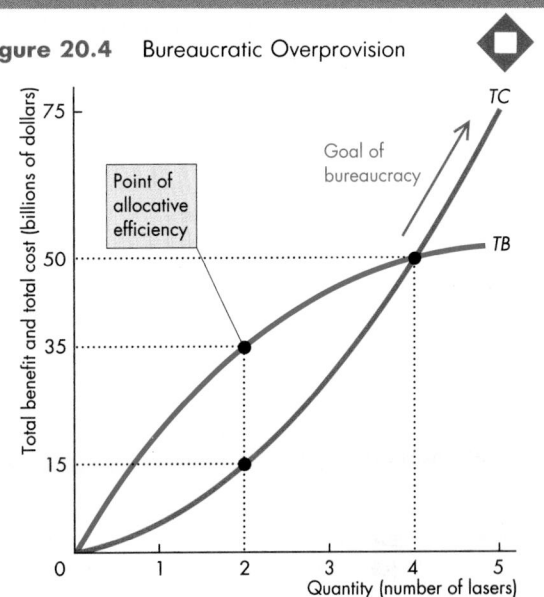

Figure 20.4   Bureaucratic Overprovision

A bureau that maximizes its budget will seek to expand output and expenditure as far as possible. For example, the Pentagon prefers 4 antimissile lasers at a cost of $50 billion to the allocatively efficient number—2 at a cost of $15 billion. The goal of the bureau is to move as far up the total cost curve as possible. If voters are well informed, politicans will not be able to deliver the taxes that enable the bureau to get beyond the point of allocative efficiency. But if some voters are rationally ignorant while others are well informed, it is possible that the bureau will be able to increase its budget above the allocatively efficient level. In general, the bureau will produce a higher quantity than the one that maximizes net benefit.

crats and ensure that the maximum budget allowed to them is that which maximizes net benefit?

If voters are well informed and if their perception of their self-interest is correct, the political party that wins the election is the one that holds the Pentagon budget to the level that provides the efficient level of defense. But there is another possible equilibrium. It is one based on the principle of voter ignorance and well-informed interest groups.

Voter Ignorance and Well-Informed Interest Groups

One of the major propositions of public choice theory is that it does not pay voters to be well-informed

The Political Economy of Tax Reform

The Making of a Miracle

They said it couldn't be done . . . couldn't be done . . . couldn't be done. Scrap the gargantuan federal tax code and write a simpler, fairer one? How naive! Drastically reduce top tax rates to their lowest levels in 58 years by throwing out the special breaks and deductions that have accrued over the past four decades? . . . Get real! Such a drastic overhaul would amount to putting the public interest ahead of special interests—in this case nearly every interest with enough clout to hire a lobbyist. And everybody knows the political process does not work that way.

Except that once in a great while the process *does* work that way. Thus it was with tax reform, a political miracle that was brought to the verge of fruition by an amazingly varied group of conservatives and liberals, Republicans and Democrats. . . .

The Tax Reform Act of 1986 is one of the few pieces of legislation that can truly be called historic. It reverses the whole direction that federal taxation has been following for decades: instead of adding exceptions and deductions, it wipes them out by the hundreds; instead of shifting the tax burden from business to individuals, it switches that load the other way. . . .

The bill by 1988 would erase the complex schedule of 15 tax rates on individual incomes, ranging from 11% to 50%, and replace them with just two: 15% and 28%.

To get these benefits, individuals will have to give up some cherished tax breaks. The bill preserves the most popular: deductions for state and local income taxes and for mortgage interest on first and second homes. But there will be no more deductions for interest on loans to buy cars, boats, clothes and furniture. Nor will there be any for sales taxes. The special deduction for families in which both husband and wife work will be eliminated, along with credits for child-care expenses. Charitable contributions will be deductible only for those who choose to send in itemized returns (at present they can be written off by users of the short form). Profits on the sale of stocks, bonds, houses and other assets, which have been subject to low capital-gains rates, will be taxed at the same rate as ordinary income: 28% tops.

One of the bill's greatest benefits will be psychological rather than monetary. It will foster a public perception that the tax laws have become fairer by levying approximately the same amount on people with similar incomes. Most significantly, it will wipe out those complex schemes that allow wealthy individuals with wily accountants to claim large paper losses through small cash investments in real estate syndicates and other tax shelters.

At the bottom of the scale, some 6 million people with incomes at or below the poverty line will be freed from paying any income tax at all, doing away with a pernicious unintended consequence of the current law: for the past several years the poor have been sending a growing share of their meager pay to Washington. About 80% of taxpayers will owe less; though many of the reductions will be small, they add up to big money. Collectively, individuals over the next five years will keep in their wallets $121.7 billion that they would have to hand over to the Internal Revenue Service under present law.

Business taxes will rise by $120 billion. (One of the principles that tax reformers settled on early was "revenue neutrality," on the theory that a radical rewrite of the tax code would be difficult enough without getting it tangled up in the debate over whether the Government should raise its total tax take in order to reduce deficits.) Although the top tax rate on business profits will drop from 46% to 34%, it will apply to far more corporate income. Scores of special breaks that benefited such industries as banking and real estate will be wiped out.

Time, August 25, 1986

The Essence of the Story

- In the summer of 1986, few believed that the federal income tax code could be reformed.

- But a coalition of conservatives and liberals, Republicans and Democrats passed the Tax Reform Act of 1986.

- That act is "revenue neutral," cutting personal taxes and increasing corporate taxes—each by about $120 million.

- The act cuts the top tax rates but eliminates many deductions, including interest on loans to buy cars and boats, state sales taxes, and child care expenses.

- Capital gains, previously taxed at a lower rate, are taxed at the same rate as other income.

- Six million low-income families no longer have to pay income taxes.

- 80 percent of taxpayers pay less under the reformed plan.

- The rate of tax on corporations declines, but the amount of profit subject to tax increases.

- Special tax breaks for banks and real estate companies are eliminated.

Background and Analysis

- Taxes influence both allocative efficiency and the distribution of income.

- The Tax Reform Act of 1986 was "revenue neutral"—a reform that left the total amount of taxes paid constant.

- Tax *rates* were lowered, but because many previously allowed deductions from income were eliminated, the tax *base* was increased.

- Lower tax *rates* on a larger tax *base* may result in greater economic efficiency and potential gains for all—serving the public interest.

- But tax reform is driven by its effects on the distribution of income—by special interests.

- According to the estimates in the article, 80 percent of taxpayers pay less tax under the new plan, and 20 percent of taxpayers pay more. (The table summarizes the main winners and losers.)

- A tax reform that benefits 80 percent of the population and harms 20 percent does not seem as miraculous as the article claims.

- It is true that each loser has more at stake in the reform than each winner and therefore will lobby harder.

- But gainers lobby, too, and members of Congress, valuing votes, pay attention to both gainers and losers.

- Further, this tax reform was a highly publicized event, and one that directly and significantly affected each voter.

- Also, the voting record of each legislator was highly publicized.

- The increase in corporate taxes to some degree obscures the redistribution of the tax burden brought about by the reform.

- Higher corporate taxes mean less income for the *owners* of corporations—for the people who invest in them.

- The reform, therefore, lowered taxes on labor income but increased taxes on income from capital.

- Thus, the winners are those whose income is primarily from labor; the losers are those whose income is primarily from capital.

- As the labor force participation rate has been increasing steadily, over the years, an increasing number of taxpayers (voters) stood to gain from such a reform.

- If this explanation for the 1986 reform is correct, it implies that, as the population ages and more people become dependent on income from capital (retirement income), the tax burden will shift from capital income toward labor income—personal income taxes will rise, and corporate income taxes will decline.

Winners and Losers from Tax Reform

Winners	Losers
(a) Direct	
80 percent of taxpayers	20 percent of taxpayers
Low-income families	High-income families using tax shelters
Families with high labor income, low capital income, and few deductions	Families with high capital income and capital gains and low labor income
One-income families	Two-income families with child care expenses
(b) Indirect	
Potentially everyone, from greater allocative efficiency resulting from lower tax rates	Tax accountants
	Charities and foundations
	Makers of cars, boats, and durable goods
	Investors in banks and real estate companies
	Providers of day care services

about the issues on which they are voting unless those issues have an immediate and direct consequence for their own income. In other words, it pays voters to be rationally ignorant. **Rational ignorance** is the decision *not* to acquire information, because the cost of acquiring the information is greater than the benefit derived from having it. For example, each voter knows that he or she can make virtually no difference to the actual defense policy pursued by the U.S. government. Each voter also knows that it would take an enormous amount of time and effort to become even moderately well-informed about alternative defense technologies and the most effective ways of achieving different levels of defense. As a result, voters see it as being in their best interests to remain relatively uninformed about the technicalities of national defense issues. (Though we are using national defense as an example, the same applies to all aspects of government economic activity).

All voters are consumers of national defense. But not all voters produce it. Only a small number are in this latter category. Those voters who produce national defense, whether they be members of the military or firms and households that work in producing defense equipment, have a direct personal interest in defense because it affects their incomes. Unlike other voters, therefore, it pays these voters to become well informed about national defense issues and to operate a political lobby aimed at furthering their own interests. These voters, in collaboration with the bureaucracies that deliver national defense, will exert a larger influence through the voting process than the relatively uninformed general voters who only consume this public good.

If the rationality of the uninformed voter and the rationality of the informed special interest group are taken into account, a political equilibrium emerges in which the scale of provision of public goods exceeds the one that maximizes net benefit.

REVIEW

Politicians implement their policies through departments and agencies that are staffed by bureaucrats. In the economic model of bureaucracy, bureaucrats pursue the objective of budget maximization. Each agency tries to persuade politicians that its own budget should be increased. The politician has to balance the need for a bigger bureau budget against the cost of losing votes through higher taxes. If voters are well-informed about the costs and benefits of the activities of a bureau, the maximum budget permitted to the bureau will be that which maximizes net benefit. If voters are rationally ignorant, the best-informed voters will be those who both produce and consume a public good. Voters who only consume a public good will be relatively uninformed. The well-informed voters, in collaboration with the bureaucracies that produce public goods, will exert a larger influence than the uninformed voters who only consume the public goods, and so the scale of provision of public goods will exceed the one that maximizes net benefit. ∎

We've now seen how voters, politicians, and bureaucrats interact to determine the scale of provision of public goods and services and the scale of redistribution, and how they deal with external costs and benefits. But public goods and services have to be paid for with taxes. How does the political marketplace determine the scale and variety of taxes that we pay? And why is it that some goods not only are untaxed but are actually subsidized by the government? We've seen one partial answer to some of these questions already—taxes and subsidies might be used as a part of the government's attempt to deal with externalities. But that is not the entire story, as we'll now see.

Taxes and Subsidies

The bulk of the government's revenue arises from income taxes. The highest tax rates are levied on such commodities as gasoline, alcoholic beverages, tobacco products, and some imported goods. Taxes on these types of items account for more than one fifth of the revenue of federal, state, and local governments. Why are some goods taxed very highly and others hardly at all? Why are some goods even subsidized? And what are the effects of taxes and subsidies on prices and on the quantities of the goods bought and sold? And who winds up paying the tax? Does the consumer pay, does the producer pay, or do they somehow share the tax between them?

Excise Taxes

An **excise tax** is a tax on the sale of a particular commodity. The tax may be set as a fixed dollar amount per unit of the commodity, in which case it is called a *specific tax*. Alternatively, the tax may be set as a fixed percentage of the value of the commodity, in which case it is called an *ad valorem tax*. The taxes on gasoline, alcoholic beverages, and tobacco products are all examples of excise taxes.

Let's study the effects of an excise tax by considering the tax on gasoline. We'll assume that the market for gasoline is competitive. The presence of monopolistic elements does affect the answer to the question that we're now examining and we'll consider what that effect is when we've worked through the competitive case.

Figure 20.5 illustrates the market for gasoline. The quantity of gasoline, measured in millions of gallons a day, is shown on the horizontal axis and the price of gasoline (measured in cents per gallon) is on the vertical axis. The demand curve for gasoline is D and the supply curve is S. If there is no tax on gasoline, its price is 60¢ a gallon and 400 million gallons of gasoline a day are bought and sold.

Let's suppose that a tax is imposed on gasoline at the rate of 60¢ a gallon. If producers are willing to supply 400 million gallons a day for 60¢ when there is no tax, then they will be willing to supply that same quantity in the face of a 60¢ tax only if the price increases to $1.20 a gallon. That is, they will want to get the 60¢ a gallon they received before, plus the additional 60¢ that they now have to hand over to the government in the form of a gasoline tax. As a result of the tax, the supply curve shifts upward by the amount of the tax and becomes the red curve labeled "$S + tax$." The new supply curve intersects the demand curve at a quantity of 300 million gallons a day and at a price of $1.10 a gallon. This situation is the new equilibrium after the imposition of the tax. Why doesn't the equilibrium occur at $1.20—the original price plus the tax? Let's find out.

Who Pays the Tax?   When a tax of 60¢ a gallon is imposed on gasoline, Fig. 20.5 illustrates that the price of gasoline increases, but only by 50¢, to $1.10. Thus the price paid by gasoline consumers increases by less than the tax. The government collects 60¢ a gallon in tax, but the consumer pays only an extra 50¢ a gallon for gasoline. Who pays the

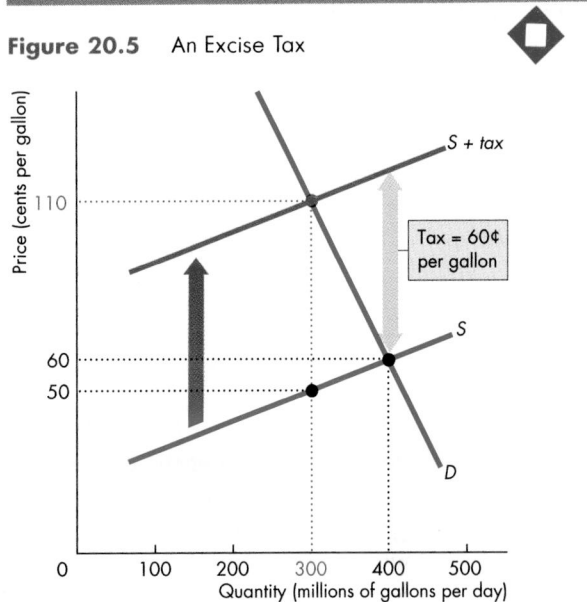

Figure 20.5   An Excise Tax

The demand curve for gasoline is D and the supply curve is S. In the absence of any taxes, gasoline will sell for 60¢ a gallon and 400 million gallons a day will be bought and sold. When a tax of 60¢ a gallon is imposed, the supply curve shifts upward to "$S + tax$." The new equilibrium price is $1.10 a gallon and 300 million gallons a day are traded. The tax is shared between the consumer, who pays 50¢, and the producer, who pays 10¢.

other 10¢? The answer must be the producer. You can see that the producer does in fact pay the missing 10¢ because the receipts of the producer fall from 60¢ a gallon to 50¢ a gallon when the quantity traded falls to 300 million gallons a day.

The way the tax payment is divided between an increase in price paid by the consumer and the fall in the price received by the producer depends on the elasticity of demand and supply. If supply is perfectly elastic—a horizontal supply curve—the rise in price will be equal to the tax. If supply is perfectly inelastic—a vertical supply curve—there will be no change in either the price or the quantity traded and the producer will pay the entire amount of the tax.

If demand is perfectly elastic, the tax will leave the price unchanged. The entire burden of the tax will fall on the producers. The producers will decrease the quantity supplied until marginal cost is below the price by the amount of the tax. The more inelastic the demand, the larger is the rise in price and the smaller is the fall in the quantity traded that results from the imposition of a tax. Furthermore, the more inelastic the demand, the larger is the fraction of the tax paid by the consumer and the smaller is the fraction borne by the producers.

Although we have just examined the effects of an excise tax on gasoline, the same basic analysis has widespread application. Taxes on alcohol and tobacco, sales taxes, and even taxes imposed in the labor market—for example, personal income taxes and social security taxes—can be analyzed in the same manner. The imposition of a tax shifts the supply curve upward by the amount of the tax. The new equilibrium is determined at a higher price and a lower quantity traded. The division of the burden of the tax between a rise in the price of the good being traded and a fall in the receipts of its producer depends on the elasticities of demand and supply.

Monopoly Markets   A monopoly industry has a higher price and smaller quantity traded than the same industry would have in competitive conditions. The monopoly determines its profit-maximizing price by making marginal revenue and marginal cost equal. The imposition of a sales tax or excise tax on a monopoly works in a manner similar to the way it works in a competitive industry. The tax represents an increase in the monopoly's marginal cost. Its marginal cost curve shifts upward by the amount of the tax. Monopoly profit is maximized by producing the output at which marginal cost plus tax equals marginal revenue. Thus the imposition of a sales tax or an excise tax on a monopoly industry has the effect of raising the price and lowering output in the same way that it does in a competitive industry.

Why Do Tax Rates Vary?

Why is the structure of taxes the way it is? Why do we tax alcohol, tobacco, and gasoline at a very high rate and some goods not at all? There are two main reasons why some commodities are taxed very highly and others hardly at all. First, the consumption of some goods, as we saw in Chapter 19, imposes external costs. By placing taxes on the purchase and consumption of such goods, people can be made to take into account the external costs they are imposing on others when they make their own consumption choices. Second, taxes create *deadweight losses*, and by levying taxes at different rates on different commodi-

ties, the deadweight loss arising from raising a given amount of revenue can be minimized. Let's look at these two explanations for variable tax rates a bit more closely.

External Costs   External costs are associated with many goods that are taxed at a high rate. For example, the high tax on gasoline in part enables road users to be confronted with the marginal social cost of the congestion that they impose on others. The high taxes on alcohol and tobacco products in part serve to confront drinkers and smokers with the external costs that their consumption habits impose on others. The impairment of long-term health that results from using these products, and the subsequent health-care costs, as well, perhaps, as a decline in their efficiency as workers, may lead to costs that are borne by others. These costs are not taken into account when a person is deciding whether or not to drink or smoke.

Some goods that have high external costs associated with their consumption are not taxed. Instead, they are made illegal. Marijuana and cocaine are important examples of such goods. Large amounts of these goods are consumed every day in the United States and the illegal markets in which they are traded generate large external costs. An alternative way of organizing these markets would be to make these drugs legal but to impose heavy taxes on them. Sufficiently high taxes would leave the quantities consumed similar to (and perhaps even smaller than) what they currently are, and would confront the users of these drugs with the marginal social cost of their actions. Such taxes would also result in a source of revenue (perhaps a large one) for the government. (Of course, matters relating to drugs have dimensions that go beyond a narrow economic calculation. Some people believe that the consumption of these drugs is so immoral that it would be equally immoral for the government, or anyone else, to legally profit from their production and consumption. These considerations, important though they are, go beyond the scope of economics.)

Let's now look at the deadweight loss that arises from taxes and the way in which this loss can be minimized.

Minimizing the Deadweight Loss of Taxes   It's easy to see that taxes create deadweight loss by returning to the example of the gasoline tax that you studied in Fig. 20.5. The deadweight loss associated with the gasoline tax is illustrated in Fig. 20.6. Without a tax, 400 million gallons of gasoline a day are consumed at a price of 60¢ a gallon. With a 60¢ tax, the price paid by the consumer rises to $1.10 a gallon and the quantity consumed declines to 300 million gallons a day. There is a loss of consumer surplus arising from this price increase and quantity decrease. There is also a loss of producer surplus. Producers now receive 50¢ a gallon for 300 million gallons compared with 60¢ a gallon for 400 million gallons in the absence of taxes. The deadweight loss —the sum of the loss of consumer surplus and producer surplus—is indicated by the gray triangle in Fig. 20.6. The dollar value of that triangle is 30 million dollars a day.[1] But how much revenue is raised by this tax? Since 300 million gallons of gasoline are sold each day and since the tax is 60¢ a gallon, total revenue from the gasoline tax is $180 million a day (300 million gallons multiplied by 60¢ a gallon). Thus to raise tax revenue of $180 million a day using the gasoline tax, a deadweight loss of $30 million a day—one sixth of the tax revenue—is incurred.

One of the main influences on the deadweight loss arising from a tax is the elasticity of demand for the product. The demand for gasoline is fairly inelastic. As a consequence, when a tax is imposed the quantity demanded falls by a smaller percentage than the percentage rise in price. In the example that we've just studied, the quantity demanded falls by 25 percent but the price increases by 83.33 percent. To see the importance of the elasticity of demand, let's consider a different commodity—orange juice. So that we can make a quick and direct comparison, let's assume that the orange juice market is exactly as big as the market for gasoline. Figure 20.7 illustrates this market. The demand curve for orange juice is D and the supply curve is S. Orange juice is not taxed, and so the price of orange juice is 60¢ a gallon— where the supply curve and the demand curve intersect—and the quantity of orange juice traded is 400 million gallons a day.

---

[1]You can calculate the area of that triangle by using the following formula:

$$\frac{\text{Base} \times \text{height}}{2}$$

Turn the triangle on its side so that its base is 60¢, the size of the tax. Its height then becomes the reduction in the quantity sold—100 million gallons a day. Multiplying 60¢ by 100 million gallons and dividing by 2 gives $30 million a day.

Figure 20.6   The Deadweight Loss from an Excise Tax

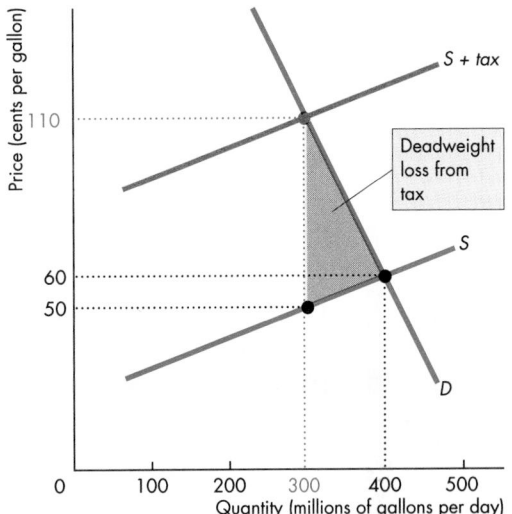

An excise tax creates a deadweight loss represented by the gray triangle. The tax revenue collected is 60¢ a gallon on 300 million gallons, or $180 million a day. The deadweight loss from the tax is $30 million a day. That is, to raise a tax revenue of $180 million a day, a deadweight loss of $30 million a day is incurred.

Now suppose that the government contemplates abolishing the gasoline tax and taxing orange juice instead. The demand for orange juice is more elastic than the demand for gasoline. It has many more good substitutes in the form of other fruit juices. The government wants to raise $180 million a day so that its total revenue is not affected by this tax change. The government's economists, armed with their statistical estimates of the demand and supply curves for orange juice that appear in Fig. 20.7, work out that a tax of 90¢ a gallon will do the job. With such a tax, the supply curve shifts upward to the curve labeled "S + tax." This new supply curve intersects the demand curve at a price of $1.30 a gallon and at a quantity of 200 million gallons a day. The price at which suppliers are willing to produce 200 million gallons a day is 40¢ a gallon. The government collects a tax of 90¢ a gallon on 200 million gallons a day, so it collects a total revenue of $180 million dollars a day—exactly the amount that it requires.

But what is the deadweight loss in this case? The answer can be seen by looking at the gray

Figure 20.7   Why We Don't Tax Orange Juice

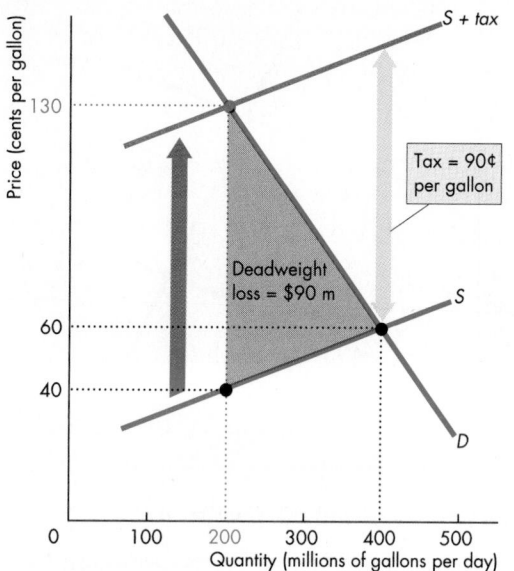

The demand curve for orange juice is *D* and the supply curve is *S*. The equilibrium price is 60¢ a gallon and 400 million gallons of juice a day are traded. To raise $180 million of tax revenue, a tax of 90¢ a gallon will have to be imposed. The introduction of this tax shifts the supply curve to "*S + tax*." The price rises to $1.30 a gallon and the quantity traded falls to 200 million gallons a day. The deadweight loss is represented by the gray triangle and equals $90 million a day. The deadweight loss from taxing orange juice is much larger than that from taxing gasoline (Fig. 20.6) because the demand for orange juice is more elastic than the demand for gasoline. Items that are taxed more heavily than items that have a low elasticity of demand have a high elasticity of of demand.

triangle in Fig. 20.7. The magnitude of that dead-weight loss is $90 million.[2] Notice how much bigger the deadweight loss is from taxing orange juice than that from taxing gasoline. In the case of orange juice, the deadweight loss is one half the revenue raised,

---

[2] This deadweight loss is calculated in exactly the same way as our previous calculation of the deadweight loss from the gasoline tax. Turning the deadweight loss triangle on its side, the base is 90¢ and the height is 200 million gallons. Using the formula for the area of the triangle—base multiplied by height divided by 2—we calculate the deadweight loss as 90¢ multiplied by 200 million divided by 2, which equals $90 million a day.

while in the case of gasoline it is only one sixth. The difference between these two markets is the elasticity of demand. The supply curves are identical in each case and the examples were also set up to ensure that the initial no-tax prices and quantities were identical. The difference between the two cases is the elasticity of demand: In the case of gasoline, the quantity demanded falls by only 25 percent when the price almost doubles. In the case of orange juice, the quantity demanded falls by 50 percent when the price only slightly more than doubles.

You can see why taxing orange juice is not on the political agenda of any of the major parties. Vote-seeking politicians seek out taxes that benefit the median voter. Other things being equal, this means that they try to minimize the deadweight loss of raising a given amount of revenue. Equivalently, they tax items with an inelastic demand more heavily than items with an elastic demand.

Let's now turn to an examination of subsidies.

Subsidies

In the aggregate, subsidies do not constitute a large fraction of government expenditure either at the federal, state, or local levels. Nevertheless, there is one industry in which subsidies constitute an important component of income— agriculture. More than 10 percent of the total receipts of grain producers, for example, are in the form of government subsidies. Let's study subsidies by examining the market for wheat.

Suppose that the wheat market is as illustrated in Fig. 20.8. The demand curve is *D* and the supply curve is *S*. Two billion bushels a year are produced at a price of $3.50 a bushel. Now suppose that the government offers wheat growers a subsidy of $1 a bushel. If suppliers are willing to supply 2 billion bushels a year for $3.50 without a subsidy, then they will be willing to supply that same quantity for $2.50 with a $1 subsidy. The supply curve for wheat, therefore, shifts downward by the amount of the subsidy. The new supply curve becomes that labeled "*S − subsidy*." The new supply curve intersects the demand curve at a price of $3 a bushel and at a quantity of 3 billion bushels a year. This price and quantity is the new equilibrium. The price of wheat falls by 50¢ a bushel. Consumers pay 50¢ a bushel less and producers' costs rise by 50¢ a bushel. The 50¢ cost increase and the 50¢ price cut are made up by the one-dollar subsidy to the producer.

Figure 20.8   Subsidies

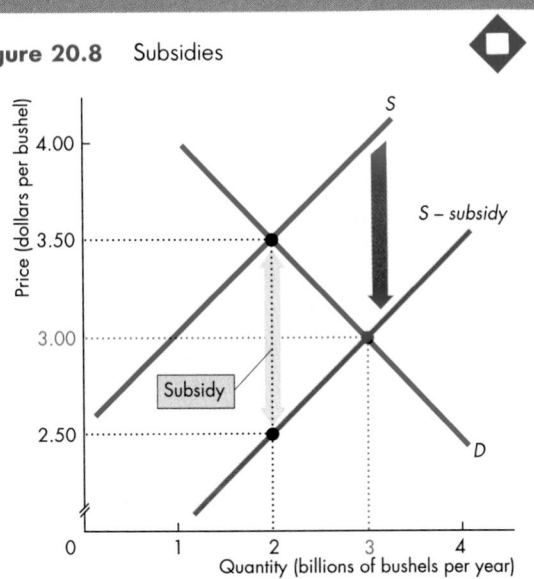

The demand curve for wheat is D and the supply curve is S. A competitive market with no taxes or subsidies produces 2 billion bushels of wheat a year at a price of $3.50 a bushel. If the government subsidizes wheat production by $1 a bushel, the supply curve shifts downward to "S−subsidy." The price of wheat falls to $3 a bushel and the quantity produced increases to 3 billion bushels a year. Wheat growers receive just enough revenue from the market, along with the subsidy, to cover their costs.

Subsidies with Quotas

In the United States, in addition to subsidies on production in the farm sector, there are also quotas. A **quota** is a limit on the quantity that a firm is permitted to produce. When a group of producers can enforce quotas, it is possible to restrict output and thereby obtain monopoly profit. We can see the effects of quotas and subsidies in Fig. 20.9. Suppose that the government establishes and enforces quotas for each producer that result in total output being 2 billion bushels a year (shown by the vertical line marked "*Quota*" in the figure). At this output level, consumers are willing to pay $3.50 a bushel for the wheat, and so that will be its market price. Producers also get a subsidy of a dollar a bushel on everything they produce so the supply curve becomes "*S − subsidy.*" With the subsidy and a market price of $3.50, producers would like to supply 4 billion bushels a year—the quantity read off from the new

red supply curve at a price of $3.50. But they're prevented from doing so by the quota.

With output restricted to 2 billion bushels of wheat, producers' costs are $3.50 a bushel. They are also selling their wheat for $3.50 a bushel. In addition, they are receiving $1 a bushel in subsidies from the government. The subsidy is like a monopoly profit.

It is interesting to contrast this situation with the one in which there is a subsidy but no quota. Without a quota, output is 3 billion bushels and marginal cost is $4 a bushel. The market price is $3 a bushel so the subsidy of $1 a bushel makes up the difference between the market price and marginal cost. Without a quota, the price plus the subsidy just cover marginal cost. With a quota, price covers mar-

Figure 20.9   Subsidies with Quotas

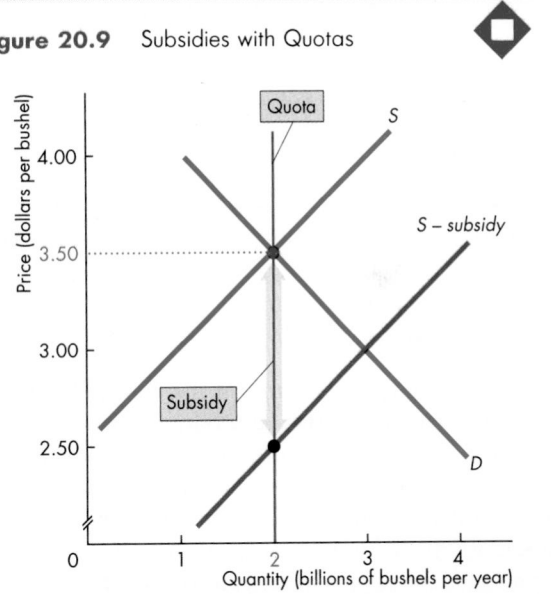

A competitive wheat market with no taxes or subsidies produces 2 billion bushels a year at a price of $3.50 a bushel—the point of intersection of the curves D and S. A subsidy of $1 a bushel shifts the supply curve to "S−subsidy." But if a quota is introduced at the same time as the subsidy, the output of each producer is restricted so that total output stays at 2 billion bushels a year, and the price remains $3.50 a bushel. With the quota, producers receive $3.50 from the market plus $1 from the government. Producers gain from the quota. The revenue from the market covers costs, so the subsidy is like a monopoly's profit.

ginal cost and the subsidy is a surplus for the producer—an excess revenue over cost.

Subsidies with quotas are clearly a good thing from the point of view of producers. But they are a bad thing from the point of view of consumers. To pay a subsidy the government has to raise taxes that create deadweight loss. So why do we have subsidies with quotas?

Why Subsidies and Quotas?   The existence of quotas and subsidies is explained by the fact that those who stand to gain from a system of quotas and subsidies are relatively well defined and easily organized into a political force. Those who stand to lose are highly diffuse and much more difficult and costly to organize. As a result, the political equilibrium that prevails is one in which a relatively small number of people gain a significant per person amount while a relatively large number of people each lose an almost unnoticeable amount.

■   We have now reviewed the structure of the government sector, market failure, and the theory of

public choice that explains how politicians, bureaucrats, and voters interact to determine the scale of provision of public goods, the extent to which taxes and subsidies are used to cope with externalities, the amount of income redistribution, and the levels of taxes and subsidies.

We have seen that a political equilibrium emerges in which no individual can improve his or her own situation by proposing or implementing a different policy. Each political party devises a program that appeals as closely as possible to half of the electorate. The parties differ in their rhetoric because of differences in the particular half of the electorate to which they appeal, but their actions are similar to each other. Bureaus grow to a size such that politicians perceive the benefit from increasing the bureaus' budgets still further is matched by the perceived cost of higher taxes and their consequences for lost votes. Voters are as well informed as it pays them to be—they are rationally ignorant.

In the next chapter, we're going to study a further range of government actions—their interventions in markets for goods and services in which there are monopoly and cartel elements.

S U M M A R Y

The Political Marketplace

There are three types of actors in the political marketplace: voters, politicians, and bureaucrats. Voters are the consumers of the outcome of the political process. They express their demands through their votes, campaign contributions, and lobbying. Public choices are made by politicians and implemented by bureaucrats. The objective of politicians is to win enough votes to be elected and then to remain in office. They do so by offering policies that are likely to appeal to a majority of voters. To appeal to a majority of voters, politicians have to appeal to the median voter. Since politicians aim for the vote of the median voter, their policies will resemble each other—they will be minimally differentiated. For example, in designing income redistribution policies, politicians transfer from the rich not only to the poor but to all those with incomes at or below the median. Redistribution will be aimed at making the median voter as rich as possible.

Bureaucrats, in pursuing their own objectives, seek to maximize the budget of their own bureau. If voters are well informed, politicians will not be able to collect taxes to enable bureaucrats to achieve budgets in excess of those that maximize net benefit. But if voters are rationally ignorant, producer interests may result in voting to support taxes that in turn support a level of provision of public goods in excess of that which maximizes net benefit. (pp. 515–528)

Taxes and Subsidies

The imposition of a tax on a good shifts the supply curve upward, raises the price of the good, and lowers the quantity traded. A tax is shared between the consumer and the producer and creates a deadweight loss. The size of the deadweight loss depends on the elasticity of demand. By taxing goods that have a low elasticity of demand, deadweight loss of raising a given amount of tax revenue is minimized. The highest tax rates are applied to goods with a low elasticity of demand.

Subsidizing a good shifts the supply curve downward, lowers the price of the good and increases the quantity traded. Subsidies combined with quotas generate additional income for producers at the expense of consumers. (pp. 528–534)

K E Y   C O N C E P T S

R E V I E W   Q U E S T I O N S

1 What are the three types of actors in the political marketplace?

2 Describe the economic functions of voters and explain how they make their economic choices.

3 Describe the economic functions of politicians and explain how they make their economic choices.

4 What is meant by "political equilibrium"?

5 What is the principle of minimum differentiation?

6 How does the principle of minimum differentiation explain political parties' policy platforms?

7 What is the median voter theorem?

8 What features of political choices does the median voter theorem explain?

9 What are the economic functions of bureaucrats and how do they make their economic choices?

10 Describe the ways in which government redistributes income.

11 Why is it rational for voters to be ignorant?

12 Explain why it is likely that the scale of provision of public goods will exceed the allocatively efficient scale.

P R O B L E M S

1 Your local city council is contemplating upgrading its system for controlling traffic signals. By installing a sophisticated computer with sensing mechanisms at all the major intersections, the council believes that it can better adjust the timing of the changes in signals and improve the speed of the traffic flow. The bigger the computer it buys, the better job it can do; the more sensors

it installs, the more intersections it can monitor and the faster the overall traffic flow that will result. The mayor and the other elected officials who are working on the proposal want to determine the scale and sophistication of the system that will win them the most votes. The city bureaucrats in the traffic department want to maximize the budget. Suppose that you are an economist who is observing this public choice. Your job is to calculate the scale of provision of this public good that maximizes net benefit—that achieves allocative efficiency.

a) What data would you need in order to reach your own conclusions?

b) What does the public choice theory predict will be the scale of provision chosen?

c) How could you, as an informed voter, attempt to influence the choice?

2 Three people—Joe, Jim, and Jon—have incomes of $1000, $500, and $250. Set up a proposed redistribution of income between these three people that will achieve majority support. Once you've determined the new distribution (after implementing your proposal), set up another scheme that will also command a majority support. Show that you can find a voting cycle.

3 A community of 9 people, identified by letters A through I, have strong views about a local factory that is polluting the atmosphere. Some of them work at the factory and don't want the government to take any action against it while others want to see the imposition of a huge tax based on the scale of pollution. The preferences of each person concerning the scale of the tax that should be imposed are as follows:

A	B	C	D	E	F	G	H	I
100	90	80	70	60	0	0	0	0

Suppose that there are two political parties competing for office in this community. What tax rate will the parties propose?

4 You are given the following information about a perfectly competitive market for cookies.

Price (dollars per pound)	Quantity demanded (pounds per month)	Quantity supplied (pounds per month)
10	0	12
8	1	10
6	2	8
4	3	6
2	4	4
0	5	0

a) What are the competitive equilibrium price and quantity traded?

b) Suppose that a 10 percent tax is imposed on cookies.

(i) What is the new price of cookies?

(ii) What is the new quantity traded?

(iii) What is the total amount of tax revenue raised by the government?

(iv) What is the deadweight loss?

c) Now suppose that cookies are not taxed but are instead subsidized by 10 percent.

(i) What happens to the price of cookies?

(ii) What happens to the quantity traded?

(iii) How much is the subsidy paid out by the government?

(iv) Suppose that along with the subsidy, a quota is imposed on cookie producers. What is the scale of the quota that will maximize profit for the producer?

Chapter 21

After studying this chapter, you will be able to:

- Define regulation

- State which parts of the economy are subject to regulation

- Describe the main trends in regulation and deregulation

- Describe the main elements of antitrust law

- Explain how antitrust law has been applied in a number of landmark cases

- Distinguish between the "public interest" and "capture" theories of regulation

- Explain how regulation of natural monopolies affects prices, outputs, profits, and the distribution of the gains from trade between consumers and producers

- Explain how the regulation of cartels affects prices, outputs, profits, and the distribution of the gains from trade between consumers and producers

S ome of the most important things that you consume are bought from regulated natural monopolies. Water, electric power, gas, cable TV, and subway services are all examples of such goods. Why are the industries that produce goods and services regulated? How are they regulated? And do the regulations work in the interests of consumers—the public interest— or do they serve the interests of the producer—special interests? ■ Regulation extends beyond natural monopoly, to cartels. For example, until 1978, the price of air transportation in the United States, and the routes that airlines could fly, were regulated by the Civil Aeronautics Board (CAB). But in 1978, domestic air travel was deregulated, and the CAB was disbanded. The government still regulates the

airline industry to ensure adequate safety standards, but air-lines are now free to choose their routes and decide their own fares. The initial result was that more airlines sprang up, prices fell, and the number of airline passengers increased dramatically. Subsequently, however, prices began to edge upward and competition lessened. ■ Regulation and deregulation are not con-fined to the airline industry. Interstate trucking, and the financial sector—banking and insurance and other financial services—were regulated in the past but in recent years were deregulated. Why do we sometimes regulate an industry and at other times deregulate that same industry? Whose interest is served by regulation and deregulation—the consumer or the producer? ■ Regulation and deregulation rep-resent just one aspect of the actions governments can take to influence the market economy. They also pass laws—antitrust laws—that block mergers between large competing companies and that result in other companies being broken up. For example, until a few years ago, if you made a long-distance phone call, you had no choice but to use the American Telephone and Telegraph Company (AT&T). Our antitrust laws were used to break up AT&T and to create a number of independent producers of long-distance telephone service. Today, after the breakup of AT&T, and also following deregulation in the phone business, you can choose your long-distance carrier, and such alternatives as MCI and U.S. Sprint compete with AT&T. The price of a long-distance phone call has gone down considerably.   ■ What are the antitrust laws? How have they evolved over the years? How are they used today? Do antitrust laws serve consumer interests—the public interest—or the special interests of producer groups?

■ This chapter studies the actions taken by government to regulate, control, and influence trading in markets for goods and services. It begins by describing the various ways in which government intervenes in monopolistic and oligopolistic markets. The chapter draws on your earlier study of how competitive, monopolistic, and oligopolistic markets work, and on your knowledge of the gains from trade—of consumer and producer surplus. It shows how consumers and producers might redistribute those gains, and identifies who stands to gain and who stands to lose from various types of government intervention. And since such intervention is supplied by politicians and bureaucrats, the chapter also looks at the economic behavior of these groups, expanding on what you learned in the previous chapter about public choice and the political "marketplace."

Market Intervention

There are two main ways in which the government intervenes in monopolistic and oligopolistic markets to influence *what, how,* and *for whom* various goods and services are produced:

• Regulation
• Antitrust law

Regulation

Regulation consists of rules administered by a government agency to restrict economic activity by determining prices, product standards and types, and the conditions under which new firms may enter an industry. In order to implement its regulations, the government establishes agencies to oversee the regula-

tions and ensure their enforcement. The first such agency to be set up in the United States was the Interstate Commerce Commission (ICC), established in 1887. Over the years since then and up to the late 1970s, regulation of the economy grew until, at its peak, almost a quarter of the nation's output was produced by regulated industries. Regulation applied to banking and financial services, telecommunications, gas and electric utilities, railroads, trucking, airlines and buses, and many agricultural products. Since the late 1970s, there has been a tendency to deregulate the U.S. economy.

Deregulation is the process of removing restrictions on prices, product standards and types, and entry conditions. In recent years, deregulation has occurred in domestic air transportation, telephone service, interstate trucking, and banking and financial services.

Antitrust Law

An **antitrust law** is a law that regulates and prohibits certain kinds of market behavior, such as monopoly and monopolistic practices. Antitrust law is enacted by Congress and enforced through the judicial system. Lawsuits under the antitrust laws may be initiated either by government agencies or by privately injured parties.

The main thrust of the antitrust law is the prohibition of monopoly practices and of restricting output in order to achieve higher prices and profits. The first antitrust law was enacted in 1890—the Sherman Act. Successive acts and amendments have strengthened and refined the body of antitrust law. Antitrust law (like all law) depends as much on decisions of the courts and of the Supreme Court as on the statutes passed by Congress. Over the 100 years since the passage of the Sherman Act, there have been some interesting turns of direction in the interpretation of the law by the courts and the vigor with which the law has been enforced. We'll study these later in this chapter.

To understand why the government intervenes in the market economy and to work out the effects of its interventions, we need to identify the gains and losses that government actions can create. These gains and losses are the consumer surplus and producer surplus associated with different output levels and prices. You've already met these concepts in Chapters 7 (pp. 167–168) and 13 (p. 332). All we need to do here, therefore, is refresh our understanding of these concepts and of the way in which their magnitudes are affected by the price at which a good is sold and the quantity traded.

Surpluses and Their Distribution

Consumer surplus is the difference between the maximum amount that consumers are willing to pay and the amount that they actually do pay for a given quantity of a good. Consumer surplus is the gain from trade accruing to consumers. *Producer surplus* is the difference between the producer's revenue and the opportunity cost of production. Producer surplus is the gain from trade accruing to producers. **Total surplus** is the sum of consumer surplus and producer surplus.

The lower the price and the larger the quantity traded, the larger is consumer surplus. The closer are the price and quantity traded to the monopoly profit-maximzing levels, the larger is producer surplus. Total surplus is maximized (in the absence of external costs and benefits) when marginal cost equals price. In this situation, allocative efficiency is achieved.

There is a conflict between maximizing producer surplus and maximizing total surplus. Monopoly firms have an incentive to restrict output below the competitive level, increasing producer surplus but reducing consumer surplus and creating deadweight loss. Thus there is a tension between the public interest of maximization of total surplus and the producer's interest of maximizing monopoly profit and producer surplus. This tension is of central importance in the economic theory of regulation. Let's now examine that theory.

The Economic Theory of Regulation

The economic theory of regulation is part of the broader theory of public choice. You have already met that theory in Chapter 20 and seen the main components of a public choice model. We're going to reexamine the main features of such a model but with an emphasis on the regulatory aspects of government behavior. We'll examine the demand for government actions, the supply of those actions, and the political equilibrium—the balancing of demands and supplies.

The Demand for Regulation

The demand for regulation is expressed through political institutions. Both consumers and producers vote, lobby, and campaign for regulations that best further their own interests. None of these activities are costless. Voters incur costs in order to acquire information on the basis of which to decide their vote. Lobbying and campaigning cost time, effort, and contributions to the campaign funds of political parties. Individual consumers and producers demand political action only if the benefit that they individually receive from such action exceeds the costs incurred by them in obtaining the action. There are four main factors that affect the demand for regulation:

- Consumer surplus per buyer
- Number of buyers
- Producer surplus per firm
- Number of firms

The larger the consumer surplus per buyer resulting from regulation, the greater is the demand for regulation by buyers. Also, as the number of buyers increases, so does the demand for regulation. But numbers alone do not necessarily translate into an effective political force. The larger the number of buyers, the greater is the cost of organizing them, so the demand for regulation does not increase proportionately with the number of buyers.

The larger the producer surplus per firm arising from a particular regulation, the larger is the demand for that regulation by firms. Also, as the number of firms that might benefit from some regulation increases, so does the demand for that regulation. But again, as in the case of consumers, large numbers do not necessarily mean an effective political force. The larger the number of firms, the greater is the cost of organizing them.

For a given surplus, consumer or producer, the smaller the number of households or firms who share that surplus, the larger is the demand for the regulation that creates it.

The Supply of Regulation

Regulation is supplied by politicians and bureaucrats. As we saw in the previous chapter, politicians choose policies that appeal to a majority of voters, thereby enabling themselves to achieve and maintain office, and bureaucrats support policies that maximize their budgets. Given these objectives of politicians and bureaucrats, the supply of regulation depends on the following factors:

- Consumer surplus per buyer
- Producer surplus per firm
- The number of persons affected

The larger the consumer surplus per buyer or producer surplus per firm generated, and the larger the number of persons affected by a regulation, the greater is the tendency for politicians to supply that regulation. If regulation benefits a large number of people significantly enough for it to be noticed and if the recipients know who is the source of the benefits, that regulation appeals to politicians and it is supplied. If regulation affects markets that benefit a large number of people but by a small amount per person, and if such benefits do not attract notice, that regulation does not appeal to politicians and it is not supplied. Regulation that bestows clear and large benefits on a small number of people may be attractive to politicians provided some of those benefits flow back and thus enable the politicians to fight more effective election campaigns.

Equilibrium

In equilibrium, the regulation that exists is such that no interest group feels it is worthwhile to use additional resources to press for changes, and no group of politicians feels it is worthwhile to offer different regulations. Being in a political equilibrium is not the same thing as everyone being in agreement. Lobby groups will devote resources to trying to change regulations that are already in place. And others will devote resources to maintaining the existing regulations. But no one will feel it is worthwhile to *increase* the resources they are devoting to such activities. Also, political parties will not agree with each other. Some support the existing regulations and others propose different regulations. In equilibrium, no one wants to change the proposals that they are making.

What will a political equilibrium look like? There are two theories of political equilibrium: one is called the public interest theory and the other the capture theory. Let's look at these two theories.

Public Interest Theory   The **public interest theory of regulation** states that regulations are supplied to satisfy the demand of consumers and pro-

ducers for the maximization of total surplus—or the attainment of allocative efficiency. Public interest theory predicts that the political process will relentlessly seek out deadweight loss and introduce regulations that eliminate it. For example, where monopoly or monopolistic practices by collusive oligopoly exist, the political process will introduce price regulation to ensure that output and price are close to their competitive levels.

Capture Theory   The **capture theory of regulation** states that the regulations that exist are those that maximize producer surplus. The key idea of capture theory is that the cost of regulation is high and that only those regulations that increase the surplus of small, easily identified groups who have low organization costs will be supplied by the political process. Such regulations will be supplied even where they impose costs on others, provided those costs are spread thinly and widely enough so that they do not have negative effects on votes.

The predictions of the capture theory of regulation are less precise than the predictions of the public interest theory. According to the capture theory, regulations benefit cohesive interest groups by large and visible amounts and impose costs on everyone else that are so small, in per capita terms, that no one feels it is worthwhile to incur the cost of organizing an interest group to avoid these costs. To make these predictions concrete enough to be useful, the capture theory needs a model of the costs of political organization.

Whichever theory of regulation is correct, the political system delivers an amount and type of regulation that best furthers the electoral success of politicians. Since we have seen that producer-oriented and consumer-oriented regulation are in direct conflict with each other, it is clear that the political process cannot satisfy both groups in any particular industry. Only one group can win. This makes the regulatory actions of government a bit like a unique product—for example, a painting by Rembrandt. There is only one original and it will be sold to just one buyer. Normally, a unique commodity is sold through an auction; the highest bidder takes the prize. Equilibrium in the regulatory process can be thought of in much the same way: The suppliers of regulation will satisfy the demands of the higher bidder. If the producer demand offers a bigger return to the politicians, either directly through votes or indirectly through campaign contributions, then the producers' interests will be served. If the consumer demand translates into a larger number of votes, then the consumers' interests will be served by regulation.

We have now completed our study of the theory of regulation in the marketplace. Let's turn our attention to an examination of the regulations that exist in our economy today.

Regulation and Deregulation

The past 20 years have seen dramatic changes in the way in which the U.S. economy is regulated by government. We're going to examine some of the more important of those changes. To begin, we'll look at what is regulated and also at the scope of regulation. Then we'll turn to the regulatory process itself and examine how regulators control prices and other aspects of market behavior. Finally, we'll tackle the more difficult and controversial questions: Why do we regulate some things but not others? Who benefits from the regulation that we have?

The Scope of Regulation

The first federal regulatory agency, the Interstate Commerce Commission (ICC), was set up in 1887 to control prices, routes, and the quality of service of interstate transportation companies—railroads, trucking lines, bus lines, water carriers, and, in more recent years, oil pipelines. Following the establishment of the ICC, the regulatory environment remained static until the years of the Great Depression. Then, in the 1930s, more agencies were established—the Federal Power Commission, the Federal Communications Commission, the Federal Maritime

Table 21.1   Federal Regulatory Agencies Controlling Prices, Entry, and Services in 1978

Organization	Year established	Controls and regulates
Interstate Commerce Commission	1887	Prices, routes, and services of railroads, trucks, bus lines, oil pipelines, and domestic water carriers
Federal Power Commission	1930	Wellhead gas prices and wholesale prices of natural gas and electricity sold for resale in interstate commerce
Federal Communications Commission	1934	Prices for telephone and telegraph service; entry into telecommunications and broadcasting
Federal Maritime Commission	1936	Fares and schedules of transoceanic freight shipments
Civil Aeronautics Board	1938	Airline passenger fares; entry of airlines into city-to-city air routes
Postal Rate Commission	1970	Classes of mail and rates for those classes; sets fees for other services
Federal Energy Regulatory Commission	1974	Wellhead crude-oil prices and refinery, wholesale, and retail prices of petroleum products; allocation levels for wholesalers and retailers of crude oil, residual fuel oil, and most refined petroleum products produced in or imported into the United States during a period of energy emergency
Copyright Royalty Tribunal	1976	Fees and charges on copyright materials

Source: Paul W. MacAvoy, The Regulated Industries and the Economy (New York: W.W. Norton, 1979), 146–147.

Commission, and, in the late 1930s, the Civil Aeronautics Board. There was a further lull until the establishment in the 1970s of the Postal Rate Commission and the Energy Regulatory Administration and finally, the Copyright Royalty Tribunal. Table 21.1 provides a summary of the federal regulatory agencies and their functions.

In the mid-1970s, almost one quarter of the economy was subject to some form of regulation, as seen in Table 21.2 (a). The most heavily regulated industries—those subject both to price regulation and to regulation of entry of new firms—were electricity, natural gas, telephones, airlines, highway freight services, and railroads (see Table 21.2b). It has been estimated that in 1975 regulation was costing the U.S. economy $100 billion a year—more than 6¢ on every dollar earned.

Regulation reached its peak in 1977. Since then, there has been a gradual and important deregulation process in place. Deregulation has had the most significant impact in the telecommunication, banking and finance, railroad, bus, trucking, and airline industries.

What exactly do regulatory agencies do? How do they regulate?

The Regulatory Process

Though regulatory agencies vary in size and scope and in the detailed aspects of economic life that they control, there are certain features common to all agencies.

First, the senior bureaucrats who are the key decision makers in a regulatory agency are appointed by the administration or Congress. In addition, all agencies have a permanent bureaucracy made up of experts in the industry being regulated and often recruited from the regulated firms. Agencies have financial resources, voted by Congress, to cover the costs of their operations.

Second, each agency adopts a set of practices or operating rules for controlling prices and other aspects of economic performance based on well-defined physical and financial accounting procedures that are relatively easy to administer and to monitor.

In a regulated industry, individual firms are free to determine the technology that they will use in production. But they are not free to determine the prices at which they will sell their output, the quantities that they will sell, or the markets that they will serve. The regulatory agency grants certification to a

Table 21.2   How Much Regulation?

(a) Regulation as a percentage of total output

	Year	
	1965	1975
Price regulation	5.5	8.8
Financial regulation	2.7	3.0
Health and safety regulation	—	11.9
Total	8.2	23.7

(b) Industries subject to price and entry regulation

Industry	Jurisdiction and extent of regulation
Electricity	Federal Energy Regulatory Commission and 49 state agencies certify service.
Natural gas	Federal Energy Regulatory Commission controls interstate transportation and 49 state agencies set rates for distribution.
Telephones	Federal Communications Commission and 50 state agencies set rates, entry, and service conditions.
Airlines	Civil Aeronautics Board regulations set fares and entry conditions before the Airline Deregulation Act of 1978; 21 state agencies set fare and entry conditions interstate.
Highway freight	Interstate Commerce Commission and 47 state agencies regulate rates; the ICC and 45 state agencies control entry into common-carrier services.
Railroads	Interstate Commerce Commission and 44 state agencies set freight rates; the ICC and 26 state agencies certify entry into the provision of rail services.

Source: Paul W. MacAvoy, The Regulated Industries and the Economy (New York: W.W. Norton, 1979), 18, 25.

company to serve a particular market and with a particular line of products, and it determines the level and structure of prices that will be charged. In some cases, the agency also determines the scale of output permitted.

To analyze the way in which regulation works, it is convenient to distinguish between the regulation

Figure 21.1   Natural Monopoly: Marginal Cost Pricing

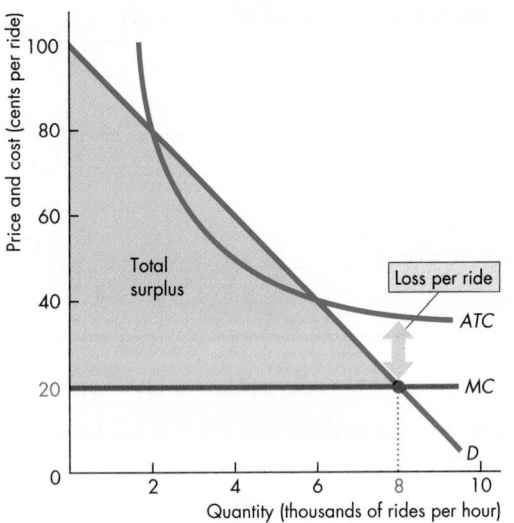

A natural monopoly is an industry in which average total cost is falling even when the entire market demand is satisfied. A natural monopoly for subway rides has a demand curve D. Marginal costs are constant at 20¢ a ride, as shown by the curve MC. Fixed costs are heavy and the average total cost curve, which includes average fixed cost, is shown as ATC. A marginal cost pricing rule that maximizes total surplus sets the price of a ride at 20¢, with 8000 rides an hour being taken. The resulting consumer surplus is shown as the green area. The producer makes a loss on each ride indicated by the red arrow. In order to remain in business, the producer must either price discriminate or receive a subsidy.

of natural monopoly and the regulation of cartels. Let's begin with natural monopoly.

Natural Monopoly

Natural monopoly was defined in Chapter 13 (pp. 316–317) as an industry in which one firm can supply the entire market at a lower price than two or more firms can. As a consequence, a natural monopoly experiences economies of scale, no matter how high an output rate it produces. Examples of natural monopolies include gas and electric utilities and subway services. It is much more expensive to have two or more competing sets of pipes, wires, and train lines serving every neighborhood than it is to have a single set.

Let's consider the example of a subway train service. The demand for the subway service and the subway's cost curves are illustrated in Fig. 21.1. The demand curve is *D*. The marginal cost curve is *MC*. Notice that the marginal cost curve is horizontal at 20¢ a ride—that is, the cost of each additional ride is a constant 20¢. The subway company has a heavy investment in track, trains, and control equipment and so has high fixed costs. These fixed costs feature in the company's average total cost curve, shown as *ATC*. The average total cost curve slopes downward because as the number of rides increases the fixed cost is spread over a larger number of rides. (If you need to refresh your memory on how the average total cost curve is calculated, take a quick look back at pp. 237–241.)

Regulation in the Public Interest   How will this industry be regulated according to the public interest theory? Recall that the public interest theory states that regulation maximizes total surplus—achieves allocative efficiency. Allocative efficiency occurs when marginal cost equals price. Equivalently, it occurs when total surplus (the green area) is maximized—when the area above the marginal cost curve and below the demand curve has reached a maximum. As you can see in the example shown in Fig. 21.1, that outcome occurs if the price is regulated at 20¢ a ride and if 8000 rides an hour are produced. Such a regulation is called a marginal cost pricing rule. A **marginal cost pricing rule** sets price equal to marginal cost. It maximizes total surplus in the regulated industry.

A natural monopoly that is regulated to set price equal to marginal cost makes an economic loss. Because its average total cost curve is falling, marginal cost is below average total cost. Because price equals marginal cost, price is below average total cost. The difference between price and average total cost is the loss per unit produced, a shown by the red arrow in Fig. 21.1. It's pretty obvious that a private subway company that is required to use a marginal cost pricing rule will not stay in business for long. How can a company cover its costs and, at the same time, obey a marginal cost pricing rule?

One possibility is price discrimination. Some natural monopolies can fairly easily price discriminate. For example, local phone companies can charge consumers a monthly fee for being connected to the telephone system and then charge a low price (perhaps even zero) for each local call. A subway company can price discriminate by offering discounts on weekly or monthly season tickets.

But a natual monopoly cannot always price discriminate. When a natural monopoly cannot price discriminate, it can only cover its total cost and follow a marginal cost pricing rule if it receives a subsidy from the government. In such a case, the government would have to raise the revenue for the subsidy by taxing some other activity. But as we saw in Chapter 20, taxes themselves generate deadweight loss. Thus the deadweight loss resulting from additional taxes has to be offset against the allocative efficiency gained by forcing the natural monopoly to adopt a marginal cost pricing rule. It is possible that deadweight loss will be minimized by permitting the natural monopoly to charge a higher price than marginal cost rather than by taxing some other sector of the economy in order to subsidize the natural monopoly. Such a pricing arrangement is called an average cost pricing rule. An **average cost pricing rule** sets price equal to average total cost. The average cost pricing solution is shown in Fig. 21.2. The subway company charges 40¢ for each ride and sells 6000 rides an hour. Consumer surplus (the green area) falls below its maximum possible amount, and deadweight loss arises, represented by the gray triangle in the figure.

Even though there is a deadweight loss, this situation may well be allocatively efficient. Recall that the subway company goes out of business if it doesn't cover its costs. If a subsidy is required to cover costs and if the subsidy requires a tax that has a deadweight loss larger than the one shown in the figure, then the average cost pricing rule is the best available.

Capturing the Regulator What does the capture theory predict about the regulation of this industry? Recall that according to the capture theory, regulation serves the interests of the producer. The interests of the producer, in this case, are best satisfied by maximizing profit. To work out the price that achieves this goal, we need to look at the relationship between marginal revenue and marginal cost. As you know, a monopoly maximizes profit by producing the output at which marginal revenue equals marginal cost. The monopoly's marginal revenue curve in Fig. 21.3 is the orange curve *MR*. Marginal revenue equals marginal cost when output is 4000 rides an hour. The subway company sells three rides at a price of 60¢ a ride (as determined by the demand curve). The subway company's average total cost is 50¢ a ride, its

Figure 21.2 Natural Monopoly: Average Cost Pricing

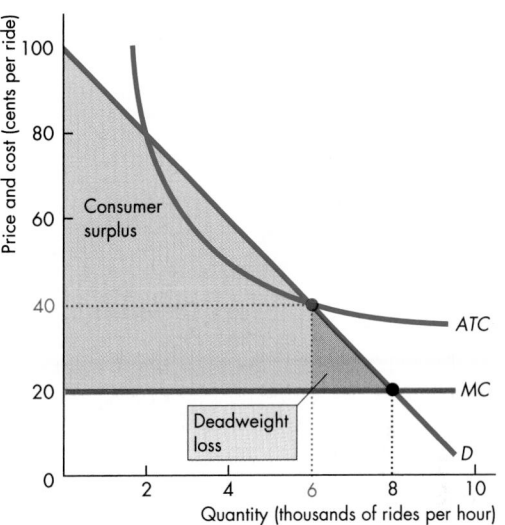

Average cost pricing sets price equal to average total cost. The Subway Company charges 40¢ a ride and sells 6000 rides an hour. In this situation the Subway Company will break even—average total cost equals price. Deadweight loss, shown by the gray triangle, is generated. Consumer surplus is reduced to the green area.

profit is 10¢ a ride, and its total profit is shown by the blue triangle. Consumer surplus shrinks (green triangle), and deadweight loss expands (gray triangle).

We have discovered that a regulation that best serves the interest of the producer will set the price at 60¢ a ride. But how can a producer go about obtaining regulation that results in this monopoly profit-maximizing outcome? To answer this question, we need to look at the way in which agencies determine the level at which to set a regulated price. The key method used is called rate of return regulation.

Rate of Return Regulation **Rate of return regulation** determines a regulated price by setting the price at a level that enables the regulated firm to earn a specified target percent return on its capital. The target rate of return is determined with reference to what is normal in competitive industries. This rate of

Figure 21.3   Natural Monopoly: Profit
                   Maximization

The subway company would like to maximize profit. To do so, marginal revenue (*MR*) is made equal to marginal cost (*MC*). At a price of 60¢ a ride, 4000 rides an hour are sold. Consumer surplus is reduced to the green triangle. The deadweight loss increases to the gray triangle. Monopoly makes the profit shown by the blue rectangle. If the producer can capture the regulator, the outcome will be the situation shown here.

return is part of the opportunity cost of the natural monopolist and is included in the firm's average total cost. By examining the firm's total cost, including the normal rate of return on capital, the regulator attempts to determine the price at which average total cost is covered. Thus rate of return regulation is equivalent to average cost pricing.

In the example that we have just been examining (Fig. 21.2), average cost pricing results at a regulated price of 40¢ a ride with 6000 rides an hour being sold. Thus rate of return regulation, based on a correct assessment of the producer's average total cost curve, results in a price and quantity that favors the consumer and does not enable the producer to maximize monopoly profit. The special interest group will have failed to capture the regulator and the outcome will be closer to that predicted by the public interest theory of regulation.

But there is an important feature of many real world situations that the above analysis does not take

into account—the ability of the monopoly firm to mislead the regulator about its true costs.

Inflating Costs   The senior managers of a firm might be able to inflate the firm's costs by spending part of the firm's revenue on inputs that are not strictly required for the production of the good. By this device, the firm's apparent cost curves exceed the true cost curves. On-the-job luxury in the form of sumptuous office suites, limousines, free baseball tickets (disguised as public relations expenses), company jets, lavish international travel, and entertainment are all ways in which managers can inflate costs.

If the subway company manages to inflate its costs and persuade the regulatory agency that its true cost curve is that shown as *ATC*(inflated) in Fig. 21.4, then the regulator, applying the normal rate of return principle, will regulate the price at 60¢ a ride. In this example, the price and quantity will be the same as those under unregulated monopoly. Though it might be impossible for firms to inflate their costs by as much as that shown in the figure, to the extent

Figure 21.4   Natural Monopoly: Inflating Costs

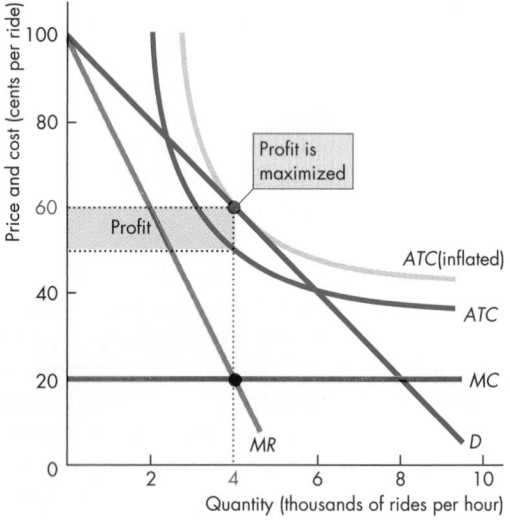

If the subway company is able to inflate its costs to *ATC*(inflated) and persuade the regulator that these are genuine minimum costs of production, rate of return regulation will result in a price of 60¢ a ride—the profit-maximizing price. To the extent that the producer can inflate costs above average total cost, the price will rise, output will fall, and deadweight loss will increase.

that costs can be inflated, the apparent average total cost curve lies somewhere between the true ATC curve and ATC(inflated). The greater the ability of the firm to pad its costs in this way, the closer its profit (measured in economic terms) approaches the maximum possible. The shareholders of this firm don't receive this economic profit. It gets used up by the managers of the firm on the self-serving activities that they have used to inflate the company's costs.

Public Interest or Capture?

It is not clear whether actual regulation produces prices and quantities that more closely correspond with the predictions of capture theory or with public interest theory. One thing is clear, however. Price regulation does not require natural monopolies to use the marginal cost pricing rule. If it did, most natural monopolies would make losses and receive hefty government subsidies to enable them to remain in business. But there are even exceptions to this conclusion. For example, many local telephone companies do appear to use marginal cost pricing for local phone calls. They cover their total cost by charging a flat fee each month for being connected to their telephone system but then permitting each call to be made at its marginal cost—zero or something very close to it.

A test of whether natural monopoly regulation is in the public interest or the interest of the producer is to examine the rates of return earned by regulated natural monopolies. If those rates of return are significantly higher than those in the rest of the economy, then, to some degree, the regulator may have been captured by the producer. If the rates of return in the regulated monopoly industries are similar to those in the rest of the economy, then we cannot tell, for sure, whether the regulator has been captured or not for we cannot know the extent to which costs have been inflated by the managers of the regulated firms.

Table 21.3 shows the rates of return in regulated natural monopolies as well as the economy's average rate of return. In the 1960s, rates of return in regulated natural monopolies were somewhat below the economy average; in the 1970s, those returns exceeded the economy average. Overall, the rates of return achieved by regulated natural monopolies are not very different from those in the rest of the economy.

We can conclude from these data either that natural monopoly regulation does, to some degree,

Table 21.3 Rates of Return in Regulated Natural Monopolies

	Years	
	1962–69	1970–77
Electricity	3.2	6.1
Gas	3.3	8.2
Railroad	5.1	7.2
Average of above	3.9	7.2
Economy average	6.6	5.1

Source: Paul W. MacAvoy, The Regulated Industries and the Economy (New York: W.W. Norton, 1979), 49–60.

serve the public interest, or that natural monopoly managers inflate their costs by amounts sufficiently large to disguise the fact that they have captured the regulator and that the public interest is not being served.

We've now examined the regulation of natural monopoly. Let's next turn to regulation in oligopolistic industries—to the regulation of cartels.

Cartel Regulation

A *cartel* is a collusive agreement among a number of firms designed to restrict output and achieve a higher profit for the members of the cartel. Cartels arise in oligopolistic industries. An oligopoly is an industry in which a small number of firms compete with each other. We studied oligopoly (and duopoly—two firms competing for a market) in Chapter 14. There we saw that if firms manage to collude and behave like a monopoly, they can set the same price and sell the same total quantity as a monopoly firm would. But we also discovered that in such a situation, each firm will be tempted to "cheat," increasing its own output and profit at the expense of the other firms. The result of such "cheating" on the collusive agreement is the unraveling of the monopoly equilibrium and the emergence of a competitive outcome with zero profit for producers. Such an outcome benefits consumers at the expense of producers.

Figure 21.5   Collusive Oligopoly

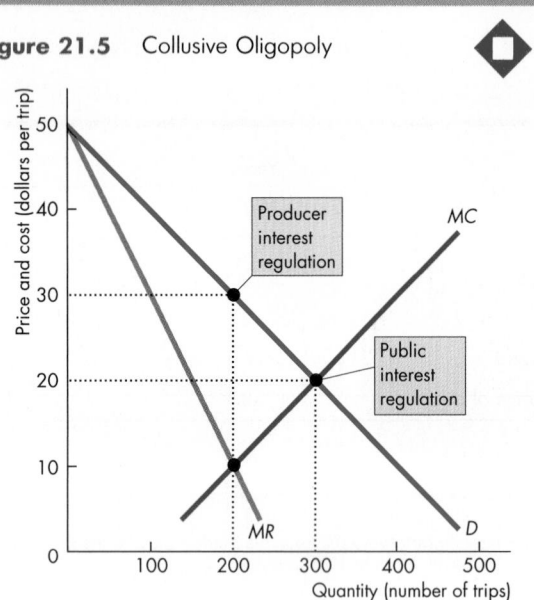

Ten trucking firms transport tomatoes from the San Joaquin valley to Los Angeles. The demand curve is *D* and the industry marginal cost curve is *MC*. Under competition, the *MC* curve is the industry supply curve. If the industry is competitive, the price of a trip will be $20 and 300 trips will be made each week. Producers will demand regulation that restricts entry and restricts the output of producers to 200 trips a week. This regulation will raise the price to $30 a trip and result in each producer making maximum profit —as if it is a monopoly. The industry marginal revenue will be equal to industry marginal cost.

How is oligopoly regulated? Does regulation prevent monopoly practices or does it encourage those practices?

According to the public interest theory, oligopoly is regulated to ensure a competitive outcome. Consider, for example, the market for trucking tomatoes from the San Joaquin valley to Los Angeles, illustrated in Fig. 21.5. The demand curve for trips is *D*. The industry marginal cost curve—and the competitive supply curve is *MC*. Public interest regulation will regulate the price of a trip at $20 and there will be 300 trips a week.

How would this industry be regulated according to the capture theory? Regulation that is in the producer interest will set the price at $30 a trip and, to ensure that that price is maintained, will restrict the number of trips to 200 a week. Each producer will make a maximum profit, and the industry marginal revenue will be equal to the industry marginal cost.

If there are 10 trucking companies, this outcome can be achieved by issuing a production quota to each trucking company restricting it to 20 trips a week so that the total number of trips in a week is 200. Penalities can be imposed to ensure that no single producer violates its quota.

What does regulation of oligopoly do in practice? Though there is disagreement about the matter, the consensus view is that regulation tends to favor the producer. Trucking (regulated by the Interstate Commerce Commission), taxicabs (regulated by cities), and airlines (regulated by the Civil Aeronautics Board) are all specific examples in which it has been calculated that increased profits have accrued to producers as a result of regulation. In some cases—and trucking is one of these—the work force, through unionization, also manages to take a large part of the total surplus.

Some further evidence in support of the conclusion that regulation sometimes increases profit is presented in Table 21.4. If regulation ensures a competitive outcome, rates of return in a regulated oligopoly will be no higher than those in the economy as a whole. As the numbers in Table 21.4 show, rates of return in airlines and trucking exceeded twice the economy average rate of return in the 1960s. In the 1970s, the rate of return in trucking remained higher than the economy average (although by a smaller margin than had prevailed in the 1960s). Airline rates of return in the 1970s fell to below the economy average. The overall picture that emerges from examining data on rates of return is mixed. The regulation of oligopoly does not always result in higher profit but there are many situations in which it does.

Further evidence on cartel and oligopoly regulation can be obtained from the performance of prices and profit following deregulation. If, following deregulation, prices and profit fall, then, to some degree, the regulation must have been serving the interest of the producer. In contrast, if, following deregulation, prices and profit remain constant, or increase, then the regulation may be presumed to have been serving the public interest. Since there has been a substantial amount of deregulation in recent years, we may use this test of oligopoly regulation to see which of the two theories better fits the facts. The evidence is mixed, but there are many cases in which deregulation has been accompanied by falling prices. Airlines, trucking, railroads, long-distance telephones, and banking and financial services are all industries in

Table 21.4   Rates of Return in Regulated Oligopolies

	Years	
	1962–69	1970–77
Airlines	12.8	3.0
Trucking	13.6	8.1
Economy average	6.6	5.1

Source: Paul W. MacAvoy, The Regulated Industries and the Economy (New York: W.W. Norton, 1979), 49–60.

which deregulation was, initially at least, associated with more competition, lower prices, and a large increase in the volume of transactions.

Interpreting the deregulation evidence, however, is made difficult by the possibility that firms in oligopoly industries will find other ways of restricting competition in a deregulated environment. There is evidence, for example, that the airlines managed to do this in the 1980s (see Reading Between the Lines, pp. 550–551.)

Making Predictions

Most industries have a few producers and many consumers. In these cases, public choice theory predicts that regulation will protect producer interests because a small number of people stand to gain a large amount and they would be fairly easy to organize as a cohesive lobby. Under such circumstances, politicians will be rewarded with campaign contributions rather than votes. But there are situations where the consumer interest is sufficiently strong and well organized and thus able to prevail. There are also cases in which the balance switches from producer to consumer, as seen in the deregulation process that began in the late 1970s.

Deregulation raises one of the hardest questions for economists seeking to understand and make predictions about regulation. Why has the transportation sector been deregulated? If the producers gained from regulation, and if the producer lobby was strong enough to achieve regulation, what happened in the late 1970s to change the equilibrium to one in which the consumer interest prevailed? We do not have a good and convincing answer to this question at the present time. One possibility—though it is an after-the-fact rationalization—is that regulation had become so costly to consumers, and the potential benefits to them from deregulation so great, that the cost of organizing the consumer voice became a cost worth paying. Furthermore, as communication technology improves, and the cost of communication falls, it is probable that the cost of organizing larger groups of individuals will also fall. If this line of reasoning is correct, we should expect to see more consumer-oriented regulation in the future. In practice, more consumer-oriented regulation means deregulation—removing the regulations that are already in place to serve the interests of producer groups.

There is another puzzling feature of the deregulation movement. Although the movement was begun by a Democratic administration (see "Talking with Alfred Kahn," which opens Part 7 on pp. 491–494), its major impetus in the 1980s has come not from the Ralph Nader consumer movement but from the Republican party and the business interests that it is perceived to support. If the regulator really has been captured and serves the interests of producers, why are producers the ones pressing hardest for deregulation? This is another question to which we don't know the answer.

Let's now leave regulation and turn to the other main method of intervention in markets—antitrust law.

Antitrust Law

Antitrust law provides an alternative way in which the government may influence the marketplace. As in the case of regulation, antitrust law can be formulated in the public interest, to maximize total surplus, or in private interests, to maximize the surpluses of particular special interest groups such as producers.

Landmark Antitrust Cases

The antitrust laws themselves are brief and easily summarized. The first antitrust law, the Sherman Act, was passed in 1890 in an atmosphere of outrage and disgust at the actions and practices of the "rob-

Airline Deregulation

Why Flying Is Unpleasant

Why are airline fares skyrocketing? Why is airline service going to the dogs? Why can't some pilots find the right runway or even the right airport? Why are some planes flying into the flight paths of others? The fashion is to blame deregulation and to search for a solution in some form of re-regulation.

This reflects both ignorance of history and an analytical failure to distinguish a disease from its symptoms. The problem lies not in deregulation but in the Reagan Administration's failure to enforce antitrust laws and build up safety regulation and oversight—all of which are needed for fair and constructive competition.

The initial results of the 1978 deregulation of routes, rates and entry were impressive: the number of scheduled carriers nearly tripled. Fares (in inflation-adjusted terms) fell 13 percent on average. The proportion of travelers flying on low-cost discount fares rose from 48 percent to 80 percent by 1982.

Productivity in the industry improved by an estimated 80 percent, with cumulative cost savings of possibly as much as $10 billion in the first several years. And air travel expanded at significantly higher annual rates, as larger numbers of people found it increasingly affordable.

Why, then, the current disenchantment? It is rooted in a profound misunderstanding of deregulation. Deregulation is not synonymous

with rambunctious, laissez-faire anarchy. If regulations barring entry to the industry are dropped and price regulation is abandoned, then they must be replaced with another regulatory mechanism—competition. And this requires that Government enforce antitrust laws so that competition is not subverted by unrestrained mergers and oligopolistic collusion.

Yet, the Reagan Administration has abandoned this responsibility. It has tolerated the most widespread merger and acquisition movement in the industry's history. In all, the Administration has countenanced 38 airline mergers and acquisitions, which have created a highly concentrated, noncompetitive industry. Once the USAir-Piedmont consolidation is completed, just eight carriers will collectively control 94 percent of the nation's airline business.

In regional markets, the impact of the absence of competition is clear. Before 1978, St. Louis was served by five airlines. While nine more carriers entered the St. Louis market after decontrol, their numbers quickly dwindled. Today, T.W.A. controls 82 percent of the city's air passenger traffic. The problem is replicated across the country. At 15 of the nation's largest airports (including Denver, Detroit, Houston, Minneapolis and Pittsburgh), either half of the business is now controlled by a single carrier or two carriers share more than 70 percent of the traffic.

The problems posed by the lack of competition have been exacerbated by a proliferation of anticompetitive practices among the airlines.

Computerized reservation systems—which are widely used by travel agents to book flights and are crucial to the ability of all carriers to compete—are dominated by two of the nation's biggest air carriers.

United's Apollo system and American Airlines' Sabre system together account for 70 percent of passenger revenues booked by travel agents nationwide. Control of these computerized systems has enabled the airlines to stifle competition in a number of ways: biasing screen displays by listing competitors' flights last, using information gained through the systems to unfair advantage and charging exorbitant rates for access to these key systems by other carriers.

Monopolization of airport terminal gates has further eroded competition. The airline oligopoly blocks potential competitors by tying up gates through exclusive long-term leases and by obstructing expansion plans by local airport authorities. In some cities, gates go unused because established carriers either refuse to lease them or demand astronomical rents. (Walter Adams is Professor of Economics at Michigan State University, and James W. Brock is Associate Professor of Economics at Miami University of Ohio.)

The New York Times, **August 6, 1987**

The Essence of the Story

- Domestic air travel was deregulated in 1978.

- In the past year or so, air fares have been rising and service quality falling.

- Deregulation is blamed for the recent developments in the airline industry.

- Deregulation is not the problem.

- Since 1978, the number of air carriers has tripled, fares have fallen, the proportion of discount fare travelers has risen, and larger numbers of people can afford air travel.

- The airline industry's problems arise from mergers and acquisitions that lower competition.

- Fifteen of the largest airports are served by one or two dominant carriers.

- There has been a proliferation of anticompetitive practices, including computerized reservation systems that manage information on flight schedules and availability and the monopolization of terminal facilities by long-term leases.

Background and Analysis

- The figure analyzes the market for air transportation out of one of the nation's 15 largest airports.

- If the airline industry were perfectly competitive, the price would be P_C and quantity Q_C, where the competitive supply curve (S) cuts the demand curve (D).

- If the industry were monopolized, the price would be P_M and the quantity traded Q_M. This quantity makes marginal revenue equal to marginal cost (the marginal cost curve is the supply curve, so MR equals S) and the price is the maximum price at which Q_M can be sold.

- When the airline industry was regulated, the price was above the competitive price, P_C. The airline industry regulation process had been "captured" by the producers and operated more in their favor than in the interests of the consumers.

- Deregulation injected competition into the industry and brought the price down toward its competitive level.

- More recently the industry has become increasingly monopolized. This monopoly movement has resulted partly from mergers and acquisitions reducing the number of competitors, and partly from the use of practices that restrict entry of new competition.

Conclusion

The conclusion is provided by the authors of the article:

" . . .Deregulation without competition does not serve the public interest. The competitive market is neither a self-perpetuating nor an immutable artifact of nature. If it is to perform its role as economic regulator, it must be protected from subversion, and that is the inescapable responsibility of government. It calls for strict antitrust enforcement, especially against oligopolistic mergers and market concentration . . ."

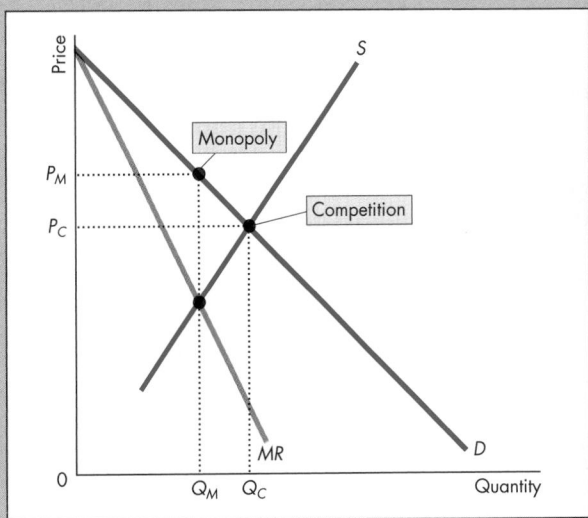

551

Table 21.5   Antitrust Laws

Name of law	Year passed	What the law prohibits
Sherman Act	1890	• Combination, trust, or conspiracy to restrict interstate or international trade
		• Monopolization, or attempt to monopolize interstate or international trade
Clayton Act	1914	• Price discrimination where effect is to substantially lessen competition or create monopoly and where such discrimination is not justified by cost differences
Robinson-Patman Amendment	1936	
Cellar-Kefauver Amendment	1950	
		• Contracts that force other goods to be bought from same firm
		• Acquisition of competitors' shares or assets if effect is to reduce competition
		• Interlocking directorships among competing firms
Federal Trade Commission Act	1914	• Unfair methods of competition and unfair or deceptive business practices

ber barons."[1] The most lurid stories of the actions of the robber barons are not of their monopolization and exploitation of consumers but of their sharp practices against each other. Nevertheless, monopolies did emerge—for example, the spectacular control of the oil industry by John D. Rockefeller. But once the Sherman Act was passed it had little effect until the early part of this century. Table 21.5 gives a summary of the main antitrust laws.

The real force of any law arises from its interpretation. Interpretation of the antitrust laws has ebbed and flowed. At times, it has appeared to favor producers and at other times consumers. Lets see how.

Table 21.6 summarizes the landmark antitrust cases. The first important cases were those of the American Tobacco Company and Standard Oil Com-

pany, decided in 1911. These two companies were found guilty of violations under the Sherman Act and ordered to divest themselves of large holdings in other companies. The breakup of John D. Rockefeller's Standard Oil Company resulted in the creation of many oil companies that today are household names—such as Exxon.

In finding these companies to be in violation of the provisions of the Sherman Act, the Supreme Court enunciated the "rule of reason." The rule of reason states that monopoly arising from mergers and agreements among firms is not necessarily illegal. Only if there is an unreasonable restraint of trade does the arrangement violate the provisions of the Sherman Act. The rule of reason was widely regarded as removing the force of the Sherman Act itself. This view was reinforced in 1920 when U.S. Steel was acquitted of violations under the act even though it had a very large (more than 50 percent) share of the U.S. steel market. Applying the "rule of reason," the court declared that "size alone is not an offense."

Matters remained much as they were in 1920 until 1940 when the *Socony-Vacuum Oil Company* case resulted in the first chink in the armor of the "rule of reason." The court found Socony-Vacuum Oil Company guilty because a combination had been formed for the purpose of price fixing. The court ruled that no consideration of reasonableness should be applied to such a case. Where the purpose of the agreement was price fixing, the automatic interpretation was to be that the agreement was unreasonable.

The "rule of reason" received its death blow in the *ALCOA* case, decided in 1945. ALCOA was judged to be in violation of the law because it was too big. It had too large a share of the aluminum market. A relatively tough interpretation of the law continued through the late 1960s. In 1961, General Electric, Westinghouse, and other electrical component manufacturers were found guilty of a price-fixing conspiracy. This case was the first one in which the executives (as opposed to the company itself) were fined and also jailed.

Tough antimerger decisions were taken in 1962 against Brown Shoe and in 1965 against Von's Grocery. In the first of these cases, Brown Shoe was required to divest itself of ownership of Kinney's—a shoe retail chain. This case is an example of the court ruling that a vertically integrated firm is capable of restraining competition. **Vertical integration** is the merger of two or more firms operating at different stages in a production process of a single good or

---

[1]Business practices of this era are discussed by Matthew Josephson, *The Robber Barons: The Great American Capitalists, 1861–1901* (New York: Harcourt Brace Jovanovich, 1934).

Table 21.6 Landmark Antitrust Cases

Case	Year	Verdict and consequence
American Tobacco Company	1911	*Guilty:* Ordered to divest themselves of large holdings in other companies; "rule of reason" enunciated—only *unreasonable* combinations guilty under Sherman Act.
Standard Oil Company	1911	
U.S. Steel Company	1920	*Not guilty:* Although U.S. Steel had a very large market share (near monopoly), mere "size alone is not an offense"; application of the "rule of reason."
Socony-Vacuum Oil Company	1940	*Guilty:* Combination was formed for purpose of price fixing; no consideration of "reasonableness" applied.
ALCOA	1945	*Guilty:* Too big—had too large a share of the market; end of "rule of reason."
General Electric, Westinghouse, and others	1961	*Guilty:* Price-fixing conspiracy; first time executives fined and jailed.
Brown Shoe	1962	*Guilty:* Ownership of Kinney, a retail chain, reduced competition; ordered to sell Kinney (Brown supplied 8% of Kinney's shoes and Kinney sold 2% of nation's shoes).
Von's Grocery	1965	*Guilty:* Merger of two supermarkets in Los Angeles would restrain competition (the merged firm would have had 7½% of the L.A. market).
IBM	1982	*Case dismissed* as being "without merit"; back to the "rule of reason"?
AT&T	1983	*Agreement* between AT&T and government that company would divest itself of all local telephone operating companies—80% of its assets.

service. For example, the merger of a firm that produces raw materials, a firm that converts those raw materials into a manufactured good, and a firm that retails the finished product will be a vertically integrated firm. The vertically integrated Brown Shoe and Kinney retail chain was ordered to be broken up even though Brown supplied only 8 percent of Kinney's shoes and Kinney sold only 2 percent of the nation's shoes.

Von's Grocery is an example of a horizontally integrated firm. **Horizontal integration** is a merger of two or more firms providing essentially the same product or service. In the *Von's Grocery* case, the court ruled that the combination of two supermarkets in Los Angeles would restrict competition even though the combined sales of the two firms would have been only 7.5 percent of total supermarket sales in the Los Angeles area.

The two most visible recent antitrust cases, and two cases that were settled in interesting ways, are those involving AT&T and IBM. Though important and highly visible cases, neither of the two was decided by the courts. The *AT&T* case was resolved by an agreement between AT&T and the Department of Justice, and the *IBM* case, after 13 years of litigation, was dismissed by the government as being "without merit."

The present attitude toward monopoly is pragmatic. AT&T's monopoly on telephone services has gone. IBM's position in the computer industry is much less secure and looks much less like a monopoly today than it did in 1967 when the Justice Department began its proceedings against that firm. Also, increased international competition has reduced the monopoly power of any particular firm or group of firms.

Regulating Long Distance Phone Rates

FCC Hopes New Regulations Will Cut Phone Rates—But Others Aren't So Sure

Since the breakup of the Bell System 3½ years ago, federal regulators have forced American Telephone & Telegraph Co. to cut long-distance rates a whopping 33.5%. But whether phone bills will go even lower under newly proposed regulation is a matter of heated debate.

Earlier this week, the Federal Communications Commission proposed removing its limit on AT&T's profits and replacing it with a price cap. FCC Chairman Dennis Patrick and AT&T executives contend that the company would have more incentive to cut costs, passing part of the savings to consumers, with the rest fattening AT&T's bottom line. Moreover, says Larry Garfinkel, an AT&T vice president, the company would be more inclined to put new technology in its network, which would generate new services.

But consumer groups are skeptical. "Based on what we know, rates go down more under profit regulation," says Fred Goldberg, the Washington counsel to the National Association of State Utility Consumer Advocates.

Monitoring Costs

Currently, AT&T's inter-state rates are set by limiting how much it can earn on its $9.1 billion investment in interstate plant and equipment. The allowed rate of return is now 12.2%. Under price regulation, the FCC would instead set a ceiling on what AT&T can charge. The ceiling would rise or fall depending on inflation, taxes, the industry's productivity, and AT&T's costs to connect to local phone companies.

The debate over which system is best centers in large part on how good the FCC is at monitoring AT&T's costs. Under profit regulation, prices should drop as technological advances reduce the company's costs. But if AT&T can keep its costs artificially high—and many people think it has—prices won't drop as fast as they could. One analyst estimates that AT&T could easily cut $2 billion of costs without affecting service.

AT&T denies it pads its costs, but acknowledges it doesn't have any incentive to cut them under profit regulation. "With price-cap regulation instead of rate-of-return, prices will go down more because we'll have the incentive to really try to be more effi-cient. We would pass some of that (savings) on to customers," says Wendell Lind, administrator of rates and tariffs for AT&T. But Mr. Goldberg says that even if AT&T does pad its costs, the current regulatory system still does a better job of ensuring that the industry's declining costs are reflected in lower rates than a price-cap approach would. FCC studies say phone rates overall have only doubled since 1935 while overall prices have risen eightfold. With price-caps tied to an inflation index, Mr. Goldberg fears the caps will effectively become price floors for future increases.

Price Cuts Since the Breakup

Percentage reductions in basic long-distance service costs since the AT&T break-up in January 1984:

May 1984	6.4
June 1985	5.6
June 1986	11.8
January 1987	11.4
July 1987	4.8

Wall Street Journal, August 6, 1987
By Janet Guyon, staff reporter
Reprinted by permission of *The WallStreet Journal*,
©Dow Jones & Company, Inc. 1987. All Rights Reserved.

The Essence of the Story

- The Bell System long-distance phone monopoly was broken in January 1984.

- Prices of long-distance phone calls fell steadily between January 1984 and August 1987.

- The long-distance phone industry is regulated by the Federal Communications Commission (FCC).

- Long-distance phone rates are regulated by allowing a maximum rate of return of 12.2 percent on capital (rate of return regulation).

- The FCC is proposing to replace rate of return regulation with a price cap—a maximum price that may be charged.

- The proposed change is controversial: Some argue that prices will be more effectively controlled by rate of return regulation than by a price cap.

Background and Analysis

Costs and Demand

- The figure analyzes AT&T's costs and demand under different regulations.

- D is the demand curve that AT&T faces.

- Average total cost, using existing technologies, is shown by the curve ATC (old). That curve is AT&T's average total cost curve including an allowed rate of return of 12.2 percent.

Rate of Return Regulation

- At the point where the average total cost curve ATC (old) cuts the demand curve at price P_1 and quantity Q_1, AT&T just makes its allowed rate of return. (Recall that the rate of return is included in the cost curve).

- Suppose that AT&T pads its costs so that they rise to the curve labeled PC for padded costs. (The padded curve is not a cost curve because a cost curve shows the minimum possible cost. Padding takes the firm off its cost curve.) With rate of return regulation, there will be

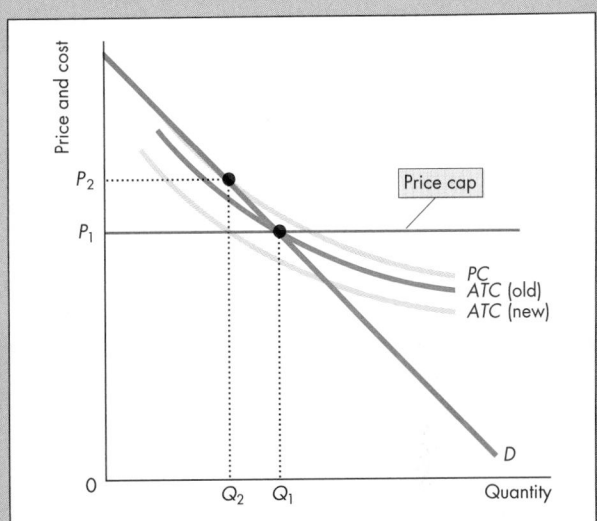

nothing to stop AT&T from raising the price to P_2 and cutting output to Q_2. Thus rate of return regulation does not provide an incentive for the producer to be economically efficient.

- Suppose that a new technology becomes available and results in costs falling to the curve labeled ATC (new). There is no incentive for AT&T to adopt the new technology because it can make its maximum permissible 12.2 percent return by using the existing technology, selling Q_1 phone calls for a price of P_1.

Price Cap

- Suppose that rate of return regulation is replaced by a price cap, with P_1 being the cap price. This regulation means that AT&T cannot charge a price higher than P_1.

- Under the price cap regulation, if AT&T produces Q_1 calls with the cost curve ATC (old), it will make exactly the same rate of return as under rate of return regulation.

- But there is now no incentive for AT&T to pad costs, for to do so will simply cause it to make losses.

(Continued on next page.)

Background and Analysis (cont.)

■ If a new technology becomes available, it pays AT&T to adopt it. If it can continue to charge P_1 and produce Q_1, it makes a higher profit—the difference between average total cost with the new technology and the cap price.

■ The theory is clear in its predictions: Rate of return regulation provides no incentive to minimize cost, while a price cap encourages cost minimization, though not necessarily ensuring that lower costs result in lower prices for consumers.

Empirical Issues

■ Though the theory makes clear predictions, experience has generated controversy.

■ In Maryland, AT&T has not been subject to rate of return regulation since mid-1986. The company made a profit of 125 percent in Maryland in the year ended March 31, 1987.*

■ After Maryland dropped rate of return regulation in mid-1986, "the cost of a 5-minute day time phone call within 100 miles dropped 27 percent."**

---

*John M. Glynn, Maryland Peoples' Council, *Wall Street Journal* (August 21, 1987).
**Wall Street Journal* (August 21, 1987).

Conclusion

■ As the *Wall Street Journal* reminds us, "It's always good to keep in mind that the folks who run consumerist organizations have a conflict with the very people they say they represent. If deregulation continues to grow in popularity with consumers, simple market competition will substitute for regulatory hearings. And when those hearing rooms are closed, consumerists will have to find other work. No wonder they are not happy with the FCC's latest proposal."†

---

†*Wall Street Journal* (August 21, 1987).

Public or Special Interest?

It is clear from the historical contexts in which antitrust law has evolved that its intent has been to protect and pursue the public interest and restrain the profit-seeking and anticompetitive actions of producers. But it is also clear from the above brief history of antitrust legislation and cases that from time to time the interest of the producer has had an influence on the way in which the law has been interpreted and applied. Nevertheless, the overall thrust of antitrust law appears to have been directed toward achieving allocative efficiency and, therefore, to serving the public interest.

It is interesting to note that there is an important difference between the way in which antitrust law and regulation are administered. Regulation is produced by a bureaucracy. Antitrust law is interpreted and enforced by the legal process—the courts. Economists are now beginning to extend theories of public choice to include an economic analysis of the law and the way the courts interpret the law. It is interesting to speculate that the legal institutions that administer antitrust law are more sensitive to the public interest than the political and bureaucratic institutions that deal with regulation.

The breakup of the AT&T monopoly is a strikingly good example of the consumer and public interest emerging and dominating that of the producer. The effects of the breakup and deregulation of long-distance telecommunications, while controversial, appear to have brought some visible benefits to consumers (see Reading Between the Lines, pp. 554–556.)

■ In this chapter, we've seen how the government intervenes in markets to affect prices, quantities, the gains from trade, and the division of those gains between consumers and producers when there is monopoly or oligopoly. We've seen that there is a conflict between the pursuit of the public interest—achieving allocative efficiency—and the pursuit of the special interests of producers—maximizing monopoly profit. The political and legal arenas are the places in which these conflicts are resolved. We've reviewed the two theories—public interest and capture—concerning the type and scope of government intervention.

S U M M A R Y

Market Intervention

There are two ways in which the government intervenes to regulate monopolistic and oligopolistic markets: regulation and antitrust law. In the United States, both of these methods are widely used. In studying regulation, we seek to understand the reasons for and the effects of regulation.

Government action can influence consumer surplus, producer surplus, and total surplus. Consumer surplus is the difference between what consumers are willing to pay for a given consumption level and what they actually pay. Producer surplus is the difference between a producer's revenue from sales and the opportunity cost of production. Total surplus is the sum of consumer surplus and producer surplus. Total surplus is maximized under competition. Under monopoly, producer surplus is increased and consumer surplus decreased, and a deadweight loss is created. (pp. 539–540)

The Economic Theory of Regulation

Consumers and producers express their demand for the regulation that influences their surpluses by voting, lobbying, and making campaign contributions. The larger the surplus that can be generated by a particular regulation and the smaller the number of people affected, the larger is the demand for that regulation. A smaller number of people are easier to organize into an effective political lobby. Regulation is supplied by politicians who pursue their own best interest. The larger the surplus per head generated and the larger the number of persons affected by it, the larger is the supply of regulation.

In equilibrium, the regulation that exists is such that no interest group feels it is worthwhile to employ scarce resources to press for further changes. There are two theories of political equilibrium: public interest theory and capture theory. Public interest theory predicts that total surplus will be maximized, thereby achieving allocative efficiency; capture theory predicts that producer surplus will be maximized. (pp. 540–542)

Regulation and Deregulation

Regulation began with the establishment of the Interstate Commerce Commission in 1887. A further expansion of regulation occurred in the 1930s. There was further steady growth of regulatory activity to the mid-1970s. Since 1978, the transportation, telecommunication, and financial sectors have been deregulated.

Regulation is conducted by regulatory agencies controlled by politically appointed bureaucrats and staffed by a permanent bureaucracy of experts. Regulated firms are required to comply with rules about price, product quality, and output levels. Two types of industries are regulated: natural monopolies and

cartels. In both cases, regulation has enabled firms in the regulated industries to achieve profit levels equal to or greater than those attained on the average in the rest of the economy. This outcome is closer to the predictions of the capture theory of regulation than to the predictions of the public interest theory. (pp. 542–549)

Antitrust Law

Antitrust law provides an alternative way in which the government can control monopoly and monopolistic practices. The law itself is brief and its interpretation has fluctuated between favoring the consumer and favoring the producer.

But the overall thrust of the law has been directed toward serving the public interest. In recent years, increased international competition has reduced monopoly power. (pp. 549–557)

KEY CONCEPTS

Key Figures and Tables

REVIEW QUESTIONS

1 What are the two main ways in which the government can intervene in the marketplace?

2 What is consumer surplus? How is it calculated and how is it represented in a diagram?

3 What is producer surplus? How is it calculated and how is it represented in a diagram?

4 What is total surplus? How is it calculated and how is it represented in a diagram?

5 Why do consumers demand regulation? In what kinds of industries are their demands for regulation greatest?

6 Why do producers demand regulation? In what kinds of industries are their demands for regulation greatest?

7 Explain the public interest and capture theories of the supply of regulation. What does each theory imply about the behavior of politicians?

8 How is oligopoly regulated in the United States? In whose interest is it regulated?

9 What are the main antitrust laws in force in the United States today?

10 What is the "rule of reason"? When was this rule formulated? How has it been applied? When was it abandoned?

P R O B L E M S

1 Cascade Springs, Inc., is a natural monopoly that bottles water from a natural spring high in the Grand Tetons. The total fixed cost incurred by Cascade Springs is $80,000 and its marginal cost is 10¢ a bottle. The demand for bottled water from Cascade Springs is as follows:

Price (cents per bottle)	Quantity demanded (thousands of bottles per year)
100	0
90	100
80	200
70	300
60	400
50	500
40	600
30	700
20	800
10	900
0	1000

What is the price of a bottle of water and how many bottles does Cascade Springs sell?

2 Does Cascade Springs maximize total surplus or producer surplus?

3 If the government regulates Cascade Springs by imposing a marginal cost pricing rule, what is the price of a bottle of water and how many bottles will Cascade Springs sell?

4 Is the regulation in problem 3 in the public interest or in the private interest?

5 If the government regulates Cascade Springs by imposing an average cost pricing rule, what is the price of a bottle of water and how many bottles does Cascade Springs sell?

6 Is the regulation in problem 5 in the public interest or in the private interest?

7 Compare consumer surplus in problem 3 with that in problem 5. Which situatin has the larger consumer surplus?

Part 8

Talking
with
James
Tobin

James Tobin has had a long and distinguished career in macroeconomics, extending the model suggested by Keynes, paying special attention to the demand for money, consumption and saving, fiscal and monetary policy, and economic growth. For most of his career, he has been at Yale University. He was a member of President John F. Kennedy's Council of Economic Advisers. For his many contributions, James Tobin received the Nobel Prize in economic science in 1981. Michael Parkin spoke with Professor Tobin about the challenges that face the economy.

Professor Tobin, you were a young boy dur- *ing the Great Depression. Do you remember that period as a time of great hardship?*

Not of personal hardship, although my grandfather lost his job and his entire fortune when the bank of which he was president went under, and my father suffered serious losses when creditors took over the office building he had constructed in 1929. My father was a journalist at the University of Illinois. In 1932, my mother became the head of the local Family Service agency. Her job kept us aware of the ravages of the Depression. Our hometown, Champaign, Illinois, was on the main rail line. Many poor people from the South, hoping for jobs and better lives in the North,

"Today, if I have to be labeled—and considering the alternatives—I'm proud to be a Keynesian."

got off the train in Champaign.

When did you first study economics?

As a Harvard sophomore in 1936. We met weekly with a tutor and discussed what we were reading or writing. My tutor was also my introductory economics teacher. He had just come back from a year in England, where he had heard a lot about a new book by John Maynard Keynes. He suggested that we read it. I was too green to understand that it was absurd for a sophomore to tackle *The General Theory of Employment, Interest, and Money*. So I plunged into it and got very excited about the book and about economics.

People usually refer to you as a Keynesian macroeconomist. Do you agree with that term?

I don't like labeling. I tried to contribute to economics, especially to macroeconomics. I tried to strengthen what we now call the microfoundations of macroeconomics. In the 1950s and 1960s we hoped that the Keynesian-Neoclassical controversy would soon be behind us, superseded by a synthesis of the two strands. Beginning with my first published article in 1940, which disagreed with Keynes about the relation between wages and employment, I wrote many pieces critical of *The General Theory*. Unfortunately, the old debates have been revived and magnified over the past two decades and we are far from

a new synthesis. Today, if I have to be labeled—and considering the alternatives—I'm proud to be a Keynesian.

How would you characterize the controversy in macroeconomics? Has it stayed the same over the years, or is it different today?

The original controversy in the 1930s and 1940s was whether a capitalist market economy possesses reliable automatic mechanisms of adjustment, which would restore equilibrium between jobs and workers and between output and capacity whenever some shock to demand pushes the economy from full employment. Orthodox economists—Keynes called them Classical—said yes. Keynes said no. Today's New Classical macroeconomists are more extreme than their old Classical predecessors. They assert that the economy is *always* in full employment equilibrium. That the economy as a whole operates like a rational maximizing individual. Keynesians believe the economy can fall out of equilibrium and that government interventions can speed up recoveries.

Given that macroeconomists still have impor-

tant disagreements, can they use any of the same approaches? Might a Keynesian, for instance, use the idea of rational expectations, which is identified with the New Classical school?

Thoughtful economists of all sorts have long incorporated rational expectations in their models, to a limited degree. They would not postulate a stable, repetitive equilibrium that depended on expectations at odds with the actual values of variables. For example, if the interest rate is 2 percent year after year, people would surely learn not to act on the expectation that it will become 4 percent. But I think it stretches credibility to assume that ordinary business people and consumers can learn to form rational expectations in volatile economic environments whose structures even econometricians cannot discern.

I think rational expectations of quantities like output and employment could have a place in Keynesian models. Those are important variables

once the New Classical assumption that markets are always clearing is abandoned.

Many economists regard the macroeconomic performance of the early 1960s as a very successful period of moderate inflation, low unemployment, and strong growth in real output. Was that the high point of macroeconomic management from which we've been sliding ever since?

Yes. I suppose I have a vested interest in believing that to be true—I helped to inaugurate the policy in 1961. And it was a pleasant period, when economists and policymakers were not as divided and combative as they are now. At the beginning of the Kennedy administration, unemployment was 7 percent, considered unacceptably high in those days. Inflation was only 1 or 2 percent, thanks in good part to the two recent Eisenhower recessions. We economists

pushed for stimulative fiscal policy. We got some, but it took some time to bring President Kennedy and Congress to accept a major initiative. We were lucky when what looked like a hesitation in the recovery before our policies were firmly in place turned out to be temporary. The administration pursued a wage-price guidepost policy, seeking to get management and labor to agree to noninflationary wage settlements and price decisions. By 1966 unemployment was down to 4 percent and inflation was still around 2 percent.

Were all the breaks good ones? Was there any bad luck?

The bad luck was the Vietnam War. Despite the advice of his Keynesian economists, President Johnson would not ask for a tax increase to finance his escalation of the war in 1966. His budget overheated the economy in the late 1960s. Unemployment fell to 3 percent, and in-

"It was a pleasant period, when economists and policy makers were not as divided as they are now."

flation rose to 4 or 5 percent. At the time 5 percent inflation was considered very serious, bad enough to induce President Nixon to introduce price controls. Today 5 percent is accepted as "zero" inflation, a reminder that attitudes are relative.

What have we learned from the events of the 1970's?

Maybe what we should have learned is that those events were exceptional. There were two enormous shocks in oil and energy prices. A major increase in an important price raises the price index, but OPEC price shocks don't happen every year and shouldn't be incorporated into projections of overall inflation. What it was proper to worry about was the inflation potential of wage increases seeking to catch up with the increases in energy prices. The 1980s indicate that under normal circumstances, we experience less severe inflation.

We've just experienced seven years of economic recovery. How did economic policy contribute?

I give the Federal Reserve high marks for monetary policy since 1982. From October 1979 until 1982, the

Fed was very monetarist. The overriding priority was to rid the economy of the temporary double-digit inflation that accompanied the second oil shock. Restrictive monetary policy and recession did bring it down to about 5 percent. The strategy worked faster than I had expected—though not so fast as the optimists were suggesting. By 1982, unemployment reached its highest level since the Depression.

In 1982, Paul Volcker, the chairman of the Fed, turned both his policy and the economy around. Monetarism was displaced by concern for macroeconomic performance. The Fed fine-tuned the recovery, reducing unemployment as long as no new inflation threatened. By 1989 unemployment was down to 5 percent, lower than the Fed and most economists thought "inflation-safe" 10 years earlier.

Fiscal policy in the 1980s has been a radical departure from any previous federal administration in peacetime. The tremendous reduction in taxes in 1981 along with the expansion of defense spending generated a series of deficits that raised federal public debt from 25 to 43 percent of GNP over the eight years of the Reagan presidency.

Reagan's fiscal policy was a massive demand stimulus. The Fed had to worry about whether it would overheat the economy. It was like having two drivers in the same car. The fiscal driver had a heavy foot on the gas pedal. The monetary driver had to keep a foot on the brake. As I said, the Fed fine-tuned the brake quite well. But the by-products of this bizarre combination of policies have been disastrous—high interest rates, low capital investment, enormous trade deficits, threatening the living standards of future Americans.

What economic principles would you share with students?

First, opportunity cost—a simple, fruitful concept. Students can learn it; most people innocent of economics don't understand it. Second, fungibility—"money mingles," a friend of mine liked to say. You can give people money, ostensibly for your own purpose, but the recipients will generally find a way to accommodate their own priorities. Third, economics students who understand the macro identities—for example, $Y = C + I + G + NX$—know more than most politicians and journalists.

"Students who understand the macro identities know more than most politicians and journalists."

Chapter 22

Inflation, Unemployment, Cycles, and Deficits

After studying this chapter, you will be able to:

- Define inflation and explain its effects

- Define unemployment and explain its benefits and costs

- Define gross national product (GNP)

- Distinguish between nominal GNP and real GNP

- Explain the importance of increases and fluctuations in real GNP

- Define the business cycle

- Describe how unemployment, stock prices, and inflation fluctuate over the business cycle

- Define the government budget deficit and the country's current account deficit

A shopping cart of groceries that today costs $80 cost only $50 in 1980, $25 in 1970, and $15 in 1950. In fact, for the past 50 years, there has hardly been a single year in which prices have not increased. The same is true of wages. An average hour of work, in 1950, earned $1.34. The same average hour earned $3.23 in 1970 and $6.66 in 1980. Today, it earns more than $10. This persistent increase in prices and wages means that firms need more dollars to pay us and we need more dollars to buy the goods and services that we consume. But does this matter? What are the effects of persistently rising prices and wages? ■ In 1988, for every 15 people with jobs, one other person was unemployed—was looking for work but

Shopping Cart Blues

could not find it. Another unknown percentage of people had become discouraged about their chances of finding jobs and had stopped looking. Although unemployment has been unusually high through most of the 1980s, its rate was modest compared with the 1930s—the years of the Great Depression. In that earlier period, one fifth of the labor force was unemployed for several years and one quarter of the labor force was unemployed in the worst year, 1933. Unemployment fluctuates but it never disappears. And yet we do talk about "full employment." How can there be "full employment" when there are people looking for work? Why is there always some unemployment? What is the cost of unemployment? And does it bring any benefits? ■ At the depths of the Great Depression, in 1933, the value of the total output of the nation was $56 billion. By 1988, 55 years later, the value of the nation's output was approaching $5 trillion (a ninetyfold increase over its 1933 level). From 1960 to 1989, the nation's output has increased tenfold in value. How much of the growth in the value of our output is real and how much of it is an illusion created by inflation? ■ Our economy does not follow a smooth and predictable course. From 1982 to 1987, the economy was on a course of sustained expansion: production grew, unemployment fell, stock prices rose, and inflation was modest. Then, in October 1987, the stock market crashed. Overnight, millions of people found themselves poorer by billions of dollars. But the economy kept on expanding. Production continued to grow and unemployment held steady. Expansions as strong and prolonged as that of the 1980s are unusual. Periods of expansion are usually punctuated by periods of contraction, and sometimes severe ones. For example, 1975 and 1982 were such times. In those years, production sagged and unemployment climbed. We call these waves of expansion and contraction business cycles. Which features of business cycles are similar from one cycle to another and which are different? Does the economy normally keep booming when the stock market crashes as it did in 1987? Or do stock market crashes sometimes signal an upcoming contraction? ■ We hear a lot these days about deficits. One of these deficits is the government's. Ever since 1980, both the U.S. federal government and the total government sector (the federal government plus state and local governments) have spent more than they have raised in taxes. To make up the difference, the government borrows. Some of that borrowing is domestic and some international. Just how big is the government's deficit? Has it been getting bigger? And is it unusual for the government to have a deficit? ■ The other deficit that we hear a lot about is our international deficit—the difference between the value of the goods and services we sell to the rest of the world and the value of our own purchases. That deficit reached almost 4 cents on every dollar that we earned in 1988. What happens when we spend more in the rest of the world than we earn? How do we make up the difference? And what are the consequences?

■ The questions that we have just posed are the subject matter of macroeconomics—that branch of economics that seeks to understand the problems of rising prices, high unemployment, fluctuating output, and government and international payments deficits. It also studies the government's attempts to cope with these problems. ■ The macroeconomic events through which we are now living are as exciting and tumultuous as any in history. Governments here and around the world face a daily challenge to find policies that will give all of us a smoother macroeconomic ride. ■ With what you learn in these chapters, you will be better able to understand these macroeconomic policy challenges and the political debate that surrounds them. We begin our study of macroeconomics by looking at inflation.

Inflation

Inflation is an upward movement in the average level of prices. Its opposite is **deflation,** a downward movement in the average level of prices. The boundary between inflation and deflation is price stability. **Price stability** occurs when the average level of prices is moving neither up nor down. The average level of prices is called the **price level** and is measured by a price index. A **price index** measures the average level of prices in one period as a percentage of their average level in an earlier period called the **base period.**

U.S. price indexes that go all the way back to 1820 have been compiled, and the story they tell is shown in Fig. 22.1. Over the roughly 170-year period shown in that figure, prices have risen almost nineteen-fold—an average annual rate of increase of 1.76 percent. But prices have not moved upward at a constant and steady pace. In some periods, such as the Civil War, World War I, and World War II, the increase was sharp and pronounced—at times exceeding 20 percent a year. In other periods, such as the 1960s and 1970s, the increase was prolonged and steady. At yet other times there have also been periods of falling prices—in the 1840s, following the Civil War, and during the Great Depression.

The Inflation Rate and the Price Level

The **inflation rate** is the percentage change in the price level. The formula for the annual inflation rate is

$$\text{Inflation rate} = \frac{\text{Current year's price level} - \text{Last year's price level}}{\text{Last year's price level}} \times 100$$

A common price index (that we'll learn more about in Chapter 23) is called the *Consumer Price Index* or simply the CPI. We can illustrate the calculation of the annual inflation rate by using this index.

Figure 22.1   The Price Level: 1820–1988

Prices, on the average, have increased nineteenfold between 1820 and 1988. In some periods, such as the Civil War and both world wars, price increases were rapid. In other periods, such as the 1970s, a period of sustained increases occurred. At yet other times, such as the years following the Civil War and during the Great Depression, prices fell.

Sources: Cost-of-living index compiled by the Federal Reserve Bank of New York, *Historical Statistics* (1960), Series E-157; Consumer Price Index, *Historical Statistics* (1960), Series E-113; and *Economic Report of the President* (1989).

In December 1987, the CPI was 105.9. In December 1988, it was 110.0. The inflation rate for 1988 is calculated using the above formula:

$$\text{Inflation rate} = \frac{110.0 - 105.9}{105.9} \times 100$$
$$= 3.9 \text{ percent}$$

The Recent Inflation Record

Recent U.S. economic history has seen some dramatic changes in the rate of inflation. The inflation rate between 1960 and 1988, as measured by the CPI, is shown in Fig. 22.2.

As you can see, the inflation rate in the early 1960s was very low, lying between 1 and 2 percent a year. The inflation rate is also relatively low today. But the 20 years between 1965 and 1985 saw some dramatic changes in inflation, which reached a peak rate of more than 13 percent a year in 1980. Between the late 1960s and 1980, inflation was on a strong upward trend. Also there have been distinct cycles in the inflation rate with peaks in 1970, 1974, and 1980, and troughs in 1972, 1976, 1983, and 1986.

Although the inflation rate has gone up and down over the years, since 1955 the price level has never fallen. The inflation rate has fallen from time to time but the price level (see Fig. 22.1 again) has increased relentlessly, year after year. The price level falls only when the inflation rate is negative, or less than zero. There has never been such a year in the period since 1955. Thus even in years like 1960 and 1987 when the inflation rate was low, the price level was rising.

Inflation and the Value of Money

When inflation is present, money is losing value. The **value of money** is the amount of goods and services that can be bought with a given amount of money. When an economy experiences inflation, the value of money falls. In other words, you cannot buy as many groceries with $50 this year as you could last year. The rate at which the value of money falls is equal to the inflation rate. When the inflation rate is high, as it was in 1980, money loses its value at a rapid pace. When inflation is low, as it was in 1961, the value of money falls slowly.

Figure 22.2   Inflation: 1960–1988

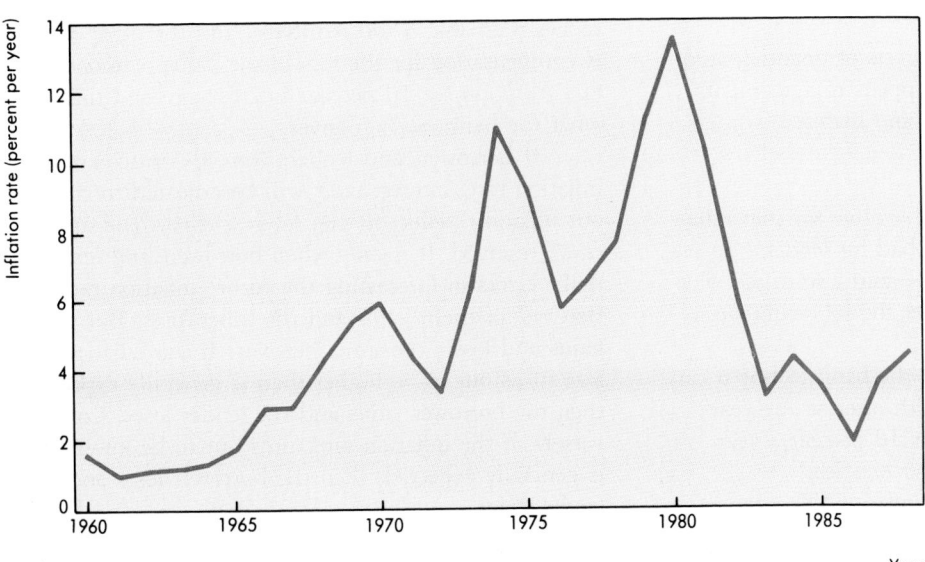

Inflation is a persistent feature of modern economic life in the United States. The inflation rate was low in the first half of the 1960s but then moved upward until 1980. After 1980, it fell dramatically. Inflation has followed a series of cycles, with peaks in 1970, 1974, and 1980 and troughs in 1972, 1976, 1983, and 1986.

Source: Historical Statistics (1960), Series E-113, and Economic Report of the President (1989).

Inflation is a phenomenon experienced in all countries. But inflation *rates* vary from one country to another. When inflation rates differ by a lot and over a prolonged period of time, the result is a change in the foreign exchange value of money. **A foreign exchange rate** is the rate at which one money exchanges for another money. For example, in January 1989, one U.S. dollar exchanged for 130 Japanese yen. The value of the U.S. dollar, in terms of the Japanese yen, has gradually fallen over recent years because our inflation rate has been somewhat higher than that in Japan. But the U.S. dollar has gained in value against such currencies as the British pound, since inflation in the United Kingdom has exceeded that here. We'll learn more about exchange rates and how they're influenced by inflation in Chapter 36.

Is Inflation a Problem?

Is it a problem if money loses its value and loses it at a rate that varies from one year to another? It is, indeed, a problem but to understand why, we need to distinguish between anticipated and unanticipated inflation. When prices are moving upward, most people are aware of that fact. They also have some notion about the rate at which they are rising. The rate at

which people (on the average) believe that the price level is rising is called the **expected inflation rate.** But expectations may be right or wrong. If they turn out to be right, the actual inflation rate equals the expected inflation rate and inflation is said to be anticipated. That is, an **anticipated inflation** is an inflation rate that has been correctly forecasted (on the average). To the extent that the inflation rate is misforecasted, it is said to be unanticipated. That is, **unanticipated inflation** is the part of the inflation rate that has caught people by surprise.

The problems arising from inflation differ depending on whether its rate is anticipated or unanticipated. Let's begin by looking at the problems arising from unanticipated inflation.

**The Problem of
Unanticipated Inflation**

Unanticipated inflation is a problem because it produces unanticipated changes in the value of money. Money is used as a measuring rod of the value in the transactions that we undertake. Borrowers and lenders, workers and their employers all make contracts in terms of money. If the value of money varies, then the amounts *really* paid and received differ from those that people intended to pay and receive when the contract was signed. Measuring value with a measuring rod whose units vary is a bit like trying to measure a piece of cloth with an elastic ruler. The size of the cloth depends on how tightly the ruler is stretched.

Let's take a look at the effects of unanticipated inflation by looking at what happens to agreements between borrowers and lenders and between workers and employers.

Borrowers and Lenders   People often say that inflation is good for borrowers and bad for lenders. To see how that conclusion is reached—and also to see why it's not always correct—consider the following situation.

Sue borrows $5000 from the bank to buy a car and agrees to repay the loan with interest one year later. The agreed interest rate is 10 percent a year. Sue repays the bank $5500 after one year.

Suppose that there is no inflation. The goods and services that can be bought with $5000 are the same after one year as they are when Sue borrows the money. In this situation, to pay the bank $500 in interest, Sue has to forgo the consumption of $500 worth of goods and services.

Now, in contrast, suppose that the economy is experiencing inflation at a rate of 10 percent a year. In this case, when the loan is repaid with interest, although the bank receives $5500, the quantity of goods and services that it can buy with that money is exactly what it could have bought with $5000 a year earlier. (With a 10 percent inflation rate, the price of a car, for example, will have risen from $5000 to $5500.) As far as Sue is concerned, although she pays the bank $500 in interest, that payment does not impose an opportunity cost on her. Over the year, the value of money has fallen. The $5000 that she borrowed is now worth only $4500 in terms of goods and services. This fall in the value of money cancels out the interest payment and leaves her having *really* paid no interest at all. Sue, the borrower, gains at the expense of the bank, the lender.

But the borrower does not always necessarily gain and the lender lose when there is inflation. Suppose that both Sue and the bank anticipate a 10 percent inflation rate. They can act to offset the decreasing value of money by adjusting the interest rate that they agree upon. In this particular case, if they agree that 10 percent is the appropriate interest rate with no inflation, they will agree to a 20 percent interest rate when they expect a 10 percent inflation rate. Let's see what happens in this case.

Sue repays the bank $6000 at the end of the year. (Of this, $5000 is the repayment of the amount borrowed and $1000 is the interest payment—20 percent of $5000.) Of the additional $1000 that Sue repays the bank, $500 is interest and the other $500 is compensation for the loss in the value of money. Sue *really* pays a 10 percent interest rate and that's what the bank *really* receives.

If borrowers and lenders correctly anticipate the inflation rate, interest rates will be adjusted to cancel out inflation's effect on the interest *really* paid and *really* received. It is only when borrowers and lenders make errors in forecasting the future inflation rate that one of them gains and the other loses. But those gains and losses can go either way. If the inflation rate turns out to be higher than is generally expected, then the borrower gains and the lender loses. Conversely, if the inflation rate turns out to be lower than is generally expected, then the borrower loses and the lender gains.

Thus it is not inflation itself that produces gains and losses for borrowers and lenders. It is an *unanticipated increase* in the *inflation rate* that *benefits borrowers* and hurts lenders and an *unanticipated decrease* in the *inflation rate* that *benefits lenders* and hurts borrowers.

In the United States in the late 1960s and 1970s, the inflation rate kept rising and to some de--gree the rise was unanticipated, so borrowers tended to gain. In the 1980s, the fall in the inflation rate was also, at least initially, unanticipated and lenders gained. On the international scene, many developing countries, such as Mexico and Brazil, borrowed large amounts of money in the late 1970s and early 1980s at high interest rates in anticipation that an inflation rate above 10 percent a year would persist. These countries are now stuck with paying the interest on these loans without the extra revenue that they expected to receive from higher prices for their exports.

Workers and Employers   Another common belief is that inflation redistributes income between workers and their employers. Some people believe that workers gain at the expense of employers and others believe the contrary.

The previous discussion concerning borrowers and lenders applies to workers and their employers as well. If inflation increases unexpectedly, then wages will not have been set high enough. Profits will be higher than expected and wages will buy fewer goods than expected. Employers gain at the expense of workers. Conversely, if the anticipated inflation rate is higher than what the actual inflation rate turns out to be, wages will have been set too high and profits will be squeezed. Workers will be able to buy more with their income than was originally anticipated. In this case, workers gain at the expense of employers.

In recent experience in the United States, unanticipated changes in the inflation rate have produced fluctuations in the buying power of earnings—that is, in the value of paychecks in terms of the goods they buy. For example, in 1974 when the inflation rate climbed to more than 10 percent a year, the buying power of earnings fell by more than 3 percent. In 1980, when the inflation rate rose to 13 percent a year, the buying power of earnings fell by almost 5 percent. These two episodes of higher inflation were largely unanticipated. The *fall* in the inflation rate in 1982 was also to some degree unanticipated and brought a corresponding *rise* in the buying power of earnings.

We've now seen the problems that unanticipated inflation can bring. Let's now turn to anticipated inflation.

The Problem of Anticipated Inflation

Anticipated inflation can be a problem for two reasons. First, it imposes an opportunity cost on holding money. Second, it encourages a wasteful increase in the volume and frequency of transactions that people undertake. Let's explore these two propositions more closely.

Opportunity Cost of Holding Money Whether you hold money in the form of notes and coins in your purse or in the form of a deposit at the bank, the opportunity cost of holding money equals the inflation rate. To make this idea clearer, compare two situations: In the first, inflation is 10 percent a year and you have $100 in the bank. At the end of the year, you still have $100 in the bank but it now buys goods that were worth only $90 at the beginning of the year. In the second situation, there is no inflation and again, you have $100 in the bank at the beginning of the year. At the end of the year, the bank charges you $10 (a 10 percent fee) on bank deposits. Now you have $90 and so, again, you can buy only $90 worth of goods.

From your point of view the two situations just described are identical. Either way you wind up at the end of the year being able to buy only $90 worth

of goods. An inflation rate of 10 percent a year reduces the value of your money by the same amount as a 10 percent fee on money holdings would. So the inflation rate is the opportunity cost of holding money. The higher the inflation rate, the greater is the opportunity cost of holding money.

Volume and Frequency of Transactions Since the inflation rate is the opportunity cost of holding money, anticipated inflation is the anticipated opportunity cost of holding money. People can avoid an anticipated cost of holding money only by economizing on the amount of money that they hold. For example, if the inflation rate is 10 percent a year and if, on the average, you keep $100 in your purse, then the opportunity cost of holding that money is $10 a year. If you hold less money—say $10 on the average—then the opportunity cost is lower—in this case, $1 a year.

But it's not easy to vary the amount of money that we hold. To do so, we have to vary the frequency with which we are paid and with which we do our shopping. For example, suppose that you have a job that pays $100 a week. If you are paid once a week and you spend all your income pretty evenly over the week, the amount of money that you hold, on the average, is $50. (You have $100 at the beginning of the week and nothing at the end of the week, averaging out at $50.) If you are paid once a month, you will have $400 on payday, nothing just before the next payday, and $200 on the average. If you are paid daily (in a five-day week) you are paid $20 a day and, on the average, you have $10 in your pocket.

Transacting at a high frequency is much less convenient and more costly than transacting at a lower frequency. But the higher the anticipated inflation, the higher is the frequency with which transactions are undertaken. This aspect of the problem of anticipated inflation is not very serious for inflation rates in the range that we have experienced in the United States. But it can be serious if the inflation rate is sufficiently high. For example, during hyperinflations (hyperinflation being a situation in which prices are rising faster than 50 percent per month), the opportunity cost of holding money is enormous. To avoid holding money that is losing its value at a rapid pace, people transact with incredibly high frequency. Firms pay out wages twice a day and as soon as they have been paid, people go off and spend their wages before they lose too much value. To buy a handful of groceries, you need a shopping cart of bank notes. Such situations are rare but they are not unknown. In Germany, Poland, and Hungary in the 1920s, the picture just painted was a reality. People who lingered too long in the coffee shop found that the price of their cup of coffee had increased between the time they placed their order and when the bill was presented.

Indexing

It is sometimes suggested that the costs of inflation can be avoided by indexing. **Indexing** is a technique that links payments made under a contract to the price level. With indexing, Sue in our example above would not agree to pay back the car loan in terms of a set number of dollars; instead, she would agree to an indexing formula for calculating the number of dollars to pay. Similarly, with indexed wages a wage contract does not specify the number of dollars that will be paid to workers; instead, it specifies an indexing formula for calculating the number of dollars. These formulas take into account the inflation rate. The amount of interest to be paid on bank deposits can also be linked to the inflation rate in order to avoid the opportunity cost of holding such deposits. Indexing is thought likely to be most important in preserving the buying power of pensions. Indexing is also used to limit the effects of inflation on long-term loans that people take to buy a home.

Adopting indexing to cope with changes in the value of money is not a simple matter for, as we will see in Chapter 23, there isn't just one unique measure of the price level and, therefore, of the inflation rate. If borrowers and lenders and workers and employers are to index their contracts, they have to agree on the price index to be used to measure the inflation rate. Such agreements are hard to reach and increase the cost of engaging in transactions.

Though indexing can be helpful in some situations, it is not a universal solution to the problem of fluctuations in the value of money. Only by somehow holding the price level constant can the costs of inflation be avoided.

Unemployment

At many times in the history of the United States, unemployment has been a severe problem. For example, in the early 1980s more than 10 million people were seeking jobs. What exactly is unemployment? How is it measured? How has its rate fluctuated? Does it have any benefits? What are its costs?

What Is Unemployment?

Employment is measured as the number of adult workers (aged 16 and over) who have jobs. **Unemployment** is the number of adult workers who are not employed and are seeking jobs. To be classified as unemployed, a person must be able and willing to work, be actively seeking work, and be without a job. Everyone who fits this description is unemployed. The **labor force** is the total number of employed and unemployed workers. The **unemployment rate** is unemployment expressed as a percentage of the labor force.

Measuring Unemployment

Unemployment is measured in the United States every month. The Bureau of Labor Statistics in the U.S. Department of Labor calculates the monthly unemployment figures and publishes them in *Employment and Earnings.* These unemployment figures are based on a survey of households called the Current Population Survey.

To be counted as unemployed in the Current Population Survey, a person must be available for work and must be in one of three categories:

1 Without work, but has made specific efforts to find a job within the previous four weeks

2 Waiting to be called back to a job from which he or she has been laid off

3 Waiting to start a new job within 30 days

Anyone surveyed who satisfies one of these three criteria is counted as unemployed. Part-time workers are counted as being employed.

There are three reasons why the unemployment level as measured by the Current Population Survey may be misleading. Let's examine these.

Unrealistic Wage Expectations   If someone is willing to work but only for a much higher wage than what is available, then it does not make sense to count that person as being unemployed. That is, if someone says that he or she is willing to work at McDonald's but only for $25 an hour, then that person is not really available for work and, therefore, is not really unemployed.

Figure 22.3   Unemployment: 1900–1988

Unemployment is a persistent feature of economic life, but its rate varies considerably. At its worst—during the Great Depression—25 percent of the labor force was unemployed. Even in recent recessions (the OPEC recession of 1975 and the Volcker recession of 1982), unemployment climbed toward the 10 percent mark. Between the late 1960s and 1982, there was a general tendency for unemployment to increase. The rate has fallen between 1983 and 1988.

Sources: Unemployment 1900–1946, *Historical Statistics* (1960), Series D-46. Unemployment 1946–1988, *Economic Report of the President* (1989).

Correcting the unemployment data to take account of wage and job expectations would result in a lower measured rate of unemployment. How much lower we do not know. A second factor works in the opposite direction.

Discouraged Workers   Many people who still fail to find a suitable job after prolonged and extensive search effort come to believe that there is no work available for them. They become discouraged and stop looking for work. Such people are called discouraged workers. **Discouraged workers** are people who do not have jobs and would like work, but have stopped seeking work. Discouraged workers are not counted as unemployed by the Current Population Survey because they have not actively sought work within the past 30 days. If discouraged workers were added to the unemployment count, the unemployment rate would be higher than the one currently measured.

Part-time Workers   As we have noted, part-time workers are counted as being employed. But many part-time workers are available for and seeking full-time work. The measured unemployment rate does not capture this element of part-time unemployment. This source of unemployment is a potentially important one.

The Unemployment Record

The U.S. unemployment record since 1900 is set out in Fig. 22.3. The dominant feature of that record is the Great Depression in the early 1930s. During that episode of our history, between 20 and 25 percent of the labor force was unemployed. Although in recent years we have not experienced anything as devastating as the Great Depression, we have experienced some high unemployment rates. Two such periods are highlighted in the figure—the OPEC recession of the mid-1970s and the Volcker recession of the early 1980s. The average unemployment rate over this 88-year period has been 6.3 percent.

The Benefits and Costs of Unemployment

Unemployment is a highly charged topic. We chart the course of the unemployment rate as a measure of the nation's economic health with the intensity that a physician keeps track of a patient's temperature. What does the unemployment rate tell us about the economic health of the nation? Is a high unemployment rate a sign of economic ill-health, or is there such a thing as too low an unemployment rate? Let's address these questions by first examining what is gained from unemployment.

The Benefits of Unemployment Try to imagine a world in which there is no unemployment. In such a world, no one would be looking for a job. Everyone who wanted a job would have one and everyone who didn't have a job would have no regrets and no intention of seeking one. When people finished school and joined the labor force, they would take the first job that came along no matter how bad it was or how ill-suited they were for it. If a steel plant in Pittsburgh closed down and laid off its workers, those workers would immediately snap up any kind of employment going.

The world that we've just considered would clearly not be a nice place in which to live and work. Workers and jobs would be badly mismatched, productivity would probably not be very high, and there would be a good deal of unhappiness and lack of job satisfaction. The world that we live in differs from this fictional world in many respects, and we'll focus on two of them.

First, in the real world, people don't usually take the first job that comes their way. Instead, they spend time searching out what they believe will be the best job available for them. By doing so, they can match their own skills and interests with the available jobs, finding a satisfying job and income. This benefit from unemployment results in substantial age differences in the incidence of unemployment. Young people (aged 16 to 19) who have recently entered the labor market take much more time to find a suitable job than do older workers. Also, younger workers change jobs more frequently in the process of trying to find the best available match. But not all unemployment takes the form of young people finding their first or second job.

Second, the real world is dynamic and ever-changing. Production and consumption change as new technologies are developed and exploited. Firms are born and die. In this process, old jobs disappear and new jobs are created. As a consequence, workers of all ages constantly face the risk of losing their current job and the prospect that a potentially better job might exist. Unemployment arising from this source has been particularly important in the United States in recent years. The rapid expansion of jobs in the high-tech computer-oriented sectors and the loss of jobs in traditional sectors such as automobiles and steelmaking have resulted in a large rate of labor turnover, which has resulted in workers moving not only from one sector of the economy to another but from one region of the country to another.

Unemployment associated with people seeking their first job and with labor turnover arising from technological change is called **frictional unemployment.** When the only unemployment is frictional unemployment, the economy is said to be at **full employment.** When the economy is at full employment and the only unemployment is frictional, the unemployment rate is called the **natural rate of unemployment.**

Measuring frictional unemployment and distinguishing frictional from other types of unemployment is controversial. Some economists believe that the natural rate of unemployment in the United States is between 5 and 6 percent of the labor force and that all unemployment in excess of 6 percent could, and should, be eliminated. Others believe that the natural rate of unemployment varies and that most of the fluctuations in the actual rate of unemployment represent fluctuations in its natural rate. We will examine the reasons for these differences of opinion in Chapter 30 (pp. 806–812).

Next, let's examine the costs of unemployment.

The Costs of Unemployment

Loss of Output and Income The most obvious cost of unemployment is the loss of output and the loss of income that the unemployed would have produced if they had had jobs. How big this cost is depends on the natural rate of unemployment. If the natural rate of unemployment is between 5 and 6 percent, as economists such as James Tobin of Yale University believe, the lost output from unemployment is enormous.

Arthur Okun of the Brookings Institution estimated that for every one percentage point rise in the unemployment rate, the nation's output of goods and services falls by 3 percentage points. More recent studies have suggested that each 1 percentage point added to the unemployment rate cuts output by 2 percentage points. If numbers in this range are correct, then the lost output resulting from high unemployment is enormous. One percent of aggregate output in the United States is $45 billion. Thus getting the unemployment rate down from 8 percent to 6 percent raises output by between $180 billion and $270 billion. On the average, every person could buy an extra thousand dollars' worth of goods and services each year if this loss could be avoided.

Those economists who believe that the natural rate of unemployment itself varies think that the lost output cost of unemployment is small. If the unemployment rate is temporarily high because a lot of technical change calls for a higher than normal amount of labor turnover, then lowering the unemployment rate will prevent the necessary reallocation of labor. To reap the full advantage of the new technologies, people need to change jobs. If they do not, both output and income will be lower than the new technologies could otherwise have achieved.

Human Capital A second, and important, cost of unemployment is the permanent damage that can be done to an unemployed worker by hindering his or her career development and acquisition of human capital. **Human capital** is the value of a person's education and acquired skills. It is measured as the amount of money that, invested at the average interest rate, would 'yield the same income as that produced by the person's acquired skills. These skills include the mechanical and mental skills that we acquire in school as well as those that we develop on the job. They also include our work habits and our ability to concentrate. Prolonged unemployment seriously lowers the value of a person's human capital. When unemployment is prolonged, human capital depreciates or deteriorates—skills lose their value.

Crime A rise in the unemployment rate usually causes an increase in the amount of crime. When people cannot earn an income from legitimate work, they sometimes turn to crime. A high crime rate is also one of the costs of high unemployment.

Human Dignity A final cost that is difficult to quantify is the loss of self-esteem that afflicts many who suffer prolonged periods of unemployment. It is probably this aspect of unemployment that makes it so highly charged with political and social significance.

Unemployment is not the only indicator of the state of the nation's economic health. Another is its gross national product. Let's now examine that.

Gross National Product

The value of all the final goods and services produced in the economy is called **gross national product** or GNP. **Final goods and services** are goods and services that are not used as inputs in the production of other goods and services, but are bought by their final user. Such goods include consumption goods and services and also new durable goods. Examples of final goods are cans of soda and cars. Examples of final services are automobile insurance and haircuts.

Not all goods and services are "final." Some are called intermediate goods and services. **Intermediate goods and services** are those used as inputs into the production process of another good or service. Examples of intermediate goods are the windshields, batteries, and gearboxes used by car producers, and the paper and ink used by newspaper manufacturers. Examples of intermediate services are the banking and insurance services bought by car producers and news printers. Whether a good or service is intermediate or final depends on who buys it and for what purpose. For example, electric power purchased by a car producer or a printer is an intermediate good. Electric power bought by you is a final good.

When we measure gross national product, we do not include the value of intermediate goods and services produced. If we did, we would be counting the same thing more than once. When someone buys a new car from the local Chrysler dealer, that is a final transaction and the value of the car is counted as part of GNP. But we must not also count as part of GNP the amount paid by the dealer to Chrysler for the car or the amount paid by Chrysler to all its suppliers for the car's various parts.

If we want to measure GNP, we have to somehow add together all the *final* goods and services produced. Obviously, we can't achieve a useful measure by simply adding together the number of cars, newspapers, kilowatts of electric power, haircuts, and automobile insurance policies. To determine GNP, we first calculate the dollar *value* of the output of each final good or service. This calculation simply involves multiplying the quantity produced of each final good or service by its price. That is, we measure the output of each good and service in the common unit of dollars. We then add up the dollar values of the outputs of the different goods to arrive at their total value, which is GNP. We measure GNP in dollars, but it is a mixture of real quantities—the numbers of final goods and services produced—and dollar quantities—the prices of the goods and services. A change in GNP, therefore, contains a mixture of the effects of changes in prices and changes in the quantities of final goods and services. For many purposes, it is important to distinguish price changes from quantity changes. To do so, we use the concepts of nominal GNP and real GNP. Let's examine these concepts.

Nominal GNP and Real GNP

Nominal GNP measures the value of the output of final goods and services using *current* prices. It is sometimes called *current dollar GNP*. **Real GNP** measures the value of the output of final goods and services using the prices that prevailed in some base period. An alternative name for real GNP is *constant dollar GNP*. Each measure refers to a specific time period, usually a year.

Comparing real GNP from one year to another enables us to say whether the economy has produced more or fewer goods and services. Comparing nomi-

nal GNP from one year to another does not permit us to compare the quantities of goods and services produced in those two years. Nominal GNP may be higher in 1990 than in 1989, but that might reflect only higher prices, not more production.

The importance of the distinction between real GNP and nominal GNP is illustrated in Fig. 22.4. Real GNP is measured by the green bars and nominal GNP is measured by the sum of the green and the red bars. The red bars show the inflation component in nominal GNP. In 1960, GNP was $515 billion. By 1988, it had grown to $4862 billion. But only part of that increase represents an increase in goods and services available—an increase in real GNP. Most of the increase came from inflation. Notice that nominal GNP increases in every year in the figure but real GNP falls in 1975 and 1982.

Real GNP—the Record

Estimates of real GNP in the United States go back to 1869. Figure 22.5 illustrates the real GNP record. Two facts stand out. First, there is a general tendency for real GNP to increase. Second, the rate of upward movement is not uniform and sometimes real GNP has actually declined. The most precipitous decline

Figure 22.4   Gross National Product: 1960–1988

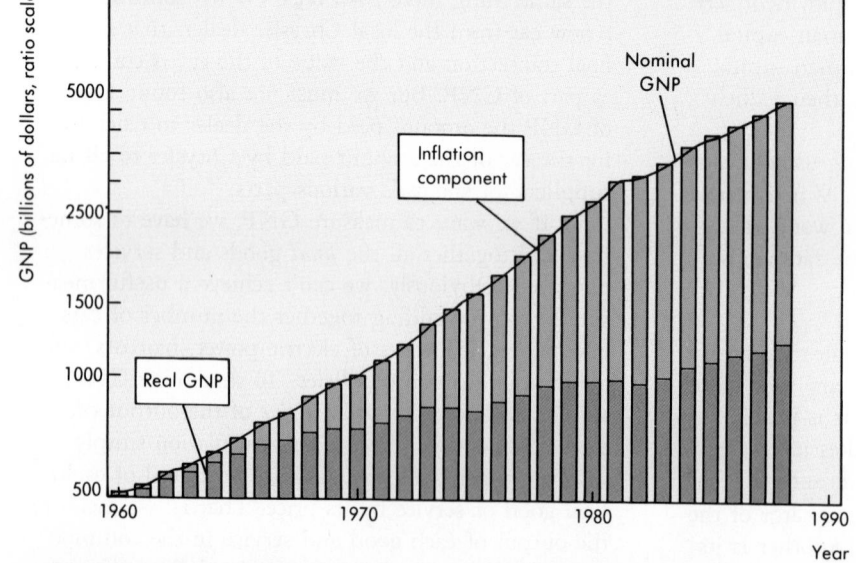

Gross national product has increased almost tenfold between 1960 and 1988. But much of that increase is the result of inflation. Real GNP, the increase in GNP attributable to the increase in the volume of goods and services produced, has increased but at a more modest pace. The figure shows how real GNP and the inflation component of nominal GNP have evolved. Nominal GNP has increased in every year, but real GNP fell in 1975 and again in 1982.

Source: Real and nominal GNP 1960–1988, Economic Report of the President (1989).

Figure 22.5   Real GNP: 1869–1988

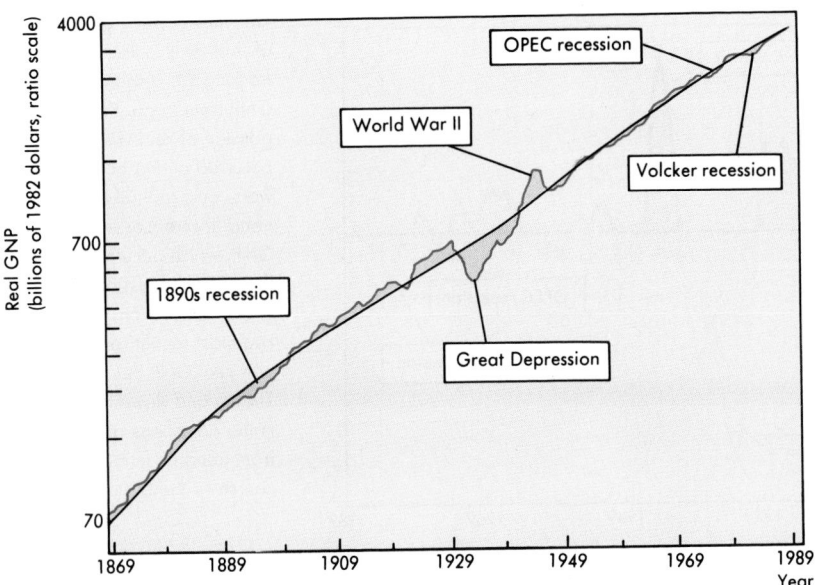

Real GNP has grown at an annual average rate of 3.3 percent between 1869 and 1988. But the growth rate has not been the same each year. In some periods, such as the years during World War II, real GNP expanded quickly. In other periods, such as the Great Depression and, more recently, the OPEC and Volcker recessions, real GNP declined. There were several periods of decline in the nineteenth century as well, one of which is marked in the figure.

Sources: The data used for real GNP 1869–1928 are an average of those presented in two sources: Christina D. Romer, "The Prewar Business Cycle Reconsidered: New Estimates of Gross National Product, 1869–1908," *Journal of Political Economy* 97 (February 1989); and Nathan S. Balke and Robert J. Gordon, "The Estimation of Prewar Gross National Product: Methodology and New Evidence," *Journal of Political Economy* 97 (February 1989). Real GNP 1929–1988, *Economic Report of the President* (1989).

occurred in the early 1930s during the Great Depression. But declines also occurred in recent times during the OPEC recession and during the Volcker recession. There were several periods during the nineteenth and early twentieth centuries when real GNP declined, one of which, the 1890s recession, is shown in the figure. There were also periods when real GNP grew extremely quickly—for example, the years during World War II.

In order to obtain a clearer picture of the changes in real GNP, we consider separately the two general tendencies that we've just identified. The first of these tendencies is the general upward movement of real GNP. This feature of real GNP is called trend real GNP. **Trend real GNP** is a measure of the general upward tendency or drift of real GNP that ignores its fluctuations. Trend real GNP rises for three reasons:

• Growing population

• Growing stock of capital equipment

• Advances in technology

These forces have produced the general upward tendency that you can see in Fig. 22.5. Trend GNP is illustrated in Fig. 22.5 as the thin black line passing through the middle of the path actually followed by real GNP in its meanderings above trend (blue areas) and below trend (red areas).

The departures of real GNP from its trend are a measure of economic fluctuations. We can measure these fluctuations as deviations from trend in real GNP. The **deviation from trend in real GNP** is the difference between the actual value of real GNP and trend real GNP. These deviations from trend appear again in Fig. 22.6. As you can see, they show distinct cycles in economic activity that correspond to the recession and depression events and the wartimes that we have already identified. They also show how, during wartime, real GNP deviates above trend.

The Importance of Real GNP

The upward trend in real GNP is the major source of improvements in living standards. The pace of this

Figure 22.6   Real GNP—Deviations from Trend

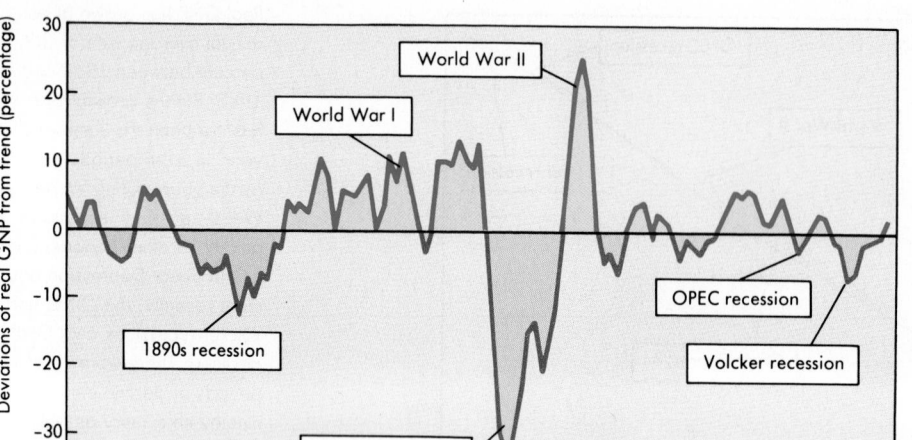

The uneven pace of increase of real GNP is illustrated by tracking the deviations of real GNP from trend. Rapid expansion of real GNP, which occurred during both world wars, puts real GNP above trend. Decreases in real GNP, which occurred during the 1890s recession, the Great Depression, and the two most recent recessions, puts real GNP below trend. The up and down movements in the deviations of real GNP from trend describe the course of the business cycle.

upward movement has a powerful effect on the standard of living of one generation compared with its predecessor. For example, if real GNP trends upward at 1 percent a year, it will take 70 years for real GNP to double. But a growth trend of 10 percent a year will double real GNP in just seven years. With an average trend increase of between 2 and 3 percent a year, which is commonly experienced in industrial countries, and which has also been the long-term experience of the United States, real GNP doubles approximately every generation (every 25 years or so).

But the upward trend in real GNP has its costs. The more quickly we increase real GNP, the faster are exhaustible resources like oil and natural gas depleted, and the more severe our environmental and atmospheric pollution problems become. Furthermore, the more quickly real GNP increases, the more we have to accept change, both in what we consume and in the jobs that we do. But increases in real GNP also bring benefits in the form of more consumption goods and services available. These benefits have to be balanced against the costs. The choices that people make to balance these benefits and costs, acting individually and through government institutions, determine the actual pace at which real GNP increases.

As we have seen, real GNP does not increase at an even pace. In some years the economy booms and in other years it busts. Are the fluctuations in real GNP important?

This question is a hard one and one on which economists disagree. Some economists believe that fluctuations are costly and that when real GNP is below trend, output is lost and when output is above trend, bottlenecks and shortages arise. With output below trend, unemployment is above its natural rate and the economy's stock of capital equipment is underused. If a downturn in real GNP can be avoided, average income and consumption levels can be increased. If large fluctuations above trend can be controlled, shortages and bottlenecks can be avoided and inflation better kept in check.

An alternative view is that most of the fluctuations in real GNP represent the best possible response to the uneven pace of technological change. At times when technological progress is rapid, capital accumulation is also rapid, so total production increases as more new-technology capital is produced. Once a boom, driven by the exploitation of new technologies, has run its course, the economy temporarily drops into low gear, ready to accelerate in the next burst of technological progress and innovation. Since we are

Figure 22.7   The Business Cycle

The business cycle has four phases: contraction, trough, expansion, and peak. Our most recent experience is used to illustrate these phases. There was a contraction from 1973 to 1975. In 1975, the trough was reached and an expansion began. That expansion reached a peak in 1978, when a new contraction set in that in turn reached a new trough in 1982. From 1982 to 1988, the economy was on a prolonged expansion.

not able to order the pace of new technology to be smooth, we are only able to smooth the pace of economic growth by delaying the implementation of new technologies. Such delays would result in never-to-be-recovered waste.

Regardless of which position economists take, they all agree that depressions as deep and long as that which occurred in the early 1930s result in extraordinary waste and human suffering. The disagreements concern the more common and gentler ebbs and flows of economic activity that have occurred in the years since World War II, which we saw earlier in Fig. 22.6.

Let's now take a more systematic look at the ebbs and flows of economic activity.

The Business Cycle

The **business cycle** is the periodic but irregular up and down movement in economic activity measured by fluctuations in real GNP and other macroeconomic variables. A business cycle is not a regular, predictable, or repeating phenomenon like the swings of the pendulum of a clock. Its timing is random and, to a large degree, unpredictable.

A business cycle is identified as a sequence of four phases:

- Contraction
- Trough
- Expansion
- Peak

These four phases are identified in Fig. 22.7. A **contraction** is a slowdown in the pace of economic activity, as occurred between 1973 and 1975 and again between 1978 and 1982. An **expansion** is a speedup in the pace of economic activity, as occurred between 1975 and 1978 and again after 1982. A **trough** is the lower turning point of a business cycle, where a contraction turns into an expansion. Troughs occurred in 1975 and 1982. A **peak** is the upper turning point of a business cycle, where an expansion turns into a contraction. A peak occurred in 1978.

A recession occurs if a contraction is severe enough. A **recession** is a downturn in the level of economic activity, defined by the Commerce Department as two successive quarters of falling real GNP. A deep trough is called a slump or a **depression.**

Unemployment and the Business Cycle

Real GNP is not the only variable that fluctuates over the course of the business cycle. Its fluctuations are matched by related fluctuations in a wide range of other economic variables. One of the most important of these is unemployment. In the contraction phase of a business cycle, the unemployment rate is rising; in the expansion phase, the unemployment rate is falling; at the peak of a business cycle, the unemployment rate is at its lowest; at the trough of a business cycle, the unemployment rate is at its highest. This relationship between the unemployment rate and the phases of the business cycle is illustrated below in Fig. 22.8.

That figure shows the deviations of real GNP from trend in the United States since 1900. The Great Depression, World War II, the OPEC recession, and the Volcker recession are labeled in the figure. The figure also shows the unemployment rate. So that we can see how these two variables line up with each other over the business cycle, the unemployment rate has been measured with its scale inverted. That is, as we move down the vertical axis on the right side, the unemployment rate increases. As you can see, fluctua-

tions in the unemployment rate closely follow those in the deviations of real GNP from trend.

The Stock Market and the Business Cycle

We have defined the business cycle as the ebbs and flows of economic activity and have measured these ebbs and flows by the deviation from trend of real GNP. We have seen that unemployment fluctuations mirror the GNP fluctuations very closely. Another indicator of the state of the economy, perhaps the most visible of all such indicators, is provided by the stock market. Every weekday evening, we are told of the day's events in the New York and Tokyo stock exchanges. Movements in share prices attract attention partly for their own sake and also partly for what they might foretell about our *future* economic fortunes.

Do stock prices fluctuate in sympathy with fluctuations in real GNP and unemployment? Is a stock price downturn a predictor of economic contraction? Is a stock price boom a predictor of economic expansion? To answer these questions, let's take a look at the behavior of stock prices and see how they relate to the expansions and contractions of economic activity.

Figure 22.8   Unemployment and the Business Cycle

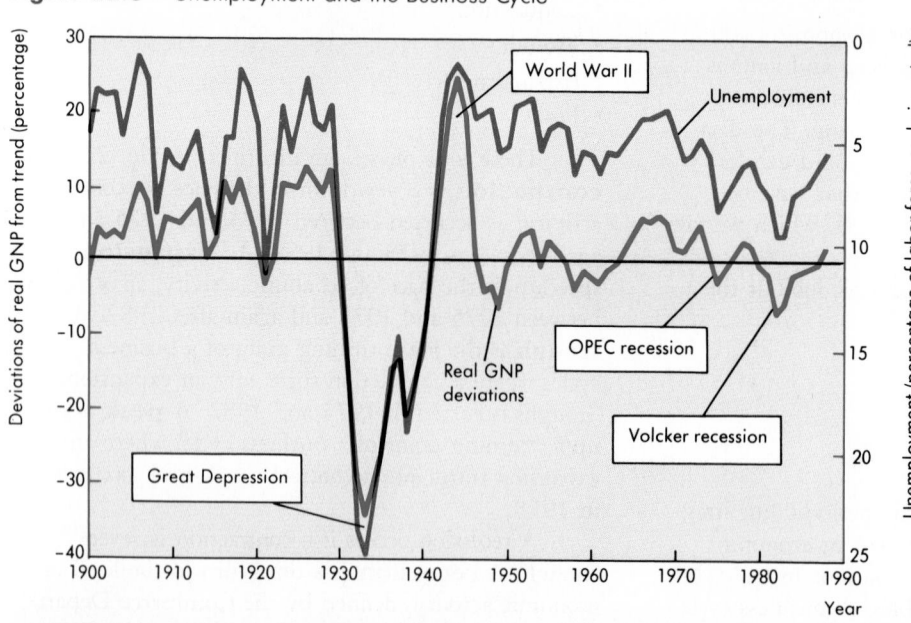

This figure shows the relationship between unemployment and the business cycle. The deviation of real GNP from trend tells us when the economy is in a contraction or expansion phase. Unemployment is plotted on the same figure but with its scale inverted. The line measuring unemployment is high when unemployment is low and low when unemployment is high. As you can see, the cycles in real GNP are closely matched by the cycles in unemployment.

Figure 22.9   Stock Prices

1929 crash

1987 crash

Year

Sources: Real stock price index, 1871–1948, Index of Common Stocks, *Historical Statistics* (1960) Series X-351; Real stock price index, 1949–1988, The Dow-Jones Industrial Average, *Economic Report of the President* (1989). The two indexes were linked to form a common index and converted to real terms using the same price index that converts nominal GNP to real GNP. The index is scaled to have an average value between 1871 and 1988 of 100.

Stock prices are among the most volatile elements of our economy. Here, real stock prices (stock prices measured to take out the effects of changes in the value of money) climbed strongly from 1870 to 1910 but with strong fluctuations. They then fell dramatically through 1920 but increased at a spectacular pace through 1929. Then came the crash that preceded the Great Depression. Stock prices began a new climb after World War II, reaching a peak in 1965. They gradually fell to a trough in 1982 after which they climbed to a new peak before the crash of October 1987.

Figure 22.9 tracks the course of inflation-adjusted stock prices since 1871. Actual stock prices have increased much more than what is indicated here because of inflation but those purely inflationary price increases have been removed so that we can see what has "really" been happening to stock prices. The most striking feature of stock prices is their extreme volatility and lack of any obvious cyclical patterns. Two stock price crashes are indicated in the figure: those of 1929 and 1987. The 1929 crash, as you can see, was a sharp one and was followed by two successive years of massive stock price decline. There have also been periods of rapid stock price increases, the most dramatic being that preceding the 1929 crash. There were also strong increases before the 1987 crash.

How do stock price changes correspond with the business cycle? The movements in stock prices through the Great Depression and the recovery from that depression suggest that the stock market provides information about where the economy is heading. The stock market moved in sympathy with, but slightly ahead of, the contraction and expansion of real GNP and the rise and fall in the unemployment rate. But do turning points in the stock market always reliably predict the turning points in the economy? The answer is no. There are some periods when the stock market and real GNP move together but there are more periods when their movements oppose each other. For example, between 1976 and 1978, the economy expanded but stock prices fell. Again, in 1984, stock prices dipped slightly while the economy expanded strongly. Finally, between 1987 and 1988, there were further examples of opposing movements in stock prices and the state of the economy.

When stock prices collapsed in October 1987, many people drew parallels between that episode and the 1929 stock price crash. In 1930, the economy collapsed. In 1988, the economy continued to grow. Why were the two episodes so different? The key answer and the key reason for the lack of a strong connection between stock price fluctuations and the business cycle is our inability to forecast the business

Figure 22.10   Inflation and the Business Cycle

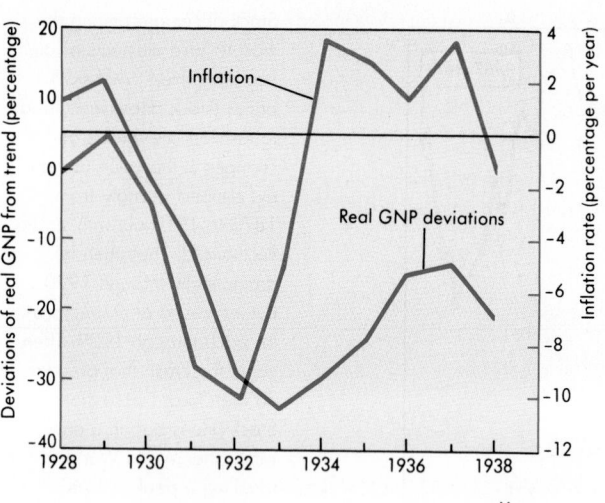

(a) The Great Depression

Inflation follows the course of the business cycle on some occasions but on others, departs from it. As shown in part (a), through the Great Depression, inflation and real GNP moved together during the contraction phase but, in the expansion phase, inflation increased much more strongly than real GNP. As shown in part (b), inflation and real GNP fluctuated closely together from 1973 to 1982. For this time period, inflation is graphed to lag behind real GNP (that is, inflation in the following year is plotted against real GNP for the current year). Since 1982, inflation has remained moderate while real GNP has expanded quickly.

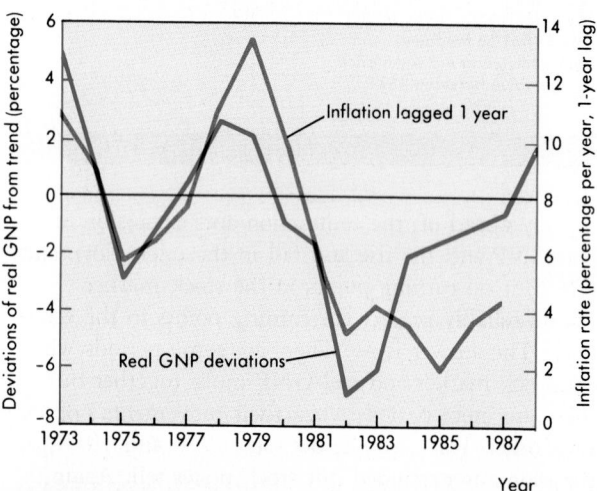

(b) OPEC and Volcker recessions

cycle. Stock prices are determined by people's expectations about future profitability of firms. Future profitability, in turn, depends on the state of the economy. Hence, stock prices are determined by expectations about the future state of the economy. But those expectations turn out to be wrong about as often as they turn out to be right. Thus stock prices are not entirely reliable predictors of the state of the economy.

Inflation and the Business Cycle

We've looked at fluctuations in real variables: real GNP, the unemployment rate, and real stock prices. We've seen that there is a strong and systematic relationship between fluctuations in real GNP and in the unemployment rate. We have also seen that there are times when there is a systematic relationship between real stock prices and the business cycle and other times when there isn't. How does inflation behave over the business cycle? Are fluctuations in its rate closely connected with business cycle fluctuations or does the inflation rate vary independently of the business cycle?

To answer these questions, let's look again at the Great Depression and at the two recent recessions and see how inflation varied during those periods. Figure 22.10(a) shows the inflation rate through the Great Depression. The state of the economy is shown by the fluctuations in real GNP. You can see from the figure that as the economy went into the contraction phase of the Great Depression, the inflation rate was also falling. In fact, inflation was negative, so the price level was falling. But the inflation rate reached its low point in 1932, a year before the trough of the business cycle. Thereafter, the inflation rate increased and at a much faster pace than the real GNP recovery. Thus through this business cycle episode, the inflation rate and the business cycle were in step with each other during the contraction phase but the inflation rate increased sharply while the economy was still in the depths of the Great Depression.

Part (b) shows the course of inflation during the business fluctuations of the 1970s and 1980s. In this figure, the inflation rate is graphed to lag behind real GNP. For example, the inflation rate plotted against 1979 is the inflation rate in 1980. As you can see, through the first contraction and expansion and the second contraction, the inflation rate closely follows the business cycle—but with a one-year time-lag. But, after 1982, as the economy goes through the long, strong expansion phase of the business cycle, the inflation rate remains low.

It is interesting to contrast the course of inflation over these recent cycles with that of the Great Depression. In both cases, there are periods during which the inflation rate falls along with economic contraction and a phase during which the inflation rate increases along with economic expansion. But there are other periods in which the inflation rate and the state of the business cycle go in their own directions. In the recovery from the Great Depression, the inflation rate moved up more quickly than the economy recovered. In the expansion of the 1980s, there was no corresponding increase in the inflation rate.

A further contrast between the two periods is important. During the Great Depression, the average inflation rate was much lower than that of the 1970s and 1980s. In the 1930s, the inflation rate fell from

0 to −10 percent per year and then increased to about 3 percent per year. In the 1970s and 1980s, inflation cycled, climbing to a peak of more than 13 percent and falling to around 2 percent.

These episodes reveal two things about inflation that need to be explained: First, much of the time, inflation moves in sympathy with the business cycle; second, there are important changes in the inflation rate and differences in the average rate of inflation that appear to be in no way connected with the business cycle phase through which the economy is passing.

We've now studied inflation, unemployment, real GNP fluctuations, and business cycles. Let's turn next to our final topic, deficits.

Government Deficit and International Deficit

I f you spend more than you earn, you have a deficit. To cover your deficit, you have to borrow or sell off some of the things that you own. Just as individuals can have deficits, so can governments and so can entire nations. These deficits—the government deficit and the international payments deficit—have attracted a lot of attention recently.

Government Deficit

The **government deficit** is the total expenditure of the government sector less the total revenue of that sector. The government sector of the economy is composed of the federal government and the state and local governments. These governments spend on a variety of public and social programs and obtain their revenue from taxes.

Sometimes the government sector is in surplus and at other times it is in deficit. Occasionally, the deficit is a very large one as it was, for example, in 1975. But deficits and surpluses have alternated. However, since 1980, the government sector has had a persistent deficit, averaging about 3 percent of gross national product.

To some degree, the balance of the government budget is related to the business cycle. When the economy is expanding quickly (in the expansion phase of the business cycle), tax receipts rise quickly and the government's spending on unemployment benefits decreases. Through this phase of the business cycle, the government usually runs a surplus. When the economy is in a contraction phase, tax receipts decline and unemployment benefits increase and the government budget goes into deficit. What is interesting about our recent budget deficit is that it has persisted despite the fact that the economy has experienced strong and prolonged expansion.

We'll study the government deficit more closely and at greater length in Chapter 34. In that chapter, we'll discuss the sources and consequences of the deficit.

International Deficit

The difference between the value of all the goods and services that we sell to other countries (exports) and the value of all the goods and services that we buy from foreigners (imports) is called our **current account balance.** If we sell more to the rest of the world than we buy from it, we have a current account surplus. If we buy more from the rest of the world than we sell to it, we have a current account deficit.

Most of the time since 1950 we have had a small current account surplus. But in recent years, a current account deficit has emerged. That deficit has been not only persistent but gradually increasing in magnitude. When we have a current account deficit, we have to borrow from the rest of the world to pay for the goods and services that we're buying in excess of the value of those that we're selling. Mirroring our current account deficit and borrowing from the rest of the world is a current account surplus and lending to the rest of the world in some other countries. The most notable country on the opposite side of our international balance sheet is Japan. That country has been operating a current account surplus and, in recent years, are increasing surplus.

The causes of these international payments surpluses and deficits and their consequences will be discussed at greater length in Chapter 36.

■ In our study of macroeconomics, we're going to find out what we currently know about the causes of inflation and of variations in its rate; we're also going to discover what we know about the causes of unemployment and business cycle fluctuations. We're going to discover why there are certain times when the stock market is a good predictor of the state of the economy and others when it is not; we're also going to discover why sometimes inflation and the business cycle move in sympathy with each other and why there are times when these variables follow separate courses. Finally, we're going to learn more about the deficits—the government deficit and the international payments deficit—and their causes, their importance, and their consequences.

The next step in our study of macroeconomics is to learn more about macroeconomic measurement —about how we measure gross national product, the price level, and inflation.

S U M M A R Y

Inflation

Inflation is an upward movement in the average level of prices. To measure the average level of prices, we calculate a price index. The inflation rate is the percentage change in the value of a price index.

Inflation is a persistent feature of economic life in the United States, but the rate of inflation fluctuates. In the early 1960s, inflation was between 1 and 2 percent a year. By 1980, its rate exceeded 13 percent a year. There was an upward trend in inflation through the 1960s and 1970s but inflation has been on a downward trend since 1980.

Inflation is a problem because it brings a fall in the value of money at an unpredictable rate. The more unpredictable the inflation rate, the less useful is money as a measuring rod for conducting transactions. Inflation makes money especially unsuitable for transactions spread out over time such as borrowing and lending or working for an agreed wage rate. The inflation rate is the opportunity cost of holding money. (pp. 567–572)

Unemployment

Unemployment is the number of adult workers (aged 16 and over) who are not employed and who are actively seeking jobs. Employment is the number of adult workers holding jobs. The labor force is the sum of those unemployed and those employed. The unemployment rate is the percentage of the labor force unemployed. Unemployment is measured each month by a survey of households.

Unemployment in the United States was not regarded as a major problem in the 1960s when its rate averaged less than 5 percent. Its rate also declined during that decade. Since 1969, unemployment has been on an upward trend and has fluctuated strongly. Its rate reached a peak in 1982 and 1983.

Unemployment has some benefits. It provides people with the time and opportunity to search out the job that best matches their own skills and temperament. It also permits an ongoing response to the ever-changing technologies in our economy.

The major costs of unemployment are the lost output and earnings that could have been generated if the unemployed had been working. Other major costs are a slowdown in the accumulation of human capital, or a rise in its depreciation rate, and, when unemployment is prolonged, crime and severe social and psychological problems for unemployed workers and their families. (pp. 572–575)

Gross National Product

The nation's total output is measured by gross national product. Gross national product is the dollar value of all the goods and services produced in the economy in a given time period. Changes in gross national product reflect both changes in prices and changes in the quantity of goods and services available. To separate the effects of prices from real quantities, we distinguish between nominal GNP and real GNP. Nominal GNP is measured using current prices. Real GNP is measured using prices for some base year.

Real GNP grows, on average, every year, so that the trend of real GNP is upward. But real GNP does not increase at a constant rate. Its rate of expansion fluctuates so that real GNP fluctuates around its trend value. Increases in real GNP bring rising living standards but not without costs. The main costs of fast economic growth are resource depletion, environmental pollution, and the need to face rapid and often costly changes in job type and location. The benefits of higher consumption levels have to be balanced against such costs. (pp. 575–579)

The Business Cycle

The business cycle is the periodic but irregular up and down movement in macroeconomic activity. The cycle has four phases: Contraction, trough, expansion, and peak. Deep troughs are called slumps or depressions.

Unemployment fluctuates closely with the deviation from trend in real GNP. When real GNP is above trend, unemployment is low; when real GNP is below trend, unemployment is high. But real stock prices do not fluctuate in a similar manner to business cycle fluctuations. Sometimes a stock market crash precedes a recession but it does not always do so.

There is no simple relationship between the inflation rate and the phase of the business cycle. Sometimes the inflation rate increases in an expansion phase and decreases in a contraction phase. But there are other times when inflation moves independently of the business cycle. Thus there are two types of forces at work generating inflation that have to be investigated—those that are related to the business cycle and those that are not. (pp. 579–583)

Government Deficit and International Deficit

The government deficit is the total expenditure of the government sector less the total revenue of that sector. To some degree the government deficit fluctuates over the course of the business cycle. But since 1980, the government sector has persistently operated with a deficit averaging about 3 percent of gross national product while the economy has experienced expansion.

A country's current account balance is the difference between the value of the goods and services that it sells to other countries and the value of the goods and services that it buys from the rest of the world. The United States normally has had a current account surplus, but in recent years, a deficit has emerged that has grown in magnitude. Mirroring our current account deficit is a current account surplus in some other countries. Japan is one of the countries that in recent years has had a large surplus. (pp. 583–584)

K E Y   C O N C E P T S

Key Figures

R E V I E W   Q U E S T I O N S

1 What is inflation?

2 What are some of the costs of inflation?

3 What, if any, are the benefits from inflation? If there are none, explain why.

4 Why doesn't inflation always benefit borrowers at the expense of lenders?

5 Explain why inflation is the opportunity cost of money holding.

6 What is the definition of unemployment?

7 How does the U.S. Department of Labor measure unemployment?

8 Why may the measured rate of unemployment understate or overstate the true extent of unemployment? What are the main costs of unemployment? Are there any benefits arising from unemployment? If so, what are they?

9 What is a business cycle? Describe the four phases of a business cycle. What was the phase of the U.S. business cycle in 1975, 1980, and 1985?

10 When the economy is in a recovery phase, what is happening to the unemployment rate? The stock market?

11 How does the inflation rate fluctuate over the business cycle?

12 Compare the fluctuations in inflation and unemployment.

PROBLEMS

1 At the end of 1989, the price index was 105. At the end of 1990, the price index was 110. Calculate the inflation rate in 1990.

2 In a noninflationary world, Joe and Mary are willing to borrow and lend at 2 percent a year. Joe expects that inflation next year will be 4 percent and Mary expects that it will be 8 percent. Would Joe and Mary be willing to sign a contract in which one of them borrows from the other? Explain why or why not.

3 Will the Cone-Heads Ice Cream Parlor be able to agree with their employees on a wage rate for next summer if the employer expects that inflation next year will be 4 percent while his employees expect that it will be 2 percent? Explain your answer.

4 Obtain data on unemployment in your home state. If your school library has the U.S. Department of Labor publication *Employment and Earnings,* you can get the data from there. Otherwise you may have to call your local newspaper business desk for the information. Compare the behavior of unemployment in your home state with that in the United States as a whole. Why do you think your state might have higher or lower unemployment than the U.S. average?

Chapter 23

*After studying this
chapter, you will be
able to:*

- Describe the circular flow
  of expenditure and
  income

- Explain why national expenditure, income, and
  product are equal to each
  other

- Explain the three ways in
  which GNP is measured—
  the expenditure ap-
  proach, the income ap-
  proach, and the output
  approach

- Explain how *real* GNP is
  measured

- Explain how the cost of
  living is measured by the
  Consumer Price Index
  (CPI)

- Distinguish between two
  measures of the price
  level—the CPI and the
  GNP deflator

- Distinguish between inflation and changes in relative prices

Every three months, the U.S. Department of Commerce publishes the latest quarterly estimates of the gross national product, or GNP—a barometer of the nation's economy. As soon as it is published, analysts pore over the data, trying, like tea readers, to understand the past and divine the future. But how do government accountants add up all the blooming, buzzing economic activity of the country to arrive at the number called GNP? And what exactly *is* GNP? ■ We saw in the last chapter that the pace of expansion of GNP fluctuates and is occasionally interrupted by a period of contraction. We described these ebbs and flows of economic activity as the business cycle. But to reveal the business cycle, we have to measure the extent

Reading the Tea Leaves

to which GNP has expanded because production has increased and the extent to which it has expanded because prices have risen. In other words, we have to distinguish between real GNP and nominal GNP. How do we go about measuring the real component of GNP and separating out the inflation component? ■ Most economic activity results in transactions taking place in markets for goods and services and factors of production. But not all economic activity results in such transactions. Some people make a living from crime. Others, although undertaking work that is legal, try to hide that fact and also try to hide the payment they receive in order to evade taxes or other regulations. And finally, some people undertake economic activity that does not take place in the marketplace at all. Fixing meals, laundering shirts, mowing the lawn, and washing the car are all examples of production activities that take place within the household. Are these activities taken into account when we measure GNP? If they are not taken into account, how important are they? And does it matter if they don't show up in GNP? ■ From economists to homemakers, inflation watchers of all types pay close attention to the monthly publication of the Consumer Price Index, or CPI. The Department of Labor publishes new figures each month, and analysts in newspapers and on TV quickly leap to conclusions. How does the government determine the CPI? How well does it measure the consumer's living costs? If oranges go up in price by 40 percent, and haircuts go up by only 4 percent, are rising orange prices causing inflation?

■ In this chapter, we're going to learn more about the macroeconomic concepts of GNP and the price level. We'll see how GNP is measured. We'll also see how the real and inflationary components of GNP are separately measured and identified. Finally, we'll learn how to calculate and interpret the CPI. We're going to begin by describing the circular flow of expenditure and income.

The Circular Flow of Expenditure and Income

The circular flow of expenditure and income provides the conceptual basis for measuring national expenditure, national income, and national product. We'll see some of the key ideas and relationships more clearly if we begin with a model economy that is simpler than the one in which we live. We'll then add some features to make our model economy correspond quite closely with that of the real economy.

Circular Flows in a Model Economy

Our model economy has just two kinds of economic institutions: households and firms. Households:

• Supply factors of production to firms
• Buy consumption goods and services from firms

Firms:

• Hire factors of production from households
• Pay profits made on their activities to households (or have losses covered by payments from households)
• Sell consumption goods and services to households

• Sell capital goods to other firms

The economy has three types of markets:

• Markets for goods and services
• Markets for factors of production
• Financial markets

The economy, and the flows that occur within it, are illustrated in Fig. 23.1. Two kinds of flows occur between households and firms. First, real objects are supplied by households to firms and by firms to households. Second, money passes between households and firms in exchange for these real objects. The real flows are shown by the red arrows and money flows by the green arrows.

The real flows from households to firms are the services of factors of production. That is, households supply factors of production—labor, capital, land, and natural resources—to firms. The real flows from firms to households are consumption goods and services. That is, firms produce popcorn and soda, movies and chocolate bars, microwave ovens and cars and sell them to households.

Moving in the opposite direction to the real flows are money flows. That is, firms pay wages to households for their labor services, interest for the use of their capital, rents for the use of their land, and profits to the owners of firms. The payments that firms make to households in exchange for factor services are the households' income. **Income** is the amount received by households in payment for the services of factors of production. Aggregate income, that is, total income for all households, is denoted by Y.

Households spend part of their income on consumption goods and services. That is, households buy popcorn and soda, movies and chocolate bars, cars and microwave ovens from firms. The aggregate, or total, expenditure by households on consumption goods and services is called **consumption expenditure,** denoted by C.

Households do not spend all their income—they save some of it. In this model economy, saving is the difference between household income and consumption expenditure. Saving gets channeled through financial markets and is indicated by S in the figure.

Firms do not sell all their output to households. First, some output may be added to inventory. For example, if General Motors produces 1000 cars and sells 950 of them to households, 50 cars will still remain unsold and GM's inventory of cars will in-

Figure 23.1   The Circular Flow of Expenditure and Income between Households and Firms

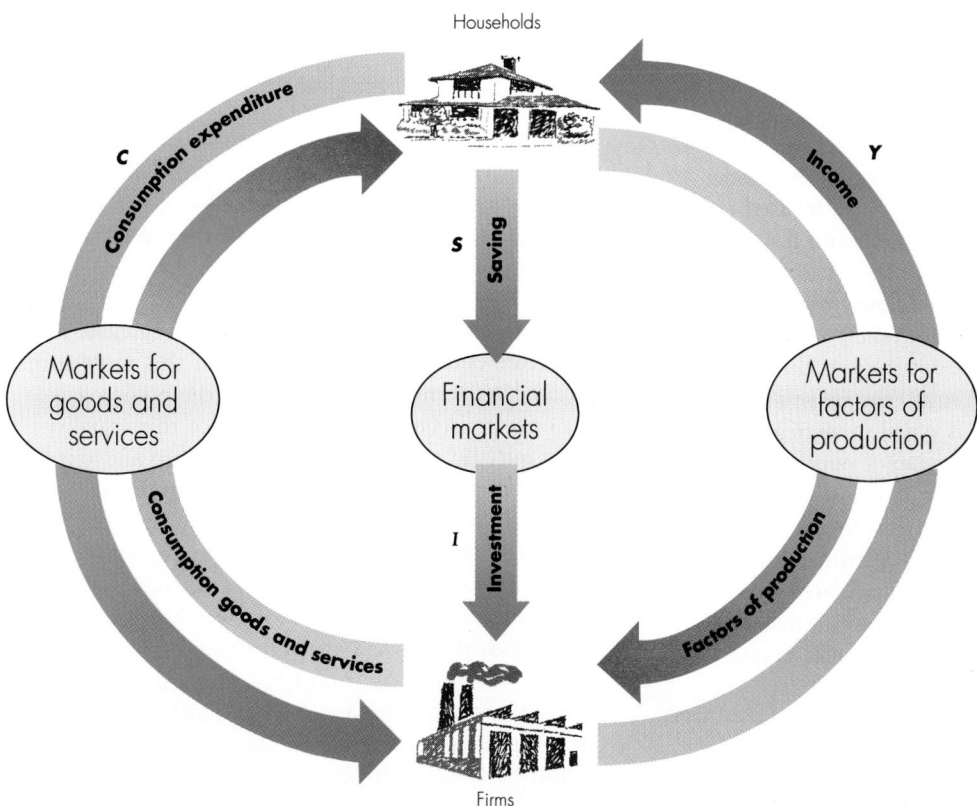

Households supply factors of production (factor flows) to firms and buy goods (goods flows) from firms. The red arrows show this circular flow of real economic activity. Money (green arrows) flows in the opposite direction to goods and factors. Households receive income (Y) from firms and make consumption expenditures (C) that flow to firms. What households don't consume, they save (S). Firms invest in new capital goods and inventories (I). The green flow of income from firms to households equals the green flow of expenditure into firms.

crease by 50. Second, some output is new capital equipment that is sold to other firms. For example, IBM sells a mainframe computer to GM. To pay for new capital and additional inventories, firms borrow from households in the financial markets. The purchase of new plant, equipment, and buildings, and additions to inventories are called **investment**. This item is indicated by I in the figure. In this economy, aggregate expenditure is the sum of consumption expenditure and investment.

Equality of Income and Expenditure   We're going to establish that aggregate income equals aggregate expenditure. To see this equality, let's focus on firms. Notice that there are three green arrows touching firms in Fig. 23.1—two pointing into firms and one pointing away. Everything that a firm receives it also pays out. The income paid to households (Y) includes the payment of wages, interest, rent, and prof-

its. The total amount received by firms is the sum of consumption expenditure (C) and investment (I). But this total is aggregate expenditure. What firms receive equals aggregate expenditure and what they pay out equals aggregate income. Since what they receive is equal to what they pay out, then

Aggregate income = Aggregate expenditure.

Equality of Expenditure, Income, and Value of Output   The value of output is the value of all the goods and services produced by firms. There are two ways in which we can value the goods and services produced by firms. One is to value them on the basis of the cost of the factors of production used to produce them. The other is to value them on the basis of what the buyers have paid for them. But we've just discovered that aggregate expenditure equals aggregate income. That is, the total amount spent on the goods and services produced equals the total amount paid for factors of production used to produce them. Thus the value of output equals aggregate income, which in turn equals aggregate expenditure. That is,

$$\frac{\text{Aggregate}}{\text{income}} = \frac{\text{Aggregate}}{\text{expenditure}} = \frac{\text{Value of}}{\text{output (GNP).}}$$

Government and Foreign Sectors   In the model economy that we've just examined, we focused exclusively on the behavior of households and firms. In real world economies, there are two other important institutions that add additional flows to the circular flow of expenditure and income: the government and the rest of the world. These institutions do not change the fundamental results that we've just obtained. Aggregate income is equal to aggregate expenditure and equal to the value of output no matter how many sectors we consider and how complicated a range of flows we consider between them. Nevertheless, it is important to add the government and the rest of the world to our model so that we can see the additional expenditure and income flows that they generate. Let's now add these two sectors to our model economy.

The government:

• Collects taxes from households and firms
• Pays benefits under various social programs to households
• Buys goods and services from firms

The rest of the world:

• Buys goods from domestic firms
• Sells goods to domestic firms

The additional flows arising from the transactions between the government, the rest of the world, and households and firms, along with the original flows that we've already considered, are illustrated in Fig. 23.2.

Let's first focus on the flows involving the government. Taxes (*TAX*) are flows of money from firms and households to the government. The diagram does not show firms paying any taxes. You can think of taxes paid by firms as being paid on behalf of the households that own the firms. For example, a tax on a firm's profit means that the households owning the firm receive less income. It is as if the households receive all the profit and then pay the tax on the

profit. This way of looking at taxes simplifies Fig. 23.2, but does not change any conclusions.

The flows of money from the government to households in the form of social benefits are called **transfer payments,** labeled *TR* in the figure. The government's purchases of goods and services from firms are shown as the flow *G*. Let's now look at the transactions with the rest of the world. These are shown in the figure as a flow of money from the rest of the world to firms for the purchase of exports (*EX*) and from firms to the rest of the world for the purchase of imports (*IM*).

Expenditure Equals Income Again   Aggregate expenditure equals aggregate income in this more complicated economy just as it does in the economy that has only households and firms. To see this equality, focus initially on the flows of money into and out of firms. We now have six arrows touching firms—four pointing toward firms and two away from them. As before, everything that a firm receives from the sale of its output is paid out as income to the owners of the factors of production that it employs and to the households that have a claim on its profits. The two arrows pointing away from firms are aggregate income (*Y*) and the payments for imports (*IM*). The four arrows pointing toward firms are consumption expenditure (*C*), investment (*I*), government purchases of goods and services (*G*), and foreigners' expenditure on domestic output, exports (*EX*). The sum of the flows into firms equals the sum of the flows out. That is,

$$Y + IM = C + I + G + EX.$$

Subtract *IM* from both sides of this equation so that

$$Y = C + I + G + EX - IM.$$

The difference between *EX* and *IM* is called net exports (*NX*). **Net exports** is the expenditure of foreigners on U.S.-produced goods minus the expenditure by U.S. residents on foreign-produced goods. The sum of the items on the right side of this equation is expenditure on domestic output. **Expenditure on domestic output** is the sum of consumption expenditure, investment, government purchases of goods and services, and net exports.

The number (represented by the letter *Y*) on the left side of the equation is aggregate income. As we found in the simple economy, aggregate income equals aggregate expenditure in this economy as well.

Figure 23.2   The Circular Flow Including Government and the Rest of the World

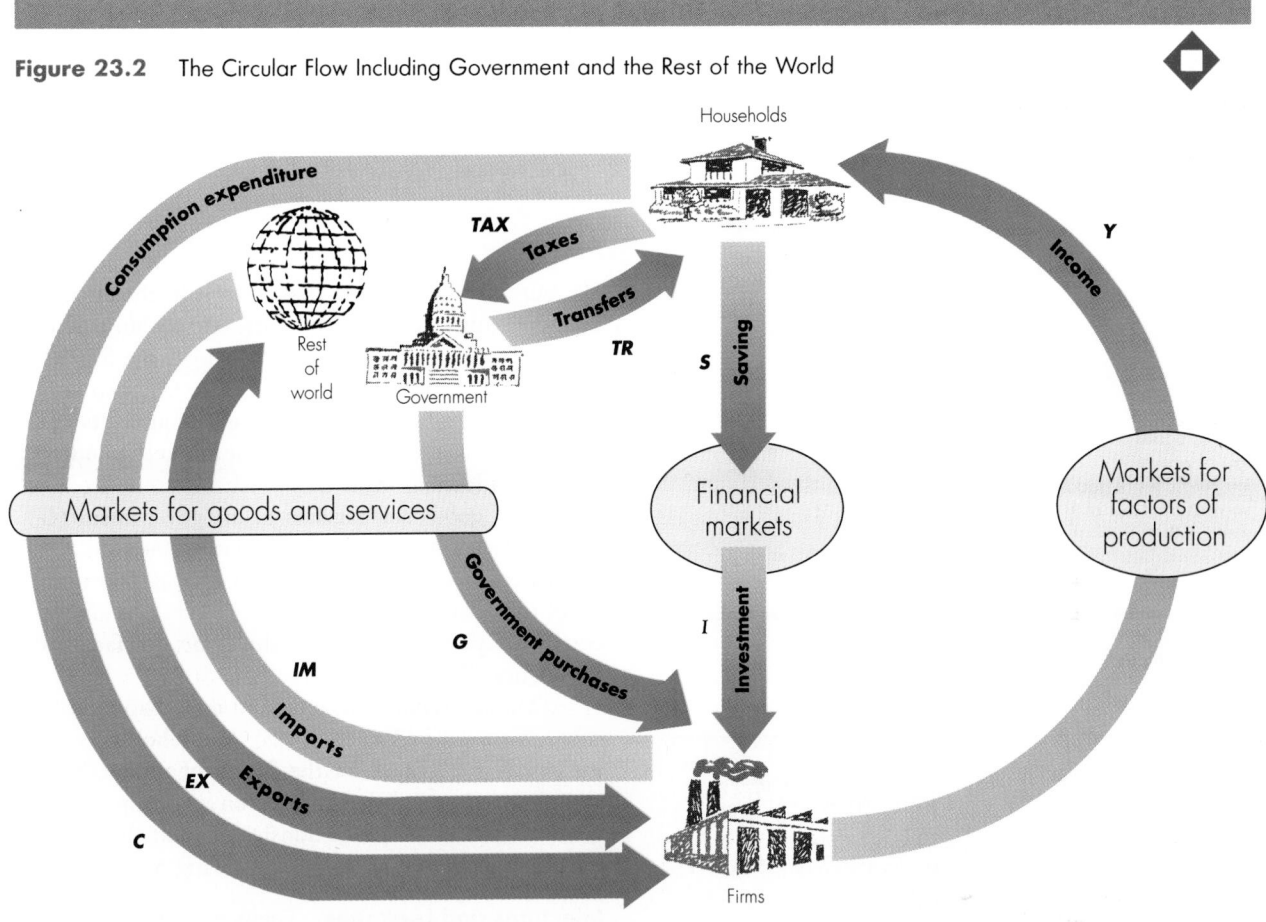

Households and firms interact not only with each other but with government and the rest of the world. Households pay taxes (*TAX*) to government and receive transfers (*TR*) from them. Government buys goods and services (*G*) from firms. Firms pay the rest of the world for foreign-produced goods and services (*IM*) and receive money from them for U.S.-produced goods and services (*EX*). Households' income (*Y*) plus transfers received from government (*TR*) are either consumed (*C*), saved (*S*), or paid in taxes (*TAX*). Therefore, $Y = C + S + TAX - TR$. The income paid out by firms (*Y*) equals the value of expenditure or output. Therefore, $Y = C + I + G + EX - IM$.

The value of output (GNP) also equals aggregate expenditure, or aggregate income. This equality occurs because we can measure the value of output either as the sum of the incomes paid to the factors of production or as the expenditure on that output.

Households   Let's next look at households in Fig. 23.2. There are two flows into households and three flows out. The flows in are income and transfer payments. The flows out are consumption expenditure, saving, and taxes. **Saving** equals disposable income minus consumption expenditure. **Disposable income** equals income plus transfer payments minus taxes. With this modified definition of saving, it is clear that everything received by households—income and transfer payments—is either spent on consumption goods, paid in taxes, or saved. That is,

$$Y + TR = C + S + TAX.$$

It is important not to confuse government transfer payments with government purchases of goods and services. The name *transfer payments* is

Table 23.1   Firms' and Households' Accounts

(a) Firms

Revenue		Expenditure	
Sale of consumption goods and services	C	Payments to factors of production	Y
Sale of capital goods	I		
Sale of goods and services to government	G		
Sale of goods and services to rest of world (EX), less Purchases of goods and services from rest of world (IM)	NX		
Total	Y		Y

(b) Households

Income		Expenditure	
Payments for supplies of factors of production	Y	Purchases of consumption goods and services	C
		Taxes paid (TAX), less Transfers received (TR)	T
		Saving	S
Total	Y		Y

Firms, shown in part (a), receive an income from the sale of consumption goods and services to households (C), capital goods to other firms (I), goods and services to government (G), and net exports (NX), or the difference between the value of their sales to the rest of the world (EX) and their purchases of goods from the rest of the world (IM). They make payments for the services of factors of production (Y). Their total income equals their total expenditure—$Y = C + I + G + NX$. Households, shown in part (b), receive an income for the supply of factors of production (Y). They buy consumer goods and services from firms (C) and pay taxes net of transfers received from the government (T). The part of their income that is not spent on consumption goods or taxes is saved (S). Consumption expenditure plus taxes plus saving is equal to income—$Y = C + T + S$.

designed to remind us that these items are simply transfers of money and, as such, are a bit like taxes except that they flow in the opposite direction—they

flow from government to households. We'll call the difference between taxes and transfers net taxes, denoted by T. We can now simplify the above equation showing the household flows to

$$Y = C + S + T.$$

Income and Expenditure Accounts

We can record the transactions shown in the circular flow diagram in a set of accounts, one for firms and one for households. Table 23.1(a) shows the firm's revenue and expenditure account. The first two sources of revenue are the sale of goods and services to households and the sale of capital goods to other firms. In addition, firms now receive revenue from the sale of goods and services to the government (G) and for their sale of goods and services (net of purchases) to the rest of the world (NX). The sum of all their sources of revenue ($C + I + G + NX$) equals the payments made to the owners of factors of production (Y).

The households' income and expenditure account is shown in Table 23.1(b): Households receive income Y in payment for the factors of production supplied and spend that income on consumption goods C, pay taxes net of transfers T, and the balancing item, as before, is household saving S.

Injections and Leakages   The flow of income from firms to households and of consumption expenditure from households to firms is the circular flow of income and expenditure. Investment, government purchases of goods and services, and exports are called **injections** into the circular flow of expenditure and income. Taxes, saving, and imports are called **leakages** from the circular flow of expenditure and income. Let's take a closer look at these leakages and injections.

We have seen from the firms' accounts that

$$Y = C + I + G + EX - IM.$$

We have also seen from the households' accounts that

$$Y = C + S + T.$$

Since the left side of these two equations is the same, it follows that

$$I + G + EX - IM = S + T.$$

If we add IM to both sides of this equation, we get

$$I + G + EX = S + T + IM.$$

The left side shows the injections into the circular flow of expenditure and income and the right side the leakages from the circular flow. *The injections into the circular flow equal the leakages from the circular flow.* The circular flow of income and expenditure, and the income and expenditure accounts of firms and households, are our tools for measuring GNP.

Let's now see how the accountants at the Department of Commerce use these concepts to measure the GNP of the United States.

U.S. National Income and Product Accounts

The Department of Commerce uses three methods to measure GNP:

- Expenditure approach
- Factor incomes approach
- Output approach

Let's look at what is involved in using these three alternative ways of measuring GNP.

The Expenditure Approach

The **expenditure approach** measures GNP by adding together consumption expenditure (C), investment (I), government purchases of goods and services (G), and net exports (NX). This approach is illustrated in Table 23.2. The numbers refer to 1988 and are in billions of dollars. The name of the item used in the *National Income and Product Accounts of the United States* (published by the Department of Commerce) appears in the first column, and the symbol we have used in our GNP equations appears in the next column. To measure GNP using the expenditure approach, we add together personal consumption expenditures (C), gross private domestic investment (I), government purchases of goods and services (G), and net exports of goods and services (NX).

Personal consumption expenditures are all the expenditures on goods and services produced by firms and sold to households. They include goods such as soda, records, books and magazines as well as services such as insurance, banking, and legal advice. They do not include the purchase of new residential houses, which is counted as part of investment.

Gross private domestic investment is expenditure on capital equipment by firms and expenditure on

---

Table 23.2   GNP: The Expenditure Approach

Item	Symbol	Amount in 1988 (billions of dollars)	Percentage of GNP
Personal consumption expenditures	C	3227	66
Gross private domestic investment	I	767	16
Government purchases of goods and services	G	965	20
Net export earnings	NX	−95	− 2
Gross national product	Y	4864	100

The expenditure approach measures GNP by adding together personal consumption expenditures, gross private domestic investment, government purchases of goods and services, and net exports. In 1988, GNP measured by the expenditure approach was $4864 billion. Two thirds of expenditure is on personal consumption of goods and services.

Source: U.S. Department of Commerce, *Survey of Current Business* (April 1989), p. 10.

new residential houses by households. It also includes the change in firms' inventories. **Inventories** are the stocks of raw materials, semifinished products, and unsold final products held by firms. Inventories are an essential input into the production process. If a firm does not hold inventories of raw materials, its production process can operate only as quickly as the rate at which new raw materials can be delivered. Similarly, if a firm does not have inventories of semifinished goods, processes at later stages of production may become disrupted as a result of breakdowns or accidents at earlier stages. Finally, by holding inventories of finished goods, firms can respond to fluctuations in sales, standing ready to meet an exceptional surge in demand.

The stock of plant, equipment, and buildings (including residential housing) is called the **capital stock.** Additions to the capital stock are investment.

Government purchases of goods and services are the purchases of goods by all levels of government—from Washington to the local town hall. This item of expenditure includes the cost of providing national defense, law and order, street lighting, and garbage collection. It does not include *transfer payments*. As we have seen, such payments do not represent a purchase of goods and services but rather a transfer of money from government to households.

Net exports of goods and services are the difference between the value of exports and imports. When IBM sells a computer to Volkswagen, the German car producer, the value of that computer is part of U.S. exports. When you buy a new Mazda RX7, your expenditure is part of U.S. imports. The difference between what the country earns by selling to the rest of the world and what it pays for goods bought from the rest of the world is the value of net exports.

Table 23.2 shows the relative importance of the four items of aggregate expenditure. As you can see, personal consumption is by far the largest component of the expenditures that add up to GNP.

The Factor Incomes Approach

The **factor incomes approach** measures GNP by adding together all the incomes paid by firms to households for the services of the factors of production they hire—wages for labor, interest for capital, rent for land, and profits. But this addition, on its own, does not give GNP. Some further adjustments have to be made. Let's see what these adjustments are, and how the factor incomes approach works.

The *National Income and Products Accounts* divide factor incomes into five components:

- Compensation of employees
- Rental income
- Corporate profits
- Net interest
- Proprietors' income

Compensation of employees is the total payments by firms for labor services. This item includes the net wages and salaries (called take-home pay) that workers receive each week or month, plus taxes withheld on earnings, plus all fringe benefits such as social security and pension fund contributions.

Rental income is the payment for the use of land and other rented inputs. It includes payments for rented housing and inputed rent for owner-occupied housing. (Inputed rent is an estimate of what homeowners would pay to rent the housing they own. By including this item in the national income accounts, we measure the total value of housing services, whether they are owned or rented.)

Corporate profits are the total profits made by corporations. Some of these profits are paid out to households in the form of dividends and some are retained by the corporations as undistributed profits.

Net interest is the total interest payments received by households on loans made by them minus interest payments made by households on their own borrowing. Interest is net in the sense that interest payments by households are netted out from interest receipts by households. This item includes, on the plus side, payments of interest by firms to households on bonds and on the minus side, households' interest payments on the outstanding balances on their credit cards.

Proprietors' income is a mixture of the elements that we have just reviewed. The proprietor of an owner-operated business supplies labor, capital, and perhaps land and buildings to the business. National income accountants find it difficult to split up the income earned by an owner-operator into its component parts—compensation for labor, payment for the use of capital, rent payments for the use of land or buildings, and profit. As a consequence, the national income accounts lump all these separate factor incomes earned by proprietorships into a single category.

Net national income at factor cost is the sum of all factor incomes. Thus if we add together the items that we have just reviewed, we arrive at this measure of aggregate income. To measure GNP using the factor incomes approach, we have to make two adjustments to *net national income at factor cost.* Let's see what these adjustments are.

Factor Cost and Market Price   When we calculate GNP using the expenditure approach, we add together expenditures on *final goods and services.* These expenditures are valued at the prices people pay for the various goods and services. The price that people pay for a good or service is called the **market price.** There is another way of valuing a good — factor cost. **Factor cost** is the value of a good measured by adding together the costs of all the factors of production used to produce it. If the only economic transactions that take place are between households and firms — if there were no government — the market price and factor cost methods of measuring value are identical. But transactions involving the government can drive a wedge between these two methods of valuation. The source of that wedge is indirect taxes and subsidies.

An **indirect tax** is a tax paid by consumers when they purchase goods and services. Examples of indirect taxes are state sales taxes and taxes on alcohol, gasoline, and tobacco products. Indirect taxes result in the consumer paying more than the producer receives for a good. For example, suppose that in your state there is a sales tax of 7 percent. If you buy a $1 chocolate bar, it costs you $1.07. The total cost, including profit, of all the inputs used to produce the chocolate bar, is $1. The market price value of the chocolate bar is $1.07. The factor cost value of the chocolate bar is $1.

A **subsidy** is a payment made by the government to producers. Examples are subsidies paid to grain growers and dairy farmers. A subsidy also drives a wedge between the market price value and the factor cost value but in the opposite direction to indirect taxes. A subsidy lowers the market price below the factor cost — consumers pay less for the good than it costs the producer to make the good.

To use the factor incomes approach to measure gross national product, we need to add indirect taxes to total factor incomes and subtract subsidies. Making this adjustment still does not quite get us to GNP. There is one further adjustment needed.

Net National Product and Gross National Product   If we total all the factor incomes and add indirect taxes less subsidies to that total, we arrive at net national product at market prices. **Net national**

product at market prices equals the sum of all factor incomes plus indirect taxes minus subsidies. What is the meaning of the words *gross* and *net* and what is the distinction between the two terms *net national product* and *gross national product*?

The difference between these two terms is accounted for by the depreciation of capital. **Depreciation** is the reduction in the value of the capital stock that results from wear and tear and the passage of time. We've seen that investment is the purchase of new capital equipment. Depreciation is the opposite — the wearing out or destruction of capital equipment. Part of investment represents the purchase of capital equipment to replace equipment that has worn out. That investment does not add to the stock of capital; it simply maintains the capital stock. The other part of investment represents additions to the capital stock — the purchase of new additional plant, equipment, and inventories. Total investment is called gross investment. **Gross investment** is the amount spent on replacing depreciated capital and on net additions to the capital stock. The difference between gross investment and depreciation is called net investment. **Net investment** is the net addition to the capital stock. Let's illustrate these ideas with an example.

On January 1, 1989, Swanky, Inc., had a capital stock consisting of three knitting machines that had a market value of $7500. In 1989, Swanky bought a new machine for $3000. But during the year the machines owned by Swanky depreciated by $1000. By December 31, 1989, Swanky's stock of knitting machines was worth $9500. Swanky's purchase of a new machine for $3000 is the firm's gross investment. The firm's net investment — the difference between gross investment ($3000) and depreciation ($1000) — is $2000. These transactions and the relationship between gross investment, net investment, and depreciation are summarized in Table 23.3.

Gross national product equals net national product plus depreciation. (Depreciation is called *capital consumption* by the national income accountants in the Department of Commerce.) Total expenditure *includes* depreciation — because it includes *gross investment.* Total factor incomes plus indirect taxes less subsidies *exclude* depreciation — because when firms calculate their profit they make an allowance for depreciation and so subtract from their gross profit their estimate of the decrease in the value of their capital stock. As a result, adding up factor incomes gives a measure of national product that is net of the depre-

Table 23.3   Capital Stock, Investment, and Depreciation for Swanky, Inc.

Capital stock on January 1, 1989 (value of knitting machines owned at beginning of year)	$7500
Gross investment (value of new knitting machine bought in 1989)	+3000
less Depreciation (fall in value of knitting machines during year 1989)	−1000
equals Net Investment	2000
Capital stock on December 31, 1989 (value of knitting machines owned at end of year)	9500

Swanky, Inc.'s capital stock at the end of 1989 equals its capital stock at the beginning of the year plus net investment. Net investment is equal to gross investment less depreciation. Gross investment is the value of new machines bought during the year and depreciation is the fall in the value of Swanky's knitting machines over the year.

ciation of the capital stock. To reconcile the factor incomes and expenditure approaches, we must add capital consumption (depreciation) to net national product. Table 23.4 summarizes these calculations and shows how the factor incomes approach leads to the same estimate of GNP as the expenditure approach. The numbers are for 1988 and are in billions of dollars. The table also shows the relative importance of the various factor incomes. As you can see, wages and salaries (compensation of employees) is by far the most important factor income.

The Output Approach

The **output approach** measures GNP by summing the value added of each firm in the economy. **Value added** is the value of a firm's output minus the value of inputs bought from other firms. Let's illustrate value added by looking at the production of a chocolate bar.

Table 23.5 takes you through the brief but sweet life of a chocolate bar. It starts with the producers of the raw materials that go into the chocolate bar. Milk, sugar, cocoa beans, and electric power are produced by farmers and an electric utility company.

Let's suppose (just for the purpose of this story) that these producers buy no inputs other than factor services—labor, capital, and land. When the chocolate producer buys milk, sugar, cocoa beans, and electric power, it pays for the value added by firms in those other sectors of the economy. The chocolate producer combines the milk, sugar, and cocoa by using equipment driven by the electric power it purchases and operated by labor that it hires to make the chocolate bars. The payment made by the chocolate producer to the labor that it hires is part of the value added in the chocolate sector of the economy.

When the chocolate producer sells the chocolate bar to a wholesaler, there is some more value added in the chocolate sector: the profit of the chocolate producer. That profit is obviously not the entire 72¢ received from the wholesaler for the chocolate bar. It

Table 23.4   GNP: The Factor Incomes Approach

Item	Amount in 1988 (billions of dollars)	Percentage of GNP
Compensation of employees	2905	60
Rental income	19	—*
Corporate profits	328	7
Net interest	392	8
Proprietors' income	324	7
Indirect taxes *less* Subsidies	390	8
Capital consumption (depreciation)	506	10
Gross national product	4864	100

*Less than 0.5%.

The sum of all factor incomes equals net national income at factor cost. GNP equals net national income at factor cost plus indirect taxes minus subsidies plus capital consumption (depreciation). In 1988, GNP measured by the factor incomes approach was $4864 billion. The compensation of employees—labor income—was by far the largest part of total factor incomes.

Source: U.S. Department of Commerce, *Survey of Current Business* (April 1989), p. 12.

Table 23.5 Value Added in the Life of a Chocolate Bar

Transaction	Total amount paid/received (dollars)	Value added (dollars)	Sector in which value is added
Chocolate producer buys milk	0.04	0.04	Dairy
Chocolate producer buys sugar	0.08	0.08	Sugar
Chocolate producer buys cocoa beans	0.08	0.08	Cocoa
Chocolate producer buys electric power	0.12	0.12	Electric
Chocolate producer pays labor	0.28	0.28	Chocolate
Chocolate producer sells to wholesaler	0.72	0.12	Chocolate
Wholesaler sells to retailer	0.80	0.08	Wholesale
Retailer sells to you	1.00	0.20	Retail
Total	$3.12	$1.00	

To produce a $1 chocolate bar, a chocolate producer buys milk, sugar, cocoa beans, and electric power from other producers. The value of these inputs into the chocolate bar are part of the product—value added—of the dairy, sugar, cocoa, and electric sectors of the economy. The chocolate producer buys labor services and sells the chocolate bar to the wholesaler at a profit. Its labor cost and profit are part of the value added in the chocolate sector. The wholesaler sells to the retailer, providing a service and adding further value to the chocolate bar. Finally, the retailer sells to you, the customer, adding further value in the form of retail services. The sum of all the amounts paid and received—$3.12—is a mixture of expenditure on intermediate goods and services and expenditure on the final good, and it has no economic meaning. The sum of the value added in each sector equals final expenditure on the chocolate bar.

is the difference between the 72¢ and all the previous expenditures. If you add up those expenditures, you will see that they total 60¢, which means that the chocolate producer's profit is 12¢. The value added in the chocolate sector is 40¢—the wages of the workers 28¢ and the profit of the producer 12¢. When the wholesaler sells the chocolate bar to the retailer, there is some more value added. That value added is 8¢ and represents the profit of the wholesaler and the payments made by the wholesaler for labor and other factors of production hired in that sector. Finally, when the retailer sells the chocolate bar to you, there is yet further value added—20¢—which represents the retailer's profit and factor costs.

If we total all the value added in the dairy, sugar, cocoa, electric, chocolate, wholesale, and retail sectors we see that they come to $1, the price paid

by you for the chocolate bar. If we add up all the amounts received and paid they total $3.12. That total has no economic meaning.

The story of the life of a chocolate bar illustrates an important distinction between expenditure on final goods and expenditure on intermediate goods.

Final Goods and Intermediate Goods In valuing output, we count only expenditure on *final goods.* The only thing that's been produced and consumed here is a $1 chocolate bar. All the other transactions involve the purchase and sale of *intermediate goods.* To count the expenditure on intermediate goods and services as well as the expenditure on the final good involves counting the same thing twice, or more than twice when there are several intermediate stages, as there are in this example. Counting both expenditure on final goods and intermediate goods is known as **double counting.**

Milk, sugar, cocoa, and electric power are all intermediate goods in the production of a chocolate bar—the final good. But the milk, sugar, cocoa, and electric power that you consume directly yourself are final goods. Thus whether a good is intermediate or final depends not on what it is but what it is used for.

When the output approach is used to measure GNP in the United States economy, the result for 1987, the latest year available, is set out in Table 23.6. The value added of all the sectors sum to the gross *domestic* product. **Gross domestic product,**

or GDP, measures the value of output *produced in* the United States. Gross *national* product is the total value of output *owned by residents* of the United States. The difference between gross *domestic* product and gross *national* product is the net investment income that U.S. residents receive from other parts of the world. For example, Americans own production plants in Japan and Europe. Japanese and European residents own production plants in the United States. Net investment income received from the rest of the world is the total payment of profits and dividends to U.S. residents on their foreign investments less the payments of interest and dividends to foreigners on their investments in the United States.

When we use the output approach to measure GNP, we do not obtain the same numerical estimate as that obtained by using the expenditure approach. The difference is called the statistical discrepancy. This discrepancy is usually small relative to the aggregates being measured—in 1987 it was $8 billion, ⅕ of 1 percent of GNP.

Table 23.6   GNP: The Output Approach

Sector	Value added in 1987 (billions of dollars)
Agriculture, forestry, and fisheries	95
Mining	85
Construction	219
Manufacturing	854
Transportation and public utilities	408
Wholesale trade	313
Retail trade	427
Finance, insurance, and real estate	775
Services	794
Government and government enterprises	535
Statistical discrepancy	− 8
Gross domestic product	4497
Net investment income from rest of world	30
Gross national product	4527

The output approach measures GNP by adding together the value added in each sector of the economy. In 1987, GNP measured by this approach was $4527 billion.

Source: U.S. Department of Commerce, *Survey of Current Business* (July 1988), p. 78.

Measured and Actual Gross National Product

Gross national product aims to measure the total value of economic activity taking place in the nation. But some productive activities are not measured and included as part of GNP. Let's review the more important of these activities.

Crime A great many people make a living by "working" in activities that are illegal. In today's economy, various forms of illegal gambling, prostitution, and drug trading are an important omitted component of economic activity.

It is impossible to measure the scale of illegal activities but guesses range between 1 and 2 percent of GNP (between $49 billion and $98 billion).

Underground Economy The **underground economy** is all economic activity that is legal but unreported. Though much of the economic activity that takes place in the underground economy is legal, the participants withhold information about the activity to evade taxes or regulations. For example, avoiding safety regulations, minimum wage laws, social security payments, or other fringe benefits are motives for operating in the underground economy. Attempts have been made to estimate the scale of the underground economy and guesses range between 5 and 15 percent of GNP ($245 billion to $735 billion).

Nonmarket Activities An enormous amount of economic activity that is perfectly legal and which no one is obliged to report takes place every day in our own homes. Changing a light bulb, cutting the grass, washing the car, laundering a shirt, painting a door, and teaching a child to catch a ball are all examples of productive activities that do not involve market transactions and that are excluded from GNP.

Is Measurement Error a Problem? Whether the factors left out of GNP are important depends on the questions being asked. Measures of GNP are used for three main purposes:

- To assess which phase of the business cycle the economy is in
- To compare standards of living at different points in time
- To compare standards of living in different countries

For business cycle questions, errors in measuring national income are probably not important at all. The ups and downs of measured economic activity are probably mirrored fairly closely by fluctuations in most of the unmeasured components. For the other two uses of GNP, measurement errors can be important. For example, in developing countries the nonmarket and underground economies are a much higher fraction of economic activity than in developed countries. This fact makes comparisons of GNP between countries such as the United States and Nigeria, for example, unreliable measures of comparative living standards unless the GNP data are supplemented with other information.

Using GNP data to gauge changes in living standards over time is unreliable, not so much because of mismeasurement of production but because of conceptual problems. Living standards depend only partly on the value of output. They also depend on the composition of output. For example, two economies may have the same GNP but one economy may produce more weapons and the other more music. Consumers will not be indifferent as to which of these two economies they live in.

Other factors affecting living standards include the amount of leisure time available, the quality of the environment, the security of jobs and homes, the safety of city streets, and so on. It is possible to construct broader measures that combine the many factors that contribute to human happiness and GNP will be one element in that measure. But it will be by no means the whole of it.

The Price Level and Inflation

To measure the price level, we use a price index. The value of a price index in the current year is the ratio of the value of a basket of goods in the current year to the value of that same basket of goods in an earlier year called the *base period,* multiplied by 100. For example, suppose that Tom buys the "basket" of goods shown in Table 23.7. That is, he buys 4 movies and 2 six-packs of soda. In the base period, the price of a movie is $6 and the price of soda is $3 a six-pack. The value of Tom's basket in the base period is $30. In the current period, a movie costs $6.75 and soda costs $4.20 a six-pack. The current value of Tom's basket is $35.40. The current value of the price index of Tom's basket is

$$(\$35.4/\$30) \times 100 = 118.$$

Notice that if the current period and the base period were one and the same, the value of the price index would be 100.

There are two main price indexes used to measure the price level in the United States today: the Consumer Price Index and the GNP deflator. The **Consumer Price Index (CPI)** measures the average level of prices of the goods and services typically consumed by an urban American family. The **GNP deflator** measures the average level of prices of all the goods and services that are included in GNP. We are now going to study the method used for determining these price indexes. In calculating the actual indexes, the Departments of Commerce and Labor process millions of pieces of information. But we can learn the principles involved in those calculations by working through some simple examples.

Consumer Price Index

The *Consumer Price Index* measures the average level of prices of the goods and services typically consumed by an urban American family. The Bureau of Labor Statistics in the U.S. Department of Labor calculates and publishes the CPI every month.

To construct this price index, the Department of Labor first selects a base period. Currently the base period is the three-year period from 1982 through 1984. It then selects a basket of goods—the quantities of approximately 400 different goods and services that were typically consumed by urban households in the base period.

Table 23.7   Calculating a Price Index

Good	1988 (base period)			1989 (current period)	
	Quantity bought	Price	Expenditure	Price	Expenditure
Movies	4	$6	$24	$6.75	$27.00
Six-packs of soda	2	3	6	4.20	8.40
			$30		$35.40

Price index for 1989 $= \dfrac{\$35.40}{\$30.00} \times 100 = 118$

A price index for 1989 is calculated in two steps. The first step is to value the goods bought in 1988, the base period, at the prices prevailing in both 1988 and 1989. The second step is to divide the value of those goods in 1989 by their value in 1988, and multiply the result by 100.

Table 23.8   The Consumer Price Index: A Simplified Calculation

Items in the basket	Base period			Current period	
	Quantity	Price	Expenditure	Price	Expenditures on base-period quantities
Oranges	5 pounds	$ 0.80/pound	$ 4	$ 1.20/pound	$ 6
Haircuts	6	11.00 each	66	12.50 each	75
Bus rides	200	0.70 each	140	0.75 each	150
Total expenditure			$210		$231
CPI	$\dfrac{\$210.00}{\$210.00} \times 100 = 100$			$\dfrac{\$231.00}{\$210.00} \times 100 = 110$	

A fixed basket of goods—5 pounds of oranges, 6 haircuts, and 200 bus rides—is valued in the base period at $210. Prices change and that same basket is valued at $231 in the current period. The CPI is equal to the current-period value of the basket divided by the base-period value of the basket multiplied by 100. In the base period the **CPI** is 100 and in the current period the **CPI** is 110.

Every month the Department of Labor sends a team of observers to more than 50 urban centers in the United States to record the prices for these 400 items. When all the data are collected, the CPI is calculated by expressing the current month's value of the base-period basket as a percentage of the base-period's value of the base-period basket.

To see more precisely how the CPI is calculated, let's work through an example. Table 23.8 summarizes our calculations.

Let's suppose that there are only three goods in the typical consumer's basket: oranges, haircuts, and bus rides. The quantities bought and the prices prevailing in the base period are shown in the table. Total expenditure in the base period is also shown: The typical consumer buys 200 bus rides at 70¢ each and so spends $140 on bus rides. Expenditure on oranges and haircuts are worked out in the same way. Total expenditure is the sum of expenditures on the three goods, which is $210.

To calculate the price index for the current period, all we need to do is to discover the prices of the goods in the current period. We do not need to know the quantities bought. Let's suppose that the prices are those set out in the table under "current period." We can now calculate the current period's value of the basket of goods by using the current period's prices. For example, the current price of oranges is $1.20 per pound, so the current period's value of the base-period quantity (5 pounds) is 5 multiplied by $1.20, which is $6. The base-period quantities of haircuts and bus rides are valued at this period's prices in a similar way. The total value in the current period of the base-period basket is $231.

We can now calculate the CPI—the ratio of this period's value of the goods to the base period's value, multiplied by 100. In this example, the CPI for the current period is 110. The CPI for the base period is by definition 100.

GNP Deflator

The *GNP deflator* measures the average level of the prices of all the goods and services that make up GNP. It is calculated as the ratio of nominal GNP to real GNP, multiplied by 100. We use the term nominal GNP, because it measures the money value of output. Real GNP is a measure of the physical volume of output arrived at by valuing the current period output at prices that prevailed in a *base period*. Currently, the base period for calculating real GNP is 1982. We refer to the units in which real GNP is measured as "1982 dollars."

The values of Table 23.9 show nominal GNP, real GNP, and the GNP deflator for selected years since 1942. As you can see, nominal GNP has increased by a much larger proportion than real GNP. In fact, nominal GNP in 1988 is 30 times what it was in 1942, while real GNP is only 3.7 times its 1942 value. The GNP deflator is 8.3 times as high in 1988 as it was in 1942.

Table 23.9   Nominal GNP, Real GNP, and the GNP Deflator

Year	Nominal GNP (trillions of dollars)	Real GNP (trillions of 1982 dollars)	GNP deflator (1982 = 100)
1942	0.16	1.08	14.7
1952	0.35	1.38	25.5
1962	0.57	1.80	31.9
1972	1.21	2.61	46.5
1982	3.17	3.17	100.0
1988	4.86	4.00	121.7

Nominal GNP measures the money value of output. Real GNP measures the physical volume of output. Nominal GNP values output in the prices that prevailed in the period in question. Real GNP values output in the prices of a common base period. In the table, goods and services produced between 1942 and 1987 are valued in the prices that prevailed in 1982. The GNP deflator is equal to nominal GNP divided by real GNP multiplied by 100. In 1982, the base period, the GNP deflator is 100. Nominal GNP in 1988 is 30 times what it was in 1942; real GNP is 3.7 times as high, and the GNP deflator is 8.3 times as high.

Sources: Economic Report of the President (1989), Tables B-1, B-2, and B-3, pp. 248–252; and U.S. Department of Commerce, *Survey of Current Business* (April 1989), pp. 10, 21.

We are going to learn how to calculate the GNP deflator by studying an imaginary economy. We will calculate nominal GNP and real GNP as well as the GNP deflator. To make our calculations simple, let's imagine an economy that has just three final goods: The consumption good is oranges; the capital good is computers; and the government purchases red tape. (Net exports are zero in this example.) Table 23.10 summarizes the calculations of nominal GNP, real GNP, and the GNP deflator in this economy.

Let's focus first on calculating nominal GNP. We'll use the expenditure approach. The table shows quantities of the final goods and their prices. To calculate nominal GNP, let's work out the expenditure on each good and then total the three

Table 23.10   Nominal GNP, Real GNP and the GNP Deflator: Simplified Calculations

Item	Current period			Base period	
	Quantity	Price	Expenditure	Price	Expenditure
Oranges	4240 pounds	$1.05/pound	$ 4,452	$1/pound	$ 4,240
Computers	5	$2100/each	10,500	$2000 each	10,000
Red tape	1060 yards	$1/yard	1,060	$1/yard	1,060
	Nominal GNP		$16,012	Real GNP	$15,300

Deflators for current period

GNP deflator

$$= \frac{\$16,012}{\$15,300} \times 100 = 104.7$$

Consumption expenditure deflator

$$= \frac{\$4,452}{\$4,240} \times 100 = 105$$

Investment deflator

$$= \frac{\$10,500}{\$10,000} \times 100 = 105$$

Government purchases of goods and services deflator

$$= \frac{\$1,060}{\$1,060} \times 100 = 100$$

An imaginary economy produces only oranges, computers, and red tape. In the current period, nominal GNP is $16,012. If the current-period quantities are valued at the base-period prices, we obtain a measure of real GNP, which is $15,300. The GNP deflator in the current period—which is calculated by dividing nominal GNP by real GNP in that period and multiplying by 100—is 104.7. Deflators for the components of GNP are calculated in a similar manner.

expenditures. Consumption expenditure (oranges) is $4452, investment (computers) is $10,500, government purchases of red tape are $1060, so nominal GNP is $16,012.

Next, let's calculate real GNP. This is calculated by valuing the current-period quantities at the base-period prices. The table shows the prices for the base period. Real expenditure on oranges for the current period is 4240 pounds of oranges valued at $1 per pound, which is $4240. If we perform the same types of calculations for computers and red tape and add up the real expenditures, we arrive at a real GNP of $15,300.

To calculate the GNP deflator for the current period, we divide nominal GNP ($16,012) by real GNP ($15,300) and multiply the result by 100. The GNP deflator that we obtain is 104.7. If the current period is also the base period, nominal GNP equals real GNP and the GNP deflator is 100. Thus the GNP deflator in the base period is 100, just as it is for the CPI.

The national income accountants also calculate deflators for consumption expenditure, investment, and government purchases of goods and services (as well as other more detailed components of GNP). We can calculate deflators for consumption expenditure, investment, and government purchases of goods and services for our imaginary economy. These deflators are calculated in a manner similar to the calculation that we have just performed. For example, the consumption expenditure deflator is calculated by dividing the current period's consumption expenditure by the real consumption expenditure and multiplying by 100. A similar calculation is performed for the other two components of GNP. In our example, the consumption expenditure deflator and the investment deflator are each 105, while the government purchases of goods and services deflator is 100. These deflators make sense when you compare them with the price changes. Oranges and computers have each increased in price by 5 percent and their deflators have moved from 100 to 105. The price of red tape has remained constant at $1 a yard and its deflator has remained constant at 100.

Inflation and Relative Price Changes

The inflation rate is calculated as the percentage increase in the price index. For example, in the case that we studied in Table 23.8, the CPI rose by 10 percent from the base period to the current period. Underlying that change in the price index are the individual changes in the prices of oranges, haircuts, and bus rides. No individual price rose by 10 percent. The price of oranges rose by 50 percent, the price of haircuts by 13.6 percent, and the price of bus rides by 7.1 percent. This example captures a common feature of the world that we live in: It is rarely the case that all prices change by the same percentage amount. When the prices of goods rise by different percentages, there is a change in relative prices. The **relative price** is the ratio of the price of one good to the price of another good. For example, if the price of oranges is 80¢ per pound and the price of a haircut is $11, the relative price of a haircut is 13¾ pounds of oranges. It costs 13¾ pounds of oranges to buy one haircut.

Prices and inflation, of course, mean a great deal to people. However, many people are confused by the difference between the inflation rate and relative price changes. Inflation and relative price changes are completely separate and independent phenomena. To see why this is true, we will work through an example showing that, for the same relative price changes, we can have two entirely different inflation rates.

We will first learn how to calculate a change in relative prices. We can calculate the percentage change in a relative price as the difference between the percentage change in the price minus the inflation rate. Let's use again the calculations that we worked through in Table 23.8, now presented in Table 23.11(a). For example, the price of oranges rises from 80¢ to $1.20, or by 50 percent. We have already calculated that prices on the average rise by 10 percent. To calculate the percentage change in relative prices, subtract the inflation rate from the percentage change in the price of each good. The price of oranges increased relative to the average price of all goods by 50 percent minus 10 percent, which is 40 percent. Bus rides fell in price relative to goods on the average by 2.9 percent. The change in relative prices on the average is zero by definition. For every good whose relative price increases by x percent there must be other goods whose relative prices fall by an average of x percent.

In Table 23.11(b), we will see that relative prices can change without inflation. In fact, part (b) illustrates the same changes in relative prices that occurred in part (a) but with no inflation. In this case, the price of oranges increases by 40 percent to $1.12, the price of haircuts increases by 3.6 percent to $11.40, and the price of bus rides falls by 2.9 percent, to 68¢. If you calculate the current and base-period values of the basket in part (b), you will find that consumers spend exactly the same at the new prices as they do at the base-period prices. There is no inflation, even though relative prices have changed.

We've now looked at two cases in which the relative price of oranges increases by 40 percent. In one, inflation is 10 percent; in the other, there is no inflation. Clearly, inflation has not been *caused by* the change in the price of oranges. In the first case, the price of each good increases by 10 percent more than it does in the second case. Singling out the good whose relative price has increased most does not help us explain why all prices are rising by 10 percent more in the first case than in the second case.

Any inflation rate can occur with any behavior of relative prices. Relative prices are determined by supply and demand in the markets for the individual goods and services. The price level and the inflation rate are determined independently of *relative* prices. To explain an increase (or decrease) in the inflation rate, we have to explain why all prices are inflating at a different rate and not why some prices are increasing faster than others. Not everyone understands this distinction (see Reading Between the Lines, p. 608).

Table 23.11   Relative Price Changes With or Without Inflation

(a) 10 percent inflation

Item	Base-period price	New price	Percentage change in price	Percentage change in relative price
Oranges	$ 0.80	$ 1.20	50.0	+40.0
Haircuts	11.00	12.50	13.6	+ 3.6
Bus rides	0.70	0.75	7.1	− 2.9

(b) No inflation

Item	Base-period price	New price	Percentage change in price	Percentage change in relative price
Oranges	$ 0.80	$ 1.12	+40.0	+40.0
Haircuts	11.00	11.40	+ 3.6	+ 3.6
Bus rides	0.70	0.68	− 2.9	− 2.9

A relative price is the price of one good divided by the price of another good. Relative prices change whenever the price of one good changes by a different percentage from the price of some other good. Relative price changes do not cause inflation. They can occur with or without inflation. In part (a), the price index rises by 10 percent. In part (b), the price index remains constant. In both parts, the relative price of oranges increases by 40 percent and that of haircuts by 3.6 percent, and the relative price of bus rides falls by 2.9 percent. The rise in the price of oranges cannot be regarded as the cause of the rise in the price index in part (a) because that same rise in the price of oranges occurs with no change in the price index in part (b).

The Consumer Price Index and the Cost of Living

Does the Consumer Price Index measure the cost of living? Does a 5 percent increase in the CPI mean that the cost of living has increased by 5 percent?

A change in the CPI measures the percentage change in the price of a *fixed* basket of goods and services. The actual basket of goods and services bought depends on relative prices and on consumers' tastes. Changes in relative prices will lead consumers to economize on goods that have become relatively expensive and to buy more of those goods whose relative prices have fallen. If chicken doubles in price but the price of beef increases by only 5 percent, people will substitute the now relatively less expensive beef for the relatively more expensive chicken. Because consumers make such substitutions, a price index based on a fixed basket will overstate the effects of a given price change on the consumer's cost of living.

Discrepancies between the CPI and the cost of living also arise from the disappearance of some commodities and the emergence of new ones. For example, suppose that you want to compare the cost of living in 1990 with that in 1890. Using a price index that has horse feed in it will not work. Though that price featured in people's transportation costs in 1890, it plays no role today. Similarly, a price index with gasoline in it will be of little use since gasoline, while relevant today, did not feature in people's spending in 1890. Even comparisons between 1990 and 1980 suffer from this same problem. Compact discs and microwave popcorn that feature in our budgets in 1990 were not available in 1980.

Substitution effects, and the arrival of new goods, make the connection between the CPI and the cost of living imprecise. To reduce the problems that arise from this source, the Bureau of Labor Statistics updates the weights used for calculating the CPI from time to time. Even so, the CPI is of limited value for making comparisons of the cost of living over long periods of time. But for the purpose for which it was devised—calculating month-to-month and year-to-year rates of inflation—the CPI does a pretty good job.

■ In Chapter 22, we examined the macroeconomic performance of the United States in recent years and over a longer sweep of history. In this chapter, we studied in some detail the methods used for measuring the macroeconomy and in particular the average level of prices and the overall level of real economic activity. In the following chapters, we're going to study some macroeconomic models—models designed to explain and predict the behavior of real GNP, the price level, employment and unemployment, the stock market, and other related phenomena. We start this process in the next chapter by examining a macroeconomic model of demand and supply—a model of *aggregate* demand and *aggregate* supply.

SUMMARY

The Circular Flow of Expenditure and Income

All economic agents—households, firms, government, and the rest of the world—interact in the circular flow of income and expenditure. Households sell factors of production to firms and buy consumption goods and services from firms. Firms hire factors of production from households and pay incomes to households in exchange for factor services. Firms sell consumption goods and services to households and capital goods to other firms. Government collects taxes from households and firms, pays benefits under various social programs to households, and buys goods and services from firms. Foreigners buy goods from domestic firms and sell goods to them.

The flow of expenditure on final goods and services winds up as somebody's income. Therefore,

Aggregate income = Aggregate expenditure.

Furthermore, expenditure on final goods and services is a method of valuing the output of the economy. Therefore,

$$\frac{\text{Aggregate}}{\text{income}} = \frac{\text{Aggregate}}{\text{Expenditure}} = \frac{\text{Value of}}{\text{output (GNP)}}$$

From the firm's accounts we know that

$$Y = C + I + G + EX - IM,$$

and from the household's accounts we know that

$$Y = C + S + T.$$

Combining these two equations we obtain

$$I + G + EX = S + T + IM.$$

This equation tells us that injections into the circular flow (left side) equal the leakages from the circular flow (right side). (pp. 590–595)

U.S. National Income and Product Accounts

Because aggregate expenditure, aggregate income, and the value of output are equal, national income accountants can measure GNP using one of three approaches: expenditure, factor incomes, and output.

The expenditure approach adds together consumption expenditure, investment, government purchases of goods and services, and net exports to arrive at an estimate of GNP.

The factor incomes approach adds together the incomes paid to the various factors of production plus profit paid to the owners of firms. To use the factor incomes approach, it is necessary to make an adjustment from the factor cost value of GNP to the market price value by adding indirect taxes and

Relative
Prices
and Inflation

Consumer Prices in July Increased by a Modest 0.2%

Gain Is Smallest for the Year as Energy Costs Moderate and Food Turns Down

In another sign of slowing inflation, the Labor Department reported today that consumer prices rose a modest two-tenths of 1 percent in July. It was the smallest monthly rise in the Consumer Price Index this year.

A downturn in food prices and moderating energy prices, always volatile factors, were largely responsible for last month's small advance, which was half of June's rate. . . .

Excluding food and energy prices, the consumer index rose three-tenths of 1 percent in July, following a two-tenths of 1 percent increase in June. . . .

Today's Labor Department report showed that food and beverage prices declined two-tenths of 1 percent in July, following a seven-tenths of 1 percent rise in June. The drop was largely the result of a turnaround in fruit and vegetable prices.

Apparel prices fell for the second consecutive month, after advancing 4.6 percent in the first five months of the year. Last month's decline of six-tenths of 1 percent was attributed principally to larger-than-usual seasonal price reductions for women's clothing and shoes.

Slower Pace for Energy Prices

Energy prices continued to advance, albeit at a much slower pace of one-tenth of 1 percent last month, following a 1.5 percent jump in June. Most of the slowdown was attributed to a decline in natural gas prices.

Housing costs rose two-tenths of 1 percent, while transportation costs increased at a more rapid rate of six-tenths of 1 percent. Used-car prices continued to advance sharply, the report said, increasing 1 percent in July and 9.4 percent in the first seven months of the year. By contrast, new-car prices were up four-tenths of 1 percent in July and eight-tenths of 1 percent so far this year.

Both medical care and entertainment costs were up five-tenths of 1 percent last month.

With July's increase, the overall Consumer Price Index covering all urban consumers now stands at 340.8, which means that a basket of goods and services that cost $10 in 1967 now costs $34.08.

The New York Times, **August 22, 1987**

by Gary Klott

The Essence of the Story

- The Consumer Price Index (CPI) for July 1987 was 340.8.

- The rise in the CPI in July 1987 was 0.2 percent, which was smaller than the previous months of 1987.

- Excluding food and energy prices, the index rose by 0.3 percent.

- Fruit and vegetable prices fell.

- There were larger-than-usual seasonal price reductions on women's clothing and shoes.

- The price of natural gas fell and energy prices rose by 0.1 percent compared with 1.5 percent in June.

- The rise in the index in July was half the rise in June.

- New car prices rose by 0.4 percent.

- Medical care and entertainment costs rose by 0.5 percent.

- Housing costs rose by 0.2 percent.

- Transportation costs rose by 0.6 percent.

- Used-car prices rose by 1 percent.

- The fall in food prices and the slower rise in energy prices "were largely responsible for" the inflation slowdown.

Background and Analysis

- This news article does not distinguish between inflation and relative price changes. It claims that the slowdown of inflation was caused by a fall in the relative prices of food and energy.

- The story is really about two independent sets of events:
  - —Relative price changes
  - —Inflation

Relative Price Changes

- In July 1987, the relative prices of fruits and vegetables, women's clothing and shoes, and natural gas fell and the relative prices of most other goods rose.

Inflation Rate

- In July 1987, the inflation rate as measured by the CPI fell to half the June inflation rate and stood at 0.2 percent.

- As you know from your study of the distinction between inflation and relative price changes (see Table 23.11) any inflation rate is possible in combination with any pattern of relative price changes. We cannot look at relative price changes and from those numbers work out why the inflation rate performed in the way that it did.

- A common way of reporting inflation is to examine the change in the inflation rate and then to look at those items in the price index that changed most in the direction of the change in the inflation rate.

- Suppose that the inflation rate had not slowed down in July but had increased slightly. Also suppose that relative price changes were exactly the same as those reported for July. How would the story on the consumer price increase have been written? The conclusion would have been that inflation increased because of the sharp rise in used-car prices, medical care and entertainment cost, new-car prices, and transportation costs in general.

- The change in the CPI is an average of the changes in the prices of the underlying goods. Since relative prices are always changing, some goods will have the fastest price rise and some the slowest price rise (or fastest fall). It is correct to describe the change in the CPI as being made up of the underlying price changes. It is incorrect to attribute cause and effect.

subtracting subsidies. It is also necessary to add capital consumption in order to arrive at GNP.

The output approach sums the value added by each firm in the economy. In using the output approach, it is necessary to be careful to avoid double counting and only measure value added rather than total sales in each sector of the economy.

Actual GNP does not measure all the economic activity in the nation. It excludes crime, the underground economy, and nonmarket activities. (pp. 595–601)

The Price Level and Inflation

There are two major price indexes that measure the price level and inflation: the Consumer Price Index and the GNP deflator.

The CPI measures the average level of prices of goods and services typically consumed by an urban family in the United States. The CPI is the ratio of the value of a base-period basket of commodities at current-period prices to the same basket valued at base-period prices, multiplied by 100.

The GNP deflator is the ratio of nominal GNP to real GNP, multiplied by 100. Nominal GNP is calculated by valuing current-period quantities produced at current-period prices. Real GNP is calculated by valuing the quantities produced in the current period at the prices that prevailed in the base period. The GNP deflator is nominal GNP divided by real GNP, multiplied by 100.

In interpreting changes in prices, we need to distinguish between inflation and relative price changes. A relative price is the price of one good in terms of another good. Relative prices are constantly changing. We cannot tell anything about the sources of inflation by studying which relative prices have changed most. Any relative price changes can occur with any inflation rate.

Because relative prices are constantly changing and causing consumers to substitute less expensive items for more expensive items and because of the disappearance of some goods and the arrival of new goods, the CPI is an imperfect measure of the cost of living, especially when comparisons across a long time span are made. (pp. 601–607)

K E Y   C O N C E P T S

Key Figures and Tables

R E V I E W   Q U E S T I O N S

1 List the components of aggregate expenditure.

2 What are the components of aggregate income?

3 Why does aggregate income equal aggregate expenditure?

4 Why does the value of output (or GNP) equal aggregate income?

5 Distinguish between government purchases of goods and services and transfer payments.

6 What are injections into the circular flow of expenditure and income?

7 What are the three methods used by the Department of Commerce to measure GNP?

8 Describe how the factor incomes approach is used to measure GNP.

9 Describe how the output approach is used to measure GNP.

10 What is the distinction between expenditure on final goods and expenditure on intermediate goods?

11 What are the main omissions from measured GNP?

12 What are the two main price indexes used to measure the price level and inflation?

13 How is the Consumer Price Index calculated?

14 How is the GNP deflator calculated?

15 Explain what a relative price change is.

16 How can relative price changes be identified in periods when the inflation rates are different?

P R O B L E M S

1 The following flows of money took place in an imaginary economy last period:

Item	Millions of $
Wages paid to labor	800,000
Consumption expenditure	650,000
Taxes paid on wages	200,000
Government payments to support the unemployed, sick, and aged	50,000
Firms' profits	200,000
Investment	250,000
Taxes paid on profits	50,000
Government purchases of goods and services	200,000
Export earnings	250,000
Saving	200,000
Import payments	300,000

a) Calculate the GNP for this economy.

b) Did you use the expenditure approach, factor incomes approach, or output approach to make this calculation?

c) Does your answer to part (a) value output in terms of market prices or factor cost? Why?

d) Calculate the value added last year.

e) What extra information do you need in order to calculate net national product?

2 A typical family in an island economy consumes only apples, bananas, and cloth. The base period is year 1. Prices in the base period are $2 per pound for apples, $3 per pound for bananas, and $5 per yard for cloth. The typical family spends $40 on apples, $45 on bananas, and $25 on cloth. In year 2, apples cost $3 per pound, bananas cost $3 per pound, and cloth costs $8 per yard. Calculate the economy's Consumer Price Index for year 2 and the inflation rate between year 1 and year 2.

3 A newspaper in the economy in problem 2, commenting on the inflation figures that you have just calculated, runs the headline "Steeply Rising Clothing Prices Cause Inflation." Write a letter to the editor pointing out the weakness in the economic reasoning of the paper's business reporter.

4 An economy has the following real GNP and nominal GNP in 1989 and 1990:

Year	Real GNP	Nominal GNP
1989	$1000 billion	$1200 billion
1990	$1050 Billion	$1386 billion

a) What is the GNP deflator for 1989?

b) What is the GNP deflator for 1990?

c) What is the inflation rate as measured by the GNP deflator between 1989 and 1990?

Chapter 24

After studying this chapter, you will be able to:

- Define aggregate demand and explain what determines it

- Explain the sources of growth and fluctuations in aggregate demand

- Define aggregate supply and explain what determines it

- Explain the sources of growth and fluctuations in aggregate supply

- Define macroeconomic equilibrium

- Predict the effect of changes in aggregate demand and aggregate supply on real GNP and on the price level

- Explain why real GNP grows

- Explain why we have inflation and why its rate varies, sometimes exploding as it did in the 1970s

- Explain the OPEC recession of 1974-75, the Volcker recession of 1981-82; and the recovery of the 1980s

I n the quarter century from 1964 to 1989, U.S. real GNP more than doubled. In fact, a doubling—or more than a doubling—of real GNP each 25 years has been routine. What forces drive our economy to grow? ■ At the same time as real GNP has been growing, our dollar has been falling in value—we've experienced persistent inflation. Today, you need $400 to buy what $100 would have bought in 1960. Most of this fall in the value of the dollar occurred in the 1970s when the price level doubled. What causes inflation? Why does it persist over many decades, and why did it explode in the 1970s? ■ The U.S. economy doesn't grow in a smooth, unperturbed expansion. Instead, it ebbs and flows over the business cycle. What makes real GNP grow

What Makes Our Garden Grow?

unevenly, sometimes speeding up and sometimes slowing or even shrinking? ■ Recent years have shown great turbulence in the economy. In 1982, the unemployment rate shot up to its highest level since the Great Depression. Since then, it has fallen dramatically. In the same period, real GNP has gone from shrinking in 1982 to extremely rapid growth in 1984 and then to more moderate but sustained growth in the subsequent four years. Can we make sense of such rapid economic change? ■ Sometimes the economy receives a sudden shock —for example, the OPEC oil embargo and price hike of 1973, or the Federal Reserve's interest rate hikes of 1980 and 1981. How do such shocks affect prices and production?

■ To answer questions like these, we need a model—a macroeconomic model. Our first task in this chapter is to build such a model. It is a model based on the general principles that we discussed in Chapter 1 (pp. 18–20). The particular macroeconomic model that we'll study in this chapter contains three key concepts:

aggregate demand, aggregate supply, and macroeconomic equilibrium. Our second task is to use this model to answer the following questions: What makes our economy grow? Why do we have inflation? Why do we have business cycles? What were the effects of the OPEC price hike and the Federal Reserve's interest rate hikes? Why did we have a deep recession in 1982? And why did the economy grow so strongly and persistently through the mid-1980s?

Aggregate Demand

The aggregate quantity of goods and services produced is measured as real GNP—GNP valued in constant dollars. The average price of all these goods and services is measured by the GNP deflator. We are going to build a model that determines the values of real GNP and the GNP deflator. The model that we will build is based on the same concepts of demand, supply, and equilibrium that we met in Chapter 4. But here the good is not tapes—it is real GNP—and the price is not the price of tapes—it is the GNP deflator.

The **aggregate quantity of goods and services demanded** is the sum of the quantities of consumption goods and services demanded by households, of investment goods demanded by firms, of goods and services demanded by governments, and of net exports demanded by foreigners. Thus the aggregate quantity of goods and services demanded depends on decisions made by households, firms, governments, and foreigners. When we studied the demand for tapes in Chapter 4, we summarized the buying plans of households in a demand schedule and a demand curve. Similarly, when we study the forces influencing aggregate buying plans, we summarize the decisions of households, firms, governments, and foreigners by using an aggregate demand schedule and an aggregate demand curve.

An **aggregate demand schedule** lists the quantity of real GNP demanded at each price level, holding all other influences on buying plans constant. The **aggregate demand curve** plots the quantity of real GNP demanded against the price level. The term **aggregate demand** is used to refer to the entire relationship between the quantity of real GNP demanded and the price level.

Figure 24.1 shows an aggregate demand schedule and aggregate demand curve. Each row of the

Figure 24.1   The Aggregate Demand Schedule and Aggregate Demand Curve

	Price level (GNP deflator)	Real GNP (trillions of 1982 dollars)
a	100	5.5
b	110	5.0
c	120	4.5
d	130	4.0
e	140	3.5

The aggregate demand curve (AD) traces the quantity of real GNP demanded as the price level varies, holding everything else constant. The aggregate demand curve is derived from the schedule in the table. Each point a through e on the curve corresponds to the row in the table identified by the same letter. Thus when the price level is 120, the quantity of real GNP demanded is 4.5 trillion 1982 dollars, illustrated by point c in the figure.

table corresponds to a point in the figure. For example, row c of the aggregate demand schedule tells us that if the GNP deflator is 120, the level of real GNP demanded is 4.5 trillion 1982 dollars. This row is plotted as point c on the aggregate demand curve.

In constructing the aggregate demand schedule and aggregate demand curve, we hold constant all the influences on the quantity of real GNP demanded other than the price level. The effect of a change in the price level is shown as a movement along the aggregate demand curve. A change in any of the other influences on the quantity of real GNP demanded results in a new aggregate demand schedule and a shift in the aggregate demand curve. First, let's concentrate on the effects of a change in the price level on the quantity of real GNP demanded.

You can see from the downward slope of the aggregate demand curve, and from the numbers that describe the aggregate demand schedule, that the higher the price level, the smaller is the quantity of real GNP demanded. Why does the aggregate demand curve slope downward?

Why the Aggregate Demand Curve Slopes Downward

It's easy to understand why the demand curve for a single good slopes downward. If the price of Coca-Cola rises, the quantity of Coca-Cola demanded falls because people switch to drinking Pepsi-Cola and other substitutes. It's also easy to understand why the demand curve for a whole class of goods and services slopes downward. If the prices of Coca-Cola, Pepsi-Cola, and all other sodas rise, the quantity of soda demanded falls because people switch from drinking soda to other substitute drinks and other goods. But it's less easy to see why the demand curve for *all* goods and services slopes downward. If the price of all goods increases and people demand less of *all* goods, what do they demand more of? What do they substitute for goods and services?

There are three types of substitutes for the goods and services that make up real GNP. They are:

- Money and financial assets
- Goods and services in the future
- Goods and services produced in other countries

People may plan to buy a smaller quantity of the goods and services that make up real GNP and hold a larger quantity of money or other financial assets. They may plan to buy a smaller quantity of goods and services today but a larger quantity at some time in the future. Also, people may decide to buy a smaller quantity of the goods and services made in the United States and buy a larger quantity of goods and services made in other countries. These decisions are influenced by the price level and those influences result in the aggregate demand curve sloping downward.

We can identify three separate effects of the price level on the quantity of real GNP demanded:

- Money and the real balance effect
- Intertemporal substitution effect
- International substitution effect

Money and the Real Balance Effect

The **real balance effect** is the influence of a change in the quantity of real money on the quantity of real GNP demanded. The **quantity of money** is the quantity of currency, bank deposits, and deposits at other types of financial institutions such as savings and loan associations and thrift institutions held by households and firms. **Real money** is a measure of money based on the quantity of goods that it will buy. Real money is measured as dollars divided by the price level. For example, suppose that you have $20 in notes and coins in your pocket and $480 in the bank. The quantity of money that you are holding is $500. Suppose that you continue to hold $500 but that the price level increases by 25 percent. Then your real money holdings decrease by 25 percent. That is, the $500 of money that you are holding will now buy what $400 would before the price level increase.

The real balance effect is the proposition that the higher the quantity of real money, the larger is the quantity of goods and services demanded—of real GNP demanded. To understand the real balance effect, let's think about how your spending plans are influenced by your real money holdings, continuing with the above example.

You have $20 in your pocket and $480 in the bank. You also own a Walkman and some tapes worth $200. Your total assets are $700. Furthermore, you have decided that you don't want to change the way you are holding your assets. You don't want to have less money and more tapes or a better Walkman, and you don't want to trade in your Walkman for an inferior product or sell some tapes in order to have more money. Given that your total assets are $700, you are as happy as you can imagine with $500 in money and $200 worth of music equipment.

Now suppose that the prices of most goods and services, and the average price level, fall. Suppose that among the prices that fall are those of tapes and Walkmans. The money that you are now holding buys more goods than it would before. You've got more real money. But your music-making equipment is now worth less than before. This change in the price level has increased your holdings of real money and decreased the value of your holdings of music-making equipment. Since you were happy before about the proportions in which you owned money and music-making equipment, you will now, in general, want to make a change. You'll want more music-making equipment and less money. You use some of your extra real money to buy a better Walkman and a bigger stock of tapes. But Walkmans and tapes are two of the goods that make up real GNP. Thus your decision to use some of your extra real money to buy more music-making equipment results in an increase in the quantity of goods and services demanded, an increase in real GNP demanded.

Of course, if only you behave in this manner, there will not be a very large effect on real GNP demanded. The real balance effect will be tiny. But if everyone else behaves like you, the aggregate quantity of goods and services demanded will be higher than before. This increase in the quantity of goods and services demanded results from a fall in the price level.

The real balance effect is the first reason why the aggregate demand curve slopes downward. A decrease in the price level increases the quantity of real money. The larger the quantity of real money, the larger is the quantity of goods and services demanded.

Intertemporal Substitution Effect   Intertemporal substitution is the substitution of goods now for goods later or of goods later for goods now. An example of intertemporal substitution is your decision to buy a new Walkman today instead of waiting until the end of the month. Another example is IBM's decision to speed up its installation of a new computer production plant. Yet another example is your decision to postpone that long-hoped-for vacation.

An important influence on intertemporal substitution is the level of interest rates. Low interest rates encourage people to borrow and spend on capital goods—plant and equipment, houses, and consumer durable goods. High interest rates discourage people from borrowing and decrease the quantity demanded of these goods.

Interest rates, in turn, are influenced by the quantity of real money. We have just seen that the quantity of real money increases if the price level falls. We've also seen that the more real money people have, the larger is the quantity of goods and services that they demand. But a change in the quantity of real money does not affect only the quantity of goods and services that people plan to buy. It also affects the amount that they are willing to lend and borrow. With more real money, people increase their supply of loans and decrease their demand for loans. An increase in the supply of loans and a decrease in the demand for them results in a fall in interest rates. And lower interest rates lead to an increase in the quantity of goods and services demanded.

This intertemporal substitution effect is the second reason why the aggregate demand curve slopes downward. A lower price level:

- Increases the quantity of real money
- Increases the amount that people plan to lend
- Decreases the amount that people plan to borrow
- Lowers interest rates
- Increases the quantity of goods and services demanded

Let's now look at the third reason why the aggregate demand curve slopes downward.

International Substitution Effect   International substitution is the substitution of domestic goods for foreign goods or of foreign goods for domestic goods. An example of international substitution is your decision to buy a General Motors car (made in Detroit) instead of a Toyota (made in Japan). Another example of international substitution is the decision by the British government to equip its armed forces with U.S.–produced weapons rather than weapons made in Great Britain. Yet another example is your decision to take a vacation in Acapulco instead of Florida.

If the U.S. price level falls, holding everything else constant, U.S.–made goods become cheaper and, therefore, more attractive relative to goods made in other countries. Americans will plan to buy more domestically produced goods and fewer imports; and foreigners will plan to buy more U.S.–made goods and fewer of their own domestically produced goods. Thus at a lower U.S. price level, people and firms will demand a larger quantity of goods and services produced in the United States. International substitution gives us the third reason for the downward slope of the aggregate demand curve.

R E V I E W

The aggregate demand curve traces the effects of a change in the price level—the GNP deflator—on the aggregate quantity of goods and services demanded—real GNP demanded. The effect of a change in the price level is shown as a movement along the aggregate demand curve. Other things being equal, the higher the price level, the smaller is the quantity of real GNP demanded—the aggregate demand curve slopes downward.

The aggregate demand curve slopes downward for three reasons: money and goods are substitutes (real balance effect); goods today and goods in the future are substitutes (intertemporal substitution effect); domestic goods and foreign goods are substitutes (international substitution effect).

These effects work in the following ways:

• Real balance effect—money decreases in real value, so people hold a larger quantity of money and buy a smaller quantity of goods and services

• Intertemporal substitution effect—the supply of loans decreases, the demand for loans increases, interest rates rise, and people buy a smaller quantity of goods and services

• International substitution effect—domestic goods become expensive relative to foreign goods, so people buy larger amounts from abroad and a smaller quantity of domestic goods and services ■

Changes in Aggregate Demand

We've just seen that real GNP demanded varies when the price level varies. The effects of a change in the price level on real GNP demanded are shown as a movement along an aggregate demand curve. But an aggregate demand schedule and aggregate demand curve describe aggregate demand at a point in time, and aggregate demand does not remain constant. There are many factors that lead to changes in aggregate demand. When any one of these factors changes, there is a shift in the aggregate demand curve. Let's review the most important of these factors. They are summarized in Table 24.1

1. Interest Rates   An increase in interest rates, other things being equal, leads to a decrease in the quantity of new capital equipment that firms plan to

Table 24.1   Aggregate Demand

Aggregate demand

Increases if:	*Decreases if:*
• Interest rates decrease	• Interest rates increase
• Expected inflation rate increases	• Expected inflation rate decreases
• Foreign exchange rate falls	• Foreign exchange rate rises
• Expected future profit increases	• Expected future profit decreases
• Quantity of money increases	• Quantity of money decreases
• Aggregate wealth increases	• Aggregate wealth decreases
• Government spending on goods and services increases	• Government spending on goods and services decreases
• Taxes decrease or transfer payments increase	• Taxes increase or transfer payments decrease
• Foreign income increases	• Foreign income decreases
• Population increases	• Population decreases

All of the above influences on aggregate demand are spread out over time and are not completely predictable.

buy and to a decrease in the quantity of new houses and durable goods that households plan to buy. We've just seen that a change in the price level, through its effect on the quantity of real money, influences the level of interest rates. A change in interest rates induced by a change in the price level changes the aggregate quantity of goods and services demanded. But, as we saw above, this change is represented as a movement along an aggregate demand curve and not as a change in aggregate demand.

However, interest rates can and do change for many other reasons. Whatever the reason for a change in interest rates, their level influences aggregate demand. Whenever interest rates change independently of changes in the price level, the aggregate demand curve shifts. For example, in recent years, there has been an enormous increase in the demand for loans by the U.S. government to cover its deficit. Such an increase in the demand for loans, other things being equal, increases interest rates and has a depressing effect on the spending plans of households and firms. But also, in recent years, there has been a large increase in the supply of loans from the rest of the world, especially from Japan and Western Europe. These increases in the supply of loans have kept interest rates moderate and prevented aggregate demand from falling.

2. Expected Inflation   An increase in the expected inflation rate, other things being equal, leads to an increase in aggregate demand. The higher the expected inflation rate, the higher is the expected price of goods and services in the future and the lower is the expected real value of money and other assets in the future. As a consequence, when people expect a higher inflation rate, they plan to buy more goods and services in the present and hold smaller quantities of money and other financial assets.

There have been changes in inflation expectations during the 1980s. At the beginning of the decade, people expected inflation to persist at close to 10 percent. But a severe recession in 1982 reduced those inflation expectations. Other things being equal, the effect of this decrease in inflation expectations was to decrease aggregate demand.

3. The Foreign Exchange Rate   We've seen that a change in the U.S. price level, other things being equal, leads to a change in the prices of our goods and services relative to the prices of goods and services produced in other countries. Another important influence on the price of our goods and services relative to those produced abroad is the *foreign exchange rate*. The foreign exchange rate affects aggregate demand because it affects the prices that foreigners have to pay for U.S.–produced goods and the prices that we have to pay for foreign-produced goods.

Suppose that the dollar is worth 125 Japanese yen. You can buy a NEC computer (made in Japan) that costs 125,000 yen for $1000. What if for $900 you can buy an Apple computer (made in the United States) that is just as good as the NEC computer costing 125,000 yen? In such a case, you will buy the Apple.

But which computer will you buy if the value of the U.S. dollar rises to 150 yen and everything else remains the same? Let's work out the answer. At 150 yen per dollar, you pay only $833.33 to buy the 125,000 yen needed to buy the NEC computer. Since the Apple computer costs $900, the NEC computer is now cheaper and you will substitute the

NEC computer for the Apple. The demand for U.S.–made computers falls as the foreign exchange value of the dollar rises. So as the foreign exchange value of the dollar rises, everything else held constant, aggregate demand decreases.

There have been large swings in the foreign exchange value of the dollar through the 1980s, leading to large swings in aggregate demand.

4. Expected Future Profit   A change in expected future profit changes firms' demands for new capital equipment. For example, suppose that there has been a recent wave of technological change that has increased productivity. Firms will expect that by installing new equipment that uses the latest technology, their future profit will rise. This expectation leads to an increase in demand for new plant and equipment and so to an increase in aggregate demand.

Profit expectations were pessimistic in 1981 and led to a decrease in aggregate demand. Expectations have been optimistic through most of the mid-1980s, leading to sustained increases in aggregate demand.

5. The Quantity of Money   The greater the *quantity of money,* the larger is aggregate demand. An easy way to see why money affects aggregate demand is to imagine what would happen if the government loaded all the army's helicopters with millions of dollars worth of new $10 bills and sprinkled these bills like confetti across the nation. We would all stop whatever we were doing and rush out to pick up our share of the newly available money. We wouldn't, though, just put the money that we picked up in the bank. We would spend some of it, so our demand for goods and services would increase. Though this story is pretty extreme, it does illustrate that a rise in the quantity of money increases aggregate demand.

In practice, the quantity of money is determined by the Federal Reserve (the Fed) using techniques that we'll study in Chapter 28. Also, in practice, changes in the quantity of money change interest rates and so have an additional influence on aggregate demand by affecting investment demand and the demand for consumer durables. When the Fed speeds up the rate at which new money is being injected into the economy, there's a tendency for interest rates to fall. When the Fed slows down the pace at which it's creating money, there's a tendency for interest rates to rise. Thus there is a second effect of the quantity of money on aggregate demand operating through its effects on interest rates.

Fluctuations in the quantity of money and in interest rates induced by those fluctuations have been some of the most important sources of changes in aggregate demand. Sustained increases in the quantity of money through the 1970s increased aggregate demand, contributing to the inflation of those years; decreases in the growth rate of the quantity of money slowed aggregate demand growth, contributing to the recession of 1981.

6. Aggregate Wealth Wealthy people consume larger quantities of goods and services than do poor people. If everyone's wealth increases, aggregate wealth also increases and so does aggregate demand. This source of changes in aggregate demand exerts a steady upward influence as wealth gradually accumulates.

7. Government Demand for Goods and Services The scale of government demand for goods and services has a direct effect on aggregate demand. If taxes are held constant, the more weapons, highways, schools, and colleges the government demands, the higher is government demand and so the higher is aggregate demand. The most important changes in government purchases of goods and services that influence aggregate demand arise from the state of international tension and conflict. In times of war, government purchases increase dramatically. In this century, increases in government purchases during World War II, the Korean War, and the Vietnam War and decreases following these episodes have exerted a large influence on aggregate demand.

8. Taxes and Transfer Payments A decrease in taxes increases aggregate demand. An increase in transfer payments—in unemployment benefits, social security benefits, and other welfare payments—also increases aggregate demand. Both of these influences operate by increasing households' *disposable* income. The higher the level of disposable income, the greater is the demand for goods and services. Since lower taxes and higher transfer payments increase disposable income, they also increase aggregate demand.

This source of changes in aggregate demand has been an important one in recent years. Through the late 1960s, there was a large increase in government payments under various social programs that led to a sustained increase in aggregate demand. During the

1980s, Reagan's supply-side tax cuts have also led to an increase in aggregate demand.

9. Foreign Income The income of foreigners affects the aggregate demand for domestically produced goods and services. For example, an increase in income in Japan and Germany increases the demand by Japanese and German consumers and producers for U.S.–made consumption goods and capital goods. These sources of change in aggregate demand have been important ones in the postwar period. The rapid economic growth of Japan and Western Europe and of some of the newly industrializing countries of the Pacific Rim, such as Korea and Singapore, has led to a sustained increase in demand for U.S.–made goods and services.

10. Population An increase in population increases aggregate demand. The more people there are, the greater the demand for housing, clothing, food, and the many other goods and services that people buy. Our population grows at about 1 percent a year, exerting a steady increase in aggregate demand.

Time Lags The effects of all the influences on aggregate demand that we have just considered do not occur in an instant or in a predictable manner. A change in any of the influences on aggregate demand affects aggregate demand for many months following the initial change. For example, if the Federal Reserve increases the money supply, there might at first be no effect on aggregate demand at all. A little later, as people reallocate their wealth, there is an increase in the supply of loans and a tendency for interest rates to fall. Later yet, some households and firms, confronted with lower interest rates, change their buying plans for consumer durables and capital goods. As more time passes, more households and firms change their plans and aggregate demand gradually increases. The total effect of the initial change in the quantity of money is spread out over many months. The next time the Federal Reserve takes exactly the same action, there is no guarantee that its effects will take place with exactly the same timing as before. The lags in the effects of influences on aggregate demand are both spread out and variable and, to a degree, unpredictable.

Now that we've reviewed the factors that influence aggregate demand, let's summarize their effects on the aggregate demand curve.

Figure 24.2   Changes in Aggregate Demand

(a) An increase in aggregate demand

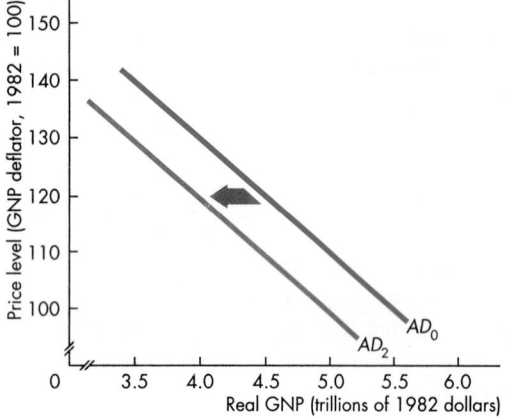

(b) A decrease in aggregate demand

The factors that increase aggregate demand (listed in Table 24.1) shift the aggregate demand curve to the right. Such a shift is illustrated by the movement from AD_0 to AD_1 in part (a). The factors that decrease aggregate demand (listed in Table 24.1) shift the aggregate demand curve to the left. Such a shift is illustrated by the movement from AD_0 to AD_2 in part (b).

Shifts of the Aggregate Demand Curve

We illustrate a change in aggregate demand as a shift in the aggregate demand curve. Figure 24.2 illustrates two changes in aggregate demand. Aggregate demand is initially AD_0 (the same curve as AD in

Fig. 24.1) In part (a), there is an increase in aggregate demand and in part (b) a decrease in aggregate demand.

The aggregate demand curve shifts to the right, from AD_0 to AD_1, as shown in part (a), if there is an increase in expected future profit, the expected inflation rate, the money supply, aggregate wealth, government spending on goods and services, foreign income, or population. A decrease in interest rates, the foreign exchange rate, or taxes also causes the same shift to the right.

The aggregate demand curve shifts to the left, from AD_0 to AD_2, as shown in Fig. 24.2(b), if there is a decrease in expected future profit, the expected inflation rate, the money supply, aggregate wealth, government spending on goods and services, foreign income, or population. An increase in interest rates, the foreign exchange rate, or taxes cause the same shift to the left.

R E V I E W

A change in the price level leads to a change in the aggregate quantity of goods and services demanded. That change is shown as a movement along the aggregate demand curve. A change in any other factor that influences aggregate demand shifts the aggregate demand curve. These other factors include:

- Interest rates
- Expected inflation rate
- Foreign exchange rate
- Expected future profit
- Quantity of money
- Aggregate wealth
- Government spending on goods and services
- Taxes and transfer payments
- Foreign income
- Population ■

Aggregate Supply

Aggregate supply is the relationship between the aggregate quantity of goods and services supplied—real GNP supplied—and the price level—the GNP deflator—holding everything else constant. In studying aggregate supply, we distinguish between two time frames: the long run and the short run.

Long-run Aggregate Supply

Long-run aggregate supply is the quantity of real GNP supplied when each firm is producing its capacity output and when there is full employment.

A firm's **capacity output** is the output at which its cost per unit produced is minimized. Each firm has a unique capacity output. The concept of capacity output can be illustrated by an automobile production line. For example, if General Motors' output is below capacity, the enormous fixed costs of its production line are spread over a smaller output and the cost of each car produced is higher than it might otherwise be. Conversely, if GM operates its production line above its capacity output, although the fixed costs are now spread over a larger output, the plant is being operated closer to its limits and machinery breakdowns and maintenance problems add to the cost of producing a car. There is a particular output that balances the gains from spreading fixed costs over a larger output against the costs of bottlenecks and increased plant breakdowns. That output is the firm's capacity output.

The second feature of long-run aggregate supply is that the economy is at *full employment*. Full employment occurs when there is a balance between the quantity of labor demanded and the quantity of labor supplied, so that the only unemployment present is frictional, arising from new labor market entrants finding a first job and from job turnover arising from technological change. In this situation, unemployment is at its natural rate.

Since there is a unique capacity output for each firm and just one natural rate of unemployment, there is a unique level of long-run aggregate supply. The level of long-run aggregate supply does not depend on the price level. If a firm's output price increases by 10 percent and if the costs that it faces also increase by 10 percent, then its capacity output remains unchanged. It operates at a constant output rate but at a higher level of input prices and output price.

The **long-run aggregate supply curve** shows the relationship between long-run aggregate supply and the price level. Since there is a unique level of long-run aggregate supply that does not vary with the price level, the long-run aggregate supply curve is vertical—labeled *LAS* in Fig. 24.3.

Figure 24.3   The Long-run Aggregate Supply Curve

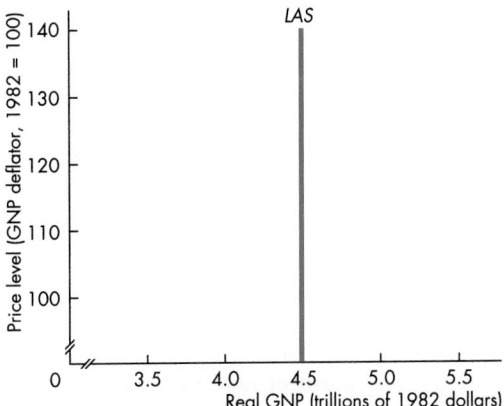

The long-run aggregate supply curve (*LAS*) shows the full-employment level of real GNP. It is independent of the price level. There is uncertainty about the position of the long-run aggregate supply curve, because we are not able to measure accurately the economy's capacity output level and its natural unemployment rate, two factors on which long-run aggregate supply depends.

Measuring Long-run Aggregate Supply   Real GNP is a measure of the *actual* quantity of goods and services produced. It is not a measure of long-run aggregate supply. We do not, at the present time, have a sure method for calculating long-run aggregate supply. Two approaches are used for estimating long-run aggregate supply, but neither of them gives a completely reliable or satisfactory answer. The two methods are as follows:

• Trend approach
• Production function approach

Trend Approach   The trend approach to estimating long-run aggregate supply calculates a smooth trend line through the actual path of real GNP. Such a trend line was used in Chapter 22 (pp. 576–577) to calculate the deviations from trend that form the business cycle. However, there are many different trend lines that could be calculated—and each would give rise to a different estimate of long-run aggregate supply. For example, if long-run aggregate supply is based on a trend line with a constant growth rate from 1869 through 1988, actual real GNP has been below long-run aggregate supply for most of the 1970s and 1980s. Conversely, using the trend calculations of Chapter 22, real GNP has fluctuated around long-run aggregate supply, falling below long-run aggregate supply in 1975 and again in 1982 but rising above long-run aggregate supply in the 1980s expansion. The trend approach for estimating long-run aggregate supply results in different estimates arising from different time periods over which the trend is asssessed.

Production Function Approach   The production function approach to estimating long-run aggregate supply uses the fact that long-run aggregate supply depends on the stock of capital equipment and the full-employment labor force. To estimate long-run aggregate supply by this method, we need an estimate of the natural unemployment rate. But, again, we do not yet have a reliable way of estimating the natural unemployment rate. As a consequence, this method produces different estimates of long-run aggregate supply based on different views of the natural unemployment rate.

Because of the impossibility, in the current state of our knowledge, of measuring long-run aggregate supply, there is uncertainty about the position of the long-run aggregate supply curve. We know that the long-run aggregate supply curve is vertical, but we do not know its exact position. This uncertainty is a source of some of the disagreements among economists and policymakers about how to conduct macroeconomic policy. We'll briefly meet some of that controversy later in this chapter and in Chapters 30 and 33.

Let's now turn to an examination of short-run aggregate supply.

Short-run Aggregate Supply

Short-run aggregate supply is the relationship between the aggregate quantity of goods and services (real GNP) supplied and the price level (the GNP deflator), holding constant the prices of the factors of production—and in particular, holding wage rates constant. We can represent short-run aggregate supply either as a short-run aggregate supply schedule or a short-run aggregate supply curve.

The **short-run aggregate supply schedule** lists quantities of real GNP supplied at each price level, holding everything else constant. The **short-run aggregate supply curve** plots the relationship between the quantity of real GNP supplied and the price level, holding everything else constant.

Figure 24.4   The Aggregate Supply Schedule and Aggregate Supply Curves

	Price level (GNP deflator)	Real GNP (trillions of 1982 dollars)
a′	110	3.5
b′	115	4.0
c′	120	4.5
d′	125	5.0
e′	140	5.0

The long-run aggregate supply curve (*LAS*) is the same as the curve in Fig. 24.3. The short-run aggregate supply curve (*SAS*) traces the quantity of real GNP supplied as the price level varies, holding everything else constant. The short-run aggregate supply curve in this figure is derived from the schedule in the table. Points a′ through e′ correspond to the rows in the table identified by those same letters. Thus when the price level is 120, real GNP supplied is 4.5 trillion 1982 dollars (point c′).

Figure 24.4 shows a short-run aggregate supply schedule and the corresponding short-run aggregate supply curve (labeled *SAS*). Each row of the table corresponds to a point in the figure. For example, row

c' of the short-run aggregate supply schedule and point c' on the curve tell us that if the price level is 120 (GNP deflator is 120) the quantity of real GNP supplied is 4.5 trillion 1982 dollars. In constructing the short-run aggregate supply schedule and the short-run aggregate supply curve, we hold constant *all* the influences on the quantity of real GNP supplied other than the price level.

The short-run aggregate supply schedule and short-run aggregate supply curve in Fig. 24.4 tell us that the higher the price level, the larger is the aggregate quantity of goods and services supplied, up to some maximum. Why does the short-run aggregate supply curve slope upward? Why does it become vertical at some output level?

The easiest way to understand why the short-run aggregate supply curve slopes upward is to consider how an individual firm responds to an increase in the price of its output, while the prices of its inputs remain constant. Suppose, for example, that car prices increase and that auto workers' wage rates and the prices of auto parts remain constant. In this situation, General Motors will increase its output and try to sell more cars. It will also hire more workers and increase the work-hours of its existing work force. Conversely, if car prices fall while auto workers' wage rates and parts prices remain constant, GM will decrease its output and offer fewer cars for sale. It will lay off workers and cut back on its parts orders.

Charles E. Wilson, president of GM in the 1950's, once said "What is good for General Motors is good for America." Without supporting or disputing that assertion, it is clear that what GM does when its output price changes while input prices remain constant, all firms do—what GM does, America does!

Thus changes in the price level, with input prices held constant, lead to changes in the aggregate quantity of goods and services supplied and to a change in the level of employment and unemployment. The higher the price level, the higher is the aggregate quantity of goods and services supplied, the higher is the level of employment, and the lower is the level of unemployment.

Why does the short-run aggregate supply curve eventually become vertical? It is because there is a physical limit to the output capacity of the economy. When the economy is on its long-run aggregate supply curve, unemployment is at its natural rate and each firm is producing its capacity output—the output that minimizes the cost per unit produced. If output prices increase while input prices stay constant, each firm increases its output above its capacity level. It does so by working its labor overtime, hiring more labor, and working its plant and equipment at a faster pace. But there is a limit to the extent to which workers will accept overtime and there is a limit to which the unemployment rate can be pushed below its natural rate. There is also a limit beyond which firms will not want to operate their plant and equipment. Once these limits have been reached, no more output can be produced no matter how high prices become, relative to costs. At that point, the short-run aggregate supply curve becomes vertical.

REVIEW

The long-run aggregate supply curve shows the relationship between real GNP supplied and the price level when each firm is producing its capacity output and when there is full employment. This level of real GNP is independent of the price level. The long-run aggregate supply curve is vertical. Its position tells us the level of real GNP when the economy is at full employment. The short-run aggregate supply curve shows the relationship between real GNP supplied and the price level, holding everything else constant. With constant input prices, an increase in the price level results in an increase in real GNP supplied. The short-run aggregate supply curve is upward-sloping. ∎

A change in the price level, with everything else held constant, results in a movement along the short-run aggregate supply curve. A change in the price level, with an accompanying change in input prices that keeps each firm producing its capacity output and keeps unemployment at its natural rate results in a movement along the long-run aggregate supply curve. But there are many other influences on real GNP supplied. These influences result in a change in aggregate supply and shifts in the aggregate supply curves.

Some factors change both long-run aggregate supply and short-run aggregate supply; others affect short-run aggregate supply but leave long-run aggregate supply unchanged. Let's examine these influences

Table 24.2 Aggregate Supply

Short-run aggregate supply and long-run aggregate supply

Increase if:	Decrease if:
• Labor force increases	• Labor force decreases
• Capital stock increases	• Capital stock decreases
• Human capital increases	• Human capital decreases
• New raw material sources are discovered	• Raw materials are depleted
• Climatic conditions improve	• Climatic conditions deteriorate
• Technology advances	
• Composition of GNP changes slowly	• Composition of GNP changes quickly
• Incentives are strengthened	• Incentives are weakened

Short-run aggregate supply also

Increases if:	Decreases if:
• Wages decrease	• Wages increase
• Raw material prices decrease	• Raw material prices increase

on aggregate supply starting with those that affect *both* long-run aggregate supply and short-run aggregate supply.

Changes in Both Long-run and Short-run Aggregate Supply

Table 24.2 sets out the main factors that influence long-run and short-run aggregate supply.

1. Labor Force The larger the labor force, the larger is the quantity of goods and services that will be produced.

2. Capital Stock The larger the stock of productive plant and equipment, the more productive will the labor force be and the greater is the output that it will be able to produce.

3. Human Capital *Human capital,* the value of the skills that people acquire in school and through on-the-job training, has an important influence on the

level of aggregate supply. The more highly trained and experienced the labor force, the greater is output.

4. Raw Materials The availability of raw materials has an important effect on output. The discovery of new and easily accessed raw materials lowers their cost and increases output. The depletion of materials has the reverse effect, lowering output.

5. Climate The climate has an obvious effect on output, especially in the agricultural sector. Ideal rainfall and sunshine can produce an increase in output while extreme climatic conditions restrict output.

6. Technology The state of technology obviously has an important effect on aggregate supply. Inventing new and better ways of doing things enables firms to produce more from any given amount of inputs. So, even with a constant population and constant capital stock, improvements in technology increase production and increase aggregate supply.

7. Changing Composition of Real GNP When the different sectors and regions of the economy grow at a similar pace, the composition of GNP remains stable. But if some sectors expand very rapidly and others decline, then the composition of GNP changes quickly. An example of a rapid change in the composition of GNP is the explosive growth in the production of electronic products in Minneapolis and the decline of steel production in Gary. The more rapidly the economy changes the composition of its output, the larger is the rate of turnover of its labor force. Job search activity increases and the natural rate of unemployment rises. Such a process leads to a decrease in aggregate supply.

8. Incentives Aggregate supply can be influenced by the incentives that people face. For example, high taxes may discourage people from working and discourage saving and the accumulation of capital. Aggregate supply falls as disincentives from high taxes rise. Another influence on incentives is the regulatory environment: Safety and environmental protection regulations that raise costs lower the quantity of goods and services produced and reduce aggregate supply.

These are the major influences on long-run aggregate supply and short-run aggregate supply. But there are two other important influences on short-run aggregate supply that do not affect long-run aggregate supply.

Changes in Short-run Aggregate Supply

The factors that change short-run aggregate supply but not long-run aggregate supply are wages and raw material prices.

1. Wages Wages affect short-run aggregate supply through their influence on a firm's costs. The higher the level of wages, the higher is a firm's costs and the lower the quantity of output the firm will want to supply at each price level. Thus an increase in wages decreases short-run aggregate supply.

2. Raw Material Prices Raw material prices affect short-run aggregate supply in the same way that wages do. An increase in raw material prices increases a firm's costs and decreases the output supplied at each price level.

Why do wages and raw material prices affect short-run aggregate supply but not long-run aggregate supply? The answer lies in the definition of long-run aggregate supply. Recall that long-run aggregate supply refers to the quantity of real GNP supplied when each firm is producing its capacity output and when there is full employment. When the economy is producing its long-run aggregate supply, any changes in wages and raw material prices are matched by an equivalent change in the price level.

Let's now summarize the factors that influence aggregate supply by examining how they lead to shifts in the long-run and the short-run aggregate supply curves.

Shifts in the Aggregate Supply Curves

If any of the events listed in Table 24.2 that increase long-run aggregate supply occur, the long-run aggregate supply curve and the short-run aggregate supply curve shift to the right. Both curves shift to the right by the same amount. Figure 24.5 illustrates these shifts. Initially, the long-run aggregate supply curve is LAS_0 and the short-run aggregate supply curve is SAS_0. These curves intersect at a price level of 120 where real GNP is 4.5 trillion 1982 dollars. An increase in the productive capacity of the economy

Figure 24.5 Changes in Aggregate Supply

Any of the factors that increase long-run aggregate supply and short-run aggregate supply (listed in Table 24.2) shift both supply curves to the right by the same amount. Such a shift is illustrated by the change from LAS_0 and SAS_0 to LAS_1 and SAS_1. The size of the horizontal shift in the short-run aggregate supply curve is the same as that in the long-run aggregate supply curve. As a result, SAS_1 intersects LAS_1 at the same price level (120) that SAS_0 intersects LAS_0.

that increases full-employment real GNP to 5.5 trillion 1982 dollars shifts both the long-run aggregate supply curve and the short-run aggregate supply curve to LAS_1 and SAS_1. Long-run aggregate supply is now 5.5 trillion 1982 dollars.

Notice that the price level at which the long-run aggregate supply and the short-run aggregate supply curves intersect remains at 120. The short-run aggregate supply curve shifts to the right by exactly the same amount as the shift in the long-run aggregate supply curve.

Next, let's look at the effect of a change in input prices. Figure 24.6 illustrates this case. Long-run aggregate supply is LAS and initially the short-run aggregate supply curve is SAS_0. These curves intersect at the price level 120. Now suppose that input prices rise by 20 percent. Since firms are willing to supply, in total, $4.5 trillion worth of output at a price level of 120, they will supply that same level of output when input prices are 20 percent higher only if they can get 20 percent higher prices.

Figure 24.6   A Change in Aggregate Supply:
A Change in Input Prices

A change in input prices shifts the short-run aggregate supply curve but leaves the long-run aggregate supply curve unaffected. If all input prices increase by 20 percent, the short-run aggregate supply curve shifts upward by 20 percent. If the original short-run aggregate supply curve is SAS_0, the new short-run aggregate supply curve is SAS_1, 20 percent above SAS_0. (Note that the price level of 144 is 20 percent higher than the price level of 120.)

Thus the short-run aggregate supply curve shifts upward. The new short-run aggregate supply curve is SAS_1. This supply curve intersects LAS at a price level of 144—20 percent above 120. The curve SAS_1 is located 20 percent above SAS_0 at every output level.

The direction in which we measure the distance between two short-run aggregate supply curves depends on the source of the shift. If short-run aggregate supply changes because of changes in the economy's productive capacity, the *horizontal* distance between the two short-run aggregate supply curves is the same as the horizontal distance between the two long-run aggregate supply curves and is the amount by which the economy's full-employment output has changed. If short-run aggregate supply changes because of a change in input prices, the *vertical* distance between the initial and the new short-run aggregate supply curves is equal to the percentage change in input prices.

R E V I E W

When firms are producing their capacity output and there is full employment, the economy is on its long-run aggregate supply curve. The long-run aggregate supply curve is vertical. When there is a change in the price level and everything else (including input prices) is held constant, the economy slides up or down its short-run aggregate supply curve. A movement along a short-run aggregate supply curve is referred to as a change in the aggregate quantity of goods and services supplied. The short-run aggregate supply curve is upward sloping. Everything that shifts the long-run aggregate supply curve also shifts the short-run aggregate supply curve. A change in input prices shifts the short-run aggregate supply curve but leaves the long-run aggregate supply curve unchanged. ∎

Next, we study macroeconomic equilibrium.

Macroeconomic Equilibrium

Our purpose in building a model of aggregate demand and aggregate supply is to determine and predict changes in real GNP and the price level. To make predictions about real GNP and the price level, we need to combine aggregate demand and aggregate supply and to determine macroeconomic equilibrium. **Macroeconomic equilibrium** occurs when the quantity of real GNP demanded equals the quantity of real GNP supplied. Let's see how macroeconomic equilibrium is determined.

Determination of Real GNP and the Price Level

We have seen that the aggregate demand curve tells us the quantity of real GNP demanded at each price level and the short-run aggregate supply curve tells us the quantity of real GNP supplied at each price level. There is one and only one price level at which the quantity demanded equals the quantity supplied. Macroeconomic equilibrium occurs at that price level. Figure 24.7 illustrates such an equilibrium at a price level of 120 and real GNP of 4.5 trillion 1982 dollars (point c, c').

Figure 24.7   Macroeconomic Equilibrium

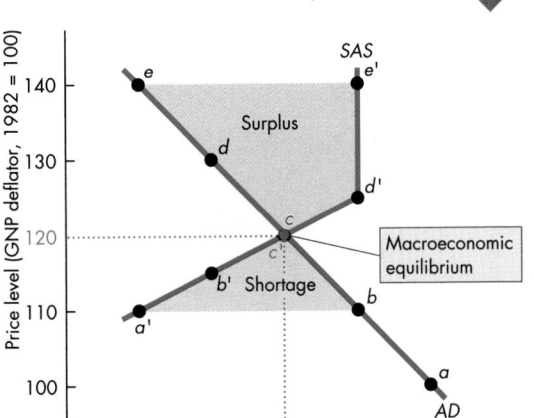

Macroeconomic equilibrium occurs when real GNP demanded equals real GNP supplied. Such an equilibrium is at the intersection of the aggregate demand curve (AD) and the short-run aggregate supply curve (SAS)—points c and c'. At price levels above 120 there is an excess of the quantity of goods and services supplied over the quantity demanded—a surplus—and prices fall. At price levels below 120 there is an excess of the quantity of goods and services demanded over the quantity supplied—a shortage—and prices rise. Only when the price level is 120 is the quantity of goods and services demanded equal to the quantity supplied. This is the equilibrium price level. The quantity of goods and services traded at this price level is the equilibrium level of real GNP—4.5 trillion 1982 dollars.

To see why this position is an equilibrium, let's work out what happens if the price level is something other than 120. Suppose, for example, that the price level is 140. In that case, real GNP demanded is $3.5 trillion (point e) but real GNP supplied is $5 trillion (point e'). There is an excess of the quantity supplied over the quantity demanded, or a surplus of goods and services. Unable to sell all their output, firms willingly accept lower prices. Prices will be cut until the excess of the quantity supplied over the quantity demanded is eliminated—at a price level of 120.

Next consider what happens if the price level is 110. In this case, firms supply $3.5 trillion worth of goods and services (point a') and households demand $5 trillion worth (point b). The quantity demanded exceeds the quantity supplied. Aware of shortages,

firms push their prices upward and continue to do so until the quantities demanded and supplied are in balance—again at a price level of 120.

Macroeconomic Equilibrium and Full Employment

Macroeconomic equilibrium does not necessarily occur at full employment. At full employment, the economy is on its long-run aggregate supply curve. Macroeconomic equilibrium occurs at the intersection of the short-run aggregate supply curve and the aggregate demand curve—at the price level where the aggregate quantity of goods and services demanded equals the aggregate quantity of goods and services supplied. Macroeconomic equilibrium can occur at, below, or above full employment. We can see this fact most clearly by considering the three cases shown in Fig. 24.8. Figure 24.8(a) is an example of full-employment equilibrium. **Full-employment equilibrium** occurs when macroeconomic equilibrium is at a point on the long-run aggregate supply curve. In the situation depicted in Fig. 24.8(a), unemployment is at its natural rate.

Figure 24.8(b) shows the economy at a macroeconomic equilibrium below full employment. Such an equilibrium is called an unemployment equilibrium. An **unemployment equilibrium** is a situation in which macroeconomic equilibrium occurs at a level of real GNP below long-run aggregate supply. The unemployment equilibrium illustrated in Fig. 24.8(b) occurs where aggregate demand curve AD_1 intersects short-run aggregate supply curve SAS_1 at a real GNP level of 4 trillion 1982 dollars and a price level of 120. The U.S. economy was in a situation similar to that depicted in part (b) in 1975, and again in 1982. (You may like to check back to Chapter 22, p. 573 and p. 578 to see that in those years, unemployment was high and real GNP was substantially below trend.)

Finally, macroeconomic equilibrium can occur at a level of real GNP above full-employment. Such an equilibrium is an above full-employment equilibrium. **Above full-employment equilibrium** is a situation in which macroeconomic equilibrium occurs at a level of real GNP above long-run aggregate supply. Figure 24.8(c) illustrates such a case. Here, the short-run aggregate supply curve is SAS_2 and the aggregate demand curve is AD_2. The price level is 120 and real GNP is 5 trillion 1982 dollars. The U.S. economy was in a situation similar to that

Figure 24.8   Macroeconomic Equilibrium and Unemployment

(a) Full-employment equilibrium

(b) Unemployment equilibrium

(c) Above full-employment equilibrium

Macroeconomic equilibrium does not necessarily occur at full employment. Part (a) shows a macroeconomic equilibrium that *is* a full-employment equilibrium. Such an equilibrium occurs when the short-run aggregate supply curve SAS_0 intersects the aggregate demand curve AD_0 on the long-run aggregate supply curve LAS. Part (b) shows an unemployment equilibrium. Such an equilibrium occurs when the aggregate demand curve AD_1 intersects the short-run aggregate supply curve SAS_1 at a level of real GNP that is below long-run aggregate supply. Part (c) shows an above full-employment equilibrium. Such an equilibrium occurs when the aggregate demand curve AD_2 intersects the short-run aggregate supply curve SAS_2 at a level of real GNP that is above long-run aggregate supply.

depicted in part (c) in 1988. In that year, unemployment was low and real GNP was above its trend value.

Fluctuations in aggregate demand and short-run aggregate supply produce fluctuations in real GNP and the price level. Let's see how these fluctuations arise, first by looking at the effects of imaginary changes in aggregate demand and aggregate supply. We'll then use the theory of aggregate demand and

aggregate supply to interpret some recent events in the U.S. economy.

The Effects of a Change in Aggregate Demand

We're going to work out what happens to real GNP and the price level following a change in aggregate demand. Let's suppose that the economy starts out at full employment and, as illustrated in Fig. 24.9, is producing $4.5 trillion worth of goods and services at a price level of 120. The economy is on the aggregate demand curve AD_0, the short-run aggregate supply curve SAS_0, and on its long-run aggregate supply curve LAS.

Now suppose that the Fed takes steps to increase the quantity of money. With more money in the economy, people increase their demand for goods and services—the aggregate demand curve shifts to the right. Suppose that the aggregate demand curve shifts from AD_0 to AD_1 in Fig. 24.9. A new equilibrium occurs, where the aggregate demand curve AD_1 intersects the short-run aggregate supply curve SAS_0. Output rises to 5 trillion 1982 dollars and the price level rises to 130. The economy is now at an above full-employment equilibrium. Real GNP is above its long-run level.

The increase in aggregate demand has increased the prices of all goods and services. Faced with higher prices, firms have increased their output rates. At this stage, prices of goods and services have increased but input prices—wage rates and raw material prices —have not changed. (Recall that as we move along a short-run aggregate supply curve, input prices are constant.)

The economy cannot stay above its long-run aggregate supply and full-employment levels forever. Why not? What are the forces at work bringing real GNP back to its long-run level and restoring full employment? First, if the price level has increased but wages have remained constant, workers have experienced a fall in the purchasing power of their wages. Furthermore, firms have experienced a fall in the real cost of labor. In these circumstances, workers demand higher wages, and firms, anxious to maintain their employment and output levels, meet those demands. If firms do not raise wages, they either lose workers or have to hire less productive ones. Second, the owners of raw materials, facing higher prices for the things that they buy, have also experienced a fall in the purchasing power of their income. They demand higher prices for their raw materials.

As input prices rise, the short-run aggregate supply curve begins to shift. It moves upward from SAS_0 toward SAS_1. The rise in input prices and the shift in the SAS curve produce a sequence of new equilibrium positions. At each point on the adjustment path, output falls and the price level rises. Eventually, input prices will have risen by so much that the SAS curve is SAS_1, by which time the aggregate demand curve AD_1 intersects SAS_1 at a full-

Figure 24.9   The Effect of a Change in Aggregate Demand

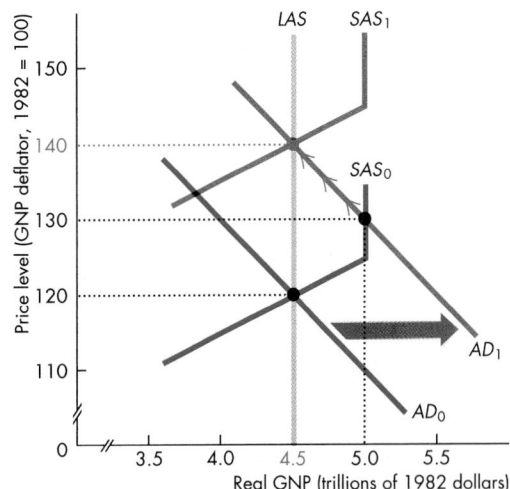

An increase in aggregate demand shifts the aggregate demand curve from AD_0 to AD_1. Real GNP increases from 4.5 trillion to 5 trillion 1982 dollars and the price level increases from 120 to 130. A higher price level induces higher wages and other input prices, which in turn cause the short-run aggregate supply curve to move upward. As the SAS curve moves upward from SAS_0 to SAS_1, it intersects the aggregate demand curve AD_1 at higher price levels and lower real GNP levels. Eventually, the price level increases to 140 and real GNP falls back to 4.5 trillion 1982 dollars—its full-employment level.

employment equilibrium. The price level has risen to 140, and output is back where it started, at its full-employment level. Real GNP is again back at its long-run level.

Throughout the adjustment process, higher input prices raise firms' costs and, with rising costs, firms offer a smaller quantity of goods and services for sale at any given price level. By the time the adjustment is over, firms are producing exactly the same amount as initially produced, but at higher prices and higher costs. The level of costs relative to prices will be the same as it was initially.

We've just worked out the effects of an increase in aggregate demand. A decrease in aggregate demand has similar but opposite effects to those that we've just studied. That is, when aggregate demand falls, real GNP falls below its long-run level and unemployment rises above its natural rate. The lower price level increases the purchasing power of wages

Figure 24.10   The Effects of a Change in Short-run Aggregate Supply

(a) No change in aggregate demand

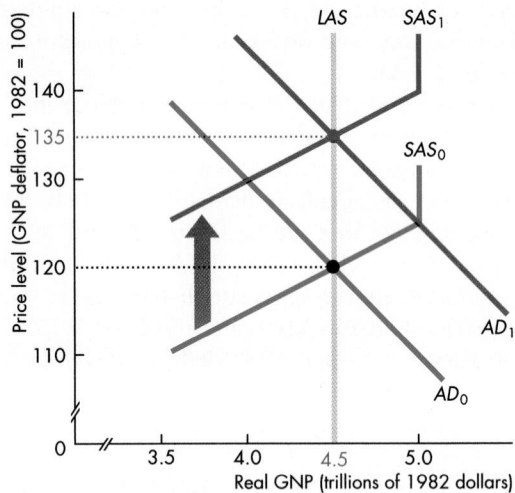

(b) An increase in aggregate demand

An increase in the price of oil shifts the short-run aggregate supply curve upward. Such a shift is illustrated as the movement from SAS_0 to SAS_1 in part (a). Real GNP falls from 4.5 trillion to 4 trillion 1982 dollars and the price level increases from 120 to 130. In the absence of any further changes in aggregate demand, input prices gradually fall, returning the economy to its initial position with a price level of 120 and real GNP of 4.5 trillion 1982 dollars. But input prices may take a very long time to fall, and in the meantime unemployment remains above its natural rate. To restore full employment, an increase in aggregate demand from AD_0 to AD_1 can be undertaken, as shown in part (b). This change in aggregate demand returns real GNP to 4.5 trillion 1982 dollars (its full-employment level) but increases the price level to 135.

and other factor incomes, and increases firms' costs relative to their prices. Eventually, as the slack economy leads to falling wages and other factor prices, the short-run aggregate supply curve shifts downward and, gradually, full employment is restored.

The Effects of a Change in Short-run Aggregate Supply

Let's now work out the effects of a change in short-run aggregate supply on real GNP and the price level. Figure 24.10 illustrates the analysis. Suppose, as shown in part (a), that the economy is initially at full-employment equilibrium. The aggregate demand curve is AD_0 and the short-run aggregate supply curve is SAS_0. The long-run aggregate supply curve is LAS. Output is 4.5 trillion 1982 dollars and the price level is 120.

Now suppose that there is an increase in the price of oil such as that imposed by OPEC in 1973. The oil price rise shifts the short-run aggregate supply curve to SAS_1. As a result of this change in short-run aggregate supply, the economy moves to a new equilibrium where SAS_1 intersects AD_0. The price level rises to 130 and real GNP falls to 4 trillion 1982 dollars.

The economy is now in a recession. Real GNP is below its long-run level and unemployment is above its natural rate. What happens after this initial effect? One possibility is that the economy may remain in a prolonged recession. With excessive unemployment, wages and raw material prices might eventually fall. If they do fall, the short-run aggregate supply curve shifts downward again to SAS_0 and full employment is eventually restored. But such a process may take a long time.

An alternative is shown in Fig. 24.10(b). Faced with a deep recession either the government or the Fed decides to stimulate aggregate demand. The government might cut taxes or increase its purchases of goods and services; the Fed might increase the money supply. If aggregate demand is stimulated so that the aggregate demand curve shifts to AD_1, full employment is restored at a real GNP level of 4.5 trillion 1982 dollars. But the price level also increases yet further to 135 in this example.

We've now studied aggregate demand, aggregate supply, and macroeconomic equilibrium. We've worked out the effects of changes in aggregate demand and aggregate supply on real GNP and the price level. Let's now put our new knowledge to work and see how it helps us understand U.S. macroeconomic performance.

Trends and Cycles in the U.S. Economy

We're now going to use our new tools of aggregate demand and aggregate supply to interpret some recent trends and cycles in the U.S. economy. We'll begin by looking at the state of the U.S. economy in 1988.

The Economy in 1988–89

Real GNP in 1988 was $4.0 trillion (measured in 1982 dollars). The price level was 122. We can illustrate this state of the U.S. economy by using the aggregate demand and aggregate supply model. Figure 24.11 shows the state of the economy in 1988. The aggregate demand curve, AD_{88}, cuts the short-run aggregate supply curve, SAS_{88}, at a price level of 122 and at a real GNP of $4.0 trillion.

We do not know, with certainty, where the long-run aggregate supply curve was in 1988. As discussed above, there is no single method for determining long-run aggregate supply. In Fig. 24.11, the long-run aggregate supply curve (LAS_{88}) is based on the assumption that long-run aggregate supply in 1988 was $3.9 trillion. Thus actual real GNP is above long-run aggregate supply, and unemployment is below its natural rate.

There was in 1988 and early 1989 a widely held expectation that the economy was not going to stay in this high level of activity. Fears of inflation and of a slowdown were widespread.

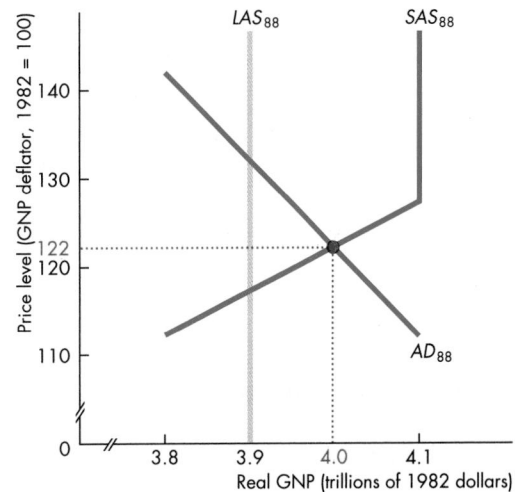

Figure 24.11   The U.S. Economy in 1988

In 1988, the U.S. economy was on the aggregate demand curve AD_{88} and the aggregate supply curve SAS_{88}. The price level was 122 and real GNP was 4.0 trillion 1982 dollars. The long-run aggregate supply curve LAS_{88} and full-employment real GNP were at 3.9 trillion 1982 dollars.

You can see why fears of inflation and an economic slowdown existed by comparing Fig. 24.11 with Fig. 24.9. In the earlier figure, we analyzed what happens when aggregate demand increases to put real GNP above its long-run level. By returning to Fig. 24.9, you will see that, in such a situation there is a tendency for wages to increase and, as they do so, for the short-run aggregate supply curve to shift upward. In the absence of any further changes in aggregate demand or in long-run aggregate supply, we can predict, using Fig. 24.11, that wage increases and increases in other input prices will shift the SAS curve upward above the SAS_{88} curve, raising the price level and lowering output.

Of course, other things are unlikely to remain constant. Several of the factors that we identified and discussed above will be shifting the long-run aggregate supply curve and short-run aggregate supply curve to the right and also other factors will be increasing aggregate demand. However, if the forces that we have just analyzed operate, although output will probably not fall, its pace of expansion will slow down.

The Tightrope Between Inflation and Recession

The Essence of the Story

■ In mid-1988, the economy was in its sixth year of expansion

■ Fearing inflation, the Federal Reserve pushed up interest rates

■ Indicators that the economy was expanding too quickly were:

—Unemployment fell to 5.4 percent in April 1988.
—Inflation (CPI) increased from a 4.4 percent annual rate in 1987 to a 6.4 percent annual rate in March 1988.
—Capacity utilization increased from 80.3 percent in March 1987, to 82.5 percent in March 1988.

■ Indicators that the economy was not expanding too quickly were:

—Wage growth remained moderate at 3.5 percent.
—Real GNP growth was moderate at 2.3 percent.

■ Economists differed in their views about the fears of inflation:

—Lyle Gramley: "We don't have an explosion of inflation, but it is clear that the inflationary process is under way."
—Richard Rahn: "Fears of inflation are greatly overblown."

Blowing Off Some Steam

With the Economy Threatening to Overheat, Greenspan Fights to Avert an Inflationary Explosion

What is going on here? By all accounts, the 5½-year-old economic expansion should be fizzling out. Already ancient by historical standards, the upswing appeared to have suffered a devastating blow when the stock market crashed last October. But, defying expectations, the economy is still running and even blowing off enough steam to inspire fears that it may actually be overheating. Forget about a recession, many economists counsel, and start worrying about inflation. Once a faint and far-off danger, rising prices may now pose the gravest threat to economic stability.

Responding to that threat is the job, as always, of Chairman Alan Greenspan and the other governors of the Federal Reserve. As the person in control of the U.S. money supply, Greenspan has the primary responsibility for preventing a price explosion. Last week he seemed to be moving decisively to cool things down by letting interest rates rise.

The crucial question is how high the Fed will let interest rates go in its efforts to slow the economy and ward off inflation.

The clearest indication that the economy might be expanding too quickly came two weeks ago, when the Labor Department reported that the unemployment rate fell from 5.6% in March to 5.4% in April, its lowest level in 14 years. While the drop was good news to anyone looking for work, many economists were alarmed because they believe that unemployment can fall only so far before inflation starts to accelerate. While no one knows precisely where this "trigger point" is, many economists think it is now no lower than 5.5%.

Current statistics provide disturbing evidence that the inflation trigger has been pulled again. In March consumer prices shot up at an annual rate of 6.4%, in contrast to a 4.4% rate for last year.

So far in 1988, the falling unemployment rate has not led to dramatic increases in wages. For the first three months of the year, workers' average hourly compensation rose by 3.5%, up only slightly from a 3.2% gain during the fourth quarter of last year.

While wage gains have remained moderate, other signs point to strong economic activity that could accelerate inflation. U.S. factories were operating at an average 82.5% of their total capacity in March, up from 80.3% a year earlier. Some industries, including chemicals and paper, are running at more than 90% of capacity. When production is so strained, shortages develop and prices are likely to surge.

While few economists consider the evidence of overheating to be conclusive, many are concerned. Says Lyle Gramley, a former Federal Reserve Board member who is now chief economist of the Mortgage Bankers Association of America: "We don't have an explosion of inflation, but it is clear that the inflationary process is under way."

Still, some economists doubt that growth is too rapid and deny that inflation is about to take off. The gross national product, they point out, expanded at a modest 2.3% annual rate during the first quarter. Concludes Richard Rahn, chief economist of the U.S. Chamber of Commerce: "Fears of inflation are greatly overblown."

Time, May 23, 1988

By Barbara Rudolph, reported by Richard Hornik/Washington and Thomas McCarroll/New York.

Background and Analysis

- In 1988, real GNP was 4.0 trillion 1982 dollars and the price level (GNP deflator) was 122. Long-run aggregate supply was 3.9 trillion 1982 dollars (Fig. a).

- Long-run aggregate supply was rising at a 2.5 percent annual rate, shifting the LAS_{88} curve to the right. Wages were rising at a 3.5 percent annual rate, shifting the SAS_{88} curve upward. Aggregate demand was rising at a 6 percent annual rate, shifting the AD_{88} curve to the right.

- A continuation of 1988 trends will shift the LAS_{88} curve to LAS_{89} and the AD_{88} curve to AD_1. The economy in 1989 will be on the aggregate demand curve AD_1 and the short-run aggregate supply curve SAS_1, (Fig. b). Real GNP will increase by 2.3 percent to 4.09 trillion 1982 dollars and the price level will rise by 3.3 percent to 126.3.

- If aggregate demand grows to AD_1 and wages increase at a faster pace, shifting the aggregate supply up to SAS_2, real GNP will be 4.0 trillion 1982 dollars (the same as 1988) and the price level will rise to 129—an inflation rate of 5.7 percent. This is the inflation fear.

(a) 1988

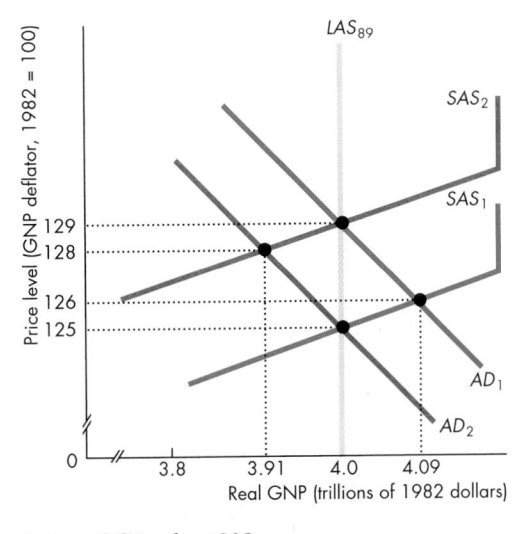

(b) Possibilities for 1989

- If the Fed restrains demand to keep inflation down, the aggregate demand curve will be AD_2. If wages do not explode, the aggregate supply curve will remain at SAS_1. Real GNP will be 4.0 trillion 1982 dollars (zero growth) and the price level will be 125 (2.5 percent inflation).

- If the Fed slows aggregate demand growth down to AD_2 but if the wage explosion is already under way and aggregate supply increases to SAS_2, then recession will occur. Real GNP will fall to 3.91 trillion 1982 dollars (a fall of 2.4 percent) but we will still get inflation of 4.9 percent, with the price level rising to 128.

- Key uncertainty and disagreement concerns the position of the LAS curve. If trend GNP growth speeds up, LAS_{89} will be farther to the right than shown in Fig. b and the SAS curve will not move to SAS_2. A rise in inflation is unlikely.

- If trend GNP growth does not speed up and long-run aggregate supply is accurately described in the figure, and if the short-run aggregate supply curve moves upward toward SAS_2, inflation will speed up and output will not grow.

Conclusion

To predict the course of inflation and real GNP, we need to predict the growth of long-run aggregate supply, the growth of short-run aggregate supply, and the growth of aggregate demand. To control inflation, the Fed forecasts where the economy is heading without any policy change and then tries to influence aggregate demand, balancing off its attempts to restrain inflation against the fear of causing recession.

Figure 24.12   Aggregate Demand and Aggregate
Supply: 1960 to 1988

Each point indicates the value of the GNP deflator and real GNP
in a given year. In 1960, these variables were determined at the
intersection of the aggregate demand curve AD_{60} and the aggregate supply curve SAS_{60}. Each point is generated by the gradually
shifting AD and SAS curves. By 1988, the curves were AD_{88} and
SAS_{88}. Real GNP had more than doubled and the price level had
increased almost fourfold. But growth and inflation did not proceed smoothly. Real GNP grew quickly and inflation was moderate in the 1960s; real GNP sagged in 1975 and again in 1982.
The 1975 recession was caused by an unusually sharp increase in
raw material (oil) prices and the 1982 recession by a slowdown in
the growth of aggregate demand engineered by the Fed's monetary policy. The period from 1982 to 1988 was one of strong,
persistent recovery. Inflation was rapid in the 1970s but slowed in
the 1980s.

Not everyone agreed, at the beginning of 1989,
that a recession and increased inflation were just
around the corner. Some took a more optimistic
view. Those taking an optimistic view believed that
the long-run aggregate supply curve would shift to
the right quickly enough to avoid recession and rising
inflation. If the accumulation of capital and the advance of technology are sufficiently strong, long-run
aggregate supply increases can prevent the type of
inflationary recession that we described in Fig. 24.9
and that would follow from the conditions described
in Fig. 24.11. Reading Between the Lines on pp.

632–633 takes a closer look at the macroeconomic
situation at the end of 1988.

Growth, Inflation, and Cycles

The economy is continually changing. If you imagine
the economy as a video, then Fig. 24.12 is a freeze-
frame. We're going to run the video again—an instant replay—but keep our finger on the freeze-frame
button, looking at some important parts of the previous action. Let's run the video from 1960.

Figure 24.12 shows the state of the economy in
1960 at the point of intersection of its aggregate
demand curve AD_{60} and short-run aggregate supply
curve SAS_{60}. Real GNP was $1.7 trillion and the
GNP deflator was 31 (around 25 percent of its 1988
level).

By 1988, the economy had reached the point
marked by the intersection of aggregate demand
curve AD_{88} and short-run aggregate supply curve
SAS_{88}. Real GNP was $4 trillion and the GNP
deflator was 122.

There are three important features of the path
followed by the economy traced by the blue and red
points:

- Expansion
- Inflation
- Cycles

Expansion   Over the years, real GNP expands. The
main force generating this expansion is an increase in
long-run aggregate supply. Long-run aggregate supply
increases because of population growth, the accumulation of capital—both physical plant and equipment
and human capital—the discovery of new resources,
and the advance of technology.

Inflation   The steady and persistent increase in prices results from a persistent increase in aggregate demand. Of all the factors that can shift the aggregate
demand curve, one—the quantity of money—is the
single most important factor leading to persistent
increases in aggregate demand and the price level.

Cycles   The pace of economic growth and inflation
is uneven. The unevenness arises because both the
expansion of short-run aggregate supply and the
growth of aggregate demand do not proceed at a
fixed, steady pace.

Let's examine the expansion, inflation, and cycles in the period since 1960 by focusing on four time periods in Fig. 24.12.

First, you can see that in the 1960s, there was a strong increase in real GNP with very small increases in prices. This was a period of steady increases in long-run aggregate supply and of moderate increases in aggregate demand.

Second, look at the period from 1973 to 1975. In 1973 and 1974, a series of massive oil price increases put the U.S. economy into a deep recession. Real GNP fell sharply in 1975 and the inflation rate hit 10 percent that year. The recession and increased inflation occurred because the increase in oil and other raw material prices shifted the short-run aggregate supply curve upward at a faster pace than the increase in aggregate demand. The result was a contraction with rising prices. Real GNP fell below its long-run aggregate supply level.

The rest of the 1970s saw sharp inflation—the price level increased quickly—but only moderate growth in real GNP. This inflation was the product of a battle between OPEC and the Fed. OPEC jacked up the price of oil. An inflationary recession ensued. Eventually, the Fed gave way and increased the money supply to bring the economy back to full employment. Then OPEC played a similar hand again, jacking up the price of oil still further. The Fed was faced with a dilemma. Should it inject more money and bring the economy back to full employment, notching up the inflation rate yet further or should it keep the growth of aggregate demand in check? The answer, delivered by Fed chairman Paul Volcker, was to keep demand growth in check.

You can see the effects of chairman Volcker's actions in the third period we're highlighting, 1979 to 1982. In this period, aggregate demand increased but not at a fast enough pace to keep up with the upward movement of the short-run aggregate supply curve resulting from wage and raw material price increases. As a consequence, by 1982 the upward movement of the short-run aggregate supply curve was so strong relative to the growth of aggregate demand that the economy went into a further deep recession.

Fourth, let's focus on the years 1982 to 1988. In this period, moderate wage growth slowed the pace of the upward movement in the short-run aggregate supply curve and sustained-but-steady growth in aggregate demand and in long-run aggregate supply kept the economy expanding and kept inflation steady. The economy moved from a recession with output well below its long-run aggregate supply level to full employment and perhaps beyond full employment.

■ This chapter has provided a model of real GNP and the GNP deflator that can be used to understand the growth, inflation, and cycles that our economy follows. The model is a useful one because it enables us to keep our eye on the big picture—on the broad trends and cycles in inflation and output. The model lacks detail. It does not tell us as much as we need to know about the components of aggregate demand— consumption, investment, government purchases of goods and services, and exports and imports. It doesn't tell us what determines interest rates or wages or even, directly, what determines employment and unemployment. In the following chapters, we're going to start to fill in that detail.

In some ways, the study of macroeconomics is like doing a large jigsaw puzzle. The aggregate demand and aggregate supply model provides the entire edge of the jigsaw. We know its general shape and size but we haven't filled in the middle. One block of the jigsaw contains the story of aggregate demand. Another, the story of aggregate supply. And when we place the two together, we place them in the frame of the model developed in this chapter, and the picture is completed.

S U M M A R Y

Aggregate Demand

Aggregate demand is the relationship between the aggregate quantity of goods and services demanded —real GNP demanded—and the price level—the GNP deflator. The aggregate demand curve slopes downward. A rise in the price level produces a movement along the aggregate demand curve, reducing the quantity of real GNP demanded. Factors that change aggregate demand shift the aggregate demand curve. (pp. 614–620)

Aggregate Supply

Aggregate supply is studied on two time frames: the long run and the short run.

Long-run aggregate supply is the quantity of goods and services supplied when each firm is producing its capacity output and when there is full employment. Long-run aggregate supply is independent of the price level.

Short-run aggregate supply is the relationship between the aggregate quantity of goods and services supplied—real GNP supplied—and the price level —the GNP deflator—with everything else held constant. The short-run aggregate supply curve slopes upward. Other things being equal, the higher the price level, the more output firms plan to sell.

The factors that change short-run aggregate supply shift the short-run aggregate supply curve. Anything that shifts the long-run aggregate supply curve also shifts the short-run aggregate supply curve. Changes in input prices shift the short-run aggregate supply curve but leave the long-run aggregate supply curve unaffected. (pp. 620–626)

Macroeconomic Equilibrium

Macroeconomic equilibrium occurs when the quantity of real GNP demanded equals the quantity of real GNP supplied. Macroeconomic equilibrium occurs at the intersection of the aggregate demand curve and the short-run aggregate supply curve. The price level that achieves that equality is the equilibrium price level; the resulting output is equilibrium real GNP.

Macroeconomic equilibrium does not always occur at full employment—at a point on the long-run aggregate supply curve. Unemployment equilibrium occurs when equilibrium real GNP is less than its long-run aggregate supply level. When equilibrium real GNP is above its long-run level, employment is above full employment.

An increase in aggregate demand shifts the aggregate demand curve to the right and increases both real GNP and the price level. If real GNP increases above its long-run level, input prices begin to increase and, as they do so, the short-run aggregate supply curve shifts upward. The upward shift of the short-run aggregate supply curve results in a yet higher price level but lower real GNP. Eventually, real GNP returns to its long-run level.

An increase in input prices shifts the short-run aggregate supply curve upward and results in a fall in real GNP and a rise in the price level. If there is no subsequent change in aggregate demand, the economy stays in a recession until input prices have fallen back to their original levels. If aggregate demand is increased to restore full employment, then the price level rises still higher. (pp. 626–631)

Trends and Cycles in the U.S. Economy

Long-term growth in the U.S. economy results from population growth, capital accumulation, and technological change. Inflation persists in the U.S. economy because of steady increases in aggregate demand brought about by increases in the quantity of money. The U.S. economy experiences cycles because the short-run aggregate supply and aggregate demand curves shift at an uneven pace.

A large hike in the price of oil in 1973 resulted in an inflationary recession in the mid-1970s. A replay in 1979 intensified the inflationary situation. Restraint in aggregate demand growth in 1980 and 1981 resulted in a severe recession in 1982. This recession resulted in lower output and a lower inflation rate. Moderate increases in input prices and steady technological advance and capital accumulation resulted in a sustained expansion in the early 1960s and again in the 1980s. (pp. 631–635)

K E Y   C O N C E P T S

Key Figures and Tables

REVIEW QUESTIONS

1 What is aggregate demand?

2 What is the difference between aggregate demand and the aggregate quantity of goods and services demanded?

3 List the main factors that affect aggregate demand. Separate them into those that make aggregate demand rise and those that make it fall.

4 Which of the following do not affect aggregate demand:

   a) Quantity of money

   b) Interest rates

   c) Technological change

   d) Human capital

5 What is aggregate supply?

6 What is the difference between aggregate supply and the aggregate quantity of goods and services supplied?

7 Distinguish between short-run aggregate supply and long-run aggregate supply.

8 Consider the following events:

   a) The labor force increases

   b) Technology improves

   c) The money wage rate increases

   d) The quantity of money increases

   e) Foreign incomes increase

   f) The foreign exchange value of the dollar increases

Sort these events into the following four categories:

Category A: Those that affect the long-run aggregate supply curve but not the short-run aggregate supply curve;

Category B: Those that affect the short-run aggregate supply curve but not the long-run aggregate supply curve;

Category C: Those that affect both the short-run aggregate supply curve and the long-run aggregate supply curve;

Category D: Those that have no effect on the short-run aggregate supply curve or on the long-run aggregate supply curve.

9 Define macroeconomic equilibrium.

10 Distinguish between macroeconomic equilibrium and full-employment equilibrium.

11 Work out the effect of a rise in the quantity of money on the price level and on real GNP.

12 Work out the effect of a rise in the price of oil on the price level and on real GNP.

13 What are the main factors generating growth of long-run aggregate supply in the U.S. economy?

14 What are the main factors generating persistent inflation in the U.S. economy?

15 Why does the U.S. economy experience cycles in aggregate economic activity?

P R O B L E M S

1 You are the President's economic advisor and you are trying to figure out where the U.S. economy is headed next year. You have the following forecasts for the *AD, SAS,* and *LAS* curves:

Price level	Real GNP demanded	Real GNP supplied in the short run	Long-run aggregate supply
(trillions of 1982 dollars)			
110	4.3	2.7	3.9
120	4.0	3.2	3.9
130	3.7	3.7	3.9
140	3.4	4.2	3.9

This year, real GNP is $3.9 trillion and the price level is 122. The President wants answers to the following questions:

a) What is your forecast of next year's real GNP?

b) What is your forecast of next year's price level?

c) What is your forecast of the inflation rate?

d) Will unemployment be above or below its natural rate?

e) Will real GNP be above or below trend? By how much?

2 Carefully draw some figures similar to those in this chapter, and use the information in problem 1, to explain:

a) What will have to be done to aggregate demand to achieve full employment?

b) What will the inflation rate be if aggregate demand is manipulated to achieve full employment?

Part 9

Talking with Robert Lucas

Robert E. Lucas, Jr., is closely associated with the development of rational expectations macroeconomics. A professor of economics at the University of Chicago, Lucas first applied his ideas about rational expectations to the Phillips curve. Michael Parkin spoke with Professor Lucas about rational expectations macroeconomics, his views on other approaches to economics, and his views of economic policy.

You applied the idea of rational expectations to macroeconomics and to expectations about inflation. How has that hypothesis changed the way we think about things?

It ties down a loose end that shouldn't have been there. Any important economic decision depends upon what you think about the future. Rational expectations is just a way of dealing with that.

What do you see as the chief criticisms of the rational expectations hypothesis?

Here's the genuine difficulty people have with the idea. You would never discover the idea of rational expectations by introspection. Rational expectations describes something that has to be true of the outcome of a much more complicated underlying process. But it doesn't describe the actual thought process people use in trying to figure out the future. Our behavior is adaptive. We try some mode of behavior. If it's successful, we do it again. If not, we try something else. Rational expectations describes the situation when you've got it right.

Can you give an example?

In economics we're mostly concerned about repetitive events and decisions of some consequence. Our capitalist economy has been operating under pretty much the same laws for 200 years now. People aren't reacting to every monetary contraction as if it's the first time it ever happened. It's just inconceivable. I think people have developed certain ways of living with regular events as best they can.

> "People aren't reacting to every monetary contraction as if it's the first time."

What do you now think of the first rational expectations model that you proposed?

Rational expectations can be used in combination with a wealth of other assumptions to produce all kinds of different models. The particular models of business cycles that Tom Sargent and I, among others, advanced in the 1970s have run

into hard times. In my case, I put a lot of emphasis on people having inadequate information about the quantity of money, and I think a lot of economists now feel that that's just too thin a reed to hang a theory of business cycles on. That it's just not that hard to get accurate information on the quantity of money, which is published every Friday. That's a criticism of a very specific model.

One of the most significant contributions of the 1980s has been real business cycle theory. How do you evaluate this approach?

Real business cycle theory asks what the time path of the economy's GNP or employment would be under the best possible macroeconomic

policy. The early authors of this approach asked themselves what fraction of actual variation in GNP you could account for if you restrict yourself to the fluctuations in the rate of technological change. Their answer was, all of it. There's nothing left over for traditional macroeconomic theory to account for. I don't think that can be right.

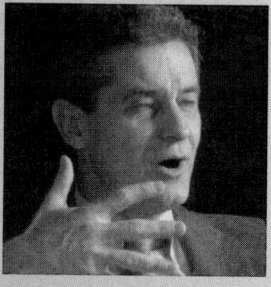

Why can't that be right?

Because you can't account for something like the events of 1929 to 1933 when real output fell by a quarter in four years, as if it resulted from the changes in the rate at which technology was decaying. The Depression didn't occur because production techniques got worse. Real business cycle theory suggests that real forces are much more important than we had thought and that the questions addressed by traditional macroeconomics are not as important as we once thought. That's the message.

TALKING WITH ROBERT LUCAS 641

How can we introduce monetary forces into a macroeconomic model that at the same time pays serious attention to real forces, one that shows fluctuations in price as well as in output?

I think that's a central unsolved problem that my 1972 paper on rational expectations, which we discussed earlier, addressed, only there I used deficiencies in people's information. There's also the approach that looks at fixed wage contracts, work done by John Taylor or Stanley Fischer. I'm much more sympathetic to that line of thought than I was 10 years ago. Why is it that people commit themselves to agreements to buy and sell at fixed nominal prices in a world where the value of a dollar is fluctuating all the time? Why would you tie your future decisions to some unit when you have no way of knowing what that unit is going to mean later on? That's a great question. No one yet knows the answer to it.

Some economists suggest that even at the level of pricing goods, not just labor and contracts, we should think of a rigidity that arises from "menu costs." The idea that you've got to publish your prices, to label the shelves, jars and bottles. And this is costly, so you won't change the price every minute. What do you think of this approach?

I think there's some truth to it. But it's criticized; It seems like a slim reed. People ask, do you mean to tell me that the Great Depression occurred because it was too much of a bother for supermarket clerks to put new price tags on the goods on their shelves? There's no question that there's something to this approach, but there's a question of how important it is. I think the details of individual price setting are very poorly understood. So when people adopt an assumption like rigid prices, I don't think we can afford to look down our noses at them.

You were a student of Milton Friedman, the architect of the movement called monetarism. How do you distinguish this approach from the kind of macroeconomics that you are responsible for creating?

I'm not that big on the distinction. I'm a monetarist. But the term does refer to several things. One aspect of what people call monetarism is just emphasis on the quantity of some monetary aggregate as a determinant of prices and of economic activity. In some ways, I think that revolution has been so successful that it doesn't seem like a revolution any more. In this day and age, no one talks about the price level, exchange rates, or interest rates without talking about the quantity of money. In that sense,

we're all monetarists. The second aspect of monetarism is a hostility toward government's continual management of the economy. The role of government, in a monetarist perspective, is to make its own behavior on fiscal or monetary policy simple and predictable and then just to let the system operate without fine-tuning. That view, I think, is absolutely right.

> "We don't want to manage the U.S. economy. And we don't think anybody else should take the job either."

In recent years, we've experienced the biggest peacetime government budget deficit ever. How have you viewed the deficit over the years?

That's an embarrassing question for me because the deficit is not having the immediate unpleasant consequences I had predicted. My handle on the deficit is this. If you think of an economy in some kind of smooth, steady state, running a deficit year in and year out, what has to make up that deficit are changes in the monetary base. So I see large deficits that occur regularly as equivalent to a large rate of growth in the monetary base, which means inflation. I don't like deficits because they signal inflation. There's not a tight year to year connection, because you can issue bonds to cover the deficit, which are a promise either to raise taxes later or to print money later. But sooner or later it's the monetary base that fills the gap between government spending and tax revenues.

At the start of the Reagan administration, Tom Sargent and I wrote newspaper articles saying that the deficit would be inflationary. Well, that just hasn't happened. I'm in the process of re-thinking about deficits. I'm sympathetic to people like Larry Kotlikoff, who suspect that the deficit might be an illusion as a result of inadequate accounting. That it just doesn't measure anything since things like future social security liabilities are arbitrarily excluded or included.

What is the context of your well-known debate with James Tobin?

Tobin views the role of macroeconomics to be to provide principles for guiding monetary and fiscal policy in order to keep the economy near what he thinks of as full employment. And he thinks if this isn't done, we'll have the Depression again. People like Sargent or Friedman or myself basically come and poke holes, saying "Look, these principles you have for managing the economy are useless." Our opponents in this debate tried to discredit us as economic managers, asking, "Would you trust the management of the U.S. economy to Lucas?" We're not asking them to. We don't want the job, and we don't think anybody else should take it either.

Chapter 25

After studying this chapter, you will be able to:

- Describe the importance and degree of fluctuation in the components of aggregate expenditure—consumption expenditure, investment, government purchases of goods and services, and net exports

- Explain how people make their consumption and saving decisions

- Explain how consumption and saving are influenced by income and wealth

- Define and calculate the average and marginal propensities to consume and save

- Explain the relationship between consumption expenditure and GNP

- Explain how firms make their investment decisions

- Explain why there are large fluctuations in investment

- Explain how export and import decisions are made and how net exports are determined

"**C**ONSUMERS IGNORE PLUNGE IN STOCKS AND SPEND FREELY" With this headline, and an almost audible sigh of relief, the *New York Times* reported the U.S. Commerce Department's first news on retail sales following the stock market crash of October 1987. "The nation's shoppers," the article said, "seem to have been largely unfazed by the stock market plunge that began in mid-October, continuing to spend freely."[1] However, by December, the headlines spoke fearfully of weak holiday season sales, and of retailers cutting prices to attract shoppers. ■ Why all the fear and trembling over what happens in the shopping aisles? Besides a few manufacturers and stores, who really cares whether people buy a lot of gifts for the holidays, or

Fear and Trembling in the Shopping Aisles

whether they continue to buy cars and VCRs after a stock market crash? How does this affect the rest of us? What makes people decide to spend less and save more? ■ It's not only consumer spending that stirs up hope and fear in the economy. "DURABLE GOODS ORDERS ROSE 8.8% IN JUNE, DRIV-EN BY AIRCRAFT, MILITARY BOOKINGS" trumpeted a *Wall Street Journal* story in mid-1988 about the Commerce Department's latest assessments of demand for capital goods.[2] "WEAK DOLLAR HELPS EXPORTS" read a *New York Times* headline in late 1987.[3] How do business investment and exports affect us? How much of the country's spending do they make up, when compared with consumer spending? Are fluctuations in these components of aggregate expenditure sources of fluctuations in our job prospects and living standards? ■ What about the government's spending on goods and services? Is the government a source of instability in the

---

[1]*New York Times* (November 14, 1987), p. 1.

[2]*Wall Street Journal* (July 27, 1988), p. 3.

[3]*New York Times* (November 13, 1987), p. 29.

economy or is the government's spending more stable than that of the private sector?

■ We have just discovered, in Chapter 24, how the interaction of aggregate demand and aggregate supply determines the price level and real GNP. In this chapter, and the following four chapters, we are going to take a closer look at the aggregate demand side of the economy. In Chapter 24, we learned some propositions about the aggregate demand curve and what makes that curve shift. That is, we catalogued the influences on aggregate demand, including the influences of taxes and government purchases and of the Fed's monetary policy. We're now going to learn more about those influences on aggregate demand, discovering why they operate in the way they do and also discovering how aggregate demand might be influenced by policy to smooth out fluctuations. Our first step in this process is to study people's spending decisions more closely.   ■ We discovered in our study of the national income accounts in Chapter 23 that when one person spends a dollar, it shows up as a dollar of income spread out among a lot of other people. The spending that people do in shopping aisles spreads out in waves across the economy, affecting millions of people. In this chapter, we study the composition of those waves and see why consumption has a big effect outside the stores. We also study the other components of aggregate expenditure— investment, government purchases of goods and services, and net exports.   ■ Our concern in this chapter is to study each of these components of aggregate expenditure in isolation. Then, in Chapter 26, we'll bring the separate elements together and see how they interact with each other to determine the levels of aggregate expenditure and GNP. When we have completed our study of these two chapters, we'll have a clearer and deeper understanding of how aggregate demand is determined and why it fluctuates.   ■ Let's begin by looking at the components of aggregate expenditure.

The Components of Aggregate Expenditure

The components of aggregate expenditure are:

• Consumption expenditure

• Investment
• Government purchases of goods and services
• Net exports (exports minus imports)

Relative Importance of the Components of Aggregate Expenditure

What are the relative magnitudes of the components of aggregate expenditure? Which is the largest component? Figure 25.1 answers these questions for the years since 1960. By far the biggest portion of aggregate expenditure is consumption expenditure, which ranges between 59 and 66 percent and averages 62 percent GNP. The smallest portion is net exports, whose average value is close to zero. Investment ranges between 14 and 20 percent of GNP and averages 17 percent. Government purchases of goods and services are slightly larger than investment, ranging between 19 and 25 percent of GNP, and averaging 23 percent.

Volatility of the Components of Aggregate Expenditure

Which of the components of aggregate expenditure fluctuate the most—which are the most volatile? Figure 25.2 answers this question. And that answer is investment and net exports. Consumption expenditure and government purchases of goods and services fluctuate much less strongly than these two items.

In studying this figure, notice that the vertical axis measures the extent to which the four components of aggregate expenditure deviate from their own trend values. The scales on which each of the four variables are measured are identical, so the up and down movements in the lines give a precise indication of the relative volatility of the four components. Note that although the fluctuations in consumption expenditure have a much smaller range than those in investment, the ups and downs of the two series move in sympathy with each other. Note also that the two big declines in investment—in 1975 and 1982—occurred at precisely the time that the economy was at the trough of severe recessions (recessions that we saw in Chapter 22, p. 579 and in Chapter 24, p. 635). Government purchases of goods and services show two dramatic increases— one in the late 1960s and another in the late 1980s. Net exports have become especially volatile in the 1980s.

Figure 25.1   The Components of Aggregate Expenditure: 1960–1988

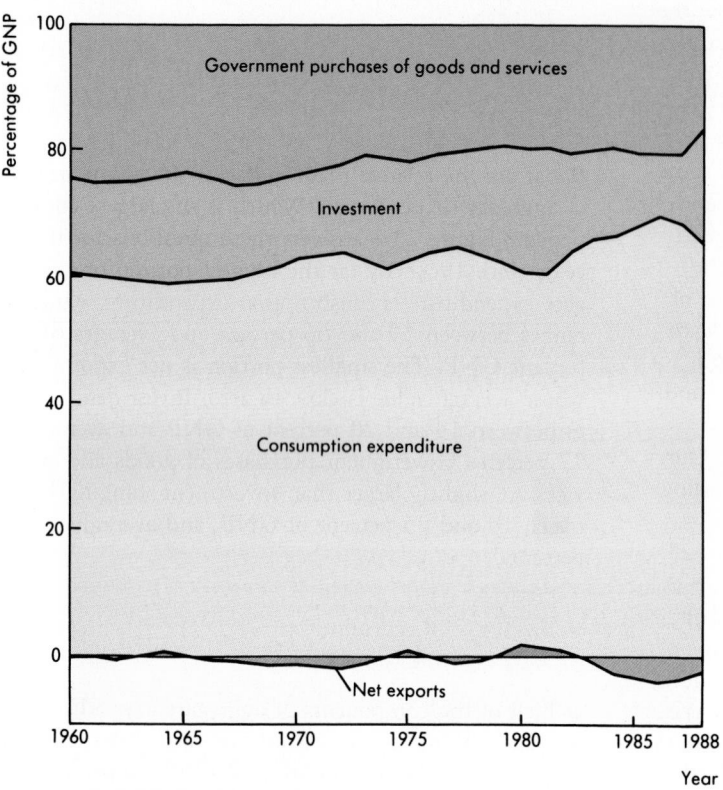

The biggest component of aggregate expenditure is consumption expenditure. It ranges between 59 and 66 percent of GNP and averages 62 percent. Investment averages 17 percent of GNP, fluctuating between 14 and 20 percent. Government purchases of goods and services range between 19 and 25 percent of GNP and average 23 percent of GNP. Net exports are the smallest item and average approximately zero.

Consumption expenditure, investment, and net exports are the private components of aggregate expenditure. Government purchases of goods and services are determined by decisions made by governments in their interactions with voters. This is the public component of aggregate expenditure. In the material that follows, we're going to study the choices that determine the private components of aggregate expenditure. Let's begin with the largest component —consumption expenditure.

Consumption Expenditure and Saving

Consumption expenditure is the value of the consumption goods and services bought by households. There are five main factors that influence a household's consumption expenditure:

- Disposable income
- Expected future income
- Stage in life
- Degree of patience
- Interest rates

Disposable Income   *Disposable income* is the total income that households receive in exchange for supplying the services of factors of production, plus transfers from the government minus taxes. A household can do only two things with its disposable income: Spend it on consumption goods and services or save it.

As a household's disposable income increases, so does its expenditure on food and beverages, clothing, housing, transportation, medical care, and on most other goods and services. That is, a household's consumption expenditure increases as its income increases.

Figure 25.2   Fluctuations in the Components of Aggregate Expenditure: 1960–1988

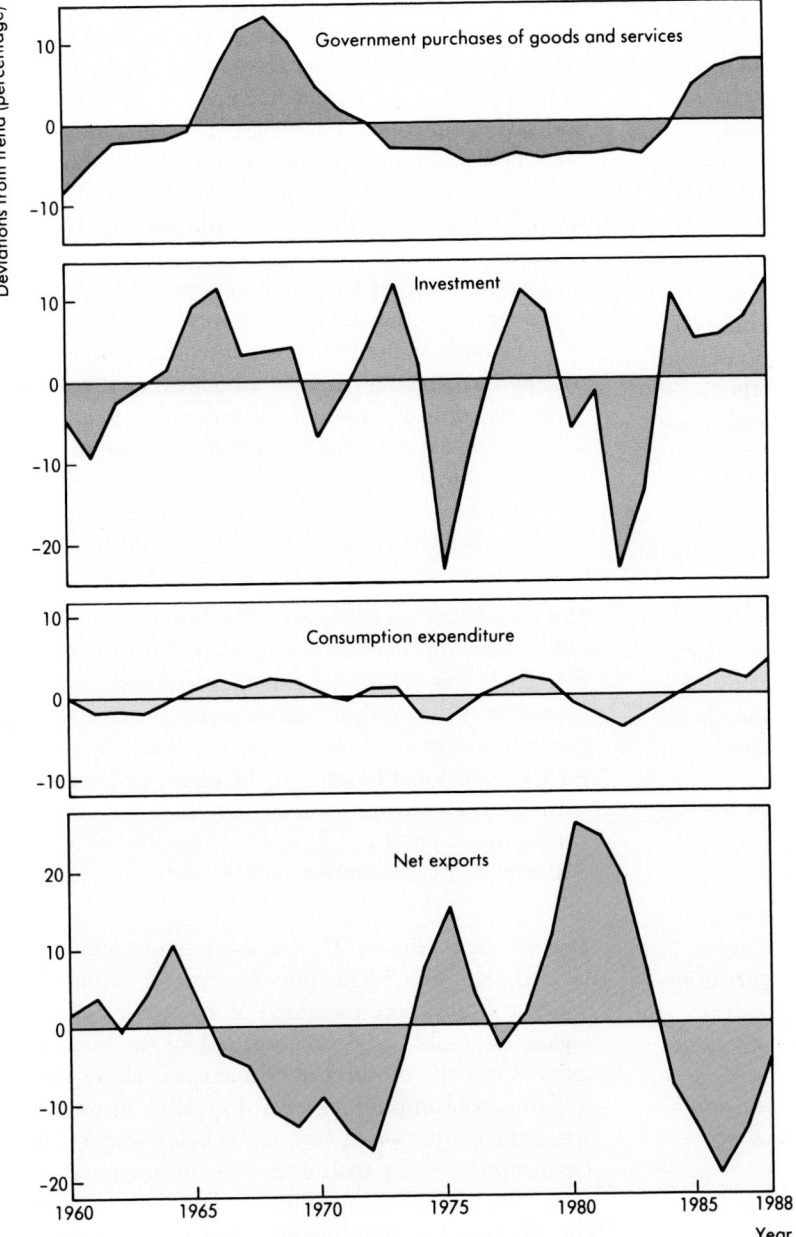

Fluctuations in the components of aggregate expenditure are shown as percentage deviations from trends. Although consumption is the biggest portion of aggregate expenditure, it is the one that fluctuates least, in percentage terms. Investment and net exports fluctuate most. Government purchases of goods and services show a strong increase above trend in the 1960s and again in the 1980s.

Expected Future Income   Other things being equal, the higher a household's expected future income, the greater is its current consumption expenditure. That is, if there are two households that each have the same disposable income in the current year, the household with the larger expected future income will spend a larger portion of current disposable income on consumption goods and services. Consider, for example, two households whose principle income earner is a senior executive in a large corporation.

One executive has just been told of an important promotion that will increase the household's income by 50 percent in the following years. The other has just been told that the firm has been taken over and that there will be no further employment beyond the end of the year. The first household buys a new car and takes an expensive foreign vacation, thereby increasing its current consumption expenditure. The second household sells the family's second car and cancels its winter vacation plans, thereby cutting back on its current consumption expenditure.

Stage in Life On the average, households that spend the largest part of their disposable income on consumption goods and services are young households with dependent children. Those who spend the smallest part of their disposable income on consumption goods and services are the elderly and retired.

Degree of Patience The degree of patience varies from one person to another and from one household to another. Some, impatient to consume, do not worry if they run into debt. Others prefer to defer consumption and save instead. These personal characteristics influence the level of a household's consumption expenditure. The more impatient the household, the larger is its consumption expenditure, other things being equal.

Interest Rates The higher the interest rate, the lower is the level of consumption expenditure. High interest rates discourage consumption by making consumer loans more expensive or by making it more attractive for a household to save and lend part of its income to others.

Of the five influences on consumption expenditure, the most important one is the level of disposable income. Let's look at the relationship between consumption expenditure and disposable income more closely.

The Consumption Function and the Saving Function

The relationship between consumption expenditure and disposable income is called the **consumption function.** The relationship between saving and disposable income is called the **saving function.** We'll first examine the consumption function and saving function for an imaginary household. Then we'll study the consumption function in the U.S. economy.

A household's consumption function and saving function are a statement about the household's consumption expenditure and saving plan at each possible level of disposable income. Figure 25.3 sets out the consumption function and saving function for the Polonius household. There are two important things to note about the Polonius household's consumption and saving functions. First, even if the Polonius household has no disposable income, it still consumes. It does so by having a negative level of saving. Negative saving is called **dissaving.** Households that consume more than their disposable income do so either by living off assets or by borrowing, a situation that cannot, of course, last forever.

Second, as the Polonius household's disposable income increases, so does the amount that it plans to spend on consumption and the amount that it plans to save. Since a household can only consume or save its disposable income, these two items always add up to disposable income. That is, consumption and saving plans are consistent with disposable income.

The Consumption Function The Polonius household's consumption function is plotted in part (a) of Fig. 25.3. The horizontal axis measures disposable income and the vertical axis measures consumption expenditure (both in thousands of dollars). The points labeled *a* through *f* in the figure correspond with the rows having the same letters in the table. For example, point *c* indicates a disposable income of $20,000 and consumption of $18,000.

The 45° Line Figure 25.3(a) also contains a line labeled ''45° line.'' This line connects the points at which consumption, measured on the vertical axis, equals disposable income, measured on the horizontal axis. When the consumption function is above the 45° line, consumption exceeds disposable income; when the consumption function is below the 45° line, consumption is less than disposable income; and at the point where the consumption function intersects the 45° line, consumption and disposable income are equal.

The Saving Function The saving function is graphed in part (b) of the figure. The horizontal axis is exactly the same as that in part (a). The vertical axis measures saving. Again, the points marked *a* through *f* correspond to the rows of the table.

There is a relationship between the consumption function and the saving function. We can see

Figure 25.3   The Polonius Household's Consumption Function and Saving Function

(a) Consumption function

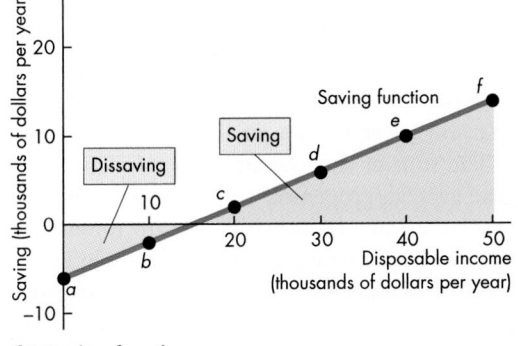

(b) Saving function

	Disposable income	Consumption expenditure	Saving
	(thousands of dollars per year)		
a	0	6	−6
b	10	12	−2
c	20	18	2
d	30	24	6
e	40	30	10
f	50	36	14

The table sets out the consumption and saving plan of the Polonius household at various levels of disposable income. Part (a) of the figure shows the relationship between consumption expenditure and disposable income (the consumption function). Part (b) shows the relationship between saving and disposable income (the saving function). Points a through f on the consumption and saving functions correspond to the rows in the table. The 45° line in part (a) is the line of equality between consumption expenditure and disposable income. The Polonius household's consumption expenditure and saving equals its disposable income. When the consumption function is above the 45° line, saving is negative (dissaving occurs) and the saving function is below the horizontal axis. When the consumption function is below the 45° line, saving is positive and the saving function is above the horizontal axis. At the point where the consumption function intersects the 45° line, all disposable income is consumed, saving is zero, and the saving function intersects the horizontal axis.

this relationship by looking at the two parts of the figure. When the saving function is below the horizontal axis, saving is negative (dissaving) and the consumption function is above the 45° line. When the saving function is above the horizontal axis, saving is positive and the consumption function is below the 45° line. When saving is zero, the saving function cuts the horizontal axis and when consumption equals disposable income, the consumption function cuts the 45° line. The level of disposable income at which the saving function cuts the horizontal axis is the same as that at which the consumption function cuts the 45° line.

The Average Propensities to Consume and to Save

The **average propensity to consume** (APC) is consumption expenditure divided by disposable income. Table 25.1(a) shows you how to calculate the average propensity to consume. Let's do a sample calculation. At a disposable income of $20,000, the Polonius household consumes $18,000. Its average propensity to consume is $18,000 divided by $20,000, which equals 0.9.

As you can see from the numbers in the table, the average propensity to consume declines as

Table 25.1   Average and Marginal
Propensities to Consume
and to Save

(a) Calculating average propensities to consume and to save

Disposable income (YD)	Consumption expenditure (C) (dollars per year)	Saving (S)	APC (C/YD)	APS (S/YD)
0	6,000	−6,000	–	–
10,000	12,000	−2,000	1.20	−0.20
20,000	18,000	2,000	0.90	0.10
30,000	24,000	6,000	0.80	0.20
40,000	30,000	10,000	0.75	0.25
50,000	36,000	14,000	0.72	0.28

(b) Calculating marginal propensities to consume and to save

Change in disposable income	ΔYD =	10,000
Change in consumption	ΔC =	6,000
Change in saving	ΔS =	4,000
Marginal propensity to consume	MPC = $\Delta C/\Delta YD$ = 0.6	
Marginal propensity to save	MPS = $\Delta S/\Delta YD$ = 0.4	

Consumption and saving depend on disposable income. At zero disposable income, some consumption is undertaken and saving is negative (dissaving occurs). The average propensities to consume and to save are calculated in part (a). As disposable income increases, so do both consumption and saving. The average propensity to consume—the ratio of consumption to disposable income—declines as disposable income increases; the average propensity to save—the ratio of saving to disposable income—increases as disposable income increases. These two average propensities sum to 1. Each additional—or *marginal*—dollar of disposable income is either consumed or saved. Part (b) calculates the marginal propensities to consume and to save. The extent to which disposable income is consumed is measured by the marginal propensity to consume and the extent to which it is saved is measured by the marginal propensity to save. The marginal propensity to consume is the change in consumption that results from a $1 change in disposable income. The marginal propensity to save is the change in saving that results from a $1 change in disposable income. The marginal propensities to consume and to save sum to 1.

disposable income rises. At a disposable income of $10,000, the household consumes more than its income, so its average propensity to consume is greater than 1. But at a disposable income of $50,000 the household consumes only $36,000, so its average propensity to consume is $36,000 divided by $50,000, which equals 0.72.

The **average propensity to save** (APS) is saving divided by disposable income. It too is calculated in Table 25.1(a). For example, when disposable income is $20,000 the Polonius household saves $2000, so that the average propensity to save is $2000 divided by $20,000, which equals 0.1. When saving is negative, the average propensity to save is negative. As disposable income increases, the average propensity to save increases.

As disposable income increases, the average propensity to consume falls and the average propensity to save rises. Equivalently, as disposable income increases, the fraction of income saved increases and the fraction of income consumed decreases. These patterns in the average propensities to consume and save reflect the fact that people with very low disposable incomes are so poor that their income is not even sufficient to meet their consumption expenditure. Consumption expenditure exceeds disposable income. As people become richer, with higher incomes, they are able to meet their consumption requirements with a lower and lower fraction of their disposable income.

The sum of the average propensity to consume and the average propensity to save is equal to one. These two average propensities add up to one because consumption and saving exhaust disposable income. Each dollar of disposable income is either consumed or saved.

You can see that the two average propensities add up to 1 by using the following equation:

$$C + S = YD.$$

Divide both sides of the equation by disposable income to obtain

$$C/YD + S/YD = 1.$$

C/YD is the *average propensity to consume* and S/YD is *average propensity to save*. Thus

$$APC + APS = 1.$$

The Marginal Propensities to Consume and to Save

The last dollar of disposable income received is called the marginal dollar. Part of that marginal dollar is consumed and part of it is saved. The division of the marginal dollar between consumption expenditure and saving is determined by the marginal propensities to consume and to save.

The **marginal propensity to consume** (MPC) is the fraction of the last dollar of disposable income that is spent on consumption goods and services. It is calculated as the increase in consumption expenditure divided by the increase in disposable income. The **marginal propensity to save** (MPS) is the fraction of the last dollar of disposable income saved. The marginal propensity to save is calculated as the increase in saving divided by the increase in disposable income.

Table 25.1(b) calculates the Polonius household's marginal propensities to consume and to save. Looking back at part (a) of the table, you can see that disposable income increases by $10,000 as we move from one row to the next—$10,000 is the change in disposable income. You can also see from part (a) that when disposable income increases by $10,000, consumption increases by $6000. The marginal propensity to consume—the change in consumption divided by the change in disposable income is therefore $6000 divided by $10,000, which equals 0.6. The Polonius household's marginal propensity to consume is constant. Out of a marginal dollar of disposable income, 60¢ is spent on consumption goods and services.

Part (b) of the table also calculates the marginal propensity to save. You can see from that part of the table that when disposable income increases by $10,000, saving increases by $4000. The marginal propensity to save—the change in saving divided by the change in disposable income—is therefore $4000 divided by $10,000, which equals 0.4. The Polonius household's marginal propensity to save is constant. It is the same at each level of disposable income. Out of the last dollar of disposable income, 40¢ is saved.

The marginal propensity to consume plus the marginal propensity to save equals one. Each additional dollar must either be consumed or spent. In this example, when disposable income increases by $1, 60¢ more is spent and 40¢ more is saved.

Marginal-Average Relationships In the calculations we have just done, the marginal propensity to consume is below the average propensity to consume, and as disposable income increases, the average propensity to consume falls.

This relationship between the marginal propensity to consume and the average propensity to consume is a feature of all marginal and average relationships. You may appreciate the relationship more clearly if you think of a baseball batting average. Suppose that Lenny Dykstra comes "up to the plate" with a batting average of .270. All his previous at bats contributed to this average. His current at bat is going to produce his marginal score. If he gets a hit, his marginal score is better than his average and his average rises. If he makes an out, his marginal score is worse than his average and his average falls.

You can see that this marginal-average relationship also holds in the case of saving. The marginal propensity to save is higher than the average propensity to save. As a consequence, as disposable income increases, so does the average propensity to save.

Saving is like a batter getting a hit: the marginal propensity to save exceeds the average propensity to save, so the average propensity increases as disposable income increases—the score from the marginal innings exceeds the average, so the average increases as the number of times at bat increases. The marginal and average propensities to consume are like making an out. The marginal propensity to consume is below the average propensity and the average propensity to consume decreases as disposable income increases—the marginal score is below the average score so the average declines as the number of times at bat increases.

Marginal Propensities and Slopes The marginal propensity to consume is equal to the slope of the consumption function. You can see this equality by looking back at Fig. 25.3. In that figure, the consumption function has a constant slope that can be measured as the change in consumption divided by the change in income. For example, when income increases from $20,000 to $30,000—an increase of $10,000—consumption increases from $18,000 to $24,000—an increase of $6000. The slope of the consumption function is $6000 divided by $10,000, which equals 0.6—the same value as the marginal propensity to consume that we've calculated in Table 25.1.

The marginal propensity to save is equal to the slope of the saving function. You can see this equality by again looking back at Fig. 25.3. In this case, when income increases by $10,000, saving increases by $4000. The slope of the saving function is $4000 divided by $10,000, which equals 0.4—the same value as the marginal propensity to save that we calculated in Table 25.1.

We've studied the consumption and saving choices of a representative household. Let's now look at the consumption expenditure of actual households in the United States and see how that expenditure varies as disposable income varies.

The U.S. Consumption Function

Data for the U.S. consumption function in 1985 are shown in Table 25.2. Each row represents disposable income and consumption expenditure averaged over a group of households. There are five such rows, each showing the average disposable income and average consumption expenditure of households comprising 20 percent of the population. The rows are arranged from the lowest to the highest income.

Consumption in the United States increases as disposable income increases. We can calculate the average and marginal propensities to consume using these data. First, let's calculate the average propensity to consume—consumption expenditure divided by

disposable income. As you can see, the lowest 20 percent income group consumes more than three times its disposable income. But the average propensity to consume declines as income increases and the 20 percent of households with the highest income has an average propensity to consume of 0.78.

Next, we'll calculate the marginal propensity to consume—the change in consumption expenditure divided by the change in disposable income. The marginal propensity to consume as disposable income increases between the lowest and second lowest income group is 0.45. As income increases through the third, fourth, and highest groups, the marginal propensity to consume is a little higher than 0.6.

We saw in the case of the Polonius household, and in the case of the baseball batting scores, that when the marginal exceeds the average, the average increases; when the marginal is below the average, the average decreases. You can see the same relationship between the marginal and average propensities here. The marginal propensity to consume is below the average propensity to consume, and as disposable income increases, the average propensity to consume declines.

Table 25.2   Disposable Income and Consumption Expenditure in the United States

	Income group	Disposable income (dollars per year)	Consumption expenditure (dollars per year)	Average propensity to consume	Marginal propensity to consume
a	Lowest 20 percent	3,462	11,006	3.18	
					.........0.45
b	Second 20 percent	10,338	14,131	1.37	
					.........0.65
c	Third 20 percent	18,131	19,183	1.06	
					.........0.67
d	Fourth 20 percent	28,178	25,932	0.92	
					.........0.63
e	Highest 20 percent	54,215	42,374	0.78	

The rows record average disposable income and average consumption expenditure for U.S. income groups ranging from the lowest to the highest 20 percent. These data are used to calculate the average and marginal propensities to consume. The average propensity to consume—consumption expenditure divided by disposable income—declines as income increases. The marginal propensity to consume—the change in consumption divided by the change in disposable income—is fairly steady and averages around 0.6.

Source: ''Consumer Expenditure Survey: Interview Survey, 1985,'' *Statistical Abstract of the United States: 1988* (1987), Table 688, p. 420.

Figure 25.4 plots the data in Table 25.2. Each point (*a* through *e*) represents a row in the table. The orange line is the U.S. consumption function that describes the average relationship between consumption expenditure and disposable income across these income groups. Notice the similarity between the U.S. consumption function in Fig. 25.4 and the Polonius household's consumption function in Fig. 25.3(a).

Shifts in the Consumption Function

We have noted that there are five main factors that influence a household's consumption expenditure, only one of which is its disposable income. Those other factors—expected future income, stage in life, degree of patience, and interest rates—influence consumption expenditure and are represented by shifts in the consumption function. For example, an increase in expected future income shifts the consumption function upward; a decrease in expected future income shifts it downward. The consumption function shifts upward as a result of a decrease in interest rates. As a family progresses through its life cycle, its consumption function shifts upward as the number of children in the household increases and as the children get older. The consumption function then shifts downward when the children leave home and as the adults in the family approach retirement age.

These factors that shift the consumption function may be very important for individual households but, on the average, do not have large effects. The average consumption function, measured across all households, is a remarkably stable economic relationship.

The Aggregate Consumption Function

Our purpose in developing a theory of the consumption function is to explain the determination of aggregate expenditure and real GNP. So far, we have studied the relationship between consumption expenditure and disposable income for a typical household, and have described the average consumption function across households in the United States. We're now going to direct our attention away from the consumption function of an individual household and of households at different income levels and examine the aggregate consumption function.

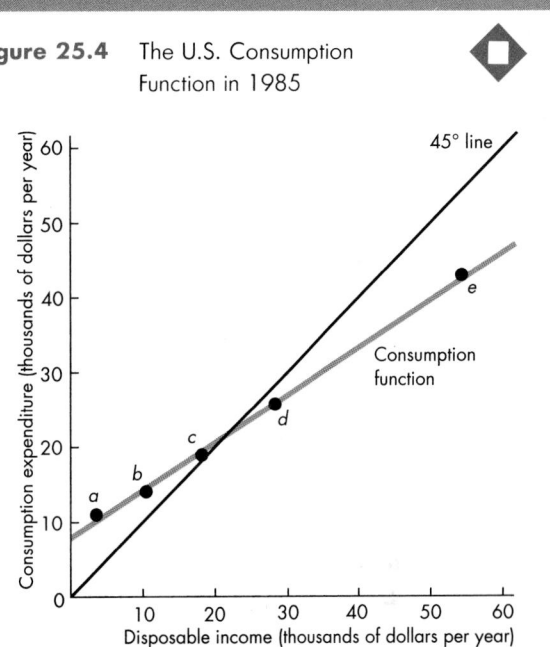

Figure 25.4   The U.S. Consumption Function in 1985

U.S. consumption function plots household consumption expenditure on the vertical axis against household disposable income on the horizontal axis. The consumption function shown here is based on disposable income and consumption expenditure data for five income groups in 1985, as shown in Table 25.2. Points a through e on the consumption function correspond to the rows in the table. For example, the highest 20 percent of households had an average income of $54,215 in 1985 and a consumption expenditure of $42,374. This consumption and disposable income is shown as point e on the consumption function in the figure.

The **aggregate consumption function** is the relationship between real consumption expenditure and real GNP. To obtain the aggregate consumption function, we first calculate the relationship between real consumption expenditure and real disposable income. This relationship is shown in Fig. 25.5(a). The vertical axis measures real consumption expenditure (in 1982 dollars) and the horizontal axis measures real disposable income (also in 1982 dollars). Each point identified by a blue dot represents real consumption expenditure and real disposable income for a particular year from 1960 to 1988. The line passing through these points is the time-series consumption function. The **time-series consumption function** is the relationship between real consumption expenditure and real disposable income over time. The slope of this consumption function,

Figure 25.5   The Aggregate Consumption Function

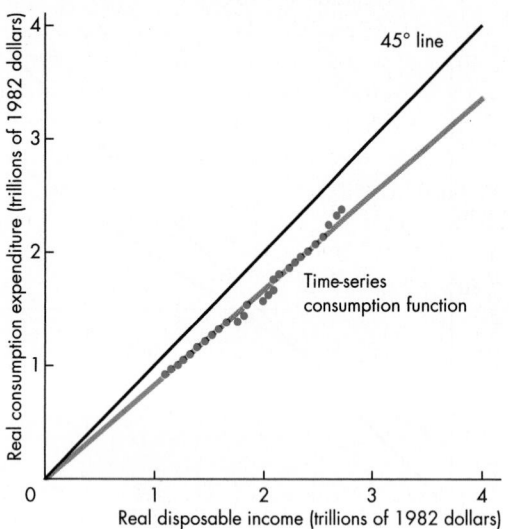

(a) Consumption as a function of disposable income

(b) Consumption as a function of real GNP

Real GNP (Y)	Disposable income (YD = 0.67Y) (trillions of 1982 dollars)	Consumption expenditure (C = 0.9YD = 0.6Y)
1.0	0.67	0.6
2.0	1.33	1.2
3.0	2.00	1.8
4.0	2.67	2.4

Part (a) shows the U.S. time-series consumption function—the relationship between real consumption expenditure and real disposable income—for each year between 1960 and 1988. Each point in the figure represents real consumption expenditure and real disposable income for a particular year. The marginal propensity to consume out of disposable income is approximately 0.9. Part (b) shows the U.S. aggregate consumption function—the relationship between real consumption expenditure and real GNP. This consumption function takes into account the fact that as real GNP increases, so do net taxes. The marginal propensity to consume out of real GNP is approximately 0.6. The connection between the time-series consumption function and the aggregate consumption function is shown in the table. The tax rate is 33⅓ percent, so that disposable income is 0.67 times real GNP. The marginal propensity to consume out of disposable income is 0.9. Combining a tax rate of 33⅓ percent with a marginal propensity to consume out of disposable income of 0.9 gives a marginal propensity to consume out of real GNP of 0.6.

and hence the marginal propensity to consume, is 0.9.

It is important to understand why this time-series consumption function looks different from the consumption function for individual households that we examined in Fig. 25.4. The individual household consumption function tells us how consumption expenditure varies with disposable income across households in a given year. The time-series consumption

function tells us how aggregate consumption expenditure varies with aggregate disposable income from one year to another. Equivalently, it tells us about the relationship between average consumption expenditure and average disposable income over time. Averaging over families with low incomes and high incomes, consumption expenditure represents 90¢ in every dollar of disposable income. There is a large amount of variation around this average and that variation is illustrated in the consumption function for individual households.

Figure 25.5(b) shows the aggregate consumption function—real consumption expenditure plotted against real GNP. To express consumption expenditure as the function of GNP, we need to establish the link between disposable income and GNP. That link is implicit in the definition of disposable income. Recall that we have defined disposable income as the difference between aggregate income and net taxes (net taxes are taxes minus transfer payments). Aggregate income is GNP. To work out the relationship between consumption and GNP, we need to know what happens to net taxes as GNP changes.

Net taxes increase as GNP increases. Almost all the taxes that we pay—personal taxes, corporate taxes, and social security taxes—increase as our incomes increase. Transfer payments, such as social security and welfare benefits, decrease as our incomes increase. (Social security benefits due to retirement do not vary with income but aggregate transfer payments do vary with income.) Since taxes increase and transfers decrease, net taxes clearly increase as incomes increase. It turns out that there is a tendency for net taxes to be a fairly stable proportion of GNP. That proportion is about one third. If one third of GNP is paid in taxes net of transfers, two thirds of GNP is available as disposable income.

The table in Fig. 25.5 sets out the relationship between real GNP, disposable income, and consumption. It incorporates the two-thirds relationship between GNP and disposable income. For example, if real GNP is $3 trillion, taxes net of transfers is $1 trillion and, therefore, disposable income is $2 trillion.

The table also tells us what consumption expenditure is. We have seen that the marginal propensity to consume out of disposable income is 0.9. That is, out of each additional dollar of disposable income, 90¢ is consumed and 10¢ is saved. Thus if disposable income is $2 trillion, consumption expenditure is nine tenths of that amount, which is $1.8 trillion.

Consumption as a function of real GNP—the aggregate consumption function—is shown in Figure 25.5(b) as the straight line passing through the dots representing actual real consumption expenditure and real GNP for the years 1960 to 1988.

The position of the aggregate consumption function depends both on the propensity to consume out of disposable income and on the relationship between disposable income and GNP. Since nine tenths (0.9) of disposable income is consumed and since two thirds (0.67) of GNP is available as disposable income, the fraction of GNP consumed is 0.6 (0.9 multiplied by 0.67, which equals 0.6). The vertical gap between the 45° line and the aggregate consumption function reflects the amount of saving and the level of taxes net of transfers. The higher the taxes, the wider is that gap and the lower is the aggregate consumption function.

The story of the development of the theory of consumption and saving is told in Our Advancing Knowledge, p. 656.

R E V I E W

Consumption is a function of disposable income. Disposable income is a stable proportion of GNP. Thus consumption is also a function of GNP. In the United States today, each additional dollar of real GNP generates, on the average, an additional 60¢ of real consumption expenditure. ▪

Let's now turn to the other main private component of aggregate expenditure, investment.

Investment

*I*nvestment is the purchase of new plant, equipment, and buildings and additions to inventories. As we saw in Fig. 25.2, this component of aggregate demand is a volatile one. What determines the level of investment and why does it fluctuate so much? For example, how does Chrysler decide how much to spend on a new car assembly plant? What determines IBM's outlays on new computer designs? How does AT&T choose what it will spend on fiber-optic communications systems? And why are there times when firms invest at a high rate and other times at a low rate?

What Determines Investment?

Obviously, thousands of factors are taken into account by Chrysler, IBM, and AT&T when they make

Consumption and Saving

Irving Fisher

By 1930, a consensus had emerged among economists concerning the determination of consumption and saving. That consensus was crystallized by Irving Fisher of Yale University in his classic work, *The Theory of Interest*, published in 1930. The accepted view was that consumption and saving depend primarily on the real interest rate. A high real interest rate causes a decrease in consumption and an increase in saving. Fisher assumed that people have to be induced to decrease their spending with the reward of a high rate of return. The higher the reward, the greater is the tendency to put off consumption and to save.

This consensus received a revolutionary challenge from John Maynard Keynes of Cambridge, England, in his book *The General Theory of Employment, Interest, and Money*, published in 1936. Keynes's idea was that consumption and saving do not depend on the interest rate but on the level of disposable income:

> The propensity to consume is a fairly stable function so that, as a rule, the amount of aggregate consumption depends on the amount of aggregate income, . . . changes in the propensity itself being . . . a secondary influence. . . . the fundamental psychological law, upon which we are entitled to depend with confidence both *a priori* from our knowledge of human nature and from the detailed facts of experience, is that men are disposed, as a rule and on the average, to increase their consumption as their income increases, but not by as much as the increase in their income. That is to say, if C is the amount of consumption and Y is income, ΔC has the same sign as ΔY but is smaller in amount, *i.e.* $\Delta C/\Delta Y$ is positive and less than unity.*

A little earlier than the time that Keynes was writing, Colin Clark, working in England, and Simon Kuznets, at the University of Chicago, were beginning to compile national income data. These data fitted Keynes's theory remarkably closely.

During the 1940s and 1950s, a large amount of additional data was being collected—but this time by government bureaus. Official national income accounts were providing additional observations of consumption and income each year and, after 1947, each quarter-year. Cross-section data—that is, data on the consumption and income of individual groups of people classified by age, race, and location—were also being collected. These new data revealed shortcomings in Keynes's theory. Even as early as the late 1940s, the

---

*John Maynard Keynes, *The General Theory of Employment, Interest, and Money* (London: Macmillan, 1936), 96.

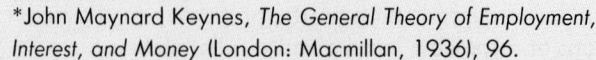

John Maynard Keynes

Keynesian theory of the consumption function began to make important forecasting errors. Also, the cross-section data showed that the fraction of income consumed varied systematically, depending on whether people were young or old, black or white, or from urban or rural areas.

The anomalies and puzzles in the data brought forth two related new theories and advances in our understanding. The first of these was the *life-cycle hypothesis* proposed by Franco Modigliani of MIT; the second was the *permanent income hypothesis* proposed by Milton Friedman, then at the University of Chicago. Modigliani's work, done jointly with a young English economist, Richard Brumberg, was published in 1954.** Friedman's work was published three years later, in 1957, in a book entitled *A Theory of the Consumption Function.*[†]

Each of these scholars suggested that consumption is determined not by income but by wealth. Other things being equal, the wealthier an individual, the more that individual will consume. Income and wealth are related to each other, but not directly on a year by year basis. A wealthy person might have a low income in a particular year. A poor person might have a big income (a windfall) in a particular year. Random fluctuations in income not associated with fluctuations in wealth will produce small, or even no fluctuations in consumption.

Modigliani's main contribution was to emphasize the relationship between an individual's stage of life and the relationship between income and wealth. Young people with secure jobs may have a small income but be wealthy in the sense that their future incomes will grow. Such people therefore tend to consume a large fraction of their current income. People in mid-life have an income that is high relative to their wealth. They consume a small fraction of their income.

Friedman's main contribution was to emphasize the distinction between permanent and transitory changes in income. Permanent changes in income have a large effect on consumption while transitory changes have a small effect. The ideas of Modigliani and Friedman resolved most of the paradoxes of both the cross-section and time-series data. Both scholars received a Nobel Prize in economics, partly for their contributions in this area.

Another revolution in economics—the rational expectations revolution—began in the 1960s and gathered momentum in the 1970s. This revolution forced economists to change their views about Modigliani's and Friedman's theories of the

(Continued on next page)

Franco Modigliani

**Franco Modigliani and Richard Brumberg, "Utility Analysis of the Consumption Function: An Interpretation of Cross-Section Data," in *Post-Keynesian Economics*, ed. K. Kurihara (New Brunswick: Rutgers University Press, 1954).

[†]Milton Friedman, *A Theory of the Consumption Function* (Princeton: Princeton University Press, 1957).

(Continued from previous page)

consumption function. An important contribution to this reformulation is one made by Robert Hall of Stanford University in 1978.[†]

The rational expectations theory of the consumption function as proposed by Hall starts from the same point as Modigliani and Friedman: consumption depends on wealth. Wealth can be thought of as depending on all future income. The more income a person is going to earn in the future, whether in wages or interest, the wealthier that person is. People do not know how much they are going to earn in the future but, to make consumption decisions today, they have to form an expectation of what that future income will be. In forming their expectations, people will use all the information that is available. Having made a best estimate of their wealth, people will make consumption plans that achieve the best (in their assessment) allocation of consumption over time.

Expectations will change only as a result of "news"—of new information not previously known. News arrives at random. As a consequence, people's estimates of how wealthy they are also changes in a random fashion. Since consumption plans depend on wealth, these plans will also vary in a random fashion.

Changes in consumption from one period to another will reflect both the working out of a consumption plan, as Modigliani and Friedman sketched, and changes in plans due to new information. As a result, changes in consumption from one year to another will be random. The average value will reflect average long-run consumption plans but their changes from year to year will reflect changes in information and expectations about future wealth. No variable, other than current consumption, should be of any value for predicting future consumption.

Robert Hall's contribution is, for the time being, the most recent milestone in the path of our evolving understanding of consumption and saving. It is by no means the last word, though. Every month new contributions on this topic, some of which will turn out to be milestones when viewed in a longer perspective, are being published in the economics journals.

Milton Friedman

[†]Robert E. Hall, "Stochastic Implications of the Life-Cycle Permanent Income Hypothesis: Theory and Evidence," *Journal of Political Economy* 86 (December 1978): 971–988.

their investment choices. But these factors can be reduced to four:

- Interest rates
- Expected inflation
- Expected profit
- Depreciation

1. Interest Rates The lower the level of interest rates, the greater is the amount of investment. Firms sometimes pay for capital goods with money that they have borrowed, and sometimes they use their own funds—called retained earnings. Regardless of the method of financing an investment project, the interest rate is part of its *opportunity cost*. The interest paid on borrowing is a direct cost. But retained earnings could be lent to another firm at the going interest rate and the interest foregone is the opportunity cost of using retained earnings to finance an investment project. The lower the interest rate, the lower is the opportunity cost of any given investment project. Some projects that would not be profitable at a high interest rate become profitable at a low interest rate. The lower the interest rate, the larger is the number of investment projects that become profitable and, therefore, the greater is the level of investment.

For example, suppose that Chrysler is contemplating building a new automobile assembly line at a cost of $100 million. The assembly line is expected to produce cars for three years and then it will be scrapped completely and replaced with a new line that produces an entirely new range of models. The expected net revenue in each of the three years is the amount shown in Table 25.3.

Net revenue is the difference between the total revenue from car sales and the costs of producing those cars. In calculating net revenue, we do not take into account the initial cost of the assembly line or the interest that has to be paid on it. We take separate account of these costs. To build the assembly line, Chrysler plans to borrow the initial $100 million, paying the interest on the amount outstanding at the end of each year, and using its expected net revenue to pay off as much of the loan as it can each year. Does it pay Chrysler to invest $100 million in this car assembly line? The answer depends on the interest rate.

Case 1 shows what happens if the interest rate is 10 percent per year. Chrysler borrows $100 million and at the end of the first year has to pay $10 million in interest. It has a net revenue of $40

Table 25.3   Investment in an Automobile Assembly Line

Cost of assembly line	$100,000,000
Expected net revenue: Year 1	40,000,000
Year 2	50,000,000
Year 3	20,000,000

Case 1: Interest rate is 10 percent per year

	Loan outstanding	Interest payment	Amount repaid
Initially	$100,000,000	—	—
End of year 1	70,000,000	$10,000,000	$40,000,000
End of year 2	27,000,000	7,000,000	50,000,000
End of year 3	–	2,700,000	29,700,000

Loss: $9,700,000

Case 2: Interest rate is 5 percent per year

	Loan outstanding	Interest payment	Amount repaid
Initially	$100,000,000	—	—
End of year 1	65,000,000	$5,000,000	$40,000,000
End of year 2	18,250,000	3,250,000	50,000,000
End of year 3	—	912,500	19,162,500

Profit: $837,500

An automobile assembly line costs $100 million to build and is expected to generate revenues of $40 million in the first year, $50 million in the second year, and $20 million in the third year. The line will then be scrapped and replaced by a new one. In Case 1, the interest rate is 10 percent a year. The revenue stream is too low to cover the total expense in this case and the project is not worth undertaking. In Case 2, the interest rate is 5 percent a year; the revenue stream is sufficient to repay the initial amount borrowed, pay all the interest, and still leave a small profit. In this case, the project is worthwhile and is undertaken. The lower the interest rate, the larger is the number of projects that are profitable.

million and so can reduce the amount of its borrowing to $70 million. At the end of the second year, it pays $7 million interest (10 percent of the $70 million loan outstanding) and uses the $50 million net revenue to reduce the outstanding loan to $27 million. At the end of the third year, Chrysler owes $2.7 million in interest payments plus the $27 million worth of outstanding loan. It therefore has to pay $29.7 million. But revenue in the third year is only $20 million, so Chrysler makes a loss of $9.7 million on this project. That is, by the end of the third year, Chrysler has to find an extra $9.7 million, compared with what would have been the case if the assembly line had not been purchased and operated.

Case 2 shows what happens if the interest rate is 5 percent per year. In this case, Chrysler pays only $5 million interest at the end of the first year and so can reduce its outstanding borrowing to $65 million. In the second year, the interest payment on the loan is $3,250,000. In this year, the loan outstanding is reduced to $18,250,000. In the third and final year of the project, the outstanding loan plus the interest on it amounts to $19,162,500, which Chrysler repays. But the project brings in $20 million in the final year, so Chrysler has $837,500 in pocket at the end of this project.

You can see that at an interest rate of 10 percent a year, it does not pay Chrysler to invest in this car assembly plant. At a 5 percent interest rate, it does pay. The lower the interest rate, the larger is the number of projects, such as the one considered here, that yield a positive net profit. Thus the lower the interest rate, the larger is the scale of investment.

2. Expected Inflation   The higher the expected inflation rate, the greater is the amount of investment. Higher expected inflation brings higher expected future net revenue. And the larger the expected future net revenue relative to the initial cost of an investment project, the larger is the return on the project.

In the Chrysler example above, the new car assembly plant costs $100 million to build in the current year regardless of the inflation rate. But the higher the inflation rate, the faster are car prices rising. Wages and other production costs also rise faster as well. The gap between car prices and wages and other production costs also rises at the same rate as the inflation rate. Thus higher inflation leads to higher net revenue and, *at a given level of interest rates,* results in more investment projects being profitable.

The effect of expected inflation on investment is opposite to that of the interest rate. There is an important consequence of these opposing effects on a firm's investment decision. It is that investment depends on the real interest rate. The **real interest rate** is the interest rate minus the expected inflation rate. That is, the real interest rate is the actual interest rate paid adjusted for the percentage change in the value of money arising from the expected inflation. You can see why it is the real interest rate that influences investment by considering again Chrysler's decision on whether to build a $100 million automobile assembly line.

We saw that with a 10 percent interest rate, it does not pay to build the assembly line; with a 5 percent interest rate, it does. Suppose that the interest rate is 10 percent (as in Case 1 of Table 25.3). But also suppose that prices are expected to rise by 5 percent a year. With rising prices, expected net revenue will also rise by 5 percent a year. With expected net revenue rising by 5 percent a year, the extra revenue enables more of the loan to be repaid each year and cuts the interest payments on the outstanding loan. The combined effect of a 10 percent interest rate and a 5 percent expected inflation rate is almost the same as the combined effect of a 5 percent interest rate and no expected inflation. That is, the profit after three years when the interest rate is 10 percent and the expected inflation rate is 5 percent is approximately the same as the case in which the interest rate is 5 percent and the expected inflation rate is zero.[4]

Thus, although investment is affected positively by lower interest rates and by higher expected inflation, we can combine these two influences into a single determinant of investment—the real interest rate. The lower the real interest rate, the higher is the level of investment.

3. Expected Profit   The higher the expected profitability of new capital equipment, the greater is the amount of investment. To see why this proposition is correct, consider Chrysler's assembly line yet again. To decide whether or not to build the assembly line, Chrysler has to work out its net revenue. To perform that calculation, it has to work out the total revenue from car sales that in turn are affected by its expectations of car prices and the share of the market that it

---

[4]This proposition is demonstrated in the appendix to this chapter on pp. 671–673.

can attain. Chrysler also has to figure out its operating costs, which include the wages of its assembly workers and the costs of the products that it buys from other producers. The larger the net revenue that it anticipates, the more profitable is the investment project that generates those net revenues, and the more likely is it that the project will be undertaken.

4. Depreciation   *Depreciation* is the wearing out of existing capital equipment. The larger the stock of capital equipment and the older that stock, the larger is the amount of capital that wears out. Worn out capital is not always replaced, but often it is. The larger the amount of capital that is depreciating, the larger the volume of investment to replace that worn out capital. Total investment (investment on new additions to plant and machinery and inventories), as well as replacement investment (investment that replaces worn out or depreciated capital) is called *gross investment*. Additions to the capital stock—that is gross investment minus depreciation—is called *net investment*.

Investment Demand

Investment demand is the relationship between the level of investment and the real interest rate. The **investment demand schedule** is a list of the quantities of planned investment at each real interest rate, holding all other influences on investment constant. The **investment demand curve** graphs the relationship between the real interest rate and the level of planned investment, holding everything else constant. Some examples of investment demand schedules and investment demand curves appear in Fig. 25.6. The investment demand schedule and the position of the investment demand curve depend on the other influences on investment—expected profit and depreciation.

To calculate its expected profit on an investment, a firm has to do its best to foresee future events. The firm has to forecast the scale of demand for its output so that it can make a forecast of its revenue from sales. It has to forecast future technological developments and future prices of its inputs so that it can forecast its costs. Sometimes the firm will be pessimistic about the future. At other times it will be optimistic. Pessimistic expectations arise when a firm foresees general business conditions to be poor or when it expects rapid technological change that makes current technology obsolete. Expectations are optimistic when the firm foresees booming business

conditions or when a new technology has become available that is not expected to be surpassed for a reasonable period of time. At yet other times, firms will be neither optimistic nor pessimistic. In such periods, profit expectations are average.

Fluctuations in firms' profit expectations are the main source of fluctuations in investment demand. The three investment demand schedules in the table in Fig. 25.6 give examples of investment demand under the three types of expectations. The first example is with average profit expectations. In this case, if the real interest rate is 6 percent a year, investment is $0.5 trillion. If the real interest rate is 4 percent a year, investment increases to $0.6 trillion. The second example is with optimistic profit expectations. In this case, investment is higher at each interest rate than it is when expectations are average. The third case is with pessimistic profit expectations. In this case, investment is lower at each interest rate than with average expectations.

The investment demand curve is shown in the figure. In part (a), the investment demand curve (*ID*) is that for average expected profit. Each point (*a* through *c*) corresponds to a row in the table. A change in the real interest rate causes a movement along the investment demand curve. Thus if the real interest rate is 4 percent a year, planned investment is $0.6 trillion. If the interest rate rises to 6 percent a year, there is a movement up the investment demand curve (see blue arrow), and planned investment falls to $0.5 trillion. If the interest rate falls to 2 percent a year, there is a movement down the investment demand curve (see blue arrow), and planned investment increases to $0.7 trillion.

The effects of profit expectations are shown in part (b). A change in profit expectations shifts the investment demand curve. The demand curve ID_0 represents average expected profit. When profit expectations become optimistic, the investment demand curve shifts to the right, from ID_0 to ID_1. When profit expectations become pessimistic, the investment demand curve shifts to the left, from ID_0 to ID_2.

The investment demand curve also shifts when there is a change in the amount of investment to replace depreciated capital. This influence leads to a steady rightward shift in the *ID* curve.

Accelerator Principle

The **accelerator principle** states that the investment demand curve shifts in response to *changes* in the level of real GNP. When real GNP rises quickly,

Figure 25.6   The Investment Demand Schedule and Investment Demand Curve

(a) The effect of a change in real interest rate

(b) The effect of a change in profit expectations

	Real interest rate (percent per year)	Real investment (trillions of 1982 dollars)		
		Average	Optimistic	Pessimistic
a	6	0.5	0.6	0.4
b	4	0.6	0.7	0.5
c	2	0.7	0.8	0.6

The investment demand schedule lists the quantities of aggregate planned investment at each real interest rate. The table shows three investment demand schedules. As the real interest rate decreases from 6 percent a year to 2 percent a year, planned investment increases from $0.5 trillion to $0.7 trillion. The investment demand curve graphs the investment demand schedule in part (a). As the real interest rate rises from 2 percent to 6 percent, there is a movement along the investment demand curve from c to a. Investment plans are affected by the state of expectations of future profit. If there is optimism about future profit, planned investment increases at each real interest rate. If there is pessimism about future profit, planned investment decreases at each real interest rate. Swings in expectations about future profit lead to shifts in the investment demand curve, as shown in part (b). With optimistic profit expectations, the investment demand curve shifts to the right to ID_1; with pessimistic expectations, it shifts to the left to ID_2.

the investment demand curve shifts to the right. When the real GNP rises slowly (or falls), the investment demand curve shifts to the left. There are two possible explanations for the accelerator principle:

- Capital stock adjustment
- Profit expectations and the business cycle

The explanation for the accelerator principle based on capital stock adjustment arises from the idea that there is a stable relationship between the *level* of real GNP and the *stock* of capital. Investment is the *change* in the *stock* of capital. A change in the *level* changes the desired *stock* of capital. To change the capital stock, investment takes place. The larger the change in real GNP, the greater is the desired change in the capital stock and, therefore, the greater is the level of investment.

The second explanation for the accelerator principle is the influence of the business cycle on profit expectations. We've already seen that profit expectations are an important factor influencing the level of investment demand. We identified three cases of profit expectations: optimistic, pessimistic, and average. Optimistic expectations are likely to occur when real GNP is rising rapidly. In such circumstances, expectations for profit in the near future are high. With the economy booming, sales are expected to rise and, with rising sales, profit is also expected to rise. Thus rapidly expanding real GNP brings optimism about future profit and higher investment demand. When real GNP is rising slowly, or when it is falling as in a recession, expectations for profit in the immediate future are pessimistic. With pessimistic profit expectations the investment demand declines. Swings in the pace of change of real GNP that generate swings in profit expectations produce fluctuations in investment demand.

R E V I E W

Investment depends on the real interest rate and on profit expectations, and on the scale of replacement of depreciated capital. Other things held constant, the lower the real interest rate, the higher is the level of investment. With optimistic profit expectations, the investment demand curve shifts to the right; with pessimistic profit expectations, it shifts to the left. Profit expectations are influenced by the business cycle. When the economy is expanding quickly, profit expectations are optimistic and investment demand is high. When the economy is expanding slowly (or contracting), profit expectations are pessimistic and investment demand is low. Investment to replace depreciated capital grows steadily over time. ∎

We've just studied the theory of investment demand. Let's now see how that theory helps us to understand the fluctuations in investment that occur in the United States economy.

Investment Demand in the United States

As we saw in Fig. 25.2, investment is one of the most volatile elements in aggregate expenditure. In some years, investment is as much as 20 percent below trend and in others more than 10 percent above trend. Let's see how we can interpret these fluctuations in investment with the theory of investment demand that we have just been studying.

We'll begin by looking at Fig. 25.7(a). It shows investment (in billions of 1982 dollars) between 1960 and 1988. It also shows the way in which investment—gross investment—is broken down between net investment and the replacement of depreciated capital—depreciation. As you can see, both depreciation and gross investment increase steadily over time. Depreciation follows a very smooth path. It reflects the fact that the capital stock grows steadily and smoothly. Net investment is the component of investment that fluctuates. You can see that fluctuation as the area between gross investment and depreciation in part (a).

The theory that we have been studying predicts that fluctuations in investment result from fluctuations in the real interest rate and in expectations of future profit. What is the relative importance of these two factors? Figure 25.7(b) partly answers this question. It leaves out of the picture the steady increase in investment arising from depreciation and focuses on net investment and the real interest rate. The real interest rate, which is measured on the right scale, is inverted. That is, the interest rate increases as we move down the right scale. Thus when the real interest rate line is close to the bottom of the figure, real interest rates are high and when the line is close to the top of the figure, real interest rates are low.

As you can see, there is a remarkably close relationship, as predicted by the theory, between net investment and the real interest rate. But there are also some important changes in net investment that are independent of changes in the real interest rate. These are caused by fluctuations in profit expectations. We can see these fluctuations more directly by looking at Fig. 25.8. The investment demand curve drawn in the graph describes the *average* relationship between net investment and the real interest rate. The blue points show the actual values of net investment and the real interest rate in *average* years. The green and purple points show years in which investment

Figure 25.7   Investment and the Real Interest Rate in the United States

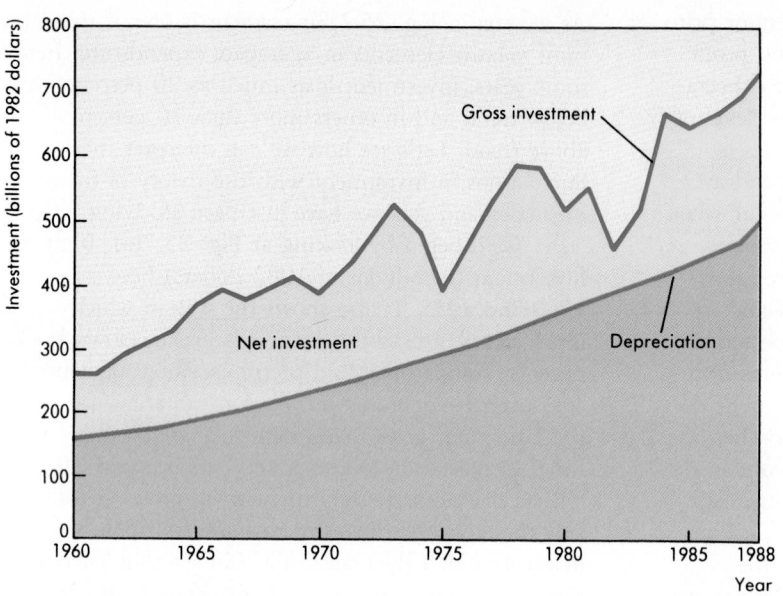

(a) Gross and net investment

In part (a), gross investment is separated into two parts— the replacement of depreciated capital (shaded green) that grows steadily and net investment (shaded blue) that fluctuates. In part (b), net investment fluctuates in sympathy with the real interest rate. When the real interest rate is high (as measured on the inverted scale on the right vertical axis), net investment is low.

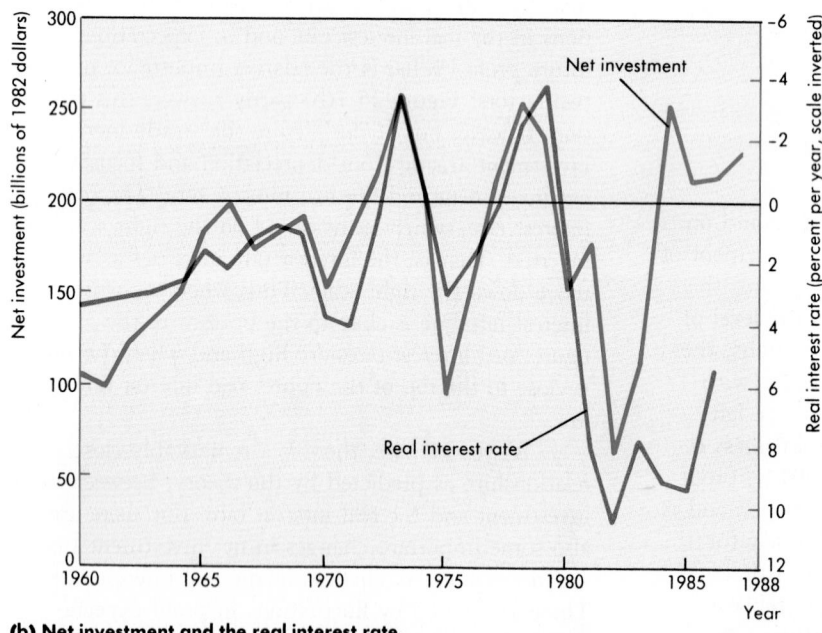

(b) Net investment and the real interest rate

demand was high and expectations optimistic, as they were in the 1980s. The red points show years in which investment demand was low and expectations pessimistic, as they were in the early 1960s and 1975.

As predicted by the theory, investment is high,

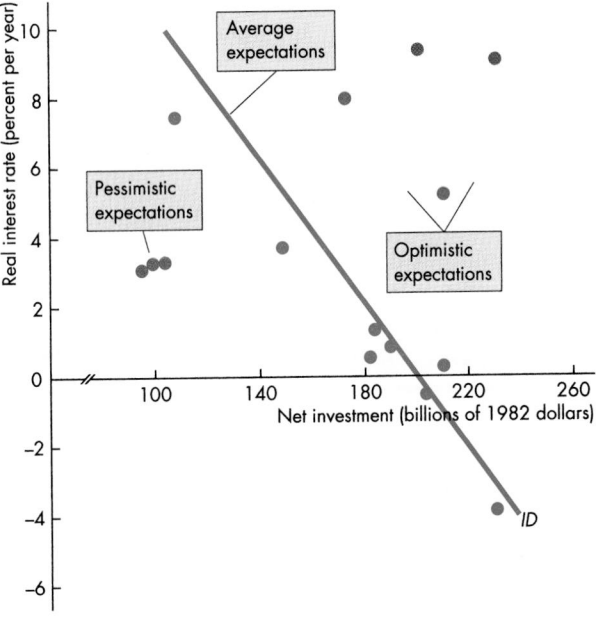

Figure 25.8 The U.S. Investment Demand Curve

With average profit expectations, the U.S. investment demand curve is *ID*. Each blue point in the figure represents a year in which expectations are average. When profit expectations are very optimistic (as they were in the 1980s), the investment demand curve lies to the right of *ID*, passing through points like the purple ones. When profit expectations are slightly less optimistic than that, the investment demand curve still lies to the right but passes through the green points. When profit expectations are pessimistic, as they were in the early 1960s and in 1975, the investment demand curve lies to the left of *ID*, passing through the red points.

on the average, when real interest rates are low. The investment demand curve slopes downward. But there are large fluctuations in investment that occur independently of changes in the real interest rate. The investment demand curve shifts. It shifts to the right (to pass through the green and purple points) in years of optimism about future profits, and it shifts to the left (to pass through the red points) in years of pessimism.

Fluctuations in the level of investment have important effects on the economy, regardless of whether they are generated by shifts in the investment demand curve or movements along it. We'll find out what some of those effects are in Chapter 29. Before doing that, we need to look at the last private component of aggregate expenditure—net exports.

Net Exports

Net exports is the expenditure by foreigners on U.S.–produced goods and services, minus the expenditure by U.S. residents on foreign-produced goods and services. That is, net exports is the value of U.S. exports minus the value of imports. *Exports* are the sale of goods and services produced in the United States to the rest of the world. *Imports* are the purchase of goods produced in the rest of the world by firms and households in the United States.

Exports

Exports are determined by decisions made in the rest of the world and are influenced by four main factors:

- GNP in the rest of the world
- Degree of international specialization
- Prices of U.S.–made goods relative to the prices of similar goods made in other countries
- Foreign exchange rates

Other things being equal, the higher the level of real GNP in the rest of the world, the greater is the demand by foreigners for U.S.–made goods and services. For example, an economic boom in Japan increases that country's demand for Boeing airplanes, Californian oranges, and Texan beef, and increases U.S. exports. A recession in Japan cuts its demand for those goods and decreases U.S. exports.

Also, the greater the degree of specialization in the world economy, the larger is the volume of exports, other things being equal. Over time, international specialization has been increasing. For example, the world aircraft industry is now heavily concentrated in the United States. While a small number of transcontinental airliners are built in France and Britain and in the Soviet Union, all the world's major airlines buy their aircraft from either Boeing or McDonnell-Douglas. Also, the United States dominates the world in the manufacture and sale of biotechnology products. But many goods and services, notably in the consumer electronics industry, that were once made in the United States in large quanti-

Figure 25.9   Net Export Schedule and Net Export Function

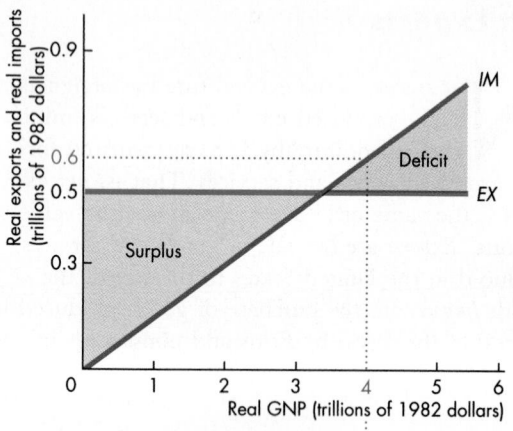

(a) Real exports and real imports

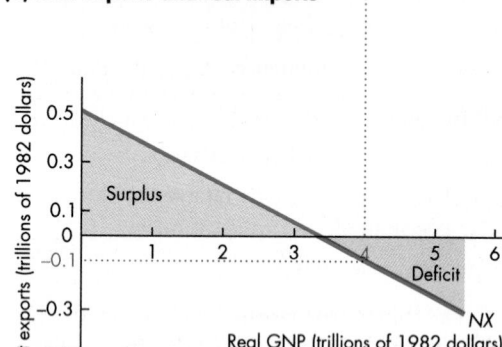

(b) Real net exports

Real GNP (Y)	Real exports (EX)	Real imports (IM)	Real net exports (EX − IM)
		(trillions of 1982 dollars)	
0	0.5	0	0.50
1.0	0.5	0.15	0.35
2.0	0.5	0.30	0.20
3.0	0.5	0.45	0.05
4.0	0.5	0.60	−0.10
5.0	0.5	0.75	−0.25

The net export schedule in the table shows the relationship between real net exports and real GNP. Real net exports is equal to real exports (EX) minus real imports (IM). Exports are independent of real GNP but imports rise as real GNP rises. In the table, imports are 15 percent of real GNP. Net exports fall as GNP rises.

Part (a) graphs the export and import schedules. Since exports are independent of real GNP, they are graphed as a horizontal line. Since imports rise as real GNP rises, they appear as an upward-sloping line. The distance between the export curve and the import curve represents net exports. Net exports are graphed in part (b) of the figure. The net export function is downward-sloping because the import curve is upward-sloping. The real GNP level at which the net export function intersects the horizontal axis in part (b) is the same as that at which the imports curve intersects the exports curve in part (a). That level of real GNP is $3.33 trillion. Below that level of real GNP there is a surplus and above it there is a deficit. In 1988, when real GNP was $4.0 trillion, imports exceeded exports and net exports were −$0.1 trillion.

ties are now made almost exclusively in Japan, Hong Kong, and other countries on the Asian rim of the Pacific Ocean.

Next, other things being equal, the lower the price of U.S.–made goods relative to the prices of similar goods made in other countries, the greater is the quantity of U.S. exports.

Finally, and again other things being equal, the lower the value of the U.S. dollar, the larger is the quantity of U.S. exports. For example, as the U.S. dollar fell in value against the German mark and the Japanese yen in 1987, the demand for U.S.–made goods by those two countries increased sharply.

Imports

Imports are determined by four main factors:

- U.S. real GNP
- Degree of international specialization
- Prices of foreign goods relative to the prices of similar goods made in the United States
- Foreign exchange rates

Other things being equal, the higher the level of U.S. real GNP, the larger is the quantity of U.S. imports. For example, the long period of sustained income growth in the United States between

1983 and 1987 brought a huge increase in U.S. imports.

Also, the higher the degree of international specialization, the larger is the volume of U.S. imports, others things being equal. For example, there is a high degree of international specialization in the production of VCRs. As a consequence, all the VCRs sold in the United States are now produced in other countries—mainly Japan and Korea.

Finally, and again other things being equal, the higher the prices of U.S.–made goods and services relative to the prices of similar foreign-made goods and services, and the higher the value of the U.S. dollar, the larger is the quantity of U.S. imports. Though high real GNP growth in the United States in 1986 and 1987 produced an increase in imports, the increase was less severe than it otherwise would have been because of the fall in the value of the U.S. dollar. The falling dollar made foreign goods more expensive and so slowed down, to some degree, the growth of U.S. imports.

Net Export Function

The **net export function** is the relationship between net exports and U.S. real GNP, holding constant real GNP in the rest of the world, prices, and the exchange rate. The net export function can also be described by a net export schedule, which lists the level of net exports at each level of real GNP, with everything else held constant. The table in Fig. 25.9 gives an example of a net export schedule.

In the table, exports are a constant $0.5 trillion regardless of the level of real GNP. Imports increase by $0.15 trillion for each $1.0 trillion increase in real GNP. Net exports, the difference between exports and imports, is shown in the final column of the table. When real GNP is $1.0 trillion, net exports are $0.35 trillion. Net exports decline as real GNP rises. At a real GNP of $3.33 trillion, net exports are

zero, and at real GNP levels higher than that, net exports become increasingly negative (imports exceed exports).

Exports and imports are graphed in Fig. 25.9(a) and the net export function is graphed in Fig 25.9(b). By comparing part (a) and part (b) you can see that when exports exceed imports, net exports are above zero (there is a surplus), and when imports exceed exports, net exports are below zero (there is a deficit). When real GNP is $3.33 trillion, there is a balance between exports and imports.

The data in Fig. 25.9 are based on the U.S. economy in 1988. In that year, real GNP was $4 trillion, exports were $0.5 trillion, imports were $0.6 trillion, and net exports were -$0.1 trillion, highlighted in the figure.

The position of the net export function depends on real GNP in the rest of the world, on the degree of international specialization, and on prices in the United States compared with those in the rest of the world. If real GNP in the rest of the world increases, the net export function shifts upward. If U.S. goods become cheap relative to goods in the rest of the world, the net export function also shifts upward. A change in the degree of international specialization has an ambiguous effect on the position of the net export function. If the United States becomes more specialized in goods for which there is an increase in world demand, the net export function shifts upward. If U.S. demand increases for goods in which the rest of the world specializes, the net export function shifts downward.

■ In this chapter, we've studied the factors that influence private expenditure decisions, looking at each item of aggregate expenditure in isolation from the others. In the next chapter, we'll study the interactions between the components of aggregate expenditure.

S U M M A R Y

The Components of Aggregate Expenditure

The components of aggregate expenditure are as follows:

- Consumption expenditure
- Investment
- Government purchases of goods and services
- Net exports

The main component of aggregate expenditure is consumption expenditure. On the average, 60 percent of total expenditure comes from consumption; investment accounts for 17 percent; and government purchases of goods and services account for 23 percent of the total. Net exports on the average are close to zero.

The components of aggregate expenditure that fluctuate most are investment and net exports. (pp. 645–646)

Consumption Expenditure and Saving

Consumption expenditure is influenced by five factors:

- Disposable income
- Expected future income
- Stage in life
- Degree of patience
- Interest rates

The most important influence on consumption expenditure is disposable income. As disposable income increases so does consumption expenditure. The relationship between consumption expenditure and disposable income is called the consumption function. As disposable income increases so too does saving. The relationship between saving and disposable income is called the saving function. At low levels of disposable income, consumption expenditure exceeds disposable income, which means that saving is negative (dissaving occurs). As disposable income rises, consumption increases but by less than the increase in disposable income. The fraction of each additional dollar of disposable income consumed is called the marginal propensity to consume. The fraction of each additional dollar of disposable income saved is called the marginal propensity to save. All the influences on consumption and saving, other than disposable income, shift the consumption and saving functions.

If we look at variations in disposable income and consumption expenditure across families, we see that for each dollar increase in disposable income, consumption increases by about 60¢, on the average. The relationship between aggregate consumption expenditure and aggregate disposable income over time is called the time-series consumption function. The time-series consumption function shows how aggregate consumption varies as disposable income varies from one year to the next. The average and marginal propensity to consume out of disposable income, on the average, is 0.9. But there is a large variation around that average across individual families.

The relationship between real consumption expenditure and real GNP is called the aggregate consumption function. To calculate the aggregate consumption function, we take into account the difference between real disposable income and real GNP. Disposable income equals GNP plus transfer payments minus taxes. Transfer payments minus taxes are a fairly stable percentage of GNP. As a result, since consumption is a fairly stable percentage of disposable income, it is also a fairly stable percentage of GNP. Taxes net of transfers are approximately one third of GNP. Since consumption is nine tenths of disposable income, consumption equals six tenths (0.6) of GNP. (pp. 646–655)

Investment

The level of investment depends on:

- Interest rates
- Expected inflation
- Expected profit
- Depreciation

The lower the interest rate, the higher is the level of investment; the higher the expected inflation rate, the greater is the level of investment. The higher the expected profit, the greater is the volume of investment. Interest rates and expected inflation have equal and opposite effects on investment. As a consequence, the two effects can be combined into a real interest rate effect. The higher the real interest rate, the lower is the volume of investment.

The main influence on investment demand is fluctuations in profit expectations. Sometimes expectations are optimistic and at other times pessimistic. Swings in the degree of optimism and pessimism lead to shifts in the investment demand curve. Swings in profit expectations are closely associated with business cycle fluctuations. When the economy is in an expansion phase, profit expectations are optimistic and investment high. When the economy is in a contraction phase, profit expectations are pessimistic and investment is low. (pp. 655–665)

Net Exports

Net exports are the difference between exports and imports. Exports are determined by decisions made in the rest of the world and are influenced by GNP in the rest of the world, the degree of international specialization, U.S. prices relative to prices of similar goods made in other countries, and the foreign exchange rate. Imports are determined by U.S. real GNP, the degree of international specialization, prices of foreign goods relative to U.S. prices of simlar goods, and the foreign exchange rate.

The net export function shows the relationship between net exports and U.S. real GNP, holding constant all the other influences on exports and imports. (pp. 665–667)

K E Y   C O N C E P T S

Key Figures and Tables

R E V I E W   Q U E S T I O N S

1 What are the components of aggregate expenditure?

2 Which component of aggregate expenditure is the largest?

3 Which components of aggregate expenditure fluctuate the most?

4 What is the consumption function?

5 What is the fundamental determinant of consumption?

6 What is the difference between disposable income and GNP?

7 What is the meaning of the term marginal propensity to consume? Why is it less than one?

8 What is the saving function? What is the relationship between the saving function and the consumption function?

9 What determines investment and why does investment increase as the real interest rate falls?

10 What is the effect of the following on U.S. net exports:

a) An increase in U.S. GNP

b) An increase in GNP in Japan

c) A rise in the price of Japanese-made cars with no change in the price of U.S.–made cars

PROBLEMS

1 You are given the following information about the Batman family (Batman and Robin):

Disposable income	Consumption expenditure
$ 0	$10,000
10,000	15,000
20,000	20,000
30,000	25,000
40,000	30,000

a) Calculate the Batmans' marginal propensity to consume.

b) Calculate the average propensity to consume at each level of disposable income.

c) Calculate how much the Batmans save at each level of disposable income.

d) Calculate the marginal propensity to save.

e) Calculate the average propensity to save at each level of disposable income.

2 A car assembly plant can be built for $10 million and it will have a life of five years. At the end of five years, the plan will have a scrap value of $1 million. The firm will have to hire labor at a cost of $1 million a year and will have to buy parts and fuel costing another $1 million. If the firm builds the plant, it will be able to produce cars that will sell for $5 million each year. Will it pay the firm to invest in this new production line at the following interest rates:

a) 2 percent a year

b) 5 percent a year

c) 10 percent a year

3 You are given the following information about a hypothetical economy: the marginal propensity to consume out of disposable income is 0.8; and taxes net of transfer payments are a quarter of national income. What is the marginal propensity to consume out of GNP in this economy?

Appendix to Chapter 25

Net Present Value and Investment

To decide whether or not to undertake an investment project, we may calculate the project's net present value.

Calculating Net Present Value

Net present value is the sum of the present value of the stream of payments and receipts generated by an investment project. The *present value* of a future sum of money is the sum which, if invested in the present, accumulates to the future sum if it earns compound interest at a given rate. If the net present value of an investment project is positive, it pays to undertake the investment. If the net present value is negative, it does not pay to undertake the investment. Let's calculate a net present value.

An investment of $2775 is expected to yield the future stream of earnings of $1000 a year for three years. Thus an initial payment of $2775 dollars results in a future receipt of $1000 in each of three years. Obviously, more comes back than is paid out. But the returns come later. To decide whether enough flows in later, we calculate the project's net present value. To calculate the net present value of a project, we use the formula

$$\text{NPV} = \frac{\$1000}{(1 + r)} + \frac{\$1000}{(1 + r)^2} + \frac{\$1000}{(1 + r)^3} - \$2775,$$

where r is the interest rate.

The higher the interest rate, the lower is the net present value. Table A25.1 sets out some calculations for three different interest rates. In part (a), an interest rate of 4 percent a year is used. In this case, the net present value is zero. Let's see how that present value is calculated by using the above formula. The initial cost of the project ($2775) is paid out today, so its present value is exactly the same as the amount spent. The first $1000 of revenue from the project is received one year in the future. Its present value is $961. That is, if $961 is invested today at an interest rate of 4 percent a year, it will accumulate to $1000 one year from today. The next $1000 is received two years hence. Its present value is $925. That is, if $925 is invested today for a two-year period at an interest rate of 4 percent a year, it will accumulate to $1000 by the end of that period. Finally, the last $1000 is received three years hence and has a present value of $889. If $889 is invested today at an interest rate of 4 percent a year, it will accumulate to $1000 after three years. Adding these present values together, and subtracting the present value of the initial cost of the project, gives the overall net present value for the project which, at an interest rate of 4 percent a year, is zero.

Part (b) calculates the net present value at a lower interest rate—2 percent. In this case, the net present value of the project is positive at $108. Part (c) calculates the net present value at an interest rate of 6 percent. This net present value is −$102.

Table A25.1   Net Present Value of an Investment Project

	Dollars paid	Dollars received	Present value (dollars)
(a) Interest rate: 4 percent per year			
Initial cost of project	2775		−2775
Receipts after 1 year		1000	961
Receipts after 2 years		1000	925
Receipts after 3 years		1000	889
Net present value: $0			
(b) Interest rate: 2 percent per year			
Initial cost of project	2775		−2775
Receipts after 1 year		1000	980
Receipts after 2 years		1000	961
Receipts after 3 years		1000	942
Net present value: $108			
(c) Interest rate: 6 percent per year			
Initial cost of project	2775		−2775
Receipts after 1 year		1000	943
Receipts after 2 years		1000	890
Receipts after 3 years		1000	840
Net present value: −$102			

At any interest rate below 4 percent a year, it pays to undertake this investment project. But at an interest rate above 4 percent a year, it does not pay to invest in the project.

Investment projects differ in their initial capital cost and in the revenue stream that they generate. To decide which projects to undertake, a firm calculates the net present value of each project using the current interest rate at which it can borrow. All those projects that have a positive net present value are undertaken and all those that have a negative net present value are rejected. The lower the interest rate at which the firm can borrow, the larger is the number of projects that have a positive net present value and so the larger is the number of projects undertaken and the larger the firm's investment.

Expected Inflation and Real Interest Rate

The real interest rate is the interest rate that people expect to earn after taking into account changes in the value of money. If you lend a dollar at an annual interest rate of r, you will have $1 + r$ dollars at the end of the year. If prices are rising at an annual rate of π, you will need $1 + \pi$ dollars at the end of the year to buy what one dollar buys today. Your $1 + r$ dollars will only really be worth $(1 + r)/(1 + \pi)$ dollars. The interest rate that you have really earned is the amount that your money is really worth— $(1 + r)/(1 + \pi)$—minus the dollar that you lent. That is, your real interest rate is:

$$\text{Real interest rate} = \frac{1 + r}{1 + \pi} - 1.$$

In this formula, r is the interest rate (sometimes called the nominal interest rate) and π is the inflation rate. You can interpret this formula most easily by considering the case where the interest rate and the inflation rate are the same. Suppose that the interest rate and the inflation rate are each 6 percent a year. Then the formula tells us that

$$\text{Real interest rate} = \frac{1.06}{1.06} - 1 = 0.$$

That is, the interest that is paid when the interest rate is 6 percent a year is only enough to compensate for the fall in the value of money, which means that no "real" interest has been paid.

Let's do one more calculation. If the interest rate is 6 percent a year and the inflation rate is 1.92 percent a year, the real interest rate is 4 percent a year. To see this, put the numbers for interest rate and the inflation rate in the formula. We obtain

$$\text{Real interest rate} = \frac{1.06}{1.0192} - 1$$
$$= .04 \text{ (or 4 percent)}.$$

Let's work out the net present value when the interest rate is 6 percent and the expected inflation rate is 1.92 percent, so that the real interest rate is 4 percent. The calculations are summarized in Table A25.2. As before, the project costs $2775. The receipts at the end of the first year are now higher because of inflation. With inflation running at 1.92 percent, receipts will be $1019. The present value of $1019 at a 6 percent interest rate is $961. That is, if $961 is invested today at an interest rate of 6 percent

Table A25.2 Present Value, Inflation, and the Real Interest Rate

Interest rate: 6 percent per year

Inflation rate: 1.92 percent per year

Real interest rate: 4 percent per year

	Dollars paid/received	Real dollars paid/received	Present value (dollars)
Initial cost of project	−2775	−2775	−2775
Receipts after 1 year	1019	1000	961
Receipts after 2 years	1039	1000	925
Receipts after 3 years	1059	1000	889

Net present value: $0

a year, it accumulates to $1019 up to one year. At the end of the second year, the firm receives $1039. That is, over a two-year period, prices have increased by 3.9 percent. The present value of $1039 two years hence is $925. That is, if $925 is invested today at an interest rate of 6 percent a year, it accumulates to $1039 after two years. With inflation continuing into the third year at the same rate, receipts increase to $1059. The present value of $1059 received three years in the future at an interest rate of 6 percent is $889. That is, if $889 is invested today at an interest rate of 6 percent a year, it accumulates to $1059 three years in the future.

Adding the present value of the income stream and subtracting the present value of the cost of the project gives the net present value of the project. That net present value is zero.

Notice that when the interest rate is 6 percent a year and inflation is 1.92 percent a year, we obtain exactly the same net present value as we did in Table

A25.1 with no inflation and an interest rate of 4 percent a year. But notice also that the real interest rate in Table A25.2 is 4 percent a year. Comparing the numbers in Tables A25.1 and A25.2, you can see that the net present value of an investment project depends on the real interest rate. That is, the project that we are considering here has a net present value of zero when the real interest rate is 4 percent a year. It makes no difference whether that real interest rate arises from an actual interest rate of 4 percent a year and no inflation or the actual interest rate of 6 percent a year and 1.92 percent inflation. Either way, the net present value of the project is zero. The lower the real interest rate, the larger is the number of projects that have a positive net present value and that are undertaken.

Investment Demand

The investment demand schedule of the firm is obtained by calculating the total cost of all the projects that have a positive net present value at each interest rate. As the interest rate falls, the number of projects that are undertaken increases and the total amount of investment undertaken increases. Thus the firm's investment demand schedule shows an increase in the amount of investment as the real interest rate falls. Adding up all the investment projects of all the firms in the economy produces the aggregate investment demand schedule.

The net present value calculation of an investment project depends on the firm's best forecast of the future stream of revenue generated by the project. If firms have optimistic expectations, a larger number of projects will have positive net present values at each interest rate. If firms have pessimistic expectations about future revenue, a smaller number of projects will have positive net present values. Thus the number of projects that are undertaken at each interest rate depends on the degree of optimism or pessimism embodied in firms' forecasts of future revenue streams. Changes in the degree of optimism and pessimism lead to shifts in investment demand schedules.

Chapter 26

After studying this chapter, you will be able to:

- Derive the aggregate expenditure function

- Distinguish between autonomous expenditure and induced expenditure

- Explain how the level of aggregate expenditure is determined

- Define and calculate the multiplier

- Explain why changes in investment, government purchases of goods and services, taxes, and exports produce changes in consumption expenditure and have multiplier effects on aggregate expenditure

- Explain the relationship between the aggregate expenditure curve and the aggregate demand curve

Bruce Springsteen breathes into a microphone at a barely audible whisper. The electronic signal picked up by the sensitive instrument travels along wires to a huge bank of amplifiers and then through high-fidelity speakers to the ears of 50,000 fans spread out across the Greek Theater in Los Angeles. Moving to a louder passage, Springsteen increases the volume of his voice and now, through the magic of electronic amplification, booms across the stadium drowning out every other sound. ▪ Coleman Young, the Mayor of Detroit, is being driven to a business meeting along one of the city's less well-repaired highways. (There are some pretty badly pot-holed highways in Detroit.) He is dictating notes to a secretary who is taking down the words in impeccable shorthand. The car's wheels are bouncing and vibrating over some of the worst highway in the nation, but its passengers are completely undisturbed, and the shorthand notes are written without a ripple, thanks to the car's efficient shock absorbers. ▪ Investment and exports fluctuate like the volume of Bruce Springsteen's voice and the uneven surface of a Detroit highway. How does the economy react to those fluctuations? Does it react like Coleman Young's limousine, absorbing the shocks and providing a smooth ride for the economy's passengers? Or, does it behave like Bruce Springsteen's amplifier, blowing up the fluctuations and spreading them out to affect the many millions of participants in an economic rock concert? ▪ And is the economic machine built to a design that we simply have to live with, or can we modify it, changing its amplification and shock absorbing powers? ▪ We are now going to explore these questions. We are going to discover that the economy contains an important amplification unit that tends to magnify the effects of fluctuations in investment and exports resulting in a larger change in aggregate

Economic Amplifier or Shock Absorber

expenditure than the change in investment or exports that initiated it. But we are also going to discover that taxes act as a kind of shock absorber. They don't provide the smooth ride of a Lincoln Continental but they do a better job than the springs of a stagecoach.

■ In Chapter 25, we studied the factors that determine the components of aggregate expenditure. We discovered that the largest component, consumption expenditure, is a remarkably stable proportion of GNP. But we also saw that consumption expenditure can be influenced by the gap between disposable income and GNP. We also discovered that the most volatile components of aggregate expenditure are investment and exports. Our goal in this chapter is to work out how fluctuations in investment and exports, and in government purchases of goods and services and taxes, influence consumption and aggregate expenditure. That is, in contrast to Chapter 25 where we studied each component of aggregate expenditure in isolation from the other, the goal of this chapter is to study how the components of aggregate expenditure interact together to determine aggregate expenditure. We begin by studying the relationship between aggregate expenditure and GNP.

Aggregate Expenditure and Real GNP

There is a relationship between real aggregate planned expenditure and real GNP. That relationship may be described by either an aggregate expenditure schedule or an aggregate expenditure curve. The **aggregate expenditure schedule** lists the level of aggregate expenditure that is generated at each level of real GNP. The **aggregate expenditure curve** is a graph of the aggregate expenditure schedule.

Aggregate Expenditure Schedule

The aggregate expenditure schedule is set out in the table of Fig. 26.1. (The data in this table and figure are examples and do not refer to the real world.

Nevertheless, they are in the same ballpark as data for the U.S. economy in the late 1980s). The table shows not only aggregate planned expenditure but also its components. To work out the level of aggregate planned expenditure, we simply add the various components together. The first column of the table shows real GNP and the second column shows the consumption expenditure generated by each level of real GNP. When real GNP is $1 trillion, so is consumption expenditure. A $1 trillion increase in real GNP generates a $0.65 trillion increase in consumption expenditure.

The next two columns show investment and government purchases of goods and services. Recall that investment depends on the real interest rate and the state of profit expectations. Suppose that those factors are constant and, at a given point in time, generate a level of investment of $0.5 trillion. This investment level is independent of the level of real GNP. It is influenced solely by the real interest rate and state of profit expectations that we are holding constant.

Government purchases of goods and services are determined by decisions made by the administration and by Congress as well as by the legislatures of state and local governments. These purchases vary from year to year but, at any given point in time, their level has been determined by past decisions. Thus we'll suppose that this item is also fixed. Its value is $0.7 trillion. That is, like investment, government purchases of goods and services are fixed at any given point in time and do not vary as real GNP varies.

The next three columns show exports, imports, and net exports. Exports are influenced by events in the rest of the world and by our prices compared with prices in other countries, as well as the foreign exchange value of our dollar. They are not directly affected by the level of real GNP. In the table, exports appear as a constant $0.45 trillion. But imports do increase as real GNP increases. In the table, a $1 trillion increase in real GNP generates a $0.15 trillion increase in imports. Net exports—the difference between exports and imports—also varies as real GNP varies. It decreases by $0.15 trillion for each $1 trillion increase in real GNP.

The final column of the table shows aggregate planned expenditure. This amount is the sum of planned consumption expenditure, investment, government purchases of goods and services, and net exports.

Figure 26.1   Aggregate Expenditure Schedule and Aggregate Expenditure Curve

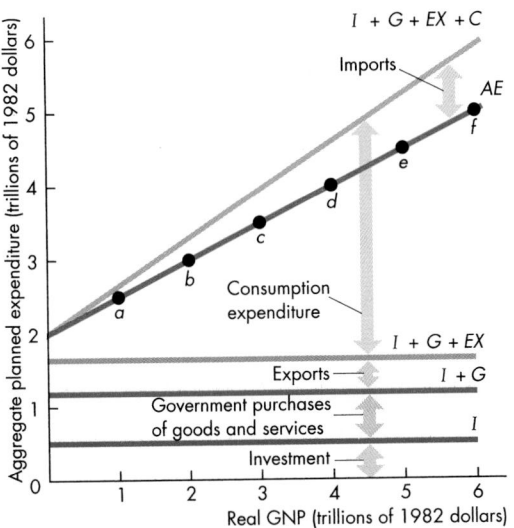

The aggregate expenditure function shows how aggregate planned expenditure varies as real GNP varies. The aggregate expenditure function may be described by an aggregate expenditure schedule (as shown in the table) or an aggregate expenditure curve (as shown in the diagram). Aggregate planned expenditure is calculated as the sum of planned consumption expenditure, investment, government purchases of goods and services, and net exports. For example, in row a of the table, if real GNP is $1.0 trillion, aggregate planned consumption is $1.00 trillion, planned investment is $0.5 trillion, planned government purchases of goods and services are $0.7 trillion, and planned net exports are $0.30 trillion. Thus when real GNP is $1.0 trillion, aggregate planned expenditure is $2.5 trillion ($1.0 + $0.5 + $0.7 + $0.30). The expenditure plans are graphed as the aggregate expenditure curve AE in the figure (the line af).

	Real GNP (Y)	**Planned Expenditure**						Aggregate expenditure (AE = C + I + G + NX)
		Consumption expenditure (C)	Investment (I)	Government purchases (G)	Exports (EX)	Imports (IM)	Net exports (NX = EX − IM)	
				(trillions of 1982 dollars)				
a	1.0	1.00	0.5	0.7	0.45	0.15	0.30	2.5
b	2.0	1.65	0.5	0.7	0.45	0.30	0.15	3.0
c	3.0	2.30	0.5	0.7	0.45	0.45	0	3.5
d	4.0	2.95	0.5	0.7	0.45	0.60	−0.15	4.0
e	5.0	3.60	0.5	0.7	0.45	0.75	−0.30	4.5
f	6.0	4.25	0.5	0.7	0.45	0.90	−0.45	5.0

Aggregate Expenditure Curve

The aggregate expenditure curve appears in the diagram in Fig. 26.1. Real GNP is shown on the horizontal axis and aggregate planned expenditure on the vertical axis. The aggregate expenditure curve is the red line labeled AE. Points a through f on that curve correspond to the rows in the table in Fig. 26.1. The AE curve is a graph of the last column, "Aggregate expenditure," plotted against real GNP.

The figure also shows the components of aggre-

gate expenditure. The constant components—investment, government purchases of goods and services, and exports—are indicated by the horizontal lines in the figure. Consumption is the vertical gap between the line labeled I + G + EX + C and that labeled I + G + EX.

To calculate the AE curve, we subtract imports from the I + G + EX + C line. Imports are subtracted because they are not expenditure on U.S. GNP. The purchase of a new car is part of consumption expenditure but if that car is a Toyota, made in Japan, expenditure on it has to be subtracted from consumption expenditure to find out how much is spent on goods produced in the United States—on U.S. GNP. Money paid to Toyota for car imports from Japan does not add to aggregate expenditure in the United States.

Autonomous and Induced Expenditure

It is useful to classify the components of aggregate expenditure into two broad groups:

• Autonomous expenditure
• Induced expenditure

Autonomous expenditure is the sum of those components of aggregate planned expenditure that are not influenced by real GNP. These autonomous components of aggregate expenditure are investment, government purchases of goods and services, exports, and that part of consumption expenditure that does not vary with real GNP. In the example in Fig. 26.1, there is $0.35 trillion of consumption expenditure even if real GNP is zero. This component of consumption expenditure is part of autonomous expenditure.

Induced expenditure is the sum of those components of aggregate planned expenditure that do vary as real GNP varies. The induced components of aggregate expenditure are that part of consumption expenditure that varies with real GNP and imports. In the example in Fig. 26.1, each $1 trillion increase in real GNP induces an additional $0.65 trillion of consumption expenditure. This is the induced part of consumption expenditure. Imports are also part of induced expenditure since they increase as real GNP increases. But imports have to be subtracted from total spending to arrive at aggregate expenditure on real GNP.

Autonomous expenditure and induced expenditure are shown in Fig. 26.2. Autonomous expenditure is made up of investment ($0.5 trillion), government purchases of goods and services ($0.7 trillion), exports ($0.45 trillion), and the autonomous component of consumption expenditure ($0.35 trillion). The sum of these items is $2 trillion. Induced expenditure increases by 50¢ for each $1 increase in real GNP. This increase is made up of 65¢ of consumption minus 15¢ of imports. For example, when real GNP is $4 trillion, aggregate expenditure is also $4 trillion (point *d* on the *AE* curve), which is

Figure 26.2   Autonomous and Induced Expenditure

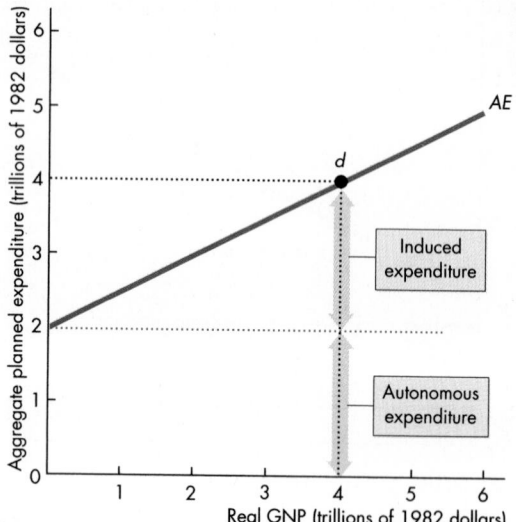

Planned autonomous expenditure, shown at the bottom of the figure, consists of investment, government purchases of goods and services, exports, and the autonomous component of consumption expenditure. Planned induced expenditure consists of the remainder of consumption expenditure minus imports. The sum of autonomous and induced expenditure is aggregate expenditure. For example, at point *d*, aggregate expenditure is $4 trillion—$2 trillion of autonomous expenditure and $2 trillion of induced expenditure.

made up of $2 trillion of autonomous expenditure and $2 trillion of induced expenditure. Autonomous expenditure remains at $2 trillion regardless of the level of real GNP, but the induced component of aggregate expenditure rises from zero when real GNP is zero to $3 trillion when real GNP is $6 trillion.

Slope of the Aggregate Expenditure Curve

What determines the slope of the aggregate expenditure curve? The answer is the extent to which expenditure is induced by an increase in real GNP. As we've just seen, an increase in real GNP of $1 increases consumption by 65¢ and increases imports by 15¢. The difference between these two, 50¢, is the increase in induced expenditure.

Recall that the fraction of the last dollar of real

GNP consumed is called the *marginal propensity to consume*. In Fig. 26.1, the marginal propensity to consume is 0.65. The fraction of the last dollar of real GNP spent on imports is called the **marginal propensity to import**. In this case, the marginal propensity to import is 0.15. The difference between these two marginal propensities is the marginal propensity to spend on domestic goods and services.

The **marginal propensity to spend on domestic goods and services** (which we'll call by the shorter term **marginal propensity to spend**) is the fraction of the last dollar of real GNP spent on domestic goods and services. In Fig. 26.2, a $1 increase in real GNP induces an increase in aggregate expenditure of 50¢ so the marginal propensity to spend is 0.5.

Notice the distinction between the marginal propensity to consume and the marginal propensity to spend. The marginal propensity to consume is the fraction of the last dollar of income spent on all goods and services regardless of where in the world they are made. The marginal propensity to spend is the fraction of the last dollar of income spent on domestically produced goods and services. It equals the marginal propensity to consume minus the marginal propensity to import.

The marginal propensity to spend equals the slope of the aggregate expenditure curve. You can see this relationship by looking again at Fig. 26.2. If real GNP increases from $1 trillion to $2 trillion, an increase of $1 trillion, aggregate expenditure increases from $2.5 trillion to $3 trillion, an increase of $0.5 trillion. The slope of the aggregate expenditure curve equals the increase in aggregate expenditure divided by the increase in real GNP—$0.5 trillion divided by $1 trillion, which equals 0.5.

R E V I E W

Aggregate expenditure is the sum of consumption expenditure, investment, government purchases of goods and services, and net exports. Aggregate expenditure is classified into two components: autonomous expenditure and induced expenditure. Investment, government purchases of goods and services, exports, and part of consumption are autonomous. The other part of consumption expenditure minus imports is induced expenditure. Autonomous expen-

diture is independent of real GNP; induced expenditure varies as real GNP varies. The higher the level of autonomous expenditure, the greater is the level of aggregate expenditure. The fraction of the last dollar of income spent on domestic goods and services is called the marginal propensity to spend. The marginal propensity to spend equals the marginal propensity to consume minus the marginal propensity to import. The larger the marginal propensity to spend, the steeper is the aggregate expenditure curve. ■

We've now seen how to calculate the aggregate expenditure schedule and aggregate expenditure curve. We've seen that aggregate planned expenditure increases as real GNP increases. But what determines the point on the aggregate expenditure curve at which the economy operates?

Equilibrium Expenditure

Equilibrium expenditure occurs when aggregate planned expenditure equals real GNP. At levels of real GNP below equilibrium, planned expenditure exceeds real GNP; at levels of real GNP above equilibrium, planned expenditure falls short of real GNP.

When Planned Expenditure Equals Real GNP

The table in Fig. 26.3 shows different levels of real GNP in our model economy. Against each level of real GNP, the second column shows aggregate planned expenditure. Only when real GNP equals $4 trillion is aggregate planned expenditure equal to real GNP. This level of expenditure is the equilibrium expenditure.

The equilibrium is illustrated in Fig. 26.3(a). The aggregate expenditure curve is *AE*. The 45° line shows points at which aggregate planned expenditure equals real GNP. Where the aggregate expenditure curve intersects the 45° line, at point *d*, equilibrium expenditure is determined.

Convergence to Equilibrium

You can perhaps get a better idea of why point *d* is the equilibrium if you consider what is happening

Figure 26.3   Equilibrium Expenditure and Real GNP

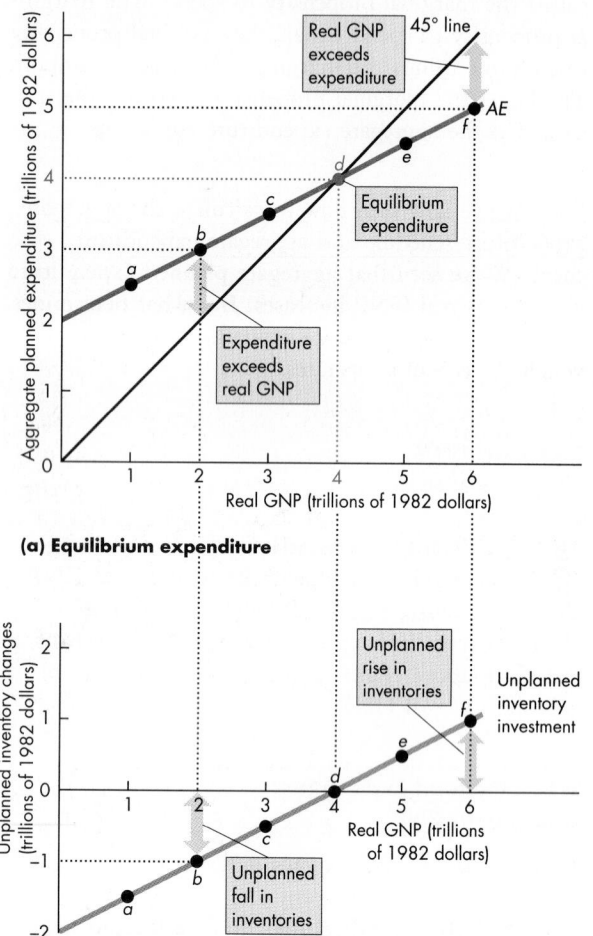

(a) Equilibrium expenditure

(b) Unplanned inventory changes

	Real GNP (Y)	Aggregate planned expenditure (AE) (trillions of 1982 dollars)	Unplanned inventory changes (Y − AE)
a	1.0	2.5	−1.5
b	2.0	3.0	−1.0
c	3.0	3.5	−0.5
d	4.0	4.0	0
e	5.0	4.5	0.5
f	6.0	5.0	1.0

The table shows the aggregate expenditure schedule. When real GNP is $4 trillion, aggregate planned expenditure equals real GNP. At real GNP levels below $4 trillion, aggregate planned expenditure exceeds real GNP. At real GNP levels above $4 trillion, aggregate planned expenditure is less than real GNP. The diagram illustrates equilibrium expenditure. In part (a), the 45° line shows those points at which aggregate planned expenditure equals GNP. AE is the aggregate expenditure curve. Actual aggregate expenditure equals real GNP. Equilibrium expenditure and real GNP are $4 trillion. That GNP level generates planned expenditure that equals GNP—$4 trillion. At GNP levels below $4 trillion, aggregate planned expenditure exceeds GNP and inventories fall—for example, point b in both parts of the figure. In such cases, firms increase output to restore their inventories and real GNP rises. At GNP levels higher than $4 trillion aggregate planned expenditure is less than GNP and inventories rise—for example, point d in both parts of the figure. In such a situation, firms decrease output to work off excess inventories and real GNP falls. Only where the aggregate planned expenditure curve cuts the 45° line is planned expenditure equal to GNP. This position is the equilibrium. There are no unplanned inventory changes and output remains constant.

when the economy is not at point *d*. Suppose that real GNP is $2 trillion. You can see from Fig. 26.3 (a) that in this situation aggregate planned expenditure is $3 trillion (point *b*). Thus aggregate planned expenditure is higher than real GNP. If aggregate expenditure was actually $3 trillion as planned, then real GNP would also be $3 trillion, since every dollar spent by one person is a dollar of income for some-

one else. But real GNP is $2 trillion. How can real GNP be $2 trillion if people plan to spend $3 trillion? The answer is that actual spending is less than planned spending. If real GNP is $2 trillion, the value of output is also $2 trillion. If people try to buy goods and services worth $3 trillion, firms' inventories fall. In this example, inventories fall by $1 trillion (point *b* in Fig. 26.3b). Since changes in inventories are part of investment, *actual* investment is lower than planned investment.

But this is not the end of the story. Firms now have lower inventories than they desire. To restore their inventories, they hire additional labor and increase output. Suppose that they increase output in the next period by enough to replenish their inventories. Aggregate output rises by $1 trillion to $3 trillion. But again, aggregate planned expenditure exceeds real GNP. When real GNP is $3 trillion, aggregate planned expenditure is $3.5 trillion (point *c* in Fig.26.3a). Again, inventories fall but this time by less than before. With an output of $3 trillion and planned expenditure of $3.5 trillion, inventories fall by only $0.5 trillion (point *c* in Fig. 26.3b). Again, firms hire additional labor, increase output, and real GNP increases yet further.

The process that we have just described of planned expenditure exceeding income, inventories falling, and output rising to restore the unplanned inventory reduction ends when real GNP has reached $4 trillion. At this level of real GNP, there is an equilibrium. There are no unplanned inventory changes and firms do not change their output.

Next, let's perform a similar experiment to that above but in reverse, starting with a level of real GNP above the equilibrium. Suppose that real GNP is $6 trillion. At this income level aggregate planned expenditure is $5 trillion, (point *f* in Fig. 26.3a), $1 trillion less than real GNP. With aggregate planned expenditure less than real GNP, inventories rise by $1 trillion (point *f* in Fig. 26.3b)—there is unplanned investment. With unsold inventories on their hands, firms cut back on production. They lay off workers, reduce the amount that they pay out in wages, and real GNP falls. If they cut back production by the amount of the unplanned increase in inventories, real GNP falls by $1 trillion to $5 trillion. At that level of real GNP, aggregate planned expenditure is $4.5 trillion (point *e* in Fig. 26.3a). Again, there is an unplanned increase in inventories, but only of one half the previous increase (point *e* in Fig. 26.3b). Again, firms will cut back production and lay off yet more workers, reducing real GNP still further. Real GNP continues to fall whenever unplanned inventories increase. As before, real GNP keeps on changing until it reaches its equilibrium level of $4 trillion.

You can see, then, that if real GNP is below equilibrium, aggregate planned expenditure exceeds real GNP, inventories fall, firms increase output to restore their inventories, and real GNP rises. If real GNP is above equilibrium, aggregate planned expenditure is less than real GNP, unsold inventories prompt firms to cut back on production, and real GNP falls.

Only if real GNP equals aggregate planned expenditure are there no unplanned inventory changes and no changes in firms' output plans. In this situation, real GNP remains constant.

R E V I E W

Equilibrium expenditure occurs when aggregate planned expenditure equals real GNP. If aggregate planned expenditure exceeds real GNP, inventories fall and firms increase output to replenish inventory levels. Real GNP increases and so does planned expenditure. If aggregate planned expenditure is below real GNP, inventories accumulate and firms cut output to lower inventory levels. Real GNP and aggregate planned expenditure decline. Only when aggregate planned expenditure equals real GNP are there no unplanned changes in inventories and no changes in output. Real GNP remains constant. ∎

We have now discovered how the equilibrium levels of real GNP and aggregate expenditure are determined. Our next task is to study the sources of *changes* in the equilibrium.

Fluctuations in Expenditure and in Real GNP

We've seen that equilibrium expenditure occurs where aggregate planned expenditure equals real GNP. For a given *AE* curve, there is only one such equilibrium—where the *AE* curve intersects the 45° line. When the *AE* curve shifts, equilibrium expenditure changes. What are the factors that shift the *AE* curve?

The position of the aggregate expenditure curve is determined by two factors:

- Autonomous expenditure
- The marginal propensity to spend

Anything that changes autonomous expenditure shifts the *AE* curve but leaves its slope unchanged. Anything that affects the marginal propensity to spend changes induced expenditure and changes the slope of the *AE* curve. Any such changes, either a change in autonomous expenditure or a change in the marginal propensity to spend, shift the *AE* curve and bring about a new equilibrium level of aggregate expenditure and real GNP. Let's look at these changes, starting with a change in autonomous expenditure.

A Change in Autonomous Expenditure

There are many possible sources of a change in autonomous expenditure: a fall in the real interest rate might induce firms to increase their planned investment. Booming business conditions may increase firms' optimism about future profits, adding yet more to their planned investment. Stiff competition in the auto industry from Japanese and European imports might force GM, Ford, and Chrysler to increase their investment in robotic assembly lines. An economic boom in Western Europe and Japan might lead to a large increase in expenditure in those countries on U.S.–produced goods—on U.S. exports. A worsening of international relations might lead the U.S. government to increase its expenditure on armaments —an increase in government purchases of goods and services. These are all examples of increases in autonomous expenditure. What are the effects of such increases on aggregate planned expenditure? And do increases in autonomous expenditure affect consumers? Will they plan to increase their consumption expenditure? Let's answer these questions.

Aggregate planned expenditure is set out in the table and illustrated in the diagram in Fig. 26.4. Autonomous expenditure initially is $2 trillion. The marginal propensity to spend out of real GNP is 0.5. Thus for each $1 trillion increase in real GNP, induced expenditure increases by $0.5 trillion. Adding induced expenditure and autonomous expenditure together gives aggregate planned expenditure. Initially, equilibrium occurs when real GNP is $4 trillion. This equilibrium can be seen in row *d* of the table, and in the figure where the aggregate planned expenditure AE_0 cuts the 45° line at the point marked *d*.

Now suppose that planned investment, government purchases, and exports increase by an aggregate amount of $0.5 trillion, so that autonomous expenditure becomes $2.5 trillion. What is the new equilib-

rium? The answer is worked out in the final columns of the table and illustrated in the diagram. When the new level of autonomous expenditure is added to induced expenditure, aggregate planned expenditure increases by $0.5 trillion at each level of real GNP. The aggregate expenditure curve shifts upward to AE_1—a parallel shift. That is, the vertical gap between AE_1 and AE_0 is $0.5 trillion at all levels of real GNP. The new equilibrium, highlighted in the table (row *e'*), occurs where AE_1 intersects the 45° line and is at $5 trillion (point *e'*). At this income level, aggregate planned expenditure equals real GNP. Autonomous expenditure is $2.5 trillion and induced expenditure is also $2.5 trillion.

Notice that equilibrium expenditure has increased by more than the increase in autonomous expenditure. Increased autonomous expenditure increases real GNP and the increase in real GNP produces an increase in induced expenditure. Aggregate expenditure increases by the sum of the initial increase on autonomous expenditure and the increase in induced expenditure.

Although we have just analyzed the effects of an *increase* in autonomous expenditure, the same analysis applies to a decrease in autonomous expenditure. If autonomous expenditure is initially $2.5 trillion, the initial equilibrium real GNP is $5 trillion. If, in that situation, there is a cut in government purchases, exports, or investment of $0.5 trillion, then the aggregate expenditure curve shifts downward to AE_0. Equilibrium real GNP falls from $5 trillion to $4 trillion. The fall in real GNP is larger than the fall in autonomous expenditure.

A Change in the Marginal Propensity to Spend

There are three main influences on the marginal propensity to spend:

- The marginal propensity to consume
- The marginal propensity to import
- The marginal tax rate

The Marginal Propensity to Consume   Some changes in households' consumption plans may change the marginal propensity to consume. We saw in the previous chapter that there are two important influences of income on consumption expenditure. First, an increase in *current* disposable income leads to an increase in consumption expenditure. Second,

Figure 26.4   An Increase in Autonomous Expenditure

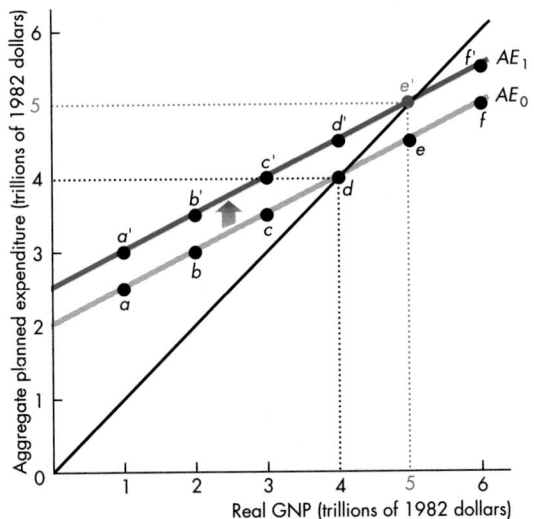

If autonomous expenditure increases from $2.0 trillion to $2.5 trillion, aggregate planned expenditure at each level of GNP also increases by $0.5 trillion. As shown in the table, the initial equilibrium expenditure of $4.0 trillion is no longer the equilibrium. At that level of GNP, aggregate planned expenditure is now $4.5 trillion. The new expenditure equilibrium is $5.0 trillion, where aggregate planned expenditure equals GNP. The increase in GNP is larger than the increase in autonomous expenditure. The figure illustrates the effect of the increase in autonomous expenditure. At each level of real GNP, aggregate planned expenditure is $0.5 trillion higher than before. The aggregate planned expenditure curve shifts upward from AE_0 to AE_1—a parallel shift. The new AE curve intersects the 45° line at e' where real GNP is $5 trillion—the new equilibrium point.

Real GNP (Y) (trillions of 1982 dollars)	Induced expenditure (N)		Original Autonomous expenditure (A_0) (trillions of 1982 dollars)	Aggregate expenditure (AE_0)		New Autonomous expenditure (A_1) (trillions of 1982 dollars)	Aggregate expenditure (AE_1)
1.0	0.5	a	2.0	2.5	a'	2.5	3.0
2.0	1.0	b	2.0	3.0	b'	2.5	3.5
3.0	1.5	c	2.0	3.5	c'	2.5	4.0
4.0	2.0	d	2.0	4.0	d'	2.5	4.5
5.0	2.5	e	2.0	4.5	e'	2.5	5.0
6.0	3.0	f	2.0	5.0	f'	2.5	5.5

an increase in *expected future* income also leads to an increase in consumption expenditure. Sometimes an increase in current income is expected to be permanent. In such a case, both current income and expected future income increase together. But sometimes an increase in current income is expected to be only temporary. In this case, current income increases but expected future income does not. The effect on consumption of an increase in income that is expected to be permanent is larger than the effect of an increase that is expected to be temporary. For this reason, the

fraction of the last dollar of income spent on consumption goods and services varies and in a way that is connected with the business cycle.

When the economy begins a period of expansion from recession, at first the increases in income are perceived by most people as being permanent. Consumption increases and a large fraction of increased income is spent on consumption goods and services—the marginal propensity to consume is high. As the expansion continues, more people start to suspect that a halt to expansion, or even a contraction, is going to occur soon—they perceive the current income increase as being temporary. In this situation, the fraction of additional income consumed falls—the marginal propensity to consume falls. When the economy actually goes into a recession and incomes fall, the decrease in income is regarded as temporary. Consumption does not fall by as large a percentage as the fall in income. In this situation, the marginal propensity to consume is low—a one dollar *decrease* in disposable income leads to a small *decrease* in consumption expenditure.

Fluctuations in the marginal propensity to consume—some of them related to the business cycle—lead to changes in the slope of the aggregate expenditure curve. The higher the marginal propensity to consume, the higher is the marginal propensity to spend and the steeper is the *AE* curve.

The Marginal Propensity to Import   We discovered in Chapter 25 that there has been a steady increase in imports as a percentage of GNP over the past 20 years. This steady increase has resulted partly from changes in international relative prices—many goods and services that are produced abroad are produced there at a lower cost than we can produce them in the United States. The increase has also resulted from a steady increase in the degree of international specialization in the production of goods and services. That is, we have become more specialized, increasing our exports, and other countries have also become more specialized, increasing their exports to us. All of these factors have increased the marginal propensity to import. The higher the marginal propensity to import, the lower is the marginal propensity to spend and the flatter is the *AE* curve.

The Marginal Tax Rate   The **marginal tax rate** is the fraction of the last dollar of income paid to the government in taxes. For individuals, there is some variation in the marginal tax rate that depends on the level of a person's income. People with very low incomes pay no taxes (and even receive net benefits from the government). As individual income increases, the marginal tax rate increases. For the economy, on the average, the marginal tax rate is calculated as the change in tax receipts of the government sector divided by the change in GNP. Other things being equal, the higher the marginal tax rate, the lower is disposable income. Thus for a given increase in GNP, disposable income increases by less, the higher is the marginal tax rate. Thus a cut in marginal tax

rates increases the marginal propensity to spend and makes the *AE* curve steeper.

We can analyze the effects of a change in the marginal propensity to consume, the marginal propensity to import, and the marginal tax rate by working out their effects on the marginal propensity to spend. We can then work out the effect of a change in the marginal propensity to spend, with a given level of autonomous expenditure, on equilibrium expenditure and on real GNP.

The Effects of a Change in the Marginal Propensity to Spend

Let's work out the effects of a change in the marginal propensity to spend on equilibrium expenditure and real GNP. Suppose that marginal tax rates have been cut, as they were under the Reagan Administration's tax reforms of the 1980s. What are the predicted effects of such a change in taxes on equilibrium expenditure and real GNP?

Suppose that a change in tax rates results in an increase in the marginal propensity to spend, from 0.5 to 0.6. The table in Fig. 26.5 lists the effects of this change in the marginal propensity to spend on induced expenditure and on aggregate planned expenditure, at each level of real GNP. Notice that the new induced expenditure (N_1) equals 0.6 times real GNP, whereas the original induced expenditure (N_0) equals 0.5 times real GNP. Aggregate planned expenditure equals induced expenditure plus the constant $2 trillion of autonomous expenditure.

The aggregate expenditure curve associated with the higher marginal propensity to spend is shown as AE_1 in the diagram in Fig. 26.5. Since autonomous expenditure has not changed, the aggregate planned expenditure curve intersects the vertical axis at the same point as the original curve, AE_0. The *AE* curve rotates upward. It does not shift in a parallel fashion; it becomes steeper. It becomes steeper because the increase in induced expenditure is larger, the higher is real GNP.

The original equilibrium real GNP is $4 trillion and the new equilibrium is $5 trillion. Starting out at $4 trillion, the higher marginal propensity to spend increases aggregate expenditure to $4.4 trillion (see row *d'* of the table). But now aggregate expenditure exceeds real GNP, so real GNP increases (by the process described in Fig. 26.3). Real GNP continues to increase until a new equilibrium is established. In

Figure 26.5   An Increase in the Marginal Propensity to Spend

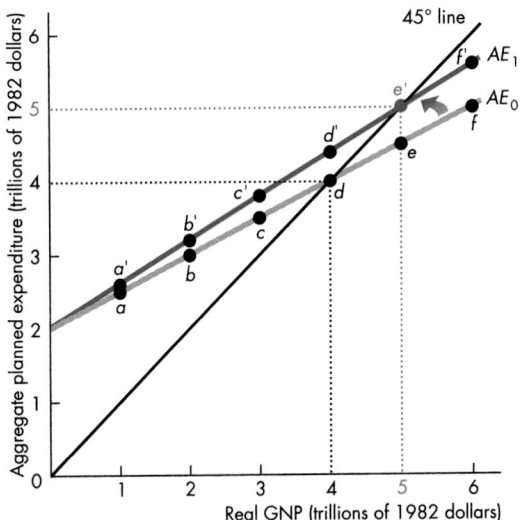

A tax cut increases the marginal propensity to spend from 0.5 to 0.6. Autonomous expenditure remains constant at $2.0 trillion but induced expenditure increases. For example, when real GNP is $2.0 trillion (row b of table), induced expenditure increases from $1.0 trillion to $1.2 trillion. In the figure, the aggregate expenditure curve shifts from AE_0 to AE_1. The aggregate expenditure curve becomes steeper because the marginal propensity to spend has increased. The new equilibrium occurs where aggregate planned expenditure equals real GNP—row e' in the table. In the diagram, the intersection of AE_1 and the 45° line determines equilibrium expenditure—$5 trillion (point e'). Alternatively, an increase in saving (an increase in thrift) would shift the aggregate expenditure curve down, say from AE_1 to AE_0, resulting in a fall in real GNP and equilibrium expenditure. The negative effect on real GNP of an increase in saving is called the paradox of thrift.

Real GNP (Y) (trillions of 1982 dollars)	Autonomous expenditure (A) (trillions of 1982 dollars)		Original Induced expenditure (N_0) (trillions of 1982 dollars)	Aggregate expenditure (AE_0)		New Induced expenditure (N_1) (trillions of 1982 dollars)	Aggregate expenditure (AE_1)
1.0	2.0	a	0.5	2.5	a'	0.6	2.6
2.0	2.0	b	1.0	3.0	b'	1.2	3.2
3.0	2.0	c	1.5	3.5	c'	1.8	3.8
4.0	2.0	d	2.0	4.0	d'	2.4	4.4
5.0	2.0	e	2.5	4.5	e'	3.0	5.0
6.0	2.0	f	3.0	5.0	f'	3.6	5.6

the process, induced expenditure increases further. Only when real GNP is $5 trillion has aggregate planned expenditure adjusted to the level required to attain a new expenditure equilibrium. You can verify this fact by noticing that at this level of real GNP, aggregate planned expenditure also equals $5 trillion. That is, induced expenditure is $3 trillion (real GNP of $5 trillion multiplied by 0.6) and when this amount is added to autonomous expenditure of $2 trillion, aggregate planned expenditure equals real GNP at $5 trillion.

The Paradox of Thrift

Thrift is another word for saving. The thriftier a household, the more it saves. Also, the thriftier a household, the wealthier it becomes. By consuming *less* than its income, a household *increases* its income. It lends what it saves and earns interest on it.

What happens if we *all* become thriftier? Does aggregate income increase? We can work out one answer to this question by using the analysis that we've just performed—but doing it in reverse.

Suppose that initially, the marginal propensity to spend is 0.6 and equilibrium real GNP and expenditure are $5 trillion—the aggregate expenditure curve is AE_1 in Fig. 26.5. Now suppose that there is an increase in thriftiness. As a result, the marginal propensity to consume falls and, consequently, the marginal propensity to spend falls, say from 0.6 to 0.5. The aggregate expenditure curve rotates downward from AE_1 to AE_0 in Fig. 26.5. Equilibrium GNP and expenditure fall to $4 trillion.

An increase in thriftiness has reduced real GNP. The fall in real GNP caused by an increase in saving is called the **paradox of thrift.** It is a paradox because an increase in thriftiness, which for an individual leads to an increase in income, leads, for the economy as a whole, to a decrease in income.

The paradox arises in this model because an increase in saving is not associated with an increase in investment. Although people save more, no one buys additional real capital. If at the same time that saving increases, there is also an increase in investment, there is no fall in income. The increased saving shifts the AE curve downward but an increase in investment shifts it upward by the same amount. The result is no change in real GNP. Thus the paradox of thrift is not so paradoxical after all. It is a consequence of increased saving without increased investment.

We have now discovered that changes in autonomous expenditure and changes in the marginal propensity to spend shift the aggregate expenditure curve and change equilibrium real GNP. But how big are the changes? What determines the magnitude of the change in aggregate expenditure brought about by a change in autonomous expenditure?

The Multiplier

Suppose that the economy appears to be heading for a recession. Profit prospects look bleak and firms are cutting investment. The government, anxious to avoid the recession, wants to take steps to prevent the level of aggregate expenditure from falling. It knows that by cutting interest rates it can encourage firms to invest more. It also knows that by increasing its own purchases of goods and services, or by cutting taxes, it can encourage a higher level of aggregate expenditure. But, for effective economic management, the government needs to know more than the direction in which to change interest rates, taxes, or its own purchases of goods and services. It needs to answer a quantitative question: By how

much must spending increase to avoid a recession? This is a hard question to answer but an important ingredient in the answer is working out the connection between a change in autonomous expenditure and the change in equilibrium aggregate expenditure. We've already seen that when autonomous expenditure changes, equilibrium expenditure and real GNP change by a larger amount. But what is the quantitative relationship between the change in autonomous expenditure and the change in equilibrium real GNP?

The **autonomous expenditure multiplier** (often abbreviated to simply the **multiplier**) is the amount by which a change in autonomous expenditure is multiplied to calculate the change in equilibrium aggregate expenditure and real GNP. To calculate the multiplier, we divide the change in equilibrium real GNP by the change in autonomous expenditure that brought about that change. Let's calculate the multiplier for the example in Fig. 26.4. Autonomous expenditure increases from $2 to $2.5 trillion and equilibrium real GNP increases from $4 trillion to $5 trillion, an increase of $1 trillion. That is,

• Autonomous expenditure increases by $0.5 trillion.
• Real GNP increases by $1 trillion.

The multiplier is:

$$\text{Multiplier} = \frac{\text{Change in equilibrium real GNP}}{\text{Change in autonomous expenditure}}$$
$$= \frac{\$1 \text{ trillion}}{\$0.5 \text{ trillion}} = 2.$$

Thus a change in autonomous expenditure of $0.5 trillion produces a change in equilibrium real GNP of $1 trillion, a change that is twice as big as the initial change in autonomous expenditure. That is, the change in autonomous expenditure leads, like Bruce Springsteen's music-making equipment, to an amplified change in equilibrium aggregate expenditure and real GNP.

There is an interesting relationship between the value of the multiplier and the marginal propensity to spend. Let's see what that relationship is.

The Multiplier and the Marginal Propensity to Spend

Table 26.1 shows how to calculate the value of the multiplier. The multiplier k is defined as

$$k = \frac{\Delta Y}{\Delta A},$$

Table 26.1 Calculating the Multiplier

	Symbols and formulas	Numbers
(a) Definitions		
Change in real GNP	ΔY	
Change in autonomous expenditure	ΔA	$500 billion
Marginal propensity to spend	ϵ	2/3
Change in induced expenditure	$\Delta N = \epsilon \Delta Y$	$\Delta N = (2/3)\Delta Y$
Change in aggregate planned expenditure	$\Delta AE = \Delta A + \Delta N$	
The multiplier (autonomous expenditure multiplier)	$k = \Delta Y/\Delta A$	
The multiplier effect	$\Delta Y = k\Delta A$	
(b) Calculations		
Aggregate planned expenditure	$AE = A + \epsilon Y$	
Change in AE curve	$\Delta AE = \Delta A + \epsilon \Delta Y$	$\Delta AE = 500 + (2/3)\Delta Y$
Change in equilibrium expenditure	$\Delta AE = \Delta Y$	
Replacing ΔAE with ΔY	$\Delta Y = \Delta A + \epsilon \Delta Y$	$\Delta Y = 500 + (2/3)\Delta Y$
Subtracting $\epsilon\Delta Y$ or $(2/3)\Delta Y$ from both sides	$\Delta Y - \epsilon\Delta Y = \Delta A$	$\Delta Y - (2/3)\Delta Y = 500$
Factoring ΔY	$\Delta Y(1 - \epsilon) = \Delta A$	$\Delta Y(1 - 2/3) = 500$
Dividing both sides by $(1 - \epsilon)$ or $(1 - 2/3)$	$\Delta Y = \dfrac{1}{1 - \epsilon}\Delta A$	$\Delta Y = \dfrac{1}{1 - 2/3}\,500$ or $\Delta Y = \dfrac{1}{(1/3)}\,500$ or $\Delta Y = 1500$
Dividing both sides by ΔA or 500 gives the multiplier	$\dfrac{\Delta Y}{\Delta A} = \dfrac{1}{1 - \epsilon}$	$\dfrac{\Delta Y}{\Delta A} = \dfrac{1500}{500} = 3$

The autonomous expenditure multiplier, or multiplier, is the ratio of the change in real GNP to a change in real autonomous expenditure. The multiplier effect is the change in real GNP brought about by a given change in autonomous expenditure—the change in autonomous expenditure multiplied by k. To calculate the multiplier, work through the steps in part (b). The multiplier formula that results is

$$\frac{\Delta Y}{\Delta A} = \frac{1}{1 - \epsilon}.$$

and its value is $k = \dfrac{1}{1 - \epsilon}$.

The letter ϵ stands for the marginal propensity to spend. The marginal propensity to spend is a fraction—lying between 0 and 1—so, $1/(1 - \epsilon)$ is greater than 1. The larger the marginal propensity to spend, the larger is the multiplier.

If the marginal propensity to spend is 0 (if ϵ equals 0), there is no induced expenditure. In such a case, the multiplier is 1. It is easy to see why. A $1

Figure 26.6   The Multiplier and the Marginal Propensity to Spend

(a) Multiplier is 2

(b) Multiplier is 3

The size of the multiplier depends on the marginal propensity to spend. The multiplier formula, $k = 1/(1 - \epsilon)$, tells us the relationship. If the marginal propensity to spend (ϵ) is 1/2, the multiplier is 2. In this case, an increase of autonomous expenditure of \$1 trillion shifts the AE curve upward from AE_0 to AE_1 in part (a). Real GNP increases from \$3 trillion to \$5 trillion. If ϵ equals 2/3, the multiplier is 3. In this case, a \$1 trillion increase in autonomous expenditure shifts the aggregate expenditure curve upward from AE_0 to AE_1 in part (b). Real GNP increases from \$3 trillion to \$6 trillion, three times the size of the increase in autonomous expenditure.

change in autonomous expenditure changes real GNP by \$1 and, with no induced expenditure changes, that is the end of the matter.

If the marginal propensity to spend (ϵ) is 0.5, \$1 of additional income induces 50¢ of additional expenditure. The multiplier is 2. This case is illustrated in Fig. 26.6(a). A \$1 trillion increase in autonomous expenditure shifts the AE curve upward from AE_0 to AE_1 and increases equilibrium real GNP from \$3 trillion to \$5 trillion. An autonomous expenditure increase of \$1 trillion increases equilibrium real GNP by \$2 trillion, so the multiplier is 2. If the marginal propensity to spend (ϵ) is two thirds (0.67), the multiplier is 3. Figure 26.6(b) illustrates this case. Here a \$1 trillion increase in autonomous expenditure shifts the AE curve upward from AE_0 to AE_1 and increases equilibrium real GNP from \$3 trillion to \$6 trillion.

Why Is the Multiplier Greater than 1?

The multiplier is greater than 1 because of induced expenditure—an increase in autonomous expenditure *induces* an increase in consumption expenditure. If GM spends \$10 million on a new car assembly line, aggregate expenditure and real GNP immediately increase by \$10 million. But that is not the end of the story. Engineers and construction workers now have more income and they spend part of the extra income on cars, microwaves, vacations, and a host of other goods and services. Real GNP now rises by the initial \$10 million plus the extra consumption expenditure induced by the \$10 million increased income. The producers of cars, microwaves, vacations, and other goods now have increased incomes and they, in turn, also spend part of their increase in

Figure 26.7   The Multiplier Process

Expenditure round	Increase in expenditure	Cumulative increase in real GNP
	(billions of 1982 dollars)	
1	500	500
2	333	833
3	222	1055
4	148	1203
5	99	1302
6	66	1368
7	44	1412
8	29	1441
9	20	1461
10	13	1474
.	.	.
.	.	.
.	.	.
All others	26	1500

Increase in real GNP (billions of 1982 dollars) — vertical axis, values 0, 500, 1000, 1500

Expenditure round — horizontal axis, 1 through 13

■ Increase in current round
▨ Cumulative increase from previous rounds

Autonomous expenditure increases in round 1 by $500 billion. Real GNP also increases by the same amount. In round 2, the round 1 increase in GNP induces an increase in real expenditure of $333 billion. At the end of round 2, real GNP has increased by $833 billion. The extra $333 billion of real GNP in round 2 induces a further increase in expenditure of $222 billion in round 3. Real GNP increases yet further to $1055 billion. This process continues until real GNP has eventually increased by $1500 billion. The table stops counting after round 10 since the extra amounts become smaller and smaller. (Perhaps you would like to run the process further on your pocket calculator. As a matter of interest, after 19 rounds you will be within $1 of the $1500 billion total, and after 30 rounds within 1 penny of that total!) The diagram shows you how quickly the multiplier effect builds up. The multiplier in this case is 3 because the marginal propensity to spend is 2/3 (see Table 26.1). The larger the marginal propensity to spend, the larger is the multiplier.

income on consumption goods and services. Additional income induces additional expenditure, which creates additional income.

This multiplier process is illustrated in Fig. 26.7. In this example, the marginal propensity to spend (ϵ) is two thirds (0.67) as in Fig. 26.6(b). In "round 1," there is an increase in autonomous expenditure of $500 billion. At that stage, there is no change in induced expenditure so total expenditure increases by $500 billion. In "round 2," the higher

income induces higher consumption expenditure. Since the marginal propensity to spend (ϵ) is two thirds (0.67), an increase in income of $500 billion induces a further increase in expenditure of $333 billion. This change in induced expenditure, when added to the initial change in autonomous expenditure, results in an increase in total expenditure of $833 billion. The "round 2" increase in income induces a "round 3" increase in expenditure. The process repeats through successive rounds recorded in the table. Each increase in income is two thirds the size of the previous increase. The cumulative increase in income gradually approaches $1500 billion. Even after 10 rounds it has almost reached that level.

As the multiplier process depicted in Fig. 26.7 is working itself out, inventories and output are being adjusted in the manner described in Fig. 26.3. But you should not think of each expenditure round depicted in Fig. 26.7 as taking place in a fixed amount of calendar time. This multiplier process can take place in a single day or even a single instant. The amount of time that it takes is not important. But what is more important is that the multiplier process is a description of the forces that keep the economy at equilibrium.

It appears, then, that the economy does not operate like the shock absorbers on Coleman Young's car. The economy's potholes and bumps are changes in autonomous expenditure—mainly brought about by changes in investment and exports. These economic potholes and bumps are not smoothed out but instead are amplified.

But the economic amplifier not only amplifies fluctuations in investment and exports. It also amplifies fluctuations in government purchases of goods and services. Because of this fact, the government can take advantage of the multiplier in order to attempt to smooth out fluctuations in aggregate expenditure. Let's see how.

Fiscal Policy Multipliers

Fiscal policy is the attempt by government to vary its purchases of goods and services and taxes to smooth the fluctuations in aggregate expenditure. Government purchases of goods and services have the same effect on aggregate expenditure as other components of autonomous expenditure. They set up a multiplier effect exactly like the multiplier effect of investment or exports. By varying government expenditure to offset changes in exports or investment the government can attempt to keep total autonomous expenditure constant (or growing at a steady rate). In practice, however, the political decision process that produces changes in government purchases of goods and services operates with a long time lag so that there is a limit to the use of this instrument of macroeconomic stabilization policy.

The government can also attempt to influence aggregate expenditure by changing taxes. The effects of a change in taxes depend on whether the taxes are

autonomous or induced. **Autonomous taxes** are taxes that do not vary directly with real GNP. Examples of such taxes are contributions for social insurance, property taxes, and estate taxes. **Induced taxes** are taxes which vary directly with real GNP. Examples of induced taxes are personal income tax and sales taxes. The scale of induced taxes determines the *marginal tax rate*. That is, the marginal tax rate is the change in induced taxes divided by the change in real GNP.

Taxes have two distinct types of effects on fluctuations in real GNP. First, the government can change taxes in an attempt to offset fluctuations in autonomous expenditure. Second, by its selection of the marginal tax rate, the government can influence directly the value of the autonomous expenditure multiplier. Let's first consider changes in taxes.

The Tax Multiplier   The **tax multiplier** is the amount by which a change in taxes is multiplied to determine the change in equilibrium expenditure that it generates. A *decrease* in taxes produces an *increase* in expenditure by increasing disposable income, so the tax multiplier is *negative*. But a $1 increase in disposable income does not increase expenditure by $1. Instead, it increases expenditure by $1 multiplied by the marginal propensity to consume. For example, if the marginal propensity to consume is 0.9, a $1 increase in disposable income increases consumption by 90¢. The tax multiplier equals the negative of the autonomous expenditure multiplier multiplied by the marginal propensity to consume. That is:

$$\text{Tax multiplier} = -\frac{\text{Marginal propensity to consume}}{(1 - \epsilon)}$$

The second way that taxes affect real GNP is through their effect on the magnitude of the autonomous expenditure multiplier. In fact, taxes act like an economic shock absorber, making the aggregate effects of fluctuations in autonomous expenditure smaller than they otherwise would be.

Induced Taxes as a Shock Absorber   To see how induced taxes act as an economic shock absorber, let's see how a change in autonomous expenditure (in investment or exports) affects aggregate planned expenditure, first with no induced taxes and then with induced taxes at a rate similar to those in place in the United States today. In an economy with no induced taxes, although there is a gap between GNP and disposable income, the size of that gap is constant—it equals the fixed amount of taxes levied by the government. If the marginal propensity to consume out of disposable income is 0.9, the marginal propensity to consume out of GNP is also 0.9. That is, each extra dollar of GNP is an extra dollar of disposable income and induces an extra 90¢ of consumption expenditure. For the minute, suppose that there are no imports so that not only is the marginal propensity to consume 0.9, but so is the marginal propensity to spend.

What is the size of the multiplier if the marginal propensity to spend is 0.9? You can answer this question by using the formula

$$k = \frac{1}{(1 - \epsilon)}.$$

Plugging in 0.9 in place of ϵ you discover that the value of the multiplier is 10. In this economy, a $1 billion change in autonomous expenditure produces a $10 billion change in equilibrium expenditure. This economy has a very strong amplifier.

Contrast the economy that we have just described with one that has induced taxes and a marginal tax rate of 0.3. Each additional dollar of real GNP creates 70¢ of disposable income. If the marginal propensity to consume remains at 0.9, a $1 increase in GNP increases disposable income by 70¢ and increases consumption by 63¢ (0.9 of 0.7 equals 0.63). In this economy, the marginal propensity to spend is 0.63. Using 0.63 in place of ϵ in the multiplier formula, you discover that the value of the multiplier for this economy is 2.7. The economy still amplifies shocks from changes in exports and investment but on a much smaller scale than the economy with no induced taxes. Thus, to some degree, induced taxes absorb the shocks of fluctuating autonomous expenditure. The higher the marginal tax rate, the greater the extent to which autonomous expenditure shocks are absorbed by taxes.

The existence of taxes and transfers that vary as income levels vary helps the shock-absorbing capacities of the economy. They don't produce the economic equivalent of the suspension of a Lincoln Continental but they do produce the economic equivalent of something better than the springs of a stagecoach.

We've now seen what determines the value of the autonomous expenditure multiplier, how the multiplier can be used by the government to influence aggregate planned expenditure by changing gov-

ernment purchases or autonomous taxes, and how, by its choice of the marginal tax rate, the government can influence the magnitude of the multiplier itself. But so far we have studied model economies with hypothetical numbers. Let's now turn to the real world. What is the size of the marginal propensity to spend in the United States? How big is the multiplier in the U.S. economy?

The Multiplier in the United States The model economy that we studied earlier in this chapter and that is illustrated in Figs. 26.1 through 26.4 has a lot of the features of the U.S. economy. In the model economy, the marginal propensity to spend is 0.5— each additional dollar of income induces 50¢ of expenditure. This marginal propensity to spend is close to that in the U.S. economy at the end of the 1980s. The marginal propensity to consume out of disposable income is 0.9 and disposable income is approximately two thirds of GNP. Putting these two facts together, consumption expenditure is six tenths of GNP. The marginal propensity to consume out of GNP is 0.6 (2/3 of 9/10 equals 6/10, or 0.6). Imports are approximately 15 percent of GNP. The marginal propensity to import is 0.15 (each dollar of income induces 15¢ of imports). Subtracting the marginal propensity to import from the marginal propensity to consume gives the marginal propensity to spend, which is 0.60 minus 0.15, or 0.45. With a marginal propensity to spend of 0.45, the multiplier is 1.82. That is,

$$k = \frac{1}{1 - 0.45} = \frac{1}{0.55} = 1.82.$$

Thus in the late 1980s, the multiplier in the United States was a little under 2.

The marginal propensity to spend has been gradually falling over time in the United States. The marginal propensity to consume out of disposable income has been constant and the relationship between disposable income and GNP has also not changed much. But the marginal propensity to import has increased gradually over the years. In the 1960s, the marginal propensity to import was about 0.05. Subtracting that number from the marginal propensity to consume gives a marginal propensity to spend of 0.55. In this case, the multiplier is 2.22. That is,

$$k = \frac{1}{1 - 0.55} = \frac{1}{0.45} = 2.22.$$

In the 1970s, the marginal propensity to import was about 0.1, the marginal propensity to spend was 0.5, and the multiplier was 2. That is,

$$k = \frac{1}{1 - 0.5} = \frac{1}{0.5} = 2.$$

The Multiplier in Recession and Recovery

We've seen that the average value of the multiplier in the U.S. economy in the late 1980s is about 1.8. Is the multiplier a highly stable number—a constant—on which we can rely? Does the multiplier take on the same value when the economy is going into a recession as when it is coming out and recovering? Or does its value vary and in some systematic way? Answers to questions such as these are important for the design of policies to keep aggregate expenditure steady. How big an increase in government spending or cut in taxes is needed to avoid a recession? How big a cut in government spending or tax hike is needed to prevent the economy from overheating?

You can see part of the answers to these questions in Table 26.2. The table calculates the multiplier for selected years and the results are shown in the final column. As we have already discovered, the multiplier has fallen in value from around 2.2 to 1.8. Its average value over the period 1960 to 1987, shown in the first row of the table, is 1.92. This value of the multiplier, along with the others in the table, is calculated by dividing the change in real GNP by the change in autonomous expenditure. In these calculations, the change in autonomous expenditure is measured as the change in the sum of investment, government purchases of goods and services, and exports. The change in induced expenditure is measured as the change in consumption minus imports.

The second and third rows of the table calculate the multiplier for two recession years. You will recall that in 1975 we experienced a sharp cut in investment following the pessimism created by the OPEC oil price hike. In 1981, we experienced a sharp cut in investment partly caused by high interest rates and partly by pessimistic profit expectations. In both of these recession years, despite there being a decrease in autonomous expenditure, induced expenditure increased. As a result, real GNP fell but by less than the fall in autonomous expenditure. In these two years, the multiplier was less than 1.

Table 26.2   The Multiplier in Selected Years

	Change in autonomous expenditure (ΔA)	Change in induced expenditure (ΔN)	Change in real GNP (ΔY)	Multiplier (k = ΔY/ΔA)
	(billions of 1982 dollars)			
1960–87	+1121.9	+1032.4	+2154.3	1.92
1974–75	−99.8	+65.5	−34.4	0.34
1981–82	−117.1	+34.3	−82.8	0.71
1982–83	+50.3	+62.8	+113.1	2.25
1983–87	+383.3	+157.2	+540.5	1.41

The average value of the multiplier from 1960 to 1987 was 1.92. In recession years (1974–75 and 1981–82), the multiplier was less than 1. In recovery years (1982-1983 and 1983-1987), the multiplier was larger than 1. The multiplier was small in recession years because the decrease in income was expected to be temporary. The multiplier was smaller in the 1980s than in the 1970s because of a large surge in imports.

Source: *Economic Report of the President* (1988), Table B2, pp. 250–51.

The final two rows of the table calculate the multiplier for two recovery periods in the 1980s. As you can see, the multipliers for both periods are larger than the multipliers for the recessions.

Why are multipliers small when the economy goes into recession and larger in recovery? The answer to this question is found in the discussion above (on pp. 682–684) about the marginal propensity to consume. At the start of a recovery, income gains are expected to be permanent and the marginal propensity to consume is high. When a cycle peak is approached, and during recessions, income changes are viewed as temporary and the marginal propensity to consume is low. When income fell in 1974–1975 and again in 1981–1982 as the economy went into recession, households regarded the income loss that they then experienced as temporary. They did not cut their consumption expenditure. Instead consumption expenditure increased but by less than it would have done in the absence of the recession. Nevertheless, the increase in consumption was a rational reaction to events interpreted as a temporary halt to an otherwise on-going period of economic growth and expansion. Because consumption expenditure did not decline, the recessions were less severe than they otherwise would have been. The multiplier was less than 1 and consumption acted, to some degree, like a shock absorber.

When a recovery gets underway and incomes increase, people regard a large part of those increased incomes as permanent. As a consequence, consumption increases to reinforce the increase in autonomous expenditure and the multiplier is larger than 1.

Although the multiplier in recovery is larger than that in recession, you can see from the numbers in the table that in the recovery years 1983–87 the multiplier was still relatively small at 1.41. What kept the multiplier small in the 1980s? The answer is the behavior of imports. Imports into the United States increased between 1983 and 1987 by $192 billion. In that same period, as you can see in the table, GNP increased by $540.5 billion. Thus the marginal propensity to import, over this period, was 0.36. For every extra dollar of GNP, our imports increased by 36¢. This incredibly high marginal propensity to import is probably temporary but was sufficient, over this recovery period, to keep the multiplier low. Extra income spent on goods made abroad is a leakage from the circular flow of income and so lowers the multiplier effect of a change in autonomous expenditure.

R E V I E W

Changes in autonomous expenditure or changes in the marginal propensity to spend change equilibrium expenditure and real GNP. The magnitude of the effect of a change in autonomous expenditure on equilibrium expenditure is determined by the multiplier. The multiplier, in turn, is determined by the value of the marginal propensity to spend. The higher the marginal propensity to spend, the larger is the multiplier. The multiplier acts like an amplifier. Fluctuations in autonomous expenditure—such as fluctuations in investment, government purchases of goods and services, or exports—change real GNP, introducing a change in consumption expenditure and having amplified effects on aggregate expenditure.

The presence of taxes and transfers lowers the value of the multiplier by lowering the marginal propensity to spend. The higher the marginal tax rate, the smaller is the change in disposable income that results from a $1 change in aggregate income, and the smaller, therefore, is the change in induced expenditure.

The multiplier in the United States is around 2. In the early 1960s, it was slightly larger than 2; in the 1970s, it was almost exactly 2; and in the late 1980s, it was a little below 2. ■

In this chapter, we have studied the aggregate expenditure curve and the determination of equilibrium aggregate expenditure and real GNP. In Chapter 24, we studied the *aggregate demand curve* and the determination of *macroeconomic equilibrium*. What is the connection between the aggregate expenditure curve and the aggregate demand curve? And what is the connection between equilibrium expenditure and *macroeconomic equilibrium?*

Aggregate Expenditure and Aggregate Demand

The aggregate demand curve is the relationship between the aggregate quantity of goods and services demanded and the price level. That is, the aggregate demand curve shows the quantity of real GNP demanded at each different price level. The aggregate expenditure curve tells us how aggregate planned expenditure varies as real GNP varies. The quantity of goods and services demanded is related to aggregate planned expenditure. Also, there is a connection between equilibrium expenditure and the aggregate demand curve. Let's explore the links between these concepts.

Aggregate Planned Expenditure and the Price Level

In studying aggregate planned expenditure, we have distinguished between autonomous expenditure and induced expenditure. Induced expenditure varies with real GNP. Autonomous expenditure does not vary with real GNP. But autonomous expenditure is not

Figure 26.8   Aggregate Planned Expenditure and Aggregate Demand

(a) Equilibrium expenditure

(b) Aggregate demand

The position of the aggregate expenditure curve depends on the price level. Suppose that when the price level is 100 the aggregate expenditure curve is AE_0, as shown in part (a). Equilibrium occurs where AE_0 intersects the 45° line at point b. The level of real GNP demanded is $4 trillion. In part (b), point b is a point on the aggregate demand curve—at a price level of 100 the aggregate quantity of goods and services demanded is $4 trillion. Suppose that when the price level increases to 150 the aggregate expenditure curve shifts downward to AE_1. Equilibrium occurs at point a (in part a), where the aggregate quantity of goods and services demanded is $2 trillion. Thus at a price level of 150 and an aggregate quantity of goods and services demanded of $2 trillion, point a is a point on the aggregate demand curve (in part b). If the price level falls to 50 and the AE curve shifts upward to AE_2, the equilibrium quantity of goods and services demanded occurs at point c where AE_2 intersects the 45° line. Point c in part (b) is another point on the aggregate demand curve. A change in the price level leads to a shift in the aggregate expenditure curve and to a movement along the aggregate demand curve.

necessarily constant. In fact, we have analyzed the effects of changes in autonomous expenditure earlier in this chapter. Also, autonomous expenditure is not independent of other economic magnitudes. For example, a change in interest rates leads to a change in the investment component of autonomous expenditure. A change in the foreign exchange rate leads to a change in the export component of autonomous expenditure. Autonomous expenditure is also influenced by the price level.

At a given price level, there is a given level of autonomous expenditure and a given level of aggregate planned expenditure. But if the price level changes, so does autonomous expenditure. An increase in the price level decreases autonomous expenditure through the three effects described in Chapter 24—the real balance effect, the intertemporal substitution effect, and the international substitution effect.

Figure 26.8 illustrates the effects of the price level on aggregate planned expenditure and the relationship between equilibrium expenditure and the aggregate demand curve. When the price level is 100, the aggregate expenditure curve is AE_0 in part (a). The curve AE_0 intersects the $45°$ line at point b where equilibrium expenditure is $4 trillion. We have generated one point on the aggregate demand curve: At a price level of 100, the aggregate quantity of goods and services demanded is $4 trillion—point b on the aggregate demand curve AD in part (b).

Now suppose that the price level increases to 150. As a result, the aggregate planned expenditure curve shifts downward. Suppose that the aggregate expenditure curve shifts to AE_1 in part (a). The curve AE_1 intersects the $45°$ line at point a, and equilibrium expenditure is $2 trillion. Thus the aggregate quantity of goods and services demanded at a price level of 150 is $2 trillion, which is point a on the aggregate demand curve in part (b). A higher price level results in a downward shift in the AE curve and generates another point on the aggregate demand curve in part (b).

Next suppose that the price level falls to 50. A lower price level results in higher aggregate planned expenditure. Suppose that the aggregate expenditure curve shifts to AE_2. The curve AE_2 intersects the $45°$ line at point c, and equilibrium expenditure is $6 trillion. Thus the aggregate quantity of goods and services demanded when the price level is 50 is $6 trillion, which is point c on the aggregate demand curve in part (b). The lower price level results in an upward shift in the AE curve, which generates another point on the AD curve. Joining points a, b, and c, we can trace out the aggregate demand curve.

We can summarize the connection between the equilibrium expenditure at each price level and the AD curve in the following way: A rise in the price level causes the AE curve to shift downward, which lowers equilibrium expenditure and produces a movement along the aggregate demand curve.

Aggregate Demand Curve and Autonomous Expenditure

The aggregate expenditure curve shifts when the price level changes. It also shifts for a thousand other reasons. It is these other sources of shift in the aggregate expenditure curve that we have been studying earlier in this chapter—for example, a change in profit expectations that shifts the investment demand curve or a change in real GNP in Japan that increases that country's demand for U.S. exports. Any factor other than the price level that shifts the aggregate planned expenditure curve also shifts the aggregate demand curve. Figure 26.9 illustrates these shifts.

Initially the aggregate planned expenditure curve is AE_0 in part (a) and the aggregate demand curve is AD_0 in part (b). The price level is 100. Now suppose that an increase in profit expectations leads to a rise in investment. Autonomous expenditure increases. If the price level remains at 100, the aggregate expenditure curve shifts upward to AE_1. This new higher AE curve intersects the $45°$ line at an equilibrium expenditure of $6 trillion. This amount is the aggregate quantity of goods and services demanded at a price level of 100, as shown by point c' in part (b). Point c' lies on a new aggregate demand curve. The aggregate demand curve has shifted to the right to AD_1.

The distance by which the aggregate demand curve shifts to the right is determined by the multiplier. The larger the multiplier, the larger is the shift in the AD curve resulting from a given change in autonomous expenditure. In this example, a $1 trillion increase in autonomous expenditure produces a $2 trillion increase in the aggregate quantity of goods and services demanded at each price level. The multiplier is 2. That is, a $1 trillion increase in autonomous expenditure shifts the aggregate demand curve to the right by $2 trillion.

A decrease in autonomous expenditure shifts the AE curve downward and shifts the aggregate demand curve to the left. You can see this effect by supposing that the economy initially is on aggregate expenditure curve AE_1 and aggregate demand curve AD_1. There is then a decrease in autonomous expenditure and the AE curve falls to AE_0. The aggregate quantity of goods and services demanded falls to $4 trillion and the aggregate demand curve shifts to the left to AD_0.

Figure 26.9   Changes in Autonomous Expenditure and
Aggregate Demand

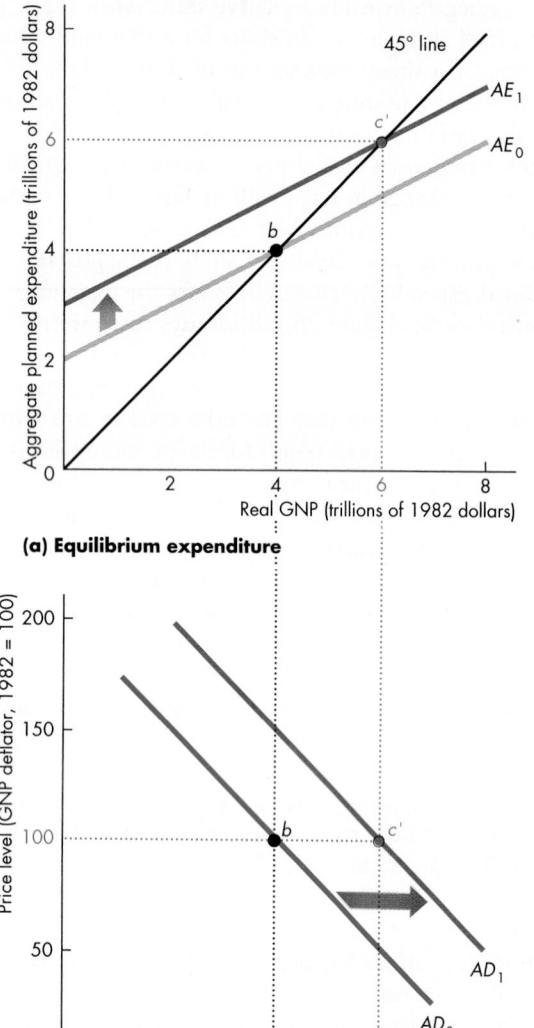

(a) Equilibrium expenditure

(b) Aggregate demand

The price level is 100. When the aggregate expenditure curve is
AE_0 (part a), the aggregate demand curve is AD_0 (part b). An
increase in autonomous expenditure shifts the aggregate expenditure upward to AE_1. The new equilibrium occurs where AE_1 intersects the 45° line at a real GNP of $6 trillion. The aggregate
demand curve shifts to the right to AD_1. The magnitude of the
rightward shift of the aggregate demand curve is determined by
the change in autonomous expenditure and the size of the multiplier.

We can summarize what we have just discovered in the following way: An increase in autonomous
expenditure arising from some source other than a
change in the price level shifts the AE curve upward
and shifts the AD curve to the right. The size of the
shift of the AD curve is determined by the change in
autonomous expenditure and the size of the multiplier.

Equilibrium GNP and the
Price Level

In Chapter 24, we learned how to determine the
equilibrium levels of real GNP and the price level as
the intersection point of the aggregate demand curve
and short-run aggregate supply curve. In this chapter,
we have put aggregate demand under a more powerful microscope and studied the factors that determine
aggregate demand and that make the aggregate demand curve shift. We have discovered that the aggregate demand curve shifts when there is a change in
autonomous expenditure and that the magnitude of
the shift depends on the size of the multiplier. But
whether a change in autonomous expenditure results
ultimately in a change in real GNP or a change in
the price level or some combination of the two depends on the slope of the short-run aggregate supply
curve at the equilibrium point. That is, everything
that we learned in Chapter 24 about the intersection
of the aggregate demand and aggregate supply curve
determining real GNP remains valid. We simply
have a richer understanding of aggregate demand
than we had in Chapter 24.

You can see the importance of aggregate supply
for determining real GNP and the price level by
considering two extreme cases—one in which the
short-run aggregate supply curve is horizontal at the
equilibrium point and the other in which it is vertical. First, suppose that the short-run aggregate supply
curve is horizontal at a price level of 100. This case,
which may be relevant for an economy in deep depression, such as the U.S. economy was in the early
1930s, is illustrated in Fig. 26.10(a). The aggregate
supply curve is SAS_H. A $1 trillion increase in auton-
omous expenditure shifts the aggregate expenditure
curve upward from AE_0 to AE_1. The increase in
autonomous expenditure also shifts the aggregate demand curve from AD_0 to AD_1. Real GNP increases
from $4 trillion to $6 trillion leaving the price level
constant at 100. This case is the same as that illustrated in Fig. 26.9.

Figure 26.10   Changes in Autonomous Expenditure, Aggregate Demand, and the Price Level

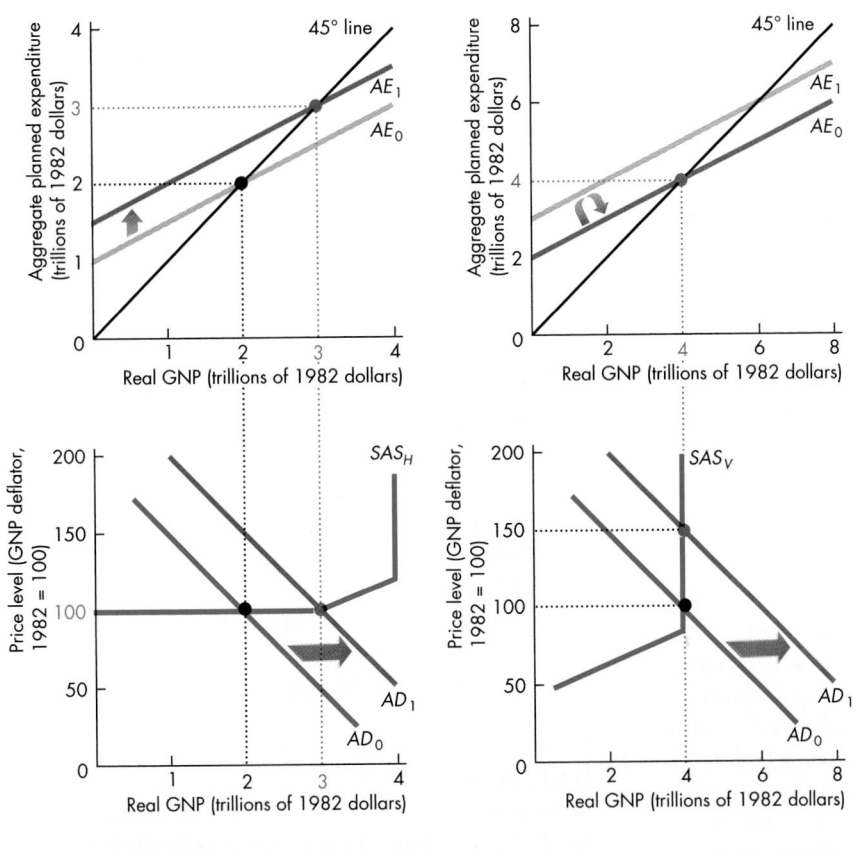

(a) Price level constant   **(b) Price level rises**

An increase in autonomous expenditure shifts the aggregate expenditure curve upward from AE_0 to AE_1 and shifts the aggregate demand curve from AD_0 to AD_1. Whether this increase in autonomous expenditure leads to an increace in real GNP, an increase in the price level, or a combination of the two depends on the slope of the short-run aggregate supply curve at the equilibrium point. If that curve is horizontal, such as SAS_H in part (a), real GNP increases and the price level remains constant. If the short-run aggregate supply curve is vertical, such as SAS_V in part (b), the price level increases and real GNP remains constant. In this case, the increase in the price level leads to a decrease in planned expenditure that shifts the aggregate expenditure curve back to AE_0. In general, the short-run aggregate supply curve is neither horizontal nor vertical but upward sloping. As a consequence, when an increase in autonomous expenditure shifts the aggregate demand curve to AD_1, the price level rises to some extent, and the higher price level causes the AE curve to shift back down toward AE_0 but not by as much as the initial upward shift.

But suppose that $4 trillion is the capacity limit of the economy and that no more output can be produced. The aggregate supply curve is vertical at $4 trillion of real GNP. Suppose also that, initially, AD_0 intersects the short-run aggregate supply curve along its vertical part. This case, which is relevant for the U.S. economy at times of above full-employment, is illustrated in Fig. 26.10(b). The aggregate supply curve is SAS_V. Again, suppose that autonomous expenditure increases by $1 trillion. The increase in autonomous expenditure shifts the aggregate expenditure curve upward to AE_1 and shifts the aggregate demand curve to AD_1. But the shift in the aggregate demand curve increases the price level from 100 to 150 and leaves real GNP unchanged. The higher price level lowers aggregate planned expenditure and shifts the AE curve back to AE_0. The initial change in autonomous expenditure has been offset by a change in the opposite direction that is induced by the higher price level. With no change in autonomous expenditure, there is no change in the aggregate expenditure curve and no change in the equilibrium quantity of goods and services demanded. The AD curve has shifted but there has also been a movement along the new AD curve, the combined effect of which is a higher price level and no change in real GNP.

The two cases that we have examined are the extremes of what is possible. In general, an increase in autonomous expenditure shifts the AE curve upward to AE_1 and shifts the demand curve to AD_1. The short-run aggregate supply curve is upward sloping—neither horizontal nor vertical—so there is an increase in the price level and an increase in real GNP. The higher price level shifts the AE curve downward from AE_1 but not as far as AE_0. The new AE curve intersects the 45° line at the same level of real GNP as that at which the aggregate demand curve AD_1 intersects the short-run aggregate supply curve.

■ We have now studied the forces that influence the components of aggregate expenditure and have analyzed the way the components interact with each other to determine aggregate expenditure and the position of the aggregate demand curve. Fluctuations in the aggregate expenditure curve and in the aggregate demand curve are caused by fluctuations in autonomous expenditure. An important element of autonomous expenditure is investment, which in turn is determined by, among other things, the level of interest rates. But how are interest rates determined? That is the question to which we turn in the next chapter.

S U M M A R Y

Aggregate Expenditure and Real GNP

Aggregate planned expenditure is the sum of planned consumption expenditure, planned investment, planned government purchases of goods and services, and planned net exports. The relationship between aggregate planned expenditure and real GNP can be represented by the aggregate expenditure schedule and the aggregate expenditure curve. Aggregate expenditure is divided into two components: autonomous expenditure and induced expenditure. Autonomous expenditure is that part of consumption expenditure that does not vary as real GNP varies plus investment, government purchases of goods and services, and exports. Induced expenditure is that part of consumption expenditure that varies as real GNP varies minus imports.

The fraction of the last dollar of real GNP spent on domestic goods and services is called the marginal propensity to spend. Equivalently, the marginal propensity to spend is equal to the marginal propensity to consume minus the marginal propensity to import. The marginal propensity to spend determines the slope of the aggregate expenditure curve. (pp. 676–679)

Equilibrium Expenditure

Equilibrium expenditure occurs when aggregate planned expenditure equals real GNP. At real GNP levels above the equilibrium, aggregate planned expenditure is below real GNP and, in such a situation, real GNP falls. At levels of real GNP below the equilibrium, aggregate planned expenditure exceeds real GNP and real GNP rises. Only when real GNP equals aggregate planned expenditure is real GNP constant and in equilibrium. The main influence bringing real GNP and aggregate planned expenditure into equality is the behavior of inventories. When aggregate planned expenditure exceeds real GNP, inventories fall. To restore their inventories, firms increase output and this action increases real GNP. When planned expenditure is below real GNP, inventories accumulate and firms cut back their output. This action lowers the level of real GNP. Only when there are no unplanned inventory changes do firms keep output constant and real GNP remains constant. (pp. 679–681)

Fluctuations in Expenditure and in Real GNP

Equilibrium expenditure is determined by autonomous expenditure and the marginal propensity to spend. Anything that increases autonomous expenditure—an increase in investment, government purchases, or in exports—increases autonomous expenditure and increases equilibrium expenditure. Equilibrium expenditure and real GNP increase by more than the increase in autonomous expenditure. Anything that increases the marginal propensity to spend also increases equilibrium expenditure. The marginal propensity to spend is affected by the marginal propensity to consume, the marginal propensity to import, and the marginal tax rate. An increase in the marginal propensity to consume, a decrease in the marginal propensity to import, or a decrease in the marginal tax rate all increase the marginal propensity to spend. An increase in saving decreases expenditure and results in lower real GNP. This effect is called the paradox of thrift (pp. 681–686)

The Multiplier

The multiplier is the amount by which a change in autonomous expenditure is multiplied to calculate the change in equilibrium expenditure. The size of the multiplier depends on the marginal propensity to spend: The larger the marginal propensity to spend, the larger is the multiplier. The government can take advantage of the multiplier to produce changes in aggregate planned expenditure by changing government purchases or autonomous taxes. Also, in its choice of the marginal tax rate, the government can influence the size of the multiplier. The higher the marginal tax rate, the lower is the marginal propensity to spend out of GNP. The multiplier in the United States fluctuates over the business cycle and has fallen over time. In the late 1980s it was about 1.8. (pp. 686–693)

Aggregate Expenditure and Aggregate Demand

The aggregate demand curve is the relationship between the aggregate quantity of goods and services demanded and the price level. The aggregate expenditure curve is the relationship between aggregate

planned expenditure and real GNP. At a given price level, there is a given level of aggregate planned expenditure and a given aggregate expenditure curve. A change in the price level changes autonomous expenditure and shifts the aggregate expenditure curve. Thus a movement along the aggregate demand curve is associated with a shift in the aggregate expenditure curve.

A change in autonomous expenditure not caused by a change in the price level shifts the aggregate expenditure curve and also shifts the aggregate demand curve. The magnitude of the shift in the aggregate demand curve depends on the size of the multiplier and on the change in autonomous expenditure.

Real GNP and the price level are determined by both aggregate demand and aggregate supply. If, at the equilibrium point, the short-run aggregate supply curve is horizontal, as it might be in a deep business-cycle trough, an increase in autonomous expenditure that shifts the aggregate expenditure and aggregate demand curves increases real GNP, and the price level remains constant. But if, at the equilibrium point, the short-run aggregate supply curve is vertical, as it might be at a business-cycle peak, an increase in autonomous expenditure shifts the aggregate expenditure curve upward and shifts the aggregate demand curve. But the price level rises and real GNP stays constant. The higher price level reduces autonomous expenditure and shifts the aggregate expenditure curve back down to its original position. (pp. 693–698)

K E Y   C O N C E P T S

Key Figures and Table

R E V I E W   Q U E S T I O N S

1 What is the aggregate expenditure function?

2 Distinguish between autonomous expenditure and induced expenditure.

3 Define the marginal propensity to spend.

4 What is the slope of the aggregate expenditure curve?

5 How is equilibrium expenditure determined? What would happen if aggregate planned expenditure exceeded real GNP?

6 What is the multiplier?

7 What is the relationship between the multiplier and the marginal propensity to spend?

8 Why is the multiplier greater than 1?

9 What is the size of the multiplier in the United States today?

10 What is the relationship between the aggregate expenditure curve and the aggregate demand curve?

11 If the price level changes and everything else is held constant, what happens to the aggregate demand curve and the aggregate expenditure curve?

12 If there is a change in autonomous expenditure not produced by a change in the price level, what happens to the aggregate expenditure curve and the aggregate demand curve?

P R O B L E M S

1 You are given the following information about a hypothetical economy: The autonomous part of consumption is $100 billion. The marginal propensity to consume out of disposable income is 0.8. Investment is $460 billion; government purchases of goods and services are $400 billion; taxes are a constant $400 billion and do not vary as income varies.

a) Calculate the equilibrium levels of GNP and consumption.

b) If government expenditure is cut to $300 billion, what is the change in GNP and the change in consumption?

c) What is the size of the multiplier?

2 Suppose that the tax laws are changed and instead of taxes being a constant $400 billion they become one eighth of GNP. Nothing else is changed from the set-up in problem 1.

a) Calculate the equilibrium levels of GNP and consumption.

b) If government expenditure is cut to $300

billion, what is the change in GNP and the change in consumption?

c) What is the size of the multiplier?

3 Suppose that the economy described in problem 1 has an absolute limit to its output of $3200 billion. At that output level its aggregate supply curve is vertical.

a) If the government increases expenditure, what happens to the economy's aggregate demand curve and aggregate expenditure curve?

b) What happens to the price level?

4 You are given three bits of information about the multiplier in an economy: Its average value is 2; in year A it is ½, and in year B it is 3½.

a) Make an educated guess about the state of this economy in year A and year B.

b) Was year A a recovery year or a recession year? Why?

c) Was year B a recovery year or a recession year? Why?

Chapter 27

Money, Banking, and Prices

After studying this chapter, you will be able to:

- Define money and state its functions

- Describe the different forms of money

- Explain how money is measured in the United States today

- Explain what a financial intermediary is

- Describe the balance sheets of the main financial intermediaries

- Explain the economic functions of commercial banks and other financial intermediaries

- Describe some of the important financial innovations of the 1980s

- Explain how banks create money

- Explain why the quantity of money is an important economic magnitude

- Explain the quantity theory of money

- Describe the historical and international evidence on the relationship between the quantity of money and the price level

Money, like fire and the wheel, has been around for a very long time. No one knows for sure how long or what its origins are. An incredible array of items have served as money—wampum (beads made from shells) were used by North American Indians; cowries (brightly colored shells) were used in India; whales' teeth were used in Fiji; tobacco was used by early American colonists; large stone disks were used in the Pacific island of Yap; cigarettes and liquor have been used in more modern times; and even cakes of salt have served as money in Ethiopia, Africa, and Tibet. The Roman army was paid in salt—an allowance called salarium (which is the origin of the word *salary*). What exactly is money?

Money Makes the World Go Around

Why has this rich variety of commodities served as money? ■ Today, when we want to buy something, we can use coins or bills, or we can write a check or present a credit card. Are all these things money? ■ When we deposit some green paper into a bank or savings and loan association (S & L), is that still money? And what happens when the bank or the S & L lends the money in our deposit account to someone else? How can we get our money back if it's been lent out? Does lending by banks and S & Ls create money—out of thin air? ■ The 1980s have seen dramatic changes in the types of accounts that banks and other financial institutions have been offering us. In the 1970s, we either had a savings account or a demand deposit (checking account). The savings account earned interest and the checking account didn't. Today, there is a wide variety of new types of accounts—NOW accounts and ATS accounts being the most prominent ones—that provide us with the convenience of a checking account and the income of a savings account. Why have these new kinds of bank accounts been developed? ■ The biggest transaction that most people ever undertake is the

Store of Value A **store of value** is any commodity that can be held and exchanged later for some other commodity or service. Most physical objects are stores of value. All financial assets, paper securities such as treasury bonds, and bank accounts are also stores of value. Services are not stores of value. Once a service has been performed, that is the end of the matter.

There are no stores of value that are completely safe and predictable. The value of a physical object, such as a house, a car, a work of art as well as the value of a paper security and even of money itself fluctuates over time. The more stable and the more predictable the value of a commodity, the better can it act as a store of value. Thus the higher and the more unpredictable the rate of inflation, the less useful is money as a store of value. It is essential that money be a store of value. Otherwise, it will not be acceptable as a medium of exchange.

The Different Forms of Money

There are four different forms that money can take:

- Commodity money
- Convertible paper money
- Fiat money
- Private debt money

Commodity Money **Commodity money** is a physical commodity valued in its own right and also used as a medium of exchange. An amazing array of items have served as commodity money at different times and places, several of which were described in the chapter opener. But the most common commodity monies have been coins made from metals such as gold, silver, and copper. The first known coins were made in Lydia, a Greek city-state, at the beginning of the seventh century B.C. These coins were made of electrum, a natural mixture of gold and silver. Commodity money has considerable advantages but some drawbacks. Let's look at these.

Advantages of Commodity Money The main advantage of commodity money is that the commodity is valued for its own sake and can be used in ways other than as a medium of exchange. This fact provides a guarantee of the value of the money. For example, gold may be used to fill teeth and make rings; silver

may be used to make tableware; cigarettes may be smoked; beads may be worn. The commodities that are most advantageous as money are the semiprecious metals such as gold and silver. Historically, these commodities were ideal because they were in constant demand by those wealthy enough to use them for ornaments and jewelry. Their quality was easily verified and they were easily divisible into units small enough to facilitate exchange.

Disadvantages of Commodity Money Commodity money has two main disadvantages. First, there is a constant temptation to cheat on the value of the money. Two methods of cheating have been commonly used— clipping and debasement. *Clipping* is reducing the size of coins by an imperceptible amount, thereby lowering their metallic content. *Debasement* is creating a coin having a lower silver or gold content (the balance being made up of some cheaper metal).

This temptation to lower the value of money led to a phenomenon known as Gresham's Law, after the sixteenth-century English financial expert Sir Thomas Gresham. **Gresham's Law** is the tendency for bad money to drive out good money. Bad money is debased money; good money is money that has not been debased. It's easy to see why Gresham's Law works. Suppose that a person is paid with two coins, one debased and the other not. Each coin has the same value if used as money in exchange for goods. But one of the coins—the one that's not debased— is more valuable as a commodity than it is as a coin. It will not, therefore, be used as money. Only the debased coin will be used as money. It is in this way that bad money drives good money out of circulation.

A second major disadvantage of commodity money is that the commodity, valued for its own sake, could be used in ways other than as a medium of exchange if it was not being used as money—the commodity used has an opportunity cost. This cost creates incentives to find alternatives to the commodity itself for use in the exchange process. One such alternative is a paper claim to commodity money.

Convertible Paper Money **Convertible paper money** is a paper claim to a commodity that circulates as a medium of exchange. The first known example of paper money occurred in China during the Ming dynasty (1368–1399 A.D.). This form of money was also used extensively throughout Europe in the Middle Ages.

It was the inventiveness of goldsmiths and their clients that led to the increase and widespread use of convertible paper money. Because gold was valuable, goldsmiths had well-guarded safes in which to keep their own gold. They also rented space to artisans and others who wanted to put their gold in safekeeping. The goldsmiths issued a receipt entitling the owner of the gold to reclaim their "deposit" on demand. These receipts were much like the coat check token that you get at a theater or museum.

Suppose that Isabella has a gold receipt indicating that she has 100 ounces of gold deposited with Samuel Goldsmith. She is going to buy a piece of land valued at 100 ounces of gold from Henry. There are two ways that Isabella might undertake the transaction. The first way is to go to Samuel, hand over her receipt and collect her gold, transport the gold to Henry, and take title to the land. Henry now goes back to Samuel with the gold and deposits it there for safekeeping, leaving with his own receipt. The second way of doing this transaction is for Isabella simply to hand over her gold receipt to Henry, completing the transaction by using the gold receipt as money. Obviously, it is much more convenient to complete the transaction in the second way, provided Henry can trust Samuel. The gold receipt circulating as a medium of exchange is money. The paper money is *backed* by the gold held by Goldsmith. Also the paper money is *convertible* into commodity money.

Fractional Backing Once the convertible paper money system is operating and people are using their gold receipts rather than gold itself as the medium of exchange, goldsmiths notice that their vaults are storing a large amount of gold that is never withdrawn. This gives them a brilliant idea. Why not lend people gold receipts? The goldsmith can charge interest on the loan and the loan is created just by writing on a piece of paper. As long as the number of such receipts created is not too large in relation to the stock of gold in the goldsmith's safe, the goldsmith is in no danger of not being able to honor his promise to convert receipts into gold on demand. By this device, *fractionally backed* convertible paper money was invented.

Between 1879 and 1933, the monetary system of the United States was one based on fractionally backed convertible paper. Until 1933, the U.S. dollar had a guaranteed value in terms of gold and could be converted into gold at a fixed value on demand.

Between 1933 and 1971, it was illegal for U.S. citizens to hold gold coins or ingots but the U.S. Treasury stood ready to convert dollars into gold at $35 per ounce of gold for foreign central banks and foreign governments. In 1971, the gold convertibility of the U.S. dollar was finally abandoned.

Even with fractionally backed paper money, valuable commodities that could be used for other productive activites are tied up in the exchange process. There remains an incentive to find a yet more efficient way of facilitating exchange and of freeing up the commodities used to back the paper money. This alternative is fiat money.

Fiat Money Fiat money is an intrinsically worthless (or almost worthless) commodity that serves the functions of money. The term *fiat* means by government order. Some of the earliest fiat monies were the continental currency issued during the American Revolution and the "greenbacks" issued during the Civil War. Greenbacks circulated until the restoration of the gold standard in 1879. Another early issue of fiat money was that of the so-called *assignats* issued during the French Revolution. These early experiments with fiat money ended in rapid inflation because the amount of fiat money created was allowed to increase at a rapid pace, causing the money to lose value.

However, provided the quantity of fiat money is not allowed to grow too rapidly, it has a reasonably steady value in terms of the goods and services that it will buy. People are willing to accept fiat money in exchange for the goods and services they sell only because they know it will be honored when they go to buy goods and services. The bills and coins that we use in the United States today—collectively known as **currency**—are examples of fiat money. Because of the creation of fiat money, people are willing to accept a piece of paper with a special watermark, printed in green ink, and worth not more than a few cents as a commodity, in exchange for $100 worth of goods and services. The small metal alloy disk that we call a quarter is worth almost nothing as a piece of metal but it pays for a local phone call and many other small commodities. The replacement of commodity money by fiat money enables the commodities themselves to be used productively. But the tokens that we use as fiat money do have an opportunity cost and important decisions have to be made in designing our bills and coins (see Reading Between the Lines on pp. 712–713).

Private Debt Money In the modern world, there is a fourth important type of money—private debt money. **Private debt money** is a loan that the borrower promises to repay in currency on demand. By transferring the entitlement to be repaid from one person to another, such a loan can be used as money. For example, you give me an IOU for $10; I give the IOU to a bookseller to buy a biography of Adam Smith; you pay the holder of the IOU $10— only now it's the bookseller holding the IOU.

The most important example of private debt money is the checkable deposit at commercial banks and other financial institutions. A **checkable deposit** is a loan by a depositor to a bank, the ownership of which can be transferred from one person to another by writing an instruction to the bank —a check—asking the bank to alter its records. We'll have more to say about this type of money shortly. Before doing so, let's look at the different forms of money and their relative importance in the United States today.

Money in the United States Today

There are three official measures of money in current use: **M1, M2,** and **M3.** They are defined in Table 27.2 and the terms used to describe the components of the three measures are set out in the compact glossary in Table 27.3.

Are All the Measures of Money Really Money?

We have defined money as a medium of exchange. The items that make up M1 fit that definition fairly closely. Currency (both coins and dollar bills of various denominations) and traveler's checks are universally acceptable in exchange for goods and services. So also are checkable deposits at banks, credit unions, and thrift institutions. The other items that make up M2 and M3 are not quite so clearly money but they have a high degree of liquidity. **Liquidity** is the degree to which an asset is instantly convertible into a medium of exchange at a known price. Assets vary in their degree of liquidity. Some are not very liquid because some minimum amount of notice has to be given before they can be converted into a medium of exchange. Others lack liquidity because they are traded on markets and their prices fluctuate, making the amount of the medium of exchange into which they can be converted uncertain. But the savings deposits

---

Table 27.2 The Three Official Measures of Money

M1

- Currency held outside banks
- Traveler's checks
- Demand deposits
- Other checkable deposits (OCDs), including NOW accounts and ATS accounts at commercial banks, credit unions, and thrift institutions.

M2

- M1
- Savings deposits
- Small time deposits
- Eurodollar deposits, noninstitutional money market mutual fund shares, and other M2 deposits

M3

- M2
- Large time deposits
- Eurodollar time deposits, institutional money market mutual fund shares, and other M3 deposits

---

M1 consists of currency (pennies, nickels, dimes, and quarters and Federal Reserve bank notes, that is, dollar bills of various denominations); and bank deposits on which a check can be written, including NOW accounts and ATS accounts. The currency component of M1 is only that held outside the banks. Currency held by banks is not part of M1. M2 is M1 plus savings accounts, small time deposits, and other very liquid assets. M3 is M2 plus somewhat less liquid assets such as large time deposits and institutional money market mutual fund shares.

---

and small time deposits that make up M2 and the large time deposits and other accounts that make up M3 are easily converted into a medium of exchange. They are highly liquid—or almost money.

The relative importance of the components of the various measures of money is shown in Fig. 27.1. As you can see, the most important parts of money in the United States are the deposits in banks and

Table 27.3   A Compact Glossary of the Components of Money

Currency	Notes issued by Federal Reserve banks and coins issued by the U.S. Treasury.
	Notes and coins in circulation and held outside the banking system.
Traveler's check	A check issued by a bank and convertible into currency on demand.
Checkable deposit	Any deposit account with a bank or other financial institution on which a check can be written. Checkable deposits include demand deposits, NOW accounts, and ATS accounts.
Demand deposit	A bank deposit that the depositor may convert into currency on demand and without notice. Checks can be written on demand deposit accounts.
NOW account	Negotiable Order of Withdrawal account—a negotiable order of withdrawal is another name for a check. (NOW accounts are not legally checking accounts. When banks were regulated and prevented from paying interest on checking accounts, NOW accounts were invented to get around the regulation.)
ATS account	Automatic-Transfer Savings account—when the balance on an ATS account rises above a pre-agreed amount, the surplus is transferred into a savings account that pays interest. When a check is written on an ATS account that takes its balance below the agreed level, funds are transferred from a savings account.
Savings deposit	A deposit that bears interest and that cannot (technically) be withdrawn on demand. (In practice, competition among banks and other financial institutions make these deposits convertible into currency on demand.)
Time deposit	A deposit with a bank that bears interest and has a fixed term to maturity. Terms may range from several months to several years, and although early withdrawal is possible, it carries a penalty charge.
Small time deposit	A time deposit that is below $100,000.
Large time deposit	A time deposit of $100,000 or more.
Eurodollars	U.S. dollar bank accounts in banks outside the United States but mainly in Western Europe. (Eurodollars were "invented" by the Soviet Union when that country wanted to deposit some proceeds from international trade in U.S. dollars but didn't want to place the funds in the United States). Some Eurodollar deposits are instantly convertible into other medium of exchange assets and are included in M2; others are time deposits and are included in M3.
Mutual fund	A financial intermediary that obtains funds by selling shares and uses the proceeds to buy a portfolio of stocks and bonds.
Money market mutual fund	A financial institution that issues shares redeemable at a fixed price by writing a check.

other financial institutions. Even though there is a remarkably large amount of currency in circulation—about $815 per person—currency is only a quarter of M1. The biggest component of M1 is checkable deposits.

It is important to understand why it is these deposits that are money and not the checks that people write when they make a payment.

Checkable Deposits Are Money but Checks Are Not   The best way to see why checkable deposits are money but checks are not is to consider what happens when someone pays for goods by writing a check. Let's suppose that Barb buys a bike for $200 from Rocky's Mountain Bikes. When Barb goes to Rocky's bike shop she has $500 in her demand deposit account at the Laser Bank. Rocky has $1000

Figure 27.1 The Three Official Measures of Money

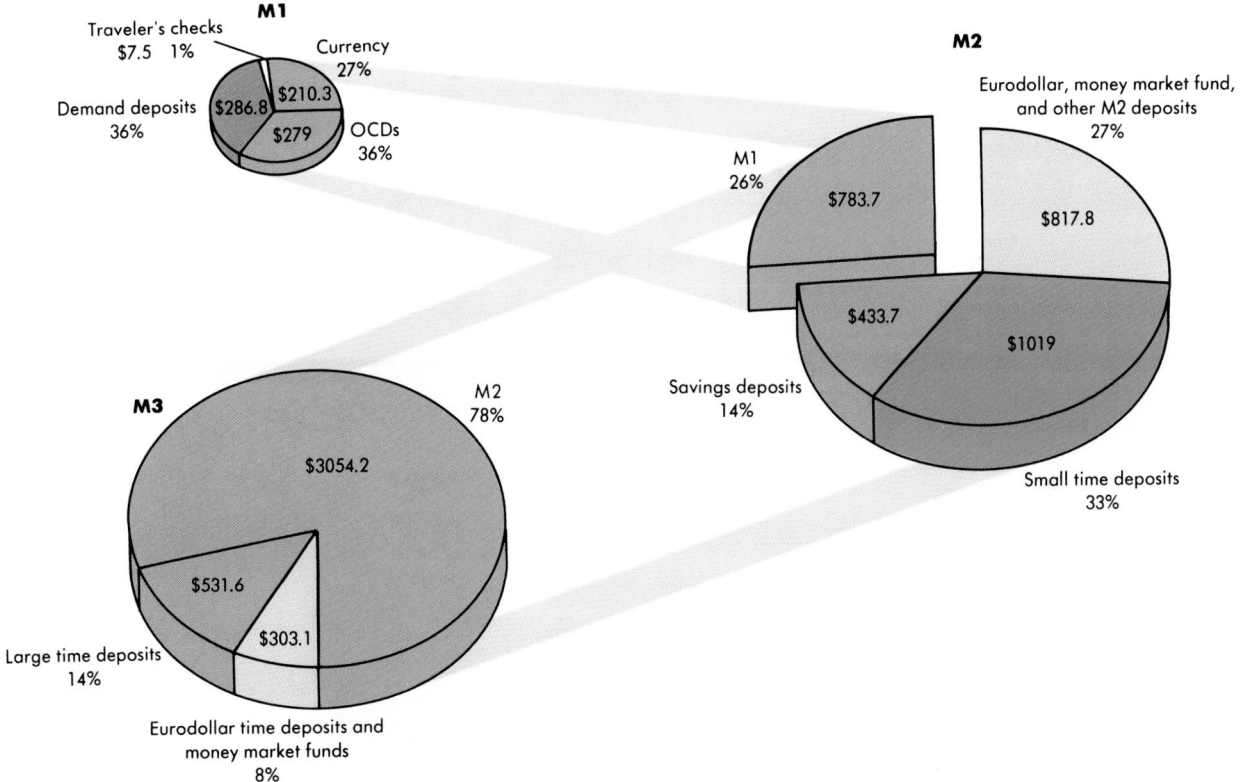

The M1 measure of money consists of all the assets that are a medium of exchange—currency, traveler's checks, demand deposits, and other checkable deposits. M1 makes up about a quarter of the M2 measure of the money supply. M2 consists of M1 plus savings deposits and small time deposits as well as noninstitutional money market fund shares. M2 constitutes nearly 80 percent of M3. M3 consists of M2 plus large time deposits, Eurodollar time deposits, and institutional money market mutual fund shares.

Source: Economic Report of the President, 1989.

in his demand deposit—at the same bank, as it happens. The total demand deposits of these two people is $1500. On June 11, Barb writes a check for $200. Rocky takes the check to Laser Bank right away and deposits it. Rocky's bank balance rises from $1000 to $1200. But the bank not only credits Rocky's account with $200, it also debits Barb's account $200 so that her balance falls from $500 to $300. The total demand deposits of Barb and Rocky are still the same as before, $1500. Rocky now has $200 more and Barb $200 less than before. These transactions are summarized in Table 27.4.

This transaction has not changed the quantity of money in existence. It has simply transferred money from one person to another. The check itself was never money. That is, there wasn't an extra $200 worth of money while the check was in circulation. The check simply served as a written instruction to the bank to transfer the money from Barb to Rocky.

In our example, Barb and Rocky use the same bank. Essentially, the same story, though with additional steps, describes what happens if Barb and Rocky use different banks. Rocky's bank will credit the check to Rocky's account and then take the check

Table 27.4   Paying by Check

LASER BANK

137 Dakota Street ● Andover, MA 01810 ● (508)555-3973

Date	Item	Debit	Credit	Balance
June 1	Opening balance			$500.00 (CR)*
June 11	Rocky's Mountain Bikes	$200.00		$300.00 (CR)

Barb's demand deposit account

LASER BANK

137 Dakota Street ● Andover, MA 01810 ● (508)555-3973

Date	Item	Debit	Credit	Balance
June 1	Opening balance			$1000.00 (CR)
June 11	Barb buys bike		$200.00	$1200.00 (CR)

Rocky Mountain Bikes demand deposit account

*CR means "credit": The bank owes the depositor.

to a check-clearing center. Barb's bank will pay Rocky's bank $200 and then debit Barb's account $200. This process can take a few days but the principles are the same as when two people use the same bank.

So, checks are not money. But what about credit cards? Isn't having a credit card in your wallet and presenting the card to pay for a bike the same thing as using money? Why aren't credit cards somehow valued and counted as part of the quantity of money?

Credit Cards Are Not Money   When you pay by check you are frequently asked to prove your identity by showing your driver's license. It would never occur to you to think of your driver's license as money. Your driver's license is just an ID.

A credit card is also an ID card but one that enables you to borrow money at the instant a purchase is made on the promise of repaying later. When you make a purchase, you sign a credit card sales slip that creates a debt in your name. You are saying: "I agree to pay for these goods when the credit card company bills me." Once you get your statement from the credit card company, you have to make the minimum payment due. To make that payment you need money—you need to have funds in your checkable deposit so that you can write a check to pay the credit card company.

R E V I E W

Money has four functions: medium of exchange, unit of account, standard of deferred payment, and a store of value. Any durable commodity can serve as money, but modern societies use fiat money and private debt money rather than commodity money. The most important component of money in the United States today is checkable deposits at banks and other financial institutions. Neither checks nor credit cards are money. A check is an instruction to a bank to transfer money from one account to another. Money is the balance in the account itself. A credit card is an ID card that enables a person to borrow at the instant a purchase is made on the promise of repaying later. When repayment is made, money (currency or a checkable deposit) is used for the payment. ■

We've seen that the most important component of money in the United States is deposits at banks and other financial institutions. Let's take a look at the banking and financial system a bit more closely.

Financial Intermediaries

We are going to study the banking and financial system of the United States by first describing the variety of financial intermediaries that operate in the United States today. Then we'll examine the operations of banks and of other financial institutions. After describing the main features of financial intermediaries, we'll examine their economic functions, describing what they produce and how they make a profit. Finally, we'll explain how money gets created.

A **financial intermediary** is a firm that takes deposits from households and firms and makes loans to other households and firms. There are five types of financial intermediaries whose deposits are components of the nation's money:

- Commercial banks
- Savings and loan associations
- Savings banks
- Credit unions
- Money market mutual funds

A compact glossary on these financial intermediaries and an indication of their relative importance is given in Table 27.5.

Let's begin by examining commercial banks.

Table 27.5   A Compact Glossary of Financial Intermediaries

Financial intermediary (approximate number)	Total assets (billions of dollars)	Main functions
Commercial banks (15,000)	2928	A private firm chartered by either the Comptroller of the Currency (of the U.S. Treasury) or a state agency to receive deposits and make loans.
Savings and loan associations (3,000)	960	Financial institutions that receive savings deposits (sometimes called shares) and checkable deposits and use the funds to make mortgage loans.
Savings banks (800)	269	Similar to savings and loan associations. They accept deposits and make mortgage loans.
Credit unions (17,000)	172	Small cooperative lending institutions often organized in a place of work or by a labor union. They take deposits and make consumer loans.
Money market mutual funds	831	Financial intermediaries that obtain funds by selling shares and using the proceeds to buy a portfolio of stocks. Shareholders can write checks against the value of their money market mutual fund shares.

Sources: Federal Reserve Bulletin (February 1989), pp. A10, A26, and A27; Economic Report of the President (1989), p. 386.

Economical Money

Loose Change

A dollar bill buys hardly more than a quarter did two decades ago. Yet while other nations have adapted their currencies to the reality of inflation (see table), Americans cling to their devalued money, pulling out wads of notes for virtually all purchases larger than a newspaper. America's dearest commonly used coin, the quarter, is worth one seventh of Britain's, the pound; the dollar bill is worth barely one-ninth of a "fiver", now Britain's smallest-denomination note.

Two congressmen from Arizona, Mr. Morris Udall and Mr. Jim Kolbe, have re-introduced legislation calling for yet another attempt to introduce a dollar coin and to phase out the production of one-dollar bills. A similar proposal in 1987 got nowhere. Despite periodic attempts since the first silver dollar was introduced in 1794, the dollar coin has never captured the public's imagination. The Treasury's most recent effort was the Susan B. Anthony dollar (featuring that famous suffragette), which was introduced in 1979 and almost immediately dropped out of circulation. People complained that its size and shape made it too easy to confuse with a quarter. At last count there were 456m Anthony dollars stored in mints and Federal Reserve banks across the country.

In Britain, by contrast, the government's introduction in 1983 of the pound coin to replace the pound note succeeded despite similar grumbling about the new coin's similarity to a 5p piece.

The Arizonans have an ulterior motive. They want the next dollar coin to be made of American-mined copper, three-fifths of which comes from Arizona. Dollar-coin advocates claim the Treasury would save $125m a year because coins, although more expensive to produce, last for decades whereas paper money wears out after a couple of years. Businesses that use coin machines to sell items such as food and tickets are also enthusiastic. As ever-fewer things cost less than a dollar, they are driven to installing bill changers at $2,400 each.

Even the blind would benefit. "The visually handicapped would be able to make small purchases without fear of accidentally parting with a large bill or of being cheated when receiving change," says Mr James Benfield, an energetic Washington lobbyist who has made the dollar coin his personal crusade. The blind, and the merely careless, are inconvenienced by the fact that American notes of different values are all the same size and colour—a defect no one is proposing to remedy.

Defenders of America's existing coins point out that at least their bulk is as modest as their value, so does not tear holes in pockets. Some of Britain's least valuable coins are as unwieldy as electric plugs. In fact, the correlation between weight and worth is poor in both countries.

Tossed salad:
Currencies great and small

	Highest coin ($ value)	Lowest note ($ value)
Australia	A$2 ($1.76)	A$5 ($4.40)
Britain	£1 ($1.77)	£5 ($8.85)
Canada*	C$1 ($0.85)	C$1 ($0.85)
West Germany	DM5 ($2.70)	DM10 ($5.41)
Japan	¥500 ($3.92)	¥1,000 ($7.80)
Sweden	Skr5 ($0.82)	Skr10 ($1.60)
United States**	quarter ($0.25)	$1 ($1.00)
Venezuela	5 bolivar ($0.13)	10 bolivar ($0.26)

*Canada ceased production of dollar notes in June 1989.
**The American mint still produces the 50-cent coin, although in small numbers. In fiscal 1988, for example, the mint produced 20m half-dollars, compared to 843m quarters.

	United States			Britain		
	25¢	10¢	5¢	£1.00	50p	20p
Size and weight Size—square centimetre*	4.62	2.52	3.53	3.98	7.07	3.60
Value per square centimetre (Cents)	5.41	3.97	1.42	44.48	12.51	9.84
Weight—grammes*	5.67	2.27	5.00	9.50	13.50	5.00
Value per gramme (Cents)	4.41	4.41	1.00	18.64	6.55	7.08

*Approximate
Sources: U.S. Treasury; Royal Mint.

The Essence of the Story

- A one-dollar bill buys about the same quantity of goods and services that a quarter did 20 years ago.

- Congressmen Udall and Kolbe want to replace the one-dollar bill with a one-dollar coin.

- The first one-dollar coin was introduced in 1794.

- The most recent one-dollar coin is the Susan B. Anthony dollar, introduced in 1979.

- People prefer the one-dollar bill and most of the one-dollar coins do not circulate as currency.

- In Britain, the one-pound note was replaced by a one-pound coin, but the move was unpopular.

- It is claimed by advocates of the one-dollar coin that it has the following advantages over the one-dollar bill: it lasts longer; it is easier to use in coin machines (bill-changing machines are expensive); it is easier for the blind to use.

- Existing U.S. coins are small and easier to use than those of some other countries—notably Britain.

Background and Analysis

- To buy goods and services that cost $1 in 1989, the following amounts were needed in earlier years:

1979	59¢
1969	30¢
1959	24¢
1949	19¢

- Coins are more expensive than notes to manufacture. If it is to be economical to use coins, their life has to be much longer than the life of a bill.

- The life of a bill is highly correlated with the frequency with which it changes hands.

- Bills that spend most of their lives in a wallet last a long time.

- Bills that change hands many times a day have a very short life.

- The smaller the denomination of a bill or coin, the more frequently it changes hands because it is used as change.

- One-dollar bills change hands with high frequency and have a life of less than a year.

- If it was economical to use a coin rather than a bill for a 25¢ transaction in 1959, then it is efficient to use a coin for a $1 transaction today.

- Many countries have adopted a coin even for denominations larger than $1 (see first table).

- U.S. coins are among the smallest and most convenient to use in the world (see comparison with British coins).

- Opponents of a $1 coin emphasize the inconvenience of carrying a larger number of coins that are heavier and bigger than a quarter.

- One solution, not discussed in the article is to withdraw the penny from circulation and introduce a dollar coin the size of a penny but perhaps gold-like or silver-like in appearance.

- Eliminating the penny makes sense for the same reasons that eliminating the one-dollar bill does.

- To buy the goods and services that cost a penny in 1989, a coin worth one quarter of a penny would have been needed in 1959. We managed without such a coin in 1959 and so, presumably, we can manage without a penny today.

- The savings from eliminating pennies would likely pay for the dollar coin.

Conclusion

Fiat money is more efficient than commodity money, but the design of the tokens that we use in our fiat money system has an important influence on the costs, benefits, and convenience of that system.

Commercial Banks

A **commercial bank** is a private firm, chartered by either the Comptroller of the Currency (in the U.S. Treasury) or by a state agency to receive deposits and make loans. There are close to 15,000 commercial banks in the United States today. The scale and scope of the operations of commerical banks can be seen by examining the balance sheet of the commercial banking sector.

A **balance sheet** is a statement that lists a firm's assets and liabilities. **Assets** are the things of value that a firm owns. **Liabilities** are the things that a firm owes to households and other firms. Such a balance sheet—that for all commercial banks in November 1988—is set out in Table 27.6. The left side (the assets) lists the items *owned* by the banks. The right side (the liabilities) lists the items that the banks *owe* to others. Let's start on the liabilities side.

Total liabilities in November 1988 were $3012 billion. These liabilities are divided roughly equally among four types of deposits. Your deposit at a bank is an asset to you but a liability for your bank. The bank has to repay you your deposit (and sometimes interest on it too) whenever you decide to take your money out of the bank.

You have met three of the banks' liabilities before in the various definitions of money: They are demand deposits, savings deposits, and time deposits. The other liabilities consist of borrowing by the banks in what is sometimes called **wholesale deposit markets**—markets for deposits among banks and other financial institutions.

Why does a bank obligate itself to pay you your money back with interest? Because it wants to use your deposit to make a profit for itself. The asset side of the balance sheet tells us what the banks did with their $3012 billion worth of borrowed resources in November 1988.

First, the banks kept some of their assets in the form of deposits at Federal Reserve banks and as cash in their vaults. (We'll study the Federal Reserve banks in Chapter 28.) The cash in a bank's vault plus its deposits at Federal Reserve banks are called its **reserves.** You can think of a commercial bank's deposit at the Federal Reserve as being similar to your deposit at your own bank. Commercial banks use these deposits in the same way that you use your bank account. A commercial bank deposits cash into or draws cash out of its account at the Federal Reserve and writes checks on that account to settle debts with other banks.

Table 27.6   The Balance Sheet of All Commercial Banks, November 1988

Assets (billions of dollars)			Liabilities (billions of dollars)	
Reserve assets			Demand deposits	627.2
Reserves with Federal Reserve banks	33.7		Savings deposits	542.2
Vault cash	28.7		Time deposits	951.2
Total reserves		62.4	Other liabilities	891.4
Liquid assets		172.7		
Investment securities		554.4		
Loans		2021.1		
Other assets		201.4		
Total		3012.0	Total	3012.0

Source: *Federal Reserve Bulletin* (March 1989).

If the banks kept all their assets in the form of deposits at the Federal Reserve and cash in their vaults, they wouldn't make any profit. But if they didn't keep *some* of their assets as cash in their vaults and as deposits at the Federal Reserve, they wouldn't be able to meet the demands for cash that their customers place on them. Nor would they be able to keep that automatic teller machine replenished every time you, your friends, and all their other customers have raided it for cash for a midnight pizza.

The bulk of a bank's borrowed resources are put to work by making loans. Some of these loans are instantly convertible into cash and with virtually no risk. These are called liquid assets. **Liquid assets**, which take their name from the concept of liquidity, are those assets that are instantly convertible into a medium of exchange with virtually no uncertainty about the price at which they can be converted. An example of a liquid asset is a U.S. government treasury bond that can be sold at a moment's notice for an almost guaranteed price.

The banks' assets also include investment securities. An **investment security** is a marketable security that a bank can sell at a moment's notice if necessary but at a price that fluctuates. An example of an investment security is a U.S. government long-term bond. Such bonds can be sold instantly but their prices fluctuate on the bond market. Banks earn a higher interest rate on their investment securities than they do on liquid assets, but they involve higher risk.

Most of the banks' assets are the loans that they have made. A **loan** is a commitment of a fixed amount of money for an agreed period of time. Most of the loans made by banks are used by corporations to finance the purchase of capital equipment and inventories. But banks also make loans to households —personal loans. Such loans are used to buy consumer durable goods such as cars or boats. The outstanding balances on credit card accounts are also bank loans.

Banks make a profit by earning interest on loans, investment securities, and liquid assets in excess of the interest paid on deposits and other liabilities. Also, banks receive revenue by charging fees for managing accounts.

Money is made up of the various liabilities of the banks. Demand deposits are an important component of the M1 measure of money—accounting for 37 percent of M1 in 1988. Demand deposits, savings deposits, and small time deposits are an important

part of the M2 measure of money. The commercial banks' total liabilities are an important component of M3. But the deposit liabilities of banks are not the only components of the nation's money. Other financial institutions also take deposits that form part— and an increasing part—of the nation's money. Let's now examine those financial institutions.

Other Financial Intermediaries

Until 1980, there was a reasonably sharp distinction between commercial banks and other deposit-taking financial institutions. But in 1980, Congress passed the Depository Institutions' Deregulation and Monetary Control Act, which made the distinctions much less clear. First, the deregulation permitted the setting up of NOW accounts and ATS accounts at all deposit-taking institutions—banks and nonbanks. At the same time, nonbank financial intermediaries were permitted to compete with commercial banks in a wider range of lending business. Another important regulatory change occurred at the beginning of the 1980s—the abolition of regulation Q. *Regulation Q* placed a ceiling on the interest rates that financial institutions could offer on deposits. With the abolition of regulation Q, a fiercely competitive environment was created in which a new group of financial instruments emerged—money market mutual funds.

The first money market mutual fund was set up in 1971 by Bruce Bent and Henry Brown, two Wall Street entrepreneurs. But low interest rates through the 1970s prevented their invention from taking off. In the 1980s, however, money market mutual funds experienced spectacular growth.

Deregulation and the development of new types of deposit accounts have led to some important changes in the composition of the nation's money. In 1960, M1 consisted of only currency and demand deposits. In the 1980s, other checkable deposits expanded while demand deposits declined. Similar dramatic changes took place in the composition of M2. Savings deposits declined while time deposits, noninstitutional money market mutual fund shares and Eurodollar deposits expanded quickly. There have been less dramatic but important changes involving M3. In 1960, M2 and M3 were almost the same concept, but the growth of large time deposits and other types of time deposits included in M3 has gradually expanded.

The Economic Functions of Financial Intermediaries

All financial intermediaries make a profit from a spread between the interest rate they pay on deposits and the interest rate at which they lend. Why can financial intermediaries borrow at a low interest rate and lend at a higher one? What services do they perform that makes their depositors willing to put up with a low interest rate and their borrowers willing to pay a higher one?

Financial intermediaries provide four main services:

- Minimizing the cost of obtaining funds
- Minimizing the cost of monitoring borrowers
- Pooling risk
- Creating liquidity

Minimizing the Cost of Obtaining Funds   Finding someone from whom to borrow can be a costly business. Imagine how troublesome it would be if there were no financial intermediaries. A firm that was looking for $1 million to buy a new production plant would probably have to hunt around for several dozen people from whom to borrow in order to acquire enough funds for its capital project. Financial intermediaries lower those costs. The firm needing $1 million can go to a single financial institution to obtain those funds. The financial institution has to borrow from a large number of people but it's not doing that just for this one firm and the million dollars it wants to borrow. The financial institution can establish an organization that spreads the cost of raising money from a large number of depositors.

Minimizing the Cost of Monitoring Borrowers
Lending money is a risky business. There's always a danger that the borrower may not repay. Most of the money lent gets used by firms to invest in projects that they hope will return a profit. But sometimes those hopes are not fulfilled. Checking up on the activities of a borrower and ensuring that the best possible decisions are being made for making a profit and avoiding a loss is a costly and specialized activity. Imagine how costly it would be if each and every household that lent money to a firm had to incur the costs of monitoring that firm directly. By depositing funds with a financial intermediary, households avoid those costs. The financial intermediary performs the monitoring activity by using specialized resources that have a much lower cost than what each household would incur if it had to undertake the activity individually.

Pooling Risk   As we noted above, lending money is risky. There is always a chance of not being repaid—of default. The risk of default can be reduced by lending to a large number of different individuals. In such a situation, if one person defaults on a loan, it is a nuisance but not a disaster. In contrast, if only one person borrows and that person defaults on the loan, the entire loan is a write-off. Financial intermediaries enable people to pool risk in an efficient way. Thousands of people lend money to any one financial intermediary and, in turn, the financial institution re-lends the money to hundreds, and perhaps thousands, of individual firms. If any one firm defaults on its loan, that default is spread across all the depositors with the intermediary and no individual depositor is left exposed to a high degree of risk.

Creating Liquidity   Financial intermediaries create liquidity. We defined liquidity earlier as the ease and certainty with which an asset can be converted into a medium of exchange. The liabilities of some financial intermediaries are themselves a medium of exchange. Others are easily convertible into a medium of exchange and so are highly liquid.

Financial intermediaries create liquidity by borrowing short and lending long. Borrowing short means taking deposits but standing ready to repay them on short notice (and on even no notice in the case of demand deposits). Lending long means making loan commitments for a prearranged, and often quite long, period of time. For example, when a person makes a deposit with a savings and loan association, that deposit can be withdrawn on seven days' notice. The S & L, however, makes a lending commitment for perhaps 20 years to someone buying a new house.

Financial Innovation

In their pursuit of a profit, financial intermediaries are constantly seeking better ways of delivering their product—of lowering the cost of obtaining funds and monitoring borrowers, of pooling risk, and of creating liquidity. They also are inventive in seeking ways of avoiding the costs imposed on them by financial regulation. The development of new financial products and methods of borrowing and lending is called **financial innovation**.

The pace of financial innovation has been remarkable in the 1980s. Some of the innovation has been aimed at reducing risk. An important example is the development of variable interest rate mortgages. Traditionally, house purchases have been financed on mortgage loans at a guaranteed interest rate. Rising interest rates brought rising borrowing costs for savings and loan assocations, and since they were committed to fixed interest rates on their mortgages, the industry incurred severe losses. The creation of variable interest rate mortgages takes some of the risk out of long-term lending for house purchases.

Other financial innovations resulted from technological change, most notably that associated with the increased use of computers and the decreased cost of long-distance communication. The spread in the use of credit cards and the development of international financial markets—for example, the increased importance of Eurodollars—are consequences of technological changes.

A good deal of financial innovation takes place to avoid regulation. The development of NOW accounts and ATS accounts, as well as the introduction of money market mutual funds are in this category. Regulation Q, which prevented banks from paying interest on checking accounts, gave the impetus to devising these new types of deposit accounts, thereby getting around the regulation.

R E V I E W

Most of the nation's money is made up of deposits in financial intermediaries. Those financial intermediaries are commercial banks, savings and loan associations, savings banks, credit unions, and money market mutual funds. In the 1980s, financial deregulation blurred the distinction between bank deposits and deposits at other financial institutions and a whole range of new types of deposit accounts was created.

The main economic functions of financial intermediaries are minimizing the cost of obtaining funds, minimizing the cost of monitoring borrowers, pooling risk, and creating liquidity. Financial intermediaries are constantly seeking new ways of making a profit and of avoiding the adverse effects of regulations on their activities. ∎

Because financial intermediaries are able to create liquidity and to create assets that are a medium of exchange—money—they occupy a unique place in our economy and exert an important influence on the quantity of money in existence. Let's see how money gets created.

How Banks Create Money

Money is created by the activities of commerical banks and other financial institutions—by all those institutions whose deposits circulate as a medium of exchange. In this section, we'll use the term "banks" to refer to all these depository institutions.

As we saw in Table 27.6, banks don't have $100 in bills for every $100 that people have deposited with them. In fact, a typical bank today has less than $1 in currency and another $1.50 on deposit at a Federal Reserve bank for every $100 deposited in it. No need for panic. Banks have learned, from experience, that these reserve levels are adequate for ordinary business needs. The fraction of a bank's total deposits that are held in reserves is called the **reserve ratio**. The value of the reserve ratio is influenced by the actions of a bank's depositors. If a depositor withdraws currency from a bank, the reserve ratio falls. If a depositor puts currency into a bank, the reserve ratio increases.

All banks have a *desired* reserve ratio. The **desired reserve ratio** is the ratio of reserves to deposits that banks regard as necessary in order to be able to conduct their business. The desired reserve ratio is determined partly by regulation (discussed in Chapter 28) and partly by what the banks regard as the minimum safety level for their reserve holdings. The difference between actual reserves and desired reserves are **excess reserves**.

Whenever banks have excess reserves, they are able to create money. When we say that banks create money, we don't mean that they have smoke-filled back rooms in which counterfeiters are busily working. Remember, most money is deposits, not currency. What they create is deposits and they do so by making loans. To see how banks create money we are going to look at a model of the banking system.

Let's suppose that the banks have a desired reserve ratio of 25 percent. That is, for each dollar deposited, they want to keep 25¢ in the form of reserves. Al, a customer of the Golden Nugget Bank, decides to reduce his holdings of currency and put $100 in his deposit account at the bank. Suddenly, the Golden Nugget Bank has $100 of new deposits and $100 of additional reserves. But with $100 of new deposits the Golden Nugget Bank doesn't want to hold onto $100 of additional reserves. It has excess reserves. Its desired reserve ratio is 25 percent so it plans to lend $75 of the additional $100 to another customer. Amy, a customer at the same bank, borrows $75. At this point, the Golden Nugget Bank has new deposits of $100, new loans of $75, and new reserves of $25. As far as Golden Nugget is concerned, that is the end of the matter. No money has been created. Al has reduced his holdings of currency by $100 and increased his bank deposit by $100, but the total amount of money has remained constant. Although that's the end of the story for the Golden Nugget Bank, it is not the end of the story for the entire banking system. What happens next?

Amy uses the $75 loan to buy a jacket from Barb. To undertake this transaction, she writes a check on her account with the Golden Nugget and Barb deposits the check in the Laser Bank. The Laser

Bank now has new deposits of $75 and an additional $75 of reserves. The total amount of money supply is now $75 higher than before.

The Laser Bank doesn't need to hang on to the entire $75 that it has just received in reserves: It needs only a quarter of that amount—$18.75. The Laser Bank lends the additional amount, $56.25, to Bob who buys some used stereo equipment from Carl. Bob writes a check on his account at the Laser Bank, which Carl deposits in his account at the Apollo Bank. The Apollo Bank now has new deposits of $56.25, so the amount of money has increased by a total of $131.25 (the $75 lent to Amy and paid to Barb plus the $56.25 lent to Bob and paid to Carl).

The transactions that we've just described are summarized in Table 27.7. But the story is still incomplete. The process that we're describing continues through the remaining banks and their depositors and borrowers, all the way down the list in that table. By the time we get down to the Pirates Bank, Ken has paid Len $5.63 for a box of computer discs and so the Pirates Bank has new deposits of $5.63 and

Table 27.7   Creating Money by Making Loans: Many Banks

Bank	Depositor	Borrower	New deposits	New loans	New reserves	Increase in money	Cumulative increase in money
Golden Nugget	Al	Amy	$100.00	$ 75.00	$ 25.00	$ 0.00	
Laser	Barb	Bob	75.00	56.25	18.75	75.00	$ 75.00
Apollo	Carl	Con	56.25	42.19	14.06	56.25	131.25
Monty Python	Di	Dan	42.19	31.64	10.55	42.19	173.44
Plato	Ed	Eve	31.64	23.73	7.91	31.64	205.08
J.R. Ewing	Fran	Fred	23.73	17.80	5.93	23.73	228.81
Ist Madonna	Gus	Gail	17.80	13.35	4.45	17.80	246.61
Rambo	Holly	Hal	13.35	10.01	3.34	13.35	259.96
Trump	Jim	Jan	10.01	7.51	2.50	10.01	269.97
Disney	Kym	Ken	7.51	5.63	1.88	7.51	277.48
Pirates	Len	Lee	5.63	4.22	1.41	5.63	283.11
			.	.	.	.	.
All others			16.89	12.67	4.22	16.89	
Total banking system			$400.00	$300.00	$100.00	$300.00	$300.00

additional reserves of that same amount. Since it needs only $1.41 of additional reserves, it makes a loan of $4.22 to Lee, who in turn spends the money. By this time, the total amount of money has increased by $283.11, the new deposits at each stage of the process listed in the first column of numbers in the table.

This process continues but with amounts that are now getting so tiny that we will not bother to keep track of them. All the remaining stages in the process taken together add up to the numbers in the second to last row of the table. The final tallies appear as the totals at the bottom of the table. Deposits have increased by $400, loans by $300, and reserves by $100. The banks have created money by making loans. The quantity of money created is $300—the same amount as the additional loans made. It's true that deposits have increased by $400, but $100 of that increase is Al's original deposit. That increase in deposits does not increase the quantity of money. The currency that Al deposited was already money. It is only the new deposits created by the lending activity of the banks that has increased the quantity of money in existence.

The ability of banks to create money does not mean that they can create an indefinite amount of money. The amount that they can create depends on the size of their reserves and on the desired reserve ratio. In this example where the desired reserve ratio is 25 percent, bank deposits have increased by four times the level of reserves. There's an important relationship between the change in reserves and the change in deposits.

The Simple Money Multiplier   The **simple money multiplier** is the amount by which an increase in bank reserves is multiplied to calculate the effect of the increase in reserves on total bank deposits. The simple money multiplier is given by:

$$\text{Simple money multiplier} = \frac{\text{Change in deposits}}{\text{Change in reserves}}.$$

In the example that we've just worked through, the simple money multiplier is 4—a $100 increase in reserves created the $400 increase in deposits.

The simple money multiplier is related to the desired reserve ratio. In our example, that ratio is 25 percent (or ¼). That is,

$$\text{Desired reserves} = (¼) \text{ Deposits}.$$

Whenever desired reserves exceed actual reserves (a

situation of negative excess reserves), the banks call in loans. When desired reserves are below actual reserves (a situation of positive excess reserves), the banks make additional loans. By adjusting their loans, the banks bring their actual reserves into line with their desired reserves, eliminating excess reserves. Thus when banks have changed their loans and reserves to make actual reserves equal desired reserves,

$$\text{Actual reserves} = (¼) \text{ Deposits}.$$

If we divide both sides of this equation by ¼, we obtain

$$\text{Deposits} = 1/(¼) \text{ Actual reserves}.$$

If there is a change in reserves when desired reserves and actual reserves are equal, bank deposits change in order to satisfy the above equation. That is,

$$\text{Change in deposits} = 1/(¼) \text{ Change in reserves}$$

But $1/(¼)$ is the simple money multiplier. It is the amount by which the change in reserves is multiplied to calculate the change in deposits. In our example, this multiplier equals 4. The relationship between the simple money multiplier and the desired reserve ratio is

$$\text{Simple money multiplier} = \frac{1}{\text{Desired reserve ratio}}.$$

Real World Money Multipliers

The money multiplier in the real world differs from the simple money multiplier that we have just calculated for two reasons. First, the desired reserve ratio of real world banks is much smaller than the 25 percent that we have used here. Second, in the real world, not all the loans made by banks return to the banks in the form of reserves. Some of them remain outside the banks in the form of currency in circulation. This tendency for some of the loans to leave the banking system is called the **currency drain.** These two differences between the real world money multiplier and the simple money multiplier that we have just calculated work in opposing directions to each other. The smaller desired reserve ratio of real world banks makes the real world multiplier larger than the above numerical example. The currency drain makes the real world multiplier smaller. We study the actual values of real world money multipliers in the next chapter.

Bank Panic and Failure

Because banks lend most of their customers' deposits, they could not pay out all their depositors on demand if they were required to do so. If one bank finds itself short of reserves, it can easily remedy the situation by borrowing from another bank. But suppose that the whole banking system is short of reserves. In such a situation, the banks are not able to pay their depositors' demands. Depositors, in turn, will become nervous about the security of their bank deposits and so will try to get even more of their money out of the bank. When the amount of currency the depositors are trying to withdraw from banks exceeds the amount that the banks have, there is a banking panic and banks fail.

The last time widespread bank panic and failure occurred in the United States was during the Great Depression in the 1930s. But before that, bank panic and failure had been routine at roughly 10-year intervals. A particularly serious and severe bank panic and failure occurred in 1907.

Panic and failure do not only affect banks. They also affect other financial institutions that lend out most of what is deposited with them and keep only small reserves of currency. In recent years, savings and loan associations have been under severe strain in this regard.

One important invention that reduces the likelihood of a failure of the financial system is deposit insurance. Bank deposits are insured by the Federal Deposit Insurance Corporation (FDIC). Deposits at savings and loan associations are insured by the Federal Savings and Loan Insurance Corporation (FSLIC). Because deposits are insured, even if depositors believe that banks and S & Ls might fail, the danger of personal loss is reduced and so a herd-like move to withdraw currency from the banks and the financial institutions is much less likely to occur.

But the most important source of stability and security for our financial system arises from the existence of the Federal Reserve System, an institution that monitors and regulates the banking and financial industry and seeks to maintain relatively stable and predictable conditions in markets for money and financial assets. We study this aspect of the financial system in Chapter 28.

Our next task in this chapter is to examine the effects of money on the economy and, in particular, the relationship between the quantity of money and the price level.

Money and the Price Level

We now know what money *is*. We also know that in a modern economy such as that of the United States today, most of the money is made up of deposits at banks and other financial institutions. We've seen that these institutions can actually create money—by making loans. Does the quantity of money created by the banking and financial system matter? What effects does it have? Does it matter whether the quantity increases quickly or slowly?

We're going to address these questions first by refreshing our understanding of the aggregate demand–aggregate supply model and recalling the role played by money in influencing real GNP and the price level. Then we're going to consider a special theory of money and prices—the quantity theory of money. Finally, we'll look at some historical and international evidence on the relationship between money and prices.

Money in the AD–AS Model

In Chapter 24, we developed a model of aggregate demand and aggregate supply in which money plays an important role in influencing the aggregate demand curve. Figure 27.2 illustrates the model. The long-run aggregate supply curve is *LAS*. Initially, the aggregate demand curve is AD_0 and the short-run aggregate supply curve is SAS_0. Equilibrium occurs where the aggregate demand curve AD_0 intersects the short-run aggregate supply curve SAS_0. The price level is 120 and real GNP is $4.5 trillion. The economy is also on its long-run aggregate supply curve and is in full-employment equilibrium.

Now suppose that there is an increase in the quantity of money. For the reasons discussed in Chapter 24 (see pp. 618–619), this increase in the quantity of money results in an increase in aggregate demand. The aggregate demand curve shifts to the right to become AD_1. The new equilibrium is at the intersection point of AD_1 and SAS_0. The price level rises to 132 and real GNP increases to $5 trillion. But this is the short-run effect of an increase in the quantity of money. Over time, the prices of factors of production increase and, as they do so, the short-run aggregate supply curve shifts upward. The upward movement of the short-run aggregate supply curve

Figure 27.2 Aggregate Demand, Aggregate Supply, and the Quantity of Money

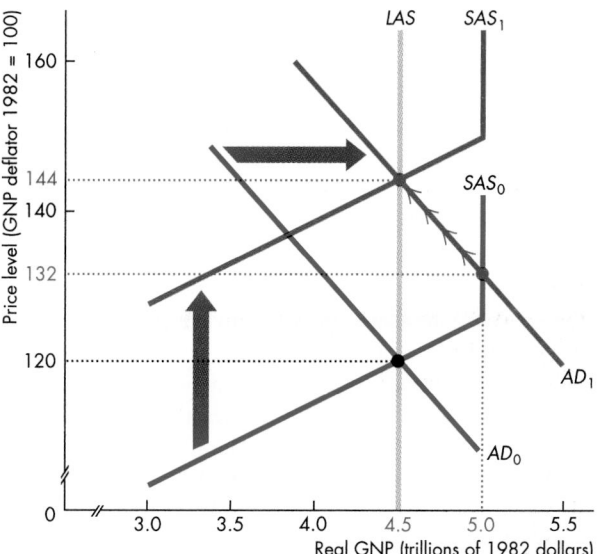

An economy's long-run aggregate supply curve is *LAS*. Initially, its short-run aggregate supply curve is SAS_0, and its aggregate demand curve is AD_0. The price level is 120 and real GNP is $4.5 trillion. An increase in the quantity of money shifts the aggregate demand curve to AD_1. The price level increases to 132 and real GNP increases to $5 trillion. The economy is at an above full-employment equilibrium. Wages and other input prices begin to rise and the short-run aggregate supply curve shifts upward toward SAS_1. As it does so, real GNP falls back to its initial level and the price level increases to 144.

leads to an ever-higher price level and lower real GNP. The long-run effect of an increase in the quantity of money occurs when the short-run aggregate supply curve has shifted upward to SAS_1, which intersects the aggregate demand curve AD_1 on the long-run aggregate supply curve *LAS*. This equilibrium is at a price level of 144 with real GNP back at its original level of $4.5 trillion.

The effects of this increase in the quantity of money have been, first, to increase both real GNP and the price level and, second, to increase the price level yet further, while returning real GNP to its original—full employment—level. That is, the short-run effect of an increase in the quantity of money is to increase both real GNP and the price level, but

the long-run effect of an increase in the quantity of money is to increase the price level only, leaving real GNP at its original level.

It is the long-run relationship between the money supply and the price level that gives rise to the quantity theory of money.

The Quantity Theory of Money

The **quantity theory of money** is the proposition that an increase in the quantity of money leads to an equal percentage increase in the price level. The original basis of the quantity theory of money is not the aggregate demand and aggregate supply model but the equation of exchange. The **equation of exchange** states the following:

$$\text{Quantity} \cdot \text{Velocity of} = \text{Price} \cdot \text{Real}$$
$$\text{of money} \quad \text{circulation} \quad \text{level} \quad \text{GNP.}$$

To understand the equation of exchange, let's start on the right side—with the price level multiplied by real GNP. You will recognize this value as nominal GNP. That is, it is simply the total amount of expenditure on final goods and services valued in current dollars. The left side of the equation of exchange can be thought of as defining the velocity of circulation. The **velocity of circulation** is the average number of times a dollar is used annually to buy the goods and services that make up GNP.

The equation of exchange is true by definition. That is, there is no independent way of going out and measuring the velocity of circulation to check whether the equation is true. Rather, the velocity of circulation is whatever number it has to be to make the equation true.

The equation of exchange becomes the quantity theory of money by making two propositions:

• The velocity of circulation is a constant.

• Real GNP is not influenced by the quantity of money

We can interpret the quantity theory of money in terms of our aggregate demand–aggregate supply model. The first proposition—that the velocity of circulation is a constant—implies that a change in the quantity of money shifts the aggregate demand curve by a very precisely stated amount. When the quantity of money increases, the aggregate demand curve shifts and its shift can be measured vertically by the percentage change in the quantity of money. For example, in Fig. 27.2, the aggregate demand curve shifts from AD_0 to AD_1. That shift, measured by the vertical distance between the two demand curves, is 20 percent. According to the quantity theory of money, a 20 percent increase in the quantity of money shifts the aggregate demand curve upward by 20 percent. The second proposition of the quantity theory of money—that real GNP is not affected by the money supply—can be interpreted as a statement about full-employment equilibrium. As you can see in Fig. 27.2, if a 20 percent increase in the quantity of money increases aggregate demand from AD_0 to AD_1, *in full-employment equilibrium* the price level also increases by 20 percent—an increase from 120 to 144 being a 20 percent increase.

There are important factors that influence the velocity of circulation that result in it not being a constant. We discuss these factors in the next chapter. Also, because changes in the money supply have a short-run effect that is different from the long-run effect, the relationship between the quantity of money and the price level is not going to be as precise as that predicted by the quantity theory of money. Nevertheless, it is interesting to ask to what extent the quantity theory of money correctly predicts the relationship between the quantity of money and the price level. Let's look at the relationship, both historically and internationally.

Historical Evidence on the Quantity Theory of Money

The quantity theory of money can be tested on the historical data of the United States by looking at the relationship between the growth rate of the quantity of money and the inflation rate. But in looking at the historical evidence, we have to remember that the quantity theory of money is a proposition about long-run effects. We don't see long-run effects in the data. We see a sequence of short-run effects. But we can sharpen our focus on long-run effects and reduce the importance of short-run effects if we consider averages over periods longer than a year.

Figure 27.3 shows the historical relationship between the growth rate of the quantity of money and the inflation rate in the United States for the 100 years between 1888 and 1988. The graph is constructed by plotting for each year the average money growth rate and inflation rate during that year

Figure 27.3   Money Growth and Inflation in the United States

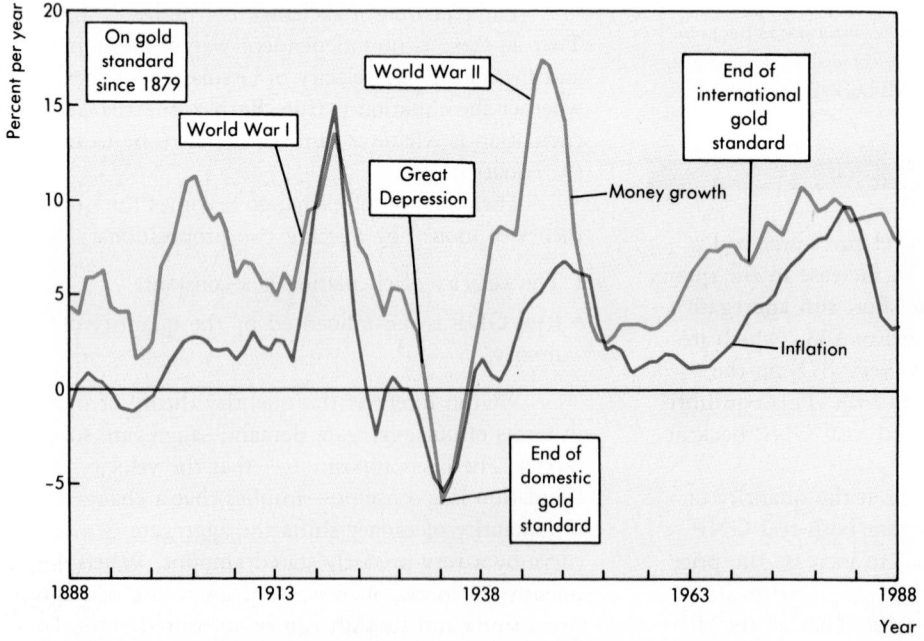

Five-year averages of money growth and inflation between 1888 and 1988 show that broad movements in the inflation rate are caused by changes in the money growth rate. But there are many independent changes in the inflation rate, indicating that money growth is not the only cause of inflation.

Sources: For 1883–1960, Milton Friedman and Anna J. Schwartz, A Monetary History of the United States (Princeton, N.J.: Princeton University Press, 1963); for 1961 –1988, Economic Report of the President, 1989.

and the previous four years—in what is called a five-year moving average. Thus for example, the points plotted for 1988 represent the average growth rate of the quantity of money for the years 1984 to 1988 and the inflation rate is the average inflation rate for that same five-year period.

Two things stand out in the figure. First, there is an unquestionable broad tendency for variations in the growth rate of the quantity of money to be associated with variations in the inflation rate. The massive buildup of inflation in the 1920s was accompanied by a huge increase in the growth rate of the quantity of money. The falling prices of the Great Depression were associated with a decrease in the quantity of money. Increasing money supply growth during World War II brought increased inflation in the immediate postwar years, and steadily increasing money supply growth through the 1960s and 1970s brought steadily rising inflation through those decades. The second striking feature of this figure is the lack of precision in the relationship between these two variables. That is, there are many sub-periods in which there are obviously other influences at work on the price level and variations in the quantity of money.

What does the international evidence tell us?

International Evidence on the Quantity Theory of Money

The international evidence on the quantity theory of money is summarized in Fig. 27.4, which shows the inflation rate and the money growth rate for 60 countries. There is an unmistakable tendency for high money growth to be associated with high inflation.

But like the historical evidence for the United States, these international data also tell us that money supply growth is not the only cause of inflation. Some countries have an inflation rate that exceeds the money supply growth rate, while others have an inflation rate that falls short of the money supply growth rate.

REVIEW

The quantity of money exerts an important influence on the price level. An increase in the quantity of money increases aggregate demand. In the short run, that increase in aggregate demand increases both the

Figure 27.4   Money Growth and Inflation in the World Economy

(a) All countries

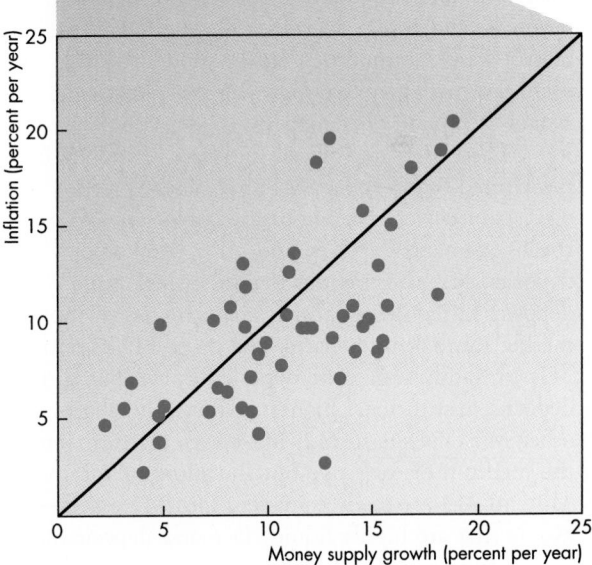

(b) Low-inflation countries

Inflation and money growth in 60 countries (all countries in part a and low-inflation countries in part b) show that money growth is one of the most important influences, though not the only influence, on inflation.

Source: Federal Reserve Bank of St. Louis, Review, May/June 1988, p.15.

price level and real GNP. In the long run, real GNP moves toward its original level and the price level continues to increase. The quantity theory of money predicts that an increase in the quantity of money produces an equivalent percentage increase in the price level. The historical and international evidence on the relationship between the quantity of money and the price level provides broad support for the quantity theory of money but also reveals important changes in the price level that occur independently of changes in the quantity of money. ■

■ In this chapter, we have studied the institutions that make up our banking and financial system. We've seen how the deposit liabilities of commercial

banks and other financial institutions comprise our medium of exchange—our money. Banks and other financial institutions create money by making loans. The quantity of money in existence has important effects on the economy and, in particular, on the price level.

In the next chapter, we're going to see how the quantity of money is regulated and influenced by the actions of the Federal Reserve System. We're also going to discover how, by its influence on the money supply, the Fed is able to influence interest rates, thereby affecting the level of aggregate demand. It is through its effects on the money supply and interest rates and their wider ramifications that the Fed is able to help steer the course of the economy.

S U M M A R Y

What Is Money?

Money has four functions. It is a medium of exchange, a unit of account, a standard of deferred payment, and a store of value. The earliest forms of money were commodities. In the modern world, we use a fiat money system. The biggest component of money is private debt money.

There are three official measures of money in the United States today: M1, M2, and M3. M1 consists of currency held outside banks, traveler's checks, demand deposits, and other checkable deposits. M2 adds savings deposits, small time deposits Eurodollar deposits, noninstitutional money market mutual fund shares, and other M2 deposits to M1. M3 adds large time deposits, Eurodollar time deposits, institutional money market fund shares, and other M3 deposits to M2. M1 serves the function of the medium of exchange but the additional items in M2 and M3 are easily converted into M1 assets—assests that are highly liquid. Demand deposits are money but checks and credit cards are not. (p.703–711)

Financial Intermediaries

The main financial intermediaries whose liabilities serve as money are commercial banks, savings and loan associations, savings banks, credit unions, and money market mutual funds. All of these institutions

take in deposits, hold cash reserves to ensure that they can meet their depositors' demands for currency, hold securities, and make loans. Financial intermediaries make a profit by borrowing at a lower interest rate than that at which they lend. All financial intermediaries provide four main economic services: They minimize the cost of obtaining funds, minimize the cost of monitoring borrowers, pool risks, and create liquidity. The continual search for profitable financial opportunities leads to financial innovation—to the creation of new financial products such as new types of deposits and loans. NOW accounts and ATS accounts are examples of some of the new financial products of the 1980s.

Banks and other financial institutions create money by making loans. When a loan is made to one person and the amount lent is spent, much of it ends up as someone else's deposit. The total quantity of deposits that can be supported by a given amount of reserves (the simple money multiplier) is equal to 1 divided by the desired reserve ratio. (pp. 711–720)

Money and the Price Level

The quantity of money affects aggregate demand. An increase in the quantity of money increases aggregate demand. In the short run, this increase in aggregate demand increases the price level and real GNP. In the long run, the price level continues to increase but real GNP returns to its original level. The quantity theory of money predicts that an increase in the money supply increases the price level by the same percentage amount. Both historical and international evidence suggest that the quantity theory of money is only correct in a broad average sense. The quantity of money does exert an important influence on the price level. But there are other important influences too. Nevertheless, other things being equal, the higher the growth rate of the quantity of money, the higher is the inflation rate. (pp. 720–724)

K E Y   C O N C E P T S

Asset, 714
Balance sheet, 714
Barter, 703
Checkable deposit, 707
Commercial bank, 714
Commodity money, 705
Convertible paper money, 705
Currency, 706
Currency drain, 719
Desired reserve ratio, 717
Double coincidence of wants, 703
Equation of exchange, 721
Excess reserves, 717
Fiat money, 706
Financial innovation, 717
Financial intermediary, 711
Gresham's Law, 705
Investment security, 715
Liability, 714
Liquid asset, 715
Liquidity, 707
Loan, 715
M1, 707
M2, 707
M3, 707

Medium of exchange, 703
Money, 703
Private debt money, 707
Quantity theory of money, 721
Reserve ratio, 717
Reserves, 714
Simple money multiplier, 719
Standard of deferred payment, 704
Store of value, 705
Unit of account, 703
Velocity of circulation, 721
Wholesale deposit market, 714

Key Figures and Tables

Figure 27.2 Aggregate Demand, Aggregate Supply, and the Quantity of Money, 721
Table 27.2 The Three Official Measures of Money, 707
Table 27.3 A Compact Glossary of the Components of Money, 708
Table 27.5 A Compact Glossary of Financial Intermediaries, 711

R E V I E W   Q U E S T I O N S

1 What is money?

2 What are the functions of money?

3 What are the three official measures of money in the United States today?

4 Are checks and credit cards money? Explain your answer.

5 What is a commercial bank? How does it make a profit?

6 What are the main items in the balance sheet of a commercial bank?

7 What are the main deposit-taking institutions other than commercial banks?

8 How do banks create money?

9 Define the simple money multiplier.

10 What does the aggregate demand–aggregate supply model predict about the effects of a change in

the quantity of money on the price level and real GNP?

11 What is the quantity theory of money?

12 What does the quantity theory of money predict about the relationship between the price level and the quantity of money?

13 What is the historical evidence on the quantity theory of money?

14 What is the international evidence on the quantity theory of money?

P R O B L E M S

1 You are given the following information about a hypothetical economy: The commercial banks have deposit liabilities of $300 billion. Their reserves are $15 billion.

a) Using Table 27.6 as a guide, set out the balance sheet of the commercial banks. Supply any missing numbers using your knowledge of the fact that total assets equal total liabilities.

b) How much money is there in this economy if households and firms hold 10 times as much in their deposits as they do in cash?

c) What is the simple money multiplier for this economy?

2 A new immigrant arrives in New Transylvania with $1000. The $1000 is put into a bank deposit. All the banks in New Transylvania have a desired reserve ratio of 10 percent.

a) What is the initial increase in the quantity of money of New Transylvania?

b) What is the initial increase in the quantity of bank deposits when the immigrant arrives?

c) How much does the immigrant's bank lend out?

d) Using a format similar to that in Table 27.7, calculate the amount lent and the amount of deposits created at each "round," assuming that all the funds lent are returned to the banking system in the form of deposits.

e) By how much has the quantity of money increased after 20 rounds of lending?

f) What is the ultimate increase in the quantity of money, in bank loans, and in bank deposits?

3 An economy has a quantity of money of $1000 and GNP is $4000. What is the velocity of circulation in this economy?

Chapter 28

The Federal Reserve, Money, and Interest Rates

After studying this chapter, you will be able to:

- Describe the structure of the Federal Reserve System (the Fed)

- Describe the tools used by the Fed to influence the money supply and interest rates

- Explain what an open market operation is

- Explain how an open market operation works

- Explain how an open market operation changes the money supply

- Distinguish between the nominal money supply and the real money supply

- Explain what determines the demand for money

- Explain the effects of financial innovations on the demand for money in the 1980s

- Explain how interest rates are determined

- Explain how the Fed influences interest rates

A young couple, planning to buy a first home, has found the perfect place. They're in luck—the year is 1960 and mortgages are plentiful at interest rates below 6 percent a year. Twenty-three years later, that same couple's daughter is looking for her first home. She too finds the perfect place, but mortgage rates have now reached 16 percent a year. Amid much gnashing of teeth, she puts off her purchase until interest rates decline again, making a mortgage affordable. Why do interest rates rise and fall? What determines interest rates? Are they determined by forces of nature? Or is somebody fiddling with the knobs somewhere? ■ You suspect that someone is indeed fiddling with the knobs. For you've just read in your newspaper:

Fiddling with the Knobs

"The Fed is prepared to continue nudging interest rates higher in order to head off the threat of inflation." And a few months earlier, you read: "The Fed doesn't plan to push interest rates lower unless it sees further weakness in the economy." What is "the Fed"? Why would the Fed want to change interest rates? And how can the Fed influence interest rates? ■ There is enough currency—coins and Federal Reserve bills—circulating in the United States for every single individual to have a wallet stuffed with $854. There is enough checking deposits in banks and other financial institutions for everyone to have $2329 in these accounts. There are enough savings accounts for everyone to have a further $9225. Of course, not many people hold as much currency, checkable deposits, and savings deposits as these averages. But these *are* the averages. Therefore, if most people don't hold this much, some people must be holding a great deal more. What determines the quantity of money that people hold? And what determines the composition in which they hold it? ■ The 1980s have seen a revolution in our banking and financial sector. At the beginning of that decade, most banks and other financial institutions offered just two kinds of deposit arrangements: a demand deposit or a savings deposit. Checks could be written on demand deposits but those deposits earned no interest; savings deposits earned interest but checks couldn't be written on those accounts. Today, we are confronted with a rich variety of deposit arrangements: checking accounts earn interest, at a rate which depends on such things as average daily balances. ATS accounts and NOW accounts provide depositors with the benefits of a savings deposit and the convenience of a checking account. How has the development of these new kinds of deposits influenced the amount of money that we hold? ■ Credit cards have been around for a long time (Diners' Club introduced the first card just after World War II). But there has been a virtual explosion in their use during the 1980s. Some people never use cash to buy gasoline or a restaurant meal or many other commonly purchased items. But you can't buy everything with a credit card. For example, you feel like a midnight snack but your favorite spot doesn't accept credit cards and you're out of cash. No problem! You head straight for the automatic teller and withdraw what you need tonight and for the next few days as well. While walking out, you wonder to yourself: How much cash would I need to hold if I didn't have quick access to an automatic teller machine? How did people get cash for midnight pizza before such machines existed? How have credit cards and computers affected the amount of money that we hold?

■ In the last chapter, we discovered that money is the currency (bills and coins) in circulation plus deposits at banks and other financial institutions. We also discovered that banks and financial intermediaries create money by making loans. Finally, we discovered that the quantity of money has an important effect on the price level. Increases in the quantity of money bring increasing prices. But we also saw that there is no precise relationship between the quantity of money and the price level—only a general tendency for the two to be correlated. ■ An important reason why the quantity of money and the price level do not have a precise relationship with each other is that the *velocity of circulation* of money fluctuates. In this chapter, we are going to discover what determines the velocity of circulation. We are going to discover that the velocity of circulation is determined by the demand for money. We are also going to

discover that interest rates are determined in the market for money by the interaction of the demand for money and the supply of money. ■ But first we are going to study the Federal Reserve System and learn how the Fed influences the quantity of money in its attempts to influence interest rates and, more generally, the overall level of aggregate demand and inflation. At the end of the chapter, we will return to the Fed and see how its operations in the late 1970s and early 1980s generated huge swings in interest rates but eventually brought inflation under control.

The Federal Reserve System

The **Federal Reserve System** is the central bank of the United States. A **central bank** is a public authority charged with regulating and controlling a country's monetary and financial institutions and markets. The Fed is also responsible for the nation's monetary policy. **Monetary policy** is the attempt to control inflation and moderate the business cycle by changing the quantity of money in circulation and adjusting interest rates. We are going to study the tools available to the Fed in its conduct of monetary policy and also work out the effects of the Fed's actions on interest rates later in this chapter. But first we'll examine the origins and structure of the Fed.

The Origins of the Federal Reserve System

The Fed was created by the Federal Reserve Act of 1913. Thus for more than 100 years of our history, we had no central bank. Central banking and a deep hostility to central power—visible in the checks and balances built into our constitution—just did not seem to mix. As a consequence, we tried to get along without a central bank for the first 137 years of our history. During this period, there was a series of severe national bank panics. In 1907, bank failures and depositors' losses were so severe that the need for a central bank became clear to almost everyone. It was the serious financial turmoil of 1907 that led to the emergence of a consensus on the need for a central bank. That consensus finally found expression in the Federal Reserve Act of 1913.

By the time that the Fed was created, most other countries already had a central bank. The first

Figure 28.1   The Federal Reserve System

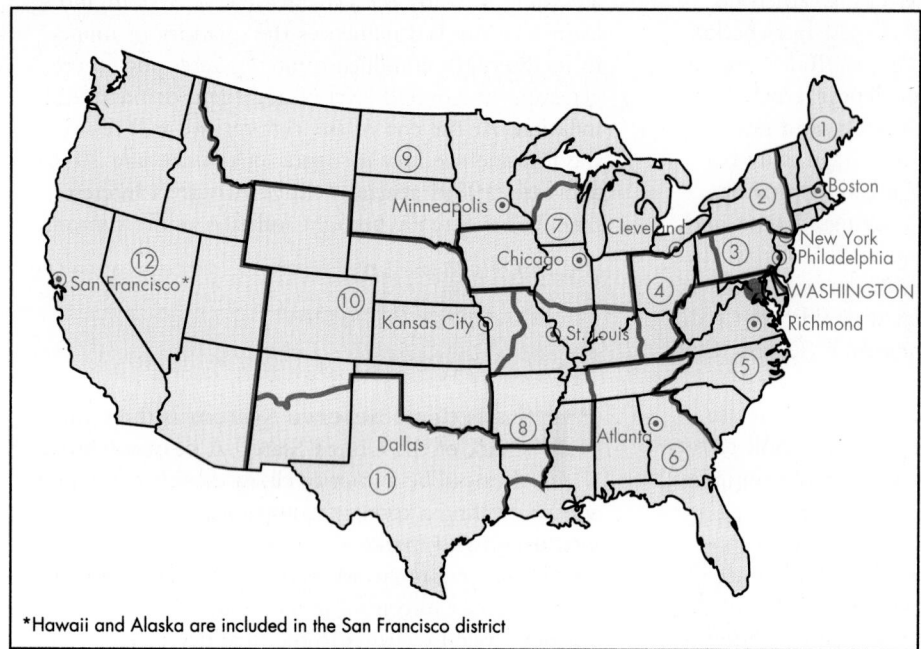

The nation is divided into 12 Federal Reserve districts, each having a Federal Reserve bank. (Some of the larger districts also have branch banks.) The Board of Governors of the Federal Reserve System is located in Washington, D.C.

(*Source: Federal Reserve Bulletin,* published monthly.)

*Hawaii and Alaska are included in the San Francisco district

— Boundaries of Federal Reserve districts
● Board of governors of the Federal Reserve
⊙ Federal Reserve bank cities

such banks were established in Sweden and England in the seventeenth century. But their origins were very different from that of the Fed. They were set up as private banks designed to solve the financial problems of monarchs. These banks gradually evolved into modern central banks, eventually becoming publicly owned corporations. Central banks, as their name suggests, concentrate the power to control and influence the banking system in a single center. In setting up the Federal Reserve System, care was taken to design a central bank that diffused and decentralized, as far as possible, responsibility for monetary policy. The result was a central bank with a unique structure unlike all other central banks. Let's examine that structure.

The Structure of the Federal Reserve System

There are three key elements in the structure of the Federal Reserve System:

- Board of Governors
- Regional Federal Reserve banks
- Federal Open Market Committee

Board of Governors   The Board of Governors of the Federal Reserve System consists of seven members appointed by the president of the United States and confirmed by the Senate. The board is located in Washington, D.C. Each member is appointed for a 14-year term and the terms are staggered so that one place on the board becomes vacant every two years. One of the members of the board is named chairman. The length of the term of the chairman is four years.

Federal Reserve Banks   There are 12 Federal Reserve banks, one for each of 12 Federal Reserve districts (see Fig. 28.1). Each Federal Reserve bank has nine directors, three of whom are appointed by the Board of Governors and six of whom are elected by the commercial banks in the Federal Reserve district. The directors of the regional Federal Reserve banks appoint the bank's president and other senior officers.

The Federal Reserve Bank of New York (or the New York Fed as it is often called) occupies a special place in the Federal Reserve System. It is the New York Fed that implements some of the Fed's most important policy decisions.

Federal Open Market Committee The **Federal Open Market Committee (FOMC)** is the main policymaking organ of the Federal Reserve System. The FOMC consists of the following members:

- The chairman of the Board of Governors
- The other six members of the Board of Governors
- The president of the Federal Reserve Bank of New York
- The presidents of four other regional Federal Reserve banks (elected on a rotating basis)

The FOMC meets once a month to review the state of the economy and to formulate detailed policy actions to be carried out by the New York Fed.

The Fed's Power Center

A description of the formal structure of the Fed gives the impression that power in the Fed resides with the Board of Governors. In practice, it is the chairman of the Board of Governors who has the largest influence on the Fed's monetary policy actions. This position has been held by some remarkable individuals. The current chairman is Alan Greenspan, who was appointed by President Reagan in 1987. His predecessor was Paul Volcker, who was appointed in 1979 by President Jimmy Carter and reappointed in 1983 by President Reagan (see "Talking with Paul Volcker," pp. 863–866).

The chairman's power and influence stem in an important way from his ability to control the agenda at and to dominate the meetings of the FOMC. His influence is yet further enhanced by virtue of his day-to-day contact with and control of a sizable staff of economists and other technical experts who provide the chairman, the Board of Governors, and the FOMC with the detailed background briefings necessary to formulate monetary policy.

Next, let's look at the actual policy tools used by the Fed.

Policy Tools

The Federal Reserve System has many responsibilities, but we'll examine its single most important responsibility—regulating the amount of money floating around in the United States and influencing the level of interest rates. How does the Fed control the money supply and influence interest rates? It does so by adjusting the reserves of the banking system. It is also by adjusting the reserves of the banking system,

Table 28.1   Required Reserves

Type of deposit	Minimum reserve required (percentage of deposits)
Very large checking accounts	12
Long-term deposits (over 1.5 years)	0
All other deposits	3

Source: *Federal Reserve Bulletin* (February 1989), p. A8.

and by standing ready to make loans to banks, that the Fed is able to prevent banking panics and bank failures. The Fed uses three main policy tools to achieve its objectives:

- Reserve requirements
- Discount rate
- Open market operations

Reserve Requirements All depository institutions in the United States (whether members of the Federal Reserve System or not) are required to hold reserves on a scale not less than that specified in regulations formulated by the Federal Reserve System. The minimum reserves that a bank is permitted to hold are called **required reserves**. Required reserves are specified as a minimum percentage of deposits of various classes. The reserve requirements in force in 1988 are set out in Table 28.1.

By increasing required reserve ratios, the Fed can create a shortage of reserves for the banking system, reducing the amount of bank lending. Reduced lending puts upward pressure on interest rates. It also lowers the money supply by a process that we describe later in this chapter (see pp. 734–740). Reserve requirements are determined by the Board of Governors.

Although reserve requirements have an important influence on the money supply and interest rates, reserve requirements are not *varied* much. That is, they are not used as an active tool for achieving *variations* in interest rates and the money supply.

Discount Rate The **discount rate** is the interest rate at which the Fed stands ready to lend reserves to

Figure 28.2   The Structure and Policy Tools of the Fed

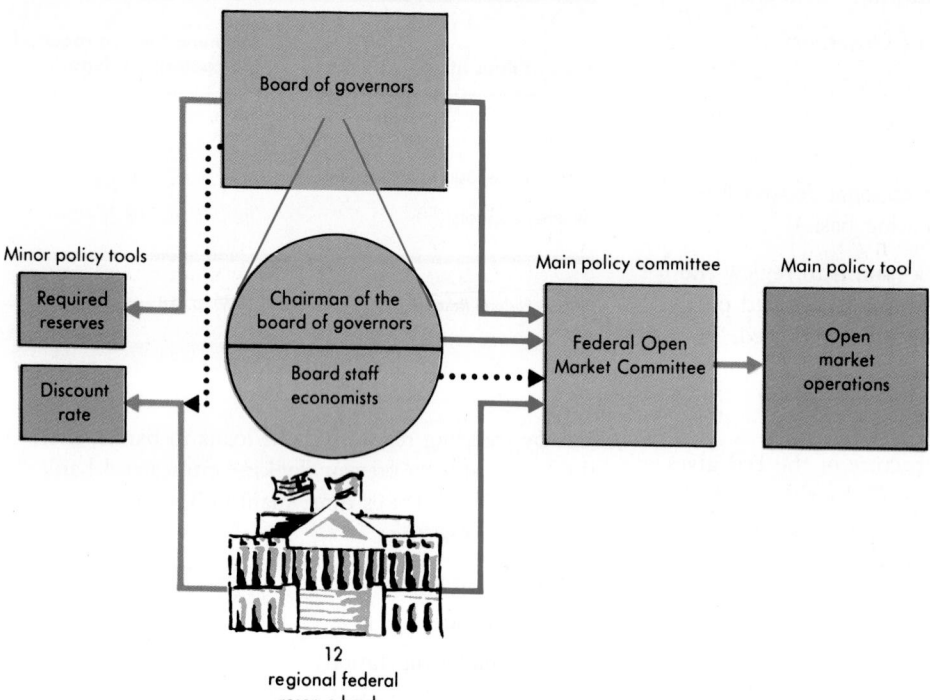

The main organs of the Federal Reserve System are the Board of Governors, the 12 regional Federal Reserve banks, and the Federal Open Market Committee. At the center of the Federal Reserve System is the chairman of the Board of Governors supported by the economists on the board's staff. The 12 Federal Reserve banks propose discount rate changes that are set with the approval of the Board of Governors. The Board of Governors sets required reserve ratios. Together, the Board of Governors and members of the regional Federal Reserve banks sit on the FOMC to determine open market operations and generally monitor the state of the economy. The Fed's policy tools are required reserve ratios, the discount rate, and open market operations. Of these, open market operations are the most important and most often used tools for influencing interest rates and the money supply.

commercial banks. The discount rate is proposed by the 12 Federal Reserve banks and determined with the approval of the Board of Governors. By increasing the discount rate, the Fed can make it more costly for banks to borrow reserves, thereby encouraging them to cut back their lending and putting upward pressure on interest rates. By lowering the discount rate, the Fed can encourage banks to borrow more reserves, thereby stimulating bank lending and putting downward pressure on interest rates in general.

The discount rate can be an effective tool of Federal Reserve policy only if the banking system is short of reserves and needs to borrow some reserves

from the Fed. If the banks are not borrowing from the Fed, the level of the discount rate has no immediate impact on the banks' behavior. But the Fed can determine whether or not the banking system has a shortage or a surplus of reserves. It does so by using open market operations.

Open Market Operations   Open market operations are the purchase or sale of U.S. government securities—U.S. treasury bills and bonds—by the Federal Reserve System designed to influence the money supply. Decisions to buy or sell government securities are made by the FOMC. They are carried out by the Federal Reserve Bank of New York. When the Fed sells government securities, they are paid for with bank deposits and bank reserves, and tighter monetary and credit conditions are created. With lower reserves, the banks cut their lending, and interest rates rise. When the Fed buys government securities, the Fed's payment for them puts additional reserves in the hands of the banks and loosens credit conditions. With extra reserves, the banks increase their lending, and interest rates fall.

The structure and policy tools of the Federal Reserve System are summarized in Fig. 28.2. The most important and powerful of the Fed's policy tools are its open market operations. In order to understand the Fed's open market operations, we first need to examine the structure of the Fed's balance sheet.

The Fed's Balance Sheet

The balance sheet of the Federal Reserve System for November 1988 is set out in Table 28.2. The assets on the left side are what the Fed owns and the liabilities on the right side are what it owes. Most of the Fed's assets are U.S. government securities. In addition, the Fed holds some gold and foreign exchange—foreign central banks' liabilities. The most important aspect of the Fed's balance sheet is on the liabilities side.

The largest liability of the Fed is Federal Reserve notes in circulation. These are the bank notes that we use in our daily transactions. Some of these bank notes are in circulation with the public and others are in the tills and vaults of banks and other financial institutions.

You may be wondering why Federal Reserve notes are considered a liability of the Fed. Bank notes are considered a liability of the bank that issues them because, when notes were invented, they gave their owner a claim on the gold reserves of the issuing bank. Such notes are *convertible paper money*. The holder of such a note could convert the note on demand into gold (or some other commodity such as silver) at a guaranteed price. Thus when a bank issued a note, it was holding itself liable to convert that note into a commodity. Modern bank notes are nonconvertible. A **nonconvertible note** is a bank note that is not convertible into any commodity and that obtains its value by government fiat—hence the term fiat money. Such bank notes are considered the legal liability of the bank that issues them but they are backed not by commodity reserves but by holdings of securities and loans. Federal Reserve notes are backed by the Fed's holdings of U.S. government securities.

The other important liability of the Fed is the deposits held there by banks. We saw these deposits as an asset in the balance sheets of the banks. The remaining liability of the Fed consists of items such as U.S. Treasury deposits (government bank accounts at the Fed) and accounts held by foreign central banks (such as the Bank of England and the Bank of Canada).

Table 28.2   The Balance Sheet of the Federal Reserve System, November 1988

Assets (billions of dollars)		Liabilities (billions of dollars)		
Gold and foreign exchange	16.5	Federal Reserve notes in circulation	224.5	
U.S. government securities	232.7	Banks' deposits	40.0	
Other assets	35.2	Monetary base		264.5
		Other liabilities		19.9
Total	284.4	Total		284.4

Source: *Federal Reserve Bulletin* (April 1989).

The two largest items on the liability side of the Fed's balance sheet make up most of the monetary base. The **monetary base** is the sum of Federal Reserve notes in circulation, banks' deposits at the Fed, and coins in circulation. Coins are issued, not by the Fed, but by the Treasury. They do not appear, therefore, as a liability of the Fed.

By buying or selling government securities, the Fed can directly determine the scale of its own liabilities and exert a considerable influence upon the monetary base. Such purchases and sales of government securities are the Fed's open market operations. Let's see how open market operations work.

How Open Market Operations Work

When the Fed conducts an open market operation in which it buys U.S. government securities, it increases the reserves of the banking system. When it conducts an open market operation in which it sells U.S. government securities, it decreases the reserves of the banking system. Let's study the effects of an open market operation by working out what happens when the Fed buys $100 million of U.S. government securities.

Open market operations affect the balance sheets of the Fed, the banks, and the rest of the economy. Table 28.3 keeps track of the changes in these balance sheets. When the Fed buys securities, there are two possible sellers: the banks or some other agents in the economy. Part (a) of the table works out what happens when banks sell the securities that the Fed buys.

When the Fed buys securities from the banks, the Fed pays for the securities by crediting the banks' deposit accounts at the Fed. The changes in the Fed's balance sheet are that its assets increase by $100 million (the additional U.S. government securities bought) and its liabilities also increase by $100 million (the additional bank deposits). The banks' balance sheet also changes but their total assets remain constant. Their deposits at the Fed increase by $100 million and their securities decrease by $100 million.

Part (b) of the table deals with the case in which the banks do not sell any securities and the Fed buys securities from agents in the rest of the economy other than the banks. The Fed's holdings of U.S. government securities increase by $100 million

and other agents' holdings of U.S. government securities go down by $100 million. The Fed pays for the securities by giving checks drawn on itself to the sellers. The sellers take the checks to the banks and deposit them. Bank deposits increase by $100 million. The banks in turn present the checks to the Fed, which credits the banks' accounts with the value of the checks. Banks' deposits with the Fed—reserves—increase by $100 million.

Regardless of which of the two cases takes place, by conducting an open market purchase of securities, the Fed increases the banks' deposits with itself—increases the banks' reserves.

If the Fed conducts an open market *sale* of securities, the events that we have just traced occur in reverse. The Fed's assets and liabilities will decrease in value and so will the reserves of the banks.

The effects of an open market operation on the balance sheets of the Fed and the banks that we've traced in Table 28.3 are not the end of the story—they are just the beginning. With an increase in their reserves, the banks are now able to make more loans—just like the banks did in Chapter 27 (pp.717–719) when Al increased his deposit at the Gold-nugget Bank. That has a big effect on the quantity of money for, again as we saw in Chapter 27, by making loans banks themselves create money. Let's see how this multiple expansion of money comes about.

The Multiplier Effect of an Open Market Operation

The **money multiplier** is the amount by which a change in the monetary base is multiplied to determine the resulting change in the quantity of money. We'll work out the multiplier effect of an open market operation for the example where the Fed buys securities from the banks. In this case, although the open market operation increases the banks' reserves, it has no immediate effect on the quantity of money. The banks are simply holding additional reserves and fewer U.S. government securities. But the banks have excess reserves. When the banks have excess reserves, the sequence of events shown in Fig. 28.3 takes place. These events are:

- Banks lend excess reserves.

- New loans are used to make payments.

- Households and firms receive payments from new loans.

Table 28.3   An Open Market Operation

(a) Banks sell securities

Effects on the balance sheet of the Fed (millions of dollars)

Change in assets		Change in liabilities	
U.S. government securities	+100	Banks' deposits (reserves)	+100

Effects on the balance sheet of the banks (millions of dollars)

Change in assets		Change in liabilities	
Banks' deposits (reserves)	+100		
U.S. government securities	−100		

(b) Banks do not sell securities

Effects on the balance sheet of the Fed (millions of dollars)

Change in assets		Change in liabilities	
U.S. government securities	+100	Banks' deposits (reserves)	+100

Effects on the balance sheet of the banks (millions of dollars)

Change in assets		Change in liabilities	
Banks' deposits (reserves)	+100	Deposits	+100

Effects on the balance sheet of other agents (millions of dollars)

Change in assets		Change in liabilities	
Deposits	+100		
U.S. government securities	−100		

- Part of the receipts are held as currency—a *currency drain*.
- Part of the receipts are deposited in banks.
- Bank reserves increase (by the same amount as the increase in deposits).
- Desired reserves increase (by a fraction—the desired reserve ratio—of the increase in deposits).
- Excess reserves decrease, but remain positive.
- The money supply increases by the amount of the currency drain and the increase in bank deposits.

The sequence just described is similar to that which we studied in Chapter 27 except that there we ignored the currency drain. The sequence repeats in a series of "rounds" but each round begins with a smaller quantity of excess reserves than did the previous one. The process continues until excess reserves have finally been eliminated.

Figure 28.3   A Round in the Multiplier Process Following an Open Market Operation

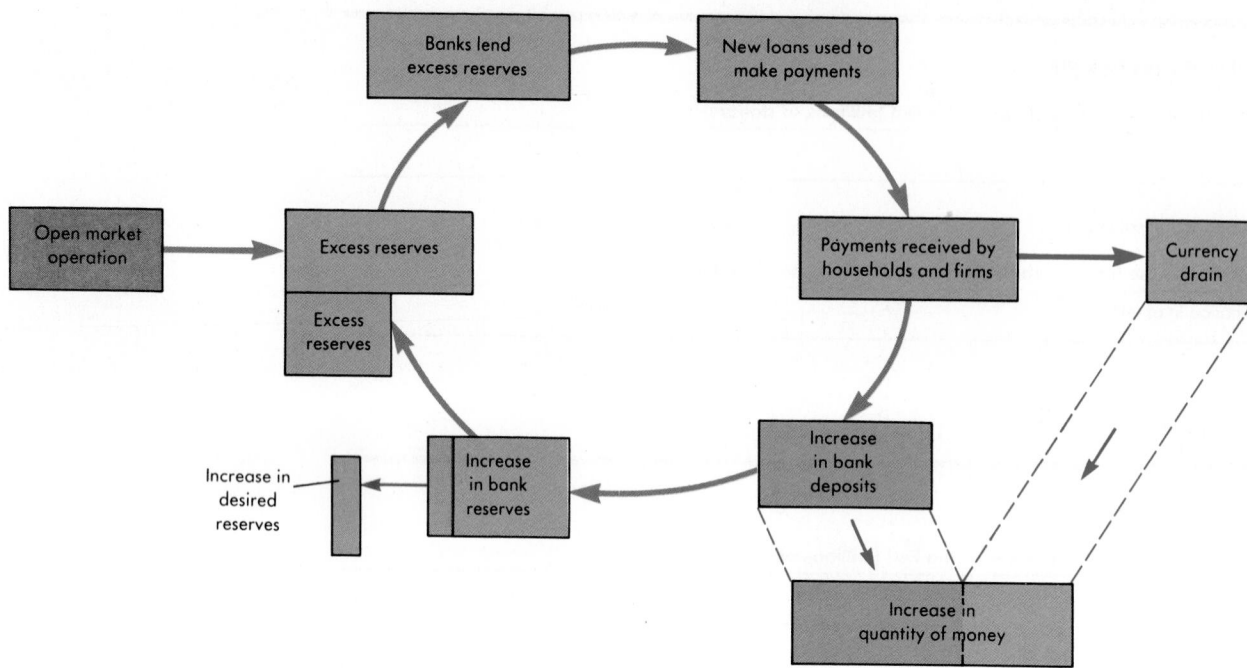

An open market purchase of U.S. government securities increases bank reserves and creates excess reserves. Banks lend the excess reserves and new loans are used to make payments. Households and firms receiving payments keep some of the receipts in the form of currency—a currency drain—and place the rest on deposit in banks. The increase in bank deposits increases banks' reserves but also increases banks' desired reserves. Desired reserves increase by less than actual reserves, so the banks still have some excess reserves, though less than before. The process repeats until excess reserves have been eliminated. There are two components to the increase in the quantity of money: the currency drain and the increase in deposits.

Table 28.4 keeps track of the magnitudes of new loans, the currency drain, the increase in deposits and reserves, the increase in desired reserves, and the change in excess reserves at each round of the multiplier process. The initial open market operation has increased the banks' reserves but, since deposits have not changed, there is no change in desired reserves. The banks have excess reserves of 100. They lend those reserves. When the money borrowed from the banks is spent, some of it returns to the banks in the form of additional deposits and some of it drains off in the form of a currency drain. In the table, we're assuming that two thirds of what the banks lend comes back to them in the form of deposits and one third drains off and is held by households and firms in the form of currency. Thus when the banks lend

the initial $100 million of excess reserves, $66.67 million comes back to them in the form of deposits and $33.33 million drains off and is held outside the banks as currency. The quantity of money has now increased by $100 million—the increase in deposits plus the increase in currency holdings.

The increased bank deposits now produce an increase in the bank's desired reserves. Assume that the desired reserve ratio is 3 percent. This means that an increase in deposits of $66.7 million generates an increase in desired reserves of $2 million. But actual reserves have increased by the same amount as the increase in deposits—$66.7 million. Therefore the banks now have excess reserves of $64.67 million. At this stage we have completed round 1. We have been around the circle shown in Fig. 28.3. The banks still

Table 28.4   The Multiplier Effect of an Open Market Operation

Round	Excess reserves at start of round	New loans	Change in deposits	Currency drain	Change in reserves	Change in desired reserves	Excess reserves at end of round	Change in quantity of money
				(millions of dollars)				
1	100.00	100.00	66.67	33.33	66.67	2.00	64.67	100.00
2	64.67	64.67	43.11	21.56	43.11	1.29	41.82	64.67
3	41.82	41.82	27.88	13.94	27.88	0.84	27.04	41.82
4	27.04	27.04	18.03	9.01	18.03	0.54	17.49	27.04
5	17.49	17.49	11.66	5.83	11.66	0.35	11.31	17.49
6	11.31	11.31	7.54	3.77	7.54	0.23	7.31	11.31
7	7.31	7.31	4.88	2.44	4.88	0.15	4.73	7.31
8	4.73	4.73	3.15	1.58	3.15	0.09	3.06	4.73
9	3.06	3.06	2.04	1.02	2.04	0.06	1.98	3.06
10	1.98	1.98	1.32	0.66	1.32	0.04	1.28	1.98
	⋮	⋮	⋮	⋮	⋮	⋮	⋮	⋮
All others	.	3.62	2.41	1.21	.	0.07	.	3.62
Total		283.02	188.68	94.34		5.66		283.02

have excess reserves but the level has fallen from $100 million at the beginning of the round to $64.67 million at the end of the round. Round 2 now begins.

When the excess reserves of $64.67 are lent, and the loans spent, two thirds—$43.11 million—come back to the banks in the form of deposits and one third—$21.56 million—drains off as currency. The quantity of money has now increased by a further $64.67 million for a total increase of $164.67 million.

The process that we've just described keeps on repeating. Table 28.4 shows the first ten rounds in this process and collapses all the remaining ones into the next to last row of the table. At the end of the process, the quantity of money has increased by slightly more than $283 million.

The accumulated increase in bank deposits, currency, and the quantity of money is illustrated in Fig. 28.4. As you can see, when the open market operation takes place (labeled as OMO in the figure), there is no initial change in either the quantity of

money or its components. Then, after the first round of bank lending, the quantity of money increases by $100 million—the size of the open market operation. In successive rounds, the quantity of money and its components continue to increase but by successively smaller amounts until, after 10 rounds, currency, deposits, and the quantity of money have almost reached the value to which they are ultimately heading.

What determines the size of the money multiplier and how big is the money multiplier in the United States?

The U.S. Money Multiplier

The money multiplier is calculated as the ratio of the quantity of money to the monetary base. That is,

$$\text{Money multiplier} = \frac{\text{Quantity of money}}{\text{Monetary base}}.$$

The size of the money multiplier depends on which definition of money we're considering. The

Figure 28.4   The Multiplier Effect of an Open Market Operation

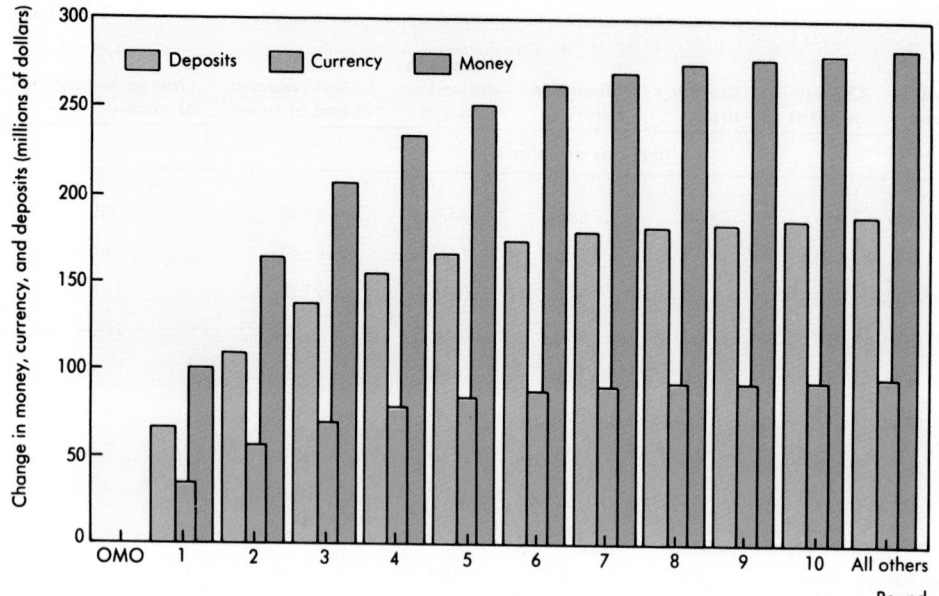

An open market operation (OMO) in which government securities are bought from the banks has no immediate effect on the money supply but creates excess reserves in the banking system. When loans are made with these reserves and the loans are used to buy goods and services, bank deposits and currency holdings increase. Each time new loans are spent, part of the loan returns to the banking system in the form of additional deposits and additional reserves. Banks continue to increase their lending until excess reserves have been eliminated. The magnitude of the resulting increase in the money supply is determined by the money multiplier.

Table 28.5   The Money Multiplier

Year	Monetary base (MB) (billions of dollars)	M1 (billions of dollars)	M2 (billions of dollars)	M3 (billions of dollars)	M1 money multiplier (M1/MB)	M2 money multiplier (M2/MB)	M3 money multiplier (M3/MB)
1984	200	552	2364	2998	2.8	11.8	14.9
1985	218	620	2563	3196	2.8	11.8	14.7
1986	241	725	2808	3491	3.0	11.7	14.5
1987	258	751	2901	3664	2.9	11.2	14.2
1988	274	784	3054	3889	2.9	11.1	14.2

Source: Federal Reserve Bulletin (February 1989), pp. 412–413.

values of the M1, M2, and M3 multipliers in the United States between 1984 and 1988 are set out in Table 28.5. As you can see, the M1 multiplier ranges between 2.8 and 3, the M2 multiplier ranges between 11.1 and 11.8, and the M3 multiplier ranges between 14.2 and 14.9. Multipliers of these magnitudes tell us that if the monetary base changes by $1 million, M1 changes by a little under $3 million, M2 changes by somewhat more than $11 million, and M3 changes by somewhat more than $14 million.

The monetary base is like the base of an inverted pyramid of money. The monetary base itself is divided into currency and reserves. Each dollar of currency creates a dollar of money. Each dollar of reserves supports a multiple of itself as money and the larger the multiple the broader the definition of money. By changing the monetary base, the Fed changes reserves. The change in reserves has a multiplier or magnification effect on the quantity of money outstanding.

Why are the money multipliers so stable? They are stable because their values depend on two ratios that themselves do not vary much. These ratios are:

- Currency holdings of households and firms as a fraction of total deposits
- Reserve holdings of banks as a fraction of total deposits

Table 28.6 shows how the money multiplier depends on these two ratios. It also provides numbers that illustrate the M1 money multiplier. Currency holdings of households and firms are approximately 0.5 times the deposits that make up M1. Equivalently, currency makes up one third of M1 and deposits two thirds (these are the values that we assumed when calculating the currency drain in the previous example of an open market operation summarized in Table 28.4). Reserve holdings are approximately 3 percent (0.03) of the deposits in M1. We used this value for the desired reserve ratio in the above calculation. Combining these ratios in the formula derived in the table shows that the M1 money multiplier is approximately 2.8. In our example in Table 28.4, an open market operation of $100 million changed the money supply by approximately $280 million—a multiplier of 2.8.

Other Policy Tools

The Fed's other policy tools—the required reserve ratio and the discount rate—also affect the quantity

Table 28.6   Calculating the Money Multiplier

	In general	Numbers for M1
1. The variables		
Currency	$= C$	
Reserves	$= R$	
Monetary base	$= MB$	
Deposits	$= D$	
Money supply	$= M$	
Money multiplier	$= mm$	
2. Definitions		
The monetary base is the sum of currency and reserves	$MB = C + R$	
The money supply is the sum of deposits and currency	$M = D + C$	
The money multiplier is the ratio of the money supply to the monetary base	$mm = M/MB$	
3. Ratios		
Currency to deposits	C/D	0.5
Reserves to deposits	R/D	0.03
4. Calculations		
Begin with the definition	$mm = M/MB$	
Use the definitions of M and MB to give	$mm = \dfrac{D + C}{C + R}$	
Divide top and bottom by D to give	$mm = \dfrac{1 + C/D}{C/D + R/D}$	$\dfrac{1 + 0.5}{0.5 + 0.03}$
		$= \dfrac{1.5}{0.53}$
		$= 2.8$

of money by changing the excess reserves of the banking system. An increase in the required reserve ratio increases the reserves that the banks hold at a given level of deposits. With no change in actual reserves, excess reserves fall. An increase in the discount rate also increases the reserves that the banks plan to hold. When it costs more to borrow reserves, the banks want to run less risk of being in that position and so plan to hold a larger quantity of reserves to reduce the likelihood of having to borrow from the Fed.

Whatever the source of a change in excess reserves, once it is present, it sets up a chain of events similar to those described earlier, following an open market operation. Thus the Fed's minor policy instruments work in a similar way to its open market operations. By changing excess reserves, they change the amount of bank lending and the quantity of money in circulation.

But reserve requirements and the discount rate also affect the size of the money multiplier. They do so by changing the banks' desired reserve ratio. As we've seen, the desired reserve ratio is one of the elements in the money multiplier. The higher the banks' desired reserve ratio, the smaller is the money multiplier. But because these policy tools are not often used, changes in the money multiplier resulting from these instruments do not often occur.

R E V I E W

The Federal Reserve System is the nation's central bank. The Fed influences the quantity of money in circulation by changing the excess reserves of the banking system. It has three instruments at its disposal: changing reserve requirements, changing the discount rate, and open market operations. The last of these is the most important and most frequently used. Open market operations not only change the excess reserves of the banking system but also set up a multiplier effect. When excess reserves are lent, some of the loans "drain" out of the banking system, but others come back in the form of new deposits. The banks continue to lend until the currency drain and the increase in their desired reserves have eliminated excess reserves. The multiplier effect of an open market operation depends on the scale of the currency drain and the size of the banks' desired reserve ratio. ∎

The Fed's objectives in conducting open market operations or taking other actions that influence the quantity of money in circulation is not simply to affect the money supply for its own sake. Their objective is to influence the course of the economy—especially the level of output, employment, and prices. But these effects are indirect. The Fed's immediate objective is to move interest rates up or down. To work out the effects of the Fed's actions on interest rates, we need to work out how and why interest rates change when the quantity of money changes. We'll discover the answer to these questions by studying the demand for money.

The Demand for Money

The amount of money we *receive* each week in payment for our labor is income—a flow. The amount of money that we hold in our wallet or in a deposit account at the bank is an inventory—a stock. There is no limit to how much income—or flow—we would like to receive each week. But there is a limit to how big an inventory of money each of us would like to hold, on the average.

The Motives for Money Holding

Why do people hold an inventory of money? Why do you carry coins and bills in your wallet, and why do you keep money in a deposit account at your neighborhood bank?

There are three main motives for holding money:

• Transactions motive

• Precautionary motive

• Speculative motive

Transactions Motive   The main motive for holding money is to be able to undertake transactions and to minimize the cost of transactions. By carrying an inventory of currency, you are able to undertake small transactions such as buying your lunch at the college cafeteria. If you didn't carry an inventory of currency, you'd have to go to the bank every lunchtime in order to withdraw enough cash. The opportunity cost of these transactions, in terms of your own lost studying or leisure time, would be considerable. You avoid those transactions costs by keeping an inventory of currency large enough to make your normal purchases over a period of perhaps a week in length.

You also keep an inventory of money in the form of deposits at the bank to make larger transactions such as paying the rent on your apartment or paying your college bookstore bill. Instead of having an inventory of bank deposits for these purposes, you might put all your assets into the stock or bond market—buying IBM shares or U.S. government securities. But if you did that, you would have to call your broker and sell some stocks and bonds each time you needed to pay the rent or the bookstore. Again, you'd have to pay the opportunity cost of such transactions. Instead, by holding larger inventories of bank deposits, those costs can be avoided.

Individual holdings of money for transactions purposes fluctuate considerably during any week or month. But aggregate money balances held for transactions purposes do not fluctuate much because, what one person is spending, someone else is receiving.

Firm's money holdings are at their peak just before the moment they pay their employees wages. Households' money holdings are at a peak just after wages have been paid. As households spend their incomes, their money holdings decline and firms' holdings of money increase. Firms' holdings of money are actually quite large and it is this fact that makes average money holdings appear to be so large. Average money holdings of households are much lower than the economy-wide averages presented in the chapter opener.

Precautionary Motive   Money is held as a precaution against unforeseen events that require unplanned purchases to be made. For example, on an out-of-town trip you carry some extra money in case your car breaks down and has to be fixed. Or, if you are shopping in the January sales, you take with you more money than you are planning on spending in case you come across a real bargain that you just can't pass up.

Speculative Motive   The final motive for holding money is to avoid losses from holding stocks or bonds that are expected to fall in value. Suppose, for example, a week before the stock market crash of October 1987, you had predicted the crash. On the Friday afternoon before the markets closed, you would have sold all your stocks and put the proceeds into your bank deposit account for the weekend. This temporary holding of money would persist until stock prices had fallen to their lowest predicted level. Only then would you reduce your bank deposit and buy stocks again.

The Influences on Money Holding

What determines the quantity of money that households and firms choose to hold? There are three important influences on this quantity:

- Prices
- Real expenditure
- The opportunity cost of holding money

The higher the level of prices, other things being equal, the larger is the quantity of money that people will want to hold. The higher the level of real expenditure, other things being equal, the larger the quantity of money that people plan to hold. The higher the opportunity cost of holding money, the smaller is the quantity of money that people plan to hold.

These influences on individual decisions about money holding translate into three macroeconomic variables that influence the aggregate quantity of money demanded:

- The price level
- Real GNP
- The interest rate

Price Level and the Quantity of Money Demanded   The quantity of money measured in current dollars is called the **nominal quantity of money**. The nominal quantity of money demanded is proportional to the price level. That is, other things being equal, if the price level (GNP deflator) increases by 10 percent, people will want to hold 10 percent more nominal money than before. What matters to people is not the number of dollars that they hold but the buying power of those dollars. Suppose, for example, that to undertake your weekly expenditure on movies and soda you carry an average of $20 in your wallet. If your income and the prices of movies and soda increased by 10 percent, you would increase your average cash holdings by 10 percent to $22.

The quantity of money measured in constant dollars (for example, in 1982 dollars) is called *real money*. Real money is equal to nominal money divided by the price level. The quantity of real money demanded is independent of the price level. If the price level as measured by the GNP deflator is 200, people will want to hold, on the average, the same quantity of real money as they would if the GNP deflator was 100. Doubling the price level doubles the quantity of nominal money demanded but leaves the quantity of real money demanded unchanged.

Real GNP and the Quantity of Real Money Demanded

An important determinant of the quantity of real money demanded is the level of real income—for the aggregate economy, real GNP. As you know, real GNP and real aggregate expenditure are two sides of the same transaction. The amount of money that households and firms demand depends on the amount of spending that they want to do. The higher the expenditure—the higher the income—the larger is the quantity of money demanded. Again, suppose that you hold an average of $20 to finance your weekly purchases of movies and soda. Now imagine that the prices of these goods and of all other goods remain constant but that your income increases. As a consequence, you now spend more and you also keep a larger amount of money on hand to finance your higher volume of expenditure.

The Interest Rate and the Quantity of Money Demanded

The higher the level of interest rates, other things being equal, the lower is the quantity of real money demanded. Equivalently, the higher the level of interest rates, the higher is the *velocity of circulation* of money. The velocity of circulation is the ratio of real GNP to the quantity of real money demanded.* It measures how much work a given amount of money does. A high velocity of circulation means that money is circulating quickly so that each dollar bill and each dollar of checkable deposits is doing a lot of work. A low velocity of circulation means that currency and checkable deposits are circulating slowly.

Though there are physical limits to how quickly money can circulate, the velocity of circulation can vary greatly. For example, suppose that four people

---

In Chapter 27, we defined the velocity of circulation using the equation of exchange:

$$MV = PY,$$

where M is the quantity of nominal money, V is the velocity of circulation, P is the price level, and Y is real GNP.

Divide this equation by P to give

$$(M/P)V = Y$$

and then divide by the real quantity of money (M/P) to give

$$V = Y/(M/P).$$

That is, the velocity of circulation is equal to the ratio of real GNP to the real money supply.

have just a single one-dollar bill between them. At 9:00 A.M., Ann is holding the dollar bill and the other three people have no money at all. Ann uses the dollar bill at 9:00 A.M. to buy two cups of coffee from Bob. Bob uses the same dollar bill at lunchtime to buy a sandwich from Chuck. Chuck uses the dollar bill in the afternoon to buy an ice-cream cone from Debbie, who in turn uses it in the evening to rent a video from Ann. Ann holds the dollar bill overnight and the same transactions sequence repeats the next day.

In this example, a single one-dollar bill has produced $4 worth of transactions in a single day—involving coffee, a sandwich, ice cream, and a video. The dollar bill has circulated quickly. A small amount of money has produced many transactions with a high velocity of circulation.

These same transactions could have occurred with a low velocity of circulation and a larger quantity of money. For example, each of the four people could have started and ended the day with a dollar, buying and selling the same goods as before. In the first example, the velocity of circulation is 4—$4 worth of expenditure is financed with a one dollar bill. In the second example, the velocity of circulation is 1—$4 worth of transactions are financed with $4 worth of money.

Does the velocity of circulation matter? Do people care how quickly they turn their money over? They do. There are both costs and benefits to having a high velocity of circulation.

The Costs of a High Velocity of Circulation   The main cost of a high velocity of circulation is that people have to transact frequently. They also may have to transact at inconvenient times. For example, in the above story when there is only one dollar, only one person holds the dollar bill at any one time, so none of the others can make a purchase until they have made their sale. Debbie couldn't rent her video until she had sold the ice cream. Chuck couldn't buy his ice cream until he had sold a sandwich, and so on. But if each person in the story starts and ends the day holding a dollar, any of the transactions could be undertaken at any time during the day. For example, it might be much more convenient for Debbie to rent the video on her way to work, before Ann has bought her breakfast, rather than having to run around to Ann's video rental shop in the late afternoon. It might be even more convenient to rent three videos at a time and hang onto them for three days, thereby visiting the video store just twice a week rather than every day. However, to do so, Debbie would need at least as much money as the price of three videos. Economizing on transactions—transacting less frequently—always requires a larger quantity of money than transacting frequently. These are the main costs of a high velocity of circulation—the increased costs of doing business.

The Benefits of a High Velocity of Circulation What are the benefits of a high velocity of circulation of money? A high velocity of circulation means that a small quantity of money is being held relative to the amount of expenditure being undertaken. The lower the quantity of money held, the greater is the quantity of other assets that can be held. Cash in your pocket doesn't earn interest. Some bank deposits do earn interest but at lower rates than other assets such as bonds and stocks. By holding less money and holding more assests that earn a higher interest rate than do bank deposits, people can increase their incomes. This is the main benefit of a high velocity of circulation—a large interest income.

Interest Rate and Opportunity Cost You already know the fundamental principle that as the opportunity cost of something rises, people try to find substitutes for it. Money is no exception to this principle. The opportunity cost of holding money is the interest that could be earned on other assets. The higher the interest rate, the higher is the opportunity cost of holding money and the more will people try to find substitutes for money and economize on their holdings of money. The main substitute for holding money is more frequent transactions. By transacting more frequently and in smaller amounts, people can undertake a given amount of economic activity with a smaller amount of real money. The higher the opportunity cost of holding money, the lower is the quantity of money demanded and the higher is the frequency of transactions. Or in other words, the higher the interest rate, the higher is the velocity of circulation.

The Demand for Real Money

The **demand for real money** is the relationship between the quantity of real money demanded and the interest rate, holding constant all other influences on the amount of money that people wish to hold. To make the demand for real money more concrete, let's consider an example. A person's demand for real money can be represented as a demand schedule for

real money. Such a schedule sets out the quantity of real money that a person wants to hold at a given level of real income for different levels of the interest rate.

Figure 28.5 sets out some numbers for the Polonius household. The household's real income is $20,000 a year. The price level is 1 or the GNP

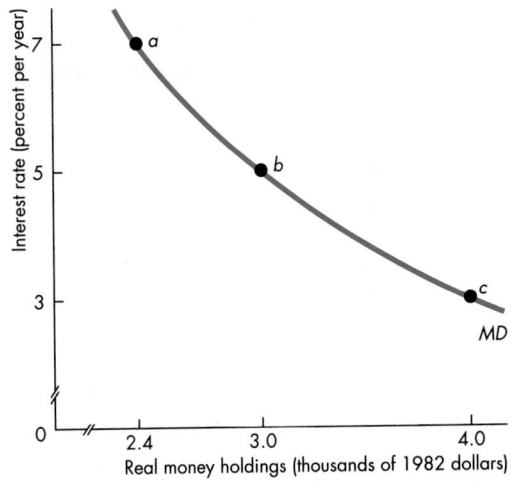

Figure 28.5   The Polonius Household's Demand for Real Money

Polonius household's real income is $20,000; price level is 1

	Interest rate (percent per year)	Real money holdings (thousands of 1982 dollars)
a	7	2.4
b	5	3.0
c	3	4.0

The table shows the Polonius household's demand schedule for real money. The lower the interest rate, the larger is the quantity of real money that the household plans to hold. The graph shows the household's demand curve for real money (MD). Points a, b, c on the curve correspond to the rows in the table. A change in the interest rate leads to a movement along the demand curve. The demand curve for real money slopes downward because the interest rate is the opportunity cost of holding money. The higher the interest rate, the larger is the interest foregone on holding another asset.

deflator is equal to 100, so the quantity of money is the same whether we measure it in nominal terms or real terms. The table tells us how the quantity of real money demanded by the Polonius household changes as the interest rate changes. For example, in row *a*, when the interest rate is 7 percent a year, the Polonius household holds $2400 of money, on the average. When the interest rate is 5 percent a year, real money holdings increase to $3000, and when the interest rate falls to 3 percent a year, real money holdings increase to $4000. The figure also graphs the Polonius household's demand curve for real money (*MD*).

The demand curve for real money slopes downward. The reason for this relationship between the amount of real money held and the interest rate is that the opportunity cost of holding money falls as the rate of interest falls. At an interest rate of 3 percent, the opportunity cost of holding money is small and the Polonius household holds a large average level of real money balances. But at an interest rate of 7 percent, the opportunity cost of holding money is high, so the Polonius household holds a smaller average level of real money.

Shifts in the Demand Curve for Real Money

The demand curve for real money shifts when:

- Real income changes
- Financial innovation occurs

Changes in Real Income An increase in real income shifts the demand curve for real money to the right and a decrease shifts it to the left. The effect of real income on the demand curve for real money is shown in Fig. 28.6. The table shows the effects of a change in real income on the quantity of real money demanded when the interest rate is constant at 5 percent. Look first at row *b* of the table. It tells us that when the interest rate is 5 percent and real income is $20,000, the quantity of real money demanded by the Polonius household is $3000. This row corresponds to point *b* on the demand curve for real money *MD*$_0$. Continuing to hold the interest rate constant, if real income falls to $12,000, the quantity of real money held falls to $2400. Thus the demand curve for real money shifts from *MD*$_0$ to *MD*$_1$ in Fig. 28.6. If the Polonius household's real income

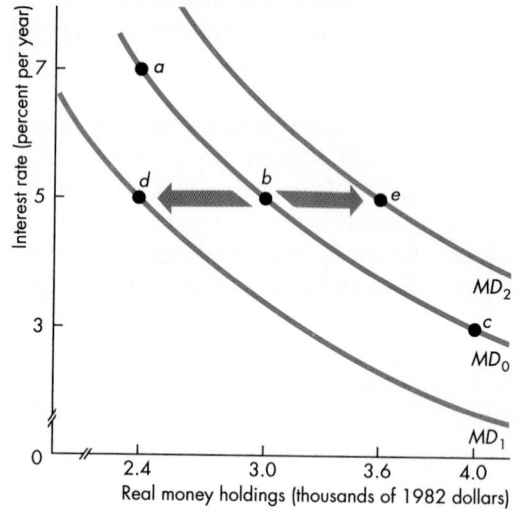

Figure 28.6   Changes in the Polonius Household's Demand for Real Money

Interest rate is 5 percent; price level is 1

	Real income (thousands of 1982 dollars)	Real money holdings (thousands of 1982 dollars)
d	12	2.4
b	20	3.0
e	28	3.6

A change in real income leads to a change in the demand for real money. The table shows the quantity of real money held by the Polonius household at three different levels of real income when the interest rate is constant at 5 percent. The graph shows the effects of a change in real income on the demand curve for real money. When real income is $20,000 and the interest rate is 5 percent, the household is at point *b* on the demand curve for real money *MD*$_0$. When real income falls to $12,000, the demand curve is *MD*$_1$ and, at a 5 percent interest rate, the household is at point *d*. When real income rises to $28,000, the demand curve shifts to *MD*$_2$. With an interest rate of 5 percent, the household is at point *e*.

increases to $28,000, the quantity of real money held by the household increases to $3600. In this case, the demand curve shifts to the right from *MD*$_0$ to *MD*$_2$.

Financial Innovation Financial innovation also results in a change in the demand for real money and a shift in the demand curve for real money. The most important such innovation in recent years has been the development of highly liquid deposits with banks and other financial institutions that make it possible for people to quickly and easily convert such deposits into a medium of exchange—into money. These innovations have been brought about partly as a result of deregulation of the financial sector (see Chapter 27, pp. 716–717) and partly by the availability of low-cost computing power.

Computers are an important part of the story of financial innovation because they have dramatically lowered the cost of keeping records and doing calculations. Interest-bearing checking accounts, for example, have to have balances and interest payments calculated on a daily basis. Doing such calculations by hand, although technologically feasible, would be very costly. Arrangements such as ATS accounts require that funds be transferred to or from a savings account when the balance on a checking account rises above or falls below a certain pre-agreed level. Again, keeping the records that make such bank accounts feasible in the precomputer age would have been prohibitively costly.

Now that banks have access to a vast amount of extremely low-cost computing power, they can offer a wide variety of deposit arrangements that make it convenient to convert non-medium of exchange assets into medium of exchange assets at extremely low cost. The development of these arrangements has led to a decrease in the demand for money.

The availability of low-cost computing power in the financial sector is also responsible, in large degree, for the widespread use of credit cards. Again, keeping the records and calculating the interest and outstanding debt required to operate a credit card system is feasible by hand but too costly to undertake. No one would find it worthwhile to use plastic cards, shuffle sales slips, and keep records if all the calculations had to be done by hand (or even by pre-electronic mechanical calculating machines). This innovation—low-cost computing power—has also lowered the demand for money. By using a credit card to make purchases, it is possible to operate with a much lower inventory of money. Instead of holding money for transactions purposes through the month, it is possible to charge purchases to a credit card, paying the credit card bill on or a day or two after payday with the consequence that the average holding of money throughout the month is much lower.

The financial innovations that we have just considered affect the demand for money. Some financial innovations have changed the composition of our money holdings but not its total amount. One of these is the automatic teller machine. On the average, we can now function efficiently with smaller currency holdings than before, simply because we can easily obtain currency at almost any time or place. Although this innovation has decreased the demand for currency and increased the demand for deposits, it has probably not affected the overall demand for real money.

R E V I E W

The quantity of money demanded depends on the price level, real GNP, and the interest rate. The quantity of nominal money demanded is proportional to the price level. Real money is the nominal quantity of money divided by the price level. The quantity of real money demanded increases as real GNP increases. The opportunity cost of holding money is the interest rate. The benefit from holding money is the avoidance of frequent transactions. The higher the opportunity cost of holding money (the higher the interest rate), the smaller is the quantity of real money demanded and the higher is the velocity of circulation.

We can represent the demand for money by a demand curve for real money. That demand curve for real money shows how the quantity of real money demanded varies as the interest rate varies. When the interest rate changes, there is a movement along the demand curve for real money. Equivalently, there is a change in the velocity of circulation of money. Other influences on the quantity of real money demanded shift the demand curve for real money. An increase in real income shifts the demand curve to the right; financial innovations that develop convenient near-money deposits shift the demand curve to the left. ∎

Now that we have studied the theory of the demand for real money, let's look at the facts about money holdings in the United States and see how they relate to real income and the interest rate.

The Demand for Money in
the United States

We've just seen that the demand curve for real money, which shows how the quantity of real money demanded varies as the interest rate varies, shifts whenever there is a change in real GNP or when there is a financial innovation influencing money holding. Because these factors that shift the demand curve for real money are changing all the time in the real world, it is not easy to "see" the demand curve for real money for a real world economy. What we can see, however, is the velocity of circulation of money. As we have just seen, a movement along the demand curve for real money is associated with a change in its velocity of circulation. The theory of the demand for real money predicts that the higher the interest rate, the lower is the quantity of real money demanded and the higher is its velocity of circulation. By examining the velocity of circulation, and comparing it with movements in the interest rate, we can check whether the theory of the demand for real money provides a good description of movements in the velocity of circulation in the United States.

Figure 28.7 shows the relationship between the interest rate and the velocity of circulation of M1 and M2. The interest rate is measured on the left vertical scale of each part of the figure and the velocity of circulation on the right scale. As you can see, there is a distinct relationship between both the velocity of circulation of M1 and M2 and the interest rate. The relationship is more pronounced in the case of the velocity of circulation of M2 in part (b). The velocity of circulation of M1 is less closely related to the movements in the interest rate than is the velocity of circulation of M2. In fact, the main feature of the velocity of circulation of M1 is its steady trend increase from 1960 to 1980. Even when interest rates fell, as they did in 1971 and 1972 and again in 1975 and 1976, the velocity of circulation of M1 continued to increase. But the fall in interest rates after 1980 was associated with a decrease in the velocity of circulation of M1 through the 1980s.

The fact that the velocities of circulation of M1 and M2 fluctuate in sympathy with fluctuations in interest rates means that the U.S. economy has a demand curve for real money that is similar to that of the Polonius household. As interest rates rise, the economy slides up its demand curve for real money and the quantity of real money demanded decreases, *other things held constant*. But in the real world, other things are not constant. Steadily growing real income

has brought an increase in the demand for real money—shifting the demand curve for real money to the right. Financial innovations have slowed that increase.

There is another aspect of the velocities of circulation of M1 and M2 that is interesting and should be noted. It concerns the range of variation in the velocities. The velocity of circulation of M2 is a remarkably stable number. Look at the range of values on the right scale of Fig. 28.7(b). As you can see, the lowest value of the M2 velocity is 1.5, the highest value is 1.7, and the average value is around 1.6. The fact that the M2 velocity varies only by a small amount means that the demand curve for real M2 is very steep. Large changes in interest rates bring about only a small change in the quantity of real M2 demanded and in its velocity of circulation. In contrast, the variation in the velocity of circulation of M1 is much larger. It ranges from less than 4 to 7. This fact means that the slope for the demand curve for real M1 is much less steep than that for real M2. An increase in the interest rate produces a much larger decrease in the quantity of M1 demanded and a much larger increase in the velocity of circulation of M1 than it does for the quantity of M2 demanded and the velocity of circulation of M2.

Why is the velocity of circulation of M1, and the quantity of M1 demanded, much more responsive to interest rate changes than M2? It is because currency and checkable deposits, the components of M1, do not themselves earn interest while the deposits that are added to M1 to make up M2 do earn interest. There is a tendency for interest rates to vary together. Thus when interest rates in general are rising, the interest rate on savings deposits is also rising. This increase in interest rates on the deposits in M2 means that people have less incentive to decrease their holdings of such deposits when interest rates in general rise. In contrast, the components of M1, which earn either no interest or a very low interest rate, become more expensive to hold—their opportunity cost increases—so the quantity of them held decreases.

We have now studied the factors that determine the demand for real money and discovered that an important determinant of the quantity of real money demanded is the opportunity cost of holding it—the interest rate. We've also studied the way in which the Fed can influence the quantity of money supplied. We're now going to combine our models of the demand side of the money market and the supply side to see how the interest rate is determined.

Figure 28.7 The Interest Rate and the Velocity of Circulation of M1 and M2

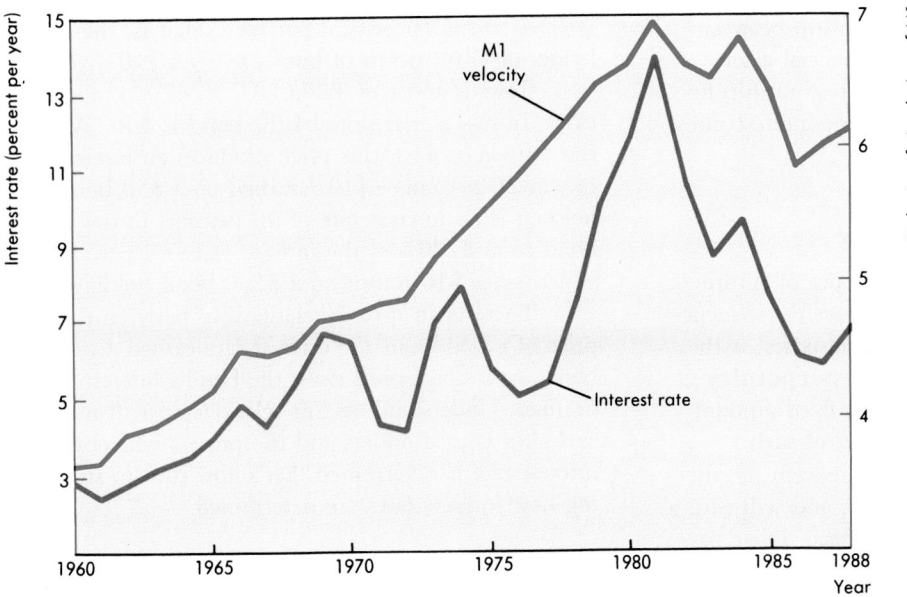

(a) M1 velocity and the interest rate

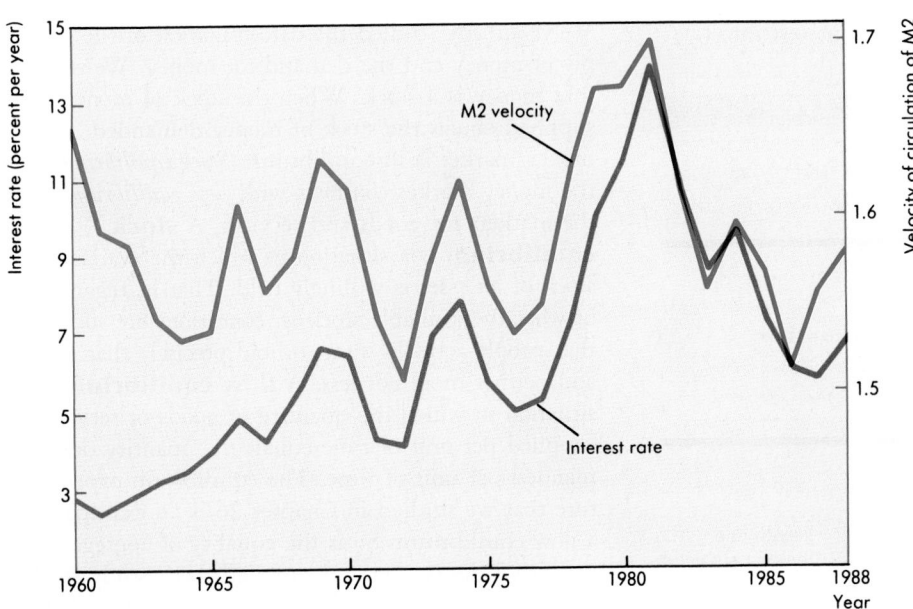

(b) M2 velocity and the interest rate

Source: Economic Report of the President, 1989.

In part (a), the velocity of circulation of M1 is measured on the right scale and interest rates on the left scale. Both the velocity of circulation of M1 and interest rates increased until 1980 and declined through the 1980s. M1 velocity is much smoother than interest rates and does not have the pronounced cycles visible in interest rates in the 1970s. The two series follow similar trends. In part (b), the velocity of circulation of M2 is measured on the right scale and interest rates on the left scale. These two variables fluctuate remarkably close together. But the range of variation in the velocity of circulation of M2 is much lower than the range of variation in interest rates (or in the range of variation of the velocity of M1, as seen in part a).

Interest Rate Determination

An interest rate is the percentage yield on a financial security such as a *bond* or a *stock*. There is an important relationship between the interest rate and the price of a financial asset. Let's spend a moment studying that relationship before analyzing the forces that determine interest rates.

Interest Rates and Asset Prices

A bond is a promise to make a sequence of future payments. There are many different possible sequences but the most simple one, for our purposes, is the case of a bond called a perpetuity. A **perpetuity** is a bond that promises to pay a certain fixed amount of money each year forever. The issuer of such a bond will never buy the bond back (redeem it); the bond will remain outstanding forever, and will earn a fixed dollar payment each year. The fixed dollar payment is called the *coupon*. Since the coupon is a fixed dollar amount, the interest rate on the bond varies as the price of the bond varies. Table 28.7 illustrates this fact.

First, the table shows the formula for calculating the interest rate on a bond. The interest rate (r)

is the coupon (c) divided by the price of the bond (p) all multiplied by 100 to convert it into a percentage. The table goes on to show some numerical examples for a bond whose coupon is $10 a year. If the bond cost $100 (row b of Table 28.7), the interest rate is 10 percent per year. That is, the holder of $100 worth of bonds receives $10 a year.

Rows a and c of Table 28.7 show two other cases. In row a, the price of the bond is $50. With the coupon at $10, this price produces an interest rate of 20 percent—$10 returned on a $50 bond holding is an interest rate of 20 percent. In row c, the bond costs $200 and the interest rate is 5 percent— which gives $10 return on a $200 bond holding.

There is an inverse relationship between the price of a bond and the interest rate earned on the bond. As a bond price rises, the bond's interest rate declines. Understanding this relationship will make it easier for you to understand the process whereby the interest rate is determined. Let's now turn to studying how interest rates are determined.

Money Market Equilibrium

The interest rate is determined at each point in time by equilibrium in the markets for financial assets. We can study that equilibrium in the market for money. We've already studied the determination of the supply of money and the demand for money. We've seen that money is a stock. When the stock of money supplied equals the stock of money demanded, the money market is in equilibrium. *Stock equilibrium* in the money market contrasts with *flow equilibrium* in the markets for goods and services. A **stock equilibrium** is a situation in which the available stock of an asset is willingly held. That is, regardless of what the available stock is, conditions are such that people actually want to hold precisely that stock and neither more nor less. A **flow equilibrium** is a situation in which the quantity of goods or services supplied per unit of time equals the quantity demanded per unit of time. The equilibrium expenditure that we studied in Chapter 26 is an example of a flow equilibrium. So is the equality of aggregate real GNP demanded and supplied. Let's study stock equilibrium and the market for money and see how it determines the level of interest rates.

The nominal quantity of money supplied is determined by the policy decisions of the Fed and by the lending actions of banks and other financial intermediaries. The real quantity of money supplied is

---

Table 28.7   The Interest Rate and the Price of a Bond

Formula for interest rate

r = interest rate, c = coupon, p = price of bond

$$r = \frac{c}{p} \cdot 100$$

Examples

	Price of bond	Coupon	Interest rate (percent per year)
a	$ 50	$10	20
b	100	10	10
c	200	10	5

equal to the nominal quantity supplied divided by the price level. At a given moment in time, there is a particular price level and so the quantity of real money supplied is a fixed amount.

The demand curve for real money depends on the level of real GNP. And on any given day, the level of real GNP may be treated as fixed. But the interest rate is not fixed. The interest rate adjusts to achieve stock equilibrium in the money market. If the interest rate is too high, people will try to hold less money than is available. If the interest rate is too low, people will try to hold more than the stock that is available. When the interest rate is such that people want to hold exactly the amount of money that is available, then a stock equilibrium prevails.

Figure 28.8 illustrates an equilibrium in the money market. The quantity of real money supplied is $3 trillion. The table sets out the quantity of real money demanded at three different interest rates when real GNP is constant at $4 trillion and the price level is constant at 1 (the price index equals 100).

At a 5 percent interest rate, the quantity of real money demanded is $3 trillion, which equals the quantity of real money supplied. The equilibrium interest rate is 5 percent. If the interest rate is above 5 percent, people will want to hold less money than is available. At an interest rate below 5 percent, people will want to hold more money than is available. At a 5 percent interest rate, the amount of money available is willingly held.

How does money market equilibrium come about? To answer this question, let's perform a thought experiment. First, imagine that the interest rate is temporarily at 7 percent. In this situation, people will want to hold only $2 trillion in real money even though $3 trillion exists. But since $3 trillion exists, people must be holding it. That is, people are holding more money than they want to. In such a situation, they will try to get rid of some of their money. Each individual will try to reorganize his or her affairs in order to lower the amount of money held and take advantage of the 7 percent interest rate by buying more financial assets. But everybody will be trying to buy financial assets, and nobody will be trying to sell them at a 7 percent interest rate. There is an excess demand for financial assets such as bonds. When there is an excess demand for anything, its price rises. So with an excess demand for financial assets, the prices of financial assets will rise. We saw earlier that there is an inverse

Figure 28.8   Money Market Equilibrium

Adjustments in the interest rate achieve money market equilibrium. If real GNP is $4 trillion, the demand for real money is given by curve MD. If the supply of real money is $3 trillion (curve MS in the figure), the equilibrium interest rate is 5 percent. At interest rates above 5 percent, the quantity of real money demanded is less than the quantity supplied, so interest rates will fall. At interest rates below 5 percent, the quantity of real money demanded exceeds the quantity supplied, so interest rates will rise. Only at 5 percent is the quantity of real money in existence willingly held.

Real GNP is $4 trillion; price level is 1

Interest rate (percent per year)	Quantity of real money demanded (trillions of 1982 dollars)	Quantity of real money supplied (trillions of 1982 dollars)
7	2	3
5	3	3
3	4	3

relationship between the price of a financial asset and its interest rate. As the price of a financial asset rises, its interest rate falls.

As long as anyone is holding money in excess of the quantity demanded, that person will try to lower his or her money holdings by buying additional financial assets. Financial asset prices will continue to rise and interest rates will continue to fall. Only when the interest rate has moved down to 5 percent will the amount of money in existence be held willingly. That is, people's attempts to get rid of unwanted excess money do not result in reducing the amount of money held in aggregate. Instead, those efforts result in a change in the interest rate that makes the amount of money available willingly held.

The thought experiment that we have just conducted can be performed in reverse by supposing that the interest rate is 3 percent. In this situation, people want to hold $4 trillion even though only $3 trillion is available. To acquire more money, people will sell financial assets. There will be an excess supply of financial assets, so their prices will fall. As the prices of financial assets fall, the yield on them—the interest rate—rises. People will continue to sell financial assets and try to acquire money until the interest rate has risen to 5 percent, where the amount of money available is the amount that they want to hold.

The determination of the equilibrium interest rate is illustrated in the diagram in Fig. 28.8. The real money supply is the vertical curve MS at $3 trillion. The demand curve for real money (MD) cuts the supply curve at an interest rate of 5 percent. At interest rates above 5 percent, there is an excess of the quantity of real money supplied over the quantity of real money demanded. At interest rates below 5 percent, there is an excess of the quantity of real money demanded over the quantity of real money supplied. The only interest rate that makes the quantity of real money available willingly held is 5 percent.

Changing the Interest Rate

Imagine that the economy is sagging and the Fed wants to encourage additional aggregate demand and spending. To do so, it wants to lower interest rates and encourage more borrowing and more investment. What does the Fed do? How does it fiddle with the knobs to achieve lower interest rates?

The Fed undertakes an open market operation, buying government securities from banks, households, and firms. As a consequence, the monetary base increases, and banks start making additional loans. The money supply increases.

Suppose that the Fed undertakes open market operations on a sufficiently large scale to increase the money supply from $3 trillion to $4 trillion. As a consequence, the supply curve of real money shifts to the right, as shown in Fig. 28.9(a), from MS_0 to MS_1, and the thought experiment that we conducted earlier now becomes a real world event. The interest rate falls as individuals attempt to reduce their money holdings and buy additional financial assets. When the interest rate has fallen to 3 percent, people are willingly holding the higher $4 trillion stock of real money that the Fed and the banking system has now created.

Conversely, suppose that the economy is overheating and the Fed fears inflation. The Fed decides to take action to slow down spending and cuts the money supply. In this case, the Fed undertakes an open market sale of securities. As it does so, it mops up bank reserves and induces the banks to cut down the scale of their lending. The banks make a smaller quantity of new loans each day until the stock of loans outstanding has fallen to a level consistent with the new lower level of reserves. Suppose that the Fed undertakes an open market sale of securities on a scale big enough to cut the real money supply to $2 trillion. Now the supply of real money curve shifts to the left, as shown in Fig. 28.9(b), from MS_0 to MS_2. With less money available, people attempt to acquire additional money by selling interest-earning assets. As they do so, asset prices fall and interest rates rise. Equilibrium occurs when the interest rate has risen to 7 percent, at which point the new lower real money stock of $2 trillion is willingly held.

The Fed in Action

All this sounds nice in theory, but does it really happen? Indeed, it does happen, and sometimes with dramatic effect. Let's look at two episodes in the life of the Fed, one from the turbulent years of the early 1980s and the other from the period since the stock market crash of 1987.

Paul Volcker's Fed   At the start of Paul Volcker's term of office as chairman of the Fed, which began in August 1979, the United States was locked in the grips of double-digit inflation. Volcker ended that inflation. He did so by forcing interest rates sharply upward from 1979 through 1981. This increase in interest rates resulted from the Fed using open market operations and increases in the discount rate to keep the banks short of reserves, which in turn held back the growth in the supply of loans and of money, relative to the growth in their demand

As we saw in Fig. 28.9(b), to increase interest rates, the Fed has to cut the real money supply. In

Figure 28.9 The Fed Changes the Interest Rate

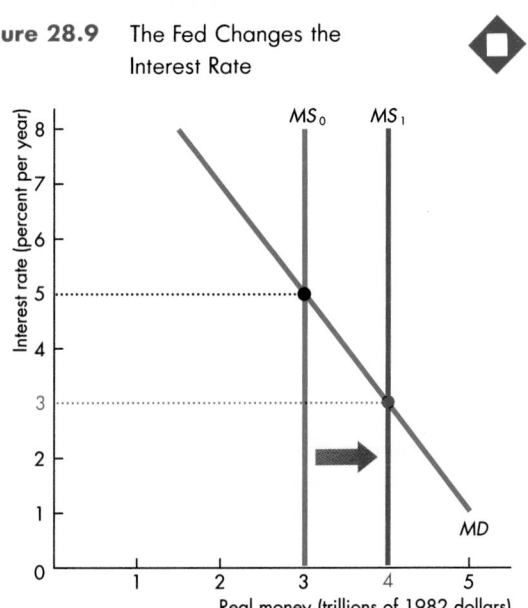

(a) An increase in the money supply

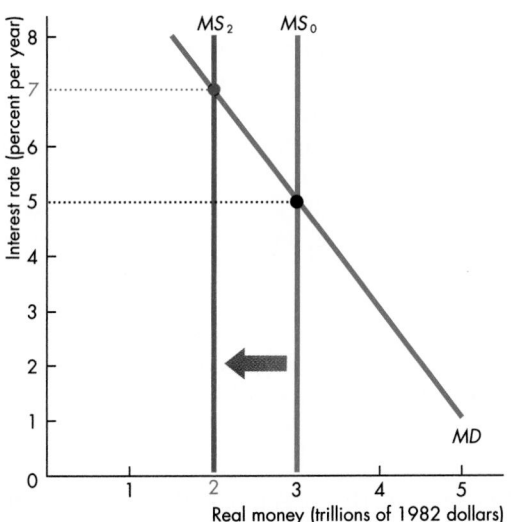

(b) A decrease in the money supply

In part (a), the Fed conducts an open market purchase of securities, increasing the money supply to $4 trillion. The real money supply shifts to the right. The new equilibrium interest rate is 3 percent. In part (b), the Fed conducts an open market sale of securities, decreasing the real money supply to $2 trillion. The money supply curve shifts to the left, and the interest rate rises to 7 percent. By changing the money supply, at a given real GNP and price level, the Fed can adjust interest rates daily or weekly.

practice, because the economy is growing and because prices are rising, a slowdown in nominal money supply growth is enough to increase interest rates. It is not necessary to actually cut the nominal money supply.

When Volcker became chairman of the Fed, the money supply was growing at more than 8 percent a year. Volcker slowed down that money supply growth to 6.5 percent in 1981. As a result, interest rates increased. The treasury bill rate—the rate at which the government borrows—increased from 10 percent to 14 percent. The rate at which the big corporations borrow increased from 9 percent to 14 percent. Mortgage rates—the rates at which home buyers borrow—increased from 11 percent to 15 percent. The economy went into recession. The money supply growth slowdown and interest rate hike cut back the growth rate of aggregate demand. Real GNP fell and the inflation rate slowed down.

Alan Greenspan's Fed   Alan Greenspan became chairman of the Fed in August 1987. In the two preceding years the money supply had grown at a rapid pace, interest rates had tumbled, and the stock market had boomed. Then, suddenly and with no warning, stock prices fell bringing fears of economic calamity and recession. This was Alan Greenspan's first test as Fed chairman.

The Fed's immediate reaction to the new situation was to emphasize the flexibility and sensitivity of the financial system and to make reserves plentiful to avoid any fear of a banking crisis. But as the months passed it became increasingly clear that the economy was not heading for any kind of a recession. Unemployment continued to fall, income growth continued to be strong, and the fears that emerged were of inflation, not recession.

Seeking to avoid a serious upturn in inflation, the Fed slowed money growth and, just as Paul Volcker had done eight years earlier, forced interest rates sharply upward. Open market operations were targeted toward creating a shortage of reserves in the banking system to slow down the growth rate of the money supply. As a consequence, during the year from May 1988 to May 1989 the M1 measure of the money supply was virtually constant and the M2 measure grew by only 2.4 percent, both down from growth rates of around 5 percent a year earlier and down from around 10 percent a year before the stock market crash. The slowdown in money supply growth had the effect implied by the model that you have been studying in this chapter. Interest rates increased throughout 1988. The interest rate on U.S. government 3-month treasury bills increased from less than 6 percent a year at the start of 1988 to almost 9 percent a year by early 1989.

As 1989 advanced, concern about inflation remained, but renewed fears of recession returned as an increasing number of signs of a slowing economy emerged

Profiting by Predicting the Fed

Day by day, even minute by minute, the Fed can influence interest rates and the money supply by its open market operations. By increasing the supply of money, the Fed can lower interest rates; by lowering the supply of money, the Fed can increase interest rates. Holders of financial assets know about the powers of the Fed. They also know about another relationship that we have worked out: The higher the interest rate, the lower is the price of a bond and the lower the interest rate, the higher is the price of a bond. They can also put these two things together and know that, if they can predict changes in monetary policy, then they can predict future interest rates and future bond prices. Predicting future bond prices is a potentially profitable activity. Predicting that interest rates are going to fall is the same as predicting that bond prices are going to rise—a good time to buy bonds. Predicting that interest rates are going to rise is the same as predicting that bond prices are going to fall—a good time to sell bonds.

Because predicting the Fed is profitable, a good deal of effort goes into that activity. But *if* people do anticipate the Fed's monetary policy changes, then bond prices and interest rates will change as soon as the Fed's actions are foreseen. By the time the Fed actually takes its actions, those actions will have no effect. The effect will have occurred in anticipation of the Fed's actions. Only changes in the money supply that were not foreseen will change the interest rate at the time that those changes occur.

At any given moment, the interest rate is determined by the demand for and the supply of money. The interest rate makes the quantity of money demanded equal to the quantity of money supplied. Changes in the interest rate occur as a result of changes in the money supply. When the money supply change is not predicted, interest rates will change at the same time as the change in the money supply. If a change in the money supply is foreseen, interest rates will start to change ahead of the change in the money supply.

■   In this chapter, we've studied the determination of interest rates and discovered how the Fed can "fiddle with the knobs" to influence interest rate levels as well as influence the quantity of money and the volume of bank lending. In Chapters 25 and 26, we discovered that the level of interest rates has an important influence on the level of investment and on aggregate expenditure and real GNP. In the next chapter, we're going to bring these two aspects of the macroeconomy together and study the wider effects of the Fed's actions—effects on investment, spending, and the level of aggregate demand.

S U M M A R Y

The Federal Reserve System

The Federal Reserve System is the central bank of the United States. The Fed consists of the Board of Governors and 12 regional Federal Reserve banks. The main policymaking committee is the Federal Open Market Committee. The Fed influences the economy by determining reserve requirements for banks and other deposit-taking institutions, by setting the discount rate—the interest rate at which it is willing to lend reserves to the banking system—

and by open market operations. By buying government securities in the market (an open market purchase), the Fed is able to increase the monetary base and the reserves available to banks. As a result, there is an expansion of bank lending and a fall in interest rates. By selling government securities, the Fed is able to decrease the monetary base and the reserves of banks and other financial institutions, thereby curtailing loans and putting upward pressure on interest rates. The overall effect of a change in the monetary base on the money supply is determined by the money multiplier, which in turn depends on the ratio of currency to deposits held by households and firms and the ratio of reserves to deposits held by banks and other financial institutions. (pp. 729–740)

The Demand for Money

The quantity of money demanded is the amount of currency, demand deposits, and other checking accounts that people hold on the average. The quantity of money demanded is proportional to the price level and the quantity of real money demanded depends on the interest rate and real GNP. A higher level of real GNP induces a larger quantity of real money demanded. A higher interest rate induces a smaller quantity of real money demanded. Fluctuations in the ratio of real GNP to real money (the velocity of circulation) are correlated with fluctuations in the interest rate. Technological change in the financial sector has also reduced the demand for money over the years. (pp. 740–747)

Interest Rate Determination

Changes in interest rates achieve stock equilibrium in the markets for money and financial assets. There is an inverse relationship between the interest rate and the price of a financial asset. The higher the interest rate, the lower is the price of a financial asset. Money market equilibrium achieves an interest rate and asset price that makes the quantity of real money available willingly held. If the quantity of real money is increased by the actions of the Fed, the interest rate falls and the prices of financial assets rise.

People attempt to profit by predicting the actions of the Fed. To the extent that they can predict the Fed, interest rates and the price of financial assets move in anticipation of the Fed's actions rather than in response to them. As a consequence, interest rates change when the Fed changes the money supply only if the Fed catches people by surprise. Anticipated changes in the money supply produce interest rate changes by themselves. (pp. 748–752)

K E Y   C O N C E P T S

R E V I E W   Q U E S T I O N S

1 What are the three main elements in the structure of the Federal Reserve System?

2 What are the three policy tools of the Fed? Which of these is the main tool?

3 If the Fed wants to cut the quantity of money, does it buy or sell U.S. government securities in the open market?

4 Describe the events that take place when banks have excess reserves.

5 What is the money multiplier?

6 Why has the money multiplier in the United States been so constant in recent years?

7 Distinguish between nominal money and real money.

8 What do we mean by the demand for money?

9 What determines the demand for real money?

10 What is the opportunity cost of holding money?

11 What happens to the interest rate on a bond if the price of the bond increases?

12 How does equilibrium come about in the money market?

13 What happens to the interest rate if the real GNP and price level are constant and there is an increase in the supply of money?

14 Explain why it pays people to try to predict the Fed's actions.

P R O B L E M S

1 You are given the following information about a hypothetical economy: The banks have deposits of $300 billion. Their reserves are $15 billion, two thirds of which are deposits with the central bank. The monetary base is $40 billion. There is no coin in this economy.

   a) Set out the balance sheet of the commercial banks. Supply any missing numbers using your knowledge of the fact that total assets equal total liabilities.

   b) What is the amount of currency in circulation?

   c) What is the money supply?

   d) What is the money multiplier?

2 Suppose that the central bank in the economy of problem 1 undertakes an open market purchase of securities of $1 million. What happens to the money supply? Explain why the money supply changes by more than the change in the monetary base?

3 You are given the following information about another imaginary economy: For each $1 increase in real GNP, the demand for real money increases by one third of a dollar, other things being equal. Also, if the interest rate increases by 1 percentage point (for example, from 4 percent to 5 percent), the quantity of real money demanded falls by $40. If the price level is 1, real GNP is $1000, and the real money supply is $133, what is the interest rate?

4 Suppose that the central bank in the economy of problem 3 wants to change the interest rate to 4 percent. By how much would it have to change the real money supply to achieve that objective?

Chapter 29

*After studying this
chapter, you will be
able to:*

- Explain the interest rate
  transmission mechanism of
  monetary policy

- Describe the other transmission mechanisms of
  monetary policy—real
  balance effect, wealth effect, and exchange rate

- Describe the time lags in
  the operation of monetary
  policy

- Define and explain crowding out

- Explain why crowding out
  weakens the effects of fiscal policy actions on aggregate demand

- Explain the effects of fiscal
  policy on the exchange
  rate and net exports

- Describe the time lags in
  the operation of fiscal
  policy

- Describe the Keynesian-
  monetarist controversy
  about aggregate demand

- Explain how the Keynes-
  ian-monetarist aggregate
  demand controversy was
  settled

Each year Congress and the state legislatures approve budgets that determine the level of government purchases of goods and services. By 1988, that total exceeded $1 trillion—about one fifth of GNP. These same legislative assemblies also determine the scale of social programs and the transfer payments associated with them as well as the rules governing the taxes that we all have to pay. In 1988, transfer payments were $0.5 trillion and taxes $1.4 trillion. Government purchases, taxes, and transfer payments are the levers of fiscal policy. How do these levers of fiscal policy influence the economy? In particular, how do they affect aggregate demand? How do they affect other variables that influence aggregate demand, such as interest rates and the exchange rate? ■ Five city blocks from the White House is the home of the board of governors of the Federal Reserve System. Here the Fed pulls the nation's monetary policy levers. At some times, such as in 1980 and 1981, the Fed has used those levers to slow down the economy—increasing interest rates, slowing money growth, and slowing the growth of aggregate demand. At other times, such as in the mid-1980s, the Fed has used its monetary policy levers to speed up the economy—lowering interest rates, speeding up money growth, and increasing aggregate demand. We've seen how the Fed's policy levers influence interest rates. But how do the effects of the Fed's actions ripple through from interest rates to the rest of the economy? How do they affect aggregate demand? ■ In the Executive Office Building—part of the White House complex —is the home of the President's Council of Economic Advisers. This council, established by the Employment Act of 1946, monitors both the fiscal policy actions of the Congress and the monetary policy actions of the Fed and attempts to keep the president and cabinet informed about the actions and plans of each branch of

Congress, the Fed, and the White House

macroeconomic policymaking and of their likely effects. Since both fiscal actions taken by the Congress
and monetary actions taken by the Fed can increase
or decrease aggregate demand, are these two methods
of changing aggregate demand equivalent to each
other? Does it matter whether a recession is avoided
by having the Fed loosen up its monetary policy or
by getting Congress to implement a tax cut? Do
changes in taxes and government purchases and
changes in the money supply have to reinforce each
other or can they offset each other? For example,
when the Fed, under Alan Greenspan, slowed down
money growth and increased interest rates in 1988 to
keep the lid on inflation in 1989, could Congress
have offset the Fed's actions by taking actions of its
own—for example, cutting taxes or increasing government purchases? Or, alternatively, if Congress cut
government purchases, creating fears of recession,
could the Fed increase the money supply and keep
GNP up, thereby avoiding recession?

■ We are going to answer these important questions
in this chapter. You already know that the effects of
monetary and fiscal policy are determined by the
interaction of aggregate demand and aggregate supply. And you already know quite a lot about these
two concepts. But this chapter gives you an even
deeper understanding of aggregate demand and the
way it is affected by the monetary policy actions of
the Fed and the fiscal policy actions of the federal
government. ■ Although this chapter is about policy issues, it is not about the *conduct* of policy. It is a
chapter about the *theory* of policy. It's important to
get the theoretical foundations straight so that when
we do come to study the conduct of policy, in
Chapters 33 and 34, we will have a firm foundation
on which to build.[1]

Money, Interest, and Aggregate Demand

We discovered in Chapter 26 (pp. 679–
681) that equilibrium expenditure depends on the level of autonomous expenditure. We also discovered that one of the components
of autonomous expenditure—investment—varies
with the interest rate. The higher the interest rate,
other things held constant, the lower is investment,

and hence the lower is autonomous expenditure and
equilibrium expenditure. In Chapter 28 (pp. 748–
750), we saw that the interest rate is determined by
equilibrium in the money market. By increasing the
quantity of money, the Fed can lower interest rates.

We're now going to bring these two sets of
results together and see how the Fed's actions influence aggregate demand.

The Interest Rate Transmission Mechanism

To study the interest rate transmission mechanism of
monetary policy, let's see how we can link together
the money market, where the interest rate is determined, and the market for goods and services, where
equilibrium expenditure is determined. First, we'll
study the economy at a given point in time and see
how equilibrium expenditure and interest rates are
determined. Then, we'll disturb that equilibrium by
changing the money supply and work out the consequences of the change.

Equilibrium Expenditure and the Interest Rate
The determination of equilibrium expenditure and
the interest rate is illustrated in Fig. 29.1. The figure
has three parts: Part (a) illustrates the money market;
part (b) shows investment demand; and part (c)
shows aggregate planned expenditure and the determination of equilibrium expenditure. Let's begin in
part (a).

The curve labeled *MD* is the demand for real
money. The position of that curve depends on the
level of real GNP. For a given level of real GNP,
there is a given demand curve for real money. Suppose that the demand curve shown in the figure is
the one that describes the demand for real money
when real GNP is $4 trillion. If real GNP is higher
than $4 trillion, the demand curve for real money is
to the right of the one shown; if real GNP is below
$4 trillion, the demand curve for real money is to the
left of the one shown.

The curve labeled *MS* is the supply curve of
real money. Its position is determined by the monetary policy actions of the Fed, the behavior of the

---

[1]It is possible to study stabilization policy in Chapters 33 and 34
without having previously studied the present chapter. But if you
do take the time and effort to study this chapter, you will find
that you have an even deeper understanding of the discussion of
policy issues in those later chapters.

Figure 29.1 Equilibrium Interest Rate and Real GNP

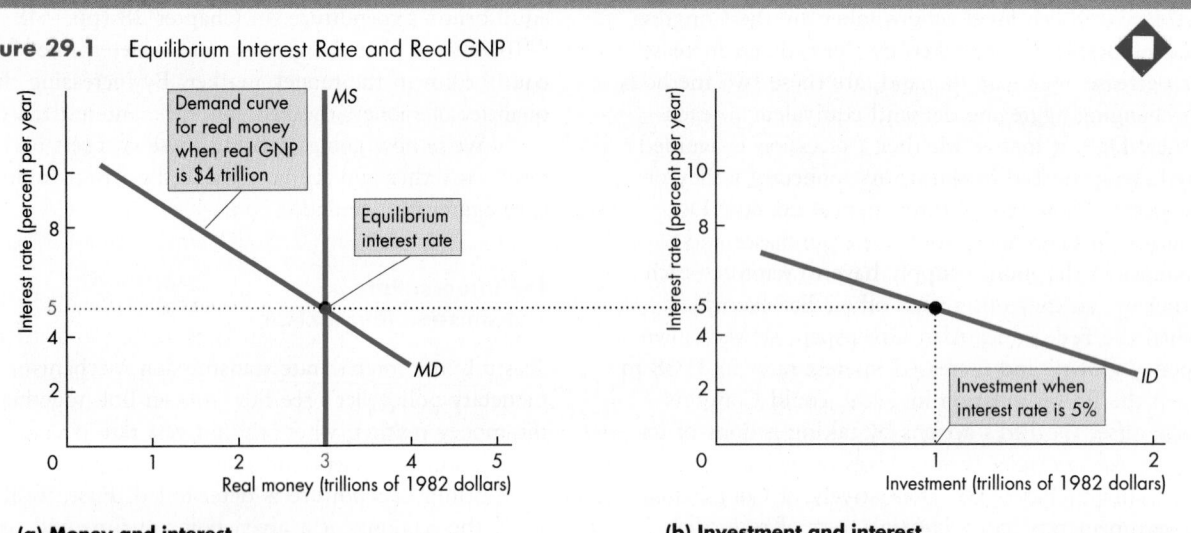

(a) Money and interest

(b) Investment and interest

(c) Expenditure and GNP

Equilibrium in the money market (part a) determines the interest rate. The money supply curve is *MS*. The demand curve for real money is *MD*. The position of the demand curve for real money is determined by real GNP. The demand curve for real money is *MD* when real GNP is $4 trillion. The investment demand curve (*ID*) in part (b) determines investment at the equilibrium interest rate determined in the money market. Investment is part of autonomous expenditure, and its level determines the position of the aggregate expenditure curve (*AE*) shown in part (c). Where the aggregate expenditure curve intersects the 45° line, equilibrium expenditure and real GNP are determined. An equilibrium occurs when real GNP and the interest rate are such that the quantity of real money demanded equals the quantity of real money supplied and aggregate planned expenditure equals real GNP.

banking system, and the price level. At a given point in time, all these influences determine a quantity of money supplied that is independent of the interest rate. Hence the supply curve for real money is vertical.

The equilibrium interest rate is determined at the point of intersection of the demand and supply curves. In the economy illustrated in Fig. 29.1, that interest rate is 5 percent.

Next, let's look at part (b) where investment is determined. The investment demand curve is *ID*. The position of the investment demand curve is determined by profit expectations and, as those ex-

pectations change, the investment demand curve shifts. For given expectations, there is a given investment demand curve. This curve tells us the level of planned investment at each level of the interest rate. But we already know the interest rate from equilibrium in the money market. When the investment demand curve is *ID* and the interest rate is 5 percent, the level of planned investment is $1 trillion.

Part (c) shows the determination of equilibrium expenditure. This diagram is similar to the one that you studied in Chapter 26 (Fig. 26.4). The aggregate expenditure curve (*AE*) tells us aggregate planned expenditure at each level of real GNP. Aggregate planned expenditure is made up of autonomous expenditure and induced expenditure. Investment is part of autonomous expenditure. In this example, investment is $1 trillion, the other components of autonomous expenditure are $0.6 trillion, and autonomous expenditure is $1.6 trillion. These amounts of investment and autonomous expenditure are shown by the horizontal lines in part (c). Investment is I and total autonomous expenditure A. Induced expenditure in this example (the induced part of consumption expenditure minus imports) equals 0.6 multiplied by real GNP. In other words, the marginal propensity to spend on real GNP is 0.6.

Equilibrium expenditure is determined at the point of intersection of the AE curve and the 45° line. Equilibrium occurs when aggregate expenditure and real GNP are each $4 trillion. That is, the level of aggregate demand is $4 trillion.

The Money Market Again   Recall that the demand curve MD, in part (a), is the demand curve for real money when real GNP is $4 trillion. We've just determined in part (c) that at the expenditure equilibrium, real GNP is also $4 trillion. What happens if the level of real GNP that we discover in part (c) is different from the value that we assumed when drawing the demand curve for real money in part (a)? Let's perform a thought experiment to answer this question.

Suppose, when drawing the demand curve for real money, we assume that real GNP is $3 trillion. In this case, the demand curve for real money is to the left of the MD curve in part (a). The interest rate will be lower than 5 percent. With an interest rate below 5 percent, investment is not $1 trillion as determined in part (b), but a higher amount. If investment is higher than $1 trillion, autonomous expenditure will be higher and the AE curve is higher than the one shown in part (c). If the aggregate expenditure curve is higher than AE, equilibrium expenditure and real GNP are larger than $4 trillion. Thus if we start with the demand curve for real money for a level of real GNP below $4 trillion, expenditure equilibrium occurs at a level of real GNP above $4 trillion. There is an inconsistency. The real GNP assumed in drawing the demand curve for real money is too low.

Next, let's reverse the experiment. Assume a level of real GNP of $5 trillion. In this case, the demand curve for real money will be to the right of the MD curve in part (a). The interest rate will be

higher than 5 percent. With an interest rate higher than 5 percent, investment is below $1 trillion and the AE curve is lower than the one shown in part (c). In this case, expenditure equilibrium occurs at a level of real GNP that is below $4 trillion. Again, there is an inconsistency. If we assume a level of real GNP of more than $4 trillion to determine the position of the demand curve for real money, expenditure equilibrium occurs at a level of real GNP that is less than $4 trillion.

Only if we use real GNP of $4 trillion to determine the position of the demand curve for real money do we get a consistent story in the three parts of this figure. If the demand curve for real money is based on real GNP of $4 trillion, the interest rate determined (5 percent) delivers investment of $1 trillion that, in turn, generates an expenditure equilibrium at the same level of real GNP that determines the position of the demand curve for real money. The situation described in Fig. 29.1 is one of stock and flow equilibrium. There is stock equilibrium in the money market and flow equilibrium in the market for goods and services.

The Effects of a Change in the Money Supply
Suppose that the economy is in the situation illustrated in Fig. 29.1. The interest rate is 5 percent, investment is $1 trillion, and real GNP is $4 trillion. Also, suppose that the Fed is concerned that the economy is overheating and that inflation is about to take off. To dampen the economy, the Fed decides to attempt to reduce aggregate demand by conducting an open market operation. The Fed sells government securities, thereby decreasing reserves in the banking system and cutting the money supply.

Suppose that the Fed cuts the real money supply by $1 trillion, from $3 trillion to $2 trillion. The real money supply curve shifts to the left from MS_0 to MS_1 in Fig. 29.2(a). The immediate effect of this action, in the money market, is an increase in interest rates from 5 percent to 7 percent. The higher interest rate leads to a fall in investment from $1 trillion to $0.2 trillion, as shown in Fig. 29.2 (b).

The fall in investment lowers autonomous expenditure and so lowers aggregate planned expenditure. The fall in aggregate planned expenditure lowers the expenditure equilibrium and lowers real GNP, and the fall in real GNP decreases the demand for real money. The decrease in the demand for real money, in turn, has further effects on the interest rate. To keep track of all these simultaneously occur-

Figure 29.2   The Effect of a Change in the Money Supply

(a) Change in money supply

(b) Change in investment

A decrease in the money supply shifts the supply curve of real money from MS_0 to MS_1 (part a). Equilibrium in the money market is achieved by an increase in the interest rate from 5 percent to 7 percent. At the higher interest rate, investment decreases (part b).

ring events, it's a good idea to break the process up and study it in two parts. That's what we'll do. First, we'll see what happens to equilibrium expenditure and real GNP if the interest rate stays at its new higher level of 7 percent. Then we'll study the adjustment process that follows as the interest rate and real GNP respond together to the decreased money supply.

Equilibrium Expenditure at a Constant Interest Rate   The real money supply decreased from $3 trillion to $2 trillion, and the real money supply curve shifted to the left from MS_0 to MS_1 in Fig. 29.2(a). The interest rate increased to 7 percent. The higher interest rate lowered investment from $1 trillion to $0.2 trillion, as shown in Fig. 29.2(b). Let's work out what happens to equilibrium expenditure and real GNP *if the interest rate remains at its new higher level of 7 percent.* With the interest rate at 7 percent, investment falls to $0.2 trillion, autonomous expenditure falls by the same amount as the fall in investment, and the aggregate planned expenditure curve shifts downward from AE_0 to AE_1 in Fig. 29.3. That is, the AE curve shifts downward by $0.8 trillion, the amount of the decrease in investment. When the aggregate expenditure curve is AE_1, equilibrium expenditure and real GNP are $2 trillion.

The economy does not immediately jump from an equilibrium real GNP of $4 trillion to one of $2 trillion. Equilibrium real GNP has changed from $4 trillion to $2 trillion and the economy begins to move in the direction of the new equilibrium. But that process takes time, and during the adjustment process other changes take place that affect equilibrium real GNP so that the economy never actually gets to the point shown in Fig. 29.3. Let's now look at those other forces and see what course the economy actually takes.

Adjustment Process

When investment decreases, the resulting decrease in aggregate planned expenditure sets up a multiplier process that gradually lowers the level of actual expenditure and real GNP. We described this process in Chapter 26 (pp. 681–682).

When aggregate planned expenditure decreases, it initially falls below real GNP. But actual expenditure equals real GNP. There is, therefore, a gap between actual expenditure and planned expenditure—a gap filled by unplanned expenditure. The unplanned expenditure is an increase in inventories. An increase in inventories is part of investment. Thus although planned investment decreases, as shown in

Fig. 29.2(b), actual investment does not decrease by as much, initially, because of the unplanned increase in inventories.

With an unplanned increase in inventories, firms are anxious to restore inventories to their desired levels. To achieve this objective, firms cut back their production. As they do so, real GNP begins to fall.

So far, we've worked out two effects of a monetary policy action that increases interest rates. The first of these effects is a decrease in *equilibrium* expenditure and real GNP. We illustrated this effect in Fig. 29.3. The second effect, that we have just described, is an unplanned increase in inventories that initiates a process of falling *actual* aggregate expenditure and real GNP. To keep track of what happens next, it is important to be clear about the distinction between actual real GNP and equilibrium real GNP. Actual real GNP is determined by actual expenditure

—planned and unplanned expenditure. Equilibrium real GNP is determined by planned expenditure—by the *AE* curve. As the economy continues to adjust to a decrease in the money supply, actual real GNP continues to fall but equilibrium real GNP increases. The falling actual real GNP and rising equilibrium real GNP converge at a new equilibrium that we're now about to discover.

The fall in actual real GNP decreases the demand for real money. As a consequence, the demand curve for real money shifts to the left and the interest rate falls. A lower interest rate increases planned investment and makes the *AE* curve start to shift upward. As the *AE* curve shifts upward, equilibrium expenditure and equilibrium real GNP increase. Let's see how the interest rate changes induced by falling real GNP bring about the new equilibrium.

Induced Interest Rate Changes   The Fed has decreased the money supply. Interest rates are 7 percent, planned investment has fallen but unplanned inventories are accumulating. Equilibrium real GNP has fallen to $2 trillion and actual real GNP, which started out at $4 trillion, is falling. Figure 29.4 illustrates where this process ends up. Let's begin in part (a), which shows money market equilibrium.

Actual real GNP begins to fall. Falling real GNP shifts the demand curve for real money to the left of MD_0. Suppose that the demand curve for real money, when real GNP is $3 trillion, is MD_1. With this demand curve and the supply curve at MS_1, the equilibrium interest rate is 6 percent.

When the interest rate is 6 percent, investment is $0.6 trillion, as shown in Fig. 29.4(b). Thus the fall in the interest rate from 7 percent to 6 percent increases planned investment from $0.2 trillion to $0.6 trillion.

The increase in planned investment from $0.2 trillion to $0.6 trillion shifts the *AE* curve upward from AE_1 to AE_2 in Fig. 29.4(c). When the aggregate expenditure curve is AE_2, equilibrium expenditure and equilibrium real GNP are $3 trillion. But this level of real GNP is precisely the level that makes the demand curve for real money MD_1. When actual real GNP has fallen to $3 trillion, the demand curve for real money has shifted to MD_1 and the interest rate has fallen to 6 percent. Investment has increased to $0.6 trillion ($I_2$) and aggregate planned expenditure has increased, so that equilibrium expenditure and equilibrium real GNP are also $3 trillion. In this situation, there is a new stock and flow equilibrium. The level of aggregate demand is $3 trillion.

Figure 29.3   The Effect of a Change in the Money Supply on Equilibrium Real GNP

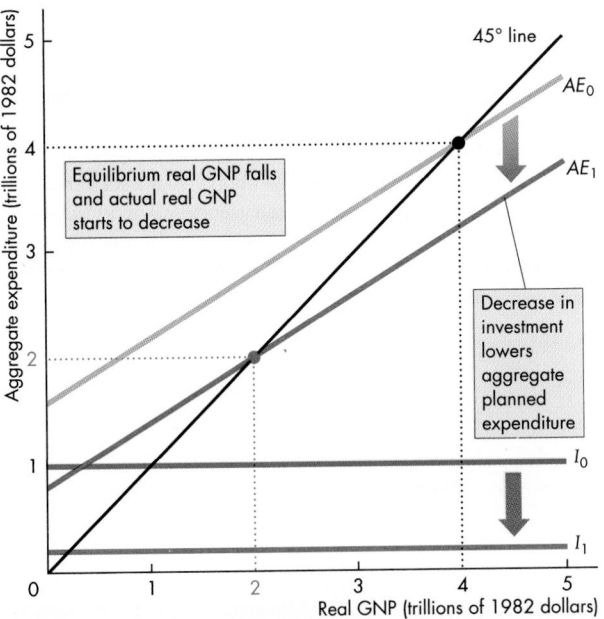

A decrease in the money supply increases the interest rate, lowers investment, and results in a fall in aggregate planned expenditure. The *AE* curve shifts downward from AE_0 to AE_1. Equilibrium real GNP falls from $4 trillion to $2 trillion. Actual real GNP starts to decrease.

Figure 29.4   The Convergence to a New Expenditure Equilibrium

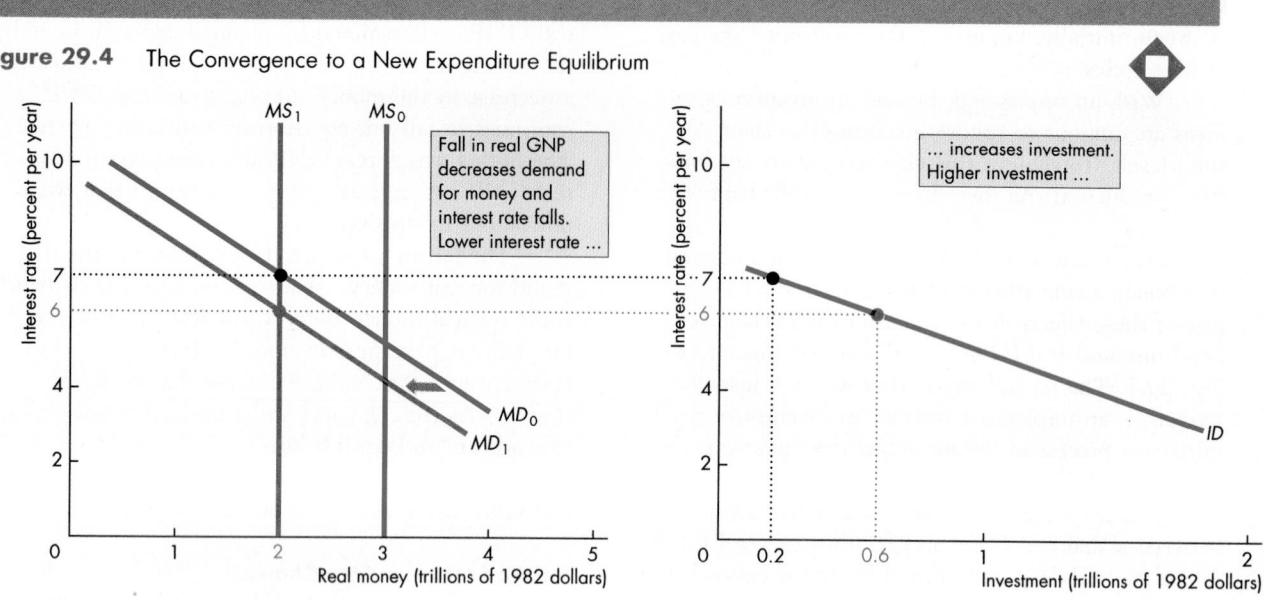

(a) Decrease in demand for money

(b) Increase in investment

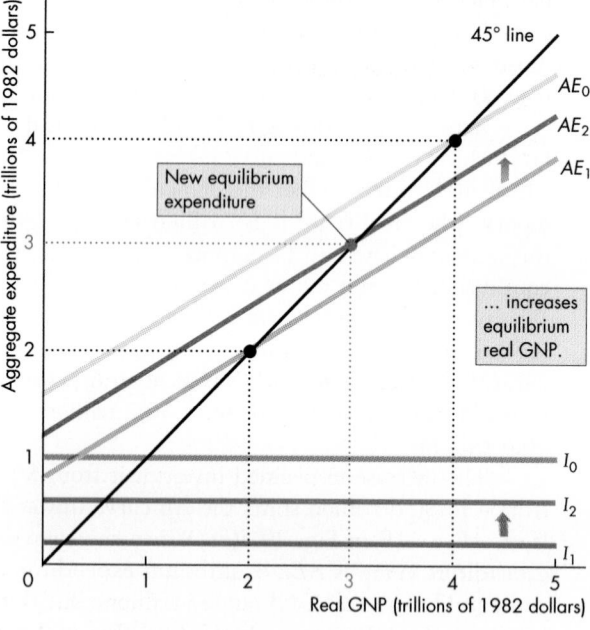

(c) New equilibrium real GNP

As real GNP falls, the demand curve for real money shifts to the left, from MD_0 to MD_1 (part a). The decrease in the demand for real money lowers the interest rate. As the interest rate falls, planned investment increases (part b). The increase in planned investment shifts the AE curve upward to AE_2 (part c). During the process of adjustment, actual real GNP falls and aggregate planned expenditure increases. A new equilibrium occurs when real GNP and aggregate planned expenditure have converged to the same value. In the figure, the new expenditure equilibrium occurs at real GNP of $3 trillion (see part c). That level of real GNP makes the demand curve for real money MD_1 (part a), which generates an interest rate of 6 percent. At that interest rate, investment is $0.6 trillion (part b), which in turn makes the aggregate expenditure curve AE_2 (in part c).

You may find it interesting to work out what would be happening in this economy if we had not picked a new equilibrium level of real GNP to start out the story described in Fig. 29.4. Let's rerun the economic video and hit the freeze-frame button at a different point.

Starting from the initial decrease in the money supply, let's freeze the picture when real GNP has fallen by only $0.5 trillion and is at $3.5 trillion. The demand curve for real money has not shifted as far to the left as MD_1 and the interest rate has not yet fallen to 6 percent. It lies somewhere between 6 and 7 percent. Planned investment is increasing but has not yet increased to $0.6 trillion. It lies somewhere between $0.2 trillion and $0.6 trillion. The aggregate expenditure curve is shifting upward but is below AE_2, lying somewhere between AE_1 and AE_2. Aggregate planned expenditure is below actual expenditure and real GNP, so real GNP is falling.

But if real GNP is falling, the demand curve for real money is shifting to the left; the interest rate is falling; planned investment is increasing; and the AE curve is shifting upward. Equilibrium real GNP is increasing. Inventories are accumulating and actual real GNP is decreasing. Equilibrium real GNP and actual real GNP meet at some point in this process. The point at which they meet is that shown in Fig. 29.4(c).

R E V I E W

To lower aggregate demand, the Fed undertakes an open market operation. It sells U.S. government securities. This action sets up the following sequence of events:

- The quantity of money decreases and the money supply curve shifts to the left.

- The interest rate increases.

- Planned investment decreases.

- Aggregate planned expenditure decreases.

- Equilibrium expenditure and equilibrium real GNP decrease.

- Unplanned inventories accumulate.

- Actual real GNP begins to fall.

- Falling real GNP shifts the demand curve for real money to the left.

- The shifting demand curve for real money decreases the interest rate.

- The falling interest rate increases planned investment.

- Increasing planned investment increases equilibrium expenditure and equilibrium real GNP.

- Falling planned real GNP and rising equilibrium real GNP converge and meet at a new stock and flow equilibrium.

- In such an equilibrium, the real GNP and interest rate that make the quantity of real money demanded equal the quantity supplied also make aggregate planned expenditure equal to real GNP. ∎

We've now seen how a change in the money supply sets up a chain of events that results in a change in investment and other components of aggregate expenditure. In the example that we have just worked through, the change in aggregate expenditure and the change in the money supply happen to be equal—a $1 trillion change in the money supply produces a $1 trillion change in aggregate demand. Such an outcome is not at all inevitable. It arises simply from the numbers that we used in the model economy that we studied. The actual effect of the money supply on aggregate demand could be much larger than that or much smaller. What determines the potency of a change in the money supply?

How Potent Is Monetary Policy?

The potency of monetary policy depends on two key factors:

- The sensitivity of the demand for real money to the interest rate

- The sensitivity of investment demand to the interest rate

Let's contrast two cases, one in which a change in the money supply has a large effect on aggregate demand (that is, monetary policy is effective) and another in which it has almost no effect (monetary policy is ineffective). Figure 29.5 illustrates the two cases. First, look at part (a). Here, the demand curve for real money is MD_A and the investment demand curve is ID_A. Initially, the money supply is MS_0 and the equilibrium interest rate is 5 percent. At that interest rate, investment is $1 trillion. An increase in the money supply shifts the supply curve of real money to the right from MS_0 to MS_1. The interest rate falls to 3 percent. The lower interest rate causes a movement along the investment demand curve and investment increases to $1.8 trillion. This increase in investment increases equilibrium expenditure and aggregate demand.

Figure 29.5   The Potency of Monetary Policy

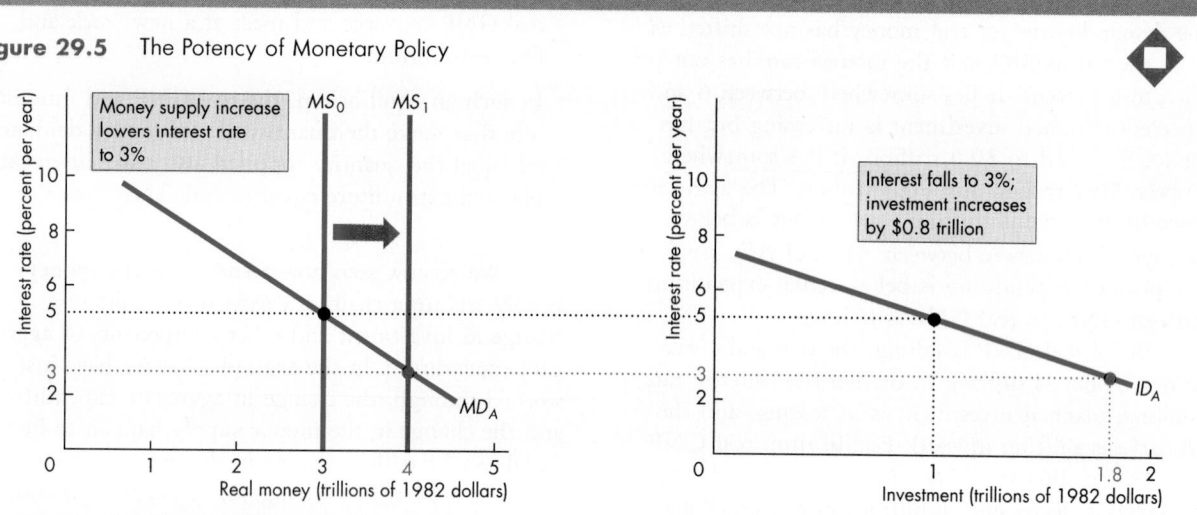

(a) Monetary policy is effective

(b) Monetary policy is ineffective

Monetary policy is effective (part a) when a change in the money supply changes interest rates and a change in interest rates changes investment. Monetary policy is ineffective (part b) when a change in the money supply has virtually no effect on interest rates and/or when the change in interest rates has almost no effect on investment. The steeper the demand curve for real money and the flatter the investment demand curve, the more powerful is the effect of a change in the money supply on the level of aggregate planned expenditure.

Now look at Fig. 29.5(b). The demand curve for real money is MD_B and the investment demand curve is ID_B. The initial situation is the same as before. The supply curve of real money is MS_0, the interest rate is 5 percent, and at that interest rate investment is $1 trillion. The money supply increases, shifting the supply curve of real money to the

right, exactly as in part (a), to MS_1. But now the interest rate barely changes. It falls to 4.9 percent. This tiny decrease in the interest rate has an even tinier effect on investment—it increases by only $5 billion. With almost no change in investment, there is almost no change in equilibrium expenditure and aggregate demand.

Why does investment increase by $0.8 trillion in part (a) and by almost nothing in part (b)? It is because of the two key factors identified above. In part (a), the demand for real money is less sensitive to the interest rate than it is in part (b). That is, for a given change in the quantity of real money, the interest rate has to change by more in part (a) to increase the quantity of real money demanded so as to restore money market equilibrium than it has to in part (b). Also, in part (a), investment demand is more sensitive to the interest rate than it is in part (b). That is, for a given fall in the interest rate, investment increases by more in part (a) than it does in part (b).

The less sensitive the demand for real money to the interest rate and the more sensitive investment demand to the interest rate, the larger is the effect of a change in the quantity of money on equilibrium expenditure and aggregate demand.

What determines the degree of sensitivity of the demand for real money and investment demand to interest rates? The answer is the degree of substitutability between money and other financial assets and in the timing of investment decisions. Because money performs a unique function that other assets do not perform — it facilitates the exchange of goods and services — money is an imperfect substitute for other financial assets. Because of this, we hold money, even though it has an opportunity cost. But the amount that we hold decreases as its opportunity cost — the interest rate — increases. The degree to which a change in the interest rate brings a decrease in the quantity of real money held depends on how close a substitute for money are other assets that do not directly serve as a medium of exchange.

The sensitivity of investment to interest rates depends on how willing people are to vary the timing of their investment. Some investment activities can be easily postponed, or brought forward in time, at low cost. Others cannot. To the extent that people do not care much about the timing of their investment, investment is highly sensitive to interest rates. To the extent that timing is of crucial importance, investment is insensitive to interest rates.

In the two situations illustrated in Fig. 29.5, a change in the money supply has *some* effect on investment. In Fig. 29.5(b) the effect is tiny but not zero. But there is a special, extreme case in which monetary policy actually has no effect at all on investment. This case occurs when the demand curve for real money is horizontal or the investment demand curve

is vertical. With a horizontal demand curve for real money, a change in the quantity of money has no effect on the interest rate. With a vertical investment demand curve, a change in the interest rate has no effect on investment and, therefore, no effect on aggregate expenditure. These cases are extreme and hypothetical but do serve to illustrate the key proposition that we have established in this section: The more sensitive the demand for real money to the interest rate and the less sensitive investment demand to the interest rate, the smaller is the effect of a change in the money supply on equilibrium expenditure and therefore, on aggregate demand.

The Lags of Monetary Policy

Monetary policy actions do not have an instantaneous effect on aggregate demand. Instead they operate with a time lag. This is, their effects are spread out over time. There are three important time lags:

- An autonomous expenditure lag
- An induced expenditure lag
- A price adjustment lag

Let's examine each in turn.

1. Autonomous Expenditure Lag   Stock equilibrium in the market for money and other assets is achieved by continuous movements in interest rates. But the effects of interest rate changes on investment plans take some time to operate. This is the autonomous expenditure lag. Most of the investment that is being undertaken at any given moment in time is the result of decisions that have been made months and sometimes years in the past. For example, when a power company decides to increase its generating capacity, it knows that the decision that it is now taking will result in a stream of investment that runs five to seven years into the future. But not all investment plans have to be made so far in advance. Decisions to buy off-the-shelf items such as automobiles, consumer durable goods, a wide variety of machine tools, computers, and a host of other equipment can be implemented within a reasonably short period.

The fact that some investment is based on long-past decisions, while other components of investment are based on more recent decisions means that the response of investment to a change in interest rates is spread out over time. For example, if interest rates increase, the purchase of a new automobile or piece of earth-moving equipment can be delayed easily and quickly. The purchase of a new electric power generating station is already under way and cannot be stopped at a reasonable cost. So investment falls, but at first by a modest amount. The fall in investment gradually becomes larger the longer interest rates stay high.

2. Induced Expenditure Lag   A fall in investment induces a fall in consumption expenditure and in equilibrium expenditure. This induced change is the multiplier effect that we studied in Chapter 26. But the multiplier effect takes time to operate, so there is a second time lag. We described the elements of this time lag in Chapter 26. Let's briefly recall them here. The chain of events begins with a change in firms' inventories. Only when firms adjust output to restore their inventories to their desired levels does real GNP change. And not until real GNP has changed is there a change in induced expenditure. A change in induced expenditure changes real GNP yet further. Eventually, the multiplier process comes to an end when aggregate planned expenditure, once again, is equal to real GNP.

3. Price Adjustment Lag   The third time lag that occurs is between a change in equilibrium expenditure and a change in prices. An increase in equilibrium expenditure shifts the aggregate demand curve to the right. With a new aggregate demand curve, the price level begins to increase. But the increase in prices is slow at first and only begins to speed up when the higher price level induces higher prices of factors of production that, in turn, start to shift the short-run aggregate supply curve upward.

Policy Formation Lag

We have described the time lags involved in the response of the economy to actions taken by the Fed. But the Fed responds to the state of the economy and there is a lag in that process too. When the Fed sees inflation increasing, its reaction is to tighten the monetary reigns, holding back on the growth rate of the money supply and permitting interest rates to nudge upward. When the Fed sees a recession on the horizon, it seeks to stimulate aggregate demand by increasing the money supply and lowering interest rates.

But the Fed cannot reach decisions instantaneously on the basis of the current performance of the economy. The current and recent performance of the economy has to be carefully assessed and a consensus established on its most likely future course. Agreement must also be reached on the Fed's goals and the best actions to take for achieving those goals.

Also, because the effects of the Fed's actions operate with long time lags, the Fed must forecast the state of the economy at the time when all the effects of its current actions will have been realized. That is, the Fed has to behave like the electric power company. The power company knows that if it is to meet the demand for electric power in 1997, it must set some plans in place here and now to build additional generating capacity that will come on stream in that year. If the time lag from the Fed's open market operation to a change in the inflation rate takes two years, the Fed's monetary policy actions in 1990 must be geared to the best available forecasts of the state of the economy in 1992. That is, the Fed, like the electric power company, must take actions today that will put in place the correct level of aggregate demand to maintain stable prices not today but two years from today.

So far, we have restricted our analysis of the effects of monetary policy to studying one channel of transmission—the interest rate channel. Let's now broaden our vision and look at some other channels whereby monetary policy influences aggregate demand.

Other Transmission Mechanisms

There are three other important transmission mechanisms of monetary policy:

- Real balance effect
- Wealth effect
- Exchange rate effect

Let's look at each of these in turn.

Real Balance Effect   The *real balance effect* is the effect of a change in the quantity of real money on the quantity of real GNP demanded. We first met the real balance effect, briefly, in Chapter 24. Let's see how it works.

An increase in the quantity of money at a given price level increases the amount of real money in the economy. With additional holdings of real money, households and firms plan to reallocate their holdings of assets of all types. They want to lower their holdings of real money and increase their holdings of other assets. Some of these other assets are real assets—capital goods. To the extent that households convert their additional real money holdings into real assets, there is an increase in investment. This increase in investment is separate from the increase resulting from a lower interest rate. Even if the interest rate does not change, a larger holding of real money balances will, in general, trigger an asset reallocation involving some additional spending on goods and services.

For example, the Fed might buy $100 million worth of government bonds from Coca-Cola Corporation. That is an open market operation that increases the monetary base and increases Coca-Cola's real money holdings. Let's suppose, to keep things simple, that no change in the interest rate has occurred at this point in time. Coca-Cola is not going to sit on this extra $100 million of money for very long. It's going to put these financial resources to work acquiring profitable assets. Some of the money may be used to take over other firms and some of it may be used directly to buy new bottling plants. To the extent that Coca-Cola buys new capital goods, there is an immediate increase in investment. If they take over other firms, these other firms have more real money and are able to increase their own investment. Gradually, investment increases as firms spend the extra real money balances that the open market operation created.

Wealth Effect The **wealth effect** is the effect of a change in real wealth on aggregate planned expenditure. An increase in the money supply can lead to an increase in wealth mainly by its effect on stock prices. To see how this effect operates, suppose that in the previous example when Coca-Cola sells some government securities to the Fed, it uses the $100 million proceeds from the sale to buy stock in other corporations. Coca-Cola's action increases the demand for the stock of some companies. That increase in demand shifts the demand curve for stock to the right and increases stock prices. Higher stock prices mean that all the existing stockholders are now wealthier. The paper assets that they are holding can now be sold for more than before. With higher wealth, some of these stockholders will sell some of their stock and buy additional consumer durable goods. To the extent that higher wealth stimulates consumption expenditure it increases aggregate demand.

The increase in stock market prices in the 1980s provides a good example of how increasing stock prices lead to increased consumption expenditure. And the stock market crash of 1987 shows how people can quickly revise their spending plans downward when they are no longer as wealthy as they thought they were. The steady increase in the demand for BMW and Jaguar cars during a stock market boom and the tailing off in the demand for such goods as a result of a stock market crash are an example of this transmission mechanism at work.

Exchange Rate Effect An increase in the money supply can lead to a depreciation of the dollar and to an increase in net exports. Since net exports are part of aggregate expenditure, this is a further channel whereby monetary policy can influence aggregate demand. This effect works in the following way.

An increase in the money supply lowers interest rates. With lower interest rates, there is a tendency for international investment flows to occur. If interest rates fall in the United States but do not fall in Japan and Western Europe, international investors will sell the now lower-yielding U.S. assets and buy the relatively higher-yielding foreign assets. As they undertake these transactions, they sell U.S. dollars and buy foreign currency. These actions decrease the demand for U.S. dollars and increase the demand for foreign currencies. The result is a lower value of the U.S. dollar relative to the values of other currencies. (This mechanism is discussed in greater detail in Chapter 36, pp. 951–970.)

With the U.S. dollar worth less, foreigners can now buy U.S. goods at a lower price and Americans have to pay a higher price for the foreign goods that they buy. The result is a net increase in the demand for U.S.–made goods as Americans switch from buying expensive imports to cheaper domestically produced goods, and foreigners switch from buying their expensive home-produced goods to cheap imports from the United States.

This process also operates in the opposite direction if the Fed undertakes a monetary policy action that lowers the money supply and increases interest rates.

Time Lags Again All these additional transmission mechanisms for the effects of monetary policy on aggregate demand, like the interest rate transmission mechanism, do not operate instantaneously. They all operate with time lags and the same factors that influence the time lags in the interest rate mechanism operate in these cases as well.

R E V I E W

A change in the money supply affects aggregate demand by changing interest rates, real money balances, wealth, and the foreign exchange rate. An increase in the money supply leads to an increase in aggregate demand and a decrease in the money supply leads to a decrease in aggregate demand. The potency of the effect of a change in the money supply depends mainly on two factors: the sensitivity of the demand for real money to interest rates and the sensitivity of investment demand to interest rates. Other things being equal, the less sensitive the demand for real money and the more sensitive investment demand to interest rates, the greater is the effect of a change in the money supply on equilibrium expenditure and aggregate demand. Monetary policy actions operate with a time lag. Interest rate changes occur fairly quickly but other changes—the change in investment and the induced change in consumption expenditure —occur more slowly. A change in aggregate demand eventually leads to a change in the price level, but that effect is drawn out even further. The Fed reacts to the state of the economy so that aggregate demand is influenced by monetary policy actions that are themselves being influenced by the evolution of the economy. ∎

Let's now turn to an examination of the effects of fiscal policy on aggregate demand.

Fiscal Policy and Aggregate Demand

We studied the effects of fiscal policy on aggregate planned expenditure and aggregate demand in Chapter 26. But the model economy that we used in that chapter is one in which the interest rate is fixed. The model that we are now studying is one in which interest rates are determined by money market equilibrium. In this model, a change in government purchases of goods and services or a change in taxes has an effect not only on aggregate planned expenditure and real GNP but also on interest rates. When we take these effects into account, it turns out that the multipliers that we calculated in Chapter 26 overstate the change in equilibrium expenditure and real GNP brought about by a fiscal policy action. Let's see why.

Fiscal and Monetary Policy Interaction: Crowding Out

When the government increases its purchases of goods and services, autonomous expenditure increases and the increased equilibrium expenditure brought about by the subsequent multiplier process increases real GNP. This increase in real GNP leads to an increase in the demand for real money. Figure 29.6 illustrates the effects of this increase in the demand for real money. In part (a), with the money supply constant at $3 trillion, the change in real income shifts the demand curve for real money from MD_0 to MD_1 and the interest rate increases from 5 percent to 6 percent. But this is not the end of the story.

As you can see by looking at part (b) of the figure, the higher interest rate lowers investment. Because investment is part of autonomous expenditure, the higher interest rate reduces autonomous expenditure. But recall that the experiment that we are conducting is one in which autonomous expenditure has increased because of an increase in government purchases of goods and services. What we have now discovered is that an increase in government purchases of goods and services increases autonomous expenditure but generates a decrease in investment, which reduces autonomous expenditure. This phenomenon is called "crowding out." **Crowding out** is the tendency for an increase in government purchases of goods and services to increase interest rates, thereby reducing investment. The increase in government purchases of goods and services crowds out investment.

Crowding out may be partial or complete. Partial crowding out occurs when the decrease in investment is less than the increase in government purchases of goods and services. This is the normal case. Increased government purchases of goods and services increase real GNP, which increases the demand for real money, and so interest rates rise. Higher interest rates decrease investment. But the effect on investment is small relative to the initial change in government purchases.

Complete crowding out occurs if the decrease in investment equals the initial increase in government purchases. For complete crowding out to occur, a small change in the demand for real money must lead to a large change in the interest rate, and the change in the interest rate must lead to a large change in investment. Although complete crowding out does not occur in practice, it is an interesting extreme case and serves to highlight the importance

Figure 29.6   Fiscal Policy and Crowding Out

(a) Fiscal policy and interest rate

(b) Crowding out

An increase in government purchases of goods and services or a tax cut increases aggregate planned expenditure and real GNP rises. Rising real GNP increases the demand for money and the demand curve for real money shifts from MD_0 to MD_1. The interest rate rises. A higher interest rate leads to a decrease in investment (part b). The decrease in investment offsets, to some extent, the initial increase in government purchases. The more steep the demand curve for real money and the less steep the investment demand curve, the larger is the crowding out effect.

of the interaction between fiscal policy and monetary policy.

Influencing the Composition of Aggregate Demand

If aggregate demand is to be increased, there is a choice of methods for increasing it. Either the money supply may be increased or fiscal policy may be expansionary (an increase in government purchases or a tax cut). If there is an increase in the money supply, as we have seen above, the increased aggregate demand comes along with lower interest rates. Lower interest rates, in turn, result in a higher level of investment. However, if aggregate demand is stimulated by fiscal policy, the increased aggregate demand comes along with higher interest rates. Higher interest rates mean lower investment. Thus the method whereby aggregate demand is increased has an important effect on its *composition*.

With an increase in aggregate demand resulting from an increase in the money supply, both investment and consumption expenditure increase while government purchases of goods and services are un-

changed. If aggregate demand is increased by an increase in government purchases of goods and services, consumption expenditure also increases but investment decreases. If the increase in aggregate demand is brought about by a tax cut, consumption expenditure increases and investment decreases. In this case, government purchases remain constant.

Politics of Monetary and Fiscal Policy

These different effects on the composition of aggregate demand resulting from different policies for changing aggregate demand are a source of tension between the various branches of government and have an important effect on the economy's long-term capacity for growth. Usually, Congress and the administration do not want the Fed to tighten monetary policy, which increases interest rates. Instead, they want to see the Fed steadily expanding the money supply, keeping interest rates as low as possible.

The Fed, on the other hand, frequently points to the importance of keeping government purchases of goods and services under control and keeping taxes sufficiently high to pay for those goods and services and argues that unless Congress increases taxes or cuts its expenditure, then a more expansionary monetary policy cannot be pursued. Some of this tension in the current debate can be seen in Reading Between the Lines (pp. 772–774).

The choice of monetary or fiscal policy affects our long-term growth prospects because the long-term capacity of the economy to produce goods and services depends on the rate at which capital is accumulated and that, in turn, depends on the level of investment. Expansionary fiscal policies lead to a decrease in investment and slow down the economy's long-term growth.

So far, we have concentrated our attention on one channel through which fiscal policy affects not only the level of aggregate demand but also its composition. There is another important channel—the exchange rate.

Fiscal Policy and the Exchange Rate

We've seen that an increase in government purchases or a decrease in taxes leads to higher interest rates. We've also seen that a change in interest rates affects the exchange rate. Higher interest rates make the dollar appreciate in value. With interest rates higher in the United States than in the rest of the world, funds flow into the United States and people around the world demand more dollars. As the dollar goes up in value, foreigners find U.S.–made goods and services more expensive and Americans find imports less expensive. Exports fall and imports rise. These changes in expenditure offset, to some degree, the initial increase in expenditure brought about by the expansionary fiscal policy.

Notice that this effect is also reversed if aggregate demand is increased by an expansion of the money supply. A higher money supply lowers interest rates. The lower interest rate makes the dollar weak —makes it fall in value. With a weaker dollar, our exports fall in price and imports from the rest of the world increase in price. Exports rise and imports fall. (We studied these exchange rate effects in Chapter 24 (p. 618) and we'll meet them again, in greater detail, in Chapter 36.)

The effects of fiscal policy, both on the level and composition of aggregate demand, do not occur instantaneously. Like monetary policy, fiscal policy operates with a time lag. Let's examine these time lags and see how they compare with those of monetary policy.

Time Lags of Fiscal Policy

Some fiscal policy actions have an immediate effect on aggregate demand. For example, a change in government purchases of goods and services has an immediate impact on the markets in which the government is buying the additional goods and services. A tax cut also has an immediate effect on disposable income, but its effect on consumption expenditure is more drawn out in time. There is a further delayed effect of fiscal policy. Rising incomes lead to an increase in the demand for real money and interest rates rise. Higher interest rates cause some crowding out of investment—investment decreases—but this effect is subject to the same time lags as those of monetary policy.

There is an important difference in the time lags of fiscal and monetary policy. Fiscal policy has an immediate effect on aggregate expenditure followed by a long drawn out effect as interest rates change and other components of aggregate expenditure adjust in response to the changing interest rates. In the case of monetary policy, there is no immediate effect on aggregate demand. The effect gradually builds up as more and more firms and households respond to the changed interest rates and other money and financial market conditions.

Fiscal policy has important policy formation lags that are longer than those for monetary policy. To implement changes in government purchases of goods and services, or in taxes, the entire legislative process must be completed. This process, involving both houses of congress and many committees, as well as interest groups and lobbies, operates on a time frame that makes fine adjustments in fiscal policy for macroeconomic stabilization purposes virtually impossible. Nevertheless, fiscal policy has important longer term effects, especially those arising from its influence on the composition of output, discussed above.

R E V I E W

An increase in government purchases of goods and services or a decrease in taxes affects aggregate demand by increasing autonomous expenditure. Higher autonomous expenditure induces an increase in consumption expenditure and a multiplier effect on equilibrium expenditure and real GNP. But higher real GNP increases the demand for real money and interest rates rise. Higher interest rates lead to a cutback in investment and a partial offsetting of the initial effects of the increased autonomous expenditure arising from the fiscal policy action. Fiscal policy affects the exchange rate, with a higher exchange rate cutting exports and stimulating imports. This, too, operates to partially offset the initial increase in autonomous expenditure brought about by the fiscal policy action.

Fiscal policy time lags differ from those of monetary policy. The initial change in fiscal policy has a quick impact on aggregate expenditure but the subsequent effects brought about by induced changes in interest rates follow the same time path as expenditure changes brought about by monetary policy. The lags in formulating and implementing fiscal policy are longer than those of monetary policy. ∎

The analysis that we have presented in this chapter of the effects of monetary and fiscal policy on aggregate demand was for several years in the 1950s and 1960s extremely controversial. It was at the heart of what was called the Keynesian-monetarist controversy. The Keynesian-monetarist controversy of today is different from that of the 1950s and 1960s and we'll see what that controversy is—a controversy about how labor markets work—in Chapter 30. But that earlier Keynesian-monetarist controversy was an interesting and important episode in the development of modern macroeconomics. Let's take a look at the essentials of the dispute and see how it was resolved.

The Keynesian-Monetarist Controversy

The Keynesian-monetarist controversy is an ongoing dispute in macroeconomics between two broad groups of economists. **Keynesians** are macroeconomists whose views about the functioning of the economy represent an extension of the theories of John Maynard Keynes, published in Keynes's *General Theory* (see Our Advancing Knowledge, pp. 656–658). Keynesians re-gard the economy as being inherently unstable and as requiring active government intervention to achieve stability. They assign a low degree of importance to monetary policy and a high degree of importance to fiscal policy. **Monetarists** are macroeconomists who assign a high degree of importance to variations in the quantity of money as the main determinant of aggregate demand and who regard the economy as inherently stable. The founder of modern monetarism is Milton Friedman (see Our Advancing Knowledge, pp. 656–658).

The nature of the Keynesian-monetarist debate has changed over the years. In the 1950s and 1960s, that debate and controversy focused almost exclusively on the relative effectiveness of fiscal policy and monetary policy in changing aggregate demand. Although it is an oversimplification, we shall be able to see the essence of the controversy if we distinguish three views:

- Extreme Keynesianism
- Extreme monetarism
- Intermediate position

Extreme Keynesianism

An extreme Keynesian is an economist who believes that a change in the money supply has no effect on the level of aggregate demand, and a change in government purchases of goods and services or in taxes has a large and predictable effect on aggregate demand.

We saw earlier in this chapter that there are two circumstances in which a change in the money supply has no effect on aggregate demand. They are:

- A vertical investment demand curve
- A horizontal demand curve for real money

If the investment demand curve is vertical, investment is completely insensitive to interest rates. In that situation, even if monetary policy changes interest rates, those interest rate changes do not affect aggregate planned expenditure and monetary policy is impotent. A horizontal demand curve for real money means that people are willing to hold any amount of money at a given interest rate—a situation called a **liquidity trap.** With a liquidity trap, a change in the quantity of money affects only the amount of money held. It does not affect interest rates. Therefore, with a liquidity trap, even if investment does not respond to interest rate changes, monetary policy

Money and the Stock Market

Is the Fed Behind the Stock Boom? Easy Money May Lead to Bloated Share Prices

Baffled by the continuing roar of the stock market? Try this theory: stock prices follow the Federal Reserve. According to this investment guide, whenever the Fed tightens monetary policy, the stock market goes down—starting about six months later. And whenever the Fed spurs the growth of the money supply, the market goes up, again after a lag of about half a year. If you can believe this, then the market explosion is easily explained; in fact, it becomes almost inevitable. In the last two years the Fed increased the money supply at the once unheard-of rates of 12 and 15 percent. H. Erich Heinemann, chief economist at Ladenburg, Thalmann & Co., says big chunks of those new dollars found their way into the stock market—and helped boost prices—simply because they had "no place else to go."

This follow-the-Fed market theory is rooted in basic monetary economics. Its proponents say that when the Fed opens the money spigot, interest rates fall and more money filters into Americans' pockets. They whittle down the "excess" by purchasing refrigerators, taking vacations and investing in stocks.

Easy money eventually causes inflation, strapping everyone for funds, and the market's joy ride ends. The father of this theory is Beryl Sprinkel, head of President Reagan's Council of Economic Advisors, who wrote three books on the subject between 1964 and 1977. Sprinkel concedes that strict monetary theory generally has failed in recent years but says, "It does seem to me that the relationship between money and stock prices is intact."

Record high

That would certainly help account for the market's otherwise inexplicable behavior so far in 1987. The outlook for the economy is for slow growth at best, yet stock prices [as measured by the Standard & Poors 500—an index of the prices of 500 common stocks] have jumped 9.5 percent already this year, adding an estimated $220 billion to the value of all stocks traded. Each day for the past two weeks the Dow Jones industrial average broke its own record high, and volume of shares traded on the New York Stock Exchange last week pierced the 1 billion level for the first time.

Market analysts say some of the 1987 surge resulted from the new tax law. Before the end of last year, investors took profits in stocks and corporations completed acquisitions completed their transactions would qualify for capital-gains treatment, which, in effect, is no longer available. Money accumulated in these deals is now being reinvested in the market. But that doesn't explain the big increase in stock prices that began in 1985. Some analysts trace that run-up to investors' continuing expectation of higher corporate profits. Low interest rates and stringent company cost cutting were expected to produce a sharp increase in profits when demand or prices, or both, increased. This scenario proved disappointing. Jerry Jordan, chief economist at First Interstate Bancorp, suggests money growth is the real reason behind the surge, noting that all other industrial economies share the American experience: rapid money growth and booming stock prices.

For many economists, the direct link between money growth and stock prices is a little too simple. Some market analysts say the theory seems to hold but perhaps

works through interest rates. Ample supplies of money reduce interest rates, which in turn boost stock prices. One reason: low interest rates on bonds persuade many investors to abandon that market for stocks. W. Lee Hoskins, senior vice president at PNC Financial Corp., has another variation. He says that a good deal of newly created money will be spent on products and services that will make corporate profits rise in the future. The market sees this and, in anticipation, bids up prices now.

Oil shock

Even the most faithful monetarists caution that the Sprinkel theory should not be an investor's sole guide. The theory failed miserably in the inflationary 1970s. Fed policy was fairly expansive then but stock prices went nowhere. Sprinkel himself says inflation always diverts money from financial assets like stocks into housing, paintings and other real assets. Another explanation for the phenomenon: the oil-price shock reduced American wealth on a massive scale and stock prices were knocked down accordingly. Today, of course, oil prices are much lower. Perhaps that's why the market is strong now.

The Essence of the Story

Background and Analysis

If the money theory of stocks is valid, however, prices should rise further. The Fed's expansive policy is likely to continue: for one thing, easy money could help the United States bring down the dollar's value. Monetarists say there will be a price to pay later. Hoskins predicts the money boom will lead to an inflation rate of about 6 percent in 1988. These warnings are familiar; according to the monetarists' charts, prices should have begun jumping in 1984. The faithful now say the usual lag between a pumping-up of the money supply and inflation has just been extended. But in the months immediately ahead, they believe, inflation will be minimal and stock prices will continue to react favorably to the steady supply of fresh money flowing into the economy. That is, unless the theory about money and stocks is all wet. But does anyone have a better one?

The M1 Connection

The stock market has followed the money supply in recent years.

Money supply is M1 less half of other interest-bearing checking accounts. Both variables are % changes in quarterly averages year to year. *Source:* Heinemann Economic Research Unit, Ladenburg, Thalmann & Co.

Newsweek, **January 26, 1987**

© 1987, Newsweek, Inc. All rights reserved. Reprinted by permission.

- In January 1987 (the time of the article), the stock market was booming and jumped 9.5 percent ($220 billion) in one month.

- In 1985 and 1986, the money supply (M1 definition) was growing quickly.

- When the money supply growth rate increases, interest rates fall, aggregate demand increases, and, eventually, inflation increases.

- Lower interest rates on bonds cause people to substitute stocks for bonds, putting additional upward pressure on stock prices.

- The connection between money growth and stock prices is not a reliable one and did not hold in the 1970s.

- If the monetary theory of stock prices is valid, prices should rise further through 1987.

- Inflation should eventually increase to about 6 percent in 1988.

- In 1985, M1 growth was 12.4 percent; in 1986, it was 17 percent. The broader definitions of the money supply, M2 and M3, were growing at around 8 percent a year during those two years.

- When the money supply increases quickly, interest rates fall to equalize the quantity of money demanded and the quantity supplied.

- Lower interest rates increase spending.

- Increased spending increases profit expectations that lead to a rise in stock prices.

- Lower interest rates on bonds lead to a substitution of stocks for bonds, further increasing the demand for stocks and increasing their prices.

- As a consequence of the above effects, an increase in the money supply leads to an increase in stock prices.

- A slowdown in money growth has the opposite effects: it increases interest rates, slows spending, lowers profit expectations, and lowers stock prices.

(Continued on next page)

- The relationship between the money supply and stock prices is a *ceteris paribus* relationship. That is, changes in the money supply lead to predictable changes in stock prices only if everything else that influences stock prices remains constant.

- But many factors, other than the money supply, influence stock prices. The most important of these is profit expectations.

- Profit expectations can be influenced by changes in aggregate supply such as those arising from changes in oil prices.

- Such events change stock prices independently of changes in the money supply.

- In 1987 (after the article was written—see figure), money supply growth rates slowed. M1 growth slowed most, but M2 and M3 growth also slowed.

- The theory of the connection between the money supply and the stock market predicts a stock market decline following the decrease in money supply growth rates, such as the stock market crash of October 1987.

- Through 1988, money supply growth rates remained steady.

- The monetary theory of the stock market predicts steady stock prices through 1988.

- But the stock market rallied again in the final half of 1988. This stock market increase was not the result of an increase in money supply growth.

- If variations in the money supply were the only cause of variations in stock prices, everyone would be able to predict stock price changes. But to profit from stock price increases or avoid loss from decreases, the demand for stocks would change as soon as the money supply changed.

- There is a connection between money growth and the stock market.

- We know the causal links between these two variables.

- But many factors other than the money supply influence the stock market.

- Because there are many other factors at work, changes in money supply growth cannot be used as a reliable predictor of stock price changes.

- If they could be so used, everyone would use them.

- In that event, stock prices would move whenever the money supply changed, and to forecast stock price changes, it would be necessary to forecast changes in the money supply.

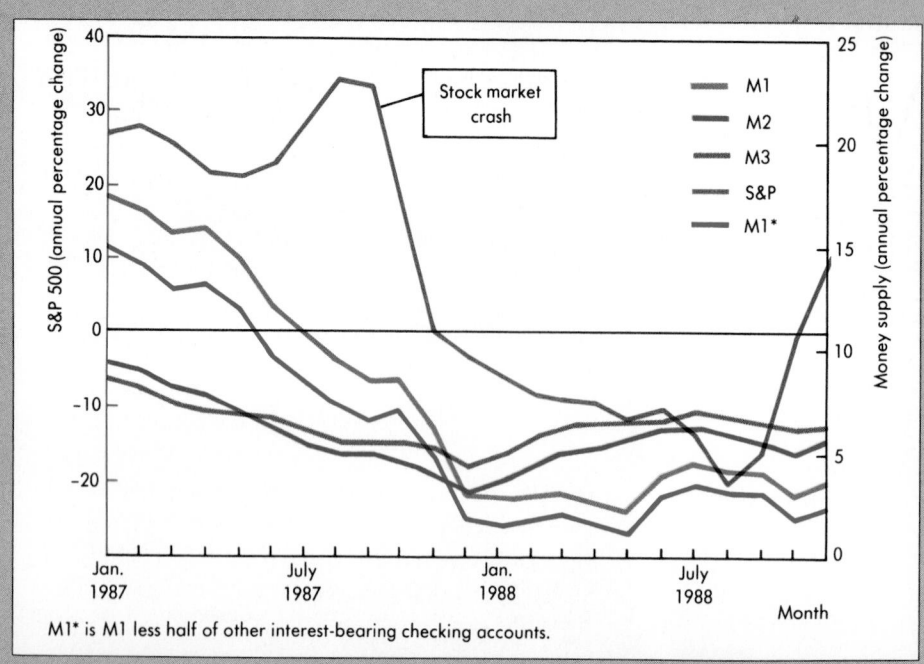

M1* is M1 less half of other interest-bearing checking accounts.

is impotent because it is unable to change interest rates in order to change investment and aggregate planned expenditure.

Extreme Keynesians believe that both of these conditions prevail. Notice that either one of these circumstances on its own is sufficient but, for good measure, extreme Keynesians suppose that both of these situations exist in reality.

Extreme Monetarism

An extreme monetarist is an economist who believes that a change in government purchases of goods and services or in taxes has no effect on aggregate demand and that a change in the money supply has a large and predictable effect upon aggregate demand. There are two circumstances giving rise to the predictions of an extreme monetarist:

- A horizontal investment demand curve
- A vertical demand curve for real money

These conditions characterize the logical possibility of complete crowding out that we described above. If an increase in government purchases of goods and services induces an increase in interest rates that is sufficiently large to reduce investment by the same amount as the initial increase in government purchases, then fiscal policy has no effect on aggregate demand. For this result to occur, either the demand curve for real money must be vertical—a fixed amount of money is held regardless of the interest rate—or the investment demand curve must be horizontal—any amount of investment will be undertaken at a given interest rate.

The Intermediate Position

The intermediate position is that both monetary and fiscal policy affect aggregate demand. Crowding out is not complete, so that fiscal policy does have an effect. There is no liquidity trap and investment does respond to interest rates, so monetary policy does indeed affect aggregate demand. This position is the one that now appears to be correct. Let's see how economists came to this conclusion.

Sorting Out the Competing Claims

The dispute between monetarists, Keynesians, and those taking the intermediate position was essentially a disagreement about the magnitudes of two macroeconomic parameters:

- The sensitivity of investment demand to interest rates
- The sensitivity of the demand for real money to interest rates

If investment demand is highly sensitive to interest rates and the demand for real money is hardly sensitive at all, then monetary policy is powerful and fiscal policy relatively ineffective and the world looks similar to the claims of extreme monetarists. If the demand for real money is highly sensitive to interest rate changes and investment demand is very insensitive, then fiscal policy is powerful and monetary policy is relatively ineffective and the world looks similar to the claims of the extreme Keynesians.

Using statistical methods to study the demand for real money and investment demand and using data from a wide variety of historical and national experiences, economists were able to settle this dispute. Neither extreme position turned out to be supported by the evidence and the intermediate position was the one that won.

An intermediate position does not always win in scientific matters. Indeed, scientific progress is at its most exciting when logically possible situations are shown, empirically, not to occur. But in this particular dispute that outcome did not arise. The demand curve for real money does slope downward. So does the demand curve for investment. Neither of these demand curves is vertical nor horizontal, which thereby rules out the positions adopted by the extreme Keynesians and extreme monetarists.

This particular controversy in macroeconomics is now behind us, but other controversies are still around. One concerns the relative magnitudes of the multiplier effects of monetary and fiscal policy. Another concerns the time lags of those effects. But the major outstanding controversy that divides modern Keynesians and monetarists concerns the working of labor markets, a controversy that we'll meet in the next chapter.

■ We have now studied the determination of aggregate demand and the way in which fluctuations in aggregate demand can be offset or produced by policy actions taken by the government and the Federal Reserve.

Our next task is to turn to the aggregate supply side of the economy and to study the determination of long-run and short-run aggregate supply, employment, and unemployment.

The appendix to this chapter, although optional, puts the discussion here into a tighter and tidier framework. If you have the time and interest, take a look at this appendix. It will certainly pay off.

S U M M A R Y

Money, Interest, and Aggregate Demand

The main transmission mechanism by which a change in the money supply affects aggregate demand is through the interest rate. A decrease in the money supply increases the interest rate. The higher interest rate decreases investment, and lower investment reduces aggregate planned expenditure. A decrease in aggregate planned expenditure causes real GNP to begin to fall. A fall in real GNP decreases the demand for real money. The demand curve for real money shifts to the left and interest rates fall. Falling interest rates lead to an increase in investment and aggregate planned expenditure starts to rise. Falling real GNP and rising aggregate planned expenditure converge at a new stock and flow equilibrium. Such an equilibrium is a situation in which real GNP and the interest rate take on values that make the quantity of real money demanded equal the quantity supplied and aggregate planned expenditure equal real GNP.

The effects of a change in the money supply on aggregate demand depend on two factors: the responsiveness of the demand for real money to the interest rate and the responsiveness of investment demand to the interest rate. The less responsive is the demand for real money and the more responsive is investment demand to the interest rate, the larger is the effect of a change in the money supply on aggregate demand.

Monetary policy operates with time lags. A change in the money supply has an immediate effect on interest rates, but its effect on expenditure plans is drawn out in time. Once expenditure has changed, a multiplier effect follows as induced expenditure increases. Higher aggregate expenditure and real GNP eventually bring faster-rising prices. After a yet further lag, the Fed reacts to the state of the economy and makes further changes in its monetary policy.

Other transmission mechanisms for monetary policy are the real balance effect, the wealth effect, and the exchange rate effect. A change in the quantity of real money has a direct effect on aggregate expenditure. A change in wealth also has a direct effect on aggregate expenditure. A change in the exchange rate changes U.S. demand for foreign-made goods and services and foreign demand for U.S.-made goods and services. (pp. 757–768)

Fiscal Policy and Aggregate Demand

A change in government purchases of goods and services has a direct effect on aggregate demand. A change in taxes has an effect on aggregate demand through its effect on disposable income. But fiscal policy changes real GNP and also changes interest rates. Therefore fiscal policy has an indirect effect on investment. An increase in government purchases of goods and services that increases aggregate planned expenditure makes real GNP begin to rise. Rising real GNP increases the demand for real money and shifts the demand curve for real money to the right. An increase in the demand for real money increases interest rates. Higher interest rates lower investment. The fall in investment resulting from an increase in government purchases offsets the expansionary effect of the initial fiscal policy action. In an extreme situation, the offset could be total. That is, the decrease in investment could be sufficient to offset the entire increase in government purchases. In practice, extreme crowding out does not seem to occur.

The mix of monetary and fiscal policy influences the composition of aggregate demand. If aggregate demand is increased as a result of an increase in the money supply, interest rates fall and investment increases. If aggregate demand is increased by an increase in government purchases of goods and services, interest rates rise and investment falls. These different effects of monetary and fiscal policy on aggregate demand lead to some political tensions. To keep aggregate demand in check and interest rates moderate, there must be a high enough level of taxes in relation to the level of government purchases.

Fiscal policy has an influence on aggregate demand through the exchange rate. A high level of government purchases of goods and services tends to increase interest rates and to make the dollar appreciate. When the dollar goes up, Americans buy more imports and foreigners buy fewer U.S.–made goods, so U.S. exports decline. There are time lags in the operation of fiscal policy but they are different from those of monetary policy. In general, fiscal policy has a bigger immediate effect than monetary policy, although it, too, has long drawn out effects. Also, the decision lags in fiscal policy are much longer than those in monetary policy. (pp. 768–771)

The Keynesian-Monetarist Controversy

The Keynesian-monetarist controversy concerns the relative effectiveness of monetary and fiscal actions in infuencing aggregate demand. The extreme Keynesian position is that only fiscal policy affects aggregate demand and monetary policy is impotent. The extreme monetarist position is the converse—that only changes in the money supply affect aggregate demand and that fiscal policy is impotent. This controversy was the central one in macroeconomics in the 1950s and 1960s. As a result of statistical investigations, we now know that neither of these extreme positions is correct and that both monetary and fiscal actions influence aggregate demand. Controversy remains about the relative effectiveness of the two sets of policy and the precise timing of their effects. (pp. 771–776)

KEY CONCEPTS

Crowding out, 768
Keynesian, 771
Liquidity trap, 771
Monetarist, 771
Wealth effect, 767

Key Figures

Figure 29.1   Equilibrium Interest Rate and Real GNP, 758
Figure 29.4   The Convergence to a New Expenditure Equilibrium, 762
Figure 29.5   The Potency of Monetary Policy, 764
Figure 29.6   Fiscal Policy and Crowding Out, 769

REVIEW QUESTIONS

1 List the alternative transmission mechanisms whereby a change in the money supply leads to a change in real GNP.

2 Set out the main steps in the interest rate transmission mechanism of monetary policy.

3 Explain why a change in the money supply has a large effect on aggregate demand if investment is highly responsive to interest rate changes.

4 Explain why monetary policy has a small effect on aggregate demand if the demand for real money is highly sensitive to the interest rate.

5 Explain how a change in stock prices is triggered by a change in the money supply.

6 Describe the time lags in the operation of monetary policy.

7 What is crowding out?

8 Why does an increase in government purchases of goods and services lead to higher interest rates?

9 What is a Keynesian?

10 What is a monetarist?

11 What are the main elements in the Keynesian-monetarist controversy about the relative effectiveness of stimulating aggregate demand by monetary policy and fiscal policy?

P R O B L E M S

1 In the economy described in Fig. 29.1, suppose there is an increase in the money supply of $1 trillion.

 a) Work out the immediate effects of this change on the interest rate.

 b) What is the effect on investment?

 c) What is the immediate effect on aggregate planned expenditure?

 d) What is the immediate effect on equilibrium real GNP?

 e) What happens to inventory accumulation?

 f) What is the interest rate and real GNP at the new stock and flow equilibrium?

2 There are two economies that are identical in every way except the following: In economy A, a change in the interest rate of 1 percentage point (for example, from 5 percent to 6 percent) results in a $100 billion change in the quantity of real money demanded. In economy B, the same change in the interest rate leads to a $1 trillion change in the quantity of real money demanded.

 a) In which economy does a change in the quantity of real money have a larger effect on equilibrium real GNP?

 b) In which economy does an increase in government purchases of goods and services have a larger effect on real GNP?

 c) In which economy is the crowding out effect the weakest?

3 The government wants to increase aggregate demand, stimulate exports, and increase investment. Explain whether it should seek to achieve this objective either by increasing government purchases of goods and services, cutting taxes, or increasing the money supply. Explain the mechanisms at work under the alternative policies that lead to your policy recommendation. What are the time lags in the effectiveness of the alternative policies?

Appendix to Chapter 29

The *IS-LM* Model of Aggregate Demand

This appendix presents the *IS-LM* model of aggregate demand. This model provides an explicit account of the derivation of the aggregate demand curve and of the effects of monetary and fiscal policy on aggregate demand. The material is not inherently difficult but it is of a higher level than the presentation in the chapter and is optional. Nevertheless, if you have the time and interest to study the appendix, you will emerge with a deeper and clearer understanding of aggregate demand and how it is influenced by monetary and fiscal policy.

Chapters 25, 26, and 28 contain the ingredients of the *IS-LM* model. First, we'll refresh our memory about equilibrium expenditure and real GNP flows; second, we'll look at money market equilibrium. Then we'll bring these two things together.

Equilibrium Expenditure and Real GNP

Aggregate planned expenditure depends on real GNP because consumption, the biggest component of aggregate expenditure, increases as real GNP increases. The equilibrium flows of aggregate planned expenditure and real GNP occur when aggregate planned expenditure equals real GNP. But aggregate planned expenditure also depends on the interest rate. The higher the interest rate, the lower is planned investment. Thus the higher the interest rate, the lower is aggregate planned expenditure.

These ideas, which were discussed in greater detail in Chapters 25 and 26, are summarized in Fig. A29.1. Let's work through this figure carefully, starting with its table.

Begin by looking at the two columns headed "Interest rate" and "Autonomous expenditure." Recall that investment is part of autonomous expenditure and that investment decreases as the interest rate rises. The table shows us how autonomous expenditure varies as the interest rate varies. For example, when the interest rate is 6 percent, autonomous expenditure is $1.2 trillion. When the interest rate falls to 5 percent, autonomous expenditure rises to $1.6 trillion.

Next, look at the last two rows of the table labeled "Induced expenditure" and "Real GNP." Recall that induced expenditure is expenditure that depends on real GNP. It is that part of consumption expenditure that depends on real GNP minus imports. The numbers here tell us how induced expenditure varies as real GNP varies. For example, if real GNP is $3 trillion, induced expenditure is $1.8 trillion. If real GNP increases to $4 trillion, induced expenditure rises to $2.4 trillion.

Finally, look at the block of table labeled "Aggregate planned expenditure." Each number in this block tells us the level of aggregate planned expenditure at a specific combination of the interest rate and

Figure A29.1   Aggregate Planned Expenditure, Flow Equilibrium, and the *IS* Curve

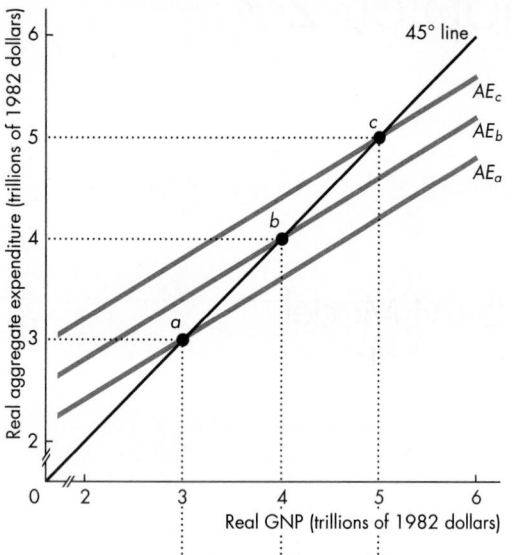

(a) Aggregate expenditure and real GNP

The table shows the aggregate planned expenditure—the sum of autonomous expenditure and induced expenditure—that occurs at different combinations of the interest rate and real GNP. For example, if the interest rate is 6 percent and real GNP is $5 trillion, aggregate planned expenditure is $4.2 trillion (top right number). Flow equilibrium—equality of aggregate planned expenditure and real GNP—is shown by the green squares. Each row a, b, and c represents an aggregate expenditure schedule, plotted as the aggregate expenditure curves AE_a, AE_b, and AE_c, respectively, in part (a). Equilibrium expenditure positions are shown in part (a), where these *AE* curves intersect the 45° line, and are marked a, b, and c, Part (b) shows these same equilibrium positions but highlights the combinations of the interest rate and real GNP at which they occur. The line connecting these points is the *IS* curve.

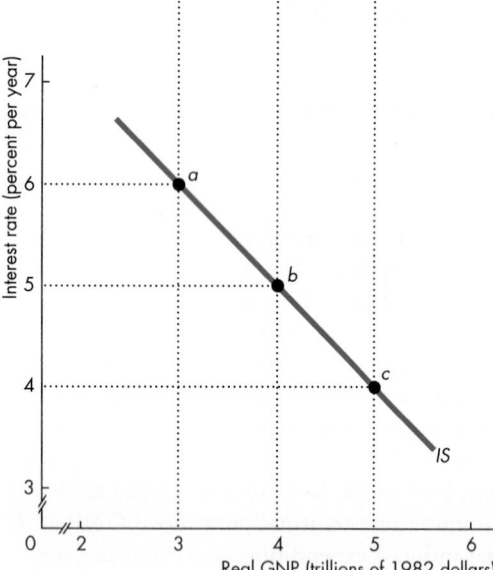

(b) The *IS* curve

	Interest rate (percent per year)	Autonomous expenditure (trillions of 1982 dollars)	Aggregate planned expenditure (trillions of 1982 dollars)		
a	6	1.2	3.0	3.6	4.2
b	5	1.6	3.4	4.0	4.6
c	4	2.0	3.8	4.4	5.0

Induced expenditure		1.8	2.4	3.0
Real GNP (trillions of 1982 dollars)		3.0	4.0	5.0

the level of real GNP. For example, row *b* tells us that when the interest rate is 5 percent and when real GNP is $3 trillion, aggregate planned expenditure is $3.4 trillion—the sum of autonomous expenditure of $1.6 trillion and induced expenditure of $1.8

trillion. The other eight numbers in the top right section of the table are arrived at in the same way. Check that you can calculate them as the sum of autonomous expenditure and induced expenditure at the appropriate interest rate and real GNP.

The green squares in the table indicate positions of equilibrium expenditure. For example, look again at row *b*. It tells us that when the interest rate is 5 percent, equilibrium expenditure is $4 trillion. At that interest rate, autonomous expenditure is $1.6 trillion. At real GNP of $4 trillion, induced expenditure is $2.4 trillion. Therefore, aggregate planned expenditure is $4 trillion, which equals real GNP. This is an expenditure equilibrium. When aggregate planned expenditure exceeds real GNP, real GNP increases. At an interest rate of 5 percent, if real GNP is $3 trillion, aggregate planned expenditure is $3.4 trillion—real GNP increases. When aggregate planned expenditure is below real GNP, real GNP falls. At an interest rate of 5 percent, if real GNP is $5 trillion, aggregate planned expenditure is $4.6 trillion—real GNP falls. At an interest rate of 5 percent, aggregate planned expenditure is equal to real GNP only when real GNP is $4 trillion. The other two green squares tell us equilibrium expenditure at interest rates of 6 percent and 4 percent.

The *IS* Curve

The *IS curve* shows combinations of real GNP and the interest rate at which aggregate planned expenditure equals real GNP. The name *IS* curve was suggested by the curve's inventor, the great English economist John Hicks. The letter *I* stands for investment and *S* stands for saving. When Hicks invented the *IS* curve, he used a model economy in which there was no government and no foreign sector so that flow equilibrium occurs when investment equals saving. The label *IS* tells us that along that curve planned investment is equal to saving in such an economy. In an economy with a government and foreign sector, the points on the *IS* curve are points at which planned injections into the circular flow of expenditure and income equal the planned leakages from the circular flow.

Figure A29.1 derives the *IS* curve. Part (a) looks familiar. It is similar to Fig. 26.4 (p. 683). The 45° line shows all the points at which aggregate planned expenditure equals real GNP. Curves AE_a, AE_b, and AE_c are aggregate planned expenditure curves. Curve AE_a represents aggregate planned expenditure when the interest rate is 6 percent (row *a* of the table). Curve AE_b shows aggregate planned expenditure when the interest rate is 5 percent (row *b*) and AE_c shows aggregate planned expenditure when the interest rate is 4 percent (row *c*).

There is just one expenditure equilibrium on each of these three aggregate planned expenditure curves. On curve AE_a, the expenditure equilibrium is at point *a*, where real GNP is $3 trillion. The expenditure equilibrium on curve AE_b occurs at point *b*, where real GNP is $4 trillion. The expenditure equilibrium on AE_c occurs at point *c*, where real GNP is $5 trillion.

Figure A29.1(b) shows each expenditure equilibrium again but highlights the relationship between the interest rate and real GNP at the expenditure equilibrium. Its horizontal axis, like Fig. A29.1(a), measures real GNP. Its vertical axis measures the interest rate. Point *a* in part (b) illustrates the expenditure equilibrium at point *a* in part (a) of the figure (or in row *a* of the table). It tells us that if the interest rate is 6 percent, the expenditure equilibrium occurs at a real GNP of $3 trillion. Points *b* and *c* in the figure illustrate the expenditure equilibrium at points *b* and *c* of part (a). The continuous line through these points is the *IS* curve.

It is often helpful to think of the relationships between two variables as one of "cause" and "effect." For example, the investment demand curve tells us the level of investment (effect) at a particular interest rate (cause). The *IS* curve is *not* a "cause and effect" relationship. Rather, it is a relationship that can be read in two ways. The *IS* curve that we have just derived tells us that if the interest rate is 6 percent, then aggregate planned expenditure equals real GNP only if real GNP is $3 trillion. But we can turn things around: If real GNP is $3 trillion, then the interest rate at which aggregate planned expenditure equals real GNP is 6 percent.

The *IS* curve shows combinations of the interest rate and real GNP at which there is an expenditure equilibrium. To determine the interest rate and real GNP, we need an additional relationship between those two variables. That second relationship between interest rates and real GNP comes from equilibrium in the money market.

Money Market Equilibrium

The quantity of money demanded depends on the price level, real GNP, and the interest rate. The quantity of money demanded is proportional to the price level. If the price level doubles, so does the quantity of money demanded. Real money is the ratio of the quantity of money to the price level. The quantity of real money demanded increases as real GNP increases and decreases as the interest rate increases.

The supply of money is determined by the actions of the Fed, the banks, and other financial intermediaries. Given those actions, and given the price level, there is a given quantity of real money in existence. Money market equilibrium occurs when the quantity of real money supplied is equal to the quantity demanded. Equilibrium in the money market is a stock equilibrium. Figure A29.2 contains a numerical example that enables us to study money market equilibrium.

Suppose that the quantity of money supplied is $3 trillion. Also, suppose that the GNP deflator is 100 so that the quantity of real money supplied is also $3 trillion. The real money supply is shown in the last row of the table. Money market equilibrium occurs when the quantity of real money demanded equals the quantity supplied—$3 trillion. The quantity of real money demanded depends on real GNP and the interest rate. The table tells us about the demand for real money. Each row tells us how much real money is demanded at a given interest rate as real GNP varies and each column tells us how much is demanded at a given real GNP as the interest rate varies. For example, at an interest rate of 6 percent and real GNP at $3 trillion, the quantity of real money demanded is $2 trillion. Alternatively, at an interest rate of 5 percent and real GNP at $4 trillion, the quantity of real money demanded is $3 trillion. The rest of the numbers in the table are read in a similar way.

Money market equilibrium occurs when the quantity of real money demanded equals the quantity supplied—$3 trillion. The green squares in the table highlight the combinations of interest rate and real GNP at which money market equilibrium occurs. If real GNP is $3 trillion, the quantity of real money demanded is $3 trillion when the interest rate is 4 percent. Thus at real GNP of $3 trillion and an interest rate of 4 percent, the money market is in equilibrium. The other two green squares tell us the interest rate at which the quantity of real money demanded is $3 trillion when real GNP is $4 trillion and $5 trillion respectively. That is, they show the interest rates at which the money market is in equilibrium.

The *LM* Curve

The *LM curve* shows the combinations of real GNP and the interest rate at which the quantity of real money demanded equals the quantity of real money supplied. The name *LM* curve, like the name *IS* curve, was invented by John Hicks. The quantity of money demanded used to be called *liquidity preference*. The label *LM,* when first used, meant that liquidity preference (*L*) is equal to the quantity of money supplied (*M*).

Figure A29.2 derives the *LM* curve. Part (a) shows the demand and supply curves for real money. The quantity supplied is fixed at $3 trillion, so the supply curve *MS* is vertical. Each of the columns of the table labeled *d, e* and *f* is a demand schedule for real money—a schedule that tells us how the quantity of real money demanded rises as the interest rate falls. There is a different schedule for each level of real GNP. These three demand schedules for real money are graphed as demand curves for real money in part (a) of the figure as MD_d, MD_e, and MD_f. For example, when real GNP is $3 trillion, the demand curve for real money is MD_d. Money market equilibrium occurs at the intersection of the supply curve and the demand curves for real money at points *d, e,* and *f* in part (a).

Figure A29.2(b) shows each money market equilibrium again but highlights the relationship between the interest rate and real GNP at which an equilibrium occurs. Points *d, e,* and *f* in part (b) illustrate the money market equilibrium represented by the green squares in the table and by those similarly labeled points in part (a). The continuous line through these points is the *LM* curve. The *LM* curve shows the interest rate and real GNP at which money market equilibrium occurs when the real money supply is $3 trillion.

Like the *IS* curve, the *LM* curve does not have a "cause and effect" interpretation. The *LM* curve illustrated in Fig. A29.2(b) tells us that if the quantity of real money supplied is $3 trillion and real GNP is $3 trillion, then for money market equilibrium the interest rate is 4 percent. It also tells us that if the quantity of real money supplied is $3 trillion and the interest rate is 4 percent, then for money market equilibrium real GNP is $3 trillion. That is, the *LM* curve shows combinations of the interest rate and real GNP at which there is money market equilibrium.

Figure A29.2   The Money Market, Stock Equilibrium, and the *LM* Curve

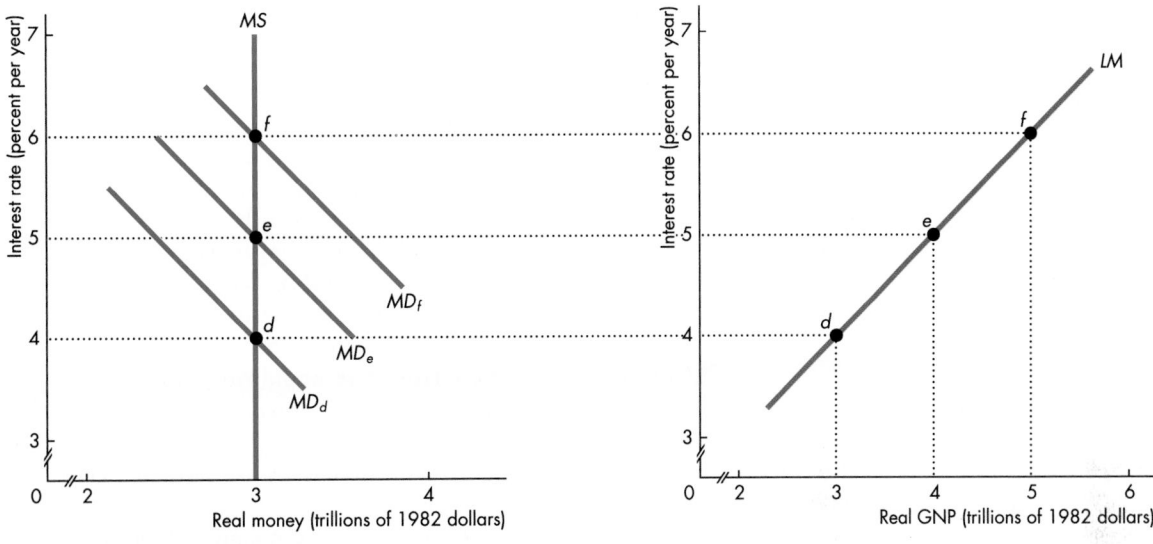

(a) Money market equilibrium

(b) The *LM* curve

The table shows the quantity of real money demanded at different combinations of the interest rate and real GNP. For example, if the interest rate is 6 percent and real GNP is $3 trillion, the quantity of real money demanded is $2 trillion (top left number). Stock equilibrium—equality between the quantity of real money demanded and supplied—is shown by the green squares. Each column *d*, *e*, and *f* represents a demand schedule for real money, plotted as the demand curves for real money *MD_d*, *MD_e*, and *MD_f*, respectively, in part (a). Money market equilibrium positions are shown in part (a), where these *MD* curves intersect the supply curve of real money (*MS*), and are marked *d*, *e*, and *f*. Part (b) shows these same equilibrium positions but highlights the combinations of the interest rate and real GNP at which they occur. The line connecting these points is the *LM* curve.

Interest rate (percent per year)	Quantity of real money demanded (trillions of 1982 dollars)		
6	2.0	2.5	3.0
5	2.5	3.0	3.5
4	3.0	3.5	4.0
Real GNP	3.0	4.0	5.0

Real money supply (trillions of 1982 dollars)	3.0	3.0	3.0
	d	*e*	*f*

The Equilibrium Interest Rate and Real GNP

We now have two relationships between the interest rate and real GNP. The first—the *IS* curve—tells us the relationship between those two variables when aggregate planned expenditure equals real GNP. The second—the *LM* curve—tells us the relationship between real GNP and the interest rate when the quantity of real money demanded equals the quantity supplied. But neither of these two relationships, on its own, determines the interest rate or real GNP. Yet together they determine *both* real GNP and the interest rate (at a given price level). Let's see how.

Figure A29.3 *IS-LM* Equilibrium

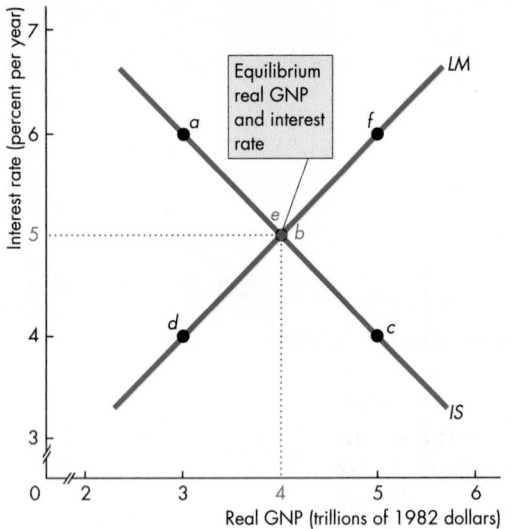

All points on the *IS* curve are points where aggregate planned expenditure equals real GNP. All points on the *LM* curve are points at which the quantity of real money demanded equals the quantity of real money supplied. The intersection of the *IS* curve and the *LM* curve determines the equilibrium interest rate and real GNP—5 percent and $4 trillion. At this interest rate and real GNP, there is flow equilibrium in the goods market and stock equilibrium in the money market.

Figure A29.3 brings together the *IS* curve and the *LM* curve to determine equilibrium real GNP and the interest rate. This equilibrium is the point of intersection of the *IS* curve and *LM* curve. Point *b* on the *IS* curve is a point of expenditure equilibrium. The interest rate and real GNP are such that aggregate planned expenditure equals real GNP. Point *e* on the *LM* curve is a point of money market equilibrium. The interest rate and real GNP are such that the quantity of real money demanded equals the quantity of real money supplied. At this intersection point, there is both flow equilibrium in the goods market and stock equilibrium in the money market. The equilibrium interest rate is 5 percent and real GNP is $4 trillion.

At all other points, there is either no expenditure equilibrium or the money market is not in equilibrium or both. At a point such as *a*, the economy is on its *IS* curve but off its *LM* curve.

With real GNP at $3 trillion and the interest rate at 6 percent, the interest rate is too high or real GNP is too low for money market equilibrium. Interest rates adjust quickly and would fall to 4 percent to bring about money market equilibrium, putting the economy at point *d*, a point on the *LM* curve. But point *d* is off the *IS* curve. At point *d*, with the interest rate at 4 percent and real GNP at $3 trillion, aggregate planned expenditure exceeds real GNP. By checking back to the table in Fig. A29.1, aggregate planned expenditure is $3.8 trillion, which exceeds real GNP of $3 trillion. With aggregate planned expenditure larger than real GNP, real GNP will increase. But as real GNP increases, so does the demand for real money and so does the interest rate. Real GNP and the interest rate would rise, and continue to do so, until the point of intersection of the *IS* and *LM* curves is reached.

The account that we have just given of what *would* happen if the economy was at a point like *a* or *d* tells us that the economy cannot be at such points. The forces that operate in such situations would be so strong that they would always push the economy to the intersection of the *IS* and *LM* curves.

The Aggregate Demand Curve

The *aggregate demand curve* traces the relationship between the quantity of real GNP demanded and the price level (the GNP deflator), holding everything else constant. Let's see how we can derive the aggregate demand curve from the *IS-LM* model. To derive the aggregate demand curve, we vary the price level and work out how equilibrium real GNP varies as we do so.

The point at which the price level enters the *IS-LM* model is in determining the quantity of real money supplied. The Fed determines the money supply as a certain number of current dollars. The higher the price level, the lower is the real value of those dollars. Because the price level affects the quantity of real money supplied, it also affects the *LM* curve.[2] Let's see how.

---

[2]In a more general version of the *IS-LM* model, the price level also affects the *IS* curve. Its effects come through the real balance effect on expenditure and the international substitution effect. In this appendix, we'll ignore those effects. In the real world, those effects reinforce the effects that we are studying here.

The Effects of a Change in Price Level on the *LM* Curve

Let's begin by asking what happens if the price level, instead of being 100, is 120—20 percent higher than before. The money supply is $3 trillion. With a GNP deflator of 100, the real money supply is also $3 trillion. But if the GNP deflator is 20 percent higher, the real money supply is 20 percent lower— $2.5 trillion. (The real money supply is $3 trillion divided by 1.2, which equals $2.5 trillion.) We can see in the table in Fig. A29.2 that the quantity of real money demanded is $2.5 trillion if real GNP is $4 trillion and the interest rate is 6 percent. Thus with a GNP deflator of 120, an interest rate of 6

percent and real GNP of $4 trillion become a point on the *LM* curve. You can see this as point *g* in Fig. A29.4(a).

Next, suppose that the GNP deflator is lower than the original case—86 instead of 100. Now the real money supply becomes $3.5 trillion (the real money supply is $3 trillion divided by 0.86, which equals $3.5 trillion). Again for money market equilibrium we can see in the table of Fig. A29.2 what happens to the interest rate at a real GNP of $4 trillion. With a GNP deflator of 86, the interest rate falls to 4 percent in order to increase the quantity of real money demanded to $3.5 trillion—equal to the real money supply. Thus with a GNP deflator of 86, an interest rate of 4 percent and real GNP of $4

Figure A29.4   Deriving the Aggregate Demand Curve

(a) *IS* and *LM* curves

(b) Aggregate demand curve

The position of the *LM* curve depends on the price level. In part (a), if the GNP deflator is 100, the *LM* curve is LM_0. If the GNP deflator increases to 120, the *LM* curve shifts to the left to LM_1. A lower real money supply requires a higher interest rate at each level of real GNP for money market equilibrium. For example, if real GNP is $4 trillion, the interest rate has to increase from 5 percent to 6 percent (point *g*). If the price level falls, the real money supply increases and the *LM* curve shifts to the right to LM_2. If real GNP is $4 trillion, the interest rate falls to 4 percent (point *h*) to maintain money market equilibrium. When the GNP deflator is 100, the *IS* and *LM* curves intersect at point *e*—at an interest rate of 5 percent and real GNP of $4 trillion. This equilibrium is shown again in part (b) at point *e* on aggregate demand curve *AD*. This point tells us that when the GNP deflator is 100, the quantity of real GNP demanded is $4 trillion. If the GNP deflator is 120, the *LM* curve is LM_1. The equilibrium interest rate is 5.5 percent and real GNP is $3.5 trillion. A second point on the aggregate demand curve is found at *j*. If the GNP deflator is 86, the *LM* curve is LM_2, the interest rate is 4.5 percent, and real GNP is $4.5 trillion. Another point on the aggregate demand curve is generated at point *k*. Joining points *j*, *e*, and *k* gives the aggregate demand curve.

trillion become a point on the *LM* curve—point *h* in Fig. A29.4(a).

The *LM* Curve Shift   The example that we have worked through tells us that there is a different *LM* curve for each price level. Figure A29.4(a) illustrates the *LM* curves for the three different price levels we have considered. The initial *LM* curve has the GNP deflator equal to 100. This curve has been relabeled as LM_0 in Fig. A29.4(a). When the GNP deflator is 120 and real GNP is $4 trillion, the interest rate that achieves equilibrium in the money market is 6 percent. This equilibrium is shown as point *g* on curve LM_1 in Fig. A29.4(a). The entire *LM* curve shifts up to LM_1 in order to pass through point *g*. When the GNP deflator is 86 and real GNP is $4 trillion, the interest rate that achieves equilibrium in the money market is 4 percent. This equilibrium is shown as point *h* on curve LM_2 in Fig. A29.4(a). Again, the entire *LM* curve shifts downward to LM_2 in order to pass through point *h*.

Now that we have worked out the effects of a change in the price level on the position of the *LM* curve, we can derive the aggregate demand curve.

The Aggregate Demand Curve Derived

The aggregate demand curve shows how aggregate expenditure varies as the price level varies. We can derive the aggregate demand curve from the *IS-LM* model. Equilibrium in the *IS-LM* model determines real GNP for a given price level such that the money market is in equilibrium and there is an expenditure equilibrium. Since there is an expenditure equilibrium, the equilibrium real GNP determined by the *IS-LM* model is also aggregate expenditure. Therefore we can derive the aggregate demand curve by determining the equilibrium real GNP in the *IS-LM* model for a variety of different price levels. Let's derive the aggregate demand curve.

Figure A29.4 shows the derivation. Part (a) shows the *IS* curve and the three *LM* curves associated with the three different price levels (GNP deflators of 86, 100, and 120). When the GNP deflator is 100, the *LM* curve is LM_0. Equilibrium is at point *e* where real GNP is $4 trillion and the equilibrium interest rate is 5 percent. If the GNP deflator is 120, the *LM* curve is LM_1. Equilibrium is at point *j* where real GNP is $3.5 trillion and the interest rate is 5.5 percent. If the GNP deflator is 86, the *LM*

curve is LM_2. Equilibrium is at point *k* where real GNP is $4.5 trillion and the interest rate is 4.5 percent. At each price level there is a different equilibrium real GNP and interest rate.

Part (b) traces the aggregate demand curve. The price level is measured on the vertical axis of part (b) and real GNP on the horizontal axis. When the GNP deflator is 100, equilibrium real GNP is $4 trillion (point *e*). When the GNP deflator is 120, equilibrium real GNP is $3.5 trillion (point *j*). And when the GNP deflator is 86, real GNP demanded is $4.5 trillion (point *k*). Each of these points corresponds to the same point in part (a). The line joining these points in part (b) is the aggregate demand curve.

Now that we have derived the aggregate demand curve and seen how it depends on flow equilibrium in the goods market and stock equilibrium in the money market, we can work out the effects on aggregate demand of changes in government purchases of goods and services, taxes, and the money supply. Let's begin with fiscal policy and work out its effects on aggregate demand.

Fiscal Policy and Aggregate Demand

A change in government purchases or in taxes shifts the *IS* curve and the aggregate demand curve. In Chapter 26, we worked out the magnitude of the change in aggregate planned expenditure resulting from a change in government purchases or in taxes when the interest rate is constant. In terms of the *IS-LM* model, these multiplier effects tell us how far the *IS* curve shifts. But the change in aggregate planned expenditure at a given interest rate is not the same thing as a change in aggregate demand. For, when aggregate planned expenditure changes, the interest rate usually changes as well and that has further effects on expenditure plans.

Figure A29.5 illustrates three different effects of a change in fiscal policy. In all three parts of the figure, the same fiscal policy action takes place. There is either a rise in government purchases or a cut in autonomous taxes that shifts the *IS* curve from IS_0 to IS_1. In part (a), the normal case, the *LM* curve is upward-sloping (LM_N). When the *IS* curve shifts, the interest rate increases and so does real GNP. But the increase in real GNP is smaller than the magnitude of the rightward shift in the *IS* curve. The reason is that the higher interest rate leads to a decrease in

Figure A29.5   Fiscal Policy and Aggregate Demand

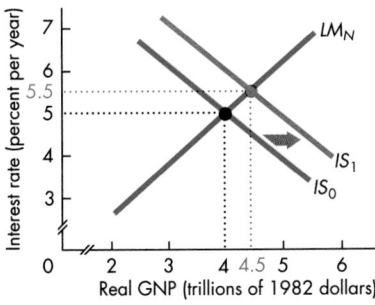

(a) Fiscal policy: normal case

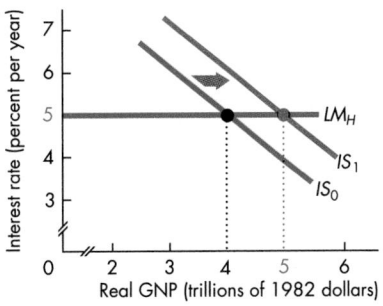

(b) Fiscal policy: maximum effect on GNP

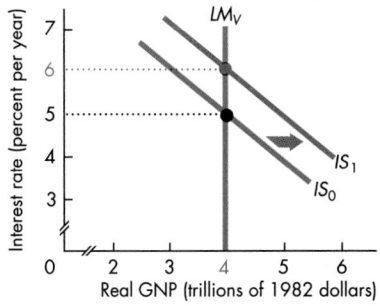

(c) Fiscal policy: no effect on GNP

An increase in government purchases or an autonomous tax cut shifts the *IS* curve to the right. The effects of fiscal policy on real GNP and the interest rate depend on the slope of the *LM* curve. In the normal case (part a), interest rates and real GNP rise. If there is a liquidity trap, the *LM* curve is horizontal (part b) and real GNP increases but interest rates stay constant. If the demand for money is insensitive to interest rates, the *LM* curve is vertical (part c) and interest rates rise but real GNP stays constant. In this case, there is complete "crowding out." The higher interest rate leads to a cut in investment that exactly offsets the initial fiscal policy action.

investment and that decrease in investment partially offsets the initial increased spending resulting from the fiscal policy action.

In part (b), the *LM* curve is horizontal (LM_H). The *LM* curve is horizontal only if there is a "liquidity trap"—a situation in which people are willing to hold any quantity of money at a given interest rate. When the *IS* curve shifts to the right, real GNP increases by the same amount as the rightward shift of the *IS* curve. Interest rates stay constant. In this case, the multiplier effect of Chapter 26 still operates.

In part (c), the *LM* curve is vertical (LM_V). In this case, although the *IS* curve shifts to the right by exactly the same amount as in parts (a) and (b), real GNP stays constant. Here, the interest rate increases. The higher interest rate leads to a decrease in investment that exactly offsets the initial increase in expenditure resulting from the fiscal policy. There is complete crowding out. Complete crowding out occurs if the demand for real money is completely insensitive to interest rates. No matter what the interest rate, the quantity of real money demanded is a constant portion of real GNP.

Part (b) of the figure corresponds to the extreme Keynesian prediction, part (c) to the extreme

monetarist prediction, and part (a) to the intermediate position.

Next, let's consider monetary policy.

Monetary Policy and Aggregate Demand

We saw earlier in this appendix that when the *LM* curve shifts because of a change in the price level, equilibrium real GNP changes and there is a movement along the aggregate demand curve. But a change in the money supply also shifts the *LM* curve. If the *LM* curve shifts because there is a change in the nominal money supply, then the aggregate demand curve shifts. The magnitude of the change in aggregate demand—the shift in the aggregate demand curve—depends on two factors: the size of the shift of the *LM* curve and the slope of the *IS* curve. Figure A29.6 shows three possible cases. In each case, the *LM* curve shifts to the right by the same amount, from LM_0 to LM_1. In part (a), the normal case, the *IS* curve is downward-sloping (IS_N). When the money supply increases, the interest rate falls and real GNP rises. The rise in real GNP results from increased investment induced by the lower interest rate.

Figure A29.6   Monetary Policy and Aggregate Demand

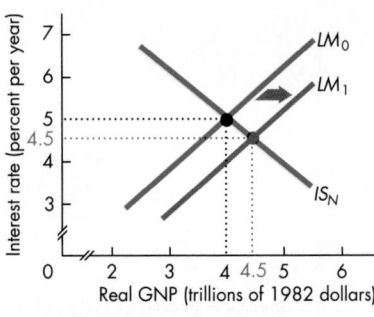

(a) Monetary policy: normal case

(b) Monetary policy: maximum effect on GNP

(c) Monetary policy: no effect on GNP

An increase in the money supply shifts the *LM* curve to the right. The effect of the monetary action on interest rates and real GNP depends on the slope of the *IS* curve. In the normal case (part a), interest rates fall and real GNP rises. The lower interest rates stimulate investment. In the special case (part b) the *IS* curve is horizontal. People don't care *when* they undertake their investment and will undertake any amount at an interest rate of 5 percent. The change in the money supply changes real GNP but leaves the interest rate constant. If investment demand is completely insensitive to interest rates (part c), the *IS* curve is vertical and a change in the money supply lowers interest rates but leaves real GNP unchanged. In this case, the lower interest rate has no effect on investment, so there is no initial injection of additional expenditure.

In part (b), the *IS* curve is horizontal (*IS_H*). This situation arises if people retime their investment whenever the interest rate rises above or falls below 5 percent. If the interest rate rises above 5 percent, all investment stops; if the interest rate falls below 5 percent, there is no limit to the amount of investment that people try to undertake. At 5 percent, any amount of investment will be undertaken. In this case, a change in the money supply shifts the *LM* curve and increases real GNP but leaves the interest rate unchanged.

In part (c), the *IS* curve is vertical (*IS_V*). This case arises if investment is completely insensitive to interest rates. People plan to undertake a given level of investment regardless of the interest cost involved. In this case, when the *LM* curve shifts, interest rates fall but the lower interest rate does not stimulate additional expenditure, so real GNP stays constant.

Part (c) corresponds to the views of extreme Keynesians. A change in the money supply has no effect on real GNP. Part (b) corresponds to the predictions of monetarists. A change in the money supply has a large and powerful effect on real GNP. Part (a) is the intermediate position.

Chapter 30

Unemployment and Aggregate Supply

After studying this chapter, you will be able to:

- Explain why real GNP and employment fluctuate together

- Explain how firms decide how much labor to employ

- Explain how households decide how much labor to supply

- Explain how wages, employment, and unemployment are determined if wages are flexible

- Explain how wages, employment, and unemployment are determined if wages are "sticky"

- Derive the short-run and long-run aggregate supply curves

- Explain the influences that shift the aggregate supply curves

As our economy ebbs and flows through the business cycle, employment and unemployment and real GNP march in close step with each other. Sometimes the U.S. economy is in a state of deep recession—real GNP has fallen and the unemployment rate is high. Such a situation prevailed in the winter of 1982. Eleven percent of the labor force was without a job. And while one third of the unemployed had been without jobs for only four weeks or less, another one third had lacked jobs for between one and three months, and one out of six had gone without work for more than six months. By 1988, the economy had experienced five years of continuous recovery and unemployment had fallen to below 6 percent.

Jobs and Incomes

Why does unemployment occur? Why, at times, are more than one in 10 people of working age looking unsuccessfully for a job? What makes the unemployment rate rise and fall? ■ In January 1988, Chrysler announced it was going to close an aged car manufacturing plant in Kenosha, Wisconsin. The workers and the mayor of Kenosha reacted angrily. Why, instead of laying off its workers, didn't Chrysler cut back on everybody's hours and negotiate a pay cut to keep the plant working? ■ The opposite of unemployment is overtime working. Many firms routinely work overtime and at times when the economy is booming most firms are in that situation. But even while some firms are paying overtime to their workers, other people are still without jobs. Why? Why don't the unemployed get jobs and the employed work normal hours for normal wages?

■ In this chapter, we'll take a close look at the U.S. labor market. We'll attempt to discover why the unemployment rate is sometimes unusually high and what brings high unemployment rates down. Our study of labor markets will take us to the heart of the current controversy in macroeconomics. That controversy is about how flexible an instrument the labor market is in bringing about changes in wages to equate the quantity of labor supplied and the quantity demanded. Some economists see the labor market as a highly flexible and sophisticated instrument that maintains equality between the quantities demanded and supplied on a continuous basis. In the view of these economists, unemployment arises mainly from frictions and from the fact that it takes time for labor to be reallocated from one sector to another, or from one region of the country to another. That is, they explain fluctuations in unemployment as fluctuations in the natural rate of unemployment. ■ Another group of macroeconomists believe that wages do not adjust quickly enough to maintain equality between the quantity of labor supplied and the quantity demanded. In the view of these economists, wages are sometimes "too high" and, as a consequence, the quantity of labor demanded is less than the quantity supplied and unemployment is above its natural rate. ■ The alignment of macroeconomists in this controversy is similar to that in the older Keynesian-monetarist controversy that we discussed in the previous chapter (pp. 771–775). Monetarists tend to take the view that wages are flexible and that unemployment is frictional or "natural." Keynesians take the view that wages are sticky and that some unemployment arises from insufficient wage flexibility. Unlike the old Keynesian-monetarist controversy, this controversy is still not settled. We have not yet found the "acid test" that enables economists on both sides of the debate to set out a research agenda that can, in principle, settle their differences. Because of this fact all we can do, in the current state of knowledge, is to set out the competing views and work out their implications. That's what we do in this chapter. ■ Our study of the labor market will complete a further block in the macroeconomic jigsaw puzzle— the aggregate supply-side block. We'll return to the short-run and long-run aggregate supply curves that you met in Chapter 24 and see how those curves are related to the labor market. We'll discover that along the long-run aggregate supply curve, the quantity of labor demanded equals the quantity supplied; and we'll see how the levels of employment and unemployment change as the economy slides along its short-run aggregate supply curve. But, to understand these connections, we must first study the relationship between employment and real GNP.

The Short-run Aggregate Production Function

A production function shows how output varies as the employment of inputs is varied. A **short-run production function** shows how output varies when the quantity of labor employed varies, holding constant the quantity of capital and the state of technology. Although production functions exist for every kind of economic activity— building dams and highways, or baking loaves of bread—the production function we will study in this chapter is the short-run *aggregate* production function. The **short-run aggregate production function** shows how real GNP varies as the quantity of labor employed is varied, holding the capital stock and state of technology constant.

The table in Fig. 30.1 records part of an economy's short-run aggregate production function. In that table, we look at the aggregate quantity of labor, measured in billions of hours a year, over the range 100 to 200. Through that range of employment, real GNP varies between $3.7 trillion and $4.1 trillion a year (measured in 1982 dollars).

The short-run aggregate production function is illustrated in the graph in Fig. 30.1. The labor input is measured on the horizontal axis and real GNP on the vertical axis. The short-run production function (*PF*) slopes upward, indicating that more labor input produces more real GNP.

The Marginal Product of Labor

The **marginal product of labor** is the additional real GNP produced by one additional hour of labor input, holding all other inputs and technology constant. We calculate the marginal product of labor as the change in real GNP divided by the change in the quantity of labor employed. Let's do such a calculation, using Fig. 30.1.

When the labor input increases from 100 to 125 billion hours, real GNP increases from $3.7 trillion to $3.9 trillion—an increase of $0.2 trillion. The marginal product of labor, over this range, is $8 an hour (0.2 trillion divided by 25 billion). Next, look at what happens at a higher level of labor input. When the labor input increases by the same 25 billion hours but from 175 billion to 200 billion

Figure 30.1   The Short-run Aggregate
Production Function

	Labor (billions of hours per year)	Real GNP (trillions of 1982 dollars per year)
a	100	3.70
b	125	3.90
c	150	4.00
d	175	4.07
e	200	4.10

The short-run aggregate production function shows the level of
real GNP at each quantity of labor input, holding constant the
stock of capital equipment and state of technology. The table lists
five points on a short-run aggregate production function. Each row
tells us the amount of real GNP that can be produced by a given
labor input. Points a through e in the graph correspond to the
rows in the table. The curve passing through these points traces
the economy's short-run aggregate production function. The marginal product of labor is highlighted in the diagram. As the labor
input increases, real GNP also increases but by successively smaller amounts. For example, a 25 billion hour increase in labor from
100 to 125 billion increases real GNP by $0.2 trillion—a margin-
al product of $8 an hour. But the same 25 billion hour increase in
labor from 175 to 200 billion hours increases real GNP by only
$0.03 trillion—a marginal product of $1.20 an hour.

hours, real GNP increases but by much less than in
the previous case—by only $0.03 trillion. Now the
marginal product of labor is only $1.20 an hour
(0.03 trillion divided by 25 billion).

The most important fact about the marginal
product of labor, apparent from the calculations that
we've just performed and visible in the figure, is that
it declines as the labor input increases. This phenomenon is called the diminishing marginal product of
labor. The **diminishing marginal product of
labor** is the tendency for the marginal product of
labor to decline as the labor input increases, holding
everything else constant. Diminishing marginal product of labor is a feature of almost every production
process. It arises because we are dealing with a *short-
run* production function. As the quantity of labor
employed is varied, all other inputs are held constant.
Thus although more labor can produce more output,
the additional labor operates the same capital
equipment—machines and tools—as a smaller labor
force would. As more people are hired, the capital
equipment is worked closer and closer to its physical
limits and output cannot be increased in proportion
to the increased labor input. This feature is present in
almost all production processes and is also present in
the relationship between aggregate employment and
aggregate output—real GNP.

The fact that the marginal product of labor
diminishes has an important influence on the demand
for labor, as we shall see shortly. But first, let's look
at some of the things that make the production
function shift.

Economic Growth and Technological Change

Economic growth is the expansion of the economy's
productive capacity. Every year, some of the economy's resources are devoted to developing new technologies to achieve greater output from a given amount
of labor input. Also, resources are devoted to building new capital equipment that incorporates the most
productive technologies available. Because capital accumulates and technology advances, the short-run aggregate production function shifts upward over time.
Figure 30.2 illustrates such a shift. The curve labeled
PF_{90} is the same as the production function in Fig.
30.1. During 1990, capital accumulates and new
technologies are incorporated into the new, and more
productive, capital equipment. Some old and less

productive capital wears out and is retired to the scrap heap. The net result is an increase in the productivity of the economy that results in an upward movement of the short-run aggregate production function to PF_{91}. When 150 billion hours of labor are employed, the economy could produce a real GNP of $4 trillion in 1990 (point c). By 1991, that same quantity of labor could produce $4.2 trillion (point c'). Each level of labor input produces more output in 1991 than in 1990.

Variable Growth Rates

Capital accumulation and technological change do not proceed at a constant pace. Sometimes they are rapid and at other times they are very slow. Also, there are times when a lot of new things are being discovered but have not yet been put into practice through innovation in production techniques. In other words, there may be periods of rapid invention but slow innovation. **Invention** is the discovery of a new technique. **Innovation** is the act of putting a new technique into operation.

Though the short-run aggregate production function usually shifts upward over time, occasionally it shifts downward—lowering the economy's production potential. Negative influences, or shocks, that make the aggregate production function shift downward are widespread droughts, major disruptions to international trade, major civil unrest, or war. A serious disruption of international trade occurred in 1974 when the Organization of Petroleum Exporting Countries (OPEC) placed an embargo on oil exports. This deprived the industrialized world of one of its most crucial raw materials. Therefore firms could not obtain all the fuel they needed, and as a result, the labor force could not produce as much output as it normally would. As a consequence of that embargo, the short-run aggregate production function shifted downward in 1974.

Let's take a closer look at the short-run aggregate production function in the United States.

The U.S. Short-run Aggregate Production Function

We can examine the short-run aggregate production function in the United States by looking at the relationship between real GNP and aggregate employment.

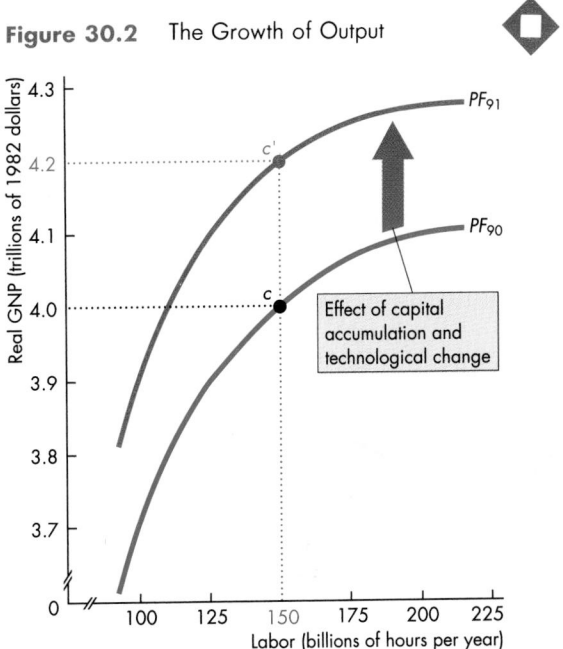

Figure 30.2   The Growth of Output

Output grows over time. The accumulation of capital and the adoption of more productive technologies makes it possible to achieve a higher level of real GNP for any given labor input. For example, between 1990 and 1991 the production function shifts upward from PF_{90} to PF_{91}. A labor input of 150 billion hours produces $4 trillion of real GNP in 1990 (point c) and $4.2 trillion in 1991 (point c').

Figure 30.3 measures real GNP on the vertical axis and the quantity of labor on the horizontal axis. The values of these two variables is plotted for each year between 1960 and 1988. For example, in 1960 real GNP is $1.7 trillion and labor hours are 136 billion; in 1988 real GNP is $4 trillion and labor hours are 211 billion.

These two points together with the other points in the figure do not all lie on the same short-run aggregate production function. Instead, they each lie on their own short-run aggregate production function. Each year the stock of capital equipment and the state of technology change so that the economy's productive potential usually is higher than in the year before. The production function for 1960 is PF_{60} and that for 1988 is PF_{88}.

The 1988 short-run production function is about 80 percent higher than the 1960 aggregate production function. This means that if employment

Figure 30.3   The U.S. Short-run Aggregate Production
Function

The points in the figure show real GNP and aggregate hours of
labor employed in the United States for each year between 1960
and 1988. For example, in 1960 labor input was 136 billion hours
and real GNP was $1.7 trillion. In 1988 labor input was 211
billion hours and real GNP was $4 trillion. The points do not lie on
one short-run aggregate production function. Instead, the short-
run aggregate production function shifts from year to year as
capital accumulates and technologies change. The figure shows
the short-run aggregate production functions for 1960 and 1988
—PF_{60} and PF_{88}. The 1988 production function is 80 percent
higher than that for 1960. For example, the 136 billion hours of
labor that produced $1.7 trillion of real GNP in 1960 would have
produced almost $3 trillion of real GNP in 1988. Similarly, the
211 billion hours of labor that produced $4 trillion of real GNP in
1988 would have produced approximately $2 trillion of real GNP
in 1960.

in 1988 had been the same as it was in 1960, real
GNP in 1988 would have been $3 trillion. Equiva-
lently, if employment in 1960 had been the same as
it was in 1988, real GNP in 1960 would have been
$2.2 trillion.

The difference between real GNP in 1988 and
in 1960 is partly accounted for by an increase in
capital stock and technological change that shifts the
short-run aggregate production function upward and
partly by an increase in employment from 136 billion
hours to 211 billion hours that produces a movement
along the new short-run production function.

REVIEW

A production function tells us how the output that
can be produced varies as inputs are varied. A short-
run production function tells us how the output that
can be produced varies as the employment of labor
varies, holding everything else constant. The short-
run aggregate production function tells us how real
GNP varies as total labor hours vary. The marginal
product of labor—the increase in real GNP resulting
from a one-hour increase of labor input—diminishes
as the labor input increases.

The short-run production function usually shifts
upward from year to year but, on occasion, it shifts
downward. Capital accumulation and technological
advances shift the short-run aggregate production
function upward. Shocks such as droughts, disruptions of international trade, or civil and political
unrest shift the production function downward. The
short-run aggregate production function in the United States shifted upward by 80 percent between
1960 and 1988.   ∎

We've just seen that the level of output in any
given year depends on the position of the short-run
aggregate production function and on the quantity of
labor employed. Even if the production function
shifts upward, it is still possible for output to fall
because of a fall in employment. For example, in
1982 employment fell by almost 4 billion hours from
its 1981 level and real GNP fell by $80 billion. To
determine the level of output, we need to understand
not only the influences on the short-run aggregate
production function but also those on the level of
employment. To determine the level of employment,
we need to study the demand for and supply of labor
and how the market allocates labor to jobs. We'll
begin by studying the demand for labor.

The Demand for Labor

The **quantity of labor demanded** is the
number of labor hours hired by all the firms
in an economy. The **demand for labor** is a
schedule or curve that shows the quantity of labor
demanded at each level of the real wage rate. The
real wage rate is the wage per hour expressed in
constant dollars—for example, the wage per hour

expressed in 1982 dollars. The wage rate expressed in *current dollars* is called the **money wage rate.** The real wage rate is the money wage rate divided by the GNP deflator and multiplied by 100. A real wage rate expressed in 1982 dollars tells us what today's money wage rate would buy if prices today were the same as in 1982. For example, if today the money wage rate is $8.40 and the GNP deflator is 112, the real wage rate is $7.50 ($8.40 divided by 112 and multiplied by 100 equals $7.50).

An example of a demand for labor schedule is shown in the table of Fig. 30.4. Row *a* tells us that at a real wage rate of $9 an hour, 100 billion hours of labor (per year) are demanded. The other rows of the table are read in a similar way. The demand for labor schedule is graphed as the demand for labor curve (*LD*). Each point on the curve corresponds to the row identified by the same letter in the table.

Why is the quantity of labor demanded influenced by the *real* wage rate? Why isn't it the *money* wage rate that affects the quantity of labor demanded? Also, why does the quantity of labor demanded increase as the real wage rate decreases? That is, why does the demand for labor curve slope downward? We're now going to answer these questions.

Diminishing Marginal Product and the Demand for Labor

Firms are in business to maximize profits. Each worker that a firm hires adds to its costs and increases its output. Up to a point, the extra output produced by the worker is worth more to the firm than the wages the firm has to pay. But each additional hour of labor hired produces less output than the previous hour—the marginal product of labor diminishes. As the amount of labor employed varies and the capital equipment employed is constant, more workers have to work the same machines and the plant operates closer and closer to its physical limits. Output increases but it does not increase in proportion to the increase in labor input. As the firm hires more workers, it eventually reaches the point where the revenue from selling the extra output produced by an additional hour of labor equals the hourly wage rate. But if the firm hires even one more hour of labor, the extra cost incurred will exceed the revenue brought in from selling the extra output. The firm will not employ that additional hour of labor. It stops at the point at which the revenue brought in by the last hour of labor input equals the wage rate.

Figure 30.4   The Demand for Labor

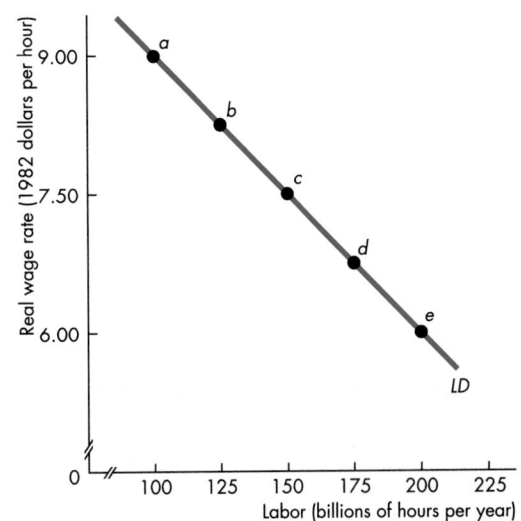

	Real wage rate (1982 dollars per hour)	Quantity of labor demanded (billions of hours per year)
a	9.00	100
b	8.25	125
c	7.50	150
d	6.75	175
e	6.00	200

The quantity of labor demanded increases as the real wage rate decreases, as illustrated by the labor demand schedule in the table and the demand for labor curve (*LD*). Each row in the table tells us the quantity of labor demanded at a given real wage rate and corresponds to a point on the labor demand curve. For example, when the real wage rate is $7.50 an hour, the quantity of labor demanded is 150 billion hours a year (*c*). The demand for labor curve slopes downward because it pays firms to hire labor so long as the marginal product of labor is greater than or equal to the real wage. The lower the real wage rate, the larger is the number of workers whose marginal product exceeds that real wage.

To see why the real wage, rather than the money wage, affects the quantity of labor demanded, let's consider an example. A soda factory employs 400 hours of labor. The additional output produced by the last hour hired is 11 bottles of soda. That is, the marginal product of labor is 11 bottles of soda per hour. Soda sells for 50 cents a bottle, so the revenue brought in from selling these 11 bottles is $5.50. Suppose the money wage rate is also $5.50 an hour. This last hour of labor hired brings in as much revenue as the wages paid out, so it just pays the firm to hire that hour of labor. The firm is paying a real wage rate that is exactly the same as the marginal product of labor—11 bottles of soda. That is, the real wage rate is equal to the money wage rate of $5.50 an hour divided by the price of soda, 50 cents a bottle.

To see why the money wage rate does not affect the quantity of labor demanded, suppose that the money wage rate and all prices double. The money wage rate increases to $11 an hour and the price of soda increases to $1 a bottle. The soda factory is in the same real situation as before. It pays $11 for the last hour of labor employed and sells the output produced by that labor for $11. The money wage rate has doubled from $5.50 to $11 an hour but nothing *real* has changed. The real wage rate is still 11 bottles of soda. As far as the firm is concerned, 400 hours is still the right quantity of labor to hire. The money wage rate has changed but the real wage rate and the quantity of labor demanded have remained constant.

To see why the real wage affects the quantity of labor demanded, let's work out what happens if the money wage rate increases to $11 an hour while the price of soda remains constant at 50 cents a bottle. The real wage rate has now increased to 22 bottles of soda—equal to the money wage of $11 an hour divided by 50 cents a bottle, the price of a bottle of soda. The last hour of labor hired now costs $11 but brings in only $5.50 of extra revenue. It does not pay the firm to hire this hour of labor. The firm cuts back the scale of its labor input until its marginal product brings in $11 of revenue. That occurs when the marginal product of labor is 22 bottles an hour— that is, 22 bottles at 50 cents a bottle sell for $11. The marginal product is again equal to the real wage rate. But to make the marginal product of labor equal to the real wage rate, the firm has to decrease the quantity of labor employed. Thus when the real wage rate increases, the quantity demanded decreases.

In the example that we've just worked through, the real wage increased because the money wage increased with a constant output price. But the same outcome occurs if the money wage remains constant

and the output price decreases. For example, if the wage rate remains at $5.50 an hour while soda falls in price to 25 cents a bottle, the real wage is also 22 bottles of soda and the soda bottling factory hires the amount of labor that makes the marginal product of labor equal to 22 bottles an hour.

Thus the quantity of labor demanded depends on the real wage, not the money wage, and the higher the real wage rate, the lower is the quantity of labor demanded.

We now know why the quantity of labor demanded depends on the real wage and why the demand for labor curve slopes downward, but what makes it shift?

Shifts in the Demand for Labor Curve   When the marginal product of each hour of labor changes, the demand for labor curve shifts. The accumulation of capital and the development of new technologies are constantly increasing the marginal product of each hour of labor. We've already seen one effect of such changes. They shift the short-run aggregate production function upward, as shown in Fig. 30.2. At the same time, they make the short-run aggregate production function *steeper*. Anything that makes the short-run production function steeper increases the marginal product of each hour of labor—increases the extra output obtained from one additional hour of labor. At a given real wage rate, firms will increase the amount of labor they hire until the revenue brought in from selling the extra output produced by the last hour of labor input equals the hourly wage. Thus as the short-run aggregate production function shifts upward, the demand for labor curve also shifts to the right.

In general, the demand for labor curve shifts to the right over time. But there are fluctuations in the pace at which the demand for labor curve shifts that match the fluctuations in the short-run aggregate production function. Fluctuations in the production function produce changes in the demand for labor, which in turn produce fluctuations in employment, real GNP, and the real wage rate.

Let's look at the demand for labor in the United States and see how it has changed over the period since 1960.

The U.S. Demand for Labor

Figure 30.5 shows the real wage rate and the quantity of labor employed in each year between 1960 and 1988. For example, in 1988 the real wage was $7.69

Figure 30.5   The U.S. Demand for Labor

The figure shows the quantity of labor employed and real wages in the United States from 1960 to 1988. For example, in 1960 the real wage was $6.75 an hour and 136 billion hours of labor were employed. In 1988 the real wage was $7.69 an hour and 211 billion hours of labor were employed. These two points (and the points for the years between them) do not lie on a single demand for labor curve. The demand for labor curve has shifted as a result of shifts in the short-run aggregate production function. The figure shows the demand curves for 1960 and 1988—LD_{60} and LD_{88}. Over time, the demand for labor curve has shifted to the right.

an hour (in 1982 dollars) and 211 billion hours of labor were employed. The figure also shows two demand for labor curves, one for 1960 and the other for 1988. Between 1960 and 1988, the production function shifted upward and the marginal product of labor increased. If the quantity of labor employed in 1988 had been the same as in 1960, 136 billion hours, the real wage rate would have been $9 per hour. If the quantity of labor employed in 1960 had been as high as that in 1988 (211 billion hours), the real wage rate in that year would only have been $5.71 per hour.

R E V I E W

The quantity of labor demanded by firms depends on the real wage rate. For an individual firm, the real wage rate is the money wage rate paid to the worker divided by the price for which the firm's output sells. For the economy as a whole, the real wage rate is the money wage rate divided by the price level. The lower the real wage rate, the greater is the quantity of labor demanded. The demand for labor curve slopes downward.

The demand for labor curve shifts because of shifts in the short-run aggregate production function. An increase in the capital stock or advances in technology embodied in the capital stock shift the short-run aggregate production function upward and increase the marginal product of labor. The demand for labor curve shifts to the right, but at an uneven pace. ∎

Let's now turn to the other side of the labor market and see how the supply of labor is determined.

The Supply of Labor

The **quantity of labor supplied** is the number of hours of labor services that households supply to firms. The **supply of labor** is a schedule or curve that shows how the quantity of labor supplied varies as the real wage varies.

A supply of labor schedule appears in the table in Fig. 30.6. Row *a* tells us that at a real wage rate of $6 an hour, 100 billion hours of labor (per year) are supplied. The other rows of the table are read in a similar way. The supply of labor schedule is graphed as the supply of labor curve (*LS*). Each point on the *LS* curve represents the row identified by the same letter in the table. As the real wage increases, the quantity of labor supplied increases. The supply of labor curve slopes upward.

But why does the quantity of labor supplied increase when the real wage increases? There are two reasons:

- Hours per worker increase
- The labor force participation rate increases

The Determination of Hours per Worker

In choosing how many hours to work, a household has to decide how to allocate its time between work and other activities. If a household chooses not to

Figure 30.6   The Supply of Labor

	Real wage rate (1982 dollars per hour)	Quantity of labor supplied (billions of hours per year)
a	6.00	100
b	6.75	125
c	7.50	150
d	8.25	175
e	9.00	200

The quantity of labor supplied increases as the real wage rate increases, as illustrated by the labor supply schedule in the table and the supply of labor curve (LS). Each row of the table tells us the quantity of labor supplied at a given real wage rate and corresponds to a point on the labor supply curve. For example, when the real wage rate is $7.50 an hour, the quantity of labor supplied is 150 billion hours a year (c). The supply of labor curve slopes upward because households work longer hours, on the average, at higher wages and more households participate in the labor force. These responses are reinforced by intertemporal substitution—the retiming of work to take advantage of temporarily high wages.

work for an hour, it does not get paid for that hour. The real hourly wage rate that the household gives up is the opportunity cost of an hour of not working.

What the household really gives up by not working is all the goods and services that it could buy with the hourly money wage. So the opportunity cost of an hour of time spent not working is the real hourly wage rate.

What happens to people's willingness to work if the real wage rate increases? Such a change has two opposing effects:

• A substitution effect
• An income effect

Substitution Effect   The substitution effect of a change in the real wage rate works in exactly the same way that a change in the price of tapes affects the quantity of tapes demanded. Just as tapes have a price, so does time. As we've just noted, the real hourly wage rate is the opportunity cost of an hour spent not working. A higher real wage rate increases the opportunity cost of time and makes time itself a more valuable commodity. This higher opportunity cost of not working encourages people to reduce their nonwork time and increase the time spent working. Thus as the real wage rate increases, more hours of work are supplied.

Income Effect   But a higher real wage rate also increases people's incomes. As you know, the higher a person's income, the greater is their demand for all the different types of goods and services. One such "good" is leisure—the time to do pleasurable things that don't generate an income. Thus a higher real wage rate also makes people want to enjoy longer leisure hours and supply fewer hours of work.

Which of these two effects dominates depends on each individual's attitude toward work and also on the real wage rate. Attitudes toward work, though varying across individuals, do not change much, on the average, over time. But the real wage rate does change and brings changes in the quantity of labor supplied. At a very low real wage rate, the substitution effect is stronger than the income effect. That is, the inducement to substitute working time for leisure time is stronger than the inducement to spend part of a larger income on longer leisure hours. As a consequence, as the real wage rate increases, the quantity of labor supplied also increases.

At a high enough real wage rate, the income effect becomes stronger than the substitution effect. The inducement to spend more of the additional income on leisure time is stronger than the incentive to economize on leisure time, now that its opportunity cost has increased.

Some people undoubtedly enjoy such a high real wage that a further increase would cause them to reduce their hours of work. But for most of us a higher real wage coaxes us to work more. Thus on the average, the higher the real wage rate, the more hours each person works.

The Participation Rate

The **labor force participation rate** is the proportion of the working age population that is either employed or unemployed (but seeking employment). For a variety of reasons, people differ in their willingness to work. Some people have better productive opportunities at home and so need a bigger inducement to quit those activities and work for someone else. Other individuals place a very high value on leisure, and they require a high real wage to induce them to do any work at all. These considerations suggest that each person has a reservation wage. A **reservation wage** is the lowest wage at which a person will supply any labor. Below that wage, a person will not work.

Those people who have a reservation wage below or equal to the actual real wage will be in the labor force, and those with a reservation wage above the real wage will not be in the labor force. The higher the real wage rate, the larger is the number of people whose reservation wage falls below the real wage; hence, the higher is the labor force participation rate.

Reinforcing and strengthening the increase in hours worked per household and the labor force participation rate is an intertemporal substitution effect on the quantity of labor supplied.

Intertemporal Substitution

Households have to decide not only whether to work but *when* to work. This decision is based not just on the current real wage but on the current real wage relative to expected future real wages.

Suppose that the wage rate is higher today than it is expected to be later on. How does this fact affect a person's labor supply decision? It encourages more work today and less in the future. Thus the higher the real wage relative to what is expected in the future (other things being constant), the larger is the supply of labor.

Temporarily high real wages are similar to a high rate of return. If wages are temporarily high, people can obtain a higher rate of return on their work effort by enjoying a smaller amount of leisure and supplying more labor in such a period. By investing in some work now and taking the return in more leisure time later, they can obtain a higher overall level of consumption of goods and services and of leisure.

We've now seen why, as the real wage rate increases, the quantity of labor supplied increases—why the supply of labor curve slopes upward. Let's next bring the two sides of the labor market together and study the determination of wages and employment.

Wages and Employment

We have discovered that as the real wage rate increases the quantity of labor demanded declines and the quantity of labor supplied increases. We now want to study how the two sides of the labor market interact to determine the real wage, employment, and unemployment.

There is disagreement about how the labor market works, and this disagreement is the main source of current controversy in macroeconomics. There are two leading theories about the labor market:

- Flexible wage theory
- Sticky wage theory

The flexible wage theory is built on the assumption that labor is traded in markets that operate much like the markets for ordinary goods and services, with the real wage continuously and freely adjusting to keep the quantity demanded equal to the quantity supplied. The sticky wage theory is based on the assumption that the dominant form of trading in the labor market is a wage contract that specifies a fixed money wage for a fixed period of time—hence the name sticky wages. Because money wages are sticky, real wages do not continuously adjust to keep the quantity of labor demanded equal to the quantity supplied. Let's look at these two theories, beginning with the simplest—the flexible wage theory.

The Flexible Wage Theory

The flexible wage theory of the labor market emphasizes the possibility of wages adjusting to achieve a continuous balance between the quantities of labor supplied and demanded. The theory is illustrated in Fig. 30.7. The demand for labor curve is *LD* and the supply of labor curve is *LS*. This market determines an equilibrium real wage rate of $7.50 an hour and a quantity of labor employed of 150 billion hours. If the real wage rate is below its equilibrium level of $7.50 an hour, the quantity of labor demanded exceeds the quantity supplied. In such a situation, wages will rise since firms are willing to offer higher and higher wages in order to overcome their labor shortages. The real wage rate will continue to rise until it reaches $7.50 an hour, at which point there will be no shortage of labor.

If the real wage rate is higher than its equilibrium level of $7.50 an hour, the quantity of labor

supplied exceeds the quantity demanded. In this situation, households are not able to get all the work that they want and firms will find it easy to hire labor. Firms will have an incentive to cut the wage and households will accept the lower wage to get a job. The real wage rate will fall until it reaches $7.50 an hour, at which point every household will be satisfied with the quantity of labor that it is supplying.

Changes in Wages and Employment   The flexible wage theory makes predictions about wages and employment that are identical to the predictions of the demand and supply model that we studied in Chapter 4. An increase in the demand for labor shifts the demand for labor curve to the right and increases both the real wage rate and the quantity of labor employed. An increase in the supply of labor shifts the supply of labor curve to the right, lowering the real wage rate and increasing employment.

The demand for labor increases over time because capital accumulation and technological change increase the marginal product of labor. The supply of labor increases over time because the working age population is steadily increasing. Rightward shifts in the demand for labor curve are generally larger than shifts in the supply of labor curve so, over time, both the quantity of labor employed and the real wage rate increase.

Aggregate Supply with Flexible Wages   In Chapter 24, we met the concept of aggregate supply and the long-run and short-run aggregate supply curves. What does the flexible wage theory of the labor market tell us about aggregate supply?

Recall the definitions of the short-run aggregate supply curve and the long-run aggregate supply curve. The short-run aggregate supply curve tells us how the quantity of real GNP supplied varies as the price level varies, holding input prices constant. The long-run aggregate supply curve tells us how the quantity of real GNP varies as the price level varies, when all input prices adjust by the same percentage as the price level.

According to the flexible wage theory of the labor market, the money wage rate adjusts to determine a real wage that brings equality between the quantity of labor demanded and quantity supplied. If the prices of all other inputs also behave in the same way as the money wage rate, then all input prices change to preserve equilibrium in the various input

Figure 30.7   Equilibrium with Flexible Wages

Equilibrium occurs when the real wage makes the quantity of labor demanded equal to the quantity supplied. This equilibrium occurs at a real wage of $7.50 an hour. At that real wage rate, 150 billion hours of labor are employed. At real wage rates below $7.50 an hour, the quantity of labor demanded exceeds the quantity supplied and the real wage rate rises. At real wage rates above $7.50 an hour, the quantity of labor supplied exceeds the quantity of labor demanded and the real wage rate falls.

Figure 30.8   Aggregate Supply with Flexible Wages

(a) Labor market

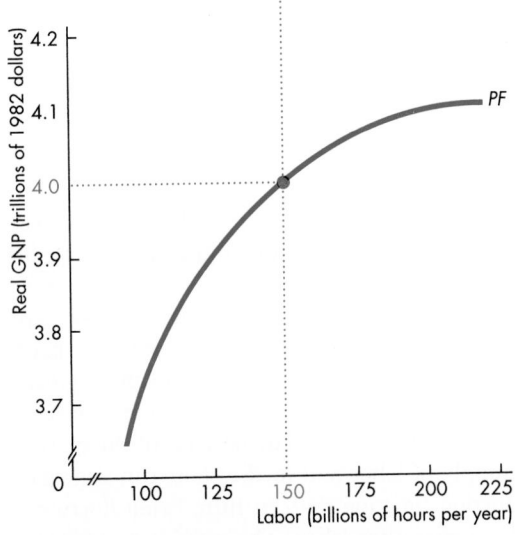

(b) Short-run aggregate production function

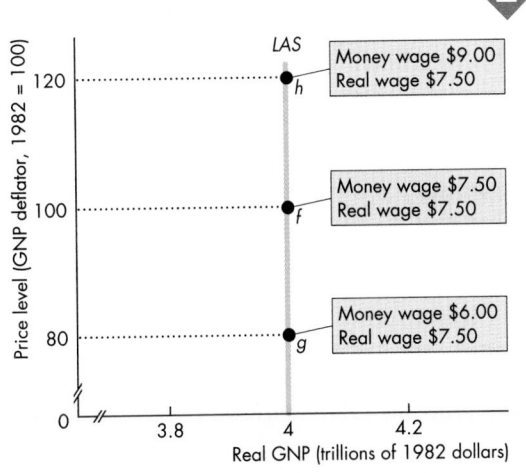

(c) Long-run aggregate supply curve

Labor market equilibrium determines the real wage and employment. The demand for labor curve (*LD*) intersects the supply of labor curve (*LS*) at a real wage of $7.50 an hour and 150 billion hours of employment (part a). The short-run aggregate production function (*PF*) and employment of 150 billion hours determine real GNP at $4 trillion (part b). Real GNP supplied is $4 trillion regardless of the price level. The long-run aggregate supply curve is the vertical line (*LAS*) in part (c). If the GNP deflator is 100, the economy is at point f. If the GNP deflator is 120, money wages rise to keep real wages constant at $7.50 an hour, employment remains at 150 billion hours, and real GNP is $4 trillion. The economy is at point h. If the GNP deflator is 80, money wages fall to keep real wages constant at $7.50 an hour, employment remains at 150 billion hours, and real GNP is $4 trillion. The economy is at point g.

markets. The aggregate supply curve generated by the flexible wage model of the labor market is the same as the long-run aggregate supply curve. It is vertical. Let's see why.

Figure 30.8 illustrates the derivation of the long-run aggregate supply curve. Part (a) shows the aggregate labor market. The demand and supply

curves shown are exactly the same as those in Fig. 30.7. And the equilibrium, a real wage of $7.50 an hour and employment of 150 billion hours, is exactly the same equilibrium that was determined in that figure.

Figure 30.8(b) shows the short-run aggregate production function. This production function is exactly the same as the one shown in Fig. 30.1. We know from the labor market (part a) that 150 billion hours of labor are employed. Part (b) tells us that when 150 billion hours of labor are employed, real GNP is $4 trillion.

Figure 30.8(c) shows the long-run aggregate supply curve. That curve tells us that real GNP is $4 trillion regardless of the price level. Let's examine the aggregate supply curve a bit closer and convince ourselves that it really is vertical.

Suppose that the price level, measured by the GNP deflator, is 100. In this case, the economy is at point f in part (c) of the figure. That is, the GNP deflator is 100 and real GNP is $4 trillion. We've determined, in part (a), that the real wage rate is $7.50. With the GNP deflator of 100, the money wage (the wage in current dollars) is also $7.50.

Let's now ask what happens to real GNP at two different price levels—a lower one and a higher one. First, suppose that the GNP deflator is not 100 but 80. If the money wage rate remains at its initial level of $7.50, the real wage rate rises and the quantity of labor supplied exceeds the quantity demanded. In such a situation, the money wage rate will fall. It falls to $6 an hour. With a money wage of $6 and a GNP deflator of 80, the real wage rate is still $7.50 ($6 divided by 80 and multiplied by 100 equals $7.50). With the lower money wage but a constant real wage rate, employment remains at 150 billion hours and real GNP is constant at $4 trillion. The economy is at point g in Fig. 30.8(c).

Next, consider what happens to real GNP if the GNP deflator is not 100 but 120 (a 20 percent higher price level). If the money wage rate stays at $7.50 an hour, the real wage rate falls and the quantity of labor demanded exceeds the quantity supplied. In such a situation, the money wage rate rises. It will keep rising until it reaches $9 an hour. At that money wage rate, the real wage is $7.50 ($9 divided by 120 and multiplied by 100 equals $7.50) and the quantity of labor demanded equals the quantity supplied. Employment remains at 150 billion hours, real GNP remains at $4 trillion, which means that the economy is at point h in Fig. 30.8(c).

Points f, g, and h in part (c) all lie on the long-run aggregate supply curve. We have considered only three price levels. We could have considered any price level and we would have reached the same conclusion: A change in the price level generates a proportionate change in the money wage rate and leaves the real wage rate unchanged. Employment and real GNP are also unchanged. The long-run aggregate supply curve is vertical.

Fluctuations in Real GNP   In the flexible wage theory of the labor market, fluctuations in real GNP arise from shifts in the long-run aggregate supply curve. Technological change and capital accumulation shift the short-run aggregate production function upward and also shift the demand for labor curve to the right. Population growth shifts the supply of labor curve to the right. These changes in economic conditions change equilibrium employment and real GNP and also shift the long-run aggregate supply curve. Most of the time these changes result in the long-run aggregate supply curve moving to the right—increasing real GNP. But the pace at which the long-run aggregate supply curve shifts to the right varies, leading to fluctuations in the growth rate of real GNP. Occasionally, the short-run aggregate production function shifts downward. When it does so, the demand for labor curve shifts to the left, employment falls, and the long-run aggregate supply curve shifts to the left, producing a recession.

R E V I E W

The flexible wage theory of the labor market maintains that the real wage rate adjusts sufficiently freely to maintain continuous equality between the quantity of labor demanded and the quantity of labor supplied. In such an economy, there is only one aggregate supply curve—the vertical long-run aggregate supply curve. Fluctuations in employment, money wages, and real GNP occur because of fluctuations in the supply of labor and in the short-run aggregate production function that, in turn, bring fluctuations in the demand for labor. The most important source of fluctuations is the uneven pace of technological change and other occasional negative influences on the short-run aggregate production function.   ∎

The labor market analysis that we have just studied leaves out one feature of real world labor markets that some economists regard as being important—money wage rates are fixed by wage contracts and do not adjust quickly. Let's now examine how the labor market works when money wages are sticky.

The Sticky Wage Theory

The sticky wage theory of the labor market emphasizes that money wage rates are fixed by wage contracts and that they are not free to adjust minute by minute to enable changes in the real wage rate to maintain a balance between the aggregate quantity of labor demanded and supplied. Economists who regard the flexible wage theory as the appropriate one argue that there are many ways in which money wages, even those that are fixed by wage contracts, can and do adjust upward or downward and that they do so quickly enough to maintain labor market equilibrium. Bonus payments and the mix of overtime and normal time work (overtime being paid at a higher wage rate) are the two principal means whereby wage flexibility is achieved. But most economists, while recognizing the scope for flexibility in wages from bonuses and special overtime wage rates, believe that these sources of flexibility are insufficient to keep the quantity of labor supplied equal to the quantity of labor demanded. Basic money wage rates, they point out, rarely adjust more frequently than once a year, so money wage rates are fairly rigid. Real wage rates change more frequently than do money wage rates because of changes in the price level, but not with sufficient flexibility to achieve continuous full employment.

The starting point for the sticky wage theory of the labor market is a theory of the determination of the money wage rate—the wage that is "sticky."

Money Wage Determination   Firms, naturally, like to pay as low a wage as possible. Workers like as high a wage as possible. But workers want to get hired and firms want to be able to find labor. Firms recognize that if they offer too low a wage there will be a labor shortage. Workers recognize that if they try to achieve too high a wage there will be a shortage of jobs—excessive unemployment. The wage that balances off these opposing forces is the equilibrium wage—the wage that makes the quantity of labor demanded equal to the quantity supplied. But if money wages are going to be set for a year or more ahead, it will be impossible to achieve a continuous balance between the quantity of labor demanded and the quantity supplied. In such a situation, how is the wage determined? It is set at a level designed to achieve an expectation or belief that, on the average, the quantity of labor demanded will equal the quantity supplied. Let's work out what that money wage rate is.

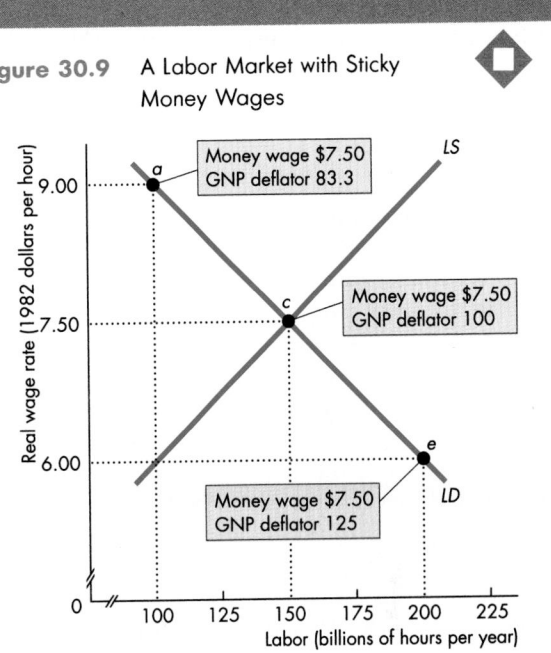

Figure 30.9   A Labor Market with Sticky Money Wages

The labor demand curve is LD and the labor supply curve is LS. The money wage is set to achieve an expected balance between the quantity of labor demanded and the quantity supplied. If the GNP deflator is expected to be 100, the money wage rate is set at $7.50 an hour. The labor market is expected to be at point c. The quantity of labor employed is determined by the demand for labor. If the GNP deflator turns out to be 100, then the real wage is equal to $7.50 and the economy operates at point c, employing 150 billion hours of labor. If the GNP deflator turns out to be 83.3, then the real wage is $9 an hour and the quantity of labor demanded falls to 100 billion hours. The economy operates at point a. If the GNP deflator is 125, then the real wage is $6 an hour and employment increases to 200 billion hours. The economy operates at point e.

If the labor demand and supply curves are the same as those that we used in Fig. 30.7, the real wage that achieves balance between the quantity demanded and quantity supplied is $7.50, as shown in Fig. 30.9. The money wage that this real wage translates into depends on the price level. If the GNP deflator is 100 and the real wage is $7.50, then the money wage is $7.50 (point c in the figure).

When firms and workers agree to a money wage rate for a future contract, they do not know what the price level is going to be. All they can do is base the contract on their best forecast of future prices. Let's suppose that firms and their workers all have the same expectations about the future. In our example, we suppose that they *expect* the GNP deflator for the coming year to be 100. That being the case, firms and workers will be ready to agree to a money wage rate of $7.50 per hour.

Real Wage Determination   The real wage rate that actually emerges depends on the *actual* price level. If the GNP deflator turns out to be 100, as expected, then the real wage rate is $7.50, as expected. In this case, employment is 150 billion hours—the quantity determined at the intersection of the labor demand and labor supply curves. But many other outcomes are possible. Let's consider two of them, one in which the price level turns out to be higher than expected and one in which it turns out to be lower than expected.

First, suppose that the GNP deflator turns out to be 125. In this case, the real wage is $6. That is, a money wage of $7.50 and a GNP deflator of 125 enables people to buy the same goods that a money wage of $6 buys when the GNP deflator is 100. Next, suppose that the GNP deflator turns out to be 83.3 instead of 100. In this case, the real wage is $9. A money wage of $7.50 with a GNP deflator of 83.3 buys the same quantity of goods that a real wage of $9 buys when the GNP deflator is 100. The three points *a, c,* and *e* in Fig. 30.9 illustrate the relationship between the price level, the money wage, and the real wage. The money wage is constant at $7.50 and the higher the price level, the lower is the real wage. If the real wage is different from $7.50, how is the level of employment determined?

Employment with Sticky Wages   The sticky wage theory assumes that the quantity of labor demanded determines employment. Households agree to supply whatever labor firms demand, provided firms pay the agreed wage. This means that the labor supply curve *LS* is used to calculate the money wage rate but does not represent a constraint on the amount of labor that firms can employ. At the money wage of $7.50, households willingly supply whatever labor firms demand for the duration of the wage contract. Since the quantity of labor demanded at the actual real wage determines employment, actual employment is determined from the demand for labor curve in Fig. 30.9. Thus when the money wage is $7.50 and the GNP deflator is 83.3, the real wage is $9 and the quantity of labor demanded and employment are 100 billion

hours (point *a* in the figure). When the money wage is $7.50 and the GNP deflator is 125, the real wage is $6 and the quantity of labor demanded and employment are 200 billion hours (point *e* in the figure).

Short-run Aggregate Supply with Sticky Wages
When money wages are sticky, the short-run aggregate supply curve slopes upward—it is the short-run aggregate supply curve that we examined in Chapter 24. Figure 30.10 illustrates why this is so. First, look at the table in that figure. The first column lists three different values of the GNP deflator—those that we have just considered above. With the money wage fixed at $7.50, the next column tells us the real wage at these three different price levels. The third column tells us how much labor will be employed at each real wage rate and the final column tells us how much real GNP that level of employment can produce. (The numbers used in this table come from the short-run aggregate production function shown in Fig. 30.1.)

First, let's consider row *c,* where the GNP deflator is 100. Recall that this was the expected value of the GNP deflator when the $7.50 wage rate was set. In this case, the real wage is $7.50 and the quantity of labor demanded equals the quantity supplied—150 billion hours. Real GNP is $4 trillion. This situation is point *c* in the figure. If the money wage rate always adjusts to keep the real wage constant at $7.50 an hour, real GNP will remain constant at $4 trillion and the economy will be on its long-run aggregate supply curve. That curve is shown in the figure as *LAS.* This is the aggregate supply curve generated by the flexible wage model.

Next look at row *a.* In this situation, the GNP deflator is below its expected level and the real wage turns out to be $9 an hour. At that real wage, only 100 billion hours of labor are demanded and real GNP is $3.7 trillion. This situation is shown as point *a* in the figure. Next look at row *e.* Here the GNP deflator turns out to be higher than expected, so the real wage is lower than expected. Employment is 200 billion hours and real GNP $4.1 trillion. This situation is point *e* in the figure. Points *a, c,* and *e* lie on the short-run aggregate supply curve (*SAS*).

The short-run aggregate supply curve cuts the long-run aggregate supply curve at the expected price level—where the GNP deflator is 100. At price levels higher than that expected, the quantity of real GNP supplied exceeds its long-run level and when

Figure 30.10   Aggregate Supply with Sticky Wages

	Price level (GNP deflator)	Real wage rate (1982 dollars)	Labor (billions of hours per year)	Real GNP (trillions of 1982 dollars per hour)
a	83.3	9.00	100	3.70
c	100.0	7.50	150	4.00
e	125.0	6.00	200	4.10

The table shows the effects of changes in the price level on real GNP supplied when the expected GNP deflator is 100 and the contracted money wage is fixed at $7.50 an hour. If the GNP deflator is 100, the real wage is also $7.50 an hour. Employment is 150 billion hours and real GNP is $4 trillion. The economy is producing at c on its long-run aggregate supply curve (LAS). At a lower price level (row a), the real wage rate increases, employment falls, and real GNP falls. This price level and real GNP are shown as point a on the graph. At a higher price level (row e), the real wage rate falls, employment increases, and real GNP increases. Point e on the graph corresponds to row e of the table. The short-run aggregate supply curve (SAS) passes through points a, c, and e.

the GNP deflator is below that expected, the quantity of real GNP supplied falls short of its long-run level.

All the factors that lead to fluctuations in long-run aggregate supply in the flexible wage theory apply to the long-run aggregate supply curve of the sticky wage theory. But in addition, employment and real GNP can fluctuate because of movements along the short-run aggregate supply curve. These movements occur because of changes in real wages. Real wages can change in the sticky wage theory when the price level moves but the contractually determined money wage rate stays constant.

R E V I E W

The sticky wage theory emphasizes the importance of labor market contracts that fix the money wage rate,

making it insensitive in the short run to price level changes. The money wage is set on the basis of expectations about the price level over the course of the wage contract. If the price level turns out to be the same as expected, the real wage is the same as it would be if wages were flexible. If the price level turns out to be lower than expected, the real wage is higher than in the flexible wage case. If the price level is higher than expected, the real wage is lower than in the flexible wage case.

The level of employment is determined by the demand for labor. When the real wage is higher than expected, employment falls; when the real wage is lower than expected, employment increases. These movements in the level of employment result in changes in the level of real GNP and are represented as movements along the short-run aggregate supply curve. A higher than expected price level lowers the real wage, increases employment, and increases real GNP; a lower than expected price level increases the real wage, lowers employment, and lowers real GNP. ∎

So far, although we have been examining models of the labor market, we have used those models to determine the level of employment and wages but have ignored unemployment. How is unemployment determined?

Unemployment

In the labor market models that we have just been studying, we have determined the real wage rate and aggregate hours of labor employed but have not said anything about *who* supplies the hours. Unemployment arises when some people in the labor force are working zero hours but are seeking work. Why does unemployment exist? Why does its rate vary?

There are four main reasons why unemployment arises:

- To vary employment, it pays firms to vary the number of workers employed rather than the number of hours per worker.
- Firms have imperfect information about people looking for work.
- Households have incomplete information about available jobs.
- Wage contracts prevent the wage adjustments that would be needed to keep the quantity of labor demanded equal to the quantity supplied.

The flexible wage theory places emphasis on the first three of these sources of unemployment. The sticky wage theory acknowledges the importance of these factors but regards the fourth factor as the most significant cause of unemployment and of variations in its rate. First, we'll examine the sources of unemployment that are present regardless of whether wages are flexible or sticky. Then we'll see how wage stickiness generates yet more unemployment.

Indivisible Labor

If it were profitable to do so, firms would vary the amount of labor they employ by varying the hours worked by each person on their payrolls. For example, suppose that a firm employs 400 hours of labor each

week and has 10 workers, each working 40 hours. If the firm decides to cut back its production and reduce employment to 360 hours, it might either lay off one worker or cut the hours of each of its 10 workers to 36 hours a week. In most production processes, the profitable reaction for the firm is to lay off one worker and keep the remaining workers' hours constant. There is an optimum or efficient number of hours for each worker. Work hours in excess of the optimum level result in decreased output per hour as workers become tired. Employing a large number of workers for a small number of hours each also lowers output per hour since workers take time to get started up and there are disruptions to the production process caused by workers leaving and arriving. It is for these reasons that labor is an economically indivisible factor of production. That is, taking account of the output produced per hour, it pays firms to hire labor in indivisible lumps. As a consequence, when the demand for labor changes, the number of people employed changes rather than the number of hours per worker.

Being fired or laid off would not be important if an equally good job could be found right away. But finding a job takes time and effort—it has an opportunity cost. Firms are not fully informed about all the potential workers available to them and households are not fully informed about all the potential jobs available to them. As a consequence, both firms and workers have to search for a profitable match. Let's examine this source of unemployment.

Job Search and Unemployment

Because households are incompletely informed about available jobs, they find it efficient to devote resources to searching for the best available job. Time spent searching for a job is part of unemployment. Let's take a closer look at this source of unemployment by examining the labor market decisions that people make and the flows that arise from those decisions. Figure 30.11 provides a schematic summary of this discussion.

Labor Market Decisions and Flows   The population is divided into two broad groups: those in the labor force and those not in the labor force. Those not in the labor force are the three groups identified at the top of the figure. These are full-time students, specialists in household production—homemakers

Figure 30.11   Labor Market Flows

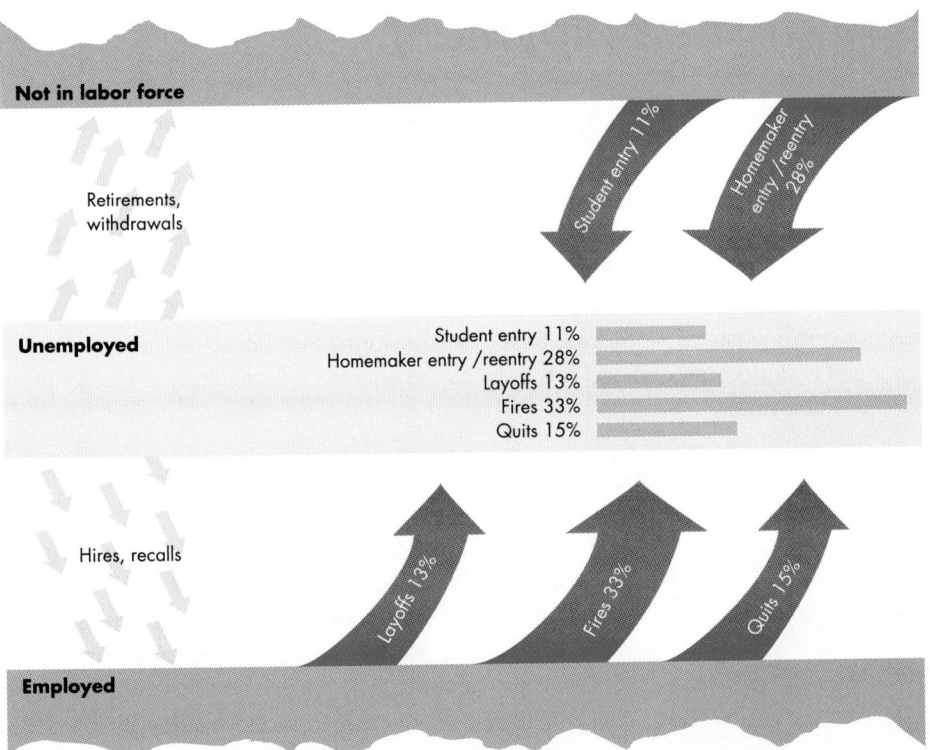

The population is divided into two groups: those in the labor force and those not in the labor force. The labor force, in turn, is divided into those employed and those unemployed. The figure shows the flows between the labor force and the rest of the population and between the employed and the unemployed. New entrants from full-time schooling flow into the unemployment pool. As these new entrants are hired, they flow out of the unemployment pool. Flows from employed to unemployed occur as a result of fires, quits, and layoffs. Flows occur in the opposite direction as a result of hires and recalls. Workers sometimes withdraw temporarily from the labor force to become homemakers or to go back to school. Sometimes they retire. Those who have temporarily withdrawn from the labor force re-enter and search for a job. They flow in through the unemployment pool. The quantity of unemployment depends on the scale of the flows and on the length of time that people remain in the unemployed category. The greater the entry flow and the greater the rate of fires, quits, and layoffs, the higher is the average rate of unemployment.

Source: Monthly Labor Review (December 1988). The data are for October 1988.

and children—and retirees. The labor force consists of two broad groups: the employed and the unemployed.

Decisions made by the demanders of labor and the suppliers of labor result in nine types of flows that change the numbers of people employed and unemployed. These flows are shown by the arrows in the figure. Let's look at each of these decisions and how the flow that results from it affects the amount of unemployment and employment.

There are two ways in which a person not in the labor force can become unemployed. Full-time students can decide to quit school, enter the labor force, and search for a job; or specialists in household production can decide to change their activities by entering or re-entering the labor force, and seeking a

Unemployment: Waste or "Natural"?

E ver since the Great Depression and the subsequent publication of Keynes's *General Theory* (see Our Advancing Knowledge on p. 656–658), most macroeconomists have believed that fluctuations in unemployment have been caused by fluctuations in aggregate demand and are an avoidable waste of resources. Sticky money wages that do not adjust to changes in aggregate demand are seen as the source of fluctuations in real GNP and unemployment.

Okun's Law

The quantitative relationship between output and unemployment is called "Okun's Law," named after Arthur Okun.

Arthur Okun (1929–1980) did his graduate work in economics at Columbia University and taught for several years at Yale. But most of Okun's professional career was spent in Washington, D.C. He became a member of Johnson's Council of Economic Advisors in 1964. He became chairman of the Council in 1968 and so became President Lyndon B. Johnson's senior economic advisor. After he left the CEA, he spent the rest of his life as a research economist at the Brookings Institution. Okun was a compassionate and articulate exponent of Keynesian macroeconomics.

The relationship that intrigued Arthur Okun is illustrated in the first figure (below). Deviations of real GNP from trend measure the output gap on the left scale. The "natural" rate of unemployment is taken as constant at 6 percent. The natural rate minus the actual rate of unemployment measures the unemployment gap on the right scale. The two gaps track each other closely, which has led economists to conclude that fluctuations in aggregate

Arthur Okun

demand produce fluctuations in out put that lead to fluctuations in unemployment. This cause-and-effect relationship is Okun's Law.

This consensus has been challenged in recent years by real business cycle theorists and by those economists focusing on sectoral shifts as sources of cyclical unemployment.

Real Business Cycle Theory

Real business cycle theory is a new branch of macroeconomics developed by Edward Prescott of the University of Minnesota, Finn Kydland of Carnegie-Mellon University, and John Long and Charles Plosser of the University of Rochester. Real business cycle theory explains aggregate fluctuations as the consequence of fluctuations in the pace of technological change. According to real business cycle theory, fluctuations in employment and real GNP are the best possible response to real changes affecting the economy.

The concept of indivisible labor, discussed in the chapter (p. 806) has been incorporated into real business cycle theories by Richard Rogerson of the University of Rochester. Gary Hansen of the University of California at Los Angeles has shown that an artificial economy incorporating these ideas, that can be run on a computer, produces fluctutations in output, employment, and unemployment similar to those that we observe in the U.S. economy.

Sectoral Shifts

The possible importance of sectoral shifts as a cause of unemployment has been suggested by David Lilien of the University of Southern California. Lilien calculated the scale of sectoral shifts by measuring the amount of labor turnover across 21 major sectors of the U.S. economy. He discovered that his measure of labor turnover was strongly correlated with the actual unemployment rate and he was able to explain most of the rise in unemployment in the 1970s. The second figure (below) illustrates Lilien's findings for the period of his study—1949 to 1980. The graph plots the actual unemployment rate and next to it is Lilien's calculation of the natural rate produced by variations in the extent of labor switching jobs across sectors of the economy. The remaining unemployment, possibly resulting from fluctuations in aggregate demand, is represented as the shaded area between these two curves and is also plotted separately in the figure.

Lilien's results and his interpretation has been challenged by Katharine Abraham (of the Brookings Institution and MIT) and Lawrence Katz (of the University of California, Berkeley) who show that sectoral shifts are correlated with aggregate demand. They argue that Arthur Okun's original conclusion—that unemployment is caused primarily by aggregate demand fluctuations—is broadly correct.

Edward Prescott

(Continued on next page)

The Keynesian
Resurgence

In recent years, there has been a burst of research activity aimed at providing a theoretical foundation for the Keynesian idea that unemployment is wasteful. Carl Shapiro of Princeton and Joseph Stiglitz of Stanford have suggested the efficiency wage hypothesis. The central idea of this hypothesis is that firms can get greater effort from their workers by paying them a higher wage. But a higher wage results in unemployment—an excess of the quantity of labor supplied over the quantity demanded. Indeed, it is the threat and fear of unemployment that generates the greater effort from workers who are paid an efficiency wage.

Assar Lindbeck (see "Talking with Assar Lindbeck," pp. 1–4), of the University of Stockholm, and Dennis Snower, of the University of London, have developed what they call the "insider-outsider" theory of employment and unemployment. Their idea is that people who have jobs don't care about people who don't and negotiate wages with their employers that preserve their own employment level but that do not enable "outsiders" to get in.

Peter Diamond of MIT has suggested that job search, of the type discussed in this chapter (pp. 806–811), can create "multiple equilibrium" levels of unemployment. If a large number of firms are looking for a large number of workers, the chances of each side finding a good match are high and unemployment is low. If a small number of firms are looking for a small number of workers, the chances of matches being made are much lower and unemployment is high. Diamond's ideas have been developed by Olivier Blanchard and Lawrence Summers of Harvard to explain the difference between European unemployment (persistently high) and U.S. unemployment (falling through the 1980s). Their idea is given the name "hysteresis." Loosely, hysteresis applied to unemployment means that the unemployment rate depends on its previous level. A large shock to the economy can create a high unemployment rate that then persists until another large shock knocks the economy back to a low unemployment rate.

The significance of the debate among economists about the causes of unemployment is not just of academic interest and importance. It is crucial for the design and conduct of macroeconomic stabilization policy. If real wages are flexible enough to ensure that all unemployment is "natural unemployment" and fluctuations in actual unemployment are fluctuations in natural unemployment, then aggregate demand policy has no role to play. There is only one aggregate supply curve—the vertical long-run aggregate supply curve. Fluctuations in real GNP, employment, and unemployment are all associated with shifts in this vertical aggregate supply curve. Monetary and fiscal policy can be used to influence aggregate demand and shift the aggregate demand curve. But these shifts will not affect real GNP, employment, and unemployment. They will only affect the price level (and inflation rate).

On the other hand, if wages are not sufficiently flexible and if some unemployment results from sticky wages, the short-run aggregate supply curve slopes upward and a role exists for managing the level of aggregate demand to achieve full employment. A fall in aggregate demand can produce a fall in real GNP and an increase in unemployment. That fall in aggregate demand can, in principle at least, be offset by an appropriate increase in the money supply, an increase in government purchases of goods and services, or a tax cut.

Economists remain a long way from agreement about the causes of unemployment and the reasons for its sometimes high and constantly fluctuating rate.

job. Initially, when such people enter the labor force, they are unemployed.

There are three ways in which employed workers may become unemployed. An employer may lay off workers temporarily; an employer may fire workers; or workers may decide to quit their current job to find a better one. Each of these decisions results in a fall in employment and a rise in unemployment.

There are four ways in which people can leave the pool of unemployment. They may decide to withdraw from the labor force temporarily (to bring up children, become homemakers, or go back to school); quit work altogether and retire; be recalled from temporary layoff; or be hired in a new job.

At any one moment, there is a stock of employment and unemployment and, over any given period, there are flows between the labor force and the rest of the population and between employment and unemployment. In October 1988, for example, there were 123.5 million people in the labor force—65.9 percent of the population. Of these, 6.5 million (5.3 percent of the labor force) were unemployed and 117 million (94.7 percent of the labor force) were employed. Of the 6.5 million unemployed, 33 percent had been fired from their previous job and about 28 percent had re-entered the labor force after a period of specializing in household production. The rest of the unemployed were in the other three categories— either new entrants (11 percent), layoffs (13 percent), or people who had voluntarily quit their previous job to seek a better one (15 percent).

Unemployment with Flexible Wages   If real wages are flexible, all the unemployment that exists arises from the sources that we have just reviewed. Furthermore, fluctuations in unemployment are caused by fluctuations in labor market flows. For example, a bulge in the birth rate, such as occurred in the early 1950s, leads, with a time lag, to a bulge in new entrants in the labor force. Such a bulge occurred in the 1970s. This bulge in new entrants produced a rise in unemployment.

Cycles in unemployment arise from the fact that the scale of hiring, firing, and job quitting ebbs and flows with the fluctuations in real GNP—with the business cycle. These labor market flows and the resulting unemployment are also strongly influenced by the pace and direction of technological change. When some sectors of the economy are expanding quickly and others are contracting quickly, labor turnover increases. This means large flows between employment and unemployment and the pool of

those temporarily unemployed increases at such a time. The relative decline of industries in the so-called "Rust Belt" and the rapid expansion of industries in the so-called "Sun Belt" are an important source of large flows of labor and of the rise in unemployment that occurred during the 1970s and early 1980s.

According to the flexible wage model of the labor market, the unemployment rate is always equal to the natural rate of unemployment. There is a balance between the quantity of labor demanded and the quantity of labor supplied. But the quantity of labor supplied is the number of hours available for work at a given moment without further search for a better job. And the quantity of labor demanded is the number of hours that firms wish to hire at a given moment in time, given their knowledge of the individual skills and talents available. In addition to supplying hours for work, households also supply time for job search. Those people that devote no time to working and specialize in job search are the ones who are unemployed.

According to the sticky wage model of the labor market, there is an additional source of unemployment that has to be added to the natural rate of unemployment that occurs in a flexible wage labor market. Let's see what it is.

Unemployment with Sticky Wages   We've already studied an economy with sticky money wages and seen how the level of employment and real GNP are determined in such an economy. Such an economy also generates unemployment, over and above that arising from the frictions that we have just considered. If the price level is lower than expected, real wages are above their equilibrium level and the quantity of labor employed is less than the quantity supplied. Unemployment increases above its natural rate. Figure 30.12 shows why.

Suppose that the expected GNP deflator is 100 and money wages are set at $7.50 an hour. The labor market is expected to be in equilibrium with 150 billion hours of employment. Now suppose that the price level turns out to be lower than expected. In particular, suppose that the GNP deflator is 83.3. As we have just seen in Fig. 30.9, this level of the GNP deflator increases the real wage to $9 an hour. At a real wage of $9 an hour, the quantity of labor demanded falls substantially short of the quantity of labor supplied. The gap between these two magnitudes is unemployment in excess of that occurring in the flexible wage model—unemployment above its natural rate. In the situation depicted in Fig. 30.12, the economy has moved down its short-run aggregate supply curve and is at the position marked *a* in Figs. 30.9 and 30.10.

If the price level turns out to be higher than expected, the real wage falls below $7.50. In this case, the quantity of labor demanded exceeds the quantity of labor supplied. But workers have contracted to supply whatever labor the firm demands at the agreed money wage. Hence the level of employment rises and unemployment falls below its natural rate. In this situation, the economy has moved up its short-run aggregate supply curve and is at the position marked *e* in Fig. 30.10.

According to the sticky wage theory, fluctuations in unemployment arise primarily from the mechanism that we have just described. Changes in the real wage rate arising from sticky money wages and changing prices result in movements along the labor demand curve and movements along the short-run aggregate supply curve.

Those economists who emphasize the role of sticky wages in generating fluctuations in unemployment usually regard the natural rate of unemployment as constant—or slowly changing. Fluctuations in the actual unemployment rate are fluctuations around the natural rate. Notice that this interpretation of fluctuations in unemployment contrasts with that of the flexible wage theory. A flexible wage model predicts that *all* changes in unemployment are fluctuations in the natural rate of unemployment.

If most of the fluctuations in unemployment *do* arise from sticky wages, aggregate demand management can moderate the size of the fluctuations in unemployment. By keeping aggregate demand steady so that the price level stays close to its expected level, the economy can be kept close to full employment.

The controversy about unemployment, and some recent attempts to improve our understanding of the phenomenon, are dealt with in Our Advancing Knowledge on pp. 808–810.

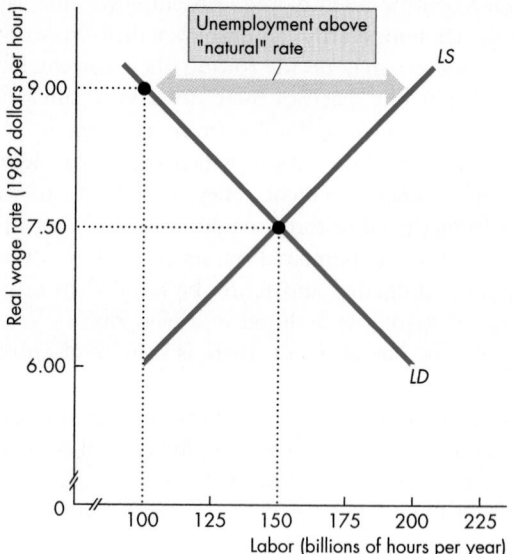

Figure 30.12   Unemployment with Sticky Money Wages

Money wages are set at $7.50 an hour in anticipation that the GNP deflator will be 100. The deflator turns out to be 83.3, so real wages are $9 an hour. At this higher real wage rate, the quantity of labor demanded falls short of the quantity of labor supplied. The horizontal gap between the demand curve (*LD*) and the supply curve (*LS*) represents unemployment in excess of the natural rate. Fluctuations in the price level, with sticky money wages, cause fluctuations in the level of unemployment.

■   We have now studied the labor market and the determination of long-run and short-run aggregate supply, employment, wages, and unemployment. Our next task is to bring together the aggregate demand and aggregate supply sides of the economy again and to see how they interact to determine inflation and business cycles. We are going to pursue these tasks in the next two chapters.

S U M M A R Y

The Short-run Aggregate Production Function

The short-run aggregate production function tells us how real GNP varies as the aggregate quantity of

labor employed varies with a given stock of capital equipment and given state of technology. As the labor input increases, real GNP increases but by diminishing marginal amounts. The short-run aggregate production function shifts as a result of capital accumulation and technological change. These factors cause the short-run aggregate production function to shift upward over time. Occasionally the production function shifts downward because of negative influences such as restrictions on international trade. The U.S. short-run aggregate production function shifted upward by 80 percent between 1960 and 1988. (pp. 791–794)

The Demand for Labor

Firms choose how much labor to demand. The lower the real wage rate, the larger is the quantity of labor hours demanded. In choosing how much labor to hire, firms aim to maximize their profits. They achieve this objective by ensuring that the revenue brought in by an additional hour of labor equals the hourly wage rate. The more hours of labor that are employed, the lower the revenue brought in by the last hour of labor. Firms can be induced to increase the quantity of labor hours demanded, either by a decrease in the price of labor—the wage rate—or by an increase in the revenue brought in—by an increase in the price of output. Both a decrease in wages and an increase in prices result in a lower real wage. Thus the lower the real wage, the higher is the quantity of labor demanded.

The relationship between the real wage and the quantity of labor demanded is summarized in the demand for labor curve, which slopes downward. The demand for labor curve shifts as a result of shifts in the short-run aggregate production function. (pp. 794–797)

The Supply of Labor

Households choose how much labor to supply. They also choose the timing of their labor supply. The higher the real wage rate, the more hours each worker supplies up to some maximum, the higher is the participation rate, and the higher is the quantity of labor currently supplied. Taking all these forces together, the higher the real wage rate, the greater is the quantity of labor supplied. (pp. 797–799)

Wages and Employment

There are two theories of labor market equilibrium, one based on the assumption that wages are flexible and the other based on the assumption that they are sticky. Under the flexible wage theory, the real wage

rate adjusts to ensure that the quantity of labor supplied equals the quantity demanded.

With flexible wages, the aggregate supply curve is vertical—the long-run aggregate supply curve. The quantity of real GNP supplied is independent of the price level. The long-run aggregate supply curve shifts as a result of shifts in the supply of labor curve and shifts in the short-run aggregate production function that lead to shifts in the demand for labor curve.

With sticky money wages, real wages do not adjust to balance the quantity of labor supplied and the quantity demanded. Money wages are set to make the expected quantity of labor demanded equal to the expected quantity supplied. The real wage depends on the money wage contracted and the price level. The level of employment is determined by the demand for labor, with households agreeing to supply the quantity demanded. Fluctuations in the price level relative to what was expected generate fluctuations in the quantity of labor demanded and in employment and real GNP. The higher the price level relative to what was expected, the lower is the real wage. The lower the real wage, the greater is the quantity of labor demanded and the greater is employment and real GNP.

With sticky money wages, the aggregate supply curve slopes upward—the short-run aggregate supply curve. The higher the price level, the higher is the quantity of real GNP supplied. (pp. 799–806)

Unemployment

The labor market is in a constant state of change—of labor turnover. Labor turnover creates unemployment. New entrants to the labor force and workers reentering after a period of household production must take time to find a job. Some people quit an existing job to seek a better one. Some are laid off and others are fired and forced to find another job. The pace of labor turnover is not constant. When technological change is expanding one sector and leading to a contraction of another sector, labor turnover increases. Finding new jobs and moving takes time and the process of adjustment may create overtime and unfilled vacancies in the expanding sector but unemployment in the contracting sector.

Even if wages are flexible, unemployment arising from labor-market turnover cannot be avoided. The rate of unemployment arising from this source is the natural unemployment rate. In labor markets with flexible wages, all the fluctuations in unemployment are fluctuations in the natural rate arising from changes in the rate of labor turnover.

   If wages are sticky, unemployment arises for all the same reasons as in the case of flexible wages and for one additional reason. With sticky wages the real wage may not move quickly enough to keep the quantity of labor demanded equal to the quantity supplied. In such a case, if the real wage rate is ''too high,'' the level of employment is below full employment and unemployment rises above its natural rate. If real wages fall ''too low,'' the quantity of labor demanded and employed rises and unemployment falls below its natural rate. (pp. 806–812)

K E Y   C O N C E P T S

Demand for labor, 794
Diminishing marginal product of labor, 792
Innovation, 793
Invention, 793
Labor force participation rate, 799
Marginal product of labor, 791
Money wage rate, 795
Production function, 791
Quantity of labor demanded, 794
Quantity of labor supplied, 797
Real wage rate, 794
Reservation wage, 799
Short-run aggregate production function, 791
Short-run production function, 791
Supply of labor, 797

Key Figures

R E V I E W   Q U E S T I O N S

1 What is the relationship between output and labor input in the short run? Why does the marginal product of labor diminish?

2 If the short-run production function shifts from 1990 to 1991 by the amount shown in Fig. 30.2, what happens to the marginal product of labor between 1990 and 1991?

3 Explain why the demand for labor curve slopes downward.

4 Given your answer to question 2, does the demand for labor curve shift between 1990 and 1991? If so, in what direction and by how much?

5 Why does the labor force participation rate rise as the real wage rate rises?

6 How is the quantity of labor currently supplied influenced by wages today relative to those expected in the future?

7 Explain what happens in a labor market with flexible wages when the marginal product of labor for each unit of labor input rises.

8 In question 7, explain what happens to the long-run aggregate supply curve.

9 What are sticky wages?

10 Explain what happens in a labor market with sticky wages when the marginal product of labor for each unit of labor input rises.

11 In question 10, explain what happens to the short-run aggregate supply curve.

12 Explain how unemployment can arise if wages are flexible.

13 Explain how unemployment fluctuates above its natural rate.

PROBLEMS

Use the following information about an economy to answer problems 1 through 6. The economy's short-run production function is:

Labor hours	Real GNP
1	20
2	38
3	54
4	68
5	80
6	90
7	98
8	104

Its demand and supply schedules for labor are:

Real wage rate	Labor hours Demanded	Supplied
6	8	2
8	7	3
10	6	4
12	5	5
14	4	6
16	3	7
18	2	8
20	1	9

1 If real wages are flexible, how much labor is employed and what is the real wage rate?

2 If the GNP deflator is 120, what is the money wage rate?

3 If real wages are flexible, what is the aggregate supply curve in this economy?

4 If money wages are sticky and if the GNP deflator is expected to be 100, what is the money rate in this economy?

5 Find three points on the short-run aggregate supply curve of this economy when money wages are at the level determined by your answer to problem 4.

6 Calculate the real wage rate at each of the three points that you have used in your answer to problem 5.

7 There are two economies, each with *constant* unemployment rates but with a great deal of labor market turnover. In economy A, there is a rapid pace of technological change. Twenty percent of the work force is either fired or quits its job every year and 20 percent is hired every year. In economy B, only 5 percent is fired or quits and 5 percent is hired. Which economy has the higher unemployment rate? Why?

8 There are two economies, Flexiland and Fixland. These economies are identical in every way except that in Flexiland, real wages are flexible and maintain equality between the quantities of labor demanded and supplied. In Fixland, money wages are sticky but wages are set so that, *on the average,* the quantity of labor demanded equals the quantity supplied.

a) Explain which economy has the higher average unemployment rate.

b) Explain which economy has the largest fluctuations in unemployment.

Chapter 31

*After studying this
chapter, you will be
able to:*

- Describe the features of
  macroeconomic
  equilibrium

- Explain the costs of wrong
  expectations about
  inflation

- Explain how expectations
  of inflation affect *actual*
  inflation

- Explain the concept of
  macroeconomic rational
  expectations

- Calculate the rational expectation of the price
  level

- Explain how inflation is
  determined

- Explain how inflation expectations affect interest
  rates

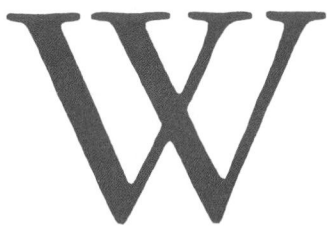

hile firms and labor unions jawboned about wages in 1973, they all agreed about one thing: Inflation in 1974 would be around 5 percent. Pay settlements came in at 8 percent. In other words, taking inflation out of the picture, they expected pay raises of 3 percent. But the unexpected happened. In 1974, inflation surged to 11 percent—far more than the average pay raise. Unanticipated inflation socked workers with the equivalent of a 3 percent pay cut. ■ What causes inflation? Why do the best made plans often go awry when it comes to inflation? How do people form expectations about inflation? How do those expectations influence the economy? ■ Suppose that by a supreme effort of self-discipline you have saved $100 for a rainy day. On January 1, 1988, you put your $100 in a 30-year U.S. treasury bond, with an annual yield of 9¼ percent. If you reinvest the interest income each year, you could have $1421 to spend in 2018. Is that a good deal? Should you run out and buy treasury bonds? That depends on what $1421 buys in the year 2018. With no inflation, your $100 would have grown into enough to buy a fairly fancy audio-video system. If inflation averages 9¼ percent, however, $1421 in the year 2018 would buy the same amount of goods as $100 did in 1988. If inflation averages 20 percent, a hamburger lunch at a diner that today costs $5.99 would cost $1421 in 2018. No matter how much you like diner food, it would not be a good deal, over 30 years, to shrink $100 into today's equivalent of $5.99. How do expectations of inflation affect interest rates? Are bondholders any better than labor unions at forecasting inflation rates?

Wanted: A Crystal Ball

■ This book will not tell you whether treasury bonds are a good deal today. To do that, we would need a crystal ball. But this chapter will help you to understand what people in the real world do in the absence of crystal balls. We will discover that the actual levels of real GNP, the GNP deflator, and interest rates all depend on inflation expectations. We're also going to discover that when expectations turn out to be wrong (as they almost always do), the forecasting errors themselves have an important influence on real GNP, employment and unemployment, and inflation.

Macroeconomic Equilibrium

Four conditions are satisfied when the economy is in *macroeconomic equilibrium*:

- Real GNP demanded equals real GNP supplied.
- Aggregate planned expenditure equals real GNP.
- Real money demanded equals real money supplied.
- Quantity of labor demanded equals quantity of labor supplied.

There are two ways in which we can describe an economy in macroeconomic equilibrium. One is in terms of the various demand and supply curves that we have studied in the previous chapters. The other is in terms of what each individual in the economy is doing. Let's first describe macroeconomic equilibrium using the analysis of the earlier chapters on the markets for goods, money, and labor.

Equilibrium in the Markets for Goods, Money, and Labor

The first condition for macroeconomic equilibrium requires that the price level be such that the aggregate demand curve intersects the aggregate supply curve. In such a situation, real GNP demanded equals real GNP supplied (Chapter 24). The second condition requires that real GNP be at a level that makes the aggregate expenditure curve intersect the 45° line (Chapter 26). The third condition requires that the interest rate be such that the quantity of money demanded equals the quantity of money supplied (Chapter 28). The fourth condition requires

that the quantity of labor employed be determined by the demand for labor curve and that households supply the quantity of labor that they wish to supply, given the wages that prevail, the information that they have about available jobs, and the wage and employment contracts that they have accepted (Chapter 30).

Macroeconomic equilibrium does not imply full employment. *Full-employment equilibrium,* a situation in which the level of unemployment equals the *natural rate of unemployment,* is one possible macroeconomic equilibrium. At such an equilibrium the economy produces its capacity output. But macroeconomic equilibrium can occur at an output level above capacity (unemployment below the natural rate) or below capacity (with unemployment above the natural rate).

The concept of macroeconomic equilibrium can be given flesh and bones by describing the actions of the people in the economy.

Individuals in a Macroeconomic Equilibrium

Macroeconomic equilibrium is a state in which no one wants to change his or her actions under the current circumstances, given all the information and options available. That is, no one finds it profitable to take different actions. The amount of consumption and investment, the quantity of money held, and the quantity of labor employed seem to each individual to be the best available, given current conditions and existing contracts. Such a situation is not necessarily one in which everyone is happy or pleased. Some people may well feel badly off or perhaps even disappointed and cheated. The most likely source of disappointment is that inflation turns out to be different from what was expected when contracts of various kinds were entered into. Workers and lenders feel cheated when inflation turns out to be higher than expected. Employers and borrowers feel cheated when inflation turns out to be lower than expected. But none of these groups can, in the circumstances they face, do any better than they are currently doing.

This description of macroeconomic equilibrium in terms of what people are doing is equivalent to the more formal definition. The price level, the interest rate, wages, and income cannot balance the quantities demanded and supplied in the economy if someone wanted to behave differently.

Figure 31.1   Equilibrium with a Given Price Level
Expectation

The long-run aggregate supply curve (LAS) and the short-run aggregate supply curve (SAS) intersect at the expected price level,
which is 100. When aggregate demand is AD, equilibrium occurs
at point a. The price level is equal to the expected price level, the
GNP deflator is 100, and real GNP is equal to its capacity level
of $4 trillion.

Our main goal in this chapter is to discover
how the price level, inflation, expectations of future
inflation, and interest rates are determined. We are
going to approach this goal by studying a model
economy in macroeconomic equilibrium. We are going to discover how, in the model economy, expectations of inflation affect actual inflation and how errors
in forecasting inflation affect real GNP. We are then
going see how the predictions that we can obtain in a
model economy help us understand the actual forces
generating inflation in the United States today.

The Effects of Price Level
Expectations

Let's begin by studying the simplest possible economy: One in which no one expects inflation and there
is no inflation. Such an economy is illustrated in Fig.
31.1. The long-run aggregate supply curve (LAS)
tells us that capacity real GNP is $4 trillion. With
no inflation expected, the GNP deflator is expected

to be 100. The short-run aggregate supply curve is
SAS. We discovered in Chapter 30 that the short-run
aggregate supply curve intersects the long-run aggregate supply curve at the expected price level. The
short-run aggregate supply curve in Fig. 31.1 intersects LAS at the expected price level of 100, at point
a. With no actual inflation, the aggregate demand
curve is AD. This curve intersects the short-run aggregate supply curve at point a—where the GNP
deflator is 100 and real GNP is $4 trillion. This
macroeconomic equilibrium is a full-employment
equilibrium. The economy is producing its capacity
level of real GNP. The GNP deflator is expected to
be 100 and actually turns out to be 100.

What happens if the people in this economy
expect inflation? The answer is that the economy gets
some inflation but not as much as was expected. In
other words, expectations of inflation are partially
self-fulfilling. To see why, let's examine how the
equilibrium shown in Fig. 31.1 is disturbed when
some inflation is expected.

Let's suppose that everyone expects 15 percent
inflation, which means that the GNP deflator is expected to rise to 115. Figure 31.2(a) shows the
effects of this expectation of inflation. The short-run
aggregate supply curve shifts upward to SAS_1. Pay
attention to the magnitude of the shift. The vertical
distance between SAS_0 and SAS_1 is the percentage
increase in the price level that people are expecting.
The new SAS curve, SAS_1, intersects the LAS curve at
the expected price level of 115.

The new equilibrium occurs at point b, where
SAS_1 intersects AD. Real GNP is $3.5 trillion and
the GNP deflator is 110. The increase in the actual
price level is less than the increase in the expected
price level. Fifteen percent inflation was expected, but
actual inflation turns out to be 10 percent. But real
GNP falls below its capacity level. The economy goes
into a recession.

You will perhaps be able to understand more
clearly the result that we have just discovered if we
turn to an example in one small part of the economy.
Let's examine the effects of an increase in the expected inflation rate on one small soda bottling plant in
Kalamazoo, Michigan. The firm and its workers agree
that inflation is going to be 15 percent next year, so
they agree to raise wages by 15 percent. With higher
wages, the firm's costs increase and the supply curve
of bottled soda shifts to the left. In agreeing to
higher wages, the firm expects to be able to sell its
output for 15 percent higher prices.

Figure 31.2   The Effects of Price Level Expectations

(a) Price level expected to rise by 15 percent

(b) Price level expected to fall by 15 percent

Long-run aggregate supply is *LAS* and aggregate demand is *AD*. Three possible expected price levels are analyzed. First, as in Fig. 31.1, the expected price level is 100, the short-run aggregate supply curve is SAS_0, and the actual price level equals the expected price level. That is, macroeconomic equilibrium is at point *a* in both parts. Second, if the expected price level is 115, the short-run aggregate supply curve becomes SAS_1 in part (a). The actual price level rises to 110 and real GNP falls to $3.5 trillion—macroeconomic equilibrium is at point *b* in part (a). Third, if the expected price level is 85, the short-run aggregate supply curve becomes SAS_2 in part (b). The actual price level falls to 90 and real GNP rises to $4.5 trillion—macroeconomic equilibrium is at point *c* in part (b). A change in the expected price level with aggregate demand constant changes the actual price level in the same direction as the change in the expected price level, but the actual price level changes by a smaller amount than does the expected price level.

In order to isolate the effects of the change in inflation expectations, we must hold everything else constant. In particular, we will keep demand constant. Nothing has happened to aggregate demand and nothing has happened to the demand for soda. The firm's supply curve of soda has shifted to the left but its demand curve for soda is unchanged. As a result, the price of soda rises and the quantity of soda sold falls. The firm cuts back on its employment, laying off some of its workers. For the soda producer, the increase in the expected price level increases its labor costs by the same percentage as prices are expected to increase. But actual prices increase by less than expected, so output and employment fall.

Next, let's work out what happens if the price level is expected to fall by 15 percent, which means that the GNP deflator is expected to fall from 100 to

85. We can see the effect in Fig. 31.2(b). With an expected price level of 85, the short-run aggregate supply curve becomes SAS_2. It intersects the long-run aggregate supply curve at the expected price level. The new equilibrium is where *AD* intersects SAS_2, at an output of $4.5 trillion and a GNP deflator of 90 (point *c*). At this equilibrium, real GNP is above its capacity level. The price level falls but not by as much as was expected. A 15 percent expected fall in the price level has resulted in a 10 percent actual fall in the price level and an increase in real GNP. The economy goes into a boom.

Again, let's look at what happens at the soda bottling plant. With the price level expected to fall, the firm and the unions agree to lower wages. Again, we're isolating the effects of a change in expectations about prices, so let's suppose that nothing happens to aggregate demand or the demand for soda. Lower wages mean lower costs, so the firm's supply curve of soda shifts to the right. The price of soda falls, but the quantity traded increases. The firm has to hire additional workers and work its plant overtime. Extra costs are incurred to produce the extra output, so the price of soda falls by less than the price level is expected to fall.

You have now seen how variations in the expected price level lead to variations in the actual performance of the economy. The higher the expected price level, other things being equal, the higher is the actual price level and the lower is real GNP. But a rise in the expected price level induces a smaller rise in the actual price level than was expected. Only when the price level equals the expected price level is the economy producing its capacity real GNP. When price level expectations are wrong, real GNP is either above or below capacity. If price level expectations are higher than the actual price level, real GNP is below capacity; and if price level expectations are lower than the actual price level, real GNP is above capacity.

The Cost of Wrong Forecasts

Our inability to know the future combined with our need to make forecasts about it inevitably impose costs on us. The more wrong we are in assessing the future price level, the more expensive our mistake will be. To see why errors in forecasting the price level are expensive, let's return to the soda bottling plant.

Wages   In the first case that we looked at, the firm and its workers expect more inflation (15 percent) than occurs (10 percent). That outcome imposes costs on both the firm and the workers. Wages increase by a larger percentage than prices. But faced with higher real labor costs, the firm cuts back on employment. Workers are laid off or given only part-time work. At the higher real wage, they would like more work but can't get it. With lower output and with costs having increased by a bigger percentage than prices, the firm makes a smaller profit.

In the second case, the firm and its workers expect a 15 percent fall in prices. They are wrong again. Prices actually fall by 10 percent. In this case, real wages fall and the firm increases its output. But to do so, it has to operate its plant at a very high rate and incur overtime costs and other costs associated with operating at the physical limits of its plant. The workers, in this situation, wind up feeling cheat-

ed. They've worked overtime to produce the extra output and, when they come to spend their wages, they discover that prices have not fallen by as much as was expected, so their wages buy a smaller quantity of goods and services than anticipated. Their real wage has fallen.

Interest Rates   Just as firms and workers incur costs from wrong forecasts of the price level, so do borrowers and lenders. Interest rates are agreed upon on the basis of some expectation of the future value of money—which, in turn, depends on the future course of the price level. If inflation turns out to be unexpectedly high, borrowers gain and lenders lose. But what borrowers gain is less than what lenders lose. Both groups will regret the scale of borrowing and lending that took place. Borrowers wish they had borrowed more and lenders wish they'd lent less. The situation is, again, symmetric. If inflation turns out to be lower than expected, lenders gain and borrowers lose. Again, both groups regret the scale of borrowing and lending. In this case, lenders wish they'd lent more and borrowers wish they'd borrowed less. Again, the gains of the lenders are not sufficient to match the losses of the borrowers.

Costs occur regardless of whether price expectations turn out to be wrong on the up side or the down side. Wrong expectations impose costs on firms and households, and the larger the forecasting error, the larger are those costs. The costs of wrong forecasts, like any other costs, are something to be minimized. These costs arise from scarcity in the same way that all other costs arise from scarcity. In this case, what is scarce is crystal balls. Nevertheless, although the costs of wrong forecasts cannot be entirely avoided, they can at least be made as small as possible.

Minimizing the Losses from Wrong Expectations

Lacking crystal balls, people cannot be right all the time. But they can use all the information available to them to make their forecasting errors as small as possible. That is, they can make a rational expectation. A **rational expectation** is a forecast based on all the available information, such that the expected forecast error is zero and the range of error is as small as possible. A rational expectation has two features. First, the range of the forecast error is as small as possible. No information that might narrow the range of uncertainty has been wasted. Given what is known, the range of uncertainty cannot be made smaller. Second, a rational expectation is correct on the average. This does not mean that a rational expectation is an accurate forecast nor that it will ever be exactly correct. Rather, it means that there is as much chance that the forecast will be too high as it will be too low, and by the same amounts. By making a forecast that consciously errs on one side or the other, people could avoid being wrong in one direction. But the cost of that would be being more wrong in the other direction. Since the costs of wrong forecasts occur regardless of whether expectations are too high or too low, the best that can be done is to make a forecast that has an equal chance of being too high or too low.

Now let's turn to the task of determining the rational expectation of the price level.

The Rational Expectation of the Price Level

How do people form expectations of the price level? And in particular, how do they form a rational expectation?

How People Form Expectations in the Real World

Different people devote different amounts of time and effort to forming expectations. Some people specialize in forecasting and even make a living by selling their forecasts. For example, investment advisors forecast the future prices of stocks and bonds. Banks, large stock and commodity brokers, government agencies, and private forecasting firms make macroeconomic forecasts about inflation. Indeed, some people, such as Henry Kaufman, have made spectacular fortunes as a result of good forecasting.

Specialist forecasters stand to lose a great deal by having wrong forecasts. They have a strong incentive, therefore, to make their forecasts as accurate as possible—minimizing the range of error and at least making them correct on the average. Furthermore, organizations that stand to lose by having wrong forecasts invest a good deal of effort in checking the forecasts of the professionals. For example, all the large banks, all the major labor unions, government

departments, and most large private-sector producers of goods and services devote a lot of effort not only to making their own forecasts but to checking their forecasts and comparing them with the forecasts of others.

But most people devote little time and effort to making forecasts. Instead, they get their forecasts either by buying them from specialists or by mimicking people who appear to have been successful.

How Economists Predict People's Forecasts

Economics is sometimes called the science of choice. It is the science that tries to predict the choices that people make in the face of scarcity. But if an important determinant of people's choices are their expectations of such phenomena as inflation, then to predict people's choices we also have to predict their expectations of inflation. How do economists set about that task? They assume that people are as rational in their use of information and in forming expectations as they are in all their other economic actions. This idea leads economists to the rational expectations hypothesis, whose origin is described in Our Advancing Knowledge on pp. 824–825. The **rational expectations hypothesis** is the proposition that the forecasts that people make are the same as the forecasts made by an economist using the relevant economic theory together with all the information available at the time the forecast is made. For example, to predict people's expectations of the price of orange juice, economists use the economic model of demand and supply, together with all the available information about the positions of the demand and supply curves for orange juice. To make a prediction about people's expectations of the price level and inflation, economists use the economic model of aggregate demand and aggregate supply. Let's see how we can use the model of aggregate demand and aggregate supply to work out a rational expectation of the price level.

Calculating a Rational Expectation of the Price Level

To calculate a rational expectation of the price level, we use the aggregate demand and aggregate supply model to forecast the state of the economy in much the same way that meteorologists use a model of the atmosphere to forecast the weather. But there is an important difference between the meteorologist's model of the atmosphere and the economist's model of aggregate demand and aggregate supply. Tomorrow's weather will not be affected by our forecast of it. We may forecast a sunny day or a torrential downpour, but the outcome is independent of that forecast. The consensus forecast of the price level, however, does affect the actual price level. If the price level is expected to be higher, the actual price level is higher. We must take this fact into account when working out a rational expectation of the price level.

We'll now calculate a rational expectation of the price level. We will use Fig. 31.3 to guide our analysis. The aggregate demand and aggregate supply model predicts that the price level is at the point of intersection of the aggregate demand and short-run aggregate supply curves. To forecast the price level, therefore, we have to forecast the positions of these curves.

Let's begin with aggregate demand. Suppose that we have forecasted all the things that influence aggregate demand, we then have a forecast of the position of the aggregate demand curve. This forecast is given by the expected aggregate demand curve (*EAD*).

Our next task is to forecast the position of the short-run aggregate supply curve, but here we have a problem. We know that the position of the short-run aggregate supply curve is determined by two things:

1 Long-run aggregate supply

2 The expected price level

The short-run aggregate supply curve intersects the long-run aggregate supply curve at the expected price level. Can you see the problem? We're trying to forecast the price level. The price level is determined at the intersection of the aggregate demand curve and short-run aggregate supply curve, but we don't know where the short-run aggregate supply curve is until we know the expected price level.

Our problem is solved by finding a forecast of the price level that makes our forecast of both the aggregate demand and short-run aggregate supply curves intersect at that same forecasted price level. The next step in that process is to forecast long-run aggregate supply.

Suppose that we have made the best forecast we can of capacity real GNP and that we expect long-run aggregate supply to be $4 trillion. Our expectation, then, is that the long-run aggregate supply curve will be *ELAS* in Fig. 31.3. We're now ready to forecast the price level. At the same time, we're going to forecast the position of the short-run aggregate

Figure 31.3   The Rational Expectation of the Price Level

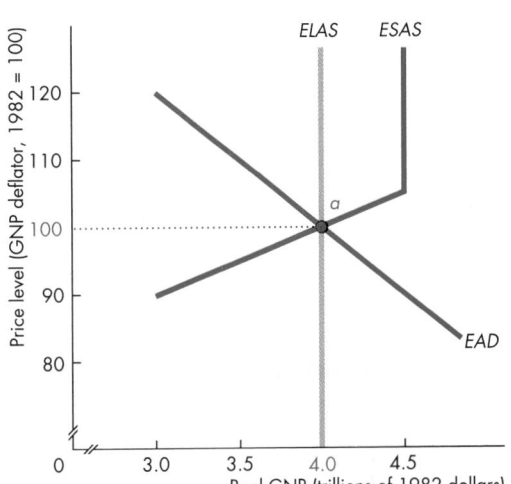

The rational expectation of the price level is the best available forecast. That forecast is constructed by forecasting the expected aggregate demand curve (*EAD*) and the expected long-run aggregate supply curve (*ELAS*). The rational expectation of the price level occurs at the point of intersection of curves *EAD* and *ELAS*. The expected short-run aggregate supply curve (*ESAS*) is such that it too passes through the intersection of curves *ELAS* and *EAD*.

supply curve. Our forecast is that the price level will be 100 and that the short-run aggregate supply curve will be *ESAS*.

R E V I E W

The rational expectation of the price level is calculated by using:

• Expected aggregate demand (*EAD*)

• Expected long-run aggregate supply (*ELAS*)

The point of intersection of the expected short-run aggregate demand curve and the expected long-run aggregate supply curve determines the rational expectation of the price level. The expected short-run aggregate supply curve (*ESAS*) passes through the point of intersection of the expected aggregate demand and expected long-run aggregate supply curves. ■

Expectations

Economists have always known that expectations are important, but it is only in the last 20 years that they have developed a satisfactory way of incorporating expectations into economic models.

In earlier times, three approaches to expectations were employed:

- Perfect foresight
- Static expectations
- Adaptive expectations

The assumption of perfect foresight amounts to giving people complete knowledge of the future. Incorporating that assumption into economic models enables economists to make predictions about what would happen if people indeed did have perfect foresight. Such predictions are not useless. They are often accurate concerning very long-term tendencies.

The assumption of static expectations is that the future will be exactly the same as the present. This assumption enables economists to build models that make predictions that would be correct if people did indeed believe that the future will be very much the same as the present. Again, such models are not completely useless. They are probably reasonable for very short-term forecasting.

The assumption of adaptive expectations is an attempt to have a more flexible version of static expectations. With adaptive expectations, expectations change in proportion to the extent to which previous expectations have been shown to be wrong. This assumption is an attractive one for it has a good deal of intuitive appeal. If you expect inflation to be 2 percent and it turns out to be 5 percent and it keeps on turning out to be 5 percent, it seems sensible to suppose that you will gradually revise your expectation upward from 2 percent to 3 percent to 4 percent and eventually to 5 percent. But adaptive expectations has the unattractive feature in that it supposes that people make expectations just on the basis of the past history of the variable that they are trying to forecast. Any knowledge that they have about the mechanisms generating inflation are ignored.

The modern theory of expectations—the rational expectations theory—was first suggested in a remarkable article* published in 1961 by John F. Muth. Born in Chicago in 1930, Muth was a young economist at Carnegie-Mellon University in Pittsburgh. (As a matter of fact, he had not yet completed his Ph.D. when his article was published.) In that article, Muth suggested that we should explore the implications of the idea that the people in our economic models form their expectations by using the very same model of the economy that the economist has invented. The idea was revolutionary but was also largely ignored.

It was not until 1970 that the idea really began to take hold. At that time, in a series of remarkable papers that have transformed macroeconomics beyond recognition, Robert E. Lucas, Jr., began to apply Muth's ideas to macroeconomic theory.

Born in Yakima, Washington, in 1937, Lucas was, in 1970, a professor of economics at Carnegie-Mellon University, the same place where Muth had made his remarkable discovery a few years earlier. Lucas at first applied his ideas to the expectations of inflation and reinterpreted the Phillips curve (see Our Advancing Knowledge on pp. 832–834). He subsequently went on to show how the concept of rational expectations is a completely general one and has widespread application. His work inspired such scholars as Thomas Sargent and Robert Barro to undertake statistical investigations of aggregate fluctuations, incorporating the rational expectations hypothesis. The rational expectations hypothesis is now the working hypothesis of almost all the current practitioners of macroeconomics.

ECONOMETRICA

JOURNAL OF THE ECONOMETRIC SOCIETY

An International Society for the Advancement of Economic Theory in its Relation to Statistics and Mathematics

CONTENTS

VOL. 29, NO. 3—July, 1961

*John F. Muth, "Rational Expectations and the Theory of Price Movements," *Econometrica* (1961), vol. 29, pp. 315–335.

Theory and Reality

The analysis that we have just conducted leads to the question: Do real people form expectations of the price level by using that same analysis? We can imagine that graduates of economics might, but it seems unrealistic to attribute such calculations to most people. Does this fact make the whole idea of rational expectations invalid?

The answer is no! In performing our calculations, we have been building an economic model. That model does not seek to describe the thought processes of real people. Its goal is to make predictions about *behavior,* not mental processes. The *rational expectations hypothesis* states that the forecasts that people make, regardless of how they make them, are on average the same as the forecasts that an economist makes using the relevant economic theory. In using the rational expectations hypothesis, economists do not deny that in reality people make decisions in very complicated ways, and possibly in ways that the decision maker couldn't even describe. To forecast that behavior, economists assume that people are rational, seeking to get as much as possible out of their scarce resources. By building models that incorporate this assumption and then making predictions using these models, economists seek to understand and predict actual behavior. Assuming that people's expectations are rational is just another example and application of the central theme of economics: If expectations are rational, they can only be improved by incurring a cost. In such a situation, the cost of a better forecast has to be offset against its benefits.

Now that we know what macroeconomic rational expectations are and how rational expectations of the price level and output are calculated, let's go on to see how actual real GNP and the actual price level are determined and compare them with their rational expectations.

Rational Expectations Equilibrium

We have now done two things in this chapter. First, we have discovered how macroeconomic equilibrium is affected by changes in the expected price level. Second, we have worked out a rational expectation of the price level.

Our next task is to bring these two things together. That is, we want to work out a macroeconomic equilibrium when the expected price level is a rational expectation—is the best forecast of the price level that is available.

We're going to illustrate and summarize our analysis in Fig. 31.4. The figure has three parts. Part (a) contains people's forecasts of the economy and parts (b) and (c) show two alternative outcomes that differ from the forecast. The forecast in part (a) is exactly the same as that seen in Fig. 31.3. The forecasted or expected price level is 100. In part (b), we work out what happens when aggregate demand turns out to be different from expected aggregate demand. The long-run aggregate supply curve (*LAS*) and the short-run aggregate supply curve (*SAS*) in part (b) are identical to the expected long-run aggregate supply curve (*ELAS*) and the expected short-run aggregate supply curve (*ESAS*) in part (a). The point at which these curves intersect—point *a*—is the same in each part of the figure and occurs when the GNP deflator is 100 and real GNP is $4 trillion.

Part (b) shows what happens when actual aggregate demand turns out to be lower than expected. Such an outcome might arise from an *unexpected* slowdown in the rate at which the Fed is creating money, an *unexpected* fall in foreign demand for U.S. exports, an *unexpected* tax increase, or an *unexpected* reduction in government purchases of goods and services. The actual aggregate demand curve is *AD*. Equilibrium is determined where the actual aggregate demand curve intersects the short-run aggregate supply curve. The GNP deflator is 95 and real GNP $3.5 trillion. With actual aggregate demand below its expected level, the price level is below its expected level and real GNP is below capacity.

Part (c) shows what happens when aggregate supply turns out to be less than expected but aggregate demand is the same as expected. The aggregate demand curve (*AD*) in part (c) is identical to the expected aggregate demand curve in part (a). But the aggregate supply curves are farther to the left in part (c) than the expected aggregate supply curves in part (a). Such a situation could arise because of an *unexpected* slowdown in capacity growth, perhaps because of *unexpectedly* slow technological change or capital accumulation. Again, the equilibrium occurs where the aggregate demand curve intersects the short-run aggregate supply curve. In this case, that equilibrium is at a GNP deflator of 110 and real GNP of $3.5 trillion. The actual price level is higher than expected

Figure 31.4   Rational Expectations Equilibrium

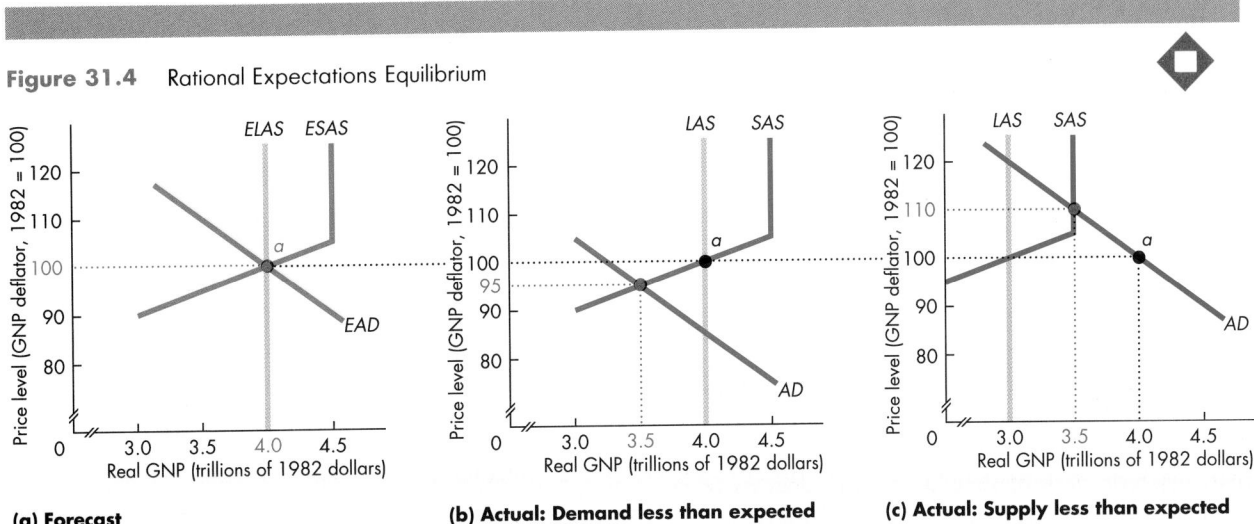

(a) Forecast   **(b) Actual: Demand less than expected**   **(c) Actual: Supply less than expected**

The rational expectation of the price level is calculated in part (a). It occurs at the intersection of curves *EAD* and *ELAS* (point a). If long-run aggregate supply turns out to be as expected but aggregate demand is lower than expected, as in part (b), real GNP falls below capacity and the price level falls below its expected level. If aggregate demand turns out to be as expected but long-run aggregate supply is lower than expected, as in part (c), the price level rises above its expected level and real GNP falls.

because short-run aggregate supply is lower than expected. With the price level higher than expected, real GNP is above its capacity level. In this particular case, the capacity level of real GNP has fallen compared with its expected value and real GNP itself has also fallen but by less than the fall in capacity GNP.

The two equilibrium positions shown in parts (b) and (c) are examples of a rational expectations equilibrium. A **rational expectations equilibrium** is a macroeconomic equilibrium based on expectations that are the best available forecasts. In a rational expectations equilibrium, the actual values taken on by real GNP and the GNP deflator are not always those forecasted, but they are affected by those forecasted. For example, in Figure 31.4(b), both the GNP deflator and real GNP are lower than expected. This outcome results from aggregate demand turning out to be lower than expected. In Fig. 31.4(c), the GNP deflator is higher than expected and real GNP is lower than expected. This outcome results from aggregate supply being lower than expected. In both cases, the outcome depends on the actual as well as the expected levels of aggregate demand and aggregate supply. If the forecasted price level had been lower than it was, real GNP would have been higher

and the actual price level (inflation rate) lower than what occurred. If the forecasted price level had been higher, real GNP would have been lower and the inflation rate higher than what occurred.

Once the events that we've just described have occurred and the economy has been observed, people are aware of what has happened and they know that their expectations were wrong. By then it is too late to do anything about it. Time has moved on and people are forming expectations for the future.

Other rational expectations equilibrium positions can occur—those resulting from long-run aggregate supply being at or above rather than below its expected level and aggregate demand being at or above rather than below its expected level. For example, if long-run aggregate supply turns out to be higher than expected, real GNP is above its expected level and the price level and inflation are below their expected levels. If aggregate demand turns out to be higher than expected, real GNP is above its expected level but, in this case, the price level and inflation are higher than expected. (Actually there are nine possible combinations arising from aggregate demand and long-run aggregate supply, each being below, at, or above their expected levels.)

Individuals in a Rational Expectations Equilibrium

The key characteristic of any economic equilibrium is that all the people in the economy, all of whom are trying to do the best they can for themselves, have reached a situation in which they cannot make a reallocation of their resources that they regard as superior to the one they have chosen.

Each household or firm sees itself as a small part of the overall economy. Those firms and households that have sufficient market power to influence prices have exerted that influence to their maximum possible advantage. But most households and firms are not able to exert a significant effect on the prices that they face. Each household and firm does its best to forecast those prices relevant to its own actions.

Armed with its best forecasts, or rational expectations, each household works out how many chickens, microwaves, and suits to buy, how much to spend on cars and plumbing, how much money to have in the bank, and how many hours a week to work. These decisions are expressed not as fixed quantities but as demand and supply schedules.

On the other side of the markets, firms, also armed with their rational expectations, determine how much new capital equipment to install (investment), how much output to supply, and how much labor to demand. Like households, firms don't express their decisions as fixed quantities. Instead, they express them as demand schedules for factors of production and supply schedules of output.

Prices, wages, and interest rates are determined in the markets for goods and services, labor, and money at levels that ensure the mutual consistency of all the plans of individual households and firms trading in these markets. The quantities demanded and supplied in each market balance.

In a rational expectations equilibrium, each person is satisfied that there is no better action he or she could currently take. But such an equilibrium is not static. The economy constantly changes. You could imagine the economy at each point that we observe as a frozen frame in a video: In the frame, the supply and demand curves in the markets for all the different goods, services, and factors of production all intersect, determining their prices and quantities at that moment. Economists try to understand what is happening by stopping the video to take a closer look at it.

Inflation

We're now going to use our macroeconomic model of aggregate demand and aggregate supply to study the causes of inflation. First, recall that inflation is the percentage rise in the price level. That is,

$$\text{Inflation rate} = \frac{\text{Current year's price level} - \text{Last year's price level}}{\text{Last year's price level}} \cdot 100.$$

Let's write this equation in symbols. We'll call this year's price level P_1 and last year's price level P_0, so that,

$$\text{Inflation rate} = \frac{P_1 - P_0}{P_0} \cdot 100.$$

This equation shows that there is a connection between the inflation rate and the price level. For a given price level last year, the higher the inflation rate, the higher is the price level this year. Let's begin our analysis of the causes of inflation by focusing on an inflation that is anticipated.

Anticipated Inflation

Let's suppose that last year the GNP deflator was 100 and real GNP was $4 trillion. Let's also suppose that the economy's capacity output last year was $4 trillion, as the economy was at full employment. Figure 31.5 illustrates the economy last year. The aggregate demand curve last year was AD_0, the aggregate supply curve was SAS_0, and the long-run aggregate supply curve was LAS. Since the economy was in equilibrium at capacity real GNP, the actual price level equaled the expected price level.

To simplify our analysis, let's suppose that at the end of last year capacity real GNP was not expected to change, so that this year's expected long-run aggregate supply is the same as last year's. Let's also suppose that aggregate demand was expected to increase, so that the expected aggregate demand curve for this year is EAD_1. We can now calculate the rational expectation of the price level for this year. It is a GNP deflator of 110, the price level at which the new expected aggregate demand curve cuts the expected long-run aggregate supply curve. Wages increase as a result of the expected increase in the price level and the short-run aggregate supply curve also increases. In particular, given that the expected price

INFLATION 829

Figure 31.5 Anticipated Inflation ◆

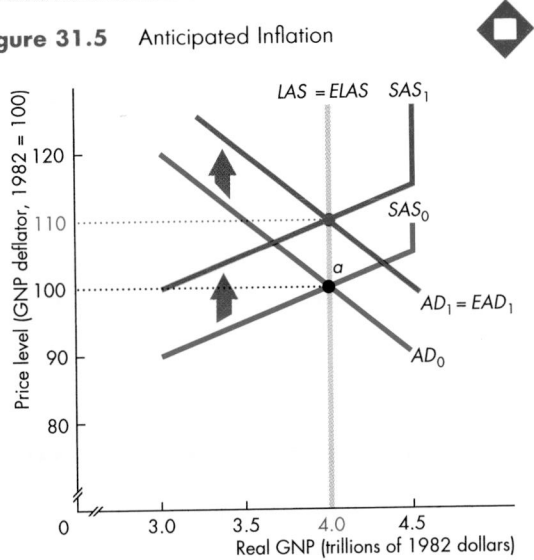

The actual and expected long-run aggregate supply curve (*LAS*) is at a real GNP of $4 trillion. Last year, aggregate demand was AD_0 and the short-run aggregate supply curve SAS_0. The actual price level was the same as that expected—a GNP deflator of 100. This year, aggregate demand is expected to rise to EAD_1. The rational expectation of the GNP deflator changes from 100 to 110. As a result, the short-run aggregate supply curve shifts up to SAS_1. Anticipated inflation is 10 percent. If aggregate demand actually increases as expected, the actual aggregate demand curve AD_1 is the same as the expected aggregate demand curve EAD_1. Equilibrium occurs at a real GNP of $4 trillion and an actual GNP deflator of 110. Inflation is 10 percent, as anticipated.

level has increased by 10 percent, the short-run aggregate supply curve for next year (SAS_1) shifts upward by that same percentage amount and passes through the long-run aggregate supply curve (*LAS*) at the expected price level.

If aggregate demand actually increases by exactly the amount expected, then the actual aggregate demand curve AD_1 is the same as EAD_1. The intersection point of the AD_1 and SAS_1 determines the actual price level—where the GNP deflator is 110. Between last year and this year, the economy experienced an increase in the GNP deflator from 100 to 110 or, equivalently, an inflation rate of 10 percent. There was no change in real GNP, so the economy's growth rate was zero.

In this example, inflation was anticipated. The price level was expected to rise from 100 to 110—there was an expected inflation rate of 10 percent. The price level did exactly what it was expected to do, so there was an actual inflation rate of 10 percent as well.

What caused the inflation? The immediate answer is the anticipated and actual rise in aggregate demand. Because aggregate demand was expected to rise from AD_0 to EAD_1, the short-run aggregate supply curve shifted up from SAS_0 to SAS_1. Because aggregate demand actually did increase by the amount that was expected, the aggregate demand curve shifted up from AD_0 to AD_1. The combination of the anticipated and actual upward shift in the aggregate demand curve produced a rise in the price level that was anticipated.

For prices to keep rising year after year—for inflation to be an ongoing phenomenon—something must be making the aggregate demand curve continue to shift upward year after year. What makes the aggregate demand curve keep shifting upward year after year? The answer is the quantity of money. Growth in the quantity of money makes the aggregate demand curve shift upward. An anticipated increase in the quantity of money shifts the aggregate demand curve upward, increases the expected price level, thereby shifting the short-run aggregate supply curve upward, and increases the price level, leaving real GNP constant. That is, for the growth of the quantity of money to cause anticipated inflation, the money supply growth itself must be anticipated. Only in this case will the economy follow the course described in Fig. 31.5. If the expected growth rate in the money supply is different from the actual growth rate, so that the expected aggregate demand curve shifts by a different amount from the actual aggregate demand curve, the inflation rate will depart from its expected level and, to some extent, there will be unanticipated inflation.

Unanticipated Inflation

The events described in Fig. 31.5 involve aggregate demand increasing by exactly the amount expected. The consequence is a fully anticipated inflation. But fully anticipated inflation is a rare phenomenon. And there are some years in which errors in forecasting inflation are especially large. For example, from 1969 to 1970 inflation accelerated in a way that was com-

Figure 31.6   An Unanticipated Rise in the Price Level

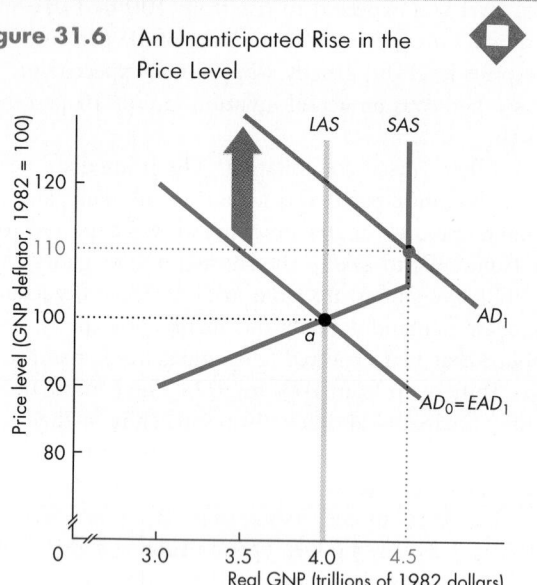

The long-run aggregate supply curve is *LAS*. Last year, the aggregate demand curve was AD_0, a level of aggregate demand that was expected, and so the short-run aggregate supply curve was *SAS*. The actual price level was the same as that expected—a GNP deflator of 100. This year, people do not expect aggregate demand to rise, so expected aggregate demand is EAD_1, which is the same as AD_0. The expected GNP deflator remains at 100 and so the short-run aggregate supply curve remains at *SAS*. No inflation is expected. Aggregate demand actually rises to AD_1, so the price level rises to 110 and real GNP rises to $4.5 trillion. The 10 percent rise in the price level is unanticipated.

pletely unforeseen in 1968. In those years, the economy boomed and real GNP rose above its capacity level. And in 1982 and 1983 the inflation rate fell by magnitudes that were completely unforeseen in 1981. In those years, the economy went into a severe recession. Let's take a closer look at unanticipated movements in prices. We'll first deal with a case in which inflation is higher than anticipated.

We'll begin with the same situation as that in Fig. 31.5. Last year the GNP deflator was 100 and real GNP was $4 trillion. Capacity real GNP was also $4 trillion. The economy is on its long-run aggregate supply curve (*LAS*) and at the point of intersection of the aggregate demand curve AD_0 and the short-run aggregate supply curve *SAS*, in Fig. 31.6. Now let's suppose that this year people expect

aggregate demand to be the same as last year. In other words, the expected aggregate demand curve is AD_0—to remind you, the aggregate demand curve AD_0 has been labeled $AD_0 = EAD_1$. Because aggregate demand is expected to remain constant at AD_0, the expected price level does not change and the short-run aggregate supply curve stays at *SAS*.

But despite people's expectations that aggregate demand will be unchanged, let's suppose that in fact aggregate demand increases to AD_1. Such a situation might arise if the Fed had pursued a tight monetary policy for several years that kept the price level constant and then, without warning, suddenly started to permit the money supply to increase at a rapid rate. The point where the aggregate demand curve AD_1 intersects the short-run aggregate supply curve *SAS* determines the price level and real GNP. The GNP deflator increases to 110 and real GNP increases to $4.5 trillion. The economy experiences 10 percent inflation (a GNP deflator of 110 compared with 100 in the previous year). But because the expected inflation rate is zero, that inflation is unanticipated.

So that you can understand what is going on in individual parts of the economy, keep the Kalamazoo soda bottling plant in mind. In the situation that we have just analyzed, with no inflation expected, wages are held steady and firm's costs stay constant. Households are happy with no wage increase because, like the firm that employs them, they too expect no increases in prices. When demand actually increases and prices rise, real wages fall. The firm scrambles to hire more labor and increase its output. The bottling plants are worked at their physical limits.

The situation that developed in the U.S. economy at the end of the 1960s is a good example of the process that we have just analyzed. In 1969 and 1970, aggregate demand increased at a faster pace than it was anticipated to do. As a consequence, inflation increased and real GNP moved above its capacity level.

Let's now consider the case in which inflation turns out to be lower than expected. We'll begin again in the same place with a GNP deflator of 100 and real GNP of $4 trillion. This initial equilibrium is shown in Fig. 31.7 at the point of intersection of the aggregate demand curve AD_0 and the short-run aggregate supply curve SAS_0.

Aggregate demand is expected to increase from AD_0 to EAD_1. As a result, the price level is expected to rise from 100 to 115. Therefore the short-run aggregate supply curve shifts up from SAS_0 to SAS_1.

Now suppose that although aggregate demand is expected to increase, it stays constant at AD_0. Such a situation would arise if the Fed had been permitting the money supply to increase at a rapid rate for several years, and then, without warning, kept the money supply constant. The aggregate demand curve, AD_1, is the same as in the previous year, AD_0. The point of intersection of the aggregate demand curve and the short-run aggregate supply curve determines real GNP and the price level. The GNP deflator increases from 100 to 110, an inflation rate of 10 percent. The GNP deflator was expected to increase from 100 to 115, an expected rate of inflation of 15 percent. The actual inflation rate is less than that anticipated. Real GNP is $3.5 trillion, which is below its capacity level. Thus when aggregate demand is expected to increase and it doesn't, actual inflation is below its expected level and actual GNP is below capacity.

The situation that we have just described is similiar to the one that occurred in 1982 and 1983. In those years, after several years of rapid money growth, the Fed tightened the reins on the money supply, slowing down the growth rate of aggregate demand. As a consequence, the inflation rate slowed down more quickly than was anticipated, real GNP went below capacity.

Here we've focused on the relationship between unanticipated inflation and real GNP. But we know that as real GNP fluctuates, so does unemployment. Thus there is also a relationship between unanticipated inflation and unemployment. That relationship is part of what is known as Phillips curve theory (see Our Advancing Knowledge on pp. 832–834).

The Quantity Theory of Money

When we looked at the relationship between money supply growth and inflation in Chapter 27 (pp. 722–723), we discovered that there is a correlation between the growth rate of the money supply and inflation, both historically in the United States and in the international data from the experience of other countries. We also discovered, however, that the correlation is not perfect. There are some important departures of the inflation rate from the growth rate of the money supply.

The analysis that we have conducted in this chapter explains these deviations. In order for an

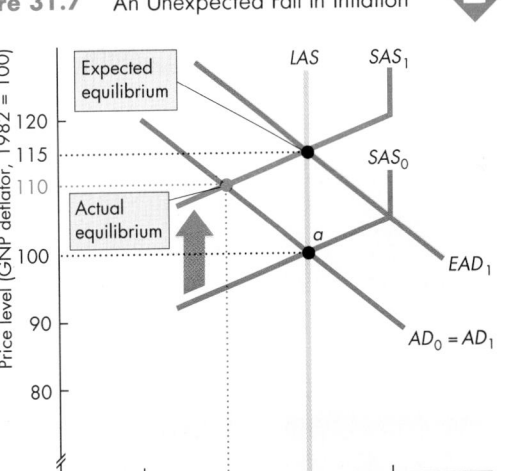

Figure 31.7   An Unexpected Fall in Inflation

Initially, the actual and expected GNP deflator is 100 and real GNP is $4 trillion—the point of intersection of AD_0, LAS, and SAS_0. Aggregate demand is expected to rise to EAD_1. The rational expectation is that the GNP deflator will increase by 15 percent to 115. The short-run aggregate supply curve shifts upward to SAS_1. Actual aggregate demand does not rise but remains at AD_0. That is, AD_1 is the same as AD_0. The new equilibrium occurs at the intersection of AD_1 and SAS_1. The GNP deflator increases to 110 and real GNP falls to $3.5 trillion. Inflation was expected to be 15 percent but turns out to be 10 percent. Real GNP falls below its capacity level.

increase in the money supply to produce an increase in the price level with no change in real GNP, that increase must be anticipated. An unanticipated increase in the money supply increases the price level and real GNP. An unanticipated slowdown in money growth lowers inflation but also lowers real GNP. It is because money supply growth in the real world is partly anticipated and partly unanticipated that the correlation between inflation and money growth is an imperfect one.

In addition, as we have seen in this chapter, changes in aggregate supply also affect the price level, independently of changes in the money supply. This is a further reason why there is a less than complete correlation between inflation and money supply growth. Let's look at the actual relationship between inflation and money growth in the United States since 1960.

The Phillips Curve

A. W. Phillips

Phillips Curve Theory

In 1958, an electrical engineer turned economist, A. W. (Bill) Phillips (1914–1975), became a household name among economists. In that year, Phillips, a native of New Zealand working at the London School of Economics, published an article displaying what is now called the **Phillips curve**—a curve that shows a negative relationship between the unemployment rate and the inflation rate.* Remarkably, that relationship, which had prevailed, on the average, over a period of 100 years, fit the experience of the 1950s almost exactly.

Following Phillips's work with United Kingdom data, Paul Samuelson and Robert Solow at M.I.T. explored the relevance of the Phillips curve for the United States and found similar patterns.

The central proposition of the Phillips curve theory is: other things remaining constant, the higher the unemployment rate, the lower is the inflation rate. Figure 1 illustrates the Phillips curve—the downward-sloping curve labeled *PC*. Along the Phillips curve, the higher the unemployment rate, the lower is the inflation rate. At point *a*, unemployment is 6 percent, and inflation is 10 percent a year.

Phillips's original idea was that the unemployment rate indicates the state of demand pressure in the economy. When unemployment is low, real GNP is above capacity, bottlenecks arise, and inflation accelerates. When unemployment is high, real GNP is below capacity, and inflation diminishes.

In the early 1960s, the Phillips curve became a central element of macroeconomics. At that time, most economists worked with the following model:

• Real GNP is determined by aggregate expenditure—at the point at which the *AE* curve cuts the 45° line, as in Fig. 26.3 (a).

• Given GNP, unemployment, is determined by Okun's Law (pp.808–810).

• Given unemployment, inflation is determined by the Phillips curve.

The Phillips curve was regarded as a menu for policy choice, a list of options for policymakers. They could opt for low unemployment, but the price was high inflation; they could opt for low inflation, but the price was high unemployment.

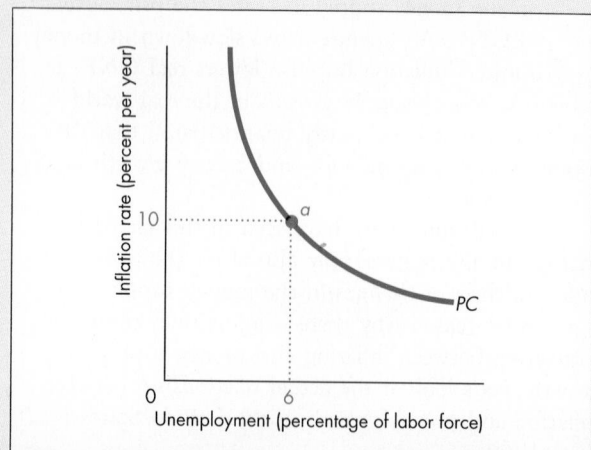

*A. W. Phillips, "The Relation Between Unemployment and the Rate of Change of Money Wages in the United Kingdom, 1861–1957," *Economica* 25 (November 1988): 283–99.

The Phelps-Friedman Hypothesis

In the mid-1960s, Edmund Phelps (now at Columbia University, then a young professor at the University of Pennsylvania) and Milton Friedman theorized that the Phillips curve could be neither a stable relationship nor a menu for policy choice. They predicted that increases in expected inflation in the late 1960s would shift the Phillips curve upward.

They suggested that the Phillips curve is a short-run relationship that holds only for a given expected inflation rate. When the expected inflation rate changes, the short-run Phillips curve shifts. Phelps and Friedman proposed that there is also a long-run Phillips curve—a relationship between inflation and unemployment that prevails when the actual inflation rate equals the expected inflation rate. The long-run Phillips curve is vertical and located at the natural rate of unemployment.

Figure 2 illustrates the short-run and long-run Phillips curves. If the expected inflation rate is 10 percent a year, the short-run Phillips curve is PC_0. If the expected inflation rate falls to 5 percent, the short-run Phillips curve shifts downward to PC_1. At points a and b, inflation is equal to its expected rate, and unemployment is equal to its natural rate of 6 percent. The distance by which the short-run Phillips curve shifts downward when the expected inflation rate falls is equal to the change in the expected inflation rate. Points a and b also lie on the long-run Phillips curve ($LRPC$). This curve tells us that in the long run unemployment equals its natural rate, but it does not tell us what inflation will be.

Variable Natural Rate of Unemployment

Until the 1970s, the natural rate of unemployment was regarded as a constant. In recent years, however, some economists have suggested that the natural rate of unemployment varies because of variations in the amount of labor market turnover arising from technological change, which in turn results in job switching from sector to sector and region to region. A change in the natural unemployment rate shifts both the short-run and the long-run Phillips curve (Fig. 3). If the natural unemployment rate increases from 6 percent to 8 percent, the long-run Phillips curve shifts from $LRPC_0$ to $LRPC_1$, and if expected inflation is constant at 5 percent a year, the short-run Phillips curve shifts from PC_1 to PC_2. Because the expected inflation rate is constant, the short-run Phillips curve PC_1 intersects the long-run curve $LRPC_0$ (point b) at the same inflation rate as the short-run Phillips curve PC_2 intersects the long-run curve $LRPC_1$ (point c).

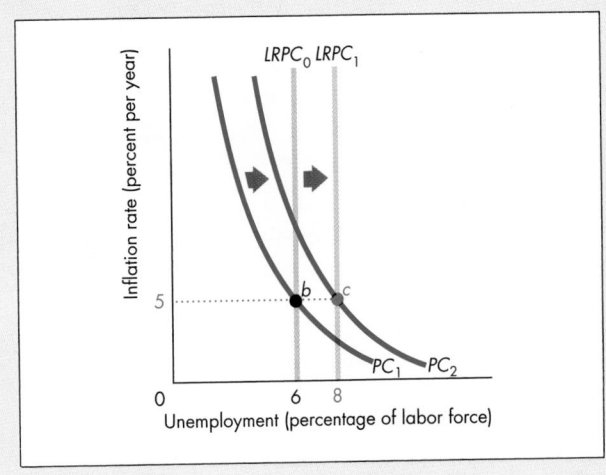

The Phillips Curve in the United States

Now let's look at the relationship between inflation and unemployment in the United States and see how we can interpret that relationship using the Phillips curve theory. Begin by looking at Fig. 4(a), a scatter diagram of inflation and unemployment since 1960. Each dot in the figure represents a combination of inflation and unemployment for a particular year. As you can see, starting in the early 1960s, unemployment gradually decreased and inflation gradually increased. In 1970, there was a sharp increase in unemployment and, at the same time, a slight increase in inflation. Then, in the early 1970s, inflation and unemployment moved in opposite directions again, at first with unemployment increasing and inflation decreasing and then with a reverse movement—a fall in unemployment and a rise in inflation. In 1974, there was a massive increase in inflation and a slight increase in unemployment. There followed a large loop of inflation and unemployment from 1974 through 1980. Then, through 1983, inflation fell dramatically as unemployment increased. Since 1983, unemployment has fallen quite sharply, while inflation has remained relatively steady.

Figure 4(b) interprets the data in terms of four short-run Phillips curves. The Phillips curve of the 1960s (discovered by Samuelson and Solow) is PC_0. At that time, the expected inflation rate was 2 percent a year and the natural unemployment rate, 5 percent. The short-run Phillips curve of the early 1970s and late 1980s is PC_1. These two periods have a natural unemployment rate similar to that of the 1960s but an expected inflation rate that is much higher than that of the 1960s. The short-run Phillips curve of the second half of the 1970s is PC_2. This was the period following the large increase in oil prices that disrupted the economy and had profound effects on both the natural rate of unemployment, which increased to 8 percent, and the expected inflation rate, which increased to around 6 percent a year. The short-run Phillips curve of the early 1980s (and also of 1975) is PC_3. In these years, both the expected inflation rate and the natural unemployment rate were high. Although in the late 1980s the economy was on the same short-run Phillips curve as in the early 1970s (PC_1), there is an important difference between these two periods. In the early 1970s, the natural unemployment rate was around 5 percent, and the expected inflation rate was around 6 percent a year, while in the 1980s, the natural unemployment rate was probably around 6 percent, with inflation expectations at about 4 percent a year. Thus, although the short-run Phillips curves for these two periods are similar, a different combination of expected inflation and natural unemployment underlies the two curves.

(4a) The time sequence

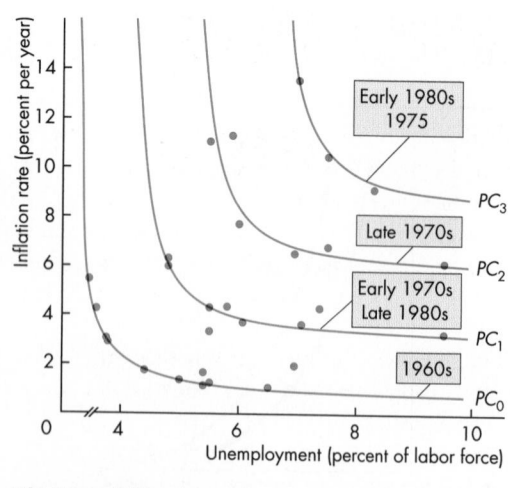

(4b) Four phillips curves

Figure 31.8   Inflation and Money Growth

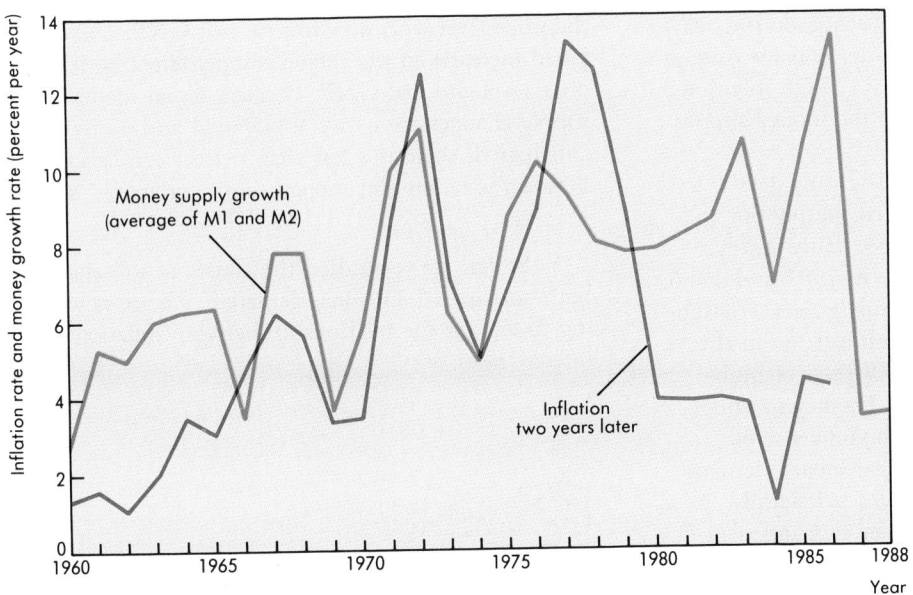

The inflation rate and the money supply growth rate are plotted alongside each other for the years 1960 to 1988. The money supply growth rate is the average of M1 and M2. The inflation rate is graphed two years behind the money supply growth rate. From the mid-1960s to the mid-1970s, inflation and money supply growth fluctuations follow each other closely. But in 1974 and 1975, the inflation rate increases much more quickly than does the money supply growth rate. In the 1980s, inflation collapsed while the money supply growth rate held steady. In the 1970s, the main influence on inflation, in addition to the money supply, was the abrupt change in the price of oil in 1974. Falling interest rates brought an increase in the quantity of money demanded in the 1980s, making it possible for the growth rate of the money supply to exceed the inflation rate through those years.

Source: Economic Report of the President (1989).

U.S. Inflation and Money Growth Since 1960

Figure 31.8 looks at the relation between inflation and money growth in the United States between 1960 and 1988. The money supply growth rate and the inflation rate are both measured on the vertical axis. The money supply growth rate shown is an average of M1 and M2. The inflation rate is graphed two years behind the money supply growth rate. As you can see, fluctuations in the money supply growth rate and fluctuations in the inflation rate two years later line up with each other remarkably closely for the 10 years from the mid-1960s to the mid-1970s.

The relationship is much less close in the 1980s. In this later period, inflation fell dramatically at a time when the money supply growth rate did not fall. Nevertheless, there was a slowdown in money growth in the late 1970s (but of a much smaller magnitude than the slowdown in inflation that occurred in the early 1980s).

Let's examine the two periods in which inflation and money supply growth move apart from each other a little more closely.

First, consider 1974 and 1975. These were years in which the inflation rate increased sharply. The money supply growth rate also increased during those years but not by nearly as much as the increase in the inflation rate. The main source of the faster rise in prices was a large negative supply shock. An oil embargo accompanied by a large increase in the price of crude oil shifted the short-run aggregate supply curve upward. As a consequence, output fell and the price level increased quickly. It is for this reason that these two years show very high inflation with no corresponding increase in the money supply growth rate.

Next, consider the 1980s. The early 1980s were years in which the inflation rate fell sharply but the money supply growth rate remained fairly steady. Later in that decade, in particular in 1985 and 1986, the money supply growth rate actually increased substantially but without triggering an increase in the inflation rate. Why were the 1980s years of high money growth and low inflation? The key to understanding this period is to recall the influence of interest rates on the quantity of real money demanded. During the 1980s, interest rates fell sharply. As a consequence, the quantity of money demanded increased. The money supply grew quickly, but because the quantity of money demanded also grew quickly, the increased money supply did not shift the aggregate demand curve very much. As a consequence, although the price level increased, its rate of increase was moderate.

Despite many influences on inflation—influences such as those just described that sometimes dominate the picture—the clear fact remains that money supply growth generally leads to inflation and that most of the ups and downs in the inflation rate are brought about by fluctuating money supply growth rates.

R E V I E W

When aggregate demand increases by the amount that is expected, a fully anticipated inflation occurs. If aggregate demand increases unexpectedly, prices rise and unanticipated inflation occurs. If aggregate demand fails to increase by as much as expected, prices may still rise but not by as much as expected. Inflation is lower than expected.

Anything that shifts the aggregate demand curve changes the price level. Unanticipated changes in aggregate demand produce unanticipated changes in the price level. Anticipated changes in aggregate demand produce anticipated changes in the price level. The source of persistent increases in aggregate demand is increases in the money supply. Anticipated increases in the money supply bring an increase in the price level with no effect on real GNP. Unanticipated increases in the money supply affect both the price level and real GNP. Because actual money supply changes are partly anticipated and partly unanticipated, there is a less than perfect correlation between inflation and money supply growth. ■

So far, we've studied the causes of inflation—both anticipated and unanticipated. We are now going to look at the relationship between inflation and interest rates.

Interest Rates and Inflation

There have been massive fluctuations in interest rates in the U.S. economy in recent years. In the early 1960s, corporations could raise long-term capital at interest rates of 4.5 to 5 percent a year. By the end of the 1960s, that interest rate had increased to almost 8 percent a year. During the 1970s, the interest rates paid by firms for long-term loans fluctuated between 7.5 and 10.5 percent. During the 1980s, interest rates hit the high teens. Why have interest rates fluctuated so much and why were they so high in the late 1970s and early 1980s?

To answer these questions it is necessary to distinguish between nominal interest rates and real interest rates. **Nominal interest rates** are those actually paid and received in the marketplace. *Real interest rates* are the rates that nominal interest rates translate into when the effects of inflation are taken into account. If the nominal interest rate is 15 percent a year and prices are rising by 10 percent a year, the real interest rate is only 5 percent a year. If you made a loan of $100 on January 1, 1989, it's true you'd have $115 to spend on January 1, 1990. But you'd need $110 to buy the same goods that $100 would have bought a year earlier. All you've really made is $5—the difference between the $110 you need to buy $100 worth of goods and the $115 that you've got.

When we studied how interest rates are determined in Chapter 28, we analyzed an economy in which the price level was constant. In such an economy, there is no difference between the nominal and real interest rate. There's just one interest rate and its level ensures that the quantity of money demanded equals the quantity of money supplied.

But we know that in the real world, the price level is rarely constant and, most of the time, it is increasing. What are the effects on interest rates of a rising price level and of expectations of the price level continuing to rise? These are the questions that we are now going to answer.

Expectations of Inflation and Interest Rates

Let's begin our exploration of the relationship between inflation expectations and interest rates by imagining two economies that are identical in every way except for one: One of the economies has no inflation and the other economy has a 10 percent inflation rate. In each case, the behavior of the price level is correctly anticipated. That is, in the first economy there is no inflation and none is expected. In the second economy, there is 10 percent inflation and a 10 percent inflation rate is expected. What is the difference in the interest rates in these two economies?

Suppose that in the zero-inflation economy the interest rate is 5 percent a year. What will the interest rate be in the second economy? The answer is 15.5 percent a year. Why?

First, let's look at things from the point of view of lenders. People who make loans recognize that the value of the money that they have lent is falling at a rate of 10 percent a year. Each year the money buys 10 percent less than it would have bought the year before. Lenders will want to protect themselves against such a loss in the value of money by asking for a higher interest rate on the loans that they make.

Let's now look at the situation from the point of view of borrowers. People who borrow recognize that in an economy that is inflating at 10 percent a year the money they use to repay what they have borrowed will be worth 10 percent less each year than it was worth the year before. They will recognize that lenders need to be protected against the falling value of money and willingly agree to a higher interest rate.

But how much higher will the interest rate be that borrowers and lenders agree to? First, they will agree to add 10 percentage points because the value of the money borrowed and lent is expected to fall at a 10 percent annual rate. Second, they will recognize

that even the interest payment will buy less at the end of the year than at the beginning of the year. To allow for that factor, they will add 10 percent of the interest rate. Since the interest rate is 5 percent when there is zero inflation, 10 percent of the interest rate is half a percentage point. So the total amount that they will agree to add to the real interest rate of 5 percent is 10.5 percentage points. Thus the nominal interest rate equals the real interest rate plus an allowance for the expected rate of inflation that is slightly higher than that expected inflation rate. The higher the expected inflation rate, the higher is the nominal interest rate. When inflation and interest rates are low, the nominal interest rate approximately equals the sum of the real interest rate and the expected inflation rate.

By considering the behavior of borrowers and lenders, you can see that it makes sense for the nominal interest rate to rise above the real interest rate by an amount slightly larger than the expected inflation rate. But when we studied the determination of interest rates in Chapter 28, we discovered that it is the demand for real money and the supply of real money that determine interest rates. But which interest rate—the nominal interest rate or the real interest rate—is it that equates the quantity of real money demanded with the quantity supplied? In Chapter 28, these two interest rates are the same because there is no inflation.

To answer this question, we need to determine the opportunity cost of holding money, for it is that opportunity cost that adjusts to make the quantity of money demanded equal to the quantity supplied. There are two components to the cost of holding money: One is the fall in the value of money resulting from inflation; the other is the real interest rate that could have been earned by reducing money holding and making loans or investing in real capital—plant and equipment. Thus

$$\begin{matrix} \text{Opportunity} \\ \text{cost of} \\ \text{holding money} \end{matrix} = \begin{matrix} \text{Expected} \\ \text{inflation} \\ \text{rate} \end{matrix} + \begin{matrix} \text{Real} \\ \text{interest} \\ \text{rate.} \end{matrix}$$

But we know the nominal interest rate is also approximately equal to the expected inflation rate plus the real interest rate. We've discovered, therefore, that the opportunity cost of holding money is the nominal interest rate. It is the nominal interest rate that adjusts in the money market to ensure that the quantity of money demanded equals the quantity available. The higher the expected inflation rate, the higher is the opportunity cost of holding money and the lower is the quantity of money people plan to hold.

Inflation and Interest Rates in the United States

What is the actual relationship between inflation and interest rates in the United States? That relationship is illustrated in Fig. 31.9. The interest rate measured on the vertical axis is that paid by large corporations on long-term bonds. Each point on the graph represents a year in recent U.S. macroeconomic history between 1960 and 1988. The blue line shows the relationship between the interest rate and the inflation rate if the real interest rate is constant at 3.2 percent, its actual average value over this period. As you can see, there is a clear correlation between the inflation rate and the interest rate. That correlation arises from the relationship that you have just reviewed. To the extent that a higher inflation rate is anticipated, it results in higher interest rates.

During the 1960s, both actual and expected inflation were moderate and so were interest rates. In the early 1970s, inflation began to increase but it was not expected to increase much and certainly not to persist. As a result, interest rates did not rise very much at that time. By the mid-1970s, there was a burst of unexpectedly high inflation. Interest rates increased somewhat but not by nearly as much as the inflation rate. During the late 1970s and early 1980s, inflation of close to 10 percent a year came to be expected as an ongoing and highly persistent phenomenon. As a result, interest rates increased to around 15 percent a year. Then in 1984 and 1985, the inflation rate fell—at first unexpectedly so. Interest rates began to fall but not nearly as quickly as the inflation rate. Short-term interest rates fell more quickly than long-term interest rates because, at that time, it was expected that inflation would be lower in the short term but not so low in the longer term.

The relationship between inflation and interest rates is even more dramatically illustrated by international experience. For example, in recent years Chile has been experiencing an inflation rate of around 30 percent with interest rates of about 40 percent. Brazil has experienced inflation rates of more than 200 percent a year with interest rates also above 200 percent a year. At the other extreme, such countries as Japan and Belgium have low inflation and low nominal interest rates.

Figure 31.9   Inflation and the Interest Rate

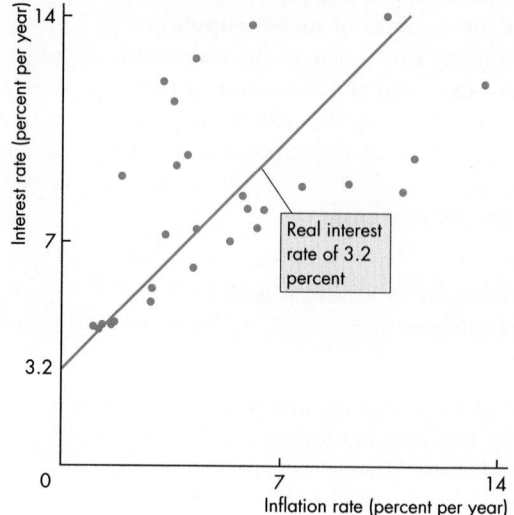

Other things being equal, the higher the expected inflation rate, the higher is the interest rate. A graph showing the relationship between interest rates and the actual inflation rate reveals that the influence of inflation on interest rates is a powerful one. Here, the interest rate is that paid by large corporations on long-term bonds. Each point represents a year in U.S. macroeconomic history between 1960 and 1988.
Source: Economic Report of the President (1989).

Money Supply and Interest Rates Again

We have seen that high nominal interest rates and high expected inflation rates go together. We have also seen that high expected inflation is the product of a high anticipated money supply growth rate. Thus a high anticipated growth rate of the money supply brings not only a high anticipated inflation rate but also high interest rates.

In Chapter 28, when we studied the effects of the Fed's actions on interest rates, we concluded that an increase in the quantity of money *lowers* interest rates. How can both of these conclusions be correct? How can an increase in the anticipated growth rate of the money supply increase interest rates while an increase in the quantity of money lowers them?

The answer lies in the time scale of the adjustments of interest rates to a change in the money supply. If the Fed takes an unexpected action that increases the quantity of money, the immediate effect of that action is to lower interest rates. Lower interest rates are needed to bring the quantity of money demanded to equality with the quantity supplied. But, if the Fed continues to increase the money supply and keeps on increasing it year after year at a faster pace than real GNP is growing, people will come to expect that increase in the money supply and the inflation that goes with it. In these circumstances, they will not be willing to make loans unless they obtain a return on them that sufficiently compensates them for the loss in the value of money due to inflation.

Thus it is an unanticipated increase in the money supply that brings a fall in interest rates. An anticipated and ongoing increase in the money supply increases interest rates. The decrease in interest rates following an increase in the money supply is an immediate but temporary response. The increase in interest rates associated with an increase in the growth rate of the money supply is a long-run response.

■   We have now completed our study of inflation and the relationship between the inflation rate and the interest rate. Our next task, which we'll pursue in Chapter 32, is to see how the same aggregate demand and aggregate supply model that we have used to understand inflation also helps us to explore and interpret fluctuations in real GNP and explain recessions and depressions.

S U M M A R Y

Macroeconomic Equilibrium

In macroeconomic equilibrium, four conditions are satisfied:

• Real GNP demanded equals real GNP supplied.

• Aggregate planned expenditure equals real GNP.

• Real money demanded equals real money supplied.

• Quantity of labor demanded equals quantity of labor supplied.

Stated another way, macroeconomic equilibrium is a state in which no one wishes to act differently under current circumstances, given the information and options available. Macroeconomic equilibrium is not necessarily full-employment equilibrium. The higher the level of aggregate demand, the higher are real GNP and the price level. The higher the expected price level, the lower is real GNP and the higher is the price level. When the actual price level equals the expected level, real GNP is at capacity output. If the price level is higher than expected, real GNP is above capacity. If the price level is lower than expected, real GNP is below capacity. Wrong price expectations are expensive. Losses from wrong expectations can be minimized by minimizing forecasting errors. The expectations that minimize those errors are rational expectations. (pp. 818–822)

The Rational Expectation of the Price Level

Different people devote different amounts of attention to forming expectations—some specialize in the activity and others simply follow someone else's forecast. The rational expectation of the price level can be found by using the theory of aggregate demand and aggregate supply to forecast the state of the economy. People do not use the theory of aggregate demand and aggregate supply explicitly to make their forecasts of the price level. They use a variety of methods. The rational expectations hypothesis states that regardless of how people actually go about calculating their expectations, on the average, the expectations that they form are the same as the forecast that an economist would make using the relevant economic theory. (pp. 822–826)

Rational Expectations Equilibrium

A rational expectations equilibrium is a macroeconomic equilibrium based on expectations that are the best available forecasts. The rational expectations equilibrium occurs at the intersection of the aggregate demand and short-run aggregate supply curves. A rational expectations equilibrium may be a full-employment equilibrium but other possibilities can occur. Aggregate demand and aggregate supply may be higher or lower than expected. The combination of these possibilities means that output may be higher or lower than capacity and the price level higher or lower than expected. Regardless of which of these states the economy is experiencing, in a rational expectations equilibrium no one would have acted differently given the state of affairs in which they made their choices. (pp. 826–828)

Inflation

Inflation is the percentage rise in the price level from one year to another. When changes in aggregate demand and aggregate supply are correctly anticipated, there is anticipated inflation. Any unanticipated changes in aggregate demand or aggregate supply produce unanticipated inflation. An unanticipated increase in aggregate demand leads to an unanticipated rise in the inflation rate and raises output above capacity. If aggregate demand rises by less than expected, there is an unanticipated fall in the inflation rate and output falls below capacity.

The inflation rate depends on all the factors that influence aggregate demand and aggregate supply. But one of those factors dominates the path of the price level—the money supply. Growth in the money supply and increases in the price level are closely related to each other. However, the other influences on aggregate demand and aggregate supply also have effects so that examining annual money supply growth rates and inflation reveals considerable independence of inflation from money supply growth from year to year. (pp. 828–836)

Interest Rates and Inflation

Expectations of inflation affect nominal interest rates. The higher the expected rate of inflation, the higher is the nominal interest rate. Borrowers will willingly pay more and lenders will successfully demand more as the anticipated rate of inflation rises. Borrowing and lending and asset-holding plans are made consistent with each other by adjustments in the real rate of interest—the difference between the nominal rate of interest and the expected rate of inflation. (pp. 836–839)

K E Y   C O N C E P T S

Nominal interest rate, 836
Rational expectation, 821
Rational expectations equilibrium, 827
Rational expectations hypothesis, 822

Key Figures

Figure 31.3   The Rational Expectation of the Price Level, 823
Figure 31.4   Rational Expectations Equilibrium, 827
Figure 31.5   Anticipated Inflation, 829
Figure 31.6   An Unanticipated Rise in the Price Level, 830
Figure 31.7   An Unexpected Fall in Inflation, 831

R E V I E W   Q U E S T I O N S

1 What are the conditions that are satisfied in a macroeconomic equilibrium?

2 For a given price level expectation, analyze the

effects on real GNP and the price level of the following:

a) A rise in the money supply

b) A rise in government purchases of goods and services

c) A rise in income taxes

d) A rise in investment demand

e) A fall in long-run aggregate supply

f) A rise in the expected price level

3 Why are wrong price expectations costly? Suggest some of the losses that an individual would suffer in labor markets as well as in asset markets.

4 Describe and illustrate the calculation of a rational expectation of the price level.

5 Draw a diagram to illustrate a rational expectations equilibrium in which real GNP is below capacity.

6 How does anticipated inflation come about?

7 What is the main factor leading to changes in aggregate demand that produces ongoing and persistent increases in the price level?

8 Review the relationship between inflation and money supply growth in the United States since 1960.

a) In which years was inflation particularly high compared with money supply growth? Why?

b) In which years was inflation particularly low compared with money supply growth? Why?

9 What is the connection between expected inflation and interest rates?

P R O B L E M S

1 An economy has the following aggregate demand and short-run aggregrate supply curves:

Price level (GNP deflator)	GNP demanded	GNP supplied
	(trillions of 1982 dollars)	
80	4	1
100	3	3
120	2	5
140	1	5

The expected price level is 100.

a) What is capacity real GNP?

b) What is actual real GNP?

c) What is the price level?

2 In the economy of problem 1, the expected price level increases to 120.

a) What is the new *SAS* curve?

b) What is the level of real GNP?

c) What is the price level?

d) Is GNP above or below capacity?

3 In 1990, the expected aggregate demand for 1991 is as follows:

Price level (GNP deflator)	Expected real GNP demanded (trillions of 1982 dollars)
120	4.0
121	3.9
122	3.8
123	3.7
124	3.6

In 1990, the level of capacity real GNP expected for 1991 is $3.8 trillion. Calculate the 1990 rational expectation of the price level for 1991.

4 The economy in problem 3 has the following short-run aggregate supply schedule:

Price level (GNP deflator)	Real GNP supplied (trillions of 1982 dollars)
120	3.2
121	3.5
122	3.8
123	4.1
124	4.4

a) Explain why this short-run aggregate supply schedule is consistent with your answer to problem 3.

b) Calculate the actual and expected inflation rate if the aggregate demand curve is expected to shift upward by 10 percent and if it actually does shift upward by that amount.

Chapter 32

Recessions and
Depressions

After studying this chapter, you will be able to:

- Describe the origins of the OPEC recession of the 1970s and the Volcker recession of the 1980s

- Describe the course of money, interest rates, and expenditure as the economy contracts

- Describe the labor market in recession

- Compare and contrast the flexible and sticky wage theories of the labor market in recession

- Describe the onset of the Great Depression in 1929

- Describe the economy in the depths of the Great Depression between 1929 and 1933

- Compare the economy of the 1930s with that of today and assess the likelihood of another Great Depression.

The 1920s were years of unprecedented prosperity for Americans. After the horrors of World War I, the economic machine was back at work, producing such technological marvels as cars and airplanes, telephones and vacuum cleaners. Houses and apartments were being built at a frantic pace. Then, almost without warning, in October 1929, came an unprecedented stock market crash. Overnight, the values of stocks and shares trading on Wall Street fell by 30 percent. In the four succeeding years, there followed the worst contraction in recorded history. By 1933, real GNP had fallen by 30 percent; unemployment had increased to a quarter of the labor force; employment was down 20 percent and prices down 25 percent.

The cost of the Great Depression, in terms of human suffering, will never be fully known. But the cost went far beyond the hardship faced by those having no jobs. Families were unclothed, hungry, and homeless, social tensions and crime increased, and the political attitudes that were to dominate the next 40 years of U.S. history were formed. What caused the Great Depression? ■ In October 1987, stock markets in the United States and throughout the world crashed. The crash was so steep and so widespread that it has been dubbed a stock market "meltdown"—conjuring up images of Three Mile Island and Chernobyl. This severe and widespread stock market crash has caused some commentators to draw parallels between 1987 and 1929—the eve of the greatest economic depression in history. Are there similar forces at work in the United States and world economies today that might bring about a Great Depression of the 1990s? ■ Although not in the same league as the Great Depression, we have experienced two severe recessions in recent history. The worst of these, and the most severe recession since the Great Depression, occurred in 1982, a year in which real GNP fell by 2.5 percent and unemployment increased to almost 11 percent. What caused the 1982 recession? ■ The other recession occurred eight years earlier, in 1974 and 1975. On that occasion, real GNP fell by 1.8 percent over two years, and unemployment rose from 4.9 percent to 8.5 percent. What caused these recessions? Are all recessions triggered in the same way or is there a variety of causes?

■ In this chapter, we're going to use the macroeconomic tools that we have studied in the previous chapters to interpret the dramatic events that we have just reviewed. We're going to unravel some of the mysteries of recession and depression and assess the likelihood of a serious depression such as that of the 1930s occurring again. We're going to begin by examining the two most recent recessions in U.S. economic history.

Two Recent Recessions

The two most recent recessions in the United States occurred in 1974–1975 and in 1982. We're going to compare and contrast the origins and mechanisms at work during these two episodes of U.S. macroeconomic history. We'll pay special attention to the labor market and to the central disagreement among economists about how the labor market works during an economic contraction. We'll conclude our examinaton of the two recent recessions by comparing and contrasting them. But let's begin with their origins.

The Origins of Recent Recessions

We'll begin by examining the forces that initiated the two recessions. Then we'll study the mechanisms whereby the effect of those forces was worked out.

The OPEC Recession In the early 1970s, the U.S. economy was progressing in an unremarkable manner. Real GNP was close to its trend value and growing at a similar rate to its long-run average growth rate. Unemployment ranged between 5 and 6 percent and inflation between 3 and 6 percent a year.

More and more people were enjoying and sharing in the benefits of sustained economic expansion.

Then, toward the end of 1973, the economy was dealt a devastating blow. The price of a barrel of oil, which had cost $2.60 on January 1, 1973, was increased to $11.65 by January 1, 1974. This massive 348 percent increase in the price of crude oil had dramatic macroeconomic effects. For the next two years, the U.S. economy went into a severe recession. The severity of the recession and its immediate cause can be seen in Fig. 32.1.[1] Before the oil price shock, the aggregate demand and short-run aggregate supply curves were AD_{73} and SAS_{73}. Real GNP was $2.8 trillion and the GNP deflator was 50. Through the subsequent two years, aggregate demand continued to increase at roughly the same steady pace that it had been increasing in the previous few years. The aggregate demand curve shifted upward to AD_{75}. If the prices of inputs—labor and raw materials—had also continued to increase at their normal pace, the short-run aggregate supply curve would have shifted upward to SAS_n. By 1975, the economy would have moved to point a. Inflation would have been about 3 percent a year and real GNP would have continued to grow at a similar pace.

But that's not how things turned out. When OPEC producers dramatically increased the price of crude oil, the prices of other fuels as well as the prices of many other raw materials increased in sympathy. Labor costs also started to increase more quickly. As a result, the short-run aggregate supply curve shifted upward all the way to SAS_{75}. This upward shift in the short-run aggregate supply curve, triggered by the oil price increase, was the single most important event producing the OPEC recession. Real GNP fell to $2.7 trillion and the GNP deflator

---

[1]In this figure, as well as in Figs. 32.2 and 32.6, we use the aggregate demand–aggregate supply model to determine equilibrium real GNP and the price level. These figures omit the long-run aggregate supply curve. There are two reasons for this. First, it is the intersection point of the short-run aggregate supply curve and aggregate demand curve that determines the actual level of real GNP and the price level. We need the long-run aggregate supply curve only to determine whether we are above or below capacity. Since we're studying recessions in this chapter, the economy is always, in some sense, moving below its capacity output level. But there is some uncertainty about how far below capacity the economy has gone—in other words, there is some disagreement about the exact position of the long-run aggregate supply curve.

Figure 32.1   The OPEC Recession

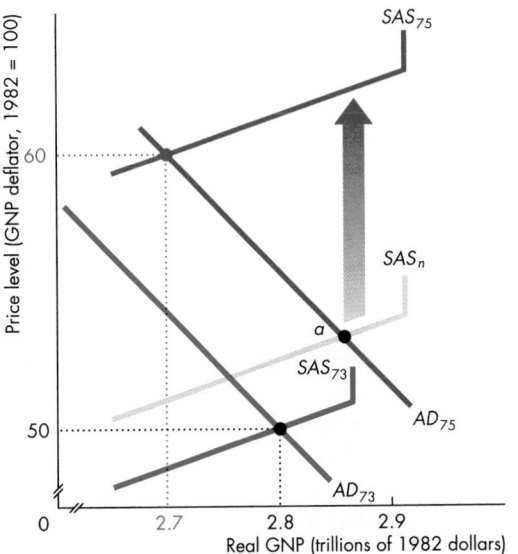

In 1973, the economy was on its aggregate demand curve AD_{73} and its short-run aggregate supply curve SAS_{73}, with real GNP at $2.8 trillion and a GNP deflator of 50. Between 1973 and 1975, aggregate demand continued to increase at a moderate pace and the aggregate demand curve shifted to AD_{75}. In the normal course of events, input prices would have increased at a moderate rate, shifting the short-run aggregate supply curve upward. The economy would have settled down at point a with an increase in real GNP and a continuation of moderate inflation. But 1974 was not a normal year. OPEC increased the price of oil by 348 percent. Other input prices and wages moved up more quickly than in a normal year. The short-run aggregate supply curve shifted up to SAS_{75}. The sharp upward movement of the SAS curve combined with the moderate upward shift of the AD curve led to stagflation—a fall in real GNP and an acceleration of inflation.

increased to 60—an inflation of close to 10 percent a year for the two years of recession. Thus during the OPEC recession, real GNP fell but the inflation rate increased. This combination of events gave rise to a new word: stagflation. **Stagflation** is a situation in which real GNP stops growing or even declines and inflation accelerates.

The events that we have just described had a dramatic impact for two quite different reasons. First, they represented a concentration of the macroeconomic evils of inflation and unemployment. Between

1973 and 1975, more than 3.5 million additional people were unemployed, and even those with jobs faced sharply rising prices and a fall in the purchasing power of their earnings. Second, these events delivered a shock to economists. Rising inflation and rising unemployment were not supposed to happen together according to the models that guided their thinking and their policy advice. (See "Our Advancing Knowledge," pp. 832–834.)

We'll return to the OPEC recession and study the mechanisms operating during that period of economic contraction. But first let's review the origins of the recession of the 1980s.

The Volcker Recession   The years 1979 to 1981 were not outstanding ones for the U.S. economy. To begin with, the economy had to endure a yet further series of increases in the price of oil in 1979—to $15 in April, to $19 in June, and finally, to $26 by the year's end. Oil prices went on increasing through 1980 and 1981 and by October 1981, crude oil cost $37 a barrel. These large and continued increases in the price of oil put great strain on the U.S. economy. Energy-intensive production activities declined and research efforts were devoted to finding more energy-efficient methods of production, transportation, and home heating.

Running alongside these energy shocks was a massive revolution in the electronics sector of the economy. Microprocessors of all kinds became cheaper, and affordable computing power found more widespread applications.

The combination of these two processes—continued increases in the price of energy and expanded applications for microprocessors—generated an unusually large reallocation of resources in the U.S. economy. Traditionally strong sectors began to grow more slowly or even to decline, and new sectors emerged with rapid growth. What came to be called the Rust Belt was the scene of relative decline, and the Sun Belt, Silicon Valley, and other areas specializing in electronics and related products (for example, Minneapolis and Massachusetts) became focal points for expansion and growth.

The years 1979 through 1981 were also times of high inflation. The price level increased by close to 10 percent during each of these years. There was a widely held belief that inflation was so entrenched that it could be anticipated to continue at this level into the foreseeable future. This, then, was the scene for the 1982 recession.

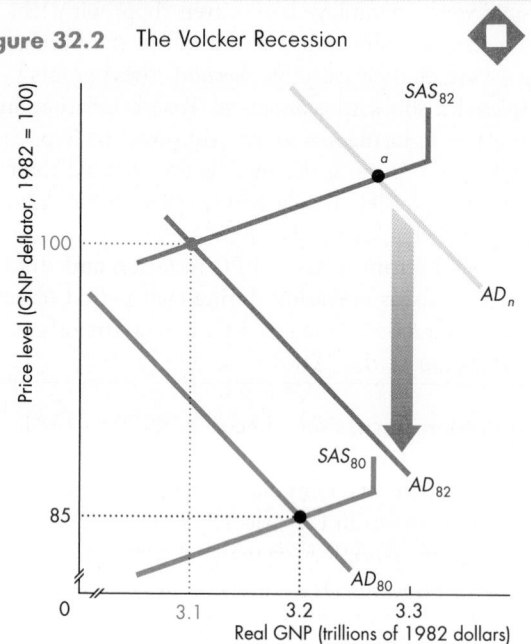

Figure 32.2   The Volcker Recession

In 1980, the economy was on its aggregate demand curve AD_{80} and its short-run aggregate supply curve SAS_{80}, with real GNP at $3.2 trillion and a GNP deflator of 85. Inflation was raging and wages and other input prices were increasing at a rapid rate to reflect the strong inflationary expectations. The aggregate supply curve shifted upward to SAS_{82}. If aggregate demand continued to increase at the pace of the late 1970s, the aggregate demand curve would have moved to AD_n and the economy would have gone to point a—a steady increase in real GNP and a continuation of inflation at around 10 percent per year. But 1982 was not a normal year. The Fed slowed down money growth and forced interest rates up. The aggregate demand curve shifted to AD_{82}. The combination of continuing high inflation expectations, shifting the SAS curve upward, and a slowdown of aggregate demand growth put the economy into recession. Real GNP fell and inflation moderated.

The origin of that recession and its magnitude are illustrated in Fig. 32.2. Aggregate demand and short-run aggregate supply in 1980 are shown by AD_{80} and SAS_{80}. Real GNP was $3.2 trillion and the GNP deflator was 85. Over the two years to 1982, with a widespread expectation that inflation was going to continue at 10 percent a year, wages and other input prices increased, shifting the short-run aggregate supply curve upward to SAS_{82}. If aggregate demand had continued increasing at the same pace as it did in the late 1970s, the aggregate demand curve

would have shifted upward to AD_n by 1982. The economy would have been at point a, with real GNP continuing to grow at its trend rate and inflation remaining at around 10 percent a year.

Events did not turn out like that. Instead of permitting aggregate demand to continue growing, the Federal Reserve Board, under Chairman Paul Volcker, applied a severe dose of monetary restraint. The Fed permitted interest rates to increase (which we'll look at in a moment) and slowed down the pace of investment. Instead of shifting to AD_n, the aggregate demand curve moved up to only AD_{82}. By slowing the growth of aggregate demand down to below the pace at which the short-run aggregate supply curve was shifting upward, the Fed put the economy into recession. Real GNP fell to $3.1 trillion and the inflation rate began to slow down. Thus a key difference between the OPEC and the Volcker recessions is that while the former was an example of stagflation, the latter saw inflation falling.

This key difference between the anatomy of the two recessions arises because of a fundamental difference in their origins. The OPEC recession was caused by an unexpectedly large shift in the short-run aggregate supply curve, itself resulting from an unexpectedly large increase in the price of inputs. This large shift in the supply curve, combined with a moderate increase in aggregate demand, lowered real GNP and increased the GNP deflator, and the inflation rate. In contrast, the 1982 recession was triggered by an unexpectedly sharp slowdown in the pace at which the Fed permitted aggregate demand to grow. The aggregate demand curve shifted by less than it would have without the policy of restraint. The lower level of aggregate demand led to both lower real GNP and a lower GNP deflator and inflation rate than what would have occurred without a policy of restraint.

Although these two recessions had very different characteristics concerning the behavior of real GNP and the price level and although they had very different origins, they have certain features that are common to all recessions—the fundamental economic mechanisms that work once an economy is in recession.

Let's now take a closer look at the recession mechanism.

Recession Mechanism

The markets in which things begin to happen first and move fastest are the markets for money and

Figure 32.3   Interest Rates and Money in Recession

(a) The OPEC recession

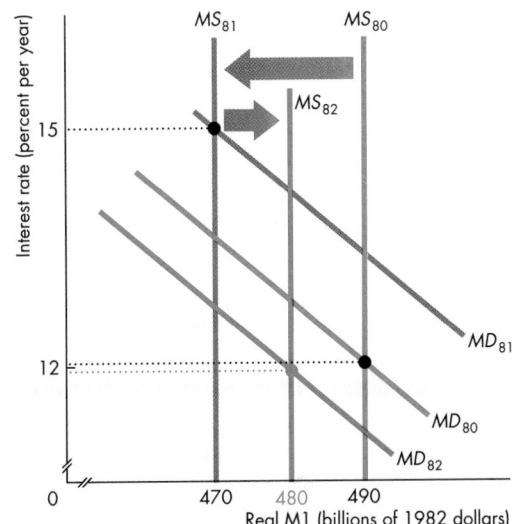

(b) The Volcker recession

Regardless of their origin, recessions are similar in the path followed by the interest rate. At first, interest rates increase and then, as the recession deepens, interest rates fall.

In 1973, interest rates were 8 percent—at the intersection of MS_{73} and MD_{73} in part (a). The inflation increase of 1973 lowered the real money supply, shifting the supply curve of real money to MS_{74}. The demand curve for real money fell only slightly to MD_{74} as a result of real GNP falling. Interest rates increased to 10 percent. By 1975, the recession was deep and the demand for real money fell because real income fell. Continued inflation lowered the real money supply but by less than the fall in the demand for real money, so interest rates fell to 6 percent.

In 1980, interest rates were just above 12 percent—at the intersection of MS_{80} and MD_{80} in part (b). The slowdown in the money supply growth rate, combined with continuing inflation, lowered the supply curve of real money in 1981 to MS_{81}. Real income continued to grow, so the demand for real money increased. The demand curve for real money shifted to MD_{81} and interest rates rose to 15 percent. The high interest rates brought on a deep recession, real GNP fell, and so did the demand for real money. The demand curve for real money shifted to MD_{82}. The slowdown in inflation resulted in the real money supply increasing and the supply curve of real money shifting to MS_{82}. Interest rates fell to just below 12 percent.

financial assets. We're going to begin our examination of the recession mechanism by examining the money market.

Money and Interest Rates   A general feature of a recession is that in its early stages, interest rates increase. But once the recession is under way, interest rates begin to fall, and by the time real GNP has reached its trough, interest rates have fallen, often to levels lower than those at the onset of the recession.

Why do interest rates behave in this manner? To find out, let's study the money market in the two recent recessions. Figure 32.3 contains the relevant analysis.

First, consider Fig. 32.3(a), which deals with the OPEC recession. In 1973, the *real money supply* (M1) was $540 billion. In 1974, the *real money supply* decreased by about 5 percent, and the supply curve of real money shifted from MS_{73} to MS_{74}. This decrease in the supply of real money and shift in the supply curve of real money occurred because the

GNP deflator increased by an amount larger than the increase in the *nominal money supply*. The demand curve for real money in 1973 was MD_{73} and the interest rate that achieved equality between the quantity of real money demanded and the quantity of real money supplied was 8 percent. The demand for real money fell in 1974 but only slightly. It fell because real GNP fell. (Recall that the demand for real money depends on real GNP. An increase in real GNP shifts the demand curve for real money to the right and a decrease in real GNP shifts that curve to the left.) Because real GNP fell only slightly in 1974, the demand curve for real money shifted only slightly to the left. The much higher price level reduced the quantity of real money supplied by considerably more than the lower real GNP decreased the demand for real money. As a consequence, the interest rate increased. In 1974, the interest rate was 10 percent— at the point of intersection of MS_{74} and MD_{74}.

Between 1974 and 1975, the money supply continued to increase but at a much slower pace than the price level was rising. As a result, the supply of real money continued to decline to MS_{75}. But by 1975, there was a large fall in real GNP which, in turn, reduced the demand for real money. The demand curve for real money shifted to the left to MD_{75}. In 1975, the economy was at the depth of recession. The demand for real money had fallen by much more than the fall in the real money supply and as a result the interest rate fell to 6 percent a year.

The money market during the Volcker recession years is illustrated in Fig. 32.3(b). In 1980, interest rates were just over 12 percent a year, at the point of intersection of MS_{80} and MD_{80}. During 1981, the GNP deflator continued to increase at around 10 percent a year. Money supply growth was slowed down and the Fed permitted the quantity of money to increase by only 6 percent. As a consequence, the real money supply fell. The fall in the real money supply shifted the real money supply curve from MS_{80} to MS_{81}. During the same year, real GNP continued to increase. As a result, the demand for real money increased and the demand curve for real money shifted to the right to MD_{81}. The combination of an increased demand for real money and a decreased supply of real money pushed interest rates up to 15 percent a year. These high interest rates began to slow down spending and pushed the economy into its recession. In 1982, real GNP fell and to a level below that of 1980. As a result of the fall in real

GNP, the demand for real money decreased and the demand curve for real money shifted to the left to MD_{82}. At the same time, the inflation rate was slowing down. The slowdown in inflation combined with growth in the money supply was sufficient to increase the quantity of real money supplied in 1982 to MS_{82}. Money market equilibrium in 1982 occurred at an interest rate of slightly below 12 percent a year.

Comparing the events in the money market in the two recessions reveals a similar path for interest rates. In both recessions, interest rates rose at first and then declined. But the source of those interest rate movements is different in each case. In the case of the OPEC recession, interest rates increased because a sharp rise in the price level cut the real money supply. Interest rates subsequently fell because of the depth of the recession and the effects of the lower real GNP on the demand for real money. Because of continued strong inflation, the supply of real money continued to decrease through 1975 in that earlier recession. In the case of the Volcker recession, the initial increase in interest rates was directly induced by Fed policy. Subsequent downward pressure on interest rates came from a fall in the demand for real money, just as in the case of the OPEC recession. In addition, however, the real money supply increased in 1982 and reinforced the effects of the decrease in the demand for real money on interest rates.

The key reason why the real money supply continued to fall through 1975 but began to increase in 1982 arises from the behavior of the price level in the two recessions. In 1985, inflation continued to be high, and to be higher than the growth rate of the nominal money supply. In 1982, the inflation rate fell substantially below the growth rate of the money supply.

It is the behavior of interest rates that gives rise to the next step in the story of recession—a fall in aggregate expenditure.

Changes in Expenditure When the economy is in a recession, real GNP falls and real aggregate expenditure also falls. (Recall that real GNP and real aggregate expenditure are equal to each other.) But the main component of aggregate expenditure that falls is investment. Investment falls for two reasons. First, an increase in real interest rates—in interest rates relative to expected inflation—increases the opportunity cost of buying new capital equipment. Second, expectations of recession lead to a revision downward of profit expectations, and that too lowers investment. For these two reasons, investment falls. During the OPEC recession, investment (in 1982 dollars) fell from $521 billion in 1973 to $383 billion by 1975. During the Volcker recession, investment fell from $509 billion in 1980 to $447 billion in 1982. Such decreases in investment have two effects. First, they represent a decrease in aggregate expenditure and in aggregate demand. Second, they result in the capital stock growing less quickly and in a slowdown in the pace of innovation of new technologies. This aspect of the investment slowdown feeds back to slow down the growth of aggregate supply. But it is the effect of decreased investment on aggregate demand that dominates.

One of the main reasons people fear recession is because it is associated with a high unemployment rate. What happens in the labor market during a recession? Why does unemployment increase during a recession? Let's now examine these questions.

The Labor Market in Recession

For illustrative purposes, we'll examine the labor market in just one of the two recent recessions—the OPEC recession. Figure 32.4 provides a summary and analysis of the main events.

The starting point to understanding what happens in the labor market during a recession is an examination of the short-run aggregate production function. (Recall that we studied the short-run aggregate production function in Chapter 30.) The short-run aggregate production function, which shows the maximum real GNP that can be produced for a given labor input, is shown in Fig. 32.4(a). Curve PF_{73} is the short-run aggregate production function for 1973, just prior to the OPEC recession. In that year, 167 billion hours of labor produced $2.8 trillion of real GNP. The effect of the OPEC oil price increase was to shift the short-run production function downward from PF_{73} to PF_{75}. Why did this happen?

There are two aspects of the oil price increase that resulted in the downward shift of the production function. First, to enforce the massive price increase, OPEC severely restricted the output of crude oil. It placed an embargo on oil exports for a period. This disruption of international trade in oil had a direct effect of lowering the availability of a key productive resource. But there was a second and perhaps even more important effect. With such an enormous in-

crease in the price of energy, energy users of all kinds sought ways of economizing on their use of this now more expensive commodity. Activities intensive in their use of energy were cut back and other activities expanded. For example, cars and airplanes designed with engines highly suitable for the cheap fuel that prevailed in the 1960s were now scrapped at a much more rapid pace than they otherwise would have been. Research and design efforts were put into making cars, planes, and all kinds of transportation and heating equipment that were more energy-efficient. This redirection of economic activity from fuel-intensive production and consumption to fuel-saving production and consumption meant that there was a severe mismatch of people and jobs. More of the labor force, even if it remained employed, had to devote its efforts to retraining and other activities that did not directly, at least initially, produce real GNP. As a consequence of these two related factors, the production function shifted downward as shown in Fig. 32.4(a).

The downward shift of the production function lowered the marginal product of labor. As we discovered in Chapter 30, the quantity of labor demanded depends on its marginal product. With a lower marginal product of labor, the demand for labor curve shifts downward. That shift is shown in Fig. 32.4(b) as the shift from LD_{73} to LD_{75}.

Labor Supply and the Sticky Wage Theory

There is not too much controversy in macroeconomics about the demand side of the labor market. But there is considerable disagreement about the supply side of the labor market and the ability of the labor market to act as a coordination mechanism to bring about an equality between the quantities of labor demanded and supplied. Modern Keynesians believe that the supply curve of labor is not very sensitive to changes in real wages, and that wages themselves are sticky and do not adjust quickly enough to maintain a continuous balance between the quantities of labor demanded and supplied. Let's interpret the labor market in the OPEC recession by using this labor market theory.

Let's suppose that in 1973 the supply of labor curve was LS_{73}, in Fig. 32.4(b). (We don't actually know the position or, with any real confidence, the slope of the labor supply curve. The curve shown here is an assumption.) With the labor supply curve LS_{73} and the demand for labor curve LD_{73}, the equilibrium in the labor market occurs at a real wage of

Figure 32.4   Sticky Wage Theory of Recession

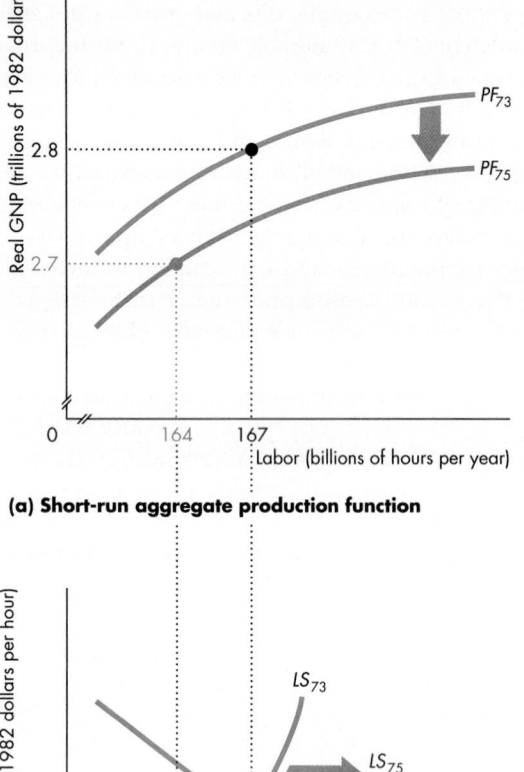

(a) Short-run aggregate production function

(b) Labor market

The OPEC oil price hike and embargo lowered the short-run aggregate production function from PF_{73} to PF_{75} in part (a). The marginal product of labor fell, so the demand for labor curve moved downward from LD_{73} to LD_{75}, as shown in part (b). Assuming that the year 1973 was one of equality between the quantity of labor demanded and the quantity supplied, the real wage rate of \$7.95 and employment of 167 billion hours in that year are at the point of intersection of LD_{73} and LS_{73}. An increase in population shifted the supply of labor curve from LS_{73} to LS_{75}. Real wages fell but not by enough to bring about equality between the quantities of labor supplied and demanded. The quantity demanded was 164 billion hours but the quantity supplied was 170 billion hours. Unemployment increased.

\$7.95 an hour with 167 billion hours of labor being employed. This represents the situation that actually prevailed in 1973. Let's assume that the actual unemployment rate in 1973 was also the natural rate of unemployment for that year. (This is an assumption, not a fact.)

Through 1974 and 1975, the population increased and, as a result, the supply of labor curve shifted to the right from LS_{73} to LS_{75}. The magnitude of the shift is determined by the percentage increase in the population. Money wages continued to increase through the recession but at a slower pace than the price level was rising. As a result, real wages decreased. By 1975, real wages had fallen to $7.65 an hour. But that fall in real wages was insufficient to maintain equality between the quantity of labor supplied and the quantity demanded. The level of employment fell to 164 billion hours—the quantity of labor demanded. That is, at a real wage rate of $7.65, and with the demand for labor curve LD_{75}, the amount of labor that firms wished to hire (to maximize their profits) was 164 billion hours. But given the assumptions made about the supply of labor curve, the quantity of labor supplied was 170 billion hours. Thus employment fell by about 3 billion hours and the amount of labor available increased by a further 3 billion hours.

The difference between the amount of labor supplied and the amount employed (and demanded) was unemployment. It represented about 3.5 percent of the quantity of labor supplied. According to the sticky wage theory of the labor market, this increase in unemployment represents an addition to the natural unemployment that prevailed before the recession's onset.

Labor Supply and the Flexible Wage Theory

Modern monetarists and real business cycle theorists disagree with the Keynesian interpretation of the labor market in recession that we have just presented. They believe that the supply curve of labor is much more responsive to a change in real wages than Keynesians believe. They acknowledge that wages don't change much, but they believe that they don't need to change much in order to maintain equality between the quantity of labor demanded and the quantity supplied. To understand the flexible wage theory, let's examine the same episode again, and interpret it in terms of this alternative economic model.

Recall that the labor market effects of recession that we've just analyzed are based on an *assumption* about the supply of labor curve. Figure 32.4 has been drawn in such a way that the labor supply curves LS_{73} and LS_{75} are fairly steep, indicating that a large change in the real wage rate evokes only a small change in the quantity of labor supplied. We are uncertain about the slope of the labor supply curve, but we're reasonably sure that the curve shifted to the right by the amount shown because we know exactly the amount by which the population increased over the relevant period. Suppose that the quantity of

labor supplied is much more responsive to a change in the real wage rate than that shown in Fig. 32.4. In particular, suppose that the supply of labor for 1973 and for 1975 are represented by the curves shown in Fig. 32.5.

Figure 32.5 is identical to Fig. 32.4(b) except that the labor supply curves do not slope upward as steeply in Fig. 32.5. Again, the labor market in 1973 is depicted as a situation in which the quantity of labor demanded equals the quantity supplied, so that the unemployment that exists is, by definition, the natural unemployment associated with job market turnover. When this supply of labor curve shifts to the right, it moves to LS_{75}. The magnitude of the shift from LS_{73} to LS_{75} is identical in this figure to the magnitude of the shift in Fig. 32.4(b). The

Figure 32.5 The Labor Market in Recession: Flexible Wage Theory

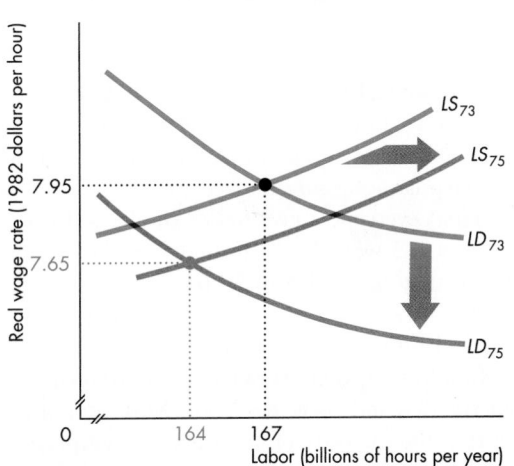

During the OPEC recession, real wages fell from $7.95 an hour to $7.65 an hour and employment fell from 167 to 164 billion hours. These movements of real wages and employment are consistent with the flexible wage theory if the labor supply curves indicate a large degree of responsiveness of the quantity of labor supplied to a change in the real wage. Such labor supply curves are LS_{73} and LS_{75}. According to the flexible wage theory, the increase in unemployment that occurred between 1973 and 1975 is interpreted as a temporary increase in the natural rate of unemployment, resulting from increased labor market turnover as people quit or were fired from jobs in energy-intensive industries and sought jobs in other parts of the economy.

demand for labor curve shifts down from LD_{73} to LD_{75}. In 1975, the demand for labor curve and the supply of labor curve intersect at a real wage rate of $7.65 and employment of 164 billion hours, exactly the values of those two variables that prevailed in 1975. The labor market shown in Fig. 32.5 agrees with the assumptions of the flexible wage theory. Wages fall and employment falls.

In the flexible wage interpretation of the labor market, nothing has been said about what happens to unemployment. The flexible wage theory of unemployment is that all unemployment arises from job market turnover. During a recession, job market turnover increases because some sectors of the economy decline quickly while others continue to expand. An increase in the amount of labor force reallocation—from the declining sectors to the expanding sectors—results in an increased amount of labor turnover and a temporarily higher unemployment rate. During the 1975 recession, the declining sectors were those that relied heavily on oil and other high-cost energy sources; the expanding sectors were those associated with developing energy-saving technologies.

Which Theory of the Labor Market Is Correct?

What exactly do economists disagree about concerning the labor market and why? The essence of the controversy is nicely summarized in Figs. 32.4(b) and 32.5. First, everyone agrees about the facts. Real wages in 1973 were $7.95 an hour, on the average. In 1975, they had fallen to $7.65, on the average. Employment in 1973 was 167 billion hours and it fell to 164 billion hours in 1975.

In addition, there is not much disagreement about the demand curve for labor. Most economists agree that the quantity of labor actually employed is determined by the profit-maximizing decisions of firms. That quantity depends on the real wage. This means that the level of employment and the real wage in any particular year are a point on the demand for labor curve. If we agree that the employment level and real wage are a point on the demand for labor curve, we can figure out where the demand for labor curve is and work out what makes it shift. Thus there is not much disagreement among economists about the slope and position of the demand for labor curve.

Where economists disagree is on the supply of labor curve. Because a large amount of labor is supplied on long-term contracts and on wages and other terms that remain fixed for the duration of the con-

tract, most economists believe that households are not normally operating on their supply of labor curve. Sometimes they are, but much of the time they are not. Furthermore, they believe that on the basis of evidence from variations in hours of work and wages, the quantity of labor supplied does not respond much to changes in real wages. In other words, they believe that the supply of labor curve is like those shown in Fig. 32.4(b).

Other economists believe that the combination of the real wage rate and the level of employment not only represents a point on the demand for labor curve but also a point on the supply of labor curve. From this assumption they infer that the quantity of labor supplied is highly responsive to wages and that the supply of labor curve looks like those in Fig. 32.5.

No one has yet suggested a test that is sufficiently clear for all economists to agree on. The Keynesian-monetarist aggregate demand controversy was eventually settled when economists were able to agree on tests of the effects of interest rates on the demand for real money and aggregate expenditure. The modern Keynesian-monetarist–real business cycle controversy will be settled only when economists can agree on, and implement, a test of their competing views about the responsiveness of the quantity of labor supplied to a change in real wages. Once such a test has been implemented, we shall be able to put this controversy behind us. But until then, professional economists and students of the subject have to live with the fact that we remain ignorant about a large and important issue at the heart of macroeconomics.

Determining which of these two theories is correct is not just a matter of academic curiosity. It is a matter of enormous importance in designing an appropriate antirecessionary policy. We discovered in Chapter 30 that if the flexible wage theory is true, the aggregate supply curve is vertical. This fact means that any attempt to bring the economy out of recession by increasing aggregate demand—for example, by lowering interest rates and increasing the money supply or by fiscal policy measures—is doomed to failure and can result only in a higher price level (more inflation). Conversely, if the sticky wage theory is correct and the labor market looks like the one depicted in Fig. 32.4(b), then the short-run aggregate supply curve looks like that shown in Figs. 32.1 and 32.2 and an increase in aggregate demand, although increasing the price level somewhat, will also increase real GNP, and bring the economy out of a recession.

Comparing the Two Recessions

The OPEC recession was caused by a shock to short-run aggregate supply. The Volcker recession was caused by a shock to aggregate demand. The OPEC recession was an example of *stagflation*—falling real GNP and rising inflation—while the Volcker recession combined falling real GNP with falling inflation.

In both recessions, money market conditions led to an initial increase in interest rates. The supply of real money declined relative to the demand for real money, and interest rates rose. Higher interest rates choked off spending and brought a lower level of aggregate demand. Real GNP fell and reduced the demand for money relative to its supply. The result was lower interest rates.

In both recessions, employment fell and unemployment increased. The real wage fell in the OPEC recession but remained roughly constant in the Volcker recession. Employment fell in both recessions because the marginal product of labor declined.

Comparing these two recessions, you can see that recessions do not have identical causes nor do they follow precisely the same course. Of these two recent recessions, one had its origins on the supply side of the economy and the other on the demand side. But, once under way, the mechanism that transmits the effects of a shock to interest rates and aggregate expenditure and also to the labor market is similar and, to a large degree, independent of the particular shock that tripped the recession mechanism.

Reading Between the Lines on pp. 854–855 takes a closer look at the process of recession in the fall of 1981, as the Volcker recession was intensifying.

Another Great Depression?

Following the most recent of the recessions that we have just studied, the U.S. economy moved into a period of long sustained recovery. In fact, that recovery has been one of the longest and strongest on record. It resulted from developments on both the demand and supply sides of the economy. On the supply side, a steady accumulation of capital and technological change, together with growth of population, increased capacity real GNP by around 20 percent between 1982 and 1987. In the first of these years, the economy was operating below capacity, but by 1987 real GNP was at or perhaps slightly above capacity. As the recovery got under way, inflation fell. At first, the drop in inflation was unanticipated and it was that fact that led to the 1982 recession. Wages were set at too high a level given what happened to prices. But lower inflation gradually came to be anticipated and, as it did so, real GNP approached and eventually exceeded its capacity level. Throughout the recovery, interest rates eased, which helped stimulate additional investment.

Although the recovery continued, there was, by the fall of 1987, widespread fear that the good times were coming to an end, at least for a while. In October 1987, these fears were strengthened by the biggest stock market crash to hit the United States economy (and, indeed, the world economy) since that of 1929, which had heralded the Great Depression. The magnitude of the 1987 crash was almost identical to the 1929 crash—the range between the high and the low was 34 percent. This similarity was so striking that many commentators concluded that the closing years of the 1980s and the early 1990s would resemble the Great Depression of the early 1930s. A book that fed such fears, and that otherwise would have passed almost unnoticed, became a bestseller.[2]

Is there going to be another Great Depression? Of course, the answer to this question is that no one knows. But we can try to assess the likelihood of such an event. Let's begin by first asking some questions. What was the Great Depression like? Just how bad did things get in the early 1930s? What would the U.S. economy look like in the 1990s if it was to have a rerun of those events? Once we've charted the broad anatomy of the Great Depression, we'll examine why it happened and consider the question of whether it could happen again and how likely such an event would be.

What the Great Depression Was Like

At the beginning of 1929, the U.S. economy was operating at capacity output and unemployment was

---

[2]Ravi Batra, *The Great Depression of 1990* (New York: Simon and Schuster, 1987). By the end of 1987, this book had been on the New York Times Best Seller List for half a year.

Monetary Policy in Action

Hard Times on Main Street

It was a protest that both spoke of frustration and a sense of enveloping helplessness. Silver-haired Chicago Businessman William H. Hoyerman, 55, walked outside the red brick entrance of his truck-body plant, General Body Co., and lowered the American flag to half-mast. He then sent letters to his suppliers and customers, exhorting them to do the same. Said he: "Let us fly our flags at half-mast in mourning for the millions of employees and businesses who are being hurt by high interest rates."

Small businesses, which are roughly defined as those firms with fewer than 500 employees, are the very backbone of the U.S. economy, accounting for more than 56% of all jobs in the American labor force. Yet all across the U.S. managers and owners of small businesses are reeling as the towering cost of money pushes one firm after another to the edge of bankruptcy and, all

too frequently, right down into the abyss of forced liquidation. During the first week of October alone, 468 U.S. companies, ranging in size from neighborhood dry cleaners to sprawling regional lumber mills, closed their doors for good, a rate that is more than double the number of a year ago and a cruel reminder to Ronald Reagan that for millions of self-employed small businessmen, supply-side economics is coming to mean pain and suffering aplenty.

Interest rates have replaced inflation as the No. 1 double-digit nightmare of businessmen everywhere, and the sheer unpredictability of the future cost of money has all but paralyzed decision making in firms both large and small. Last week short-term interest rates moved a notch downward, as several of the nation's largest banks dropped their prime rate to 18%. But long-term rates for corporate bonds and other such investments actually showed signs of inching upward a touch.

Meanwhile, Economist Henry Kaufman of the New York investment banking firm of Salomon Brothers, whose pessimistic year long predictions of ever higher rates have proved unnervingly accurate, delivered yet another gloomy forecast. He warned a group of corporate financial officers in New York that Government borrowing will propel the cost of money to new and higher peaks in the next six months or so. Said he: "A noose is now tightening around the credit markets."

With the cost of money high, business conditions have begun to deteriorate, and hardest hit are the smaller firms.

The current interest-rate squeeze first made itself felt nearly two years ago among auto dealers and home-builders. Now, it is rippling through the rest of the economy, causing failures from garment wholesalers to furniture dealers, from small manufacturers to Main Street retailers.

Time, **October 26, 1981**
By Alexander L. Taylor III, reported by J. Madeleine Nash/Chicago and Sara White/Boston, with other U.S. bureaus

The Essence of the Story

Background and Analysis

In the fall of 1981:

- Interest rates were close to 20 percent a year.

- The high cost of loans led to a sharp rise in the number of firms going out of business—double the number a year earlier.

- Small firms (those employing fewer than 500 people) were especially hard hit.

- These firms accounted for 56 percent of jobs.

- Forecasting experts predicted even higher rates in the coming six months.

- What started as a slowdown in auto and home sales two years earlier came to affect the whole economy.

- In 1980, the Fed pushed interest rates upward in an attempt to slow inflation.

- Higher nominal interest rates and falling inflation led to an increase in real interest rates.

- High real interest rates led to a fall in investment in houses and automobiles (investment demand schedule of Chapter 25), and led to layoffs and unemployment in those sectors (labor market analysis of Chapter 30).

- Lower spending in the durable goods sector led to lower incomes and lower spending on other goods (the multiplier of Chapter 26).

- Some firms cut back production but others that could not cover their costs went out of business.

- More workers lost their jobs, unemployment increased further, and the economy went into deeper recession.

- By the fall of 1981, the recession was severe and widespread—touching all the firms on Main Street.

only 3.2 percent of the labor force. But, as that eventful year unfolded, increasing signs of economic weakness began to appear. The most dramatic events occurred in October when the stock market collapsed, losing more than one third of its value in only two weeks. The four years that followed were years of monstrous economic depression—depression so severe that it came to be called the Great Depression.

The dimensions of the Great Depression can be seen in Fig. 32.6. That figure shows the situation on the eve of the Great Depression in 1929 when the

Figure 32.6   The Great Depression

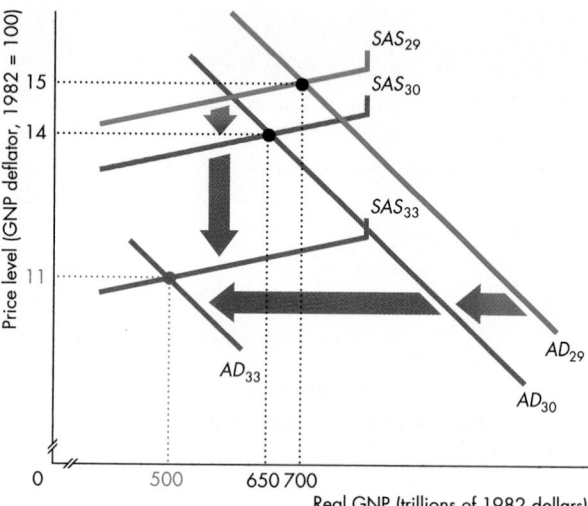

In 1929, real GNP was $700 billion and the GNP deflator was 15—at the intersection of AD_{29} and SAS_{29}. Increased pessimism and uncertainty resulted in a drop in investment and in the demand for durables, resulting in a fall in aggregate demand to AD_{30}. To some degree, this fall was anticipated and wages fell, so the short-run aggregate supply curve shifted downward to SAS_{30}. Real GNP fell by 7 percent and the price level fell. In the next three years, the money supply collapsed as a result of bank failures and investment and consumption expenditure collapsed as the outlook continued to be ever more bleak. By 1933, aggregate demand had shifted down to AD_{33}. Again, to some degree, the fall in aggregate demand was anticipated, so wages fell and the short-run aggregate supply curve continued to move down to SAS_{33}. By 1933, real GNP had fallen to $500 billion (about 70 percent of its 1929 level) and the GNP deflator had fallen to 11 (73 percent of its 1929 level).

economy was on its aggregate demand curve (AD_{29}) and short-run aggregate supply curve (SAS_{29}). Real GNP was $700 billion and the GNP deflator was 15. (Real GNP at the end of the 1980s is some 5.7 times its 1929 level and the GNP deflator about 8 times its level of that year).

In 1930, there was widespread expectation that prices would fall, and wages fell. With lower wages, the short-run aggregate supply curve shifted downward from SAS_{29} to SAS_{30}. But aggregate demand fell by a larger amount than expected to AD_{30}. In 1930, the economy went into recession as real GNP fell by about 7 percent. The price level also fell by a similar amount. (It was not unusual at that time for prices occasionally to fall). When the price level is falling, the economy is experiencing *deflation*.

If the normal course of events had ensued in 1930, the economy might have remained in its depressed state for several months and then started a recovery. But 1930 was not a normal year. For the subsequent three years, the economy was further bombarded with huge negative demand shocks (the sources of which we'll look at in a moment). The aggregate demand curve shifted to the left all the way to AD_{33}. With a depressed economy, the price level was expected to fall and wages fell in line with those expectations. The money wage fell from 55¢ an hour in 1930 to 44¢ an hour by 1933. As a result of lower wages, the aggregate supply curve shifted downward from SAS_{30} to SAS_{33}. But the size of the downward shift of the short-run aggregate supply curve was much less than the drop in aggregate demand. As a result, the aggregate demand curve and the short-run aggregate supply curve intersected in 1933 at a real GNP of $500 billion and a GNP deflator of 11. Real GNP had fallen by almost 30 percent from its 1929 level and the price level had fallen by more than 25 percent.

Although the Great Depression brought enormous hardship, the distribution of that hardship was very uneven. A quarter of the work force had no jobs at all. Also at that time, there were virtually no organized social security and unemployment programs in place. So, for many families, there was virtually no income. But the pocketbooks of the other 75 percent of the labor force barely noticed the Great Depression. It's true that wages fell (from 57¢ an hour in 1929 to 44¢ an hour in 1933). But at the same time, the price level fell and by just about exactly the same percentage amount as the fall in wages. Hence, real wages remained constant. Thus those who had jobs continued to be paid a wage rate that had roughly the same buying power at the end of the Great Depression as in 1929.

You can begin to appreciate the magnitude of the Great Depression if you compare it with the two recessions that we studied earlier in this chapter. Between 1973 and 1975, real GNP fell by 1.75 percent. From 1981 to 1982, it fell by 2.5 percent. In comparison, in 1930, real GNP fell by more than 7 percent and from 1929 to 1933, it fell by close to 30 percent. A 1990s Great Depression of the same magnitude would lower income per person to its level of more than 20 years ago.

Why the Great Depression Happened

The late 1920s were years of economic boom. New houses and apartments were built on an unprecedented scale, new firms were created, and the capital stock of the nation expanded. But these were also years of increasing uncertainty. The main source of increased uncertainty was international. The world economy was going through tumultuous times. The patterns of world trade were changing as Britain, the traditional economic powerhouse of the world, began its period of relative economic decline and new economic powers such as Germany and Japan, as well as the United States, began to emerge. International currency fluctuations and the introduction of restrictive trade policies by many countries (see Chapter 35) further increased the uncertainty faced by firms. There was also domestic uncertainty arising from the fact that there had been such a strong boom in recent years, especially in the capital goods sector and housing. No one believed that that boom could continue but there was great uncertainty as to when it would end and how the pattern of demand would change.

This environment of uncertainty led to a slowdown in consumer spending, especially on new homes and household appliances. By the fall of 1929, the uncertainty had reached a critical level and contributed to the stock market crash. The stock market crash, in turn, heightened people's fears about economic prospects in the foreseeable future. Fear fed fear. Investment collapsed. The building industry almost disappeared. An industry that had been operating flat out just two years earlier was now building virtually no new houses and apartments. It was this drop in

investment, and a drop in consumer spending on durables, that led to the initial leftward shift of the aggregate demand curve from AD_{29} to AD_{30} in Fig. 32.6.

At this stage, what became the Great Depression was no worse than many previous recessions had been. What distinguishes the Great Depression from other previous recessions (and subsequent ones) are the events that followed between 1930 and 1933. But economists, even to this day, have not come to agreement on how to interpret those events. One view, argued by Peter Temin,[3] is that spending continued to fall for a wide variety of reasons—including a continuation of increasing pessimism and uncertainty. According to Temin's view, the continued contraction resulted from a leftward shift in the investment demand curve and a fall in autonomous expenditure. Milton Friedman and Anna J. Schwartz have argued that the continuation of the contraction was almost exclusively the result of the subsequent worsening of financial and monetary conditions.[4] According to Friedman and Schwartz, it was a severe cut in the money supply that lowered aggregate demand, prolonging the contraction and deepening the depression.

Although there is disagreement about the causes of the contraction phase of the Great Depression, the disagreement is not about the elements at work but the degree of importance attached to each. Everyone agrees that increased pessimism and uncertainty lowered investment demand, and everyone agrees that there was a massive contraction of the real money supply. Temin and his supporters assign primary importance to the fall in autonomous expenditure and secondary importance to the fall in the money supply, while Friedman and Schwartz and their supporters assign primary responsibility to the money supply and regard the other factors as being of limited importance.

Let's look at the contraction of aggregate demand a bit more closely. Between 1930 and 1933, there was a massive 20 percent contraction in the nominal money supply. This fall in the money supply

---

[3] Peter Temin, *Did Monetary Forces Cause the Great Depression?* (New York: W. W. Norton, 1976).

[4] This explanation was developed by Milton Friedman and Anna J. Schwartz in *A Monetary History of the United States 1867–1960* (Princeton: Princeton University Press, 1963), Ch. 7.

was not directly induced by the actions of the Fed. The monetary base hardly fell at all. But the bank deposits component of the money supply suffered an enormous collapse. It did so primarily because a large number of banks failed. The primary source of bank failure was unsound lending in the boom running up to the onset of the Great Depression. Fueled by increasing stock prices and booming business conditions, bank loans expanded. But after the stock market crash and the downturn, many borrowers found themselves in hard economic times. They could not pay the interest on their loans and they could not meet the agreed repayment schedules. Banks had deposits that exceeded the realistic value of the loans that they had made. When depositors withdrew funds from the banks, the banks lost reserves and many of them simply couldn't meet their depositors' demands to be repaid.

Bank failures feed on themselves and create additional failures. Seeing banks fail, people become anxious to protect themselves and so take their money out of the banks. Such were the events of 1930. The quantity of notes and coins in circulation increased and the volume of bank deposits declined. But the very action of taking money out of the bank to protect one's wealth accentuated the process of banking failure. Banks were increasingly short of cash and unable to meet their obligations.

Bank failure and the massive contraction of the money supply had two effects on the economy. First, the bank failures themselves brought financial hardship to many producers, increasing the business failure rate throughout the economy. At the same time, a sharp drop in the money supply kept interest rates high. Not only did nominal interest rates stay high, real interest rates increased sharply. The real interest rate is (approximately) the difference between the nominal interest rate and the expected inflation rate. During the Great Depression, inflation was negative—the price level was falling. Thus the real interest rate equaled the nominal interest rate plus the expected rate of deflation. With high real interest rates, investment remained low.

What role did the stock market crash of 1929 play in producing the Great Depression? It certainly created an atmosphere of fear and panic, and probably also contributed to the overall air of uncertainty that dampened investment spending. It also reduced the wealth of stockholders, encouraging them to cut back on their consumption spending. But the direct effect of the stock market crash on consumption, although a contributory factor to the Great Depression, was not the major source of the drop in aggregate demand. It was the collapse in investment arising from increased uncertainty that brought the 1930 decline in aggregate demand.

But the stock market crash was a predictor of severe recession. It reflected the expectations of stockholders concerning future profit prospects. As those expectations became pessimistic, the prices of stocks were bid lower and lower. That is, the behavior of the stock market was a consequence of expectations about future profitability and those expectations were lowered as a result of increased uncertainty.

Can It Happen Again?

Since, even today, we have an incomplete understanding of the causes of the Great Depression, we are not able to predict such an event or to be sure that it cannot occur again. But there are some important differences between the economy of the 1990s and that of the 1930s that make a severe depression much less likely today than it was 60 years ago. The most important features of the economy that make a severe depression less likely today are as follows:

- Bank deposit insurance
- The Fed's role as lender of last resort
- Taxes and government spending
- Multi-income families

Let's examine these in turn.

Bank Deposit Insurance   As a result of the Great Depression, the federal government established, in the 1930s, the Federal Deposit Insurance Corporation (FDIC). The FDIC insures bank deposits for up to $100,000 per deposit so that most depositors need no longer fear bank failure. If a bank fails, the FDIC pays the deposit holders. With federally insured bank deposits, the key event that turned a fairly ordinary recession into the Great Depression is most unlikely to occur. It was the fear of bank failure that caused people to withdraw their deposits from banks. The aggregate consequence of these individually rational acts was to cause the very bank failures that were feared. With deposit insurance, most depositors have nothing to lose if a bank fails and so have no incentive to take actions that are likely to give rise to that failure.

Lender of Last Resort The Fed is the lender of last resort in the U.S. economy. If a single bank is short of reserves, it can borrow reserves from other banks. If the entire banking system is short of reserves, banks can borrow from the Fed. By making reserves available (at a suitable interest rate), the Fed is able to make the quantity of reserves in the banking system respond flexibly to the demand for those reserves. Bank failure can be prevented, or at least contained, to cases where bad management practices are the source of the problem and widespread failures of the type that occurred in the Great Depression prevented.

It is interesting to note that during the weeks following the October 1987 stock market crash, Fed Chairman Alan Greenspan used every opportunity available to remind the American banking and financial community of the Fed's ability and readiness to maintain calm financial conditions.

Taxes and Government Spending The government sector was a much less important part of the economy in 1929 than it has become today. On the eve of that earlier recession, government purchases of goods and services were less than 9 percent of GNP. In contrast, today they are more than 20 percent. Government transfer payments were less than 6 percent of GNP in 1929. These items have grown to more than 15 percent of GNP at the present time.

A larger level of government purchases of goods and services means that when recession hits, a large component of aggregate demand does not decline. It is government transfer payments, however, that is the most important economic stabilizer. When the economy goes into recession and depression, more people qualify for unemployment compensation and social security. As a consequence, although disposable income decreases, the extent of the decrease is moderated by the existence of such programs. Consumption expenditure, in turn, does not decline by as much as it would in the absence of such government programs. But limited decline in consumption spending further limits the overall decrease in aggregate expenditure, thereby limiting the magnitude of an economic downturn.

Multi-income Families At the time of the Great Depression, families with more than one wage earner were much less common than they are today. The labor force participation rate in 1929 was around 55 percent. Today, it is 66 percent. Thus even if the unemployment rate increased to around 25 percent today, close to 50 percent of the adult population would actually have jobs. During the Great Depression, less than 40 percent of the adult population had work. Multi-income families have greater security than single-income families. The chance of both (or all) income earners in a family losing their jobs simultaneously is much lower than the chance of a single earner losing work. With greater family income security, family consumption is likely to be less sensitive to fluctuations in family income that are seen as temporary. Thus when aggregate income falls, it does not induce a cut in consumption. For example, during the OPEC and Volcker recessions as real GNP fell personal consumption expenditure actually increased.

For the four reasons we have just reviewed, it appears the economy has better shock-absorbing characteristics today than it had in the 1920s and 1930s. Even if there is a collapse of confidence leading to a fall in investment, the recession mechanism that is now in place will not translate that initial shock into the large and prolonged fall in real GNP and rise in unemployment that occurred 60 years ago.

Because the economy is now more immune to severe recession than it was 60 years ago, even a stock market crash of the magnitude that occurred in 1987 had barely noticeable effects on spending. A crash of a similar magnitude in 1929 resulted in the near collapse of housing investment and consumer durable purchases. In the period following the 1987 stock market crash, investment and spending on durable goods hardly changed.

None of this is to say that there might not be a deep recession or even a great depression in the 1990s. But it would take a very severe shock to trigger one.

■ We have now completed our study of the working of the macroeconomy. We've studied the macroeconomic model of aggregate demand and aggregate supply and we've learned a great deal about the workings of the markets for goods and services, labor, and money and financial assets. We have applied our knowledge to explaining and understanding the problems of unemployment, inflation, and business cycle fluctuations.

In the next part of the book we will study two aspects of macroeconomic policy—the policies that governments can take to stabilize the economy and the policy toward the government's budget deficit.

SUMMARY

Two Recent Recessions

The two most severe recessions in recent U.S. history occurred in 1974–1975 and 1982. The first recession was caused by the actions of OPEC. At the end of 1973 and the beginning of 1974, OPEC increased the price of oil and, for a period, placed an embargo on the export of oil. These events resulted in a severe upward movement in the short-run aggregate supply curve. The aggregate demand curve shifted upward also but not by as much as that of the short-run aggregate supply curve. As a consequence, real GNP fell and the price level increased at an accelerating pace. The phenomenon gave rise to a new economic term — stagflation.

The Volcker recession resulted from a fall in the growth of aggregate demand, triggered by the monetary policy of the Federal Reserve. In its attempt to beat inflation, the Fed unexpectedly slowed the growth of aggregate demand. Wages increased on the presumption that inflation would continue at close to 10 percent a year, and those wage changes shifted the short-run aggregate supply curve upward. But the upward shift of the short-run aggregate supply curve was much larger than that of the aggregate demand curve. As a consequence, real GNP declined but the inflation rate moderated. In both recessions interest rates increased at first and subsequently declined.

There is controversy about the behavior of the labor market during a recession. According to the sticky wage interpretation of events, the quantity of labor supplied is not very responsive to changes in real wages and wages themselves do not fall much in a recession. As a result, when the economy goes into recession, the quantity of labor supplied exceeds the quantity demanded. According to the flexible wage interpretation of events, the quantity of labor supplied is highly responsive to changes in real wages. When the economy goes into recession, real wages fall a little, and by enough to keep the quantity of labor demanded equal to the quantity supplied. Unemployment increases but the increase arises from increased job search activity associated with a higher degree of labor turnover. Macroeconomists have not yet found the acid test that enables them to resolve their dispute about the labor market mechanism in recession. (pp. 844–853)

Another Great Depression?

The Great Depression that began in 1929 lasted longer and was more severe than any before it or since. The Great Depression started with increased uncertainty and pessimism that brought a fall in investment (especially in housing) and spending on consumer durables. Increased uncertainty and pessimism also brought on the stock market crash. The crash added to the pessimistic outlook and further spending cuts occurred. There then followed a near total collapse of the financial system. Banks failed and the money supply fell, resulting in a continued fall in aggregate demand. Expectations of falling prices led to falling wages but the fall in aggregate demand continued to exceed expectations and real GNP continued to decline.

The Great Depression itself produced a series of reforms that make a repeat of such a depression much less likely. The most important of these were the Fed's willingness to act as lender of last resort and the introduction of federal bank deposit insurance, both of which reduced the risk of bank failure and financial collapse. Higher taxes and government spending have given the economy greater resistance against depression and the increased labor force participation rate provides a greater measure of security, especially for families with more than one wage earner. For these reasons, an initial even large change in either aggregate demand or aggregate supply is much less likely to translate into an accumulative depression than it did in the early 1930s. Thus even a stock market crash as severe as the one that occurred in 1987 does not lead to a collapse in aggregate demand. (pp. 853–859)

KEY   CONCEPTS

Stagflation, 845

Key Figures

Figure 32.1   The OPEC Recession, 845

Figure 32.2   The Volcker Recession, 846
Figure 32.4   The Labor Market in Recession: Sticky Wage Theory, 850
Figure 32.5   The Labor Market in Recession: Flexible Wage Theory, 851

REVIEW   QUESTIONS

1 When did the Great Depression, the OPEC recession, and the Volcker recession occur?

2 What triggered the OPEC recession?

3 Which of these recessions was a period of stagflation?

4 Compare the movements in interest rates in the OPEC recession and the Volcker recession.

5 Describe the changes in employment and real wages in the OPEC recession. With which theory of the labor market are these changes in real wages and unemployment consistent?

6 Describe the changes in real GNP, employment and unemployment, and the price level that occurred during the Great Depression years of 1929 to 1933.

7 What were the main causes of the onset of the Great Depression in 1929?

8 What events in 1931 and 1932 led to the continuation and increasing severity of the fall in real GNP and the rise in employment?

9 What four features of today's economy make it less likely now than in 1929 that a Great Depression will occur?

PROBLEMS

1 Analyze the changes in the interest rate during the OPEC recession by drawing a diagram of the money market showing shifts in the demand and supply curves for real money. What policy changes could have prevented interest rates from rising? What would the effects of such actions have been on real GNP and the price level?

2 During the OPEC recession, real wages fell from $7.95 an hour to $7.65 an hour. Employment fell from 167 billion hours to 164 billion hours. Illustrate these changes in the labor market by drawing demand and supply curves for labor in 1973 and 1975. Draw two diagrams, one that illustrates these changes in wages and employment if the flexible wage theory is true, and one that illustrates these changes if the sticky wage theory is true.

3 During the Volcker recession, real wages did not fall. They held steady at $7.70 an hour. Employ-

ment fell from 187 to 183 billion hours. How can these events be explained by the sticky wage theory? By the flexible wage theory?

4 Compare and contrast the events that took place between 1929 and 1933 with those of 1974–1975 and 1982.

5 List all of the features of the U.S. economy in 1990 and 1991 that you can think of that are consistent with a pessimistic outlook for the 1990s.

6 List all of the features of the U.S. economy in 1990 and 1991 that you can think of that are consistent with an optimistic outlook for the 1990s.

7 How do you think the U.S. economy is going to evolve over the next year or two? Explain your predictions, drawing on the pessimistic and optimistic factors that you have listed in the previous two questions and on your knowledge of macroeconomic theory.

Part 10

Talking
with
Paul
Volcker

Paul Volcker served as chairman of the board of governors of the Federal Reserve System from 1979 to 1987, a time when double-digit inflation was gripping the U.S. economy. Michael Parkin spoke with Mr. Volcker about his experience as chairman of the Fed and about his vision and concerns for the future of the economy.

Mr. Volcker, what originally attracted you to economics?

I was an undergraduate immediately after the Second World War. I think a lot of people at the time got interested in economics because of the experience of the Depression and the war years. They thought things must be able to work better than they had during the Depression, and they were filled with a zeal for doing better. That was part of my thinking, but just as important, economics seemed to me, of all the social sciences, to have a little more precision. I thought I could combine this practical logical structure with an instinct for public service. In retrospect, I'm sure I overestimated the logic and coherence!

What are the economic principles that you learned in school that have proved useful in your professional life?

Some economic principles are eternally useful. All that business about "no free lunch" remains a valid observation—although we in the public sector sometimes wonder! Economics does teach you the discipline of understanding that the direct immediate effects of some action may not be the full story—that without close analysis and study you may have unintended and unanticipated effects later on. Those later "side effects" may be greater than the immediate effects. Finally, the concept of looking at the margin—at incremental effects—is very important in terms of actual policy.

> "Economics does teach you that the immediate effects of some action may not be the full story."

Is a background in economics, familiarity with economic principles, mandatory for a chairman of the Federal Reserve?

I haven't been able to detect any correlation in performance between chairmen that were economists and those who were not. The chairman doesn't have to be a trained economist if he or she has a staff of very good economists. Without that, you'd really be in trouble.

There must be as many opinions about what the Fed should be doing as there are economists. How do these controversies among macroeconomists affect the Fed's job? Are they relevant for the conduct of monetary policy?

Oh, I think they're relevant. The internal technical debate doesn't make that much difference. But to the extent that economists' positions on public policy influence public opinion and differ widely, you lack a consensus against which to conduct policy. In a political context, some of these different points of view become politicized. That's part of the environment in which the Fed must operate.

The one advantage when you're the chairman of the Federal Reserve Board is that you can sometimes influence—or can lead yourself and everyone else into thinking that you can influence—the nature of the consensus about economic policy, as it is actually reflected in public opinion.

There has certainly not been consensus about the consequences of the Fed's policy in fighting inflation during the late 1970s and early 1980s, while you were chairman. When you embarked on your war against inflation, did you expect to be presiding over the longest peacetime recovery in U.S. history?

I thought then, and think now, that inflation is the enemy of sustained expansion. But dealing with these things always turns out to be more difficult, more complicated, and to take longer than you expect. I guess I did misjudge how long we could put up with internal government deficits and external trade imbalances.

What were you missing?

In part I think there is a much more fluid international capital market than we had recognized. I would not have guessed that the United States could borrow, or that the Japanese would be willing to lend, so much money year after year without more uncertainty about the dollar. I would not have guessed that the value of the dollar could come down from its high level as much as it has without more disturbance in interest rates and inflation. We've been very fortunate in being able to manage that big a decline in the value of the dollar with as little inflation as we've had.

Did your war on inflation cost more in human terms than you had thought?

Probably—stopping inflation is never easy. What I object to is that people said that the Federal Reserve caused the recession in the early 1980s and all its pain and suffering. But, in my view, we were going to have the pain anyway. It was just a question of when and how. We thought it would be less if we dealt with the inflation earlier rather than later.

One of my predecessors, Bill Martin, once described the Fed's job as taking away the punch bowl just when the party's getting good.

You avoid the hangover that way, or reduce it anyway.

Do you bring the punch bowl back if the party starts to fade?

My critique of Federal Reserve history is not that it was always too harsh and brought all these expansions to an end when they could have gone on forever. But sometimes the Fed was overeager to get the party started. Once you get in a recession, the pressures on the Fed are very strong. Even after you come out of the recession, the temptation is to overstimulate. But policy only works with a lag and the lags catch up with you. You're off to another jolly party again. We tried to avoid this last time, I think with some success.

We've talked a bit about the government's budget deficit. Did the government's need to finance its budget deficit affect your job as chairman of the Fed?

I do not believe that the Federal Reserve was forced into inflationary financing. In retrospect, the government's budget deficit position did not in fact appear to impair our ability to achieve a record expansion. But if you look at whether the expansion can be carried on for another seven years, you have to get concerned about our relatively low level of investment, our low productivity, and our dependence on foreign lending and investment. None of these can be dealt with by monetary policy alone. Fiscal policy gives you an expansionary thrust, which

"Inflation is the enemy of sustained expansion."

then has to be countered by tighter monetary policy—by higher interest rates. This leaves you with a vulnerable economy, increasingly dependent on money borrowed from overseas.

"A major policy challenge is to find a way of cutting the growth of consumption."

Our economic relationship with other countries also includes the exchange of goods and services. In recent years we have been experiencing a substantial decline in net exports. What do you see as the principal cause of the external trade deficit?

It's an internal imbalance between our ability to produce and our propensity to spend. Our spending is mostly consumption, personal and public. Investment is, at

best just so-so for a period of expansion. So a major policy challenge is to find a way of cutting consumption. On the other hand, there are imbalances in the opposite direction in other economies. The Japanese are doing a good job in beginning to deal with this problem. But it is true that there is a bias in the trading world toward less openness. If you took a snapshot of the world trading scene, you'd have to agree that the United States is by far the most open market of all, and our trading partners are more

closed. How do you deal with that complaint? You can't ignore how these imbalances are aggravated by our own internal economic policies, our own consumption.

What will improve the situation?

We've got to contain domestic spending and we've got to see foreign

markets open up so that foreign expenditure for our goods increases. Of course, just opening foreign markets wouldn't induce any change in our own spending by itself. Moreover, changing our spending *pattern* can't be done just by monetary policy, by high interest rates. Monetary policy won't move spending from consumption into investment. That means you've got to bring fiscal policy to bear. More taxes or less spending or both. But now you've got a lot of political choices. You'll have to make some political bargains in order to get expenditure cuts.

When a college student seeks your advice on the choice of a career, what do you suggest?

I'd strongly encourage him or her to consider a career in public service. There are so many important jobs for people in the government. Who do we look to for the solution of problems like AIDS? The government. Who's going to solve the drug problem, if anyone can? The government. We need young people who recognize the challenge and excitement and satisfaction of service to the public. Without their contributions, we will have a serious problem in this country.

Chapter 33

Stabilizing the Economy

After studying this chapter, you will be able to:

- Describe the goals of macroeconomic stabilization policy

- Describe the key players whose actions influence economic stability

- Explain how the state of the economy affects the popularity of the government

- Explain how the government and the Federal Reserve can influence the economy

- Distinguish between fixed rules and feedback rules for stabilization policy

- Explain the debate among economists between fixed rules and feedback rules

- Review the stabilization successes and failures of the recent past and the challenges of the present and future

P eople panic when things go very wrong and turn to their political leaders for reassurance and action. Thus it was, in the depths of the Great Depression, that our grandparents turned to Franklin Delano Roosevelt to deliver them from that economic holocaust and establish a New Deal that would banish such horrors forever. Fifty years later, when Ronald Reagan arrived in Washington, his political agenda was to undo what he saw as the shackles of the New Deal, leaving free people in free markets to find their own economic progress and prosperity. But when the U.S. and world stock markets crashed on a mild and sunny October Monday in 1987, after 59 consecutive months of economic expansion, the cry went out again—"Who's in charge?"

Who's in Charge?

Who *is* in charge of the U.S. economy? When the stock market crashes, what can and what does government do about it? What does the government do about less dramatic macroeconomic ills such as high inflation, high unemployment, and slow and variable real GNP growth? ■ In 1976, with unemployment close to 8 percent and inflation high by historical standards, the electorate rejected the Republican administration that had been in power for the previous eight years and elected Democrat Jimmy Carter as President. Four years later, with unemployment not much lower and inflation substantially higher, the electorate dismissed Jimmy Carter and elected Ronald Reagan. In 1984, with unemployment still high but inflation having dramatically fallen, the electorate endorsed Ronald Reagan, returning him to power in a landslide election. In 1988, the economy was enjoying its sixth year of continuous expansion, low unemployment, and low inflation. Under these circumstances, George Bush, the candidate of the incumbent party, was able to secure a relatively easy victory over Michael Dukakis. How important was the economy in determining that and earlier election outcomes? And what aspects of the economy do voters care about? Do they mainly fear unemployment, worrying little about inflation? Or is inflation the source of nightmares and unemployment less important? ■ Although we all want security—security of employment, security of lifetime savings that will not be wiped out—how much security can the government actually provide? And how much insecurity is induced by our political system and the stabilization policies that it pursues? ■ The second half of the 1980s has been a period of unimagined prosperity and macroeconomic stability. How was this stability and prosperity achieved? What was the price that had to be paid to achieve it? And what are the stabilization policy challenges that face the United States as we move forward into the 1990s?

■ In this chapter, we're going to study the problems of stabilizing the U.S. economy—of avoiding inflation, high unemployment, and wildly fluctuating levels and growth rates of economic activity summarized in real GNP. At the end of the chapter, you will have a clearer and deeper understanding of the macroeconomic policy problems facing the United States today and of the political debate that surrounds us concerning those problems.

The Stabilization Problem

The stabilization problem is to deliver a macroeconomic performance that is as smooth and predictable as possible. Solving this problem involves specifying targets to be achieved and then devising policies that result in getting as close as possible to those targets.

Macroeconomic Policy Targets

The targets of stabilization policy are the specific values of macroeconomic variables that policymakers seek to achieve. There are five main macroeconomic policy targets:

• Unemployment at its natural rate
• Steady growth in real GNP
• Low and predictable inflation
• Stable exchange rates between the dollar and foreign currencies
• Balanced international trade

We defined the first three variables that are targets of macroeconomic policy in Chapter 22. There we discovered that keeping unemployment close to its natural rate and keeping real GNP growth steady avoids the costs of excessive unemployment and of excessive bottlenecks in the economy. When unemployment is above its natural rate, output is lost, there's a slowdown in the accumulation of human capital, and, if unemployment is high and prolonged, serious psychological and social problems arise for the unemployed workers and their families. When unemployment falls below its natural rate, labor and other resources do not move to their highest value uses as quickly as they otherwise would. We also discovered in Chapter 22 that low and predictable inflation increases the usefulness of money as a measuring rod for conducting transactions, especially those that are spread out over time, such as borrowing and lending or working for an agreed wage.

The fourth target of macroeconomic policy—stable exchange rates between the dollar and other foreign currencies—is not so much a goal of U.S. stabilization policy but a goal of world stabilization policy. To understand some U.S. stabilization policy actions that have occurred in recent years, we cannot ignore the importance of this international goal. But we will not study global stabilization policy until we get to Chapter 36.

The fifth target of macroeconomic policy is also an international target. It is the attainment of a balance of trade with the rest of the world that is close to zero. Like the exchange rate targets, we cannot ignore this target of macroeconomic policy if we want to understand the contemporary stabilization policy problem. We'll return to this aspect of policy in Chapter 36.

The five targets of macroeconomic stabilization policy are not independent of each other. As we have already seen, in Chapter 22, unemployment and real GNP fluctuate in sympathy with each other. Similarly, inflation and the foreign exchange value of the dollar move together, although as we shall see in Chapter 36, movements in these two variables are not as precisely linked as those of real GNP and unemployment. Nevertheless, other things being equal, if the inflation rate goes up by 1 percent, the dollar loses 1 percent of its value against the currencies of other countries. Finally, the balance of trade deficit fluctuates with the state of the economy, although its movements depend on a large number of other factors, including the state of the world economy.

The links between the five macroeconomic policy targets make it useful, for many purposes, to divide the targets into two groups:

• Real targets
• Nominal targets

The **real targets** of macroeconomic policy are unemployment at its natural rate, steady growth in real GNP, and balanced international trade. The **nominal targets** of macroeconomic policy are low and predictable inflation and stable exchange rates.

Macroeconomic Performance Indexes

There are various ways in which macroeconomic performance can be summarized. The ones that we'll consider are indexes that combine, in some way, the real targets and the nominal targets of macroeconomic policy. All the indexes can be stated in terms of a combination of unemployment (real target) and inflation (nominal target). The different indexes place different weights on these two variables. Let's begin by considering one of the best known indexes, although one that has absolutely no scientific basis— the so-called Misery Index.

Misery Index   The **misery index** (MI) is an index of macroeconomic performance equal to the sum of the inflation rate and the unemployment rate. That is,

MI = Inflation rate + Unemployment rate.

An increase in the misery index is "bad," and a decrease in the misery index is "good." The weights attaching to inflation and unemployment in the misery index are equal. That is, an increase in the inflation rate of 1 percentage point is just as bad as an increase in the unemployment rate of 1 percentage point. The misery index was devised as a political slogan by the Democrats in 1975 during the closing years of the Ford administration. It was subsequently used by the Republicans themselves against President Jimmy Carter.

The idea behind the misery index is that it provides a measure of the extent to which the real and nominal macroeconomic policy targets have been missed. The higher the inflation rate, the less is the success in achieving low and predictable inflation and a stable dollar. The higher the unemployment rate, the less is the success in keeping unemployment close to its natural rate and in keeping real GNP growth steady.

A second index of macroeconomic performance, and one that does have some scientific basis, is based on voter behavior.

Voter Behavior   The effects of economic performance on voter behavior have been studied most thoroughly by Ray Fair of Yale University. By studying the outcome of all the presidential elections between 1916 and 1984, Fair discovered the following:

• For each 1 percentage point increase in the real GNP growth rate, the incumbent political party gets a 1 percentage point increase in voter share.
• For each 3 percentage point increase in the inflation rate, the incumbent political party gets a 1 percentage point decrease in voter share.

This real GNP growth is three times as important as inflation in its effects on votes.

We can use Fair's discovery to make a voter unpopularity index (UPI) as follows:

UPI = Inflation rate − 3 × Real GNP growth rate.

Politicians seek to make the UPI as low as possible— that is, they seek to avoid unpopularity. The idea behind this index is similar to that of the misery index. It combines the real and nominal aspects of macroeconomic performance into a single index that tells us whether performance is better or worse as indicated by its effects on voter behavior. The higher the inflation rate and the lower the real GNP growth rate, the more unpopular is the government. Real GNP growth is three times as important as inflation in determining voter behavior.

In order to compare the unpopularity index with the misery index, we need a relationship between unemployment and real GNP growth. We saw such a relationship—Okun's Law—in Our Advancing Knowledge, pp. 808–810. Okun's Law states that for each 2 percentage point fall in real GNP relative to trend, the unemployment rate increases by 1 percentage point, other things being equal. Using Okun's law together with Fair's voter popularity findings, the unpopularity index becomes

UPI = Inflation rate+ 6 × Unemployment rate.

What this equation tells is that, on the average, voters care six times as much about unemployment of a given percentage as they do about inflation of that same percentage, other things being equal. This means that if the unemployment rate increases by 1

Figure 33.1   Indexes of Macroeconomic Performance

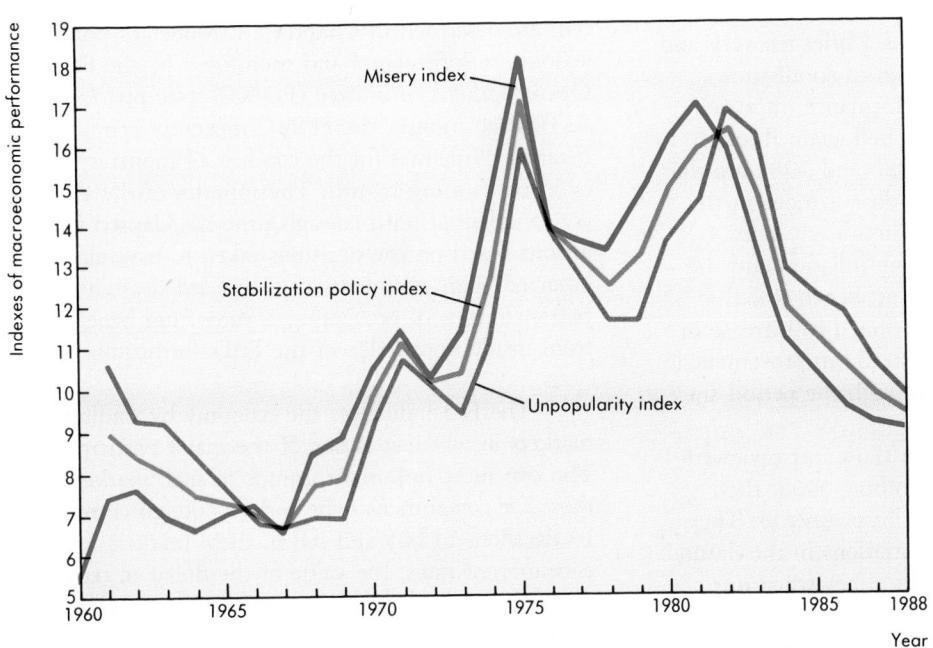

The voter popularity of an administration depends in part on macroeconomic performance. The more strongly the economy grows and the lower the inflation rate, the more popular is an administration. Three indexes of performance are graphed here. The misery index, which was invented for political purposes, is simply the sum of inflation and unemployment. An unpopularity index, which is based on election results, measures voter unpopularity. A stabilization policy index measures the closeness with which nominal GNP targets are achieved.

percentage point, to maintain its popularity the government would have to find a way of lowering the inflation rate by 6 percentage points. Thus unemployment matters a great deal for electoral popularity. If inflation increases by 1 percentage point, the government would have to find a way of lowering the unemployment rate by one sixth of one percentage point in order to maintain its popularity.

A third index of macroeconomic performance is based on nominal GNP.

Nominal GNP Target   James Tobin of Yale University and John Taylor of Stanford University have suggested that a useful operating goal for macroeconomic policy is to keep the growth rate of nominal GNP steady. Nominal GNP is the current dollar value of the final goods and services produced. Thus nominal GNP increases when real GNP increases and when prices increase. The following simple equation tells us the connection between nominal GNP, real GNP, and inflation:

$$\text{Nominal GNP growth rate} = \text{Real GNP growth rate} + \text{Inflation rate}.$$

If the inflation rate increases by 1 percentage point, nominal GNP growth would remain steady if the real GNP growth rate falls by 1 percentage point. Thus the goal of stabilizing the growth rate of nominal GNP puts equal weight on inflation and real GNP growth. The nominal GNP target, then, is a bit like Fair's voter unpopularity, except that the weight placed on real GNP growth is not three times that placed on inflation but equal to that placed on inflation. We can use Okun's Law to compare a nominal GNP target with the misery index. Using Okun's Law with a nominal GNP target gives a stabilization policy index (SPI):

$$\text{SPI} = \text{Inflation rate} + 2 \times \text{Unemployment rate}.$$

A comparison of SPI and MI shows that a nominal GNP target places twice as much importance on unemployment as does the misery index.

Performance Indexes Since 1960   The macroeconomic performance of the United States since 1960, as measured by the three performance indexes that we have just reviewed, is set out in Fig. 33.1. (All the indexes have been scaled to have the same average values.) As you can see, all three indexes tell the same broad story. Macroeconomic performance improved between 1961 and 1967. It then deteriorated sharply through 1971. There was a brief recovery and then a further strong deterioration to an all-time worst performance in 1975. Performance improved through 1978 and then deteriorated again through 1980 and 1981. Notice that 1980 and 1981 are the only years in which the indexes do not move in the same direction as each other. (The misery index, which places the largest weight on inflation and the smallest weight on unemployment, began to fall while the other two indexes continued to increase in 1981.) All three indexes show steady improvement in macroeconomic performance through the period since 1981.

Of course, indexes such as those just reviewed have limitations. They tell us nothing about the distribution of economic misery or prosperity. They also do not take into account variations in the natural rate of unemployment. There are times when unemployment is high because an unusually large amount of reallocation of labor and other resources is taking place. At such times the high unemployment rate reflects the fact that a larger number of people are voluntarily relocating to their highest value jobs. Such indexes also do not take into account the extent to which inflation is anticipated or unanticipated. As we've seen, this distinction makes a crucial difference to the costs of inflation and the people on whom those costs fall.

Nevertheless, although the indexes that we've reviewed are crude, they all point in a similar direction. And the state of the economy, as summarized in such indexes, has an important effect on the actions of policymakers.

But who are the policymakers?

The Key Players

There are three key players that formulate and execute macroeconomic stabilization policy:

- The Board of Governors of the Federal Reserve System
- The Congress
- The Administration

The Federal Reserve Board

The *Federal Reserve System* is the nation's central bank. The main features of the Federal Reserve System are described in Chapter 28. Monetary policy actions are formulated and monitored by the Federal Open Market Committee (FOMC), (see pp. 730–733). Each month, the FOMC meets to formulate detailed guidelines for the conduct of monetary policy in the coming month. The minutes of the FOMC are confidential until enough time has elapsed for the actions based on the decisions taken to have already occurred. This confidentiality is regarded as an important means of preventing anyone from benefiting from inside knowledge of the Fed's forthcoming actions.

The Fed influences the economy by trading in markets in which it is one of the major participants. The two most important groups of such markets are those for government debt and for foreign currency. Its decisions to buy and sell in these markets influence interest rates, the value of the dollar in terms of foreign currencies, and the amount of money in the economy. These variables that the Fed can directly influence in turn affect the conditions on which the millions of firms and households in the economy undertake their own economic actions. But the Fed itself operates under severe constraints—constraints imposed by the spending and taxing decisions made by Congress.

The Congress

The House of Representatives and the Senate and various committees of Congress implement the nation's fiscal policy. Fiscal policy has three elements:

- Spending plans
- Tax laws
- Deficit

All three elements of fiscal policy are brought together in the federal budget. The **federal budget** is a statement of the federal government's financial plan, itemizing programs and their costs, tax revenues, and the proposed deficit or surplus.

The expenditure side of the budget is a list of programs, together with the amount that the government plans to spend on each program and a forecast of the total amount of government expenditure. Some expenditure items in the federal budget are directly controlled by government departments. Others arise from decisions to fund particular programs, the total cost of which depends on actions that Congress can forecast but not directly control. For example, social security expenditure depends on the state of the economy and on how many people qualify for support. Farm subsidies depend on farm costs and prices.

Congress makes decisions about government revenue by enacting tax laws. As in the case of some important items of government expenditure, Congress cannot control with precision the amount of tax revenue that it will receive. Congress makes the tax laws, but the amount of tax paid is determined by the actions of the millions of people and firms who make their own choices about how much to work and spend and save.

The difference between the expenditure on government programs and the taxes received is the government deficit. (We will discuss the deficit in detail in Chapter 34.) Every year since 1969, the federal government has spent more than it has received and, in the early 1980s, an unusually large gap between outlays and revenues arose.

The emergence and persistence of the federal government deficit have led to a variety of creative ideas on the part of Congress to keep spending in check or to increase revenue. One idea, proposed by Senators Gramm, Rudman, and Hollings, and incorporated into the Gramm-Rudman-Hollings Act of 1985, is to impose automatic spending cuts if the deficit does not follow a predetermined path that will ultimately result in a balanced budget by 1993.

Another way of balancing the federal budget is to increase government revenue. But there is disagreement and two competing views about how this objective might be achieved. One, supported by former President Ronald Reagan, is that tax reform and lower tax rates will increase revenue by stimulating economic activity, increasing the incomes on which taxes are paid by enough to ensure that lower tax rates, combined with higher incomes, bring in higher revenue. The other view is that revenue can only be increased by increasing tax rates and introducing new taxes.

The Administration

The role of the administration in formulating and implementing macroeconomic stabilization policy is to give advice and attempt to persuade. Even the president of the United States has severely limited powers when it comes to stabilizing the economy.

The president can attempt to influence the chairman and members of the Board of Governors of the Federal Reserve System, persuading them to take whatever stabilization policy actions the administration deems appropriate. The president can also try to influence Congress and the outcome of congressional debates. And the president carries some important carrots and sticks that enhance his influence. For example, he appoints the chairman (for four years) and members of the Federal Reserve Board (for 14 years). But once he has appointed them, he cannot remove them until their fixed term of office is complete. This fact means that an administration often has to live with a Federal Reserve Board appointed largely by the preceding administration.

The president's influence on Congress arises from his power of veto. But with government spending bills, the president only has the power to take the entire bill or to leave it. He does not have a line-item veto, as do many state governors. That is, the president cannot decide to veto certain items in a budget proposed by Congress. He either approves the entire package or rejects the entire package. In practical terms, this means that the president does not have a veto on financial bills. To veto a half billion dollar dam project would require also vetoing the entire defense budget.

Each year, the president prepares an economic report that reviews the state of the economy and sets out the president's goals and ambitions for the future. The report is accompanied by the annual report of the president's Council of Economic Advisors (CEA). Established in the Employment Act of 1946, the CEA consists of a small group of economists who work closely with the president, keeping him informed and advised of economic developments and of policy developments in the Fed and Congress. The CEA, together with the president, take a view on the appropriate combination of monetary and fiscal policy actions and also offer opinions on the actions of the two branches of policymaking, paying special attention to consistency of the policies with each other.

At the head of the CEA is its chairman. Almost always the chairman is a highly distinguished economist, often with an academic background. The current chairman is Michael Boskin, on leave from his regular job as a professor of economics at Stanford University. Usually, the CEA and its chairman operate quietly in the background. Occasionally, however, the chairman becomes embroiled in public debate. The most notable such occasion arose in 1984 when

Ronald Reagan's CEA chairman, Martin Feldstein, a Harvard professor, vocally and publicly expressed his concern about the administration's attitude toward the large, and seemingly permanent, federal deficit. But such public disagreements are rare and most of the time the CEA works in close harmony with the president.

We've now reviewed the effects of macroeconomic performance on political popularity and have also described the key players in the policymaking game. Let's now turn our attention to the methods used for stabilizing the economy.

Alternative Means Used to Stabilize the Economy

There are obviously many different monetary and fiscal policies that can be pursued. To understand the policies that *are* adopted, it is convenient to classify all possible policies into two broad categories:

• Fixed rules
• Feedback rules

Fixed Rules and Feedback Rules

A **fixed rule** specifies an action to be pursued independently of the state of the economy. There are many examples of fixed rules in everyday life. Perhaps the best known one is that which keeps the traffic flowing by having us all stick to the right. The best known fixed rule for stabilization policy is one that has long been advocated by Milton Friedman (see Our Advancing Knowledge, pp. 878–879). He proposes setting the quantity of money growing at a constant rate year in and year out, regardless of the state of the economy. As we have seen, inflation persists because continual increases in the money supply raise aggregate demand. Friedman proposes allowing the money supply to grow at a rate that would hold the *average* inflation rate at zero.

A **feedback rule** specifies how policy actions respond to changes in the state of the economy. An everyday example of a feedback rule is that governing your actions in choosing what to wear and whether or not to carry an umbrella. You base those actions on the best available forecast of the day's temperature and rainfall. (With a fixed rule, you either always or never carry an umbrella.) A stabilization policy feedback rule is one that changes policy instruments such as the money supply, interest rates, or even taxes, in response to the state of the economy. For example, the Fed pursues a feedback rule if an increase in unemployment causes it to engage in an open market operation aimed at increasing the money supply growth rate and lowering interest rates. The Fed also pursues a feedback rule if an increase in the inflation rate triggers an open market operation aimed at cutting the money supply growth rate and raising interest rates.

The key distinction between a fixed rule and a feedback rule is that with a fixed rule, policy instruments are set without regard to whether the economy is depressed or booming, or moving into recession or recovery, while with a feedback rule, policy instrument settings are changed in direct response to the state of the economy.

Expectations and Policy Rules

We saw in Chapter 31 that inflation expectations play an important role in determining the actual inflation rate and the level of real GNP. Expectations of inflation in turn depend in part on expectations about changes in aggregate demand. These expectations in turn depend on expectations about stabilization policy. But expectations about stabilization policy obviously depend on the stabilization policy rules that are being pursued. If the Fed pursues a fixed rule, such as Friedman's constant money supply growth rate rule, the Fed's actions will be expected to keep aggregate demand growing at its average rate. (Other factors might be expected to speed up or slow down the growth rate of aggregate demand, but the Fed's own actions will not be expected to have such an effect.) Alternatively, if the Fed always lowers interest rates and speeds up the growth of aggregate demand when unemployment rises to some trigger point and always increases interest rates and slows the growth of aggregate demand when inflation rises to some trigger point, then forecasts about the future growth of aggregate demand will incorporate the effects of the forecasted change in the Fed's monetary actions.

Let's study the effects of a fixed rule and a feedback rule for the conduct of stabilization policy by examining how real GNP (and employment and unemployment that move with real GNP), and the price level behave under two alternative rules.

The Two Rules Compared

We'll study an economy that starts out at full employment and has no inflation. Figure 33.2 illustrates this situation. The economy is on aggregate demand curve AD_0 and short-run aggregate supply curve SAS. These curves intersect at a point on long-run aggregate supply curve LAS. The GNP deflator is 100 and real GNP is $4 trillion. Now let's see what happens if there is a change in aggregate demand. Suppose that there is an unexpected and temporary fall in aggregate demand.

Perhaps there is a wave of pessimism about the future that results in a fall in investment demand, or perhaps there is a recession in the rest of the world that leads to a fall in exports. Regardless of the origin of the fall in aggregate demand, the aggregate demand curve shifts to the left, to AD_1 in the figure. Because the fall in aggregate demand is unanticipated, expected aggregate demand remains at AD_0, so the expected GNP deflator remains at 100. The short-run aggregate supply curve stays at SAS. Aggregate demand curve AD_1 intersects the short-run aggregate supply curve SAS at a GNP deflator of 90 and a real GNP of $3 trillion. The economy is in a depressed state. Real GNP is below its long-run level and unemployment above its natural rate.

The fall in aggregate demand from AD_0 to AD_1 is not permanent. But, at the same time, it is not purely temporary—aggregate demand gradually increases back to its original level of AD_0. That is, as confidence in the future improves, firms' investment picks up or as economic recovery proceeds in the rest of the world, exports gradually rise, and so the aggregate demand curve gradually returns to AD_0, but it takes a good deal of time to do so.

We are going to work out how the economy responds under two alternative monetary policies during the period in which aggregate demand gradually increases to its original level: a fixed-rule policy with the money supply constant and a feedback-rule policy that stimulates aggregate demand by increasing the money supply. Figure 33.3 illustrates the analysis.

First, we'll consider what happens with a fixed rule.

Fixed Rule   When aggregate demand falls to AD_1, the money supply growth rate is held constant. (In

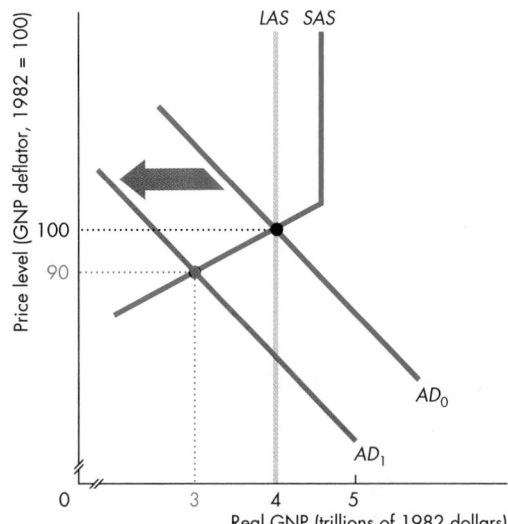

Figure 33.2   A Fall in Aggregate Demand

The economy starts out at full employment on aggregate demand curve AD_0 and short-run aggregate supply curve SAS, with the two curves intersecting on the long-run aggregate supply curve LAS. Real GNP is $4 trillion and the GNP deflator is 100. A fall in aggregate demand (due to pessimism about future profits, for example) unexpectedly shifts the aggregate demand curve to AD_1. Real GNP falls to $3 trillion, and the GNP deflator falls to 90. The economy is in a depressed state.

this example, the growth rate of the money supply is zero, so the money supply remains constant.) No special measures are taken to bring the economy back to full employment. But recall that we are assuming that aggregate demand gradually increases because of other factors and eventually returns to AD_0. As it does so, real GNP and the GNP deflator gradually increase. The GNP deflator gradually returns to 100 and real GNP to its long-run level of $4 trillion, as shown in Fig. 33.3(a). Throughout this process, the economy experiences more rapid growth than usual but beginning from a state of excess capacity. Unemployment remains high until the aggregate demand curve has returned to AD_0.

Let's contrast this adjustment with what occurs under a feedback-rule monetary policy.

Feedback Rule   Under the feedback rule that we are analyzing, the money supply increases whenever there

Figure 33.3   Two Monetary Policies

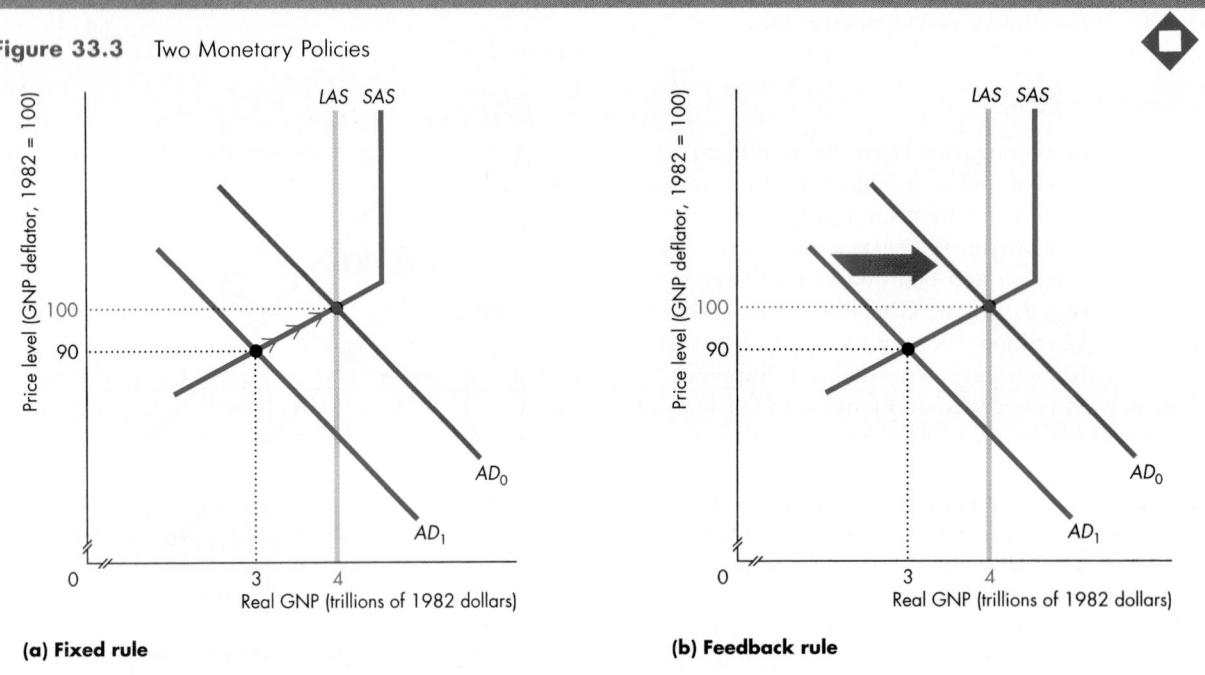

(a) Fixed rule   **(b) Feedback rule**

The economy is in a depressed state with a GNP deflator of 90 and real GNP of $3 trillion. The short-run aggregate supply curve is at *SAS*. A fixed-rule monetary policy (part a) leaves the aggregate demand initially at AD_1, so the GNP deflator remains at 90 and real GNP at $3 trillion. As other influences on aggregate demand gradually increase, the aggregate demand curve shifts back to AD_0. As it does, real GNP rises back to $4 trillion and the GNP deflator increases to 100. A feedback-rule monetary policy (part b) increases the money supply, shifting the aggregate demand curve instantly from AD_1 to AD_0. Real GNP returns to $4 trillion and the GNP deflator returns to 100. The money supply is then gradually decreased as the other influences on aggregate demand increase its level. As a result, the aggregate demand curve is kept steady at AD_0 and real GNP stays at $4 trillion.

is a fall in aggregate demand and decreases whenever there is a rise in aggregate demand. When aggregate demand falls to AD_1, the Fed increases the money supply to shift the aggregate demand curve back to AD_0, as shown in Fig. 33.3(b). As the other forces that increase aggregate demand kick in, the Fed gradually cuts back on the money supply, holding the aggregate demand curve steady at AD_0. Real GNP jumps back to its full-employment level and the GNP deflator jumps back to 100.

Under a fixed-rule policy, the economy goes into a recession and stays there for however long it takes the aggregate demand curve to return to its original position. Under a feedback-rule policy, the economy is pulled out of its recession quickly by the policy action. The price level and real GNP fall and rise by exactly the same amounts in the

two cases, but real GNP stays below its long-run level for longer with a fixed rule than it does with a feedback rule.

So Feedback Rules Are Better?

Isn't it obvious that a feedback rule is better than a fixed rule? Can't the Fed use a feedback rule to keep the economy close to full employment with a stable price level? Of course, unforecasted changes—such as the fall in aggregate demand in our example—will knock the economy from time to time. But by responding with an active change in the quantity of money, can't the Fed minimize the damage from such a shock? It certainly appears to be so from our analysis.

Despite the appearance of the superiority of a feedback rule, many economists remain convinced that a fixed rule works best. These economists assert the following:

- Feedback rules require greater knowledge of the economy than we have.
- Feedback rules introduce unpredictability.
- Feedback rules generate bigger fluctuations in aggregate demand.
- Aggregate supply shocks, not aggregate demand shocks, cause most economic fluctuations.

We'll look briefly at the first three assertions and then, at greater length, at the fourth.

Knowledge of the Economy   Although the aggregate demand–aggregate supply model of the economy provides us with a useful tool for both understanding and predicting aggregate fluctuations, it is not a precise tool. We can predict the general direction in which the economy will move following a change in one of the factors that influence aggregate demand or aggregate supply. But we cannot predict, with any certainty, either the magnitude of a change or its precise timing. The multiplier effects of monetary and fiscal policy actions take place over a prolonged period of time and are influenced by far more factors than can be kept track of.

Also, we have a limited knowledge of the precise way in which the labor market works. The degree of wage flexibility and the economy's capacity level of real GNP and natural rate of unemployment are all magnitudes that can only be estimated and about which there is uncertainty and disagreement.

Lacking a precise model of the economy that makes exact predictions about the quantitative effects of policy actions and of other exogenous influences, we are not able to design feedback rules that can be guaranteed to smooth out fluctuations. We may easily end up designing rules that make fluctuations more severe. For example, suppose that whenever the inflation rate increases, the money supply growth rate is decreased. If it takes between one and two years for the change in the money supply growth rate to have its full effects on real GNP and the price level, by the time those effects are being felt the economy may already have moved into a contraction phase of the business cycle. If that is so, the slowdown in money supply growth will accentuate the contraction, making the recession more severe than it otherwise would have been.

The second problem with the feedback rules is that they can introduce unpredictability. Let's see how.

Predictability of Feedback Rules   To make decisions about long-term contracts for employment (wage contracts) and for borrowing and lending, people have to anticipate the future course of prices—the future inflation rate. To make a forecast of inflation, it is necessary to forecast aggregate demand. Suppose that people anticipate that aggregate demand is going to rise less quickly next year. In view of this anticipation, firms and workers agree to a slower rate of wage increase. The short-run aggregate supply curve shifts upward less quickly as a result of the expectation of slower growth in aggregate demand. If aggregate demand *actually* slows down, as anticipated, inflation also slows but firms continue to produce at their capacity output levels and there is full employment. A correctly anticipated slowdown in the growth of aggregate demand has resulted in a slowdown in inflation but with no slowdown in output growth and no increase in unemployment.

Contrast this case with one in which there is an *un*anticipated slowdown in aggregate demand. Aggregate demand is anticipated to continue growing at its current rate but, in fact, it slows down. With this anticipation, firms and workers agree to keep money wages rising at their current rate. As a consequence, the short-run aggregate supply curve shifts upward. When aggregate demand fails to increase at the expected rate, real GNP falls below its long-run level, unemployment rises above its natural rate, and there is a slowdown in inflation. The economy goes into recession because money wages have been set too high for the level of aggregate demand that has actually come about.

Why might aggregate demand growth slow down unexpectedly? There are many possible reasons but one is that the Fed may unexpectedly slow down the growth rate of the money supply, forcing interest rates up and lowering investment. Such an action by the Fed would slow inflation but would also push real GNP below its long-run level and increase unemployment. If the Fed sticks to a rock-steady, fixed rule for increasing the money supply, then the Fed itself cannot be a contributor to unexpected fluctuations in aggregate demand. To the extent that the Fed's actions are unpredictable, they lead to unpredictable fluctuations in aggregate demand. These fluctuations, in turn, produce fluctuations in real GNP, employment, and unemployment.

The Quantity Theory and Monetarism

T he quantity theory of money has had a long and checkered history. Its first statement—that a change in the quantity of money brings about a proportional change in the price level—was made by the French philosopher Jean Bodin in the early seventeenth century. Its first clear statement in the English language was by David Hume. Hume was an extraordinary philosopher and economist who lived in Edinburgh, Scotland, from 1711 to 1776. (He died the year when Adam Smith's *Wealth of Nations* was published.) Hume was a close friend of Adam Smith and had enormous influence on him.

A milestone in the development of the quantity theory of money was the contribution of Henry Thornton, a British monetary economist and legislator who lived in London from 1760 to 1815. While a member of the British Parliament, Thornton wrote his impressive *An Enquiry into the Nature and Effects of the Paper Credit of Great Britain.* In this book, he developed the notion of the quantity of money and its velocity of circulation, the two key elements in the modern statement of the quantity theory of money.

David Hume

The first major American contribution to the development of the quantity theory was that by Irving Fisher (see Our Advancing Knowledge, p. 656). Born in Saugerties, New York, in 1867, Fisher spent his entire professional career at Yale University, where he also received his B.A. and Ph.D. His book, *The Purchasing Power of Money,* published in 1911, provided extensive evidence on the long-run proportionality between the quantity of money and the general level of prices.

The quantity theory of money was never popular with everyone. It was particularly unpopular with John Maynard Keynes (see Our Advancing Knowledge, p. 656). Keynes argued that there was but the loosest connection between the quantity of money and the price level. He described the lack of a connection with the ancient proverb, "there's many a slip twixt cup and lip." Keynes' views on the lack of a connection between money and the price level was so forcefully expressed that he was able to attract a very large following and his views became the dominant views in the 1950s and early 1960s.

Throughout the postwar years, Milton Friedman (see Our Advancing Knowledge, p. 657) had been quietly working away on his version of the quantity theory of money. In a monumental work with Anna J. Schwartz, *A Monetary History of the United States 1867–1960,* published in 1963, the role and importance of money in explaining fluctuations in the U.S. economy was argued and established. Then, in 1967, Friedman published what was to become a landmark paper, "The Quantity Theory of Money: A Restatement." In that paper, Friedman argued that the quantity theory of money, in its modern form, is a theory about the demand for money. There is, argued Friedman, a stable demand curve for real money and the demand for real money depends on the interest rate (the opportunity cost of holding money) and real income. Variations in the nominal money supply can produce short-run variations in real GNP and interest rates but, in the long run, all their effects are felt only on the price level.

Stemming from his views about the importance of money in influencing aggregate expenditure, Friedman formulated what has become a famous rule—the "*k* percent rule." Friedman said pick a number *k* equal to the average growth rate of real GNP and make the money supply grow steadily year after year at that rate. On the average, inflation will be zero. The economy will fluctuate but the fluctuations will be as small as they can possibly be made and smaller than those arising from active attempts to stabilize aggregate demand. Friedman's views were given the name "monetarism" by Karl Brunner, another proponent of Friedman's version of monetary theory and another advocate of steady money supply growth rules.

Brunner arrived in the United States in the 1950s from Switzerland and spent his teaching and research career at UCLA, Ohio State University, and the University of Rochester. Brunner and his lifelong collaborator Alan H. Meltzer (of Carnegie-Mellon University) founded the "Shadow Open Market Committee." This committee meets to make recommendations about monetary policy and open market operations that parallel those of the Federal Open Market Committee, the group making the real decisions.

Today, monetarism has a large following among economists working in central banks and advising governments, not only here in the United States but around the world. One of the leading younger monetarists, Michael Darby of UCLA, was a member of the administration's team of economists at the Reagan White House.

The quantity theory of money has always had its dissenters. Modern critics of the quantity theory of money include Thomas Sargent of Stanford's Hoover Institution, Bruce Smith of the University of Western Ontario, and Neil Wallace of the University of Minnesota. These scholars argue that the quantity of money is not the important variable for determining the general price level except in special circumstances. Only because there are legal tender laws and legal restrictions on bank reserve holdings does the quantity of money take on a special significance. More generally, they argue that it is the total value of outstanding government debt that is the important nominal magnitude for determining the general price level. Tests of their views remain controversial and more will have to be undertaken before it can be said that the foundations of the quantity theory of money have been destroyed.

There is more scope for the Fed's actions to be unpredictable when it is pursuing a feedback rule rather than a fixed rule, for in such a situation it is necessary to predict the future values of the variables to which the Fed reacts. Consequently, the feedback rule for monetary policy can create more unpredictable fluctuations in aggregate demand than a fixed rule. Economists disagree whether those bigger fluctuations offset the potential stabilizing influence of the predictable changes the Fed makes. No agreed measurements have been made to settle this dispute. Nevertheless, the unpredictability of the Fed is an important fact of economic life. Even in congressional testimony, Federal Reserve Board chairmen are reluctant to make the Fed's actions and intentions entirely plain. (It has even been suggested that two former chairmen of the Federal Reserve Board, the pipe-puffing Arthur Burns and the cigar-puffing Paul Volcker, carried their own smokescreens around with them as if to exemplify the mysteriousness and unpredictability of the Fed.)

It is not surprising that the Fed seeks to keep some of its actions behind a smokescreen. First, the Fed wants to maintain as much freedom of action as possible and so does not want to state with too great a precision the rules that it will follow in any given circumstances. Second, the Fed is part of a political process and, although constitutionally independent of the federal government, it is not immune to subtle influence. For at least these two reasons, the Fed does not specify feedback rules that are as precise as the one that we have analyzed in this chapter and so cannot deliver an economic performance that has the stability that we generated in the model economy.

If it is difficult for the Fed to pursue a predictable, feedback stabilization policy, it is probably impossible for Congress. Since the stabilization policy of Congress is formulated in terms of spending programs and tax laws and since those programs and laws themselves are the outcome of a political process that is constrained only by the Constitution, there can be no effective way in which a predictable feedback fiscal policy can be adhered to.

Variability of Aggregate Demand with Feedback Rules

Some economists argue that aggregate demand will not only be more unpredictable but will also fluctuate more with a feedback rule. The main thrust of the argument is that stabilization policies affect aggregate demand with a time lag that is long and impossible to predict. As a consequence, any policy action taken today will be inappropriate for the state of the economy at that uncertain future date when the policy's effects will be felt.

For example, when the Fed puts on the monetary brake, the first action is that interest rates increase. Some time later, higher interest rates produce a slowdown in investment and the purchases of consumer durable goods. Some time yet later still, this fall in expenditure reduces income, which in turn induces lower consumption expenditure. The sectors in which the spending cuts occur vary, and so does the impact on employment. It can take anywhere from nine months to two years for an initial action by the Fed to cause a change in employment, real GNP, and the inflation rate. Thus to smooth the fluctuations in aggregate demand, the Fed needs to take actions today, based on a forecast of what will be happening over a period stretching more than a year into the future. It is no use taking actions a year from today to influence the situation that then prevails. It's too late. Any actions taken then will have their effect yet two additional years into the future.

If the Fed were good at economic forecasting and based its policy actions on its forecasts, it is possible that it could deliver the type of ideal aggregate demand—smoothing performance that we assumed in the model economy that we studied earlier in this chapter. But if the Fed takes policy actions that are based on today's economy rather than on the forecasted economy a year in the future, then those actions will often be inappropriate ones. When unemployment is high and the Fed puts its foot on the accelerator, it speeds the economy back to full employment. But the Fed is not able to ease off the accelerator and gently tap the brake, holding the economy at its full-employment point. Instead, the accelerator pedal is left hard down as the economy races through the full-employment point and starts to experience shortages and inflationary pressures. Eventually, when inflation increases and unemployment falls below its natural rate, the Fed steps on the brake, pushing the economy back below full employment. The Fed's own reactions to the current state of the economy become one of the major sources of fluctuations in aggregate demand and the major factor that people have to forecast in order to make their own economic choices.

We noted that a fourth reason why economists do not agree on monetary policy is that they do not agree about the sources of aggregate fluctuations.

Those advocating feedback rules believe most fluctuations come from aggregate demand. Those advocating fixed rules believe that aggregate supply fluctuations are the dominant ones. Let's now see how aggregate supply fluctuations affect the economy under a fixed rule and a feedback rule, for monetary policy and see why those economists who believe that aggregate supply fluctuations are the dominant ones also favor a fixed rather than a feedback rule.

Stabilization Policy and Aggregate Supply

There are two reasons why aggregate supply fluctuations can cause problems for a stabilization feedback rule:

- Cost-push inflation

- Slowdown in growth or fall in capacity real GNP

In either of these situations, the economy experiences *stagflation*. Let's study the effects of alternative policies to deal with this problem.

Cost-Push Inflation

Cost-push inflation is inflation that has its origins in cost increases. The two most important potential sources of cost-push inflation are wage increases and increases in raw material prices (such as the increases in the price of oil that occurred in the 1970s and the early 1980s). To proceed, a cost-push inflation must be accommodated by an increase in the money supply—which in turn increases aggregate demand. A monetary policy feedback rule makes cost-push inflation possible. A fixed rule makes such inflation impossible. Let's see why.

Consider the economy that is shown in Fig. 33.4. Aggregate demand is AD_0, short-run aggregate

Figure 33.4   Monetary Policy and Aggregate Supply: A Wage Increase

(a) Fixed rule

(b) Feedback rule

The economy starts out on AD_0 and SAS_0, with a GNP deflator of 100 and real GNP of $4 trillion. A labor union (or a key supplier of raw materials) forces up wages (or the price of the raw materials), shifting the short-run aggregate supply curve to SAS_1. Real GNP falls to $3 trillion and the GNP deflator increases to 120. With a fixed money supply rule (part a), the Fed makes no change to aggregate demand. The economy stays depressed until wages (or raw material prices) fall again, and the economy returns to its original position. With a feedback rule (part b), the Fed injects additional money, increasing aggregate demand to AD_1. Real GNP returns to $4 trillion (full employment) but the GNP deflator increases to 130. The economy is set for another round of cost-push inflation.

supply is SAS_0, and long-run aggregate supply is LAS. Real GNP equals its capacity level of \$4 trillion and the GNP deflator is 100.

Now suppose that a number of labor unions, or the key suppliers of an important raw material such as oil, try to gain a temporary advantage by increasing the price at which they are willing to sell their services—by increasing wages or by increasing the price of the raw material. To make the exercise interesting, let's suppose that the people in question control a significant portion of the economy. As a consequence, when they increase the wage rate or the price of oil, the short-run aggregate supply curve shifts upward from SAS_0 to SAS_1.

Fixed Rule Figure 33.4(a) shows what happens if the Fed follows a fixed rule for monetary policy. With a fixed rule, the Fed pays no attention to the fact that there has been an increase in wages or raw material prices. The money supply growth rate will not be changed. (In this example, with a zero money supply growth rate, the money supply itself will remain constant.) The short-run aggregate supply curve will have shifted upward to SAS_1 and aggregate demand will stay at AD_0. The price level will rise to a GNP deflator of 120, and real GNP will fall to \$3 trillion. The economy is experiencing stagflation. Until such time as those responsible for increased wages or raw material prices reverse their action, the economy will be depressed and will remain depressed. This decrease in wages or raw material prices may take a long time to come about. Eventually, however, the low level of real GNP and associated high level of unemployment will bring about a lowering of wages —of those very wages whose increase caused the initial problem. Eventually, the short-run aggregate supply curve will shift back downward to SAS_0. The GNP deflator will fall to 100 and real GNP will increase to \$4 trillion.

Feedback Rule Figure 33.4(b) shows what happens if the Fed operates a monetary feedback rule. The starting point is the same as before—the economy is on SAS_0 and AD_0 with a GNP deflator of 100 and real GNP of \$4 trillion. Wages are increased and the short-run aggregate supply curve shifts upward to SAS_1. The economy goes into a recession with real GNP falling to \$3 trillion and the price level increasing to 120. The Fed's monetary feedback rule is to increase the money supply growth rate and to increase aggregate demand when real GNP is below

capacity. So, with real GNP at \$3 trillion, the Fed pumps up the money supply growth rate and shifts the aggregate demand curve to AD_1. The price level increases to 130 and real GNP returns to \$4 trillion. The economy moves back to full employment but at a higher price level. The unionized workers or the raw material suppliers, who saw an advantage in forcing up their wages or prices before, will see the same advantage again. Thus the short-run aggregate supply curve will shift up once more and the Fed will chase it with an increase in aggregate demand. The economy will be in a freewheeling inflation.

Incentives to Push Up Costs You can see that there are no checks on the incentives to push up costs if the Fed pursues a feedback rule of the type that we've just analyzed. If some group sees a temporary gain from pushing up the price at which they are selling their own resources and if the Fed always accommodates to prevent unemployment and slack business conditions from emerging, then cost-push elements will have a free rein.

But when the Fed pursues a fixed-rule policy, the incentive to attempt to steal a temporary advantage by increasing wages or prices is severely weakened. The cost of higher unemployment and lower output is a consequence that each group will have to face and recognize.

Thus a fixed rule is capable of delivering a steady inflation rate (or even zero inflation) while a feedback rule, in the face of cost-push pressures, will leave the inflation rate free to rise and fall at the whim of whichever group believes a temporary advantage to be available from pushing up its wage or price.

Slowdown in Capacity Growth

Some economists believe that fluctuations in real GNP (and in employment and unemployment) are caused not by fluctuations in aggregate demand but by fluctuations in the growth rate of long-run aggregate supply. These economists have developed a new theory of aggregate fluctuations called real business cycle theory. **Real business cycle theory** is a theory of aggregate fluctuations based on flexible wages and random shocks to the economy's aggregate production function. The word "real" draws attention to the idea that it is real things—random shocks to the economy's real production possibilities—

rather than nominal things—the money supply and its rate of growth—that are, according to that theory, the most important sources of aggregate fluctuations.

According to real business cycle theory, there is no useful distinction to be made between the long-run aggregate supply curve and the short-run aggregate supply curve. Because wages are flexible, the labor market is always in equilibrium at the natural rate of unemployment. The vertical long-run aggregate supply curve is also the short-run aggregate supply curve. Fluctuations occur because of shifts in the long-run aggregate supply curve. Normally, the long-run aggregate supply curve shifts to the right— the economy expands. But the pace at which the long-run aggregate supply curve shifts to the right varies. Also, on occasion, the long-run aggregate supply curve shifts to the left, bringing a decrease in aggregate supply and a fall in real GNP.

Economic policy that influences the aggregate demand curve has no effect on real GNP. But it does affect the price level. However, if a feedback policy is used to increase aggregate demand every time real GNP falls, and if the real business cycle theory is correct, the feedback monetary policy will make price level fluctuations more severe than they otherwise would be. To see why, consider Fig. 33.5.

Imagine that the economy starts out on aggregate demand curve AD_0 and long-run aggregate supply curve LAS_0, at a GNP deflator of 100 and with real GNP equal to $4 trillion. Now suppose that long-run aggregate supply falls to LAS_1. (An actual fall in long-run aggregate supply could occur as a result of a severe drought or other natural catastrophe or perhaps as the result of a disruption of international trade such as the OPEC embargo of the 1970s.)

Fixed Rule   With a fixed rule for the money supply, the fall in the long-run aggregate supply has no effect on the Fed and no effect on aggregate demand. The aggregate demand curve remains AD_0. Real GNP falls to $3 trillion and the GNP deflator increases to 120.

Feedback Rule   Now suppose that the Fed uses a feedback rule. In particular, suppose that when real GNP falls, the Fed increases the money supply to increase aggregate demand. In this example, the Fed increases the money supply and shifts the aggregate demand curve to AD_1. The Fed's goal is to bring real GNP back to $4 trillion. But the long-run aggregate

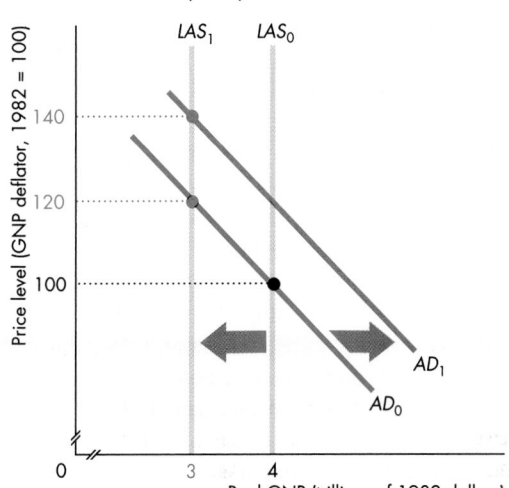

Figure 33.5   Monetary Policy and Aggregate Supply: A Capacity Decrease

A fall in capacity output shifts the long-run aggregate supply curve from LAS_0 to LAS_1. Real GNP falls to $3 trillion and the GNP deflator rises to 120. With a fixed money supply rule, aggregate demand stays at AD_0, and that is the end of the matter. With a feedback rule, the Fed increases the money supply, intending to increase real GNP. Aggregate demand moves to AD_1, but the long-run result is an increase in the price level—the GNP deflator rises to 140—with no change in real GNP.

supply curve has shifted and so capacity output has fallen to $3 trillion. The increase in aggregate demand cannot bring forth an increase in output if the economy does not have the capacity to produce that output. So, real GNP stays at $3 trillion but the price level rises still further—the GNP deflator goes to 140.

You can see that in this case the attempt to stabilize real GNP using a feedback monetary policy has no effect on real GNP but generates a substantial price level increase.

We've now seen some of the shortcomings of using feedback rules for monetary policy. Some economists believe that these shortcomings are serious and urge the Fed to implement a fixed rule. Others, regarding the potential advantages of feedback rules as greater than their costs, urge the Fed to continue to pursue such policies.

Controlling Inflation by Announcing Monetary Policy

Those who favor feedback rules often argue that not only should the Fed seek to vary its actions in light of current economic conditions but it should also seek to minimize the damage it does by clearly announcing the policy actions that it intends to follow. This argument has a special appeal when applied to slowing down inflation. When the Fed in fact slowed down inflation in 1981, we all paid a very high price. The Fed's monetary policy action was unpredicted and, as a result, occurred in the face of wages that had been set at too high a level to be consistent with the growth of aggregate demand that the Fed subsequently allowed. The consequence was high unemployment. Couldn't the Fed have lowered inflation without causing unemployment by telling people far enough ahead of time that it did indeed plan to slow down the growth rate of aggregate demand? Wouldn't wages then have increased less quickly, enabling inflation to be cured at much lower cost in terms of increased unemployment? In graphic terms, couldn't the Fed, by announcing its intentions, have made the short-run aggregate supply curve shift by the same amount as the Fed intended to shift the aggregate demand curve, keeping the two curves intersecting along the long-run aggregate supply curve?

The answer appears to be no. The main reason why is that people form their expectation of the Fed's action (like they form expectations about anyone's actions) on the basis of actual behavior, not on the basis of stated intentions. How many times have you told yourself that it is your firm intention to take off ten unwanted pounds, or to keep within your budget and put a few dollars away for a rainy day, only to discover that, despite your very best intentions, your old habits win out in the end?

Forming expectations about the Fed's behavior is no different except, of course, it is more complex than forecasting your own behavior. And it has as little to do with the Fed's stated intentions as your behavior does with your intentions. To form expectations about the Fed's actions, people look at its past actions, not its stated intentions. Based on such observations—called Fed-watching—they try to work out what the Fed's policy is, to forecast its future actions, and to forecast the effects of those actions on aggregate demand and inflation.

Stabilizing the U.S. Economy in the 1980s and 1990s

As the 1980s opened, the main stabilization problem facing the U.S. economy was that of eradicating a near 10 percent inflation that was beginning to look like a permanent feature of life. Let's look at the way in which the Fed got rid of that inflation.

The Fed's Finest Hour?

The U.S. economy in early 1981 could be compared to an overweight jogger: It was running in agony. While the economy was growing moderately, interest rates and inflation were high. Worst of all, people had resigned themselves to expect that prices would rise by about 10 percent a year forever.

In the closing months of 1980, the Fed had already put its foot firmly on the monetary brake, forcing interest rates up to more than 20 percent a year. But from January to April of 1981, the Fed eased off the brake and gently tickled the gas pedal. Then, in May 1981, the Fed slammed on the brake again. It was at this time that the Fed declared war on inflation. Foremost in the decision was Paul Volcker. Volcker's Fed slammed on the brakes of the economy by holding the growth rate of the money supply below the growth rate of the demand for money. Given less money than was being demanded, interest rates increased sharply and were held high for almost six months. With high interest rates, people spent less. To an economy expecting continual injections of money and continued inflation, the restriction was like withdrawl from an addiction.

The economy crashed. As industries suffered and people lost their jobs, observers began comparing the recession to the Great Depression. The White House and Congress pressured the Fed, and Volcker in particular, to ease up. Volcker, however, in congressional testimony, talked only of the importance of beating inflation.

The tremendous shock inflicted by the Fed knocked most of the inflation—and inflationary expectations—out of the economy (see Chapter 32, pp. 845–846). That done, the Fed stepped on the gas again and allowed the money supply to grow fast enough to keep interest rates falling and the economy growing. The economy enjoyed a powerful recovery with surprisingly low inflation from 1982 through 1989. Volcker had put the economy on a course that was to lead to the longest peacetime period of sustained expansion in U.S. economic history.

Paul Volcker became a villain to some. But to many more, even to farmers and to housebuyers who were hurt by his policies, he became a hero. People delighted in learning about the modesty and humanity of this powerful man. (Popular magazine articles portrayed Volcker living in his small Washington apartment, smoking cheap cigars, and taking his heap of dirty shirts to his daughter to be laundered.)

Many economists now say that Volcker achieved his goals. But while some economists believe that the economy needed his strong-arm methods, others feel that the Fed inflicted unnecessary pain. With delicate monetary tools at his disposal, critics claim, Volcker dropped the scalpel in favor of the hatchet.

Whatever the pros and cons of the particular episode, monetary policy did lower the inflation rate and the economy was put on its longest sustained peacetime recovery path ever. It is keeping that recovery going and preventing a renewed inflation that constitutes the major challenge of the 1990s. Let's now look at that challenge.

The Fed on a Tightrope

Although the Fed is not a circus act, it is a very experienced tightrope walker. Let's look at the balancing act confronting the Fed during the recovery years of the 1980s. Throughout this period, the Fed has been trying to promote the two broad policy goals that we've just noted. On the one hand, it wanted to nourish and sustain an economic recovery, keeping real GNP growth strong at around 3 percent a year on the average, and keeping unemployment close to its natural rate. On the other hand, it wanted to keep a tight rein on inflation. Having gone through an agonizing recession to snuff out inflation in the early 1980s the Fed did not want to see prices again climbing out of control. But keeping inflation under control requires keeping the growth of aggregate demand in check, and thereby running the risk of killing the recovery and touching off recession.

So, the Fed's tightrope act through the recovery years of the 1980s was to keep aggregate demand growing at a pace that balanced the needs of the growing economy and the fears of rekindling infla-

tion. If the money supply grew too slowly, it would snuff out the recovery; if it grew too fast, it would lead to inflation.

To balance on its tightrope, the Fed leaned first in one direction and then the other. During the early years of the recovery, from 1982 to 1987, the Fed leaned in the direction of permitting the money supply and aggregate demand to grow fast enough to take up the slack in the economy . But throughout this period, it kept money growth steady and on a steadily falling growth path. That is, the money supply grew, but at steadily declining rates.

By the fall of 1987, when the stockmarket crashed, the Fed was ready to ease off its gradual slowdown in money supply growth, fearing an impending recession, However, as the months passed and the feared recession kept failing to arrive, the Fed's concerns slowly turned from recession to inflation. With unemployment continuing to fall toward the 5 percent mark, and with signs of an upturn in inflation, the Fed became more and more convinced that it was about to fall off the tightrope into inflation and started leaning, gently and tentatively, in the opposite direction. It became more willing to risk falling off the tightrope into recession to avoid what it saw as the larger risk of falling off into inflation.

Unlike the circus tightrope walker, the Fed will probably never become completely sure-footed. For, the tightrope which the Fed has to walk is one that is constantly changing: The tension on the rope changes without warning and the winds that blow around it are constantly changing in force and direction. And, they change also without warning. Although not much is certain in the world of economics, one of the things about which we can be sure is that there will be many more recessions and inflationary upturns. The Fed will, from time to time, fall off that tightrope. (See Reading Between the Lines, pp. 886–887.)

■ We've now examined the main issues of stabilization policy. We've seen how fixed and feedback rules operate under differing assumptions about the behavior of the economy and why economists take different views on using these rules. Finally, we have looked at recent stabilization policy.

In the next chapter, we examine what many people believe is our economy's single most serious problem—the government's budget deficit.

Going for a Soft Landing

Tension Grows as President and Aides Push the Fed to Ease Its Credit Policy

WASHINGTON—Fasten your seat belts. The much-heralded "soft landing" may include some hard knocks—not just in the economy, but at the White House.

Economic growth so far this year has skidded to a 1.7% annual rate. And the Federal Reserve's latest forecast suggests that growth will slow further, hovering between 1% and 1.5% through the middle of next year. That's just the sort of "soft landing" many economists and Wall Street investors hope for.

But behind that benign-sounding expression lies a painful truth: Even a soft landing—with its benefits of avoiding both a recession and a surge in inflation—would inflict a lot of pain. It could throw half a million people onto the unemployment rolls, according to Data Resources Inc. . . . And it could shave $800 off the annual income of the average American family. . . .

Mounting Pressures
For the White House, . . . the Fed's projection isn't good enough. With mid-term congressional elections approaching and other pressures mounting, the administration needs more than a soft landing. It needs a perfect landing. . . .

The Bush team has made no secret of its view that a Fed-engineered soft landing isn't necessary to keep inflation under control. The administration's current forecast shows real growth softening only slightly, to a 2.6% pace next year, and then returning to 3%-plus in subsequent years. [Michael Boskin, the chairman of the President's Council of Economic Advisers,] says such a forecast is "consistent with stabilizing, and eventually falling, inflation." And Budget Director Richard Darman insists that "neither a recession or a soft landing is inevitable."

But in the battle over economic policy, the Fed holds most of the cards. Administration officials have little power to influence the economy over the next year and a half, but the Fed can do a great deal by manipulating short-term interest rates. If the central bank is determined to slow economic growth to less than 2%, it can.

Indeed, many economists believe that the Fed's tight-money policies earlier this year have already set the stage for not just a soft landing but a full-fledged recession. And at least one Fed official agrees.

Crash Landing?
"The next six months or so are cooked," says Fed Governor Martha Seger, who has tended to favor an easier monetary policy than most other governors. "It's going to be very difficult to land the aircraft in a nice, gentle way. Instead, we may take a wing off." . . .

Because the effects of the Fed's actions usually take months to work their way through the economy, the economic outlook for the next six months has largely been determined by credit-policy moves already taken. Similarly, the current easing probably won't have much effect until 1990. "Whatever we do now," Ms. Seger says, "I don't think it will affect the rest of the year very much."

In the past, episodes of rising interest rates have often been followed by recessions. The usual sequence of events: As the economic expansion ages, inflation begins to accelerate. The Federal Reserve responds by pushing up rates to rein in inflation. But, unable to foresee the future, the Fed makes a "mistake," pushes too far and squeezes the economy into recession.

The Wall Street Journal, July 31, 1989

Alan Murray, staff reporter

- Real GNP growth slowed to a 1.7 percent annual rate in the first half of 1989, and at mid-year, the Fed was forecasting 1 percent to 1.5 percent real GNP growth through mid-1990.

- Such a slowdown would increase unemployment, lower incomes, and make the administration less popular.

- With mid-term elections approaching, the White House wanted the Fed to ease its credit policy and keep real GNP growing at 2.6 percent in 1990 and over 3 percent in subsequent years, in the belief that such real GNP growth does not pose an inflation problem.

- But the Fed is the key actor in determining the course of monetary policy, and its actions take time to have an effect.

- Tight monetary policies early in 1989 pushed up interest rates and set the stage for a slowdown that could turn into a recession.

- Whatever the Fed's actions are in the rest of 1989, they could not affect economic growth during 1990, but if the Fed tightened further and if inflation accelerated, the economy could be pushed into recession.

Background and Analysis

- Three views of GNP and unemployment for 1990 are a "soft landing" (path *a* in Fig. 1), a "perfect landing" (path *b*), and a "crash landing"—recession (path *c*).

- Fears of slowdown and recession stemmed in part from the Fed's monetary policy (Fig. 2).

- Money growth was high and encouraged economic expansion through 1986, but money supply growth rates began to decline through 1987.

- Monetary policy was loosened again following the stock market crash of October 1987 but was further tightened by mid-1988 and, more severely, in the first half of 1989, as is evident in Fig. 2.

- Despite tight monetary policy and rising interest rates, real interest rates remained moderate into 1989 because of rising inflation (Fig. 3).

- Fed monetary policy began to ease in mid-1989, and interest rates started to fall.

- No one can predict with certainty the course of the economy over the next six to twelve months. The slowdown in money supply growth and rising interest rates pointed to a slowdown in the growth of demand and to a soft landing or even recession. But moderate *real* interest rates suggested that the landing could be very soft —as desired by the administration.

- Whether real GNP can grow indefinitely at over 3 percent without triggering an upturn in inflation depends on the source of that growth. Capital accumulation and a fast pace of technological change that increase capacity real GNP, shifting the long-run aggregate supply curve to the right at a rate of 3 percent or more each year, would permit continued expansion, with constant or even falling inflation, as foreseen by the White House.

- If long-run aggregate supply does not increase at such a pace, and if the Fed loosens its monetary policy to increase the growth rate of aggregate demand, the result will be higher inflation, not faster output growth.

Figure 1

Figure 2

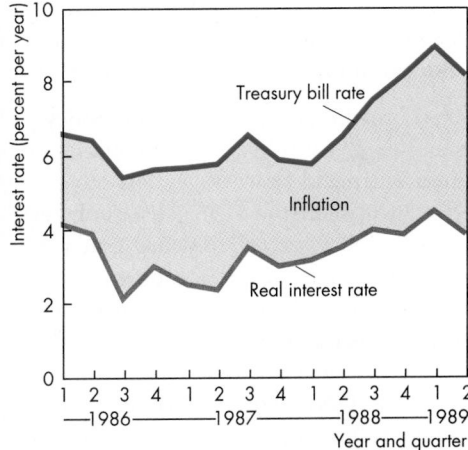

Figure 3

SUMMARY

The Stabilization Problem

The targets of macroeconomic policy fall into two categories: real and nominal. The real targets are to keep unemployment at its natural rate, achieve steady and sustained growth in real GNP, and maintain balanced international trade. The nominal targets are to achieve low and predictable inflation and stable exchange rates between the dollar and foreign currencies. Indexes of macroeconomic performance combine the real and nominal targets into a single measure. Three such measures are the misery index, an unpopularity index based on voter behavior, and a stabitization policy index based on a nominal GNP growth target. All three indexes paint a similar picture of U.S. macroeconomic performance: steady improvement through the 1960s; sharp deterioration through 1975; slight improvement and further deterioration through 1981; and steady improvement through the 1980s. (pp. 869–872)

The Key Players

The key players in the formulation and execution of macroeconomic policy are the Federal Reserve Board, Congress, and the Administration. The Federal Reserve Board makes the nation's monetary policy. Congress makes the fiscal policy, and the Administration, through its advice and persuasion, seeks to coordinate the use of separate branches of policy. (pp. 872–874)

Alternative Means Used to Stabilize the Economy

There are two broad types of stabilization policy: fixed rules and feedback rules. Since expectations about aggregate demand affect wages and other costs, and therefore affect short-run aggregate supply, expectations about policy, as well as actual policy actions, influence the course of the economy.

Fixed-rule policy permits the aggregate demand curve to fluctuate as a result of all the independent forces that influence demand. As a result, there are fluctuations in real GNP and the price level. Feedback-rule policy adjusts the money supply to offset the effects of other influences on aggregate demand. An ideal feedback rule would keep the economy at full employment, with stable prices.

Some economists argue that feedback rules require greater knowledge of the economy than we have, introduce unpredictability, generate bigger fluctuations in aggregate demand, and are ineffective in the face of the most prominent type of shock—an aggregate supply shock. Feedback rules are unpredictable because it is not possible for the Fed or Congress to specify with great clarity and precision ahead of time exactly how their policies will react to the state of the economy. Feedback rules induce greater variability in aggregate demand because actions are based on the current state of the economy and only have their effects many months later when the economy is in a different state from that which triggered the policy action. (pp. 874–881)

Stabilization Policy and Aggregate Supply

Two types of aggregate supply shock generate stabilization problems: cost-push inflation and changes in capacity real GNP. A fixed rule minimizes the threat of, and problems associated with, cost-push inflation. A feedback rule validates cost-push inflation and leaves the price level and inflation rate free to pursue whatever course they are pushed in. If capacity real GNP falls (or its growth rate slows down), a fixed rule results in lower output (and higher unemployment) and a higher price level. A feedback rule that increases the money supply to stimulate aggregate demand results in an even higher price level and higher inflation. Output (and unemployment) follows the same course as with a fixed rule. (pp. 881–884)

Stabilizing the U.S. Economy in the 1980s and 1990s

The main stabilization problem in 1980 was eliminating a severe inflation. To remove inflation, the Fed engineered a severe slowdown in the growth rate of aggregate demand by generating a sharp rise in interest rates. The result was an unanticipated fall in aggregate demand and a severe recession. The main problem as the U.S. economy enters the 1990s is to ensure a continuation of moderate inflation and sustained growth that characterized the 1980s. (pp. 884–885)

K E Y   C O N C E P T S

Cost-push inflation, 881
Federal budget, 872
Feedback rule, 874
Fixed rule, 874
Misery index, 870
Nominal targets, 870
Real business cycle theory, 882
Real targets, 870

Key Figures

Figure 33.3   Two Monetary Policies, 876
Figure 33.4   Monetary Policy and Aggregate Supply: A Wage Increase, 881
Figure 33.5   Monetary Policy and Aggregate Supply: A Capacity Decrease, 883

R E V I E W   Q U E S T I O N S

1 What are the goals of macroeconomic stabilization policy?

2 Describe three ways of measuring macroeconomic performance.

3 What are the main institutions that formulate and execute macroeconomic policy?

4 What is the distinction between a fixed rule and a feedback rule?

5 Analyze the effects of a decrease in aggregate demand that is temporary if a fixed money supply rule is employed.

6 Analyze the behavior of output and the price level in the face of a permanent decrease in aggregate demand under a fixed monetary rule and a feedback monetary rule.

7 Why do economists disagree with each other on the appropriateness of fixed and feedback rules?

8 Analyze the effects of a rise in the price of oil on real GNP and the price level if the Fed employs a fixed monetary rule.

P R O B L E M S

1 The economy is experiencing 10 percent inflation and 7 percent unemployment. Set out policies for the Fed and Congress to pursue that will lower both inflation and unemployment. Explain how and why your proposed policies will work.

2 The economy is booming and inflation is beginning to rise, but it is widely agreed that a massive recession is just around the corner. Weigh the advantages and disadvantages of the Fed pursuing a fixed and a feedback rule monetary policy.

3 You have been hired by the president to draw up a plan that will maximize the chance of his being re-elected.

a) What are the macroeconomic stabilization policy elements in that plan?

b) What do you have to make the economy do in an election year?

c) How important is it to keep inflation in check?

d) How important is it to prevent unemployment from rising?

e) What policy actions would help the president achieve his objective?

(In dealing with this problem, be careful to take into account the effects of your proposed policy on expectations and the effects of those expectations on actual economic performance.)

Chapter 34

After studying this chapter, you will be able to:

- Explain why, during the 1980s, the federal government spent more each year than it raised in taxes

- Distinguish between debt and the deficit

- Distinguish between the *nominal* deficit and the *real* deficit

- Explain why the deficit appears to be larger than it really is

- Describe the different means available for financing the deficit

- Explain why the deficit makes the Fed's job harder

- Explain why a deficit can cause inflation

- Explain why a deficit can be a burden on future generations

- Describe the measures that are being taken to eliminate the deficit

Every year since 1982, the U.S. government has spent at least $100 billion more than it has raised in taxes. This enormous gap between government spending and taxes, called the deficit, is a larger proportion of the U.S. economy than has ever occurred except in time of war. Why do we have deficits? Why is the deficit so large? ■ The deficit is large. In fact, it is so large that Governor Michael Dukakis, during the 1988 presidential election campaign, observed that during the eight years of Ronald Reagan's presidency, the total debt of the U.S. government increased by more than in the entire previous 204 years since the Declaration of Independence. Is the deficit really so large? How can we gauge the scale of the deficit when there is so much inflation going on? How big is the deficit when we adjust for changes in the value of money? ■ Some countries, such as Bolivia, Chile, Brazil, and Israel, have had large government deficits and runaway inflations. In an earlier era, following World War I, Germany suffered an enormous budget deficit as a result of being required to make payments to France in compensation for damage inflicted during the war. That deficit produced a hyperinflation—an inflation of more than 50 percent per month. The fact that deficits have, at other times and places, produced extraordinary inflations raises the question for us today: Will the U.S. government's deficit lead to a renewed outburst of inflation? Does the deficit somehow make it harder, or even impossible, for the Fed to control the money supply and keep inflation in check? ■ When we incur a personal debt, that debt has to be repaid. Thus when we incur a debt, we incur a self-imposed burden to repay the debt with interest. This fact leads to worries that when the nation incurs a debt as a result of a government deficit, a burden is being placed not just on ourselves later but on our children and grandchildren. Does a

Spendthrift Uncle Sam

government deficit create a burden on future generations?   ■ There are two ways in which we can approach any problem: Pretend it doesn't exist or try to identify its nature and solve it. How are we approaching the deficit? Are we sticking our heads in the sand like ostriches or are we taking steps that are calculated to eliminate the deficit in a reasonably short time span? What are the prospects for the future of the deficit?

■ In this chapter, we're going to study what perhaps became the hottest economic topic of the 1980s. We're going to examine the origins of the deficit, gauge its true scale, and explain why deficits are feared and why they constitute a problem. We'll also discuss some of the measures that are being taken to eliminate the deficit. Because the deficit is a hot economic and political topic, the public debate on it has generated more heat and smoke than light. In this chapter, we'll clear away some of the rhetorical smoke, lower the temperature, and try to answer the questions posed above. By the time you're through with this chapter, you'll be able to explain what the deficit is all about.

The Sources of the Deficit

What exactly is the deficit? The federal government's **budget surplus** or **deficit** is the difference between the taxes it receives and its total expenditure in a given period of time. Normally the period of time over which we measure the government's surplus or deficit is a year. The government's total expenditure is the sum of government purchases of goods and services, transfer payments, and interest on the government's debt. If taxes exceed expenditure, the federal government has a surplus. If expenditure exceeds taxes, the government has a deficit. Thus we can define the government's surplus/deficit as follows:

$$\text{Surplus/deficit} = \text{Taxes} - \text{Expenditures}.$$

If the surplus/deficit is zero, in other words if taxes and expenditures are equal, the government's budget is balanced. A **balanced budget** is a government budget that is in neither surplus nor deficit.

Government debt is the total amount of borrowing that the government has undertaken and the total amount that it owes to households, firms,

Figure 34.1   The Deficit

The figure records the surplus (above the balanced budget line) and the deficit (below the balanced budget line) from 1960 to 1988. The deficit that first emerged in the early 1970s has become large and persistent.

Source: Economic Report of the President, 1989.

Figure 34.2   The Government Debt

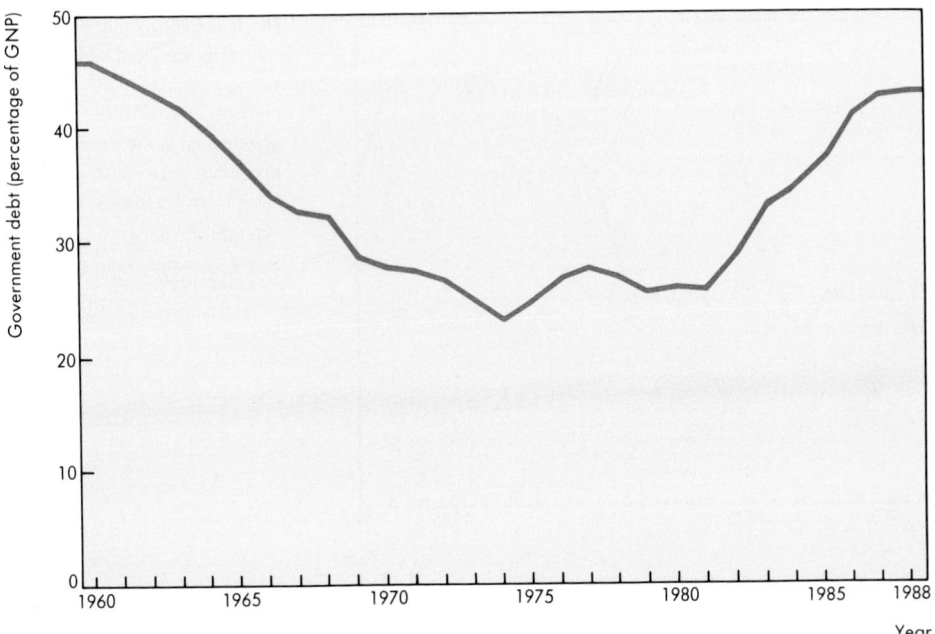

Government debt (the accumulation of past deficits less past surpluses) declined through 1973 but then started to move upward. After a further brief decline in the late 1970s, it exploded in the 1980s.

Source: Economic Report of the President, 1989.

and foreigners. Government debt is a stock. It is the accumulation of all the past deficits, minus all the past surpluses. Thus if the government has a deficit, its debt is increasing. If the government has a surplus, its debt is decreasing. If the government has a balanced budget, its debt is constant.

The Federal Budget
Since 1960

The federal government's deficit, measured as a percentage of GNP, is shown in Fig. 34.1. The deficit is shown as a percentage of GNP, rather than in billions of dollars, so that we can see its importance in relation to the scale of the economy—because of economic growth and inflation, GNP in 1988 was almost ten times what it was in 1960.

The scale on which we measure the surplus/deficit records a surplus as a positive number and a deficit as a negative number. The zero line in the graph indicates a balanced budget. Thus as the deficit gets larger, the line on the deficit graph goes further below zero—the balanced budget line.

As Fig. 34.1 illustrates, the last time the U.S. federal government had a budget surplus was in 1969. Before that time, with the exception of periods of war, the federal government's budget has been more or less in balance. A small deficit began to appear in the early 1970s, and by 1975 the deficit exceeded 4 percent of GNP. The deficit declined to less than 1 percent of GNP by 1979. A larger deficit then started to appear in the early 1980s, and although in the closing years of the 1980s the deficit began to shrink again, it remained throughout most of the 1980s at close to 4 percent of GNP, and one of the nation's most discussed economic issues.

The effect of the deficit on the government's debt is shown in Fig. 34.2. As you can see, debt as a percentage of GNP declined through 1974, when it reached its lowest point since World War II. It increased slightly in the 1970s and dramatically between 1981 and 1986. In the late 1980s, its growth continued but at a more moderate rate.

Why has the government deficit grown? The immediate sources of the deficit can be seen in Fig. 34.3. As you can see, throughout the 1960s, taxes

Figure 34.3   Taxes and Expenditure

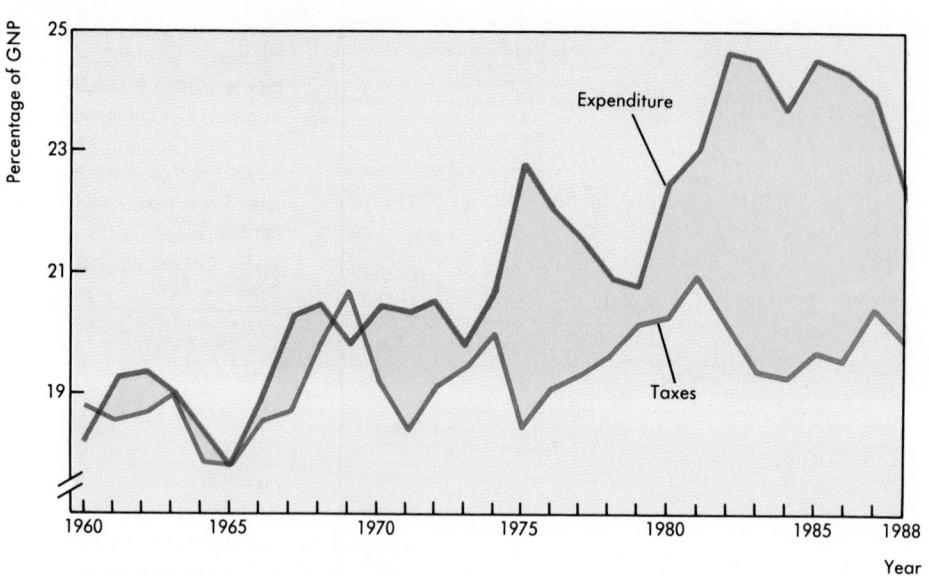

The figure shows that the deficit has arisen from continued strong increases in the percentage of GNP spent by the government in the face of taxes that have remained much more steady as a percentage of GNP.

Source: Economic Report of the President, 1989.

and expenditures fluctuated more or less in line with each other. In 1969, when a small surplus emerged, taxes increased and spending decreased. But starting in 1970, spending started to increase much more quickly than taxes, with particularly sharp increases in spending in 1975 and again in 1980–1982.

Which elements of government spending are the ones that have increased most sharply? And why haven't taxes kept pace with the rising spending? Let's answer these questions by looking at taxes and spending in a bit more detail.

Taxes

There are four broad categories of taxes:

• Personal income taxes
• Corporate income taxes
• Indirect taxes
• Social security taxes

Personal Income Taxes   Personal income taxes are the taxes paid by individuals on their labor and capital incomes. These taxes have fluctuated between 8 and 10 percent of GNP and have averaged around 9 percent of GNP. There has been no tendency for

the total amount paid in personal income taxes to rise or fall over the 1970s and 1980s.

Corporate Income Taxes   Corporate income taxes are the taxes that companies pay on their profits. In the 1960s, these taxes averaged 4 percent of GNP. But they have fallen gradually over the years until, by the middle 1980s, they represented only 2 percent of GNP.

Indirect Taxes   Indirect taxes are taxes on the goods and services that we buy and include the customs duties that we pay when we import goods from other countries. As in the case of corporate income taxes, these taxes also have decreased (as a percentage of GNP) over the years. In 1960, they stood at 2 percent of GNP and by the middle 1980s they had fallen to 1.5 percent.

Social Security Taxes   Social security taxes are the taxes that are paid by employees and employers to finance the social security programs. These taxes, in contrast to the others that we have just considered, have increased steadily over the past 30 years. In 1960, they represented 3.5 percent of GNP, but by 1988 they had climbed to more than 8 percent.

Total Taxes   When all four of the components of taxes are added together, we find that their total has remained a remarkably stable percentage of GNP—standing at about 19 percent. As we have just noted, personal income taxes have themselves remained almost constant, averaging 9 percent of GNP. Social security taxes have increased, but the effect of that increase on total taxes has been offset by decreases in revenue from corporate income taxes and indirect taxes.

Next let's consider spending.

Expenditure

We will examine government expenditure by dividing it into four categories:

- Defense purchases
- Other purchases of goods and services
- Transfer payments
- Interest payments

Defense Purchases   Defense is the biggest item in the federal government's shopping basket for goods and services. In 1960 it cost 9 percent of GNP. After falling slightly in the middle 1960s, defense purchases returned to their 1960 level throughout the years of the Vietnam War. During the 1970s, defense spending declined, but it increased again in the 1980s.

Other Purchases of Goods and Services   Other purchases, although important, are the small-change items bought by the federal government and cost a steady 1.5 to 2 percent of GNP. These items have not changed in importance during the past 30 years.

Transfer Payments   Transfer payments are the largest element of spending. They include payments of social security and welfare benefits to households and subsidies to farms and other producers. Payments in these categories have increased persistently throughout the past 30 years and increased sharply between the late 1960s when they represented 5 percent of GNP and the early 1980s when they stood at 10 percent of GNP.

Interest Payments   Interest payments are the amounts paid by the government to the holders of its bonds—its outstanding debt. In 1971, this item was around 1 percent of GNP. But as a large deficit emerged during the second half of the 1970s, the total amount of government borrowing began to increase. Increased borrowing led to increased interest payments on that debt. By the 1980s, the federal government's interest payments had grown to 3 percent of GNP—three times their importance in 1971.

Total Spending   Total spending steadily increased throughout the 1970s and 1980s, and once a persistent deficit had emerged, that deficit began to feed on itself. The deficit led to increased borrowing; increased borrowing led to higher interest payments; and higher interest payments led to a larger deficit. That is the story of the 1980s.

A Personal Analogy   Perhaps you will see more clearly why the deficit feeds on itself if you think in more personal terms. Suppose that each year, you spend more than you earn. Suppose that you keep on doing this. Your debt, let's say at the bank, rises each year. Therefore, you owe the bank more in interest each year as a result of having a bigger debt outstanding. The government is in exactly the same situation. But the government doesn't just borrow from banks. It borrows from anyone who buys the bonds that it issues—households, firms, the Fed, and foreigners. The government has been running a deficit continuously since 1970, so its outstanding debt has been rising and the interest payments on that debt have also been rising.

The Deficit and the Business Cycle

There is an important relationship between the size of the deficit and the stage of the business cycle through which the economy is passing. This relationship is illustrated in Fig. 34.4. This figure tracks the deficit against the business cycle—as measured by deviations of GNP from trend. As you can see, the last time the federal government had a surplus, the economy was experiencing boom conditions—real GNP was substantially above trend. The deficits of the 1970s, all the way through to 1982, followed the business cycle. The years in which the deficit became especially large were years of severe recession—the OPEC recession of 1975 and the Volcker recession of 1981 to 1982. Why does the deficit become larger when the economy goes into recession? Part of the answer lies on the spending side and part on the taxes side of the government's account.

Figure 34.4   The Business Cycle and the Deficit

The business cycle (deviations of GNP from trend) and the deficit move together. A recession leads to lower taxes, higher transfer payments, and a higher deficit. A recovery leads to higher taxes, lower transfer payments, and a lower deficit. Despite the strong recovery of the 1980s, the deficit has persisted.

Source: Economic Report of the President, 1989.

The scale of government spending and taxes depends on the state of the economy. The government passes tax laws defining tax *rates,* not *dollars* to be paid in taxes. As a consequence, the taxes that the government collects depend on the level of income: If the economy is in a recovery phase of the business cycle, tax collections rise; if the economy is in a recession phase of the business cycle, tax collections fall.

Spending programs behave similarly. Many government programs are related to the state of well-being of individual citizens and firms. For example, when the economy is in a recession, unemployment is high, economic hardship from poverty increases, and a larger number of firms and farms experience hard times. Government transfer payments increase to respond to the increased economic hardship. When the economy experiences boom conditions, expenditure on programs to compensate for economic hardship declines.

In light of both of these factors, the deficit rises when the economy is in a depressed state and falls when the economy is in a state of boom. In order to take into account these facts, economists have developed a modified deficit concept called the cyclically adjusted deficit. The **cyclically adjusted deficit** is the deficit that would occur if the economy were at full employment. To measure the cyclically adjusted deficit, we calculate what taxes and expenditures would be if the economy were at full employment.

The formula established by the Department of Commerce[1] for determining the effect of the business cycle on the deficit has two key elements:

- Each one-percentage-point increase in the unemployment rate increases the federal deficit by $30 billion.

- Each $100 billion decrease in current dollar GNP increases the deficit by $35 billion.

The Deficit in Recovery

Since 1982, the economy has been in a prolonged and strong recovery. According to the formula for calculating the effect of the business cycle on the deficit, the deficit should have fallen dramatically through these years. But it has not done so. It has persisted at around 3 percent of GNP. It is the

---

[1]Thomas M. Holloway, "The Economy in the Federal Budget: Guides to the Automatic Effects," *Survey of Current Business* 64, 7 (July 1984): 102–5.

persistence of a large deficit, even in the face of strong economic recovery, that leads some observers to express grave concern about the potential effects of an ongoing deficit on the long-term health of the economy. Since we have a deficit of about 3 percent of GNP with the economy in a boom condition, any recession that now hits us will increase the deficit. To figure out roughly by how much, we can use the Department of Commerce's two rules. Suppose that GNP falls by 2 percent (about $80 billion) and that the unemployment rate increases by 2 percentage points. The fall in GNP will increase the deficit by $28 billion, the rise in the unemployment rate will increase the deficit by $60 billion, so the deficit will increase by $88 billion and soar to more than 5 percent of GNP.

R E V I E W

The federal government deficit has emerged because spending has increased much more strongly in the 1970s and 1980s than taxes. Taxes have fluctuated but around a constant average value. In contrast, spending has trended upward. In the 1980s, defense spending and transfer payments moved upward. So did debt interest payments. The deficit has been feeding on itself. A higher deficit has led to higher borrowing, which in turn has led to higher interest payments and a yet higher deficit.

The deficit is related to the business cycle. Other things being equal, the stronger the economy, the lower is the deficit. In the economic recovery of the 1980s, the relationship between the state of the economy and the deficit was broken—the deficit remaining large with the economy in a strong recovery. If a deep recession were to occur now, the deficit would climb to more than 5 percent of GNP. ■

We've now seen where the deficit came from and how it relates to the business cycle. We've also seen that not only is the deficit large but has persisted, despite the fact that the economy has undergone a strong and prolonged recovery. But is the deficit really as bad as it looks? Can it really be true that in eight years the national debt increased by more than in the entire previous history of the nation? These are important questions to which we'll now turn our attention.

The Real Deficit

Inflation distorts many things, not least of which is the deficit. To remove the inflationary distortion from the measured deficit, we need a concept of the real deficit. The **real deficit** is the change in the real value of outstanding government debt. The real value of outstanding government debt is equal to the market value of the debt divided by the price level. We are going to see how we can calculate the real deficit and how such a calculation changes our view of the size of the government's deficit. But before we do that, let's consider real deficits in more personal terms by examining the real deficit of a family.

The Real Deficit of a Family

In 1960, a young couple (perhaps your parents) ran a deficit to buy a new house. The deficit took the form of a mortgage. The amount borrowed to cover the deficit—the difference between the cost of the house and what the family had available to put down as a deposit—was $30,000. Today, the children of that couple are buying their first house. To do so, they also are incurring a deficit. But they're borrowing $120,000 to buy their first house. Is the $120,000 deficit (mortgage) of the 1990 house-buyer really four times as big as the deficit (mortgage) of the 1960 house-buyer? In dollar terms, the 1990 borrowing is indeed four times as big as the 1960 borrowing. But in terms of what money will buy, these two debts are almost equivalent to each other. Inflation in the years between 1960 and 1990 has raised the prices of most things to about four times what they were in 1960. Thus a mortgage of $120,000 in 1990 is really the same as a mortgage for $30,000 in 1960.

When a family buys a new home and finances it on a mortgage, it has a deficit in the year in which it buys the home. But in all the following years, until the loan has been paid off, the family has a surplus. That is, each year the family pays to the lender a sum of money, part of which covers the interest on the outstanding debt, but part of which *reduces* the outstanding debt. The reduction in the outstanding debt is the household's surplus. Inflation has another important effect here. Because inflation brings higher prices, it also brings a lower real value of outstanding debts. Thus the real value of the mortgage declines by the amount paid off each year plus the amount wiped out by inflation. Other things being equal, the higher the inflation rate, the faster is the mortgage really paid off, and the larger is the household's real surplus.

The Government's Real Deficit

This line of reasoning applies with equal force to the government. Because of inflation, the government's deficit is not *really* as big as it appears. To see how we can measure the deficit and correct for the distortion of inflation, we'll work through a concrete numerical example. First, look at Case A in Table 34.1.—a situation in which there is no inflation. Government expenditure, excluding debt interest, is $17 billion and taxes are $20 billion. Thus if the government didn't have interest to pay, it would have a surplus of $3 billion. But the government has outstanding debt of $50 billion and interest rates are running at 4 percent. Thus the government must pay $2 billion of debt interest (4 percent on $50 billion). When we add the $2 billion of debt interest to the government's other spending, we see that the government's total expenditure is $19 billion, so the government has a $1 billion surplus. The government's debt falls to $49 billion—the $50 billion outstanding at the beginning of the year is reduced by the surplus that the government has run. Ignore the last two rows of Table 34.1 for the moment.

Next, let's look at this same economy with exactly the same spending, taxes, and debt but in a situation in which there is a 10 percent inflation rate—Case B in Table 34.1. With 10 percent inflation, the market interest rate will not be 4 percent, but 14 percent. The reason why the interest rate is higher by 10 percentage points is that the real value of outstanding debt declines by 10 percent a year. Lenders—the households, firms, and foreigners that are buying government debt—know that the money that they will receive in repayment of the loans they are making to the government will be worth less than the money that they are lending out. The government also recognizes that the money that it will use to repay its debt will have a lower value than the money that it borrows. Thus the government and the people from whom it borrows readily agree to a higher interest rate that compensates for these foreseen changes in the value of money. So, with a 14 percent interest rate, the government has to pay $7 billion in debt interest—14 percent of $50 billion. When the $7 billion of debt interest is added to the govern-

Table 34.1   How Inflation Distorts the Deficit

	Case A	Case B
Government expenditure (excluding debt interest)	$17 billion	$17 billion
Taxes	$20 billion	$20 billion
Government debt	$50 billion	$50 billion
Market interest rate	4%	14%
Inflation rate	0%	10%
Real interest rate	4%	4%
Debt interest paid	$ 2 billion	$ 7 billion
Surplus(+)/deficit(−)	+$ 1 billion	−$ 4 billion
Government debt at end of year	$49 billion	$54 billion
Real government debt at end of year	$49 billion	$49 billion
Real surplus(+)/deficit(−)	+$ 1 billion	+$ 1 billion

Inflation distorts the measured deficit by distorting the debt interest payments made by the government. In this example, the real interest rate is 4 percent and government debt is $50 billion, so debt interest in real terms is $2 billion. With no inflation, Case A, the actual debt interest paid is also $2 billion. At 10 percent inflation, Case B, interest rates rise to 14 percent (in order to preserve a real interest rate of 4 percent), and debt interest increases to $7 billion. The deficit increases by $5 billion from a surplus of $1 billion to a deficit of $4 billion. This deficit is apparent, not real. With 10 percent inflation, the real value of the government's debt falls by $5 billion, offsetting the deficit of $4 billion, and resulting in a $1 billion real surplus.

ment's other spending, total expenditure is $24 billion, $4 billion more than taxes. Therefore the government has a deficit of $4 billion. At the end of the year, the government's debt will have increased from $50 billion to $54 billion.

The difference between the two situations that we've just described is a 10 percent inflation rate. Nothing else is different. What the government is actually spending and receiving is the same and the real interest rate is the same in the two cases. But at the end of one year, government debt has increased to $54 billion in Case B and has fallen to $49 billion in Case A. But the real debt is the same in the two cases. You can see that by keeping in mind that although government debt increases to $54 billion in Case B, the prices of all things have increased by 10 percent. If we deflate the government debt in Case B to express the debt in constant dollars instead of current dollars, we see that real government debt has actually fallen in Case B to $49 billion. ($54 billion divided by 1.1—1 plus the proportionate inflation rate—equals $49 billion.) Thus even in Case B, the real situation is that there is a surplus of $1 billion. Inflation makes it appear that there is a $4 billion deficit when really there is a $1 billion surplus.

The numbers in Table 34.1 are, of course, hypothetical. They deal with two imaginary situations. But the calculations that we've just done provide us with a method of adjusting the U.S. government deficit to eliminate the effects of inflation and reveal the real deficit. How important is it to adjust the U.S. deficit for inflation in order to obtain an inflation-free view of the deficit?

The Real and Nominal Deficit in the United States

Figure 34.5 provides an answer to the above question. The nominal and real deficits (or surpluses) of the United States are plotted alongside each other. As you can see, although a large nominal deficit emerged after 1975, the real deficit, even in 1975, was less than 1 percent of GNP. In the late 1970s through 1981, there was really a surplus. But since 1981, the real deficit has been large, although not quite as large as the nominal measure of the deficit.

The reason why the large nominal deficits of the late 1970s were not real deficits is that inflation was high during those years. Only when inflation declined in the mid-1980s, while interest rates remained high, did a large and persistent real deficit emerge. You can see then that the distinction between the real and nominal deficit is an important practical distinction. Taking into account the distinction dramatically changes our view of the scale and seriousness of the deficit in the United States today. But it does not remove our concern. Looking at the deficit in real terms tells us that the emergence of a deficit is a relatively recent phenomenon. It is also, however, a serious phenomenon. We have now been running a real deficit since 1982 on a scale that has averaged close to 3 percent of GNP.

Let's now go on to examine some of the effects of a deficit.

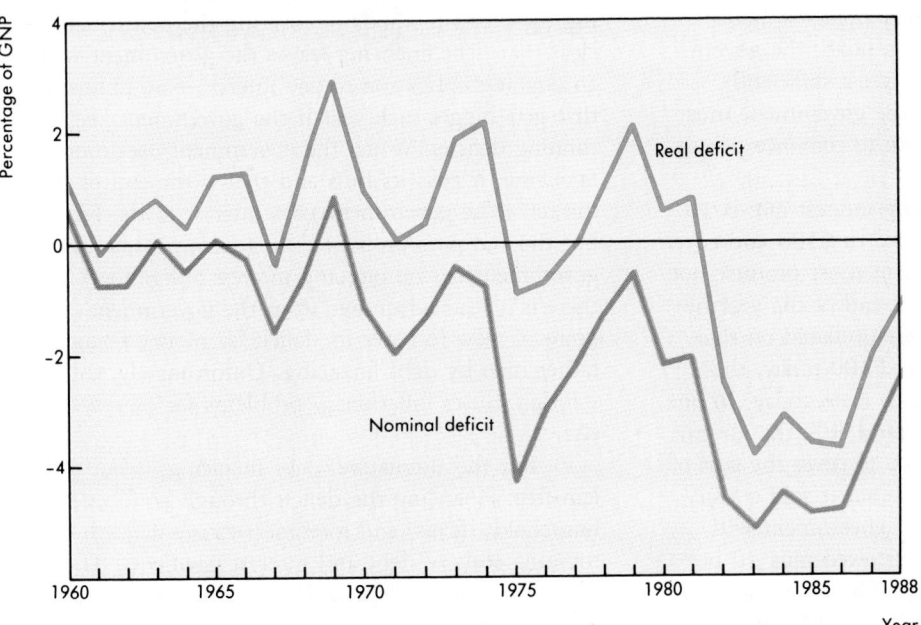

Figure 34.5 The Real Deficit and the Nominal Deficit

The real deficit removes the effects of inflation from interest rates and from the outstanding value of government debt. The real deficit and the nominal deficit follow a similar path, but the real deficit is lower than the nominal deficit (or the real surplus is higher than the nominal surplus). Only when real interest rates became high in the 1980s did a serious and persistent real deficit arise.

Source: Economic Report of the President (various years). The real deficit is my calculation. The inflation rate of the GNP deflator was used to convert the federal government deficit into real terms.

Deficits and Inflation

Many people fear government deficits because they believe deficits lead to inflation. Do deficits cause inflation? That depends on how the government finances the deficit.

Financing the Deficit

To finance its deficit, the government sells bonds. But the effects of bond sales depends on who buys the bonds. If they are bought by the Fed, they bring an increase in the money supply. If they are bought by anyone other than the Fed, they do not bring a change in the money supply. When the Fed buys government bonds, they pay for them by creating new money (see Chapter 28, p. 734). We call such financing of the deficit money financing. **Money financing** is the financing of the government deficit by the sale of bonds to the Federal Reserve System which results in the creation of additional money. All other financing of the government's deficit is called debt financing. **Debt financing** is the financing of the government deficit by selling bonds to anyone (household, firm, or foreigner) other than the Federal Reserve System.

Let's look at the consequences of these two ways of financing the deficit, starting with debt financing.

Debt Financing   First, suppose that the government borrows money by selling treasury bonds to households and firms. In order to sell a bond, the government must offer the potential buyer a sufficiently attractive deal. In other words, the government must offer a high enough rate of return to convince people to lend their money.

Let's suppose that the going interest rate is 10 percent. In order to sell a bond worth $100 and cover its deficit of $100, the government must promise not only to pay back the $100 at the end of the year but also to pay the interest of $10 accumulated on that debt. Thus to finance a deficit of $100 today, the government must pay $110 a year from today. In one year's time, in order simply to stand still, the government would have to borrow $110 to cover the cost of repaying, with interest, the bond that it sold a year earlier. Two years from today the government will have to pay $121—the $110 borrowed plus 10 percent interest ($11) on that $110. The process continues with the total amount of debt and total interest payments mushrooming year after year.

Money Financing   Next, consider what happens if instead of selling bonds to households and firms, the government sells treasury bonds to the Fed. There are two important differences in this case compared with the case of debt financing. First, the government winds up paying no interest on these bonds; second, additional money gets created.

The government ends up paying no interest on bonds bought by the Fed because the Fed, although an independent agency, pays its residual profits to the government. Thus other things being equal, if the Fed receives an extra million dollars from the government in interest payments on government bonds held by the Fed, the Fed's profits increase by that same million dollars and flow back to the government. Second, when the Fed buys bonds from the government, it uses newly created money to do so. This newly created money flows into the banking system in the form of an increase in the monetary base and enables the banks to create yet additional money by making additional loans (see Chapter 27 and Chapter 28).

As we studied in Chapter 24 and Chapter 31, an increase in the money supply causes an increase in aggregate demand. Higher aggregate demand eventually brings a higher price level. Persistent money financing leads to continuously increasing aggregate demand and to inflation.

Debt Financing vs. Money Financing   In comparing these two methods of covering the deficit, it is clear that debt financing leaves the government with an ongoing obligation to pay interest—an obligation that gets bigger each year if the government keeps running deficits. When the government uses money financing, it pays its bills and that is the end of the matter. (The government pays interest to the Fed, but the Fed pays profits to the government, so the government has no ongoing interest obligation.) Thus there is a clear advantage from the government's point of view to cover its deficit by money financing rather than by debt financing. Unfortunately, this solution causes inflationary problems for everybody else.

But the alternative, debt financing, is not problem-free. Financing the deficit through bond sales to households, firms, and foreigners causes a mushrooming scale of debt and interest payments. The larger the scale of debt and interest payments, the bigger the deficit problem becomes, and the greater is the temptation to end the process of debt financing and begin to finance the deficit by selling bonds to the Fed—money financing. This ever-present temptation is what leads many to fear that deficits are inflationary even when they are not immediately money financed. It has even been suggested, recently, that debt financing is more inflationary than money financing. Let's examine this proposition more closely.

Unpleasant Arithmetic

To study the effects of financing a government deficit with debt issue versus money creation, suppose that the government has a deficit of a given size, which it plans to maintain indefinitely. Initially, the government covers its deficit by creating money. Consequently, the economy experiences inflation. The inflation rate depends on the deficit's size. The larger the deficit, the larger is the sum of money that will have to be created and the faster will aggregate demand increase. The faster aggregate demand increases, other things being equal, the higher will be the inflation rate.

Suppose the economy is experiencing steady inflation as a result of a money-financed deficit and the government tries to slow the inflation by slowing down the growth rate of the money supply and covering its deficit by selling bonds to the public. It makes no changes in its spending and taxing policies, so the deficit, excluding debt interest, remains constant. The deficit, including debt interest, begins to grow. Furthermore, everyone understands this fact. The people to whom the government wants to sell bonds fully realize that with an ongoing deficit financed by bond sales, the deficit will have to increase to cover the additional interest payments arising from the growing national debt. They will also reason that at some point, the amount of government debt outstanding will have grown so large that the interest burden on it will be larger than the government is willing to pay. At that point, they continue to reason, the government will do what it can do here and now—cover its deficit by money financing. But the key difference is that to cover the deficit here and now by money financing only requires that the deficit, excluding debt interest, be money financed. The longer the government attempts to cover its deficit by debt financing, the larger is the deficit (the original deficit plus the additional interest burden) that will ultimately have to be paid for by creating money.

Thus people continue to reason, at some future time the government will resort to creating money and there will be rapid inflation. At that time, the government bonds that are being bought today will lose value at such a rapid rate as to make them almost worthless. Hence, if government bonds are going to be bought today, the interest rate on them must be sufficient to compensate for the foreseen future loss in their value resulting from the future inflation that will eventually arise. And, in anticipation of a fall in the value of money, people will reduce the amount of money that they plan to hold here and now. This reduction in the demand for money will lead to an increase in the demand for goods and so to rising prices.

This argument was first advanced by Thomas Sargent (of the Hoover Institution at Stanford University) and Neil Wallace (of the University of Minnesota). They called their calculations unpleasant monetarist arithmetic. It is unpleasant arithmetic because deferring the date at which a deficit is financed by money creation worsens the inflation that will ensue. It is unpleasant *monetarist* arithmetic because it constitutes a direct attack on the central proposition of monetarism—inflation is caused by the growth rate of the money supply. If the money supply growth rate is contained, inflation will not erupt. The unpleasant monetarist arithmetic calculations point out that the deficit must be sufficiently small to provide confidence in the ability and willingness of the government and the Fed to continue to keep money supply growth in line with the growth in the economy's capacity to produce goods and services. A deficit that is too large to reinforce that expectation will be inflationary.

But for the deficit to be the problem that Sargent and Wallace say it is, it must be a truly persistent phenomenon. A deficit that is large and that lasts even for a decade does not inevitably have to produce inflation. If expectations are widely held that the deficit is going to be brought under control at some reasonably near future date, then the unpleasant arithmetic, although correct, is not relevant.

We have now reviewed the relationship between deficits and inflation. Deficits are not inevitably inflationary. But the larger the deficit and the longer it persists, the greater the pressures and the greater the temptations to cover the deficit by creating money, thereby generating inflation.

Another common view about the deficit is that it places a burden on future generations. Let's now examine that view.

A Burden on Future Generations?

It is a common and popular cry that "we owe it to our children to control the deficit." Is this popular view correct? How would the deficit burden future generations?

We've already examined one way in which the deficit might leave a burden on future generations—the burden of inflation. But when people talk about the deficit as a burden on future generations, they usually mean something other than inflation.

For example, somebody has to pay the interest on the huge national debt that the deficit creates. The government will pay the interest with money it takes from the people as taxes. Taxes will have to be raised. Won't those taxes burden future generations?

Wait, though: Don't the people who pay the taxes also receive the interest? If so, how can the deficit be a burden to future generations? It might be a burden to some members of the future generation, but it must be a benefit to others, so that in the aggregate it evens out.

Although in the aggregate the interest paid equals the taxes collected, there may be important redistribution effects. For example, one feature of our present deficit is that some government debt is being bought not by Americans but by European and Japanese investors. So part of the future burden of the current deficit is that future American taxpayers will have to provide the resources with which to pay interest to foreign holders of U.S. government debt.

There's another way in which today's deficit can make people poorer tomorrow: By slowing today's pace of investment and reducing the stock of productive capital equipment available for future generations. This phenomenon is called crowding out.

Crowding Out

Crowding out is the tendency for an increase in government purchases of goods and services to bring a decrease in investment (see Chapter 29, pp. 768–769). If crowding out does occur, and if government purchases of goods and services are financed by government debt, the result is that the economy has a larger stock of government debt and a smaller stock of real capital. Unproductive government debt replaces productive real capital.

Whether or not crowding out actually occurs is a controversial issue. Let's see why it might be im-portant. In order for crowding out to occur, a deficit has to result in lower investment, so that future generations have a smaller capital stock than they otherwise would have had. This drop in investment will lower their income and, in a sense, be a burden to them. (They will still be richer than they were but not as rich as they would have been if they had a larger stock of productive machines.) Let's examine how the deficit might be a burden to future generations as a result of lowering investment today.

As we studied in Chapter 25, the scale of investment depends on its opportunity cost. That opportunity cost is the real interest rate. Other things being equal, the higher the real interest rate, the less firms will want to invest in new plant and equipment. For a government deficit to crowd out investment, it must be the case that a deficit causes interest rates to rise. Some people believe that a deficit does increase interest rates because the government's own borrowing represents an increase in the demand for loans with no corresponding increase in the supply of loans. Figure 34.6 shows what happens in this case. Part (a) shows the demand and supply curves for loans. Initially, the demand for loans is D_0 and the supply of loans is S_0. The real interest rate is 3 percent, and the quantity of loans outstanding is $1 trillion. Part (b) shows investment. At a real interest rate of 3 percent, investment is $0.8 trillion. Now suppose that the government runs a deficit. To finance its deficit, the government borrows. There is an increase in the demand for loans. The demand curve for loans shifts from D_0 to D_1. There is no change in the supply of loans, so the real interest rate increases to 4 percent and the quantity of loans increases to $1.2 trillion. Notice that the increase in loans that occurs in equilibrium is smaller than the increase in the demand for loans. That is, the demand curve shifts to the right by a larger amount than the increase in loans that actually occurs. The higher interest rate brings a decrease in investment and a lower capital stock. Thus the increased stock of government debt crowds out some productive capital.

Does a deficit make real interest rates rise as shown in Fig. 34.6? Many economists believe so, and they have some pretty strong evidence to point to. Real interest rates in the United States in the 1980s, in precisely the years in which we have had a large real deficit, have been higher than at any time in history. Furthermore, there is a general tendency for real interest rates and the real deficit to fluctuate in sympathy with each other.

Figure 34.6 The Deficit, Borrowing, and Crowding Out

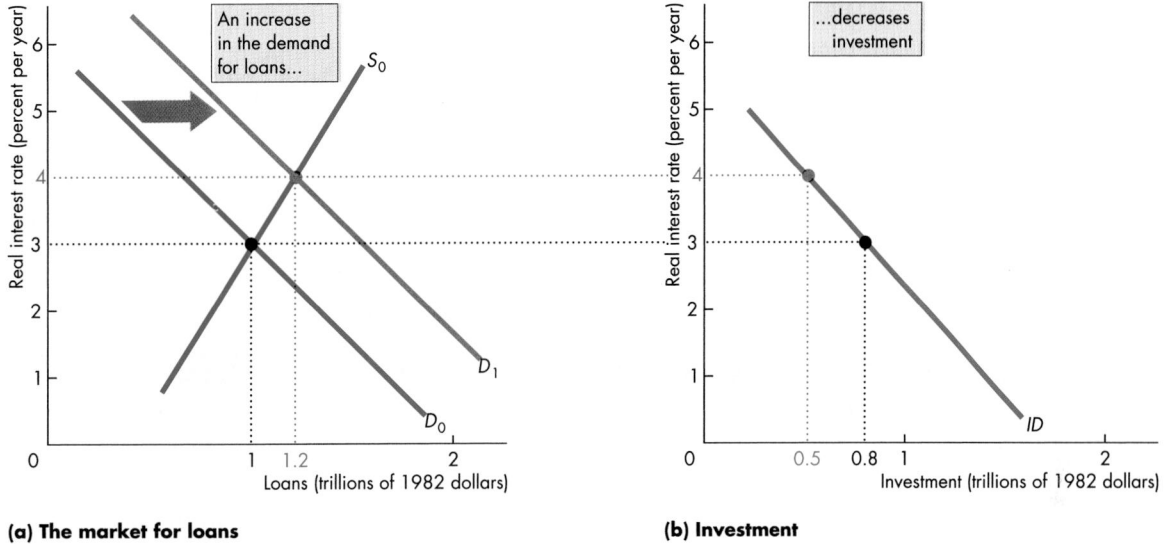

(a) The market for loans

(b) Investment

Part (a) shows the market for loans. The demand for loans is D_0 and the supply is S_0. The quantity of loans outstanding is $1 trillion and the real interest rate is 3 percent. Part (b) shows the determination of investment. At an interest rate of 3 percent, investment is $0.8 trillion. The government runs a deficit and finances the deficit by borrowing. The government's increase in demand for loans shifts the demand curve to D_1. The interest rate rises to 4 percent and the equilibrium quantity of loans increases to $1.2 trillion. The higher interest rate leads to a decrease in investment in part (b). The government deficit crowds out capital accumulation.

It is this relationship in the data that leads some economists to predict that a higher real deficit means higher real interest rates, lower investment, and a smaller scale of capital accumulation. Because of its effects on real interest rates, the real deficit and the accumulation of paper debt crowds out the accumulation of productive physical capital. As a consequence, future output will be lower than it otherwise would have been and so the deficit burdens future generations.

Ricardian Equivalence

Some economists do not believe that deficits crowd out capital accumulation. On the contrary, they argue, debt financing and paying for government spending with taxes are equivalent. The level of purchases of goods and services matters but not the way in which it is financed.

The first economist to advance this idea (known as Ricardian equivalence) was the great English economist David Ricardo (see Our Advancing Knowledge, pp. 904–905). Recently, Ricardo's idea has been given a forceful restatement by Robert Barro of Harvard. Barro argues as follows: If the government increases its purchases of goods and services but does not increase taxes, people are smart enough to recognize that higher taxes are going to have to be paid later in order to cover the higher spending and interest payments on the debt that is being issued today. In recognition of having to pay higher taxes later, people will cut their consumption now, increasing their saving so as to ensure that when the higher taxes finally are levied by the government, sufficient wealth has been accumulated to meet those tax liabilities without a further cut in consumption. The scale of increased saving matches the scale of increased government spending.

David Ricardo and the Deficit

T he economic landscape of England at the end of the eighteenth century was an exciting and rapidly changing one. Britain had left the Gold Standard in 1797, and by 1799, the price of gold was rising rapidly; equivalently, the value of paper money was falling rapidly. That same year, a 27-year-old stockbroker, on a weekend visit to Bath, happened upon a copy of *The Wealth of Nations* (see Our Advancing Knowledge, pp. 22–23), a book of which he was to become "a great admirer." The young man in question was David Ricardo (1772–1832), possibly the greatest economist of his time.

Born in London in 1772 into a devout Jewish family, Ricardo began his career at the age of 14, working for his father, a wealthy stockbroker. At 21, Ricardo displeased his father in the extreme by marrying a Quaker and was banished from the family business and disinherited. Continuing to work on his own as a stockbroker, Ricardo demonstrated real brilliance, amassing a fortune of £775,000—equivalent to $2.4 *billion* in today's money.

David Ricardo

Ricardo made important contributions to explaining a host of economic problems and issues, ranging from the value of money to the theory of value, exchange, and international trade, and laid the foundations of modern public finance theory. His most significant work was *On the Principles of Political Economy*, published in 1817. Though Ricardo was an eminently practical man, this book, and much of his other writing, dealt with abstract and difficult matters of theory—matters that remain controversial even today among historians of economic thought.

But, theoretical as it is, much of Ricardo's work has practical consequences. His contribution that has the most relevance for us today is that on public debt and on what has come to be called Ricardian equivalence. The idea of Ricardian equivalence was set out in a brief paper entitled "Funding System," which was first published in the relatively obscure *Supplement to the Fourth, Fifth and Sixth Editions of the Encyclopedia Britannica.*

Although the words used by him are open to several interpretations, Ricardo is usually held to have asserted in that article that, if people take full account of the future tax burden that will have to be imposed in order to pay the interest on public debt, then financing government purchases with current taxes is equivalent to financing it with debt and paying interest on that debt in perpetuity. But Ricardo also expressed his belief that people do not in fact make such rational calculations when making decisions on whether to consume or save.* As a consequence, tax-financing of government purchases leads to lower private consumption and lower interest rates than does debt-financing.

Interest in Ricardo's work was revived in the mid-1970s by Robert Barro (then at the University of Chicago, now at Harvard University). Using a model economy in which each generation takes account of the effects of its own actions on the consumption possibilities of the succeeding generation, Barro showed some of the conditions under which Ricardo's equivalence theorem holds.** But, as Barro pointed out, almost every other model in use in the mid-1970s assumed that debt and taxes were *not* equivalent.

The issue of Ricardian equivalence took on an extremely practical note when, in the early 1980s, President Reagan proposed cutting taxes in the face of an already-large deficit. Some economists claimed that Ricardian equivalence was a valid description of the U.S. economy and that a tax cut that increased the deficit would have no adverse effects. Interest rates would *not* increase, and private saving would increase to finance the increased amount of government debt outstanding. Others (and the majority) claimed that Ricardian equivalence was an abstract idea of little or no practical relevance and that a tax cut would stimulate aggregate demand, resulting in a deficit that would create a debt to burden on future generations. In the majority, and among Barro's most vocal critics, were Martin Feldstein, chairman of President Reagan's Council of Economic Advisers, and Nobel Laureate James Buchanan.

A series of studies of the issue, undertaken during the 1980s, has failed to come to a decisive conclusion, although one of the most recent of these studies, by Paul Evans[†] of Ohio State University, suggests that U.S. consumers are indeed Ricardian—that Ricardian equivalence is a "reasonable approximation." But the issue has yet to be settled.

---

*Gerald P. O'Driscoll, Jr., "The Ricardian Nonequivalence Theorem," *Journal of Political Economy* 85, 1 (1977): 207–210.

**Robert J. Barro, "Are Government Bonds Net Worth?" *Journal of Political Economy* 82, 6 (1974): 1095–1117.

†Paul Evans, "Are Consumers Ricardian? Evidence for the United States," *Journal of Political Economy* 96, 5 (1988): 983–1004.

Figure 34.7   Ricardian Equivalence

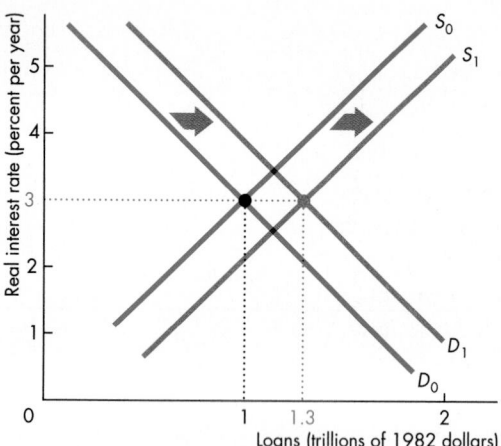

Initially, the demand for loans is D_0 and the supply of loans is S_0. The equilibrium quantity of loans is $1 trillion and the real interest rate is 3 percent. An increase in the government deficit, financed by borrowing, increases the demand for loans, shifting the demand curve to D_1. Households, recognizing that the increased government deficit will bring increased future taxes to pay the additional interest charges, cut their consumption and increase their saving. The supply curve of loans also shifts to the right to S_1. The equilibrium quantity of loans increases to $1.3 trillion, but the real interest rate stays constant at 3 percent. There is no crowding out of investment.

Figure 34.7 illustrates this case. Initially the demand for loans is D_0 and the supply of loans S_0. The real interest rate is 3 percent and the quantity of loans outstanding is $1 trillion. The government runs a deficit and finances that deficit by borrowing. The demand curve for loans shifts to the right to D_1. At the same time, using the reasoning of Ricardo and Barro, there is a cut in consumption and an increase in the supply of loans. The supply curve shifts to the right to S_1. The quantity of loans increases from $1.0 to $1.3 trillion and the real interest rate stays constant at 3 percent. With no change in the real interest rate, there is no crowding out of investment.

Some economists argue that Ricardian equivalence breaks down because people only take into account future tax liabilities that will be borne by themselves and not by their children and their grandchildren. Proponents of the Ricardian equivalence proposition argue that it makes no difference whether future tax liabilities are going to be borne by those currently alive, or by their descendants. If the taxes are going to be borne by children and grandchildren, the current generation takes into account those future taxes and adjusts its own consumption so that it can make bequests on a large enough scale to enable those taxes to be paid.

Laying out the assumptions necessary for Ricardian equivalence leaves most economists convinced that the proposition cannot be empirically relevant. Yet there is a perhaps surprising amount of evidence in its support. In order to interpret the evidence, it is important to be clear that Ricardian equivalence does *not* imply that real interest rates are not affected by the level of government purchases of goods and services. A high level of government purchases, other things being equal, brings a higher real interest rate. The Ricardian equivalence proposition implies that real interest rates are not affected by the way in which a given level of government purchases is financed. Regardless of whether it is financed by taxes, or by borrowing, real interest rates will be the same.

Figure 34.8 presents some evidence that provides support for Ricardian equivalence. It plots the real interest rate against the percentage of GNP spent by the government. As you can see, that percentage has been steadily increasing over the years. But the cycles in government spending match the cycles in the real interest rate.

Whether it is the deficit or the level of government purchases of goods and services that affects real interest rates remains unclear. If people do take into account future tax burdens (and not just their own but their children's and grandchildren's future tax burdens), then saving will respond to offset the deficit and the deficit itself will have little or no effect on real interest rates and capital accumulation. If people ignore the implications of the deficit for their own and their descendants' future consumption possibilities, the deficit will indeed increase real interest rates. The jury remains out on this question.

Eliminating the Deficit

Measures to eliminate the deficit can attack the problem on either the revenue side or the expenditure side. That is, there are two ways to eliminate the deficit:

Figure 34.8   Government Purchases and the Real Interest Rate

According to Ricardian equivalence, debt and taxes are equivalent and real interest rates are influenced by the level of government purchases of goods and services but not by the way in which those purchases are financed. Fluctuations in real interest rates are brought about by fluctuations in the level of government purchases. The recent history of government purchases as a percentage of GNP and real interest rates in the United States provides an interpretation of recent high real interest rates that is consistent with the Ricardo neutrality view. The alternative view is that debt and taxes are *not* equivalent and that real interest rates are influenced by the real deficit. Economists are still trying to devise decisive tests to discriminate between the two views.

Source: Economic Report of the President, 1989.

- Reducing expenditure
- Increasing revenue

Reducing Expenditure

There are four main proposals for reducing federal government expenditure:

- Cutting revenue to force spending cuts
- Line-item veto
- Gramm-Rudman-Hollings Act
- Balanced budget amendment

Cutting Revenue to Force Spending Cuts The approach adopted by the Reagan administration toward the deficit, and one advocated by Milton Friedman, is based on the view that Congress behaves like an undisciplined child. The child wants more candy. Give the child a dollar, and the child will buy more candy. Take a dollar away from the child, and the child will scream, but will eventually find a way of managing without candy. Revenue was certainly cut back in the 1980s. As you can see by looking back at Fig. 34.3, taxes as a percentage of GNP declined each year through 1984. They increased (again as a percentage of GNP) in the subsequent years but did not return to their 1981 peak levels. It is impossible to say what the exact effects of these revenue cuts were on spending. It does seem likely, however, that the revenue decrease was in part responsible for keeping the lid on the growth of expenditure and social programs through the 1980s. But, as we have seen, it has not reduced spending to the level of taxes. If this method works, it works on a time frame that is more drawn out than most people regard as sensible.

Line-Item Veto   In order to give the administration more power to help bring spending under control, it has been suggested that the president be given a line-item veto. A **line-item veto** is a veto power vested in the executive branch to eliminate any specific item in a budget. Many state governors have a line-item veto but the President of the United States does not. When Congress passes a bill calling for expenditures and taxes, the president must either sign the bill into law in its entirety or veto it in its entirety. He cannot eliminate particular items.

Some people believe that giving the president this power would bring a sharper and more precise scalpel to bear on the spending-cutting process. But it has to be borne in mind that the budget itself emerges as a result of compromise and is Congress's own best attempt to balance competing claims on public resources. If the president had such a veto power, there would likely be an increase in lobbying effort on the executive branch itself and there would be no guarantee that the president would be tougher on spending than is Congress.

Gramm-Rudman-Hollings   In an attempt to impose budget discipline by the legislative process, Senators Gramm, Rudman, and Hollings sponsored an act of Congress that sets guidelines for automatic spending cuts in the event that Congress is not able to bring in a budget that satisfies a target reduction path for the deficit. Since Congress makes the budget and since Congress also legislates the target path of the deficit reduction, the Gramm-Rudman-Hollings Act can be viewed as a kind of self-declared target that Congress seeks to meet. But over and above this, the idea of specifying a target is that Congress can itself do a more disciplined job if it specifies global objectives that are independent of the individual spending lines that add up to that total. It can then eliminate or pare down individual lines if the global objectives are missed.

Balanced Budget Amendment   Many want to go further than a congressional self-imposed balanced budget strategy. They want to amend the Constitution of the United States to include a formula for

requiring the federal government to balance its budget. Many economists, including Nobel laureates Milton Friedman and James Buchanan, advocate a balanced budget amendment to the Constitution.

Those favoring a balanced budget amendment argue two things. First, the process of debating and achieving the amendment would itself increase the level of awareness of the importance of financial discipline on the federal government. Second, once such an amendment were in place, Congress would have a cast-iron excuse for not satisfying all the many claims and demands imposed upon it and would, in effect, be able to take refuge behind the balanced budget law. Those who argue against such an amendment argue that it is difficult, if not impossible, to frame the law in such a way as to make it effective.

Throughout modern history, government expenditure has tended to increase not only in total but as a percentage of GNP. The federal government of the United States has done better than most governments to contain the growth of government expenditure. In some European countries, governments spend close to 50 percent of GNP. At its peak, that percentage increased to more than 53 percent in the Netherlands in 1983.

Many elements of government expenditure have a built-in tendency to increase. Two of these are education and health care. High income people spend a larger fraction of income on these items than do those with low incomes. If the government plays a significant role in the provision of these two goods, it is inevitable that government purchases and transfer payments, expressed as a percentage of GNP, will gradually rise. Only by removing from the domain of government certain responsibilities can the government's share of GNP be effectively contained. Thus in many European countries the government is getting out of a wide variety of activities involving the manufacture and provision of services. The Thatcher government in Britain, for example, is even trying to get out of the health care business, or at least limit its involvement in that sector. There is less scope for such "privatization" in the United States, for we have not taken the route of the Europeans in this regard.

Thus there is little scope for significant cuts in government expenditure as long as we maintain our global defense obligations and our obligations under social security and other programs such as social insurance, education, welfare, and health maintenance for the poor and the elderly.

It is because of the difficulty of making significant inroads into government spending that many take the view that the only way to eliminate the deficit is to increase government revenue. Let's now examine that option.

Increasing Revenue

Two approaches to increasing revenue have been proposed:

- Increase tax rates
- Decrease tax rates

Sound paradoxical? Not really, when you remember that what the government wants to do is to increase its tax *revenue*. **Tax revenue** is the product of the tax rate and the tax base. A **tax rate** is the percentage rate of tax levied on a particular activity. The **tax base** is the activity on which a tax is levied. For example, the tax base for personal income tax is earned income minus some specified allowances. The tax rates are 15 percent and 28 percent (depending on income level).

There is ambiguity and disagreement about whether an increase in tax rates increases or decreases tax revenues. The source of the disagreement is something called the Laffer curve. The **Laffer curve** (named after Arthur Laffer, who first proposed it) is a curve that relates tax revenue to the tax rate. Figure 34.9 illustrates a hypothetical Laffer curve. The tax rate ranges between zero and 100 percent on the vertical axis. Tax revenue, measured in billions of dollars, is shown on the horizontal axis. If the tax rate is zero, then no taxes are raised. That is why the curve begins at the origin. As the tax rate increases, tax revenue also increases but only up to some maximum—*m* in the figure. In this example, once the tax rate has reached 40 percent, the tax revenue is at its maximum. If the tax rate increases above 40 percent, tax revenue falls. Why does this happen?

Revenue falls because there is a fall in the scale of the activity that is being taxed. Suppose that the item in question is gasoline. With no tax, lots of people drive gas-guzzling cars and consume billions of gallons a week. If gasoline is taxed, its price increases and the quantity bought declines. At first, the quantity bought falls by a smaller percentage than the percentage increase in tax, and the tax revenue rises. But there comes a point at which the fall in the quantity demanded rises by a bigger

Figure 34.9   The Laffer Curve

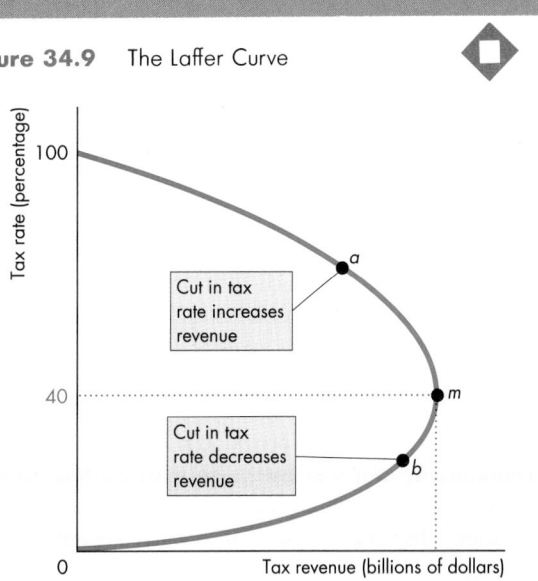

The Laffer curve shows the relationship between a tax rate and tax revenue. If the tax rate is 0 percent, the government collects no tax revenue. As the tax rate increases, the government's tax revenue also increases, but up to some maximum (*m*). As the tax rate continues to increase, tax revenue declines. At a tax rate of 100 percent, the government collects no revenue. Higher taxes act as a disincentive. The more heavily taxed is an activity, the less that activity is undertaken. When the percentage decrease in the activity is less than the percentage increase in the tax rate, we are at a point such as *b* and tax revenue rises. When the percentage decrease in the activity exceeds the percentage increase in the tax rate, we are at a point such as *a* and tax revenue decreases.

percentage than the rise in taxes. At that point, tax revenue begins to decline. People sell their gas-guzzlers, buy smaller cars, join car pools, and use public transportation. The tax rate goes up, but the tax base goes down and tax revenue declines.

You can now see that whether a cut in the *tax rate* increases or decreases *tax revenue* depends on where we are on the Laffer curve. If we're at a point such as *a* in Fig. 34.9, a decrease in the tax rate results in an increase in tax revenue. But if we're at point *b,* a decrease in the tax rate results in a decrease in tax revenue. To increase tax revenue from point *b,* we have to increase the tax rate.

Economists, and other observers, argue about where we are on the Laffer curve for each of the various taxes. Some people suspect that for the very highly taxed commodities such as gasoline, tobacco products, and alcohol, we are on the "backward-bending" part of the Laffer curve, so that an increase in the tax rate would decrease tax revenue. But hardly anyone believes this to be the case for the big revenue-raising taxes such as personal income taxes and sales taxes. It is much more likely, in the case of those taxes, that an increase in tax rates would increase tax revenue.

The second approach to increasing revenue is to reform taxes, lowering high marginal tax rates and perhaps introducing new taxes at low rates on activities not previously taxed.

The search for changes in taxes that will bring higher tax revenue is a permanent feature of our economic life and will always be with us, regardless of whether or not there is a deficit. But in a deficit situation, that search takes on a much greater urgency.

■ We have now completed our study of macroeconomics and of the challenges and problems of stabilizing the economy. In this study, our main focus has been the economy of the United States. Occasionally, we have taken into account the linkages between the United States and the rest of the world, but international economic relations have not been our main concern. In the remaining chapters we are going to shift our focus and study some vital international issues. First, in Chapter 35, we examine the international exchange of goods and services. Second, in Chapter 36, we study the financing of international trade and the determination of the value of our dollar in terms of other currencies. Third, we turn our attention to the problems of the poor developing countries of the Third World. Fourth, and finally, we examine economic systems different from our own, such as those employed in the Soviet Union and China.

S U M M A R Y

The Sources of the Deficit

The U.S. federal government deficit has arisen because the percentage of GNP spent by the federal government has grown more quickly than the percentage collected in taxes. The last time taxes exceeded expenditure was in 1969 and the deficit, although fluctuating, has tended to get larger, especially through the 1980s. The main elements of spending that have increased are transfer payments and debt interest. After a period of decline, defense spending has also increased in recent years. But the main persistent source of an increasing deficit in the 1980s has been the increasing debt interest.

The deficit fluctuates in sympathy with the business cycle. When the economy is in a recovery, taxes increase and transfer payments decrease as a percentage of GNP. The deficit declines. When the economy goes into recession, taxes decrease and transfer payments increase as a percentage of GNP, and so the deficit increases.

Adjusting the deficit for the effects of the business cycle results in the cyclically adjusted deficit. After cyclical adjustment, the current deficit is large. That is, the deficit is large, despite the fact that the economy has had a long, strong recovery. It is this fact that makes the current deficit a serious problem. (pp. 892–897)

The Real Deficit

Inflation distorts the deficit by overstating the real interest burden carried by the government. Adjusting the deficit for this fact and measuring the real deficit reveals that the deficit has become a persistent problem only since 1981. The cycles in the deficit remain the same, whether measured in real or current dollar terms. (pp. 897–899)

Deficits and Inflation

If deficits are money financed, they cause inflation. If they are debt financed, whether or not they cause inflation depends on how permanent they are. A temporary debt-financed deficit will have no inflationary effects. A permanent debt-financed deficit leads to inflation. It does so because the build-up of debt leads to a build-up of interest payments and a yet higher deficit. At some future date, the deficit will be money financed and the amount of money created will be larger, the longer the deficit persists and the more debt is issued. Fear of future inflation leads to a demand here and now for less government debt and less money. As a consequence, interest rates and inflation increase in anticipation of a future (and perhaps distant future) increase in money creation to finance the deficit. (pp. 900–901)

A Burden on Future Generations?

Whether the deficit is a burden on future generations is a controversial issue. Some economists believe that the deficit causes real interest rates to rise, thereby lowering investment and the amount of capital that we accumulate. As a consequence, future output will be lower than it otherwise would have been and future generations will be "burdened" with the effects of the deficit.

Other economists argue that government expenditure affects interest rates but the way in which that expenditure is financed does not. They suggest that if government spending is financed by borrowing, people will recognize that future taxes will have to increase to cover both the spending and the inter-

est from the accumulated debt. And, in anticipation of those higher future taxes, saving will increase and consumption will decrease in the present. Thus the burden of increased government expenditure—not the burden of the deficit—is spread across all generations. (pp. 902–906)

Eliminating the Deficit

The deficit can be eliminated by either reducing expenditure or increasing revenue, or by a combination of the two. There are four main proposals for reducing expenditure: cut revenue and wait for Congress to gradually bring spending into line; give the president a line-item veto; pursue target spending cuts such as those proposed in the Gramm-Rudman-Hollings Act; introduce a constitutional amendment requiring the Congress to balance the federal budget. Increasing revenue could result from either increasing tax rates (if we are on the upward-sloping part of the Laffer curve) or decreasing tax rates (if we are on the backward-bending part of the Laffer curve). (pp. 906–910)

K E Y   C O N C E P T S

R E V I E W   Q U E S T I O N S

1 What were the main changes in taxes and government spending associated with the emergence of the federal government deficit?

2 Trace the events since 1980 that resulted in a continued increase in the federal government's deficit.

3 What is meant by the cyclically adjusted deficit?

4 Distinguish between the real deficit and the nominal deficit.

5 In calculating the real deficit, which of the following would you do?

a) Value the interest payments in real terms and take into account the change in the real value of government debt.

b) Calculate the interest payments in nominal terms and take into account the change in the real value of government debt.

c) Calculate the interest payments in real terms but ignore the change in the real value of outstanding government debt.

6 Explain how debt financing a deficit results in mushrooming interest payments.

7 Explain how, in a modern sophisticated financial system, the government finances its deficit by creating money.

8 Review the ways in which the deficit can be a burden on future generations.

9 Why do some economists argue that taxes and government debt are equivalent to each other so that the deficit does not matter?

10 What are the four main proposals for reducing government expenditure?

11 Why do some economists think that government revenue can be increased by cutting tax rates?

P R O B L E M S

1 You are given the following information about an economy: When unemployment is at its natural rate, which is 5.5 percent, government spending and taxes are each 20 percent of GNP. There is no inflation. For each 1 percentage point increase in the unemployment rate, government spending increases by 1 percentage point of GNP and taxes fall by 1 percentage point of GNP.

Suppose that the economy experiences a cycle in which the unemployment rate takes the following values.

Year	1	2	3	4	5	6	7
Unemployment rate	5	6	7	6	5	4	5

a) Calculate the actual deficit (as a percentage of GNP) for each year.

b) Calculate the cyclically adjusted deficit for this economy.

2 Government expenditure, excluding debt interest, in an economy is $8.5 billion. Taxes are $10 billion. The government has a $25 billion outstanding debt. Interest rates are 24 percent and there is a 20 percent inflation rate. Calculate the following:

a) The debt interest that the government pays

b) The government's budget surplus or deficit

c) The value of the government debt outstanding at the end of the year

d) The government's real deficit

e) The real value of its debt outstanding at the end of the year

Part 11

Anne Krueger pioneered the study of the effects of international trade protection on economic growth and development. Currently professor of economics at Duke University, she served for five years as vice president for economics and research at the World Bank. Michael Parkin talked with Professor Krueger about her experiences and insights into the role of trade policy.

Professor Krueger, what led you into economics?

I started out in political science and found that most of the things I wanted to understand were economics. I got waylaid into economics and never got back.

There are two broad views about trade and development. One is that free trade permits resources to go to their highest value use, enhancing and accelerating development. The other is that people or countries "learn by doing," and need protection until they're mature. What's your view?

As you're asking it, the choice is either doing nothing or else inhibiting trade. I think the whole insight of the past 30 years has been that trade restriction actually inhibits the learning by doing. There probably is lots of learning—by governments on how to operate effectively, and by individuals on how to do their business. If you impose trade restrictions,

Talking with Anne Krueger

"Every protectionist says 'I am for free trade . . . But this is special.'"

what people learn is how to try and circumvent the trade restrictions. They learn how to do other things that do not contribute to higher productivity or standards of living.

Can you then give us a thumbnail sketch of what we have learned about the contribution of good trade policy toward the development process?

The evidence is fairly overwhelming that the economic costs of a highly protectionist policy are substantial. If you have high levels of protection for domestic industries, you will find yourself with a wasteful regime and very slow growth. The evidence that there are very high costs for import substitu-

tion is strong. My view is that the incentive side of the story is terribly important. And by incentive I do mean competition, not simply the reward. I mean the knowledge that if you just sit around and your firm takes losses, it may go under. This is perhaps the most powerful incentive there is. In short, the intellectual case for free trade is so overwhelming that every protectionist starts by saying "I am for free trade . . . But this is special and here's why."

We're holding this conversation the day after a general election in Canada, in which the people of Canada endorsed the free trade agreement between the United States and Canada. How important is that agreement?

It's potentially more important in the long run than the short run. It's not obvious that all the trade restrictions are going to be removed. Some of them will gradually be relaxed and some will not be intensified. I think there's still a big question about what's going to come out of the multilateral negotiations that started in 1986 under the auspices of the General Agreement on Tariffs and Trade. That will make a huge difference to how important the U.S.–Canadian trade pact will be. A great deal still depends on Europe 1992, on how the European Economic Community works out. And what happens to the bilateral U.S.–Canadian pact if the U.S. signs a U.S.–Australia or a U.S.–Japan pact. I think the world trading system is in a state of flux. The U.S.–Canada agreement represents a recognition that trade is too important not to be given its due. But there's a lot else going on.

Suppose the United States did enter into bilateral pacts with Japan and Australia. How would that affect the U.S.–Canada deal?

If the Canadians, for example, relax their protection of a domestic industry in order to have better access to the U.S. market for wheat, and the United States turns around and offers the better access to the U.S. market to Australia, then the Canadians have lost part of what they bargained for. And then, too, you'll have a U.S.–Canada bilateral commission and presumably also a U.S.–Australia bilateral commission. What happens when their rulings are inconsistent?

How serious is the debt problem for developing countries? Was there an international crisis?

Debt is an assessor of everything you've done in the past. If you borrowed and used the loan to finance productive activities that generate earnings streams, there's no problem unless you hit an unpleasant surprise. If, on the other hand, you borrow because you're spending beyond your income, when you have to pay the loan back, sometime in the future, you're going to have to cut your expenditures relative to your income. In the late 1970s, many developing countries were spending perhaps more than they should have and had great difficulties, when the worldwide recession hit in the early 1980s because many of them

had excessive domestic programs, or programs that had low rates of return on investment. Then when the cost of borrowing went up, simultaneously, their export earnings fell and they couldn't cut their imports fast enough, their debt almost doubled. Mexico was the first very big debtor and, of course, had lots of oil revenue. The only trouble was that Mexico knew how to spend it faster than it could discover new oil fields.

Not all countries borrowed so much. India and Pakistan, whatever else they did, did not borrow a great deal and did not have great difficulties with debt repayments. Other countries, like Korea, Taiwan, Singapore, and Colombia, borrowed but put the loans to productive use.

At the World Bank, we were looking at the debt problem from the developing countries' viewpoints. The commercial banks that made the loans thought about their bottom lines. But the idea that all the countries would default at the same time and bring about an international financial crisis I really think is close to inconceivable.

You were a pioneer in the development of "rent seeking," the concept not the practice! How did you hit on this important idea?

I was studying trade regimes in India and Turkey, and I discovered everywhere that the local people were using resources that could have been used productively

> "Debt is an assessor of everything you've done in the past."

> "It took my friend about 10 hours to turn my $10 into $200."

in order to try to get their share of something the government had placed under restriction. For example, the government of India used to assign all importers who applied for licenses to import, say, copper to produce utensils, a certain ceiling on how much copper they could import, according to their capacity. The government couldn't figure out why these producers kept expanding their factories. Now the bigger their capacity, the more copper they could import, right? So it paid to expand, just to get hold of more copper, even though they'd never use their bigger factories. That's rent seeking.

You've done some interesting direct observations on rent seeking, haven't you?

Indeed. I was once staying in a hotel in India and encountered a bellboy who studied economics at night. He was very entrepreneurial in his spare time. He wanted to borrow $10 in U.S. currency. I said I would lend him the money if I could come along with him to see how he made money out of the $10 during the day by rent seeking. He said, "You'll have to ride on the back of my motor scooter, O.K?" I said, "Fine, if you'll buy my lunch."

What sort of things did he do?

We engaged in about 40 transactions. Mostly small stuff, but with a little money in U.S. currency you could buy this and sell that and buy some more stuff and so on and so forth. If you rode a motor scooter, nobody noticed you, so you could do things that you couldn't otherwise. For example, there were prohibitions on selling liquor on certain days of the week in certain states. So the bellboys would go into another state to pick up beer and then sell it in the local hotels for quite a profit. There were other things. Sulfur was not allowed across state lines and price differentials were very large. It took my friend about 10 hours to turn my $10 into $200. And we had a nice lunch.

What advice do you give a student interested in working in international or development issues?

The obvious part is to get your union card by going to graduate school. I guess I'd argue for a couple of years of applied experience in between college and graduate school. Or the Peace Corps. I've seen lots of people go off into the Peace Corps and come back transformed. One of the hardest things in the generally wealthy United States or Canada is to teach young people that economics is called the dismal science because it recognizes that resources are not unlimited. And the hardest thing in the world is to convince people that in this magnificent economic phenomenon, our magnificent living standards haven't come for free and you can't take them for granted. Any economist who really understands that is already halfway there.

Chapter 35

After studying this chapter, you will be able to:

- Describe the trends and patterns in international trade

- Explain comparative advantage

- Explain why all countries can gain from international trade

- Explain how prices adjust to bring about balanced trade

- Explain how economies of scale and diversity of taste lead to gains from international trade

- Explain why trade restrictions lower the volume of imports and exports, and lower our consumption possibilities

- Explain why we have trade restrictions even though they lower our consumption possibilities

S ince ancient times, people have strived to expand their trading as far as technology allowed. The maritime nations of southern Europe, the Middle East and North Africa had flourishing trades in the Mediterranean 5000 years ago. Roman coins have been found in the ruins of ancient Indian cities. Marco Polo opened up the silk route between Europe and China in the thirteenth century. Merchants of Venice imported goods from the entire known world in the fifteenth century. Adventurers such as Christopher Columbus paved the way for the beginnings of trade between Europe and the Americas. Today, container ships laden with cars and machines and Boeing 747s stuffed with fresh fruit, fresh New Zealand lamb, and French cheeses ply the sea

Silk Routes and Rust Belts

and air routes, carrying billions of dollars worth of goods and services. Why do people go to such great lengths to trade with those in other nations? What does the pattern of international trade look like today? And what have been the recent trends in international trade? ■ International trade obviously brings enormous benefits. It enables us to consume fresh tropical fruit that doesn't grow here; to use raw materials such as chromium that are not found here; to buy low cost electrical energy generated by Canadian water power; to buy a wide range of manufactured goods such as cars, VCRs, TVs, and textiles that are available at lower prices from other countries. It also enables producers—workers and the firms that employ them—in export industries to earn more by expanding the markets for their products. ■ But international trade also has its costs. In recent years, a massive increase in the penetration of the foreign car industry into the United States has brought about a severe contraction of our own car-producing sector. Jobs in Detroit and other car-producing cities have disappeared, creating what has come to be called the Rust Belt. Do the benefits of international trade make up for the cost of jobs displaced by foreign competition? Could we, as politicians often claim, improve our economy by restricting imports? ■ The rich countries of the European Communities, Japan, and the United States import vast quantities of raw materials from Third World countries and from resource-rich developed countries such as Australia and Canada. To pay for these raw material imports, the rich countries sell manufactured goods to these countries. Do resource suppliers become poorer when they sell their bauxite, coal, and copper to the rich countries and buy farm combines and commercial jets in return? ■ The wages earned by the workers in the textile and electronics factories of Singapore, Taiwan, and Hong Kong are incredibly low compared with wages in the United States. Obviously, these countries can make manufactured goods much more cheaply than we can. How can we possibly compete with countries that pay their workers a fraction of U.S. wages? Are there any industries, besides perhaps the Hollywood movie industry, where we have an advantage? ■ The United States is a major actor in international economic affairs and, on many occasions, has taken initiatives that have had an enormous impact on world prosperity—sometimes for good but sometimes for ill. Perhaps its darkest hour was in 1930 when Congress passed the Smoot-Hawley Act, an act that increased taxes on imports to 60 percent, provoking widespread retaliation from the world's major trading countries. As a consequence, within two years, international trade almost dried up. In contrast, its finest hour came after World War II, when a process of trade liberalization brought about the creation of the General Agreement on Tariffs and Trade (GATT). The result this time was one of rapid world recovery from the devastation of war and an unprecedented expansion of world trade. What are the effects of trade restrictions? Why don't we have completely unrestricted international trade?

■ In this chapter, we're going to learn about international trade. We'll begin by looking at some facts about international trade, examining the patterns of imports and exports and trends in the main items that the United States buys from and sells to other countries. Then we will discover how *all* nations can gain by specializing in producing the goods and services at which they have an advantage compared with other countries and by exchanging some of their output with each other. We'll discover that all countries can compete, no matter how high their wages.

We will also explain why, despite the fact that international trade brings benefits to all, countries restrict trade. We'll discover who suffers and who benefits when international trade is restricted.

Patterns and Trends in International Trade

The goods and services that we buy from people in other countries are called **imports.** The goods and services that we sell to people in other countries are called **exports.** What are the most important things that we import and export? Most people would probably guess that a rich nation such as the United States imports raw materials and exports manufactured goods. While that is one feature of U.S. international trade, it is not its most important feature. The vast bulk of our exports *and* imports is manufactures. We sell earth-moving equipment, airplanes, supercomputers, and scientific equipment and we buy TVs, VCRs, blue jeans, and T-shirts. Also, we are a major exporter of agricultural products and raw materials. We also import and export a huge volume of services. Let's look at the international trade of the United States in a recent year.

U.S. International Trade

Table 35.1 classifies U.S. international trade in four major categories of goods—agricultural products, industrial supplies and materials, manufactures, and miscellaneous goods—and services. The first column gives the value of U.S. exports and the second column U.S. imports. The third column tells us the balance of trade in the various categories. The **balance of trade** is the value of exports minus the value of imports. If the balance is positive, then the value of exports exceeds the value of imports and the United States is a **net exporter.** But if the balance is negative, the value of imports exceeds the value of exports and the United States is a **net importer.**

Trade in Goods Two thirds of U.S. international trade is trade in goods. One third is trade in services. Of the categories of goods traded, by far the most important is manufactures. But the total value of exports of manufactures is less than imports—the

Table 35.1   U.S. Exports and Imports in 1988

Category	Exports	Imports	Balance
	(billions of dollars)		
Agricultural products	38.1	24.9	13.2
Industrial supplies and materials (excluding agricultural)	83.7	122.4	−38.7
Manufactures	169.1	286.1	−117.0
Miscellaneous goods	28.4	13.1	15.3
Services	210.5	195.2	−15.3
Total	529.8	641.7	−111.9

Source: Survey of Current Business (June 1989), vol. 69, pp. 50, 72, 74.

Table 35.2   U.S. Exports and Imports of Goods in 1988: Some Large Individual Items

Item	Exports	Imports	Balance
	(billions of dollars)		
Grains	15.4	0	15.4
Chemicals	26.0	12.4	13.6
Aircraft	20.6	7.5	13.1
Machinery	89.9	93.4	−3.5
Automobiles	32.5	87.9	−55.4
Fuels	9.5	43.4	−33.9
Manufactured consumer goods	24.2	96.4	−72.2

Source: Survey of Current Business (June 1989), vol. 69, pp. 72, 74.

United States is a net importer of manufactured goods. The United States is a net exporter of agricultural products and miscellaneous goods. In all other categories, it is a net importer.

Table 35.2 highlights some of the major items of imports and exports of goods. As you can see, the United States exports large quantities of machinery and cars. These are both larger than the exports of grains. However, the United States also imports large quantities of machinery, cars, and car parts. The United States is a small net importer of machinery, but it is a large net importer of cars and manufactured consumer goods. The country's biggest single net export is grains.

Trade in Services   One third of U.S. international trade is not of goods but of services. You may be wondering how a country can "export" and "import" services. Let's look at some examples.

Suppose that you decide to vacation in France, traveling there on an Air France flight from New York. What you buy from Air France is not a good, but a transportation service. Although the concept may sound odd at first, in economic terms you are importing that service from France. Since you pay U.S. money to a French company in exchange for a service, it doesn't matter that most of your flight time is over the Atlantic Ocean. For that matter, the money you spend in France on hotel bills, restaurant meals, and other things are also classified as the import of services. Similarly, the vacation taken by a French student in the United States counts as an export of services to France.

When we import TV sets from South Korea, the owner of the ship that carries those TV sets might be Greek and the company that insures the cargo might be British. The payments that we make for the transportation and insurance to the Greek and British companies are also payments for the import of services. Similarly, when an American shipping company transports Californian wine to Tokyo, the transportation cost is an export of a service to Japan.

Whenever you look at a photograph or see a movie that features a major city such as Hong Kong, Tokyo, or London, although you're looking at a foreign country, you see many familiar names: American Express, Citicorp, McDonald's, to mention just a few. These American corporations are producing goods and services in foreign countries for the citizens of those countries. Such corporations are exporting the services of U.S. capital to the rest of the world. The income that they receive for these services are payments made by foreigners for the services imported from the United States. Similarly, many foreign corporations establish plants in the United States or buy established firms. For example, Toyota has established car-making facilities in the United States. Robert Campeau, a Canadian financier, has bought retail interests in the United States, including Blooming-dale's. The income that we pay to these foreign corporations on their investments in the United States are part of our imports of services from foreigners.

The importance of the various components of trade in services is set out in Table 35.3. As you can see, the income from assets (that is, income we receive from our foreign operations and that we pay to foreigners for their economic activity here) is the biggest component of services traded. But transportation and travel are also very important.

Geographical Patterns The United States has important trading links with almost every part of the world except for Eastern Europe—which includes the Soviet giant—where trade is almost nonexistent. As you can see from Table 35.4, the bulk of our international trade is with Canada, Japan, the countries of the European Communities (notably West Germany and Britain), Latin America, and the newly industrializing countries of Asia such as Singapore, South Korea, and Taiwan.

Trends in Trade

International trade has become an increasingly important part of our economic life. In 1950, we exported less than 5 percent of total output and imported only 4 percent of the goods and services that we consumed ourselves. Over the years since then, that percentage has steadily increased and today it is more than double its level of 1950.

On the export side, all the major commodity categories have shared in the increased volume of international trade. Machinery, food, and raw materials have remained the most important components of exports and have roughly maintained their share in total exports.

But there have been dramatic changes in the composition of imports. Food and raw material imports have declined steadily. Imports of fuel increased dramatically in the 1970s but declined in the 1980s. Imports of machinery of all kinds, after being a fairly stable percentage of total imports until the middle 1980s, now approaches 50 percent of total imports.

There have been important trends in the overall balance in U.S. international trade in recent years. That overall *balance of trade* (of goods and services) is shown in Fig. 35.1. As you can see, the balance fluctuates around zero, but in the years since 1982 there has been a large excess of imports over exports

Table 35.3   U.S. Trade in Services in 1988

	Exports	Imports	Balance
		(billions of dollars)	
Travel and transportation	57.0	59.6	−2.6
Other services	35.2	15.4	19.8
Income from assets	107.8	105.5	2.3
Military services	10.6	14.7	−4.1
Total	210.6	195.2	15.4

Source: *Survey of Current Business* (June 1989), vol. 69, pp. 62, 63.

Table 35.4   U.S. Exports and Imports in 1988: Geographical Patterns

	Exports	Imports	Balance
		(billions of dollars)	
Canada	73.6	84.4	−10.8
Japan	37.1	89.8	−52.7
European Communities	74.5	85.6	−11.1
Latin America	43.6	51.4	−7.8
Other Western Europe	12.0	16.6	−4.6
Eastern Europe	3.8	2.2	1.6
Other Asia and Africa	67.9	113.0	−45.1
Australia, New Zealand, South America	6.8	3.5	3.3
Total	319.3	446.5	−127.2

Source: *Survey of Current Business* (June 1989), vol. 69, pp. 68–70.

(a negative balance of trade). The country with which we have the largest trade deficit is Japan.

Balance of Trade and International Borrowing

When people buy more than they sell, they have to finance the difference by borrowing. When they sell

Figure 35.1   The U.S. Balance of Trade

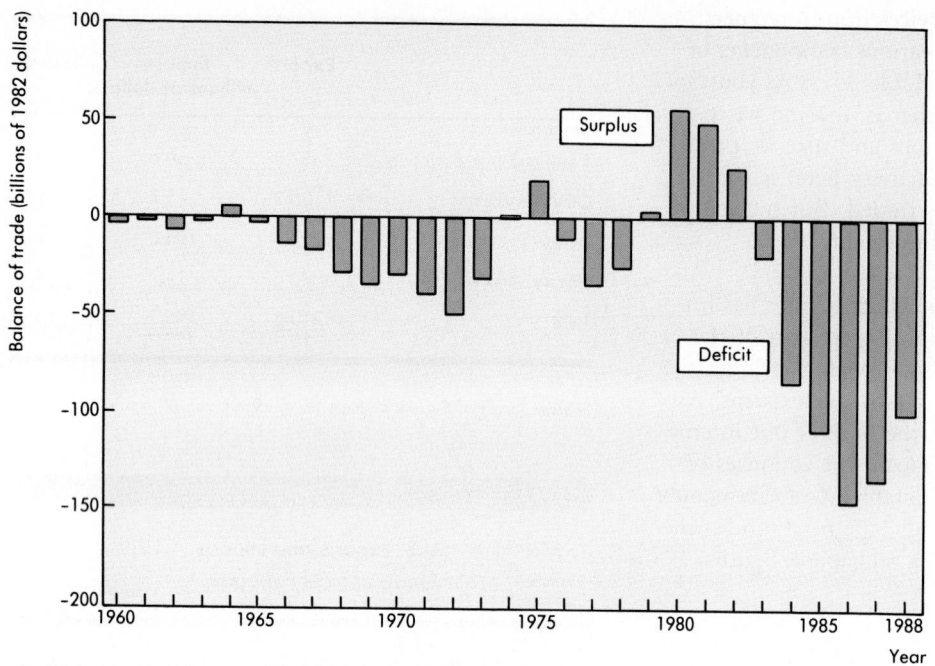

The balance of trade has fluctuated around zero, but since 1982 imports have grown more quickly than exports and a huge deficit has emerged.

Source: Economic Report of the President (1989), p. 311.

more than they buy, they can use the surplus to make loans to others. This simple principle that governs the income and expenditure and borrowing and lending of individuals and firms is also a feature of our balance of trade. If we import more than we export, we have to finance the difference by borrowing from foreigners. When we export more than we import, we make loans to foreigners to enable them to buy goods in excess of the value of the goods they have sold to us.

This chapter does not cover the factors that determine the balance of trade and the scale of international borrowing and lending that finance that balance. It is concerned with understanding the volume, pattern, and directions of international trade rather than its balance. So that we can keep our focus on these topics, we'll build a model in which there is no international borrowing and lending—just international trade in goods and services. We'll find that we are able to understand what determines the volume, pattern, and direction of international trade and also establish its benefits and the costs of trade restrictions within this framework. This model can be expanded to include international borrowing and lending, but such an extension does not change the conclusions

that we'll reach here about the factors that determine the volume, pattern, and directions of international trade. Let's now begin to study those factors.

Opportunity Cost and Comparative Advantage

L et's apply the lessons that we learned in Chapter 3 about the gains from trade between Jane and Joe, to the trade between nations. We'll begin by recalling how we can use the production possibility frontier to measure opportunity cost.

Opportunity Cost in Pioneerland

Pioneerland (a fictitious country) can produce grain and cars at any point inside or along the production possibility frontier shown in Fig. 35.2. (We're holding constant the output of all the other goods that Pioneerland produces.) The Pioneers (the people of

Pioneerland) are consuming all the grain and cars that they produce and they are operating at point *a* in the figure. That is, Pioneerland is producing and consuming 15 billion bushels of grain and 8 million cars each year. What is the opportunity cost of a car in Pioneerland?

We can answer that question by calculating the slope of the production possibility frontier at point *a*. For, as we discovered in Chapter 3 (pp. 53–55), the slope of the frontier measures the opportunity cost of one good in terms of the other. To measure the slope of the frontier at point *a*, place a straight line tangential to the frontier at point *a* and calculate the slope of that straight line. Recall that the formula for the slope of a line is the change in *y* divided by the change in *x* as we move along the line. Here, *y* is billions of bushels of grain and *x* is millions of cars. So the slope (opportunity cost) is the change in the number of bushels of grain divided by the change in the number of cars. As you can see from the red triangle in the figure, at point *a*, if the number of cars produced increases by 2 million, grain production decreases by 18 billion bushels. Therefore, the slope is 18 billion divided by 2 million, which equals 9000. To get one more car, the people of Pioneerland must give up 9000 bushels of grain. Thus the opportunity cost of 1 car is 9000 bushels of grain. Equivalently, 9000 bushels of grain cost 1 car.

Opportunity Cost in Magic Empire

Now consider the production possibility frontier in Magic Empire (another fictitious country and the only other country in our model world). Figure 35.3 illustrates its production possibility frontier. Like the Pioneers, the Magicians (the people in Magic Empire) consume all the grain and cars that they produce. Magic Empire consumes 18 billion bushels of grain a year and 4 million cars, at point *a'*.

We can do the same kind of calculation of opportunity cost for Magic Empire that we have just done for Pioneerland. At point *a'*, 1 car costs 1000 bushels of grain, or, equivalently, 1000 bushels of grain costs 1 car.

Comparative Advantage

Cars are cheaper in Magic Empire than in Pioneerland. One car costs 9000 bushels of grain in Pioneerland but only 1000 bushels of grain in Magic Empire. But grain is cheaper in Pioneerland than in

Figure 35.2   Opportunity Cost in Pioneerland

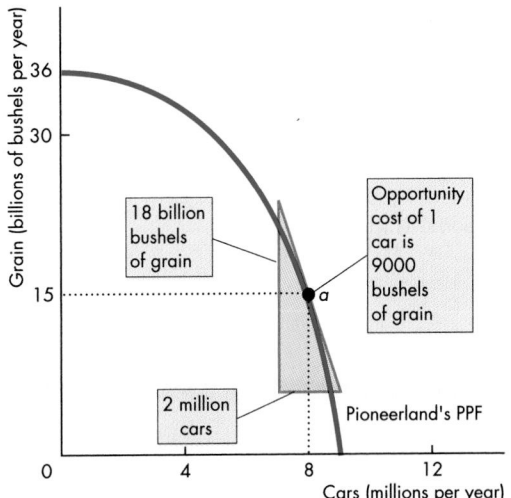

Pioneerland produces and consumes 15 billion bushels of grain and 8 million cars a year. That is, it produces and consumes at point a on its production possibility frontier. Opportunity cost is measured as the slope of the production possibility frontier. At point a, 2 million cars cost 18 billion bushels of grain. Equivalently, 1 car costs 9000 bushels of grain or 9000 bushels cost 1 car.

Figure 35.3   Opportunity Cost in Magic Empire

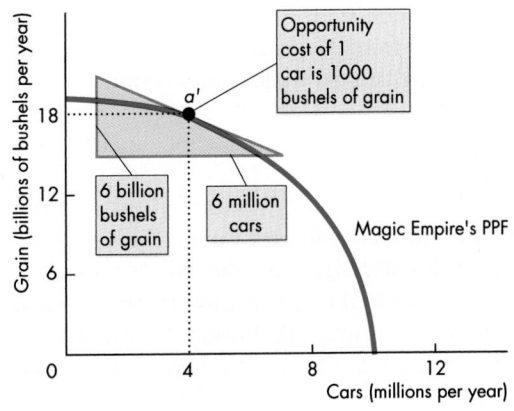

Magic Empire produces and consumes 18 billion bushels of grain and 4 million cars a year. That is, it produces and consumes at point a' on its production possibility frontier. Opportunity cost is measured as the slope of the production possibility frontier. At point a', 6 million cars cost 6 billion bushels of grain. Equivalently, 1 car costs 1000 bushels of grain or 1000 bushels cost 1 car.

Magic Empire—9000 bushels of grain costs only 1 car in Pioneerland while that same amount of grain costs 9 cars in Magic Empire.

Magic Empire has a comparative advantage in car production. Pioneerland has a comparative advantage in grain production. A country has a **comparative advantage** in producing a good if it can produce that good at a lower opportunity cost than any other country. Let's see how opportunity cost differences and comparative advantage generate gains from international trade.

The Gains from Trade

The Basic Idea

If Magic Empire bought grain for what it costs Pioneerland to produce it, then Magic Empire could buy 9000 bushels of grain for 1 car. That is much lower than the cost of growing grain in Magic Empire, for there it costs 9 cars to produce 9000 bushels of grain. If the Magicians buy at the low Pioneerland price, they will reap some gains.

If the Pioneers buy cars for what it costs Magic Empire to produce them, they will be able to obtain a car for 1000 bushels of grain. Since it costs 9000 bushels of grain to produce a car in Pioneerland, the Pioneers would gain from such an activity.

In this situation, it makes sense for Magicians to buy their grain from Pioneers and for Pioneers to buy their cars from Magicians. Let's see how such profitable international trade comes about.

Reaping the Gains from Trade

We've seen that the Pioneers would like to buy their cars from the Magicians and that the Magicians would like to buy their grain from the Pioneers. Let's see how the two groups do business with each other, concentrating attention on the international market for cars.

Figure 35.4 illustrates such a market. The quantity of cars traded internationally is measured on the horizontal axis. On the vertical axis we measure the price of a car but it is expressed as its opportunity cost—the number of bushels of grain that a car costs. If no international trade takes place, that price in Pioneerland is 9000 bushels of grain, indicated by

Figure 35.4   International Trade in Cars

As the price of a car decreases, the quantity of imports demanded by Pioneerland increases—Pioneerland's import demand curve for cars is downward-sloping. As the price of a car increases, the quantity of cars supplied by Magic Empire for export increases—Magic Empire's export supply curve of cars is upward-sloping. Without international trade, the price of a car is 9000 bushels of grain in Pioneerland (point a) and 1000 bushels of grain in Magic Empire (point a'). With free international trade, the price of a car is determined where the export supply curve intersects the import demand curve—at a price of 3000 bushels of grain. At that price, 4 million cars a year are imported by Pioneerland and exported by Magic Empire. The value of grain exported by Pioneerland and imported by Magic Empire is 12 billion bushels a year, the quantity required to pay for the cars imported.

point *a* in the figure. Again, if no trade takes place, that price is 1000 bushels of grain in Magic Empire, indicated by point *a'* in the figure. The points *a* and *a'* in Fig. 35.4 correspond to the points identified by those same letters in Figs. 35.2 and 35.3.

The lower the price of a car (in terms of bushels of grain), the greater is the quantity of cars that Pioneers import from Magicians. This fact is illustrated in the downward-sloping curve that shows Pioneerland's import demand for cars.

The Magicians respond in the opposite direction. The higher the price of cars (in terms of bushels of grain), the greater is the quantity of cars that Magicians export to Pioneers. This fact is reflected in Magic Empire's export supply of cars—the upward-sloping line in the figure.

The international market in cars determines the equilibrium price and quantity traded. This equilibrium occurs where the import demand curve intersects the export supply curve. In this case, the equilibrium price of a car is 3000 bushels of grain. Four million cars a year are exported by Magic Empire and imported by Pioneerland. Notice that the price at which cars are traded is lower than the initial price in Pioneerland but higher than the initial price in Magic Empire.

Balanced Trade

Notice that the number of cars exported by Magic Empire—4 million a year—is exactly equal to the number of cars imported by Pioneerland. How does Pioneerland pay for its cars? By exporting grain. How much grain does Pioneerland export? You can find the answer by noticing that for 1 car Pioneerland has to pay 3000 bushels of grain. Hence, for 4 million cars they have to pay 12 billion bushels of grain. Thus Pioneerland's exports of grain are 12 billion bushels a year. Magic Empire imports this same quantity of grain.

Magic Empire is exchanging 4 million cars for 12 billion bushels of grain each year and Pioneerland is doing the opposite, exchanging 12 billion bushels of grain for 4 million cars. Trade is balanced between these two countries. The value received from exports equals the value paid out for imports.

Changes in Production and Consumption

We've seen that international trade makes it possible for Pioneers to buy cars at a lower price than they can produce them for themselves. It also enables Magicians to sell their cars for a higher price, which is equivalent to saying that Magicians can buy grain for a lower price. Thus everybody seems to gain. Magicians buy grain at a lower price and Pioneers buy cars at a lower price. How is it possible for everyone to gain? What are the changes in production and consumption that accompany these gains?

An economy that does not trade with other economies has identical production and consumption possibilities. Without trade, the economy can only consume what it produces. But with international trade an economy can consume different quantities of goods from those that it produces. The production possibility frontier describes the limit of what a country can produce but it does not describe the limits to what it can consume. Figure 35.5 will help you to see the distinction between production possibilities and consumption possibilities when a country trades with other countries.

First of all, notice that the figure has two parts, part (a) for Pioneerland and part (b) for Magic Empire. The production possibility frontiers that you saw in Figs. 35.2 and 35.3 are reproduced here. The slopes of the two black lines in the figure represent the opportunity costs in the two countries when there is no international trade. Pioneerland produces and consumes at point a and Magic Empire produces and consumes at a'. Cars cost 9000 bushels of grain in Pioneerland and 1000 bushels of grain in Magic Empire.

With international trade, Magic Empire can sell cars to Pioneerland for 3000 bushels of grain each. Pioneerland can buy cars from Magic Empire for that same price. Thus both countries can exchange cars for grain or grain for cars at a price of 3000 bushels of grain per car.

With international trade, the producers of cars in Magic Empire can now get a higher price for their output. As a result, they increase the quantity of car production. At the same time, grain producers in Magic Empire are now getting a lower price for their grain and so they reduce production. Producers in Magic Empire adjust their output until the opportunity cost in Magic Empire equals the opportunity cost in the world market. This situation arises when Magic Empire is producing at point b' in Fig. 35.5(b).

But the Magicians do not consume at point b'. That is, they do not increase their consumption of cars and decrease their consumption of grain. They sell some of their car production to Pioneerland in exchange for some of Pioneerland's grain. But to see how that works out, we first need to check in with Pioneerland to see what's happening there.

In Pioneerland, cars are now less expensive and grain more expensive than before. As a consequence, producers in Pioneerland decrease car production and increase grain production. They do so until the opportunity cost of a car in terms of grain equals the cost on the world market. They move to point b, in part (a). But the Pioneers do not consume at point b. They exchange some of their additional grain production for the now cheaper cars from Magic Empire.

The figure shows us the quantities consumed in the two countries. We saw in Fig. 35.4 that Magic

Figure 35.5   Expanding Consumption Possibilities

(a) Pioneerland

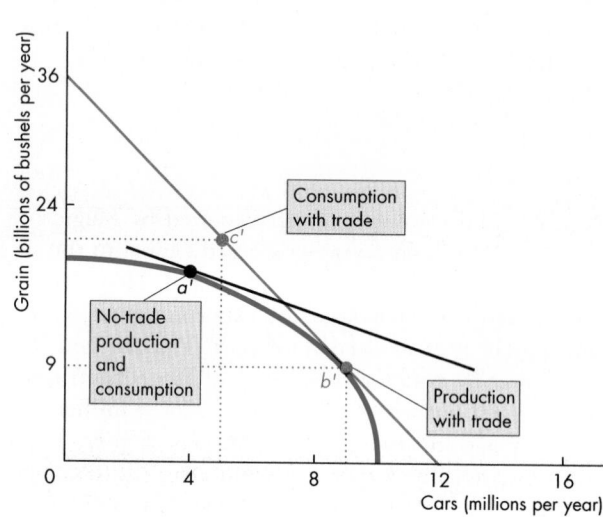

(b) Magic Empire

With no international trade, the Pioneers produce and consume at point *a* and the opportunity cost of a car is 9000 bushels of grain (the slope of the black line in part a). Also, with no international trade, the Magicians produce and consume at point *a'* and the opportunity cost of 1000 bushels of grain is 1 car (the slope of the black line in part b).

Goods can be exchanged internationally at a price of 3000 bushels of grain for 1 car along the red line. In part (a), Pioneerland decreases its production of cars and increases its production of grain, moving from *a* to *b*. It exports grain and imports cars, and it consumes at point *c*. The Pioneers have more of both cars and grain than they would if they produced all their own consumption goods—at point *a*. In part (b), Magic Empire increases car production and decreases grain production, moving from *a'* to *b'*. Magic Empire exports cars and imports grain, and it consumes at point *c'*. The Magicians have more of both cars and grain than they would if they produced all their own consumption goods—at point *a'*.

Empire exports 4 million cars a year and Pioneerland imports those cars. We also saw that Pioneerland exports 12 billion bushels of grain a year and Magic Empire imports that grain. Thus Pioneerland's consumption of grain is 12 billion bushels a year less than it produces and its consumption of cars is 4 million a year more than it produces. Pioneerland consumes at point *c* in Fig. 35.5(a).

Similarly, we know that Magic Empire consumes 12 billion bushels of grain more than it produces and 4 million cars fewer than it produces. Thus Magic Empire consumes at *c'* in Fig. 35.5(b).

Calculating the Gains from Trade

You can now literally "see" the gains from trade in Fig. 35.5. Without trade, Pioneers produce and consume at *a* (part a)—a point on Pioneerland's production possibility frontier. With international trade, Pioneers consume at point *c* (in part a)—a point *outside* the production possibility frontier. At point *c*, Pioneers are consuming 3 billion bushels of grain a year and 1 million cars a year more than before. These increases in consumption of cars and grain, beyond the limits of the production possibility frontier, are the gains from international trade.

But Magicians also gain. Without trade, they consume at point a' (part b)—a point on Magic Empire's production possibility frontier. With international trade, they consume at point c'—a point outside the production possibility frontier. With international trade, Magic Empire consumes 3 billion bushels of grain a year and 1 million cars a year more than without trade. These are the gains from international trade for Magic Empire.

Gains for All

When Pioneers and Magicians trade with each other, potentially everyone can gain. Domestic sellers add the net demand of foreigners to their domestic demand, and so their market expands. Buyers are faced with domestic supply plus net foreign supply and so have a larger total supply available to them. As you know, prices increase when there is an increase in demand and they decrease when there is an increase in supply. Thus the increased demand (from foreigners) for exports increases their price and the increased supply (from foreigners) of imports decreases their price. Gains in one country do not bring losses in another. Everyone, in this example, gains from international trade.

Absolute Advantage

Suppose that in Magic Empire, fewer workers are needed to produce any given output of either grain or cars than in Pioneerland. In this situation, Magic Empire has an absolute advantage over Pioneerland. A country has an **absolute advantage** if its output per unit of inputs of all goods is higher than that of another country. With an absolute advantage, isn't it the case that Magic Empire can outsell Pioneerland in all markets? Why, if Magic Empire can produce all goods using fewer factors of production than Pioneerland, does it pay Magic Empire to buy *anything* from Pioneerland?

The answer is that the cost of production in terms of the factors of production employed is irrelevant for determining the gains from trade. It does not matter how much labor, land, and capital are required to produce 1000 bushels of grain or a car. What matters is how many cars must be given up to produce more grain or how much grain must be given up to produce more cars. That is, what matters is the opportunity cost of one good in terms of the

other good. Magic Empire may have an absolute advantage in the production of all things, but it cannot have a comparative advantage in the production of all goods. The statement that the opportunity cost of cars in Magic Empire is lower than in Pioneerland is identical to the statement that the opportunity cost of grain is higher in Magic Empire than in Pioneerland. Thus *whenever opportunity costs diverge, everyone has a comparative advantage in something.* All countries can potentially gain from international trade.

REVIEW

When countries have divergent opportunity costs, they can gain from international trade. Each country can buy goods and services from another country at a lower opportunity cost than it can produce them for itself. Gains arise when each country increases its production of those goods and services in which it has a comparative advantage (of goods and services that it can produce at an opportunity cost that is lower than that of other countries) and exchanges some of its production for that of other countries.

All countries gain from international trade. Everyone has a comparative advantage at something. ∎

Gains from Trade in Reality

The gains from trade that we have just studied between Pioneerland and Magic Empire in grain and cars are taking place in a model economy—in an economy that we have imagined. But these same phenomena are occurring every minute of every day in real-world economies. We buy cars made in Japan and American producers of grain and lumber sell large parts of their output to Japanese households and firms. We buy cars and machinery from European producers and sell airplanes and computers to Europeans in return. We buy shirts and fashion goods from the people of Hong Kong and sell them machinery in return. We buy TV sets and VCRs from South Korea and Taiwan and sell them financial and other services as well as manufactured goods in return.

Thus much of the international trade that we see in the real world takes precisely the form of the trade that we have studied in our model of the world economy. But as we discovered earlier in this chapter, a great deal of world trade is heavily concentrated among industrial countries and primarily involves the international exchange of manufactured goods. Thus the type of trade that we have just analyzed—exchanging cars for grain—although an important and clearly profitable type of trade, is not the most prominent type. Why do countries exchange manufactured goods with each other? Can our model of international trade explain such exchange?

A Puzzle

At first thought, it seems puzzling that countries would trade manufactured goods. Consider, for example, America's trade in cars and auto parts. Why does it make sense for the United States to produce cars for export and at the same time to import large quantities of cars from Canada, Japan, Korea, and Western Europe? Wouldn't it make more sense to produce all the cars that we buy here in the United States? After all, we have access to the best technology available for producing cars. Auto workers in the United States are surely as productive as their fellow workers in Canada, Western Europe, and the Pacific countries. Capital equipment, production lines, robots, and the like used in the manufacture of cars are as available to American car producers as they are to any others. This line of reasoning leaves a puzzle concerning the sources of international exchange of similar commodities produced by similar people using similar equipment. Why does it happen?

Diversity of Taste   The first part of the answer to the puzzle is that people have a tremendous diversity of taste. Let's stick with the example of cars. Some people prefer a sports car, some prefer a limousine, some prefer a regular full-size car, and some prefer a compact. In addition to size and type of car, there are many other dimensions in which cars vary. Some have low fuel consumption, some have high performance, some are spacious and comfortable, some have a large trunk, some have four-wheel drive, some have front-wheel drive, some have manual transmission, some have automatic transmission, some are durable, some are flashy, some have a radiator grille that looks like a Greek temple, others look like a wedge. People's preferences across these many dimensions vary.

The tremendous diversity in tastes for cars means that people would be dissatisfied if they were forced to consume from a limited range of standardized cars. People value variety and are willing to pay for it in the marketplace.

Economies of Scale   The second part of the answer to the puzzle is economies of scale. *Economies of scale* are the tendency, present in many production processes, for the average cost of production to be lower, the larger the scale of production. In such situations, larger and larger production runs lead to ever lower average production costs. Many manufactured goods, including cars, experience economies of scale. For example, if a car producer makes only a few hundred (or perhaps a few thousand) cars of a particular type and design, they have to use production techniques that are much more labor-intensive and much less automated than those actually employed to make hundreds of thousands of cars in a particular model. With low production runs and labor-intensive production techniques, costs are high. With very large production runs and automated assembly lines, production costs are much lower. But to obtain lower costs, the automated assembly lines have to produce a large number of cars.

It is the combination of diversity of taste and economies of scale that produces such a large amount of international trade in similar commodities. Diversity of taste and the willingness to pay for variety does not guarantee that variety will be available. It could simply be too expensive to provide a highly diversified range of different types of cars, for example. If every car bought in the United States today was made in the United States and if the present range of diversity and variety was available, production runs would be remarkably short. Car producers would not be able to reap economies of scale. Although the current variety of cars could be made available, it would be at a very high price, and perhaps at a price that no one would be willing to pay.

But with international trade, each manufacturer of cars has the whole world market to serve. Each producer specializes in a limited range of products and then sells its output to the entire world market. This arrangement enables large production runs on the most popular cars and feasible production runs even on the most customized cars demanded by only a handful of people.

The situation in the market for cars is also present in many other industries, especially those producing specialized machinery and specialized machine tools. Thus international exchange of similar but slightly differentiated manufactured products is a highly profitable activity.

This type of trade can be understood with exactly the same model of international trade that we studied earlier. Although we normally think of cars as a single commodity, we simply have to think of sports cars and sedans and so on as different goods. Different countries, by specializing in a few of these "goods" are able to enjoy economies of scale and, therefore, a comparative advantage in their production.

You can see that comparative advantage and international trade bring gains regardless of the goods being traded. When the rich countries of the European Communities, Japan, and the United States import raw materials from the Third World and from Australia and Canada, the rich importing countries gain and so do the exporting countries. When we buy cheap TV sets, VCRs, shirts, and other goods from low wage countries, both we and the exporters gain from the exchange. It's true that if we increase our imports of cars and produce fewer cars ourselves, jobs in our car-producing sector disappear. But jobs in other sectors, sectors in which we have a comparative advantage and supply to other nations, expand. *After the adjustment is completed,* those whose jobs have been lost find employment in the expanding sectors and usually at higher wages than they had previously. They buy goods produced in other countries at even lower prices than those at which they were available before. The gains from international trade are not gains for some at the expense of losses for others.

But changes in comparative advantage that lead to changes in international trade patterns can take a long time to adjust to. For example, the increase in automobile imports and the corresponding relative decline in domestic car production has not immediately brought increased wealth for displaced auto workers. Better jobs take time to find and often people go through a period of prolonged search putting up with inferior jobs and lower wages than they had before. Thus only in the long run does everyone potentially gain from international specialization and exchange. Short-run adjustment costs, that can be large and relatively prolonged, may be borne by groups that have lost their comparative advantage.

Partly because of the costs of adjustment to changing international trade patterns, but partly also for other reasons, governments intervene in international trade restricting its volume. Let's examine what happens when governments restrict international trade. We'll contrast restricted trade with free trade. We'll see that free trade brings the greatest possible benefits. We'll also see why, in spite of the benefits of free trade, governments sometimes restrict trade.

Trade Restrictions

Governments restrict international trade in order to protect domestic industries from foreign competition. The restriction of international trade is called **protectionism.** There are two main protectionist methods employed by governments:

• Tariffs
• Nontariff barriers

A **tariff** is a tax that is imposed by the importing country when a good crosses an international boundary. A **nontariff barrier** is any action other than a tariff that restricts international trade. Examples of nontariff barriers are quantitative restrictions and licensing regulations limiting imports. We'll consider nontariff barriers in more detail below. First, let's look at tariffs.

The History of Tariffs

Average tariff levels in the United States today are quite modest compared with their historical levels. As you can see from Fig. 35.6, tariff levels have averaged around 40 percent through most of U.S. history. During certain periods, such as the 1830s and, with the passage of the Smoot-Hawley Act in the Great Depression years of the 1930s, they reached 60 percent.

Today, average tariffs represent only 4 percent of total imports and only 6 percent of that part of imports that are subject to a tariff. But some sectors have high tariffs. The sector with the highest tariffs is textiles and footwear. Ninety-two percent of all our imports of textiles and footwear are protected at an average rate of more than 10 percent. For example, when you buy a pair of blue jeans for $20, you are paying about $5 more than you would have to if there were no trade restrictions on textiles. If you buy a $20,000 automobile, you are paying close to $5000 more than the free trade price would be. Other

Figure 35.6   U.S. Tariffs: 1821–1985

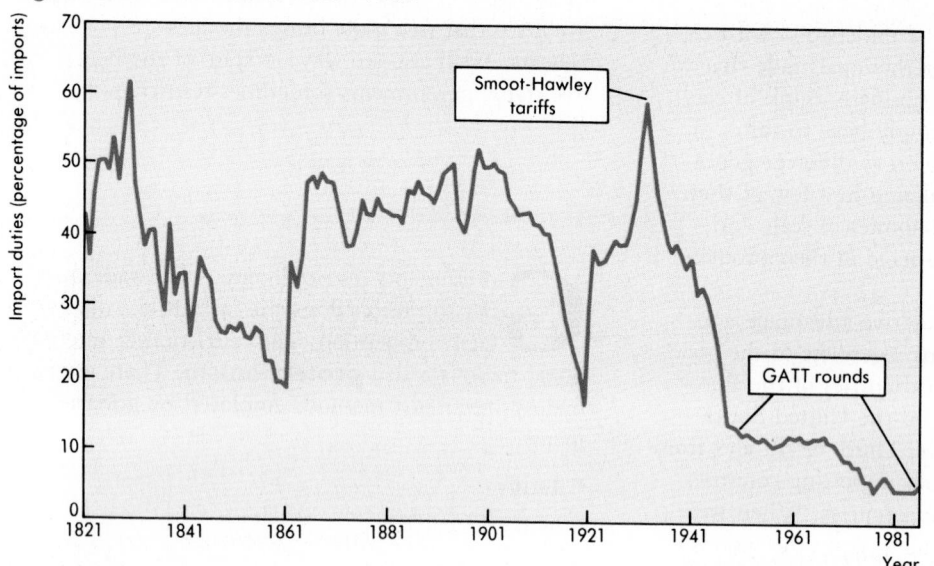

Tariffs in the United States have for most of its history, averaged around 40 percent. On occasion, they have increased to 60 percent. Since World War II, tariffs have steadily declined and are now at the lowest levels they have ever been.

Source: Historical Statistics of the United States, Series no. U-20.

sectors protected by tariffs are agricultural products, energy and chemicals, minerals and metals. Almost all the meat and cheese that you consume costs significantly more because of protection than it would with free international trade.

The temptation, on governments, to impose tariffs is a strong one. First, tariffs provide revenue to the government. Second, they enable the government to satisfy special interest groups in import-competing industries. But, as we've seen, free international trade brings enormous benefits. Because free trade brings benefits and because the temptation to restrict trade is so great, countries have attempted to enter into a multilateral agreement whose goal is the enhancement of free international trade—the General Agreement on Tariffs and Trade (GATT). The **General Agreement on Tariffs and Trade** is an international agreement designed to limit government intervention to restrict international trade. It was negotiated immediately following World War II and was signed in October 1947. Its goal is to liberalize trading activity and to provide an organization to administer more liberal trading arrangements. GATT itself is a small organization that is located in Geneva, Switzerland.

Since the formation of GATT, several rounds of negotiations have resulted in general tariff reductions (see Table 35.5). One of these, the Kennedy Round that began in the early 1960s, resulted in large tariff cuts. Yet further tariff cuts resulted from the Tokyo Round that took place between 1973 and 1979. The Uruguay Round, currently in progress, is attempting to achieve less restricted international trade in services and agricultural products, two large and important areas excluded from all previous GATT negotiations.

In addition to the multilateral agreements under GATT, the United States is a party to several important bilateral trade agreements. One of these is the Canada–United States free trade agreement that became effective on January 1, 1989 (see Reading Between the Lines, pp. 932–933). Under this agreement, barriers to international trade between Canada and the United States will be virtually eliminated after a 10-year phasing-in period. Less ambitious, but important, is the United States–Mexico Framework, a consultative mechanism to review trade and investment issues and to negotiate the removal of trade barriers. Within Western Europe, trade barriers among the member countries of the European Communities will have been completely eliminated by 1992, creating the largest unified tariff-free market in the world.

How Tariffs Work

To analyze how tariffs work, let's return to the example of trade between Pioneerland and Magic Empire. Suppose that these two countries are trading cars and grain in exactly the same way that we analyzed before. Magic Empire exports cars and Pioneerland exports grain. The volume of car imports into Pioneerland is 4 million a year and cars are selling on the world market for 3000 bushels of grain. Let's sup-

Figure 35.7   The Effects of a Tariff

Pioneerland imposes a tariff on car imports from Magic Empire. The tariff increases the price that Pioneers have to pay for cars. It shifts the supply curve of cars in Pioneerland upward. The distance between the original supply curve and the new one is the amount of the tariff. The price of cars in Pioneerland increases and the quantity of cars imported decreases. The government of Pioneerland collects a tariff revenue of $4000 per car—a total of $8 billion on the 2 million cars imported. Pioneerland's exports of grain decrease since Magic Empire now has a lower income from its exports of cars.

pose that grain costs a dollar a bushel so, equivalently, cars are selling for $3000. Figure 35.7 illustrates this situation. The volume of trade in cars and their price are determined at the point of intersection of Magic Empire's export supply curve of cars and Pioneerland's import demand curve for cars.

Now suppose that the government of Pioneerland, perhaps under pressure from car producers, decides to impose a tariff on imported cars. In particular, suppose that a tariff of $4000 per car is imposed. (This is a huge tariff, but the car producers of Pioneerland are pretty fed up with competition from Magic Empire.) What happens?

The first part of the answer is obtained by studying the effects on the supply of cars in Pioneerland. Cars are no longer going to be available at the Magic Empire export supply price. The tariff of $4000 must be added to that price—the amount paid to the government of Pioneerland on each car

Table 35.5   Summary of U.S. Tariffs

		Percentage tariff rate on U.S. imports	
		Dutiable imports	Total imports
1930	Smoot-Hawley— "high point" of retaliatory protection during the Depression	53	18
1947	Setting up of GATT		
1947–1956	GATT negotiating rounds: Geneva in 1947, Annecy in 1949, Torquay in 1951, Geneva in 1956— agreements on tariff rates and modest tariff cuts	25	9
1961	Dillon Round of tariff negotiations—further modest tariff cuts		
1967	Kennedy Round of tariff negotiations—significant tariff cuts	12	7
1979	Tokyo Round of negotiations—further tariff cuts	6	4
1988	Uruguay Round of negotiations—in progress		

Source: Based on John Whalley, *Trade Liberalization among Major World Trading Areas* (Cambridge, Mass.: MIT Press, 1985), Table 1.3, p. 16.

Winners and Losers

North Americans Ponder How They Will Fare after Free Trade Becomes a Reality

Norm Dyck, 47, sours a little as he contemplates the prospects of greater free trade between the U.S. and Canada, which could become a reality by the end of the year. A slim, bespectacled wheat farmer, Dyck owns a 1,000-acre homestead near Debolt, Alta., a farming community about 560 miles north of the Canadian–U.S. border. In his view, free trade will soon lead to a flood of cheap U.S. wheat pouring into Canada's domestic market. Says Dyck: "This is not time to expand production." This spring, he plans to plant 800 of his acres in grass and clover rather than wheat, in anticipation of falling wheat prices.

On the other side of Canada, executives at Hydro-Québec, the province's government-owned electrical utility, can barely hide their delight at the prospects contained in the version of the free-trade pact signed by President Ronald Reagan and Prime Minister Brian Mulroney in January. As a supplier of 16.4 billion kilowatt-hours of electricity to Northeastern U.S. markets —$351.8 million worth in 1987—Hydro-Québec has been worrying that Washington will restrict the firm's access to U.S. customers. Clauses in the Canada–U.S. free-trade agreement would explicitly ban any such barriers to the export of Canadian energy supplies. Says Jacques Guevremont, Hydro-Québec vice president for external sales: "We were already operating in a pretty free market. Now we'll be operating in one that's completely open."

South of the 49th parallel, in Peoria, Ill., salesmen for giant Caterpillar, Inc., are also anticipating a future bonanza from the trade treaty. Under the agreement, a 10% Canadian tariff on earth-moving equipment would be phased out over the next eight years, offering new sales opportunities for the U.S. firm. Says William Lane, a Caterpillar spokesman: "It will definitely make our products more competitive in Canada."

Out in Montana, Cattle Rancher Jimme Wilson, 56, has mixed feelings. On his 1,200-acre ranch in a mountainous section of Sanders County, Wilson keeps 400 Herefords, some of which he would like to sell in Canada. Currently he cannot, because Canadian agricultural regulations restrict the importation of live animals from the U.S., in part through costly quarantine rules. Only some of the regulations would be loosened under the free-trade accord. Most of the rules are "just an excuse" to keep out U.S. livestock, says Wilson.

With equal parts of consternation and anticipation, U.S. and Canadian businessmen are beginning to realize that the prospective free-trade accord could bring about dramatic changes in the economic lives of the two countries. The promise of the treaty is of a "win-win" future for both. Under the pact, most remaining tariffs and duties would be removed on almost $150 billion worth of mutual trade, a move that in turn should expand what is already the world's largest two-way trading relationship. U.S. exports to Canada reached $61.5 billion last year, or 26% of the U.S. worldwide total, while Canadian exports to the U.S. came to $73.7 billion, or 78% of Canada's shipments abroad.

Time, **March 14, 1988**

by Edward Desmond, reported by Beth Austin and Peter Stoler

The Essence of the Story

- U.S. exports to Canada in 1987 were $61.5 billion — 26 percent of U.S. total exports.

- Canadian exports to the United States in 1987 were $73.7 billion — 78 percent of Canada's total exports.

- A free-trade agreement between the United States and Canada will remove the remaining tariffs and expand what is already the world's largest two-way trading relationship.

- Many predictions were being made in 1988 about the consequences of the Free Trade Agreement:

  — Wheat prices will fall, cutting Canadian wheat production.
  — A completely free market in electricity will be created in the United States and Canada.
  — Exports of earth-moving equipment will increase as the 10 percent Canadian tariff is phased out.
  — Nontariff barriers such as quarantine rules for cattle will limit the extent of free trade in livestock.
  — Large changes in economic life in both countries will produce gains for all.

Background and Analysis

- With tariffs, international trade is restricted.

- International trade in earth-moving equipment is an example (see figure)

- Under free trade, the quantity of earth movers exported by the United States and imported by Canada is Q_2. The price at which this trade takes place is P_2.

- Canada imposes a 10 percent tariff on earth-moving equipment imports.

- The supply curve facing Canada is the U.S. export supply curve plus the 10 percent tariff.

- The quantity of Canadian imports of earth-moving equipment is Q_1 and the price paid by Canadian buyers is P_1.

- American producers sell such equipment for a price of C.

- The difference between P_1 and C is the tariff collected by the Canadian government on each earth mover.

- The removal of tariffs results in an increased volume of trade — from Q_1 to Q_2 — a lower price for importers — from P_1 to P_2 — and a higher price for exporters, from C to P_2.

- The removal of the tariff shifts the supply curve faced by Canada downward — to the red curve.

- The situation shown in the figure is identical for exporters of all goods, whether U.S. or Canadian.

- The introduction of free trade brings an expansion in export industries and a contraction in import competing industries — making large changes in economic life as foreseen by U.S. and Canadian businesses.

- The removal of tariffs does not bring complete free trade. Nontariff barriers remain. An example is the quarantine rules on moving live animals across the U.S.–Canadian border. Such rules restrict international trade even though that is not their initial or main intent.

- To reap the gains from trade, exporting industries must expand. This expansion can occur only if importing industries contract.

- At the time of the change to free trade, exporters are happy but importers complain.

- Eventually, those moving from import industries will find jobs in the expanding export sector and share in the gains from freer international trade.

933

imported. As a consequence, the supply curve in Pioneerland shifts in the manner shown in Fig. 35.7. The new supply curve becomes that labeled "Magic Empire's export supply of cars plus tariff." The vertical distance between Magic Empire's export supply curve and the new supply curve is the tariff imposed by the government of Pioneerland.

The next part of the answer is found by determining the new equilibrium. Imposing a tariff has no effect on the demand for cars in Pioneerland and so has no effect on Pioneerland's import demand for cars. The new equilibrium occurs where the new supply curve intersects Pioneerland's import demand curve for cars. That equilibrium is at a price of $6000 a car and with 2 million cars a year being imported. Imports fall from 4 million to 2 million cars a year. At the higher price of $6000 a car, domestic car producers increase their production. Domestic grain production decreases to free up the resources for the expanded car industry.

The total expenditure on imported cars by the Pioneers is $6000 a car multiplied by the 2 million cars imported ($12 billion). But not all of that money goes to the Magicians. They receive $2000 a car or $4 billion for the 2 million cars. The difference—$4000 a car or a total of $8 billion for the 2 million cars—is collected by the government of Pioneerland as tariff revenue.

Obviously, the government of Pioneerland is happy with this situation. It is now collecting $8 billion that it didn't have before. But what about the Pioneers? How do they view the new situation? The demand curve tells us the maximum price that a buyer is willing to pay for one more unit of a good. As you can see from Pioneerland's import demand curve for cars, if one more car could be imported, someone would be willing to pay almost $6000 for it. Magic Empire's export supply curve of cars tells us the minimum price at which additional cars are available. As you can see, one additional car would be supplied by Magic Empire for a price only slightly more than $2000. Thus since someone is willing to pay almost $6000 for a car and someone is willing to supply one for little more than $2000, there is obviously a gain to be had from trading an extra car. In fact, there are gains to be had—willingness to pay exceeds the minimum supply price—all the way up to 4 million cars a year. Only when 4 million cars are being traded is the maximum price that a Pioneer is willing to pay equal to the minimum price that is acceptable to a Magician. Thus restricting

international trade reduces the gains from international trade.

It is easy to see that the tariff has lowered Pioneerland's total import bill. With free trade, Pioneerland was paying $3000 a car and buying 4 million cars a year from Magic Empire. Thus the total import bill was $12 billion a year. With a tariff, imports have been cut to 2 million cars a year and the price paid to the foreign country has also been cut to only $2000 a car. Thus the import bill has been cut to $4 billion a year, a "saving" of $8 billion a year. Doesn't this fact mean that Pioneerland's balance of trade has changed? Is Pioneerland now importing less than it is exporting?

To answer that question, we need to figure out what's happening in Magic Empire. We've just seen that the price that Magic Empire receives for cars has fallen from $3000 to $2000 a car. Thus the price of cars in Magic Empire has fallen. But if the price of cars has fallen, the price of grain has increased. With free trade, the Magicians could buy 3000 bushels of grain for one car. Now they can buy only 2000 bushels for a car. With a higher price of grain, the quantity demanded by the Magicians decreases. As a result, Magic Empire's import of grain declines. But so does Pioneerland's export of grain. In fact, Pioneerland's grain industry suffers from two sources. First, there is a decrease in the quantity of grain sold to Magic Empire. Second, there is increased competition for inputs from the now expanded car industry. Thus the tariff leads to a contraction in the scale of the grain industry in Pioneerland.

It seems paradoxical at first that a country imposing a tariff on cars would hurt its own export industry, lowering its exports of grain. It may help to think of it this way: Foreigners buy grain with the money they make from exporting cars. If they export fewer cars, they cannot afford to buy as much grain. In fact, in the absence of any international borrowing and lending, Magic Empire has to cut its imports of grain by exactly the same amount as the loss in revenue from its export of cars. Grain imports into Magic Empire will be cut back to a value of $4 billion, the amount that can be paid for by the new lower revenue from Magic Empire's car exports. Thus trade is still balanced in this post-tariff situation. Although the tariff has cut imports, it has also cut exports, and the cut in the value of exports is exactly equal to the cut in the value of imports. The tariff, therefore, has no effect on the balance of trade—it reduces the volume of trade.

The result that we have just derived is perhaps one of the most misunderstood aspects of international economics. On countless occasions, politicians and others have called for tariffs in order to remove a balance of trade deficit or have argued that lowering tariffs would produce a balance of trade deficit. They reach this conclusion by failing to work out all the implications of a tariff. Because a tariff raises the price of imports and cuts imports, the easy conclusion is that the tariff strengthens the balance of trade. But the tariff also changes the *volume* of exports as well. The equilibrium effects of a tariff are to reduce the volume of trade in both directions and by the same value on each side of the equation. The balance of trade itself is left unaffected.

Learning the Hard Way   Although the analysis that we have just worked through leads to the clear conclusion that tariffs cut both imports and exports and make everyone worse off, we have not found that conclusion easy to accept. Time and again in our history we have imposed high tariff barriers on international trade (as Fig. 35.6 illustrates). Whenever tariff barriers are increased, trade collapses. The most vivid historical example of this interaction of tariffs and trade occurred during the Great Depression years of the early 1930s when in the wake of the Smoot-Hawley tariff increases and the retaliatory tariff changes that other countries introduced as a consequence, world trade almost dried up.

Let's now turn our attention to the other range of protectionist weapons—nontariff barriers.

Nontariff Barriers

There are two important forms of nontariff barriers:

- Quotas
- Voluntary export restraints

A **quota** is a quantitative restriction on the import of a particular good. It specifies the maximum amount of the good that may be imported in a given period of time. A **voluntary export restraint** is an agreement between two governments in which the government of the exporting country agrees to restrain the volume of its own exports. Voluntary export restraints are often called VERs.

Nontariff barriers have become important features of international trading arrangements in the period since World War II and there is now general agreement that nontariff barriers are a more severe impediment to international trade than tariffs.

It is difficult to quantify the effects of nontariff barriers in a way that makes them easy to compare with tariffs, but some studies have attempted to do just that. Such studies attempt to assess the tariff rate that would restrict trade by the same amount as the nontariff barriers do. With such calculations, nontariff barriers and tariffs can be added together to assess the total amount of protection. When we add nontariff barriers to tariffs for the United States, the overall amount of protection increases more than threefold. Even so, the United States is the least protectionist country in the world. Total protection in the European Communities is higher, and higher still in other developed countries and Japan. The less developed countries and the so-called newly industrializing countries have the highest protection rates of all.

Quotas are especially important in the textile industries, where there exists an international agreement called the Multifibre Arrangement, which establishes quotas on a wide range of textile products. Agriculture is also subject to extensive quotas. Voluntary export restraints are particularly important in regulating the international trade in cars between Japan and the United States.

How Quotas and VERs Work

To understand how nontariff barriers affect international trade, let's return to the example of trade between Pioneerland and Magic Empire. Suppose that Pioneerland imposes a quota on car imports. Specifically, suppose that the quota restricts imports to not more than 2 million cars a year. What are the effects of this action?

The answer is found in Fig. 35.8. The quota is shown by the vertical red line at 2 million cars a year. Since it is illegal to import more than that number of cars, car importers buy only that quantity from Magic Empire producers. They pay $2000 a car to the Magic Empire producer. But what do they sell their cars for? The answer is $6000 each. Since the import supply of cars is restricted to 2 million cars a year, people with cars for sale will be able to get $6000 each for them. The quantity of cars imported equals the quantity determined by the quota.

Importing cars is now obviously a profitable business. An importer gets $6000 for an item that costs only $2000. Thus there is severe competition

Figure 35.8   The Effects of a Quota

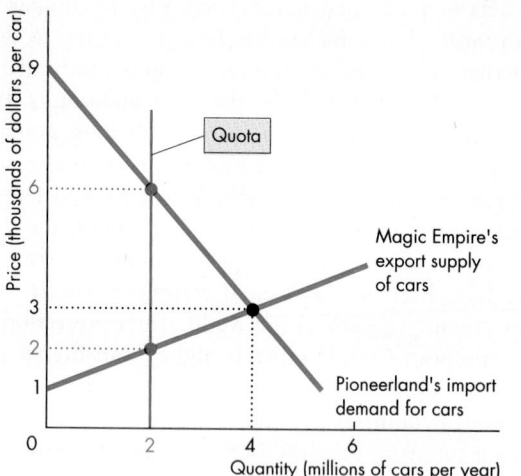

Pioneerland imposes a quota of 2 million cars a year on car imports from Magic Empire. That quantity appears as the vertical red line marked "Quota." Since the quantity of cars supplied by Magic Empire is restricted to 2 million, the price at which those cars will be traded increases to $6000. Importing cars is profitable since Magic Empire is willing to supply cars at $2000 each. There is competition for import quotas—rent seeking.

among car importers for the available quotas. It is the pursuit of the profits from quotas that Anne Krueger calls "rent seeking" (see "Talking with Anne Krueger," pp. 913–916).

The value of imports—the amount paid to Magic Empire—declines to $4 billion, exactly the same as in the case of the tariff. Thus with lower incomes from car exports and with a higher price of grain, the Magicians cut back on their imports of grain in exactly the same way they did under a tariff.

The key difference between a quota and a tariff lies in who gets the profit represented by the difference between the import supply price and the domestic selling price. In the case of a tariff, that difference goes to the government. In the case of a quota, that difference goes to the person who has the right to import under the import-quota regulations.

A voluntary export restraint is like a quota arrangement where quotas are allocated to each exporting country. The effects of voluntary export restraints are similar to those of quotas but differ from them in that the gap between the domestic price and the export

price is captured not by domestic importers but by the foreign exporter. The government of the exporting country has to establish procedures for allocating the restricted volume of exports among its producers.

Paying with Your Shirt!   Two of the most heavily protected industries in the United States today are apparel and textiles. It has been estimated that the total protection on these industries, most of which takes the form of quotas, costs the average American family between $200 and $400 a year. Despite this fact, the House of Representatives passed a new act (the Textile and Apparel Trade Act) in 1975 which, if it had become law, would have increased protection in those industries even further, adding $300 to $400 a year in additional costs for the average household.[1] Taking all protection together, it has been estimated that the cost per year to an individual U.S. family is more than $1000.[2]

Another way of looking at the cost of protection is to calculate the cost per job saved. It has been estimated, for example, that to protect one job in the textile industry costs $46,000 a year; one job in the footwear industry costs close to $80,000 a year, and one job in the carbon, steel, and auto industries costs more than $80,000 a year. In all these cases, it costs many times more to save a job through international trade barriers than the wages of the workers involved.[3]

R E V I E W

When a country opens itself up to international trade and trades freely at world market prices, it expands its consumption possibilities. When trade is restricted, some of the gains from trade are lost. A country may be better off with restricted trade than with no trade but not as well off as it could be if it engaged in free trade. A tariff reduces the volume of imports,

---

[1] For more on this topic, see "Expanding Trade and Avoiding Protectionism," *Economic Report of the President* (1988), pp. 127–162.

[2] Murray Weidenbaum and N. Munger, "Protection at Any Price?" *Regulation* (July/August 1983), pp. 14–18.

[3] Keith E. Maskus, "Rising Protectionism and U.S. International Trade Policy," *Economic Review* (July/August 1984), Federal Reserve Bank of Kansas City, pp. 3–17.

but it also reduces the volume of exports. Under both free trade and restricted trade (and without international borrowing and lending), the value of imports equals the value of exports. With restricted trade, both the total value of exports and the total value of imports are lower than under free trade, but trade is still balanced. ∎

Why Quotas and VERs Might Be Preferred to Tariffs

At first sight, it seems puzzling that countries would ever want to use quotas and even more puzzling that they would want to use voluntary export restraints. We have seen that the same domestic price and the same quantity of imports can be achieved by using any of the three devices for restricting trade. However, a tariff provides the government with a source of revenue; a quota provides domestic importers with a profit; and a voluntary export restraint provides the foreigner with a profit. Why, then, would a country use a quota or a voluntary export restraint rather than a tariff?

There are three possible reasons. First, a government can use quotas to reward its political supporters. Under a quota, licenses to import become tremendously profitable. So the government bestows riches on the people to whom it gives licenses to import. Second, quotas are more precise instruments for holding down imports. As demand fluctuates, the domestic price of the good fluctuates but not the quantity of imports. You can see this implication of a quota by going back to Fig. 35.8. Suppose that the demand for imports fluctuates. With a quota, these demand fluctuations simply produce fluctuations in the domestic price of the import but no change in the volume of imports. With a tariff, fluctuations in demand lead to no change in the domestic price but to large changes in the volume of imports. Thus if for some reason the government wants to control the quantity of imports and does not care about fluctuations in the domestic price, it will use a quota. Third, different branches of government have jurisdiction over different aspects of international trade restriction. Congress has the power to impose tariffs. The administration has the power to impose nontariff barriers. Thus changing tariffs is a slow and cumbersome matter requiring the passage of an act of Congress. In contrast, nontariff barriers can be changed quickly provided the administration is persuaded of the need for the change.

Why would a government use voluntary export restraints rather than a tariff or quota? The government may want to avoid a tariff or quota war with another country. If one country imposes a tariff or a quota, that might encourage another country to impose a similar tariff or quota on the exports of the first country. Such a tariff and quota war would result in a much smaller volume of trade and a much worse outcome for both countries. A voluntary export restraint can be viewed as a way of achieving trade restrictions to protect domestic industries but with some kind of compensation to encourage the foreign country to accept that situation and not retaliate with its own restrictions. Finally, VERs are often the only form of trade restriction that can be legally entered into under the terms of the General Agreement on Tariffs and Trade.

Dumping and Countervailing Duties

Dumping is the selling of a good in a foreign market for a lower price than in the domestic market or for a lower price than its cost of production. Such a practice can arise from discriminating monopoly seeking to maximize profit. An example of alleged dumping has occurred with Japanese sales of steel to the United States. Under current U.S. law and under GATT, dumping is illegal and antidumping duties may be imposed on foreign producers if U.S. producers can show that they have been injured by dumping.

Countervailing duties are tariffs that are imposed to enable domestic producers to compete with subsidized foreign producers. Often, foreign governments subsidize some of their domestic industries. Two examples are the Canadian pork and lumber industries. Under current U.S. law, if American producers can show that a foreign subsidy has damaged their market, a countervailing duty may be imposed.

Why Is International Trade Restricted?

There are many reasons why international trade is restricted. We've just seen two reasons—to offset the effects of dumping and of foreign subsidies. Even in these cases, it does not obviously benefit a country to protect itself from cheap foreign imports. However, more generally, we've seen that international trade benefits a country by raising its consumption possibilities. Why do we restrict international trade when such restrictions lower our consumption possibilities?

The key reason is that consumption possibilities increase *on the average* but not everyone shares in the gain and some people even lose. Free trade brings benefits to some and costs to others, with total benefits exceeding total costs. It is the uneven distribution of costs and benefits that is the principal source of impediment to achieving more liberal international trade.

Returning to our example of international trade in cars and grain between Pioneerland and Magic Empire, the benefits from free trade accrue to all the producers of grain and those producers of cars who would not have to bear the costs of adjusting to a smaller car industry. The costs of free trade are borne by those car producers and their employees who have to move and become grain producers. The number of people who gain will, in general, be enormous compared with the number who lose. The gain per person will, therefore, be rather small. The loss per person to those who bear the loss will be large. Since the loss that falls on those who bear it is large, it will pay those people to incur considerable expense in order to lobby against free trade. On the other hand, it will not pay those who gain to organize to achieve free trade. The gain from trade for any one individual is too small for that individual to spend much time or money on a political organization to achieve free trade. The loss from free trade will be seen as being so great by those bearing that loss that they *will* find it profitable to join a political organization to prevent free trade. Each group is optimizing—weighing benefits against costs and choosing the best action for themselves. The anti–free trade group will, however, undertake a larger quantity of political lobbying than the pro–free trade group.

Compensating Losers

If, in total, the gains from free international trade exceed the losses, why don't those who gain compensate those who lose so that everyone is in favor of free trade? To some degree, such compensation does take place. It also takes place indirectly as a consequence of unemployment compensation arrangements. But, as a rule, only limited attempts are made to compensate those who lose from free international trade. The main reason why full compensation is not attempted is that the costs of identifying the losers would be

enormous. Also, it would never be clear whether or not a person who has fallen on hard times is suffering because of free trade or for other reasons, and perhaps reasons largely under the control of the individual. Furthermore, some people who look like losers at one point in time may, in fact, wind up gaining. The young auto worker who loses his job in Michigan and becomes a computer assembly worker in Minneapolis resents the loss of work and the need to move. But a year or two later, looking back on events, he counts himself fortunate. He's made a move that has increased his income and given him greater job security.

It is because we do not, in general, compensate the losers from free international trade that protectionism is such a popular and permanent feature of our national economic and political life.

Political Outcome

The political outcome that emerges from this activity is one in which a modest amount of restriction on international trade occurs and is maintained. Politicians react to constituencies pressing for protection and find it necessary, in order to get re-elected, to support legislative programs that protect those constituencies. The producers of protected goods are far more vocal and much more sensitive swing-voters than the consumers of those goods. The political outcome, therefore, leans in the direction of maintaining protection.

The politics of trade can be seen easily today. The United States restricts imports of sugar by quota. Who profits from the quotas? Not the foreign exporters. Whereas voluntary export restraints give exporters like Toyota and Honda big profits, quotas do not help foreign producers. In this case, the quotas have brought real economic and political suffering to Central American and Caribbean countries which produce sugar. The U.S. sugar growers, on the other hand, benefit from the quotas.

Do sugar growers participate in politics? They certainly do, as surfaced in a debate among Democratic candidates during the presidential primaries in 1988. Missouri congressman Richard Gephardt was campaigning for the Democratic nomination for president on a platform of trade restrictions. One of his opponents, Massachusetts governor Michael Dukakis, questioned Mr. Gephardt on contributions to his campaign from the sugar industry.

Mr. Gephardt defended his willingness to take money from corporate and labor groups, arguing that those who contributed to him did not always agree with him.

"Don't give us this establishment stuff," Mr. Dukakis retorted, "when you're out there taking their money."

Mr. Gephardt in turn challenged the Governor for accepting money from companies that did business with Massachusetts.

"These two guys have eliminated themselves," Mr. Jackson cut in. "I am the choice."

The Reverend Jesse Jackson went on to demonstrate his understanding of the economics of politics, observing that "lobbyists would lose their jobs if they gave their money continuously against the interests they were working for."[4]

■ You've now seen how free international trade enables everyone to gain from increased specialization

_____

[4]*New York Times* (March 1, 1988), p. B7.

and exchange. By producing goods at which we have a comparative advantage and exchanging some of our own production for that of others, we expand our consumption possibilities. Placing impediments on that exchange when it crosses national borders restricts the extent to which we can gain from specialization and exchange. By opening our country up to free international trade, the market for the things that we sell expands and the price rises. The market for the things that we buy also expands and the price falls. All countries gain from free international trade. As a consequence of price adjustments, and in the absence of international borrowing and lending, the value of imports adjusts to equal the value of exports.

In the next chapter, we're going to study the ways in which international trade is financed and also learn why international borrowing and lending that permits unbalanced international trade arises. We'll discover the forces that determine the U.S. balance of payments and the value, in terms of foreign currency, of our dollar.

S U M M A R Y

Patterns and Trends in International Trade

Large flows of trade take place between rich and poor countries. Resource-rich countries exchange natural resources for manufactures, and resource-poor countries import their resources in exchange for their own manufactures. However, by far the biggest volume of trade is in manufactures exchanged among the rich industrialized countries. The biggest single U.S. export item is machinery. However, its biggest single net export is grain. Trade in services has grown in recent years. Total trade has also grown over the years. The U.S. balance of trade fluctuates around zero, but since 1982 the United States has had a balance of trade deficit. (pp. 919–922).

Opportunity Cost and Comparative Advantage

When opportunity costs differ between countries, the country with the lowest opportunity cost of producing a good is said to have a comparative advantage in

that good. Comparative advantage is the source of the gains from international trade. A country can have an absolute advantage, but not a comparative advantage, in the production of all goods. Every country has a comparative advantage in something. (pp. 922–924)

The Gains from Trade

Countries can gain from trade if their opportunity costs differ. Through trade, each country can obtain goods at a lower opportunity cost than it could if it produced all goods at home. Trading allows consumption to exceed production. By specializing in producing the good in which it has a comparative advantage and then trading some of that good for imports, a country can consume at points outside its production possibility frontier. Each country can consume at such a point.

In the absence of international borrowing and lending, trade is balanced as prices adjust to reflect the international supply and demand for goods. The world price is established at the level that balances the production and consumption plans of the trading parties. At the equilibrium price, trade is balanced and domestic consumption plans exactly match a combination of domestic production and international trade.

Comparative advantage explains the enormous volume and diversity of international trade that takes place in the world. But much trade takes the form of exchanging similar goods for each other—one type of car for another. Such trade arises because of economies of scale in the face of diversified tastes. By specializing in producing a few goods, having long production runs, and then trading those goods internationally, consumers in all countries can enjoy greater diversity of products at lower prices. (pp. 924–929)

Trade Restrictions

A country can restrict international trade by imposing tariffs or nontariff barriers—quotas and voluntary export restraints. All trade restrictions raise the domes-

tic price of imported goods, lower the volume of imports, and reduce the total value of imports. They also reduce the total value of exports by the same amount as the reduction in the value of imports.

All trade restrictions create a gap between the domestic price and the foreign supply price of an import. In the case of a tariff, that gap is the tariff revenue collected by the government. But the government raises no revenue from a quota. Instead, domestic importers who have a license to import increase their profit. A voluntary export restraint resembles a quota except that a higher price is received by the foreign exporter.

Governments restrict trade because restrictions help the producers of the protected commodity and the workers employed by those producers. Because their gain is sufficiently large and the loss per consumer sufficiently small, the political equilibrium favors restricted trade. Politicians pay more attention to the vocal and active concerns of the few who stand to lose than to the quieter and less strongly expressed views of the many who stand to gain. (pp. 929–939)

K E Y   C O N C E P T S

Key Figures

R E V I E W   Q U E S T I O N S

1 What are the main exports and imports of the United States?

2 How does the United States trade services internationally?

3 Which items of international trade have been growing the most quickly in recent years?

4 What is comparative advantage? Why does it lead to gains from international trade?

5 Explain why international trade brings gains to all countries.

6 Distinguish between comparative advantage and absolute advantage.

7 Explain why all countries have a comparative advantage in something.

8 Explain why we import and export such large quantities of certain similar goods—such as cars, for example.

9 What are the main ways in which we restrict international trade?

10 What are the effects of a tariff?

11 What are the effects of a quota?

12 What are the effects of a voluntary export restraint?

13 Describe the main trends in tariffs and nontariff barriers.

14 Which countries have the largest restrictions on their international trade?

15 Why do countries restrict international trade?

P R O B L E M S

1 a) Using Fig. 35.2, calculate the opportunity cost of cars in Pioneerland at the point on the production possibility frontier at which 4 million cars are produced.

b) Using Fig. 35.3, calculate the opportunity cost of a car in Magic Empire when it produces 8 million cars.

c) With no trade, Pioneerland produces 4 million cars and Magic Empire produces 8 million cars. Which country has a comparative advantage in the production of cars?

d) If there is no trade between Pioneerland and Magic Empire, how much grain is consumed and how many cars are bought in each country?

2 Suppose that the two countries in problem 1 trade freely.

a) Which country exports grain?

b) What adjustments will be made to the amount of each good produced by each country?

c) What adjustment will be made to the amount of each good consumed by each country?

d) What can you say about the price of a car under free trade?

3 Compare the total production of each good produced in problems 1 and 2.

4 Compare the situation in problems 1 and 2 with that analyzed in this chapter (pp. 922–926). Why does Magic Empire export cars in the chapter but import them in problem 2?

5 The following figure depicts the international market for soybeans.

a) What is the world price of soybeans if there is free trade between these countries?

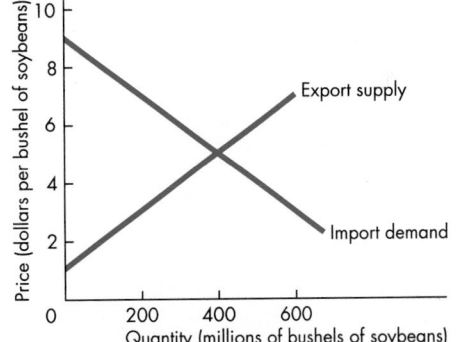

b) If the country that imports soybeans imposes a tariff of $2 per bushel, what is the world price of soybeans and what quantity of soybeans gets traded internationally? What is the price of soybeans in the importing country? Calculate the tariff revenue.

6 If the importing country in problem 5a imposes a quota of 300 million bushels, what is the price of soybeans in the importing country? What is the revenue from the quota and who gets this revenue?

7 If the exporting country in problem 5a imposes a VER of 300 million bushels of soybeans, what is the world price of soybeans? What is the revenue of soybean growers in the exporting country? Which country gains from the VER?

8 Suppose that the exporting country in problem 5(a) subsidizes production by paying its farmers $1 a bushel for soybeans harvested.

a) What is the price of soybeans in the importing country?

b) What action might soybean growers in the importing country take? Why?

Chapter 36

The Balance of Payments and the Dollar

After studying this chapter, you will be able to:

- Explain how international trade is financed

- Describe a country's balance of payments accounts

- Explain what determines the amount of international borrowing and lending

- Explain why the United States changed from being a lender to being a borrower in the mid-1980s

- Explain how the foreign exchange value of the dollar is determined

- Explain why the foreign exchange value of the dollar has fluctuated in the 1980s

- Explain the effects of changes in the exchange rate

- Explain what determines interest rates and why they vary so much from one country to another

Foreigners are buying American assets at an astonishing rate: Carnation Foods, the canned concentrated milk producer, was bought by Swiss business interests for $3 billion; Doubleday, the publisher, was bought by West Germans for $0.5 billion. Allied Stores, which owns Brooks Brothers, was bought by Canadians for $3.5 billion. Smith and Wesson, that most American of gun manufacturers, was bought by the British for $0.1 billion. Sohio gasoline stations were bought out by British Petroleum for $7.6 billion. Chesebrough-Pond's, the makers of cleansing cream and Q-tips, were bought by a Dutch and British firm for $3.1 billion. Dunes Hotel and Country Club, one of Las Vegas's best known gambling and entertainment centers, is now owned by the Japanese. Tycoons such as Britain's Gordon White, Canada's Robert Campeau, West Germany's Mark Wossner, Australia's George Herscu, and Japan's Shigeru Kobayashi are roaming the United States with a giant shopping cart and loading it up with everything in sight, from high-rise buildings in Manhattan to shopping malls in Los Angeles. ■ What is causing this foreign invasion of the United States? Why are foreigners finding U.S. businesses and real estate such attractive investments? This phenomenon is a very new one. Until the mid-1980s, Americans were the major buyers of foreign business interests. What has happened in the late 1980s to reverse this longstanding pattern? ■ In 1971, one U.S. dollar was enough to buy 360 Japanese yen. At the end of 1988, that same dollar bought only 120 yen. But the slide from 360 to 120 yen was not a smooth one. At certain times, the dollar held its own or even rose in value against the Japanese currency, as it did, for example, in 1982. But at other times, the dollar's slide was precipitous, as in the period since 1985. The dollar has not fallen in value only against the Japanese currency. It has fallen

For Sale: America

against the German mark and the Swiss franc. But the dollar has gained in value in terms of the Canadian dollar, the British pound, and the French franc.   ■ What does the value of the dollar have to do with the prices of the things that we buy—with the price of an English tweed coat, a Korean VCR, a Japanese car, or a foreign vacation? Do Eddie Bauer mountain jackets sold in Canada cost the same as the identical jacket sold in the United States? What makes our dollar fluctuate in value against other currencies? Why have the fluctuations been particularly extreme in recent years? Is there anything we can do to stabilize the value of the dollar?   ■ The world is becoming ever more integrated. In October 1987, when Wall Street crashed, so also did the stock markets of Japan and Western Europe. But despite the fact that the world is getting smaller, there are enormous differences in the interest rates at which people borrow and lend around the world. For example, at the close of 1988, the United States government was paying almost 10 percent per year on its long-term borrowing. At that same time, governments in Australia and Spain were paying more than 13 percent and in Canada, Italy, and the United Kingdom almost 11 percent. But in West Germany the government was paying only 6 percent, and in Japan and Switzerland barely more than 4 percent. How can interest rates around the world diverge so widely? Why don't loans dry up in low interest rate countries with all the money flooding to countries where interest rates are high? Why aren't interest rates made the same everywhere by the force of such movements?

■ During the 1980s, the issues of international economics have become important matters for millions of Americans. We're going to study these issues in this chapter. We're going to discover why the U.S. economy has become such an attractive target for foreign investors; why the United States has such a huge trade deficit with the rest of the world; why the dollar fluctuates so much against the values of other currencies; and why interest rates in the United States are so high compared with those in Japan, Germany, and Switzerland but still relatively low compared with those in most other countries.   ■ We're going to study the market forces that link countries together and that determine the values of their currencies, balance of payments, and interest rates.

Financing International Trade

When 47th Street Photo in New York City imports Minolta cameras, it does not pay for those cameras with U.S. dollars—it uses Japanese yen. When Saks Fifth Avenue imports Fila track suits, it pays for them using Italian lire. And when a French construction company buys an earth mover from Caterpillar, Inc., it uses U.S. dollars. Whenever we buy things from another country, we use the currency of that country in order to make the transaction. It doesn't make any difference what the item being traded is—it might be a consumer good or a capital good, a building, or even a firm.

We're going to study the markets in which transactions in money—in different types of currency—take place. But first we're going to look at the scale of international trading and borrowing and lending and at the way in which we keep our records of these transactions. Such records are called the balance of payments accounts.

Balance of Payments Accounts

A country's **balance of payments accounts** record its international trading, borrowing, and lending. There are in fact three balance of payments accounts:

• Current account

• Capital account

• Official settlements account

The **current account** records the receipts from the sale of goods and services to foreigners, the payments for goods and services bought from foreigners, and gifts and other transfers (such as foreign aid payments), received from and paid to foreigners. By far the largest items in the current account are the receipts from the sale of goods and services to foreigners (the value of exports) and the payments made for goods and services bought from foreigners (the value of imports). Net transfers are relatively small items. The **capital account** records all the international borrowing and lending transactions. The capital account balance records the difference between the amount that a country lends to and borrows from the rest of the world. The **official settlements account** shows the net increase or decrease in a country's holdings of foreign currency.

Table 36.1 shows the U.S. balance of payments accounts in 1988. As you can see from the table, the United States had a current account deficit of $126.6 billion in 1988. How do we pay for our current account deficit? That is, how do we pay for imports the value of which exceeds the value of our exports? We pay by borrowing from abroad. The capital account tells us by how much. We borrowed $219.3 billion but made loans of $85.7 billion. Thus our total borrowing, net of our foreign lending, was $123.0 billion. (Note that there is also a statistical discrepancy shown in the capital account. Actually, this discrepancy represents a combination of capital and current account transactions such as unidentified borrowing from abroad, illegal international trade—for example, the import of illegal drugs—and transactions not reported in order to illegally evade tariffs or other international trade protection measures.)

Table 36.1   U.S. Balance of Payments Accounts in 1988

	(billions of dollars)
Current account	
Imports of goods and services	−641.7
Exports of goods and services	529.8
Net transfers	−14.7
Current account balance	−126.6
Capital account	
Foreign investment in the United States	219.3
U.S. investment abroad	−85.7
Statistical discrepancy	10.6
Capital account balance	123.0
Official settlements account	
Increase in official U.S. reserves	3.6

Source: *Survey of Current Business* (June 1989) vol. 69, pp. 62–63.

The difference between our net borrowing from abroad and our current account deficit is the change in U.S. official reserves. **Official reserves** are the government's holdings of foreign currency. In 1988, those reserves increased by $3.6 billion (the difference between $123.0 billion and $126.6 billion).

The numbers in Table 36.1 give a snapshot of the balance of payments accounts in 1988. In that year, the United States had a large current account deficit and huge amounts of international borrowing. Is 1988 a typical year? By the late 1980s, it had become typical but it is certainly out of line with our longer history. Figure 36.1 shows part of that history going back to 1960. As you can see in part (a), the current account balance is almost a mirror image of the capital account balance. Changes in our foreign currency holdings (part b) are very small compared with the balances on these other two accounts.

You will perhaps obtain a better understanding of the balance of payments accounts and the way in which they are linked together if you consider the income and expenditure, borrowing and lending, and bank account of an individual.

Individual Analogy   An individual's current account records the income from supplying the services of factors of production and the expenditure on goods and services. Consider, for example, Joanne. She earned an income in 1989 of $25,000. Joanne has $10,000 worth of investments that earned her an income of $1000. Joanne's current account shows an income $26,000. Joanne spent $18,000 buying goods and services for consumption. She also bought a new house, which cost her $60,000. So Joanne's total expenditure was $78,000. The difference between her expenditure and income is $52,000 ($78,000 minus $26,000). This amount is Joanne's current account deficit.

To pay for expenditure of $52,000 in excess of her income, Joanne either has to use the money that she has in the bank or take out a loan. In fact, Joanne took a mortgage of $50,000 to help buy her house. This was the only borrowing that Joanne did, so her capital account surplus was $50,000.

With a current account deficit of $52,000 and a capital account surplus of $50,000, Joanne is still $2000 short. She got that $2000 from her own bank account. Her cash holdings decreased by $2000.

Joanne's supply of factors of production is analogous to a country's supply of exports. Her purchases of goods and services, including her purchase of a

Figure 36.1   The Balance of Payments

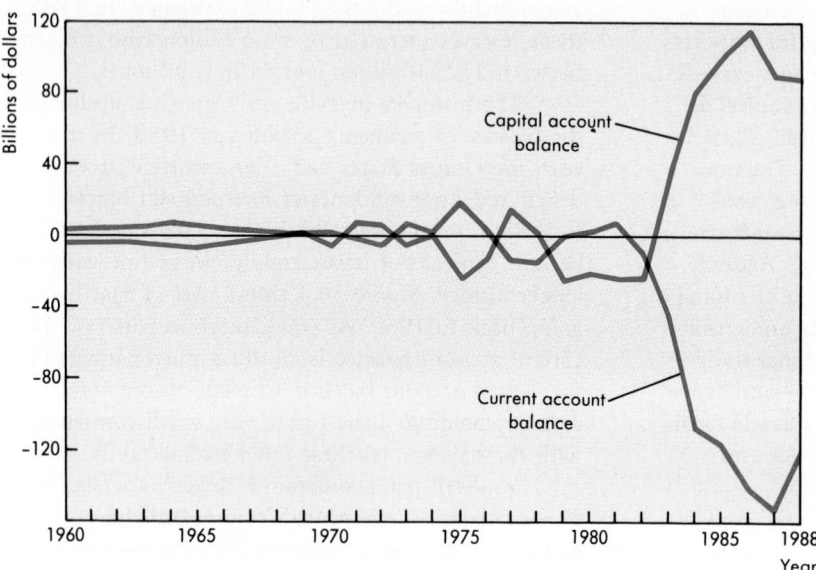

(a) Current and capital account balances

Part (a) shows the current account balance. This balance was positive (exports greater than imports) all through the 1960s. In the 1970s, there were fluctuations around a zero balance. In the 1980s, an enormous deficit arose. The capital account balance mirrors the current account balance. When the current account balance is positive, the capital account balance is negative—we lend to the rest of the world—and when the current account balance is negative, the capital account balance is positive—we borrow from the rest of the world. Part (b) shows the changes in the country's official holdings of foreign currency. Fluctuations in these holdings are small compared with fluctuations in the current account balance and the capital account balance.

Source: Economic Report of the President (1989), pp. 424–425.

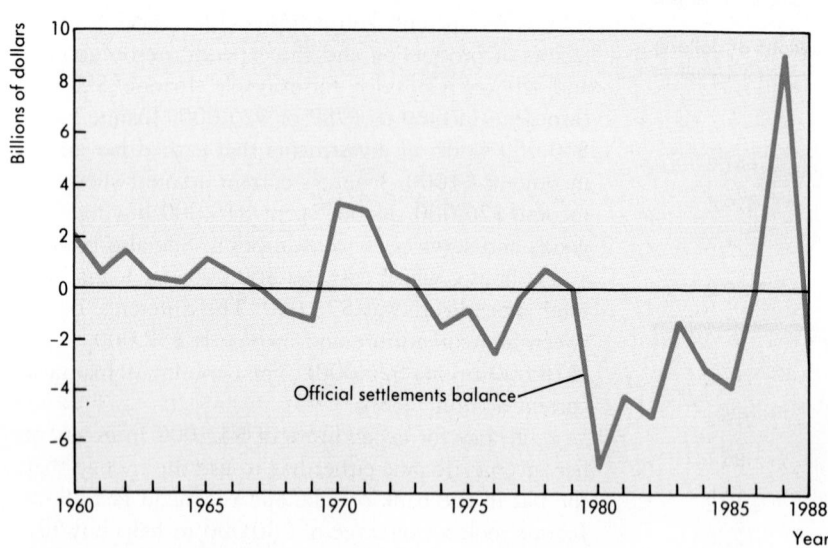

(b) Official settlements balance

house, are analogous to a country's imports. Joanne's mortgage—borrowing from someone else—is analogous to a country's foreign borrowing. Joanne's purchase of the house is analogous to foreign investment.

The change in her own bank account is analogous to the change in the country's official reserves.

Later in this chapter, we will study the factors that influence the official settlements balance, but for now we'll concentrate on the current account and the capital account.

Borrowers and Lenders, Debtors and Creditors

A country that is borrowing more from the rest of the world than it is lending to it is called a **net borrower.** Similarly, a **net lender** is a country that is lending more to the rest of the world than it is borrowing from it. A net borrower might be going deeper into debt or might simply be reducing its net assets held in the rest of the world. The total stock of foreign investment determines whether a country is a debtor or creditor. A **debtor nation** is a country that during its entire history has borrowed more from the rest of the world than it has lent to it. It has a stock of outstanding debt to the rest of the world that exceeds the stock of its own claims on the rest of the world. A **creditor nation** is a country that has invested more in the rest of the world than other countries have invested in it. The United States is a creditor nation but, in recent years, it has become a net borrower. A creditor nation is one whose net receipts of interest on debt are positive—payments made to it exceed the payments that it makes.

At the heart of the distinction between a net borrower/net lender and a debtor/creditor nation is the distinction between flows and stocks. Borrowing and lending is a flow. It is an amount borrowed or lent per unit of time. Debts are stocks. They are amounts owed at a point in time. The flow of borrowing and lending changes the stock of debt. But the outstanding stock of debt depends mainly on past flows of borrowing and lending, not on the current period's flows. The current period's flows determine the *change in* the stock of debt outstanding.

The United States is a newcomer to the ranks of net borrower nations. As you can see by glancing back at Fig. 36.1, throughout the 1960s and most of the 1970s, the United States had a surplus on its current account and a deficit on its capital account. Thus the country was a net lender to the rest of the world. It was not until 1983 that it became a significant net borrower. Since then, borrowing has increased each year and, by the end of the 1980s, exceeded $100 billion a year.

The United States is not the only net borrower nation. It is in the company of poorer countries that are at an earlier stage of economic development, such as South Korea, the Philippines, and Singapore. But unlike the United States, these countries not only are net borrowers, they are also debtor nations. That is, their total stock of borrowing from the rest of the world exceeds their lending. The debt of these developing countries has grown from less than a third to more than a half of their gross national product during the 1980s and has given rise to what has been called the "third world debt crisis."

The majority of countries are net borrowers. But a small number of countries are huge net lenders. Examples of net lenders are the oil-rich countries, such as Kuwait and Venezuela, and successful developed economies, such as Japan and West Germany.

Should the United States be concerned about the switch from being a net lender to a net borrower? The answer to this question depends mainly on what the net borrower is doing with the borrowed money. If borrowing is financing investment that in turn is generating economic growth and higher income, borrowing is not a problem. If the borrowed money is being used to finance consumption, then higher interest payments are being incurred and, as a consequence, consumption will eventually have to be reduced. The more the borrowing and the longer it goes on, the greater is the reduction in consumption that will eventually be necessary (see "Talking with Anne Krueger," pp. 913–916). We'll see below whether the United States is borrowing for investment or for consumption.

Current Account Balance

What determines the current account balance and the scale of a country's net foreign borrowing or lending?

To answer that question, we need to begin by recalling and using some of the things that we learned about the national income accounts. Table 36.2 is going to refresh your memory and summarize the necessary calculations for you. Part (a) lists the national income variables that are needed, with their symbols. Their values in the United States in 1988 are also shown.

Part (b) presents two key national income equations. First, equation (1) reminds us that gross national product is the sum of consumption expenditure, investment, government purchases of goods and services, and net exports (the difference between exports and imports). Equation (2) reminds us that aggregate income is used in three different ways. It can be consumed, saved, or paid to the government

Table 36.2   Determination of the Current Account Balance and Net Foreign Borrowing

	Symbols and equations	United States in 1988 (billions of dollars)
(a) Variables		
Gross national product (GNP)	Y	4,864
Consumption expenditure	C	3,228
Investment	I	767
Government purchases of goods and services	G	965
Exports of goods and services	EX	520
Imports of goods and services	IM	614
Saving	S	760
Taxes, net of transfer payments	T	878

(b) National income and expenditure			
Aggregate expenditure	(1)	$Y = C + I + G + EX - IM$	
Uses of income	(2)	$Y = C + S + T$	
Difference between (1) and (2)	(3)	$0 = I - S + G - T + EX - IM$	

(c) Surpluses and deficits			
Current account	(4)	$EX - IM = (T - G) + (S - I)$	$520 - 614 = -94$
Government budget		$T - G$	$878 - 965 = -87$
Private sector		$S - I$	$760 - 767 = -7$

in the form of taxes (net of transfer payments). Equation (1) tells us how our expenditure generates our income. Equation (2) tells us how we dispose of that income.

Part (c) of the table takes you into some new territory. It examines surpluses and deficits. We'll look at three surpluses/deficits—those of the current account, the government's budget, and the private sector. To get at these surpluses and deficits, first subtract equation (2) from equation (1) in Table 36.2. The result is equation (3). By rearranging equation (3), we obtain a relationship for the current account—exports minus imports—that appears as equation (4) in the table.[1]

Notice that the current account, in equation (4), is made up of two components. The first is taxes minus government spending and the second is saving minus investment. These items are the surpluses/deficits of the government and private sectors. Taxes (net of transfer payments) minus government purchases of goods and services is the budget surplus or

---

[1]In the national income accounts, the difference between exports and imports is called *net exports*. There are some slight differences in the way these numbers are calculated in national income accounts and balance of payments accounts but, for most purposes, you can regard net exports and the current account balance as meaning the same thing.

deficit. If that number is positive, the government's budget is a surplus, and if the number is negative, it is a deficit. The **private sector surplus or deficit** is the difference between saving and investment. If saving exceeds investment, the private sector has a surplus to lend to other sectors. If investment exceeds saving, the private sector has a deficit that has to be financed by borrowing from other sectors. As you can see from our calculations, the current account deficit is equal to the sum of the other two deficits—the government's budget deficit and the private sector deficit. In the United States in 1988, the most important of these other two deficits was the government budget deficit. The private sector was almost in balance and the $94 billion current account deficit was accounted for almost exclusively by the $87 billion government budget deficit.

Bookkeeping and Behavior

The calculations that we've just performed are really nothing more than bookkeeping. We've simply ma-nipulated the national income accounts and discovered that the current account deficit is just the sum of the deficits of the government and private sectors. But what determines those other two deficits? Why, for example, isn't the private sector in a surplus equal to the government's budget deficit so that the current account deficit is zero? Does an increase in the budget deficit always bring an increase in the current account deficit?

Government Budget and Current Account   You can see the answer to this question by looking at Fig. 36.2. In that figure, the government's budget balance is plotted alongside the current account balance. As you can see, these two balances move in close sympathy with each other. There is a clear tendency for the current account deficit to become larger when the budget deficit becomes larger. But the two series are not identical to each other. There are independent variations in the private sector deficit that loosen the connection between the government's budget deficit and the current account deficit. Let's see why.

Figure 36.2   Current Account and Government Budget

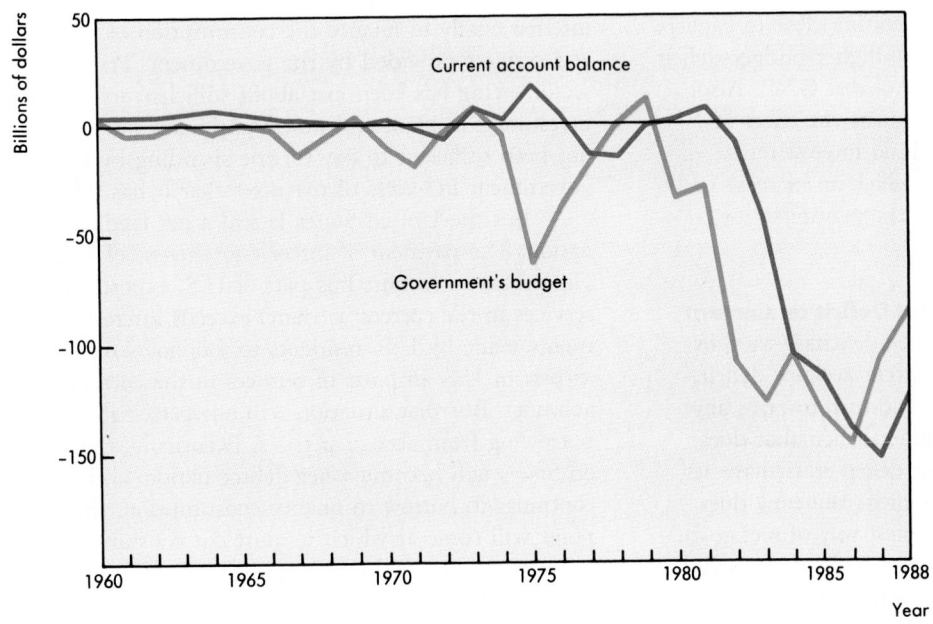

The current account and the government budget move in sympathy with each other. As the government budget deficit grew larger during the 1980s, so did the current account deficit.

Source: Economic Report of the President (1989), pp. 424–425.

Effects of Government Deficit on Private Sector Surplus   It is not surprising that there are fluctuations in the private sector surplus/deficit. As we've just seen, that variable is the gap between saving and investment. As we learned in Chapter 25, one of the main influences on the level of saving is disposable income. Anything that increases disposable income, other things being equal, increases saving and increases the private sector surplus. In that same chapter, we learned that investment depends on the interest rate and on expectations of future profits. Again, other things being equal, anything that lowers interest rates or increases future profit expectations increases investment and decreases the private sector surplus.

But when the government changes its taxes or spending—changing its budget deficit—there are some effects on income and interest rates that, in turn, influence private sector saving and investment and the private sector surplus/deficit. An increase in government purchases of goods and services or a tax cut—either of which will increase the budget deficit—tend to increase GNP and the interest rate. The higher GNP stimulates additional saving, but the higher interest rate dampens investment plans. Thus to some degree, an increased government budget deficit induces an increased private sector surplus. But the effect of the budget deficit on the private sector surplus occurs only if the government's actions do indeed stimulate higher income and higher interest rates. When the economy is operating close to capacity, as it is most of the time, the higher budget deficit does not produce a higher level of real GNP. Also, internationally mobile capital lessens the effect of increased government spending on interest rates. Thus the two mechanisms by which an increase in the budget deficit can increase the private sector surplus can be relatively weak.

Effects of Government Budget Deficit on Current Account Deficit   Since the three deficits—the government budget deficit, the current account deficit, and the private sector deficit—add up to zero, any change in the government budget deficit that does not influence the private sector deficit must have its effect on the current account deficit. But how does that effect come about? The easiest way of seeing the effect is to consider what happens when there is full employment. An increase in government purchases of goods and services or a tax cut leads to an increase in aggregate planned expenditure and an increase in aggregate demand. But with the economy at full

employment there is no spare capacity to generate a comparable increase in output. Part of the increased demand for goods and services, therefore, spills over into the rest of the world and imports increase. Also, part of the domestic production going for export is diverted to satisfy domestic demand. Exports decrease. The rise in imports and the fall in exports increases the current account deficit. The excess of imports over exports leads to a net increase in borrowing from the rest of the world.

Of course, the economy does not operate precisely at full employment. Nor does foreign capital flow in at a fixed interest rate. Thus the linkage between government budget deficit and the current account deficit is not a precise one. It is, nevertheless, a remarkably strong relationship, as we saw in Fig. 36.2.

Government policies designed to eliminate a current account deficit cannot achieve their objective if they do not take account of the effects of the government budget on the current account. (See Reading Between the Lines, pp. 952–953.)

Is U.S. Borrowing for Consumption or Investment?   We noted above that whether international borrowing is a problem or not depends on what that borrowing is used for. You can see that in recent years the United States has been borrowing internationally to finance the consumption of goods and services provided by the government. Private sector saving has been just about sufficient to pay for investment in plant and new equipment, but it has not been sufficient to pay for the spending by the government in excess of the taxes that it has collected.

But the United States is still a net creditor nation. The payment of interest to citizens of the United States (counted as part of U.S. exports of services in the current account) exceeds interest payments made by U.S. residents to foreigners (counted as part of U.S. imports of services in the current account). But that situation will not persist if net borrowing from abroad persists. Eventually, the United States will become a net debtor nation, and if it continues to borrow to finance consumption, the point will come at which it must cut consumption in order to pay the interest on its increasing amount of foreign debt.

Spreading Risks   Although foreign investors are lending to the United States to finance the government's budget deficit, they are not simply buying government bonds. Furthermore, although our own private sector saving is almost equal to investment, we are not the only people buying new capital equipment in the United States. Foreigners lend to the government and they buy private sector firms and open new firms. We use some of our savings to pay for the purchase of new capital equipment but we also use some savings to lend to the government. It is for these reasons that the dramatic events described in the chapter opener are taking place.

R E V I E W

When we buy goods from the rest of world, or invest in the rest of the world, we use foreign currency. When foreigners buy goods from us or invest in the United States, they use U.S. currency. We record international transactions in the balance of payments accounts. The current account shows our exports and imports of goods and services and net transfers to the rest of the world. The capital account shows our net foreign borrowing or lending. The official settlements account shows the change in the country's holdings of a foreign currency. In the late 1980s, the U.S. current account moved into a large deficit and the capital account moved into a large surplus — the country became a net borrower. The current account deficit is equal to the sum of the government budget deficit and the private sector deficit. In the United States, the private sector deficit is close to zero and the current account deficit is almost equal to the government budget deficit. We are borrowing from the rest of the world to pay for the consumption of goods and services provided by the government in excess of the taxes that we pay. ■

Foreign Exchange and the Dollar

When we buy foreign goods or invest in another country, we have to obtain some of that country's currency to make the transaction. When foreigners buy U.S.–produced goods or invest in the United States, they have to obtain some U.S. dollars. We get foreign currency and foreigners get U.S. dollars in the foreign exchange market. The **foreign exchange market** is the market in which the currency of one country is exchanged for the currency of another. The foreign exchange market is not a place like a downtown flea market or produce market. The market is made up of thousands of people — importers and exporters, banks, and specialists in the buying and selling of foreign exchange called foreign exchange brokers. The foreign exchange market opens on Monday morning in Tokyo, which is still Sunday evening in New York. As the day advances, markets open in Zurich, London, New York, and finally, Los Angeles and San Francisco. Before the west coast markets have closed, Tokyo is open again for the next day of business. The sun never sets on the foreign exchange market. Dealers around the world are continually in contact using computers linked by telephone. On any given day, billions of dollars change hands.

The price at which one currency exchanges for another is called a **foreign exchange rate.** For example, in November 1988, one U.S. dollar bought 121 Japanese yen. The exchange rate between the U.S. dollar and the Japanese yen was 121 yen per dollar. Exchange rates can be expressed either way. We've just expressed the exchange rate between the yen and the dollar as a number of yen per dollar. Equivalently, we could express the exchange rate in terms of dollars per yen. That exchange rate, in November 1988, was $0.008264 per yen. (In other words, a yen was worth slightly less than a penny).

The actions of the foreign exchange brokers make the foreign exchange market highly efficient. Exchange rates are almost identical no matter where in the world the transaction is taking place. If U.S. dollars were cheap in London and expensive in Tokyo, within a flash someone would have placed a buy order in London and a sell order in Tokyo, thereby increasing demand in one place and increasing supply in another, moving the prices to equality.

Foreign Exchange Regimes

Foreign exchange rates are of critical importance for millions of people. They affect the costs of our foreign vacations and our imported cars. They affect the number of dollars that we end up getting for the oranges and beef that we sell to Japan. Because of its importance, governments pay a great deal of attention to what is happening in foreign exchange markets and, more than that, take actions designed to achieve

The Making of a Mishmash

Congress Rushes to Pass a Sweeping Bill

Talk about spoiling the broth. Imagine trying to prepare dinner with 199 cooks watching every move. Something like that is happening on Capitol Hill, where a mammoth conference committee is trying to reconcile differences in the omnibus trade bills passed last year by the House and Senate. Under the direction of two Democratic leaders—Representative Dan Rostenkowski of Illinois and Senator Lloyd Bentsen of Texas—the 199 members of the committee, along with 300 or so staffers and 100 briefcase carriers sent over by the White House, have been meeting in 17 subgroups in an all-out effort to get a comprehensive piece of legislation on President Reagan's desk by April. The goal is to pass a bill that will bolster U.S. industry and reduce the trade deficit, which hit a record $171.2 billion in 1987. The danger is that the law will wind up as a potpourri of protectionist measures that serve special interests but hurt consumers and do nothing to boost the competitiveness of U.S. companies.

The issue of what to do about trade has long pitted the White House against Congress. The Reagan Administration philosophically embraces free trade, but the President has been under pressure from Capitol Hill to protect U.S. business interests. Rather than give Congress an excuse to pass protectionist legislation, the White House has taken a fairly tough line, bringing 17 actions since 1985 against nations deemed to be engaging in unfair trade practices. The most dramatic censure came last year, when the Administration imposed $300 million worth of sanctions against Japanese products after deciding Tokyo had reneged on parts of an agreement under which it would, among other things, import more U.S. computer chips.

The White House has angered Congress on several occasions by turning down pleas for import relief, most notably from the shoe industry. Many Democrats, and a few Republicans as well, are pushing for provisions in the trade bill that would force the Administration to retaliate automatically against unfair foreign traders. The President, though, has vowed to veto any bill that would take away his discretion on when to impose trade sanctions. The conflict has left the Democrats with a dilemma. Explains Rostenkowski: "We need a bill so tough that our trading partners can't ignore it, but so fair that the President wants to sign it."

Perhaps the most disturbing aspect of the trade bill is that many members of Congress are using it as a vehicle to promote their pet projects. Speaking last week at a committee hearing, Treasury Secretary James Baker praised Congress for being willing to compromise on sweeping issues such as what to do in response to unfair foreign trade practices. But Baker complained pointedly about the lack of "willingness to jettison amendments that sometimes are supported by only one member." In the same vein, Representative Robert Kastenmeier, a Wisconsin Democrat, castigated his colleagues: "A trade bill should be used to set trade policy, not provide some kind of discount Casbah for special interests."

Members of Congress have many motivations for championing causes that benefit only a few parties. Sometimes they may firmly believe in the worthiness of the proposals, or they may have been convinced by an effective lobbying campaign. Just as often, though, they may be out to please their constituents or those who have made major contributions to their campaigns. Both House and Senate versions of the free trade bill are larded with proposals of questionable merit and purpose. A few examples:

• Senator Max Baucus, a Democrat from the sheep-raising state of Montana, at first introduced a measure to set quotas on imported lamb. The idea was watered down in committee negotiations, but a provision that survives calls for federal payments to lamb producers if they are damaged by imports.

• A section of the trade bill known to Capitol Hill pundits as the "Timex provision" would lower the tariffs on imported watches and watch parts. The measure is sponsored by Representative Beryl Anthony, an Arkansas Democrat whose state has a Timex manufacturing plant. The company also assembles watches in foreign factories for import into the U.S.

• A measure introduced by Representative Don Bonker, a Washington Democrat, would protect certain kinds of U.S. wood products by restricting competing imports. In particular, the measure subjects grooved or pegged plywood, used for wall paneling and in making furniture, to higher tariffs. Washington's lumber industry has been hit hard by a surge in imported wood products.

• The Senate version of the trade bill contains a complex five-page proposal concerning patent protection for drugs that appears designed to benefit a single product. The provision would in effect enable Warner-Lambert, a pharmaceutical firm, to receive a five-year extension of the patent on Lopid, a cholesterol-reducing drug. The measure was introduced by Senator Dennis DeConcini, an Arizona Democrat who chairs the Subcommittee on Patents, Copyrights and Trademarks. Warner-Lambert reportedly hired a team of Washington lobbyists and lawyers to help DeConcini draft the proposal.

Most of these provisions, and many more like them, would provide a windfall for some but could damage consumers and taxpayers.

Time, March 28, 1988

by Gordon Bock and Jerome Cramer

The Essence of the Story

- In the spring of 1988, a conference committee of the House of Representatives and the Senate worked to produce a bill on international trade issues.

- The goal of the bill is to help U.S. industry and to reduce the deficit in U.S. international trade.

- The bill contains many detailed measures that hurt consumers and do not strengthen the competitiveness of U.S. companies: Examples are protection for lamb farmers, watchmakers, lumber firms, and pharmaceutical producers.

- Congress is protectionist and the administration supports free trade, so there is tension between the two branches of government.

- To discourage protectionist legislation, President Reagan took tough action against trade practices deemed to be unfair—for example, imposing sanctions against the Japanese for their unwillingness to import a larger quantity of U.S. computer chips.

- But President Reagan did not take all the actions requested of him and angered Congress on several occasions, notably by his refusal to protect the shoe industry.

- The omnibus trade bill is designed to limit the powers of the president and enhance those of Congress.

Background and Analysis

- Congress cannot balance U.S. international trade by using protectionist measures.

- The current account balance is defined by the equation:

$$\text{Current account balance} = \text{Exports} - \text{Imports} = (\text{Savings} - \text{Investment}) + \left(\text{Taxes} - \frac{\text{Government}}{\text{spending}}\right)$$

- Savings and investment are determined mainly by the level of GNP and interest rates and by expectations about the future state of the economy.

- The gap between savings and investment is not directly or importantly affected by protectionist laws.

- Taxes minus government spending is equal to the government budget deficit. This deficit is controlled by the actions of Congress.

- By increasing taxes or cutting government spending, Congress can directly influence the current account balance.

- By introducing protectionist measures, allegedly to remove a trade deficit, Congressmen can divert attention from the true purpose of their protectionist legislation—to compensate individuals and groups who in turn provide political support thereby preserving the delicate balance of political equilibrium.

what they regard as desirable movements in exchange rates. There are three ways in which the government can operate the foreign exchange market—three regimes. They are:

- Fixed exchange rate
- Flexible exchange rate
- Managed exchange rate

A **fixed exchange rate** is an exchange rate the value of which is pegged by the country's central bank. For example, the U.S. government could adopt a fixed exchange rate by defining the U.S. dollar to be worth a certain number of units of some other currency and with the Fed taking actions designed to maintain that announced value. We'll study what those actions are below.

A **flexible exchange rate** is an exchange rate the value of which is determined by market forces in the absence of central bank intervention. A **managed exchange rate** is an exchange rate the value of which is influenced by central bank intervention in the foreign exchange market. Under a managed exchanged rate regime, the central bank's intervention does not seek to keep the exchange rate fixed at a pre-announced level.

Recent Exchange Rate History

At the end of World War II, the major countries of the world set up the International Monetary Fund. The **International Monetary Fund** (IMF) is an international organization that monitors balance of payments and exchange rate activities. The IMF is located in Washington, D.C. It came into being as a result of negotiations between the United States and the United Kingdom during World War II. In July 1944, at Bretton Woods, New Hampshire, 44 countries signed the Articles of Agreement of the IMF. At the centerpiece of those agreements was the establishment of a worldwide system of fixed exchange rates between currencies. The anchor for this fixed exchange rate system was gold. One ounce of gold was defined to be worth 35 U.S. dollars. All other currencies were pegged to the U.S. dollar at a fixed exchange rate. For example, the Japanese yen was set at 360 yen per dollar; the British pound was set to be worth $4.80. Although the fixed exchange rate system established in 1944 served the world well during the 1950s and early 1960s, it came under increasing strain in the late 1960s and, by 1971, the order had

almost collapsed. In the period since 1971, the world has operated a variety of flexible and managed exchange rate arrangements. Some currencies have increased in value, and others have declined. The U.S. dollar is among the currencies that have declined. The Japanese yen is the currency that has had the most spectacular increase in value.

Figure 36.3(a) shows what has happened to the exchange rate of U.S. dollars in terms of Japanese yen since 1970. As you can see, the value of the dollar has fallen—the dollar has depreciated. **Currency depreciation** is the fall in the value of one currency in terms of another currency.

Just as the dollar has fallen in value in terms of the yen, so the yen has risen in value in terms of the dollar. The increase in the value of one currency in terms of another currency is called **currency appreciation.** You can see the appreciation of the yen and the depreciation of the dollar as the mirror image of each other in the two parts of Fig. 36.3.

Although the U.S. dollar has depreciated in terms of the Japanese yen, it has not depreciated, on the average, in terms of all other currencies. To calculate the value of the U.S. dollar in terms of other currencies on the average, a trade-weighted index is calculated. The **trade-weighted index** is the value of a basket of currencies where the weight placed on each currency is related to its importance in U.S. international trade. An example of the calculation of the trade-weighted index is set out in Table 36.3. In this example, we suppose that the United States trades only with three countries: Canada, Japan, and Great Britain. Fifty percent of the trade is with Canada, 30 percent with Japan, and 20 percent with Great Britain. In year 1, the U.S. dollar is worth either 1.25 Canadian dollars, 100 Japanese yen, or 0.50 British pounds. Imagine putting these three currencies into a "basket" worth 100 U.S. dollars, where 50 percent of the value of the basket is in Canadian dollars, 30 percent in Japanese yen, and 20 percent in British pounds. In year 1, the index number for the basket is 100. Suppose that in year 2, the exchange rates change in the way shown in the table. The Canadian dollar stays constant, the Japanese yen goes up in value, so that only 90 Japanese yen can be bought for one U.S. dollar, and the British pound goes down in value, so that one U.S. dollar buys 0.55 British pounds. What is the change in the value of the basket? The percentage changes in the value of the U.S. dollar against each currency are calculated in the table. The dollar goes down against the Japanese

Figure 36.3   Exchange Rates

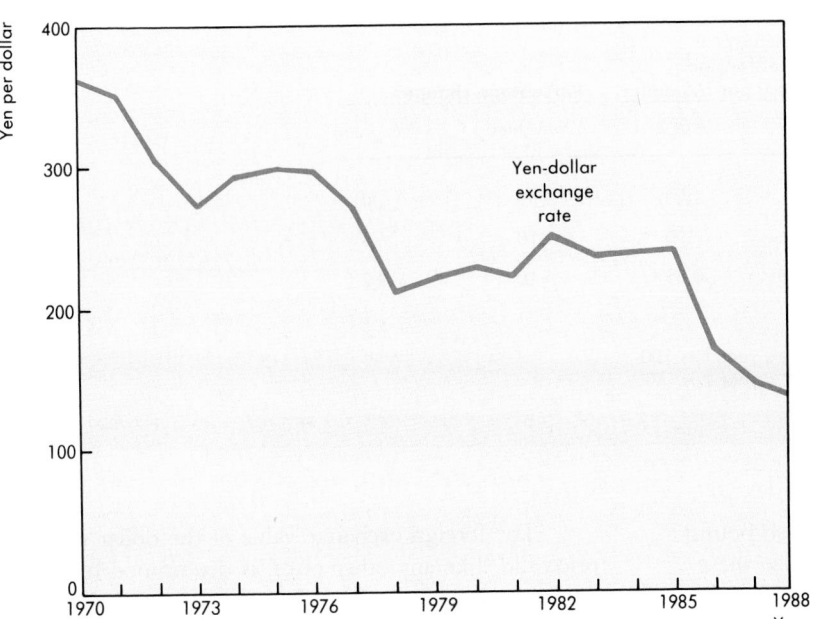

(a) Yen-dollar exchange rate

The exchange rate is the price at which two currencies can be traded. Part (a) shows the yen–dollar exchange rate expressed as yen per dollar. The dollar has fallen in value—depreciated—against the yen. Part (b) shows the yen–dollar exchange rate as cents per 100 yen. The price of yen in terms of U.S. cents has increased—the yen has appreciated against the dollar. An index of the value of the U.S. dollar against all currencies is also shown in part (b). The U.S. dollar appreciated on the average against all currencies although it depreciated slightly between 1985 and 1988.

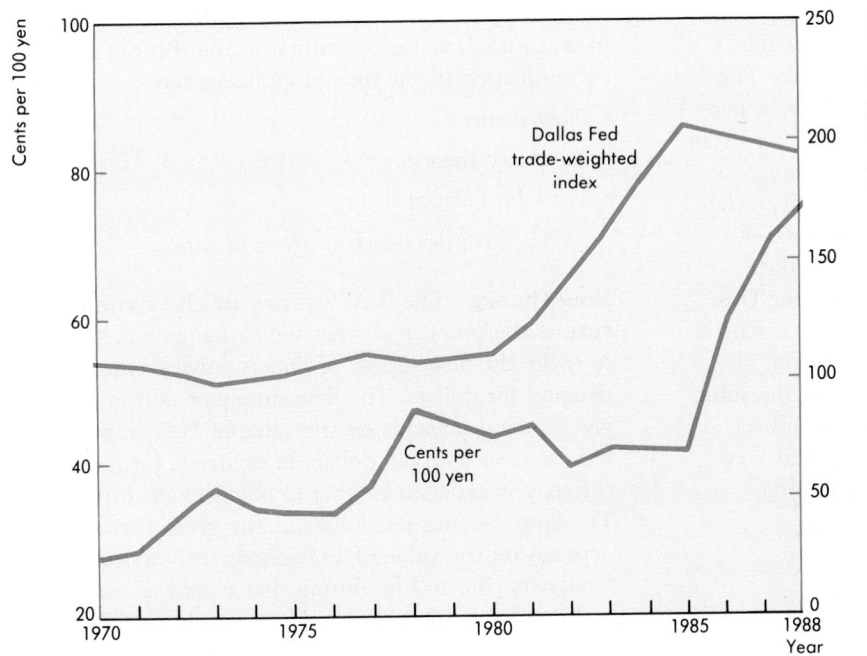

(b) The yen and other currencies

Sources: Economic Report of the President (1989), p. 431; and Federal Reserve Bank of Dallas, *Dallas Fed* (May 1989).

Table 36.3   Trade-Weighted Index Calculation

Currency	Trade weights	Exchange rates (units of foreign currency per U.S.dollar)		Percentage changes	
		Year 1	Year 2	Unweighted	Weighted
Canadian dollar	0.5	1.25	1.25	0	0
Japanese yen	0.3	100	90	−10	−3
British pound	0.2	0.50	0.55	+10	+2
Total	1.0				−1

Trade-weighted index: year 1 = 100
year 2 = 99

yen by 10 percent and up against the British pound by 10 percent. Applying the trade weights to these percentage changes, we can calculate the weighted average change in the value of the U.S. dollar. Since the weight on the Japanese yen is 0.3 and that on the British pound is 0.2, the yen is more important than the pound. That is, a larger fraction of the basket's value consists of yen than of pounds. The weighted average value of the basket falls by 1 percent. The trade-weighted index declines by 1 percent and is 99.

In this example, the U.S. dollar has depreciated on the average against the other three currencies.

The calculations that we have just worked through used hypothetical numbers. How the U.S. dollar has actually fluctuated against other currencies on the average in recent years is shown in Fig. 36.3(b). As you can see, during the 1970s the value of the U.S. dollar remained steady against other currencies; from 1980 to 1985 it appreciated very strongly; and after 1985 it depreciated slightly.

Exchange Rate Determination

What determines the foreign currency value of the dollar? Why has the dollar depreciated against the yen since 1970? Why was that depreciation particularly spectacular after 1985? Why did the dollar temporarily appreciate against the yen in 1982?

The foreign exchange value of the dollar is a price and, like any other price, is determined by demand and supply. But what exactly do we mean by the demand for and supply of dollars? There are, in fact, three different senses in which we can speak of the supply of and demand for dollars and all three have featured, at various times, in the theories of the determination of the foreign exchange rate:

• Flow theory

• Monetary theory

• Portfolio balance theory

Let's consider each of these in turn.

Flow Theory   The **flow theory of the exchange rate** is the proposition that the exchange rate adjusts to make the flow supply of dollars equal to the flow demand for dollars. The flow supply of dollars in any given period depends on the value of U.S. imports. U.S. residents supply dollars in exchange for foreign currency in order to be able to buy foreign imports. The flow demand for dollars in any given period depends on the value of U.S. goods (exports) that foreigners plan to buy during that period of time. In addition to the flow demand and supply resulting from imports and exports, there is also a net flow demand or supply resulting from international borrowing and lending. According to the flow theory of the exchange rate, the value of the exchange rate adjusts to keep the flow demand for a currency equal to its flow supply.

The flow theory of the foreign exchange rate has a serious shortcoming. It does not explain how the net flows associated with international borrowing and lending are determined. In fact, those flows result from people's decisions about which assets to hold. People have to choose whether to hold domestic or foreign assets and they also have to choose the currency in which their assets will be denominated. But these choices are choices about stocks, not flows. The decision to *change* the assets held results in *flows* but those *flows are the consequence of decisions about stocks.* Thus in considering the determination of the exchange rate, even if we approach the matter from the point of view of the flow supply and demand for a currency, we cannot avoid considering the demand for a currency as a stock to hold rather than as a flow. The emphasis on the demand for a stock of currency gives rise to the other two theories of the exchange rate. Let's now turn to them.

Monetary Theory   The **monetary theory of the exchange rate** is the proposition that the exchange rate adjusts to make the stock of a currency demanded equal to the stock supplied. The stock of a currency is identical to the *quantity of money.* In Chapter 28, we saw how the quantity of money in the United States—the quantity of U.S. dollar money—is determined by the behavior of the banking system and the actions of the Fed. The quantity of money in Japan—the quantity of yen money—is determined by similar actions of the Bank of Japan; the quantity of Canadian dollar money is determined by similar actions of the Bank of Canada, and so on. According to the monetary theory, the exchange rate adjusts to ensure that the quantity of money in each currency supplied equals the quantity demanded.

Some international finance economists regard the monetary theory of the exchange rate as too narrow and suggest that a broader asset aggregate should be considered. This consideration gives rise to the portfolio balance theory.

Portfolio Balance Theory   The **portfolio balance theory of the exchange rate** is the proposition that the exchange rate adjusts to make the stock of financial assets denominated in units of that currency demanded equal to the stock supplied. For example, the quantity of U.S. dollars supplied is the quantity of U.S. dollar–denominated securities. This total includes securities issued by the government and by firms. It also includes the U.S. money supply. But the money supply is just one part of the total stock of U.S. dollar-denominated assets. The exchange rate adjusts to make the total quantity of U.S. dollar-denominated assets demanded equal to the quantity supplied.

In studying the forces that determine the exchange rate, we'll work with this third and broadest theory—the portfolio balance theory. Let's now examine the forces that influence the quantity of dollar-denominated assets demanded and supplied.

The Demand for U.S. Dollar Assets   The law of demand applies to dollar assets just as it does to anything else that people value. The quantity of dollar assets demanded increases when the price of dollars in terms of foreign currency falls and decreases when the price of dollars in terms of foreign currency rises. There are two separate reasons why the law of demand applies to dollars. First, there is a transactions demand. The lower the value of the dollar, the larger is the demand for U.S. exports and the lower is our demand for imports. Hence the larger also is the amount of trade financed by dollars. Foreigners demand more dollars to buy U.S. exports and we demand fewer units of foreign currency and more dollars as we switch from importing to buying U.S.–produced goods.

Second, there is a demand arising from expected capital gains. Other things being equal, the lower the value of the dollar today, the higher is its expected rate of appreciation (or the lower is its expected rate of depreciation). Hence the higher is the expected gain from holding dollar assets relative to the expected gain from holding foreign currency assets. Suppose that you expect the dollar to be worth 110 Japanese yen at the end of one year. If today the dollar is worth 120 yen, you're expecting the dollar to depreciate by 10 yen. Other things being equal, you will not plan to hold dollar assets in this situation. Instead, you will plan to hold yen assets. But if today's value of the dollar is 100 yen, then you're expecting the dollar to appreciate by 10 yen. In this situation, you will plan to hold dollar assets and take advantage of the expected rise in their value. Holding assets in a particular currency in anticipation of a gain in their value arising from a change in the exchange rate is one of the most important influences on the quantity demanded of dollar assets and of foreign currency assets. The more a currency is expected to appreciate, the greater is the quantity of assets in that currency that people want to hold.

Figure 36.4   The Demand for Dollar Assets

The quantity of dollar assets that people demand, other things held constant, depends on the exchange rate. The lower the exchange rate (the smaller the number of yen per dollar), the larger is the quantity of dollar assets demanded. The increased quantity demanded arises from an increase in the volume of dollar trade (the Japanese buy more American goods and we buy fewer Japanese goods) and an increase in the expected appreciation (or decrease in the expected depreciation) of dollar assets.

Figure 36.4 shows the relationship between the foreign currency price of the U.S. dollar and the quantity of dollar assets demanded—the demand curve for dollar assets. When the foreign exchange rate changes, other things being equal, there is a movement along the demand curve.

Any other influence on the quantity of dollar assets that people want to hold results in a shift in the demand curve. Demand either increases or decreases. These other influences are:

• The volume of dollar-financed trade
• The U.S. price level
• The price levels in other countries
• The interest rates on dollar assets
• The interest rates on foreign currency assets
• The expected future value of the dollar

Table 36.4 summarizes the above discussion of the influences on the quantity of dollar assets that people demand.

Supply of Dollar Assets . The supply of dollar assets is determined primarily by the actions of the government—the Federal Reserve. The supply also depends crucially on the foreign exchange rate regime in operation. First, under a fixed exchange rate regime, the supply curve of dollar assets is horizontal at the chosen exchange rate. The government and the Fed stand ready to supply whatever quantity of dollar assets is demanded at the fixed exchange rate.

Under a managed exchange rate regime, where the government wants to smooth fluctuations in the exchange rate, the supply curve of dollar assets is upward-sloping. The higher the foreign exchange rate, the larger is the quantity of dollar assets supplied. Under a flexible exchange rate regime, a fixed quantity of dollar assets is supplied, regardless of their price. As a consequence, under a flexible exchange rate regime, the supply curve of dollar assets is vertical.

Table 36.4   The Demand for Dollar Assets

The law of demand

The quantity of dollar assets demanded

Increases if:	Decreases if:
• The foreign currency value of the dollar falls	• The foreign currency value of the dollar rises

Changes in demand

The demand for dollar assets

Increases if:	Decreases if:
• Dollar-financed trade increases	• Dollar-financed trade decreases
• The price level rises	• The price level falls
• The price level in other countries falls	• The price level in other countries rises
• Interest rates on dollar assets rise	• Interest rates on dollar assets fall
• Interest rates on foreign currency assets fall	• Interest rates on foreign currency assets rise
• The dollar is expected to strengthen	• The dollar is expected to weaken

The supply of dollar assets changes over time as a result of the following:

- The government's budget
- The Fed's monetary policy

If the government has a budget deficit, the supply of dollar assets increases. If the government has a budget surplus, the supply of dollar assets decreases. The supply of dollar assets increases whenever the Fed increases the money supply and decreases when the Fed reduces the money supply.

The above discussion of the influences on the supply of dollar assets is summarized in Table 36.5.

The Market for Dollar Assets   Let's now bring the demand and supply sides of the market for dollar assets together and determine the exchange rate. Figure 36.5 illustrates the analysis.

Fixed Exchange Rate   First, consider a fixed exchange rate regime such as that from 1944 to 1971. This case is illustrated in Fig. 36.5(a). The supply curve of dollars is horizontal at the fixed exchange rate of 200 yen per dollar. If the demand curve is D_0, the quantity of dollar assets is Q_0. An increase in demand to D_1 results in an increase in the quantity of dollar assets from Q_0 to Q_1 but no change in the yen price of dollars.

Flexible Exchange Rate   Next look at Fig. 36.5(b), which shows what happens under a flexible exchange rate regime. In this case, the quantity of dollar assets supplied is fixed at Q_0, so the supply curve of dollar assets is vertical. If the demand curve for dollars is D_0, the exchange rate is 200 yen per dollar. If the demand for dollars increases from D_0 to D_1, the exchange rate increases to 300 yen per dollar.

Managed Exchange Rate   Finally, consider a managed exchange rate regime, which appears in Fig. 36.5(c). Here, the supply curve is upward-sloping. When the demand curve is D_0, the exchange rate is 200 yen per dollar. If demand increases to D_1, the yen value of the dollar rises but only to 225 yen per dollar. Compared with the flexible exchange rate case, the same increase in demand results in a smaller increase in the exchange rate when it is managed. The reason for this is that the quantity supplied increases in the managed exchange rate case.

Table 36.5   The Supply of Dollar Assets

Supply

Fixed exchange rate regime

The supply curve of dollar assets is horizontal at the fixed exchange rate.

Managed exchange rate

In order to smooth fluctuations in the price of the dollar, the quantity of dollar assets supplied by the Fed increases if the foreign currency price of the dollar rises and decreases if the foreign currency price of the dollar falls. The supply curve of dollar assets is upward sloping.

Flexible exchange rate

The supply curve of dollar assets is vertical.

Changes in supply

The supply of dollar assets

Increases if:	Decreases if:
• The U.S. government has a deficit	• The U.S. government has a surplus
• The Fed increases the money supply	• The Fed decreases the money supply

Exchange Rate Regime and Official Settlements Balance   There is an important connection between the foreign exchange rate regime and the balance of payments. The official settlements account of the balance of payments records the change in the country's official holdings (by the government and the Fed) of foreign currency. Under fixed exchange rates (as shown in Fig. 36.5a), every time there is a change in the demand for dollar assets, the Fed must change the quantity of dollar assets supplied to match it. When the Fed has to increase the quantity of dollar assets supplied, it does so by offering dollar assets (bank deposits) in exchange for foreign currency (foreign bank deposits). In this case, the official holdings of foreign exchange increase. If the demand for dollar assets decreases, the Fed has to decrease the quantity of dollar assets supplied. The Fed does so by buying dollars back and using its foreign exchange holdings to do so. In this case, official holdings of foreign

Figure 36.5   Three Exchange Rate Regimes

(a) Fixed exchange rate

(b) Flexible exchange rate

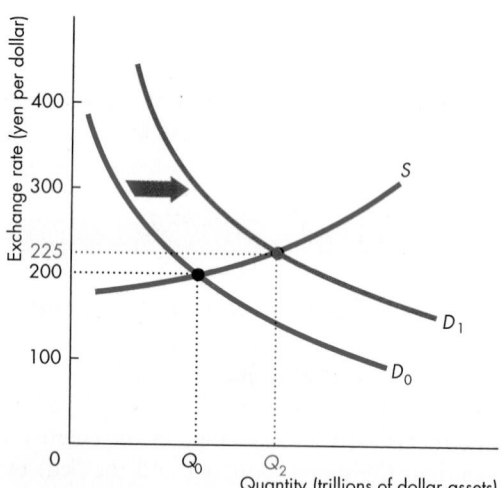

(c) Managed exchange rate

Under a fixed exchange rate regime (part a), the Fed stands ready to supply dollar assets or to take dollar assets off the market (supplying foreign currency in exchange) at a fixed exchange rate. The supply curve for dollar assets is horizontal. Fluctuations in demand lead to fluctuations in the quantity of dollar assets outstanding and to fluctuations in the nation's official holdings of foreign exchange. If demand increases from D_0 to D_1, the quantity of dollar assets increases from Q_0 to Q_1. Under a flexible exchange rate regime (part b), the Fed fixes the quantity of dollar assets so that their supply curve is vertical. An increase in the demand for dollar assets from D_0 to D_1 results only in an increase in the value of the dollar—the exchange rate rises from 200 to 300 yen per dollar. The quantity of dollar assets remains constant at Q_0. Under a managed exchange rate regime (part c), the Fed has an upward-sloping supply curve of dollar assets, so that if demand increases from D_0 to D_1, the dollar appreciates but the quantity of dollar assets supplied also increases—from Q_0 to Q_2. The increase in the quantity of dollar assets supplied moderates the rise in the value of the dollar but does not completely prevent it as in the case of fixed exchange rates.

exchange decrease. Thus with a fixed exchange rate, fluctuations in the demand for dollar assets result in fluctuations in official holdings of foreign exchange.

Under a flexible exchange rate regime, there is no government or Fed intervention in the foreign exchange market. Regardless of what happens to the demand for dollars, no action is taken to change the

quantity of dollar assets supplied. Therefore there are no changes in the country's official holdings of foreign exchange. In this case, the official settlements balance is zero.

With a managed exchange rate, official holdings of foreign exchange have to be adjusted to meet fluctuations in the demand but in a less extreme manner than under fixed exchange rates. As a consequence, fluctuations in the official settlements balance are smaller in a managed exchange rate regime than in a fixed exchange rate regime.

Up to 1970, the United States operated a fixed exchange rate, but so did all the other countries in the world. Furthermore, the United States was the largest country in the system. The task of keeping exchange rates fixed under that system was left to the individual smaller countries. Thus it was the Japanese government and Bank of Japan that were charged with the responsibility of maintaining the yen-dollar exchange rate; the British government and the Bank of England were charged with maintaining the exchange rate of the British pound. Since 1971, the United States has been on a managed exchange rate regime but, on occasion, it has come close to having a flexible exchange rate.

Why Is the Exchange Rate So Volatile?

We've seen times, especially recently, when the dollar–yen exchange rate has moved dramatically. On most of these occasions, the dollar has depreciated spectacularly, but on some occasions it has appreciated strongly.

The main reason why the exchange rate fluctuates so remarkably is that fluctuations in supply and demand are not always independent of each other. Sometimes a change in supply will trigger a change in demand that reinforces the effect of the change in supply. Let's see how these effects work by looking at two episodes.

1981 to 1982 Between 1981 and 1982, the dollar appreciated against the yen, rising from 220 to 250 yen per dollar. Figure 36.6(a) explains why this

Figure 36.6   Why the Exchange Rate Is So Volatile

(a) 1981 to 1982

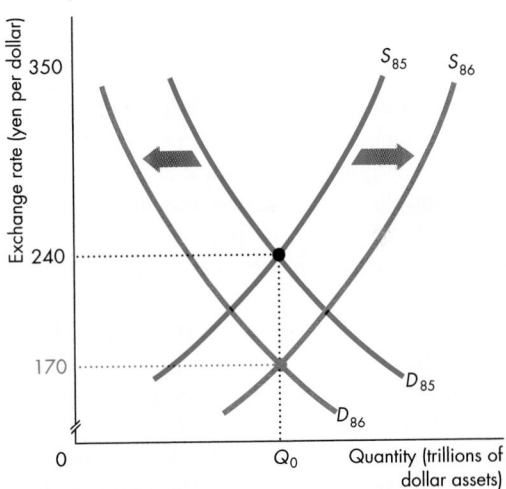

(b) 1985 to 1986

The exchange rate is volatile because shifts in the demand and supply curves for dollar assets are not independent of each other. Between 1981 and 1982 (part a), the dollar appreciated from 220 to 250 yen per dollar. This appreciation arose because the supply curve of dollar assets shifted to the left and higher interest rates induced an increase in demand for dollars assets, shifting the demand curve to the right. The result was a large increase in the foreign exchange value of the dollar. Between 1985 and 1986 (part b), the Fed permitted the quantity of dollar assets to increase to sustain the long economic recovery. The supply curve shifted to the right. At the same time, interest rates decreased and expectations of further declines in the value of the dollar shifted the demand curve to the left. The result was a steep fall in the exchange rate, from 240 yen to 170 yen per dollar between 1985 and 1986.

happened. In 1981, the demand and supply curves were those labeled D_{81} and S_{81}. The foreign exchange value of the dollar was 220 yen—where the supply and demand curves intersect. The period between 1981 and 1982 was one of severe recession. This recession was brought about in part by the Fed pursuing a very restrictive monetary policy. The Fed permitted interest rates to rise sharply, cutting back on the supply of dollar assets. The direct effect was a shift in the supply curve from S_{81} to S_{82}—a decrease in the supply of dollars. But higher U.S. interest rates induced an increase in demand for dollars to take advantage of the higher interest rates. As a result the demand curve shifted from D_{81} to D_{82}. These two shifts reinforced each other, increasing the yen price of the dollar to 250 yen.

1985 to 1986   There was a spectacular depreciation of the dollar in terms of yen from 240 yen per dollar in 1985 to 170 yen per dollar in 1986. This fall came about in the following way. First, in 1985, the demand and supply curves were those labeled D_{85} and S_{85} in Fig. 36.6(b). The yen price of the dollar— the price at which these two curves intersect—was 240 yen per dollar. From 1982 to 1985, the U.S. economy had been on a recovery. But it was a recovery through which a budget deficit of increasing severity was emerging. Thus with a large government deficit, the supply of dollar assets was increasing. The Fed was also loosening up its monetary policy, permitting money supply growth rates to be rapid enough to keep the recovery going. The direct effect of these actions was an increase in the supply of dollar assets from S_{85} to S_{86}. But interest rates in the United States began to fall, and expectations of future declines in the value of the dollar also became widely held. As a consequence, the demand for dollar assets decreased from D_{85} to D_{86}. The result of this combined increase in supply and decrease in demand was a dramatic fall in the value of the dollar to 170 yen in 1986.

R E V I E W

There are three possible foreign exchange rate regimes: fixed, flexible, and managed. Under a fixed exchange rate regime, the government and the Fed peg the exchange rate but the official settlements account of the balance of payments has to carry the burden of holding the exchange rate constant. A decrease in the demand for U.S. dollar assets and an increase in the demand for foreign currency assets has to be met by lowering the country's official holdings of foreign currency. Under a flexible exchange rate regime, the government and the Fed do not intervene in the foreign exchange markets. The official settlements balance is zero and the country's official holdings of foreign currency remain constant. Under a managed exchanged rate regime, the Fed smooths exchange rate fluctuations to a degree but less strongly than under fixed exchange rates. Under a flexible or managed exchange rate regime, the exchange rate is determined by the demand for and supply of dollar assets. Fluctuations in supply often induce reinforcing fluctuations in demand, bringing severe fluctuations in the exchange rate.   ■

Arbitrage, Prices, and Interest Rates

Arbitrage is the activity of buying low and selling high in order to make a profit on the margin between the two prices. Arbitrage has important effects on exchange rates, prices, and interest rates. An increase in the quantity of purchases forces the buying price up. A decrease in the quantity of sales forces the selling price down. The prices move until they are equal and there is no arbitrage profit available. An implication of arbitrage is the law of one price. The **law of one price** states that any given commodity will be available at a single price.

The law of one price has no respect for national borders or currencies. If the same commodity is being bought and sold on either side of the Detroit River, it doesn't matter that one of these transactions is being undertaken in Canada and the other in the United States and that one is using U.S. dollars and the other Canadian dollars. The forces of arbitrage bring about one price. Let's see how.

Arbitrage

Consider the price of a floppy disk that can be bought in either the United States or Canada. We will ignore taxes, tariffs, and transportation costs in order to keep the calculations simple, for these factors do not affect the fundamental issue.

Suppose that we can buy floppy disks in the United States for US$10 a box. Suppose that this same box of disks is available in Canada for C$15 a box. (The symbol US$ stands for the United States dollar and C$ for the Canadian dollar.) Where would it pay to buy disks—in Canada or in the United States? The answer depends on the relative costs of Canadian and U.S. money. If a U.S. dollar cost C$1.50, then it is clear that the price of the disks is the same in both countries. Americans can buy a box of disks in the United States for US$10 or they can use US$10 to buy C$15 and then buy the disks in Canada. The cost will be the same either way. The same is true for Canadians. Canadians can use C$15 to buy a box of disks in Canada or can use C$15 to buy US$10 and then buy the disks in the United States. Again, there is no difference in the price of the disks.

Suppose, however, that a U.S. dollar is less valuable than in the above example. In particular, suppose that a U.S. dollar costs C$1.40. In this case, it will pay to buy the disks in the United States. Canadians can buy US$10 for C$14 and therefore can buy the disks in the United States for C$14 a box compared with C$15 in Canada. The same comparison holds for Americans. Americans can use US$10 to buy C$14 but that would not be enough to buy the disks in Canada since the disks cost C$15 there. It therefore pays Americans also to buy the disks in the United States.

If the situation described above did prevail, there would be an advantage in switching the purchases of disks from Canada to the United States. Canadians would cross the border to buy their disks in the United States and keep on doing so until the Canadian price had fallen to C$14. Once that had happened, Canadians would be indifferent between buying their disks in Canada and in the United States. Arbitrage would have eliminated the difference in prices in the two countries.

Perhaps you are thinking that this is a pretty crazy example since Canadians don't rush down to the United States every time they want to buy a box of floppy disks. But the fact that there is a profit to be made means that it would pay someone to organize the importing of disks into Canada from the United States, thereby increasing the number of disks available there and lowering their price. The incentive to undertake such a move would be present as long as disks were selling for a higher price in Canada than in the United States.

Purchasing Power Parity

Purchasing power parity occurs when money has equal value across countries. (The word *parity* simply means equality. The phrase *purchasing power* refers to the *value of money*. Thus *purchasing power parity* directly translates to *equal value of money*.) Purchasing power parity is an implication of arbitrage and of the law of one price. In the floppy disk example, when US$1 is worth C$1.40, US$10 will buy the same box of floppy disks that C$14 will buy. The value of money, when converted to common prices, is the same in both countries. Purchasing power parity thus prevails in that situation.

Purchasing power parity theory predicts that purchasing power parity applies to all goods and to price indexes, not just to a single good such as the floppy disk that we considered above. That is, if any goods are cheaper in one country than in another, it will pay to convert money into the currency of that country, buy the goods in that country, and sell them in another. By such an arbitrage process, all prices are brought to equality.

One test of the purchasing power parity theory that has been proposed is to calculate what is called the real exchange rate between two countries. The **real exchange rate** is the ratio of the price index in one country to the price index in another. The prices in the second country are converted to prices in the first, using the exchange rate between the two currencies. For example, the real exchange rate between the U.S. dollar and the Japanese yen is calculated by using the following formula:

$$\text{Real exchange rate between U.S. dollar and Japanese yen} = \frac{\text{GNP deflator in U.S.}}{\text{GNP deflator in Japan}} \times \text{Yen per dollar}$$

To calculate the real exchange rate between the U.S. dollar and all other currencies, an index of the real exchange rate is calculated. This index is a weighted average of the real exchange rates between the U.S. dollar and every other currency, where the weights reflect the importance of each other currency in U.S. international trade. Its calculation is similar to that of the trade-weighted index of the nominal exchange rate illustrated in Table 36.3. The real exchange rate for the U.S. dollar, which is published by the Federal Reserve Bank of Dallas each month, moves around considerably. Between 1971 and 1978, the real exchange rate fell by 25 percent. From its low point in 1978 to its peak in 1985, the real exchange rate increased by 43 percent. From 1985 to 1988, the real exchange rate fell again, this time by about 25 percent.

These large movements of the real exchange rate lead some economists to conclude that the purchasing power parity theory is wrong. They argue that if the purchasing power parity theory were correct, the real exchange rate index would remain close to 100. Any increase in the GNP deflator in the United States not matched by an equal percentage increase in the GNP deflator in Japan would be accompanied by a depreciation of the U.S. dollar against the Japanese yen. The result would be an equal percentage change in U.S. prices, when valued in Japanese yen, and in Japanese prices. Thus the real exchange rate index would remain at 100.

There is an important problem with this view of the implications of purchasing power parity for the real exchange rate. It arises from the fact that many goods are not easily traded internationally. For example, it's lunch time in Provo, you are hungry and doughnuts are your thing. You don't have much choice but to buy your doughnut right there. You can't take advantage of the fact that doughnuts are cheaper in Houston and begin an arbitrage operation. Doughnuts are examples of nontraded goods. A **nontraded good** is one that cannot be traded over long distances. Sometimes it is technically possible to undertake such a trade but prohibitively costly. In other cases, it is simply not possible to undertake the trade.

There are many examples of nontraded goods. Almost all the public services provided by the government are nontraded. You can't buy cheap streetsweeping services in Seoul and sell them at a profit in San Francisco. Many location-specific services, such as fast food, are also in this category. When goods cannot be traded over long distances, the goods are strictly different goods. A fresh doughnut in Provo is as different from a fresh doughnut in Houston as it is from a pancake across the street.

Arbitrage operates to bring about equality in prices of identical goods, not different goods. It does not operate to bring about equality between prices of similar-looking goods in widely differing locations. For this reason, tests of the purchasing power parity theory based on real exchange rates are faulty. In fact, for real exchange rates to stay constant, every time the exchange rate changes, the prices of all goods will also have to change—the dollar will have to fall against all currencies and the doughnut! (See Reading Between the Lines, pp. 966–968.)

"On the foreign-exchange markets today, the dollar fell against all major currencies and the doughnut."

Drawing by Mankoff; ©1987 The New Yorker Magazine, Inc.

An additional factor that influences the real exchange rate is the existence of tariffs, taxes, and other restrictions on international trade. Such restrictions weaken the forces of arbitrage and prevent the same price from arising for the same commodity, in different countries.

Arbitrage does not only occur in markets for goods and services. It also occurs in markets for assets. As a result, it brings about another important equality or parity—interest rate parity.

Interest Rate Parity

Interest rate parity occurs when interest rates are equal across countries once the differences in risk are taken into account. Interest rate parity is a condition brought about by arbitrage in the markets for assets—markets in which borrowers and lenders operate.

At the beginning of this chapter, we noted some facts about interest rates in different countries. Those facts seem to suggest that interest rates are *not* equal in different countries. To make things concrete, let's look at a specific example. On November 15, 1988, it was possible to borrow money from a bank in Tokyo at an interest rate of 3.4 percent a year. On that same day, banks in New York were accepting three-month deposits at an interest rate of 9 percent per year. Aren't these unequal interest rates? Isn't it possible for someone to borrow, say, a million dollars in Tokyo at an interest rate of 3.4 percent and put that money on deposit in a bank in New York, earning an interest rate of 9 percent and thereby profiting from the 5.6 percentage point difference between the two interest rates? Such a transaction, done for a year, would produce a profit of $56,000, not bad for a few minutes work! Also, apparently the denial of interest rate parity!

In fact, as you're about to discover, interest rates in Japan and the United States are almost equal—at least close enough to equality that you could not profit from the transactions just described.

The key to understanding why the interest rates are equal is to realize that when you borrow in Japan, you are borrowing *yen*. When the loan is due, you are committing yourself to repaying a certain number of *yen*. When you lend money in the United States—such as by placing it on deposit in a bank—you are lending *dollars* and the bank is obliged to repay *dollars*. It's a bit like borrowing apples and lending oranges. But if you're borrowing apples and lending oranges, you've got to convert the apples to oranges. When the loans become due, you've got to convert oranges back into apples. The prices at which you do these transactions affect the interest rates that you pay and receive.

Let's look a bit more closely at the $1 million borrowing and lending operation that you might have done on November 15, 1988, and see how much you would have made (or lost) on the deal. Table 36.6 summarizes the events. Part (a) lists some data from November 15, 1988. It shows that commercial banks in Tokyo are lending at an interest rate of 3.4 percent on that day. Commercial banks in New York are taking three-month deposits at an interest rate of 9 percent. (These are annual interest rates.) On that day, you can sell yen on the foreign exchange market at 122 yen per dollar. That's the price at which you can convert the yen that you borrowed into the dollars that you are going to lend. (Like the price at which you can sell oranges for apples.)

At the end of three months, you are going to have to convert dollars back into yen to repay your bank loan and the interest on it. There are two ways in which you can do that transaction. You can wait until February 15, 1989, and take your chances on the exchange rate between the dollar and the yen that prevails on that day. If you choose to do that, you will certainly be taking some risks. If the dollar appreciates in that three-month period, you will stand to gain. If the dollar depreciates, you will stand to lose. But there is another way in which you can get the yen that you need to repay your bank loan on February 15. You can enter into a contract on November 15, 1988, at a price agreed on that day to

Table 36.6 International Borrowing and Lending

(a) Data on November 15, 1988

Commercial bank lending rate in Tokyo	3.4% per year
Commercial bank 3-month deposit rate in New York	9.0% per year
Price at which Japanese yen can be sold	122 yen per dollar
Price at which Japanese yen can be bought for delivery in three months	120 yen per dollar

(b) Transactions on November 15, 1988

Borrow	122	million yen in Tokyo
Sell	122	million yen in exchange for $1 million
Deposit	$1	million in a 3-month deposit account in New York
Buy	123.04	million yen for delivery in 3 months at 120 yen per dollar (no money needed now)

(c) Transactions on February 15, 1989

Receive	$1.0225	million from bank—deposit plus interest
Pay	$1.0253	million for forward yen contract
Loss	$0.0028	million ($2800)

buy a certain number of yen to be delivered on February 15, 1989. Such a contract is called a forward contract. A **forward contract** is a contract entered into at an agreed price to buy or sell a certain quantity of any commodity (including currency) at a specified future date. Forward contracts are traded on markets, and their prices are determined by supply and demand in the same manner that any actual commodity is traded. There are forward markets in most agricultural products and in raw materials, as well as currencies and stocks and bonds. The exchange rate in a forward contract is called a **forward exchange rate.** On November 15, 1988, the foreign exchange rate at which Japanese yen could be bought in the forward market for delivery three months in the future (on February 15, 1989) was 120 yen per dollar.

Part (b) of Table 36.6 sets out the transactions that you could have undertaken on November 15, 1988. You borrow 122 million yen in Tokyo and sell

Big Mac Currencies

On the Hamburger Standard

Depressing though it may be to gourmets, the "Big Mac" hamburger sold by McDonald's could well oust the basket of currencies as an international monetary standard. After all, it is sold in 41 countries, with only the most trivial changes of recipe. That ought to say something about comparative prices. Think of the hamburger as a medium-rare guide to whether currencies are trading at the right exchange rates.

Big-Mac-watchers will rely on the theory of purchasing-power parity (PPP) for currencies. This argues that an exchange rate between two currencies is in equilibrium (i.e., at PPP) when it equates the prices of a basket of goods and services in both countries—or, in this case, that rate of exchange which leaves hamburgers costing the same in each country. Comparing actual exchange rates with PPPs is one indication of whether a currency is under- or over-valued.

The Economist's correspondents around the world have been gorging themselves in a bid to test Mac-PPPs. In Washington, a Big Mac costs $1.60; in Tokyo, our Makudonarudo correspondent had to fork out Y370 ($2.40). Dividing the yen price by the dollar price yields a Mac-PPP of $1=Y231; but on September 1st, the dollar's actual exchange rate stood at Y154. The same method gives a Mac-PPP against the D-mark of DM2.66, compared with a current rate of DM2.02. Conclusion: on Mac-PPP grounds, the dollar looks undervalued against the yen and the D-mark.

Sterling is different. The Mac-PPP for the pound is $1.45 (69p to the dollar), within a whisker of the actual rate of around $1.49. But the pound's Mac-PPP against the D-mark is DM3.86, suggesting that sterling is undervalued at DM3.02. British industrialists, who squeal about the pound's current "strength", will now like hamburgers even less.

The Australian dollar appears to have been heavily oversold; it is 34% below its Mac-PPP rate against the American dollar. Meanwhile, the Irish pound seems to be spot on. However, our correspondent in Ireland has uncovered an opportunity for arbitrage. This month, a Big Mac can be enjoyed in Dublin for just 20 tokens

Big Mac Currencies: Hamburger prices round the world				
Country	Price* in local currency	Implied** purchasing power parity of the dollar	Actual exchange rate Sept. 1st	% over (+) or under (−) valuation of US$
Australia	A$1.75	1.09	1.64	+50
Belgium	BFr90	56	42	−25
Brazil	Cz$2.5	7.80	13.80	+78
Britain	£1.10	0.69	0.67	−3
Canada	C$1.89	1.18	1.39	+18
France	FFr16.4	10.30	6.65	−35
Hongkong	HK$7.60	4.75	7.80	+64
Ireland	IR£1.18	0.74	0.74	−1
Japan	¥370	231	154	−33
Holland	Fl4.35	2.72	2.28	−16
Singapore	S$2.80	1.75	2.15	+23
Spain	Ptas280	163	133	−18
Sweden	SKr16.5	10.30	6.87	−33
United States	$1.60	—	—	—
West Germany	DM4.25	2.66	2.02	−24

Source: McDonald's.
*Prices may vary slightly between branches. **Foreign price divided by dollar price.

The Economist, September 6, 1986

The Essence of the Story

Background and Analysis

from milk cartons.

The hamburger standard provides the United States with strong evidence for its contention that Asian NICs (newly industrialising countries) ought to upvalue their currencies; they are more or less tied to the dollar, so their exchange rates have barely budged during the past 18 months. A hamburger costs 64% more in Washington than in Hongkong—i.e., on Mac-PPP grounds the dollar is 64% overvalued against the Hongkong dollar. It is also 23% too high against the Singapore dollar.

Caveat Hamburger

The hamburger standard has its limitations. Using purchasing-power parities to forecast movements in exchange rates can produce misleading results. For instance, price differences between countries can be distorted by taxes, transport costs, property costs or such things as the famously high retail mark-ups in Japan and West Germany.

A more serious objection is that a PPP simply indicates where exchange rates should be in the long run if price levels were the only difference between countries. In fact, there are many other differences. So even though PPPs are handy for converting living standards (GDP per person) into a common currency, they are not necessarily the best way to judge the exchange rate needed to bring the current account of the balance of payments into "equilibrium". Confused? Some economics can be hard to digest.

- The Big Mac hamburger is sold in 41 countries but local prices vary.

- The price of a Big Mac in 15 countries—in local currencies—is shown in the table in the article.

- The purchasing power parity theory (PPP) predicts that Big Macs will cost the same in each country—when the prices are converted to a common currency.

- Equivalently, the PPP theory predicts that the ratio of prices in local currencies will equal the exchange rate between the currencies.

- The ratios of local prices to the U.S. price are shown in the table (in column headed "Implied Purchasing Power Parity of the Dollar"), which, if PPP holds, should equal the actual currency exchange rate.

- The actual price of Big Macs varies from 35 percent more than in the United States (France) to 78 percent less than in the United States (Brazil), implying that the French franc is 35 percent undervalued and the Brazilian cruzeiro is 78 percent overvalued.

- Cost differences might lead to departures from PPP.

- PPP is a long-run theory and not a good guide to the exchange rate needed to make the balance on the current account of the balance of payments equal to zero.

- The Big Mac is a non-traded good. Although its food content is almost identical everywhere in the world, that is only a small part of the total product.

- The Big Mac is a fast meal that includes food, location, and service.

- In the United States, less than one quarter of the total value of a Big Mac is food and more than three quarters is the costs of the location and delivery of the service.

(Continued on next page)

Background and Analysis (cont.)

- Prices of nontraded goods vary according to local demand and supply conditions. In the case of a Big Mac, the prices on September 1, 1986, expressed in U.S. dollars, are set out in the table.

- In France, Japan, and Sweden—the highest priced countries—Big Macs are sold only in the high-rent, high-density central city areas. Rent costs are high. These are also high wage countries. In Canada, Singapore, Australia, Hong Kong, and Brazil, the labor cost of producing hamburgers is lower than in the United States and so is the rent cost.

- Although the food components are potentially traded goods, international restrictions on trade, especially in meat products, prevent the equalization of price of even the food component.

- Exchange rates are determined by the demand for and supply of the various currencies.

- The current account balance is determined by saving, investment, and the government budget.

- The current account balance is not determined by the exchange rate and there is no relationship between PPP and a zero current account balance.

- To assess whether arbitrage is working to produce the law of one price, traded goods whose transport costs are negligible must be compared.

Conclusion

- The hamburger standard exercise is a good idea but applied to the wrong type of good.

Country	Price in local currency	Exchange rate	Local price in dollars	Ratio of local price to U.S. price
France	FFr16.4	6.65	2.47	1.54
Japan	Y370	154	2.40	1.50
Sweden	SKr16.5	6.87	2.40	1.50
Belgium	BFr90	42	2.14	1.34
West Germany	DM4.25	2.02	2.10	1.31
Spain	Ptas260	133	1.95	1.22
Holland	Fl4.35	2.28	1.91	1.19
Britain	£1.1	0.67	1.64	1.03
United States	$1.6	1	1.60	1.00
Ireland	IR£1.18	0.74	1.59	1.00
Canada	C$1.89	1.39	1.36	0.85
Singapore	S$2.8	2.15	1.30	0.81
Australia	A$1.75	1.64	1.07	0.67
Hong Kong	HK$7.6	7.8	0.97	0.61
Brazil	Cz2.5	13.8	0.18	0.11

those yen at 122 yen per dollar in exchange for $1 million. You deposit that $1 million in a bank in New York on a three-month deposit account. That's the end of your cash transactions on that day. At the same time, you enter into a forward contract, buying enough yen for delivery on February 15, 1989, to repay your bank loan and the interest on it. At an interest rate of 3.4 percent per year, you'll need 123.04 million yen on February 15, 1989. So you enter into a contract now to buy those 123.04 million yen at an agreed price of 120 yen per dollar.

Part (c) tells us what happens on February 15, 1989. You receive your million dollars back from the bank, together with a quarter of a year's interest ($22,500). The total amount of dollars you have is $1.0225 million. You pay for your forward yen contract, which costs you $1.0253 million. (Divide the 123.04 million yen that you need by 120 yen per dollar, the price that you agreed to in the forward market back in November, and you'll see that the answer is $1.0253 million.) Notice that you have paid out a bit more than you received. You have actually lost $2800 on this transaction—about a quarter of 1 percent of the total amount involved.

Suppose that the interest rates in Tokyo and New York and the exchange rate and the forward exchange rate had been slightly different. Suppose that instead of making a loss, this set of transactions had turned a profit. How long would the profit opportunity exist? You and millions of people like you would be borrowing from banks in Japan, converting yen into dollars, depositing the money in New York, and taking out forward contracts to get the yen back to repay your yen loan at the end of the transaction period. Even if you could make only a few thousand dollars on a $1 million contract, there would be nothing to stop you from entering into a $10 million or a $100 million contract, which means that you would make a large income in the process.

But now think about what is going to happen to interest rates and exchange rates as you and everyone else attempt to profit. With an increased demand for loans from banks in Japan, the interest rate there is going to increase. With an increased supply of deposits to the banks in New York, the interest rate there is going to decrease. As more people offer yen in exchange for dollars, the exchange rate is going to increase—more yen will have to be offered for a dollar. And as more people try to buy yen in the forward market, the number of yen per dollar in that market will decline. Every one of these changes re-

duces the possibility of making a profit by borrowing in Tokyo and lending in New York and these forces would operate until that profit opportunity had been wiped out. They will not operate to reverse the profit—that is, to make it profitable to borrow in New York and lend in Tokyo. In such a situation, the reverse forces would be at work, again removing profit from international borrowing and lending actions.

In the situation that we've just described, interest rate parity prevails. The interest rate in Tokyo—when the expected change in the price of the yen between November and February is taken into account—is almost identical to that in New York. It costs 3.4 percent per year to borrow yen in Tokyo but it costs 9 percent per year to borrow yen, convert them into dollars, and then convert them back into yen at a later date. It is in this sense that interest rates are equal. The dollar interest rate in Tokyo is the same as the dollar interest rate in New York. The yen interest rate in New York is the same as the yen interest rate in Tokyo.

A World Market

Arbitrage in asset markets operates on a worldwide scale and keeps the world capital markets linked in a single global market. This market is an enormous one. It involves borrowing and lending through banks, in bond markets, and in stock markets. The scale of this international business was estimated by Salomon Brothers, an investment bank, at more than $1 trillion in 1986. It is because of international arbitrage in asset markets that the fortunes of the stock markets around the world are so closely linked. A stock market crash in New York makes its new low-priced stocks look attractive compared with high-priced stocks in Tokyo, Hong Kong, Zurich, Frankfurt, and London. As a consequence, investors make plans to sell high in these other markets and buy low in New York. But before many such transactions can be put through, the prices in the other markets fall to match the fall in New York. Conversely, if the Tokyo market experiences rapid price increases and markets in the rest of the world stay constant, investors seek to sell high in Tokyo and buy low in the rest of the world. Again, these trading plans will induce movements in the prices in the other markets to bring them into line with the Tokyo market. The action of selling high in Tokyo will lower the prices there and the action of buying low in

Frankfurt, London, and New York will raise the prices there.

■   You've now discovered what determines a country's current account balance and the value of its currency. The most important influence on the current account balance is the government budget deficit. A country in which taxes are less than government spending is likely to be one that has a deficit in its trade with the rest of the world. The value of a country's currency is determined by the demand and supply for that currency and is strongly influenced by monetary actions. A rapid increase in the supply of a currency will result in a decline in its value relative to other currencies.

You've also learned how international arbitrage links prices and interest rates together in different countries. International arbitrage does not occur in markets for nontraded goods, so there are variations in real exchange rates. But arbitrage operates in markets for traded goods and is especially powerful in markets for assets. Arbitrage in asset markets keeps interest rates equal around the world. Differences in national interest rates reflect the expectations of changes in exchange rates. Once these differences in exchange rates are taken into account, interest rates are equal across countries.

In the final two chapters, we're going to look at some further global economic issues. First, in Chapter 37, we'll examine the problems faced by developing countries as they seek to grow. Then, in Chapter 38, we'll look at countries that operate with economic systems that are different from our own—the command economies of the Soviet Union, Eastern Europe, and the People's Republic of China and the economy of Japan.

S U M M A R Y

Financing International Trade

International trade, borrowing, and lending are financed using foreign currency. A country's international transactions are recorded in its balance of payments accounts. The current account records receipts and expenditures connected with the sale and purchase of goods and services, as well as net transfers to the rest of the world; the capital account records international borrowing and lending transactions; the official settlements account shows the increase or decrease in the country's foreign currency holdings.

Historically, the United States has been a net lender to the rest of the world but, in the mid-1980s, that situation changed and it became a huge net borrower. Nevertheless, total U.S. investment in the rest of the world exceeds foreign investment here.

The current account deficit is equal to the government budget deficit plus the private sector deficit. The private sector deficit is small and fluctuations in the trade balance arise mainly from fluctuations in the government's budget. As the government budget deficit has grown in the 1980s, so the trade deficit has also grown. (pp. 944–951)

Foreign Exchange and the Dollar

Foreign currency is obtained in exchange for domestic currency in the foreign exchange market. The foreign exchange market operates 24 hours a day around the world. Central banks often intervene in foreign exchange markets. There are three types of foreign exchange rate regimes: fixed, flexible, and managed. When the exchange rate is fixed, the government declares a value for the currency in terms of some other currency and the Fed takes actions to ensure that that price is maintained. To fix the exchange rate, the Fed has to stand ready to supply dollars and take in foreign currency or to remove dollars from circulation in exchange for foreign currency. The country's reserves of foreign currency fluctuate to maintain the fixed exchange rate.

A flexible exchange rate is one in which the central bank takes no actions to influence the value of its currency in the foreign exchange market. The country's holdings of foreign currencies remain constant and fluctuations in demand and supply lead to fluctuations in the exchange rate.

A managed exchange rate is one in which the central bank takes actions to smooth fluctuations that would otherwise arise but does so less strongly than under a fixed exchange rate regime.

In a flexible or managed exchange rate regime, the exchange rate is determined by the demand for and supply of dollars. The demand for dollars depends on the volume of dollar trade financed, the price level in the U.S. and in other countries, the interest rates on dollar assets, the interest rates on foreign currency assets, and expected changes in the value of the dollar.

The supply of dollars depends on the exchange rate regime. Under fixed exchange rates, the supply curve is horizontal; under flexible exchange rates, the supply curve is vertical; under managed exchange rates, the supply curve is upward-sloping. The position of the supply curve depends on the government's budget and the Fed's monetary policy. The larger the budget deficit or the more rapidly the Fed permits the money supply to grow, the further to the right the supply curve moves. Fluctuations in the exchange rate occur because of fluctuations in demand and supply and sometimes these fluctuations are large. Large fluctuations arise from interlinked changes in demand and supply. A shift in the supply curve often produces an induced change in the demand curve that reinforces the effect on the exchange rate. (pp. 951–962)

Arbitrage, Prices, and Interest Rates

Arbitrage—buying low and selling high—keeps the prices of goods and services that are traded internationally close to equality across all countries. Arbitrage also keeps interest rates in line with each other.

Some goods are not traded internationally—nontraded goods. International arbitrage does not bring the prices of such goods into equality. For this reason, there are fluctuations in a country's real exchange rate—the purchasing power of the dollar at home compared with its purchasing power abroad.

Interest rates around the world look unequal, but the appearance arises from the fact that loans are contracted in different currencies in different countries. To compare interest rates across countries, we have to take into account changes in the values of currencies. Countries whose currencies are appreciating have low interest rates; countries whose currencies are depreciating have high interest rates. If the rate of currency depreciation is taken into account, interest rates are equal. (pp. 962–970)

K E Y   C O N C E P T S

Key Figures and Tables

R E V I E W   Q U E S T I O N S

1 What are the transactions recorded in a country's current account, capital account, and official settlements account?

2 What is the relationship between the balance on the current account, the capital account, and the official settlements account?

3 Distinguish between a country that is a net borrower and one that is a creditor. Are net borrowers always creditors? Are creditors always net borrowers?

4 What is the connection between a country's current account balance and the government's budget deficit and the private sector deficit?

5 Why do fluctuations in the government budget balance lead to fluctuations in the current account balance?

6 Distinguish among the three exchange rate regimes: fixed, flexible, and managed.

7 Review the main influences on the quantity of dollars that people demand.

8 Review the influences on the supply of dollars.

9 How does the supply curve of dollars differ under the three exchange rate regimes?

10 Why does the dollar fluctuate so much?

11 What is arbitrage?

12 How does arbitrage lead to purchasing power parity?

13 Why do real exchange rates fluctuate?

14 What is interest rate parity?

15 How does interest rate parity come about?

P R O B L E M S

1 The citizens of Pioneerland, whose currency is the choo, conduct the following transactions in 1980:

	Billions of choos
Imports of goods and services	250
Exports of goods and services	397
Borrowing from rest of world	80
Lending to the rest of the world	20
Increase in official holdings of foreign currency	3

a) Set out the three balance of payments accounts for Pioneerland.

b) Does Pioneerland have a flexible exchange rate?

2 You are told the following about Ecoland, a country with a flexible exchange rate whose currency is the turky:

	Billions of turkies
GNP	50
Consumption expenditure	30
Government purchases of goods and services	12
Investment	11
Exports of goods and services	10
Government budget deficit	2

Calculate the following for Ecoland:

a) Imports of goods and services

b) Current account balance

c) Capital account balance

d) Taxes (net of transfer payments)

e) Private sector deficit/surplus

3 A country's currency appreciates and its official holdings of foreign currency increase. What can you say about the following:

a) The exchange rate regime being pursued by the country

b) The country's current account

c) The country's official settlements account

4 The interest rate on bank loans in Pioneerland is 11 percent a year. The interest rate on bonds in Ecoland is 4 percent a year. In the foreign exchange market, turkies can be bought for choos at a rate of 8 choos per turky. In the forward market, turkies can be bought for delivery in one year at a rate of 9 choos per turky.

a) How much would you gain or lose if you borrowed 1 million choos and invested the proceeds of the loan in Ecoland bonds, covering your transaction in the forward market?

b) In which direction will the choo/turky exchange rate and the interest rates in Pioneerland and Ecoland be moving?

Part 12

Talking
with
Janos
Kornai

Janos Kornai is professor of economics at Harvard University and department head of the Institute of Economics at the Hungarian Academy of Sciences. Professor Kornai divides his time between Cambridge and Budapest. His books and publications have been translated into 17 languages and include *Overcentralization in Economic Administration, Economics of Shortage,* and *Contradictions and Dilemmas.* Michael Parkin spoke with Dr. Kornai about how socialist economies work and the changes that are taking place in the socialist world.

Professor Kornai, why did you become an economist?

My interest in economics started very early and has always been part of my concern for political and social issues. When I was younger, I was attracted to the ideals and goals of socialism, and my research reflected that. Since then I have become more critical of socialist political economy and have become interested in alternative economic theories and in the kind of economics practiced in the West.

We're observing remarkable changes in socialist countries— Hungary, China, the Soviet Union, Poland, in both political and economic spheres. What do you think is driving these changes?

On the surface, events like the death of a leader can trigger the desire to reform the system. But more fundamentally, it's because of deep dissatisfaction with the system —dissatisfaction of the party apparatus and leadership as well as popular discontent. But these changes won't be finished overnight. Yugoslavia, for example, has been moving away from what I call classical socialism—the traditional socialism associated with Lenin, Stalin, and Mao—for 40 years!

"The maximal state associated with classical socialism is not sustainable."

tries are moving away from a highly centralized, bureaucratic society —what I like to call a maximal state. By contrast, Britain under Labour governments was very far from a maximal state, so privatization under Conservative governments in Britain is different from reforms in Eastern Bloc countries.

Do you see any connection between these reforms and the deregulation and privatization that's occurring in the United States and Europe?

They're not totally distinct. They're parallel in that they are both movements in the direction to what political philosophy calls the minimal state. But of course they're not starting at the same point and that makes quite a difference. Reforming socialist coun-

Do you see any long-term patterns of socialist economies tending to go from maximal to minimal states?

It is still early to know that. But my impression is that the maximal degree associated with classical socialism is not sustainable for many reasons. I'll mention just a few. It's terribly expensive for a society to monitor everyone's activity. Next, growth gives rise to increasing complexity—not only producing more goods, but more differentiated products. For example, in Maoist China, everyone wore the same blue uniform, so it was easy to plan their production.

But in a modern economy there are billions of goods and services. That makes complete centralization hopeless. The economy just can't keep up and there are shortages of many goods. I agree with F. A. Hayak, who argued that you need a market with free enterprise just to make use of decentralized human knowledge.

Some Western economists emphasize the role of the rational central planner in classical socialist economies, but does this ideal exist in the real world?

First let's consider whether this planner is just a single person. In fact, it never is just one individual, but the whole hierarchy of party officials, civil servants, and managers of state-owned firms. This huge apparatus is not a monolithic group, with uniform preferences, but a set of people with conflicting interests. The conflicts are revealed in the fights among interest groups, lobbies, and in various factions of the party.

As for the idea of a *rational* central planner, rationality includes the notion of stable preferences. But if you look, for example, at the history of socialist China, you'll immediately observe that Mao's own policy goals changed radically several times. His preferences were clearly *not* stable. Finally, let's emphasize *planner*— I can speak about this process from my personal experience in designing some of the models that were used to make plans. Planning theory assumes that you use the full information available to make the best possible calculations. But the planner is a human being with certain bureaucratic and personal interests who may not disclose certain information if it's not in his or her best interest. That planner, again, is part of a multilevel hierarchy, and may have to bargain with a superior about how ambitious the plan will be. In short, planning is a complicated social process, rather than a few wise people with

well-defined goals and preferences constructing an ideal plan.

Shortages of consumer goods are quite common in centralized socialist economies. What is the effect of chronic shortages on the economy?

There are immediate effects on the lives of people in their capacity as consumers. You can't spend your income according to your preferences. If you want pork, but it's chronically unavailable, you're forced to buy herring instead. This kind of forced substitution leads to a decrease in consumer welfare. If you've ever experienced a seller's market—at an airline ticket counter, for example—you know how it feels to be at the seller's

mercy. Turning to production, there's no incentive to improve quality, no competition to drive innovation. Shortages have a very serious effect, therefore, in reducing efficiency.

Does the concept of forced substitution change the practical definition of "demand" in shortage economies?

Yes, indeed. There's an assumption underlying the textbook concept of demand familiar to most American college students, namely, that goods are available. But what if you want to buy apples and you can't find them anywhere in the city, or only on Mondays? Sooner or later, a consumer who grows up in a shortage economy gets used to these supply

"Planning is a complicated social process, rather than a few wise people constructing an ideal plan."

constraints and stops demanding apples. You have to take these supply constraints and consumer expectations into account when figuring out the demand for apples.

Market economies co-ordinate the plans of buyers and sellers, demanders and suppliers, through prices. How is this coordination achieved in socialist economies?

Price is still an important factor in the choices consumers make. Supply may constrain purchases, but households are very sensitive to the prices of meat or milk, for example. Households are also sensitive to wage differentials in their supply of labor. It's in the supply of goods that price is much less important. Instead, the instructions of central planners determine which goods are produced and how much. Other centralized mechanisms that are used as signals include rationing and licensing. An important decentralized signal is inventories and back-orders. If you're used to having a two-year waiting list for cars, for example, and it suddenly shoots up to four years, then you know you have more customers than you're used to supplying. Finally, there's the concept—

"The time is ripe for a wider synthesis in methodology."

introduced by Albert Hirschman—of *voice*. In a market economy, if you don't like a certain shop, well, you can take your business elsewhere. But you can also use your *voice* to complain. The latter is an important signal in socialist economies as well. Except if your voice is too loud!

You have been trained in both Marxian and Neoclassical economic theory. What principles guide your work?

My goal has always been to understand the deep answers to important questions about how economic systems work, not just to find a comfortable analytic framework. Marxian economics frequently gives the wrong answers but to important questions. Ne-

oclassical economics, on the other hand, can give you very precise answers, but the questions themselves may or may not be important. Young economists, working with the conventional Neoclassical toolkit do not get from the underlying theory a good guide for choosing the right research strategy. They may easily miss the point and be tempted to use this powerful intellectual apparatus for addressing irrelevant issues, with a good chance that they can still impress their colleagues. They should instead start to use the Neoclassical analytical methods only *after* having identified the problem, the situation, the economic actors' motivations, and the social constraints. The time is ripe for a wider synthesis in methodology.

Chapter 37

Growth and Development

After studying this chapter, you will be able to:

- Describe the international distribution of income

- Explain the importance of economic growth

- Explain how the accumulation of capital and technological progress brings higher per capita incomes

- Describe the impediments to economic growth in poor countries

- Explain the possible effects of population control, foreign aid, free trade, and demand stimulation on economic growth and development

- Evaluate policies designed to stimulate economic growth and development

In 1984, people all over the United States saw images of starving Ethiopian children on their television screens. In a surge of sympathy, they donated millions of dollars, most visibly through a rock concert benefit called Live Aid. The people of many other countries also responded generously. While the flow of aid didn't eliminate the hunger, it saved many thousands of lives.

■ A success? Only, sadly, in the short run. Three years later, Ethiopia was as poor as ever, and it again suffered a devastating famine. The *average* person in Ethiopia has an income that is equivalent to about two dollars a week. And Ethiopia, like all other countries, has an unequal distribution of income, so the poorest people in that country have much less than two dollars a week. These poorest of the world's people have no shelter, they wear rags for clothes, and they spend most of their lives in hunger. Why are so many countries, like Ethiopia, chained to poverty? Why are there such differences in income between the poorest and richest countries? Does foreign aid help these countries? Why hasn't it alleviated their poverty? ■ As World War II ended, Hong Kong emerged from occupation by the Japanese as a poor colony of Britain. Occupying a cluster of overcrowded rocky islands with few natural resources, Hong Kong, today, is a city of vibrant, hardworking, and increasingly wealthy people. Its exports flow through the world and, with astonishing speed, its people are bootstrapping themselves out of poverty. A similar story can be told of Singapore. Two and a half million people crowded into an island city nation have, by their dynamism, transformed their economy, increasing their average income sixfold since 1960. How do some countries manage to unshackle themselves from poverty? What do they have that other poor countries lack? Can their lessons be applied elsewhere?

■ Rich countries are not all equally wealthy. At the end of World War II, per

Feed the World

capita income in Japan was a mere 17 percent of that in the United States; France's was 47 percent and Germany's 40 percent of the levels that prevailed here. Yet, today, per capita income—income per person—in these three countries is almost the same as that of the United States. How did countries like the United States, Japan, France, and West Germany get to be wealthy? Why have Japan and several European countries grown more quickly and caught up to the United States in the past few decades?

■ The world's population has passed 5 billion inhabitants. These billions of people are unevenly distributed over the earth's surface. More than 4 billion live in the world's poor countries and only 1 billion in the rich industrial countries. It is estimated that by the year 2020, world population will exceed 8 billion with close to 7 billion living in the poor countries and only 1.4 billion in the industrial countries. The governments of poor countries are constantly seeking new and more effective methods of containing their population growth rates, though with limited success. In 1988, China revised its forecasts of its own population, predicting that by the turn of the century, population targets will have been exceeded by an amount equal to more than one half of the population of the United States. Why is the population growth rate so rapid in poor countries? What are the effects of rapid population growth on economic growth and development?   ■ In a typical year in the mid-1980s, $85 billion worth of aid was given by rich countries to developing countries. The United States provided more than a third of all foreign aid. Other large donors were Japan, France, West Germany, the United Kingdom, Belgium, and Canada. The recipients of this aid were the poor countries of Africa, Latin America, and Asia. What are the effects of foreign aid on economic growth and development?

■ Some poor countries try to encourage growth and development by protecting their domestic industries from international trade and foreign competition. Other countries adopt an outward-looking orientation, engaging in free trade with the rest of the world. What kind of international trade policy gives a developing country the best chance of rapid and sustained economic growth?

■ In this chapter, we'll study the questions just posed. They are all aspects of one of those "big" questions posed in Chapter 1: What causes differences in wealth among nations, making the people in some countries rich and in others poor? We don't fully understand the answer to this question. But there are some things that we do know. We'll review that knowledge in this chapter. We'll also review some of the ideas people have advanced about what can be done to speed up the growth of poor countries. Some strategies truly help poor countries, but others have mixed results and may even hurt their development.

The International Distribution of Income

When we studied the distribution of U.S. income, we discovered that there is a great deal of inequality. In 1982, the poorest 20 percent earned 5 percent of total income while the richest 20 percent earned 43 percent. As we will see, the differences in income within a country, large though they are, look insignificant when compared with the differences among the nations. Let's see how income is distributed among the nations of the world.

Poorest Countries

The poorest countries are sometimes called underdeveloped countries. An **underdeveloped country** is a country in which there is little industrialization, limited mechanization of the agricultural sector, very little capital equipment, and low per capita income. In many underdeveloped countries, large numbers of people live on the edge of starvation. Such people devote their time to producing the meager supplies of food and clothing required for themselves and their families. They have no surplus to trade with others or to invest in new tools and capital equipment. One of the most publicized of the poor countries is Ethiopia, where thousands of people spend their lives trekking across parched landscapes in search of meager food supplies.

Just how poor are the poorest countries? Those countries whose per capita incomes range between 4 and 9 percent of those in the United States contain 27 percent of the world's people who earn only 6 percent of world income. These poorest of countries are located mainly in Africa.

Developing Countries

A **developing country** is one that is poor but is accumulating capital and developing an industrial and commercial base. The developing countries have a large and growing urban population and have steadily growing incomes. The per capita income level in such countries ranges between 10 and 30 percent of that in the United States. These countries are located in all parts of the world but many are found in Asia, the Middle East, and in Central America. Seventeen percent of the world's people live in these countries and earn 11 percent of world income.

Newly Industrialized Countries

Newly industrialized countries (often called NICs) are countries in which there is a rapidly developing broad industrial base and per capita income is growing quickly. Today their per capita income levels approach 50 percent of those in the United States. Examples of such countries are Trinidad, Israel, and South Korea. Three percent of the world's people live in the newly industrialized countries and earn 3 percent of world income.

Industrial Countries

Industrial countries are countries that have a large amount of capital equipment and in which people undertake highly specialized activities, enabling them to earn high per capita incomes. These are the countries of Western Europe, the United States and Canada, Japan, Australia, and New Zealand. Seventeen percent of the world's people live in these countries and they earn 49 percent of world income.

Oil-Rich Countries

A small number of oil-rich countries have very high per capita incomes despite the fact that they are, in most other respects, similar to the poorest countries or developing countries. These countries have little industry, and indeed little of anything of value to sell to the world, except oil. Four percent of the world's people live in these countries and they earn 4 percent of world income. But that income is very unequally distributed within the countries: Most of the people in these countries have incomes similar to those in the poorest countries, but a small number of people are extremely rich—indeed, among the richest people in the world.

Communist Countries

Close to 33 percent of the world's people live in communist countries and they earn 28 percent of world income. A **communist country** is a country in which there is limited private ownership of productive capital and of firms, limited reliance on the market as a means of allocating resources, and in which government agencies plan and direct the production and distribution of most goods and services. Rapid changes are taking place in many of these countries at the present time. We describe the economies of these countries, and the changes that are taking place, in Chapter 38.

Per capita incomes in the communist countries vary enormously. In China, per capita income is around 15 percent of that in the United States. China is a developing country. Per capita income in the German Democratic Republic (East Germany), and industrial countries, is almost 70 percent of that of the United States. Other industrialized communist countries are Czechoslovakia, Poland, Hungary, and the Soviet Union. Some communist countries, such as Romania, Yugoslavia, and Bulgaria, have per capita incomes similar to those of the newly industrialized countries. Thus within the communist countries, there is a great deal of variety in income levels and the degree of economic development.

The World Lorenz Curve

A **Lorenz curve** plots the cumulative percentage of income against the cumulative percentage of population. If income is equally distributed, the Lorenz curve is a 45° line running from the origin. The degree of inequality is indicated by the extent to which the Lorenz curve departs from the 45° line of equality. Figure 37.1 shows two Lorenz curves: one curve depicts the distribution of income among families in the United States, and the other depicts the distribution of average per capita income across countries.

As you can see, the distribution of income among countries is more unequal than the distribution of income among families within the United States. Forty percent of the world's people live in countries whose incomes account for less than 10

Figure 37.1   The World Lorenz Curve, 1980

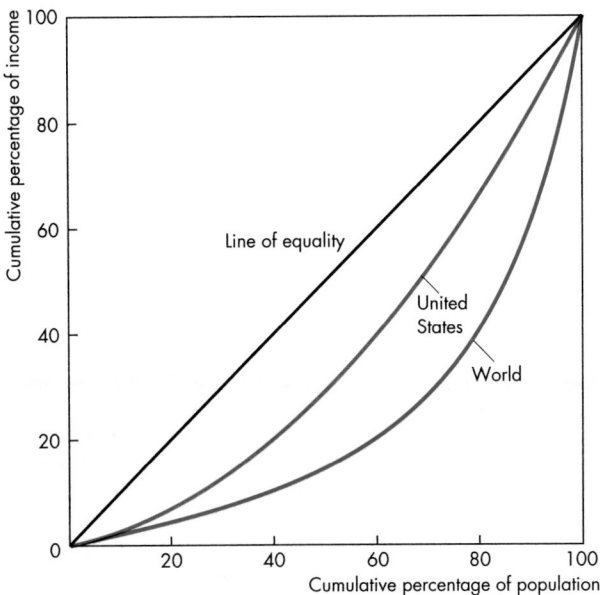

The cumulative percentage of income is plotted against the cumulative percentage of population. If income were distributed equally across countries, the Lorenz curve would be a straight diagonal line. The distribution of per capita income across countries is even more unequal than the distribution of income among families in the United States.

Sources: Robert Summers and Alan Heston, "Improved International Comparison of Real Product and Its Composition: 1950–1980," *Review of Income and Wealth,* Series 30 (June 1984): 207–262; and *Statistical Abstract of the United States: 1987,* 107th ed.

percent of the world's total. The richest 20 percent of the people live in countries whose incomes account for 55 percent of the world's total income. Inequality in income is even more severe than that apparent in Fig. 37.1, for the world Lorenz curve tells us only how unequal average incomes are among countries. Inequality within countries is not revealed by the world Lorenz curve.

Such numbers provide a statistical description of the enormity of the world's poverty problem. To better appreciate the severity of the problem, imagine that your family has an income of 30 cents a day for each person. That 30 cents has to buy housing, food, clothing, transportation, and all the other things consumed. Such is the lot of more than a quarter of the world's people.

Although there are many poor people in the world, there are also many whose lives are undergoing dramatic change. They live in countries in which rapid economic growth is taking place. As a result of economic growth and development, millions of people now enjoy living standards undreamt of by their parents and inconceivable to their grandparents. Let's look at the connection between income levels and the rate of economic growth.

Growth Rates and Income Levels

Poor countries can and do grow into rich countries. Poor countries become rich countries by achieving high growth rates of real per capita income over prolonged periods of time. Over the years, a small increase in the growth rate like compound interest, pays large dividends. A slowdown in the growth rate, maintained over a number of years, can result in a huge loss of real income.

The importance of economic growth and its effects on income levels are vividly illustrated by our own recent experience. In the United States in the early 1960s, aggregate income, measured by real GNP, was growing at around 4 percent a year. After 1965, GNP growth slowed down. The path actually followed by U.S. GNP growth is shown in Fig. 37.2(a). The path that would have been followed if the pre-1965 growth trend had been maintained is also shown in that figure. By 1990, U.S. real GNP was $2 trillion below—40 percent below—what it would have been if the 1965 growth rate had been maintained.

When poor countries have a slow growth rate and rich countries a fast growth rate, the gap between the rich and the poor widens. Figure 37.2(b) shows how the gap between the United States and many poor countries, such as Ethiopia, has widened over the years.

For a poor country to catch up to a rich country, it is necessary for its growth rate to exceed that of the rich country. In 1980, per capita income in China was 14 percent of that in the United States. In the 1980s, the United States experienced an average per capita income growth rate of 1.5 percent a year. If that growth rate is maintained and if per capita income in China also grows at 1.5 percent a year, China will remain at 14 percent of U.S. income levels

Figure 37.2   Growth Rates and Income Levels

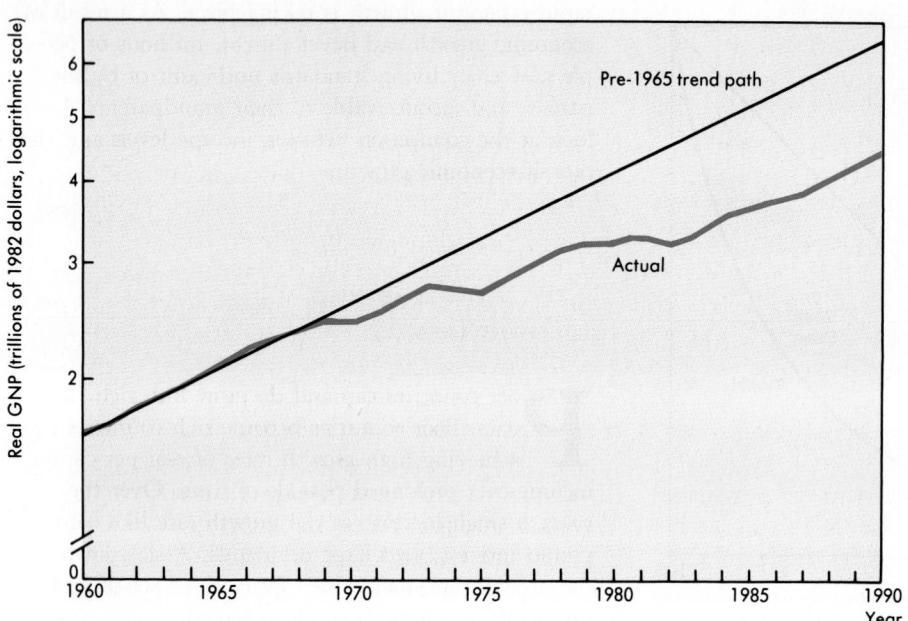

(a) U.S. output loss from growth slowdown

A fall in the growth rate of real income in the United States after 1965 (part a) has resulted in GNP being almost $2 trillion (40 percent) below what it would have been if the pre-1965 trend had continued. Small changes in the growth rate, maintained over a long period of time, produce large differences in income levels. Steady growth in the United States, compared with almost none in Ethiopia (part b), results in a gradually widening gap between the rich and the poor.

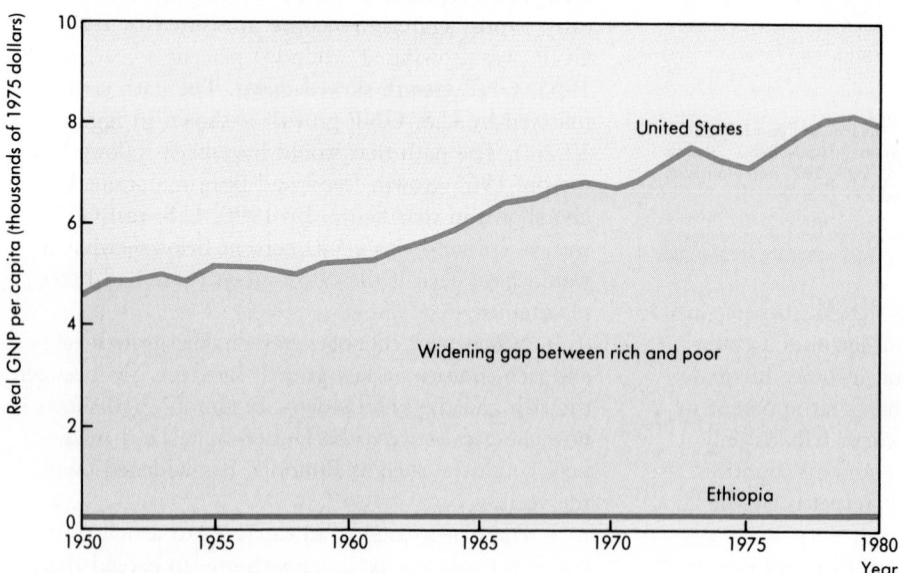

(b) The gap widens between rich and poor

Source: International Monetary Fund, *International Financial Statistics* (1988).

forever. The gap will remain constant. If per capita income in the United States were to grow at 1.5 percent and if China could maintain a per capita income growth rate at twice that level—3 percent per year—China would catch up to the United States in per capita income levels in the first part of the twenty-*second* century, around 2115. If China could do even twice as well as that—maintaining a 6 percent per year growth rate in per capita incomes— the people of China would have income levels as high as those in the United States within your own life- time—in the mid 2030s. If China could pull off a miracle and make per capita incomes grow at 12 percent a year, it would take just 20 years to catch up to the United States.

Growth rates as high as 10 or 12 percent are not unknown. Japan grew in excess of 10 percent a year, on the average, for almost 20 years following World War II. Recently China has, indeed, experi- enced per capita income and growth of 12 percent a year, a rate which, if sustained, doubles per capita income every six years. Even the poorest countries in the world—those with per capita incomes of only 4 percent of those of the United States—would catch the United States in a matter of 30 or 40 years if they could achieve and maintain growth rates of this level.

The key, then, to achieving high per capita income is to attain and maintain a high rate of economic growth. That is how today's rich countries attained their high living standards. The poor coun- tries of today will join the rich countries of tomorrow only if they can find ways of attaining and maintain- ing rapid growth.

Clearly, the question of what determines a country's economic growth rate is a vital one. What does determine a country's economic growth rate? Let's turn to an examination of this crucial question.

Inputs, Technological Progress, and Economic Growth

In the aggregate, income equals the value of out- put. Thus to increase average income, a country has to increase its output. A country's output depends on its resources or inputs, and the tech- niques it employs for transforming inputs into out-

puts. This relationship between inputs and outputs is the *production function*. There are three inputs:

- Land
- Labor
- Capital

Land includes all the natural, nonproduced in- puts such as land itself, the minerals under it, and all other nonproduced inputs. The quantity of these in- puts is determined by nature and countries have no choice but to put up with whatever natural resources they happen to have. Countries cannot achieve rapid and sustained economic growth by increasing their stock of natural resources. But countries can and do experience fluctuations in income as a result of fluctu- ations in the prices of their natural resources. Further- more, there are times at which those prices are rising quickly and such periods bring temporary income growth. The late 1970s is an example of a period in which resource-rich countries experienced rapid income growth as a result of rising commodity prices. But to achieve long-run, sustained income growth, countries have to look beyond their natural resources.

One such source of increased output is a sus- tained increase in *labor* inputs. That is, a country can produce more output over the years simply because its population of workers grows. But for each succes- sively larger generation of workers to have a higher *per capita* income than the previous generation, per capita output must increase. Population growth, on its own, does not lead to higher per capita output. The input most responsible for rapid and sustained economic growth is capital. There are two broad types of capital—physical and human. *Physical capi- tal* includes such things as highways and railways, dams and irrigation systems, tractors and plows, fac- tories, trucks and cars, and buildings of all kinds. *Human capital* is the accumulated knowledge and skills of the working population. As individuals accu- mulate more capital, their incomes grow. As nations accumulate more capital per worker, labor productivi- ty and output per capita grow.

To study the behavior of per capita output, we use the per capita production function. The **per capita production function** shows how per capi- ta output varies as the per capita stock of capital varies, in a given state of knowledge about alternative technologies. Figure 37.3 illustrates the per capita production function. Per capita output is measured on

Figure 37.3   The per Capita Production Function

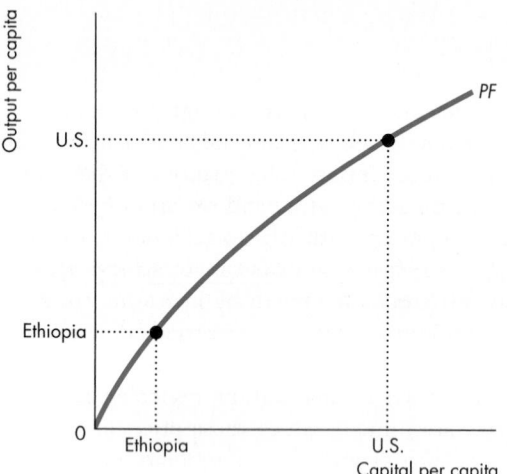

The per capita production function *PF* traces how per capita output varies as the stock of per capita capital varies. If two countries use the same technology, but one country has a larger capital stock, that country will also have a higher per capita income level. For example, suppose that Ethiopia and the United States each use the same technology. Ethiopia has a low per capita capital stock and low level of output per capita. The United States has a large per capita capital stock and a large per capita output rate.

the vertical axis and the per capita stock of capital on the horizontal axis. Curve *PF* shows how per capita output varies as the amount of per capita capital varies. A rich country such as the United States has a large amount of per capita capital and a large per capita output. A poor country such as Ethiopia has hardly any capital and very low per capita output.

Capital Accumulation

By accumulating capital, a country can grow and move along its per capita production function. The greater the amount of capital (per capita), the greater is output (per capita). But the fundamental *law of diminishing returns* applies to the per capita production function. That is, as capital per capita increases, output per capita also increases but by decreasing increments. Thus there is a limit to the extent to which a country can grow merely by accumulating capital. Eventually, the country reaches the point at

which the extra output from extra capital is simply not worth the effort of accumulating more capital. At such a point, it pays the country to consume rather than to increase its capital stock.

But no country has yet reached such a point because the per capita production function is constantly shifting upward as a result of improvements in technology. Let's see how technological change affects output and growth.

Technological Change

Although rich countries have much more capital per capita than poor countries, that is not the only difference between them. Typically, rich countries use more productive technologies than do poor countries. That is, even if they have the same per capita capital, the rich country produces more output than the poor country. For example, a farmer in a rich country might use a ten horsepower tractor, whereas a farmer in a poor country might literally use ten horses. Each has the same amount of "horsepower" but the output achieved using the tractor is considerably more than that produced by using ten horses. The combination of better technology and more per capita capital accentuates still further the difference between the rich and poor countries.

Figure 37.4 illustrates the importance of the difference that technological advance makes. Imagine that the year is 1790 and both the United States and Ethiopia (then called Abyssinia) use the same techniques of production and have the same per capita production function, PF_{1790}. With a larger per capita stock of capital, the United States produces a higher level of per capita output in 1790 than does Ethiopia. By 1990, technological advances adopted in the United States, but not in Ethiopia, enable the United States to produce more output from given inputs. The per capita production function in the United States shifts upward to PF_{1990}. Output per capita in the United States in 1990 is much higher than it was in 1790 for two reasons. First, the per capita stock of capital equipment has increased dramatically; second, the techniques of production have improved, resulting in an upward shift in the production function.

The faster the pace of technological advance, the faster the production function shifts upward. The faster the pace of capital accumulation, the more quickly a country moves along its production function. Both of these forces lead to increased per capita output. A poor country becomes a rich country, partly by moving along its production function and partly by adopting better technology, thereby shifting its production function upward.

The importance of the connection between capital accumulation and output growth is illustrated in Fig. 37.5. Capital accumulation is measured by the percentage of output represented by investment. (Recall that investment is the purchase of new capital equipment.) The figure shows what has been happening to investment over time in developing countries and industrial countries and in the two extreme cases of developing countries—Singapore and Ethiopia. As you can see in part (a), the developing countries have been steadily increasing the percentage of income invested, while in industrial countries that percentage has declined slightly. Fast-growing Singapore invests more than 40 percent of its income. Slow-growing Ethiopia invests less than 15 percent of its income. The source of Singapore's dramatic growth and of Ethiopia's almost static income level can be seen in part (b).

Figure 37.4   Technological Change

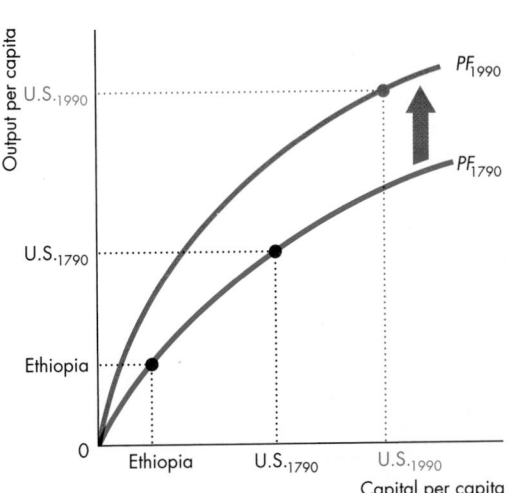

In 1790, the United States and Ethiopia have the same production function, PF_{1790}. By 1990, technological change has shifted the production function upward in the United States to PF_{1990}. Per capita income in the United States has increased from $U.S._{1790}$ to $U.S._{1990}$, partly because of an increase in the per capita capital stock and partly because of an increase in productivity arising from the adoption of better technology.

REVIEW

There is enormous inequality in the world. The poorest people in the poorest countries live on the edge of starvation. The poorest fifth of the world's people consume less than one twentieth of total output and the richest fifth consume more than half the total output. Nations become rich by establishing and maintaining high rates of economic growth over prolonged periods. Economic growth results from the accumulation of capital and the adoption of increasingly efficient technologies. The more rapidly capital is accumulated and the more rapid is the pace of technological change, the higher the rate of growth of output. Small changes in growth rates maintained over a long period of time make large differences to income levels. ∎

Obstacles to Economic Growth

The prescription for economic growth seems straightforward: Poor countries can become wealthy by accumulating capital and adopting the most productive technologies. But if the cure for abject poverty is so simple, why haven't more poor countries become rich? Why are there so many poor people in the world today?

We do not know the answers to all these questions. If we did, we would be able to solve the problem of economic underdevelopment and there wouldn't be any poor countries. But we do understand some of the reasons for poverty and underdevelopment. Let's see what they are.

Population Growth

One of the impediments to economic development and rapid and sustained growth in per capita income is rapid population growth. In the past 20 years, world population has been growing at an average rate of 2 percent per year. At a population growth rate this high, world population doubles every 37 years. That population stood at more than 5 billion at the end of 1988. But the pattern of population growth is uneven. Rich industrial countries have relatively low population growth rates—often less than a half a

Figure 37.5   Investment Trends

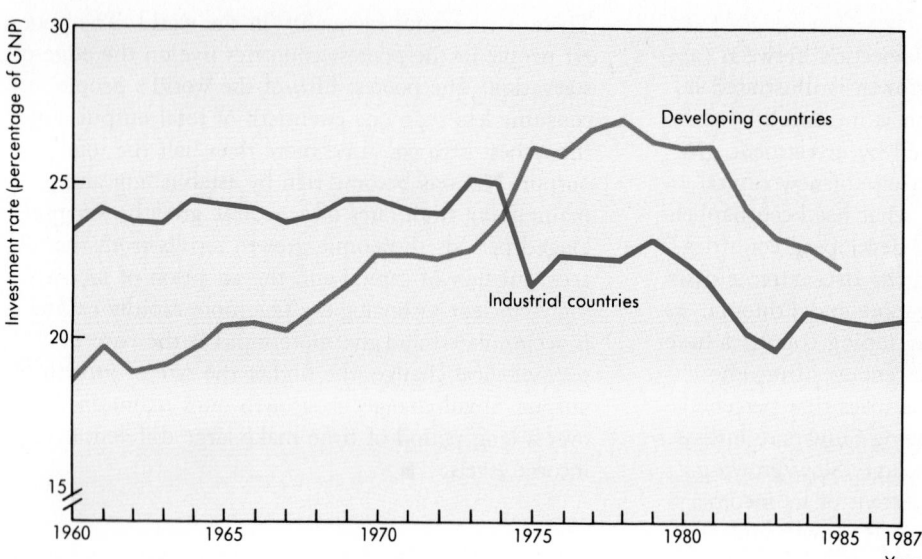

(a) Investment rates in industrial and developing countries

The rate of investment in developing countries increased from 1960 to 1977 and subsequently decreased. Investment in industrial countries was steady during the 1960s and early 1970s but fell after 1974 (part a). Investment in Singapore has increased dramatically while that in Ethiopia has been almost constant (part b). High investment in Singapore has led to rapid growth, while low investment in Ethiopia has led to low growth.

Source: International Monetary Fund, *International Financial Statistics* (1988).

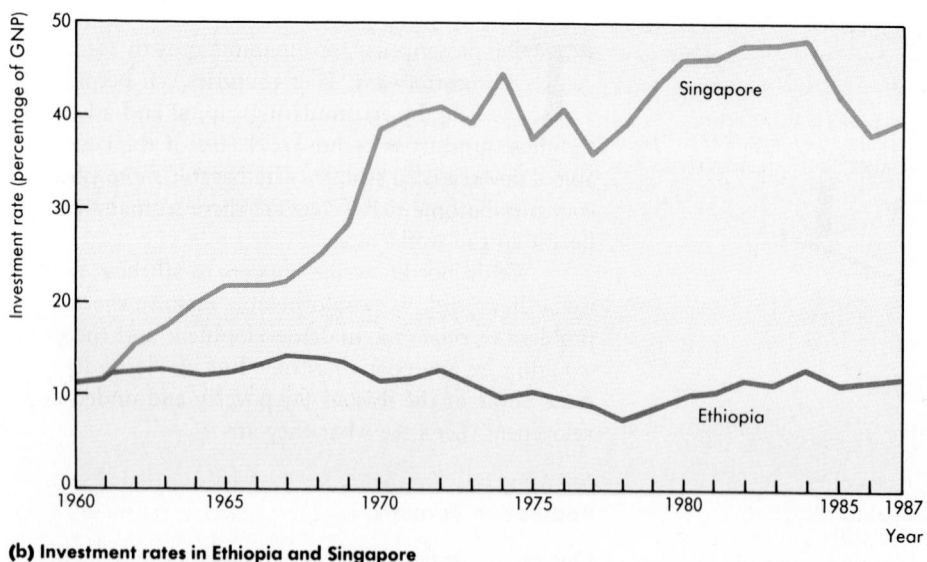

(b) Investment rates in Ethiopia and Singapore

percent a year—while the poor, underdeveloped countries have high population growth rates—in some cases exceeding 3 percent a year.

Why is fast population growth an impediment to economic growth and development. Doesn't a larger population give a country more productive resources, permit more specialization, more division of labor, and therefore yet greater output? These benefits do indeed stem from a large population. But when the population is growing at a rapid rate and when a country is poor, there are two negative effects on economic growth and development that outweigh the benefits of a larger population. They are:

- An increase in the proportion of dependents to workers
- An increase in the amount of capital devoted to supporting the population rather than producing goods and services

Some facts about the relationship between the number of dependents and population growth are shown in Fig. 37.6. The number of dependents is measured, on the vertical axis, as the percentage of the population under 15 years of age. As you can see, the higher the population growth rate, the larger is the percentage of the population under 15. In countries such as the United States, where the population growth rate is less than 1 percent per year, about one person in five (20 percent) is under the age of 15. In countries such as Ethiopia that have rapid population growth rates (3 percent per year or higher), close to one half (50 percent) of the population is under the age of 15.

Let's see why there is a connection between the population growth rate and the percentage of young people in the population. A country might have a steady population because it has a high birth rate and an equally high death rate. But the same steady population growth could occur with a low birth rate and a low death rate. Population growth rates increase when either the birth rate increases or the death rate decreases. Historically, it is a fall in the death rate with a relatively constant birth rate that has led to population explosions. The fall in the death rate mainly takes the form of a fall in the infant mortality rate, and it is this phenomenon that results in an enormous increase in the proportion of young people in the population.

In a country with a large number of young people, capital resources are directed toward providing schools, hospitals, roads, and housing rather than irrigation schemes and industrial capital projects. Such a use of scarce capital resources is obviously not wasteful and does bring great benefits, but it does not add to the economy's capacity to produce goods and services out of which yet additional capital accumulation can be provided.

Low Saving Rate

There is a further obstacle to rapid and sustained economic growth and development. It is the fact that

Figure 37.6   Population Growth and Number of Dependents

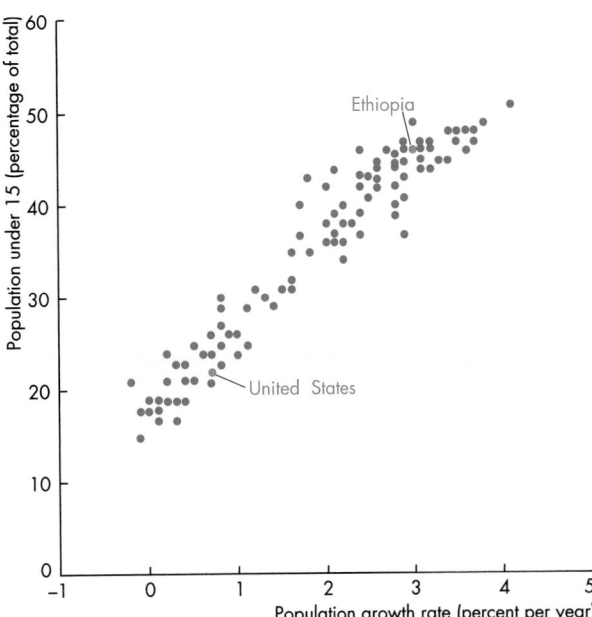

Each point represents a country. It shows the percentage of the population that is under 15 years of age (measured on the vertical axis) and the population growth rate (measured on the horizontal axis). The number of young people in the population is strongly influenced by the population growth rate. In slow-growing countries such as the United States, about a fifth of the population is under the age of 15, while in fast-growing countries such as Ethiopia more than 40 percent of the population is under the age of 15.

Source: World Population Data Sheet of the Population Reference Bureau, Inc., Washington, D.C. (1988).

poor people have such a low level of income that they consume most of it undertaking a tiny volume of saving. Saving is the source of finance for capital accumulation and, as we have seen, capital accumulation is itself one of the main engines of economic growth. Let's investigate the connection between capital accumulation and saving.

As we saw in Chapter 23 (pp. 593–594), there are just three things that people can do with their income: Consume it, save it, or pay it in taxes. That is,

Income = Consumption + Saving + Taxes.

We also saw in Chapter 23 (p. 592) that, in aggregate, the value of output equals income. An economy's output consists of consumption goods, capital goods, goods and services bought by the government, and net exports (exports minus imports). Expenditure on capital goods is investment, and expenditure on goods and services bought by the government is called government purchases of goods and services. Thus,

$$\text{Income} = \text{Consumption} + \text{Investment} \\ + \text{Government purchases} + \text{Net exports.}$$

The first of the above equations tells us that income minus consumption is equal to saving plus taxes. The second equation tells us that income minus consumption is equal to the value of investment plus government purchases plus net exports. Using these two equations then, we see that

$$\text{Saving} + \text{Taxes} = \text{Investment} \\ + \text{Government purchases} \\ + \text{Net exports.}$$

The difference between government purchases and taxes is the government budget deficit. Net exports are the balance of payments current account deficit—known more simply as the current account deficit. We can rearrange the last equation, therefore, as

$$\text{Investment} = \text{Saving} + \text{Current account deficit} \\ - \text{Government budget deficit.}$$

There are three influences on the pace at which a country can accumulate capital (can invest): saving, the government budget, and borrowing from the rest of the world. Other things being equal, the larger the volume of saving, the smaller the government budget deficit (the larger the government budget surplus), and the larger the current account deficit, the faster is the pace of capital accumulation.

The fraction of income that people save depends on the income level. Very poor people save nothing. As income rises, some part of income is saved. The higher the income level, the higher is the proportion of income saved. These patterns in the relationship between income and saving crucially affect the pace at which a country can grow.

Saving is by far the most important component in the sources of financing investment. But in general, the larger the amount of saving, the larger also is the amount of resources available from the rest of the world through the country's current account deficit. Furthermore, the countries with the least resources are those in which the government runs a deficit, thereby restricting yet further the amount available for capital accumulation through investment.

Let's now look at a third impediment to rapid growth and development, the burden of international debt.

International Debt

Poor countries often go into debt with the rest of the world. Loans have to be repaid and interest has to be paid on the loans outstanding. To make debt repayments and interest payments, poor countries need a net export surplus. That is, a country needs a current account surplus. As we have just seen, when a country has a current account deficit, that deficit provides additional financial resources to domestic saving, enabling the country to accumulate capital at a faster pace than would otherwise be possible. A country that has a current account surplus is one that is accumulating capital at a slower pace than its domestic saving permits. Such a country uses part of its saving to accumulate capital—and thereby increases productivity—and uses the other part to pay interest on or repay loans from the rest of the world.

A poor country that borrows heavily from the rest of the world and uses the borrowing to invest in productive capital will not become overburdened by debt provided the growth rate of income exceeds the interest rate on the debt. In such a situation, debt interest can be paid out of the higher income and there is still some additional income left over for additional domestic consumption or capital accumulation. Countries that borrow from the rest of the world and use the resources for consumption or invest in projects that have a low rate of return—lower than the interest rate on the debt—are the ones that become overburdened by debt.

The burden of international debt became particularly onerous for many developing countries during the 1980s. For example, the Latin American countries have accumulated external debts of almost half a trillion dollars. Many of these debts were incurred during the 1970s when raw material prices were rising quickly. From 1973 to 1980, the prices of most raw materials increased on the average by close to 20 percent per year—a rate much higher than the interest rates on the foreign debt being accumulated. In such a situation, raw material producing countries, hungry for capital, borrowed on an enormous scale. In the early 1980s, raw material prices collapsed. Huge debts had been incurred, but the revenue with which to repay those debts was not coming in. To add a further burden, interest rates increased sharply during the 1980s. Today, because of the combination of sagging raw material prices and higher interest rates, many poor countries have a crippling burden of international debt.

The Underdevelopment Trap

The obstacles to economic development are so severe that some economists have suggested that there is a kind of poverty trap that applies to countries—the underdevelopment trap. The **underdevelopment trap** is a situation in which a country is locked into a low income situation that reinforces itself. A low level of capital per worker (both physical and human capital) results in low output per worker. Low productivity in turn produces low per capita income. Low per capita income results in low saving. With low saving, there is a low rate of capital accumulation. Capital accumulation can barely keep up with population growth, so the stock of capital per worker remains low and the cycle repeats itself.

Overcoming the Obstacles to Economic Development

To disturb an equilibrium, some external force has to be applied. To break out of the equilibrium trap of underdevelopment, a variety of forces have been suggested:

- Population control
- Foreign aid
- Removal of trade restrictions
- Demand stimulation

Let's look at each of these in turn.

Population Control

Almost all developing countries use population control methods as part of their attempt to break out of the underdevelopment trap. Population control programs have two key elements: the provision of low-cost birth control facilities and the provision of incentives encouraging people to have a small number of children. These methods meet with some, but limited, success. One of the most highly publicized programs of population control is that employed in China. In that country, families are strongly discouraged from having more than one child. Despite this policy, the population of China continues to grow and forecasts, released in 1989, suggest that by the year 2000 the population will have grown above its target level by an amount equal to one half of the entire population of the United States.

Thus important though they are, population control methods are not the most likely to yield success in the fight against underdevelopment and poverty.

Foreign Aid

The idea that foreign aid helps economic development arises from a simple consideration. If a poor country is poor because it has too little capital, then by giving it aid, it can accumulate more capital and achieve a higher per capita output. Repeated applications of foreign aid year after year can enable a country to grow much more quickly than it could if it had to rely exclusively on its own domestic saving. On this line of reasoning, the greater the flow of foreign aid to a country, the faster it will grow.

Some economists suggest that foreign aid will not necessarily make a country grow faster. They argue that such aid consolidates the position of corrupt and/or incompetent politicians and that these politicians and their policies are two of the main impediments to economic development. Most people who administer foreign aid do not take this view. The consensus is that foreign aid does indeed help economic development. But it is also agreed that foreign aid is not a major factor in influencing the pace of development of poor countries. Its scale is simply too small to make a decisive difference.

A factor that has made a decisive difference in many countries is international trade policy. Let's now turn to an examination of the effects of international trade on growth and development.

Trade and Development

There is a continual cry in the rich countries for protection from imports produced with "cheap labor" in the underdeveloped countries. Other people complain that buying from underdeveloped countries

Figure 37.7   International Trade and Economic Development

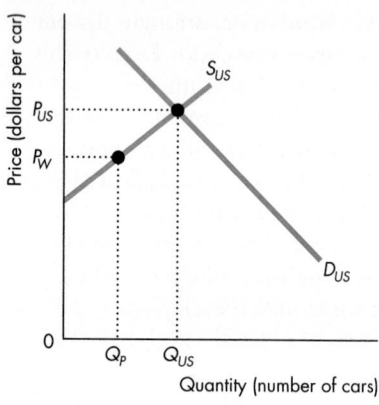

(a) U.S. production and demand

(b) Mexican production

(c) U.S. car market with free trade

The market for cars in the United States (part a) has demand curve D_{US} and supply curve S_{US}. The price of cars is P_{US} and the quantity produced and bought is Q_{US}. Mazda builds an automobile plant in Mexico and the supply curve of cars from that plant is S_M (part b). If the United States prohibits the import of cars from Mexico, the U.S. automobile market remains unchanged and Mexican output is zero. If the United States permits free international trade in cars with Mexico, the price in the U.S. market is P_W (part c) and the total quantity of cars bought in the United States is Q_W. (W stands for "with trade"). Parts (a) and (b) show that at price P_W, Q_M cars are produced in Mexico and Q_P (P for "production") in the United States. Free international trade permits poor countries to sell their output for a price higher than they would otherwise receive and rich countries to buy goods for a price lower than they would otherwise pay.

"exploits" low-wage workers. As a consequence, countries introduce tariffs, quotas, and voluntary restrictions on trade (see Chapter 35). How do such restrictions affect underdeveloped countries and how does the removal of such restrictions affect their growth and development?

To answer this question, consider the following example (which is illustrated in Fig. 37.7). Imagine a situation (such as that prevailing in the 1950s) in which the United States produces virtually all its cars. The automobile market in the United States is shown in part (a). The demand for cars is shown by curve D_U and the supply by curve S_U. The price of cars is P_U and the quantity produced and bought is Q_U.

Suppose that Mazda builds an automobile production plant in Mexico. The supply curve of cars produced in Mexico is shown in Fig. 37.7(b) as the curve S_M. What happens in the United States depends on U.S. international trade policy.

First, suppose that the United States restricts the import of cars from Mexico. To make things as clear as possible, let's suppose that there is a complete ban on such imports. In this case, Mexico produces no cars for export to the United States. The price of cars in the United States remains at P_U, and the quantity traded remains at Q_U.

In contrast, let's see what happens if the United States engages in free trade with Mexico. (A trade accord between the United States and Mexico has, in fact, recently been negotiated). To determine the price of cars and the quantities produced and consumed in the United States, and the quantity produced in Mexico for export to the United States, we need to consider Fig. 37.7(c). The demand curve for cars in the United States remains D_U but the supply curve becomes S_W. This supply curve is made up of the sum of the quantities supplied both in the United States and Mexico at each price. Equilibrium is achieved in the U.S. market at a price of P_W and a quantity traded of Q_W. To see where these cars are produced, go back to parts (a) and (b) of the figure. Mexico produces Q_M, the United States produces Q_P and these two production levels sum to Q_W.

Mazda's Mexican plant increases its output of cars and its workers generate an income. The output of cars is decreased in the United States. By permitting unrestricted trade with underdeveloped countries, rich countries gain by being able to consume goods that are imported at lower prices than would be possible if only domestic supplies were available. Developing countries gain by being able to sell their output for a higher price than would prevail if they had only the domestic market available to them.

Some of the most dramatic economic growth and development success stories have been based on reaping the gains from relatively unrestricted international trade. Countries such as Hong Kong and Singapore have opened their economies to free trade with the rest of the world and dramatically increased their living standards by specializing and producing goods and services at which they have a *comparative advantage*—which they can produce at a lower opportunity cost than other countries (see "Talking with Anne Krueger," pp. 913–916).

Aggregate Demand Stimulation and Growth

It is often suggested that growth and development can be stimulated by expanding aggregate demand. The suggestion takes two forms. Sometimes it is suggested that if the rich countries stimulate their own aggregate demand, their economies will grow more quickly and, as a consequence, commodity prices will remain high. High commodity prices help poor countries and so stimulate their income growth and economic development. (Reading Between the Lines, pp. 992–994, provides a recent example of this line of reasoning.) It is also often suggested that poor countries can make themselves grow faster by stimulating their own level of aggregate demand.

Can stimulating aggregate demand in the rich countries help the poor countries? Can aggregate demand stimulation in poor countries help them grow? The answers to both of these questions are almost certainly no, but let's see why. As we discovered when we studied the theory of aggregate demand and aggregate supply in Chapter 24, changes in aggregate income can occur as a result of either a change in aggregate demand or a change in aggregate supply. But aggregate demand changes affect output and income in the short run only. That is, when wages and other input prices are fixed, a change in aggregate demand changes both output and the price level. But in the long run, a change in aggregate demand leads to a change in the prices of goods and services and of factors of production. Once input prices have adjusted in response to a change in aggregate demand, income returns to its capacity level. Changes in per capita capacity income can be brought about only by changes in per capita productivity—which in turn is brought about by changes in the stock of per capita capital and in the state of technology.

This macroeconomic model of aggregate demand and aggregate supply applies to all countries, rich and poor alike. If rich countries stimulate aggregate demand by persistently permitting aggregate demand to grow at a pace faster than capacity growth, they will generate inflation. If they permit aggregate demand to grow at a pace similar to the growth of capacity, prices will be stable. In recent history, we have seen rich countries generating rapid inflation and moderate inflation. The 1970s was a decade of rapid inflation. During that decade, commodity prices also increased quickly, enabling many developing countries to increase the pace of capital accumulation and income growth. The 1980s were a decade of moderate inflation. It is this decade that brought falling raw material prices and the burden of large international debt for many developing countries.

Don't the facts of the 1970s and 1980s support the conclusion that rapid aggregate demand growth and inflation in the rich countries help the poor countries? They do not. Rather, they provide an example of what can happen, over a limited time period, when there is a previously unexpected increase or decrease in the growth rate of aggregate demand. In the 1970s, there was an unexpectedly rapid increase in aggregate demand. As a consequence, many countries experienced increasing inflation and increasing output growth. In the 1980s, there was an unexpectedly severe contraction of aggregate demand in the rich countries, notably in the United States, resulting in falling inflation and a slowdown in output growth (and in some countries, including the United States, a fall in output). Unexpected fluctuations in the inflation rate can produce fluctuations in output growth—precisely what happened in the 1970s and 1980s. But sustained aggregate demand growth and sustained steady inflation

Deflation and Development

Concerted Effort Urged to Raise World Trade

A United Nations report has urged industrial nations to promote worldwide growth by co-ordinating their economic policies without delay and said deflation is now the biggest threat to prosperity.

"The defeat of inflation is a major achievement," Kenneth Dadzie, head of the UN Conference on Trade and Development, said in a foreword to the Geneva-based body's annual report on the state of the world economy.

But resulting deflation has now become a menace to stability, the Ghanaian UN official said. Deflationary forces now constitute "the single most pervasive threat to world prosperity."

While welcoming a trend toward increased co-ordination of industrialized countries' economic strategies over the past year, Mr. Dadzie said not all accepted the need to stimulate global growth and cut real interest rates.

The recent collapse in oil and tin prices is the latest manifestation of deflation. Real non-oil commodity prices as a whole, despite a recent increase for coffee, had plunged to the lowest level since the Great Depression of the 1930s.

Deflation was "sapping the vitality of much of the world economy, developing countries in particular, and eroding the fabric of international trade and finance, leaving in its trail widespread unemployment, protectionism and insolvency."

Mr. Dadzie cautioned against relying on prospective cuts in the United States' record budget deficit, the oil price decline and the depreciation of the U.S. dollar to remedy the situation.

"The combined impact of these factors is unlikely to raise the momentum of growth in the world economy," he said. Lower crude prices, for one, would help net importers but sharply strain debtor countries heavily dependent on energy exports.

"As a whole, developing countries are net oil exporters and will lose $50-billion (U.S.) in net export revenues in 1986."

"The 171-page report forecast a 2.9 per cent growth in output among developed market-economy countries next year, up only marginally over 1986.

It said Japan and North America would lead the way with growth rates of 3.5 per cent next year, with Western Europe and others lagging behind with 2.5 per cent next year.

Third World growth was expected to average 2.7 per cent, slightly above 1986, ranging from South Asia's 4.9 per cent to a fall of 0.6 per cent among the least developed African states.

Only the Communist economies of eastern Europe would enjoy a significant gain of 4.2 per cent, compared with 3.2 last year. China, which posted an exceptionally rapid 13 per cent in 1985, would slide progressively back to 7 per cent in 1987.

Mr. Dadzie called for multilateral development finance institutions to step up net lending.

The report said Third World nations had borne the brunt of deflation, with low commodity prices severely damaging export earnings, debt-servicing ability and growth.

Toronto Globe Mail, August 12, 1986
Reprinted by permission of Reuters.

The Essence of the Story

The United Nations' Conference on Trade and Development (UNCTAD) has issued an annual report on the state of the world economy:

- It predicts that world output growth in 1987 will be 2.9 per cent.

- It asserts that deflation in the industrial countries has damaged the developing countries by lowering the following:

  —Commodity prices
  —Export earnings
  —Ability to pay debt interest
  —Output growth

- It urges the industrial countries to embark on a program of coordinated aggregate demand expansion.

UNCTAD's head, Kenneth Dadzie, says:

- Inflation has been defeated.

- Real commodity prices are at historically low levels.

- Deflation is blocking output growth and is causing reduced international trade and investment, unemployment, protectionism, and bankruptcy

- The combined effects of a cut in the U.S. budget deficit, a lower value for the U.S. dollar, and a lower oil price will not raise world output growth.

- Output growth will be stimulated only if real interest rates are cut.

Background and Analysis

Facts

- During the year's before the news article was written, inflation had been cut significantly in industrial countries:

	1980	1984
United States	13.5	4.3
Canada	10.2	4.3
United Kingdom	18.0	5.0
Japan	8.0	2.3

and in some developing countries, but in most developing countries it had increased:

	1980	1984
Africa	14.2	20.1
Asia	12.5	7.1
Europe	35.5	33.9
Middle East	17.2	16.2
Latin America	55.1	146.3

- Commodity prices fell in the early 1980s. Some prices in 1984, expressed as a percentage of their 1980 levels, are:

Food	73.6
Beverages	98.4
Agricultural raw materials	88.8
Metals	73.1
Oil	99.3
All commodities	82.2

Assertions

- Low real commodity prices hurt developing countries by lowering their export earnings, hampering their ability to repay their debts, and slowing their output growth.

Correct: Commodities form a large part of the output of developing countries. Low real commodity prices, therefore, lower the value of the output of these countries and lower the volume of capital and other imports that they can buy with a given volume of exports. Lower export earnings slow down growth and make it harder to service debts.

(Continued on next page)

Background and Analysis (cont.)

Conclusion

■ Real commodity prices are low because of deflation in the developed countries. A new, concerted effort to stimulate aggregate demand will raise real commodity prices again.

Probably wrong: Output growth has been low in the developed countries and unemployment has been high. Output and employment are determined, though, by aggregate demand *and* aggregate supply. Only the unanticipated fluctuations in aggregate demand have real effects. Much of the depressed state of the developed countries is likely associated with aggregate supply-side disturbances. In any case, real commodity prices are not well-correlated with the business cycle. As the figure illustrates, when the industrial countries were booming in the 1960s and early 1970s, real commodity prices were falling. The recession of the mid-1970s saw commodity prices rise very

high. Only in the 1980s have real commodity prices fallen in line with the fall in output in the rich countries.

Real commodity prices are altered by supply and demand for individual commodities. Some commodity prices rise and some fall even when the average prices are steady. For example, over the past 25 years, the price of zinc (commonly used in computers and electronic technology) has steadily increased while the price of iron has steadily declined. There is no simple connection between real commodity prices and the state of aggregate demand in developed countries. In fact, correctly anticipated, demand expansion in the developed countries would raise prices (and inflation) in those countries and have minimal effects on the developing countries.

■ Coordinated aggregate demand expansion in the rich countries would lower real interest rates and stimulate development throughout the world.

Certainly wrong: Aggregate demand stimulation using fiscal policy would almost certainly raise real interest rates. Aggregate demand expansion using monetary policy might lower real interest rates temporarily but would have no lasting effect on real interest rates and, if associated with higher inflation, would raise nominal interest rates.

UNCTAD is advocating a policy of aggregate demand stimulation. Pursuing the policy recommended by UNCTAD would certainly produce higher prices and perhaps renewed inflation in the developed countries and would do little to help the plight of the developing world.

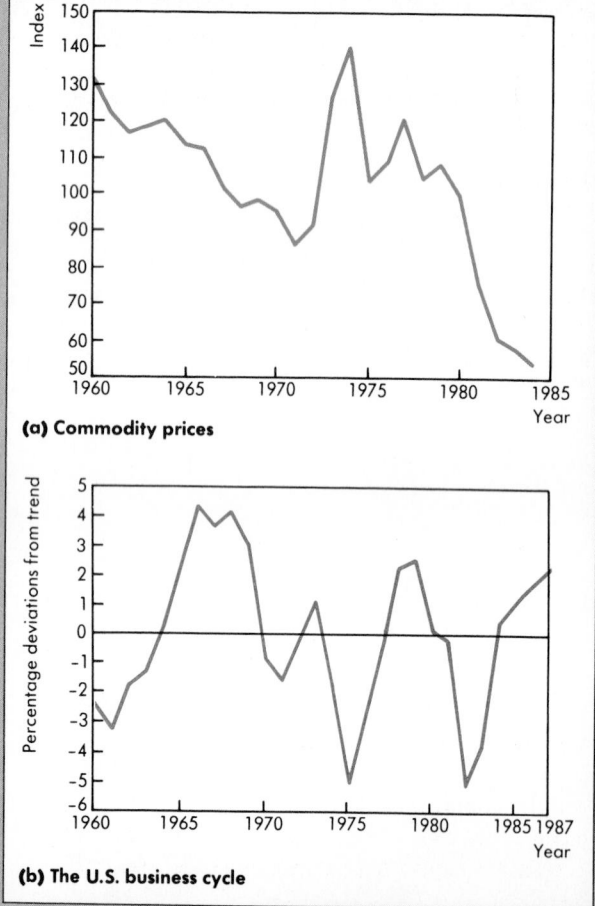

(a) Commodity prices

(b) The U.S. business cycle

are not capable of producing sustained growth in output.

Developing countries can make aggregate demand grow at a rapid or a moderate rate. The more rapidly aggregate demand grows, relative to the growth of capacity, the higher is the inflation rate. Some developing countries inflate quickly and others slowly. But there is virtually no connection between the pace of their development and the rate of inflation. As Fig. 37.8 illustrates, fast-growing Singapore that invests more than 40 percent of its income in capital equipment each year has a moderate inflation rate, while the average-growing Ghana has the highest inflation rate of the developing countries—a rate in excess of 100 percent a year. Slow-growing Ethiopia that invests only 10 percent of its income has had a moderate inflation rate. Each blue dot in the figure shows the investment percentage and inflation rate in a developing country. As you can see, the dots do not form a clear relationship between these variables. Thus the pace at which a developing country stimulates aggregate demand, while affecting its inflation rate, has no appreciable effect on the growth rate of real income or the pace of economic development.

■ We've seen that to grow quickly, a country must accumulate capital at a rapid pace. To do so, it must achieve a high savings rate and undertake foreign borrowing that is used in high-return activities. The most rapidly growing developing countries have a high pace of captial accumulation and obtain a high return on their captial by pursuing a free trade policy, thereby ensuring that they produce those goods and services in which they have a comparative advantage.

Figure 37.8   Inflation and Economic Growth

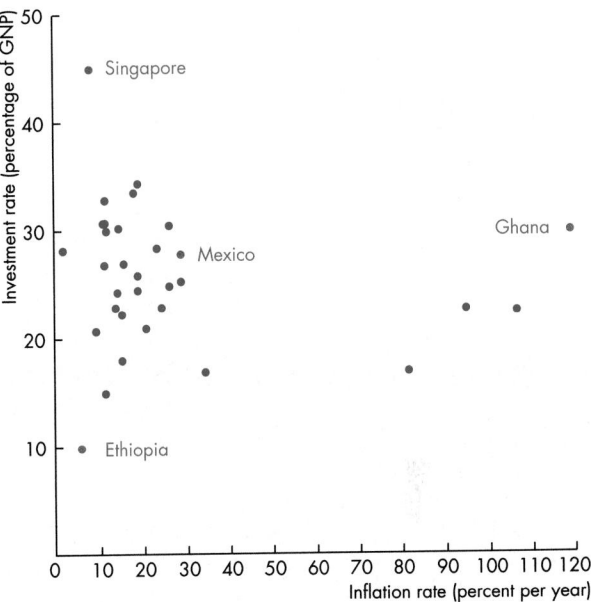

Each point in the figure represents a country. It shows the country's investment level (as a percentage of GNP) plotted against the annual inflation rate. The data are for 1960 to 1985. There is no discernible connection between a country's inflation rate and its pace of investment and economic growth. Fast-growing Singapore has a low inflation rate, as does slow-growing Ethiopia. Medium-growth Ghana has the highest inflation rate in the developing world.

Source: International Monetary Fund, *International Financial Statistics* (1988).

SUMMARY

The International Distribution of Income

There is enormous inequality in the international distribution of income. The poorest countries have average per capita income levels of 4 percent to 9 percent of that in the United States. Half of the world's population earns only 15 percent of world income and the richest 20 percent of the world's population earns 55 percent of income. (pp. 979–981)

Growth Rates and Income Levels

Poor countries become rich by achieving and maintaining for prolonged periods high rates of per capita income growth. Rich countries grow at about 1.5 percent per year. Poor countries that have a slower growth rate than that fall further behind. Poor countries that achieve a growth rate higher than 1.5 percent close the gap on the rich countries. High and sustained growth makes a dramatic difference in a short time span. If China can achieve and maintain a per capita income growth rate of 6 percent per year, the per capita income of China will catch up with that of the United States by the mid 2030s. (pp. 981–983)

Inputs, Technological Progress, and Economic Growth

Per capita income growth results from the growth in per capita capital and in technological change. The greater the fraction of income invested in new capital equipment and the faster the pace of technological change, the higher is the rate of economic growth. (pp. 983–985)

Obstacles to Economic Growth

There are three major obstacles to sustained economic growth and development: rapid population growth, a low saving rate, and an international debt burden. Rapid population growth results in there being a large proportion of young dependents in the population. Low saving results in a low rate of capital accumulation. A large international debt burden re-

sults in some savings having to be used to pay debt interest rather than to accumulate capital and improve productivity.

Low income results in low saving, which in turn results in low investment and thus low income growth. Many poor countries are caught in what appears to be an underdevelopment trap. (pp. 985–989)

Overcoming the Obstacles to Economic Development

The main techniques for overcoming the obstacles to economic development are the implementation of population control measures, foreign aid, and the removal of trade restrictions. Of these, the most dramatic success stories have almost always involved rapid expansion of international trade.

The stimulation of aggregate demand, either by rich or poor countries, cannot contribute, in the long run, to economic growth and development. If aggregate demand grows at the same rate as capacity, prices are stable; if aggregate demand grows at a faster rate than capacity, prices rise—there is inflation. The rate of inflation does not appear to have a major influence on the rate of economic growth and development. (pp. 989–995)

K E Y   C O N C E P T S

R E V I E W   Q U E S T I O N S

1 Describe the main differences between the richest and poorest countries.

2 Compare the distribution of income among families in the United States with the distribution of

income among countries in the world. Which distribution is more unequal?

3 How long will it take a poor country such as China to catch up with a rich country such as the

United States if the United States grows at 1.5 percent per year and if China grows at the following rates:

a) 1.5 percent per year

b) 3 percent per year

c) 6 percent per year

d) 12 percent per year

4 What determines a country's per capita income level? What makes the per capita income level change?

5 Give an example of a country in which rapid economic growth has occurred and one in which slow economic growth has occurred. Which country has the highest investment rate?

6 Review the obstacles to economic growth.

7 Why is rapid population growth an obstacle to economic growth?

8 Describe the underdevelopment trap.

9 What are the main ways in which poor countries try to overcome their poverty?

10 Why does free trade stimulate economic growth and development?

11 Why does demand stimulation not improve a country's rate of economic growth and its development?

P R O B L E M S

1 A poor country has 10 percent of the income of a rich country. The poor country achieves a growth rate of 10 percent per year. The rich country is growing at 5 percent per year. How many years will it take income in the poor country to catch up with that of the rich country?

2 Siliconia is a poor country with no natural resources except sand. Per capita income is $500 a year and this entire income is consumed. Per capita income is constant—there is no economic growth. The government has a balanced budget and there are no exports or imports. Then, one day, the price of silicon increases and Siliconia is able to export sand at a huge profit. Exports soar from zero to $400 (per capita). Per capita income increases to $1000 a year and per capita consumption increases to $600 a year. There are still no imports and Siliconia has a balance of payments current account surplus of $400 per capita.

a) What happens to investment and the growth rate in Siliconia?

b) If Siliconia imports capital goods equal in value to its exports, what will be its investment?

c) What will be its current account balance?

d) If the government of Siliconia runs a budget deficit of $100 (per capita), what will be its investment?

Chapter 38

Comparing Economic Systems

After studying this chapter, you will be able to:

- Explain why the economic problem of scarcity is common to all economic and political systems

- Describe the various political systems that have been proposed to deal with the economic problem

- Explain the difference between capitalism and socialism

- Describe the varieties of capitalism in the United States, Japan, and Western Europe

- Describe the main features of the economy of the Soviet Union

- Explain the economic restructuring—or *perestroika*—being undertaken in the Soviet Union

- Describe the economic reforms being undertaken in China

- Assess the efficiency of alternative economic systems

From Moscow and Beijing to Washington, London, and Tokyo, dramatic changes are taking place in the way governments manage their nations' economies. ■ In Moscow, it is called *perestroika*—restructuring. At the June 1987 meeting of the Central Committee of the Communist party, Mikhail Gorbachev presented his model for the "radical restructuring of economic management" in the Soviet Union. He preached his message in meetings with ordinary Russians, and proclaimed the virtues of "working an extra bit harder" with an almost religious intensity. In his book, *Perestroika,* which became a best seller even in the United States, he described the origins and the first steps being taken to implement his *"perestroika* revolution." ■ In Beijing,

Perestroika

widespread reforms in the Chinese economic system are being encouraged and implemented. In that country, the goal declared by the architect of the modern Chinese economy, Deng Xiaoping, is to build "a socialist nation with Chinese characteristics" that will embody "one country and two systems."

The two systems are the socialist system of China and the Soviet Union, and the capitalist system of the United States, Western Europe, and Japan. ■ Changes in government economic management are less dramatic in Washington, London, and Tokyo than those in the Soviet Union and China. But change, nevertheless, is in the air. In the United States, that change has taken the form of a steady process of deregulation, a process begun during the years when Jimmy Carter was president and given greater momentum during the Reagan years. In Great Britain, and many other Western European countries, deregulation has been accompanied by the selling off of state-operated businesses such as railroads, telecommunications, and public utilities to private enterprise. In Japan, change is taking place that results in a greater liberalization of the Japanese economy and of its international trading and financial relations.   ■ What are the main differences in the economic systems of the Soviet Union and China, and of the United States, Western Europe, and Japan? What exactly are capitalism and socialism? Why are the socialist countries undergoing such massive changes in their methods of economic management? Why are countries in Western Europe and Japan privatizing large parts of their economies? How do the alternative economic systems of capitalism and socialism perform? Can a single country successfully combine the two different economic systems?

■ In this chapter, we're going to describe some of the key differences in the economic systems of the world's major countries. We will learn how capitalist and socialist economies operate. We'll examine some of the diversity among the capitalist economies—the United States, Japan, and Western Europe. We'll study the economic system of the Soviet Union and see why *perestroika* is taking place. We'll examine the reforms in China and describe its economic goals. Finally, we'll compare the performances of the alternative economic systems.

The Fundamental Economic Problem

The first thing that we learn when we begin to study economics is that the source of all economic problems is the universal fact of *scarcity*. In embarking on a study of comparative economic systems, it will be worthwhile to review and reinforce our understanding of the implications of scarcity.

Scarcity

Scarcity arises because we all want to consume more goods and services than the available resources make possible. The *production possibility frontier* describes the limits of what we can produce—it separates the attainable from the unattainable (see Chapter 3, pp. 51–53). Our consumption possibilities are maximized if we arrange our economic affairs in such a way that we produce at a point on our production possibility frontier. The first aspect of solving the economic problem, therefore, involves getting onto the frontier itself.

Getting onto the Production Possibility Frontier

If we operate at a point on the production possibility frontier rather than at some point inside it, we produce more of all goods. We cannot take it for granted, however, that we will automatically operate on the frontier. We might waste resources. Resources are wasted, for example, if we produce more of some perishable commodity at a given moment than can be quickly consumed. Some of the commodity rots and may as well not have been produced. Therefore the resources used to produce that commodity are wasted.

Another more subtle form of waste arises if productive resources are combined in a way that makes the cost of production higher than it needs to be. For example, electricity can be generated by using either coal, oil, or nuclear power as the energy source. If the cost of producing a megawatt of electricity is lowest using nuclear power, but instead coal and oil are used, then productive resources are wasted. Don't lose sight, however, that in economics the word "cost" includes all costs. In the case of power production, the costs include environmental costs such as pollution, the hazard of nuclear accident and contamination, and many other costs not borne by the producer of electricity.

Different economic systems use different methods to get the economy to a point on its production possibility frontier. We will look at those methods in the next section. Once the economy is on its production possibility frontier, no more of any one good can be produced without producing less of some other good. It is this fact that gives rise to the concept of *opportunity cost*. The opportunity cost of producing one more unit of any particular good is the amount of some other good or goods forgone. Because it is only possible to produce more of one good by producing less of another good, a second aspect of solving the economic problem involves getting to the right point on the frontier.

Producing the Right Quantities of Goods and Services

Determining how much of each of the various goods and services to produce requires that people's preferences of the alternatives be taken into account. For example, if people place a high value on clean air and a low value on quick and convenient transportation, we would produce fewer cars and highways and have more stringent methods of controlling exhaust emission. If people value vacations on the moon highly and place little or no value at all on any of the other things that we currently produce and consume, then we would use an enormous amount of our resources to build lunar transportation systems and holiday resorts! If we all become addicted to fruit and ice cream and refuse to eat meat, Burger King and McDonald's fast-food outlets would either go out of business or radically change their mix of products. Baskin Robbins would be booming.

The way in which individual preferences influence the quantities of goods and services produced varies from one economic system to another. As we'll see shortly, our own economic system takes individual consumers' preferences as the dominant force determining what is produced. But there are other systems in which individual preferences play a limited role and those of the government's planning agency play the dominant role.

Getting onto the production possibility frontier and choosing the right point on it are two aspects of solving the economic problem. There is a third aspect —determining the distribution of economic well-being.

The Distribution of Economic Well-Being

An economy could be at a point on the production possibility frontier and further, that point could be one that exactly reflects consumers' preferences concerning the values of the various goods. At that point, production of more of any one good and less of any other good would make somebody worse off. There are, however, many such points possible, each of which is associated with a different distribution of economic well-being. One such point would be where everyone is equally well off. Another is where 90 percent of the population is almost starving and the other 10 percent are living in enormous luxury. Economic systems, in effect, make decisions about who gets what. Some economic systems favor, in principle at least, considerable equality in the distribution of economic well-being. Other systems favor equality of opportunity but pay little attention to the distribution that results from equal opportunities.

REVIEW

The best we can do in the face of scarcity is to get ourselves onto the production possibility frontier. The point on the frontier that we go to depends on whose preferences determine which goods and services the economy produces and on how the economic system distributes well-being. No economic system can abolish the economic problem. Each system, at best, can only help people cope with scarcity. ■

Let's see how different economic systems cope with the fundamental economic problem.

Alternative Economic Systems

Economic systems vary in two dimensions:

- Who owns capital and land
- Who allocates of resources

Figure 38.1 summarizes the possibilities. Capital and land may be owned entirely by individuals, entirely by the state, or by a mixture of the two. Resources may be allocated entirely by markets, entirely by government economic planners, or by a mixture of the two. The two highlighted corners of the figure represent two idealized extreme cases: capitalism and socialism.

Capitalism is an economic system based on the private ownership of capital and land and on market allocation of resources. **Socialism** is an economic system based on state ownership of capital and land and on a centrally planned allocation of resources. **Central planning** is a method of allocating resources by command. It involves plans being made by a central planning authority and then communicated to the various production and distribution organizations in the country. The plans are monitored by a large team of bureaucrats. Hardly any country has ever used an economic system that precisely corresponds to one of these extreme types, but the United States and Japan come close to being capitalist economies and the Soviet Union and China to being socialist economies.

Figure 38.1   Alternative Economic Systems

Resources allocated by	Capital owned by		
	Individuals	Mixed	State
Markets	**Capitalism** USA Japan		**Market socialism**
Mixed		Great Britain Sweden	Yugoslavia Hungary
			China USSR
Planners	**Welfare state capitalism**		**Socialism**

Under capitalism, individuals own capital—farms and factories, plant and equipment—and resources are allocated by markets. Under socialism, the state owns capital and resources are allocated by a planning and command system. Market socialism combines state ownership of capital with a market allocation of resources. Welfare state capitalism combines private capital ownership with a high degree of state intervention in the allocation of resources.

Some countries combine private and state ownership and market allocation and planning in unusual ways. **Market socialism** (also called **decentralized planning**) is an economic system that combines socialism's state ownership of capital and land with capitalism's market allocation of resources. Yugoslavia and Hungary are examples of market socialist economies. In such economies, the planners communicate a set of prices to the various production and distribution organizations and then leave those organizations free to produce whatever quantities they choose at those prices. Another combination is welfare state capitalism. **Welfare state capitalism** combines capitalism's private ownership of capital and land with a heavy degree of state intervention in the allocation of resources. Sweden, the United Kingdom, and other Western European countries provide examples of such economies.

Since all the economic systems in Fig. 38.1 are made up of a combination of capitalism and socialism, let's examine these two extreme types a bit more closely.

Capitalism

Let's describe a country that has a pure (hypothetical) form of capitalism. Such a country is one in which a concern for individual liberty is paramount. Its foundation is the establishment and enforcement of individual property rights. Each individual owns what he or she has produced or legitimately acquired. Resources are legitimately acquired as a result of buying them from a willing seller or receiving them as a gift. These are the only ways in which resources can be transferred between individuals. Any other method of transferring resources is illegal. Preventing illegal transfers is the only proper role of the state. No other economic action by any individual or group of individuals may be blocked by the force of the state. All individuals are free to form coalitions or groups to buy and sell whatever goods and services they choose and in whatever quantities they choose.

Governments may be viewed as coalitions among individuals that provide certain types of goods and services. Furthermore, if a government can offer better terms than any other coalition so that people choose to trade with it rather than with some other group, then a government may legitimately undertake economic actions. A government may not, however, coerce individuals in any way other than to prevent them from attempting to violate other people's property rights.

In capitalist economies, the allocation of resources is determined by individual choices expressed through markets. *What* is produced is determined by consumers' preferences; *how* goods are produced is determined by profit-maximizing firms; *for whom* goods are produced is determined by individual decisions on the supply of factors of production and by the market-determined prices at which those factors of production trade.

Socialism

Socialism is an economic system based on the political philosophy that the private ownership of capital and land enables the rich (owners of capital and land) to exploit the poor (workers who have no capital and land). To avoid such exploitation, capital and land are owned by the state. Individuals are permitted to own only their *human capital* and capital equipment used for consumption purposes such as consumer durable goods. All other capital is owned by the state. Thus the state owns all factories and farms and the plant and equipment to operate them. All labor works for the state and all consumption goods and services are produced by and bought from the state.

Under socialism, some people are wealthier than others (and have higher incomes than others), but gross inequalities of wealth arising from the ownership of massive industrial and commercial complexes are not permitted. The principles governing the distribution of income are "from each according to his ability, to each according to his contribution." That is, the state pays each individual a wage that reflects the state's own opinion of the value of the output of the individual.

A variant of socialism is communism. **Communism** is an economic system based on the state ownership of capital and land, on central planning, and on distributing income in accordance with the rule "from each according to his ability, to each according to his need." The word communism is commonly used to describe Eastern European and Soviet-style socialism. In ordinary speech, the words

communism and socialism are virtually interchangeable. It is worthwhile keeping the two words distinct, however, when thinking about economic systems.

In socialist (and communist) economies, resources are allocated not by markets but by central planners and it is their preferences and priorities that determine *what, how,* and *for whom* the various goods and services are produced.

The Pros and Cons of Capitalism

Advantages of Capitalism The major advantages of capitalism arise because each individual's judgment about his or her own well-being is paramount in determining what economic actions take place. Each individual decides how much work to do and for whom to work, how to spend time away from work, and how to dispose of the income made from selling his or her resources. Individual incentives are strong. Adam Smith wrote:

> As every individual . . . endeavors as much as he can both to employ his capital in the support of domestic industry and so to direct that industry that its produce be of the greatest value; every individual necessarily labors to render the annual revenue of society as great as he can. . . . He intends only his own gain, and he is in this, as in many other cases, led by an invisible hand to promote an end which was no part of his intention.[1]

Adam Smith went on to reject any detailed state intervention in economic life:

> The statesman, who should attempt to direct private people in what manner they ought to employ their capitals, would not only load himself with a most unnecessary attention, but assume an authority which could safely be trusted, not only to no single person, but to no counsel or senate whatever, and which would nowhere be so dangerous as in the hands of a man who had the folly and presumption enough to fancy himself fit to exercise it.

Disadvantages of Capitalism A major disadvantage of capitalism is seen, even by those who support this economic system, as arising from the fact that

---

[1]Adam Smith, *The Wealth of Nations* (New York: Random House, 1937) 423.

the historical distribution of endowments is arbitrary and indeed is the result of massive illegitimate transfers. For example, the European colonizers of North America took land from the native people of this continent. Because there have in the past been illegitimate transfers—violations of private property rights—the current distribution of wealth has no legitimacy. If there were no large inequality in the distribution of wealth, its historical origins would not be a matter of much concern. But the fact that wealth is distributed very unequally leads most people to the conclusion that there is a role for state intervention to redistribute income and wealth.

A further disadvantage of capitalism arises from the belief that some people do not, in fact, know what is good for them and will, if left to their own devices, make the wrong choices. We all agree that children should not be permitted to exercise complete freedom of choice. Most people would also extend some restrictions to the mentally ill, the senile, and to those who are addicted (or even potentially addicted) to dangerous drugs. Some advocates of socialism go further, arguing that socialist planners are able to make better choices than people would make for themselves.

We have reviewed some arguments against capitalism that might be used to persuade people that such a system is not desirable. But there is a more fundamental problem with capitalism: It has an internal contradiction.

The Contradiction   Private property rights can be enforced only if the state has a monopoly on coercion. If the state were simply competing with others to enforce property rights, then every time a disagreement arose between two parties each would hire its own enforcers to settle the dispute. Battles would ensue. Only when a single supplier of coercive power has emerged victorious can private property rights be successfully enforced without indulging in a process of open physical violence and conflict. The state is the monopolist in the provision of coercion for enforcing property rights. But once the state has achieved that monopoly position, there is no way of preventing it from expanding its range of coercive activities further. There is no check on those individuals who hold offices of state and who exercise the state's powers. Furthermore, there is no way of preventing private individuals and coalitions of private individuals from attempting to persuade the state to use its powers in a broader manner.

Whether it is because of the persuasiveness of the arguments against capitalism or because of the fundamental internal contradiction in the system, capitalism is a hypothetical rather than an actual economic system. No country ever has or ever will experience that pure form of economic organization. It is a philosophical ideal or reference point against which to compare actual systems. If we could have such a system and if we could remedy the historical violations of property rights, then many people would agree that we would have done the best we could to solve the economic problem. But such a solution is simply not available to us. It is for this reason that most capitalist economies include some element of state ownership and control of economic activity.

The Varieties of Capitalism

There is no unique model of capitalism. Most of this book illustrates and elaborates the principles of economics, using examples drawn from the largest and most important capitalist economy—the United States. But not all capitalist economies follow the U.S. model. In this section, we take a quick look at some of the key differences among the capitalist economies and some of the trends that are emerging in those countries.

Japan

Japan's economic performance since World War II is known as the "Japanese economic miracle." Emerging from war with per capita incomes less than one fifth of those in the United States, Japan has transformed itself into an economic giant whose per capita income now approaches that of our own. The most spectacular growth period occurred in the 25 years from 1945 to 1970, when per capita income increased eightfold. Today, the Japanese have a dominant position in world markets for cars and computers, audio and video equipment and a whole range of "high-tech" commodities. The camera-laden Japanese tourist is now as common a sight in London, Paris, and Rome as the North American tourist. And there are many more Japanese visitors to North America than Americans visiting Japan. What has led to this transformation of Japan into one of the world's most powerful and richest economies?

There are four features of the Japanese economy that appear to be responsible for its dramatic success:

- Reliance on free-market, capitalist methods
- Self-disciplined, hardworking, loyal, and cooperative people
- Small scale of government
- Pro-business government intervention

The economic system in Japan is like that in the United States. People are free to pursue their ideas, to own firms, to hire labor and other inputs, and to sell their outputs in relatively free markets.

The Japanese people have a long tradition of loyalty and a strong work ethic. As a consequence, Japanese workers are loyal to their employers and firms are loyal to their workers. This cooperative atmosphere is one that results in hard work and high productivity.

The Japanese government is the smallest in the capitalist world. The total scale of government is less than one fifth of the economy. That is, average taxes and government spending account for slightly less than one fifth of GNP. This contrasts with close to 30 percent in the United States and more than 40 percent in some Western European capitalist countries. Small scale of government means that taxes are low and therefore, do not constitute a major discouragement to work and to saving and accumulating capital. To the extent that the Japanese government does intervene in the economy, that intervention is pro-business.

The main vehicle of government intervention is the **Ministry of International Trade and Industry** (MITI)—a government agency responsible for stimulating Japanese industrial development and international trade. In the years immediately following World War II, MITI encouraged the development of basic industries such as coal, electric power, shipbuilding, and steel. It used tariffs and quotas to protect these industries in their early stages of development, subsidized them, and ensured that capital resources were abundantly available for them. MITI is almost entrepreneurial in its activities. During the 1960s, with the basic industries in place, MITI turned its attention to helping the chemical and lighter manufacturing industries. In the 1980s, it helped Japanese industry dominate the world computer market.

MITI not only is active in fostering the growth and development of certain industries, but it also helps speed the decline of those industries that are not contributing to rapid income growth. For example, in the mid-1970s when the price of oil increased dramatically, the smelting of bauxite to create aluminium became inefficient in Japan. Within two years, Japan's bauxite-smelting industry had been closed down, and Japan was importing all its aluminium from Australia. By identifying industries for profitable growth and those for profitable decline, MITI helps speed the adjustment process in reallocating resources to take maximum advantage of technological change and trends in prices.

The result of Japan's economic system and government economic intervention has been a high rate of capital accumulation. There has also been a high rate of accumulation of human capital, especially in the applied sciences. Going along with a high rate of capital accumulation—both physical and human—has been a high rate of technological advance and with no inhibitions about using the best technologies available, wherever in the world they might have been developed.

Welfare State Capitalism

Capitalism in Western Europe is more heavily tinged with socialism than in either the United States or Japan. It is welfare state capitalism. The countries of Western Europe, many of which now belong to the European Communities, are basically capitalist market economies in the sense that most productive resources are owned by private individuals and most resources are allocated by individuals trading freely in markets for both goods and services and factors of production. But the scale of government, and the degree and direction of government intervention, is much larger in these countries than in the United States and Japan.

Government expenditure and taxes range between 40 and 50 percent of GNP in European countries. Tax rates this high create disincentives that result in less effort and lower saving rates than in countries with lower taxes. The European countries also have a large, nationalized industry sector. A **nationalized industry** is an industry owned and operated by a publicly owned authority that is directly responsible to the government. Railways, airlines, gas, electricity, telephones, radio and television broadcasting, coal, steel, banking and finance, and even automobiles are among the list of industries that are either wholly or partly publicly owned in some

European countries. Nationalized industries are often managed on a command rather than market principle and usually are less efficient than privately owned, competitive firms.

Increasingly in recent years, European governments have been selling state-owned enterprises. The process of selling state-owned enterprises is called **privatization.** There has also been a retreat, in some countries, from very high tax rates. European countries have noticed the economic success of Japan and the United States and, right or wrong, have drawn the conclusion that the greater reliance on capitalism in those economies is, in part, responsible for their economic success. That conclusion is reinforced by a widespread belief that the socialist methods employed by the Soviet Union and China are no longer serving those countries well. Let's take a closer look at socialism—first in the Soviet Union and then in China.

The Soviet Union

The Soviet Union, or the Union of Soviet Socialist Republics, was founded in 1917 following the Bolshevik revolution led by Vladimir Ilyich Lenin. The Soviet Union is a vast, resource-rich, and diverse nation. Its land area is three times that of the United States; its population is approaching 300 million; it has vast reserves of coal, oil, iron ore, natural gas, timber, and almost every other mineral resource; it is a nation of enormous ethnic diversity, with Russians making up only 50 percent of the population. The remaining population includes many European, Asian, and Arabic ethnic groups.

History

A compact economic history of the Soviet Union appears in Table 38.1. Although the nation was founded in 1917, its modern economic management system was not put in place until the 1930s. The architect of this system was Joseph Stalin. The financial, manufacturing, and transportation sectors of the economy had been taken into state ownership and control by Lenin. Stalin added the farms to this list. He abolished the market and introduced a command planning mechanism, initiating a series of five-year plans that placed their major emphasis on setting and

Table 38.1   A Compact Summary of Key Periods in the Economic History of the Soviet Union

Period	Main economic events/characteristics
1917–1921 (Lenin)	• Bolshevik revolution • Nationalization of banking, industry, and transportation • Forced requisitioning of agricultural output
1921–1924 (Lenin)	• New Economic Policy (NEP), 1921 • Market allocation of most resources
1928–1953 (Stalin)	• Abolition of market • Introduction of command planning and five-year plans • Collectivization of farms • Emphasis on capital goods and economic growth • Harsh conditions
1953–1970 (Khrushchev to Brezhnev)	• Steady growth • Increased emphasis on consumer goods
1970–1985 (Brezhnev to Chernenko)	• Deteriorating productivity in agriculture and industry • Slowdown in growth
1985– (Gorbachev)	• *Perestroika*—reforms based on increased accountability

attaining goals for the production of capital goods. The production of consumer goods was given a secondary place and personal economic conditions were harsh. With emphasis on the production of capital goods, the Soviet economy grew quickly.

By the 1950s, after Stalin's death, steady economic growth continued but the emphasis in economic planning gradually shifted away from capital goods toward consumer goods production. In the 1960s, the growth rate began to sag and by the 1970s and early 1980s, the Soviet economy was running into serious problems. Productivity was actually declining, especially in agriculture but also in industry. Growth stopped and, on some estimates, per capita income in the Soviet Union began to fall.

It was in this situation that Mikhail Gorbachev came to power with plans to restructure the Soviet economy, based on the idea of increased individual accountability and rewards based on performance.

Although the Soviet economy is now undergoing a major restructuring process, its essential organization is that established in the 1930s by Stalin. Let's see what that organization is.

Planning and Command System

There are two parallel organizations in the Soviet Union: the state and the Communist party. Power resides in the Communist party. The most important policy-making body in the Soviet Union is the Politburo, a small group of party officials appointed by

the Central Committee of the Communist party, in turn appointed by the Party Congress, as shown in Fig. 38.2. The Party Congress, made up of delegates from all levels of the party and all regions of the country, exercises only nominal control over the Central Committee and the Politburo.

These organs of the Communist party parallel the state institutions. The Soviet parliament is the Supreme Soviet. This body meets infrequently and appoints a Presidium to conduct work between sessions. The Council of Ministers is the government bureaucracy. This bureaucracy controls 60 ministries responsible for detailed aspects of production. The figure provides a sample of the names and responsibilities of some of the 60 ministries. Twenty committees report to the Council of Ministers and of these, two play a central role in economic planning

Figure 38.2 Organization Chart of the Soviet Union

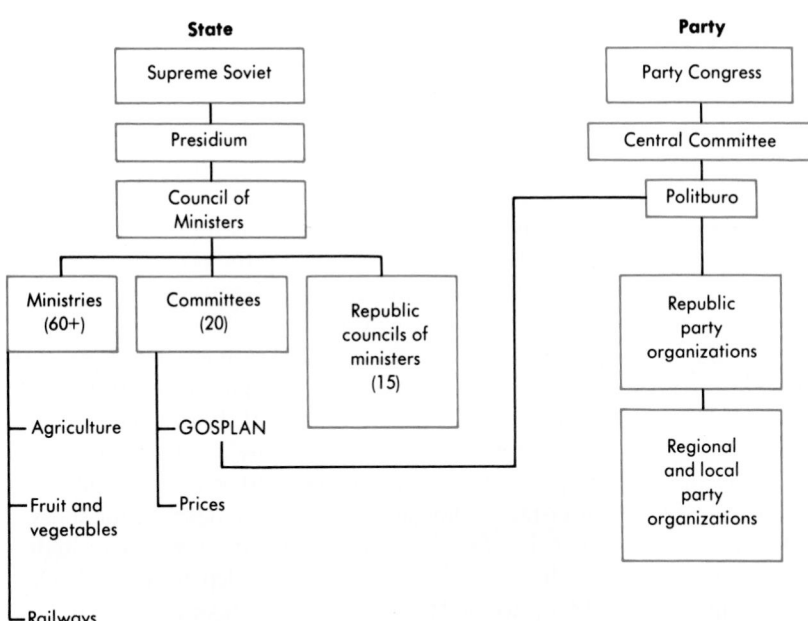

Two parallel organizations—the state and the party—manage the Soviet economy. Although the two organizations are parallel, the party is the dominant partner. GOSPLAN—the State Committee for Economic Planning—has direct links to the Politburo, the chief organ of party power. Economic plans are administered by ministries that deal with each sector of the economy. Plans are also monitored by regional and local party organizations. This chart shows only the tip of a bureaucratic iceberg. Each of the 15 republics of the Soviet Union has an organization similar to that shown here and each local region within each republic has yet another similar organization.

and control. The first of these is the State Committee for Economic Planning, whose acronym, in Russian, is GOSPLAN. **GOSPLAN** is the committee responsible for drawing up and implementing the state's economic plans. The second important economic committee is one that determines prices. Also reporting to the Council of Ministers are the Councils of Ministers of the 15 republics of the Soviet Union.

The organization chart shown in Fig. 38.2 is just the tip of a bureaucratic iceberg, for each of the 15 republics of the Soviet Union has a set of institutions that almost exactly parallels the institutions of the central government just described. This organizational form is also replicated at the regional level and then, yet again, at the local level. Thus there are ministries and party organizations whose influence stretches deep into the most detailed aspects of economic life in the Soviet Union.

The Communist party of the Soviet Union exercises control over the state by three main methods:

- GOSPLAN reports to the Politburo
- Party approves all major projects
- Party controls appointments

The detailed plans for economic activity, drawn up by GOSPLAN (and described below), are reported to and approved by the Politburo. The party exercises detailed day-to-day control over all major projects and production activities through its regional and local organizations. The Communist party's most powerful tool for influencing the Soviet economy is its control over all major appointments in the state bureaucracy, in industry, and in the military.

State Enterprises   The **state enterprise** is the basic production unit in the Soviet economy. An enterprise is run by a state-appointed director who is in charge of all the enterprise's operations but is required to follow the instructions imposed by the state's economic plans. State enterprises operate in both the industrial and agricultural sectors of the economy and the enterprise manager plays a key role in the fulfillment of plans. Soviet managers are rewarded through a complex system of performance-related payments.

Planning at GOSPLAN   Every five years, GOSPLAN draws up a five-year plan. The **five-year plan** is a broad outline of the general targets and directions set for a period of five years. Each year, GOSPLAN

draws up an annual plan. The **annual plan** is a month-by-month set of targets for output, prices, inputs, investment, and money and credit flows. The plans are approved by the Politburo and the Council of Ministers and then communicated to the individual enterprises—farms and factories—that produce the goods and services. Enterprises are overseen both by the ministries that are responsible for the various industries and by local party organizations.

The annual plan is organized around five basic balances:

1 Consumer goods
2 Labor
3 Credit
4 Capital goods
5 Materials

1. Consumer Goods Balance   Consumer goods balance is the achievement of a balance between the quantities supplied and demanded for each individual category of consumer goods and services. Soviet planners have three ways of achieving consumer goods balance: changing output, changing incomes, changing prices. Figure 38.3 illustrates these three possibilities. The demand for some good (say, shoes) is D_0; the quantity of shoes that the planners intend to produce is Q_0; the supply curve is S_0; and the cost of producing shoes is C. If the price of shoes is set by the planners at C, there will be an excess of the quantity demanded over the quantity supplied—equal to Q_1 minus Q_0. The planners will not have achieved consumer goods balance in the market for shoes. They can achieve a balance by increasing production to Q_1, in which case the supply curve will shift to the right to S_1 (part a). They can also achieve a balance by imposing higher income taxes, thereby reducing after-tax income and lowering the demand for shoes (part b). They will have to increase taxes by enough to shift the demand curve to the left from D_0 to D_1. At a price of C, the quantity of shoes demanded equals the quantity supplied (Q_0).

In practice, although these two methods of achieving consumer goods balance are available to the Soviet planners, they are not the main methods used. The easiest way of achieving consumer goods balance, and the one most frequently used, is to adjust the price. Soviet planners adjust prices by imposing turnover taxes. The **turnover tax** in the Soviet Union is a tax on a consumer good designed to make its market price high enough to achieve a balance be-

Figure 38.3 Consumer Goods Balance

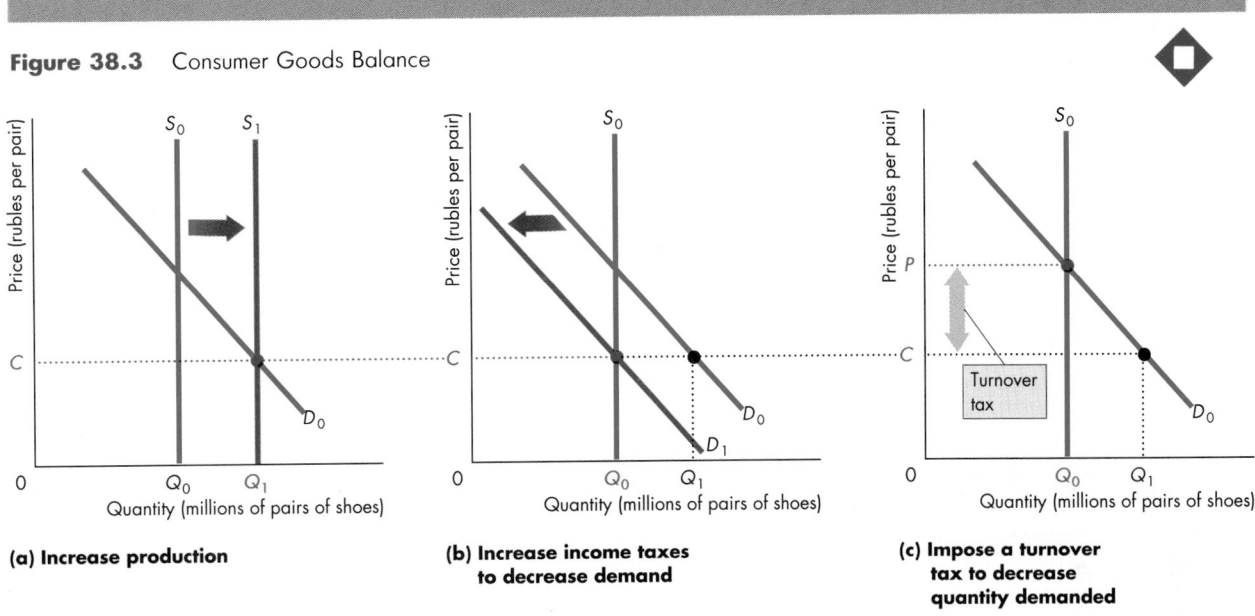

(a) Increase production

(b) Increase income taxes to decrease demand

(c) Impose a turnover tax to decrease quantity demanded

The cost of producing a consumer good (say, shoes) is C. The demand for shoes is D_0, and the quantity produced is Q_0. Three ways of achieving consumer goods balance are available. In part (a), the decision to increase output results in a shift in the supply curve to S_1. When the price is C and the quantity of shoes produced and consumed is Q_1, consumption goods balance is achieved. In part (b), income taxes are increased, reducing after-tax income. The demand for shoes decreases and the demand curve shifts to the left to D_1. The price is C and the quantity of shoes produced and consumed is Q_0. In part (c), the planners impose a turnover tax on shoes. A tax equal to the difference between P and C is imposed, raising the price of shoes to P. The quantity demanded decreases to Q_0 and consumer goods balance is achieved. The Soviet planner uses the turnover tax more frequently than the other two methods for achieving consumer goods balance.

tween the quantity demanded and quantity supplied. In this example (Fig. 38.3c), a turnover tax sufficient to increase the price to P ensures consumer goods balance in the market for shoes.

2. *Labor Balance* Labor balance is the achievement of a balance between the quantities supplied and demanded for each individual category of labor services. It is achieved, in the short run, by adjusting wage rates. Large differentials in wages—larger than those common in the United States—are necessary to achieve labor balance. In the long run, labor balance is also influenced by the planners' ability to direct resources allocated to education and training, favoring the acquisition of skills in short supply.

3. *Credit Balance* Credit balance is the achievement of a balance between the quantities of credit supplied

and demanded. The banking system in the Soviet Union is owned and controlled by the state. Credit balance is achieved by the state banking system making available the credit that the planners have decided is required.

4. *Capital Goods Balance* Capital goods balance is the achievement of a balance between the quantities supplied and demanded of each type of capital good. The central planners decide how to allocate the scarce capital goods available and, through their control of credit, influence the demand for capital goods by individual production enterprises.

5. *Materials Balance* Materials balance is the achievement of a balance between the quantities demanded and supplied for each and every raw material and intermediate good used in the production of final

Table 38.2 Materials Balance

| Material | Quantity Supplied | | | Quantity demanded | | | | |
| | | | | Intermediate goods | | | Final goods | |
	Production	Inventories	Imports	Coal	Electric power	Nylon	Domestic	Foreign
Coal (tons)	490	10	0	50	300	50	75	25
Electric power (kilowatt-hours)	10,000	0	0	2,000	1,000	1,500	5,500	0
Nylon (yards)	20,000	200	2,000	0	0	0	22,200	0

Materials can be supplied from production, inventories, or imports. They are demanded as an input in the production of intermediate goods, for final domestic consumption, or export. Plans are drawn up to ensure that the quantity supplied equals the quantity demanded. To achieve materials balance, Soviet planners can increase production, decrease inventories, increase imports, decrease the quantity demanded as an intermediate good, decrease final demand, or decrease exports. Reductions in final domestic demand are the main method employed for achieving materials balance.

consumer goods and capital goods. This balancing exercise is the most complex aspect of Soviet planning. There are literally billions of raw materials and intermediate goods and the detailed plans for the material balances fill 70 volumes, or 12,000 pages, each year.

An example of a simplified materials balance schedule is set out in Table 38.2. There are just three materials. (The actual Soviet plans consider more than 30,000 separate materials at the central planning level, and a further 50,000 at the regional and local levels.) There are three sources of any material used in the production process: production, inventories, and imports. There are three broad categories of uses of any raw material or produced input: an intermediate input into the production of other goods, final domestic use either for consumption or investment purposes, and exports. For each material, a detailed plan showing the balance between the quantity supplied and quantity demanded is drawn up. For example, the first row of the table shows that 490 tons of coal are produced and 10 tons are taken from inventory. The quantity supplied is 500 tons of coal. The quantity demanded is made up of 50 tons as inputs in the coal industry itself, 300 tons to produce electric power, 50 tons to extract chemicals that are

converted into nylon, 75 tons for domestic heating, and the 25 tons exported. The total quantity demanded is 500 tons. The plan for coal balances. The second row of the table shows the plan for electric power and the third row that for nylon.

Table 38.2 shows a balance between the quantity demanded and the quantity supplied of each material. Suppose that there is an excess of the quantity demanded over the quantity supplied of electric power. What can the Soviet planners do in such a situation? They can plan to produce more electric power or they can plan to produce less coal and less nylon, thereby reducing the amount of electric power demanded, or they can reduce the quantity of electric power for final domestic use. The Soviet planners usually choose the last of these options. If they were to increase the output of electric power, there would then be an increase in the quantity of coal demanded in the electric power industry. The increase in the quantity demanded of coal would result in a shortage in the coal sector that would require further adjustments in that sector. To balance the quantity supplied and quantity demanded of electric power by reducing the amount going to some other industry would result in that industry failing to achieve its targets.

The Market Sector   Although the economy of the Soviet Union is a planned one, a substantial amount of economic activity takes place outside the planning and command economy. The most important component of the market sector is in agriculture. It is estimated that there are 35 million private plots worked by rural households. These private plots constitute less than 3 percent of the agricultural land of the Soviet Union but produce close to 25 percent of total agricultural output and a third of all the meat and milk produced. Some estimates suggest that the productivity on private plots is 40 times that of state enterprise farms and collective farms.

There are other economic activities undertaken by Soviet citizens outside the planning systems. Many of these are legal but some are not. Often they involve the illegal buying and selling of goods brought in illegally from abroad.

Perestroika   At the June 1987 meeting of the Central Committee of the Communist party, Mikhail Gorbachev announced the first step in his reform plan, now universally known as *perestroika*. The key elements in this plan are:

- Increased independence for state enterprises
- Reform of accounting methods to calculate enterprises' full cost, revenue, and profit
- Requirement that each enterprise achieve the "highest end results" (maximum profits)
- The establishment of a direct link of income to performance
- Reduction in the power of central planners, relieving them of "interference in day-to-day activities"
- Reform of planning and pricing
- Decreased reliance on command system of management and increased role for individual incentives

Gorbachev spoke of the need to "create a powerful system of motives and stimuli [to] encourage workers to reveal their capability, work fruitfully [and] use productive resources most effectively." Remarkably, he declared that "there is only one criterion of justice [in the distribution of income]: whether or not it is earned."[2] Gorbachev even talked of abolishing job security and of closing down unprofitable state enterprises.

---

[2]Mikhail Gorbachev, *Perestroika: New Thinking for Our Country and the World* (New York: Harper & Row, 1987).

By the standards that have prevailed in the Soviet Union since 1928, Gorbachev's plans are revolutionary. They call for a redistribution of economic power and as such they are likely to meet a great deal of resistance. But to the extent that they contain the basis for improved economic performance, they also have a large number of supporters. How quickly and how far the Soviet Union will be able to travel along the road charted by Mikhail Gorbachev, we cannot yet say. But the direction that the Soviet economy is now taking is exciting and at least holds out the promise of a more efficient, productive, and prosperous Soviet Union.

We'll assess the performance of the Soviet economy and compare its performance with that of capitalist economies later in this chapter. But first, let's look at the other socialist giant, China.

China

China is the world's largest nation, with a population of more than a billion people. Chinese civilization is ancient and has a splendid history, but the modern nation—the People's Republic of China—dates only from 1949. A compact summary of key periods in the economic history of the People's Republic is presented in Table 38.3.

Modern China began when a revolutionary Communist movement, led by Mao Zedong, captured control of China, forcing the country's previous leader, Chiang Kai-shek (Jiang Jie-shi) onto the island of Formosa—now Taiwan. Like the Soviet Union, China is a socialist country. But unlike the Soviet Union, China is largely nonindustrialized—it is a developing country.

During the early years of the People's Republic, the country followed the Soviet model of economic planning and command. Urban manufacturing industry was taken over and operated by the state and the farms were collectivized. Also, following the Stalin model of the 1930s, primary emphasis was placed on the production of capital equipment.

The Great Leap Forward

In 1958, Mao Zedong set the Chinese economy on a sharply divergent path from that which the Soviet Union had followed. Mao called his new path the Great Leap Forward. The **Great Leap Forward**

Table 38.3   A Compact Summary of Key Periods in the Economic History of the People's Republic of China

Period	Main economic events/characteristics
1949	• People's Republic established under Mao Zedong
1949–1952	• Economy centralized under new communist government
	• Emphasis on heavy industry and "socialist transformation"
1952–1957	• First five-year plan
1958–1960	• The Great Leap Forward: an economic reform plan based on labor-intensive production methods;
	• Massive economic failure
1966	• Cultural Revolution: revolutionary zealots
1976	• Death of Mao Zedong
1978	• Deng's reforms: under leadership of Deng Xiaoping, liberalization of agriculture and introduction of individual incentives
	• Growth rates accelerated
1989	• Democracy movement; government crackdown

was an economic plan based on small-scale, labor-intensive production. The Great Leap Forward paid little or no attention to linking individual pay to individual effort. Instead, a revolutionary commitment to the success of collective plans was relied upon. The Great Leap Forward was an economic failure. Productivity increased, but so slowly that living standards hardly changed. In the agricultural sector, massive injections of modern, high-yield seeds, improved irrigation, and chemical fertilizers were insufficient to enable China to feed its population. The country became the largest importer of grains, edible vegetable oils, and even raw cotton.

The popular explanation within China for poor performance, especially in agriculture, was that the country had reached the limits of its arable land and that its population explosion was so enormous that

agriculture was being forced to use substandard areas for farming. The key problem was that the revolutionary and ideological motivation for the Great Leap Forward degenerated into what came to be called the Cultural Revolution. Revolutionary zealots denounced productive managers, engineers, scientists, and scholars, and banished them to the life of the peasant. Schools and universities were closed and the accumulation of human capital was severely disrupted.

1978 Reforms

By 1978, two years after the death of Mao Zedong, the new Chinese leader, Deng Xiaoping, proclaimed major economic reforms. Collectivized agriculture was abolished. Agricultural land was distributed among households on long-term leases. In exchange for a lease, a household agreed to pay a fixed tax and contracted to sell part of its output to the state. But the household made its own decisions on cropping patterns, the quantity and types of fertilizers and other inputs to use, and also hired its own workers. Private farm markets were liberalized and farmers received a higher price for their produce. Also, the state increased the price that it paid to farmers, especially for cotton and other nongrain crops.

The results of the reforms of Deng Xiaoping have been astounding. Annual growth rates of output of cotton and oil-bearing crops increased a staggering fourteenfold. Soybean production, which had been declining at an annual rate of 1 percent between 1957 and 1978, now started to grow at 4 percent a year. Growth rates of yields per acre also increased dramatically. By 1984, a country that six years earlier had been the world's largest importer of agricultural products became a food exporter!

The reforms not only produced massive expansion in the agricultural sector. Increased rural incomes brought an expanding rural industrial sector that, by the middle 1980s, was employing a fifth of the rural population.

Reform of the manufacturing sector has provided stronger incentives for enterprise managers and a greater degree of independence for making production decisions. These reforms, similar to those now being proposed by Gorbachev in the Soviet Union, have resulted in rapid growth in industrial output. China has gone even further and is encouraging foreign investment and joint ventures. In addition, China is experimenting with formal capital markets and now has a stock market.

Motivated partly by political considerations, China is proclaiming the virtues of what it calls the "one country, two systems" approach to economic management. The political source of this movement is the existence of two capitalist enclaves in which China has a close interest—Taiwan and Hong Kong. China claims sovereignty over Taiwan. As such, it wants to create an atmosphere in which it becomes possible for China to be "reunified" at some future date. Hong Kong, a British crown colony, is currently leased by Britain from China and that lease terminates in 1997. When the lease expires, Hong Kong will become part of China. Anxious not to damage the economic prosperity of Hong Kong, China is proposing to continue operating Hong Kong as a capitalist economy. With Hong Kong and Taiwan as part of the People's Republic of China, the stage will be set for the creation of other capitalist "islands" in such dynamic cities as Shanghai.

Whether China has invented a new economic system—one country, two systems—is too early to say. And the violent suppression of the democracy movement in Tiananmen Square in the summer of 1989 further clouds our view of where China is heading. But the experiment in comparative economic systems currently going on in China is one of the most exciting that the world has seen. Economists of all political shades of opinion will closely watch its outcome, and its lessons will be of enormous value for future generations—whatever those lessons turn out to be.

Comparing Capitalism and Socialism

We have now defined capitalist and socialist economic systems and have described the economic organization of some of the leading examples of the alternative types. In this final section, we'll use some of the economic models that we have studied to analyze the workings of capitalist and socialist economic systems. We'll also compare the performances of the two systems in practice.

To make our comparison of the working of a capitalist and socialist economy as clear as possible, we're going to study a model economy. The model economy, under capitalism, will have perfect competition and no external economies or diseconomies. We'll study the same economy under socialism.

Capitalism

Under capitalism, individual households choose the quantities of productive resources to supply and the quantities of goods and services to demand. Each firm seeks to make the biggest possible profit and to produce at the lowest possible cost. The demand for a good or service is summarized by its market demand curve. The market demand curve also shows the value placed on each extra unit of the good. The supply of the good is summarized by the market supply curve. The supply curve also shows the marginal cost of producing each unit of the good. The equilibrium price and quantity are determined where the supply and demand curves intersect.

Figure 38.4 illustrates a market in a perfectly competitive capitalist economy—the market for shoes. The demand curve for shoes (D) and the supply curve of shoes (S) intersect at quantity Q_C and price P_C. At this price and quantity, the perfectly competitive capitalist economy achieves *allocative* efficiency. The value placed on the last pair of shoes

Figure 38.4   Prices and Quantities Under Capitalism

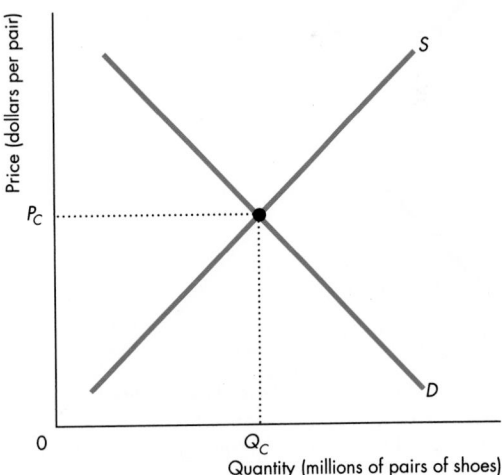

The preferences and choices of households determine the demand for shoes (curve *D*). The profit-maximization decisions of firms determine the supply of shoes (curve *S*). With a perfectly competitive shoe market, capitalism produces quantity Q_C at price P_C. If there are no external costs and benefits, this outcome achieves allocative efficiency.

produced (P_C) is the same as the marginal cost of producing them.

What happens under socialism?

Socialism

Now imagine that the economy whose market for shoes is depicted in Fig. 38.4 is taken over by a socialist government. Instead of operating under a capitalist system, it is now operated under centralized socialist planning. Let's see how the shoe market will perform under this new system of economic control. Figure 38.5 illustrates the shoe market in a socialist economy.

Consumers still have their views about the value they place on goods and services, so the demand for shoes is represented by the same demand curve. There is a difference, however, on the supply side.

Figure 38.5 Prices and Quantities under Socialism

Consumers determine the demand for shoes (curve *D*). Socialist managers determine the supply of shoes (curve *S_S*). Socialist managers have less incentive than capitalist entrepreneurs to supply goods at least cost, so the supply curve *S_S* lies to the left of the capitalism supply curve *S*. The central planning process sets a target output of shoes for the economy of *Q_S*. To achieve a balance of the quantity demanded and the quantity supplied, a tax is imposed on shoes to raise the price to *P_S*. Socialism delivers a lower quantity of shoes traded and a higher price of shoes than does capitalism.

Under socialism, firms do not own the means of production, and so the individual manager of a plant has no incentive to maximize profit and minimize cost. The manager's income is determined by the central planner and the manager receives a bonus if the firm achieves its target output, but there is no incentive for output to be produced in the most efficient possible way. On the contrary, the manager has an incentive to produce inefficiently. To see this, we need to consider how production targets are determined under socialism.

The central planner sets targets for total output and allocates those targets to the different production plants. The target output rate for any individual plant depends on what that plant has historically been able to produce. Therefore it always pays for a manager of a plant to pretend that his plant can produce less than what in fact it can. Therefore the supply curve under socialism is, in general, to the left of the supply curve under capitalism. The line labeled S_S in Fig. 38.5 is a possible supply curve for shoes under socialism, given the supply curve S under capitalism.

The gap between the socialist and capitalist supply curves is waste or inefficiency. The gap arises because the manager of the socialist factory has little incentive to produce the target output at minimum cost, and a high incentive to hide the true potential of his plant so that he will be assigned an easier production target.

The next big difference between capitalism and socialism concerns the way in which prices and quantities are determined. The quantity supplied is determined partly by the plans of the central planners and partly by the actions of the individual enterprises and the incentives that they face. Suppose that the outcome of the planning process is a quantity of shoes produced of Q_S. To achieve a balance between the quantity demanded and quantity supplied, the socialist planners will have to introduce a tax on shoes, raising their price to P_S. At this price, there is a balance between the quantity demanded and quantity supplied.

Central planning with state ownership produces a smaller quantity of shoes, Q_S compared with Q_C, at a higher price, P_S compared with P_C, than the perfectly competitive capitalist economy. This inferior performance has arisen from two sources: inefficient production resulting in higher average cost and production of the wrong quantity. Part of this problem is addressed by market socialism, but part is not. Let's see the difference that market socialism makes.

Market Socialism

Again, in order to compare the different systems, we will continue to look at the same economy and its shoe market. The demand for shoes remains as before and is shown again in Fig. 38.6. Again, the socialist manager has less incentive than the capitalist manager to maximize profit and produce at least cost, so his supply curve is S_S rather than the capitalist supply curve S. But the price is now determined in a decentralized manner in the market for shoes. The supply curve S_S and the demand curve D intersect at price P_{MS} and at quantity Q_{MS}. This price is higher than the competitive capitalist price and the quantity is smaller, but more shoes are produced and sold at a lower price under market socialism than under centrally planned socialism, as depicted in Fig. 38.5.

To get the economy to produce the capitalist quantity of shoes at the capitalist price, incentives have to be put in place at the individual firm level to encourage socialist factory managers to produce at least cost and be as efficient as capitalist managers.

Perestroika in the Model Economy

You can interpret *perestroika* in this model economy. Under the central planning methods of Stalin, the Soviet economy is producing too few shoes at too high a price. It is the situation depicted in Fig. 38.5. By moving to the decentralized planning that countries such as Hungary and Yugoslavia employ, the socialist economy can do better, lowering the price and increasing the quantity produced, as shown in Fig. 38.6. Such a move is one part of *perestroika*. But the socialist economy can do even better still, provided it can place strong enough incentives at the factory level to achieve maximum profits and produce efficiently. If that does prove to be possible, the socialist economy will be able to lower the price and increase the quantity produced to equal the competitive capitalist levels.

Inefficiencies in Capitalism

In the previous model economies, elements of inefficiency in capitalism have been ignored. That does not mean that they are not present in the real world. Capitalist economies do not function like the perfectly competitive ideal. There are external costs and benefits, monopoly elements, taxes and subsidies, all of which move the economy away from the competi-

Figure 38.6   Prices and Quantities under Market Socialism

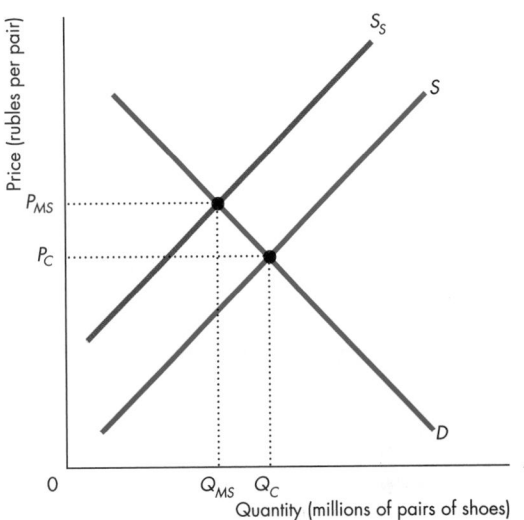

The market socialist demand and supply curves are the same as they are under socialism. The price of shoes is set in a decentralized way, so that the quantity demanded and the quantity supplied are equal. If the price is set too low, the central planner will gradually increase it. If the price is set too high, the central planner will gradually decrease it. On the average, the price is P_{MS} and the quantity traded is Q_{MS}. A smaller quantity of shoes is traded and at a higher price than in a perfectly competitive capitalist economy. But more shoes are traded and at a lower price than under socialism.

tive ideal. But these problems are present in socialist economies as well. They do not directly enter into an evaluation of the two systems. Thus we cannot compare the performance of capitalist and socialist economies merely by looking at an idealized, perfectly competitive model.

The ultimate test of capitalism and socialism comes not in a comparison of models, but of actual performance. How have socialist economies performed and how does that performance compare with that of capitalist economies?

Economic Growth and Average Living Standards

One way of comparing the success of alternative economic systems is to look at their capacity to deliver

Table 38.4   Annual Growth Rates in the United States, Japan, and the Soviet Union

Years	Annual growth rate (percentage)		
	United States	Japan	Soviet Union
1840–1885	4.4		
1885–1905	3.7	5.7	3.3 (1885–1913)
1905–1929	3.4	7.4	
1929–1950	2.8		5.4 (1928–1937)
1950–1960	3.2	11.5	6.0 (1940–1960)
1960–1970	4.0		5.1
1970–1979	3.1		4.0
1980–1986	3.1		4.0

Source: Paul R. Gregory and Robert C. Stuart, *Soviet Economic Structure and Performance*, 2nd ed. (New York: Harper & Row, 1981).

economic growth and high standards of living. Table 38.4 tells us what has happened in the United States, Japan, and the Soviet Union over 140 years of history. As you can see, throughout this period, the United States has experienced steady and sustained economic growth rates of between 3 and 4 percent a year. This growth rate has produced a living standard for Americans that is the highest in the world. Impressive though the American growth performance has been, Japan, another capitalist economy, has done better. By growing in excess of 10 percent a year in many of the postwar years, it has transformed itself from a war-devastated country in 1945 to one of the richest industrial giants in the world today.

Compare these performances with that of the Soviet Union. The Soviet Union was a capitalist country until the revolution in 1917. It was, however, a very poor country and most people worked in the agricultural sector. Eleven years after the Revolution, in 1928, the Soviet Union instituted central planning and established its first five-year plan. Since that date, Soviet economic growth has been impressive. The growth rates are set out in Table 38.4. As you can see, Soviet growth rates are larger than those of the United States. They are not as high, however,

as those of Japan. Nevertheless, they have resulted in the Soviet Union having, by 1978, a per capita gross national product that approached one half that of the United States.

The Soviet Union achieved its rapid growth primarily by squeezing consumption and focusing on capital accumulation and investment. In the United States, consumption and investment have grown at roughly the same rate over the long term. In the Soviet Union, consumption has grown at a pace that is approximately one half that of the growth rate of investment. During the first two five-year plans (the period from 1928 to 1937), consumption grew by only 0.7 percent a year while GNP grew by 5.4 percent a year and investment grew by 14.5 percent a year. Not until the late 1960s did consumption and investment in the Soviet Union grow at a similar pace. Thus although the Soviet Union has grown quickly, it has done so at enormous cost—Soviet planners have squeezed consumption to a point that capitalist countries would not have tolerated.

The growth performance of China also provides interesting evidence on the performance of a socialist economy. Figure 38.7 illustrates the rise in per capita income since 1965. During the Cultural Revolution of the 1960s, per capita income actually fell. The growth rate increased quickly in the late 1960s, but it then became modest until Deng's reforms of the late 1970s. Following those reforms, per capita income began to grow at a rate that, if maintained, will double the standard of living every ten years. Thus when China has relied most heavily on socialist methods, its growth rate has been negative or slow, and when it has relied on capitalist methods, its growth rate has increased.

Productivity   How productive are the socialist economies? We have noted that there is less incentive for managers under socialism to use the least-cost method of production and be efficient than there is under capitalism. Calculations by Soviet experts suggest that national income per unit of productive resources used in the Soviet Union is slightly less than 50 percent of what it is in the U.S. economy and only 65 percent of the productivity of France, West Germany, and the United Kingdom.[3]

[3]Paul R. Gregory and Robert C. Stuart, *Soviet Economic Structure and Performance*, 2nd ed. (New York: Harper & Row, 1981).

Figure 38.7   Economic Growth in China

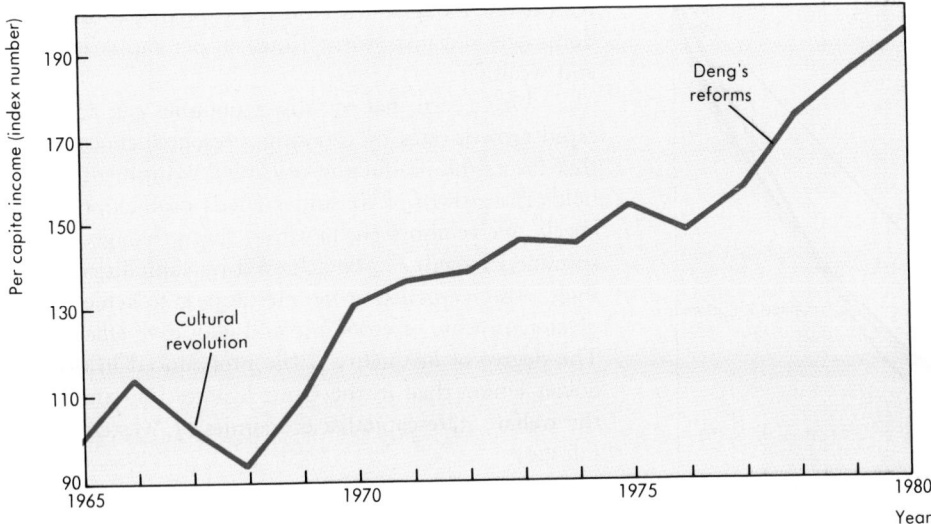

The growth of per capita income in China is strongly influenced by the economic system. During the Cultural Revolution, per capita income fell. Under a central planning and command mechanism in the early 1970s, per capita income grew at a moderate pace. Under capitalist methods of production in agriculture following the 1978 reforms, per capita income growth increased dramatically.

Source: International Monetary Fund, *International Financial Statistics* (1988).

From the available evidence, it appears as if socialism is substantially less successful than capitalism at producing high living standards. Does it, however, produce greater equality in the distribution of income?

Income Inequality under the Two Systems

There is considerable inequality of income and wealth in our own economy. Is the same true of the socialist economies of Eastern Europe and the Soviet Union? The answer appears to be yes. The Soviet Union has not published much data on the distribution of income among individuals and families. But from the evidence that is available it appears that the distribution of wage income in the Soviet Union is about the same as that in the capitalist economies of Western Europe and North America. But the overall distribution of income also depends on the distribution of income from the ownership of capital. Comparing this overall distribution of income is possible only in approximate terms, as Fig. 38.8 shows. The broad conclusion that emerges from the studies that have been done is that the overall distribution of

after-tax income in the Soviet Union is about as equal as the distribution in the welfare state economies of Western Europe, such as the United Kingdom, and more equal than other capitalist economies, such as the United States.

Ceteris Paribus   Making comparisons between countries is a bit like trying to compare apples and oranges. They differ in so many respects that it is hardly clear that we have been able to isolate the factors responsible for differences in their performances. One important difference between nations is their cultural history and the customs and habits of their people. Ideally, we'd like to be able to compare the performances of countries in which these historical and cultural factors are similar. That is, we'd like to be able to hold all these other things constant.

A few comparisons between socialist and capitalist economies are available that do almost satisfy this *ceteris paribus* condition. Examples are East Germany and West Germany, and North Korea and South Korea. East Germany and West Germany are historically and culturally similar and, at the end of World War II, were in per capita terms almost the same. West Germany became a capitalist economy

Figure 38.8   Socialist and Capitalist Lorenz Curves

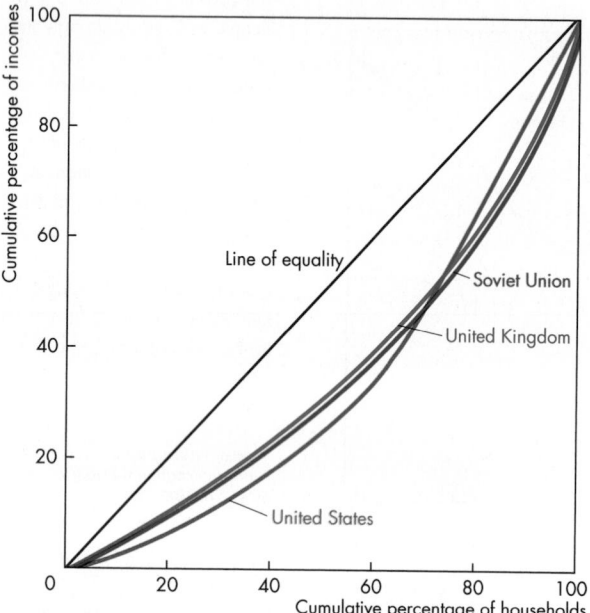

The degree of income inequality is illustrated by the Lorenz curve. If a given percentage of households have that same given percentage of income, incomes are distributed equally. The further the Lorenz curve is from the line of equality, the greater the degree of inequality. The Lorenz curves for the Soviet Union and the United Kingdom show that those two countries have an almost identical distribution of income and one that is more equal than that in the United States.

and East Germany a socialist one. Today, per capita income in West Germany exceeds that in East Germany by a sizable margin. At the end of the Korean War, in 1953, North Korea and South Korea embarked upon opposite roads. North Korea adopted the socialist model and South Korea the capitalist one. South Korea had fewer resources than North Korea, but today South Korea, a capitalist country, dominates socialist North Korea in per capita income and wealth.

We've seen that socialist economies can achieve rapid growth rates by choosing a resource allocation that favors the production of capital equipment and holds the growth of consumer goods production in check. We've also seen, however, that prolonged and sustained growth can be achieved by capitalist economies. Also, capitalist economies appear to achieve a greater measure of economic and allocative efficiency. The degree of inequality is less pronounced in the Soviet Union than in the United States but similar to the welfare state capitalist economies of Western Europe.

■ This comparison of the economic performance of socialist and capitalist economies seems to favor capitalism. A practical consequence of this comparison is the universal movement that is now taking place toward greater reliance on private enterprise and market mechanisms and less emphasis on government intervention, regulation, and control. For the moment, right or wrong, the view is increasingly widely held that capitalism works and socialism does not. The evidence generated by the variety of experiments conducted since World War II appears to support that conclusion. But it is the hallmark of a good scientist to maintain an open and skeptical mind even in the face of strong evidence. A great deal of work is required and no doubt more will be done before the final verdict on the superiority of one economic system over another is delivered.

S U M M A R Y

The Fundamental Economic Problem

No economic system can abolish the fundamental economic problem of scarcity. Each system attempts to get the economy onto its production possibility frontier, choose a point on the frontier, and distribute the gains from economic activity. (pp. 1000–1001)

Alternative Economic Systems

Economic systems vary in two dimensions—who owns capital and land and who allocates resources. Under capitalism, capital and land are privately owned and resources are allocated by markets. Under socialism, capital and land are owned by the state and resources are allocated by a command planning system.

Capitalism is based on the political philosophy that individual liberty is paramount. Individual preferences guide the production of goods and services. Socialism is an economic system based on the political philosophy that the private ownership of capital and land enables the wealthy to exploit the poor. The goods and services produced under socialism reflect the preferences not of individual consumers but of central planners.

Welfare state capitalism combines private ownership of capital and land with a large degree of state intervention. Market socialism combines state ownership of capital with market-determined prices.

All countries employ economic systems that contain some elements of capitalism and socialism. The United States and Japan come closest to being capitalist economies and the Soviet Union and China are examples of socialist economies. The countries of Western Europe employ welfare state capitalism, while Eastern European countries such as Hungary and Yugoslavia employ market socialism. (pp. 1001–1004)

The Varieties of Capitalism

The capitalist economy whose performance has been most spectacular is Japan. Its performance has been based on a strong reliance on the free market and capitalist methods of production, a small scale of government and low taxes, and pro-business government intervention. Japan's Ministry of International Trade and Industry (MITI) has taken an active and entrepreneurial role in protecting and subsidizing industries identified as priority growth areas and fostering the decline of inefficient industries.

Capitalism in Western Europe has larger elements of socialism than capitalism in Japan or the United States. Government expenditure and taxes are higher and many industries are publicly owned or nationalized. In recent years, European welfare states have been retreating from state ownership and high taxes. (pp. 1004–1006)

The Soviet Union

The Soviet Union is a vast, resource-rich nation that uses a socialist economic system with a central planning and command mechanism. Soviet planning is managed by GOSPLAN and is based on a series of detailed plans for consumer goods, labor, credit, capital goods, and materials. Targets are specified for production enterprises and enterprises are encouraged to achieve their targets by a complex system of incentives. They are also monitored by local officials of the Communist party and of state ministries. Since 1987, the Soviet Union has embarked upon a process of economic restructuring called *perestroika*. This restructuring involves a move away from central planning and command toward decentralized incentives and market prices. (pp. 1006–1011)

China

Since the foundation of the People's Republic of China, economic management has been through turbulent changes. At first, China used the Soviet system of central planning. It then introduced the Great Leap Forward, which in turn degenerated into the Cultural Revolution. China at first grew quickly with heavy reliance on state planning and capital accumulation, but growth slowed and, at times, per capita income actually fell. In 1978, China revolutionized its economic management, placing greater emphasis on private incentives and markets. As a consequence, productivity grew at a rapid rate and per capita income increased.

When Hong Kong becomes part of China at the end of this century, and if Taiwan is reunified with China, as the Chinese wish, these two islands will be permitted to remain capitalist. Furthermore, China is establishing what are, in effect, capitalist zones within China. Recent political events cast a serious shadow across the Chinese economy and raise doubts about its future course. But if the Chinese experiment continues, it will become an exciting real-world laboratory test of alternative economic systems. (pp. 1011–1013)

Comparing Capitalism and Socialism

The historical record of capitalism and socialism shows that socialism is capable of achieving high growth rates of per capita income. But it does so at the cost of squeezing consumption to levels below those that would be tolerated in capitalist economies. The most spectacular growth performance has been achieved by capitalist economies or by socialist economies when they have relaxed their central planning and command mechanisms and relied on decentralized incentives and markets. Productivity is higher in capitalist economies than in socialist economies. The distribution of income is more equal in socialist economies than in some capitalist economies but it is similar to that in welfare state capitalist countries. (pp. 1013–1018)

KEY CONCEPTS

Key Figures and Tables

REVIEW QUESTIONS

1 What are the three aspects of the economic problem that any economic system has to tackle?

2 What are the main economic systems? Set out the key features of each.

3 How does capitalism solve the economic problem? What determines how much of each good to produce?

4 How does socialism solve the economic problem? What determines how much of each good to produce?

5 How does market socialism determine the price and quantity of each good?

6 Give examples of countries that are capitalist, socialist, market socialist, and welfare state capitalist. (Do not cite those countries that appeared in Fig. 38.1).

7 Describe the capitalist economy of Japan. What are the sources of its dramatic success?

8 Describe the role of the Ministry of International Trade and Industry (MITI) in Japan. Compare and contrast capitalism in Western Europe with that in the United States and Japan. Describe the planning and command system in the Soviet Union.

9 How does GOSPLAN achieve consumer goods balance?

10 How does GOSPLAN achieve materials balance?

11 What are the main components of *perestroika*?

12 Review the main episodes in China's economic management since 1949.

13 Compare the economic growth performance of the United States, the Soviet Union, and Japan. What do we learn from this comparison?

14 Compare the degree of income inequality in socialist and capitalist economies. Why is the distribution of income more unequal in the United States than in the Soviet Union?

15 What might we learn from the current "one-country, two-systems" experiment that is going on in China?

Glossary

Above full-employment equilibrium   A situation in which macroeconomic equilibrium occurs at a level of real GNP above long-run aggregate supply.

Absolute advantage   A person has an absolute advantage in production if that person can produce more of all goods than anyone else. A country has an absolute advantage if its output per unit of inputs of all goods is higher than that of another country.

Accelerator principle   A principle stating that the investment demand curve shifts in response to *changes* in the level of real GNP.

Agent   A person who works for a principal and performs various activities, some of which are not observable by the principal. *See also* Principal.

Aggregate consumption function   The relationship between real consumption expenditure and real GNP.

Aggregate demand   The relationship between the aggregate quantity of goods and services demanded—real GNP demanded—and the price level—the GNP deflator—holding everything else constant.

Aggregate demand curve   A curve showing real GNP demanded at each price level, holding everything else constant.

Aggregate demand schedule   A list showing the quantity of real GNP demanded at each price level, holding everything else constant.

Aggregate expenditure curve   A graph of the aggregate expenditure schedule.

Aggregate expenditure schedule   A list of the amount of planned expenditure on real GNP that occurs at each level of real GNP.

Aggregate quantity of goods and services demanded   The sum of the quantities of consumption goods and services demanded by households, of investment goods demanded by firms, of goods and services demanded by governments, and of net exports demanded by foreigners.

Aggregate supply   The relationship between the aggregate quantity of goods and services supplied—real GNP supplied—and the price level—the GNP deflator—holding everything else constant.

Allocative efficiency   The situation that occurs when no resources are wasted—when no one can be made better off without someone else's being made worse off.

Annual plan   A plan of the Soviet government specifying month-by-month targets for output, prices, inputs, investment, and money and credit flows.

Anticipated inflation   An inflation rate that has been, on the average, correctly forecasted.

Antitrust law   A law prohibiting certain kinds of market activity, such as monopoly and monopolistic practices.

Arbitrage   The activity of buying low and selling high in order to make a profit on the margin between the two prices.

Asset   Anything of value that a household, firm, or government owns.

Assortative mating   Marrying within one's own socioeconomic group.

Assumptions   The foundation on which a model is built.

Autonomous expenditure   The sum of those components of aggregate planned expenditure that are not influenced by real GNP.

Autonomous expenditure multiplier   The amount by which a change in autonomous expenditure is multiplied to calculate the change in equilibrium aggregate expenditure and real GNP.

Autonomous taxes   Taxes that do not vary directly with real GNP.

Average cost pricing rule   A rule that sets the price equal to average total cost.

Average fixed cost   Total fixed cost per unit of output—total fixed cost divided by output.

Average product   Total product per unit of variable input.

Average propensity to consume   The ratio of consumption expenditure to disposable income.

Average propensity to save   The ratio of saving to disposable income.

Average revenue   Total revenue divided by the quantity sold. Average revenue also equals price.

Average revenue product   Total revenue divided by the quantity of the factor hired.

Average revenue product curve   A curve that shows the average revenue product of a factor at each quantity of the factor hired.

Average total cost   Total cost per unit of output—total cost divided by output.

Average variable cost   Total variable cost per unit of output—total variable cost divided by output.

Axes   The scale lines on a graph.

Balanced budget   A government budget that is in neither surplus nor deficit.

Balance of payments accounts   A country's record of international trading, borrowing, and lending.

Balance of trade   The value of exports minus the value of imports.

Balance sheet   A list of assets and liabilities.

Barriers to entry   Restrictions on the entry of new firms into an industry.

Barter   The direct exchange of goods for goods.

Base period   The period against which the current period is compared in a price index.

Bequest   A gift from one generation to the next.

Bilateral monopoly   A market structure in which a single buyer and a single seller confront each other.

Binding arbitration   A process in which a third party—an arbitrator—determines wages and other employment conditions.

Black market   An illegal trading arrangement in which buyers and sellers do business at a price higher than the legally imposed price ceiling.

Bond   A legally enforceable obligation to pay specified sums of money at specified future dates.

Bond market   The market in which the bonds issued by firms and governments are traded.

Bond yield   The interest on a bond, expressed as a percentage of the price of the bond.

Break-even point   An output rate at which total revenue equals total cost (and at which profit is zero).

Budget equation   An equation that states the maximum possible consumption of one good, given income, prices, and consumption of other goods.

Budget line   The limits to a household's consumption choices.

Budget surplus or deficit   The difference between tax revenue and expenditure in a given period of time. If tax revenue exceeds expenditure, the government has a budget surplus. If expenditure exceeds tax revenue, the government has a budget deficit.

Bureaucrats   Appointed officials who work at various levels in government departments.

Business cycle   The periodic but irregular up-and-down movement in economic activity measured by fluctuations in real GNP and other macroeconomic variables.

Capacity   The output rate at which a plant's average total cost is at a minimum.

Capacity output   The output at which the firm's cost per unit produced is minimized.

Capital   The real assets—equipment, buildings, tools, and other manufactured goods used in production—owned by a household, firm, or government.

Capital account   A record of a country's international borrowing and lending transactions.

Capital accumulation   The growth of capital resources.

Capital goods   Goods that are added to capital resources.

Capital-intensive technique   A method of production that uses a relatively large amount of capital and a relatively small amount of labor to produce a given quantity of output.

Capitalism   An economic system based on the private ownership of capital and land used in production and on market allocation of resources.

Capital resources   Goods that have been produced and can now be used in the production of other goods and services.

Capital stock   The stock of plant, equipment, and buildings (including residential housing).

Capture theory of regulation   A theory of regulation that states that the regulations that exist are those that maximize producer surplus.

Cartel   A group of producers who enter into a collusive agreement to restrict output in order to raise prices and profits.

Central bank   A public authority charged with regulating and controlling a country's monetary and financial institutions and markets.

Central planning   A method of allocating resources by command.

Ceteris paribus   Other things being equal, or other things remaining constant.

Change in demand   A shift of the entire demand curve that occurs when some influence on buyers' plans, other than the price of the good, changes.

Change in quantity demanded   A movement along a demand curve that results from a change in the price of the good.

Change in quantity supplied   A movement along the supply curve that results from a change in the price of the good.

Change in supply   A shift in the entire supply curve that occurs when some influence on producers' plans, other than the price of the good, changes.

Checkable deposit   A loan by a depositor to a bank.

Choke price   The price at which it no longer pays to use a natural resource.

Closed economy   An economy that has no links with any other economy.

Closed shop   An arrangement (illegal since the passage of the Taft-Hartley Act in 1947) in which only union members may be hired.

Collective bargaining   A process of negotiation between representatives of employers and unions.

Collusive agreement   An agreement between two (or more) producers to restrict output in order to raise prices and profits.

Command mechanism   A method of determining *what*, *how*, and *for whom* goods and services are produced, based on the authority of a ruler or ruling body.

Commercial bank   A financial intermediary that takes deposits and makes loans.

Commissions and royalties   A compensation rule based on the value of sales.

Commodity money A physical commodity valued in its own right and also used as a medium of exchange.

Common stock Stock that entitles its holder to vote at stockholders' meetings but gives a claim to dividends only if the directors vote to pay one. Such a dividend is paid at a variable rate, determined by the directors and varying according to the firm's profits.

Communism An economic system based on state ownership of capital and land, on central planning, and on distributing income in accordance with the rule "from each according to ability, to each according to need."

Communist country A country in which there is limited private ownership of productive capital and of firms and limited reliance on the market as a means of allocating resources, and in which government agencies plan and direct the production and distribution of most goods and services.

Comparable worth The payment of equal wages for different jobs that are judged to be comparable.

Comparative advantage A person has a comparative advantage in producing a good if he or she can produce that good at a lower opportunity cost than anyone else. A country has a comparative advantage in producing a good if it can produce that good at a lower opportunity cost than any other country.

Compensation rule A formula for calculating a person's income.

Competition A contest for command over scarce resources.

Complement A good that is used in conjunction with another good.

Constant returns to scale Technological conditions under which the percentage increase in a firm's output is equal to the percentage increase in its inputs.

Consumer equilibrium A situation in which a consumer has allocated his or her income in a manner that maximizes utility.

Consumer Price Index (CPI) An index that measures the average level of prices of the goods and services typically consumed by an urban American family.

Consumer surplus The difference between the value of a good and its price.

Consumption The process of using up goods and services.

Consumption expenditure The aggregate expenditure by households on consumption goods and services.

Consumption function The relationship between consumption expenditure and disposable income.

Consumption goods Goods that are used up as soon as they are produced.

Contraction A business cycle phase in which there is a slowdown in the pace of economic activity.

Convertible paper money A paper claim to a commodity (such as gold) that can be converted into the commodity at a guaranteed price. The paper claim circulates as a medium of exchange.

Convertible stock Stock that entitles its holder to receive a fixed coupon payment, as a bondholder does, and to convert the stock into a fixed number of shares of common stock.

Cooperation People working with others to achieve a common end.

Cooperative equilibrium An equilibrium resulting from each player responding rationally to the credible threat of the other player to inflict heavy damage if the agreement is broken.

Coordinates Lines running from a point on a graph perpendicularly to the axes.

Coordination mechanism A mechanism that makes the choices of one individual compatible with the choices of others.

Corporation A firm owned by one or more limited liability stockholders.

Cost Total payment made by a firm for the services of factors of production.

Cost-push inflation Inflation that has its origins in cost increases.

Countervailing duty A tariff that is imposed to enable domestic producers to compete with subsidized foreign producers.

Coupon payment The amount paid each year to the holder of a bond.

Craft union A group of workers who have a similar range of skills but work for different firms and industries.

Creditor nation A country that has invested more in the rest of the world than other countries have invested in it.

Cross elasticity of demand The percentage change in the quantity demanded of a good divided by the percentage change in the price of a substitute or complement.

Crowding out The tendency for an increase in government purchases of goods and services to increase interest rates, thereby reducing—crowding out—investment expenditure.

Currency Bank notes and coins.

Currency appreciation The increase in the value of one currency in terms of another currency.

Currency depreciation The fall in the value of one currency in terms of another currency.

Currency drain The tendency for some of the funds loaned by banks and financial institutions to remain outside the banking system and circulate as currency in the hands of the public.

Current account A record of receipts from the sale of goods and services to foreigners, the payments for goods and services bought from foreigners, and gifts and other transfers (such as foreign aid payments) received from and paid to foreigners.

Current account balance The value of all the goods and services that we sell to other countries minus the value of goods and services that foreigners buy from us.

Curve Any relationship between two variables plotted on a graph, even a linear relationship.

Cyclically adjusted deficit The deficit that would occur if the economy were at full employment.

Deadweight loss A measure of allocative inefficiency as the reduction in consumer and producer surplus resulting from restricting output below its efficient level.

Debt financing The financing of the government deficit by selling bonds to anyone (household, firm, or foreigner) other than the Federal Reserve System.

Debtor nation A country that, during its entire history, has borrowed more from the rest of the world than it has loaned to it. It has a stock of outstanding debt to the rest of the world that exceeds the stock of its own claims on the rest of the world.

Decentralized planning *See* Market socialism.

Decision maker Any person or organized group of persons who make economic choices.

Decreasing returns to scale Technological conditions under which the percentage change in a firm's output is less than the percentage change in the scale of inputs; sometimes called diseconomies of scale.

Deflation A downward movement in the average level of prices.

Demand The entire relationship between the quantity demanded of a good and its price.

Demand curve A graph showing the relationship between the quantity demanded of a good and its price, holding everything else constant.

Demand for labor A schedule or curve showing the quantity of labor demanded at each level of the real wage rate.

Demand for real money The relationship between the quantity of real money demanded and the interest rate, holding constant all other influences on the amount of money that people wish to hold.

Demand schedule A list of the quantities demanded at different prices, holding everything else constant.

Depreciation The fall in the value of capital or the value of a durable input resulting from its use and from the passage of time.

Depression A deep business cycle trough.

Deregulation The removal of rules restricting prices, product standards and types, and entry conditions.

Derived demand Demand for an input not for its own sake but in order to use it in the production of goods and services.

Desired reserve ratio The ratio of reserves to deposits that banks regard as necessary in order to conduct their business.

Developing country A country that is poor but is accumulating capital and developing an industrial and commercial base.

Deviation from trend in real GNP The difference between the actual value of real GNP and trend real GNP.

Diminishing marginal product of labor The tendency for the marginal product of labor to decline as the labor input increases, holding everything else constant.

Diminishing marginal rate of substitution The general tendency for the marginal rate of substitution to diminish as the consumer moves along an indifference curve, increasing the consumption of good x and decreasing the consumption of good y.

Diminishing marginal return A situation in which the marginal product of the last worker hired falls short of the marginal product of the second last worker hired.

Diminishing marginal utility The decline in marginal utility that occurs as more and more of a good is consumed.

Discount rate The interest rate at which the Fed stands ready to lend reserves to commercial banks.

Discounting The conversion of a future sum of money to its present value.

Discouraged workers People who do not have jobs and would like to work but have stopped seeking work.

Disposable income Income plus transfer payments minus taxes.

Dissaving Negative saving; a situation in which consumption expenditure exceeds disposable income.

Distribution after taxes and transfers The income distribution that takes account of taxes levied and transfers made by the government.

Dominant strategy A strategy in a game that is the unique best action regardless of the action taken by the other player.

Dominant strategy equilibrium A Nash equilibrium in which there is a dominant strategy for each player in a game. *See also* Nash equilibrium.

Double coincidence of wants A situation that occurs when person A wants to buy what person B is selling and person B wants to buy what person A is selling.

Double counting Counting the expenditure on both the final good and the intermediate goods and services used in its production.

Dumping The sale of a good in a foreign market for a lower price than in the domestic market or for a lower price than its cost of production.

Duopoly A market structure in which two producers of a commodity compete with each other.

Durable input A factor of production that is not entirely used up in a single production period.

Economic activity What people do to cope with scarcity.

Economic depreciation The change in the market price of a durable input over a given period. Economic depreciation over a year is calculated as the market price of the input at the beginning of the year minus its market price at the end of the year.

Economic efficiency A state in which the cost of producing a given output is as low as possible.

Economic growth The persistent expansion of production possibilities.

Economic rent An income received by the owner of a factor over and above the amount required to induce that owner to offer the factor for use.

Economics The study of how people use their limited resources to try to satisfy unlimited wants.

Economic theory A generalization that enables us to understand and predict economic choices.

Economies of scale   *See* Increasing returns to scale.

Economies of scope   Decreases in average total cost made possible by increasing the number of different goods produced.

Economizing   Making the best use of scarce resources.

Economy   A mechanism that allocates scarce resources among competing uses.

Efficient market   A market in which the actual price embodies all currently available relevant information.

Elastic demand   Elasticity is greater than 1; the quantity demanded of a good drops by a larger percentage than its price rises.

Elasticity of demand   *See* Price elasticity of demand.

Elasticity of supply   The percentage change in the quantity supplied of a good divided by the percentage change in its price.

Employment   The number of adult workers (age 16 and older) who have jobs.

Endowment   The resources that people have.

End-state theory of distributive justice   A theory of distributive justice that examines the fairness of the outcome of economic activity.

Entry   The act of setting up a new firm in an industry.

Equation of exchange   An equation that states that the quantity of money multiplied by the velocity of circulation of money equals the price level multiplied by real GNP.

Equilibrium   A situation in which everyone has economized—that is, all individuals have made the best possible choices in the light of their own preferences and given their endowments, technologies, and information—and in which all choices have been coordinated and made compatible with all other choices. Equilibrium is the solution or outcome of an economic model.

Equilibrium expenditure   Aggregate planned expenditure that equals real GNP.

Equilibrium price   The price at which the quantity demanded equals the quantity supplied. At this price, opposing forces exactly balance each other.

Equity or equity capital   The owner's stake in a business.

Excess capacity   A state in which output is below that at which average total cost is at a minimum.

Excess reserves   The difference between a bank's actual reserves and its desired reserves.

Excise tax   A tax on the sale of a particular commodity. The tax may be set as a fixed dollar amount per unit of the commodity, in which case it is called a *specific tax*. Alternatively, the tax may be set as a fixed percentage of the value of the commodity, in which case it is called an *ad valorem tax*.

Exhaustible natural resources   Natural resources that can be used only once and that cannot be replaced once used.

Exit   The act of closing down a firm and leaving an industry.

Expansion   A business cycle phase in which there is a speedup in the pace of economic activity.

Expected inflation rate   The rate at which people, on the average, believe that the price level is rising.

Expenditure   The amount spent for the purchase of a good. It equals the price of the good multiplied by the quantity bought.

Expenditure approach   A measure of GNP obtained by adding consumption expenditure, investment, government purchases of goods and services, and net exports.

Expenditure on domestic output   The sum of consumption expenditure, investment, government purchases of goods and services, and net exports.

Exports   The goods and services that one country sells to people in other countries.

External benefits   Those benefits accruing to people other than the buyer of a good.

External costs   Those costs borne not by the producer but by other members of society.

External diseconomies   Factors outside the control of a firm that raise its costs as industry output rises.

External economies   Factors beyond the control of a firm that lower its costs as industry output rises.

Externality   A cost or benefit arising from an economic transaction that falls on a third party and that is not taken into account by those who undertake the transaction.

Factor cost   The cost of all the factors of production used to produce a good or service.

Factor incomes approach   A measure of GNP obtained by adding together all the incomes paid by firms to households—wages, interest, rent, and profits.

Factor market   A market in which the factors of production are bought and sold.

Factors of production   The economy's productive resources—land, labor, and capital.

Fair Labor Standards Act   An act making it illegal to hire an adult worker for less than $3.35 an hour.

Federal budget   A statement of the federal government's financial plan, itemizing programs and their costs, revenues, and proposed deficit or surplus.

Federal Open Market Committee (FOMC)   The main policy-making organ of the Federal Reserve System.

Federal Reserve System   The central bank of the United States.

Feedback rule   A rule that states how various policy instruments will respond to the state of the economy.

Fiat money   An intrinsically worthless (or almost worthless) commodity that serves the functions of money.

Final goods and services   Goods and services that are not used as inputs in the production of other goods and services but are bought by their final user.

Financial assets   Paper claims of the holder against another household or firm.

Financial innovation   The development of new financial products and methods of borrowing and lending.

Financial intermediary A firm whose principal business is taking deposits from households and firms, making loans to other households and firms, and buying securities.

Firm An institution that buys or hires factors of production and organizes them to produce and sell goods and services.

Fiscal policy The attempt by government to vary its purchases of goods and services and taxes to smooth the fluctuations in aggregate expenditure.

Five-year plan A plan of the Soviet government specifying in broad outline general targets and directions for a period of five years.

Fixed cost A cost that is independent of the output level.

Fixed exchange rate A regime in which a country's central bank declares that its currency will be maintained at a certain fixed value in terms of some other currency.

Fixed inputs Those inputs whose quantity used cannot be varied in the short run.

Fixed rule A rule put in place and maintained regardless of the state of the economy.

Flexible exchange rate An exchange rate whose value is determined by market forces, in the absence of central bank intervention.

Flow A quantity measured over a period of time.

Flow equilibrium A situation in which the quantity of goods or services supplied per unit of time equals the quantity demanded per unit of time.

Flow theory of the exchange rate The proposition that the exchange rate adjusts to make the flow supply of dollars equal to the flow demand for dollars.

Foreign exchange market The market in which the currency of one country is exchanged for the currency of another.

Foreign exchange rate The rate at which one money exchanges for another money.

Forward contract A contract entered into at an agreed-upon price to buy or sell a certain quantity of any commodity (including currency) at a specified future date.

Forward exchange rate The exchange rate in a forward contract.

Four-firm concentration ratio The percentage of the value of sales accounted for by the largest four firms in an industry.

Free rider Someone who consumes a good without paying for it.

Free-rider problem The tendency for the scale of provision of a public good to be too small—to be allocatively inefficient—if it is privately provided.

Frictional unemployment Unemployment arising from new entrants into the labor market and job turnover caused by technological change.

Full employment A situation in which all unemployment is frictional.

Full-employment equilibrium A situation in which macroeconomic equilibrium is at a point on the long-run aggregate supply curve.

Game theory A method of analyzing strategic behavior.

General Agreement on Tariffs and Trade (GATT) An agreement that limits government taxes and restrictions on international trade.

GNP *See* Gross national product

GNP deflator A price index that measures the average level of the prices of all the goods and services that make up GNP. It is calculated as the ratio of nominal GNP to real GNP, multiplied by 100.

Goods and services All the valuable things that people produce. Goods are tangible, and services are intangible.

Goods market A market in which goods and services are bought and sold.

GOSPLAN The Soviet planning committee responsible for drawing up and implementing the state's economic plans.

Government An organization that provides goods and services to households and firms, and redistributes income and wealth.

Government debt The total amount of borrowing that the government has undertaken and the total amount that it owes to households, firms, and foreigners.

Government deficit The total expenditure of the government sector minus the total revenue of that sector.

Government firm A firm that is owned and operated by a government.

Government license A license that controls entry into particular occupations, professions, or industries.

Great Leap Forward An economic plan for postrevolutionary China based on small-scale, labor-intensive production motivated by revolutionary zeal.

Gresham's law The tendency for bad money to drive out good money. Bad money is debased money; good money is that which has not been debased.

Gross domestic product The value of output produced in the United States.

Gross investment The value of new capital equipment purchased in a given time period; the amount spent on replacing depreciated capital and on net additions to the capital stock.

Gross national product (GNP) The value of all the final goods and services produced in the economy.

Historical cost Cost that values resources at the prices actually paid for them.

Horizontal integration The merger of two or more firms providing essentially the same product or service.

Hotelling principle The proposition that the market for a stock of a natural resource is in equilibrium when the price of the resource is expected to rise at a rate equal to the interest rate.

Household Any group of people living together as a decision-making unit.

Household production The production of goods and services for consumption within the household.

Human capital The accumulated skill and knowledge of human beings; the value of a person's education and acquired skills.

Human resources The muscle power and brain power of human beings.

Implications The outcome of a model that follows logically from its assumptions.

Implicit rental rate The rent that a firm implicitly pays to itself for the use of the durable inputs that it owns.

Imports The goods and services that we buy from people in other countries.

Imputed cost An opportunity cost that does not involve an actual expenditure of cash.

Incentive An inducement to an agent to behave in a particular way.

Income The amount received by households in payment for the services of factors of production.

Income effect The effect of a change in income on the quantity consumed.

Income elasticity of demand The percentage change in the quantity demanded divided by the percentage change in income.

Increasing marginal returns A situation in which the marginal product of the last worker hired exceeds the marginal product of the second last worker hired.

Increasing returns to scale Technological conditions under which the percentage increase in a firm's output exceeds the percentage increase in its inputs. Under these conditions, reductions in the cost of producing a unit of a good occur as the scale of output increases.

Indexing A technique that links payments made under a contract to the price level.

Indifference curve A line showing all possible combinations of two goods among which the consumer is indifferent.

Indirect tax A tax paid by consumers when they purchase goods and services. Examples are state sales taxes and taxes on alcohol, gasoline, and tobacco products.

Individual demand The relationship between the quantity demanded by a single individual and the price of a good.

Induced expenditure The sum of those components of aggregate planned expenditure that do vary as real GNP varies.

Induced taxes Taxes whose amount varies directly with real GNP.

Industrial country A country that has a large amount of capital equipment and in which people undertake highly specialized activities, enabling them to earn high per capita incomes.

Industrial union A group of workers with a variety of skills and job types but who work for the same firm or industry.

Inelastic demand Elasticity is between 0 and 1; the quantity demanded of a good drops by a smaller percentage than its price rises.

Inferior good A good the demand for which decreases when income increases.

Inflation An upward movement in the average level of prices.

Inflation rate The percentage change in the price level.

Injections Expenditures that add to the circular flow of expenditure and income—investment, government purchases of goods and services, and exports.

Innovation The act of putting a new technique into operation.

Intellectual property The intangible product of creative effort, protected by copyrights and patents. This type of property includes books, music, computer programs, and inventions of all kinds.

Interest rate parity A situation in which interest rates are equal across all countries once the differences in risk are taken into account.

Intermediate goods and services Goods and services that are used as inputs into the production of another good or service.

International Monetary Fund (IMF) An international organization that monitors the balance of payments and exchange rate activities.

International substitution The substitution of domestic goods for foreign goods or of foreign goods for domestic goods.

Intertemporal substitution The substitution of goods now for goods later or of goods later for goods now.

Invention The discovery of a new technique.

Inventories Stocks of raw materials, semifinished products, and finished goods held by firms.

Investment The purchase of new plant, equipment, and buildings, and additions to inventories in a given time period.

Investment bank A bank that trades in firms' equities and bonds.

Investment demand The relationship between the level of investment and the real interest rate.

Investment demand curve A curve showing the relationship between the real interest rate and the level of planned investment, holding everything else constant.

Investment demand schedule The list of quantities of planned investment at each interest rate, holding everything else constant.

Investment security A marketable security that a bank can sell at a moment's notice.

Isocost equation An equation that states the relationship between the quantities of inputs that can be hired for a given total cost.

Isocost line A line that shows all the combinations of capital and labor that can be bought for a given total cost.

Isocost map A map that shows a series of isocost lines, each for a different total cost.

Isoquant A curve that shows the different combinations of labor and capital required to produce a fixed quantity of output.

Isoquant map A map that shows a series of isoquants, each for a different output.

Joint unlimited liability The liability of each and every partner for the full debts of a partnership.

Keynesian A macroeconomist whose beliefs about the functioning of the economy represent an extension of the theories of John Maynard Keynes. A Keynesian regards the economy as inherently unstable and as requiring active government intervention to achieve stability. A Keynesian assigns a low degree of importance to monetary policy and a high degree of importance to fiscal policy.

Labor *See* Human resources.

Labor force The total number of employed and unemployed workers.

Labor force participation rate The proportion of the working age population that is either employed or unemployed but seeking employment.

Labor-intensive technique A method of production that uses a relatively large amount of labor and a relatively small amount of capital to produce a given quantity of output.

Labor union An organized group of workers whose purpose is to increase wages and influence other job conditions.

Laffer curve A curve that relates tax revenue to the tax rate.

Land Natural resources of all kinds.

Law of diminishing marginal rate of substitution A law stating that the marginal rate of substitution of capital for labor falls as the amount of capital decreases and the amount of labor increases.

Law of diminishing returns The general tendency for marginal product to eventually diminish as more of the variable input is employed, holding the quantity of fixed inputs constant.

Law of one price A law stating that any given commodity will be available at a single price.

Leakages Income that is not spent on domestically produced goods and services—savings, taxes (net of transfer payments), and imports.

Least-cost technique The combination of inputs that minimizes total cost of producing a given output.

Legal monopoly A monopoly that occurs when a law, license, or patent restricts competition by preventing entry.

Liability A debt—something that a household, firm, or government owes.

Limited liability The limitation of liability of the firm's owners for debts only up to the value of the initial investment.

Linear relationship The relationship between two variables depicted by a straight line on a graph.

Line-item veto A veto power vested in the executive branch of the government, which allows it to eliminate any specific item in a budget.

Liquid asset An asset that is instantly convertible into a medium of exchange with virtually no uncertainty about the price at which it can be converted.

Liquidity The degree to which an asset is instantly convertible into cash at a known price.

Liquidity trap A situation in which the demand curve for real money is horizontal at a given interest rate and

in which people are willing to hold any amount of money at that interest rate.

Loan A commitment of a fixed amount of money for an agreed-upon period of time.

Lobbying The activity of bringing pressure to bear on government agencies or institutions through a variety of informal mechanisms.

Local A subunit of a union that organizes individual workers.

Lockout The refusal by a firm to operate its plant and employ its workers.

Long run A period of time in which the quantities of all inputs can be varied.

Long-run aggregate supply The quantity of real GNP supplied when each firm is producing its capacity output and when there is full employment.

Long-run aggregate supply curve A curve showing the relationship between long-run aggregate supply and the price level.

Long-run average cost curve A curve that traces the relationship between the lowest attainable average total cost and output when all inputs can be varied.

Long-run cost The cost of production when a firm uses the economically efficient plant size.

Long-run demand curve The demand curve that describes the response of buyers to a change in price after all possible adjustments have been made.

Long-run demand for labor The relationship between the wage rate and the quantity of labor demanded when all inputs can be varied.

Long-run elasticity of demand for labor The percentage change in the quantity of labor demanded divided by the percentage change in the wage rate when all inputs are varied.

Long-run supply curve The supply curve that describes the response of the quantity supplied to a change in price after all technologically possible adjustments to supply have been made.

Lorenz curve A curve that shows the cumulative percentage of income or wealth against the cumulative percentage of population.

Loss The difference between a firm's revenue and cost when cost exceeds revenue.

M1 A measure of money that sums currency held outside banks, traveler's checks, demand deposits, and other checkable deposits, such as NOW and ATS accounts.

M2 A measure of money that sums M1, savings deposits, small time deposits, Eurodollar deposits, noninstitutional money market mutual fund shares, and other M2 deposits.

M3 A measure of money that sums M2, large time deposits, Eurodollar time deposits, institutional money market mutual fund shares, and other M3 deposits.

Macroeconomic equilibrium A situation in which the quantity of real GNP demanded equals the quantity of real GNP supplied.

Macroeconomics The branch of economics that studies the economy as a whole. Macroeconomics is concerned with aggregates and averages of behavior rather than with detailed individual choices.

Managed exchange rate   An exchange rate regime under which the central bank's intervention does not seek to keep the exchange rate fixed at a preannounced level.

Marginal benefit   The increase in total benefit resulting from a one-unit increase in the scale of provision of a public good.

Marginal cost   The increase in total cost resulting from a one-unit increase in output.

Marginal cost pricing rule   The rule that sets price equal to marginal cost; maximizes total surplus in the regulated industry.

Marginal private cost   The marginal cost directly incurred by the producer of a good.

Marginal product   The change in total product resulting from a one-unit increase in a variable input.

Marginal product of capital   The change in total product resulting from a one-unit increase in the quantity of capital employed, holding the quantity of labor constant.

Marginal product of labor   The change in total product (output) resulting from a one-unit increase in the quantity of labor employed, holding the quantity of all other inputs constant.

Marginal propensity to consume   The fraction of the last dollar of disposable income that is spent on consumption goods and services.

Marginal propensity to import   The fraction of the last dollar of real GNP spent on imports.

Marginal propensity to save   The fraction of the last dollar of disposable income that is saved.

Marginal propensity to spend on domestic goods and services (marginal propensity to spend)   The fraction of the last dollar of real GNP spent on domestic goods and services.

Marginal rate of substitution   The rate at which a person will give up one good in order to get more of another good and at the same time remain indifferent.

Marginal rate of substitution of capital for labor   The decrease in capital per unit increase in labor that keeps output constant.

Marginal revenue   The change in total revenue resulting from a one-unit increase in the quantity sold.

Marginal revenue product   The change in total revenue resulting from employing one more unit of a factor.

Marginal revenue product curve   A curve that shows the marginal revenue product of a factor at each quantity of the factor hired.

Marginal social benefit   The dollar value of the benefit from one additional unit of consumption, including the benefit to the buyer and any indirect benefits accruing to any other member of society.

Marginal social cost   The cost of producing one additional unit of output, including the costs borne by the producer and any other costs indirectly incurred by any other member of society; the marginal cost incurred by the producer of a good, together with the marginal cost imposed as an externality on others.

Marginal tax rate   The fraction of the last dollar of income paid to the government in taxes (net of transfer payments by the government).

Marginal utility   The additional utility or change in utility resulting from the last unit of a good consumed.

Marginal utility per dollar spent   The marginal utility obtained from the last unit of a good consumed divided by the price of the good.

Market   Any arrangement that facilitates buying and selling (trading) of a good, service, factor of production, or future commitment.

Market activity   The supplying of labor through the market. *See also* Nonmarket activity.

Market constraints   The conditions under which a firm can buy its inputs and sell its output.

Market demand   The relationship between the total quantity of a good demanded and its price.

Market distribution   The distribution of income that would prevail in the absence of government policies.

Market failure   The inability of an unregulated market to achieve, in all circumstances, allocative efficiency.

Market mechanism   A method of determining *what, how*, and *for whom* goods and services are produced, based on individual choices coordinated through markets.

Market price   The price that people actually pay for a good or service. Such prices include indirect taxes but are net of subsidies.

Market socialism   An economic system that combines socialism's state ownership of capital and land with capitalism's market allocation of resources.

Maturity structure   The distribution of future dates on which bonds are to be redeemed.

Median voter theorem   The proposition that political parties will pursue policies that maximize the net benefit of the median voter.

Medium of exchange   Anything that is generally acceptable in exchange for goods and services.

Merger   Combining assets of two firms to form a single new firm.

Microeconomics   The branch of economics that studies the decisions of individual households and firms and the way in which individual markets work. Microeconomics also studies the way in which taxes and government regulation affect economic choices.

Minimum wage law   A regulation that makes it illegal to trade labor below a specified wage.

Ministry of International Trade and Industry (MITI)   A Japanese government agency responsible for stimulating Japanese industrial development and international trade.

Misery index   An index of macroeconomic performance equal to the sum of the inflation rate and the unemployment rate.

Mixed economy   An economy that relies partly on a command mechanism and partly on a market mechanism to coordinate economic activity.

Mixed good   A good that lies between a private good and a pure public good.

Momentary supply curve   The supply curve that describes the immediate response of the quantity supplied to a change in price.

Monetarist   A macroeconomist who assigns a high degree of importance to variations in the quantity of money as the main determinant of aggregate demand and who regards the economy as inherently stable.

Monetary base   The sum of the Federal Reserve notes in circulation, banks' deposits at the Fed, and coins in circulation.

Monetary exchange   A system in which some commodity or token serves as the medium of exchange.

Monetary policy   An attempt to control inflation and moderate the business cycle by changing the quantity of money in circulation and adjusting interest rates.

Monetary theory of the exchange rate   The proposition that the exchange rate adjusts to make the stock of a currency demanded equal to the stock supplied.

Money   A medium of exchange.

Money financing   The financing of the government deficit by the sale of bonds to the Federal Reserve System, which results in the creation of additional money.

Money multiplier   The amount by which a change in the monetary base is multiplied to determine the resulting change in the quantity of money.

Money wage rate   The wage rate expressed in current dollars.

Monitoring   The observation of the actions of an agent by a principal.

Monitoring costs   The costs of observing the actions of an agent.

Monopolistic competition   A market type in which a large number of firms compete with one another by making similar but slightly different products.

Monopoly   The sole supplier of a good, service, or resource that has no close substitutes. Monopoly arises from the existence of a barrier preventing the entry of new firms.

Monopsony   A market structure in which there is only a single buyer.

Multiplier   *See* Autonomous expenditure multiplier.

Nash equilibrium   The outcome of a game in which the strategy chosen by player A is the best possible response to the strategy of player B and in which player B's strategy is the best possible response to the strategy of player A.

Nationalized industry   An industry owned and operated by a publicly owned authority directly responsible to a government.

Natural monopoly   A monopoly that occurs when there is a unique source of supply for a raw material or when one firm can supply the entire market at a lower price than two or more firms can.

Natural rate of unemployment   The unemployment rate when the economy is at full employment and the only unemployment is frictional.

Natural resources   The nonproduced factors of production with which we are endowed—all the gifts of nature, including land, water, air, and all the minerals they contain.

Negative relationship   A relationship between two variables that move in opposite directions.

Net benefit   Total benefit minus total cost.

Net borrower   A country that is borrowing more from the rest of the world than it is lending to it.

Net exporter   A country whose value of exports exceeds its value of imports.

Net exports function   The relationship between net exports and U.S. real GNP, holding constant real GNP in the rest of the world, prices, and the exchange rate.

Net exports   The expenditure by foreigners on U.S.-produced goods minus the expenditure by U.S. residents on foreign-produced goods.

Net financial assets   Financial assets minus financial liabilities.

Net importer   A country whose value of imports exceeds its value of exports.

Net investment   Net additions to the capital stock—gross investment minus depreciation.

Net lender   A country that is lending more to the rest of the world than it is borrowing from it.

Net national income at factor cost   The sum of all factor incomes—compensation of employees, rental income, corporate profits, net interest, and proprietors' income.

Net national product at market prices   The sum of all factor incomes plus indirect taxes minus subsidies.

Net present value   The sum of the present values of payments spread over several years.

Net present value of an investment   The present value of a stream of marginal revenue product generated by the investment minus the cost of the investment.

Newly industrialized country   A country in which there is a rapidly developing broad industrial base and per capita income is growing quickly.

Nominal GNP   The output of final goods and services valued at current prices.

Nominal interest rate   The interest rate actually paid and received in the marketplace.

Nominal quantity of money   The quantity of money measured in current dollars.

Nominal targets   Macroeconomic policy targets of low and predictable inflation and stable foreign exchange rates.

Nonconvertible note   A bank note that is not convertible into any commodity and that obtains its value by government fiat—hence the term *fiat money*. *See also* Fiat money.

Nonexhaustible natural resources   Natural resources that can be used repeatedly without depleting what is available for future use.

Nonmarket activity   Leisure and nonmarket production activities, including education and training.

Nontariff barriers Any action, other than a tariff, that restricts international trade.

Nontraded good A good that cannot be traded over long distances.

Normal good A good the demand for which increases when income increases.

Normative statement A statement about what *ought* to be. An expression of an opinion that cannot be verified by observation.

Not-for-profit firm An organization that chooses or is required to have equal costs and revenue.

Official reserves The government's holdings of foreign currency.

Official settlements account An account showing the net increase or decrease in a country's holdings of foreign currency.

Oligopoly A market type in which a small number of producers compete with one another.

Open economy An economy that has economic links with other economies.

Open market operation The purchase or sale of government securities by the Federal Reserve System, designed to influence the money supply.

Open shop An arrangement in which no requirement is placed on an individual worker to join a union.

Opportunity cost The best alternative forgone.

Optimizing Balancing benefits against costs to do the best within the limits of what is possible.

Origin The zero point that is common to both axes on a graph.

Output approach A measure of GNP obtained by summing the value added of each firm in the economy.

Overutilized capacity When a plant produces more than the output at which average total cost is at a minimum.

Paradox of thrift The fact that an increase in saving leads to an increase in the income of an individual but may lead to a decrease in aggregate expenditure and real GNP. The paradox arises because an increase in saving occurs with no increase in investment.

Partnership A firm with two or more owners who have unlimited liability.

Patent An exclusive right granted by the government to the inventor of a product or service.

Payoff The score of each player in a game.

Payoff matrix A table that shows the payoffs resulting from every possible action by each player for every possible action by each other player.

Peak The upper turning point of a business cycle—the point at which the economy is turning from expansion to contraction.

Per capita production function A curve showing how per capita output varies as the per capita stock of capital varies, with a given technology.

Perfect competition A state that occurs in markets in which a large number of firms sell an identical product; there are many buyers; there are no restrictions on entry;

firms have no advantage over potential new entrants; and all firms and buyers are fully informed about the prices of each and every firm.

Perfectly competitive firm's supply curve A curve that shows how a perfectly competitive firm's output varies as the market price varies.

Perfectly elastic demand Elasticity is infinity; the quantity demanded becomes zero if the price rises by the smallest amount, and the quantity demanded becomes infinite if the price falls by the smallest amount.

Perfectly inelastic demand Elasticity is zero; the quantity demanded does not change as the price rises.

Perfect price discrimination The practice of charging each consumer the maximum price that he or she is willing to pay for each unit bought.

Perpetuity A bond that promises to pay a certain fixed amount of money each year forever.

Phillips curve A curve that shows a negative relationship between the unemployment rate and the inflation rate, holding everything else constant.

Physical limits The maximum output that a plant can produce.

Piece rate A compensation rule based on the output of a worker.

Political equilibrium A situation in which the choices of voters, politicians, and bureaucrats are all compatible and in which no one group of agents will be better off by making a different choice.

Politicians Elected officials in federal and state government—from chief executives (the president, state governor, or mayor) to members of the legislature (state and federal senators and representatives).

Portfolio balance theory of the exchange rate The proposition that the exchange rate adjusts to make the stock of financial assets denominated in units of that currency demanded equal to the stock supplied.

Portfolio choice A choice concerning which assets and liabilities to hold.

Positive relationship A relationship between two variables that move in the same direction.

Positive statement A statement about what *is*. Something that can be verified by careful observation.

Poverty An income level measured by a poverty index first calculated by the Social Security Administration in 1964.

Preferences A ranking of likes and dislikes and the intensity of those likes and dislikes.

Preferred stock Stock that conveys no voting rights but gives a prior claim on dividends at a fixed rate, regardless of the profit level.

Present value The value in the present of a future sum of money; equal to the amount which, if invested today, will grow as large as that future sum, taking into account the interest it will earn.

Price discrimination The practice of charging some customers a higher price than others for an identical good or of charging an individual customer a higher price on a small purchase than on a large one.

Price-earnings ratio   The current price of a share divided by the current profit per share.

Price effect   The effect of a change in the price on the quantity of a good consumed.

Price elasticity of demand   The percentage change in the quantity demanded of a good divided by the percentage change in its price.

Price index   A measure of the average level of prices in one period as a percentage of their level in an earlier period.

Price level   The average level of prices as measured by a price index.

Price stability   A situation in which the average level of prices is moving neither up nor down.

Price taker   A firm that cannot influence the price of its product.

Principal   An individual who sets a compensation rule to motivate an agent to choose activities advantageous to the principal.

Principle of minimum differentiation   The tendency for competitors to make themselves almost identical in order to appeal to the maximum number of clients or voters.

Private debt money   A loan that a borrower promises to repay in currency on demand.

Private enterprise   An economic system that permits individuals to decide on their own economic activities.

Private good   A good or service each unit of which is consumed by only one individual.

Private property right   A legally established title to sole ownership of a scarce resource.

Private sector surplus or deficit   The difference between saving and investment.

Privatization   The process of selling state-owned enterprises to private individuals and firms.

Process theory of distributive justice   A theory of distributive justice that examines the fairness of the *mechanism* or *process* that results in a given distribution.

Producer surplus   The difference between a producer's revenue and the opportunity cost of production.

Product differentiation   Making a product slightly different from that of a competing firm.

Production   The conversion of natural, human, and capital resources into goods and services.

Production function   A relationship showing how output varies as the employment of inputs is varied.

Production possibility frontier   The boundary between attainable and unattainable levels of production.

Professional association   An organized group of professional workers, such as lawyers, dentists, or doctors, that seeks to influence the compensation and other labor market conditions affecting its members.

Profit   The difference between a firm's revenue and cost when revenue exceeds cost.

Profit maximization   Making the largest possible profit.

Profit sharing   A compensation rule that allocates a certain fraction of a firm's profit to its employees.

Progressive income tax   An income tax at a marginal rate which rises with the level of income.

Property   Anything of value that is owned.

Property rights   Social arrangements that govern the ownership, use, and disposal of economic resources.

Proportional income tax   An income tax that is at a constant rate regardless of the level of income.

Proprietorship   A firm with a single owner who has unlimited liability.

Protectionism   The restriction of international trade.

Public choice theory   A theory predicting the behavior of the government sector of the economy as the outcome of the individual choices made by voters, politicians, and bureaucrats interacting in a political marketplace.

Public franchise   An exclusive right granted to a firm to supply a good or service.

Public interest theory   A theory predicting that government action will take place to eliminate waste and achieve an efficient allocation of resources.

Public interest theory of regulation   A theory of regulation that states that regulations are supplied to satisfy the demand of consumers and producers for the maximization of total surplus—or the attainment of allocative efficiency.

Purchasing power parity   A situation that occurs when money has equal value across countries.

Pure public good   A good each unit of which is consumed by everyone and from which no one can be excluded.

Quantity demanded   The amount of a good or service that consumers plan to buy in a given period of time.

Quantity of labor demanded   The number of labor hours hired by all the firms in an economy.

Quantity of labor supplied   The number of hours of labor services that households supply to firms.

Quantity of money   The quantity of currency, bank deposits, and deposits at other types of financial institutions, such as savings and loan associations and thrift institutions, held by households and firms.

Quantity supplied   The amount of a good or service that producers plan to sell in a given period of time.

Quantity theory of money   The proposition that an increase in the quantity of money leads to an equal percentage increase in the price level.

Quantity traded   The quantity actually bought and sold.

Quota   A restriction on the quantity of a good that a firm is permitted to produce or that a country is permitted to import.

Rank-tournament compensation rule   A compensation rule under which the payment to an agent depends on the agent's rank in a tournament.

Rate of return regulation   A regulation that sets the price at a level that enables the regulated firm to earn a specified target percentage return on its capital.

Rational choice   The best possible course of action from the point of view of the individual making the choice.

Rational expectation   The best forecast that can be made on the basis of all the available and relevant information. A rational expectation is one in which the expected forecast error is zero and the range of error is as small as possible.

Rational expectations equilibrium   A macroeconomic equilibrium based on expectations that are the best available forecasts.

Rational expectations hypothesis   The hypothesis that the forecasts people make, regardless of how they make them, are on the average the same as the forecasts that an economist makes using the relevant economic theory.

Rational ignorance   The decision not to acquire information, because the cost of acquiring the information is greater than the benefit derived from having it.

Rawlsian theory of fairness   A theory of distributive justice that gives the biggest income possible to the least well off.

Real assets   Land, buildings, plant and equipment, inventories, and consumer durable goods.

Real balance effect   The influence of a change in the quantity of real money on the quantity of real GNP demanded.

Real business cycle theory   A theory of aggregate fluctuations based on flexible wages and random shocks to the economy's aggregate production function.

Real deficit   The change in the real value of outstanding government debt.

Real exchange rate   The ratio of the price index in one country to the index in another. Real GNP The output of final goods and services valued at prices prevailing in the base period.

Real income   Income expressed in units of goods. Real income in terms of a particular good is income divided by the price of that good.

Real interest rate   The interest rate minus the expected inflation rate.

Real money   The quantity of goods that a given amount of money will buy.

Real targets   Macroeconomic policy targets of unemployment at its natural rate, steady growth in real GNP, and balanced international trade.

Real wage rate   The wage rate per hour expressed in constant dollars.

Recession   A severe contraction, defined by the Commerce Department as two successive quarters of falling real GNP.

Redemption date   The date on which the final payment on a bond is made.

Redemption value   The amount paid to a bondholder on the redemption date of a bond.

Regressive income tax   An income tax at a marginal rate which falls with the level of income.

Regulation   Rules enforced by a government agency to restrict economic activity by determining prices, product standards and types, and the conditions under which new firms may enter an industry.

Relative price   The ratio of the price of one good to the price of another, is expressed as the number of units of one good that one unit of another good will buy.

Rent ceiling   A regulation making it illegal to charge a rent higher than a specified level.

Rent seeking   The activity of attempting to create a monopoly.

Required reserves   The minimum reserves that a bank is permitted to hold.

Reservation wage   The lowest wage rate at which a person or household will supply any labor to the market. Below that wage, a person will not work.

Reserve ratio   The fraction of a bank's total deposits that are held in reserves.

Reserves   Cash holdings in a bank's vault plus the bank's deposits with the Federal Reserve.

Residual claimant   An agent who receives the firm's profits and is responsible for its losses.

Returns to scale   Increases in output that result from increasing all the inputs by the same percentage.

Revenue   The amount received from the sale of a good. Revenue equals the price of the good multiplied by the quantity sold.

Right-to-work law   A law allowing an individual to work at any firm without joining a union.

Saving   Income minus consumption. Saving is measured in the national income accounts as disposable income (income less taxes) minus consumption expenditure.

Saving function   The relationship between saving and disposable income.

Scarcity   The universal state in which wants exceed resources.

Scatter diagram   A diagram that plots the value of one economic variable associated with the value of another.

Search activity   The time and effort spent in searching for someone with whom to do business.

Self-sufficiency   A state that occurs when people produce only enough for their own consumption.

Share   A fraction of the stock of a corporation.

Short run   A period of time in which the quantities of some inputs are fixed and others can be varied.

Short-run aggregate production function   The relationship showing how real GNP varies when the quantity of labor employed varies, holding the capital stock and state of technology constant.

Short-run aggregate supply   The relationship between the aggregate quantity of goods and services supplied (real GNP supplied) and the price level (the GNP deflator), holding everything else constant.

Short-run aggregate supply curve   A curve showing the relationship between the quantity of real GNP supplied and the price level, holding everything else constant.

Short-run aggregate supply schedule   A list showing the quantity of real GNP supplied at each price level, holding everything else constant.

Short-run demand curve   The demand curve that describes the initial response of buyers to a change in the price of a good.

Short-run demand for labor The relationship between the wage rate and the quantity of labor demanded when the firm's capital input is fixed and labor is the only variable input.

Short-run elasticity of demand for labor The percentage change in the quantity of labor demanded divided by the percentage change in the wage rate when labor is the only variable input.

Short-run industry supply curve A curve that shows how the total quantity supplied in the short run by all firms in an industry varies as the market price varies.

Short-run production function The relationship showing how the maximum output attainable varies when the quantity of labor employed varies, holding the quantity of capital and the state of technology constant.

Short-run supply curve The supply curve that describes the response of the quantity supplied to a change in price when only *some* of the technologically possible adjustments have been made.

Shutdown point The point at which a firm's maximum profit is the same regardless of whether the firm produces a positive amount of output or produces nothing—temporarily shuts down.

Simple money multiplier The amount by which an increase in bank reserves is multiplied to calculate the effect of the increase in reserves on total bank deposits, when there are no losses of currency from the banking system.

Single-price monopoly A monopoly that charges the same price for each unit of output.

Slope The change in the value of y divided by the change in the value of x (where y is measured on the vertical axis and x is measured on the horizontal axis of a graph).

Socialism An economic system based on state ownership of capital and land and on a centrally planned allocation of resources.

Specialization The production of only one good or a few goods.

Stagflation A situation in which real GNP stops growing or even declines and inflation accelerates.

Standard of deferred payment An agreed-upon measure in which contracts for future receipts and payments are written.

State enterprise The basic production unit of the Soviet economy.

Stock A quantity measured at a point in time.

Stock equilibrium A situation in which the available stock of an asset is willingly held.

Stock exchange An organized market for trading in stock.

Stock market The market in which the equities of firms are traded.

Stock yield The income from a share in the stock of a firm, expressed as a percentage of the price of the share.

Store of value Any commodity that can be held and sold at a later time.

Strategic interaction Acting in a way that takes into account the expected behavior of others and the mutual recognition of interdependence.

Strategies All the possible actions of each player.

Strike The refusal of a group of workers to work under the prevailing conditions.

Subsidy A payment made by the government to producers.

Substitute A good that may be used in place of another good.

Substitution effect The effect of a change in price on the quantities consumed when the consumer remains indifferent between the original and the new combinations of goods consumed.

Sunk costs The historical cost of buying plant and machinery that have no current resale value.

Supply The entire relationship between the quantity supplied of a good and its price.

Supply curve A graph showing the relationship between the quantity supplied and the price of a good, holding everything else constant.

Supply of labor A schedule or curve showing how the quantity of labor supplied varies as the real wage varies.

Supply schedule A list of quantities supplied at different prices, holding everything else constant.

Takeover The purchase of the stock of one firm by another firm.

Tariff A tax on an import by the government of the importing country.

Tastes A person's attitudes or preferences toward different goods and services.

Tax base The activity on which a tax is levied.

Tax multiplier The magnitude by which a change in taxes is multiplied to determine the change in equilibrium expenditure and real GNP that it generates.

Tax rate The percentage rate at which a tax is levied on a particular activity.

Tax revenue The product of the tax rate and the tax base.

Team production A production process in which each individual in a group specializes in mutually supportive tasks.

Technique Any feasible way of converting inputs into output.

Technological efficiency A state in which it is not possible to increase output without increasing inputs.

Technological progress The development of new and better ways of producing goods and services.

Technology A method for converting resources into goods and services.

Theory of distributive justice A set of principles against which we can test whether a particular distribution of economic well-being is fair.

Time rates A compensation rule based on the number of hours an individual works.

Time-series consumption function The relationship between real consumption expenditure and real disposable income over time.

Time-series graph A graph showing the value of a variable on the y-axis plotted against time on the x-axis.

Tit-for-tat strategy A strategy in which a player cooperates in the current period if the other player cooperated in the previous period but cheats if the other player cheated in the previous period.

Total benefit The total dollar value that people place on a given level of provision of a public good.

Total cost The sum of the costs of all the inputs used in production.

Total fixed cost The cost of all fixed inputs used in production.

Total product The total quantity produced by a firm in a given period of time.

Total product curve A graph showing the maximum output attainable with a given amount of capital as the amount of labor employed is varied.

Total surplus The sum of consumer surplus and producer surplus.

Total variable cost The cost of variable inputs used in production.

Trade-weighted index The value of a basket of currencies in which the weight placed on each currency is related to its importance in U.S. international trade.

Transactions costs The costs arising from finding a trading partner, negotiating an agreement about the price and other aspects of the exchange, and ensuring that the terms of the agreement are fulfilled.

Transfer earnings The income required to induce the supply of a factor of production.

Transfer payment A payment made by the government to households under social programs.

Trend A general tendency for a variable to rise or fall.

Trend real GNP A measure of the general upward tendency, or drift, of real GNP that ignores its fluctuations.

Trigger strategy A strategy in which a player cooperates if the other player cooperates but plays the Nash equilibrium strategy forever thereafter if the other player cheats.

Trough The lower turning point of a business cycle—the point at which the economy turns from contraction to expansion.

Turnover tax A Soviet tax on a consumer good designed to make its market price high enough to achieve a balance between the quantity demanded and the quantity supplied.

Unanticipated inflation Inflation that catches people by surprise.

Underdeveloped country A country in which there is little industrialization, limited mechanization of the agricultural sector, very little capital equipment, and low per capita income.

Underdevelopment trap A situation in which a country is locked into a low per capita income situation that reinforces itself.

Underground economy All economic activity that is legal but unreported.

Unemployment The number of adult workers who are not employed and are seeking jobs.

Unemployment equilibrium A situation in which macroeconomic equilibrium occurs at a level of real GNP below long-run aggregate supply.

Unemployment rate Unemployment expressed as a percentage of the labor force.

Union shop An arrangement in which a firm may hire nonunion workers, but in order for such workers to remain employed, they must join the union within a brief time period specified by the union.

Unit elastic demand An elasticity of 1; the quantity demanded of a good and its price change in equal proportions.

Unit of account An agreed-upon measure for stating the prices of goods and services.

Unlimited liability The legal responsibility for all debts incurred by a firm up to an amount equal to the entire wealth of its owner.

Utilitarian theory The theory that the fairest outcome is the one that maximizes the sum of all individual utilities in society.

Utility The benefit or satisfaction that a person obtains from the consumption of a good or service.

Utility maximization The attainment of the greatest possible utility.

Value The maximum amount that a person is willing to pay for a good.

Value added The value of a firm's output minus the value of the inputs bought from other firms.

Value of money The amount of goods and services that can be bought with a given amount of money.

Variable cost A cost that varies with the output level.

Variable inputs Those inputs whose quantity used can be varied in the short run.

Velocity of circulation The average number of times a dollar is used annually to buy the goods and services that make up GNP.

Vertical integration The merger of two or more firms operating at different stages in the production process of a single good or service.

Voluntary export restraint A self-imposed restriction by an exporting country on the volume of its exports of a particular good; often called VER.

Voters The consumers of the outcome of the political process.

Wants People's unlimited desires or wishes for goods and services.

Wealth Total assets of a household, firm, or government minus its total liabilities.

Wealth effect The effect of a change in real wealth on aggregate planned expenditure.

Welfare state capitalism An economic system combining capitalism's private ownership of capital and land with a heavy degree of state intervention in the allocation of resources.

Wholesale deposit market The market for deposits among banks and other financial institutions.

x-axis The horizontal scale on a graph.

x-coordinate A line running, horizontally, from a point on a graph to the *y*-axis; called the *x*-coordinate because its length is the same as the value marked off on the *x*-axis.

y-axis The vertical scale on a graph.

y-coordinate A line running, vertically, from a point on a graph to the *x*-axis; called the *y*-coordinate because its length is the same as the value marked off on the *y*-axis.

Index

Key concepts and pages where they are defined appear in boldface.

Year	Gross national product Y	=	Personal consumption expenditures C	+	Gross private domestic investment I	+	Government purchases of goods and services G	+	Net exports NX	Growth rate of GNP (percent change)	Unemployed (percent of civilian labor force)
					(billions of 1982 dollars)						
1929	709.6		471.4		139.2		94.2		4.7		3.2
1933	498.5		378.7		22.7		98.5		−1.4	−2.1	24.9
1939	716.6		480.5		86.0		144.1		6.1	7.9	17.2
1940	772.9		502.6		111.8		150.2		8.2	7.8	14.6
1941	909.4		531.1		138.8		235.6		3.9	17.7	9.9
1942	1,080.3		527.6		76.7		483.7		−7.7	18.8	4.7
1943	1,276.2		539.9		50.4		708.9		−23.0	18.1	1.9
1944	1,380.6		557.1		56.4		790.8		−23.8	8.2	1.2
1945	1,354.8		592.7		76.5		704.5		−18.9	−1.9	1.9
1946	1,096.9		655.0		178.1		236.9		27.0	−19.0	3.9
1947	1,066.7		666.6		177.9		179.8		42.4	−2.8	3.6
1948	1,108.7		681.8		208.2		199.5		19.2	3.9	3.4
1949	1,109.0		695.4		168.8		226.0		18.8	.0	5.5
1950	1,203.7		733.2		234.9		230.8		4.7	8.5	5.2
1951	1,328.2		748.7		235.2		329.7		14.6	10.3	3.2
1952	1,380.0		771.4		211.8		389.9		6.9	3.9	2.9
1953	1,435.3		802.5		216.6		419.0		−2.7	4.0	2.8
1954	1,416.2		822.7		212.6		378.4		2.5	−1.3	5.4
1955	1,494.9		873.8		259.8		361.3		.0	5.6	4.3
1956	1,525.6		899.8		257.8		363.7		4.3	2.1	4.0
1957	1,551.1		919.7		243.4		381.1		7.0	1.7	4.2
1958	1,539.2		932.9		221.4		395.3		−10.3	−.8	6.6
1959	1,629.1		979.4		270.3		397.7		−18.2	5.8	5.3
1960	1,665.3		1,005.1		260.5		403.7		−4.0	2.2	5.4
1961	1,708.7		1,025.2		259.1		427.1		−2.7	2.6	6.5
1962	1,799.4		1,069.0		288.6		449.4		−7.5	5.3	5.4
1963	1,873.3		1,108.4		307.1		459.8		−1.9	4.1	5.5
1964	1,973.3		1,170.6		325.9		470.8		5.9	5.3	5.0
1965	2,087.6		1,236.4		367.0		487.0		−2.7	5.8	4.4
1966	2,208.3		1,298.9		390.5		532.6		−13.7	5.8	3.7
1967	2,271.4		1,337.7		374.4		576.2		−16.9	2.9	3.7
1968	2,365.6		1,405.9		391.8		597.6		−29.7	4.1	3.5
1969	2,423.3		1,456.7		410.3		591.2		−34.9	2.4	3.4
1970	2,416.2		1,492.0		381.5		572.6		−30.0	−.3	4.8
1971	2,484.8		1,538.8		419.3		566.5		−39.8	2.8	5.8
1972	2,608.5		1,621.9		465.4		570.7		−49.4	5.0	5.5
1973	2,744.1		1,689.6		520.8		565.3		−31.5	5.2	4.8
1974	2,729.3		1,674.0		481.3		573.2		.8	−.5	5.5
1975	2,695.0		1,711.9		383.3		580.9		18.9	−1.3	8.3
1976	2,826.7		1,803.9		453.5		580.3		−11.0	4.9	7.6
1977	2,958.6		1,883.8		521.3		589.1		−35.5	4.7	6.9
1978	3,115.2		1,961.0		576.9		604.1		−26.8	5.3	6.0
1979	3,192.4		2,004.4		575.2		609.1		3.6	2.5	5.8
1980	3,187.1		2,000.4		509.3		620.5		57.0	−.2	7.0
1981	3,248.8		2,024.2		545.5		629.7		49.4	1.9	7.5
1982	3,166.0		2,050.7		447.3		641.7		26.3	−2.5	9.5
1983	3,279.1		2,146.0		504.0		649.0		−19.9	3.6	9.5
1984	3,501.4		2,249.3		658.4		677.7		−84.0	6.8	7.4
1985	3,618.7		2,354.8		637.0		731.2		−104.3	3.4	7.1
1986	3,717.9		2,446.4		639.6		761.6		−129.7	2.7	6.9
1987	3,853.7		2,513.7		674.0		781.8		−115.7	3.7	6.1
1988	4,014.4		2,598.4		715.8		785.1		−74.9	4.4	5.5

Sources: GNP: 1929–1984, *Economic Report of the President*, 1989, Table B-2; 1985–1988, *Survey of Current Business*, July 1989, p. 40. Unemployment: 1929–1949, *Historical Statistics*, Series D-47; 1950–1988, *Economic Report of the President*, 1989, Table B-39. (The two series differ slightly.)

Year	GNP deflator (1982 = 100)	GNP deflator (percent change)	Consumer Price Index (1982–84 = 100)	CPI (percent change)	M1	M2	M1	M2
					(billions of dollars)		(percentage change)	
1929	14.6							
1933	11.2	−2.2						
1939	12.7	−.8						
1940	13.0	2.0						
1941	13.8	6.2						
1942	14.7	6.6						
1943	15.1	2.6						
1944	15.3	1.4						
1945	15.7	2.9						
1946	19.4	22.9	19.5					
1947	22.1	13.9	22.3					
1948	23.6	7.0	24.1	14.4				
1949	23.5	−.5	23.8	8.1				
1950	23.9	2.0	24.1	−1.2				
1951	25.1	4.8	26.0	1.3				
1952	25.5	1.5	26.5	7.9				
1953	25.9	1.6	26.7	2.7				
1954	26.3	1.6	26.9	0.7				
1955	27.2	3.2	26.8	−0.4				
1956	28.1	3.4	27.2	1.5				
1957	29.1	3.6	28.1	3.3				
1958	29.7	2.1	28.9	2.8				
1959	30.4	2.4	29.1	.7	140.0	297.8		
1960	30.9	1.6	29.6	1.7	140.7	312.4	0.5	4.9
1961	31.2	1.0	29.9	1.0	145.2	335.5	3.2	7.4
1962	31.9	2.2	30.2	1.0	147.9	362.7	1.9	8.1
1963	32.4	1.6	30.6	1.3	153.4	393.3	3.7	8.4
1964	32.9	1.5	31.0	1.3	160.4	424.8	4.6	8.0
1965	33.8	2.7	31.5	1.6	167.9	459.4	4.7	8.1
1966	35.0	3.6	32.4	2.9	172.1	480.0	2.5	4.5
1967	35.9	2.6	33.4	3.1	183.3	524.4	6.5	9.2
1968	37.7	5.0	34.8	4.2	197.5	566.4	7.7	8.0
1969	39.8	5.6	36.7	5.5	204.0	589.6	3.3	4.1
1970	42.0	5.5	38.8	5.7	214.5	628.1	5.1	6.5
1971	44.4	5.7	40.5	4.4	228.4	712.7	6.5	13.5
1972	46.5	4.7	41.8	3.2	249.4	805.3	9.2	13.0
1973	49.5	6.5	44.4	6.2	263.0	861.0	5.5	6.9
1974	54.0	9.1	49.3	11.0	274.4	908.5	4.3	5.5
1975	59.3	9.8	53.8	9.1	287.6	1,023.2	4.8	12.6
1976	63.1	6.4	56.9	5.8	306.5	1,163.7	6.6	13.7
1977	67.3	6.7	60.6	6.5	331.4	1,286.7	8.1	10.6
1978	72.2	7.3	65.2	7.6	358.7	1,389.0	8.2	8.0
1979	78.6	8.9	72.6	11.3	386.1	1,500.2	7.6	8.0
1980	85.7	9.0	82.4	13.5	412.2	1,633.1	6.8	8.9
1981	94.0	9.7	90.9	10.3	439.1	1,795.5	6.5	9.9
1982	100.0	6.4	96.5	6.2	476.4	1,954.0	8.5	8.8
1983	103.9	3.9	99.6	3.2	522.1	2,185.2	9.6	11.8
1984	107.7	3.7	103.9	4.3	551.9	2,363.6	5.7	8.2
1985	110.9	3.0	107.6	3.6	620.1	2,562.6	12.4	8.4
1986	113.8	2.6	109.6	1.9	725.4	2,807.7	17.0	9.6
1987	117.4	3.2	113.6	3.6	750.8	2,901.0	3.5	3.3
1988	121.3	3.3	118.4	4.2	790.3	3,069.4	5.1	5.5

Source: Economic Report of the President, 1989, Tables B-3, B-60, B-61, B-67.